Communications
in Computer and Information Science 257

Tai-hoon Kim Hojjat Adeli
Haeng-kon Kim Heau-jo Kang
Kyung Jung Kim Akingbehin Kiumi
Byeong-Ho Kang (Eds.)

Software Engineering, Business Continuity, and Education

International Conferences ASEA, DRBC and EL 2011,
Held as Part of the Future Generation
Information Technology Conference, FGIT 2011,
in Conjunction with GDC 2011,
Jeju Island, Korea, December 8-10, 2011
Proceedings

Springer

Volume Editors

Tai-hoon Kim
Hannam University, Daejeon, Korea
E-mail: taihoonn@empas.com

Hojjat Adeli
The Ohio State University, Columbus, OH, USA
E-mail: adeli.1@osu.edu

Haeng-kon Kim
Catholic University of Daegu, Korea
E-mail: hangkon@cu.ac.kr

Heau-jo Kang
Mokwon University, Daejeon, Korea
E-mail: hjkang@mokwon.ac.kr

Kyung Jung Kim
Woosuk University, Jeollabuk-do, Korea
E-mail: kkjung00@hanmail.net

Akingbehin Kiumi
University of Michigan-Dearborn, Dearborn, MI, USA
E-mail: kiumi@umich.edu

Byeong-Ho Kang
University of Tasmania, Hobart, Australia
E-mail: byeong.kang@utas.edu.au

ISSN 1865-0929 e-ISSN 1865-0937
ISBN 978-3-642-27206-6 ISBN 978-3-642-27207-3 (eBook)
DOI 10.1007/978-3-642-27207-3
Springer Heidelberg Dordrecht London New York

Library of Congress Control Number: 2011943002

CR Subject Classification (1998): D.2, C.2, H.4, F.3, I.2, H.3

Typesetting: Camera-ready by author, data conversion by Scientific Publishing Services, Chennai, India

Printed on acid-free paper

Springer is part of Springer Science+Business Media (www.springer.com)

Foreword

Advanced software engineering and its applications, disaster recovery and business continuity and education and learning are all areas that attract many professionals from academia and industry for research and development. The goal of the ASEA, DRBC and EL conferences is to bring together researchers from academia and industry as well as practitioners to share ideas, problems and solutions relating to the multifaceted aspects of these fields.

We would like to express our gratitude to all of the authors of submitted papers and to all attendees for their contributions and participation.

We acknowledge the great effort of all the Chairs and the members of Advisory Boards and Program Committees of the above-listed event. Special thanks go to SERSC (Science and Engineering Research Support Society) for supporting this conference.

We are grateful in particular to the speakers who kindly accepted our invitation and, in this way, helped to meet the objectives of the conference.

December 2011 | Chairs of ASEA 2011, DRBC 2011 and EL 2011

Preface

We would like to welcome you to the proceedings of the 2011 International Conference on Advanced Software Engineering and Its Applications (ASEA 2011), Disaster Recovery and Business Continuity (DRBC 2011) and Education and Learning (EL 2011) — the partnering events of the Third International Mega-Conference on Future-Generation Information Technology (FGIT 2011) held during December 8–10, 2011, at Jeju Grand Hotel, Jeju Island, Korea.

ASEA, DRBC and EL are focused on various aspects of advances in software engineering and its application, disaster recovery and business continuity, education and learning. These conferences provide a chance for academic and industry professionals to discuss recent progress in the related areas. We expect that the conferences and their publications will be a trigger for further related research and technology improvements in this important subject.

We would like to acknowledge the great efforts of the ASEA 2011, DRBC 2011, and EL 2011 Chairs, International Advisory Board, Committees, Special Session Organizers, as well as all the organizations and individuals who supported the idea of publishing this volume of proceedings, including the SERSC and Springer.

We are grateful to the following keynote, plenary and tutorial speakers who kindly accepted our invitation: Hsiao-Hwa Chen (National Cheng Kung University, Taiwan), Hamid R. Arabnia (University of Georgia, USA), Sabah Mohammed (Lakehead University, Canada), Ruay-Shiung Chang (National Dong Hwa University, Taiwan), Lei Li (Hosei University, Japan), Tadashi Dohi (Hiroshima University, Japan), Carlos Ramos (Polytechnic of Porto, Portugal), Marcin Szczuka (The University of Warsaw, Poland), Gerald Schaefer (Loughborough University, UK), Jinan Fiaidhi (Lakehead University, Canada) and Peter L. Stanchev (Kettering University, USA), Shusaku Tsumoto (Shimane University, Japan), Jemal H. Abawajy (Deakin University, Australia).

We would like to express our gratitude to all of the authors and reviewers of submitted papers and to all attendees, for their contributions and participation, and for believing in the need to continue this undertaking in the future.

Last but not the least, we give special thanks to Ronnie D. Caytiles and Yvette E. Gelogo of the graduate school of Hannam University, Korea, who contributed to the editing process of this volume with great passion.

This work was supported by the Korean Federation of Science and Technology Societies Grant funded by the Korean Government.

December 2011

Tai-hoon Kim
Hojjat Adeli
Haeng-kon Kim
Heau-jo Kang
Kyung Jung Kim
Akingbehin Kiumi
Byeong-Ho Kang

Organization

General Co-chairs

Haeng-kon Kim	Catholic University of Daegu, Korea
Heau-jo Kang	Prevention of Disaster with Information Technology RIC, Korea
Kyung Jung Kim	Woosuk University, Korea

Program Co-chairs

Tai-hoon Kim	GVSA and University of Tasmania, Australia
Akingbehin Kiumi	University of Michigan-Dearborn, USA
Byeong-Ho Kang	University of Tasmania, Australia

Publicity Co-chairs

Tao Jiang	Huazhong University of Science and Technology, China
June Verner	University of New South Wales, Australia
Silvia Abrahao	Camino de Vera, Spain
Muhammad Khurram Khan	King Saud University, Saudi Arabia

Publication Chairs

Byungjoo Park	Hannam University, Korea
Rosslin John Robles	University of San Agustin, Philippines
Maricel B. Salazar	University of San Agustin, Philippines
Yvette E. Gelogo	Hannam University, Korea
Ronnie D. Caytiles	Hannam University, Korea
Martin Drahansky	University of Technology, Czech Republic
Aboul Ella Hassanien	Cairo University, Egypt

International Advisory Board

Aboul Ella Hassanien	Cairo University, Egypt
Byeong-Ho Kang	University of Tasmania, Australia
Ha Jin Hwang	Kazakhstan Institute of Management, Economics and Strategic Research (KIMEP), Kazakhstan
Jose Luis Arciniegas Herrera	Universidad del Cauca, Colombia
Tien N. Nguyen	Iowa State University, USA

Wai Chi Fang	National Chiao Tung University, Taiwan
Young-whan Jeong	Korea Business Continuity Planning Society, Korea
Adrian Stoica	NASA Jet Propulsion Laboratory, USA
Samir Kumar Bandyopadhyay	University of Calcutta, India

Program Committee

Abdelouahed Gherbi
Abdelwahab Hamou-Lhadj
Agustín Yagüe
Ami Marowka
Ashfaqur Rahman
Abdullah Al Zoubi
Ali Moeini
Amine Berqia
Andrew Goh
Anita Welch
Asha Kanwar
Birgit Oberer
Bulent Acma
Carmine Gravino
Chamseddine Talhi
Chia-Chu Chiang
Chima Adiele
Cheah Phaik Kin
Chitharanjandas Chinnapaka
David Guralnick
Dinesh Verma
Doo-Hwan Bae
Emilia Mendes
Emiliano Casalicchio
Erol Gelenbe
Fabrizio Baiardi
Fausto Fasano
Florin D. Salajan
Francisca Onaolapo Oladipo
Gabriele Bavota
Giuseppe Scanniello
Gongzhu Hu
Harvey Siy
Hironori Washizaki
Hyeon Soo Kim
Istvan Siket
Jennifer Pérez Benedí
Jiro Tanaka
Jonathan Lee
Jongmoon Baik
Jose L. Arciniegas
Joseph Balikuddembe
Juan Garbajosa
Jacinta Agbarachi Opara
Jeton McClinton
John Thompson
Karel Richta
Kendra Cooper
Kin Fun Li
Kurt Wallnau Khitam Shraim
Mads Bo-Kristensen
Marga Franco i Casamitjana
Michel Plaisent
Mohd Helmy Abd Wahab
Laszlo Vidacs
Laurence Duchien
Lerina Aversano
Lirong Dai
Luigi Buglione
Maria Bielikova
Maria Tortorella
Mokhtar Beldjehem
Morshed Chowdhury
Mona Laroussi
Olga Ormandjieva
Osman Sadeck
Pankaj Kamthan
Philip L. Balcaen
Praveen Ranjan Srivastava
Rattikorn Hewett
Ricardo Campos
Rita Francese
Robert Glass
Robin Gandhi

Rocco Oliveto
Rüdiger Klein
Ramayah Thurasamy
Robert Wierzbicki
Rozhan Mohammed Idrus
Rudolf Ferenc
Salahuddin Al Azad
Satoshi Takahashi
Shawkat Ali
Simin Nadjm-Tehrani
Silvia Abrahao
Sokratis Katsikas
Sandro Bologna
Snjezana Knezic
Stefan Brem
Stefan Wrobel
Stella Lee
Sapna Tyagi
Satyadhyan Chickerur
Selwyn Piramuthu
Sheila Jagannathan
Sheryl Buckley
Soh Or Kan
Takanori Terashima
Teodora Ivanusa
Tokuro Matsuo
Tae-Young Byun
Toor, Saba Khalil
Yana Tainsh
Vincenzo Deufemia
Wuwei Shen
Yijun Yu

Special Session Organizers

Yong-Kee Jun
Shouji Nakamura
Toshio Nakagawa
Woo Yeol Kim
R. Young-chul Kim

Table of Contents

Erratum

A Novel Web Pages Classification Model Based on Integrated Ontology

Bai Rujiang, Wang Xiaoyue, and Hu Zewen

Institute of Scientific & Technical Information, Shandong University of Technology, Zibo 255049, China
{brj,wangxy,hzw}@sdut.edu.cn

Abstract. The main existed problem in the traditional text classification methods is can't use the rich semantic information in training data set. This paper proposed a new text classification model based SUMO (The Suggested Upper Merged Ontology) and WordNet ontology integration. This model utilizes the mapping relations between WordNet synsets and SUMO ontology concepts to map terms in document-words vector space into the corresponding concepts in ontology, forming document-concepts vector space, based this, we carry out a text classification experiment. Experiment results show that the proposed method can greatly decrease the dimensionality of vector space and improve the text classification performance.

Keywords: Ontology integration, Text classification model, Word vector space, Concept vector space.

1 Introduction

With the rapid development of computer technology and internet, the increase velocity of digital document information gross is very fast, so the large scale text processing has became a challenge that we face at present. A core difficulty of mass text processing is the high-dimensionality of feature space. The traditional text classification algorithms based on machine learning or statistics, such as K-nearest neighbor (KNN),support vector machine (SVM), neural network algorithm, naïve bayes algorithm etc, although are of some advantages, such as simpleness and easy to learn, fast training velocity, high classification performance etc[1], these algorithms mainly aim at the small scale corpus, utilize word vector space to carry out the training of text classification model. Obviously, text classification methods using only words as features exhibit a number of inherent deficiencies[2]:

① Multi-Word Expressions with an own meaning like "HIV (Human Immunodeficiency Virus)" are chunked into pieces with possibly very different meanings, such as in this example, concept "HIV" is separated into three different meanings words: Human, Immunodeficiency and Virus that easily make documents classify into the wrong category.

T.-h. Kim et al. (Eds.): ASEA/DRBC/EL 2011, CCIS 257, pp. 1–10, 2011.

② Synonymous Words like "Computer", "Pc", "Laptop", "Notebook", "Desktop", "Dell", "Lenovo", "HP" etc are mapped into different features.
③ Polysemous Words are treated as one single feature while they may actually have multiple distinct meanings.
④ Lack of Generalization: there is no way to generalize similar terms like "gold" and "silver" to their common hypernym "precious metal".

In order to solve the existed problems in the traditional text classification methods based bag-of-words vector space and semantic vector space. This paper takes SUMO and WordNet as research objects, proposes a text classification model based on SUMO and WordNet ontology integration. This model firstly carries an integration to WordNet and SUMO ontology by using the mapped relations between WordNet synsets and SUMO ontology concepts, forming integrated ontology library containing WordNet synsets and corresponding SUMO ontology concepts; Then based this integrated ontology library, maps the traditional high-dimensionality word vector space into the low-dimensionality concept vector space to carry the training of text classification model.

The rest of the paper is organized as follows. In section 3, we introduce the concept of semantic pattern. In section 4, an automatic text classification model based on semantic pattern vector space is given. In section 5, in order to verify performance of model, we make a text classification experiment. Finally, we make a conclusion and point out the directions of future work.

2 Text Classification Model Based SUMO and WordNet Ontology Integration

According to the above works, we propose a kind of novel automatic text classification model based on SUMO and WordNet ontology integration (as shown in Figure.1). The proposed mode is composed of the following four parts: ① The construction of integrated ontology library; ② The mapping of word vector space to concept vector space; ③ the generality of concept vector space; ④ the training and experience of classification model. The basic processes of model operation are as follows: Firstly, we compile the regular expressions to extract WordNet synsets ID, synsets, and the corresponding SUMO ontology concepts, forming integrated ontology library containing one to one mapping relations between WordNet synsets and corresponding SUMO ontology concepts; Then based on this integrated ontology library, map the different feature terms in the traditional word vector space into the corresponding synset fields in the integrated ontology library, afterwards, map the synset fields into SUMO ontology concepts, afterwards, map the concrete concepts into the general concepts, forming the low-dimensionality concept vector space to carry out the training of text classification model; Finally, carry out the same processing to test corpus and form concept vector space to carry out text classification experience and results evaluation.

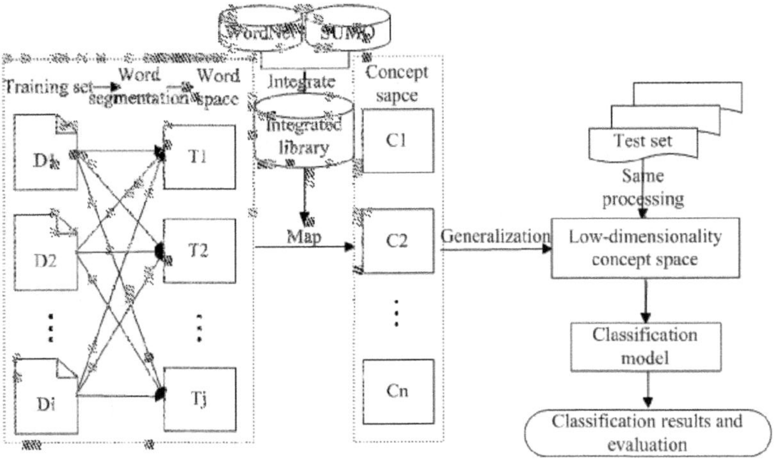

Fig. 1. Text semantic classification model based SUMO and WordNet ontology integration

2.1 The Construction of Integrated Ontology Library

We design an integration algorithm to carry out an integration to WordNet synsets and the corresponding SUMO ontology concepts, forming integrated ontology library containing one to one mapping relations between WordNet synsets and corresponding SUMO ontology concepts . The basic processes of the integrated algorithm are as follows: Firstly, acquire the mapping files between WordNet synsets and SUMO ontology concepts from http://sigmakee.cvs.sourceforge.net/sigmakee/KBs/WordNetMappings/WordNet; Then compile the regular expressions according to the mapping characteristics between synsets and concepts; Finally, utilize regular expressions to extract synsetID, synsets and the corresponding SUMO ontology concepts from the acquired mapping files, and save them into the constructed mapping table: "WSMap".

The core codes of integrated algorithm are as follows:

```
The core codes of integrated algorithm
 Input: The mapping files;
 Output: The mapping table: "WSMap"
0 $strs1=file($filename);       //grant the name of the
mapping file to variable: "strs1"
1 $con="/.+@/";
2 $synID="/^[0-9]{8}/";       //regular expression of
extract synset ID
3 $syset="/([a-z]{2,}_*[a-z]*)+/";       // regular
expression of extract synsets
4 $concep="/&%([a-zA-Z]{2,}_*[a-z]*)+/";
5  $concep1="/[a-zA-Z]{2,}/";       // regular expression
of extract concepts
```

```
6 for($i=0;$i<count($strs1);$i++)   //carry out a
circulation to every line in file
{$line[$i]=trim($strs1[$i]);  //after trimming space save
into array: “$line[$i]”
preg_match_all($con,$line[$i],$cons);  //extract contents
that regular expression: “$con” represents from $line[$i]
and save them into array: “$cons”
preg_match_all($concep,$line[$i],$conce); //extract
contents that regular expression: “$concep” represents
from $line[$i] and save them into array: “$conce”
$c=$cons[0][0];  //initialize array $cons and grant it to
variable: “$c”
$d=$conce[0][0];  // initialize array $conce and grant it
to variable: “$d”
preg_match_all($synID,$c,$synid);  //match contents that
$synID represents from $c and grant them to synset ID
array: “$synid”
preg_match_all($syset,$c,$synset);  // match contents
that $syset represents from $c and grant them to synsets
array: “$synset”
preg_match_all($concep1,$d,$concept); // match contents
that $concep1 represents from $d and grant them to
concept array: “$concept”
$set=serialize($synset[0]);   //serialize $synset and
grant it to variable: “$set”
$ids=$synid[0][0];  $cs=$concept[0][0]; //initialize
array: “$synid” and $concept and grant them to
variables: “$ids” and “$cs”
$sql="INSERT INTO `WS`.` WSMap`
(`synID` ,`synset` ,`concept`)VALUES ('$ids', '$set','$cs') on
duplicate key update synID='$ids'";  // save the ex-
tracted contents into “WSMap”   }
```

Some results of “WSMap” are shown in Figure 2.

synID	synset	concept
00001740	a:1:{i:0;s:6:"entity";}	Physical
00001930	a:1:{i:0;s:15:"physical_entity";}	Physical
00002137	a:2:{i:0;s:11:"abstraction";i:1;s:15:"abstract_ent...	Physical
00002452	a:1:{i:0;s:5:"thing";}	CorpuscularObject
00002684	a:2:{i:0;s:6:"object";i:1;s:15:"physical_object";}	CorpuscularObject
00003553	a:2:{i:0;s:5:"whole";i:1;s:4:"unit";}	CorpuscularObject
00003993	a:1:{i:0;s:8:"congener";}	familyRelation
00004258	a:2:{i:0;s:12:"living_thing";i:1;s:13:"animate_thi...	CorpuscularObject
00004475	a:2:{i:0;s:8:"organism";i:1;s:5:"being";}	Organism
00005787	a:1:{i:0;s:7:"benthos";}	Organism
00005930	a:1:{i:0;s:5:"dwarf";}	Human
00006024	a:1:{i:0;s:11:"heterotroph";}	Organism
00006150	a:1:{i:0;s:6:"parent";}	parent
00006269	a:1:{i:0;s:4:"life";}	Organism
00006400	a:1:{i:0;s:5:"biont";}	Organism
00006484	a:1:{i:0;s:4:"cell";}	Cell
00007347	a:3:{i:0;s:12:"causal_agent";i:1;s:5:"cause";i:2;s...	Agent
00007846	a:6:{i:0;s:6:"person";i:1;s:10:"individual";i:2;s:...	Human
00015388	a:6:{i:0;s:6:"animal";i:1;s:13:"animate_being";i:2...	Animal
00017222	a:3:{i:0;s:5:"plant";i:1;s:5:"flora";i:2;s:10:"pla...	Plant

Fig. 2. Some results in “WSMap”

2.2 The Mapping of Word Vector Space to Concept Vector Space

Generally, a concept can contain the meaning of many words , concepts are the abstract of words, so we can't directly map words into concepts, we need a bridge. WordNet synsets almost covers all the natural language words, besides, there existed the mapping relations between WordNet synsets and SUMO ontology concepts, which can be taken as a bridge to map words into concepts. So we design a mapping algorithm based on the constructed mapping table: "WSMap" in section 2.1, which can map words into SUMO ontology concepts by the synset field in the "WSMap" .

The concrete descriptions of the mapping algorithm are as follows:

Input: the constructed mapping table: "WSMap" in section 2.1 and the document-word vector space: Di=(T1,Wi1;T2,Wi2; ;Tj, Wij), where Wij denotes term Tj in the document Di.

Step1. For each term Tj in the document-word vector space, carrying out a judgement sentence: "is term Tj existed in the synset field of WSMap?". If existed, replacing term Tj with the corresponding concept field in the WSMap, the weight Wij of term Tj is taken as concept's weight; if not exsited, removing term Tj; exit for. At last, forming a new document-concept vector space: Di =(C1,Wi1;C2,Wi2; ;Cn, Win), where Win denotes the weight of concept Cn in the document Di;

As the many-to-many relations among term Tj, synset field and concept field, there are very many repeated concepts in the mapped document-concept vector space. Generally speaking, the higher concepts' repeated frequency is, concepts can reflect the subjects of documents or classes more, the higher concepts' weight should be. So in the next step, we mainly make a statistic to the frequency that concepts repeat, remove the repeated concepts from the document-concept vector space, readjust the weight of concepts.

Step2. For each concept Cn in the document-concept vector space, firstly, combining the same concepts as a concept and assigning it to the variable Ck; Then making a statistic to the repeated frequency of Ck and assigning it to the variable CFk; Finally utilizing the following formula to compute the weight of concept Ck:

$$CW_{ik} = \left(\sum_{n=1}^{CF_k} W_{in} + CF_k \right) \Big/ \sqrt{\sum_{n=1}^{CF_k} W_{in}^2 + CF_k^2} \tag{1}$$

where CWik denotes the weight of the concept Ck in the document Di, denotes the weight sum of the concept Ck and the same concepts as it (as terms of mapping into concepts are different, even the same concepts, their weights are also different, so in the process of removing the repeated concepts, we make the weight sum of the same concepts as the weight of the combined concept Ck) , CFk indicates not only the frequency of concept Ck, but also the number of the same concepts, the denominator is the normalization factor;

Output: the low-dimensional document-concept vector space after removing the repeated concepts and readjusting concepts' weight: Di=(C1,CWi1;C2, CWi2; ;Ck,CWik).

2.3 The Generalization of Concept Vector Space

There existed the hypernymy- hyponymy relations among concepts, so we need to carry out a generalization to concept vector space. The basic processes of the generalization are as follows:

① input the concept description file of SUMO ontology: "SUMO.owl", utilize the Image_GraphViz.class[7] in the GraphViz.php file to visualize the "SUMO.owl" and form the hierarchy structure map of ontology concepts(OC-HSM); For each concept Ck in the document-word vector space, we carry out a judgement

② sentence: "is the concept Ck existed in the OC-HSM?". If not existed, we reserve the original concept Ck, then carry out a judgement to the next concept; if existed, we acquire the layer of concept Ck and grant it to the variable: L(Ck), then we judge whether the concept Ck exists the direct epigyny concept in the L(Ck)-r(r is a adjustive parameter of layer) layer, if existed, replace concept Ck with the epigenous concept Cm, and utilize the following formula to compute the weight of concept Cm:

$$CSW_{im} = Log_{10}(CW_{ik} + \frac{1}{L(C_k) - r} \times p) \tag{2}$$

Where CSWim is the weight of concept Cm, Log10 is the normalization function, $\frac{1}{L(C_k)-r}$ is the layer weight of concept Cm , p is the adjustive parameter; If not existed, we reserve the original Ck and utilize the following formula to adjust the weight of concept Ck:

$$CSW_{ik} = Log_{10}(CW_{ik} + \frac{1}{L(C_k)} \times p) \tag{3}$$

At last, forming the lower-dimensionality concept vector space: Di=(C1,CSWi1; C2,CSWi2; ;Cm,CSWim).

As the many-to-many relations between hypogyny concepts and epigyny concepts, there are very many repeated concepts in the process of the generalization of concepts. Generally speaking, the higher concepts' repeated frequency is, the more subconcepts of reflecting this concept subject are, the stronger the differentiation degree of the class of this concepts, the higher the weight of this concept should be. So in the next step, we mainly make a statistic to the frequency that concepts repeat, remove the repeated concepts from the document-concept vector space: Di=(C1,CSWi1; C2,CSWi2; ;Cm,CSWim), readjust the weight of concepts.

Step2. For each concept Cm in the document-concept vector space, firstly, combining the same concepts as a concept and assigning it to the variable Cl; Then making a statistic to the repeated frequency of Cl and assigning it to the variable CFl; Finally utilizing the following formula to compute the weight of concept Cl:

$$CCSW_{il} = \left(\sum_{m=1}^{CF_l} CSW_{im} + CF_l \right) \Bigg/ \sqrt{\sum_{m=1}^{CF_l} CSW_{im}^2 + CF_l^2} \quad (4)$$

where CCSWil denotes the weight of the concept Cl in the document Di, $\sum_{m=1}^{CF_l} CSW_{im}$ denotes the weight sum of the concept Cl and the same concepts as it, CFl indicates not only the frequency of concept Cl, but also the number of the same concepts, the denominator is the normalization factor;

Output: the lower-dimensionality document-concept vector space: Di=(C1,CCSWi1;C2,CCSWi2; ;Cl,CCSWil).

2.4 Classification Experiment and Evaluation

Once the training and testing document corpus have been represented as vector space model, we select a kind of text classification algorithm, such as support vector machine (SVM), k-Nearest-Neighbor (KNN), Naïve Bayes et al, carry out the training of text classification model. Then based on the trained text classification model, we classify the testing document corpus into their appropriate categories. Finally, we select a kind of evaluation index, such as Accuracy, Recall, precision and F1 value et al to carry out an evaluation to the results of classification.

3 Experiment and Result Analysis

3.1 Experiment Design

Experiment Data Set. We used the second version: "20news-bydate.tar.gz" of the 20 Newsgroups data set as experimental data set (available at: http://people.csail.mit.edu/~jrennie/20Newsgroups/). This version is divided into 20 classes by news topic. We select 8 classes from 20 classes as class labels, the class names of 8 classes are as follows: alt.atheism, comp.graphics, comp.os.ms-windows.misc, comp.sys.ibm.pc.hardware, comp.sys.mac.hardware, comp.windows, x,misc.forsale, rec.autos, their class labels are respectively setted as N1 ,N2 ,N3 ,N4 ,N5 ,N6 ,N7 ,N8. We respectively extract 300 news documents as experimental training set from the training set of every class in 8 classes, extract 100 news documents as experimental test set from the test set of every class in 8 classes, so the size of training set is 2400 news documents, test set is 800 news documents.

Experiment Method. We use SVM as the learning algorithm of text classification, carry out a contrast experiment to the classification accuracy of the following two document representation model: the traditional word vector space model (WVS) and the proposed concept vector space model (CVS). In the experiment, we set the type of SVM as the C-support vector classification (C-SVC), the penalty value C of SVM as 3.0, the kernel type of SVM as the linear kernel function.

Experiment Evaluation Index. We use the most common evaluation index: Accuracy, Recall(R), Precision(P), F1 value to evaluate the performance of two kind of vector space model.

3.2 Experimental Result Analysis

Experimental results are shown in Table 1 and Figure 3. Table 1 shows the Recall(R), Precision (P), F1 value and their overall average of two kinds of classifiers when the size of train set is 960. We can see from TABLE 1 that CVS-based SVM classifier is of the higher Recall, Precision, F1 value and the lower dimensionality than WVS-based SVM classifier. Such as, compared with the traditional WVS-based SVM classifier, the overall average of Recall, Precision or F1 value of CVS-based SVM classifier respectively increased from 55.75%, 56.03%, 55.89% to 82.61%, 84.52%, 82.19%, respectively having a 26.86%, a 28.49% and a 26.30% relative increase. By carrying out a semantic processing to the traditional bag-of-words vector space and converting them into the concept vector space, the dimensionality of vector space also has decreased from 11178 to 3360, having a 7872 decrease.

Figure 3 shows the comparison of the classification accuracy of two kinds of classifier under the different train set size. As we see from Figure 3, compared with the traditional WVS-based SVM classifier, the classification accuracy of CVS-based SVM classifier have a great improvement, the overall average accuracy of 10 experiments with two kinds of classifiers has increased 19.06% to 67.19%, having a 48.13% increase. When the train set size reaches to 960 news texts, the classification performance of two kinds of classifiers is the optimal, at this point, the accuracy of WVS-based SVM classifier is 55.75%, the accuracy of CVS-based SVM classifier is 82.61%, having a 26.86% increase.

Table 1. the comparison of classification performance of two kinds of classifiers (the size of train set: 960)

Class labels	WVS-based (Dimensionality: 11178)			CVS-based (Dimensionality: 3360)		
	R	P	F1	R	P	F1
N_1	82.00%	96.47%	88.65%	81.33%	69.95%	75.21%
N_2	93.00%	51.96%	66.67%	99.00%	100.00%	99.50%
N_3	74.00%	73.27%	73.63%	98.74%	83.76%	90.64%
N_4	63.00%	63.64%	63.32%	56.90%	90.00%	69.72%
N_5	57.00%	48.31%	52.30%	100.00%	89.39%	94.40%
N_6	43.00%	40.57%	41.75%	87.96%	62.99%	73.41%
N_7	14.00%	18.42%	15.91%	76.25%	86.50%	81.05%
N_8	20.00%	55.56%	29.41%	60.68%	93.57%	73.62%
Overall	55.75%	56.03%	55.89%	82.61%	84.52%	82.19%

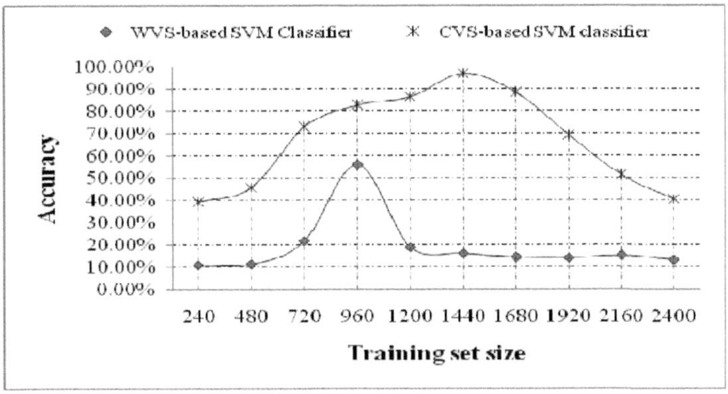

Fig. 3. The comparison of the classification accuracy of two classifiers under different train set size

4 Conclusions and Future Research Directions

For solving the existed problems in the traditional bag-of-words vector space model and the current vector space model of intensifying semantic information. We proposed a new text classification model based SUMO and WordNet ontology integration, this model utilizes the mapping relations between WordNet synsets and SUMO ontology concepts to map terms in document-words vector space into the corresponding concepts in ontology, forming the lower-dimensionality document-concept vector space, based this, we carry out a text classification experiment. Experimental results show that, compared with the traditional text classification method based on the bag-of-words vector space, the classification performance of our proposed method have a great improvement, the dimensionality of vector space also have a great decrease.

Our future research directions are to apply our proposed model in the layer classification of texts and further improve the classification performance of our proposed model and the the effect of the reduction of vector space dimensionality when the size of train set is comparatively large.

Acknowledgements. This work was supported by the National Social Science Foundation of China (10BTQ047), the Humanities and Social Sciences Project of the Ministry of Education of China (09YJA870019), the Technology Innovation Project of the Ministry of Culture of China, the Provincial Natural Science Foundation of Shandong of China (No. 2009ZRB02141).

References

1. Yang, Y.: An Evaluation of Statistical Approaches to Text Category. Journal of Information Retrieval 1(1/2), 67–88 (1999)
2. Bloehdorn, S., Hotho, A.: Boosting for Text Classification with Semantic Features. In: Mobasher, B., Nasraoui, O., Liu, B., Masand, B. (eds.) WebKDD 2004. LNCS (LNAI), vol. 3932, pp. 149–166. Springer, Heidelberg (2006)

3. Song, W., Park, S.C.: Genetic algorithm for text clustering based on latent semantic indexing. Computers and Mathematics with Applications 57, 1901–1907 (2009)
4. Litvak, M., Last, M., Kisilevich, S.: Classification of Web Documents Using Concept Extraction from Ontologies. In: Gorodetsky, V., Zhang, C., Skormin, V.A., Cao, L. (eds.) AIS-ADM 2007. LNCS (LNAI), vol. 4476, pp. 287–292. Springer, Heidelberg (2007)
5. Carpineto, C., Michini, C., Nicolussi, R.: A Concept Lattice-Based Kernel for SVM Text Classification. In: Ferré, S., Rudolph, S. (eds.) ICFCA 2009. LNCS (LNAI), vol. 5548, pp. 237–250. Springer, Heidelberg (2009)
6. Jian, Z., Chunping, L.: WordNet- based Concept Vector Space Model for Text Classification. Computer Engineering and Applications, 174–178 (2006)
7. Image_GraphViz[EB/OL] (March 10, 2010), http://pear.php.net/package/Image_GraphViz/download

AgentSpeak (L) Based Testing of Autonomous Agents

Shafiq Ur Rehman[1] and Aamer Nadeem[2]

[1] Faculty of Computing,
Riphah International University, Islamabad
shafiq.rehman@riu.edu.pk
[2] Center for Software Dependability
Mohammad Ali Jinnah University, Islamabad
anadeem@jinnah.edu.pk

Abstract. Autonomous agents perform on behalf of the user to achieve defined goals or objective. Autonomous agents are often programmed using AgentSpeak language. This language is rich enough to provide necessary support to gain proper functionality within certain environment. Testing of agents programmed in AgentSpeak language is a challenging task. In this paper testing of agents programmed in AgentSpeak has been proposed by deriving AgentSpeak code into goal-plan diagram. Certain coverage criteria have been defined based on the goal-plan diagram. Test cases meeting the defined coverage criteria are used to test the AgentSpeak program with respect to expected functionality.

Keywords: AgentSpeak (L), Autonomous Agent Testing.

1 Introduction

Agent systems are used widely to operate in dynamic environment. Agents perceive their environment and respond accordingly to meet their goal. Autonomy is the agent's ability to operate independently, without the need for human guidance or intervention [1]. The term autonomy refers to the goal oriented behavior. Autonomous agents are programmed to perform automatically in order to achieve certain goal. All of their activities converge towards achieving their defined goal.

AgentSpeak is the language used to program agent's expected behavior within certain environment. Belief, desires and intentions are used in AgentSpeak to express certain states of the agent and it operational knowledge. Agent needs some environmental knowledge to start its operation within a certain environment. Belief base contains the initial beliefs an agent has about itself, operational environment and other agents [2]. Beliefs can be added or deleted as new information or knowledge is perceived and also update as some new state is achieved by the agent. Belief base can be used to check the current state of the agent and retrieve relevant details required for the operation. Agent has certain goal referred to as achieve goal and test goal, achieve goal change the state of the system after certain operation while test goals are used to retrieve information from the belief base [3]. Goals are achieved by successful execution of the plans in AgentSpeak (L). Intentions are active plans that are used to achieve certain goal. A plan consists of a triggering event, used to initiate the plan. Events can be external, by perceiving the environment and internal, triggered as part

T.-h. Kim et al. (Eds.): ASEA/DRBC/EL 2011, CCIS 257, pp. 11–20, 2011.

of an active plan. Every plan has precondition or context which should be satisfied before execution of the plan; context is checked from the belief base [3].

Our aim in this paper is to test the AgentSpeak program; we will represent the behavior of the AgentSpeak program in form of a diagram. An agent achieves its goal with the help of plans written in AgentSpeak language. Main goal may have some sub-goals contributing their part in achieving the objective. A goal-plan diagram is used to describe the behavior of the agent showing all relevant sub-goal and actions to be performed during the execution. We are aiming to define our own coverage criteria that are used to test the autonomous agent based on selected testing criteria.

Section two covers background, section three describes related work and section four describes our proposed approach for testing autonomous agents. Section five describes conclusion and future directions for our proposed approach.

2 Background

This section gives an overview of different types of agents. Earlier BDI agents have been widely used for performing tasks, later AgentSpeak (L) language has been introduced covering additional properties for agent programming including working of agent in multi-agent environment.

2.1 BDI Agents

In this subsection we give an overview of BDI agents. Belief-Desire-Intentions (BDI) properties are used to program intelligent agents. BDI agents have been widely used since last two decades and various researchers have explored their behavior [2]. It does not support the efficient theorem proven for BDI logic [2]. BDI agents are deployed in continuous changing environment; there are also various implementation of BDI agent [20, 21, and 22].

2.2 AgentSpeak (L)

This subsection describes the semantics of AgentSpeak (L). AgentSpeak (L) is a language used to program autonomous agents [4]. Testing of AgentSpeak (L) program is getting its importance to attain the desired goals. Rao gives the idea of AgentSpeak (L) language syntax. AgentSpeak (L) agent is developed by containing several plans used to achieve defined goals. To properly understand the AgentSpeak (L) plan, meeting the certain goals we include a simple example containing two agents r1 and r2 [4]. The purpose of both agents is to clean an area from garbage, where r1 collects the garbage found on the territory and takes it towards the position where r2 is located, r2 burns the garbage and r1 resumes its searching for garbage from the position where he found the garbage.

Belief base has the knowledge about the current position of the r2 and makes sure that r1 agent's intention is to check the slot for the garbage is set to true. Fig. 1 shows the actual syntax of the cleaner agent r1. R1 starts with initial beliefs and time to time beliefs are added and deleted as program executes, -b and +b are used to add and delete the beliefs respectively. Achieve goal and test goal are represented by ! and ? signs respectively [3].

```
Agent r1
Beliefs
pos(r2,2,2).
checking(slots).

Plans
+pos(r1,X1,Y1) : checking(slots) & not garbage(r1)                 (p1)
   <- next(slot).

+garbage(r1) : checking(slots)                                      (p2)
   <- !stop(check);
      !take(garb,r2);
      !continue(check).

+!stop(check) : true                                                (p3)
   <- ?pos(r1,X1,Y1);
      +pos(back,X1,Y1);
      -checking(slots).

+!take(S,L) : true                                                  (p4)
   <- !ensure_pick(S);
      !go(L);
      drop(S).

+!ensure_pick(S) : garbage(r1)                                      (p5)
   <- pick(garb);
      !ensure_pick(S).

+!ensure_pick(S) : true <- true.                                    (p6)

+!continue(check) : true                                            (p7)
   <- !go(back);
      -pos(back,X1,Y1);
      +checking(slots);
      next(slot).

+!go(L) : pos(L,X1,Y1) & pos(r1,X1,Y1)                              (p8)
   <- true.

+!go(L) : true                                                      (p9)
   <- ?pos(L,X1,Y1);
      move_towards(X1,Y1);
      !go(L).
```

Fig. 1. Syntax of cleaner agent r1 in AgentSpeak (L) [4]

Plan is the major part in AgentSpeak (L). AgentSpeak plan consists of triggering event, context and set of actions [6]. Plan is triggered with any triggering event; context of plan should be true before the plan start. Jason Interpreter has been used to execute the AgentSpeak (L) program [6]. To execute the agent, user needs to create the environment which is created in Java [19].

3 Related Work

This section gives a brief overview of the existing testing work done to test the quality of autonomous agents. Bordini *et al.* presented a framework to verify multi agent programs written by applying BDI properties and also claimed to add missing properties to verify the AgentSpeak program [4]. AgentSpeak (F) code has been translated into Java code as it is very close to agent programming and then apply SPIN or JPF2 model to check the results [4].

Zhang *et al.* presented an automated unit testing approach for a single agent by using testing framework used to develop agent system. Testing framework caters the different sequence of agent program execution. Fault directed testing approach is used by first Identifying appropriate units of the agent and test the unit with the defined mechanism [5]. It considers the plan as a single unit then it is checked whether the plan is triggered by the appropriate event or not, checks its precondition, cycles in plan and plan completeness etc. [5].

Zheng and Alagart proposed a method for conformance testing of agent's BDI properties as alternative to formal verification [8]. Test cases are generated to check the implementation with respect to specification. Low *et al.* [11] presented method to automatically generate test cases for multi agent system based on BDI properties, nodes and plan based criteria are covered for test case generation. Different plan and node coverage criteria subsume each other, numbers of test cases generated for each criterion and subsumption hierarchy are used to select best criterion.

Winikoff and Cranefield [12] discussed the implication of analyzing the size of behavior space for BDI agent and found that failure handling has larger impact on size of behavior space. Goal-plan tree can transform sequence of actions, which is a combination of "and" or "or" predicates. Either one plan can be activated or all sub-plans are activated and successful execution of plan produces execution trace of the selected goal while in case of failure all remaining plans are executed for the respective goal.

Goal-plan diagram for the AgentSpeak (L) have not been used to test the agent's behavior although the idea of goal-plan tree has been explored by [13] and [14]. Our focus is on testing AgentSpeak (L) program by first transforming the AgentSpeak (L) program into relevant goal-plan diagram, and then applying our identified coverage criteria to test AgentSpeak (L) programmed agent's behavior with test data.

4 Proposed Approach

In this section we discuss our proposed approach for testing of autonomous agents which are programmed in AgentSpeak (L). Fig. 2 describes the overall architecture of proposed technique for testing an AgentSpeak (L) program.

Our proposed technique has three main processes namely goal/plan generator, test path generator and test data generator. Goal/plan generator generates goal/plan diagram by using AgentSpeak (L) program. Different coverage criteria will be used as input to test path generator, coverage criteria have been defined in section 4.2.1, based on those coverage criteria, test paths are generated meeting the specified coverage criteria. Test cases are meant to make the context of selected plan true by making desired changes in belief base. Test data generator will take test paths as input and produce test cases, based on the test case design. The subsequent subsections describe the detail of the three main processes of our approach.

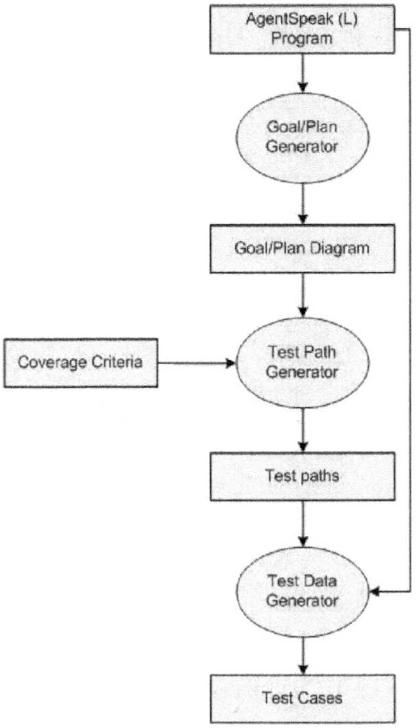

Fig. 2. Proposed technique architecture

4.1 Goal/Plan Generator

In this subsection we discuss first process of our proposed approach, i.e. goal/plan generator. Goal/plan generator helps to identify different plans associated with each goal. Dependencies between different sub-goals are also presented in graphical form. Goal/plan generator takes AgentSpeak (L) program as input and goal/plan diagram is produced as output of this process.

We support our discussion with cleaner agent example. Syntax of cleaner agent r1 written in AgentSpeak (L) has been transformed into goal-plan diagram in Fig. 3. Goal-plan diagram of agent r1 consists of 16 node representing different goal and plans. Rectangle shape represents the plans and goals are represented with rounded rectangles. The graph in Fig. 4 contains two types of nodes, one for the goal representation and other for plan representation. The idea of goal-plan diagram has been taken from [12, 13, 14] as they represent goal-plan tree for Prolog language. One goal may have more than one plan and executes a specific plan depending upon the context conditions. Plan nodes also store the relevant context conditions and triggering event as they are mandatory for each plan described in AgentSpeak (L). Graphical representation inform of goal/plan diagram for the AgentSpeak (L) program makes it convenient to identify and trace a path and validate the path with some given test data.

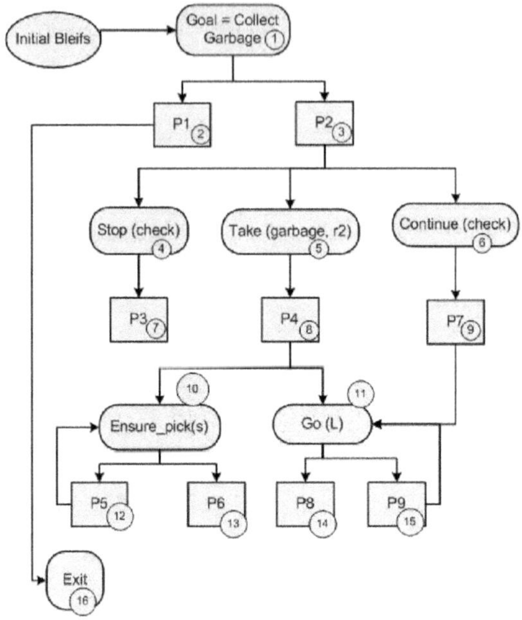

Fig. 3. Goal-plan diagram for agent r1

4.1.1 AgentSpeak (L) Plan Execution

Plans are executed to achieve goals. Whenever agent starts its execution, it will have some perceived environmental information stored in its belief base. Different plans are executed to achieve the defined goal.

Start→ Belief set → Plan → Goal

An agent have more than one plan which are executed subsequently to achieve different sub-goal, which ultimately support the achievement of main or root goal.

4.2 Test Path Generator

In this subsection we describe second process of our proposed approach named Test Path Generator. Test path generator take goal/plan diagram and coverage criteria as input and generates test paths for the program. Goal/plan diagram is generated with goal/plan generator and coverage criteria have been defined in following section.

4.2.1 Test Coverage Criteria

Our aim of this paper is to test the AgentSpeak program, for this purpose we have developed goal-plan diagram represented in fig. 4 showing dependencies between different goals and plans of AgentSpeak. We have defined following test coverage criteria based on the goal-plan diagram to test AgentSpeak program.

1) Top level goal coverage
2) All achievement goal coverage
3) All plans coverage
4) All paths coverage

Set of test case (TC) and set of test paths (TP) are used to cover different test coverage criteria, following is the precise details of every defined coverage criteria.

4.2.1.1 Top Level Goal Coverage. First criterion is top level goal coverage which is defined as: *A set of test case (TC) is said to satisfy top level goal coverage criterion if it achieves the top level goal of the goal plan diagram.*

In our example AgentSpeak (L) program the top level goal, in case of agent r1 is to collect garbage. It is not necessary that all nodes are covered in meeting first coverage criteria.

4.2.1.2 All Achievement Goal Coverage. Achievement goal are the state of system that agent want to achieve which is defined as: *A set of test cases (TC) is said to satisfy all achievement goal coverage criterion if each achievement goal is covered by at least one test case.*

In case of Agent r1, we have five achievement goals need to be covered in achievement goal coverage criteria. While meeting the all achievement goal coverage criterion, test cases will be used to cover all achievement goals of agent r1.

4.2.1.3 All Plans Coverage. A Plan is a sequence of actions an agent will take or trigger sub-plans in order to achieve certain goal. This coverage criterion is defined as: *A set S of test cases (TC) are said to satisfy all plans coverage criterion if each plan in the program is executed by at least one test case.*

AgentSpeak (L) language syntax has different plans to achieve the certain goals. Different plan supports different goals. Agent r1 has 9 plans used to achieve different achievement goals. All plan coverage criteria will test the AgentSpeak program in such a way that all plans must be covered at least once.

4.2.1.4 All Paths Coverage. A path in goal/plan diagram may contain more than one plan and combines their context conditions which have to be true for successful traverse of a path. This criteria is defined as: *A Set S of test paths (TP) is said to satisfy all path coverage criterion if every path of goal/plan diagram is included in S.*

Goal-plan diagram contains more than one path to meet the desired functionality. Different path contained in goal-plan diagram will be explored with different test cases. Goal-plan diagram of agent r1 represented in fig. 4 has different paths of execution. Achieve goal ensure_pick and go both have recursion in their plans. Path covering node 10 and 12 of fig. 4 may have more than one repetition or cycle in any path extracted from goal-plan diagram, same is the case for the node 11 and 14.

Path 1: 1-2-16
Path 2: 1-2-3-4-7-5-8-10-13-11-14-6-9-11-14
Path 3: 1-2-3-4-7-5-8-10-12-10-13-11-15-11-14-6-9-11-15-11-14
....

4.3 Test Data Generator

Test path generated by test path generator are used as the input along with AgentSpeak (L) program to test data generator. Test data generator generates test data to traverse the path on AgentSpeak (L) code. Test data consists of inputs for the plan execution e.g. triggering events. Each path is having path conditions which must be met in order to successful trace of path. AgentSpeak (L) plans have predicate which are combined to form a path condition for a respective path.

We propose to use evolutionary approach which support automatic and dynamic test data generation satisfies any given path [23, 24]. Genetic algorithms are used for test data generation instead of classical testing approaches because autonomous agents have dynamic behavior and control flow graph of agent cannot be formed. Environment may behave differently in different interactions. Belief perception make is possible to perceive the changes made to the environment. Chromosome consists of input values required for AgentSpeak (L) program testing. Chromosome has two parts one containing necessary belief addition/deletion in order to make context true and second part contains goal to be achieved. Any path in goal/plan diagram consists of different plans and each plan needs some inputs which are generated by chromosome. Input can be by perception or from belief base and fitness of each test case depends upon the context conditions involved in each path.

Chromosome designing and fitness function definition has its importance for successful testing. Test data generator process of our approach generates the test cases which are applied to AgentSpeak (L) program with different test path to successfully test the agent's behavior.

5 Conclusion and Future Directions

In this paper we have presented a novel approach to test autonomous agent which are programmed in AgentSpeak (L). AgentSpeak language has been used to program the desired behavior of autonomous agent. A goal-plan diagram has been developed showing the dependencies between different goals and plans of AgentSpeak (L) program. A plan is initiated upon any triggering event and will start execution with the belief base, meeting the context conditions. Belief base will change after every internal or external event occurrence.

We have defined some coverage criteria, based on those coverage criteria; AgentSpeak (L) program will be tested. We are aiming to design test case using genetic algorithm, chromosome structure and other necessary steps used to properly design the test case and test the AgentSpeak (L) in future. Test case designing will be purely based on the concept of deriving goal-plan diagram from the AgentSpeak (L) program. Test cases meeting the different defined coverage criteria will be designed. Chromosome designing will be important task to accomplish. We are looking to enhance our proposed testing technique based on the defined coverage criteria to properly test the AgentSpeak (L) program.

References

1. Alonso, F., Fuertes, J.L., Martinez, L., Soza, H.: Towards a set of Measures for Evaluating Software Agent Autonomy. In: Eighth Mexican International Conference on Artificial Intelligence, doi:978-0-7695-3933-1/09, 10.1109/MICAI.2009.15
2. Rao, A.S.: AgentSpeak(L): BDI agents speak out in a logical computable language. In: Van de Velde, W., Perram, J.W. (eds.) MAAMAW 1996. LNCS (LNAI), vol. 1038, pp. 42–55. Springer, Heidelberg (1996)
3. Bordini, R.H., Hübner, J.F., Wooldridge, M.: Programming Multi-Agent Systems in AgentSpeak using Jason. John Wiley & Sons Ltd., The Atrium
4. Bordini, R.H., Fisher, M., Visser, W., Wooldridge, M.: Verifiable Multi-agent Programs. In: Dastani, M.M., Dix, J., El Fallah-Seghrouchni, A. (eds.) PROMAS 2003. LNCS (LNAI), vol. 3067, pp. 72–89. Springer, Heidelberg (2004)
5. Zhang, Z., Thangarajah, J., Padgham, L.: Automated Unit Testing For Agent Systems. In: 2nd International Working Conference on Evaluation of Novel Approaches to Software Engineering, ENASE 2007 (2007)
6. Bordini, R.H., Hübner, J.F.: BDI Agent Programming in AgentSpeak Using Jason. In: Toni, F., Torroni, P. (eds.) CLIMA 2005. LNCS (LNAI), vol. 3900, pp. 143–164. Springer, Heidelberg (2006)
7. Tonella, P.: Evolutionary Testing of Classes. In: Proceedings of the 2004 ACM SIGSOFT international Symposium on Software Testing and Analysis, ISSTA 2004. ACM, New York (2004)
8. Zheng, M., Alagart, V.S.: Conformance Testing of BDI Properties in Agent-based Software System. In: Proceedings of the 12th Asia-Pacific Software Engineering Conference, APSEC 2005 (2005), doi:0-7695-2465-6/05
9. Miller, T., Padgham, L., Thangarajah, J.: Test Coverage Criteria for Agent Interaction Testing. In: Weyns, D., Gleizes, M.-P. (eds.) AOSE 2010. LNCS, vol. 6788, pp. 91–105. Springer, Heidelberg (2011)
10. Weerasooriya, D., Rao, A., Ramamohanarao, K.: Design of a Concurrent Agent-Oriented Language. In: Wooldridge, M.J., Jennings, N.R. (eds.) ECAI 1994 and ATAL 1994. LNCS (LNAI), vol. 890, pp. 386–401. Springer, Heidelberg (1995)
11. Low, C.K., Chen, T.Y., Ronnquist, R.: Automated test case generation for BDI agents. Autonomous Agents and Multi-Agent Systems 2(4), 311–332 (1999)
12. Winikoff, M., Cranefield, S.: On the testability of BDI agents. In: European Workshop on Multi-Agent Systems (2010)
13. Burmeister, B., Arnold, M., Copaciu, F., Rimassa, G.: BDI-agents for agile goal-oriented business processes. In: Proceedings of the Seventh International Conference on Autonomous Agents and Multiagent Systems (AAMAS), pp. 37–44. IFAAMAS (2008)
14. Shaw, P., Farwer, B., Bordini, R.: Theoretical and experimental results on the goal-plan tree problem. In: Proceedings of the Seventh International Conference on Autonomous Agents and Multiagent Systems (AAMAS), pp. 1379–1382. IFAAMAS (2008)
15. Nguyen, C. D., Perinirini, A., Tonella, P.: Automated continuous testing of multi-agent systems. In: Proceedings of the Fifth European Workshop on Multi-Agent Systems (EUMAS) (2007)
16. Bordini, R.H., Fisher, M., Pardavila, C., Wooldridge, M.: Model checking AgentSpeak. In: Proceedings of the Second International Joint Conference on Autonomous Agents and Multiagent Systems (AAMAS), pp. 409–416. ACM Press (2003)
17. Raimondi, F., Lomuscio, A.: Automatic verification of multi-agent systems by model checking via ordered binary decision diagrams. J. Applied Logic 5(2), 235–251 (2007)

18. Bresciani, P., Giorgini, P., Giunchiglia, F., Mylopoulos, J., Perini, A.: Tropos: An Agent-Oriented Software Development Methodology, Technical Report # DIT-02-0015
19. Bordini, R.H., Hübner, J.F.: Jason: A Java-based interpreter for an extended version of AgentSpeak, `http://jason.sourceforge.net`
20. Burmeister, B., Sundermeyer, K.: Cooperative problem-solving guided by intentions and perception. In: Werner, E., Demazeau, Y. (eds.) Decentralized A.I. 3. North Holland, Amsterdam (1992)
21. Georgeff, M.P., Lansky, A.L.: Procedural knowledge. In: Proceedings of the IEEE Special Issue on Knowledge Representation, vol. 74, pp. 1383–1398 (1986)
22. Müller, J.P., Pischel, M., Thiel, M.: Modelling Reactive Behaviour in Vertically Layered Agent Architectures. In: Wooldridge, M.J., Jennings, N.R. (eds.) ECAI 1994 and ATAL 1994. LNCS (LNAI), vol. 890, pp. 261–276. Springer, Heidelberg (1995)
23. Michael, C.C., McGraw, G.E., Schatz, M.A., Walton, C.C.: Genetic Algorithms for Dynamic Test Data Generation. In: Proceedings of 12th IEEE International Conference on Automated Software Engineering, 1997, pp. 307–308 (1997), doi:10.1109/ASE.1997.632858
24. Pargas, R.P., Harrold, M.J., Peck, R.R.: Test-Data Generation Using Genetic Algorithms. Journal of Software Testing, Verification and Reliability (1999)

A Flexible Methodology of Performance Evaluation for Fault-Tolerant Ethernet Implementation Approaches

Hoang-Anh Pham, Dae Hoo Lee, and Jong Myung Rhee

Dept. of Information and Communication Engineering, Myongji University, Korea
{anhph,dhlee,jmr77}@mju.ac.kr

Abstract. In this paper, we propose a flexible methodology which is applicable to performance evaluation for various Fault-Tolerant Ethernet (FTE) implementation approaches including two conventional approaches, the software-based and the hardware-based ones. Then, we present performance analysis results in terms of fail-over time for a redundant Ethernet network device by using our methodology.

Keywords: Fault-Tolerant Ethernet (FTE), Fail-over Time, Performance Evaluation.

1 Introduction

Fault tolerance is a key design issue required by mission-critical systems. In this paper, we focus on a fault-tolerant Ethernet (FTE) implementation for mission-critical network-based systems. Various research, development, and standardization efforts have been made to add fault-tolerance capabilities to Ethernet-based networks. The approach for FTE implementation depends on the network architecture. In general, there are three distinct network models, introduced by Song et al [1] for FTE implementation. Among these, in our research, we deal with the single network with redundant cables model on which there are at least two conventional approaches that an Ethernet based network can be used to adapt to failure including hardware-based approach and software-based approach. The advantages and disadvantages of two conventional approaches were discussed in [3].

Fail-over time for fault detection and fault recovery is a key factor for FTE design and implementation [4]. For each mission-critical system, there is an upper limit of fail-over time to satisfy the performance requirement. Performance analysis for FTE implementation allows us to determine the fail-over time whether it meets the performance requirements.

In this paper, we propose a methodology for FTE performance evaluation. Our methodology is independent of and applicable to various approaches for FTE implementation. The remainder of this paper is organized as follows. In Section 2 we present the framework of our methodology for FTE performance evaluation. In Section 3 we present a study on performance analysis to determine the fail-over time of a redundant Ethernet network device. Finally, we summarize our work and future study in Section 4.

T.-h. Kim et al. (Eds.): ASEA/DRBC/EL 2011, CCIS 257, pp. 21–25, 2011.

2 A Flexible Methodology for FTE Performance Evaluation

2.1 Network Model for FTE Performance Evaluation

Our methodology is based upon a network model depicted in Fig. 1. The model consists of three nodes: (1) FTE Node; (2) Data Generator node; and (3) Evaluator node. They are inter-connected via a switch which can support mirroring function.

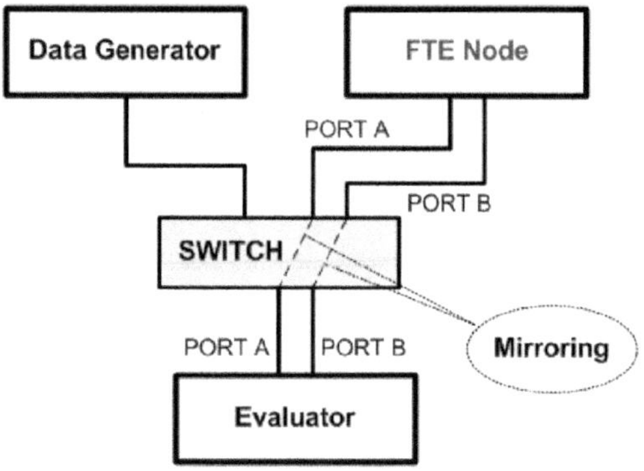

Fig. 1. Network Model for FTE Performance Evaluation

The FTE implementation, which needs to be evaluated, is installed at the FTE Node. As previously mentioned, in our research we deal with the network model in which each FTE node has redundant network connections [1,3]. In Fig. 1, the FTE Node has two network connections via PORT A and PORT B respectively. The FTE function depends on the specific approach for FTE implementation.

For software-based approach, both network ports used in the FTE Node appears as two single network devices to the application layer. A software or middleware will create a virtual interface by bonding two physical network devices. The FTE software performs the algorithms for fault detection and fault recovery.

For hardware-based approach, both network ports are accommodated in a single network device, for example, multi-port network interface card (NIC) that appears to the application layers at the FTE Node as a single network interface. The corresponding firmware is provided for fault detection and fault recovery.

The performance is evaluated based on data analysis. The data is sent by the Data Generator node and received by the FTE Node. The data analysis depends on the specific approach for FTE implementation being used in the FTE Node. For various approaches, various tools for data analysis are needed to be developed for performance evaluation. Therefore, in order to minimize that effort, we propose an intermediary node which is called Evaluator shown in Fig. 1.

The Evaluator node has two single network ports corresponding to two network ports in the FTE Node. PORT A and PORT B at the Evaluator are configured as the mirrors of PORT A and PORT B in the FTE Node, respectively. Therefore, the data stream arriving at the Evaluator is similar to the data stream arriving at the FTE Node. Instead of doing data analysis directly on the FTE Node, the data analysis has been made at the Evaluator which is independent of the FTE approach being used in the FTE Node.

2.2 Data Analysis for Performance Evaluation in Terms of Fail-Over Time

At the FTE Node, let us assume that PORT A is active at the beginning. Then PORT B is on standby and it is activated when there is fault on PORT A. The fail-over time includes the time for fault detection on PORT A and the time for fault recovery to activate PORT B becoming new active port.

According to our methodology, the data stream generated by the Data Generator is sent to the FTE Node of which the data stream is only received on the active port. When there is fault on the current active port, the data stream is redirected to standby port after it was activated as new active port.

Again the data analysis has been performed in the Evaluator instead of the FTE Node because the data stream arriving at the FTE Node is similar to data stream arriving at the Evaluator. A software toolkit has been developed for monitoring incoming packets which arrive at the two network interfaces at the Evaluator. This toolkit helps us to detect when the data stream was redirected from the active port to standby port.

Fig. 2 shows an illustration to determine fail-over time. The last data (packet) received on PORT A at time T_K immediately before there is fault on PORT A. The first data (packet) received on PORT B at time T_M immediately after PORT B has become active port. Then, the fail-over time T_{fot} can be practically approximated as follows:

$$T_{fot} = T_M - T_K \tag{1}$$

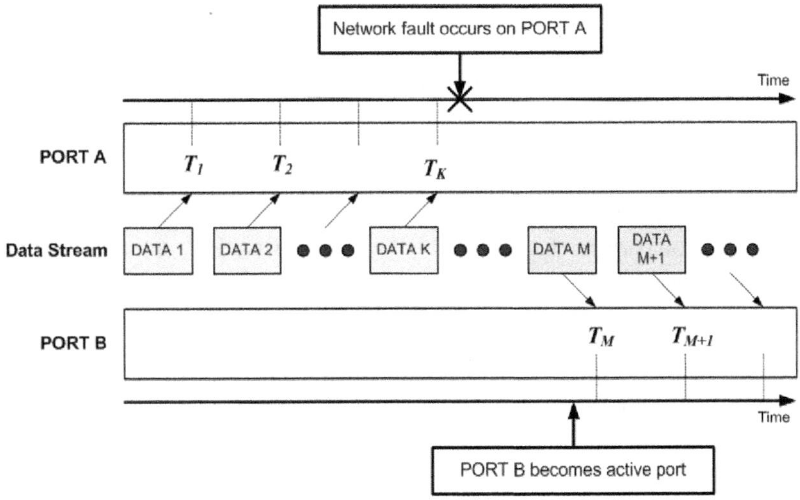

Fig. 2. Illustration to determine fail-over time

Performing the same scenarios with various data patterns generated by the Data Generator is to get the average value of fail-over time.

3 Experiment

In this section, we present experimental results on performance analysis in terms of fail-over time for a redundant network device Intel PRO1000MT which supports two ports in a single NIC and FTE function.

Based on the proposed network model shown in Fig. 1, Intel PRO1000MT was installed in the FTE Node. The Cisco Catalyst 3560 series switch has been used for our experiment. The TCP and UDP applications have been developed for data transmission at the Data Generator and for data reception at the FTE Node. The toolkits for packet monitoring and data analysis have been also developed and used at the Evaluator.

By applying our methodology to determine the fail-over time which is illustrated in Fig. 2, the experimental results in terms of fail-over time of Intel PRO1000MT are presented in Table 1. Our results are compatible to the results presented by Kim et al [5] who also evaluated same device.

Table 1. Experimental results for fail-over time of Intel PRO1000MT

Fail-over time (millisecond)	
Max	509
Min	233
Average	338

4 Conclusion

In this paper we have proposed a methodology for FTE performance evaluation. Because the Evaluator in our methodology is independent of the FTE approaches being used at the FTE Node, our methodology is flexible and applicable to various approaches for FTE implementation. Further, the performance evaluation on the FTE Node can be performed under various platforms meanwhile there is no needs to modify the tool for data analysis at the Evaluator. It is fair and reasonable to do performance comparison for various FTE implementation approaches by same methodology and framework.

In this paper, only the performance evaluation in terms of fail-over time has been presented. However, the proposed methodology can be easily extended to develop other analysis tools for evaluating other network performance metrics [6-7]. For example, based on the illustration shown in Fig. 2, the number of packet loss during the fail-over switching from PORT A to PORT B can be determined. Then, the network throughput can be measured as the ratio of the number of received packets to the number of transmitted packets.

Acknowledgments. This work was supported by the Agency for Defense Development (ADD) and by the Defense Acquisition Program Administration (DAPA), Republic of Korea.

References

1. Song, S., Huang, J., Kappler, P., Freimark, R., Gustin, J., Kozlik, T.: Fault-Tolerant Ethernet for IP-Based Process Control Networks. In: Proc. of the 25th Anunal IEEE International Conference on Local Computer Network (LCN 2000), pp. 116–125 (November 2000)
2. Huang, J., Song, S., Li, L., Kappler, P., Freimark, R., Gustin, J., Kozlik, T.: An open Solution to Fault-Tolerant Ethernet: Design, Prototyping, and Evaluation. In: Proc. of IEEE International Performance, Computing, and Communications Conference, pp. 461–468 (February 1999)
3. Pham, H.A., Rhee, J.M., Kim, S.M., Lee, D.H.: A Novel Approach for Fault-Tolerant Ethernet Implementation. In: Proc. of the 4th International Conference on Networked Computing, and Advanced Information Management (NCM 2008), vol. 1, pp. 58–61 (September 2008)
4. Rhee, J.M., Pham, H.A., Kim, S.M., Ko, Y.M., Lee, D.H.: Issues of Fail-over Switching for Fault-tolerant Ethernet Implementation. In: Proc. of IEEE International Conference on New Trends in Information and Service Science (NISS 2009), pp. 710–714 (July 2009)
5. Kim, H.S., Choi, Y.C., Sung, W.H.: Gigabit-Ethernet based Redundant Network Performance Analysis. In: Agency for Defense Development (ADD), Rep. of Korea
6. Sauers, B.: Understanding High Availability. Hewlett-Packard Company (1996)
7. RFC-2544, Benchmarking Methodology for Network Interconnect Devices (March 1999)

Behavioral Subtyping Relations for Timed Components

Youcef Hammal

LSI, Department of Computer Science, USTHB University, Algiers, Algeria
hammal@lsi-usthb.dz

Abstract. This paper deals with the behavioral substitutability of active components where services availability is a critical criterion for safety-properties preservation. Some timed subtyping relations are given and discussed in relation with the compatibility issue of active components.

1 Introduction

Software components are always refined and changed to depict intended behaviors of new components linked by refinement/substitution relationships to their predecessors. However, we have to ensure full services availability in new critical-safety components in such a way that their combination does not lead the system to erroneous statuses. For this end, we propose to enhance the subtyping relations of components defined yet in [7] with timing constraints such that these would cope efficiently with service availability issue in respect of both untimed and timed semantics. The substitutability relations are based on "*strong*" variants of branching bisimulation we propose to strengthen the service availability requirements when comparing behavioral graphs of components (i.e., transition systems).

We then analyze, at the specification level, the notion of behavioral consistency of the resulting substitutability relations since this is a key topic to the verification of safety-critical systems. Indeed, software systems always evolve throughout the product life cycle; objects and components are transformed as requirements change, bugs are discovered and fixed [2]. Evolution implies the removal of previous components and addition of new ones refined and augmented with new services. However, besides any potential benefits of inheritance and refinement in terms of implementation reuse, the refinement process may raise two kinds of problems in the new behavior: unavailability of previously provided services and violation of global correctness properties that were previously respected.

According to Liskov behavioral substitution principle [8], the substitutability problem can be defined as the verification of the following two criteria [8,2]:

1. The *containment* criterion that requires every behavior of the old object to be also a behavior of the new one. In other terms, a refined object must continue to supply all services (actions) which the basic ancestor was offering.
2. Whereas the second criterion is about *compatibility* requiring that correctness properties which were previously proven must remain valid in the new yielded system. In fact, a fragment viewed in isolation, cannot be meaningfully checked and its validity can only be expressed in terms of reasonable assumptions made by users of the entire system.

T.-h. Kim et al. (Eds.): ASEA/DRBC/EL 2011, CCIS 257, pp. 26–35, 2011.

Substitutability checking should go beyond asserting that traces of a previous object are prefixes of some traces of the new one since traces based subtyping relations are too weak and do not handle safety properties. Thus, many efforts focus on use of failures based preorders [3,5,6,9] to deal with this issue. Nevertheless, these relations are not too strong to check faithfully substitutability of active components whose parallel behaviors may deeply alter the service availability and correctness properties.

Accordingly, we propose new subtyping relations that are based on strong branching bisimulations of [7] to cope efficiently with service availability when dealing with refinement and inheritance of state-based objects. Moreover, we address the issue of substitutability in the timed context where previous subtyping relations become no more adequate because of timing constraints. So we propose fitting relations based on new timed variants of branching bisimulation. Notice that components may be modeled using high level formalisms such as Petri nets, StateCharts or Formal Description Techniques which semantics are provided with transitions systems. On the other hand, interaction protocols (depicted by UML sequence diagrams, modal/temporal logics ...) capture various safety and liveness properties of components [2,8].

The paper is structured as follows: Section 2 proposes new optimal subtyping relations for active components in respect of the untimed semantics. Next, Section 3 shows how these relations cope well with compatibility issues. In Section 4, we present and discuss news subtyping relations within the timed context. The conclusion is given in Section 5 where some remarks and future works are outlined.

2 Behavioral Substitutability within Untimed Context

2.1 Preliminary Concepts

We henceforth denote by the symbol $|[.]|$ the semantics function that maps each component model C into a labeled transition system (LTS) $G=|[C]|=<Q,\rightarrow,\Sigma,q_0>$ where:

- Q is the set of all reachable configurations of the component (referred to also as states or statuses) with the starting node q_0 as its initial configuration.
- $\rightarrow \subseteq Q\times\Sigma\times Q$ is the set of transitions between nodes labeled with actions of Σ. The extended transition $(===\omega==> / \omega\in\Sigma^*)$ denotes a chain of basic transitions labeled with names of actions which form the word ω.
- Σ is a set of actions (i.e., services). An action may be either of the form $g?e$ or $g!e$ (simplified into respectively $e?$ and $e!$) where g denotes a gate which the component C uses as an interaction point either to provide or to require services. The set Σ of any component may contain a τ-action denoting new services to be concealed when the updated component is plugged into the old component environment.

We propose below, a new variant of the branching bisimulation we use in defining substitutability relations [7] and comparing efficiently components in respect of services availability. Moreover, such a bisimulation deals well with unobservable actions which we get from hiding new services with regard to clients of old components.

Definition 1. *A Strong branching bisimulation is a symmetric relation* $R \subseteq Q_1 \times Q_2$, *such that for every* $(p,q) \in Q_1 \times Q_2$, pRq *if and only if:* $\forall a \in \Sigma \cup \{\tau\}$, $\forall p' \in Q_1$:

$p \xrightarrow{a} p'$ *then either* $a = \tau$ *and* $p'Rq$ *or* $\exists q' \in Q_2$: $q \xrightarrow{a} q'$ *and* $p'Rq'$.

Two graphs G_1 *and* G_2 *are strongly branching bisimilar* ($G_1 \approx_{sbr} G_2$) *if* $\exists R$, $q_0^1 R\, q_0^2$.

Note that two states p and q are equivalent if they can perform the same observable actions in order to reach pairs of states always equivalent. If some state p' can be attained by one τ-step from p then it should be also equivalent to the state q and preserve the same capabilities as p (see Fig.1). Such a condition cannot be guaranteed by the classical branching bisimulation (see Fig.2). This strong constraint is due to the fact that an unobservable action is not an internal one under control of the only involved component. In our setting, it represents some new service that is visible to clients of the previous component. So, even if it is called (by new clients) old clients shall still be able to use previous services which were available before the τ-progress.

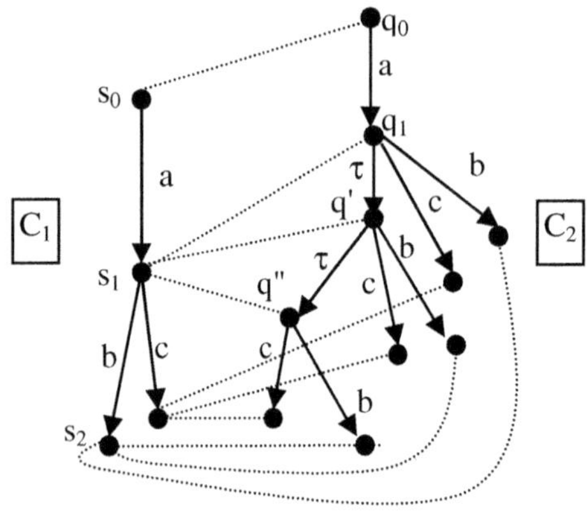

Fig. 1. Strong branching Bisimulation

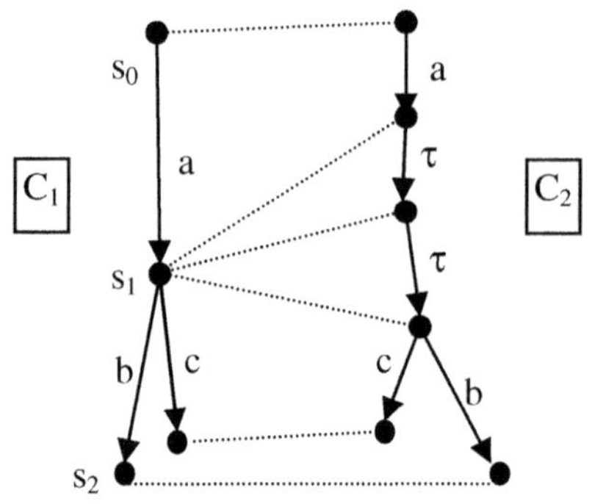

Fig. 2. Branching Bisimulation

As the strong branching bisimulation is weaker than the strong bisimulation and stronger than the branching one, we easily deduce the next hierarchy between them:

Property 1. *Let* $\approx$ *and* $\approx_{br}$ *denote respectively the classical strong bisimulation and branching bisimulations. Then, we have:* $\approx \Rightarrow \approx_{sbr} \Rightarrow \approx_{br}$.

Considering results on compositionality of strong and branching bisimulations [4], we can straightforwardly derive from Property 1 the following one. Let G, G_1, and G_2 denote behavioral models of components and || denote the parallel operator.

Property 2. $\forall G, G_1 \sim G_2 \Rightarrow G||G_1 \sim G||G_2$ *for all equivalence relation* $\sim \in \{\approx, \approx_{sbr}, \approx_{br}\}$.

2.2 Optimal Behavioral Subtyping Relations

The rationale behind behavioral substitutability is that (reactivity) capabilities of a previous component should be always preserved and often augmented in the refined one. As a result, Component signature changes raising a question about how this modification would be done. In our opinion, despite the way a component internal structure is refined, the main concern is to preserve and augment provided services (reactions to triggering events) making it possible to continue to fulfill any request related to previous services from its environment (i.e. old clients). Thus, substitutability checking consists of asserting that behaviors of old and new components are equivalent modulo an adequate subtyping relation provided that new added services (added actions) are suitably concealed to old users of the refined component.

We naturally discard the strong bisimulation because it does not take into consideration the unobservable action τ which models added services we have to hide. Note that τ-actions are not under control of only its owner component but also that of its environment because these actions require cooperation of both the two parts. That's why we introduced a variant of branching bisimulation taking care of these τ-actions.

Let C_1, and C_2 be two components. $\Sigma(C_i)$ denotes the set of actions performed by a component C_i $(i=1,2)$. $\|[Ci]\|$ is the transition system modeling the basic behavior of C_i which we produce thanks to the underlying semantics rules of the modeling language.

We use the hiding operator (note it H) as defined in process algebras to hide actions related to new services, making them unobservable to some clients who still use old services of the refined component. However, new unobservable events are different from internal actions because while the latter are completely under component control, the former events are under control of both the involved component and its environment (i.e. all cooperating components). Accordingly, we handle only unobservable actions since internal events of a component do not affect its external behavior (availability of services) with regards to its users.

Let $N = \Sigma(C_2) - \Sigma(C_1)$ be the set of new services. $H_N(\|[C]\|)$ denotes the behavior model of C where all actions of N are relabeled to τ.

$$H_N(e) = \begin{cases} e & if\ e \notin N \\ \tau & if\ e \in N \end{cases}$$

Below, we give the optimal subtyping relation based on the strong branching bisimulation ($\approx_{sbr}$) making it more faithful in terms of preservation of capabilities for active components [7].

Definition 2. *$C_2 \prec_{sbr} C_1$ if and only if $H_N(\|[C_2]\|) \approx_{sbr} \|[C_1]\|$.*

This definition aims to ensure that the component C_2 behaves as C_1 (in respect of their cooperating environments) whichever the status that C_2 could reach.

Example: The component C_2 depicted by the statechart of Fig.3(b) is a subtype of the component C_1 depicted by the statechart of Fig.3(a) because their behavioral graphs (illustrated respectively by Fig.3(d) & 3(c)) are related (i.e. $\|[C_1]\| \approx_{sbr} H_{\{(e4?;a4!)\}}\|[C_2]\|$).

Every time C_1 is able at a status p_1 (see Fig.3(c)) to interact with its environment (by performing an action $e_2?/a_2!$) and reach some stable status p_2, C_2 should also be able at q_1 (see Fig.3(d)) to do the same interaction and reach an equivalent status to p_2 (q_2 or q'_2) even though after performing an unobservable activity ($e_4?/a_4!$). In this case the intermediate status (q_4) of C_2 should as well be equivalent to the status p_1 of C_1 by offering the same actions $\{e_2?/a_2!, e_3?/a_3!\}$. Indeed, unobservable actions in C_2 have not to affect its capability at the reached status q_4 to simulate what can achieve the earlier component C_1 at its source status p_1. So, intermediate statuses should preserve directly all services that were previously offered or required at the status p_1.

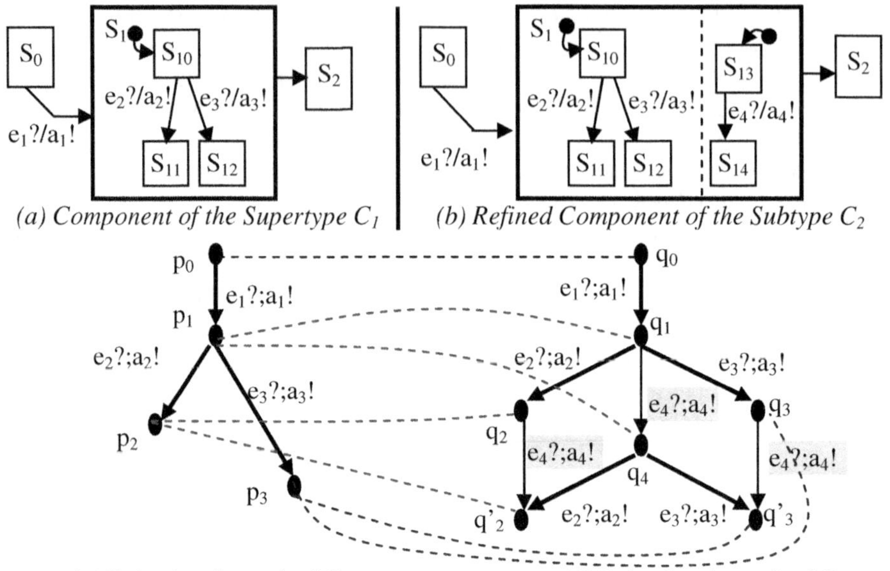

(a) Component of the Supertype C_1 *(b) Refined Component of the Subtype* C_2

(c) Behavioral graph of C_1 *(d) Behavioral graph of* C_2

Fig. 3. Strong Subtyping Relation

On the other hand, a weaker version of our strong subtyping relation given in the following definition agrees much with the subtyping relations of [3,5,6,9].

Definition 3. $C_2 \prec_{br} C_1$ *if and only if* $H_N(\|[C_2]\|) \approx_{br} \|[C_1]\|$.

C_2 behaves as C_1 in respect of C_1 clients but with possibly loss of service availability at some intermediate statuses (see Fig.2). Every time that component C_1 is able from a status s_1 to interact with its environment (by offering or requiring a service e) and reach a stable status s_2, C_2 is also able to perform the same interaction e and then reach an equivalent status of s_2 even though after performing unobservable activities. But, intermediate statuses in C2 are said equivalent to the starting point s_1 of C_1 because they indirectly offer the same actions (i.e. after doing some τ-actions). As intermediate statuses are stable, this means that C_2 may refuse at these points to provide old services to (i.e. react to request events from) any client which still requires them.

3 Compatibility of Subtyping Relations

A system specification is normally given in terms of both behavioral models of its components and assumptions about their intended interactions. We can make use of any state or logic based language to depict interactions properties as pointed out in [7]. As a result, we have to carry out the adequacy checking between new components behaviors and interaction assumptions (i.e., specifications) of old ones [2,7,8].

Our approach sees properties (specifications) as processes which are combined with the component graph and then compared to it. With this intention, we give two definitions of synchronization products between graphs; the first definition compels a full synchronization and the second one allows interleaving of τ-actions too.

Definition 4. *A full synchronization product* $\otimes_f$ *of two graphs* G^1 *and* G^2 *yields a new transition system* $G = <Q, \rightarrow, \Sigma, q_0>$ *such that:* $Q = Q^1 \times Q^2$, $\Sigma = \Sigma^1 \cup \Sigma^2$, $q_0 = (q^1_0, q^2_0)$ *and* $\rightarrow = \{ (p^1,p^2) \xrightarrow{a} (q^1,q^2) \,/\, (p^1 \xrightarrow{a} {}^1q^1) \wedge (p^2 \xrightarrow{a} {}^2q^2) \}$

Definition 5. *A* τ*-synchronization product* $\otimes_\tau$ *of two graphs* G^1 *and* G^2 *yields a new transition system* $G = <Q, \rightarrow, \Sigma, q_0>$ *such that:* $Q = Q^1 \times Q^2$, $\Sigma = \Sigma^1 \cup \Sigma^2$, $q_0 = (q^1_0, q^2_0)$ *and* $\rightarrow = \{(p^1,p^2) \xrightarrow{a} (q^1,q^2) \,/\, (a \neq \tau \wedge (p^1 \xrightarrow{a} {}^1q^1) \wedge (p^2 \xrightarrow{a} {}^2q^2)) \vee (a = \tau \wedge (p^1 \xrightarrow{\tau} {}^1q^1) \vee (p^2 \xrightarrow{\tau} {}^2q^2) \}$.

On checking adequacy, we say that a component C *strongly fulfills* (note it $\models$) its specification (denoted *Spec*) if the full synchronization product of their behavioral models is strongly branching bisimilar to the specification model.

Definition 6. $C \models$ *Spec if and if* $\|[Spec]\| \otimes_f \|[C]\| \approx_{sbr} \|[Spec]\|$.

We say as well that a component C *weakly fulfills* (note it $\models_\tau$) its specification *Spec* if the τ-synchronization product of their behavioral models is branching bisimilar to the specification model.

Definition 7. $C \models_\tau$ *Spec if and if* $\|[Spec]\| \otimes_\tau \|[C]\| \approx_{br} \|[Spec]\|$.

Next, we present some results about compatibility checking between old and new components with reference to interaction assumptions with their environment [7].

Theorem 1. *If* $C_2 \prec_{br} C_1$ *then* $C_1 \models$ *Spec implies* $H_N(C_2) \models_\tau$ *Spec.*
If $C_2 \prec_{sbr} C_1$ *then* $C_1 \models$ *Spec implies* $C_2 \models$ *Spec.*

Proofs. See [7].

When C_2 is a strong subtype of C_1 then whenever C_1 strongly fulfills any specification (property) C_2 does it too. Furthermore, if C_2 is only a weak subtype of C_1 then the fulfillment of *Spec* by C_2 is consequently weakened.

4 New Subtyping Relations within Timed Context

4.1 Preliminary Concepts

The timed behavioral model of a component C is obtained by augmenting each potential transition of the component with a time value depicting the available instant at which it could fire. Such timed graphs might be computed from high level models such as timed automata [1] using inference rules of their operational semantics.

Let $\|[C]\|_T$ be the timed transition system related to C: $\|[C]\|_T = <Q, \rightarrow, \Sigma, q_0>$ where Q is the set of the component statuses (the graph nodes) and $\rightarrow \subseteq Q \times \Sigma \times \Re^{\geq 0} \times Q$ are transitions between nodes such that each transition is labeled with an action ($a \in \Sigma$) that occurs at an absolute instant $d \in \Re^{\geq 0}$ (denoted by $p \xrightarrow{a\,@\,d} p'$)

Subsequently, we can give the timed version of the strong branching bisimulation.

Definition 8. *A timed strong branching bisimulation is a symmetric relation* $R \subseteq Q_1 \times Q_2$, *such that for every* $(p,q) \in Q_1 \times Q_2$, pRq *if and only if:* $\forall a \in \Sigma \cup \{\tau\}$, $\forall p'$:

$p \xrightarrow{a@d} p'$ *then either* $a=\tau$ *and* $p'Rq$

or $a \neq \tau$ *and* $\exists q' \in Q_2$, $d' \in \Re$: $q \xrightarrow{a@d'} q'$ *and* $p'Rq'$ *and either* $(d'=d)$ *or* $(d'<d$ *and* $\exists q_1,\ldots,q_n,q'' \in Q_2$, $\exists d_1 \leq \ldots \leq d_n \leq d$ *such that:* $q \xrightarrow{\tau@d_1} q_1 \ldots q_{n-1} \xrightarrow{\tau@d_n} q_n \xrightarrow{a@d} q''$ *and* $p'Rq''$ *and* $\forall i=1..n$: $pRq_i)$.

Graphs G_1 & G_2 *are strongly timed branching bisimilar* ($G_1 \approx_{tsbr} G_2$) *if* $q_0^1 \approx_{tsbr} q_0^2$.

As in the untimed case, two LTS states *p* and *q* are equivalent if they can perform the same observable actions in order to reach pairs of states which are always equivalent. If we can obtain some state p' by one τ-step from *p* then *p'* should be also equivalent to the *q*. Moreover, if the state *p* can do some action ($a \neq \tau$) at an instant *d*, then its equivalent state *q* can do the same action "*a*" either at the same instant *d* or at instant $d'<d$ but as well the same action indirectly at *d* after achieving some τ-actions.

This constraint is so far due to the fact that an unobservable action represents a new service that is not visible to clients of the previous component. So though it occurs, these clients should always be able to use the old service which was available before the τ-progress and at the same time instants.

4.2 Strong Timed Subtyping Relation

Behavioral substitutability of components is based in the timed context on the idea that the refined component should offer the same reactivity capabilities of its previous component at the same time occurrences even if the new component is enhanced by some new functions.

Therefore, we adapt Definition 2 of the subtyping relation by using our timed version ($\approx_{tsbr}$) of strong branching bisimulation making it more faithful in terms of preservation of capabilities even throughout time progress.

Definition 9. $C_2 \prec_{tsbr} C_1$ *if and if* $H_N(\|[C_2]\|_T) \approx_{tsbr} \|[C_1]\|_T$.

The main target of this definition is to ensure that C_2 behaves as C_1 (in respect of an old client) whatever the status and the time that the component C_2 has reached.

Proposition 1. $C_2 \prec_{tsbr} C_1$ *implies* $C_2 \prec_{sbr} C_1$.

Proof sketch. *To prove this property, it is enough to prove that:* $\|[C_1]\|_T \approx_{tsbr} \|[C_2]\|_T$ *implies* $\|[C_1]\| \approx_{sbr} \|[C_2]\|$ *.This is can be achieved inductively by proving that if* $(p \approx_{tsbr} q)$ *then* $(p \approx_{sbr} q)$.

Hence, we assume that $p \approx_{sbr} q$ *and we prove that for each pair of transitions* $p \xrightarrow{a@d} p'$ *and* $q \xrightarrow{a@d} q'$ *we have* $p' \approx_{sbr} q'$

<u>*First case (definition of* $\approx_{tsbr}$*):*</u> *if* $p \xrightarrow{a@d} p'$ *and* $a=\tau$ *then* $p' \approx_{tsbr} q$

However, inference rules of the operational semantics of timed automata [1] allow us to deduce that we have in $\|[C_1]\|$ *the transition* $p \xrightarrow{a} p'$.

Considering the hypothesis $p \approx_{sbr} q$ *we obtain* $p' \approx_{sbr} q$ *even though after a* τ*-action in respect of Definition 1 of* $\approx_{sbr}$.

<u>*Second case:*</u> *If* $p \xrightarrow{a\,@\,d} p'$ *and* $a \neq \tau$ *then either* $(\exists q': q \xrightarrow{a\,@\,d} q'$ *and* $p'Rq')$ *or* $(\exists q', d': q \xrightarrow{a\,@\,d'} q'$ $(d' < d)$ *and* $p'Rq'$ *and* $\exists q_1, \ldots, q_n, q'' \in Q_2$, $\exists d_1 \leq \ldots \leq d_n \leq d$ *such that:* $q \xrightarrow{\tau\,@\,d_1} q_1 \ldots q_{n-1} \xrightarrow{\tau\,@\,d_n} q_n \xrightarrow{a\,@\,d} q''$ *and* $p'Rq''$ *and* $\forall i=1..n: pRq_i)$.

However, with regards to inference rules of the operational semantics of timed automata [1], we will have in $\|[C_1]\|$ *the transition* $p \xrightarrow{a} p'$ *and in* $\|[C_2]\|$ *the transition* $q \xrightarrow{a} q'$ *(which occur at instant* $d' < d$*). Considering the premise* $p \approx_{sbr} q$ *and Definition 1, we get* $p' \approx_{sbr} q'$*. Moreover, all statuses reached through* τ*-actions in* $\|[C_2]\|$ *before executing a, are equivalent to p (i.e. they have the same capabilities as p).*

Remark: In view of Proposition1, we deduce immediately that Theorem 1 (about consistency of subtyping relations) holds also in the timed case.

4.3 Consistency with Temporal Specifications

Time and duration constraints are usually given as formulas of the form "ϕ: $\#a - \#b \leq d$" where "$\#a$" (resp. $\#b$) denotes the occurrence instant of action "a" (resp."b"). We denote by "$C \models \phi$" the assumption that in each path of the graph $\|[C]\|_T$, the distance between the occurrence times of some actions a and b is always less or equal than d.

Proposition 2. *Let* $C_2 \prec_{tsbr} C_1$*. If* ϕ *contains actions only of* C_1, $C_1 \models \phi$ *implies* $C_2 \models \phi$.

Proof sketch. *We have* $C_1 \models \phi$ *and we assume that* $C_2 \not\models \phi$*. Then, there should be some path* π *in* $H_N(\|[C_2]\|_T)$ *such that:* π: $q_1 \xrightarrow{a\,@\,d_1} q_2 \ldots q_{n-1} \xrightarrow{b\,@\,d_n} q_n$ *and* $d_n - d_1 > d$ *with possibly some transitions labeled with* τ*-actions between* q_2 *and* q_{n-1}.

As $C_2 \prec_{tsbr} C_1$ *(i.e.,* $H_N(\|[C_2]\|_T) \approx_{tsbr} \|[C_1]\|_T$*) and following Definition 8, we deduce that an equivalent path* π' *exists in* $\|[C_1]\|_T$ *such that:* π': $p_1 \xrightarrow{a\,@\,d_1} p_2 \ldots p_{m-1} \xrightarrow{b\,@\,d_m} p_m$ $(m \leq n) \wedge q_1 \approx_{tsbr} p_1 \wedge q_2 \approx_{tsbr} p_2 \wedge$ *for each i=2..n-1 we have two cases:*

- *There is one transition* $q_i \xrightarrow{x\,@\,di} q_{i+1}$ $(i=2..n-1)$ *with* $x \neq \tau$ *and* $q_i \approx_{tsbr} p_k$ $(2 \leq k \leq m)$*. So, we have in* π' *a transition* $p_k \xrightarrow{x\,@\,d_k} p_{k+1}$ *with* $q_{i+1} \approx_{tsbr} p_{k+1}$ *and* $d_i = d_k$ *(according to* $\approx_{tsbr}$*).*

– *There is a sequence of transitions* q_i===τ@d===>$q_{j-1}\xrightarrow{x\,@\,d_j} q_j$ *(i=2..n-1) with* $x\neq\tau$ *and* $q_i\approx_{tsbr} p_k$ $(2\leq k\leq m)$*. So, we have in* π' *a transition* $p_k\xrightarrow{x\,@\,d_k} p_{k+1}$ *with* $q_j\approx_{tsbr} p_{k+1}$ *and* $d_j=d_k$ *according to* $\approx_{tsbr}$*.(Moreover, for all l such that* $i+1\leq l\leq j-1$ *we have* $q_l\approx_{tsbr} p_k$ *such that* $d_l\leq d_k$*).*

By running inductively these two cases, we deduce finally that $q_n\approx_{tsbr} p_m$ *and* $d_n=d_m$*. Consequently,* $d_m - d_1= d_n - d_1>d$ *and hence we obtain* $C_1 \not\models \phi$ *which contradicts our premise.*

4.4 Weak Timed Subtyping Relation

We give below a weak version of the aforementioned timed subtyping relation using simulation preorders.

Definition 10. *A strong timed simulation is an asymmetric relation* $\lesssim_1\ \subseteq Q_1\times Q_2$*, such that for every* $(p,q)\in Q_1\times Q_2$*,* $p\lesssim_1 q$ *(q strongly simulates p) if and only if:* $\forall a\in\Sigma\cup\{\tau\}$*,* $\forall p' : p\xrightarrow{a\,@\,d} p'$ *then either* $a=\tau$ *and* $p'\lesssim_1 q$ *or* $\exists q'\in Q_2$*:* $q\xrightarrow{a\,@\,d} q'$ *and* $p'\lesssim_1 q'$*.*

Definition 11. *A weak timed simulation is an asymmetric relation* $\lesssim_2\ \subseteq Q_1\times Q_2$*, such that for every* $(p,q)\in Q_1\times Q_2$*,* $p\lesssim_2 q$ *(q weakly simulates p) if and only if:* $\forall a\in\Sigma\cup\{\tau\}$*,* $\forall p' : p\xrightarrow{a\,@\,d} p'$ *then either* $a=\tau$ *and* $p'\lesssim_2 q$

or $\exists q'\in Q_2$*,* $d'\in\Re$*:* $q\xrightarrow{a\,@\,d'} q'$ *and* $p'\lesssim_2 q'$ *and either (d'=d) or (d'<d and* $\exists q_1,\ldots,q_n,q''\in Q_2$*,* $\exists d_1\leq\ldots\leq d_n\leq d$ *such that:* $q\xrightarrow{\tau\,@\,d_1} q_1\ldots q_{n-1}\xrightarrow{\tau\,@\,d_n} q_n\xrightarrow{a\,@\,d} q''$ *and* $p'\lesssim_2 q''$ *and* $\forall i=1..n$*:* $p\lesssim_2 q_i$*).*

A graph G_2 strongly simulates G_1, $(G_1\lesssim_1 G_2)$ when $q_0^1\lesssim_1 q_0^2$.
A graph G_2 weakly simulates G_1, $(G_1\lesssim_2 G_2)$ when $q_0^1\lesssim_2 q_0^2$.

Definition 12. C_2 *is a (weakly timed) subtype of* C_1 $(C_2\prec_{wtbr}C_1)$ *if and only if* $H_N(\|[C_2]\|_T)\lesssim_1\|[C_1]\|_T$ *and* $\|[C_1]\|_T\lesssim_2 H_N(\|[C_2]\|_T)$*.*

The refined component strongly simulates its predecessor but this latter weakly simulates the former one. Indeed, faithful preservation of old capabilities is more suited in one forward direction.

Proposition 3. $C_2\prec_{wtbr} C_1$ *implies* $C_2\prec_{sbr} C_1$*.*

The proof of this proposition is similar to that of Proposition 1.

Remark: Following Proposition 3, Theorem 1 about consistency of subtyping relations holds as well in this weak timed case.

5 Conclusion

In this paper, we have presented a new approach for substitutability checking based on strong assumptions of service availability and correctness properties mainly in reactive and time constrained systems. We have dealt with this issue with respect to the untimed and timed semantics. In all cases, the new services in refined components are concealed in respect of old clients. However, our subtyping relations preserve the availability of old services even though the control is in some intermediate states along a chain of τ-steps. Moreover, we have proved that new components continue preserve properties that old components fulfill in interaction with their environment.

Concerning future works, we plan to proceed to the timing constraints analysis in asynchronous transition systems in relation to two fields: temporal consistency analysis and scheduling issue. We plan as well to find out what effects of step semantics on substitutability of components.

References

1. Alur, R., Dill, D.: A theory of timed automata. Theoretical Computer Science 126, 183–235 (1994)
2. Sharygina, N., Chaki, S., Clarke, E., Sinha, N.: Dynamic Component Substitutability Analysis. In: Fitzgerald, J.S., Hayes, I.J., Tarlecki, A. (eds.) FM 2005. LNCS, vol. 3582, pp. 512–528. Springer, Heidelberg (2005)
3. Fischer, C., Wehrheim, H.: Behavioural Subtyping Relations for Object-Oriented Formalisms. In: Rus, T. (ed.) AMAST 2000. LNCS, vol. 1816, pp. 469–483. Springer, Heidelberg (2000)
4. van Glabbeek, R.: The linear time–branching time spectrum. In: Handbook of Process Algebra, pp. 3–99 (1999)
5. Hameurlain, N.: Behavioural subtyping and Property Preservation for Active Objects. In: Proc. of FMOODS 2002 (2002)
6. Hameurlain, N.: On Compatibility and Behavioural substitutability of Component Protocols. In: Proc. of Intl. Conference Software Engineering & Formal Methods, SEFM 2005 (2005)
7. Hammal, Y.: Substitutability Relations for Active Components. In: Proc. of the 4th Workshop on Formal Aspects of Component Software, France, September 19-21 (2007)
8. Liskov, B.H., Wing, J.M.: A Behavioral Notion of Subtyping. ACM Transactions on Programming Languages and Systems 16(6), 1811–1841 (1994)
9. Wehrheim, A.: Checking Behavioural subtypes via Refinement. In: Proc. of FMOODS 2002 (2002)

A Quantitative Analysis of Semantic Information Retrieval Research Progress in China

Xiaoyue Wang, Rujiang Bai, and Liyun Kang

Institute of Scientific & Technical Information, Shandong University of Technology, Zibo 255049, China
{wangxy,brj,kangly}@sdut.edu.cn

Abstract. The main goal of this paper is to mine the research progress and future trends in semantic information retrieval in China. Totally 550 papers about the semantic information retrieval papers were collected from CNKI academic database. Bibliometric analysis method and social network analysis software were employed. We drew the annual numbers of table, the paper sources distribution table, the authors distribution table, the themes distribution table and co-occurrence network of high-frequency keywords. Though these tables and graphics, the main conclusion is that semantic information retrieval research are relatively weak force in China. We should construct many research groups on semantic information retrieval and followed by international development.

Keywords: semantic information retrieval, information retrieval, semantic web, ontology.

1 Introduction

At present, information retrieval, regardless of the use of metadata or the use of full-text retrieval of information resources, are based on matching text strings. However, the statistical sense of the word form matching is difficult to achieve effective retrieval of information resources used at the same time, the natural language of uncertainty greatly limits the retrieval precision and recall rates. Semantic retrieval as a new information retrieval technology, which can understand and knowledge in the knowledge based on the reasoning of accurate and comprehensive information resources to retrieve. Semantic retrieval of information resources is concerned about the potential of semantics, rather than remain in the text surface, thus ensuring the quality of information retrieval. Semantic retrieval is actually based on the concept of matching the search [1], is for keyword-based matching retrieval of their argument. Semantic Web development and application of ontologies for the semantic retrieval research and development has opened up a new path. With the development of Semantic Web technologies, semantic search has become a hotspot, its designed to overcome the limitations of traditional search technology to support knowledge retrieval [2]. Currently, research in the context of the Semantic Web ontology-based semantic retrieval has become a hotspot, domestic semantic retrieval research is still in its infancy, so the semantic retrieval research for quantitative analysis and summary of important practical significance and significance.

T.-h. Kim et al. (Eds.): ASEA/DRBC/EL 2011, CCIS 257, pp. 36–45, 2011.

In this paper, bibliometric of the domestic statistics related to semantic retrieval research papers to reveal the status of research in this area, research focus and development trends, and prospects for its development trend.

2 Data Sources and Analysis Methods

The data collected from "China Academic Journal Full-text database (CJFD)" "Chinese dissertation Full-text database", "Chinese conference papers Full-text database ". A total of 550 retrieved documents. There are 537 papers after screened. Table 1 shows the screened papers.

Table 1. Data samples retrieved

database	Search terms	Search words	Period	Numbers
China Academic Journal Full-text database (CJFD)	subject	Semantic retrieval	1995-2010	347
Chinese dissertation Full-text database	titles	Semantic retrieval	1999-2010	56
Chinese conference papers Full-text database	subject	Semantic retrieval	2000-2010	134

<Retrieval time: 2011.6.9>

After these research papers collected. In order to have an intuitive understanding of the current research situation, we plotted the distribution of the annual number of tables, paper source distribution table and he authors distributed table. At the same time, sort out the data for statistical sample pretreatment, using Bibexcel statistical occurrence frequency of data words and construct high-frequency words co-occurrence matrix, and then, using Ucinet and Netdraw software for data analysis and visualization capabilities to draw high Keywords co-occurrence frequency network can view. This co-occurrence network diagram with the main distribution table, thereby thematic analysis of research to understand the semantic retrieval research focus and focus, an accurate grasp of the current research status and level.

3 Statistical Results and Analysis

3.1 Distribution of Annual Statistics

Semantic retrieval-related papers published age distribution, to a certain extent, can reflect the status of semantic retrieval research and development speed. 537 papers selected in this paper the specific age distribution in Table 2.

Table 2 Statistics show that the semantic retrieval of relevant papers showing the distribution of the annual number of significant growth and phase characteristics. Thus domestic semantic retrieval can be divided into three stages: (1) the initial phase (1995-2000): This stage retrieves the domestic semantic horizon, not much research,

Table 2. Distribution of the number of published semantic retrieval papers by annual

Year	Number	Percent (%)
1995	1	0.19
1996	1	0.19
1997	0	0
1998	0	0
1999	1	0.19
2000	2	0.38
2001	11	2.05
2002	14	2.61
2003	10	1.86
2004	28	5.21
2005	45	8.38
2006	70	13.03
2007	97	18.06
2008	107	19.93
2009	99	18.44
2010	51	9.50
total	537	100

accounting for 0.95%. (2) the steady development phase (2001-2003): This phase fluctuations in the overall number of research papers is not, in the steady stage of development, accounting for 6.52% of total, indicating that paying attention to the academic study of semantic retrieval. (3) surge phase (2004-2010): semantic search-related proliferation of research papers, the annual amount of basically published a document a rapid increase in the number of papers at this stage to the statistics about the total number of 92.53%, indicating that the semantic retrieval in recent years into the hot spots of the study period. The reason, as the exponential growth of information resources, particularly in mass rapid growth of unstructured data sources, statistical significance based on the traditional word-based matching information retrieval approaches have failed to meet the search requirements, researchers have begun to shift the study of semantic retrieval.

It can also be seen from Table 2, the domestic research on the semantic retrieval starting point began to develop rapidly in 2001, indicating that the domestic research in this area is still in a relatively short history, still in its infancy, research space and are more difficult large.

3.2 Statistical Distribution by the Source Papers

Semantic retrieval of papers related to statistical analysis is to understand the source of semantic retrieval and effective distribution of research methods, it is beneficial for the semantic retrieval research data collection, collation and research, thus contributing to the area to conduct a comprehensive, in-depth study, paper source distribution is shown in table 3.

Table 3. Papers Source Distribution Table

Source	Number	Percent (%)
China Academic Journal Full-text database	347	61.62
Chinese dissertation Full-text database	56	10.43
Chinese conference papers Full-text database	134	27.95

As can be seen from Table 3 the amount of academic journals published papers in an absolutely dominant position, accounting for 61.62% of total published papers, but the amount of conference papers are also published of the total accounted for 27.95%, indicating that the semantic retrieval research by academics highly valued, published from dissertations can be seen that the proportion of the amount of semantic retrieval research attention began to be graduate, has started to become graduate thesis topics of the target.

To further understand the semantic retrieval research group of core journals, 347 academic journal on statistics, found mainly on published in 152 journals, including the top 12 journals in Table 4, 7.89% of total number of published, papers were included 146, accounting for 42.07% of total papers, indicating that more than 40% of papers published in less than 8% of the small number of journals, the 12 journals that semantic retrieval is to study the core journals. Table 4 also shows the semantic retrieval research focuses on computer journals and LIS journals.

Table 4. Top 12 journals

ID	Title	Published papers	Percent (%)
1	Library and Information Technology	24	6.92
2	Computer Engineering and Applications	15	4.32
3	Computer Engineering	14	4.03
4	Computer Technology and Development	14	4.03
5	Computer Science	13	3.75
6	Computer Engineering and Design	12	3.46
7	Journal Information	12	3.46
8	Information Science	11	3.17
9	Micro-computer information	9	2.59
10	Computer Applications	8	2.31
11	Intelligence Theory and Practice	7	2.02
12	Library and Information	7	2.02

3.3 Distribution Statistics by Authors

Scientific papers to measure the level of cooperation commonly used indicator is the cooperation rate, the rate may reflect the areas of cooperation in other areas of intersection with the situation and the depth of field of study. This semantic retrieval of statistical data in the field of co-authors in Table 5.

Table 5. Situation of co-authors

co-authors	1	2	3	4	5	6	7
The number of published papers	137	158	132	65	30	13	2

In the 537 research papers, the independent author of 137, accounting for 25.51% of the total, 2 and 3 have 290 partners, accounting for 54% of the total number of authors published papers, four or more partners 110, accounted for 20.48% of total papers. Collaboration paper 400, paper co-operation was 74.49%, of which there are two papers in collaboration with seven. Semantic retrieval research shows a high level of cooperation is a need for interdisciplinary exchange and cooperation in comprehensive fields of study.

The statistics show that by 1324 the total number of people, which published papers in four and more than 13 people (not limited to the first author), the total number of 0.98% of total published papers 54, accounting for 10.06% of total published papers specific distribution in Table 6.

Table 6. Published 4 and more papers distribution table

Authors name	Papers	Affiliation
Chun-Sheng Ding	6	Nanjing University of Science
Dou Yong Xiang	4	Xi'an University of Electronic Science and Technology
Cheng Cheng	4	Anhui University
Gan Win	4	Nanjing University of Science
Jiao Yuying	4	Wuhan University
Zhang Lu	4	Wuhan University
Gu Germany visit	4	Nanjing University of Science
Guo Li	4	Chinese Academy of Sciences
YAO Tian Fang	4	Shanghai Jiao Tong University
Dongfeng Cai	4	Shenyang Institute of Aeronautical Engineering
Zhou Xiangdong	4	Fudan University
Shi Bole	4	Fudan University
Zhang Liang	4	Fudan University

3.4 Statistical Analysis of the Distribution

Search keyword is the paper's logo, the word is to express the theme of the concept of natural language words can be simple, direct, more comprehensive overview of the core research content paper [3]. In this paper, 537 research papers keywords statistics are summarized as follows in Table 7. Statistics of words can reflect the research focus, while the total collection of keyword analysis can now determine the links between words in order to better study the subject of analysis. Thematic analysis to some extent can reflect the semantic search a hot research area and focus will help to understand its current status and level of research and help researchers to correctly predict trends in the field and direction.

Frequency of use Bibexcel software four times and four times in the above words twenty-two matching, statistical co-occurrence frequency of its output high-frequency words co-occurrence matrix, and then use Ucinet software and Netdraw software to draw words co-occurrence network, take a total of more than 2 times the current number of nodes to display, high-frequency words were now to be the network can view, shown in Figure 1. Nodes in the figure the greater the extent that the higher centers; the thickness of the connection between the nodes between nodes reflects the frequency of the current, line frequency, the higher the more rough, then the closer the links between nodes.

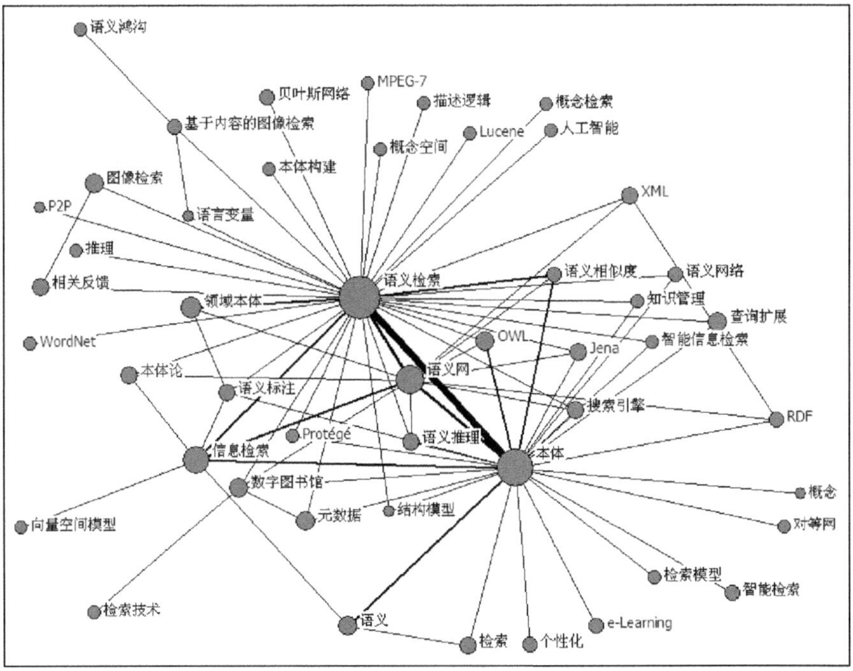

Fig. 1. High-frequency words co-occurrence visual network

From Fig.1 , Table 7 and the background matrix combination, domestic scholars in the semantic retrieval research focuses on semantics, ontology and retrieval applications. In the Semantic Web environment, the research is based on ontology in order to achieve semantic retrieval can be applied to the semantic retrieval system is the main line. In the semantic level, semantic retrieval research is focused on the Semantic Web, semantic similarity, semantic annotation and so on. Among them, the Semantic Web is a research priority, the Semantic Web as information resource description, storage and semantic-based reasoning and information security providing a set of

Table 7. Subject statistics about semantic research papers

Research class	subject	Keywords count
Theory research	semantic	Semantic retrieval （190） 、semantic web （82） 、semantic relevance （28） 、semantic annotation （26） 、semantic reasoning （9） 、semantic index （8） 、latent semantic （8） 、semantic model （7） 、image senmaitc （6） 、latent semantic index （5） 、high level semantic （4）
	ontology	ontology （207） 、Area ontology （30） 、XML(27)、OWL （18） 、conception （15） 、ontology theory （11） 、RDF （11） 、construct ontology （4） 、conception network （4）
Application research	Information retrieval	Information retrieval （98） 、image retrieval （41） 、digital library （15） 、search expansion （14） 、relevance back （13） 、SVM （12） 、meta data （11） 、intelligence search （10） 、search engineering （9） 、knowledge manager （8） 、retrieval model （6） 、knowledge search （6） 、knowledge service （5） 、intelligence knowledge search （5） 、knowledge extraction （4） 、conception search （4） 、search technology （4）

safeguards. Semantic search around the body of research focused on the domain ontology, ontology language (XML, OWL, RDF), the concept and so on. At present, how to build a comprehensive body of knowledge is the focus of the current semantic retrieval and difficult [4]. In applied research, semantic retrieval as information retrieval, a new technology, search technology designed to overcome the traditional limitations of string-based matching to support intelligent retrieval, knowledge retrieval. Table 7 also shows that semantic retrieval can be applied to digital libraries, knowledge management and other specific applications

4 Semantic Retrieval Research Status and Future Trends

4.1 Semantic Retrieval Research

Through the semantic retrieval research papers on quantitative analysis, we can see that the semantic retrieval research is still in its infancy, research space and are more difficult. We concluded that the current status and semantic retrieval research focused on the problems faced in the following areas.

(1) Study start later and lack of comprehensive research methods
Number of papers from the annual statistics table shows the distribution of the domestic research on the semantic retrieval starting point began to develop rapidly in 2001, also dating back about 10 years, explaining the short history of research in this area, still in its infancy . February 2001 with the formal launch of the W3C Semantic Web Activity, Semantic retrieval network environment into the mainstream of network research and development [5]. Semantic search techniques and methods, especially for the semantic retrieval of network information resources is the field of information retrieval research priorities and hot spots, but has yet to form a complete research methods. Only by strengthening the knowledge base to build the ontology, semantic web, semantic layer of natural language processing, semantic similarity calculation, semantic annotation and other specific aspects of research, a scientific comprehensive study methodology in order to make rapid and sound development of the semantic retrieval research.

(2) The gap between theoretical and applied research
With the rapid development of Semantic Web and the wide application of ontologies, semantic retrieval has been developed. From the above statistical analysis of topics can be seen, semantic web and semantic retrieval ontology constitute the two pillars of theoretical research, semantic retrieval research in these areas has also made great progress. However, the semantic retrieval research in the theory advanced in applied research, the semantic retrieval system is currently seen in both the retrieval process and the mode of introduction of new elements, but also to a large extent similar to the traditional retrieval system [6]. To truly different from traditional information retrieval systems, and can be applied to the actual semantic retrieval system, the depth of excavation should be the semantics behind the word form, explore the retrieval based on semantic matching technology to support the concept of retrieval, knowledge retrieval to a greater extent the intelligent retrieval. Meanwhile, the search system to quickly and accurately determine the user's query request implicit semantics is an important problem to solve this problem of query recall and precision rate is critical [7].

(3) There are weak research group
In the semantic retrieval research subject is to promote the development of the direct agents of the semantic search, semantic search research and development constitute the most important mechanism of intrinsic motivation, therefore, semantic retrieval strength is directly determines the semantic retrieval research status and future of internal. With the Semantic Web development, although the semantic search has become a hotspot, but the distribution of the table can be seen from the author, at present, the semantic retrieval research efforts are relatively weak, mainly in one of the few institutions of higher learning in the. As a result, should further strengthen the semantic retrieval research, and enable the rapid development of semantic search to be to best meet people's urgent need for efficient retrieval.

4.2 Semantic Retrieval Development Trends

Semantic retrieval compared to traditional information retrieval, mainly in its progress to express and deal with information content-based semantic matching and semantic reasoning, to effectively improve the retrieval efficiency. The growing mass of unstructured data in the context of semantic retrieval than traditional information retrieval demonstrated the superiority is bound to cause more and more attention. In order to realize the semantics used in the actual retrieval system, semantic retrieval research priorities and trends summed up mainly includes the following aspects.

(1) Build a comprehensive database of knowledge
Semantic representation of the ontology bear the mission-critical, in order to improve the semantic retrieval recall and precision rates, and must rely on the comprehensive body of scientific and rational knowledge. Build a comprehensive database of knowledge related to: ontology language, ontology creation and storage problems, ontology design and technology knowledge base, ontology compatibility conflicts, knowledge of domain ontology construction method and other issues. Establishment of a comprehensive ontology of knowledge is a very difficult thing, this is the current semantic search technology problems to be solved [8].

(2) The need to strengthen the semantic retrieval of semantic natural language processing
User issues a query request, the retrieval system to quickly and accurately determine the user's query request implicit semantics is an important problem to solve this problem of query recall rate and precision is essential. Complex natural language greatly limits the retrieval precision and recall rate, reasonable and effective natural language processing is very important. Natural language processing is not only the concept of extraction, but should be at a higher level understanding of natural language semantics, where the key is the information resource for semantic annotation, semantic indexing and reasoning in the semantic annotation based on the full use of information and full text information, According to the semantics of natural language allows a more accurate search results.

(3) Further strengthen the scientific and effective reasoning mechanism
Ontology-based semantic retrieval system in addition to using the Jena inference engine or a third party's own inference engine, can also be defined according to application needs its own rules of inference. Retrieval system based on user interests, add personalized inference rules to meet different needs, so that the results more comprehensive and accurate. With domain ontology, semantic retrieval of description logic-based reasoning and fuzzy description logic, description logic based ontology to improve reasoning reasoning effect, expand the scope of its inference algorithm, access to semantic information retrieval with text to enhance the user queries demand accuracy [9].

5 Conclusion

Vast amounts of unstructured data in the context of rapid growth, as people's increasing demand for information and social information, knowledge, intelligence, information retrieval technology has been progress, from the development of information retrieval based on keywords to the current semantic retrieval. Currently under study and use of information retrieval technology can be divided into three categories [10]: full-text search, data retrieval and semantic retrieval. Of these, only semantic retrieval is based on the knowledge, semantic matching, to improve retrieval precision and recall rates have a very good performance [11]. Although the semantic retrieval research is still in its infancy, but as people continued to deepen their research, semantic retrieval in information retrieval play an increasingly important role.

Acknowledgments. This work was supported by Shandong Provincial Natural Science Foundation(ZR2009GM015), National Social Science Foundation(10BTQ047), Young Teacher Development Support Program of Shandong University of Technology.

References

1. Li, Z., Tao, W.: Semantic retrieval. Information Science 20(11), 1190–1192 (2002)
2. Huang, M., Lai, M.: Semantic retrieval Research. Library and Information Service 52(6), 63–66 (2008)
3. Xu, Y.X.: Zhang is more flat, Li Xiaofei based on key words and Information Science Research. Statistical Analysis of Intelligence 28(11), 38–41 (2009)
4. Wang, X., Hu, Z., Bai, R., Mou, Y.: Automatic semantic retrieval and visualization model based on the integrated ontology library. Journal of Computational Information Systems 6(1), 139–145 (2010)
5. Zhang, X.: Semantic Web and Semantic Web-based information retrieval. Intelligence (8), 413–420 (2002)
6. Mei, X.: Semantic search in a number of key issues. PhD thesis, Beijing University of Posts and Telecommunications (2007)
7. Kerschberg, L., Kim, W., Scime, A.: A Personalizable Agent for Semantic Taxonomy-Based Web Search. In: Truszkowski, W., Hinchey, M., Rouff, C.A. (eds.) WRAC 2002. LNCS, vol. 2564, pp. 3–34. Springer, Heidelberg (2003)
8. Wen, H., Yue, W.: 1998-2008 study abroad application of quantitative analysis and ontology visualization of the modern library and information technique (12), 25–30 (2009)
9. Wen, M.K., Lu, Z.-D., Sun, X., Li, R.: Semantic search reviews of Computer Science 35(5), 1–4 (2008)
10. Guarino, N., Masolo, C., Vetere, G.: OntoSeek: Content-Based Access to the Web. IEEE Intelligent Systems 14(3), 70–80 (1999)
11. Gu visit. Semantic Web environment for semantic retrieval ontology-based applied research. Master's thesis, Nanjing University of Technology (2005)

Applying Evolutionary Approaches to Data Flow Testing at Unit Level

Shaukat Ali Khan and Aamer Nadeem

Center for Software Dependability, Mohammad Ali Jinnah University (MAJU), Islamabad, Pakistan

shaukatali74@hotmail.com, anadeem@jinnah.edu.pk

Abstract. Data flow testing is a white box testing approach that uses the dataflow relations in a program for the selection of test cases. Evolutionary testing uses the evolutionary approaches for the generation and selection of test data. This paper presents a novel approach applying evolutionary algorithms for the automatic generation of test paths using data flow relations in a program. Our approach starts with a random initial population of test paths and then based on the selected testing criteria new paths are generated by applying a genetic algorithm. A fitness function evaluates each chromosome (path) based on the selected data flow testing criteria and computes its fitness. We have applied one point crossover and mutation operators for the generation of new population. The approach has been implemented in Java by a prototype tool called ETODF for validation. In experiments with this prototype, our approach has much better results as compared to random testing.

Keywords: Data Flow Testing, Genetic Algorithm, Test Paths, Coverage Criteria, Mutation, Crossover.

1 Introduction

Software testing is the process of executing a program with the intent of finding errors [21]. It is an important and expensive phase of software development lifecycle. Software test case design is the most important and crucial part of software testing. Test case design approaches have been broadly categorized into two major categories, i.e., white box testing and black box testing. With black box testing, test cases are derived from specification of the program under test and in white box testing test cases are derived from code of the program. Black box testing tests the functionality of the system while white box testing checks the logic of the program. White box testing is further categorized into control flow and data flow testing. Control flow testing uses control flow graph for testing [20]. In control flow graph, a node corresponds to a code segment; nodes are labeled using letters or numbers. An edge corresponds to flow of control between code segments; edges are represented as arrows. There is an entry and exit point in a control flow graph. Control flow testing criteria include statement coverage, decision coverage, condition coverage etc. Data flow testing uses the dataflow relations in a program for the generation and selection

T.-h. Kim et al. (Eds.): ASEA/DRBC/EL 2011, CCIS 257, pp. 46–55, 2011.

of test cases. Data flow testing verifies the definition and usage of program variables in desired way. The purpose of data flow testing is to identify the data flow anomalies in the software. Most of the data flow anomalies can be identified by static analysis of the program. The purpose of data flow testing is to find faults due to incorrect use of variables as well as due to anomalies. Dynamic data flow testing uses different coverage criteria for the execution of different paths in data flow testing [21]. Automated test case design is the most challenging task in structural testing of software. Different approaches have been developed for automated test case design and data generation in structural testing [20] [21].

Evolutionary algorithms [13] have been applied to software testing for automated generation of test cases and test data. The application of evolutionary algorithms to software testing for generation of test data is known as evolutionary testing. They include genetic algorithms, particle swarm optimization, ant colony model etc. Evolutionary algorithms have been applied in software testing at various levels from procedural to object oriented programming. Application of evolutionary testing is mostly on control flow testing. In this paper, we have proposed a novel approach that uses the genetic algorithm for the generation for test paths in data flow testing at unit level. We have applied evolutionary approaches to data flow testing for the generation of test paths. Our approach has two phases, the first phase consists of test paths generation using genetic algorithm while the second phase involves identifying the infeasible. This paper presents the first phase of our approach of path selection using a genetic algorithm. The approach has been implemented in Java language by a prototype tool called ETODF for validation. In experiments with this prototype, our approach has much better results as compared to random testing [10][11][12].

The rest of the paper is organized as follows: Section 2 elaborates the survey of different techniques proposed for Software testing using evolutionary approaches, section 3 describes the proposed approach based on data flow testing using evolutionary approaches and Section 4 represents the tool ETODF and section 5 is related with experiments and testing results as in comparison with random testing. Section 6 concludes the paper and presents the future work.

2 Related Work

Tonella [16] performed the unit testing of classes using genetic algorithm. In this approach test cases are generated for unit testing of classes using genetic algorithm. Test cases are designed in the form of chromosomes, each chromosome contains information regarding which objects to create, which methods to invoke and which values to use as inputs. The recombination and mutation operators are designed for proposed algorithm to achieve maximum coverage.

McMinn and Holcombe [9] proposed a solution for the state problem in evolutionary testing using ant colony model. The presence of states in test object can render impossible the search for test objects using evolutionary algorithms. McMinn and Holcombe [9] also proposed an extended chaining approach for the solution of state problem in evolutionary testing. The basic idea of the chaining approach is to find a sequence of statements, involving internal variables, which needs to be executed prior to the test goal.

Watkins [17] performed various experiments to compare different fitness functions proposed by different researchers. They suggested that branch predicate and inverse path probability approaches were the best fitness function as compared to other approaches.

Wegener et al. [18] [19] proposed an automatic structural testing environment in their work. The testing environment has many components and each component is specialized for a particular functionality. This environment provides automatic test for structural testing. They also proposed the same environment for automatic testing of embedded systems.

Baresel et al. [1] suggest some modifications in fitness function design to improve evolutionary structural testing. A well constructed function can increase the chance of finding the solution and reach a better coverage of the software under test and result in a better guidance of the search and thus in optimizations with less iteration.

McMinn [10] provides a comprehensive survey on evolutionary testing approaches and discusses the application of evolutionary testing. The author discusses the different approaches in which evolutionary testing has been applied and also provides future directions in each individual area.

Evolutionary approaches are mostly used in the area of automated test data generation [8] [11] [13] [14] [15] [17]. Cheon et al. [3] [4] proposed a specification based fitness function for evolutionary testing of object oriented program. They also proposed automation of Java program testing at unit level using evolutionary approaches. Dharsana et al. [5] generate test cases for Java based programs and also performed optimization of test cases using genetic algorithm. Jones et al. [6] performed automatic structural testing using genetic algorithm in their approach. Bilal and Nadeem [2] proposed a state based fitness function for object oriented programs using genetic algorithm.

3 Proposed Approach

We have proposed a novel approach for the data flow testing of programs using evolutionary approaches at unit level. We have applied genetic algorithm with one point cross over and mutation for generating test paths in our proposed approach. Genetic algorithm is a well known evolutionary approach successfully applied to a variety of problems for optimization [11] [12].

Our approach starts with random population of test paths for a given program and then genetic algorithm has been applied for generating new population. Our proposed approach takes data flow graph of a program, variable whose values to be tested, dynamic data flow coverage criteria , number of iterations , if specified otherwise it uses the default value, and coverage requirement in percent as input. First of all, our algorithm generates random population of test paths between one and number of nodes in a graph. This ensures that the length of each path will not be greater than the number of nodes in a data flow graph of a program. The length of a path is dependent upon the number of nodes in a data flow graph. Figure 1 shows the algorithm of proposed approach.

```
Input    DFG: Data flow graph of program.
         Variable: Input variable for dataflow coverage.
         Coverage _Criteria: Any data flow based coverage criteria.
         Coverage _Requirement: Coverage requirement in terms of number of paths.

Output   Paths: Set of paths satisfying coverage criteria for input variable.
         Coverage _Percentage: Percentage variable coverage for criteria coverage.

TestPathGeneration (DFG, Variable, Coverage _Criteria, Coverage _Requirement)
TargetsToCover: = targets (Coverage _Criteria, Variable, Coverage_Requirement)
CurPathPopulation: =generateRandomPopulation (popSize)
Attempts: =0
Final_Paths[]:=null          //Containing final population of paths
While (TargetsToCover! =ø and ExecutionTime () < MAX_TIME)
          Attempts:=Attempts+1
For(i=0 ;i<popSize; i++)     // Calculating fitness of each chromosome
  Boolean Fitness_Chromosome:=Calculate fitness of each chromosome [i]
  If(Fitness_Chromosome)
    If(!(final_paths.contains(chromosome[i])))  //checking duplication
    Final_Paths=Final_Paths+ chromosome[i]
    End If
  End If
End For
Float Coverage_Percentage =Cal_Pop_Fitness(Final_Paths, Coverage_Requirement)
If(Coverage_Percentage >= Coverage_Requirement)
  Break;  //Coverage achieved
End If
Sort population based on fitness
Select parents for new generation
Perform recombination on current population for new generation
Perform mutation on new population
CurPathPopulation: = new population
End While
Final_Paths: Test paths that satisfy test requirements
Coverage_Percentage:= Percentage of input variable coverage for criteria coverage.
Return (Final_Paths, Coverage_Percentage)
End
```

Fig. 1. Algorithm for Test path Generation

After generating random paths, then they are sorted in ascending order as data flow graph is a directed graph from start node to exit node. After sorting, each path is checked for validness. Validation is a process that validates the path by checking whether the path exists in program or not. If the actual path exists in the graph then the path is declared as valid otherwise the path will not take part in further processing in the current cycle. The invalid path takes part in recombination and mutation. After recombination and mutation, its possibility that invalid path becomes valid because of change in its structure. Figure 2 shows the fitness function for chromosome.

After sorting of test paths and validness, each valid path is evaluated against fitness function. Fitness function takes data flow graph, data flow coverage criteria, variable whose values are to be tested and test path as input for evaluation purpose. Fitness function evaluates the test paths using data flow coverage criteria and returns its fitness in the form of true and false. If the path is considered as fit after evaluation then this path becomes the member of global fit population of paths. After fitness evaluation, if the path is evaluated as fit then the process of duplication check is performed on the path with global population list if the path is already in the global population of paths then this path is ignored and will not be added in the global population of paths otherwise it becomes the member of global population of paths.

After evaluation of each test path (chromosome), the process of recombination (crossover) is applied by selecting chromosomes based on their fitness. We are applying single point cross over in our approach. Crossover selects genes from parent chromosomes and creates a new offspring. The single point crossover chooses random crossover point and the part before this point is copied from the first parent and the part after the crossover point is copied from the second parent. Two cases of recombination are possible here.

Input *DFG:* Data flow graph of program.
Chromosome: chromosome representing path
Coverage _Criteria: Any data flow based coverage criteria.
Variable: whose values are to be tested.

Output
Fitness_value: Fitness value of the chromosome.

ComputeFitness (DFG, Coverage _Criteria, Chromosome, Variable)

```
Valid: =checkValidness (DFG, Chromosome)
Fitness:=false
  Satisfied=Check path on DFG according to the coverage criteria using
              semantic stored at each node of the graph
  If (Satisfied)
  Fitness:=true
  End if
Return (Fitness)
END
```

Fig. 2. Algorithm for Fitness of chromosome

One case is that, if two chromosomes have same length then after calculating length of each chromosome, a random cross over point is selected between one and length of chromosomes. The material of two chromosomes are then exchanged in such a way that the part before crossover point is copied from the first parent and the part after the crossover point is copied from the second parent. In the second case, if two paths are of unequal length, it is possible as we have not fixed the size of test path (chromosome); the chromosomes are of unequal size. In the case, where two chromosomes have unequal lengths, the length of each chromosome is calculated and the crossover point is selected between one and the length of smaller chromosome. The material of two chromosomes is then exchanged in such a way that the part before crossover point is copied from the first parent and the part after the crossover point is copied from the second parent and after crossover, we have two off springs of unequal length while in first case, we have two off springs of equal length after recombination. A random point is selected which is seven in this example and then the material of two parents are exchanged at this point to produce the new off springs.

After recombination, mutation is introduced in the population. Mutation is used to maintain diversity in the population. In our approach, mutation simply changes any node in the path. After recombination and mutation, the sorting of each chromosome takes place and duplicate nodes are removed from the chromosome as a part of the sorting process. A random number is generated and then node is replaced with another random number generated between one and length of the chromosome. The selected node is replaced with the newly generated random number.

After each cycle, the global population is checked for required coverage level. If required coverage level is achieved then the execution stops and final results is displayed which contains test paths that satisfy the coverage criteria, number of iterations to achieve the coverage and the coverage percentage. If the coverage level doesn't achieve after all iterations, the execution stops and percentage of coverage along with test paths and number of iterations are displayed. Figure 3 shows the algorithm for population fitness.

Chromosome is composed of different nodes forming the paths. Each chromosome represents one path from DFG consists of different nodes. Each node in the path is gene as different nodes form the path and each path is known as chromosome.

Input *Total_Paths:* number of paths required
Final_ Population: Final population of fit chromosome

Output *Fitness_value:* Fitness value of the population

ComputeFitness (Total_Paths, Final _Population)

1. Fitness_value=(Final_Population.length /Total_Paths) *100;
2. Return (Fitness_value)

Fig. 3. Algorithm for Fitness of population

Our approach has two phases; in first phase test paths are generated using genetic algorithm while second phase involves identifying the infeasible paths from the selected path. Infeasible paths are those paths for which there are no input to execute the path. For identification of infeasible paths, we will execute all the paths with some test data. If the execution of path is not possible with input data, then path is said to be infeasible.

4 The Tool *ETODF*

The proposed approach is implemented in a prototype tool called ETODF (Evolutionary Testing of Data Flow) in Java. The prototype tool uses the genetic algorithm for the generation of test path with single point cross over and mutation. The high level architecture of the tool is depicted in Figure 4.

ETODF takes data flow graph as input and stores the graph after analyzing and applying semantic on each node. The semantic analyzer and preserver is the most important part of the ETODF. The semantic analyzer reads the data flow information from input file and associates this information with each node of the graph using the parser object which stores the actual graph. The nodes are now able to process the data flow coverage criteria if applied on nodes in a path.

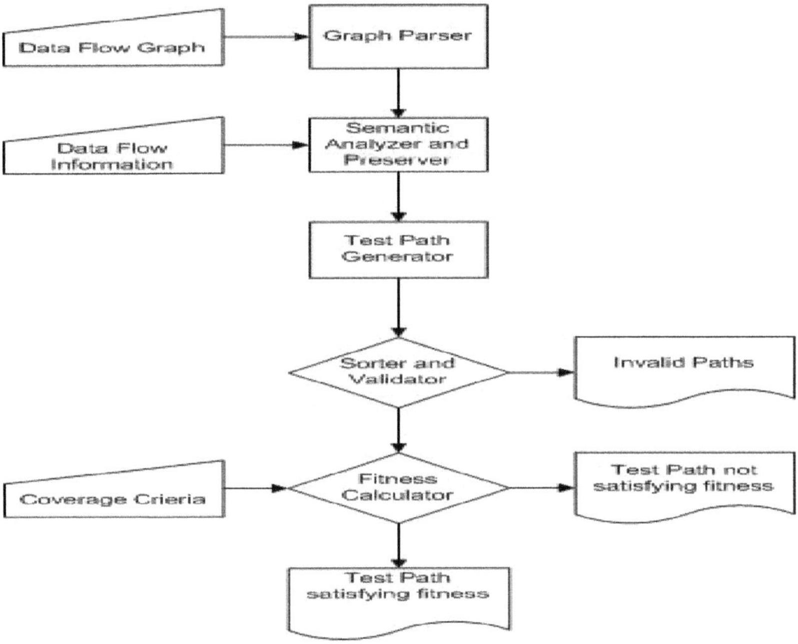

Fig. 4. High Level Architecture of ETODF

The test path generator is an important component of ETODF which first generates the test path randomly and genetic algorithm are used for path generation from second iteration onwards. The test paths are sorted by the sorter component of the ETODF and then each path is validated using semantics of the graph for validness. In this step the invalid paths are sorted out from the test paths.

The valid paths are passed to the fitness calculator which calculates the fitness of each path using the data flow coverage criteria. After evaluation, path that satisfy the coverage criteria are added in the global list while those which do not satisfy the coverage criteria remains in the population and may be used in the recombination and mutation for next iteration.

5 Experimental Results

Experimental results have been obtained using proposed methodology by applying prototype tool ETODF on procedural code at unit level. We have used All Def Uses criteria for our experiment and compare the results with random testing, although this is a very simple example with int and double data types but we believe that our approach has much better results for complex examples as well. In experiments with this prototype, our approach has much better results as compared to random testing.

```
public static void calculateBill (int Usage)
  {
  double Bill = 0;
  if (Usage > 0)
  {
  Bill = 40;
  }
  if(Usage > 100)
  {
  if(Usage <= 200)
  {
  Bill = Bill + (Usage - 100) * 0.5;
  }
  else
  {
  Bill = Bill + 50 + (Usage - 200) * 0.1;
  if(Bill >= 100)
  {
  Bill = Bill * 0.9;
  }
  }
  }
  }
```

In this example, there are two variable 'Bill' and 'Usage'. We have applied the ETODF on both these variables and compared the results to random testing. Our approach has much better results as compared with random testing. Table 1 Summarize the results obtained from approaches, our proposed approach and random testing.

For the generation of five test cases, random testing had taken forty three iterations while ETODF takes only twelve iterations. Similarly for ten test cases random testing took seventy one iterations while ETODF took only twenty one iterations. We argue that our approach will perform even better for large and complex programs as well .

Table 1. Comparison of Random testing and ETODF

Total Iterations	Test Paths Required	Random Testing		ETODF	
		Iterations	Coverage	Iterations	Coverage
100	5	43	100%	12	100%
100	10	71	100%	21	100%
100	15	100	80%	51	100%

6 Conclusion and Future Work

This paper presents a novel approach applying evolutionary algorithms for the automatic generation of test paths using data flow relations in a program. Our approach starts with a random initial population of test paths and then based on the selected testing criteria new paths are generated by applying a genetic algorithm. A fitness function evaluates each chromosome (path) based on the selected data flow testing criteria and computes its fitness. The approach has been implemented in Java by a prototype tool called ETODF for validation. In experiments with this prototype, our approach has much better results as compared to random testing.

We will extend this concept to other levels of testing i.e. integration testing and system testing. Currently we have compared our experimental with random testing only. In future, we will also carry out complete empirical case study for the verification of our approach using all data flow coverage criterion and compare the experimental results with other approaches like hill climbing, tabu search etc.

References

1. Baresel, A., Sthamer, H., Schmidt, M.: Fitness Function Design to improve Evolutionary Structural Testing. In: Proceedings of the Genetic and Evolutionary Computation Conference (GECCO 2002), New York, USA (July 2002)
2. Bashir, M.B., Nadeem, A.: A State based Fitness Function for Evolutionary Testing of Object-Oriented Programs. In: Lee, R., Ishii, N. (eds.) Software Engineering Research, Management and Applications 2009. SCI, vol. 253, pp. 83–94. Springer, Heidelberg (2009), doi:10.1007/978-3-642-05441-9
3. Cheon, Y., Kim, M.Y., Perumandla, A.: A Complete Automation of Unit Testing for Java Programs. In: The 2005 International Conference on Software Engineering Research and Practice (SERP), Las Vegas, Nevada, USA (June 2005)
4. Cheon, Y., Kim, M.: A specification-based fitness function for evolutionary testing of object-oriented programs. In: Proceedings of the 8th Annual Conference on Genetic and Evolutionary Computation, Washington, USA (July 2006)

5. Dharsana, C.S.S., Askarunisha, A.: Java based Test case Generation and Optimization Using Evolutionary Testing. In: International Conference on Computational Intelligence and Multimedia Applications, Sivakasi, India (December 2007)
6. Jones, B., Sthamer, H., Eyres, D.: Automatic structural testing using genetic algorithms. Software Engineering Journal 11(5), 299–306 (1996)
7. Liaskos, K., Roper, M., Wood, M.: Investigating data-flow coverage of classes using evolutionary algorithms. In: Proceedings of the 9th Annual Conference on Genetic and Evolutionary Computation, London, England (July 2007)
8. McGraw, G., Michael, C., Schatz, M.: Generating software test data by evolution. IEEE Transactions on Software Engineering 27(12), 1085–1110 (2001)
9. McMinn, P., Holcombe, M.: The State Problem for Evolutionary Testing. In: Cantú-Paz, E., Foster, J.A., Deb, K., Davis, L., Roy, R., O'Reilly, U.-M., Beyer, H.-G., Kendall, G., Wilson, S.W., Harman, M., Wegener, J., Dasgupta, D., Potter, M.A., Schultz, A., Dowsland, K.A., Jonoska, N., Miller, J., Standish, R.K. (eds.) GECCO 2003. LNCS, vol. 2724, pp. 2488–2497. Springer, Heidelberg (2003)
10. McMinn, P.: Search-based Software Test Data Generation: a Survey. Journal of Software Testing, Verifications, and Reliability 14(2), 105–156 (2004)
11. Pargas, R., Harrold, M., Peck, R.: Test-data generation using genetic algorithms. Software Testing. Verification and Reliability 9(4), 263–282 (1999)
12. Roper, M.: Computer aided software testing using genetic algorithms. In: 10th International Software Quality Week, San Francisco, USA (May 1997)
13. Sthamer, H.: The automatic generation of software test data using genetic algorithms, PhD Thesis, University of Ghamorgan, Pontyprid, Wales, Great Britain (1996)
14. Seesing, A., Gross, H.: A Genetic Programming Approach to Automated Test Generation for Object-Oriented Software. International Transactions on Systems Science and Applications 1(2), 127–134 (2006)
15. Tracey, N., Clark, J., Mander, K., McDermid, J.: Automated test-data generation for exception conditions. Software—Practice and Experience, 61–79 (January 2000)
16. Tonella, P.: Evolutionary Testing of Classes. In: Proceedings of the ACM SIGSOFT International Symposium of Software Testing and Analysis, Boston, MA, pp. 119–128 (July 2004)
17. Watkins, A.: The automatic generation of test data using genetic algorithms. In: Proceedings of the Fourth Software Quality Conference, pp. 300–309. ACM (1995)
18. Wegener, J., Baresel, A., Sthamer, H.: Evolutionary test environment for automatic structural testing. Information and Software Technology Special Issue on Software Engineering using Metaheuristic Innovative Algorithms 43, 841–854 (2001)
19. Wegener, J., Buhr, K., Pohlheim, H.: Automatic test data generation for structural testing of embedded software systems by evolutionary testing. In: Proceedings of the Genetic and Evolutionary Computation Conference (GECCO 2002), pp. 1233–1240. Morgan Kaufmann, New York (2002)
20. Lee, C.: A Practitioner's Guide to Software Test Design. STQE Publishing (2004)
21. Beizer, B.: Software Testing Techniques. International Thomson Computer Press (1990)

Volume-Rendering of Mitochondrial Transports Using VTK*

Yeonggul Jang[1], Hackjoon Shim[2], and Yoojin Chung [1,**]

[1] Department of Computer Science and Engineering
Hankuk University of Foreign Studies
Kyonggi, 449-791, Republic of Korea
chungyj@hufs.ac.kr
[2] Yonsei University College of Medicine
Cardiovascular Research Institute
50 Yonsei-ro, Seodaemun-gu
Seoul 120-752, Republic of Korea

Abstract. Mitochondria is an important organelle for maintaining cells such as neurons' physiological processes. Mitochondrial transport is known to be strongly related to neurodegenerative disease of the central nervous system such as Alzheimer's disease and Parkinson's disease. Recently a novel micro-fluidic culture platform enabled *in-vivo* mitochondrial being imaged using a confocal microscope. However, automated analysis of these images is still infeasible because of the low signal-to-noise ratio and formidable amount of image data. Noticing that three dimensional (3-D) visualization techniques have been useful to handle these limitations, we develop a volume-rendering tool using the Visualization Toolkit (VTK), which facilitates analysis of mitochondrial transports and comprehension of the correlations with characteristics of neurons.

Keywords: Volume-rendering, mitochondrial transports, VTK.

1 Introduction

Neuro-degenerative diseases of the central nervous system (CNS), e.g., Alzheimer's disease, Parkinson's disease, and multiple sclerosis, have been an intensely researched area due to their fatality and fast growing prevalence [1-3]. It is postulated that these diseases are linked to defective axonal transport in the CNS neurons. Live cell microscopy of the neurons that have been fluorescently labeled with mitochondria have been used to investigate the relationship between the state of axonal transport and health of the neurons. Unfortunately, detailed quantitative analysis of the motions and morphological changes to mitochondria has been difficult due to lack of

* This research was supported by Basic Science Research Program through the National Research Foundation (NRF) funded by the Ministry of Education, Science, and Technology (2009-0069549).

** Corresponding author.

T.-h. Kim et al. (Eds.): ASEA/DRBC/EL 2011, CCIS 257, pp. 56–60, 2011.

appropriate image processing methods. This paper describes a new automated image analysis tool that can be used to track and analyze fluorescent images taken by live-cell microscopy.

A novel micro-fluidic cultural platform devised by Taylor *et al.* [4, 7] has accelerated studies on mitochondria transport. Furthermore, it allows for acquisition of time-lapse fluorescent images which display *in vivo* mitochondrial transport. However, analysis using these image sequences is still challenging, because most of those researches [1-3, 4, 7] have been done manually or at most semi-automatically.

In this paper, we develop a volume-rendering tool for analysis of mitochondrial transports using the Visualization Toolkit (VTK) [6]. Volume-rendering aids in visualization. We visualized time-lapse two dimensional (2D) images of mitochondria movement in 3D that is plotted in time axis using volume-rendering. We use time-lapse images acquired from neurons growing in a micro-fluidic device [4, 7]. VTK is an open-library package that is specialized for analyzing medical images [6].

In section 2, we explain the concept and implementation of volume-rendering. In section 3, we show experimental result and final remarks.

2 Volume-Rendering

Volume-rendering aids in visualization by representing the images and setting opacity and color according to intensity. We visualized time-lapse 2D images of mitochondria movement in 3D that is plotted in time axis using volume-rendering. Volume-rendering sets opacity and color using OTF(Opacity transfer function) and CTF(color transfer function), respectively. On the other hand, setting opacity not only has function that can see desired intensity wide, but can be used to obtain previously rendered segmentation image.

2.1 Implementation of Volume-Rendering

To use volume-rendering, it need to implement OTF and volume-rendering pipeline. We represent the range of OTF using static box provided by MFC and OTF function using Draw function provided by View and control it using mouse event.

The pipeline of volume-rendering consists of visualization modeling and graphic modeling. Visualization modeling makes 3D from time-lapse 2D images acquired from neurons growing in a micro-fluidic device and graphic modeling displays 3D actor in 2D screen using rendering.

* Visualization modeling
- vtkImageData: it is information to be transformed to graphic data.
- vtkVolumeRayCastMapper: it makes ray-cast representation of object in volume-rendering.

* Graphic modeling
- vtkVolume: it represent object displayed in screen in volume-rendering. It can set opacity and color of object.

- vtkRenderer: it represents a 2D image which is determined by a camera, a light and an actor in 3D space.
- vtkRenderWindow: it manages the rendered 2D image and connects it to a window screen.

This pipeline starts from visualization modeling. Time-lapse 2D images acquired from neurons become input to vtkImageData. We connect vtkimagedata to raycastmapper to get its ray-cast representation and make volume by registering raycastmapper to vtkvolume. Then, visualization modeling finishes and graphic modeling starts.

We decide opacity and color for intensity values in a specific range using user-setting OTF and CTF. We decide OTF and CTF functions using vtkPiecewiseFunction and vtkColorTransferFunction which are member functions of vtkVolumeProperty and then connect vtkVolumeProperty to volume. Finally, we add the volume to vtkRenderer, which is connected to vtkRenderWindow, finally. Then, all pipeline process ends.

3 Experiment and Discussion

Now, our experimental results are described. The size of data in one frame used in our experiment is 476 x 401 and an image consists of 100 frames. Fig. 1 shows the effect of OTF in volume-rendering.

Fig.1 (a) is the result of assigning opacity to all intensity in image and Fig.1 (b) is the result of assigning opacity only to intensities where mitochondria are in image.

Fig. 2 shows mitochondria in time-lapse 2D images acquired from neurons: (a), (b), and (c) are the 27 th, the 33 th and the 46th frames in time-lapse image.

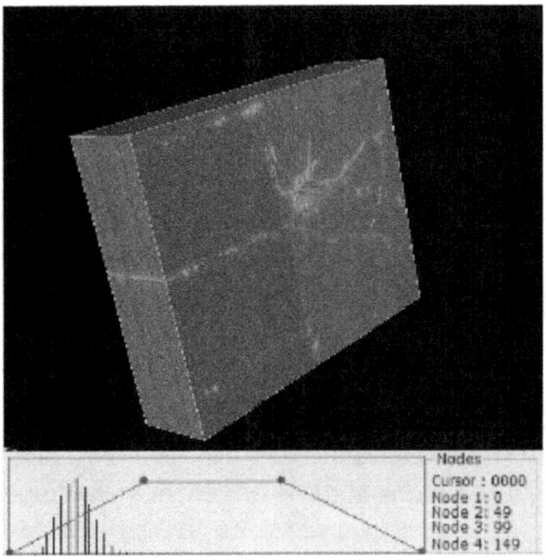

(a)

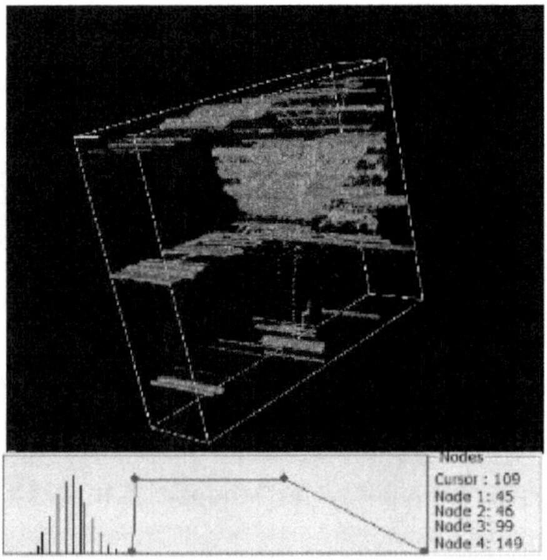

(b)

Fig. 1. Effect of OTF in volume-rendering: (a) result of assigning opacity to all intensity (b) result of assigning opacity to intensities where mitochondria are

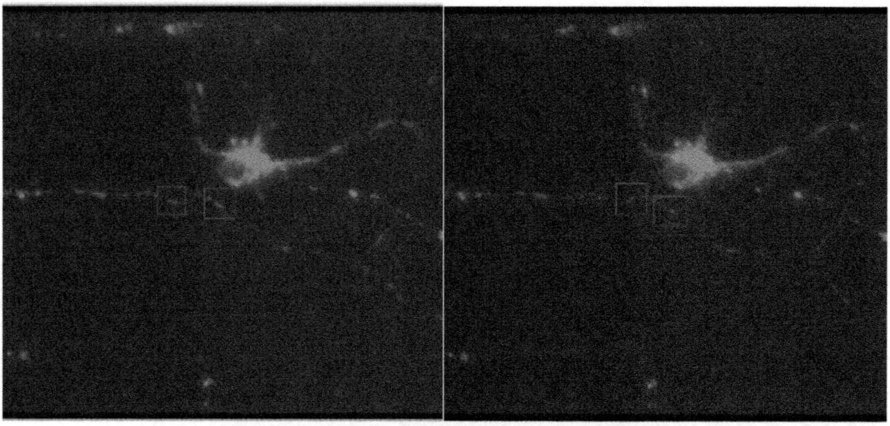

(a) The 27th frame (b) The 33th frame

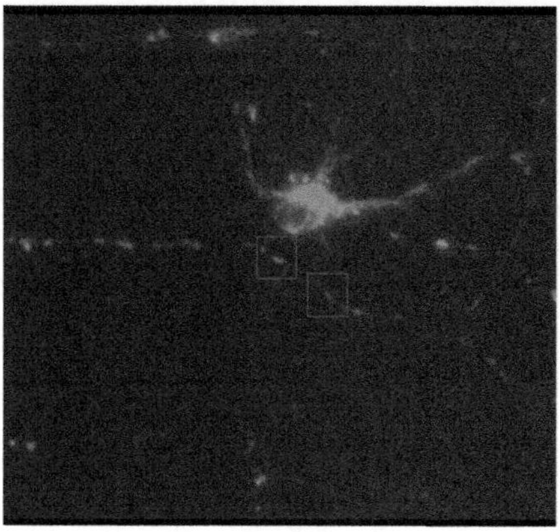

(c) The 46th frame

Fig. 2. Mitochondria in time-lapse 2D images acquired from neurons

Fig. 3 shows moving mitochondria of image. Moving objects are represented as diagonal lines and stopping objects as straight lines. In Fig. 3, stationary mitochondria constitute straight linear segments along the temporal axis, because their locations are fixed as time elapses. However, the positions of moving mitochondria change with passing time, and thus, they are represented by slanted elongated segments. The degree of being slanted of a moving mitochondrion is proportional to its speed. That is to say, if a mitochondrion moves faster, it will move more in a fixed time interval, and its path will be more slanted. Thus, if the microscopic movie images are examined by the above 3D visualization using intuitive user interaction, the differentiation between stationary and moving mitochondria will be possible. Not only this differentiation but also more detailed analysis of mitochondrial transports, such as speed and moving distances, become plausible with the proposed method.

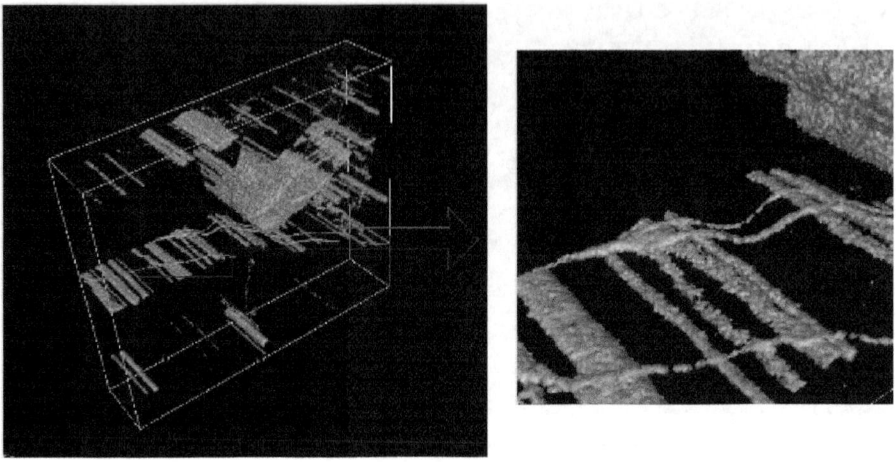

Fig. 3. Moving mitochondria of Fig 1 in volume-rendering

In this paper, we described volume-rendering tool to visualize time-lapse 2D images of mitochondria movement in 3D that is plotted in time axis and it can help to find moving mitochondria. But, it may miss some mitochondria because intensity of some mitochondria is not higher than that of background. Future research should try to solve this problem.

References

1. Malaiyan, L.M., Honick, A.S., Rintoul, G.L., Wang, Q.J., Reynolds, I.J.: Zn2+ inhibits mitochondrial movement in neurons by phosphatidylinositol 3-Kinase activation. Journal of Neuroscience 25(41), 9507–9514 (2005)
2. Cheng, D.T.W., Honick, A.S., Reynolds, I.J.: Mitochondrial trafficking to synapses in cultured primary cortical neurons. Journal of Neuroscience 26, 7035–7045 (2006)
3. Reynolds, I.J., Santos, S.: Rotenone inhibits movement and alters morphology of mitochondria in culture forebrain neurons. Society Neuroscience Abstract 31, 1017–1019 (2005)
4. Taylor, A.M., Blurton-Jones, M., Rhee, S.W., Cribbs, D.H., Cotman, C.W., Jeon, N.L.: A Microfluidic Culture Platform for CNS Axonal Injury, Regeneration and Transport. Nature Methods 2(8) (August 2005)
5. Miller, K.E., Sheetz, M.P.: Axonal mitochondrial transport and potential are correlated. Journal of Cell Science 117, 2791–2804 (2004)
6. Kitware, Inc., The VTK User's Guide: Updated for VTK 4.4, Kitware, Inc. (2004)
7. Park, J.W., Vahidi, B., Taylor, A.M., Rhee, S.W., Jeon, N.L.: Microfluidic culture platform for neuroscience research. Nature Protocols 1(4), 2128–2136 (2006)

Model Checking of Transition-Labeled Finite-State Machines

Vladimir Estivill-Castro[1] and David A. Rosenblueth[2]

[1] School of Information and Communication Technology
Griffith University
http://vladestivillcastro.net
[2] Instituto de Investigaciones en Matemáticas Aplicadas y en Sistemas
Universidad Nacional Autónoma de México
http://leibniz.iimas.unam.mx/~drosenbl/

Abstract. We show that recent Model-driven Engineering that uses sequential finite state models in combination with a common sense logic is subject to efficient model checking. To achieve this, we first provide a formal semantics of the models. Using this semantics and methods for modeling sequential programs we obtain small Kripke structures. When considering the logics, we need to extend this to handle external variables and the possibilities of those variables been affected at any time during the execution of the sequential finite state machine. Thus, we extend the construction of the Kripke structure to this case. As a proof of concept, we use a classical example of modeling a microwave behavior and producing the corresponding software directly from models. The construction of the Kripke structure has been implemented using `flex`, `bison` and `C++`, and properties are verified using `NuSMV`.

Keywords: Model-driven engineering, embedded software, Model-checking, Kripke structures, sequential finite-state machines, common sense logics.

1 Introduction

Model-driven engineering (MDE) is a powerful paradigm for software deployment with particular success in embedded systems. The domain models created are intended to be automatically converted into working systems, minimizing the potential faults introduced along the more traditional approaches that translate requirements into implementation. MDE offers traceability of the requirements to implementation, enabling validation and verification. Because software modeling is the primary focus, and there is an emphasis in automation, it has been suggested [15] that MDE can address the inabilities of third-generation languages to alleviate the complexity of releasing quality software for diverse platforms and to express domain concepts effectively.

Recently, a flexible tool to model the behavior of autonomous robotics systems has been finite state machines where transitions are labeled with statements that must be proved by an inference engine [3]. The modeling capability of these

T.-h. Kim et al. (Eds.): ASEA/DRBC/EL 2011, CCIS 257, pp. 61–73, 2011.

Transition-Labelled Finite State Machines (FSMs) has been shown [2] to be remarkably expressive with respect to other paradigms for modeling behavior, like Petri Nets, Behavior Trees and even standard finite-state machines like those of executable UML [11] or StateWorks [17]. If models of behavior are to be automatically converted into deployed systems, it is of crucial importance to verify the correctness of such models. Model checking promises to precisely enable this. Our aim here is to provide efficient and practical model-checking techniques to verify these new sequential finite state machines. We define one path to enable the model-checking of the behavior of robots expressed as finite state machines. We will describe the Finite-State Machines with transitions labeled by Boolean expressions and we will provide a semantics for it by describing the behavior in terms of sequential programs [7, Section 2.2]. Sequential programs are converted into first-order representations [7, Section 2.1.1] and these into Kripke structures. The technology for verifying properties in Kripke structures is well established. This step is perhaps direct since logics to express properties of the model are well understood as well as the algorithms to perform the validation and there are solid implementations. We will be concerned with only the sequential part of the behavior.

1.1 Sequential Finite-State Machines

An important sub-class of our models are sequential finite-state machines which we can represent visually to facilitate their specification, but which have a precise semantics. In fact, our sequential finite-state machines are a language for sequential programs and therefore, a natural approach is to describe their semantics as sequential programs [10].

A sequential finite-state machine consist of the following elements:

1. A set S of *states*, one of which is designated as the initial state $s_0 \in S$.
2. Each state s_i has associated with it a finite (and possibly empty) list $L_i = \langle t_{i1}, t_{i2}, \ldots, t_{i,it} \rangle$ of *transitions*. A transition t_{ij} is a pair (e_{ij}, s_j), where e_{ij} is a Boolean expression (a predicate that evaluates to `true` or `false`) and s_j is a state (i.e. $s_j \in S$) named the *target* of the transition. For all the transitions in L_i, the state $s_i \in S$ is called the *source*.
3. Each state has three *activities*. These activities are labeled **On-Entry**, **On-Exit**, and **Internal**, respectively. An activity is either an *atomic statement* P (and for the time being the only atomic statement is the assignment $x := e$) or a compound statement $P = \langle P_1; P_2; \ldots P_t \rangle$ where each P_k is an atomic statement.

Note that sequential finite-state machines have a very similar structure to UML's state machines [11] and OMT's state diagrams [14, Chapter 5].

Because of its structure, a sequential finite-state machine can be encoded by two tables. The first table is the *activities table* and has one row for each state. The columns of the table are the state identifier, and columns for the **On-Entry**, **On-Exit**, and **Internal** activities. The order of the rows does not matter except that the initial state is always listed as the last. The second table of the sequential finite-state machine is the *transitions table*. Here, the rows are triplets of the form (s_i, e_{ij}, s_j) where s_i is the source state, e_{ij} is the Boolean expression and s_j is the target state. In this table, all rows for the same source state must appear, for historical reasons, in the reverse order than that prescribed by the list L_i. Sequential finite-state machines can also be illustrated by state diagrams.

1.2 The Corresponding Sequential Program

The intent of a sequential finite-state machine model is to represent a single thread of execution, by which, on arrival to a state, the **On-Entry** statement (atomic or compound) is executed. Then, each Boolean expression in the list of transitions out of this state is evaluated. As soon as one of them evaluates to `true`, we say the transition *fires*, and the **On-Exit** statement is executed, followed by repeating this execution on the target state. However, if none of the transitions out of the state fires, then the **Internal** activity is performed followed by the re-evaluation of the outgoing transitions in the corresponding list order.

Note again the importance of the transitions out of a state being structured in a list. This means that the sequential finite-state machine is not the same as the finite-state automaton usually defined in the theory of computer languages. In particular, there is no need for the Boolean expression to be exclusive. That is, $e_{ij} \wedge e_{ij'}$ may be `true` for two different target states s_j and $s_{j'}$ out of the same source state s_i. Also, there is no need for the Boolean expressions to be exhaustive. That is $\bigvee_{j=1}^{j=it} e_{ij}$ may be false (and not necessarily true).

The procedure in Fig. 1 provides an operational semantics of a sequential finite-state machine viewed as sequential program.

1.3 From Sequential Programs to Kripke Structures

Thus, a sequential finite-state machine is just a special sequential program and we can apply a transformation [7] to obtain its corresponding Kripke structure, which can be verified. The crucial element is to make an abstraction identifying all possible breakpoints in a debugger for the program. These break points are actually the values for a special variable `pc` called the *program counter*.

However, what is the challenge? Under the transformation $\mathcal{C}$ [7, Section 2.2], the number of states of the Kripke structure grows quickly. For example, the direct transformation of a sequential finite-state machine with three states, two Boolean variables and four transitions results in $2^2 \times 3^2 \times 2 \times 2 \times 20 = 2,880$. Therefore, an automatic approach to generate the Kripke structure is needed and perhaps more interestingly, an alternative approach that can perhaps obtain a more succinct and efficient approach. Observe, however, that we only need to consider as break points (labels) the following points in the execution:

1. after the execution of the **OnEntry** activities in the state,
2. after the evaluation of each Boolean expression labeling the transitions,
3. after the execution of the internal activities of the state, and
4. after the execution of the **OnExit** activities of the state (which corresponds to a break point before the **OnEntry** activities of the next state).

```
current_state ← s0; {Initial state is set up}
fired ← true ; {Default arrival to a state is because a transition fired}
{Infinite loop}
while ( true ) do
  if ( fired ) then
    {On arrival to a state execute On-Entry activity}
    execute ( current_state.on_Entry ) ;
  end if

  {If the state has no transitions out halt}
  if ( ∅ == current_state.transition_List ) then
    halt;
  end if
  {Evaluate transitions in order until one fires or end of list}
  out_Transition ← current_state.transition_List.first;
  fired ← false;
  while ( out_Transition ≤ current_state.transition_List.end AND NOT fired ) do
    if ( fired ← evaluate (current_state.out_Transition) ) then
      next_state ← current_state.out_Transition.target;
    end if
    out_Transition ← current_state.transition_List.next;
  end while
  {If a transition fired, move to next state, otherwise execute Internal activities}
  if ( fired) then
    execute ( current_state.on_Exit ) ;
    current_state ← next_state;
  else
    execute ( current_state.Internal ) ;
    fired ← false;
  end if
end while
```

Fig. 1. The interpretation of a sequential finite-state machine

Now, by exploring all the execution paths, we obtain the corresponding Kripke structure. If the machine has $\|V\|$ variables, and the largest domain of these is d, then the interpreter for the sequential finite state machine can be adjusted to a traversal in the graph of the Kripke structure. The number of nodes of the graph is the number of states of the Kripke structure and will be $4 \times \|V\|^d$.

2 Building the Kripke Structure for NuSMV

The conversion of the model of a sequential FSM (or equivalently the transitions table and the activities table) into a Kripke structure description conforming to the `NuSMV` [5] syntax is as follows.

Generation rule 1. *Input files for* `NuSMV` *start with the line* `MODULE main`, *thus this is printed automatically. Then, a variables section starts with the keyword* `VAR`, *and here every variable used in the FSM is declared together with its range of values. Moreover, a variable* `pc` *standing for program counter is declared. The* `pc` *variable has a discrete range made of the following. For each state (listed in the activities table) with name* NAME, *there will be at least two values in the domain of the variable* `pc`; *namely* BEFORENAME, *and* AFTERONENTRYNAME.

The BEFORENAME value of `pc` corresponds to when the sequential program is about to commence execution of activities corresponding to the state NAME, (and also to the departure of execution from the previous state, so there is no need for a value for pc equal to AFTERONEXITNAME).

The AFTERONENTRYNAME. value of pc corresponds to when the sequential program has completed execution of the **OnEntry** activity of the state NAME.

Also, for each transition out of state NAME labeled with a Boolean expression B_i the range of pc will include the values AFTEREVALUATEBINAMETRUE and AFTEREVALUATEBINAMEFALSE.

Generation rule 2. *The initial states of the Kripke structure are specified in a section labeled* INIT *by a predicate holding exactly at such states.*

Generation rule 3. *If the sequential FSM has more than one initial state and it can start at any of these, then the* INIT *section of the Kripke structure will have a disjunction*

pc =BEFORES1 | pc =BEFORES2,

indicating that all Kripke states where the pc *is before an initial state of the sequential FSM are initial states of the Kripke structure.*

The Kripke structure corresponding to the sequential FSM is described by specifying its transition in the section TRANS of the NuSMV input. In particular, a case statement is used. Each entry in the case statement corresponds to a Boolean predicate that describes a state of the Kripke structure, such as:

x = 0 & y = 1 & pc =BEFORESTART

The transitions in the Kripke structure are indicated by using the NuSMV function next after a colon : specifying the case statement, and using the symbol | for 'or' to indicate alternative transitions. For example,

```
x = 1 & y = 0 & pc =BeforeStart : next(x) = 1 & next(y) = 0 & next(pc) =BeforeStart
                                | next(x) = 0 & next(y) = 0 & next(pc) =AfterOnEntryStart;
```

describes two transitions in the Kripke structure: a self-loop in the state with x = 1 & y = 0 & pc =BEFORESTART and a transition to the Kripke state x = 0 & y = 0 & pc =AFTERONENTRYSTART. The approach in [7, Section 2.1.1] always places a self-loop (that leaves all variables intact) to model the possible execution in a multi-tasking environment where the execution may be delayed indefinitely.

Generation rule 4. *For every Kripke state* NAME *where the* pc *has value* BEFORENAME, *there will be two departing transitions, one is the self-loop. The second transition will affect the variables by the execution of the* **OnEntry** *action and move the* pc *variable to* AFTERONENTRYNAME.

Generation rule 5. *A Kripke state with* pc=AFTERONENTRYNAME *will produce a self-loop and also another transition resulting of evaluating the first Boolean expression corresponding to the first transition in the sequential finite state machine. Because a Boolean expression is evaluated, none of the variables except* pc *changes value. If the Boolean expression evaluates to* true, *then the variable* pc *changes to* pc= AFTEREVALUATEB1STARTTRUE; *otherwise, when the Boolean expression evaluates to* false, *then* pc= AFTEREVALUATEB1STARTFALSE.

Generation rule 6. *A Kripke state with* pc=AFTEREVALUATEBINAMETRUE *will produce a self-loop and also another transition resulting of executing the* **OnExit** *statement of the state* NAME *of the sequential FSM. The target state in the Kripke structure of this transition will have the variables modified by the execution of the statement in the* **OnExit** *part and the variable* pc *set to a value* BEFORETARGET *where* TARGET *is the state of the sequential FSM that is the target of the transition that fired.*

Generation rule 7. *A Kripke state with* pc=AFTEREVALUATEBINAMEFALSE *will produce a self-loop and if B_i is the Boolean expression, but for any other FSM-transition except the last transition, the second Kripke transition is the result of evaluating the next Boolean expression labeling the next FSM-transition.*

3 Applying Model-Checking to FSM+DPL

A classical example on modeling software behavior has been a microwave oven (e.g., [16]). This example also appears in the literature of requirements engineering (e.g., [8]). Recently, the modeling tool FSM+DPL that consists of finite-state machines whose transitions are labeled with queries to the inference engine of DPL has been applied to the microwave oven example, producing shorter and clearer models that Petri Nets, Behavior Trees or other approaches also using finite-state machines [2]. It was also shown that these models could be directly converted into executable implementations (using different target languages, in one case Java and in the other C++ and on independent platforms, in one case a Lego-Mindstorm and in the other a Nao robot). They have been effective in modeling behavior of robots for RoboCup 2011 [9].

We illustrate here that the FSM+DPL approach is also receptive to be formally verified using the machinery of model checking using Kripke structures. We use the generic methodology developed in the previous sections for sequential FSM, but we will require an extension to handle external variables. To illustrate the general approach, we reproduce some parts a microwave model with FSM+DPL [3]. Here, a part of the model is the sequential finite-state machines. One of these FSM is illustrated in Fig. 2a. Associated with each of these machines is the corresponding code for a logic (formally a theory). The logic used

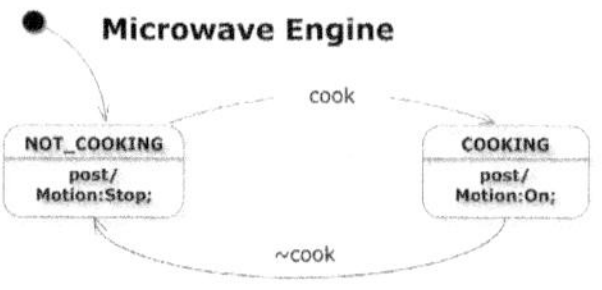

(a) A 2-state machine for controlling tube, fan, and plate.

```
name{MICROWAVECOOK}.
input{timeLeft}.
input{doorOpen}.
C0: {}          => ~cook.
C1: timeLeft =>    cook. C1 > C0.
C2: doorOpen =>  ~cook. C2 > C1.
output{b cook, "cook"}.
output{b ~cook, "dontCook"}.
```

(b) DPL for the 2-state machine in Fig. 2a controlling engine, tube, fan, and plate.

(c) Sequential FSM with Boolean expressions that models the behavior of the motor in the microwave.

Fig. 2. Simple 2-state machines control most of the microwave is DPL [13], which is an implementation of a variant of *Plausible Logic* [1,4,12]. The theory for the engine, tube, fan and plate (see Fig. 2b) can be thought of as the declarative description of an expert on whether we should `cook` or `not cook`. These are labeled as outputs. The expert would like to have information about whether there is `timeLeft` and/or whether `doorOpen` is true or false (that is, whether the door is open or not). This is not absolutely necessary; however, these desirable inputs are labeled as such. The actual inference rules are described by rules. The implementation of DPL compiles (translates) the theory to equivalent `C` Boolean expressions, or more simply to Boolean expressions. For example, using the the DPL tool with the `+c` option translates the theory about cooking in Fig 2b to `!doorOpen && timeLeft`. The corresponding finite-state machines are as in Fig. 2c.

Generation rule 8. *A FSM+DPL models is first translated to a sequential FSM with Boolean expressions in the transitions.*

We now proceed to outline the transformation of this resulting sequential FSM into the corresponding Kripke structure. Here we have the Boolean variables `timeLeft`, `doorOpen`, and `motor`.

There is an important difference in that now `timeLeft` and `doorOpen` are *external variables*. That is, the sequential program equivalent to this sequential FSM cannot modify the values of these variables. Instead, it is an external agent who does. We model this using the tools of parallel computation illustrated also in [7, Section 2.1]. We will start with a Kripke structure where:

1. such a change to external variables cannot be undetected by the corresponding sequential program, and
2. computational statements in the **OnEntry**, **OnExit** or **Internal** activities and evaluation of Boolean expressions labeling transitions are atomic.

Now, recall (Rule 1) that for each state NAME in the sequential FSM we have a state in the Kripke structure named BEFORENAME for a valuation with `pc`= BEFORENAME. For each state of our sequential FSM, first we execute the assignment of the **OnEntry** component and then we enter an infinite loop where we evaluate a Boolean expression. When the variable `pc` is just after the execution of the **OnEntry** activity we have the value AFTERONENTRYNAME.

We will model the loop of the semantics of the sequential FSM state execution with a substructure in the Kripke structure we call a *ringlet*. This essentially corresponds to the alternation of two actions in the sequential program and four states of the Kripke structure (refer to Fig. 3) using the standard transformation [7]. Three of the states are named as before, but here we introduce one to handle the external agent affecting the variables before an atomic evaluation of the Boolean expression labeling a transition.

BEFORENAME**:** The Kripke state corresponds to the label of the sequential program just before the execution of the programming statement in the **OnEntry** component.

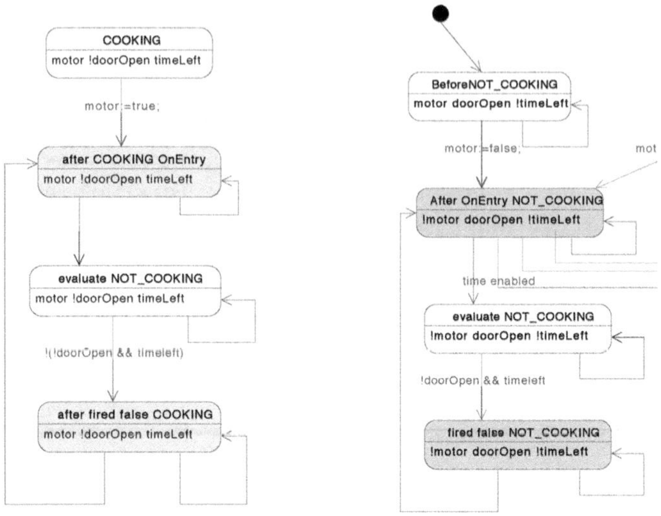

(a) One ringlet, representing the sequential program going through the loop of evaluating one state in the sequential state machine.

(b) Another ringlet, for state NOT_COOKING and valuation `motor`, `doorOpen`, `! timeLeft`

Fig. 3. Sections of the Kripke structure for the example of Fig. 2

AFTERONENTRYNAME: This Kripke state reflects the effect of the programming statement in the variables (in the case from Fig. 2a, there can only be one variable, the `motor` variable). In our diagrams, these Kripke states have a background color to reflect the arrival there by the execution of a statement in the sequential program.

BEFOREEVALUATIONBINAME: This state in the Kripke structure represents the same valuation for the variables. In a ringlet, it represents that after the previous programmed action of the sequential FSM the external agent did not affect the value of any of the external variables.

AFTEREVALUATIONBITRUE: As before, this Kripke state represents that the evaluation of the Boolean expression in the sequential FSM (and therefore in the sequential program) evaluated to true. This also does not change the valuation of the variables because it just evaluates a Boolean expression. It will also have a background color to indicate that the Kripke structure arrives here because of the action of the sequential FSM. From here the machine moves to perform the **OnExit** activities.

AFTEREVALUATIONBIFALSE: As before, this Kripke state represents that the evaluation of the Boolean expression in the sequential FSM (and therefore in the sequential program) evaluated to false. This also does not change the valuation of the variables because it just evaluates a Boolean expression. It will also have a background color to indicate that the Kripke structure arrives here because of the action of the sequential FSM. If this is the last transition, it will go to perform the **Internal** activities; otherwise, it will go to the next AFTEREVALUATIONBITRUE.

Figure 3a illustrates the ringlet for the sequential FSM in the state of `COOKING`, in particular the moment when we commence with an assignment of the variables `motor` and `timeLeft` set to `true` but the variable `doorOpen` set to `false`. We have colored red the transitions resulting from the sequential program actions. We have also labeled the transition with the assignment or the Boolean expression in red; these labels are only comments. In Fig. 3a, this transition is the execution of `motor:=true`. Therefore, the second Kripke state has a new assignment for the values. Transitions appearing in black in the Kripke structure identify labels of the sequential program and are part of the construction of the Kripke structure from labeled sequential programs as before. A similar portion of the Kripke structure, for the sequential FSM state of `NOT_COOKING` and with an assignment of the variables `motor`, `doorOpen`, to `true`, but `timeLeft` to `false`, appears in Fig. 3b. Here, however, the programming statement that will be executed is `motor:=false`, and the transition guarding the state `NOT_COOKING` in the sequential FSM is `!doorOpen && timeLeft`. Thus, the final Kripke structure has at most $2 \times 4 \times 8 = 64$ states.

We now explain other transitions of the Kripke structure that model the external variables. Figure 4 illustrates part of the Kripke structure. It shows four of the eight initial states of the Kripke structure. Each initial state of the sequential FSM should be the first Kripke state of a four-state ringlet. However, some Kripke structure states for the `NOT_COOKING` state of the sequential FSM do not have a ringlet. This is because the assignment in the **OnEntry** part modifies the value of `motor` to `false`, making the ringlet impossible.

Now, after the execution of the assignment statement and also after the evaluation of the Boolean expression by the sequential program, the external variables `doorOpen` and `timeLeft` may have been modified.

We will model the modification of external variables with magenta transitions outside a ringlet before the evaluation of Boolean expression in sequential FSM. One such transition links an AFTERONENTRY Kripke state to a BEFOREEVALUATION Kripke state. In this way, the sequential FSM must traverse a ringlet at least once and notice the change of the external variables. Therefore, there will be three transitions out of the second state of every ringlet in the Kripke structure. This corresponds to:

1. the value of `doorOpen` being flipped (from `true` to `false` or vice versa),
2. the value of `timeLeft` being flipped, and
3. the values of both `doorOpen` and `timeLeft` being flipped.

In Fig. 4 we only show these transitions out of the leftmost ringlet.

The above description shows that we can construct a Kripke structure with no more than 64 states that completely captures the model of sequential FSM with transitions labeled by DPL and that involve external variables. To automatically construct such Kripke structures we have implemented a `C++` program that uses `flex` and `bison` to scan and parse the activities and transitions table

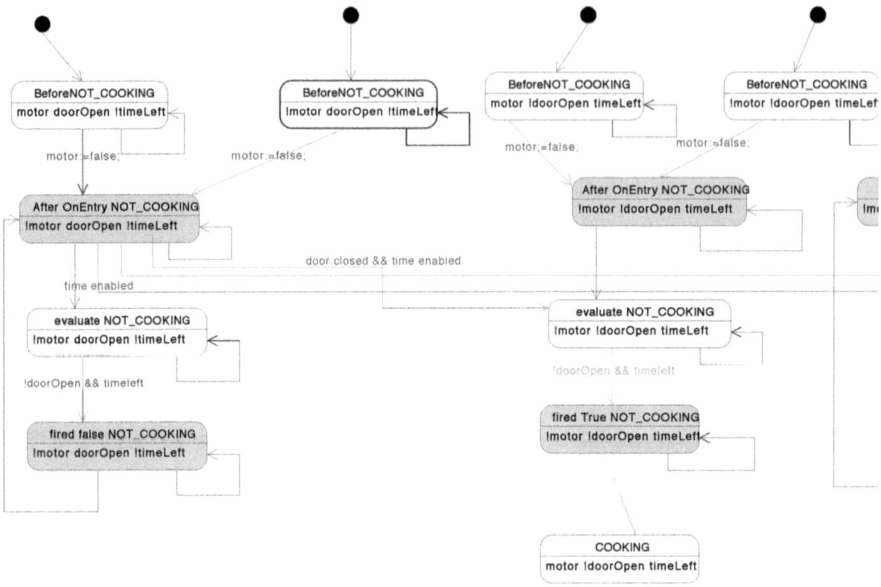

Fig. 4. Partial view of the Kripke structure for the Sequential FSM with external variables of Fig. 2c

of a sequential finite-state machine. As output, it produces the corresponding Kripke structure in a format suitable for NuSMV.

3.1 The Model-Checking Case Study

To complete the demonstration that the FSM+DPL model-driven approach can be subject to model-checking by our proposal here, we now discuss some properties verified using our implementation of the constructor of the derived Kripke structure in combination with NuSMV.

In particular, an important property is the safety requirement that "*necessarily, the oven stops three transitions in the Kripke structure after the door opens*". In CTL (Computation-Tree Logic [6]) this is the following formula:

```
AG((doorOpen=1 & motor=1 -> AX AX AX(motor=0))     (1)
```

Another illustrative property for which NuSMV return favorable verification is the following. "*It is necessary to pass through a state in which the door is closed to*

Table 1. Faulty state table. The statements on the **OnEntry** sections are in the wrong state with respect to the correct model in Fig. 2c.

State ID	**On-Entry**	**On-Exit**	**Internal**
COOKING	`motor:= false;`	∅	∅
NOT_COOKING	`motor:= true;`	∅	∅

reach a state in which the motor is working and the machine has started". The CTL formula follows.

```
!E[ !(doorOpen=0) U (motor=1 & !(pc=BeforeNOT_COOKING)) ]      (2)
```

Observe that these properties can be used for effective verification of the model. For example, Table 1 is an erroneous table for the model of Fig. 2c since (by accident or as a result of a programming mistake) the assignments in the states of the sequential FSM are in the opposite state. This makes both Property (1) and Property (2) false in the derived Kripke structure. Also, in the second one, the reader may find it surprising that we have a condition on the `pc`. However, if this condition is removed, `NuSMV` will determine that the property is false, and will provide as a trace an initial state of the Kripke structure. The reason is that the Kripke structure construction assumes that the FSM can commence execution in any combination of the variables, and of course, one such combination is to have the door closed and the motor on. However, the property proves that if the sequential FSM is allowed to execute, then it will turn the motor off and from then on, the motor will only be on when the door is closed.

Another important property is the safety requirement that "*necessarily, the oven stops three transitions in the Kripke structure after the time elapses* ". In CTL this is the following formula.

```
AG((timeLeft=0 & motor=1) -> AX AX AX(motor=0))      (3)
```

This property is equivalent to "*the microwave will necessarily stop whether the door opens or the time expires, immediately after the* `pc` *advances no more than one ringlet*".

Certain properties also show the robustness of the model. A property like "*cooking may go on for ever*" (coded as `AG(motor=1 -> EX motor=1)`) is false; naturally, because opening the door or the time expiring halts cooking. However,

```
AG( (doorOpen=0 & timeLeft=1 & motor=1 & !(pc=BeforeNOT_COOKING))
    ->EX(doorOpen=0 & timeLeft=1 & motor=1) )
```

indicates that, from a state which is not an initial state, as long as the door is closed, and there is time left, cooking can go on for ever.

4 Final Remarks

Our Kripke structure conversion is efficient in that, if the sequential finite state machine has n states and an average of m transitions per state, then our Kripke structure has a number of Kripke states bounded by $(4n+m)f(k)$. That is, the Kripke structure complexity is linear in the number of states and the number of transitions of the sequential FSM. The potential complexity challenge is on the number of the variables used in the sequential FSM (both internal and external). This is because the function $f(k)$ can be exponential in k where k is the number of variables involved. In a sense, this has the favor of fixed-parameterized complexity, with the number of variables as the parameter. The number of transitions in the Kripke structure is also linear in n and m, but potentially exponential in the number of external variables. Hence, the Kripke structure has a number of transitions linear in its number of states, so that the Kripke structure as a graph is rather sparse. In summary, the models produced by this approach could be considered efficient.

Acknowledgments. We thank many colleagues from the Mi-PAL team that have enabled the design and implementation of many facilities that constitute the infrastructure to enable Transition-Labelled Finite State Machines into a practical modeling-driven engineering method for developing behaviors on autonomous mobile robots. We also thank Miguel Carrillo for fruitful discussions on the microwave oven example, as well as the facilities provided by IIMAS, UNAM. DR was supported by grant PAPIIT IN120509.

References

1. Billington, D.: The Proof Algorithms of Plausible Logic form a Hierarchy. In: Zhang, S., Jarvis, R. (eds.) AI 2005. LNCS (LNAI), vol. 3809, pp. 796–799. Springer, Heidelberg (2005)
2. Billington, D., Estivill-Castro, V., Hexel, R., Rock, A.: Non-monotonic reasoning for requirements engineering. In: Proc. 5th Int. Conference on Evaluation of Novel Approaches to Software Engineering (ENASE), Athens, Greece, July 22-24, pp. 68–77. SciTePress — Science and Technology Publications, Portugal (2010)
3. Billington, D., Estivill-Castro, V., Hexel, R., Rock, A.: Modelling Behaviour Requirements for Automatic Interpretation, Simulation and Deployment. In: Ando, N., Balakirsky, S., Hemker, T., Reggiani, M., von Stryk, O. (eds.) SIMPAR 2010. LNCS, vol. 6472, pp. 204–216. Springer, Heidelberg (2010)
4. Billington, D., Rock, A.: Propositional plausible logic: Introduction and implementation. Studia Logica 67, 243–269 (2001) ISSN 1572-8730
5. Cimatti, A., Clarke, E., Giunchiglia, F., Roveri, M.: NuSMV: a new symbolic model checker. Int. J. on Software Tools for Technology Transfer 2 (2000)
6. Clarke, E.M., Emerson, E.A.: Design and Synthesis of Synchronization Skeletons using Branching Time Temporal Logic. In: Kozen, D. (ed.) Logic of Programs 1981. LNCS, vol. 131, pp. 52–71. Springer, Heidelberg (1982)
7. Clarke, E.M., Grumberg, O., Peled, D.: Model checking. MIT Press (2001)
8. Dromey, R.G., Powell, D.: Early requirements defect detection. TickIT Journal 4Q05, 3–13 (2005)
9. Estivill-Castro, V., Hexel, R.: Module interactions for model-driven engineering of complex behavior of autonomous robots. In: Dini, P. (ed.) ICSEA 6th Int. Conf. on Software Engineering Advances, Barcelona. IEEE (to appear, October 2011)
10. Manna, Z., Pnueli, A.: Temporal verification of reactive systems:Safety. Springer, Heidelberg (1995)
11. Mellor, S.J., Balcer, M.: Executable UML: A foundation for model-driven architecture. Addison-Wesley Publishing Co., Reading (2002)
12. Rock, A., Billington, D.: An implementation of propositional plausible logic. In: 23rd Australasian Computer Science Conference (ACSC 2000), January 31-February 3, pp. 204–210. IEEE Computer Society (2000)
13. Rock, A.: The DPL (decisive Plausible Logic) tool. Technical report (continually) (in preparation), `www.cit.gu.edu.au/~arock/`

14. Rumbaugh, J., Blaha, M.R., Lorensen, W., Eddy, F., Premerlani, W.: Object-Oriented Modelling and Design. Prentice-Hall, Inc., Englewood Cliffs (1991)
15. Schmidt, D.C.: Model-driven engineering. IEEE Computer 39(2) (2006)
16. Shlaer, S., Mellor, S.J.: Object lifecycles: modeling the world in states. Yourdon Press, Englewood Cliffs (1992)
17. Wagner, F., Schmuki, R., Wagner, T., Wolstenholme, P.: Modeling Software with Finite State Machines: A Practical Approach. CRC Press, NY (2006)

Development of Intelligent Effort Estimation Model Based on Fuzzy Logic Using Bayesian Networks

Jahangir Khan[1], Zubair A. Shaikh[2], and Abou Bakar Nauman[1]

[1] Department of Computer Science and IT
Sarhad University of Science and Information Technology Peshawar 25000, Pakistan
[2] Department of Computer Science
FAST-National university of Computer and Emerging Sciences, Karachi, Pakistan
{jahangir.csit,abubakar.csit}@suit.edu.pk,
zubair.shaikh@nu.edu.pk

Abstract. Accuracy gain in the software estimation is constantly being sought by researchers. On the same time new techniques and methodologies are being employed for getting capability of intelligence and prediction in estimation models. Today the target of estimation research is not only the achievement of accuracy but also fusion of different technologies and introduction of new factors. In this paper we advise improvement in some existing work by introducing mechanism of gaining accuracy. The paper focuses on method for tuning the fuzziness function and fuzziness value. This document proposes a research for development of intelligent Bayesian Network which can be used independently to calculate the estimated effort for software development, uncertainty, fuzziness and effort estimation. The comparison of relative error and magnitude relative error bias helps the selection of parameters of fuzzy function; however the process can be repeated n-times to get suitable accuracy. We also present an example of fuzzy set development for ISBSG data set in order to elaborate working of proposed system.

Keywords: Effort estimation, New development, Re development, statistical analysis, ISBSG data set, Bayesian networks.

1 Introduction

Effort estimation is also replaced by the term cost estimation due to the proportionality in effort and cost. Different factors, techniques and tools are used for both the size and effort estimates[1]. Size estimates are used as an input for effort estimates. There exist several estimation methods, with each one claiming gains in accuracy and application[2,3]. Now researchers are proposing using mixture or collection of estimation models and techniques to produce sufficient reliability in the estimates[4]. On the same time a debate is still on for the estimation models to consider the software engineering as process oriented or problem solving domain. This is influencing the researchers in creating new estimation methods to cater both of the camps i.e. Process and Problem solving. Estimation methods like Expert opinion,

T.-h. Kim et al. (Eds.): ASEA/DRBC/EL 2011, CCIS 257, pp. 74–84, 2011.

Analogy based estimation; Algorithmic models and predictive models are considered to have good reputation and are being used independently and collectively. COCOMO [5] has been an established model with all of its variations, however in recent times there have been indicated some limitations of this model. For example the COCOMO is based on only 63 projects, where are models like ISBSG [6] are based on more than 4000 projects, which make ISBSG models are more reliable. On the other hand there have been proposed many refinements in the original COCOMO model. Thus it can be concluded that software estimation is an vibrant area of research and new methods and combination of existing methods is always a need.

2 Techniques

Estimation Techniques

The estimation techniques for hardware were developed in 1960's, however due to the dissimilarity of software with hardware and the lesser understanding of software, the emergence of estimation technologies in software is 20-30 years late. These techniques developed by different researchers at different times with different perspectives[2,3]. This variety resulted in a wide range of techniques and tools catering various factors and processes. Today the reviews [2,3,7] represent comprehensive information on size and effort estimation tools and methods. Researches by Putnam , Boehm and Jorgensen are milestones in the area of software estimation [2]. The size estimation covers the methods to estimate the size of software. Function point, Use case point and Line of Code are some major methods for estimating size. Cost estimation covers Effort, Human Resource, Schedule and time required for software development. Different statistical, mathematical and human based models are used in both types of estimations. In some cases mathematical functions were developed e.g. Function Point, COCOMO, to incorporate the quantitative values of basic factors and estimate the effort in terms of a number. Some statistical techniques were also developed which plot the available information on regression line and develop a trend line for the effort. In some cases the experience was considered the basic element of estimation and methods were developed for experts to give their judgment of estimation on any project. In the broader aspect these categories can be made

- Mathematical / algorithmic models
- Expertise based
- Learning based.

These models are either theoretical i.e. uses formulae based on global assumptions, where as some are empirical i.e. based on the data of previous projects.

Mathematical Techniques

As discussed above, quite a few software estimation models have been developed in the last few decades. As evident by the name, the Mathematical models are based on meta-models of factors and their values. These models are based on regression e.g.

OLS, Robust regression or power formulas, comprising of different variables like Line of code, number of functional requirements etc. The values for these variables are either collected directly from the available project information or selected from available expectation list. In some models the Log of variables is also used which changes the impact of the factor on the total result. Some famous models are placed in this category like Function point, COCOMO.

Expertise Based Costing Techniques

As discussed above the values for different factors are either collected form available data or expected values are used, which shows that at some point one has to guess the values. In the same line the whole cost estimation is done with judgment by some experts. In this type of techniques the experts give their opinion about the expected effort or cost of the project after analyzing available requirements and information. In some techniques like Expertise-based techniques are useful in the absence of quantified, empirical data and are based on prior knowledge of experts in the field. Based on their experience and understanding of the proposed project, experts arrive at an estimate of the cost/schedule/quality of the software under development. The obvious drawback to this method is that an estimate is only as good as the expert's opinion. This model is also selected to implement the learning for previous project experience. However it is observed that human estimators are not consistent in their estimations. They can also be biased. It is also argued that fate of a large project can not be left alone on the intuition of human estimator. There exists a strong need to develop computer based systems to help the estimation process [7,8,9]. Examples of Expertise-based techniques include the Delphi technique, Rule-based.

Learning-Oriented Techniques

The need for learning from prior and current knowledge is addressed by learning oriented techniques which are generally based on neural networks and case-based reasoning. One of the most recognized models was present by Witting [10]. The model works with a cycle of estimation and feedback. The feedback was based on the MARE (Mean Absolute Relative Error of estimation in the cycle, on the basis of estimation error the model estimation values were adjusted and then estimation is conducted again. This type of "Iterative Development" of estimation model is also used recently in [11]. These models do acknowledge the use of latest data in the estimation process. The research given below is one of the significant developments in intelligent software effort estimation.

Adaptive fuzzy logic-based framework for software development effort prediction [11]
o Highlighted the need for adaptive learning in Estimation models o Proposed a fuzzy logic based estimation model. o The model is trained by latest data

Development of a Hybrid Cost Estimation Model in an Iterative Manner [12]
o Highlighted the need for calibration of estimation model. o Proposed the framework for calibration in iterative manner. o Calibrated the causal model. o Factors of calibration are increased with each iteration (The term iteration is used for calibration cycle)
Handling imprecision in inputs using fuzzy logic to predict effort in software development [13]
• Fuzzy logic based system • Based on COCOMO • Size and Cost drivers measurement
Handling imprecision and uncertainty in software development effort prediction: A Type 2 Fuzzy Logic Based Networks [14]
• Type-2 fuzzy logic • Effort estimation framework • Uncertainty management

Hybrid or Composite techniques are also available in estimation, these are composed of more than one techniques discussed above, e.g. the Bayesian techniques. Bayesian techniques include both Bayesian networks and Bayesian estimates of values of coefficients of any mathematical model [15,16]. There is a variety of Bayesian network models proposed by researchers in the area of software project management [17-27]. These models can be categorized in four types, however each model and categories are overlapped.

1. Project Management Models
2. Effort Estimation Models
3. Iterative Project Models
4. Defect prediction Models

3 Knowledge Gap

It is note-able that although there has been research evidence in the area of intelligent software effort estimation, however the work on ISBSG data base [27-41] for development of intelligent models has not been conducted. There is only single research [27] which deals in development of Fuzzy logic based model implemented in Bayesian networks as reviewed in table 1. Even that only one research had not made universal model but a proof of concept. We thus conclude that there is strong need of research in the area of fuzzy sets development for ISBSG database as well as the implementation of fuzzy sets using Bayesian networks. ISBSG is a large data set and development of Fuzzy rules and fuzzy sets for this database is itself a great task. Thus it is proposed that a research to be carried out to develop an fuzzy logic based intelligent effort estimation model for effort estimation based on ISBSG data set.

Table 1. ISBSG data Sets

S/No	Title of Research papers and Authors	M D	D S	BN	F S
1	"Development of Simple Effort Estimation Model based on Fuzzy Logic using Bayesian Networks"[27]	Y	N	Y	Y
2	"Improvement Opportunities and Suggestions for Benchmarking" C Gencel, L Buglione, A Abran [28]	N	N	N	N
3	"Using Chronological Splitting to Compare Cross- and Single-company Effort Models: Further Investigation" C. Lokan & E. Mendes, January [29]		Y	N	N
4	"Investigating the Use of Chronological Splitting to Compare Software Cross-company and Single-company Effort Predictions" C. Lokan & E. Mendes[30]		Y	N	N
5	"Replicating Studies on Cross- vs. Single company Effort Models using the ISBSG Database" E. Mendes & C. Lokan[31]		Y	N	N
6	"Impact of Base Functional Component Types on Software Functional Size based Effort Estimation" L Buglione, C Gencel[32]	Y	N	N	N
7	"Performance calculation and estimation with QEST/LIME using ISBSG r10 data" L Buglione, A Abran [33]	Y	N	N	N
8	"The value and validity of software effort estimation models built from a multiple organization data set" Kefu Deng[34]	Y	N	N	N
9	"Evaluation of a black-box estimation tool: a case study" A Abran, I. Ndiaye and P. Bourque[35]	Y	N	N	N
10	"An Algorithm for the Generation of Segmented Parametric Software Estimation Models and its Empirical Evaluation" Juan J. Cuadrado-Gallego, Miguel-Angel Sicilia[36]	Y	N	N	N
11	"ISBSG Software Project Repository & ISO 9126: An Opportunity for Quality Benchmarking" Laila Cheikhi, Alain Abran, Luigi Buglione[37]	N	N	N	N
12	"Convertibility of Function Points to COSMIC-FFP: Identification and Analysis of Functional Outliers" Jean-Marc Desharnais, Alain Abran, Juan Cuadrado [38]	N	N	N	N
13	"An empirical study of process related attributes in segmented software cost estimation relationships" Juan J. Cuadrado-Gallego, Miguel-A´ngel Sicilia, Miguel Garre, Daniel Rodrýguez[39]	N	N	N	N
14	"A Replicated Comparison of Cross-company and Within-company Effort Estimation Models using the ISBSG Database" E. Mendes, C. Lokan, R. Harrison, C. Triggs[40]		Y	N	N
15	"Segmented Parametric Software Estimation Models: Using the EM Algorithm with the ISBSG 8 Database" M. Garre, J.J. Cuadrado, M.A. Sicilia, M Charro, D Rodríguez[41]	Y		N	N
16	"Advances in Statistical Analysis from the ISBSG Benchmarking Database" Luca Santillo, Stefania Lombardi, Domenico Natale[42]		N	N	N
17	"Sensitivity of results to different data quality meta-data criteria in the sample selection of projects from the ISBSG dataset" [43]	N	Y	N	N
18	"Applying moving windows to software effort estimation" Chris Lokan , Emilia Mendes [44]	Y	Y	N	N

Model Development: MD, Data Subsets: DS, Bayesian Nets: BN, Fuzzy Sets: FS

4 Fuzzy Set Example

To include more significant factors in fuzzy sets, four factors (Development Type, Organizational Split, Language Type and Architecture) are analyzed. The data is classified on the basis of categorical data of these factors. The values of the factors are coded according to the scheme given below in table 2.

Table 2. Codes for categorical data in [52]

Development Type	Organizational Split	Language	Architecture
EN: Enhancement	IN: In house development	3GL	CS: Client Server
MIX: New Development, Partial Development, Default	OS: Out sourced development	4 GL	SA: Stand Alone
RE: Re development	MIX: Mixture of both, Other, Not provided	MIX: 2 GL, Application, Not provided	OTH: Other, Multi -tier, Not provided

The table listed at [52] provides the significant statistics of productivity. This table can be used to select type of project and get the productivity measure. For example, one can apply the following fuzzy rule to get the productivity by consulting the table (The table is placed on following web link due to limitation of space available) and get the following Statistics.

IF Development Type = Enhancement AND In House Project = Yes AND Architecture = Client Server AND Language = 3rd Generation THEN Productivity = 11.2278

N	Mean	Variance	Skewness	Median
18	11.2278	290.236	3.194	5.1000

However there are some limitations in the above mentioned example, first its is very passive task to consult the table every time. Secondly there can be issues to accuracy. Thirdly there is lack of adaptation or learning of this mechanism. Meanwhile when we reach at the value of productivity e.g. 11.22 in the above example, should we relay on the crisp value as the variance is 290.23. Recalling the nature of categorical data such as Development type and Continuous data such as productivity, the need of fuzzy distributions e.g triangular to map multiple categories of data over a crisp value is understandable. Thus we advocate the need of fuzziness instead of deterministic nature of factor values given in table 1.

We propose a research to identify critical factors of software estimation and learn suitable fuzzy functions to develop an estimation model based on large scale data set. This research will result in development of an intelligent effort estimation model. It is proposed to develop an estimation model based on a list of significant factors and training the values as shown in fig.1

The proposed [43] model is to extend in terms of number of factors as well as in the capability of learning the fuzziness. The model would also be extension of adaptive in terms of variation in selected factors, as well as in terms of choice of Bayesian Network as implementation tool.

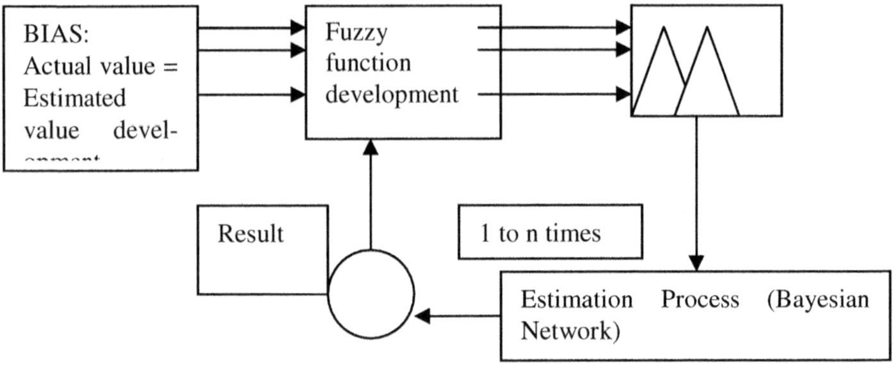

Fig. 1. Intelligent effort estimation model in Bayesian Network, This process is to be carried out N times to get suitable accuracy

$$a = Productivity \times [1 - fuzziness]$$
$$b = Productivity \times [1 + fuzziness]$$

Let fuzziness = 0.3 and Productivity = 11.23 we get the coordinates

$$a = 11.23 \times [1 - 0.3] = 7.86$$
$$b = 11.23 \times [1 + 0.3] = 14.59$$

This means the triangular distribution for size 11.23 is in fig. 2

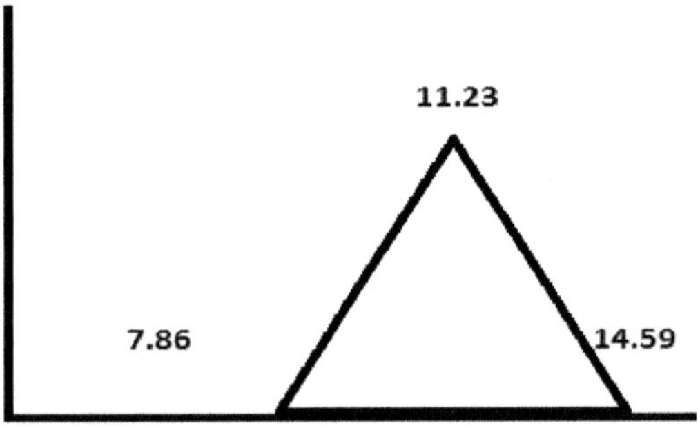

Fig. 2. Triangular distribution for size

However the a and b coordinates can be changed according to the approach given below.

Approach

1. Select a batch of data
2. Estimate the effort with initial value for triangular fuzziness and fuzzification
3. Compare the BIAS
4. If Bias is – ve, change the value of b

   If Bias is +ve, change the value of a
5. Repeat the step 2 to 4 for next batches of data

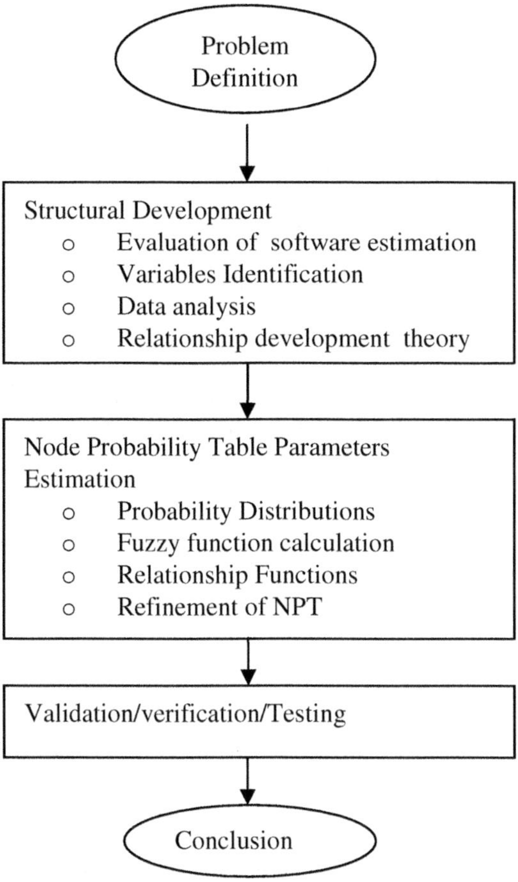

5 Conclusion

The aim of this proposed research framework is Development of reliable and intelligent software estimation model using ISBSD data set. The prime objectives are the selection of critical factors, calculation of fuzzy function, development of Bayesian network and implementation and testing of this proposed model. This article presents preliminary phase of our proposal that a model should be and can be developed for effort estimation based on fuzzy sets constructed from ISBSG data set. The future work requires selection of factors, calculation of fuzzy sets and implementation of Bayesian network. We have highlighted that existing models don't provide fuzzy sets on ISBSG dataset. We have also investigated that existing intelligent effort estimation systems don't have capability of active learning. It has also been proposed how fuzzy sets can be developed and interpreted using ISBSG dataset.

References

1. Royce, W.: Software Project Management, A Unified Frame work. Pearson Education (2000)
2. Gray, A.R., MacDonell, S.G.: A comparison of techniques for developing predictive models of software metrics. Information and Software Technology 39, 425–437 (1997)
3. Boehm, B., Abts, C., Chulani, S.: Software development cost estimation ap-proaches-—A survey. Annals of Software Engineering 10, 177–205 (2000)
4. Azzeh, M., et al.: Software Effort Estimation Based on Weighted Fuzzy Grey Relational Analysis. ACM (2009)
5. Bohem, B., et al.: Cost models for future life cycle processes: COCOMO2.0. Annals of Software Engineering 1 (1995)
6. ISBSG data release 10 (2007), http://www.isbsg.org (accessed on February 18, 2009)
7. Trendowicz, A., Münch, J., Jeffery, R.: State of the Practice in Software Effort Estimation: A Survey and Literature Review. In: Huzar, Z., Koci, R., Meyer, B., Walter, B., Zendulka, J. (eds.) CEE-SET 2008. LNCS, vol. 4980, pp. 232–245. Springer, Heidelberg (2011), doi:10.1007/978-3-642-22386-0_18
8. Li, J., Ruhe, G.: Decision Support Analysis for Software Effort Estimation by Analogy. In: Third International Workshop on Predictor Models in Software Engineering (PROMISE 2007) (2007)
9. Larman, C.: Agile and Iterative Development: A Manager's Guide. Addison Wesley (2003)
10. Witting, G., Finnie, G.: Estimating software development effort with connectionist models. In: Proceedings of the Information and Software Technology Conference, pp. 469–476 (1997)
11. Trendowicz, A., Heidrich, J., Münch, J., Ishigai, Y., Yokoyama, K., Kikuchi, N.: Development of a hybrid cost estimation model in an iterative manner. In: ICSE 2006, Shanghai, China, May 20-28 (2006)
12. Ahmeda, M.A., Saliub, M.O., AlGhamdia, J.: Adaptive fuzzy logic-based framework for software development effort prediction. Information and Software Technology 47, 31–48 (2005)
13. Verma, H.K., Sharma, V.: Handling imprecision in inputs using fuzzy logic to predict effort in software development. In: 2010 IEEE 2nd International Advance Computing Conference (IACC), February 19-20 (2010), references cited: 25
14. Ahmed, M.A., Muzaffar, Z.: Handling imprecision and uncertainty in software development effort prediction: A type-2 fuzzy logic based framework. Journal Information and Software Technology 51(3) (March 2009) cited 2, acm
15. Jensen, F.V.: An Introduction to Bayesian Networks. UCL Press (1996)
16. Murphy, K.: A Brief Introduction to Graphical Models and Bayesian Networks (1998)

17. Fenton, N.E., Krause, P., Lane, C., Neil, M.: A Probabilistic Model for Software Defect Prediction, citeseer, manuscript available from the authors (2001)
18. Pendharkar, P.C., Subramanian, G.H., Rodger, J.A.: A Probabilistic Model for Predicting Software Development Effort. IEEE Transactions on Software Engineering 31(7), 615–624 (2005)
19. Martin, N., Fenton, N.E., Nielson, L.: Building large-scale Bayesian networks. Journal of Knowledge Engineering Review 15(3) (2000)
20. Bibi, S., Stamelos, I.: Software Process Modeling with Bayesian Belief Networks. In: IEEE Software Metrics 2004, Online proceedings (2004)
21. Shamsaei, A.: M.Sc. Project report, Advanced Method in computer science at the University of London (2005)
22. Hearty, P., Fenton, N.E., Marquez, D., Neil, M.: Predicting Project Velocity in XP using a Learning Dynamic Bayesian Network Model. IEEE Transactions on Software Engineering 35(1) (January 2009)
23. Fenton, N.E., Marsh, W., Neil, M., Cates, P., Forey, S., Tailor, M.: Making Resource Decisions for Software Projects. In: Proceedings of the 26th International Conference on Software Engineering (ICSE 2004) (2004)
24. Fenton, N.E., Neil, M., Marsh, W., Hearty, P., Marquez, D., Krause, P., Mishra, R.: Predicting software defects in varying development lifecycles using Bayesian Nets. Information and Software Technology 49(1) (2007)
25. Khodakarami, V., Fenton, N., Neil, M.: Project scheduling: Improved approach incorporating uncertainty using Bayesian networks. Project Management Journal (2009)
26. Mendes, E.: Predicting Web Development Effort Using a Bayesian Network. In: Proceedings of 11th International Conference on Evaluation and Assessment in Software Engineering, EASE 2007, April 2-3, pp. 83–93 (2007)
27. Nauman, A.B., Aziz, R.: Development of Simple Effort Estimation Model based on Fuzzy Logic using Bayesian Networks. IJCA Special Issue on Artificial Intelligence Techniques - Novel Approaches & Practical Applications (3), 4–7 (2011)
28. Gencel, C., Buglione, L., Abran, A.: Improvement Opportunities and Suggestions for Benchmarking. In: Proceedings of IWSM/MENSURA 2009, Amsterdam, Netherlands, November 4-6, pp. 144–156 (2009)
29. Lokan, C., Mendes, E.: Using Chronological Splitting to Compare Cross- and Single-company Effort Models: Further Investigation. In: 32nd Australasian Computer Science Conference, ACSC 2009, Wellington, New Zealand (January 2009)
30. Lokan, C., Mendes, E.: Investigating the Use of Chronological Splitting to Compare Software Cross-company and Single-company Effort Predictions. In: EASE 2008, 12th Inter-na-tional Conference on Evaluation and Assessment in Software Engineering, Bari, Italy (June 2008)
31. Mendes, E., Lokan, C.: Replicating Studies on Cross- vs. Single-company Effort Models using the ISBSG Data-base. Empirical Software Engineering 13(1), 3–37 (2008)
32. Buglione, L., Gencel, C.: Impact of Base Functional Component Types on Software Functional Size based Effort Estimation. In: Jedlitschka, A., Salo, O. (eds.) PROFES 2008. LNCS, vol. 5089, pp. 75–89. Springer, Heidelberg (2008)
33. Buglione, L., Abran, A.: Performance calculation and estimation with QEST/LIME using ISBSG r10 data. In: Proceedings of the 5th Software Measurement European Forum (SMEF 2008), Milan, Italy, May 28-30, pp. 175–192 (2008) ISBN 9-788870-909999
34. Deng, K.: The value and validity of software effort estimation models built from a multiple organization data set, Masters thesis, University of Auckland (2008)

35. Abran, A., Ndiaye, I., Bourque, P.: Evaluation of a black-box estimation tool: a case study. Software Process Improvement and Practice 12, 199–218 (2007)
36. Cuadrado-Gallego, J.J., Sicilia, M.-A.: An Algorithm for the Generation of Segmented Parametric Software Estimation Models and its Empirical Evaluation. Computing and Informatics 26, 1–15 (2007)
37. Cheikhi, L., Abran, A., Buglione, L.: ISBSG Software Project Repository & ISO 9126: An Opportunity for Quality Bench-marking. European Journal for the Informatics Professional 7(1), 46–52 (2006)
38. Desharnais, J.-M., Abran, A., Cuadrado, J.: Convertibility of Function Points to COSMIC-FFP: Identification and Analysis of Functional Outliers (2006), http://www.cc.uah.es/cubit/CuBITIFPUG/MENSURA2006.pdf
39. Cuadrado-Gallego, J.J., Sicilia, M.-A., Garre, M., Rodrýguez, D.: An empirical study of process related attributes in segmented software cost estimation relationships. The Journal of Systems and Software 79, 353–361 (2006)
40. Mendes, E., Lokan, C., Harrison, R., Triggs, C.: A Replicated Comparison of Cross-company and Within-company Effort Estimation Models using the ISBSG Database
41. Garre, M., Cuadrado, J.J., Sicilia, M.A., Charro, M., Rodríguez, D.: Segmented Parametric Software Estimation Models: Using the EM Algorithm with the ISBSG 8 Database
42. ISBSG Productivity table, https://sites.google.com/a/suit.edu.pk/csitresearch/

A Prolog Based Approach to Consistency Checking of UML Class and Sequence Diagrams

Zohaib Khai[1], Aamer Nadeem[1], and Gang-soo Lee[2]

[1] Center for Software Dependability,
Mohammad Ali Jinnah University (MAJU), Islamabad, Pakistan
raja_zohaibkhai@yahoo.com, anadeem@jinnah.edu.pk
[2] Department of Computer Engineering,
Hannam University, Korea
gslee@hannam.ac.kr

Abstract. UML is an industrial standard for designing and developing object-oriented software. It provides a number of notations for modeling different system views, but it still does not have any means of meticulously checking consistency among the models. These models can contain overlapping information which may lead to inconsistencies. If these inconsistencies are not detected and resolved properly at an early stage, they may result in many errors in implementation phase. In this paper, we propose a novel approach for consistency checking of class and sequence diagrams based on Prolog language. In the proposed approach, consistency checking rules as well as UML models are represented in Prolog, then Prolog's reasoning engine is used to automatically find inconsistencies.

Keywords: UML, Sequence Diagram, Class Diagram, Prolog, Constraints, Consistency checking.

1 Introduction

In system development lifecycle, design phase plays an important role as a basis for implementation. During design phase system is modeled in such a way as to bridge the gap between analysis and implementation phase. It is desirable to be able to detect model inconsistencies at an early stage, so that the inconsistencies will not be propagated to code or customer deliverables, such as, documentation [9]. If design phase is modeled properly then process of up-gradation and maintenance of system becomes easy.

An important quality of design is that it should be understandable. To increase the design understandability different design methods and notations have been developed. But for the past few years Unified Modeling Language (UML) [1] is accepted as an industrial standard for object-oriented system modeling. The software design is usually represented as a collection of UML diagrams. UML is a very flexible modeling language as it provides number of notations for modeling different system perspectives, e.g., static view (class diagram) and dynamic view (sequence diagram).

T.-h. Kim et al. (Eds.): ASEA/DRBC/EL 2011, CCIS 257, pp. 85–96, 2011.

It also has a wide range of tools covering up all the features of system modeling for complete and comprehensive representation.

Cost of software development also decreases by performing consistency checking between different UML artifacts. Especially after the emergence of MDA [21] object-oriented code can be generated from UML models. So, for reliable and correct code generation UML artifacts need to be consistent for which model consistency checking is desirable. Similarly modifications in model are relatively simple as compared to the changes in source code. After modifications in model, once again consistency checking is required to validate models.

In this paper we present an approach that transforms UML models into Prolog [3] to perform consistency checking. Use of Prolog is motivated by the fact that it is a declarative programming language that provides beneficial assistance representing arbitrary concepts based on inference rules. It is also quite expressive for the types of consistency rules we deal with.

2 Inconsistency and Consistency Checking Types

This section describes the consistency checking types as given by Mens et al. [12].

2.1 Consistency Checking Types

Vertical Consistency. Consistency checking is performed between diagrams of different versions or abstraction-levels. Syntactic and semantic consistencies are also included in it.

Horizontal Consistency. Consistency checking is performed between different diagrams of same version.

Evolution Consistency. Consistency checking is performed between different versions of a same UML-artifact.

Inconsistencies we consider include both structural, which appears in class diagram, and behavioural that appears in sequence diagram. Classes of inconsistencies used below are taken from [17]. In current paper we deal with the type of consistency known as horizontal consistency. Inconsistencies that can occur are described in next section.

2.2 Inconsistency Types

Dangling Feature Reference [17]. This type of inconsistency occurs when message in sequence diagram references to a method that does not exists in class diagram.

Multiplicity Incompatibility [17]. This type of inconsistency takes place when the link in sequence diagram does not follow the multiplicity constraints defined by corresponding association in class diagram.

Dangling Association Reference [17]. This type of inconsistency occurs when a link is defined between objects in sequence diagram and it has no association between classes of corresponding objects.

Classless Connectable Element [17]. This type of inconsistency occurs when object's lifeline in sequence diagram refers to the class that does not exist in class diagram.

3 Related Work

In this section, the existing UML model consistency checking techniques are discussed. For consistency checking many techniques transform the UML model in some intermediate form, by applying the rules presented in different techniques.

Straeten et al [2, 11] present a technique for consistency detection and resolution using DL (Description logic) [14]. The authors present an inconsistency classification. A UML profile is also developed to support consistency of UML artifacts and then LOOM tool [15] is used for translation of developed profile into DL. Consistency checking is performed for messages, associations and classes but not for constraints and multiplicity.

Krishnan [4] presents an approach for consistency checking based on translation of UML diagrams in state predicates. Only UML behavior diagrams are covered. After translation, PVS (prototype verification system) a theorem prover as well as a model checker is used to perform consistency checking.

Muskens et al [5] present an approach for intra and inter phase consistency checking, which makes use of Partition Algebra using verification rules. Consistency checking is performed by deriving the rules from one view and imposing them on the other view. Consistency checking is performed for associations, messages and constraints.

Egyed [6] introduces a consistency checking technique known as View-Integra. In this technique the diagram to be compared is transformed in such a way that it becomes conceptually close to the diagram with which it is going to compare. Consistency checking is performed between same artifacts, one is original and other one is transformed. Technique is partially automated.

Ehrig et al [7] propose a technique to perform consistency checking between sequence and class diagram based on Attributed Typed Graphs and their transformation. Consistency checking is performed for existence checking (means all classes used in sequence diagram exist in class diagram), visibility checking (visibility of classes, attributes and operations, all should be visible to sequence diagram) and multiplicity checking. Their approach is not supported by any tool support.

Briand et al. [8, 18] propose an approach for change impact analysis based on UML models. This technique is applied before changes are implemented to estimate the effect of change. Some rules are formally defined using OCL to determine the impact of change on different versions of models. A prototype tool is implemented which also executes consistency checking rules defined.

Paige et al. [10] present an approach to formalize and describe the implementation of consistency constraints between two views of BON (Business Object Notation) i.e. class and collaboration diagram. PVS theorem prover is used to automate the proofs. Consistency checks performed includes sequencing consistency checks (order of message calls), class existence and routine (operation) existence.

Storrle [16] proposes a Prolog based model representation and query interface for analysis of models in MDD (Model Driven Development) setting. Models and queries are represented on the basis of representation defined for Prolog clauses. Queries are used for identifying elements, properties and sub-models of models.

4 Proposed Approach

The proposed approach is an idea of checking consistency of two UML diagrams, i.e., class diagram and sequence diagram. For this purpose, UML models as well as consistency rules are represented in Prolog and then reasoning is performed in Prolog. Our technique provides better coverage of the models and can also be extended to check consistency between OCL constraints of both UML artifacts. Flow diagram of proposed approach is given in Figure 1.

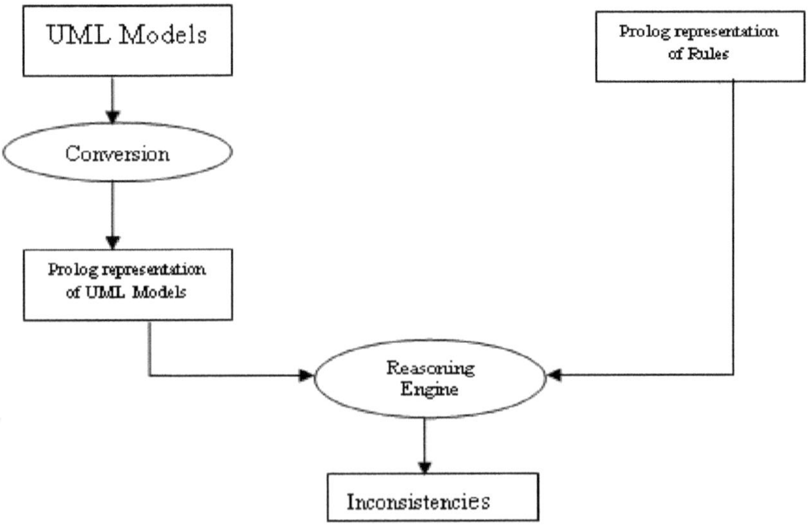

Fig. 1. Flow diagram of Proposed Approach

4.1 Representation of UML Models in Prolog

Class Diagram

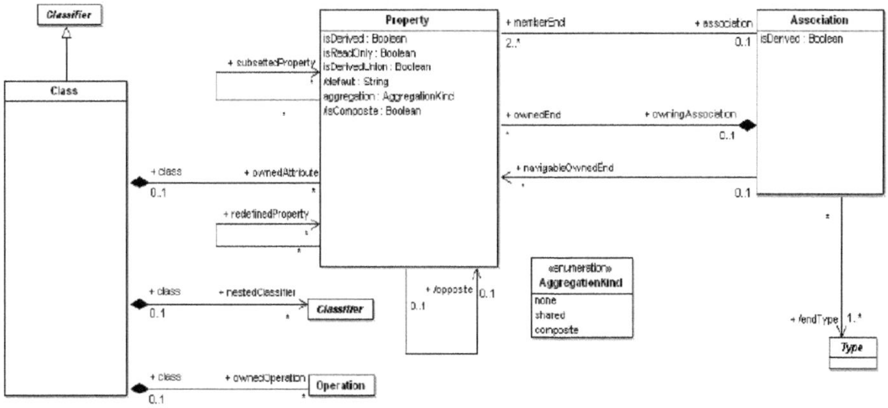

Fig. 2. Partial UML Meta-model for Class diagram [1]

This section deals with Prolog representation of UML class diagram. Figure2 shows partial meta-model of UML class diagram [1]. Class diagram consist of attributes, operations, associations and multiplicity constraints along with class name. Every element of class diagram is assigned an identifier which is a number. These assigned identifiers are used so that relationships between different elements can be created. General format of rules is as follows.

Predname(id(s) , Element(s)-details).

class(Classid , Classname). (1)

'class' used at start is predicate name after that 'Classid' is the unique id assigned to the class and 'Classname' is the actual name of class.

attribute(Attrid , Attrname, Attr-type, Classid). (2)

'attribute' written at the start is predicate name, first thing after brackets is 'Attrid' which is identifier of attribute, second is 'Attrname' i.e. attribute name, third is 'Attr-type' i.e. type of attribute and at fourth place 'Classid' is identifier of class to whom this attribute belongs.

Operation(Opid , Opname , [Parameter(s)-id] , Classid). (3)

'operation' is predicate name, then 'Opid' is operation identifier, 'Opname' is operation name, '[parameters]' is list of parameters and 'Classid' is same as in (1).

parameter(Pid ,Pname, Ptype). (4)

Keyword 'parameter' is predicate name, Pid is parameter identifier, 'Pname' is name of parameter and 'Ptype' refers to the type of parameter, it can either refers to primitive types or to a class.

association(Associd , ClassAid , ClassBid). (5)

Keyword 'association' is predicate name, 'Associd' is identifier for association. 'ClassAid' and 'ClassBid' are identifiers for the association ends.

Multiplicity(Associd , Classid , Lowval , Upval). (6)

Keyword 'multiplicity' is name of predicate, from 'Associd' and 'Classid', we come to know the association and class to which multiplicity constraints belongs. 'Lowval' & 'Upval' contains actual values of multiplicity.

Sequence Diagram

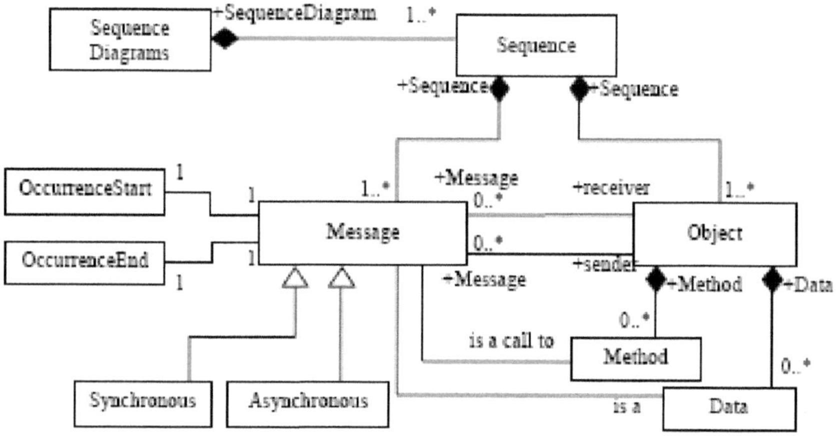

Fig. 3. UML Meta-model for Sequence diagram [19]

This section contains details of Prolog representation of sequence diagram elements. Figure 3 shows meta-model of sequence diagram [19]. Elements of sequence diagram are objects and operation/method call. Similarly identifiers are assigned to different elements of sequence diagram.

object(Objid , Objname, Classid, Multiobj). (7)

Keyword 'object' is actually name of predicate. 'Objid', 'Objname' and 'Classid' are object identifier, object name and class identifier respectively. 'Multiobj' has value of T(true) or F(false), which tells whether multiple instances exist or not.

mcall(Msgid ,Opname ,[Parameter-list] ,Sndobjid ,Recobjid). (8)

Keyword 'mcall' stands for method-call is predicate name. 'Msgid', 'Opname' and [Parameter-list] are for message identifier, operation name and parameter-list of operation respectively. 'Sndobjid' and 'Recobjid' is sending object name and receiving object name.

Below is an example of class and sequence diagram representation according to our proposed representation of UML model in Prolog. Both diagrams are taken from [20].

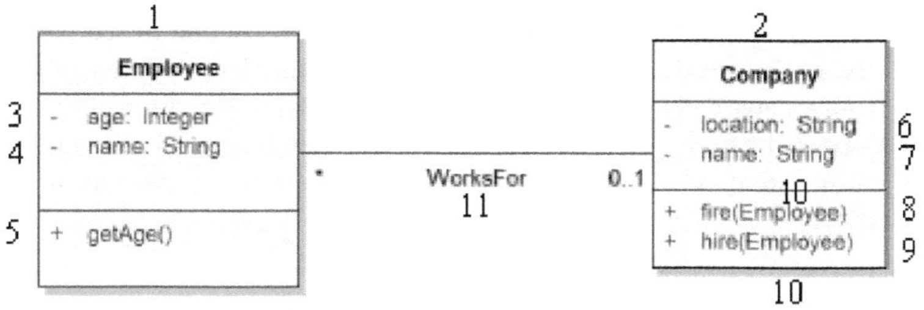

Fig. 4. Example Class Diagram [20]

```
class(1, Employee).
attribute(3, age, integer, 1).
attribute(4, name, String, 1).
operation(5, getAge, [ ], 1).
class(2, Company).
attribute(6, location, String, 2).
attribute(7, name, String, 2).
operation(8, fire,[10], 2).
operation(9, hire, [10], 2).
parameter(10, Employee, Employee).
association(11, 1, 2).
multiplicity(11, 1, 0, 1).
multiplicity(11, 2, 0, n).
```

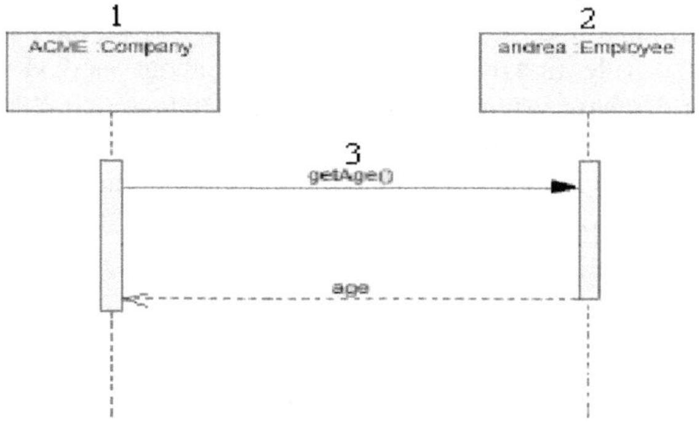

Fig. 5. Example Sequence Diagram [20]

```
object(1, ACME, 2, F).
object(2, Andrea, 1, T).
mcall(3, getAge, [ ], 1, 2).
```

4.2 Consistency Checking Rules

In this section we have proposed some rules for consistency checking of UML models based on Prolog predicate.

Classless Connectable Element. Occurs when object's lifeline in sequence diagram refers to the class that does not exist in class diagram. Here object's information is brought from database using object clause and from that information class identifier is extracted and compared with all class predicates in database to check class existence. In case of negative results of comparison an error message is returned defining inconsistency.

```
objcl_exist_rule(ClCele):-
        object(Objid,_,_,_),
        object(Objid,N,Classid,_),
        ((\+class(Classid,_),
        ClCele="Error: 301");
        fail.
```

Dangling Feature Reference. Occurs when message call in sequence diagram refers to method that does not exist in class diagram. In this rule using method call clause, required information is brought from database and from that information object identifier is extracted to find out the related object. Finally operation existence in corresponding class is checked on the basis of information taken from object. If operation does not exist an error message is returned.

```
op_exist_rule(DfRef):-
        mcall(Msgid,_,_,_),
        mcall(Msgid,Opname,_,Recobjid),
        object(Recobjid,_,Classid,_),
        ((\+operation(_,Opname,_,Classid),
        DfRef="Error: 302");
        fail.
```

Dangling Association Reference. Occurs when there is link between objects in sequence diagram while no association between corresponding classes of class diagram. In this rule first required information about method call and object is gathered from database using 'mcall' and 'object' clauses and then on the basis of gathered information comparison is made to check existence of association between classes. If association does not exist an error message is returned.

```
assoc_exist(DaRef):-
        mcall(Msgid,_,_,_),
        mcall(Msgid,_,Sndobjid,Recobjid),
        object(Sndobjid,_,ClassA,_),
        object(Recobjid,_,ClassB,_),
        ((\+association(_,ClassA,ClassB),
        DaRef="Error: 303");
        fail.
```

Multiplicity Incompatibility. Occurs when multiplicity constraints of both artifacts are not matching. In this rule required information is collected from database using ‘mcall’, ‘object’ and ‘association’ clauses. From gathered information, receiving object is checked whether it’s a multi-object or not and on the basis of this further comparison is made to check the multiplicity constraints. If constraints are non-matching then an error message is returned containing details of inconsistency.

```
mlp_in_rule(MulIn):-
        mcall(Msgid,_,_,_),
        mcall(Msgid,_,Sndobjid,Recobjid),
        object(Sndobjid,_,ClassAid,_),
        object(Recobjid,_,ClassBid,BMulti),
        association(Associd,ClassAid,ClassBid),
        ((BMulti == t,
        multiplicity(Associd,ClassBid,_,UpvalB),

        ((UpvalB =< 1,
        MulIn="Error: 304");
        (UpvalB > 1)));

        (BMulti == f,
        multiplicity(Associd,ClassBid,_,UpvalB),

        ((UpvalB < 1,
        MulIn="Error: 304b");
        (UpvalB =:= 1)))),
        fail.
```

5 Automation

Technique proposed in current paper is automatable. For automation of technique certain steps are to be followed. First UML models are converted so that information contained in models can be represented in prolog. This is done by generating XMI of each model, which is by default generated, with each model, in existing CASE tools(e.g. Togeather). Then from XMI relevant information or information to be matched is extracted and represented in the form of Prolog predicates, which are of first order.

After model conversion to prolog predicates, consistency rules from rule database along with converted models are presented to reasoning engine. Reasoning engine performs reasoning on prolog predicates generated from models based on consistency rules and return error code of inconsistencies if any.

6 Evaluation

In this section, evaluation of existing techniques presented in section 3 and our proposed technique is performed. Evaluation is performed on the basis of inconsistency types described in section 2. Result of evaluation is presented below in the form of a table.

Table 1. Comparison of Existing Related Techniques

Inconsistency Types → / Techniques ↓	DFR	MI	DAR	CCE	CI
Simmonds et al (2004), Straeten et al (2003)	Yes	No	Yes	Yes	No
Krishnan, P. (2005)	Yes	No	No	Yes	No
Muskens et al (2005)	Yes	No	Yes	No	Yes
Egyed, A. (2001)	Yes	No	Yes	Yes	No
Ehrig et al (2000)	Yes	Yes(partial)	Yes	Yes	No
Briand et al (2006, 2003)	Yes	No	No	Yes	No
Paige et al (2002)	Yes	No	No	Yes	No
CCSP	Yes	Yes	Yes	Yes	No

Table 2. Abbreviations used in Table1

Abbreviation Used	Value
DFR	Dangling Feature Reference
MI	Multiplicity Incompatibility
DAR	Dangling Association Reference
CCE	Classless Connectable Element
CI	Constraint Incompatibility
CCSP	Consistency checking of Class & Sequence diagram using Prolog

7 Conclusion and Future Work

UML is an industrial standard for designing and developing object-oriented software. To obtain consistent and correct information from UML artifacts, consistency checking of artifacts is required. Also consistency checking plays very important role in reliable and correct code generation in MDD setting, as correct code is generated only if models are consistent. In this paper we present a prolog based consistency checking technique for two different artifacts of UML, Proposed technique provides better diagram coverage and also covers more inconsistency types. Further work can be done by including more elements of both artifacts. More artifacts can also be added by covering all elements of those artifacts to avoid skipping minor details in models.

Ackmowledgement. This work was supported by the Security Engineering Research Center, under research grant from the Korean Ministry of Knowledge Economy.

References

1. Object Management Group. Unified Modeling Language specification version 2.1.2. formal/2007-11-01 (November 2007)
2. Simmonds, J., Van Der Straeten, R., Jonckers, V., Mens, T.: Maintaining consistency between UML models using description logic. In: Proceedings Langages et Modèles à Objets 2004, RSTI série L'Objet, vol. 10(2-3), pp. 231–244. Hermes Science Publications (2004)
3. Clocksin, W.F., Mellish, C.S.: Programming in Prolog, 2nd edn. Springer, Heidelberg (1984)
4. Krishnan, P.: Consistency Checks for UML. In: The Proc. of the Asia Pacific Software engineering Conference (APSEC 2000), pp. 162–169 (December 2000)
5. Muskens, J., Brill, R.J.: Generalizing Consistency Checking between Software Views. In: Proceedings of 5th Working IEEE/IFIP Conference on Software Architecture (WICSA 2005), pp. 169–180 (2005)
6. Egyed, A.: Scalable consistency checking between diagrams -The VIEWINTEGRA Approach. In: Proceedings of the 16th International Conference on Automated Software Engineering, San Diego, USA (November 2001)
7. Ehrig, H., Tsiolakis, A.: Consistency analysis of UML class and sequence diagrams using Attributed Typed Graph Grammars. In: Proceedings of joint APPLIGRAPH/ GETGRATS workshop on Graph Transformation systems, Berlin (March 2000)
8. Briand, L.C., Labiche, Y., O'Sullivan, L., Sowka, M.M.: Automated Impact Analysis of UML Models. Journal of Systems and Software 79(3), 339–352 (2006)
9. Paige, R.F., Ostroff, J.S., Brooke, P.J.: A Test-Based Agile Approach to Checking the Consistency of Class and Collaboration Diagrams, UK Software Testing Workshop, University of York, September 4-5 (2003)
10. Paige, R.F., Ostroff, J.S., Brooke, P.J.: Checking the Consistency of Collaboration and class Diagrams using PVS. In: Proc. Fourth Workshop on Rigorous Object-Oriented Methods. British Computer Society, London (March 2002)
11. Straeten, R.V.D., Mens, T., Simmonds, J.: Maintaining Consistency between UML Models with Description Logic Tools. In: ECOOP Workshop on Object-Oriented Reengineering, Darmstadt, Germany (July 2003)
12. Mens, T., Straeten, R.V.D., Simmonds, J.: A Framework for Managing Consistency of Evolving UML Models. In: Yang, H. (ed.) Software Evolution with UML and XML, ch.1. Idea Group Inc. (March 2005)
13. Usman, M., Nadeem, A., Tai-hoon, K., Cho, E.-S.: A Survey of Consistency Checking Techniques for UML Models. Advanced Software Engineering and Its Applications, pp. 57–62. ASEA, Hainan Island (2008)
14. Baader, F., McGuinness, D., Nardi, D., Patel-Schneider, P.: The Description Logic Handbook: Theory, Implementation and Applications. Cambridge University Press (2003)
15. MacGregor, R.M.: Inside the LOOM description classifier. ACM SIGART Bulletin 2(3), 88–92 (1991)
16. Störrle, H.: A PROLOG-based Approach to Representing and Querying UML Models. In: Cox, P., Fish, A., Howse, J. (eds.) Intl. Ws. Visual Languages and Logic (VLL 2007). CEUR-WS, vol. 274, pp. 71–84. CEUR (2007)
17. Straeten, R.V.D.: Inconsistency management in model-driven engineering using description logics. PhD thesis, Department of Computer Science, Vrije Universiteit Brussel, Belgium (September 2005)

18. Briand, L.C., Labiche, Y., O'Sullivan, L.: Impact Analysis and Change Management of UML Models. In: Proceedings of the 19th International Conference Software Maintenance (ICSM 2003), pp. 256–265. IEEE Computer Society Press, Amsterdam (2003)
19. Ouardani, A., Esteban, P., Paludetto, M., Pascal, J.: A Meta-modeling Approach for Sequence Diagrams to Petri Nets Transformation within the requirement validation process. In: The 20th annual European Simulation and Modeling Conference, ESM 2006 conference, LAAS, Toulouse, France (2006)
20. Baruzzo, A.: A Unified Framework for Automated UML Model Analysis. PhD thesis, Department of Mathematics and Computer Science, University of Udine, Italy (July 2006)
21. Object Management Group (OMG), MDA Guide, Version 1.0.1 (2003), http://www.omg.org/docs/omg/03-06-01.pdf

A UML Profile for Real Time Industrial Control Systems

Kamran Latif[1], Aamer Nadeem[2], and Gang-soo Lee[3]

[1] Department of Software Engineering,
International Islamic University (IIU), Islamabad, Pakistan
klatif007@yahoo.com
[2] Center for Software Dependability,
Mohammad Ali Jinnah University (MAJU), Islamabad, Pakistan
anadeem@jinnah.edu.pk
[3] Department of Computer Engineering,
Hannam University, Korea
gslee@hannam.ac.kr

Abstract. A model is a simplified representation of the reality. Software models are built to represent the problems in an abstract way. Unified modeling language is a popular modeling language among software engineering community. However, due to the limitations of unified modeling language it does not provide complete modeling solution for different domains, especially for real time and industrial control system domains. The object-oriented modeling of real time industrial control systems is in its growing stage. In this research we have evaluated the existing profiles for modeling real time industrial control systems. We have identified limitations of the existing modeling notations and proposed a new profile which overcomes the existing limitations. Our profile is based on unified modeling language's standard extension mechanism and the notations/symbols used are according to international electrotechnical committee standard.

Keywords: Real Time UML Profiles, Industrial Control System.

1 Introduction

Real Time Systems (RTS) have been defined as "the systems which must produce a response within a strict time limit, regardless of the algorithm employed" [1]. The correctness of the results in RTS depends on time; if results are correct but received after the specified time then they are treated as incorrect. While functional and timing correctness are the main focus of RTS, these systems have certain additional characteristics, e.g., temporal behavior, dynamic handling of priorities, synchronization, adaptive scheduling etc., required to achieve timing correctness. These characteristics may vary from system to system, e.g., Peter identifies concurrency, time, determinism and reliability as characteristics of reactive Real Time Industrial Control Systems (RT-ICS) [2]. Similarly Rob identifies time, interrupt driven and scheduling, as distinguishing features of real time and non real time systems [3]. However, Ekelin and

T.-h. Kim et al. (Eds.): ASEA/DRBC/EL 2011, CCIS 257, pp. 97–107, 2011.

Jonsson identify a comprehensive list of general purpose constraints, of the real time industrial control systems [4].

Industrial processes are a series of systematic mechanical or chemical operations [5]. The operations performed in Industrial Control System (ICS) strictly obey the temporal requirements. In the early days, the industrial operations were controlled using relays, electronic switches for turning a device on or off. With the introduction of Programmable Logic Controllers (PLCs) in the late 1960's [6], the relay logic was replaced with PLC. PLCs are the backbone of the today's industrial automation.

Modeling is a simplified representation of the reality. Software models are built to represent the problems in an abstract way. Different modeling languages exist for software modeling, e.g., Unified Modeling Language (UML), Modeling and Analysis of Real-time and Embedded Systems (MARTE), System Modeling Language (SysML). Unified Modeling Language (UML) is one of the most popular languages for object oriented software modeling. Model Driven Architecture (MDA) is an OMG standard [7], which aims to help development of software systems by the use of models. Automating the industrial processes is a difficult task. The software has the great responsibility of controlling the input/output devices. Late discovery of flaws and violation of timing constraints seriously affect the product's quality and cost.

Existing notations for modeling ICS provide isolated solutions for customized needs, e.g., Petri nets, State Machines, Flow charts, decision tables, K-Maps etc. A flowchart has the limitation of modeling concurrent processes. No established notation except UML provides complete solution for modeling different views of the system. UML is familiar among different group of peoples working in the project, e.g., engineers and users. In industrial automation, object oriented modeling technique is in its initial stage [8].

UML does not provide complete solution for modeling real-time system especially for ICS. Due to the limitations of UML, many UML profiles have been introduced for real time systems.

The main objective of this research work is to introduce a new UML profile which overcomes the limitations of the existing notations for modeling real time industrial control systems.

Rest of this paper is organized as follows: section 2 is about existing work regarding UML modeling of real time systems, section 3 describes the main research contribution in which we describe the UML profile for real time industrial control system. In section 4 we present a case study that has been modeled using the proposed UML profile. In section 5 we conclude our work and identify the future work.

2 Related Work

UML is an object oriented graphical modeling language in the field of software engineering, used for designing general purpose software models. The UML is a defacto standard for object oriented software paradigm modeling [9]. Although UML 2.x supports some real time features [10][11], e.g., timing diagram and two data types Time and TimeExpresion [9], but still it lacks in modeling different real time domains, specially RT-ICS. Authors in the literature have reviewed these profiles from different perspectives, e.g., Vogel Heuser et al in [8], and Abdelouahed Gherbi et al. in [9], point out that UML/SPT lacks rigorous formal semantics. RTS also have some domain specific notations, which limit the UML and its profiles for modeling specific RTS domains. OMG has adopted following real time profiles.

1. OMG Systems Modeling Language (SysML)
2. UML Profile for System on a Chip (SoC)
3. UML Profile for Schedulability, Performance and Time (SPT)
4. UML Profile for Modeling and Analysis of Real-time and Embedded Systems (MARTE)
5. UML Profile for Quality of Service (QoS)

SysML is a graphical modeling language based on UML 2.0 with extensions and minor changes [12]. SysML qualifies the basic parameters for modeling real-time systems. Timing, interaction overview, and communication diagrams are not included in the SysML [13]. It lacks support for time [14], bit logic, counters, interrupts, call subroutine and ICS domain specific modeling notations.

In order to design an SoC model, a minimal set of extensions for a UML profile is introduced [15][16]. The designers can create both class and structure diagrams with the help of SoC profile elements [15]. SoC profile is mainly used for modeling system on chip design. As SoC profile is meant for system on chip domain modeling therefore it lacks in other RTS characteristics modeling. It cannot capture different types of time that are required for RTS. It does not account for scheduling and bit logic. No stereotype is available to support subroutine (Function Block) modeling.

SPT profile provides a set of stereotypes to annotate the UML models. Structure of the SPT profile is based on General Resource Modeling (GRM) and Analysis Modeling [9]. Certain drawbacks exist to model more complex systems (distributed systems, hierarchical schedulers, etc). Specific semantic is not properly defined. It does not support state machine-based modeling. Also it does not support bit logic feature of real-time systems.

MARTE profile is an advancement of SPT profile [14]. MARTE facilitates modeling specifications, design, verification/validation stages of system development life cycle. MARTE modeling artifacts provide support for real time modeling. MARTE provides extensive support for schedulability analysis. MARTE provides partial support for modeling of RT-ICS characteristics, but it lacks in modeling bit logic and call subroutine characteristics. Another major problem with MARTE is that it does not provide domain friendly stereotypes/notations for RT-ICS. For example, the interrupt notation used in MARTE [17] is symbolically different then used in ICS domain modeling. The detailed evaluation of the above mentioned profiles is given in [18].

The limitations discussed above regarding ICS domain modeling, led us to introducing a new UML profile, which fulfils the requirements of ICS characteristics modeling, and has the notations/ symbols according to the International Electrotechnical Committee (IEC) 61131-3 [19] standard.

3 UML Profile for Real Time Industrial Control System

The aim of the proposed profile is to provide a language for describing ICS dynamic process flow. The profile is defined using the standard extensibility mechanism of the UML. UML provides an extension mechanism for adding new properties and restricting existing UML meta classes. According to this mechanism, stereotypes, tagged values and constraints are used to define new features. In a profile, coherent set of extensions are grouped together [20]. Stereotypes represent specific metaclasses, tagged values represent standard meta attributes, and profiles are specific kinds of packages [21]. As the control logic programming is sequential in nature, therefore, we have used activity diagram to represent the dynamic behavior of the model. We have introduced stereotypes with icons to annotate the action part of the activity diagram. This annotation not only helps in describing the model in detail but also in defining its properties and tagged values, helps in automatic generation of the code from the model. Figure 1 shows the extension of UML metaclass "Action" with stereotypes.

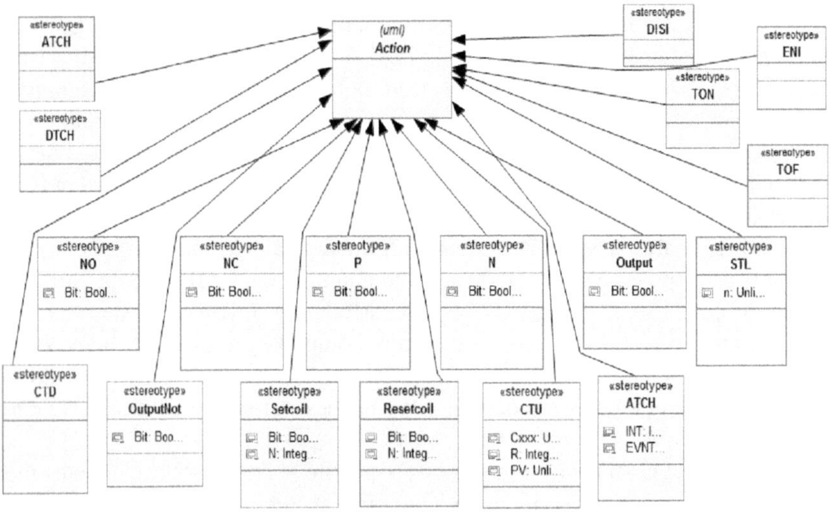

Fig. 1. RT-ICS Profile

The stereotypes that are defined in this profile are summarized in table 1.

Table 1. RT-ICS Profile Stereotypes

Stereotype	Base Class
Normal Open (NO)	Action
Normal Close (NC)	Action
Positive Transition (P)	Action
Negative Transition (N)	Action
Output	Action
OutputNot	Action

Table 1. (*Continued*)

SetCoil	Action
ResetCoil	Action
Count Up (CTU)	Action
Count Down (CTD)	Action
Attach Interrupt (ATCH)	Action
Detach Interrupt (DTCH)	Action
Enable Interrupt (ENI)	Action
Disable Interrupt (DISI)	Action
Conditional Return from Interrupt (RETI)	Action
On Delay Timer (TON)	Action
Off Delay Timer (TOF)	Action
Subroutine Call (STL)	Action

3.1 Designing of Bit Logic Stereotype

There are several Bit logic operations used in the industrial control systems. Normal Open is kind of bit logic operation (action). The symbol used to represent this action is shown in figure 2.

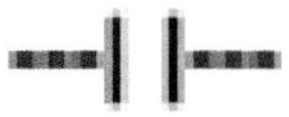

Fig. 2. Normal Open Symbol

The symbol shown in Figure 2 is according to IEC 61131-3 standard. The semantic of Normal Open operation state that the object's initial state is normal open. Table 2 shows the explicit modeling of Normal Open stereotype. Similarly Normal Close is another type of bit logic operation. The explicit modeling of Normal Close stereotype is also shown in table 2.

Table 2. Explicit modeling of Bit Logic Stereotypes

Stereotype	Icon	Extends	Representation	Semantics	Constraints
Normal Open « NO »	---| |---	Action	---| |--- <<NO>> A	Indicates that the state of the item in the action box is "Normal Open"	None
Normal Close « NC »	---|/ |---	Action	---|/ |--- <<NC>> A	Indicates that the state of the item in the action box is "Normal Close"	None

All other stereotypes in this profile have been defined similarly.

3.2 Tool Support

As we have used UML standard extension mechanism which ensures common framework for notations and semantic related concerns, therefore it is possible to use any tool which supports UML standard extension mechanism for designing and modeling of our proposed approach. However, we have used Papyrus UML tool [22] for designing and modeling of our proposed approach. Papyrus is an open source UML modeling tool. It provides an efficient graphical user interface for model development. Papyrus is an eclipse project. Eclipse is created by IBM and eclipse.org is a consortium that manages and directs Eclipse development. Eclipse is a Java based open source development platform. Papyrus addresses the two main features required for UML modeling i.e. modeling and profiling. As it is an open source it provides plug-ins for code generations, e.g., Java, C++ and C. Selection of papyrus tool has two fold benefits for us, one from modeling and profiling perspective, and other from code generation perspective.

4 Case Study

Traffic Lights System was first invented in America in 1918 with three color lights, Green, Yellow and Red. Now-a-days, modern traffic lights are controlled through PLCs. Today's traffic light systems are complex in nature due to the influence of a number of factors, e.g., traffic congestion, pedestrian conflicts, multi-way (more than four) intersections etc. The discussion about the nature of traffic control system is beyond the scope of this case study. In order to simplify the process for understanding purpose, we consider a simple traffic light control system with four way intersection and a congestion control. Our main objective is to apply our designed profile for modeling of traffic light control system. Figure 3 shows an abstract model of the traffic lights.

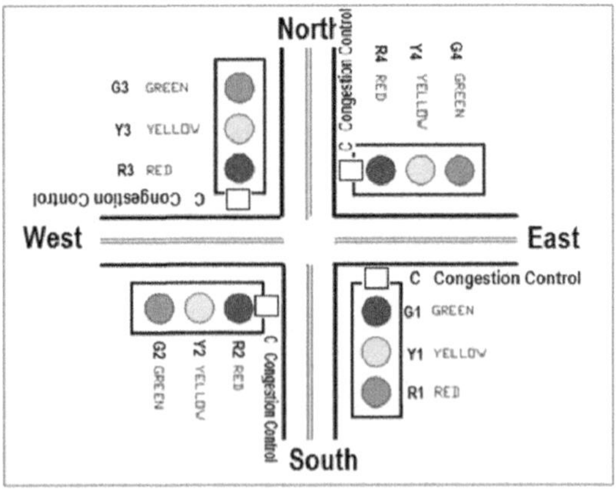

Fig. 3. Traffic Light System Model

We have constructed following three models for traffic light control system.

4.1 Functional Model (Use Case Diagram)

Use case diagram represents the functional model. Fig 4 depicts the use case diagram for traffic control system.

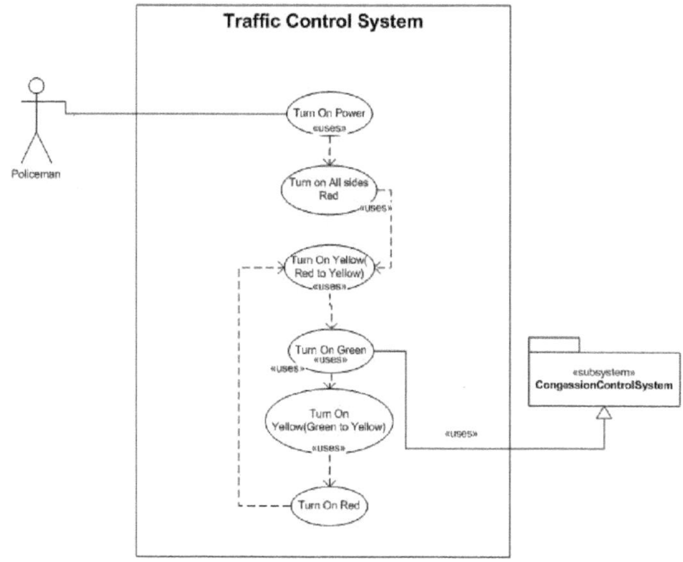

Fig. 4. use case diagram of traffic control system

4.2 Structural Model (Class Diagram)

Structure diagram represents different kinds of devices (objects), e.g., switches, timers and lights participating in the model, and their relationships. Figure 5 shows the structural model of traffic control system.

4.3 Interaction Model (Activity Diagram)

Control problem is a combination of input/output events and their logical combinations (AND, OR), which can easily be represented with activity diagram, therefore representing the control flow using activity diagrams is easier. Table 3 shows turn on green light of north side, use case of the interaction model.

4.4 Generation of Activity Flow

Input/output actions in use case diagram are mapped with the action class of the activity diagram. If the two actions are ANDed or ORed then Join and Fork classes of the activity diagram are used respectively. The action class of the activity diagram is annotated with the RT-ICS profile to represent the current state of the object. Figure 6 shows the normal activity flow without applying RT-ICS profile and figure 7 shows the activity flow with RT-ICS profile applied respectively.

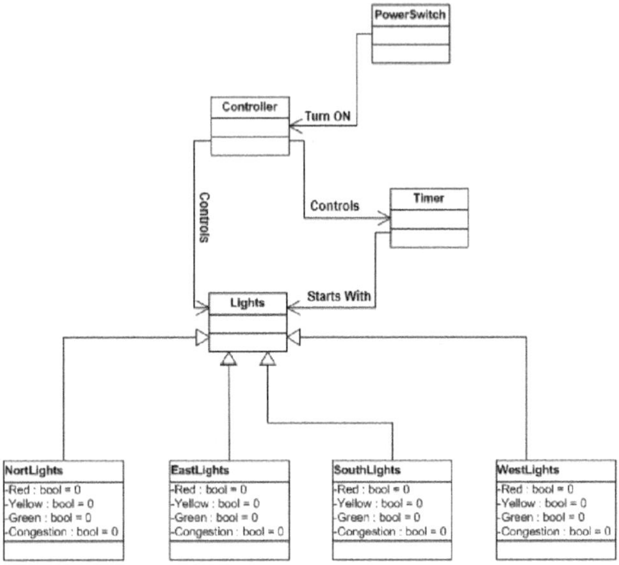

Fig. 5. Structural model of traffic control system

Table 3. Use Case: Turn On Green Light (North Side)

Pre Conditions	• North side, activation switch(NSW) on. • All other sides, red lights on. • North side Yellow light timer (NYT1) elapsed (Yellow light timer switch must be off).
Post Conditions:	• North side, Green Light(NG) on. • North side, Green Light timer(NGT) on.
Course of Action.	
Input Actions	• Check North side Yellow light timer switch; must be in normal open state. • Check North side normal green light timer switch; must be in normal close state. • Check North side green light congestion timer switch; must be in normal close state. • Check north side congestion control switch; must be in normal close state.
Output Actions.	• Turn on north side green light. • Turn on north side green light normal timer (10 Seconds)
Alternate Flow	
Input Action	• At step 3 check north side congestion timer (NGTc) switch for normal open state.
Output Action	• Turn on north side green light congestion timer (for 20 seconds)

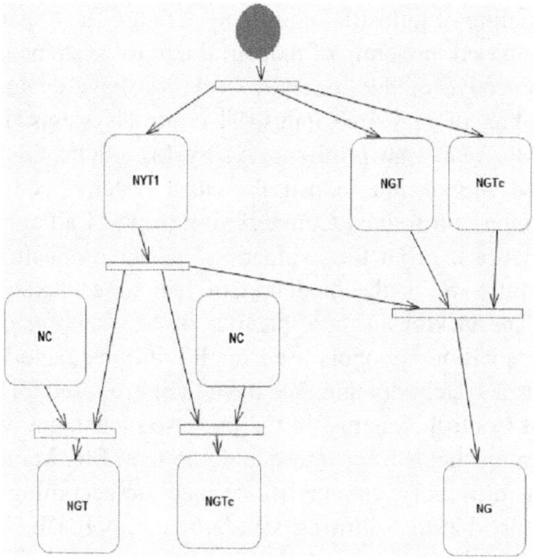

Fig. 6. Activity flow of Use case

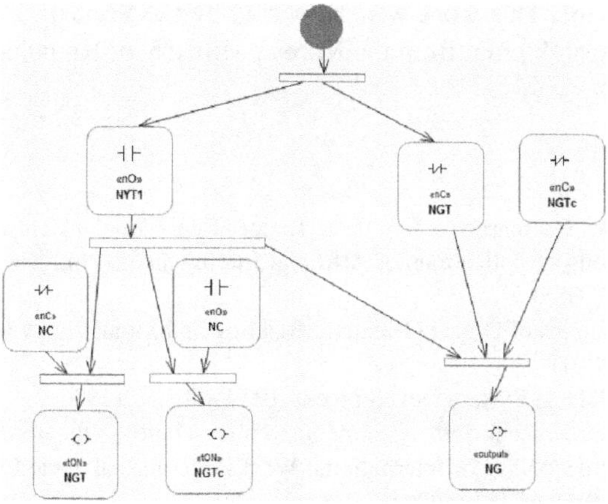

Fig. 7. Activity flow of use case after applying RT-ICS profile

The difference between the two diagrams is that in Figure 6 we cannot identify the state of the object, while in figure 7 with applying RT-ICS profile, the objects state is clear.

5 Conclusion and Future Work

Time to market and quality of the products are the challenges of today's industries. In order to cope with these challenges automation of the industries is the real need. Modeling plays an important role in automating the processes. The traditional technique for modeling of industrial control system are flow chart based. The Object-oriented paradigm based modeling of industrial control systems is at its infancy stage. To achieve the objective of this research work, we have evaluated OMG real time profiles for modeling of real time industrial control systems. For this purpose, we have selected OMG real time profiles, i.e., SysML, SOC, SPT and MARTE. Our evaluation is based on real-time industrial control system's constraints, i.e., Bitlogic, Concurrency, Timing constraints, Counters, Interrupts, Call subroutine and ICS domain friendly notations. From the evaluation, we have concluded that none of the existing profiles fully meets the modeling of real time characteristics of industrial control systems. The lacking in these profiles is, less support of ICS characteristics modeling and the notations/symbols used for RT-ICS characteristics are not friendly for industrial control system domain. We have then proposed a UML profile for modeling of Industrial Control Systems. In the proposed technique we have used UML's standard extension mechanism for introducing new profile. Main features of this profile are: it is domain friendly; stereotypes defined are according to IEC standard, variety of tool support due to following standardized approach, supports all real time characteristics required for ICS modeling. As a future work RT-ICS profile can be used to generate code from the model.

Ackmowledgement. This work was supported by the Security Engineering Research Center, under research grant from the Korean Ministry of Knowledge Economy.

References

1. O'Reilly, C.A., Cromarty, A.S.: 'Fast' is not 'Real-Time' in Designing Effective Real-Time AI Systems. Applications of Artificial Intelligence II, Int. Soc. Of Optical Engineering, 249–257 (1985)
2. Peter, F.: Principles of Object Oriented Modeling and Simulation with Modlica 2.1. Wiley-IEEE Press (2004)
3. Rob, W.: Real Time System Development. BH Publisher (2006)
4. Cecilia, E., Jan, J.: Real time system constraints: where do they come from and where do they go? In: Proceedings of International Workshop on Real Time Constraints, Alexandria, Virginia, USA, pp. 55–57 (1999)
5. Bee Dictionary, Industrial Process, `http://www.beedictionary.com/meaning/induration`
6. Melore, P.: PLC History, `http://www.plcs.net/chapters/history2.htm`
7. OMG, About OMG, `http://www.omg.org/gettingstarted/gettingstartedindex.htm`
8. Vogel-Heuser, B., Friedrich, D., Katzke, U., Witsch, D.: Usability and benefits of UML for plant automation – some research results. ATP International Journal 3 (2005)
9. Abdelouahed, G., Ferhat, K.: UML Profiles for Real-Time Systems and their Applications. Journal of Object Technology 5(4), 149–169 (2006)
10. Kirsten, B.: Using UML 2.0 in Real-Time Development: A Critical Review. In: SVERTS, San Francisco, USA, pp. 41–54 (2003)
11. Gérard, S., Terrier, F.: UML for Real-Time. In: UML for Real: Which Native Concepts to Use, pp. 17–51. Kluwer Academic Publishers (2003)
12. OMG, Specification for SysML (2008), `http://www.omg.org/spec/SysML/1.1/`

13. Sanford, F., Alan, M., Rick, S.: OMGSysML Tutorial, International Council System Engineering(INCOSE) (2008), http://www.uml-sysml.org/documentation/sysml-tutorial-incose-2.2mo
14. Jareer, H.A., Roger, S.W.: Modeling Real Time Tolapai Based Embedded System Using MARTE. In: Proceedings of the 14th WSEAS International Conference on Computers: part of the 14th WSEAS CSCC Multi Conference, Wisconsin, USA, vol. I, pp. 356–361 (2010)
15. UML Profile for System on Chip, SoC specifications (2006)
16. OMG Specifications for System on Chip Profile (2006), http://www.omg.org/spec/SoCP/
17. OMG Specification for MARTE Profile (2009), http://www.omg.org/spec/MARTE/1.0/
18. Latif, K., Basit, M.A., Rauf, A., Nadeem, A.: Evaluation of UML – Real Time Profiles for Industrial Control Systems. In: Proceedings of International Conference on Information and Emerging Technologies, pp. 1–5. IEEE, Karachi (2010)
19. Programmable controllers – Part 3: Programming languages, IEC, IEC 61131-3, Edition 2.0 (2003-2005)
20. Mueller, W., Rosti, A., Bocchio, S., Riccobene, E., Scandurra, P., Dehaene, W., Vanderperren, Y.: UML for ESL design: basic principles, tools, and applications. In: IEEE/ACM International Conference on Computer-Aided Design, pp. 73–80. ACM, New York (2006)
21. OMG Unified Modeling Language (OMG UML), Superstructure, V2.1.2 (2007), http://www.omg.org/spec/UML/2.1.2/Superstructure/PDF
22. Papyrus: Welcome to Papyrus UML web site, http://www.papyrusuml.org/

A Safe Regression Testing Technique for Web Services Based on WSDL Specification

Tehreem Masood[1], Aamer Nadeem[1], and Gang-soo Lee[2]

[1] Center for Software Dependability,
Mohammad Ali Jinnah University (MAJU), Islamabad, Pakistan
tehreem_maju@yahoo.com, anadeem@jinnah.edu.pk
[2] Department of Computer Engineering,
Hannam University, Korea
gslee@hannam.ac.kr

Abstract. Specification-based regression testing of web services is an important activity which verifies the quality of web services. A major problem in web services is that only provider has the source code and both user and broker only have the XML based specification. So from the perspective of user and broker, specification based regression testing of web services is needed. The existing techniques are code based. Due to the dynamic behavior of web services, web services undergo maintenance and evolution process rapidly. Retesting of web services is required in order to verify the impact of changes. In this paper, we present an automated safe specification based regression testing approach that uses original and modified WSDL specifications for change identification. All the relevant test cases are selected as reusable hence our regression test selection approach is safe.

Keywords: Regression testing, web services, specification testing, test case selection.

1 Introduction

Web services have become center of attention during the past few years. It is a software system designed to support interoperable interaction between different applications and different platforms. A system in which web services are used is named as web services based system. Web services use standards such as Hypertext Transfer Protocol (HTTP), Simple Object Access Protocol (SOAP) [13], Universal Description, Discovery, and Integration (UDDI), Web Services Description Language (WSDL) and Extensible Markup Language (XML) [3] for communication between web services through internet [1].

Maintenance is the most cost and time consuming phase of software life cycle, it requires enhancement of previous version of software to deal with the new requirements or problems. As modifying software may incur faults to the old software, testing is required. It is very difficult for a programmer to find out the changes in software manually, this is done by making comparison of both previous test results

T.-h. Kim et al. (Eds.): ASEA/DRBC/EL 2011, CCIS 257, pp. 108–119, 2011.

and current test results being run. Now the changed or modified software needs testing known as regression testing [2].

Regression testing is performed during and after the maintenance to ensure that the software as a whole is working correctly after changes have been made to it. Basic regression testing steps includes change identification in modified version of the system, impact of changes on other parts of the system, compatibility of both changed part and indirectly affected part with the baseline test suite, removing invalid test cases and selecting a subset of baseline test suite that is used for regression testing [2].

Significant research has been carried out on testing of web services [12] but there is limited amount of work on regression testing of web services. Most of the existing approaches for regression testing of web services are code based but no work is available on specification based regression testing of web services.

In web services, only web service provider has the source code and both web service broker and user only have the specification. Provider is not willing to share the source code [1]. So from the perspective of broker and user, specification based regression testing is needed. A change may occur in web service functionality or behavior with no interface change, specification will not change. But if a change occurs in interface, specification will also be changed [6]. Our focus is interface change. Further details about changes are explained in section III.

WSDL plays very important role in web services. It is an XML document used to describe web services. It has four major elements that are Types, Messages, PortType and Binding [8]. The main concern of our approach is Type element of WSDL specification [8]. WSDL specification uses an XML Schema [14], which is used to define types used by web service. XML schema defines simple types and complex types [14]. For simplicity, we will only consider higher level complex types. Complex type within a complex type is not considered because the depth of the tree increases.

We have applied boundary value analysis [10] on data type level changes and selected reusable test cases [11]. Test suite classification of Leung and white [11] is used in this paper. The proposed approach selects all the relevant test cases as reusable test cases which is explained by the help of an example. Safety is defined as all the relevant test cases are used [2].

The remaining paper is organized as follows: Section II includes related work in the area of regression testing of web services. Section III discusses the proposed approach for selective regression testing. In the end conclusion of the paper is presented in Section IV.

2 Related Work

Ruth, *et al.* [4] presented an approach to apply a safe regression test selection technique to Java web services. Their approach is based on Java-based control flow graph named as Java Interclass Graph (JIG).They have created JIG by performing static and dynamic analysis of code. They identified dangerous edges by comparing old and new JIG. Then they compared the table of edges covered by the tests with the set of dangerous edges to identify the tests to be performed. They provided a simulation tool.

Ruth, *et al.* [5] presented a framework to apply a safe regression test selection technique to generic web services. There technique is based on control flow graph for service involved in the regression testing activity. The idea is that Control Flow Graphs (CFG) should be able to highlight the changes that can cause regression testing. They also discussed that publishing test cases is useful.

Penta, *et al.* [6] used test cases as a contract between service provider and system integrator. They considered dynamicity as an important characteristic of service-based applications, and performed online tests, i.e., to execute tests during the operation phase of the service-based application. They discussed their approach with respect to some scenarios and used some QoS assertions for performing service regression testing. They didn't focus the changes in the specifications. They provided a toolkit for generating XML-encoded test suite.

Khan and Heckel [7] presented a model-based approach for regression testing of web services. They identified changes and impact of changes by using models that are used to describe the service interface. For external behavior they used finite state automatons and for data dependencies, bipartite dependency graph is used where the nodes represents methods and classes. Then a method for test case selection is presented.

3 Proposed Approach

In web services, a change may occur in web service functionality or behavior and interface is not changed, in this case specification will not change and old test cases can be used. But if a change occurs in interface, specification will also be changed. In this case, some required old test cases can be selected and there is a need to develop some new test cases for regression testing [6]. The proposed approach focuses on interface change.

A WSDL specification has four major elements which are messages, types, binding and port type [8]. A message provides an abstract definition of the data which is being transmitted. A binding is used to define format of message and protocol details for operations and messages. A port type represents a set of abstract operations. A type is used to provide a data type definition, used to describe the exchanged message which is then used by a web service. WSDL specification uses an XML Schema which is used to define types used by web service [14].

Figure 1 shows the overall architecture of our proposed approach for specification based regression testing of web services. The major components of our approach are parser, comparator and regression test selector. Original WSDL specification of web service is named as baseline WSDL, when initially a web service is build. Modified WSDL specification is named as delta WSDL, when a web service is changed. Major components are explained below.

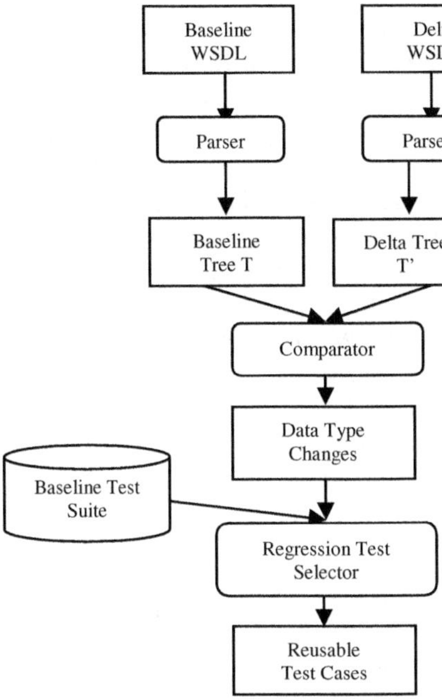

Fig. 1. Abstract Model of the proposed approach

```
Input: Wsdl specification     output: baseline and
delta tree
Step 1:
Select type element of WSDL specification.
Step 2:
Select element to be modeled as root node. Select
name of element as its attribute along with its
value enclosed with an equal sign.
Step 3:
If complex type of the root element exists then
an outgoing directed edge is formed from root
node which is connected to a complex type node
having name as its attribute along with its value
enclosed with an equal sign.
Step 4:
For each sub element of complex type, a new node
is generated, having element as name of the node
and a number of the element.
Associate all attributes and their values with
their respective nodes, in the same sequence as
described in the schema.
Step 5:
Repeat step 4 for all the sub elements of complex
type
```

Fig. 2. Algorithm for generating tree of datatype

3.1 Parser

As described earlier, the main concern of our approach is Type element of WSDL specification. It provides a data type definition for describing messages exchanged. WSDL uses an XML schema to describe types used by Web service [14]. XML Schema defines simple types and complex types. Simple types include either built in primitive data types or derived data types and data type facets. Built in primitive types include string, float, etc. Derived data types include integer, etc. Complex type is any user defined data type. A facet is a constraint which is used to set the values for a simple type like length, minInclusive, etc [14]. Here we are taking facets as attributes of sub elements. Parser takes original and modified WSDL specifications as input and generates tree for type element of the WSDL specification. An algorithm for generating trees for both original and changed WSDL specifications is given in Fig 2. If any attribute of element, complex type and sub element have no value specified in XML schema then the attribute value is considered as null.

Example: MortgageIndex

MortgageIndex is a Web service used to provide monthly, weekly and Historical Mortgage Indexes. There are many possible Adjustable Rate Mortgage (ARM) indexes. Some common mortgage indexes are 12-Month Treasury Average (MTA), Treasury bill (T-Bill), etc [9]. For example if a borrower thinks that interest rates are going to rise in the future, the T-Bill index would be a more economical choice than the one-month LIBOR index because the moving average calculation of the T-Bill index creates a lag effect.

This web service has four basic operations, i.e., GetCurrentMortgageIndexByWeek, GetCurrentMortgageIndexMonthly, GetMortgageIndexByMonth, GetMortgageIndexByWeek. Here we are taking one operation for explanation which is GetMortgageIndexByMonth. This operation takes month and year as input and provides ARM indexes for the specified values. Both month and year are of type int [9]. XML schema for this operation is provided in Fig 3.

```
Example: XML Schema
<s:element name="GetMortgageIndexByMonth">
<s:complexType>
<s:sequence>
<s:element maxOccurs="1" minOccurs="1" name="Month" type="s:int" maxInclusive
="12" minInclusive ="1" />
<s:element maxOccurs="1" minOccurs="1" name="Year" type="s:int" maxInclusive
="2007" minInclusive ="1990"/>
</s:sequence>
</s:complexType>
</s:element>
<s:element name="GetMortgageIndexByMonthResponse">
<s:complexType>
<s:sequence>
<s:element minOccurs="1" maxOccurs="1" name="GetMortgageIndexByMonthResult"
type="tns:MonthlyIndex"/> </s:sequence>
</s:complexType>
</s:element>
```

Fig. 3. Original XML Schema for Element GetMortgageIndexByMonth [9]

A runtime view of the operation GetMortgageIndexByMonth is shown in Fig 4.

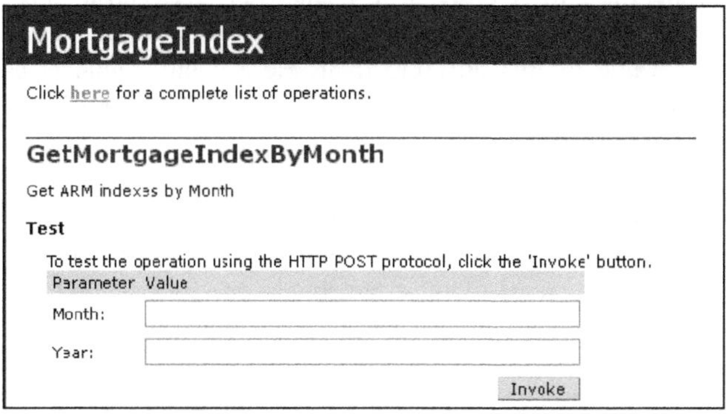

Fig. 4. A runtime view of GetMortgageIndexByMonth

The resulting baseline tree generated from the original schema is shown in Fig 5.

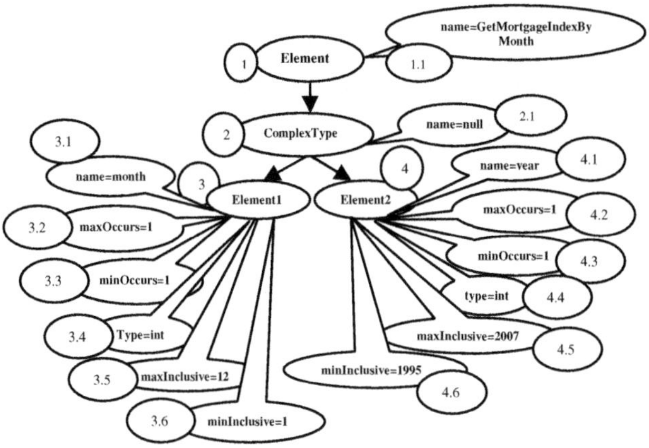

Fig. 5. Baseline tree T for complex datatype

Baseline tree for complex Datatype of Fig 3 is shown in Fig 5. In Fig 5 an oval shape represents a node e.g. here Element, ComplexType, Element1 and Element2 are nodes. An oval callout represents attributes and facets of simple type e.g. name, minOccurs, maxOccurs and type are attributes and minInclusive, maxInclusive are facets of simple type int. Here facets are also considered as attributes. The procedure for generating tree from schema as shown in Fig 3 is explained below.

In this example, first parser takes element of the type and generates a tree for it. A node shape is drawn and named it as Element. Then an attribute shape is attached with this element and enclosed the name as an attribute and a value of this attribute in it. For example here attribute is name and value is GetMortgageIndexByMonth. So Name= GetMortgageIndexByMonth is written inside the attribute shape. Then the next element is complex type, a node shape is drawn and named it as complex type. Then draws an outgoing directed edge from the root node and connect it to the new node. Then an attribute shape is attached with this new node and enclosed the name as its attribute and value of this attribute in it. Here a null value is assigned to the attribute name of ComplexType as it has no name specified in Fig 3. In Fig 3 there are two sub elements of ComplexType. First sub element is month. Now as its type is int which is a primitive data type, a new node is drawn and named it as Element1. Then an outgoing directed edge is drawn from ComplexType node to this new node. Then attribute shapes are attached with this new node for every attribute of Element 1 and enclosed the name and values of these attributes one by one. For example here 1st attribute is minOccurs having value 1, so in the attribute shape minOccurs =1 is written. Similarly all other attributes are drawn. Repeat the same procedure for the all other sub elements of ComplexType. For naming scheme circle having 1value is attached with the root node, as it is the first node of the tree. 1.1 is attached with the attribute name of root node. 2 is attached with the 2nd node named as complex type. 2.1 is attached with the attribute name of complex type node. Same is the case with other nodes and attributes. The resulting baseline tree model for element GetMortgageIndexByMonth generated by applying the above steps is shown in Fig 5. Now suppose a change occurs in the attributes of element2 (year) described in Fig 3. The changed schema is described in Fig 6. Here the values of the attributes minInclusive and maxInclusive are changed to 1995 and 2000 respectively. Remaining schema is same. Then the tree is generated from the modified schema by applying the same steps presented in Fig 2. As the only change is in the values of minInclusive and maxInclusive of element2 (year), so only these attribute values are changed in the resulting delta tree.

Example: XML Schema

```
<s:element name="GetMortgageIndexByMonth">
<s:complexType>
<s:sequence>
<s:element maxOccurs="1" minOccurs="1" name="Month" type="s:int" maxInclusive
="12" minInclusive ="1" />
<s:element maxOccurs="1" minOccurs="1" name="Year" type="s:int“ maxInclusive
=“2000" minInclusive =“1995"/>
</s:sequence>
</s:complexType>
</s:element>
<s:element name="GetMortgageIndexByMonthResponse">
<s:complexType>
<s:sequence>
<s:element minOccurs="1" maxOccurs="1" name="GetMortgageIndexByMonthResult"
type="tns:MonthlyIndex" />
</s:sequence>
</s:complexType>
</s:element>
```

Fig. 6. Modified XML schema

The resulting delta tree generated from the modified schema is shown in Fig 7.

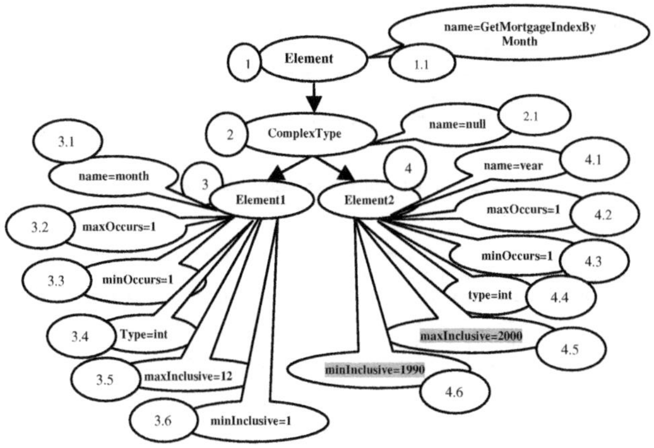

Fig. 7. Delta tree T' for complex datatype

3.2 Comparator

We define data type changes in our approach. Type element of the WSDL specification provides a data type definition for describing messages exchanged. In Fig 8 e is used for representing the root element of complex type in baseline tree and e' is used for representing the root element of complex type in delta tree. c is used to represent complex type in baseline tree and c' is used to represent complex type in delta tree. ei is the instance of sub element of complex type in baseline tree and ej is the instance of sub element of complex type in delta tree. 1st the root element attribute name and value of Fig 5 and Fig 7 are compared, as here they are same so step 2 is executed. In step 2 name and value of the complex type attribute are compared, as they are also same, so we execute step 3 and 5.

In step 3 we check the sub elements of complex type one by one, 1st element of complex type node of Fig 5 and Fig 7 when compared, they are same, and so step 4 is executed for its every attribute. In step 4 all attribute names and values are compared one by one, they are same so check if there is any other element of the complex type. As there is another sub element denoted by element2, so the name and value of element2's attribute of both Fig 5 and Fig 7 are compared, as they are same so step 4 is executed for its every attribute. In step 4 all the attribute names and values are compared one by one, in this case two values of attributes maxInclusive and minInclusive are different so this change is detected by comparator shown in Table 1. 1st is the change in the attribute maxInclusive value and 2nd is the change in the attribute minInclusive of Element 2.

```
Input: baseline and delta tree Output: changes
Variables: e denotes root node of baseline tree
e'denotes root node of delta tree
c denotes complex type node of baseline tree
c' denotes complex type node of delta tree
ei denotes instance of sub element of complex type in
baseline tree
ej denotes instance of sub element of complex type in
delta tree.
Step 1:
Compare e.name and e'.name. If matched then If
e.value==e'.value then execute step 2 else root node
deleted from baseline tree. If e.name! =e'.name and
e.value==e'.value then content of the attribute
changed. Execute step 2. Else If e.name! =e'.name and
e.value! =e'.value then root node deleted.
Step 2:
Compare c.name and c'.name. If matched then If
c.value==c'.value then execute step 3, 5 else complex
type node deleted from baseline tree. If c.name!
=c'.name and c.value==c'.value then content of the
attribute changed. Execute step 3, 5. Else If c.name!
=c'.name and c.value! =c'.value then complex type node
deleted.
Step 3: Check_subElement (c, c')
   For each child ei of c
   For each child ej of c'
Compare ei.name and ej.name. If matched then If
ei.value==ej.value then execute step 4 for every
attribute else sub element node deleted from baseline
tree. Execute step 4. If ei.name! =ej.name and
ei.value==ej.value then content of the attribute
changed. Execute step 4. Else If ei.name! =ej.name and
ei.value! =ej.value then attribute deleted from base-
line tree. Execute step 4 for every attribute.
Step 4:
Compare attribute name and value. If matched then
repeat step 4 for other attributes Else attribute
changed. Repeat step 4 for other attributes.
Step 5: Check_subElementAdded (c, c')
   For each child ej of c
   For each child ei of c'
   If ej.name==ei.name then If ej.value==ei.value then
matched else sub element added in delta tree. If
ei.name! =ej.name and ei.value==ej.value then content
of the attribute changed. Else If ei.name! =ej.name
and ei.value! =ej.value then attribute added in delta
tree.
```

Fig. 8. Change detection algorithm

The detected changes are shown below in Table 1.

Table 1. Detected changes

4.5 changed
4.6 changed

3.3 Regression Test Selector

Finally regression test selector takes baseline test suite and data type changes as input, and categorizes the test suite. Baseline test suite is categorized into obsolete and reusable test cases [11]. Obsolete test cases are those test cases that are invalid for the delta version. They are invalid because the elements may be changed or deleted from the baseline version. Reusable test cases are those test cases that are still valid for the delta version after applying boundary value conditions. We perform boundary value analysis for test case selection [10]. Criteria that we are using for boundary value analysis is max value, min value, max-1, min+1 and 1 random value which should be greater than min value and less then max value. For example by applying these conditions on specification shown in Fig 3, we get for month: 1,2,11,12,7 and for year: 1990, 1991, 2006, 2007 and 1998. First of all baseline test suite for original specification tree T is shown in Table 2 by applying the above boundary value conditions. Every value of month is combined with every value of year.

Table 2. Baseline test suite

TC1=1,1990	TC10= 7,1991	TC19= 12,2007
TC2=2,1990	TC11=1,2006	TC20= 7,2007
TC3=11,1990	TC12=2,2006	TC21= 1,1998
TC4=12,1990	TC13= 11,2006	TC22= 2,1998
TC5= 7,1990	TC14= 12,2006	TC23= 11,1998
TC6=1,1991	TC15= 7,2006	TC24= 12,1998
TC7=2,1991	TC16= 1,2007	TC25= 7,1998
TC8= 11,1991	TC17= 2,2007	
TC9=12,1991	TC18= 11,2007	

Algorithm of regression test selector is shown in Fig 9. Now for the modified tree T' in Fig 7, again boundary value analysis is performed for checking the usability of baseline test suite. The resulting reusable test cases are shown in Table 3.

```
Step 1:
Perform boundary value analysis on the boundaries of
delta version
Step 2:
Compare new boundaries with the baseline boundaries
Step 3:
Select test cases from the baseline test suite that
are still valid for delta version named as reusable
test cases.
Step 4:
Discard the obsolete test cases from the baseline test
suite that are no longer valid for the delta version.
```

Fig. 9. Test case selection algorithm

Now the boundary values for year become 1995, 1996, 2000, 1999, 1997. The test cases that are still valid from the baseline test suite after applying the changed boundary value conditions are shown in Table 3 which is known as reusable test cases.

Table 3. Reusable test cases

TC21=1,1998
TC22=2,1998
TC23= 11,1998
TC24=12,1998
TC25= 7,1998

A regression test suite is considered as safe, if it includes all the test cases covering the whole changed part of the system as well as the whole indirectly affected part of the system. A safe regression test suite can have other test cases from the baseline test suite that are covering the unchanged part of the system. Here all the relevant test cases are used as reusable test cases. Hence our test case selection approach is safe.

Case 1: Attribute changed

If values of any attribute change then there can be impact on test cases. Check the type attribute of sub element and min and max inclusive or any other range attribute if there. If value of attribute name of root element is changed then it means old element is deleted. Check other attributes as well. If value of attribute name of complex type is changed then it means old complex type is deleted. Check other attributes as well. If value of all attributes of all sub elements. E.g. name, type, minOccurs, maxOccurs, minInclusive, maxInclusive etc is changed then it means value is changed. If maxInclusive and minInclusive values are changed then test cases will be selected from the baseline test suite according to the new values of the minInclusive and maxInclusive. If type value is changed then check the compatibility of new type with the previous one.

Case 2: Types: Check the compatibility of old and new types.
e.g. If int is changed to float and minInclusive and maxInclusive values are same then test cases will be selected according to min and max inclusive values but if there is no max and min inclusive values then test cases will not be selected from baseline test suite. If float is changed to int and minInclusive and maxInclusive values are same then test cases will be selected according to min and max inclusive values but if there is no max and min inclusive values then test cases will not be selected from baseline test suite. If int is changed to string, then test cases will not be selected from baseline test suite. If string is changed to int, then test cases will not be selected from baseline test suite. Same is the case with other types.

Case 3: Node

Deleted: If any node is deleted, then all its attributes are also deleted. If complex type node is deleted, then all its attributes are also deleted and all baseline test cases will be removed

Added: If any node is added, then check its attributes and values. Select test case according to the new values.

4 Conclusion

In this paper, we presented a specification based regression test selection approach for web services based on WSDL specification of web service. The proposed approach is a safe regression testing technique as it selected all test cases which exercise the modified parts of web service. A proof-of-concept tool has also been developed to support our approach.

Acknowledgement. This work was supported by the Security Engineering Research Center, under research grant from the Korean Ministry of Knowledge Economy.

References

1. Gottschalk, K., Graham, S., Kreger, H., Snell, J.: Introduction to web services architecture. IBM Systems Journal 41(2), 170–177 (2002)
2. Binder, R.: Testing Object-Oriented Systems: Models, Patterns and Tools. Addison-Wesley Professional (2000)
3. Extensible Markup Language (XML) 1.1 (2nd edn.), – World Wide Web Consortium (2006), http://www.w3.org/TR/xml11/
4. Ruth, N.M., Lin, F., Tu, S.: Applying Safe Regression Test Selection Techniques to Java Web Services. International Journal of Web Services Practices 2(1-2), 1–10 (2006)
5. Ruth, M., Tu, S., Oh, S., Loup, A., Horton, B., Gallet, O., Mata, M.: Towards automatic regression test selection for Web services. In: 31st Annual International Computer Software and Applications Conference (COMPSAC 2007), Beijing, China, pp. 729–736 (July 2007)
6. Penta, M.D., Bruno, M., Esposito, G., Mazza, V., Canfora, G.: Web services regression testing. In: Baresi, L., Di Nitto, E. (eds.) Test and Analysis of Web Services, pp. 205–234. Springer, New York (2007)
7. Khan, T.A., Heckel, R.: A methodology for model based regression testing of web services. In: Testing: Academic and Industrial Conference - Practice and Research Techniques (TAICPART), pp. 123–124 (2009)
8. Web Services Description Language (WSDL) 2.0, part 1: Core Language (2007), – World Wide Web Consortium, http://www.w3c.org/TR/wsdl20/
9. WebserviceX.NET. -MortgageIndexWebService, http://www.webservicex.net
10. Jorgensen, P.C.: Software Testing: A Craftsman's Approach. CRC Press, Inc. (2002)
11. Leung, H.K.N., White, L.: Insights into regression testing: software testing. In: Proceedings of Conference on Software Maintenance, pp. 60–69 (October 1989) ISBN: 0-8186-1965-1
12. Bares, L., Nitto, E.D.: Test and Analysis of Web Services. ACM Computing Classification. Springer, Heidelberg (2007) ISBN 978-3-540-72911-2
13. Simple Object Access Protocol (SOAP) 1.2, Part 0, Primer: – World Wide Web Consortium (2007), http://www.w3.org/TR/soap12-part0/
14. XML Schemas- Part 2, Datatypes – World Wide Web Consortium http://www.w3.org/TR/xmlschema-2/

Evaluating Software Maintenance Effort: The COME Matrix

Bee Bee Chua[1] and June Verner[2]

[1] University of Technology, Sydney, Australia
[2] Keele University, UK

Abstract. If effort estimates are not easily assessed upfront by software maintainers we may have serious problems with large maintenance projects, or when we make repeated maintenance changes to software. This is particularly problematic when inaccurate estimates of the required resources leads to serious negotiation issues. The development of a Categorisation of Maintenance Effort (COME) matrix enables an overall summary of software maintenance changes and maintenance effort to be shown, upfront, to software practitioners. This can occur without any consideration or use of other effort estimation techniques whose results, when used to estimate effort, can appear complicated and it may not be clear how accurate their estimates may be.

We use a simple approach to categorizing maintenance effort data using five steps. We use regression analysis with Jorgensen's 81 datasets to evaluate the selected variables to find out the true efficacy of our approach: 1) adaptive changes and functional changes with maintenance effort predicted from low to high, 2) high predicted effort when updating KSLOC for software maintenance changes, 3) find that more lines of source codes do not imply that more software maintenance effort is needed, 4) find no significant relationship when we consider the age of the application and 5) find that at least 20 application sizes between KSLOC of 100, 200, 400 and 500 have a low predicted software maintenance effort.

Our experiment shows that using the COME matrix is an alternative approach to other cost estimation techniques for estimating effort for repeated requirement changes in large software maintenance projects.

Keywords: Software Maintenance, Software Maintenance Effort, The COME Matrix.

1 Introduction

Estimating software maintenance effort based on defect correction or modification is not a simple task for software estimators. Software maintenance effort is usually based on analogy [1]. Whether the approach is reliable or not, very little research has scientifically shown estimation accuracy for analogy. There is also very little empirical research investigating the estimation of human errors when the approach is used [2, 3].

T.-h. Kim et al. (Eds.): ASEA/DRBC/EL 2011, CCIS 257, pp. 120–136, 2011.

The key focus of this paper is on the introduction of a matrix to help software practitioners find a method to better estimate software maintenance effort for a large quantity of maintenance changes.

Following a comprehensive review of the software maintenance literature, several important factors were identified.

1) There is a no complete set of variables to identify software maintenance parameters, for example, parameters such as application size and age, maintenance environment and characteristics of the software maintainers. These variables, which can be used to help with effort estimation, are not readily available to the software maintenance team because they are not aware that these variables are useful and most are not visible to them during maintenance estimation.
2) The important variables are not easily collected prior to software maintenance, because some of the parameters require additional information based on conditions in the software maintenance environment.
3) There is very little research into aspects of software maintenance effort distribution, except for the research in [4,5,6,7,8], which focus on understanding proportional distribution of maintenance tasks, and the correlation between maintenance size, and software maintenance effort.
4) Some software maintenance estimation models like the ACT model [8], SMPEEM (Software Maintenance Project Effort Estimation Model) [9], and COCOMO 2.0 (Cost Constructive Model) [10, 11] lack enabling processes for estimating appropriate software maintenance effort with an acceptable degree of accuracy.

This study proposes a Categorisation of Maintenance Effort (COME) matrix as an evaluative, guide for software practitioners estimating software maintenance effort for similar projects. The matrix is useful in terms of providing software maintenance effort for software practitioners from explicit data for repeated maintenance changes, by grouping change types into different software maintenance effort levels.

We first introduce, in the next section, related work on software maintenance, estimation distribution, and models for software maintenance. We then follow with details of the COME matrix procedure in Section 3 and outline the application of the matrix in Section 4. Section 5 provides the results when we test the dependent and independent variables with the COME matrix. Section 6 discusses the COME results based on regression analysis and the implications for maintenance effort distribution. Section 7 provides an overview of the matrix challenges and Section 8 concludes the paper.

2 Related Work

We discuss related work by first considering the categorization of software maintenance effort, and then provide an evaluation of effort estimation models.

2.1 Categorization of Software Maintenance Effort

Extensive research on the effort estimation of software maintenance includes work by Lientz et al. [12,13] and Stark et al. [4]. They focused on effort distribution for software maintenance releases; other researchers such as Yang et al. [5], Martin et al. [14] and Nosek et al. [15] focused on building estimation effort models for analysing the effects of software maintenance releases and the effort of software maintainers. Milicic et al. [8] and others categorised software maintenance effort by evaluating both the project life cycle and project size. Another group of researchers, Yang et al. [5], estimated effort by analysing products by their data structures and field attributes, whereas Martin et al. [14] estimated maintenance effort by a count of requirements (by change types, impact and effects).

The quantification of software maintenance effort is normally measured by percentages rather than values. Lientz et al. [12] show that 65% of maintenance effort is allocated to perfective maintenance, 18% to adaptive maintenance, 17% to perfective maintenance and the remaining effort to preventive maintenance.

A similar study conducted by Boehm [10] discusses how software maintenance effort is distributed. He concluded that a high focus of maintenance effort was from: 1) enhancement for users (41.8%), 2) accommodating input changes into input data files (17.4%) and, 3) emergency program fixes (12.4%). A medium range of software maintenance effort focuses on 4) routine debugging (9.3%), 5) accommodating changes to hardware and operating systems (6.3%), 6) improving documentation (5%) and 7) improving code efficiency (5%); little effort in relation to software maintenance was spent on 8) other (3.4%).

2.2 Evaluating Models of Effort Estimation

Following an extensive review of software maintenance literature we highlight five effort estimation models. The table below describes related models that use methods based on size for estimating maintenance effort, rather than software development effort.

Table 1 shows that Function Point Analysis (FP) is the most popular software size method used by researchers when compared with SLOC (Source Lines Of Code) or OP (Object Points) methods when we consider the following five models:1) Function Point model [16], 2) ACT (Annual Change Traffic) [15] model, 3)COCOMO model [11], 4) COCOMO 2.0 model [10], and 5) SMPEEM (Software Maintenance Project Effort Estimation Model) [9].

Table 1. Software maintenance Effort Estimation models

Models	Size	Software Development Effort	Software Maintenance Effort
Function Point	Function Point	√	√
ACT	FP	X	√
COCOMO	SLOC¸FP, OP	√	√
COCOMO 2.0	SLOC¸FP, OP	√	√
SMPEEM	FP	X	√

Unlike software development effort estimation, software maintenance effort estimation is different in nature, and some issues may not be easily resolved using the approaches commonly adopted by software practitioners for estimating the software effort required.

1. The Function Point model was developed by Albrecht [16]. It defines five basic function types to estimate the size of the software. Two data types are internal logical files (ILF) and external interface files (EIF), and the remaining three transactional function types are external inputs (EI), external outputs (EO) and external enquiries (EQ). It relies heavily on a VAF (Value Adjustment Factor) to calculate EFP (Enhanced Function Points). Because the VAF includes data communications, distributed processing, performance, etc., it is not always applicable to the maintenance environment and cannot be measured objectively [9].
2. The ACT model [8] provides an annual maintenance cost estimation based on historical data provided by an organisation. The distribution of effort is activity-based, and does not support data analysis well enough to help practitioners understand how the effort is distributed [8]. The model is not appropriate for software maintenance effort, as it has a critical risk in that attributes are not considered quantitatively.
3. COCOMO and COCOMO 2.0 were developed by Boehm et al. [10, 11]. COCOMO 2.0 is an updated version of COCOMO. Both use highly intensive algorithmic computations; the implication is that a mathematical formula is needed to calculate effort before its application. The models take into account scale factors like precedentedness, development flexibility, architecture/risk resolution, team cohesion and process maturity as inputs and uses effort multipliers which include the required software reliability, database size, product complexity, required reusability, documentation, etc. However, these models require a large amount of data in order to provide accurate estimations, and the result is subject to the correct data being provided. The models are not suitable for small projects because Source Lines Of Code (SLOC) must be at least 2K. The analysis of distribution effort is usually grouped by an understanding of the business-domain, requirements-domain and technology-domain rather than software maintenance effort.
4. SMPEEM helps a project manager to estimate software maintenance effort by including a people factor, product factor and process factor. Because the model has been evaluated in small maintenance projects in which productivity factors were relatively low, there is not enough scientific evidence to conclude that the model is suitable for calculating productivity factors in large-scale maintenance projects, or that adjustment of VAF is needed.

Because influencing variables can impact software maintenance effort estimates, these software maintenance models are designed to calculate maintenance effort much more reliably and accurately. Unfortunately, the models are very data-dependent using influencing variables for inputs to calculate or determine an output, that is, the expected software maintenance effort. A challenge when using the models is that the actual cost of software maintenance effort can only be finalised upon the complete calculation of estimates, and this might possibly exceed the budget.

It is important to have an overall software maintenance effort estimate early, even if maintenance is to start later. This gives software practitioners time to prepare and plan. For software projects that have fixed budgets or schedules, having an early estimate of maintenance effort can minimise estimation errors and risks later. Our purpose is to focus on software maintenance effort distribution to 1) be used as a benchmark for overall estimation effort, and, 2) study which maintenance changes are required between a short duration and a long duration.

In contrast, this study is not an attempt to validate Jorgensen's results [6]. The objective is to introduce a matrix evaluation framework, the COME matrix. The purpose of this matrix is to show a categorisation of software maintenance effort in which the variables identified are software maintenance changes, software maintenance activity, size in KSLOC and application characteristics (age and size). These five variables are aligned in response to changes made by the maintenance tasks in each application. As a result, they are evaluated for the purpose of gaining an understanding of their effect on maintenance effort. In addition, another aim is to determine the type of software maintenance changes, in association with other variables, for which the predicted software maintenance effort is between a short and long duration for each maintenance change.

3 Software Maintenance Effort Dataset

The dataset we use originated from an empirical study by Jorgensen [6]. His work in [6] was an attempt to investigate the accuracy of maintenance task effort using prediction models. Jorgensen applied several estimation models such as regression analysis, neutral networks and pattern recognition to the dataset with the aim of determining which of these estimation models had the greatest prediction accuracy. The empirical results show that the use of prediction models can increase prediction accuracy as an instrument to support expert estimates, and help in analysing the variables which affect the maintenance process; such findings are useful for justifying investments because of their sophistication.

3.1 COME Matrix Steps

We analysed attributes from the data set and found attributes related to the metrics useful for developing the COME matrix. The following steps describe the application of the COME matrix.

Step 1: A set of variables are extracted from the data. See Table 2.

Step 2: The given dataset, software maintenance effort, is grouped under classes of 0.1, 0.2, 0.5, 1, 2, 5, 7, 10, 20 and 25 hours.

Step 3: Table 3 shows a detailed breakdown of each class of effort for software maintenance change types where the status of updates, inserted and deleted number of lines of source code are estimated by project leaders.

Table 2. Metrics for distributing effort by software maintenance changes

Metric	Type	Description
Size	number	Thousands of Source Lines of Code
Application Size	number	Thousands of Source Lines of Code
Application Age	Number	Total number of years
Maintenance Type	Preventive, Corrective, Adaptive, Perfective Functionality	Refer to references [4,12,13,16]
Maintenance task	number	Thousands of Source Lines of Code updated, deleted and added
Software Maintenance Effort	number	Person hours, effort of the maintenance task in maintenance days

The following (Table 3) shows the COME matrix for the distribution in the study of patterns of software maintenance effort by software maintenance changes by their sizes and types. The relevant attributes are noted in a spreadsheet; symbols used in this table are E (Effort in maintenance days), A1 (Application Size), A2 (Application Age), SMCT: (Software Maintenance Change Types), SMA (Software Maintenance Activity), 1. Update, 2. Insert, 3.Delete, 4. Insert and Update, 5.Insert and Delete, and 6. Insert, Update and Delete and KLOC.

Table 3. An Analytical matrix for patterns of variables in distributed ratio of software maintenance effort by type of changes

E	A1	A2	SMCT 1. Perfective 2. Adaptive . 3. Corrective 4. preventive 5. Functional	SMA 1 update 2. insert 3. delete 4. insert and update 5. insert and delete 6 insert, update and delete	KLOC
0.1	30	1	1	1	1
0.1	40	1	1	2	4
0.1	40	1	1	1	1
0.1	40	1	2	1	3
0.1	50	9	3	1	30
0.1	110	5	3	1	5
0.1	110	5	3	1	3
0.1	165	3	3	1	1
0.1	165	3	3	2	11

Table 3. (*Continued*)

0.1	165	3	4	1	10
0.1	210	12	2	1	1
0.1	320	8	3	1	1
0.1	320	8	3	1	5
0.1	320	8	3	1	1
0.1	350	17	3	1	1
0.1	500	8	3	1	1
0.2	165	3	3	1	2
0.2	400	18	3	1	6
0.2	400	18	1	1	2
0.5	64	2	5	2	10
0.5	64	2	3	2	6
0.5	400	9	3	1	4
0.5	400	9	3	2	6
0.5	400	9	3	1	6
1	40	1	3	1	5
1	40	1	3	1	1
1	40	1	3	1	1
1	40	1	3	1	3
1	40	1	3	1	10
1	45	1	3	1	20
1	50	9	2	1	100
1	50	9	3	1	25
1	100	6	5	1	85
1	100	6	3	1	50
1	320	8	1	2	40
1	400	18	5	2	100
1	400	18	5	2	15
1	400	18	5	2	15
1	400	18	1	1	15
1	400	18	1	1	100
1	410	3	2	1	20
1	500	8	3	2	15
2	12	21	2	2	75
2	13	2	2	2	10
2	40	1	3	1	15
2	70	13	1	1	200
2	70	13	3	I	300
2	100	6	5	2	50
2	100	6	2	6	20
2	165	3	2	1	10
2	400	9	5	1	300
2	400	18	3	5	6

Table 3. (*Continued*)

2	400	18	3	2	5
2	500	8	2	1	30
5	12	21	2	1	200
5	60	5	2	4	80
5	110	5	2	4	400
5	320	8	2	2	435
5	400	9	2	5	350
5	400	18	2	5	200
5	500	8	2	2	435
5	500	8	5	2	300
5	500	8	5	2	20
7	70	13	5	2	1000
7	100	6	2	4	1000
7	165	3	5	2	2100
7	500	8	2	1	25
10	60	5	2	1	400
10	165	3	1	2	250
10	400	18	4	3	5
10	500	8	2	1	500
10	500	8	3	1	170
20	30	1	5	4	200
20	400	18	2	5	200
20	400	18	3	1	5
25	20	3	5	2	500
25	70	13	5	2	700
25	110	5	2	2	500
25	500	8	5	2	1500

Step 4: To analyze the patterns of distributed effort from the count of software maintenance changes; similar maintenance change types for each effort class are grouped together and determine the total count presented in table 4.

Step 5: Our matrix (Table 4), shows maintenance changes for each effort class estimated for corrective, preventive, adaptive and perfective maintenance. It also provides explicit information on a particular maintenance change type that may require more or less effort and duration.

4 The Application of the COME Matrix

Table 4 shows the COME matrix for analyzing the pattern of software maintenance effort by the count of software maintenance changes and abbreviations in this matrix:

ESM Effort: Estimated Software Maintenance Effort measured in maintenance days,
SMCT: Software Maintenance Change Type,
SMCD: Software Maintenance Change Description and
TNR: Total number of records

Table 4. A matrix for analyzing the pattern of distributed efforts by the count of software maintenance changes

ESM Effort	SMCT	SMCD	TNR
0.1	C1	Corrective	10
0.1	P1	Perfective	3
0.1	P2	Preventive	1
0.1	A1	Adaptive	2
0.2	C1	Corrective	2
0.2	P1	perfective	1
0.5	F1	Functional	1
0.5	C1	corrective	4
1	F1	functional	4
1	C1	corrective	9
1	A1	adaptive	2
1	P1	perfective	3
2	F1	functional	2
2	C1	corrective	4
2	A1	adaptive	5
2	P1	perfective	1
5	F1	functional	2
5	A1	adaptive	7
7	F1	functional	2
7	A1	adaptive	2
10	A1	Adaptive	2
10	P1	perfective	1
10	P2	Preventive	1
10	C1	Corrective	1
20	F1	functional	4
20	A1	adaptive	2
20	C1	Corrective	1
25	F1	functional	1
25	A1	Adaptive	1

The aim of using the COME matrix is to provide software practitioners with an overview of predicted effort when grouping software maintenance changes. The goal is to provide software practitioners, especially novices, trying to estimate a correct variable of effort for the current change, with a review of effort for similar kinds of software maintenance changes.

To properly understand each variable in COME, our plan is to test the variables in Table 3 by conducting a regression analysis using a statistical analysis tool to evaluate the independent variables, and their effects on the predicted effort. That is, the dependent variable as the primary focus for clarity and understanding.

In the next section, we discuss the results generated by a statistical tool applied to each independent variable against the dependent variable, and highlight the significant effect and influences of the independent variables on the dependent variable. The results that are analysed for software practitioners to provide them with an understanding of how predicted effort is affected by the independent variables in applications and projects.

5 Result and Analysis

Six variables in Table 3 were input into the statistical analysis tool for a regression analysis test. Figures were generated from that tool based on curve estimation. Table 5 shows software maintenance effort classified as an independent variable and the dependent variables classified as maintenance change type, maintenance activity, KLOC and application characteristics (age and size). The following diagram shows the independent and dependent variables.

Table 5. Independent variables influenced on dependent variable

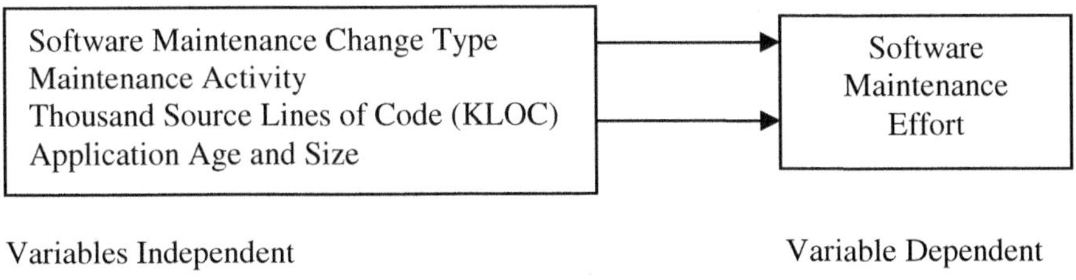

5.1 Dependent Variable 1: Software Maintenance Change Type

Software maintenance change type is the first variable that we investigate regarding its effects on predicted maintenance effort. For instance, we are interested to find out which group of software maintenance changes belongs to the predicted classes of maintenance effort: 0.1 hours, 5 hours, 10 hours, 15 hours and 25 hours.

Figure 1 shows the results analyzed from a group of software maintenance changes and their software maintenance effort. From the figure, we can see that adaptive changes are especially critical and the amount of effort required is 0.1, 0.5, 5, 7, 10, 20 and 25 hours. This is a good distribution of effort across five types of maintenance changes. Functional maintenance changes require more effort to fix. They can consume between 20 and 25 hours of effort and time.

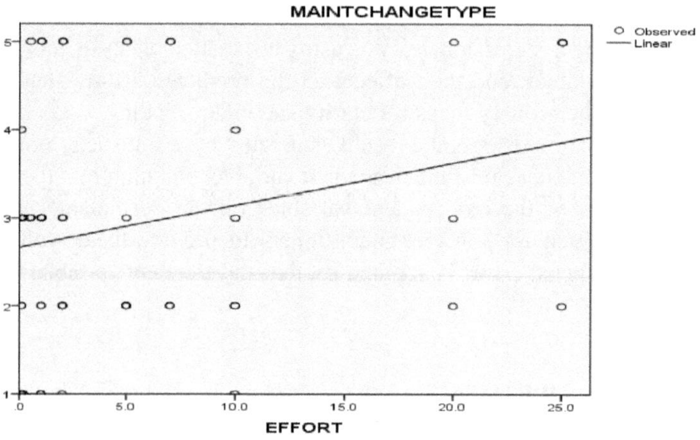

Fig. 1. Software maintenance changes types against effort classes

Adaptive changes and functional changes follow next. Corrective changes are especially time-consuming in relation to serious error corrections which are difficult to fix. Clearly, 20 maintenance hours were assigned to this group.

5.2 Independent Variable 2: Software Maintenance Activity

The second variable is software maintenance activity. From the 81 software maintenance changes, we would like to know which change activity types belong to predicted effort classes of 0.1 hour, 5 hours, 7 hours, 10 hours , 15 hours , 20 hours and 25 hours and which software maintenance changes require less effort as well as what effort the other software maintenance changes require.

Figure 2 below, shows the result of software maintenance effort for each change activity. A small amount of software maintenance effort, between 0.1 and 0.4 hours, was required for single code updates, single code insertion and multiple code insertion and deletion. Single code updates are one of the main activities frequently requiring 0.1 hour, 5 hours, 7 hours, 10 hours, 20 hours and 25 hours.

A significant effort of between 20 hours and 25 hours was spent on single code updates, multiple code insertions and updates, and multiple code insertion and deletion. The six software maintenance activities are documented in the dataset as tasks commonly mentioned for software maintainers regardless of application size and age.

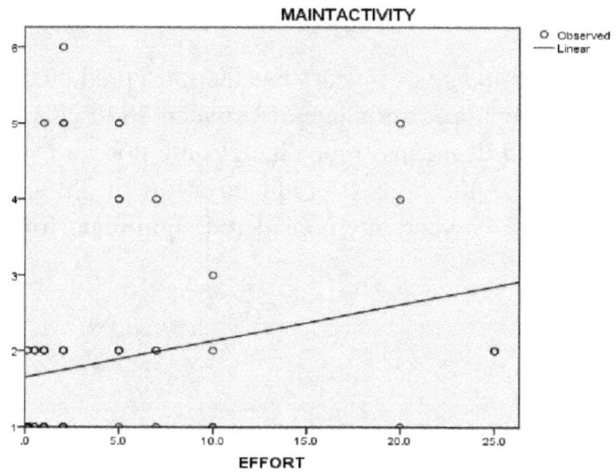

Fig. 2. Types of maintenance activity against effort classes

5.3 Independent Variable 3: Thousand Source Lines of Code (KSLOC)

The number of KSLOC inserted, deleted or modified with respect to software maintenance change activity against predicted effort was not formally measured. Figure 3 shows the software change activity of insertion and deletion of between 5 to 10 hours of predicted effort is focused largely on 500 KSLOC. On that basis, we can confirm that the 500 KSLOCs are poorly written and there was not enough testing to catch the defects early.

Interestingly, Figure 3 shows no concrete evidence that the grater the number of lines of code in the software maintenance activity, the more maintenance effort is expected. For example, we found that 2,000 KSLOCs have a predicted effort of 7 hours.

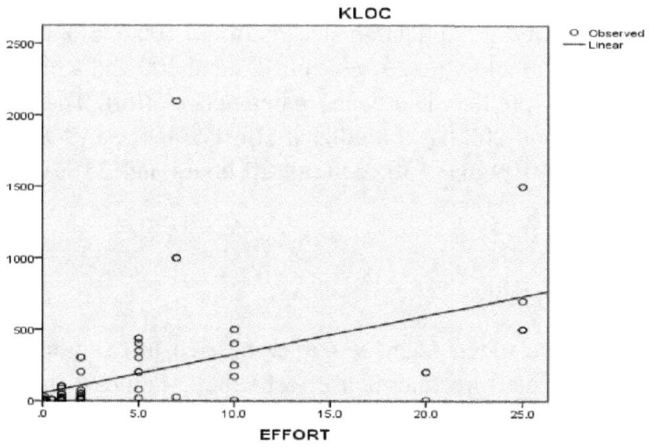

Fig. 3. KLOC against effort

5.4 Independent Variable 4: Application Age

From figure 4, an application age of 5 years has the ratio predicted of 0.1 to 0.5, 5, 10 and 25. We can tell that an application age of between 18 to 22 years has a predicted effort range from 0.5 and 5. It means some changes are not very difficult and complicated to fix and resolve. On the highest predicted effort of 25, application ages of 3 years, 5 years, 8 years and 12 years are considered significant for major correctional changes.

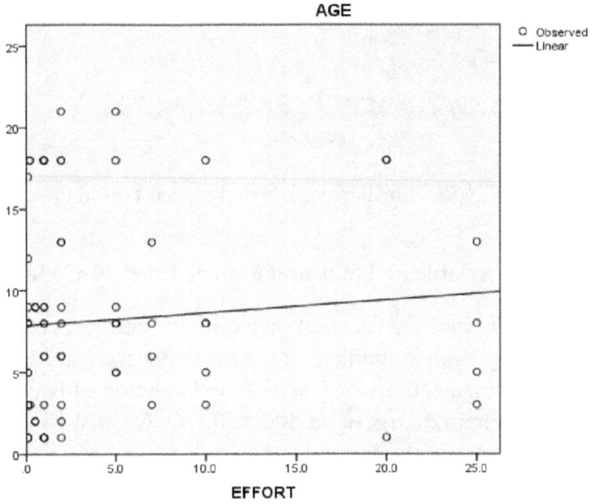

Fig. 4. Application age against effort

5.5 Independent Variable 5: Application Size

Figure 5 shows a diversity of application sizes between 100 and 500KSLOC. At least 20 application sizes are at a low range between 100 and 200 and a high range between 400 and 500 have a low predicted software maintenance effort. The majority application size between 100 and 200 has a predicted effort of between 5 and 10 hours. Application sizes between 100 and 150 required 20 hours and 25 hours for fixing the software.

5.6 Combing all Variables

The combination of five independent variables is used to examine the relationship between the maintenance efforts and their effectiveness. Figure 6 shows a fairly good coefficient on an effort interval of 0.1, 0.3, 0.5, 10, 20 and 25. In other words, it is possible to make a distinction on software maintenance effort from low to high when the five variables are combined

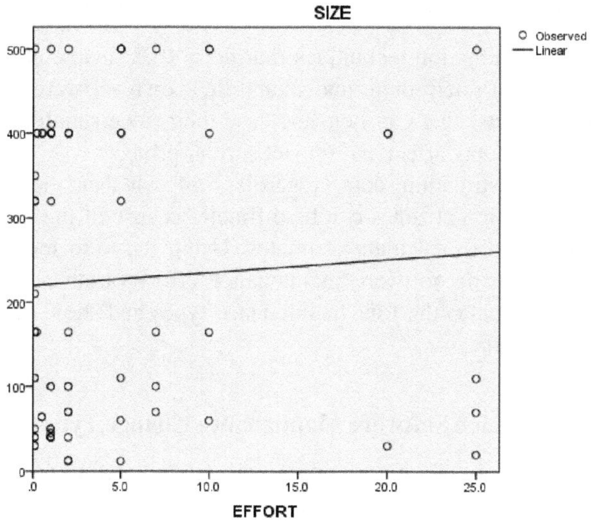

Fig. 5. Application Size against effort

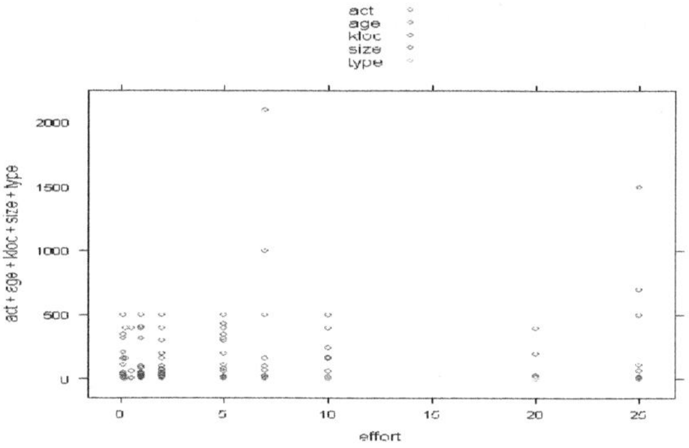

Fig. 6. A combination of the five independent variables against effort

6 Discussion

In this section, we briefly discuss how the results derived from this study can contribute to 1) improving transparency for software maintenance teams with regard to the distribution of estimation variables where software estimation efforts can be a) analyzed using the ratio study of patterns of similar software maintenance effort for the five maintenance types and b) the effects they have, 2) focusing on each software maintenance change type's strengths and identifying its impact on a range of software maintenance effort, 3) predicting costs based on software maintenance productivity rates with the aim of reducing incorrect estimates for similar software maintenance changes in future projects.

6.1 Viable Data Transparency of Estimated Variable Distributed Efforts

There is a lack of estimation techniques that do not use mathematical equations for software maintainers to help them understand their own software maintenance effort data from past projects, that can help increase their understanding of how software maintenance changes may affect and impact similar projects.

With regard to estimation data, regardless of whether they are incorrect or inconsistent, justification at times can be difficult because of the lack of sufficient or appropriate input data to calculate estimates. Using the ratio method to investigate estimation patterns using software maintenance effort variables of can create data transparency in relation to the four maintenance types and show the effects that they have on overall projects.

6.2 Focusing on Each Software Maintenance Change Type Strength

Maintenance is a time-consuming, costly, and challenging task. In order to reduce unnecessary maintenance cost and time, an early identification of maintenance types and their effects on software maintenance effort can improve the quality and cost of requirements, design, testing and coding. For example, as far as we know, with regard to corrective maintenance changes and functional changes, the significant numbers reported either mostly relate to errors in logic, design, bugs fixed and enhancement needed by users to comply with rules and practices within the business domain, technology domain and technical domain. These changes must be included as part of the software maintenance effort regardless of whether or not they require minimal or effort.

7 Matrix Challenges

There are several challenges to using the COME matrix and they are categorized by: 1) suitability, 2) reliability, 3) applicability, 4) validity and 5) compatibility. Each is briefly discussed below:

1. Suitability: In the given dataset, data are highly dependent, with a total number of 81 maintenance records which support our analysis and show that the results are promising in the context of understanding estimated variables in relation to software maintenance changes. On a small dataset, the challenge could be a significant lack of ability to demonstrate similar classification groups.
2. Reliability: A few simple and easy to understand steps drive the use the COME matrix for any level of IT professional including new and experienced users.
3. Applicability: The dataset came from an environment in which the programming language is a 3rd Generation Language. In today's IT environment, new and fast programming languages in different environments are less dependent on software size based on Source of Lines Of Code, Function Points or Object Points. More companies are using Use Cases or other methods to estimate software size [18]. Hence the need for COME matrix to be used with more datasets with different languages.

4. Validity: There is a validity threat with the COME matrix suggesting that it may not be seen as the most effective solution for performing better estimates when compared with the four most common estimation models: analogous models, top-down models, model-based, algorithmic-model-based, etc. Foundationally, there is no algorithmic equation that applies to this matrix; hence from that perspective, it could be difficult to convince the prediction and estimation community of its usefulness.
5. Compatibility: No identical matrix found in the academic literature is exactly based on our approach. Similar kinds of matrices emphasize quality control with respect to the review process of code inspections.

8 Conclusions

There are several contributions from using a COME matrix. The first contribution is that it is practical and simple to use. Unlike other formal cost estimation models, no pre-determined criteria or conditions must be assigned, prior to estimates, of effort or cost. This means that novice practitioners will find it easy to implement without having to learn and understand software maintenance effort concepts. The other contribution is that historical maintenance data from existing software maintenance projects can be used for evaluating software maintenance efforts and to find repeated maintenance changes. However, the analysis of maintenance effort distribution between individuals and groups is not possible because these variables are not easily documented in a dataset.

This study is useful for especially large maintenance projects where there are often repeated maintenance changes which are assessed and estimated by software maintainers. Because the process of effort estimation is considered complicated, an understanding of the variables, including software maintenance and effort must be firstly acquired by study, analysis and interpretation by estimators. Without adequate knowledgeable and skilled estimators, no good and proper estimation is possible.

The introduction of the COME matrix, a method which can be used to evaluate the effort required for maintenance work, can help to predict and find which maintenance change types have a low effort distribution, medium effort distribution or high effort distribution. A comprehensive study based on Jorgensen's maintenance dataset has been carried out, and the COME matrix has been applied to evaluate its efficacy. The matrix 1) shows classes of effort for a group of maintenance changes and 2) identifies low effort, medium effort and large effort for those changes.

The COME matrix provides a step forward in the study of maintenance effort estimation, providing a blueprint to help practitioners better understand maintenance effort and its characteristics, and helps us to further in our study of software maintenance.

References

1. Song, Q.B., Shepperd, J.M.: Predicting software effort A grey relational analysis based method. Journal of Expert System and Application 38(6), 7302–7316 (2011)
2. Jørgensen, M., Halkjelsvik, T.: The effects of request formats on judgment-based effort estimation. Journal of Systems and Software 83(1), 29–36 (2010)
3. Jørgensen, M., Gruschke, T.M.: The Impact of Lessons-Learned Sessions on Effort Estimation and Uncertainty Assessments. IEEE Trans. Software Eng. 35(3), 368–383 (2009)
4. Stark, G.E., Oman, P., Skillicorn, A., Ameele, A.: An examination of the effects of requirements changes on software maintenance releases. Journal of Software Maintenance: Research and Practice 11(5), 293–309 (1999)
5. Yang, Y., Li, Q., Li, M.S., Wang, Q.: An Empirical Analysis on Distribution Patterns of Software Maintenance Effort. In: Proceedings of International Conference on Software Maintenance (ICSM), pp. 456–459 (2008)
6. Jorgensen, M.: Experience With the Accuracy of Software Maintenance Task Effort Prediction Models. IEEE Transactions on Software Engineering 21(8), 674–681 (1995)
7. Osborne, W.M., Chikofsky, E.J.: Fitting Pieces to the Maintenance Puzzle. Proceedings of the IEEE Software 7(1), 11–12 (1990)
8. Milicic, D., Wohlin, C.: Distribution Patterns of Effort Estimations. In: Proceedings of EUROMICRO conference, pp. 422–429 (2004)
9. Ahn, Y., Suh, J., Kim, S., Kim, H.: The software maintenance project effort estimation model based on function points. Journal of software Maintenance and Evolution Research and Practice 15(2), 71–85 (2003)
10. Boehm, B.W., Clark, B., Horowitz, E., Westland, C., Madachy, R., Selby, R.: Cost models for future software life cycle process:COCOMO 2.0. Annals of Software Engineering Special Volume on Software Process and Product Measurement (1995)
11. Boehm, B.W.: Software Engineering Economic, pp. 596–599. Prentice-Hall, Englewood Cliff (1981)
12. Lientz, B.P., Swanson, E.B.: Software Maintenance Management: A Study of the Maintenance of Computer Application Software in 487 Data Processing Organizations. Addison-Wesley, Reading (1980)
13. Leintz, B.P., Swanson, E.B.: Problems in application software maintenance. Communications of the ACM 24(11), 763–769 (1981)
14. Martin, J., McClure, C.: Software Maintenance The Problems and its Solutions. Prentice-Hall, Englewood Cliffs (1983)
15. Nosek, J.T., Prashant, P.: Software Maintenance Management: Changes in the last Decade. Journal of Software Maintenance Research and Practice 2(3), 157–174 (1990)
16. Albrecht, A.J.: Measuring Application Development Productivity. In: Proceedings Share/Guide IBM Applications Development Symposium, Monterey, CA (1979)
17. Low, G.C., Jeffery, D.R.: Function points in the estimation and evaluation of the software process. IEEE Transactions on Software Engineering 16(1), 64–71 (1990)
18. Jones, T.C.: Measuring programming quality and productivity. IBM System Journal 17(1), 39–63 (1978)

COSMIC Functional Size Measurement Using UML Models

Soumaya Barkallah, Abdelouahed Gherbi, and Alain Abran

Departement of Software and IT Engineering
École de technologie supérieure (ÉTS), Montréal, Canada

Abstract. Applying Functional Size Measurement (FSM) early in the software life cycle is critical for estimation purposes. COSMIC is a standardized (ISO 19761) FSM method. COSMIC has known a great success as it addresses different types of software in contrast to previous generations of FSM methods. On the other hand, the Unified Modeling Language (UML) is an industrial standard software specification and modeling language. In this paper, we present a literature survey and analysis of previous research work on how to apply COSMIC functional size measurement using UML models. Moreover, we introduce a UML-based framework targeting the automation of COSMIC FSM procedures. In particular, we discuss the motivation and the rationale behind our approach, which consists in extending UML through the design of a specific UML profile for COSMIC FSM to support appropriately functional size measurements of software using UML models.

Keywords: Functional Size Measurement (FSM), COSMIC (ISO 19761), UML, Metamodeling, UML profiles.

1 Introduction

Project management needs functional size measurements in order to determine the size of the software to be build. These measures are essential to build reliable estimation and productivity models [1]. In addition, this provides more accurate control over the software development early in its life cycle. To this end, several methods of measuring the size of software have been designed and used. In particular, functional measures have known a great success in contrast to *length* measures, which are highly dependent on the technology used. The main benefit of FSM (Functional Size Measurement) methods is to quantify the software from its user's perspective, disregarding all quality and technical criteria [10].

Functional size measurement has been initially introduced in the seminal work of Allan Albrecht [3]. In this work, the Function Point analysis (FPA) method has been defined. FPA has then been increasingly used as well as been extensively studied. Subsequently, multiple generations of size measurement methods have been derived from Albrecht's method, such as IFPUG FPA, MK-II FPA and NESMA FPA [1]. A main limitation of these methods is, however, an inconsistency with software applications other than management information systems (MIS). In order to overcome this

T.-h. Kim et al. (Eds.): ASEA/DRBC/EL 2011, CCIS 257, pp. 137–146, 2011.

limitation, the Common Software Measurement International Consortium team [19] has proposed the COSMIC. This method can be applied to different domains including embedded software, real time software, business application software and hybrids software (Business and real time) [9].

From the software development perspective, modeling is increasingly considered a key activity in approaches to software engineering. In this regard, the Unified Modeling Language (UML) [24] is an industrial standard which is extensively used to specify various aspects of the software including the early user requirements, the system's structure, its dynamic behavior and the deployment. Therefore, there is a strong research interest in investigating how to enable software functional size measurement using UML models. In this context, several research initiatives have focused on sizing the software starting with its UML-based specification/design models. These approaches have in common the objective to automate the measurement procedure.

In this paper we aim, first, at reporting on a comprehensive study on the main previous research proposals focusing on functional size measurement from UML models. In particular, we focus on COSMIC method. Second, we present in this paper the motivations and the rationale underlying our approach to enable automating the COSMIC functional size measurement using UML models. The main idea sustaining our approach is the design of a UML-based modeling framework which allows the software engineer to annotate its UML models with information pertaining to COSMIC functional size measurement. To this end, a specific UML profile based on the main concepts of COSMIC will be defined.

The remaining part of this paper is organized as follows. In Section 2, we provide an overview of the COSMIC method. Section 3 is devoted to surveying the main research proposals to apply UML to the COSMIC method. We present an analysis of these proposals in Section 4. We highlight our approach to applying COSMIC functional size measurement on UML models in Section 5. We conclude the paper and outline our future work in Section 6.

2 Overview of COSMIC

COSMIC [9] is a method for measuring the functional size of software. This method is maintained and promoted by the Common Software Measurement International Consortium (i.e. The COSMIC group)[19]. This is a world-wide group of experts in the field of metrics. COSMIC become an ISO standard (ISO 19761) for measuring the functional size of software since March 2003.

The COSMIC measurement method applies a set of rules on the software functional processes as defined by its users to produce the functional size. This means that functional user requirements (FUR) are essential for measuring the functional size of a piece of software. The COSMIC method also differs from the IFPUG method [22] in terms of granularity, since it has a finer level of granularity at the level of the functional sub-processes [15]. COSMIC method can be applied to different types of software. In contrast, traditional methods measure only the functional size of MIS applications. The IFPUG method applies measurement only from the "human" user's

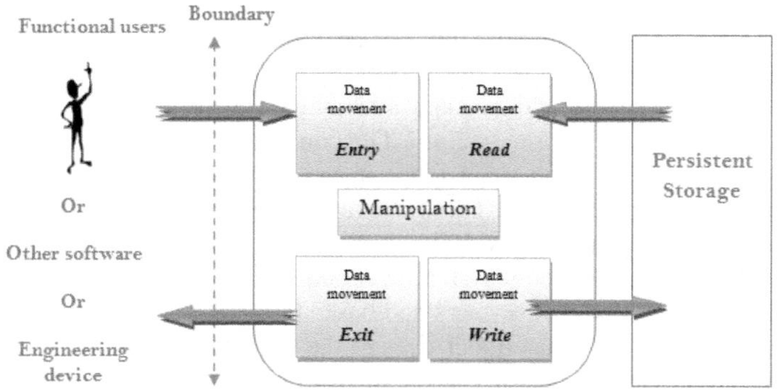

Fig. 1. COSMIC Data Movements and their interactions

perspective, while the COSMIC method measure from various viewpoints including human, other software or other equipments, interacting with the software [3].

Figure 1 illustrates the main concepts pertaining to the COSMIC FSM method. COSMIC expresses the functional user requirements by means of functional processes. The latter are divided into sub-processes that can be a data movement or a data manipulation. The COSMIC method identifies four types of data movements ("E": Entry, "X": Exit, "R":Read and "W":Write).

When the functional user triggers an event, a functional process will send a data group through the data movement *"Entry"* across the boundary of the software. The set of attributes of the data transferred will inform the software that an event was occurred. In contrast, software responds the user through the data movement *"Exit"* across the boundary. Error messages generated by the software are also considered as an 'exit'. Once information is input to the software, it will be processed and may be stored in the persistent storage. Moving the given data group from the functional process to persistent storage is called *"Write"*. Subsequently, information required by a functional process will be read from the storage where it was recorded. This data movement is called *"Read"*.

Each data movement of a single data group represents a single unit of COSMIC. This COSMIC unit of meas0ure is called COSMIC Function Point (CFP). The total size of a single functional process is the sum of these CFP as described below.

Size (functional process i) = CFP (Entries i) + CFP (Exits i) + CFP (Reads i) + CFP (Writes i)

3 COSMIC Functional Size Measurement Using UML Models

3.1 Mapping between COSMIC and UML Concepts

Bévo et al. [5] have established a mapping which consists in associating the COSMIC-related concepts with UML ones. The latter are essentially the different

UML diagrams. In particular, the concept of functional process in COSMIC is mapped to a UML use case. The different data movements (read, write, entry or exit) are considered as UML scenarios. It is worth mentioning that each UML use case is a set of scenarios. Data groups are mapped into UML classes within the class diagram and data attributes correspond to class attributes. The boundary of the software is represented in [5] by a use case diagram. The concept of COSMIC user is close to the UML actor. Finally, the authors consider that two COSMIC concepts do not have any corresponding concept in UML. These are layers and triggering event. The application of the mapping proposed by Bévo et al. in [5] was illustrated by an MIS case study, which is a control access system to a building. The functional size of the system was calculated based on use cases and based on scenarios. It is worth mentioning that, in this case study, the functional sizes of the software measured differently yielding two different results. The two different functional size represent in fact a single assessment but with different degrees of granularity.

3.2 Using Sequence Diagram to Address the Granularity Problem of Use Cases

In Jenner [7], which is an extension of the mapping presented in Bévo et al. [5], the mapping of COSMIC functional processes UML scenarios is refined. The extension proposed in [7] consists in using the UML sequence diagram. Consequently, a functional process matches with a sequence diagram and each data movement corresponds to an interaction message in this sequence diagram. A proposal for automation process to count the functional size using a CASE tool as well as the Rational Rose is proposed in [8] even though this automation process is not clear.

3.3 Using RUP for the Automation of COSMIC-Based Functional Size Measurement

Azzouz et al. proposes in [4] to automate the functional size measurement with COSMIC using the Rational Unified Process (RUP) and Rational Rose as environments for their implementation. To enable this automation, a mapping between the concepts related RUP and those related COSMIC has been established, based on those proposed by by Bévo et al. and Jenner. One distinguishing characteristic however, which we will discuss further in Section 5, is the introduction of a new UML stereotype to capture the concept of triggering event. Nevertheless, the concept of software layer had no UML equivalent and should be identified manually [4]. The proposal was verified with only one case study but not yet tested on a wide scale.

3.4 Extracting UML Concepts for FSM Automation Purposes

Vilus et al. present in [11] a method to extract instances of concepts in a specification with UML in order to facilitate the measurement of functional size. Their work comes within the context of FSM automation. This proposal complements the work of Bévo [13]. The authors developed a prototype (MetricXpert) that enables the automation of

FSM from specification done with a CASE tool as well as Rational Rose [12]. The prototype uses XMI files in which the MOF (Meta Object Facility) meta-models are exported and stores all the related measurement concepts extracted in a specific data base. The prototype was experimented using three case studies but presents a margin of error which is about 20 percent [13].

3.5 Measurement Based on the Use Case Model

Habela et al. [16] focuses on using the UML use case model to support the software measurement based on COSMIC. The authors argue that regardless of the complexity of data groups, it is more interesting to base the measurement process on data attributes. The authors present an approach which consists in using detailed scenarios to facilitate the measurement of functional size units. Interestingly, they emphasize the problem of redundancy. They suggest using the different links between use cases provided by UML such as «include» and « extend» relationships and generalizations to avoid repetition in the measurement procedure. The use case template proposed includes different elements such as business rules, preconditions and post-conditions.

3.6 Using UML Models for Measurement Considering Data Manipulations

The research in [14] proposes to use UML use case and sequence diagrams in order to measure the functional size of software. In addition, the authors propose to take into account software complexity measures in the measurement process. In particular, the authors emphasize to not only consider the data movement but also the integration of data manipulation in the COSMIC measurement. Accordingly, data movements are mapped to messages in a UML sequence diagram and data manipulation as error messages with their associated conditions in the same diagram. As a result, it becomes easy to calculate the functional size by aggregating all messages exchanged in the sequence diagram. This proposal takes into account data movements as well as data manipulations in the measurement procedure. It's challenging to look at the impact of data manipulation on the COSMIC measurement. However, it seems that the proposal is not supported by a tool to implement this procedure. This approach remains therefore theoretical and requires a lot of work to integrate the data manipulation in the measurement.

3.7 Measuring the Functional Size of the Use Case Diagram

Asma Sellami et al. present in [10] a specific technique to measure the functional size of UML use case diagrams. The authors consider that use case diagrams represent functional processes as they describe the behavior of the software as perceived by its functional users. The authors used a specific format to document the use case structure. The total size of the use case diagram is obtained by aggregating the functional size of the different scenarios which compose it. A set of rules was applied to the measurement procedure to take into account the inclusion, extension and inheritance relations between use cases. In this work, the authors argue that UML sequence and class diagrams are related to the use case diagram, thus the proposed model for measuring the functional size of use case diagram can be applied for measuring these diagrams. The approach was verified using a business application.

This proposal presents an interesting approach to measure the functional size of use case diagrams by applying a set of rules based on a specific use case format. The given procedure aims to gather in one way the measurement of the functional size of various UML diagrams. Currently, different proposals for measuring the size of these diagrams exist but are treated differently. The FSM process proposed is simple to implement; however, it requires further work to make more explicit the proposed process to be easily applicable.

3.8 A Requirements Space to Show How UML Can Support FSM

Van den Berg et al. [21] consider that UML is well adapted to specify user requirements. They propose a requirements space to show that FURs can be supported by the Unified Modeling language at the different levels of refinements which specify them. This requirements space consists in defining a number of UML diagrams that are consistent at each level. The authors argue that actors and the system boundary can be specified using the use case diagram. In addition, they propose to use the class diagram to measure data structures and used attributes. Finally, the authors suggest using the activity diagram to represent functional processes based on the concept of flow of events.

The approach proposed was supported by a small case study ("The Hotel Case"). The measurement phase is based on the activity diagram which describes the different use cases. For each use case, the authors show how to calculate the number of data movements. The total size is then obtained by aggregating all these data movements. However, the rationale behind the choice of the activity diagram is not explicit.

3.9 On the Usability of UML to Support the COSMIC Measurement

Lavazza et al. [20] also discuss how UML can be used to support the COSMIC measurement. The presented approach is illustrated through a case study in the field of embedded and real time systems ("the rice cooker controller"). The authors also use a mapping between all the COSMIC concepts and corresponding UML concepts. In particular, use case diagrams are used to represent the boundary of the software to be measured, business users and other external elements exchanging data with the application. In addition, the components diagram to identify persistent data groups and interfaces between the application and external components. The concept of triggering event is mapped onto an UML element within the component diagram. Finally, they consider that the sequence diagram is relevant to specify functional processes and data movements. Moreover, they show how to using use case and components diagrams can help to identifying non-functional users. Lavazza et al. concluded that UML can be used to build models that are relatively easy to measure. In addition, the mapping established between all the concepts of UML and COSMIC helps to build models oriented measure (for the modeler) on the one hand and to apply the COSMIC measurement rules in a simpler way (for the measurer).

4 Analysis

The literature survey on the issue of how to apply COSMIC functional size measurement using UML models, has identified nine relevant proposals [4], [5], [7], [10], [11], [14], [16], [20] and [21].

Most of these proposals have in common using UML diagrams as artifacts representing software whose functional size it to be measured. Not surprisingly, these diagrams include mainly UML sequence and Use Case diagrams as these are traditionally used to specify the software requirements. Other diagrams such as class diagram, the activity diagram, the component diagram have also been considered in some proposals. Table 1 summarizes the main features of these proposals with respect to the application domain and the UML artifacts used. In addition, we distinguish the proposals which have been automated and the tool used to support the automation accordingly.

It is worth noting that most of the proposals targeted management information system (MIS). This is remarkable considering the applicability of the COSMIC method to various domains such as real-time and embedded systems domain.

Table 1. Summary of the proposals related-COSMIC and based on UML models

Proposal	Application Domain	UML concept	Automation	Tool supporting Automation
Bévo et al. [5]	MIS	Use case, scenarios and class diagrams	Yes	Metric Xpert
Jenner et al. [7]	MIS	Use case and sequence diagrams	Yes	A tool was proposed to facilitate estimations
Azzouz et al. [4]	Real Time	Use case, scenario and class diagrams	Yes	RUP COSMIC-FFP
Luckson et al. [11]	MIS and Real Time	Meta-model MOF	Yes	Metric Xpert
Habela et al. [16]	MIS	Use case Diagram	No	None
Van den Berg [21]	MIS	Use case, activity and class diagrams	No	None
Levesque et al. [14]	MIS	Use case and sequence diagrams	No	None
Sellami et al. [10]	MIS	Use case, sequence and class diagrams	No	None
Lavazza et al. [20]	Real Time	Use case, component, class and sequence diagrams	No	None

Finally, most of the studies aimed at automating the functional size using COSMIC. To this end, different tools supporting this automation have been proposed such as the RUP COSMIC-FFP tool integrated within the rational rose environment [23] and the Metric Xpert tool [12]. The latter enables the partial automation of the functional size. There is very limited evidence available as to which extent these automation tools are validated. Therefore, as far as automation tools supporting the COSMIC functional size measurement are concerned, there is still a need to be satisfied.

5 A UML-Based Modeling Framework to Support the COSMIC FSM Method

An interesting finding, which emerges from our study presented in the previous section, is that none of the proposals considered extending UML to support more adequately and specifically the COSMIC FSM method. Our objective in an ongoing research project is to investigate this idea specifically. It is worth mentioning however, that Azzouz et al. defined a new UML stereotype to model the triggering event COSMIC concept. This is, nevertheless, a very limited extension.

The Unified Modeling Language (UML) is a very generic modeling language. UML has been designed with built in extensibility mechanisms. These mechanisms range from defining new stereotypes, to the definition of UML profiles. These are specific versions of UML adapted to the particularities of a particular domain such as the real-time domain [18]. One direct advantage is to enable experts of a particular domain to undertake their activities in their domain (using their concepts, terminologies, signs, etc) while using UML.

Our objective, therefore, in this research project is to design a UML-based framework targeting the automation of COSMIC FSM procedures. Such a framework requires a specific version of UML to support adequately COSMIC. A building block of this framework is an extension of UML in the form of a specific UML profile.

A key step towards the design of this profile is to capture the relevant concepts of the COSMIC domain in a domain model which will represent the meta-model of the profile. This meta-model will capture the main concepts of COSMIC domain along their different relationships. Furthermore, different constraints on this meta-model will have to be uncovered and formally described. This will be achieved using an appropriate formal language such as OCL.

Finally, the meta-model will be mapped to UML using new stereotypes. These will be used to annotate UML models with information pertaining to functional size measurements.

6 Conclusion and Future Work

In this paper, we have reported on the previous research initiatives devoted to investigating the issue of how to apply COSMIC functional size measurement using UML models. Most of these initiatives aimed at automating the functional size using COSMIC. To this end, different tools supporting this automation have been proposed. There is very limited evidence available as to which extent these automation tools are validated. Therefore, as far as automation tools supporting the COSMIC functional size measurement are concerned, there is still a need to be satisfied.

One particular and interesting finding of our study is that none of the proposals considered extending UML to support more adequately and specifically the COSMIC FSM method. The objective of our ongoing research project is to investigate this idea specifically. In particular, we aim at the design of a UML-based framework targeting the automation of COSMIC FSM procedures. Such a framework requires a specific UML profile. We have presented in this paper the rationale and motivation behind our approach.

References

1. Abran, A.: Software Metrics and Software Metrology. Wiley, IEEE Computer Society, Hoboken, Los Alamitos (2010)
2. Khelifi, A.: Un référentiel pour la mesure des logiciels avec la norme ISO 19761(COSMIC-FFP): une étude exploratoire. Thèse de doctorat présentée à l'École de Technologies Supérieure (2005), `http://s3.amazonaws.com/publicationslist.org/data/gelog/ref-275/963.pdf`
3. Abran, A., Dumke, R.: COSMIC Function Points: Theory and Advanced Practices, p. 334. CRC Press, Boca Raton (2011)
4. Azzouz, S., Abran, A.: A proposed measurement role in the Rational Unified Process (RUP) and its implementation with ISO 19761: COSMIC-FFP. Presented in Software Measurement European Forum - SMEF 2004, Rome, Italy (2004)
5. Bévo, V., Lévesque, G., Abran, A.: Application de la méthode FFP à partir d'une spécification selon la notation UML: compte rendues premiers essais d'application et questions. Presented at International Workshop on Software Measurement (IWSM 1999), Lac Supérieur, Canada, September 8-10 (1999)
6. Beatriz, M., Giovanni, G., Oscar, P.: Measurement of Functional Size in Conceptual Models: A Survey of Measurement Procedures based on COSMIC. Presented in MENSURA 2008, pp. 170–183 (2008)
7. Jenner, M.S.: COSMIC-FFP and UML: Estimation of the Size of a System Specified in UML – Problems of Granularity. Presented in the 4th European Conference on Software Measurement and ICT Control, Heidelberg, pp. 173–184 (2001)
8. Jenner, M.S.: Automation of Counting of Functional Size Using COSMIC-FFP in UML. Presented in the 12th International Workshop Software Measurement, pp. 43–51 (2002)
9. Abran, A., Desharnais, J.-M., Lesterhuis, A., Londeix, B., Meli, R., Morris, P., Oligny, S., O'Neil, M., Rollo, T., Rule, G., Santillo, L., Symons, C., Toivonen, H.: The COSMIC Functional Size Measurement Method- Measurement Manuel. Version 3.0.1 (2009)
10. Sellami, A., Ben-Abdallah, H.: Functional Size of Use Case Diagrams: A Fine-Grain Measurement. In: Fourth International Conference on Software Engineering Advances, ICSEA 2009, pp. 282–288 (2009)

11. Luckson, V., Lévesque, G.: Une méthode efficace pour l'extraction des instances de nconcepts dans une spécification UML aux fins de mesure de la taille fonctionnelle de logiciels. In: The Seventeenth International Conference Software & Systems Engineering & their Applications, ICSSEA 2004, Paris, Novembre 30-Décember 2 (2004)
12. Bévo : Analyse et formalisation ontologique des procedures de measures associées aux method de mesure de la taille fonctionnelles des logiciels: de nouvelles perspectives pour la mesure. Doctoral thesis, in UQAM, Montréal (2005)
13. Laboratory for research on Technology for Ecommerce LATECE, http://www.latece.uqam.ca/fr/c_projets.html
14. Levesque, G., Bévo, V., Cao, D.T.: Estimating software size with UML models. In: Proceedings of the 2008 C3S2E Conference, Montreal, pp. 81–87 (2008)
15. Maya, M., Abran, A., Oligny, S., St pierre, D., Désharnais, J.-M.: Measuring the functional size of real-time software. In: ESCOM-ENCRESS-1998, Rome (Italy), May 27-29 (1998)
16. Habela, P., Glowacki, E., Serafinski, T., Subieta, K.: Adapting Use Case Model for COSMIC-FFP Based Measurement. In: 15th International Workshop on Software Measurement – IWSM 2005, Montréal, pp. 195–207 (2005)
17. Aldawud, O., Elrad, T., Bader, A.U.: Profile for Aspect-Oriented Software Development. In: Proceedings of 3rd International Workshop on Aspect Oriented Modeling with UML at the 2nd International Conference on Aspect-Oriented Software Development (AOSD), Boston, United States (2003)
18. Catalog of UML Profile Specifications: http://www.omg.org/technology/documents/profile_catalog.htm
19. Official web site of the COSMIC group: http://www.cosmicon.com/
20. Lavazza, L., Del Bianco, V.: A Case Study in COSMIC Functional Size Measurement: the Rice Cooker Revisited, IWSM/Mensura, Amsterdam, November 4-6 (2009)
21. Van den Berg, K.G., Dekkers, T., Oudshoorn, R.: Functional Size Measurement applied to UML-based user requirements. In: Proceedings of the 2nd Software Measurement European Forum (SMEF 2005), Rome, Italy, March 16-18, pp. 69–80 (2005)
22. Official web site of the IFPUG group, http://www.ifpug.org/
23. Saadi, A.: Calcul avec Iso 19761 de la taille de logiciels développés selon Rational Unified Process. Master thesis. In: UQAM, Montréal (2003)
24. Official web site of the Object Management Group, UML section, http://www.uml.org/

Identifying the Crosscutting among Concerns by Methods' Calls Analysis

Mario Luca Bernardi and Giuseppe A. Di Lucca

Department of Engineering - RCOST, University of Sannio, Italy
{mlbernar,dilucca}@unisannio.it

Abstract. Aspect Oriented Programming allows a better separation and encapsulation of the (crosscutting) concerns by means of the "aspects". This paper proposes an approach to identify and analyze the crosscutting relationships among identified concerns with respect to the concerns' structure (in terms of source code elements) and their interactions due to the calls among methods. The approach has been applied to several software systems producing valid results.

Keywords: Aspect Mining, Aspect Oriented Programming, Software Evolution, Reverse Engineering, Software Comprehension.

1 Introduction

In this paper we present an extension to the approach proposed in [1], [2] to identify the (crosscutting) concerns implemented by code components (at class and method level) scattered and tangled along the type hierarchy of an OO system. The main improvement is the analysis of the methods' call graph to identify more and new crosscutting relationships among the identified concerns.

Due to the manner in which the crosscutting concerns are usually implemented in OO systems, there are two main ways that introduce the scattering and tangling of code components in them. A first one, we refer it as static crosscutting[1], is due to the (scattered and tangled) declarations of substitutable[2] methods and types, that are generated by means of static relationships (inheritance, implementation or containment). For instance, Figure 2-(a) shows a small type hierarchy where methods m_1 and m_2 (declared by interface I_1) are scattered in classes X_1 and X_2. The same happens for the method h, declared by interface I_3, that is scattered directly, in X_5 and X_6 by implementation of interface I_3 and indirectly, in X_1 and X_2 by containment of fragments X_5 and X_6.

The other way of introducing scattering and tangling, we refer it as dynamic crosscutting [6], is related to the control flow that (at run-time) can be crosscut by some additional behaviour executed whenever predefined events occur (during program execution). This kind of (dynamic) crosscutting can be introduced

[1] A definition and discussion on static and dynamic crosscutting, their properties and their differences is in [6].

[2] As stated by the Liskov substitution principle (LSP).

T.-h. Kim et al. (Eds.): ASEA/DRBC/EL 2011, CCIS 257, pp. 147–158, 2011.

by means of scattered and tangled method invocations. Indeed, an invocation to a method alters the run-time control flow by adding the behaviour of the called method to the calling one. Thus, when a method of a Concern is invoked by several other methods belonging to different other Concerns, the behaviour of the invoked Concern is dynamically scattered (at run-time) within the Concerns associated to the callers. Similarly, when a method makes calls to other methods belonging to different Concerns, the behaviour of such Concerns is tangled together within the calling method. For instance the Figure 2-(a) shows a simple type hierarchy in which some calls are highlighted as stereotyped dependencies. The method h calls both the method m_1 of I_1 and the method p_1 of I_3. These calls generate, during method h execution, the dynamic tangling of the behaviour executed by thc called methods m_1 and p_1 [3].

The approach presented in [1], [2] is based on a meta-model to represent Concerns at class level as sets of Type Fragments (i.e. a portion of a Type in terms of its members and relationships). Section 2 summarizes the process allowing the identification of Type Fragments and their association to Concerns. The crosscutting among the identified Concerns is then found by looking for: (*i*) the Type Fragments scattered and tangled within the identified concerns, due to the static structure of declarations specifying the system's Type hierarchy; and (*ii*) the calls among methods belonging to Type Fragments assigned to different concerns. The latter is the main extension with respect [1], [2] presented in this paper.

The paper is structured as follows. Section 2 shortly describes the meta-model defined to represent the structure of an OO system by its Concerns, the Concerns' mining approach and the (extended) method used to perform the crosscutting analysis given a concern meta-model instance. Section 3 illustrates results form a case study carried out on some Java systems. In Section 4 some relevant related works are discussed. Finally Section 5 contains conclusive remarks and briefly discusses future work.

2 Concerns Mining and Crosscutting analysis

In the following we, first, briefly describe the proposed meta-model and the static crosscutting analysis defined in [1], [2], then we present the approach extensions to identify the dynamic crosscutting.

In [1], [2] a model is defined to represent the static structure of an OO system in terms of its Concerns. Figure 1 shows, as a UML class diagram, such model with the extension made to represent the Calls among Methods.

The OO system is modeled as a set of Types (i.e. Value, Reference Types, and Array[4]) where Reference Types (i.e. Interfaces and Classes) are composed by Reference Type Fragments (that can be Class- or Interface- Fragments). Reference

[3] Actually the concrete method that is tangled at run-time could be any of substitutable methods specified by implementers of I_1 (i.e. X_1 and X_2) and I_3 (namely X_5 and X_6).

[4] Array types are threated as separated types since they must specify the type of the array components.

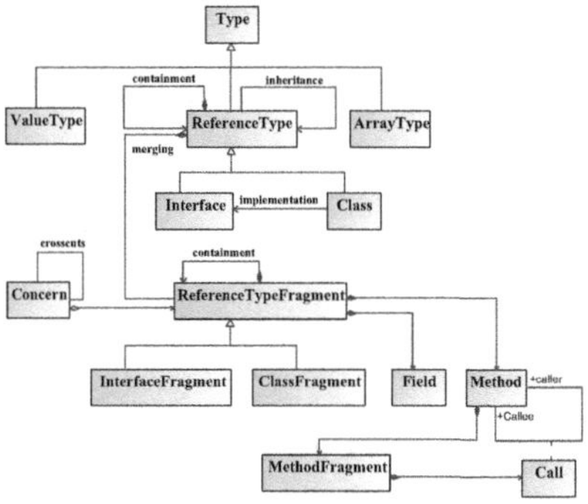

Fig. 1. A meta-model to represent Concerns implementation in Java systems

Type Fragments are composed of Fields and Methods. A Concern is represented by mean of a set of ReferenceTypeFragments (in the paper, for brevity, we refer to them also as Type Fragments or just as Fragments). Hence a Concern aggregates Fragments of (potentially different) types. Conversely, each type can be made up of Fragments aggregated by different Concerns. Similarly to Types that are composed by Type Fragments, methods are composed by Method Fragments, i.e. blocks of statements. A method can invoke another method by a Call statement, introducing a call relationship between the caller and callee methods. Such a call imply also a call relationship between the Type Fragments which the caller and callee belong to and hence between the Concerns those fragments are associated to. The model is able to represent different Concerns separately viewing the complete system as the composition of all the Concerns. An analysis of an instance of the model allows to identify the crosscutting among the Concerns due to (*i*) the tangling and scattering of the ReferenceTypeFragments associated to each Concern and (*ii*) the tangling and scattering due to the calls among different Concerns.

2.1 Static Concerns Mining

The static concerns identification process starts with a static code analysis of the system Type Hierarchy, looking at inheritance, implementation and containment relationships. Each Type introducing a new external behavior [5] is associated (initially) to a separate Concern; such a Type is said the "Seed" of the Concern.

The Figure 2-(a) shows an example consisting of three hierarchies rooted in the Interfaces "I_1", "I_2" and "I_3". Following the paths from the roots down to leaves, all the Types are to be considered. The three roots "I_1", "I_2" and "I_3" introduce basic behaviour (i.e. methods) for their abstractions and hence are considered Seeds of as many as Concerns. The Classes X_1,X_2,X_3,X_4,X_5, and X_6 are not Seeds since they doesn't introduce any new member.

[5] At this aim any Reference Type that introduces, in all paths from a root to a leaf of the type hierarchy graph, the declaration of a new set of members is to be identified.

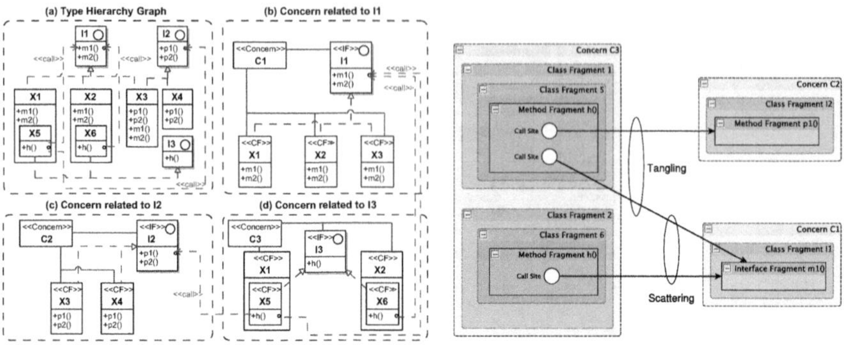

Fig. 2. A simple Type Hierarchy, the detected Concerns' Seeds and the Type Fragments composing the Concerns (Left) - Tangling and Scattering due to some calls (Right)

Initially each Seed is associated to one Concern. At the end of the traversal, each Concern will be associated to the Fragments of all the Types that implement the corresponding single Seed. The traversal of the hierarchy type graph starts from the leaves and goes up to the roots. Each type t encountered during the traversal is analysed to detect which Seeds it implements. For each Seed r, implemented by t, a Type Fragment $f_r(t)$ is created and added to the Concern c associated to the Seed r.

The sub-figures 2-(b,c,d) show the results of the traversal on the example of Figure 2-(a) for the three Concerns (C_1, C_2 and C_3) associated to the Seeds I_1, I_2 and I_3. In the figure, the UML stereotypes "IF" and "CF" are, respectively, for "Interface Fragment" and "Class Fragment". For each Seed, starting from the leaves, the Fragments are created for each Type that is (or contains a type) substitutable with the considered seed. For example, the classes X_1 and X_2 generate the two fragments $C_1.X_1$ and $C_1.X_2$ (in concern C_1) including the methods declared by the Seeds I_1 (because of direct Seed implementation) and two fragments $C_3.X_1$ and $C_3.X_2$ (in Concern C_3) because of type containment of a nested fragments $C_3.X_1.X_5$ and $C_3.X_2.X_6$ both implementing the Seed I_3). Note that the three Seeds (I_1, I_2 and I_3) generate only three fragments each in a different Concern (since, as already pointed out, a Seed is entirely assigned to a single Concern).

A Concern (e.g. Persistence) can be referred to more Seeds, each Seed implementing that Concern in a different context (e.g. the Persistence of different specific objects). Thus, when a group of Seeds participate to implement a same (abstract) Concern, their associated (specific) Concerns can be merged together into a more abstract one. Just as an example, if we have different Seeds each associated to a different Persistence Concern of a specific a class of objects, all these Concerns can be associated to the more general "Persistence" Concern. The automatic Hierarchical Agglomerative Clustering (HAC) algorithm defined in [1] is used to group Seeds on the base of a combination of a structural and a lexical distance.

2.2 Crosscutting Analysis

The crosscutting relationships among the identified Concerns are identified by a static analysis of the structural Concern model and of the 'dynamic' information of the Calls among them. The latter is an extension to the approach in [1], [2].

Static Crosscutting Analysis. A static crosscutting matrix is traced down by the relationships among the type fragments located in different Concerns. The matrix reports on both rows and columns, by the same order, the Concerns defined after the clustering step. It is generated by traversing the concern model instance, identifying the scattering and tangling at fragment level, for each couple of concerns. A matrix value F_{ij} represents the number of fragments that are tangled between the Concern in row i and the one in column j. The matrix is symmetrical as the definition of crosscutting we consider (equivalent to that provided by Kiczales [8] and its formalization provided by Ostermann [9]). Given such definition, scattered Concerns are, within our model, the Concerns containing at least two Type Fragments. Then two Concerns C_x and C_y are crosscutting if and only if: (*i*) they both contain more than one Type Fragment (hence generating scattering) and (*ii*) there are at least two Type Fragments $f \in C_x$ and $g \in C_y$, with the same fully qualified name (this means that the two Concerns are introducing members or relationships on the same Type, thus generating tangling).

Dynamic Crosscutting Analysis. This analysis is based on the identification of Dynamic Concerns' Interactions due to the calls among the methods in Fragments assigned to different Concerns. The entire system source code is parsed and a context-insensitive call graph, reporting for each call its possible targets, is built using Rapid Type Analysis (RTA). For each call $X.a \longmapsto Y.b$, an analysis is performed to detect the Concerns to which the caller method a and callee method b are assigned by looking at internal fragments structure of types X and Y. Thus we obtain an inter-fragment call $c_1.X.a \longmapsto c_2Y.b$: it expresses that Concern c_1 calls the Concern c_2 since the target method b belongs to a fragment of the type Y assigned to the Concern c_2 and the calling method a belongs to the fragment of X assigned to the Concern c_1. Two cases can happen:

- the caller/callee methods belong to fragments assigned to the same Concerns ($c_1 \equiv c_2$);
- the caller/callee methods are assigned to fragments of different Concerns ($c_1 \neq c_2$);

While the concern model contains the calls of both types, the crosscutting analysis ignores the calls of the former case focusing only on scattered and tangled inter-fragments calls assigned to different Concerns, being our interest in identifying the dynamic crosscutting relationships among different Concerns.

In the example of Figure 2-a, the method h of class X_5 calls the method m_1 of interface I_1 and the method p_1 of interface I_3. Moreover, the method h of class X_6 calls the method m_1 of interface I_1. These calls are reported to the corresponding fragments in Figure 2 (b), (c) and (d): the call $X_5.h \longmapsto I_2.p_1$ is from the fragment $C_3.X_5$ towards the fragment $C_2.I_2$ and hence a call is between concerns C_3 and C_2. Similarly the scattered calls $X_5.h \longmapsto I_1.m_1$ and $X_6.h \longmapsto I_1.m_1$ imply calls between the fragments $C_3.X_1.X_5$ and $C_3.X_2.X_6$ as sources and the fragment $C_1.I_1$ as target, resulting in calls between concerns C_3 and C_1.

The information about the calls among fragments is then used to find dynamic crosscutting according to the following definition:

Definition. Between two concerns C_x and C_y a dynamic crosscutting relationship is if and only if: (*i*) there exists a method in the system containing at least one call towards C_x and another towards C_y and (*ii*) there are (scattered) calls in different methods towards at least C_x or C_y.

From the example of Figure 2 we can derive the inter-fragment calls, as exemplified in the right side of the same figure: there are two calls tangling together the Concerns C_1 and C_2 and at least one of such calls also participate to scattering of set of calls towards C_1. This means that, by the given definition, C_1 and C_2 are (dynamically) crosscutting Concerns. The matrix Call Crosscutting Matrix (CCM)[6] is built to report information related to dynamic crosscutting.

The rows and columns of CCM report the concerns with the same order. Each row is divided in two parts labelled respectively by 'S' (Scattering) and 'T' (Tangling). For each pair of Concerns, a cell i, j of the matrix, reports:

- in the 'S' sub-row, the number of fragments assigned to the Concern on the row i containing at least a call to the Concern on the column j (this indicates scattering at statement level);
- in the 'T' sub-row, the number of system's method containing at least a call to both the Concern on the row i and to the Concern on the column j (this indicates tangling at statement level).

The matrix provides an overall picture of the dynamic crosscutting among the static Concerns identified in the system. Of course, this is not a complete dynamic crosscutting representation because crosscutting Concerns that have not also a static structure (in terms of system modules) are not considered.

3 Case Study

In order to assess and validate the proposed approach several OO systems have been analysed, with the support of the ConAn tool [3].

In this paper, due to space constraints and to keep the discussion focused, we present results only for the JHotDraw 6.01b system, a graphical editor framework designed to show good use of design patterns. The Seed identification step produced 83 Seeds, 48 related to Interfaces and 35 to Classes. Each Seed is

[6] An instance of the matrix is showed in Table 1-(b).

associated to a Concern containing the Type Fragments implementing it. The clustering phase resulted in 30 Concerns generated by merging together the ones associated to the Seeds that have been clustered together. A validation to assess the quality of the clustering was done by inspecting the source code and the type hierarchy graph. Summarizing, the manual validation step identified 30 Concerns; of these, 28 concerns were also identified by the automatic approach and the two missing ones were obtained removing the Seeds wrongly clustered from the bad clusters.

More details on the results of the static crosscutting concern mining process are reported in [1]. We just report in Table 1-(a), for convenience and in the sake of completeness, the static crosscutting matrix (on its rows are the names of the concerns resulting after the Clustering phase). The call graph of the entire system was calculated and call information were added to those contained in the static concern model instance. The Table 1-(b)) shows an excerpt of the Call Crosscutting Matrix (CCM). In the CCM, the rows reporting a greater number of cells with a positive value (both for 'S'and 'T' sub-rows) highlights the most relevant cases of crosscutting among identified concerns, since the values indicate the interactions (in terms of dynamic tangling and scattering) between the concern on the row with the ones on the columns.

Looking at the Table 1-(b) it is possible to identify the concerns with the highest number of scattered and tangled calls: the rows from 1 to 7 ("Entity Enumerations", "Tooling", "Commands", "Event Handling", "Entities Handles", "Entities Holders" and "Undo/Redo"), and the ones from 21 to 23 ("Editors", "Figures" and "Drawable Elements") and 28 ("Connectors") correspond to the most crosscutting concerns.

It's interesting to discuss how such dynamic crosscutting information are related the static crosscutting (Table 1). For several concerns not generating static crosscutting (the ones with an empty row, and an empty symmetric column, in Table 1), the CCM matrix shows a high number of scattered and tangled calls. This means that interaction among each of these concerns pairs is mainly done dynamically. It is the case for the "Entity Enumerations" Concern: in the static crosscutting matrix it has an empty row while in the Table 1-(b) it is invoked together with almost all the other Concerns in the system (looking at the tangling row). Another interesting case is related to the "Factories" Concern. From the structural point of view it doesn't generate any static crosscutting: no Factory participate by means of static relationships to any other Concern (its row in the static matrix is empty). But Factory methods are invoked by several other Concerns to create the needed objects, as reported in the CCM at the tangling row. In this case there are many calls to Factory method tangled with calls to the most crosscutting Concerns in the system.

The Concern "Persistence" in JHotDraw is one of the cases in which most of crosscutting is only static and structural. Persistence methods are injected by means of the Storable role in all entities that need to be persistent. For this reason there are few dynamic interactions with the other Concerns. The only notable exception is the Persistence-Figures case, since several Persistence fragments

Table 1. Static (a) and Dynamic (b) Crosscutting Matrix of JHotDraw 6.01b system

	CONCERNS	1	2	3	5	7	8	9	10	11	12	14	16	17	18	19	20	22	23	27	28	29	30
1	Animations							1								2			1				
2	Commands											2									6		
3	Connectors																		3				
5	Content Producers																		4				
7	Drag'N'Drop											1	1										1
8	Draw Application								2														
9	Drawable Elem.	1										2				2			2				
10	Editors						2					4										2	
11	Entities Handles																				3		
12	Entities Holders											3				4			3				
14	Event Handling	2				1		2	4		3		1			11	1	1	11	1		2	6
16	Figure Helpers					1						1											2
17	Figure Selections														1								
18	Figure Traversing													1									
19	Figures	2						2			4	11					2		31				
20	Layouting											1				2			5				
22	Palette Buttons											1											
23	Persistence	1		3	4			2			3	11				31	5						
27	Tooling											1									7		
28	Undo / Redo		6							3										7			
29	Version Request.								2			2											
30	Views					1						6	2										

Not crosscutting:	Desktop (6) , Entity Enumerators (13) , Factories (15) , Painting (21) , Resource Manager (24) , Strategies (25) Storage Formats (26)

(a)

Inter-fragment Calls		1	2	3	4	5	6	7	11	18	21	22	23	27	28	29
1 Entity Enumerations	S								1							
	T		7	5	4	4		27	8			56	19	3	28	
2 Toolings	S	5			14	3	8	19	3		17	32	18		29	2
	T	7		1	13	3	2	22	2		23	35	20	1	38	2
3 Commands	S	5					6	11	1		7	2	4		22	
	T	5	1				3	10			7	2	4		25	
4 Entities Holders	S											9				
	T	4	13					6	1		3	16	4		2	
5 Entities Handles	S	1						10			1	18			6	4
	T	4	3					8	4		1	18			8	4
6 Event Handling	S		6	3							3	15			3	
	T		2	3				4			4	16	3		4	
7 Undo/Redo	S	22	6		2							17	10		21	
	T	27	22	10	6	8	4		2		9	26	14		39	1
11 Factories	S															
	T	8	2		1	4		2			1	16	4		8	
18 Persistence	S	1			3				2			13	1	4		1
	T															
21 Editors	S		7	1					1			4	6	1	11	
	T		23	7	3	1	4	9	1			9	9	1	21	
22 Figures	S	19							20				9	1	1	4
	T	56	35	2	16	18	16	26	16		9		33	6	31	14
23 Drawable Elements	S	1							3			3				
	T	19	20	4	4		3	14	4		9	33			40	
27 Layouting	S	3										4				
	T	3	1								1	6				
28 Views	S	11	5	1		2	1		8		2	9	15			
	T	28	38	25	2	8	4	39	8		21	31	40			2
29 Connectors	S											8				
	T		2			4		1				14			2	

(b)

(i.e. 13 scattered fragments in Table 1-(b)) invoke Figures methods. This confirm the decentralized design of Persistence Concern: each Figure class implements its own Persistence methods (i.e. read and write) and often these invoke, in turn, other Figure's methods to obtain internal state. Persistence can be migrated to AOP by means of an aspect implementing the core logic of the Concern and capturing Persistence requests dynamically (instead of simply delegating to each

Table 2. An excerpt of relevant Commands, View and Undo inter-fragment calls

Caller		Callee	
Concern	**Method**	**Concern**	**Method**
Command	figures.GroupCommand::execute()	**Undo/Redo**	util.Undoable::setAffectedFigures(FigureEnumeration)
	figures.UngroupCommand::execute()		util.Undoable::setAffectedFigures(FigureEnumeration)
	standard.SendToBackCommand::execute()		util.Undoable::setAffectedFigures(FigureEnumeration)
			util.Undoable::getAffectedFigures()
	standard.AlignCommand::execute()		util.Undoable::setAffectedFigures(FigureEnumeration)
	standard.ChangeAttributeCommand::execute()		util.Undoable::setAffectedFigures(FigureEnumeration)
			util.Undoable::getAffectedFigures()
	standard.SelectAllCommand::execute()		util.Undoable::setAffectedFigures(FigureEnumeration)
	standard.BringToFrontCommand::execute()		util.Undoable::setAffectedFigures(FigureEnumeration)
			util.Undoable::getAffectedFigures()
	util.UndoCommand::execute()		util.Undoable::undo()
			util.Undoable::isRedoable()
			util.Undoable::getDrawingView()
	util.UndoableCommand::execute()		util.Undoable::isUndoable()
	util.RedoCommand::execute()		util.Undoable::redo()
			util.Undoable::isUndoable()
			util.Undoable::getDrawingView()
	util.UndoableCommand::getUndoActivity()		util.UndoableAdapter::UndoableAdapter(DrawingView)
	standard.BringToFrontCommand::execute()	**View**	framework.DrawingView::selection()
			framework.DrawingView::drawing()
			framework.DrawingView::checkDamage()

concrete class to implement its own Persistence logic). This centralized design (as opposed to the one highlighted by our analysis) reduces code duplication and the degree of static crosscutting while increasing the chances of reusing common Persistence behaviour among concrete classes.

In the following is presented a more detailed discussion about how the most crosscutting concerns interacts among themselves looking at both static crosscutting information and inter-fragment calls. Due to space constraints in the following are discussed only interactions among the Concerns Command/Tooling and Undo/Redo, as a case of crosscutting that has both a static component (based on type containment) and a dynamic one (based on scattered calls from different type fragments of both concerns).

Commands, Tooling and Undo/Redo. The "Commands", "Tooling" and "Undo/Redo" Concerns are implemented by means of a mixture of both static and dynamic crosscutting. This static crosscutting is well highlighted in the Table 1 looking at Undo/Redo column: there are 6 types containing both Commands and Undo/Redo fragments and 7 types containing both Tooling and Undo/Redo fragments. The inspection of the static concern model shows that Undo/Redo fragments (implementing the Undoable seed) are always inner fragments within Command and Tooling ones. By looking at the inter-fragment calls (Table 2 shows the subset of interest) it can be seen how the methods of the Undoable inner fragments are dynamically invoked by:

- the core Undo/Redo fragment in the UndoableCommand type, when the delegating execute() method obtains an instance of the inner Undoable by invoking the getUndoActivity of the wrapped command (this because it is a Command decorator used to add undo/redo functionality to existing commands);

– the outer Command fragment, each time it has to set the inner Undoable state needed to undo the command (this always happens during execute() method execution);

The "execute()" methods of almost all Commands fragments invoke methods (see the Table 2) of the Undoable fragments (isRedoable,isUndoable, setAffectedFigures, getAffectedFigure and undo). The table also shows that there is tangling between Undo/Redo and Views: this is showed only for BringToFront command (the last row) but it happens for almost all "execute()" methods affecting views. The command obtains a view object from the inner undoable in order to change its state (and eventually rolling it back when undo() is called). This is reported in the CCM matrix looking at the UndoRedo—View tangling and scattering cells that report, respectively, 39 tangled calls towards both concerns and 21 scattered calls from UndoRedo fragments towards Views' ones.

The crosscutting calls between "Commands" and "UndoRedo" are very interesting. Each Command fragment contains an inner UndoableActivity invoking it during all operations that require to save the state and eventually to perform the undo operation.

These information help the comprehension on how Commands and Undo/Redo concerns are structured and interacts at run-time. Such knowledge is very useful, for example, to migrate the concerns towards AOP: just looking at the model of the concerns it's easy to see that inter-type declarations could be used to inject the inner UndoActivity classes in the Command hierarchy (improving static crosscutting of both concerns). Similarly to improve dynamic crosscutting, the explicit calls of execute() methods towards their inner classes should be implicitly triggered by advices bounded to pointcuts defined in the Undo/Redo aspects.

4 Related Work

The proposed approach is related to work about aspect mining techniques with which share the aim to identify crosscutting concerns in existing (not AOP) systems. Most techniques for both static and dynamic crosscutting mining are static ones and perform source code analyses and manipulations. Others techniques focus on executing the code elaborating the data gathered at run-time (dynamic techniques). Hybrid techniques, exploiting both structural and run-time information, are also used to improve the quality of those static and dynamic approaches. In [4], Marin et. al. propose an integration technique that combines together a metric based approach (fan-in analysis [7]), a token-based one, exploiting identifier lexical analysis, and the approach proposed in [12] that exploits dynamic analysis. The approach proposed in [13] by Tonella and Ceccato focuses on crosscutting concerns produced by the scattered implementation of methods declared by interfaces that do not belong to the principal decomposition. Such interfaces, called "aspectizable" are identified and automatically migrated to aspects. The authors goal is a bottom-up refactoring strategy to migrate code modules into aspects. Our approach is instead oriented to obtain a structural and behavioral model of concerns and to study crosscutting relationships among them. From this point of view our approach is more suitable for program comprehension or re-documentation tasks. However it cannot be used yet to drive automatic refactoring (since no dependencies analysis at method level is performed).

In [5] an automatic static aspect mining approach that exploits the control flow graphs of the system is proposed. The approach searches for recurring execution patterns based on different constraints applied to calling contexts. This approach, as our inter-fragment calls mining approach, focuses on calls as the main way of interaction among (crosscutting) concerns.

In [11], Shepherd et. al. also used an agglomerative hierarchical-clustering algorithm to group methods. This approach share, with static part of our approach, the usage of agglomerative hierarchical-clustering. However in our case the clustering is applied to type fragments instead of methods; moreover it depends on a distance matrix built from a combination of structural and lexical information.

The main differences among all such techniques and our proposal is related to how concerns are identified. Our approach identify concerns by means of static crosscutting and then studies interactions among them (due to dynamic crosscutting). This provide a complete representation of both static and dynamic crosscutting for identified concerns. Conversely, the discussed approaches, identify concerns only by dynamic crosscutting producing an interaction model that lacks of structural information.

An approach to model concerns in source code that influenced the definition of our meta-model was proposed in [10] by Robillard and Murphy. Anyway our concern model takes into account the kind of relationships of a Java system and hence is dependent on language constructs of object-oriented single inheritance languages. While this can restrict the range of applicability (with respect to the approach proposed in [10] that is independent from language) it allows to reason about details of the structure of the system, explicitly taking into account all kind of modules, their members and their relationships (inheritance, implementation, overriding and type containment).

5 Conclusions and Future Work

An approach to identify dynamic concerns in existing OO systems and the crosscutting relationships among them has been proposed by extending previous work. The approach is based on the analysis of the Type Hierarchy to identify the concern seeds (types enriching their inherited external interface) and the fragments of each Type participating to the implementation of these seeds. The process exploits a meta-model to represent the concerns in the system as sets of type and methods fragments. The current model takes into account also the invocations towards type fragments of different concerns. Such information integrates the ones about the static structure of the system in order to obtain a representation of the control flow among the identified concerns in the system and of the dynamic crosscutting relationships among them. This knowledge is very useful to understand how concerns are structured and how they interact among themselves. In particular the analysis of the call relationships allows the identification of dynamic crosscutting that can not be identified by just structural analysis. However, it is also valuable when planning system refactoring towards AOP since it provides a detailed picture of concerns actual design letting developers to reason about possible improvements.

Future work will be mainly oriented towards using the mined Concern model (both static and dynamic parts) in order to support source code refactoring towards aspects. Moreover an empirical assessment of the entire approach will also be performed on larger systems.

References

1. Bernardi, M.L., Di Lucca, G.A.: A Role-based Crosscutting Concerns Mining Approach to Evolve Java Systems Towards AOP. In: Proc. of ESEC-FSE IWPSE-EVOL 2009, Amsterdam, The Netherlands, August 24-28. ACM, New York (2009)
2. Bernardi, M.L., Di Lucca, G.A.: Analysing Object Type Hierarchies to Identify Crosscutting Concerns. In: Lee, Y.-h., Kim, T.-h., Fang, W.-c., Ślęzak, D. (eds.) FGIT 2009. LNCS, vol. 5899, pp. 216–224. Springer, Heidelberg (2009)
3. Bernardi, M.L., Di Lucca, G.A.: The ConAn Tool to Identify Crosscutting Concerns in Object Oriented Systems. In: Proc. of 18th International Conference on Program Comprehension, Braga, Portugal, June 30-July 2. IEEE Comp. Soc. Press, Los Alamitos (2010) ISBN: 978-1-4244-7604-6
4. Ceccato, M., Marin, M., Mens, K., Moonen, M., Tonella, P., Tourwe, T.: A qualitative comparison of three aspect mining techniques. In: Proc. of 13th International Workshop on Program Comprehension (2005)
5. Krinke, J.: Mining Control Flow Graphs for Crosscutting Concerns. In: Proc. of 13th Working Conference on Reverse Engineering, October 23 - 27, pp. 334–342. IEEE Computer Society, Washington, DC (2006)
6. Laddad, R.: AspectJ in Action. Manning Publications (September 2003) ISBN: 1930110936
7. Marin, M., van Deursen, A., Moonen, L.: Identifying Aspects Using Fan-In Analysis. In: Proc. of 11th Working Conference on Reverse Engineering, November 8 - 12, pp. 132–141. IEEE Computer Society, Washington, DC (2004)
8. Masuhara, H., Kiczales, G.: Modeling Crosscutting in Aspect-Oriented Mechanisms. In: Proc of 17th European Conference on Object Oriented Programming, Darmstadt (2003)
9. Mezini M., Ostermann K., "Modules for crosscutting models" , In Proc. of ADA Europe International Conference on Reliable Software Technologies, Toulouse , France, 2003, vol. 2655, pp. 24-44, ISBN 3-540-403760
10. Robillard, M.P., Murphy, G.C.: Representing concerns in source code. ACM Trans. Softw. Eng. Methodol. 16(1), 3 (2007)
11. Shepherd, D., Palm, J., Pollock, L., Chu-Carroll, M.: Timna: a framework for automatically combining aspect mining analyses. In: Proc. of 20th IEEE/ACM International Conference on Automated Software Engineering, ASE 2005, Long Beach, CA, USA. ACM, New York (2005)
12. Tonella, P., Ceccato, M.: Aspect Mining through the Formal Concept Analysis of Execution Traces. In: Proc. of 11th Working Conference on Reverse Engineering, November 8 - 12, pp. 112–121. IEEE Computer Society, Washington, DC (2004)
13. Tonella, P., Ceccato, M.: Refactoring the Aspectizable Interfaces: An Empirical Assessment. IEEE Trans. Softw. Eng. 31(10), 819–832 (2005)

A Pattern-Based Approach to Formal Specification Construction*

Xi Wang[1], Shaoying Liu[1], and Huaikou Miao[2]

[1] Department of Computer Science, Hosei University, Japan
[2] School of Computer Engineering and Science, Shanghai University, China

Abstract. Difficulty in the construction of formal specifications is one of the great gulfs that separate formal methods from industry. Though more and more practitioners become interested in formal methods as a potential technique for software quality assurance, they have also found it hard to express ideas properly in formal notations. This paper proposes a pattern-based approach to tackling this problem where a set of patterns are defined in advance. Each pattern provides an expression in informal notation to describe a type of functions and the method to transform the informal expression into a formal expression, which enables the development of a supporting tool to automatically guide one to gradually formalize the specification. We take the SOFL notation as an example to discuss the underlying principle of the approach and use an example to illustrate how it works in practice.

1 Introduction

Formal methods have made significant contributions to software engineering by establishing relatively mature approaches to formal specification, refinement, and verification, and their theoretical influence on conventional software engineering has been well known. The notion of pre- and post-conditions have been introduced into some programming languages to support the "design by contract" principle [1][2]; many companies have tried or actually used some formal methods in real software projects; and many practitioners have become more interested in formal methods nowadays than before (e.g., in Japan).

However, we also need to clearly understand the situation that despite tremendous efforts over the last thirty years in transferring formal methods techniques to industry, the real applications of formal methods in industry without academics' involvement are still rare, and many companies used them once and never return since, which are often not reported in the literature. For example, in Japan several companies have tried Z and VDM, but few of them have shown

* This work is supported in part by Okawa Foundation, Hosei University, Science and Technology Commission of Shanghai Municipality under Grant No. 10510704900 and Shanghai Leading Academic Discipline Project(Project Number: J50103). It is also supported by the NSFC Grant (No. 60910004) and 973 Program of China Grant (No. 2010CB328102).

T.-h. Kim et al. (Eds.): ASEA/DRBC/EL 2011, CCIS 257, pp. 159–168, 2011.

a positive sign toward the future use of the same method again. One of the major reasons is that the practitioners find it hard to express their ideas properly in formal notations, not need to mention formal verification. This may sound difficult to accept for a formal method researcher or a person with strong mathematical background, but it is the reality in the software industry where vast majority of developers and designers may not even receive systematic training in computer science.

In this paper, we put forward a pattern-based approach to dealing with this challenge. It adopts the three-step approach in SOFL (Structured Object-oriented Formal Language) [3], which builds specification through informal, semi-formal and formal stages. Based on a set of inter-related patterns, guidance will be generated for specifying functions in terms of pre- and post-conditions step by step from semi-formal to formal stage, which enables developers to work only on the semantic level without struggling with complicated formal notations. These patterns are pre-defined, each providing an informal expression to describe certain function and the formalization method of such expression. Consider the statement "Alice belongs to student list", a corresponding pattern for "belong to" relation may suggest a formal expression, such as *Alice inset student_list* or *Alice in elems(student_list)*, depending on the type of *student_list* being defined as a set type or sequence type (in the context of VDM and SOFL). This is only a simple example; the real application is of course more complex and would ask for further information from the developer during the construction process. Although researchers proposed many patterns to help handle commonly occurred problems on specification constructions, such as the well-known design patterns [4], developers have to understand the provided solutions before they can apply them to specific problems. By contrast, our patterns are hidden from developers; it is the understandable guidance that interacts with developers, which is produced based on patterns in our approach. We have also discussed the structure of individual patterns with an example, and demonstrated how the structure serves to establish well-defined informal expressions and formalize them by a real example. Such process is not expected to be fully automatic due to the need for human decisions, but it is expected to help the developer clarify ambiguities in the informal expression and select appropriate formal expressions.

Our proposed approach can be applied to any model-based formal specification notations. In this paper, we use SOFL language as an example for discussion. The reader who wishes to understand its details can refer to the book [3].

The remainder of this article is organized as follows. Section 2 gives a brief overview on related work. Section 3 describes the pattern-based approach. Section 4 presents an example to illustrate the approach. Finally, in Section 5, we conclude the paper and point out future research.

2 Related Work

Many reports about the use of patterns in specifications are available in the literature. For informal specifications, several books [4][5] about UML based object-oriented design with patterns are published, aiming at promoting design patterns among practitioners to help create well crafted, robust and maintainable systems. Meanwhile, researchers are still improving their usabilities by specifying pattern solutions with pattern specification languages [6][7]. For formal specifications, Stepney *et al.* describe a pattern language for using notation Z in computer system engineering [8]. The patterns proposed are classified into six types, including presentation patterns, idiom patterns, structure patters, architecture patterns, domain patterns, development patterns. Each pattern provides a solution to a type of problem. Ding *et al.* proposed an approach for specification construction through property-preserving refinement patterns [9]. Konrad *et al.* [10] created real-time specification patterns in terms of three commonly used real-time temporal logics based on an analysis of timing-based requirements of several industrial embedded system applications and offered a structured English grammar to facilitate the understanding of the meaning of a specification. This work is complementary to the notable Dwyer et al.'s patterns [11].

In spite of enthusiasm in academics, specification patterns are not yet widely utilized in industry mainly because of the difficulties in applying them. As can be seen from the related work, the patterns they established force their users to make a full understanding of them before selecting and applying appropriate ones. Statistical data shows that large amount of patterns have been developed, whereas users may not fully understand how to leverage them in practice [12]. Our approach treats patterns as knowledge that can be automatically analyzed by machines to generate comprehensible guidance for users. Thus, developers need neither to be educated on the patterns nor to be trapped in tedious and sophisticated formal notations; they can only focus on function design and make critical decisions on the semantic level.

3 Mechanism for Formal Specification Construction

3.1 Pattern Structure

Pattern is introduced to convey feasible solutions to re-occurred problem within a particular context, which is intended to facilitate people who face the same problem. Its structure varies depending on the specific situation it applies to and our pattern is defined as:

name	The name of the pattern
explanation	Situations or functions that the pattern can describe
constituents	A set of elements necessary for applying the pattern to write informal or formal statements
syntax	Grammar for writing informal expressions using the pattern
solution	Method for transforming the informal expression written using the pattern into formal expressions

To illustrate the structure, we explain each item through an example pattern shown in Figure 1 where $dataType(x)$ denotes the data type of variable x and $constraint(T)$ denotes certain property of variables of type T.

```
name: alter
explanation: For describing the change of variables or parts of variables
constituents:            semi-formal elements: obj
                         formal elements: decompose: Boolean, specifier, onlyOne: Boolean, new
  rules for guidance:
    1. if(dataType(obj) = basic type)  then  decompose = false
    2. if(deompose = false)  then  specifier = onlyOne = Null ∧ new = customValue ∧ dataType(new) = dataType(obj)
    3. dataType(obj)  →  specifier  /* determining the definition of specifier by the data type of the given obj */
         set of T (T is a basic type)    ① →    T | constraint(T) | specifier ∪ specifier
         set of T (T is a composite type with n fields f1, ···, fn)
                                         ② →    T | constraint(T) | constraint(fi) | specifier ∪ specifier   (1 ≤ i ≤ n)
                               T → T'    ③ →    (T → T' | constraint(dom) | constraint(rng) | constraint(dom, rng) |
                                                   specifier1 ∪ specifier1) ∗ (dom | rng | dom ∧ rng)
              composite type with n fields f1, ···, fn
                                         ④ →    fi | specifier ∪ specifier     (1 ≤ i ≤ n)
                                         ······
    4. constraint(specifier)  →  onlyOne  /* determining the value of specifier by the given specifier  */
           specifier(2) = dom ∧ rng    ① →    false
           specifier(1) = (dom = v) ∧ (specifier(2) = dom ∨ specifier(2) = rng)   ② →   true
                                         ······
    5. if(onlyOne = true)  then  (∃!x)(x ∈ obj ∧ specifier(x) ∧ dataType(new) = dataType(x))
         else  new is a mapping:  {x: obj | specifier(x)}  →  {originBased(p), customValue}
    ······    /* originBased(p): applying pattern p,  customValue: an input value */
  syntax: alter obj
  solution:  (dataType(obj), decompose, constraint(specifier), onlyOne, constraint(new))  →   formalization result
               initial ① →  obj = alter(~obj) /* applied before specifying formal elements if the pattern is not reused*/
               (any, false, any, any, dataType(new) = given)   ② →        new
               (any, false, any, any, new = originBased(p))   ③ →       p(obj)
               (set of T, true, any, true, any)   ④ →  let   x inset obj and specifier(x)
                                                           in   union(diff(obj, {x}), alter(x, false, Null, Null, new))
         (set of T, true, any, false, any)   ⑤→   "let X = {xi: obj | specifier(xi)}
                                                    in  union(diff(obj, X)," forall[y: new] | "alter(xi, false, Null, Null, y)""")"
          composite type with n fields f_1, ···, f_n, true, any, false, any)
                                ⑥→     "modify(obj," forall[f_i: specifier] | "f_i → alter(obj.f_i, false, Null, Null, new(f_i))"")"
         (map, true, (specifier(1) = {(dom = v_1), ···, (dom = v_n)} ∧ specifier(2) = rng, false, any)
                                ⑦→    "override(obj, {" forall[x_i: specifier] | "v_i → alter(obj(v_i), false, Null, Null, new(x_i))""})"
                                ······
```

Fig. 1. Pattern "alter"

Item *name* is a unique identity based on which the pattern will be referenced. For the example pattern, the name "alter" is the identity.

Item *explanation* informally describes the potential effect of applying the pattern and suggests the situations where the pattern can be used. We can also find such item in pattern "alter", which tells that if one needs to depict modification on certain variable, pattern "alter" should be the choice.

Item *constituents* lists necessary elements to be clarified for writing expressions using the pattern and rules for guiding the clarification process. These elements can be divided into *semi-formal* and *formal* ones. The former are required to be designated when constructing well-defined informal expressions for semi-formal specifications while the latter only need to be specified during the formalization of the informal expressions. To avoid potential errors in specifications, each designated value v is required to be legal, which means v is a combination of constants and variables that can be found in the data definition part of the specification. After all the elements are legally specified, a *concrete constituents* is obtained where each element is bounded with a concrete value.

From Fig 1, we can see five elements listed in the *constituents* of pattern "alter". Element *obj* indicates the object intended to be modified; *decompose* is of boolean type meaning to replace the whole given *obj* by a new value if it is designated as true and to modify parts of the given *obj* if it is designated as false; *specifier* denotes the description of the parts to be altered within *obj*; *onlyOne* is of boolean type meaning there exists only one part consistent with the description in *specifier* if it is designated as true; *new* indicates the new values for replacing the corresponding parts to be altered.

The followed section "rules for guidance" includes two kinds of rules for guiding the process of specifying the listed five elements. One is represented as *if-then* statement that indicates certain conclusion when certain condition holds. For example, rule 1 states that if the given *obj* is of basic type, element *decompose* will be automatically set as false. This is obvious since a variable of basic type will not contain any smaller unit and therefore cannot be altered by replacing parts of it. The other kind of rules are represented as mappings, such as rule 3.

Item *syntax* establishes a standard format to write informal expressions using the pattern. For the example pattern, "*alter obj*" is valid to describe the modification on certain object when writing semi-formal specifications.

Item *solution* includes a method for producing a suggested formalization result according to the obtained *concrete constituents*. We define it as a mapping $constraint(constituents) \rightarrow string$ where $constraint(constituents)$ denotes properties of elements in *constituents*. Each property corresponds to a formalization result and a given *concrete constituents* that satisfies certain property will lead to the corresponding formalization result. For pattern *alter*, properties are represented through five sub-properties: the data type of *obj*, the value of *decompose*, properties of *specifier*, the value of *onlyOne* and properties of *new*. Let's take mapping 2 as an example where *any* denotes that whatever value is acceptable. It demonstrates the formalization result for all the *concrete constituents* satisfying the property that *decompose* is false and the value of the given *new* is of $customValue$ type.

As can be seen from pattern alter, some pattern names appear in the structure, such as the expression with "*alter*" in the *solution* item and "$originBased(p)$" in the *constituents* item, which means that the corresponding patterns will be reused when applying pattern "alter". Most reused patterns are attached with element information presented as: $p.name(arg_1, arg_2, ..., arg_m)(m <= n)$ where $p.name$ is the name of certain pattern p with n elements and $arg_1, arg_2, ..., arg_m$ are values of its first m elements listed in the *constituents* item.

3.2 Construction Method

Well-defined pattern structure establishes a foundation for our construction method which adopts the pattern notation for semi-formal specifications and applies the involved patterns to the formalization process. As shown in Fig 2, this method guides users through two stages: completion of semi-formal specifications and formalization of complete semi-formal specifications.

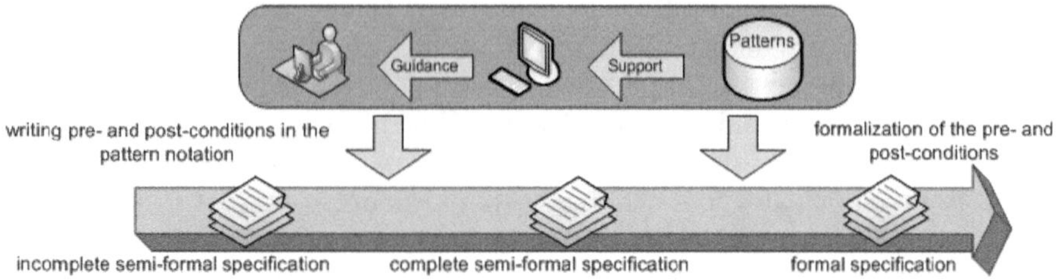

Fig. 2. Overview of the pattern-based approach

Since this paper focuses on building formal expressions, we assume that in incomplete semi-formal specifications, all the necessary types, variables, process names, process inputs and outputs are already defined. The main goal of the first stage is to help write pre- and post-conditions in pattern notation. Formal notations can also be used since they are able to logically combine single statements in pattern notation into a composite fragment to convey more complex meanings, meanwhile, the use of both languages allows expert users to choose a preferred one in writing specifications.

In the semi-formal stage, each pre- or post-condition is considered as a union of function units each described by certain pattern and different guidance will be given for different users towards building up each unit.

If the user is not familiar with the pattern notation, he will only be required to provide a general intention first by selecting patterns. This task is easy because: (1) pattern names are written in natural language and allows the selection to be easily done on semantic level, (2) the unique meaning of each pattern name differentiates itself from others and therefore avoids wrong selection, (3) the *explanation* items can help confirm the decision.

After a pattern p is selected, the user will be asked to specify its *semi-formal elements* in the order they are listed in the *constituent* item. The process of specifying each element e_i is as follows:

- If certain rules for determining the value of e_i have been activated, designate e_i according to the rules and begin to specify the element next to e_i.
- Otherwise, ask the user to specify e_i according to its definition given in p and the definition determined by certain activated rules if there is any. In case the designated value is illegal, the user will be informed and corrections can be done by defining the value as types or variables in the specification or replacing it with a legal one.
- All the rules in the "rules for guidance" item of p are examined with respect to the value of e_i and the activated ones are marked for later use.

Once the *semi-formal elements* of p have been specified, a corresponding informal expression is generated automatically on the basis of the *syntax* item of p and added to the corresponding pre- or post-condition.

Advanced users can choose to directly write expressions in pattern notation for pre- and post-conditions. Each atomic expression written with a pattern $p\prime$ will be checked based on the *syntax* item of $p\prime$ to extract information of *semi-formal elements*. For each element e designated as v:

1. If v is empty, i.e., value of e cannot be found in the expression, ask the user to specify e and insert the value to the expression according to syntax.
2. If v is illegal or does not conform to certain activated rules that determine the value or definition of e, ask the user to redefine v or replace it with a legal one conforming to the definition determined by all activated rules.
3. Examine all the rules in the "rules for guidance" item with respect to v and mark the activated ones for later use.

In this way, a valid expression can then be produced based on the original one and added to the corresponding pre- and post-condition.

One can choose from the above two alternative supporting strategies for each function unit and when each process of the specification is attached with a pre- and post-condition, the semi-formal specification is completed.

The user will be subsequently brought to the second stage where all the pre- and post-conditions are formalized sequentially. Since formal expressions are directly used for formal specifications, we only consider the formalization of expressions in pattern notation. For each atomic expression written with a pattern p, the user will be guided to specify formal elements of p by applying the same strategy for specifying *semi-formal elements*. Suppose that the obtained *concrete constituents* satisfies one of the conditions $constraint_i$ in the *solution* item of p, the expression will be formalized as $p.solution(constraint_i)$. The informal parts of the formalization result will be further formalized by repeating the above steps until no pattern notation is included.

In the same way, all the pre- and post-conditions can be formalized and the construction process will be finished resulting in the final formal specification.

4 Case Study: A Banking System

A relative small example of a banking system is used to illustrate our method. It provides four services for customers: *deposit*, *withdraw*, *information display* and *currency exchange*. For the sake of space, we take the description process of the function *currency exchange* as an example which exchanges certain amount of source currency to corresponding amount of target currency on accounts.

Assume that the user has entered semi-formal stage and finished defining types and variables as indicated in Fig 3, as well as process names, inputs and outputs. Corresponding to the example function, process *Exchange* takes the type and amount of the source currency as inputs and produces a notice if the operation is successfully done. We take the most important function unit, updating account information, as an example to show how our approach works.

In case that the developer is not familiar with our pattern notation, he will be asked to select a pattern to express his general intention. Since the essential of the function unit is to modify an object of the system, the user can easily find the

```
type
Amount = real;
Date = nat0 * nat0 * nat0;
CurrencyType = {<JPY>, <USD>, <CNY>};
OperationType = {<deposit>,<withdraw>};
Balance = map CurrencyType to Amount;
Currency_pair = composed of
                origin: CurrencyType
                dest: CurrencyType
               end;
Exchange_Rate = map Currency_pair
               to real;
```

```
Transaction = composed of
                 date: Date
                 operationType: OperationType
                 currencyType: CurrencyType
                 amount: Amount
                end;
Account = composed of
             number: string
             password: string
             balance: Balance
             transaction: seq of Transaction
            end;
```

```
var
ext #account_store:
      set of Account;
ext #today: Date;
ext #rate_store:
      Exchange_Rate;
```

Fig. 3. Definition of types and variables of the example specification

pattern *alter* as the best choice. As soon as the decision is made, the only *semi-formal element obj* is required to be clarified. The object to be altered is obvious and the user can also easily response with variable *account_store* which stands for the account datastore. Confirming that *account_store* is a legal input, an informal expression can be generated as "*alter account_store*" according to the *syntax* item of pattern *alter* and added to the semi-formal specification shown in Fig 4. Of course, advanced developers can directly write "*alter account_store*" in the semi-formal specification without guidance.

```
process Exchange(inf: string, currency: Currency_pair, amount: real) notice: string | warning: string
ext rd rate_store;
ext wr account_store;
post if (amount <= 0) then warning = "The required amount is invalid."
     else alter account_store and notice = "Successful operation"
end-process;
```

Fig. 4. Process *Exchange* in the semi-formal specification of the banking system

The complete semi-formal specification invokes the formalization process and formalizing process *Exchange* is actually formalizing "*alter account_store*". According to mapping 1 in the *solution* item of *alter*, the origin expression is transformed into $account\_store = alter(\tilde{\ }account\_store)$ where $alter(\tilde{\ }account\_store)$ needs further formalization. By the proposed method for specifying elements, Table 1 is obtained (column "reason" explains how the corresponding value generates). Notice that the obtained *concrete constituents* shown in Table 1 satisfies the property described in mapping 4 in the *solution* item; according to the formalization result it maps to, $alter(\tilde{\ }account\_store)$ is formalized into:

$$\begin{aligned}&let\ x\ inset\ \tilde{\ }obj\ and\ x.accountNo = inf\\&in\ \ union(diff(\tilde{\ }obj, \{x\}), alter(x, false, Null, Null, originBased(alter)))\end{aligned}$$

There still exists an expression with "*alter*" which can be transformed into "$alter(x)$" according to mapping 3 in the *solution* item. Again, during the

Table 1. The designated formal elements for the expression $alter(\tilde{}account\_store)$

formal element	reason	value
$decompose$	altering specific accounts instead of the whole $account\_store$	true
$specifier$	"rules for guidance" rule 3 mapping 2	$accountNo = inf$
$onlyOne$	only one account is allowed to be active and receive currency exchange service at one time	true
new	"rules for guidance" rule 5	originBased($alter$)

Table 2. The designated elements for the expression $alter(x)$

element	reason	value
obj	already specified	x
$decompose$	altering balance and transaction of x instead of the whole x	true
$specifier$	"rules for guidance" rule 3 mapping 4	$\{balance, transaction\}$
$onlyOne$	there are two specific parts to be altered including field $balance$ and $transaction$	false
new	"rules for guidance" rule 5	$\{balance$ →originBased($alter$), $transaction$ →originBased($alter$)$\}$

formalization of $alter(x)$, Table 2 is derived. Mapping 6 in the *solution* item of $alter$ is then activated, which formalizes the expression $alter(x)$ as follows:

$$modify(x, balance \rightarrow alter(x.balance, false, Null, Null, originBased(alter)) \\ transaction \rightarrow alter(x.transaction, false, Null, Null, originBased(addTo)))$$

Still, expressions involving $alter$ and $addTo$ (one of the patterns we designed) need to be formalized. By repeating the above procedures, process *Exchange* is formalized as shown in Fig 5.

```
process Exchange(inf: string, currency: Currency_pair, amount: real) notice: string | warning: string
ext rd rate_store;
ext wr account_store;
post if (amount <= 0) then warning = "The required amount is invalid."
     else account_store =
          let x inset ~account_store and x.number = inf
          in union(diff(~account_store, {x}),
                      modify(x, balance → override(x.balance,
                                     currency.origin → x.balance(currency.origin) - amount)
                                     currency.dest → x.balance(currency.dest) + amount/rate_store(currency)),
                                    transaction → conc(x.transaction, [today, <withdraw>, currency.origin, amount],
                                                      [today, <deposit>, currency.dest, amount/rate_store(currency)])))
          and notice = "Successful operation"
end-process;
```

Fig. 5. Process *Exchange* in the formal specification of the example banking system

5 Conclusion

Trying to attack the obstacles to the application of formal specification techniques by practitioners in industry, this paper presents a method for guiding developers to gradually formalize semi-formal specifications based on specification patterns that are designed to be applied by machines to help formal specification construction. While we found this approach useful and effective, further improvements of the method are necessary.

Individual patterns need to be expanded and more patterns need to be created to handle more complex situations. Besides, the self-learning mechanism for updating the pattern-based knowledge base is also one of our future researches.

References

1. Meyer, B.: Eiffel: The Language. Prentice Hall Object-Oriented Series (1991)
2. Burdy, L., Cheon, Y., Cok, D., Ernst, M., Kiniry, J., Leavens, G.T., Rustan, K., Leino, M., Poll, E.: An Overview of JML Tools and Applications. International Journal on Software Tools for Technology Transfer 7(3), 212–232 (2005)
3. Liu, S.: Formal Engineering for Industrial Software Development. Springer, Heidelberg (2004)
4. Gamma, E., Helm, R., Johnson, R.: Design Patterns: Elements of Reusable Object-Oriented Software. Addison-Wesley Professional (1994)
5. Larman, C.: Applying UML and Patterns: An Introduction to Object-Oriented Analysis and Design and Iterative Development, 3rd edn. Prentice Hall (2004)
6. France, R.B., Ghosh, S.: A uml-based pattern specification technique. IEEE Transactions on Software Engineering 30, 193–206 (2004)
7. Soundarajan, N., Hallstrom, J.O.: Responsibilities and rewards : Specifying design patterns. In: 26th International Conference on Software Engineering, pp. 666–675 (2004)
8. Stepney, S., Polack, F., Toyn, I.: An Outline Pattern Language for Z: Five Illustrations and Two Tables. In: Bert, D., Bowen, J.P., King, S., Walden, M. (eds.) ZB 2003. LNCS, vol. 2651, pp. 2–19. Springer, Heidelberg (2003)
9. Ding, J., Mo, L., He, X.: An approach for specification construction using property-preserving refinement patterns. In: 23th Annual ACM Symposium on Applied Computing, pp. 797–803. ACM, New York (2008)
10. Konrad, S., Cheng, B.H.C.: Real-time specification patterns. In: 27th International Conference on Software Engineering, pp. 372–381. ACM, New York (2005)
11. Dwyer, M.B., Avrunin, G.S., Corbett, J.C.: Pattern in property specifications for finite-state verification. In: 21th International Conference on Software Engineering, pp. 411–420. ACM, New York (1999)
12. Manolescu, D., Kozaczynski, W., Miller, A.: The growing divide in the patterns world. IEEE Software 24(4), 61–67 (2007)

A Replicated Experiment with Undergraduate Students to Evaluate the Applicability of a Use Case Precedence Diagram Based Approach in Software Projects

José Antonio Pow-Sang[1], Ricardo Imbert[2], and Ana María Moreno[2]

[1] Departamento de Ingeniería, Pontificia Universidad Católica del Perú,
Av. Universitaria 1801, San Miguel, Lima 32, Peru
japowsang@pucp.edu.pe
[2] Facultad de Informática, Universidad Politécnica de Madrid,
Campus de Montegancedo, 28660 Boadilla del Monte (Madrid), Spain
{rimbert,ammoreno}@fi.upm.es

Abstract. The Use Case Precedence Diagram (UCPD) is a technique that addresses the problem of determining the construction sequence or prioritization of a software product from the developer's perspective. This paper presents a replicated controlled experiment with undergraduate students. The results obtained from this experiment confirm the results obtained in previous studies with practitioners in which the proposed approach enables developers to define construction sequences more precisely than with other ad-hoc techniques. However, unlike previous studies with practitioners, qualitative evaluation of the UCPD based on the Method Adoption Model (MAM), where the intention to use a method is determined by the users' perceptions, shows that the relationships defined by the MAM are not confirmed with the results obtained with undergraduate students.

Keywords: UCPD, requirements precedence, software engineering experimentation, Method Adoption Model, controlled experiment.

1 Introduction

As an established practical fact, it is known that the data tables for any information system developed with relational databases are classified into one of these two types: Master Table, if the table contains data which seldom changes (e.g. customer information), and Transaction Table, if the table contains data which is frequently modified (e.g. the sales order for a customer). Based on this table classification, three types of use cases [5,9] can be identified: (1) use cases that deal with master table maintenance, (2) use cases that deal with transaction table maintenance, and (3) use cases that deal with data reporting.

According to a previous study [10], most of the developers consider the following requirements sequence based on their construction easiness (without user's restriction): use cases that maintain master tables, use cases that maintain transaction tables and, finally, use cases that present reports.

T.-h. Kim et al. (Eds.): ASEA/DRBC/EL 2011, CCIS 257, pp. 169–179, 2011.

Even though there are several approaches to determine software construction sequence that consider which requirement must be constructed first based on a simple requirements prioritization scheme, most of them do not take into consideration the developer's perspective in terms of ease of construction to define such priorities. The Use Case Precedence Diagram (UCPD) [10] is a technique based on use cases and its objective is to determine software construction sequences taking into consideration the developer's perspective in terms of ease of construction to define software requirements priorities.

This paper presents a replicated experiment of a previous study [11] in order to evaluate the applicability of the UCPD in software development projects and to compare the results obtained with practitioners and undergraduate students. The replicated experiment presented in [11] had some slight modifications from the original work presented in [10].

The rest of the paper is organized as follows: Section 2 details UCPD to define software requirements construction sequences, Section 3 presents the background scenario for the empirical study; Section 5 shows the obtained results for the experimental study; Section 6 discusses the threats of validity of this study. Finally, a summary will conclude the chapter.

2 Use Case Precedence Diagrams and the Construction Sequence

As an addition to the existing relations between use cases (include, extend, and generalization), UCPD proposes the inclusion of a new relation: precedence. The concept of this diagram was taken from [12], who proposed the use of a similar diagram, specifying the relations "precedes" and "invoke" to determine user requirements. Fig. 1 shows an example of a UCPD.

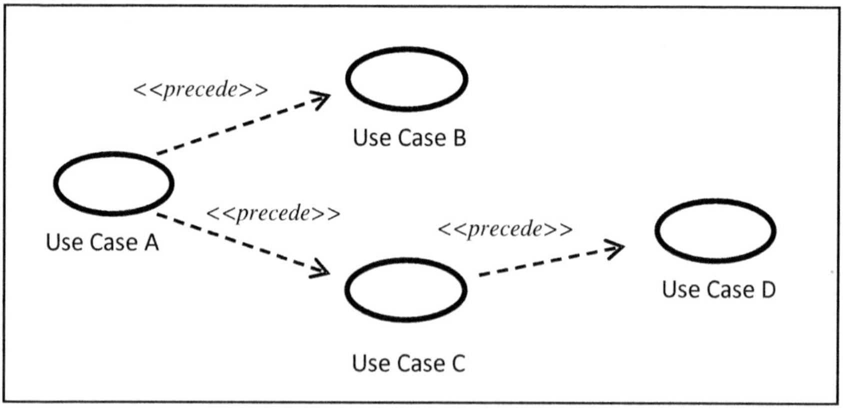

Fig. 1. Example of Use Case Precedence Diagram

In order to obtain precedence relations between use cases, the following rules must be considered:

Rule 1. *A use case U1 precedes another use case U2 if there is a precondition that corresponds to the execution of a scenario in U1 that must be fulfilled before executing a scenario of U2.* For instance, to execute a scenario from the "Maintain Customer Information" use case, the actor must have been validated by the system (i.e. execute a login). Hence, the "Login" use case precedes the "Maintain Customer Information" use case. This is shown in Fig. 2.

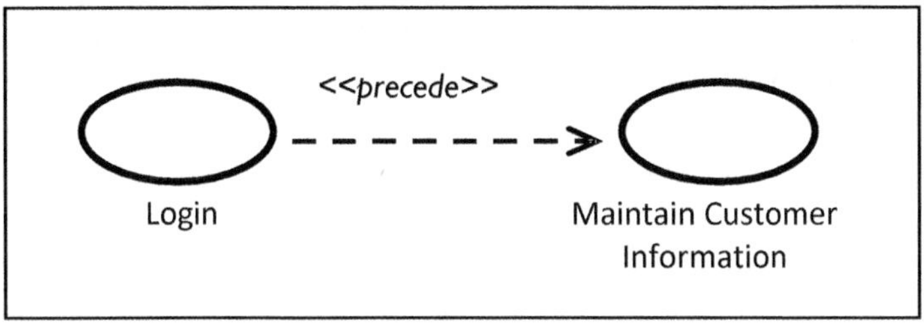

Fig. 2. Precedence rule 1 - diagram example

Rule 2. *A use case U1 precedes another use case U2 if a U2 needs information that is registered by U1.* For instance, to enter a sales order for a customer, the information of the customer should have been previously entered. Having two use cases "Maintain Customer Information" and "Enter Sales Order for a Customer", the former precedes the later. This is shown in Fig. 3.

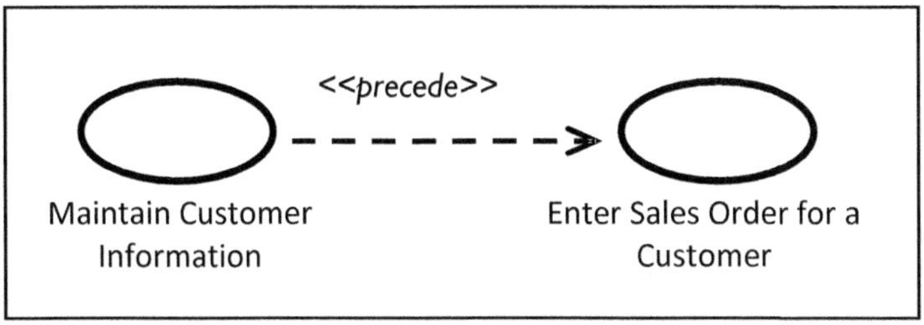

Fig. 3. Precedence rule 2 - diagram example

It is important to note that in the UCPD, Included and Extended Use Cases have not been considered since they can be part of other use cases that refer to them. Based on this UCPD, a construction sequence is defined. The use cases that are on the left side of the diagram will be implemented before the ones that are on the right side. For instance, in Fig. 1, "Use case A" will be implemented before "Use case C".

3 Experimental Design

The previous controlled experiment [11] was performed with graduate students who were practitioners with at least 2 years in software development projects. This experiment was slightly modified from the experiment presented in [10] and had the same design from the experiment presented in [11].

Using the Goal/Question/Metric (GQM) template for goal-oriented software measurement [2], this experiment was defined as follows: **Analyze**: Ad-hoc construction planning versus precedence diagram based construction planning **For the purpose of**: Compare **With respect to**: their accuracy **From the point of view of**: the researcher **In the context of**: undergraduate students and considering that the developer is free to select the sequence to construct use cases (there is no user constraint).

The research question was: Does our approach provide more accurate results than informal approaches when determining the sequence to construct use cases?

3.1 Variable Selection

The independent variable was the technique utilized by subjects to define the construction sequence of use cases. The dependent variable was accuracy: the agreement between the measurement results and the true value.

For this experiment, it was considered as "true value" the fact that the easiest construction sequence for use cases is "master-transaction-reports", as identified in the in previous studies [10,11].

3.2 Subjects

In this experiment were involved 35 undergraduate students from the Informatics Engineering program at PUCP. Unlike the previous experiment presented in [10], it was not necessary to deliver a use case training class in order to standardize the knowledge of all participants. The students had taken a course in a previous semester in which they reviewed all concepts related to UML and software requirements specifications using use cases, and therefore already knew how to specify requirements with use cases.

3.3 Materials and Case Studies

The materials used in the experiment were two case studies and three questionnaires (in the experiment presented in [10], four questionnaires were used). The first case study corresponds to the elaboration of a sales system for a restaurant, and the second corresponds to the elaboration of an enrollment registration system for a high school. Both case studies are information systems.

For each case study, the following documentation was delivered: the use case diagram, the description for each use case along with its preconditions, and the information, in terms of classes or entities, that is needed by each use case.

Two questionnaires (1 & 2) corresponds to questions in which subjects have to decide between two use cases and answer which one they would construct first. For instance, for the first case study, one of the questions included was:

Would you construct "Maintain request notes" before "Register Sale"?

a) Yes *b) No* *c) Indifferent*

Fig. 4. First case study – question sample

There are also other types of questions that allow the selection among the following use case type pairs: master-transaction, transaction-transaction, master-reports, and transaction-reports.

The third questionnaire was to know a practitioner's opinion regarding the easiness and usefulness of our technique, and the easiest way to construct software between master, transaction, and report use cases.

Further details of the case studies and used instruments can be found at: http://macareo.pucp.edu.pe/japowsang/precedence/usecase.html

3.4 Tasks Performed during the Experiment

The practitioners had to apply the first case study with their ad-hoc techniques and the second one with UCPD. We applied two different case studies with similar characteristics (both are information systems) in order to mitigate the learning effects. Table 1 shows the tasks carried out in the session by the graduate students.

Table 1. Tasks carried out by the subjects

Task Nº	Description
1	Receive case study 1 and questionnaire 1
2	Fill in questionnaire 1
3	Receive case study 2 and questionnaire 2
4	Elaborate use case precedence diagram for case study 2
5	Fill in questionnaire 2
6	Fill in questionnaire 3

Unlike the experiment presented in [10], participants did not apply UCPD to the case study 1. For statistical purposes, it is only needed that students had to apply the technique to the case study 2.

The session lasted approximately one hour and the practitioners performed 45 minutes on average to complete all the tasks. Even though it was not part of this study to know which technique demanded less time, we could observe that they spent less than 10 minutes to elaborate our proposed UCPD.

4 Results

In this experiment, all participants answered that the easiest sequence to develop software was *master-transaction-report*.

4.1 Quantitative Results

Table 2 presents the results obtained from the case studies. A significance level of $\alpha=0.05$ was established to statistically test the obtained results. In order to compare these results, the number of correct answers of the participants was tested.

Table 2. Descriptive statistics - Sequence of use case construction

Variable	Ad-hoc (Case Study 1)	UCPD (Case Study 2)
Observations	35	35
Minimum of correct answers	2	3
Maximum of correct answers	7	7
Mean	4.743	6.029
Std. Deviation	1.379	1.071

The Shapiro-Wilk test [13] was applied in order to determine whether the number of correct answers with each technique followed a normal distribution. According to the results of the Shapiro-Wilk test, the samples obtained do not follow a normal distribution. Due to these results, a parametric test could not be used and the Wilcoxon signed rank test [14] was chosen for this purpose. The statistical hypotheses formulated to test both techniques were:

- Ho: The distributions of the ad-hoc and UCPD are not significantly different.
- Ha: The distribution of the ad-hoc sample is shifted to the left of the distribution of the UCPD.

Table 3. Wilcoxon signed rank test results ad-hoc vs. UCPD

Variable	Result
V	69.00
Expected value	301.00
Variante (V)	3640.00
p-value (one-tailed)	<0.0001

Since the computed p-value was lower than the significance level $\alpha=0.05$, the null hypothesis Ho was rejected. It means that it is empirically corroborated that UCPD produces more accurate assessments than ad-hoc techniques. The results are similar to the results obtained with practitioners [10,11].

4.2 Qualitative Results

Although the results obtained in the controlled experiment were satisfactory, there is a need also to assess users' response to the new procedure and their intention to use it in the future. That is why the third questionnaire was based on the Method Adoption Model (MAM) [7].

MAM was proposed by Moody and it is an adaptation of the Technology Acceptance Model defined by Davis [4]. MAM explains and predicts the adoption of methods. The constructs of the MAM are the following:

- *Perceived Ease of Use:* the extent to which a person believes that using a particular method would be effort-free.
- *Perceived Usefulness:* the extent to which a person believes that a particular method will be effective in achieving the intended objectives.
- *Intention to Use:* the extent to which a person intends to use a particular method.

A questionnaire including one question for each constructor of the MAM was designed. Each answer had to be quantified on a five point Likert-type scale [6]. To use only one question for each constructor could have been considered as a disadvantage, but there are some studies that have applied this same approach in other fields such as medicine with appropriate results [3]. The intention was to create a user-friendly questionnaire.

The statistical hypotheses to test the user's perception about UCPD are the following:

- Ho: $\mu \leq 3$, $\alpha = 0.05$
- Ha: $\mu > 3$

"μ" is the mean response obtained in the questions related to user's perception about UCPD. If the mean response is greater than 3 it can be considered as a positive perception by the participants, because a 1 to 5 Likert-type scale was used in the questionnaires.

Table 4 presents the results obtained with the questions related to perceived ease of use, perceived usefulness and intention to use. A significance level of α=0.05 was established to statistically test the obtained results with undergraduate students.

Table 4. Wilcoxon signed rank test results ad-hoc vs. UCPD

Variable	P. Ease of Use	P. Usefulness	Intention to Use
Observations	35	31	35
Minimum	3	3	2
Maximum	5	5	5
Mean	3.971	4.486	4.4
Std. Deviation	0.618	0.658	0.736

Because the variables Perceived Ease of Use, Perceived Usefulness and Intention to Use are ordinal, a parametric test could not be used. The Wilcoxon signed rank test was chosen to test the statistical hypothesis defined previously. Table 5 presents the results obtained with the Wilcoxon test.

Table 5. Wilcoxon signed rank test results for MAM constructs

Variable	P. Ease of Use	P. Usefulness	Intention to Use
W	406	528	553
p-value	<0.001	<0.001	<0.001

Since the computed p-values were lower than the significance level α =0.05, the null hypothesis Ho had to be rejected for all samples. It means that we can empirically corroborate the practitioners perceived UCPD as easy to use and useful. In addition, they have the intention to use UCPD. The results are similar to the results obtained with practitioners [10,11].

4.3 MAM Evaluation

To assess the relationships between variables proposed in the MAM, we must use the correlation coefficient, similar to the studies conducted by Davis [4] and Adams et. al [1].

According Muijs [8] in order to determine if there is a degree of relationship between two ordinal variables, the Spearman's correlation coefficient must be used.. The Likert-scale used in the questionnaires is ordinal, for this reason Spearman's correlation (Spearman's rho) had to be used to evaluate MAM. The rules of thumb to determine the strength of a relationship proposed by Muijs are the following:

<0. +/-1 weak
<0. +/-3 modest
<0. +/-5 moderate
<0. +/-8 strong
>= +/-0.8 very strong.

Fig.5 presents Spearman's rho (ρ) and the strength for each relationship for the sample obtained in the controlled experiment with practitioners [11] and the sample obtained in this replicated controlled experiment with undergraduate students.

It can be observed that usefulness and ease of use were significantly and strongly correlated to each other for practitioners (ρ=0.624, p-value=0.017) but they were not correlated to each other for undergraduate students (modestly correlated). Usefulness and intention to use were significantly correlated to each other for both type of participants (undergraduate students and practitioners). Ease of use and intention to use were only moderately correlated to each other for practitioners (ρ=0.368, p-value=0.195).

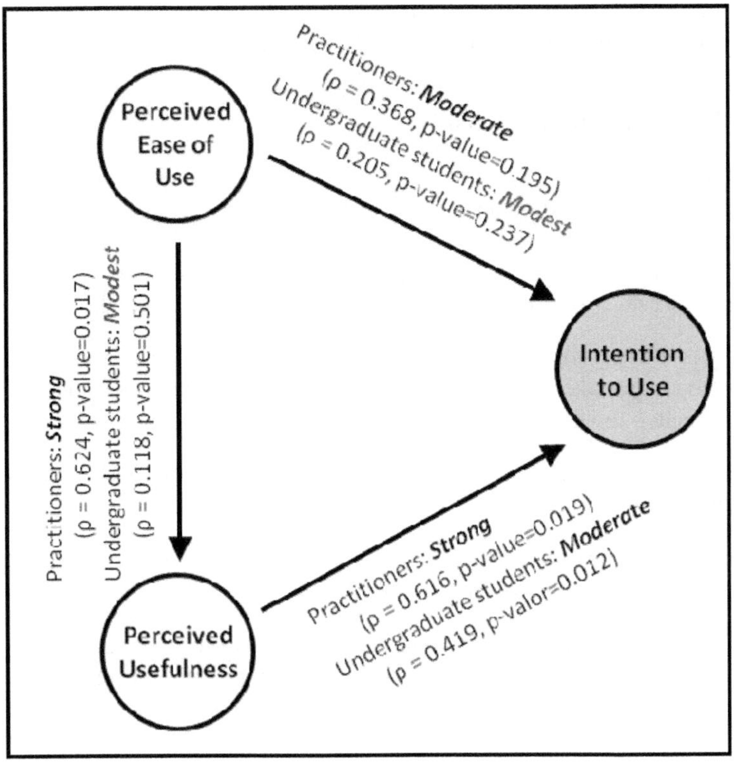

Fig. 5. Spearman's rho and strength for MAM's relationships

It means that we can empirically corroborate that the perceived ease of use has a positive effect on the perceived usefulness of UCPD and the perceived ease of use and perceived usefulness has a direct and positive effect on intention to use UCPD using the practitioners' sample, but not with the undergraduate students' sample.

5 Discussion

In this section, various threats to the validity of the empirical study are discussed, together to the way carried out to alleviate them.

5.1 Threats to Construct Validity

The construct validity is the degree to which the independent and the dependent variables are accurately quantified by the measurement instruments used in the study. The questionnaires allowed measuring quantitatively the precision of the ad-hoc and UCPD techniques through the correct number of answers. In addition, the questions considered the construction selection among a fixed set of use case type pairs:

master-transaction, transaction-transaction, master-reports, and transaction-reports. This allowed comparing the obtained results for both case studies.

5.2 Threats to Internal Validity

The internal validity is the degree to which conclusions can be drawn about cause - effect of independent variables on the dependent variables. From the results of the experiment, we could conclude that an empirical evidence of the existing relationship between the independent and the dependent variables does exist. Different aspects that could threaten the internal validity of the study have been tackled:

Differences among subjects. The subjects had similar knowledge about use cases, because they had taken a course in a previous semester in which they reviewed all concepts related to UML and requirements management.

Learning effects. The application of two different case studies cancelled the learning effect due to similarities.

Knowledge of the universe of discourse. the same case studies were used (with the same type of information system) for all subjects.

Fatigue effects. Each practitioner took one hour on average per session to apply both case studies and answer questionnaires. So, fatigue was not relevant.

Persistence effects. The practitioners had never done a similar experiment before.

Subject motivation. The practitioners were motivated because they wanted to know about new techniques to improve their work as part of their Master's studies.

5.3 Threats to External Validity

One threat to external validity was identified which limited the ability to apply any such generalization: the materials. In the experiment, case studies that can be good representations of real life cases have been used. Although the subjects came from a business environment, more empirical studies with real life cases from software companies must be performed.

6 Conclusions

The Use Case Precedence Diagram is a technique to be used to determine software requirement construction sequences from the developer's perspective. The results obtained in a replicated experiment with undergraduate students show that our approach has more significant advantages over the utilization of ad-hoc techniques to determine the sequence to construct use cases. Results obtained with undergraduate students are similar to the ones obtained in previous controlled experiments with practitioners.

The Use Case Precedence Diagram is perceived as easy to use and useful for all of the undergraduate students. Also, the participants of this study acknowledged having the intention to use UCPD in next software development projects. These results do not disagree with the quantitative results.

Although the perceptions of UCPD are positive for all the undergraduate students, the relationships defined in the MAM could be only empirically confirmed with the the practitioners' sample of a previous study.

Many researchers comment the benefits to use undergraduate students for research studies. However, it should be noted that in some situations, similar to this study, the results obtained with undergraduate students should be taken with caution and it is important to replicate those studies with practitioners, in order to get confdent results,.

References

1. Adams, D., Nelson, R., Todd, P.: Perceived usefulness, ease of use, and usage of information technology: a replication. MIS Quarterly (1993)
2. Basili, V.R., Caldiera, G., Rombach, H.D.: Goal Question Metric Paradigm. In: Marciniak, J.J. (ed.) Encyclopedia of Software Engineering. Wiley (1994)
3. Cepeda, M.S., Chapman, C.R., Miranda, N., Sanchez, R., Rodriguez, C.H., Restrepo, A.E., Ferrer, L.M., Linares, R.A., Carr, D.B.: Emotional Disclosure Through Patient Narrative May Improve Pain and Well-Being: Results of a Randomized Controlled Trial in Patients with Cancer Pain. Journal of Pain and Symptom Management 35(6), 623–631 (2008)
4. Davis, F.D.: Perceived Usefulness, Perceived Ease of Use and User Acceptance of Information Technology. MIS Quarterly, 319–340 (1989)
5. Jacobson, I.: Object-Oriented Software Engineering. A Use Case Driven Approach. Addison-Wesley, USA (1992)
6. Likert, R.: A technique for the measurement of attitudes. Archives of Psychology (1931)
7. Moody, D.L.: Dealing with Complexity: A Practical Method for Representing Large Entity Relationship Models, PhD. Thesis, Department of Information Systems,University of Melbourne, Australia (2001)
8. Muijs, D.: Doing Quantitative Research in Education with SPSS. Sage Publications, USA (2004)
9. Object Management Group, OMG Unified Modeling Language, USA (2008), http://www.uml.org
10. Pow-Sang, J.A., Nakasone, A., Imbert, R., Moreno, A.M.: An Approach to Determine Software Requirement Construction Sequences based on Use Cases. In: Proceedings Advanced Software Engineering and Its Applications-ASEA 2008, Sanya, China. IEEE Computer Society (2008)
11. Pow-Sang, J.A.: A Replicated Experiment to Evaluate the Applicability of a Use Case Precedence Diagram-based Approach in Software Development Projects, In: Software Engineering Methods, Modeling and Teaching, Universidad de Medellín (2011)
12. Rosenberg, D., Scott, K.: Use Case Driven Object Modeling with UML. Addison-Wesley, Massachusets (1999)
13. Shapiro, S., Wilk, B.: An Analysis of Variance Test for Normality (Complete Samples). Biometrika 52(3/4), 591–611 (1965), http://www.jstor.org/stable/2333709
14. Wilcoxon, F.: Individual Comparisons by Ranking Methods. Biometrics Bulletin 1(6), 80–83 (1945), http://www.jstor.org/stable/3001968

Automated Requirements Elicitation for Global Software Development (GSD) Environment

M. Ramzan[1], Asma Batool[1], Nasir Minhas[1], Zia Ul Qayyum[1], and M. Arfan Jaffar[2]

[1] UIIT-PMAS Arid Agriculture University, Rawalpindi, Pakistan
[2] Gwangju Institute of Science and Technology, Korea
ramzan.muhammad@gmail.com, asma.batool86@gmail.com.pk
{nasirminhas,zia}@uaar.edu.pk, arfanjaffar@gist.ac.kr

Abstract. Global software development (GSD) outsourcing is a modern business strategy for producing high quality software at low cost. Most of the problems in Global software development (GSD) occur due to the lack of communication between stakeholders, time zone issues, cultural differences, etc. In this paper, our main emphasis will be to improve the Value-based requirement elicitation (VBRE) steps in GSD environment and also to overcome the major GSD environment problems while taking the process of requirement elicitation from valued stakeholders. Though this model works for every kind of project but specifically for generic software.

Keywords: Requirements Engineering, Global Software Development, Value Based Requirements Engineering.

1 Introduction

Global Software Development (GSD) is an approach in which software development is performed in spite of cultural, temporal and geographical boundaries [1]. Global Software Development is considered as unexplored area which differentiates organizational forms in a very unique way from traditional global arrangements followed by many multinational corporations [18].

In GSD environment the software life cycle activities are distributed among teams across different limitations. GSD environment offers highly skilled personnel from different locations even on low cost, and, motivates many organizations to shift their business from one location to multiple locations where they get minimal cost, expenditure, quality work and around the clock service (24/7) [14]. Due to dispersed locations of teams, there are several risks/problems involved in GSD environment. Majorly include communication issues (time zone difference, distinct backgrounds, lack of informal communication, etc.), strategic issues (problem in task allocation), cultural issues, technical issues (problem in information and artifacts sharing), and knowledge management (poor documentation, etc) [2]. Requirement elicitation is also a question mark while working in GSD environment due to different locations of teams. This gets very tough job and causes problems such as incomplete requirements, misunderstanding of requirements, etc. GSD environment follows complete basic principles and steps of

T.-h. Kim et al. (Eds.): ASEA/DRBC/EL 2011, CCIS 257, pp. 180–189, 2011.

Software Engineering (SE) starting from requirement elicitation to maintenance of product. In today's era, there are different kinds of parameters involved in Software Development.

A Value Based Software Engineering (VBSE) has become known with the objective of incorporating value considerations into the full range of existing and known SE approaches, and of developing an overall framework [3]. The initial theory of value-based software engineering is '4+1' and whole value-based software engineering is rotating around that theory. In this theory, engine lays in the center of all other four theories which determines that which values are important, and how the success is assured [3]. The method of finding out the reasons of software and then compiling them in proper document format to make it readily available for analysis and subsequent implementation is called Requirement Engineering (RE) [11]. Value represents the degree of importance or, in other words, value can be said as the amount that is fairly equivalent of anything else. In Value Based Requirement Engineering (VBRE), interests/goals of stakeholders are taken into account which may vary and conflict based on their perspectives of the environment [3]. Requirements engineers need to understand the creation of value for certain Software Company while also considering customer's requirements [15].

Requirement gathering/elicitation is the first and major step in SE and the whole process of software development is based on this step. Requirement elicitation is the practice of obtaining the requirements of a system from users, customers and other stakeholders [4]. Thomas Satty [12] proposed statistical based technique called 'The Analytic Hierarchy Process (AHP)' for multi-criteria complex decision making problems. It can be used to value stakeholders on the basis of different parameters [13], like strength, influence, attitude, engagement level, experience, region etc. Requirement elicitation is non-trivial because one can never say that he has gathered complete requirements from the customer by just querying that what system should do. It includes face to face meetings, questionnaires, prototyping, use cases etc. Therefore, there are numerous difficulties and problems involved in this process.

In [5], we have found that this paper addresses only the problems that are being faced during requirement elicitation while working in GSD environment and also, value based requirement elicitation are not taken into account at all. In this paper, we will present motivation towards value based requirement elicitation and present how value based requirement elicitation step can be made easy. We have got few steps from existing model to perform in a better way and to produce better results for the valued requirements. We will also present a model to elicit requirements based on stakeholder's importance.

2 Related Work

Different scholars/authors have proposed different solutions to GSD environment problems such as Sang Won Lim, Taek Lee, Sangsoo Kim and Hoh Peter proposed a solution in The Value Gap Model: Value-Based Requirements Elicitation[10], and Gabriela N. Aranda, Aurora Vizcaíno, Alejandra Cechich, Mario Piattini proposed solution in Strategies to Minimize Problems in Global Requirements Elicitation[5].

The primary calculation of success of a software system is the extent to which it meets the purpose for which it was developed. Broadly speaking, software systems requirements engineering (RE) is the process of discovering that purpose, by identifying stakeholders and their needs, and documenting these in a form that is amenable to analysis, communication, and subsequent implementation [11].

The critical success factor for software organizations is their ability to build a product that fulfills customer requirements and offers high value that provides enhanced comfort of market success [6] and [7]. As the end result/objective of a software organization is to increase the ROI, so there is a need to make the relationship between technical decisions and business strategy clear and unambiguous that leads to the value [8]. Boehm argues that [7], software engineering (SE) is largely practiced in a value neutral way, i.e. every requirement is considered and valued equally, even though not all requirements are equal.

There can be many ways to integrate different location's attributes/characteristics with another location [9]. "Globalization" has become very major topic now-a-days and also has brought many advantages along for software development field [1]. Global Software Development (GSD) is a way in which the software development is performed beyond the boundaries such as contextual, organizational, cultural, temporal, geographical and political [1]. GSD environment needs more attention because in traditional software development, we do not give more attention to the factors which cause the different time zone, distance and cultural boundaries. Early rectification of the detections may improve the software development, reduce the cost and time consumption [16]. In GSD environment the software life cycle activities are distributed among teams across different boundaries. There is a need to globalize software development process in order to save time, cost and resources [9]. GSD environment offers highly skilled personnel with low cost. It is one of the reasons behind shifting software industry from co-located development to GSD [14]. This shifting brought some new challenges in software development. The problems arising from the geographical, temporal and socio-cultural distance are the main challenges for GSD environment. GSD environment erg to reduce these complexities and also needs to enhance the ability to focus on coordination of resources [17]. Sang [10] took SOA (Service Oriented Architecture) example to minimize the user value and system value. He claims that, initially, system value is higher than user value and fulfills users' requirements. But with the passage of time, when user feels enhancements and changes in already developed service, then user value becomes higher than system value and user expectations are more. Then requirement gathering was performed against components based on user inputs i.e. which component is more important for certain user/group of users. The limitation of this model is that it works only for SOA based applications and limited to web services only.

Aranda [5] argues that different steps can be performed to reduce the problems in GSD such as trainings to minimize the cultural differences, use of ontologies to reduce country wise problems such as different languages etc., use of asynchronous technology to overcome time zone difference etc. Here, the limitation with this solution is that, it works very well for simple requirement elicitation and does not consider value based requirement elicitation. Analytic Hierarchy Process (AHP) introduced by Thomas Satty [12] i.e. statistical based technique for multi-criteria complex decision making problems. It can be used to value stakeholders on the basis of different parameters [13], like strength, influence, attitude, engagement level, experience, region etc. In this approach, the stakeholders are filtered out in pair-wise fashion to determine the extent of how one of the stakeholders is more important than the others. For n number of stakeholders, AHP makes n (n-1) / 2 comparisons at each hierarchy level. In proposed model, we are working on value based software engineering and valuing our stakeholder using AHP in order to get their requirements efficiently. This model will cater every kind of project that is being developed by globally distributed teams but specifically for generic software.

3 Proposed Method

In today's era, while talking about GSD environment, software decisions have pretty much significant effect on most software's cost, schedule & value and gradually more in future. And value-neutral software decisions can dangerously humiliate project outcomes. Now-a-days, in software engineering, there is much different kind of parameters involved to which value-neutral cannot deal with and results in failure if applied. For example, value-neutral approach cannot handle most of the sources of software project failure. It is also difficult to make financially responsible decisions using value-neutral methods because it treats every parameter equally. Therefore, financial matters cannot be given high priority/importance while using value-neutral methods. As many organizations are switching from local software development to global software development (outsourcing) and also value based requirements elicitation is a new concept in this field, we have decided to work to combine value based requirements elicitation and GSD. In past , most of the research so far done in GSD environment, the focus mostly remains to overcome the general GSD environment challenges such as communication, cultural difference time zone etc. Our focus is to take value base requirement elicitation in GSD. For the GSD environment, that will make the global phenomena of GSD environment more prominent and effective.

Requirement elicitation is not only a major step in software engineering but also a key factor. And we will be targeting this key factor in our proposed model to elicit requirements from our valued stakeholders in an easy way out. We have taken few steps from existing model to modify it according to VBRE in order to produce better results in GSD environment. Complete architecture of the proposed framework ensures the filtration

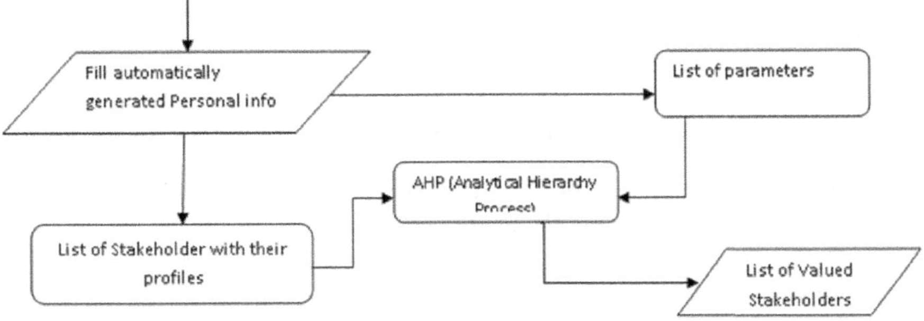

Fig. 1. Generation of Value Stakeholders (STEP 1)

of valued stakeholders and removes the GSD issues if faced by those stakeholders and then elicitat requirements from those valued stakeholders. Overall structure of our proposed framework is consisting of 5 steps as shown in figure 1 and figure 2. Basically these 5 steps show the flow of our work that how it will work. Each of these 5 steps, perform a valid functionality in proposed framework. We will discuss each and every step one by one in detail below.

3.1 Step 1(Value Assignment to Stakeholders)

The objective is to filter out the valued stakeholders from the complete list of all stakeholders by applying Analytical Hierarchy Process (AHP) against few parameters. For this purpose first we maintain a user profile of each stakeholder that contains information about that stakeholder. That information would be about culture, temporal difference, communication, timings etc. And now will define parameters against stakeholders e.g. time of availability, culture difference, role of stakeholder, mean of communication, strengths, weakness etc. We will extract all this information from personal information questionnaire. When stakeholder will login to our system by putting his user name and password which is assigned to them, personal information questionnaire automatically send to all of them. This questionnaire will be same for all stakeholders and plays important role in identifying personal information and parameters; those will help us out in valuing stakeholders.

3.2 Step 2 (Gather Informal Requirements/ Initial Requirements)

After the identification of valued stakeholders, now the objective is to elicit valued requirements from valued stakeholders. In this phase, we will discuss existing technique/model that has been used to remove the challenges of GSD if faced during elicitation process. The input of this phase is a list of valued stakeholders and output will be the requirements in raw form that have been gathered from those stakeholders through electronic means. Stakeholder will select his/her project from different projects which are present at that time on our system. Then he is free to ask any type of question about his/her project and he can also describe his requirements in Word file relevant to that project but within threshold time. Threshold time is defined for the purpose of GSD environment as; we are trying to provide our users a time controlled system. This session will be closed for stakeholders after threshold time. They can login to observe the set of requirements place by different stakeholders and to see whether a refined questionnaire is uploaded or not by the management but cannot fix any of their requirements after threshold time.

3.3 Step 3 (Requirement Engineering Phase)

We can say step 3 is a requirement engineer's phase. In this step, all set of requirements place by valued stakeholders are gathered at one place. At this time requirement engineer will purify those requirements according to project needs and will make an experienced questionnaire according to project scope which meets effectively the demands of all stakeholders. Now system analyst or team lead will check that questionnaire, construct it

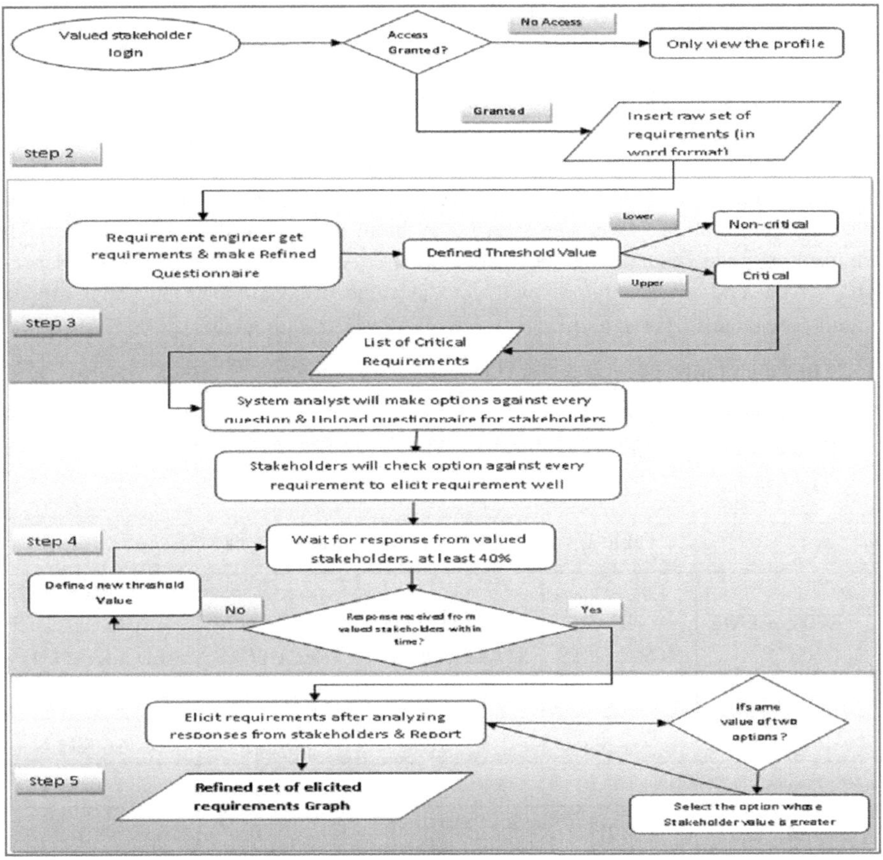

Fig. 2. Elicitation of valued requirements from valued Stakeholders

more polished if needs and build options against every requirement so that, stakeholder can choose any one of them. After embedment's questionnaire uploaded for valued stakeholders and notifies them also through mail. We will send them questionnaires to fill and revisit their feedback in that questionnaire. It's assumed that system analyst or team lead can make questionnaire more distinguished, but it's up to project needs, any one of your employee who can work well and competently on that project you can place him/her on questionnaire improvement.

3.4 Step 4 (Stakeholders' Feedback)

If we get response from them within the specified threshold, good enough and we can proceed further to our model design. But, in case, we don't get response from them within specific period of time, then we'll analyze the received feedback. If that is below average, then we will extend our threshold limit and will wait until and unless we get at least average number of responses from valued stakeholders.

3.5 Step 5 (Final Report and Graph Generation)

After getting response from stakeholders, we'll check all the requirements and figure out that how many stakeholders have selected a same option against certain requirement. . If same value occurs for two options of one requirement, we will prefer the option whose stakeholder value is more than the other one. The following formula will be applied if one unnecessary option of requirements is selected by at least one valued stakeholder and some important options have been selected by more than one ordinary stakeholder. The formula is applied by selecting the number of frequency and value of stakeholders by AHP. At the end, ultimately, we will get the value of requirements by applying this formula (see table 1). For example we have considered a requirement i.e.

R1: In which form you want to take the employees report?

☐ Tabular ☐ Charts
☐ Textual ☐ Graphical
☐ Diagram

Table 1. Selecting Value Based Requiremnts

REQUIREMENT	NO. OF RESPONSES	VALUE OF STAKEHOLDER	RELATIVE FREQUENCY	WEIGHTED VALUED REQUIREMENT
Options 1	12	45	0.5217	23.4782
Option 2	5	76	0.2173	16.5217
Option 3	1	54	0.0434	2.34782
Option 4	0	32	0	0
Option 5	5	88	0.2173	19.1304
Sum=	23		1	

Different stakeholder will give different response against this requirement. So our formula will calculate the number of responses and gives us better response which suits well according to our project. At the end report will be generated which shows the valued requirements in a sequence of their values. Figure 2 shows the graphical representation of the table 1.

After executing all of the above steps, we will have responses and feedbacks from valued stakeholders. Now, after analyzing those feedbacks and responses gathered through questionnaires and GUI based forms, we can elicit valued requirements in better way. We have referred the existing model (Gabriela et. al. 2008) to remove GSD problems. This technique will be used if GSD related issues are faced. If there are cultural differences that are medium or high, then training sessions will be conducted to bring awareness to the stakeholders about other's cultures to remove the cultural differences between stakeholders. There can be plus points in other's cultures

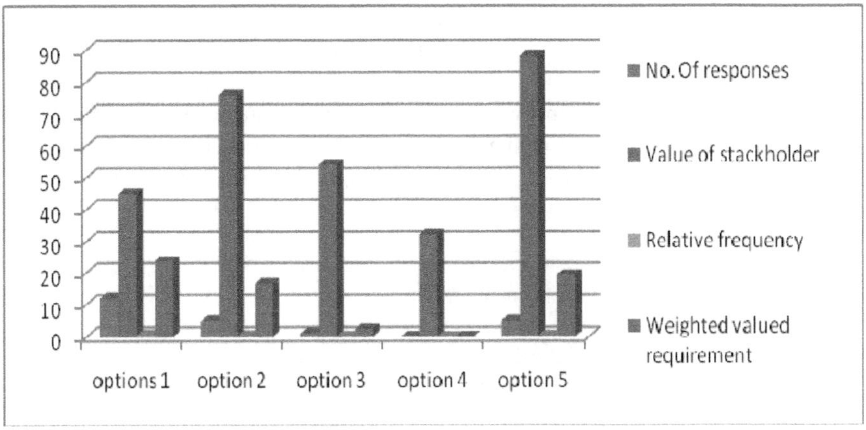

Fig. 3. Graphical Representation of Valued Requirements

that can be adopted. Theoretical evaluation of model All the research in requirements engineering that has taken place up till now is either based on no value or if value is considered, then used value neutral method. In value neutral technique, every requirement has been given equal importance whereas in reality and also according to current era, it is not true and feasible. There was no mechanism to give importance to certain stakeholders and, therefore, every stakeholder had the same importance level. Furthermore, the questionnaires those were used to send to stakeholders in order to elicit requirements from them, was the same for each and every stakeholders. We have used existing model to overcome the problems faced in requirements elicitation while working in GSD environment. We have devised a mechanism to filter out valued stakeholders from a bunch of raw data gathered based on few characteristics. Then we send stakeholders questionnaires. And, finally, elicit valued requirements from valued stakeholders. In short, this model works on value based software engineering and values every entity/requirement according to needs. This model is not only important because of work in value based requirements elicitation, but also overcomes the challenges of GSD environment.

4 Case Study

AHP (Analytical Hierarchy Process) is a strong and flexible decision making technique which helps in setting main concerns and reaching most favorable decisions in situations when quantitative and qualitative aspects have already been taken into consideration.

AHP is a methodology that helps out in filtering the alternatives against certain criteria. Generally, it takes an alternative such that the number of input, and asks the criteria to process and filter that input. We have used 123AHP tool to filter out and valuing stakeholders. We have passed stakeholders, and number of stakeholders to this tool to value them. Plus we will be passing the criteria/parameters against which this tool will return us the valued stakeholders.

The internal process of this tool is explained in the section below. First of all, this will ask the important parameters/ criteria and then compare each parameter/ criteria with other parameters/ criteria (e.g. P1 > P2). Then, each parameter will be compared with every stakeholder/alternative to identify how much certain stakeholder/alternative have importance on other stakeholders/alternative against that parameter (e.g. S1 > S2) (see figure 4). At the end of this process, this tool will return the result in the following way and we will get a list of valued stakeholders.

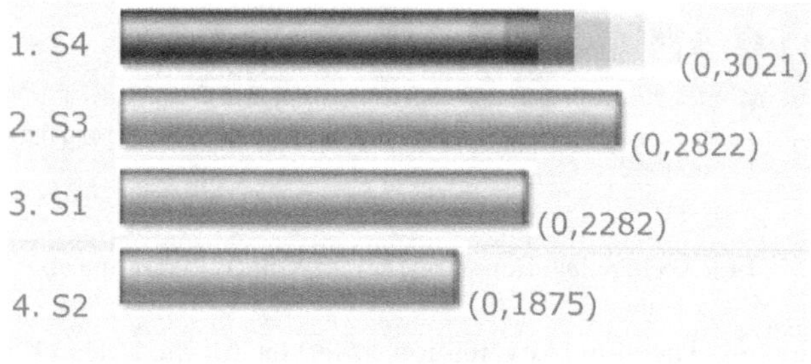

Fig. 4. AHP results

5 Conclusions and Future Work

At requirement engineering process while working in GSD environment, requirement elicitation is difficult, and different stakeholders have different opinions and expectations about the system. Problem occurs when stakeholders are not valued. Requirement gathering is a very tough job when teams are at dispersed locations. This model will minimize the difficulties and hurdles faced during requirement engineering process in GSD environment. Through this model, one can get clear picture of stakeholder's requirement. In future work, we will prove worth and validation of our model through case study to formulate in detail. Our main emphasis will be to generate questionnaires based forms in order to get requirements efficiently from valued stakeholders that will show how easily and efficiently we can elicit requirements.

References

[1] Ali Khan, A., Ullah Muhammad, Z.: Exploring the Accuracy of Existing Effort Estimation Methods for Distributed Software Projects (2009)
[2] Mohagheghi, P.: Global Software Development: Issues, Solutions, and Challenges (2004)
[3] Barry, B.: Value-Based Software Engineering (2003)
[4] Ian, S., Sawyer, P.: Requirements engineering A good practice guide. J. Wiley and Sons (1997)
[5] Aranda, N., Vizcaíno, A., Cechich, A., Piattini, M.: Strategies to minimize problems in Global Requirement elicitation (2008)

[6] Aurum, A., Wohlin, C., Porter, A.: Aligning Software Engineering Decisions. International Journal on Software Engineering and Knowledge Engineering (IJSEKE) 16(6), 795–818 (2006)
[7] Biffl, S., Aurum, A., Boehm, B., Erdogmus, H., Grunbacher, P. (eds.): Value-Based Software Engineering. Springer, Heidelberg (2005)
[8] Boehm, B.W., Sullivan, K.J.: Software Economics: A Roadmap. In: Proceedings of The Future of Software Engineering Conference, pp. 319–343 (2000)
[9] Šmite, D.: Global Software Development Projects in One of the Biggest Companies in Latvia: Is Geographical Distribution a Problem. The SPIP Journal 11, 61–76 (2006)
[10] Won Lim, S., Lee, T., Kim, S., Peter, H.: The Value Gap Model: Value-Based Requirements Elicitation
[11] Nuseibeh, B., Easterbrook, S.: Requirements Engineering: A Roadmap (2000)
[12] Satty, L.T.: The Analytic Hierarchy Process. McGraw-Hill, New York (1980)
[13] Aum, A.: Engineering and managing software requirements. Springer, Heidelberg
[14] Lehtonen, I.: Communication Challenges in Agile Global Software Development (2009)
[15] Aurum, A., Wohlin, C.: A Value-Based Approach in Requirements Engineering: Explaining Some of the Fundamental Concepts (2007)
[16] Zowghi, D.: Does Global Software Development Need a Different Requirements Engineering Process? (2003)
[17] Šmite, D., Borzovs, J.: Managing Uncertainty in Globally Distributed Software Development Projects. University of Latvia, Computer Science and Information Technologies, vol. 733, pp. 9–23 (2008)
[18] Smite, D.: Doctoral Thesis: Global Software Engineering Improvement, University of Latvia (2007)

Optimization of Transaction Mechanism on Java Card

Xiaoxue Yu, Dawei Zhang

School of Computer and Information Technology
Beijing Jiaotong University
Haidian District, Beijing, China 100044
Zhang_david2000@163.com

Abstract. Reliable update of data is very important on Java Card. Transaction mechanism ensures the data integrity on cards, but such transaction mechanism is very time consuming. Therefore, this paper presents an optimized transaction mechanism based on high object locality on Java Card. At first, we define the concept of object access and storage locality in applet transactions and then the transaction memory scheme based on hash table is designed for new value logging method. Secondly, we design the read and write access method for transactions based on access locality. At last, we optimize the commit process based on storage locality in order to reduce the number of EEPROM writing. The test results show that this optimized mechanism expands the transaction capacity and improves the execution speed of Java Card applets.

Keywords: Transaction, smartcards, Java Card.

1 Introduction

Java Card is a smart card that is capable of running programs written in Java. Applets written in Java can be compiled on computers and then downloaded onto Java Card. Multiple applets can be deployed on a single Java Card and new ones can be added to it even after it has been issued to the end user [1]. Java Card has been widely used in e-ID, e-Bank and e-Ticket etc.

There are two kinds of memory on Java Card. One is persistent memory which includes ROM, EEPROM or Flash. Another is transient memory (RAM). If the card loses power, data in transient memory is lost whereas data in persistent memory is preserved. ROM is used to store Java Card Virtual Machine (JCVM) which supports the installation, run and deletion of applets on cards. RAM is used to allocate the runtime stack for applets. Persistent memory such as EEPROM is used to store long-lived data which consist of applets' components, persistent objects, object handlers and other management data structures for JCVM. Transaction mechanism is important for reliable update of data in persistent memory [1][2][3]. Java Card provides transaction mechanism to protect the data integrity on cards. At first, it must ensure the correct transition between consistent states of applets. For example, when the new applet is added to the card the Java Card Virtual Machine will execute the applet's `install()` method to register and install it. The procedure of register and install must be transactional. The system must be restored to the initial state if the installation

T.-h. Kim et al. (Eds.): ASEA/DRBC/EL 2011, CCIS 257, pp. 190–199, 2011.

failed. Secondly, it must offer transaction functionality to all applets on cards. This mechanism is implemented by API in Java Card. Programmers can initiate a transaction by calling `JCSystem.beginTransaction()`, commit a transaction by `JCSystem.commitTransaction()` and abort a transaction by `JCSystem.abortTransaction()`.

Therefore, the transaction task is twofold [3]. First, the system is required to ensure that all updates in transactions are performed atomically; second, it must perform crash recovery to provide stability: the system must recover to a consistent state if a transaction fails.

The improvement of transaction performance is critical because such transaction mechanisms are very time consuming. The bottleneck for this optimization is limited resources on smart cards. The size of persistent and transient memory is very limited. For example, the RAM size is 6K and EEPROM size is 80K in Infineon SLE66CLX800PE [4]. JCVM will occupy the most of them. Available memory for transaction (especially RAM) is very limited. Furthermore, the writing operation of EEPROM is 1,000 times slower than to RAM and the number of EEPROM writing is limited [4]. Both of RAM and EEPROM will be used in the transaction scheme. But RAM should be used as more as possible to improve the speed and endurance of Java Card. The transaction scheme must be carefully designed with limited memory capacity and different memory characteristics.

This paper is organized as follows. We summarize the related work in section 2. The analysis of object locality in Java Card transactions is given in section 3. The transaction memory scheme is designed based on new value logging method in section 4. Section 5 discusses the new value logging method based on access locality in detail. The test evaluation between the traditional mechanism and our optimized mechanism is given in section 6 and finally the conclusion in section 7.

2 Related Work

Several papers have discussed the Java Card transaction schemes in detail [5][6]. In paper [6], various choices of possible implementation are discussed in detail, including different log schemes, their impact on performance, memory usage and possible optimizations. Paper [6] shows that the new value logging scheme has a better transaction performance on smart cards with 1 Kbyte and 16 Kbyte EEPROM. In case of new value logging, each value for a store operation is saved in the transaction buffer while the original value remains at the affected location. All logging items will be written to the affected location while committing a transaction. The performance of new value logging can be improved significantly if the transaction buffer is cached in RAM and written out lazily to EEPROM on overflow. Therefore new value logging is better than old value logging [6].

Although the memory characteristics and simple access pattern of Java Card are discussed in this paper, the data relativity is not considered. Java is an object oriented language. The data, which are defined as fields of class, will be assembled in distinct objects. In paper [6], the updates will be logged at the granularity of a single access which is an instance field more often than not. Each logging item will be written to the EEPROM separately while committing a transaction. This method ignores the high locality of data storage [7] so that it will increase the number of EEPROM writing and costs a longer time.

In papers [7-11], the high locality of Java Card objects is discussed, which means Java Card has internally a rule about the locality of EEPROM writing address. EEPROM is organized in pages (e.g. 64 bytes per page in SLE66CLX800PE [4]). One write operation will affect the whole page in spite of the number of written bytes. In other words, writing one byte or ten bytes in the same page will cost the same time. Therefore those papers present a method to add a caching buffer while writing data to EEPROM, whereby the physical relativity of data is considered. We define this relativity as storage locality and will discuss it further in section 3.

In our opinion, there are still two key issues which are not considered in the related work:

- The data relativity in Java semantics is important for transaction performance, which is called access locality in this paper. Namely, some of the accessed data in a transaction will be stored in the same Java object. This characteristic is prevalent because of the object oriented features in Java. We will discuss it in section 3.
- The granularity of new value logging scheme must be considered carefully. The granularity of a single access ignores the data locality in transactions. In this paper, the granularity of logging scheme is object and corresponding caching method is given so as to accelerate the transaction process.

  We designed the new transaction mechanism based on the above analysis. Our optimization design consists of:
- The concept of Object Locality, which consists of access and storage locality, is clearly given in this paper. We consider both the data physical relativity and semantics relativity in Java Card transactions. Based on the object locality the granularity of logging items is an object rather than a single access in our design. The new value logging method with object granularity is implemented. Both RAM and EEPROM buffer are used to expand the transaction capacity.
- We have more available RAM for transactions than previous work [6] thanks to the development of smart cards. It is possible for us to optimize the commit procedure by grouping objects into a page and log changes lazily at the granularity of page in our implementation. This optimization will reduce the number of EEPROM writings and improve the commit speed further.

We have described this idea in poster paper [12].This paper optimized our previous work further. First, we use the hash table instead of queue in [12] to store transaction buffer and design the new transaction memory scheme so that the search speed is accelerated. Second, we design the new read & write access algorithm based on this new scheme in detail. Third, we optimize our previous commit method so as to reduce the number of EEPROM writing.

3 Object Locality in Java Card Transactions

Java is an object oriented language. The data, which are defined as fields of class, will be assembled in distinct objects. Java Card supports a subset of standard Java language because of limited resources. The applets' structure which includes several objects is very compact in general because Java Card will often be used as an e-ID in e-Ticket, e-Bank etc. and the programming logic is not so complex. Furthermore, the semantics of transactions on Java Card is very compact, too. So the program codes have a high object locality in Java Card transactions.

In this paper, the object locality consists of access locality and storage locality.

The objects in heap are stored in EEPROM on smart cards. There is physical relativity, which is represented by storage locality, between those objects in the same applet. The storage locality means that generally speaking, the objects modified in one transaction are stored in EEPROM closer to each other. The objects in one transaction are generally in the same applet, which are created one by one in `install()` method. The creation sequence decides their relative locations in our heap management. If they are created closer in the creation sequence their storage locations in EEPROM are closer, too. For example, we consider the class `Purse` consists of two fields, `Balance` and `TransNo` and the class `TransLog` consists of three fields, `SerialNo`, `TransAmount` and `TransTerminal`. The object `purse` and `log` will be created one by one and stored as depicted in figure 1 when the installation completes.

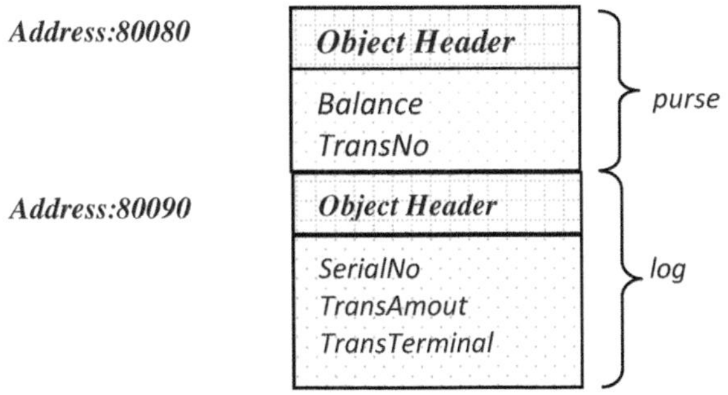

Fig. 1. Object Storage Locality

The access locality means that generally speaking, the codes will access several instance fields in one object consecutively in one transaction. For example, the transaction sample of ePurse deposit is shown as follows:

```
JCSystem.beginTransaction();
purse.Balance += depositAmount;
purse.TransNo++;
log.SerialNo = purse.TranNo;
log.TransAmount = transAmout;
JCSystem.commitTransaction();
```

In this example, the codes access object fields in purse and log consecutively. Access locality represents the data relativity in Java semantics.

4 Transaction Memory Scheme

There are two schemes for the logging of write accesses during a transaction, e.g. either new value or old value logging [6]. In this paper, we choose the new value logging scheme in our transaction mechanism but implement the optimized logging structure based on access locality. At the same time, two transaction buffers, RAM and EEPROM buffers are designed so as to expand the commit capacity.

4.1 Transaction Buffer in RAM

In our scheme, the transaction buffer is cached in RAM and written out lazily to EEPROM on some conditions in order to reduce the number of EEROM writing. The caching method between RAM and EEPROM will be discussed in section 5.

Another important issue should be considered is the granularity of logging entry. With respect to the object access locality, our scheme logs at the granularity of a single or part of object based on access locality. Furthermore, we use the hash table to store logging items in the transaction buffer. We use the three low bits of object handles as a hash value. The hash table of RAM buffer is depicted in figure 2.

Hash Value	Pointer
0	xx
…	xx
8	xx

Fig. 2. Structure of RAM transaction buffer

The pointer in figure 2 is the address of the logging entry. The structure of the logging entry is depicted in figure 3.

Handle	Page	Offset	Length	Value	Next

Fig. 3. Structure of logging entry

In the Object logging entry, 'Page' indicates which page this object is located. The commit algorithm will use this field to merge the objects in the same page when committing a transaction. 'Next' is the pointer to the next entry when the hash collision happens.

The RAM buffer needs to be written to EEPROM buffer when:

- The buffer is overflow during a transaction. At this time, we can write the old logging entries to the EEPROM buffer with enough size and log the new entry in the RAM.
- When committing a transaction, we must write the entries in RAM buffer to the EEPROM buffer at first and then write each entry to their original locations.

4.2 Transaction Buffer in EEPROM

The transaction buffer in EEPROM has a similar structure to RAM buffer but its size is large enough for common transactions. The structure is depicted in figure 4.

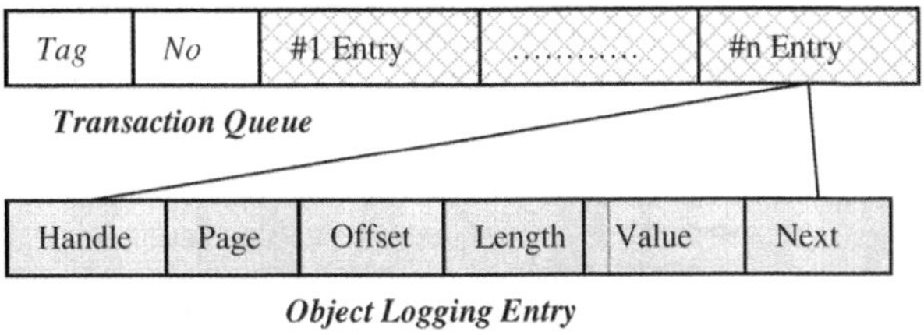

Fig. 4. Structure of EEPROM transaction buffer

In the transaction queue, the No represents the number of entries in the queue and the Tag represents the status of the transaction buffer. If all the data in the queue are ready to commit, set Tag to 1. Otherwise, set Tag to 0. In fact the Tag will only be set to 1 during a transaction commit process as discussed in section 5.

5 New Value Logging Method

In case of new value logging, each value for a store operation to a given location is saved in the transaction buffer during the transaction while the original value remains at the affected location. The read, write access and commit method during a transaction will be discussed in the following subsections.

5.1 Read and Write Access Based on Access Locality

While reading a field in object, we calculate the hash value with three low bits of object handlers and then use offset to locate the field in buffer. If hash collision happens, we also need to use object handle to search the queue. Every read access property can be represented by (handle, offset, length). When searching in buffer, we will use handle and offset to decide match or not. If not found (return NULL), read access program will get the value from objects on heap. Otherwise, get the value in buffer. This research algorithm based on the object granularity is approximately ***O(1)***, which is better than the ***O(n)*** of traditional algorithm.

Write access is a little complicated. At first program will search the logged entry in two buffers. If found and the entry is in RAM, update the value in entry directly. If not found and RAM buffer is enough, add the new entry in RAM. We will discuss other situations separately:

- If not found and RAM buffer is not enough, we will write the entries in RAM to the EEPROM buffer and add the new entry in RAM.
- If found and entry in EEPROM, we will write the entries in RAM to the EEPROM buffer and load the found entry to RAM.

The write access algorithm is depicted in figure 5.

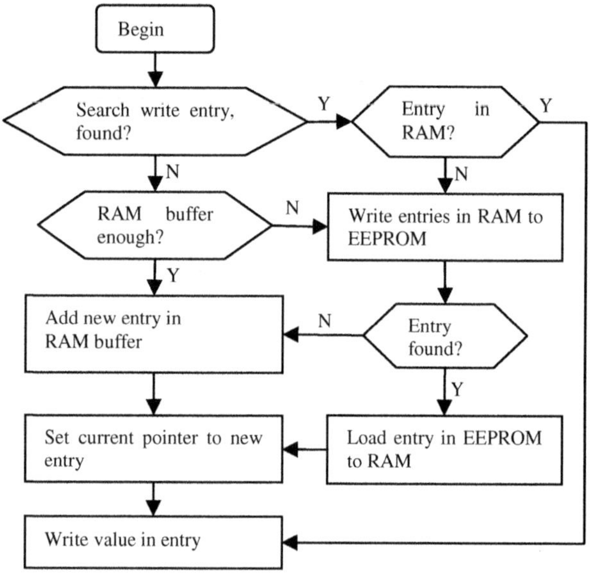

Fig. 5. Write Access Algorithm

When adding a new object entry, if the size of object fields is less than 32 (entry length limit), the whole object will be loaded in the entry. Otherwise the 32 bytes around the access point will be loaded. According to access locality rules, we needn't often access the heap based on the cached granularity of object so that the write access process will be accelerated.

5.2 Commit Method Based on Storage Locality

When committing a transaction, we need to write the RAM buffer into the EEPROM buffer at first and then write every logging entry to its original location on heap. As discussed in section 2, the storage locality means that generally speaking, the objects modified in one transaction are stored in EEPROM closer to each other. So before we write every logging entry to EEPROM buffer, we will merge the neighboring entries in the same page, backup to the EEPEOM buffer and then write to the target location. We choose the merging size is 64 bytes because SLE66CLX800PE EEPROM page size is 64 bytes.

The optimized commit process shown as follows:

```
TransactionCommit()
{
while (there are still pages not backuped in RAM ) {
    Read the original page in heap to RAM;
    Merge the logging entry into this page;
    Backup this page into EEPROM buffer;
  }
Set Tag = 1;
For every page in EEPROM buffer Do
  Write each page to destination location;
Set Tag = 0;
}
```

6 Test Results

This optimized transaction mechanism was implemented on smart card - Infineon SLE66CLX800PE with 6K RAM and 80K EEPROM. The test cases run at contact-based clock 30MHZ. The RAM transaction buffer size is 128 bytes and EEPROM buffer is 512 bytes. In order to analyze the performance gain of our optimization, we developed the new value logging method with single access granularity according to [6], which is called traditional method.

Our tests consist of two scenarios. First, we test the transaction during applets installation,. The test cases are the sample applets from Sun Java Card Development Kit [13]. Second, we test the application-oriented transaction which is a service transaction, e.g. electronic purse, electronic ticket etc. We developed three test cases according to the industrial standard in China [14][15] where the e-cash transaction is similar to EMV standards[16].

In the first scenario (installation), we choose 8 Applets. The comparison on execution time of `install()` between traditional and optimized method is shown in table 1.The execution time of install reduced approximately 32% based on our optimized mechanism.

In the second scenario (service), the test results of EEPROM writing are shown in table 2. The number of writing in optimized mechanism reduced about 81% on average.

Secondly, the test results about execution time (ms) of transaction commit are shown in Figure 7. The execution time of transaction commit reduced approximately 54% based on our optimized scheme.

Table 1. Comparison on install time (ms)

Applet	Traditional	Optimized	Reduced
Wallet	115	75	35%
JavaPurse	207	136	34%
Channels Demo	103	60	42%
JavaLoyalty	90	60	33%
PhotoCard	139	95	32%
odSample	95	52	45%
NullApplet	23	23	0%

Table 2. Comparison on EEPEOM writing

Applet	Traditional	Optimized	Reduced
Electronic Purse(EP)	16	3	81%
Electronic Ticket(ET)	10	2	80%
Health Care(HC)	12	2	83%

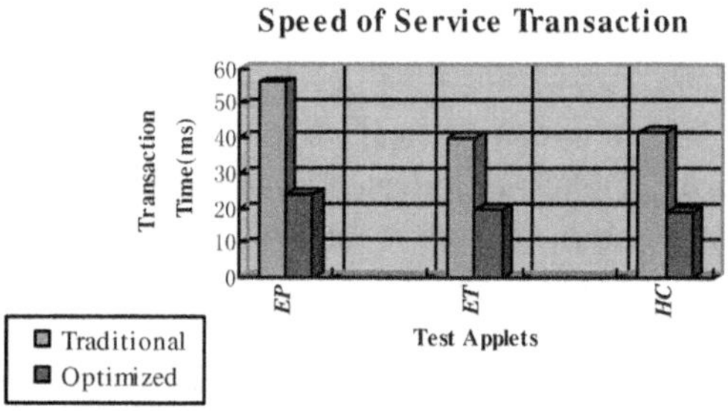

Fig. 6. Comparison on transaction time

This performance gain is better than our previous work [12] where the execution time of install reduced approximately 33% and the execution time of transaction commit reduced approximately 45%.

7 Conclusion and Future Work

Transaction mechanism is important for reliable update of data on multi-application cards like Java Card. The improvement of transaction performance is not trivial because of limited resources on smart cards. This paper analyses the object access and storage locality in applet transactions and presents an optimized transaction mechanism based on high object locality on Java Card. The test results show that the execution time of Applet installation reduced approximately 37% and the time of service transaction reduced approximately 54% based on our optimized mechanism.

References

1. Sun Microsystems Inc., Java Card 3.0.1 Platform Specification (2008), `http://java.sun.com/javacard/3.0.1/specs.jsp`
2. Chen, Z.: Java Technology for Smart Cards: Architecture and programmer's guide. Addison-Wesley, Reading (2001)
3. Gray, J.: The Transaction Concept: Virtues and Limitations. In: Proceedings of the 7th International Conference on Very Large Database Systems, pp. 144–154 (1981)
4. Infineon. SLE66CLX800PE Data Book (2006)
5. Oestreicher, M., Ksheeradbhi, K.: Object Lifetimes in Java Card. In: Proceedings of the 1st USENIX Workshop on Smart Card Technology, p. 15 (May 1999)
6. Oestreicher, M.: Transactions in Java Card. In: Proceedings of the 15th Computer Security Applications Conference, pp. 291–297 (1999)
7. Jin, M.-S., Choi, W.-H., Yang, Y.-S., Jung, M.-S.: A Study on Fast JCVM with New Transaction Mechanism and Caching-Buffer Based on Java Card Objects with a High Locality. In: Enokido, T., Yan, L., Xiao, B., Kim, D.Y., Dai, Y.-S., Yang, L.T. (eds.) EUC-WS 2005. LNCS, vol. 3823, pp. 91–100. Springer, Heidelberg (2005)
8. Won-Ho Choi, C.: A novel buffer cache scheme using java Card object with high locality for efficient java Card applications. In: Proceedings of International Conference on Convergence and Hybrid Information Technology 2006, pp. 500–510 (2006)
9. Jin, M.-S., Jung, M.-S.: A high Performance Buffering of Java Objects for Java Card Systems with Flash Memory. In: Zhou, X., Sokolsky, O., Yan, L., Jung, E.-S., Shao, Z., Mu, Y., Lee, D.C., Kim, D.Y., Jeong, Y.-S., Xu, C.-Z. (eds.) EUC Workshops 2006. LNCS, vol. 4097, pp. 908–918. Springer, Heidelberg (2006)
10. Jin, M.-S., Choi, W.-H., Yang, Y.-S., Jung, M.-S.: The Research on How to Reduce the Number of EEPROM Writing to Improve Speed of Java Card. In: Yang, L.T., Zhou, X.-s., Zhao, W., Wu, Z., Zhu, Y., Lin, M. (eds.) ICESS 2005. LNCS, vol. 3820, pp. 71–84. Springer, Heidelberg (2005)
11. Loinig, J., Steger, C., Weiss, R., Haselsteiner, E.: Java Card Performance Optimization of Secure Transaction Atomicity Based on Increasing the class Field Locality. In: Proceedings of the 3rd IEEE International Conference on Secure Software Integration and Reliability Improvement, pp. 342–347 (2009)
12. Zhang, D., Han, Z., Jin, W.: Optimized Java Card Transaction Mechanism Based on Object Locality. In: Proceedings of the 25th ACM Symposium on Applied Computing, pp. 550–551 (2010)
13. Sun Microsystems Inc., Java Card Development Kit (2008), `http://java.sun.com/javacard/`
14. People's Bank of China, PBOC bank card specification, Beijing (2002)
15. Ministry of Housing and Urbal-Rual Development of China, Application technology for construction cause IC card, Beijing (2005)
16. EMV (2008), `http://www.emvco.com/specifications.aspx`

SOCF: Service Oriented Common Frameworks Design Pattern for Mobile Systems with UML

Haeng-Kon Kim

Department of Computer Information & Communication Engineering,
Catholic University of Daegu, Kyungbuk, 712-702, South Korea
hangkon@cu.ac.kr

Abstract. The field of mobile applications and services continues to be one of the most rapidly evolving areas of communications. Modeling of domain-dependent aspects is a key prerequisite for the design of software for mobile systems. Most mobile systems include a more or less advanced model of selected aspects of the domain in which they are used. However, the traditional development approach to business applications, data base and general software is not suitable for mobile devices of the different paradigms. In this paper, we discuss the creation of such a model and its relevance for technical design of mobile software applications. The paper also reports from an empirical study where a methodology that combines both of these approaches was introduced and employed for modeling of the domain-dependent aspects that were relevant for the design of a mobile software component. The resulting models of domain-dependent aspects are presented, and the experiences from the modeling process are discussed. It strongly focus on the lightweight mobile service oriented common framework architectures for business applications running on mobile devices. It is concluded that a dual perspective based on both of the conventional approaches is relevant for capturing the aspects that are necessary for creating the domain-dependent models that are integrated in a mobile software system. As an architect, you are often challenged -- by client enterprise architects and IT stakeholders - to articulate Service-Oriented Architecture (SOA) patterns and service components in a nonproprietary, product-agnostic way. In this paper, use Unified Modeling Language (UML) models to describe the SOA architecture pattern and its associated service components. You also learn about the service components of the SOA pattern in the context of industry-standard UML formats to help stakeholders to better understand the components that constitute an SOA.

Keywords: Service oriented common framework, design pattern, mobile system, UML, RUP.

1 Introduction

Mobile software development challenge the modelling activities that precede the technical design of a software system. The context of a mobile system includes a broad spectrum of technical, physical, social and organizational aspects. Some of these aspects need to be built into the software. Selecting the aspects that are needed

T.-h. Kim et al. (Eds.): ASEA/DRBC/EL 2011, CCIS 257, pp. 200–211, 2011.

is becoming increasingly more complex with mobile systems than we have previously seen with more traditional information systems.

Lyytinen and Yoo[1] identify several drivers towards more and more mobile environments which they term the nomadic information environments. These include: mobility where the computing service follows the user rather than the user comes to the computing service, digital convergence where the standardization of services across platforms increases accessibility and networking, and mass scale where devices and mobile services will be available at significantly lower costs.

Both of these approaches are necessary in sorftware development. Yet the challenges of each approach when developing software for mobile systems are staggering, and combining the two is even more demanding. Most business applications require performing significant amounts of data processing, either locally or through high-speed networks. However, currently most of existing cell phones cannot fulfill these requirements. The main obstacles that limit the development of business applications on mobile devices remain to be unreliable network performance and limited data storage. Multiple attempts to overcome the limited capacity of mobile phones have failed, because technologies used for desktop applications don't work well on mobile phones. Business data objects have to be requested from the back-end application and stored for processing on a mobile device, which has significantly lower resources than any enterprise system. At the same time, the mobile framework must provide a comprehensive user experience as well as a convenient application implementation model for developers. Hence, business application development for mobile devices requires an innovative approach to Web Service invocation, data exchange, transformation, and interfacing with the user. The basic requirements for such a mobile solution should include the following: 1) timely, robust and easy access to Service-Oriented Architecture (SOA) system, 2) transparency between connected, occasionally-connected, and disconnected modes, 3) loose-coupling system designed to combine services on demand, 4) lightweight application composition and development and, 5) low total cost of ownership.

In this paper, we are specifically focusing on the former approach, i.e modeling of the domain-dependent aspects that will be built into the software. The purpose is to explore to what extent conventional approaches to modeling of domain-dependent aspects are relevant for and how they can be combined in the design of mobile software systems. In this paper, we propose a lightweight SOA-based architecture for mobile devices using the following techniques: 1) minimizing the amount of data transferred to and stored on the mobile device by using the knowledge of business processes and data access statistics to identify only the data required by the user, 2) a highly compressed XML format to transfer and store data, 3) reducing the amount of information contained in SOAP messages to increase efficiency of SOA-services invocation, 4) performing pro-active loading of data from the server, taking into account the client's service-invocation schedule, and 5) providing asynchronous connectivity to the back-end system, thus allowing applications to fully function in a disconnected mode.

2 Related Works

Software engineering methods that deal with modeling have different focus and perspective, and Avison and Fitzgerald [5] distinguish between process modeling, data modeling and object modeling.

2.1 Process Modeling

Process modeling base design of a software system on a model of the way in which a specific work process is carried out. The aim is that the software system will partly or fully automate the work process that is modeled.

A typical methodology within this approach is "Structured Analysis and Structured Design" (SASD). The first presentation of data flow modeling which was the core of this approach was DeMarco[6] that came out in 1979 and the first coherent method was Yourdon [7] from 1982. A more recent version is [8].

2.2 Data Modeling

Data modeling was developed as an abstract approach to database design as opposed to a direct focus on physical design. The classical reference is Date that was fist published in 1977, and it is now in the eight edition. This approach focused on the data that were processed in the user organization, and it was closely related to the relational database as the implementation platform and diagramming techniques of which the entity-relationship model was most prominent.

2.3 Object Modeling

The concept of classes and the idea of focusing on classes and objects stem from Simula programming language developed by Nygaard and Dahl[9]. In 1975, the concepts were also proposed for modelling through the Delta system description language that extended Simula. In the early 1980s, Jackson launched the Jackson System Development method (JSD) for analysis and design. The basic concept is "entity" but the term is clearly inspired by object-oriented thinking. Since classes and objects are not clearly differentiated, it is not possible to describe structural connections. The method's strength is that it introduces an event concept for describing entity dynamics. None of these methods gained substantial influence as modeling approaches.

The first significant methods for object-oriented analysis and design emerged around 1990. One stream of methods originated from object-oriented programming. A different stream of work originated from system development.

For business applications as well as for technical applications object-oriented modelling has become a dominant paradigm. The advancement of UML and several strong object-oriented programming languages like Java, C++ and C# have pushed further in that direction.

2.4 Modeling for Technical Design

The three approaches approaches presented above all provide methodological guidance for turning the results of the modeling activities into a technical design. In this sense, they build the aspects that have been modeled into the system.

The process modeling approach takes its point of departure in the way users work. This relates more generally to a focus on this domain:

- *Application domain:* The individual persons or roles and the organization that administrates, monitors, or controls a problem domain.

The application domain is where the users are and do whatever they do when they use the system. For an air traffic control system, the application domain is in the control tower where the controllers perform their air traffic control. The controllers monitor the traffic on the screen, decide on interventions, and direct the flights in their air space.

With the process modeling approach, the domain-dependent aspects are elicited from the application domain and built into the system through the activities in which the software functions are designed.

The data modeling approach takes a different point of departure by focusing on the data that people work with in the user organization. It has been argued that this was a much more stable foundation for software design than the way in which the users worked.

The data modeling approach relates more generally to a focus on this domain:

- *Problem domain:* The part of the context that is administrated, monitored or controlled by a system.

The problem domain is part of what is outside the system (i.e., in the context). For an air traffic control system the problem domain is that part of the context constituted by flights, departures, aircrafts, aircrafts' positions and trajectories, changed altitude, changed speed, etc. Everything that the controller in the tower needs to know about to control the air space effectively is in the problem domain. With the data modeling approach, the domain-dependent aspects are elicited from the problem domain and built into the system through the activities in which the database and the related software are designed.

The object modeling approach is more varied. Some of the methods, in particular the early ones, are focusing on the problem domain. The RUP methods is completely opposite as it departs from use cases which are descriptions of the application domain.

Rumbaugh et al.[12] is the only classic object-oriented method that emphasizes both the problem domain and the application domain. Two of the three fundamental models are the class diagram, emphasizing the problem domain, and a description of functions by means of data-flow diagrams from structured analysis, emphasizing the application domain. This dual focus is an interesting and innovative approach. Unfortunately, the description of functions is not related to the object-oriented model. System developers with experience using the Rumbaugh method also point out that constructing the functional model is rarely worth while.

2.5 Software for Mobile Systems

The overview above illustrate that popular software engineering methods have a strong focus on technical aspects and the representation of information in the system. Yet they have very little in particular to offer in modelling context for mobile systems. Rational Unified Process[11], for example, offers several principles of which none address how to model the context of a mobile system. Microsoft Solutions Framework, as another example, offers a set of principles for software engineering, but, again, has nothing in particular to say on modeling the context of a mobile system.

The literature on human-computer interaction has a stronger emphasis on the context of computerized systems. The basic literature deals with user interface design from a general point of view. They provide extensive guidelines and techniques for user interaction design but nothing specific on design of mobile systems and very little on modelling of domain-dependent aspect as a basis for technical design.

Some of the literature in human-computer interaction deals specifically with user interaction design for mobile systems. There is a general textbook on design of user interaction for mobile systems. This textbook has a strong focus on mobile systems but significantly less on the modelling of domain-dependent aspects and very little emphasis on the relation to software engineering and technical design of software.

A common characteristic of this literature is that they work with various domain models, but there is very little about the relation to other models that are made for design of technical aspects, including the representation of information about the relevant domains.

There is some literature that deals with technical design of context-aware systems. For example, Anagnostopoulos formulate a set of requirements for what should be modelled in designing mobile systems: context data acquisition (e.g., from sensors), context data aggregation, context data consistency, context data discovery, context data query, context data adaptation, context data reasoning, context data quality indicators, and context data integration. Baumeister et al. [13]extend UML with mobile objects, locations, and mobile activity. They formulate the extension in terms of stereotypes and end by providing a modified metamodel for UML.

3 SOCF: Service Oriented Common Frameworks Design Pattern for Mobile Systems with UML

3.1 Logical SOA Reference Architecture

The SOA pattern is represented in a UML product-agnostic manner in Figure 1. In its simplest form, the SOA pattern consists of a decoupled Enterprise Service Bus (ESB) that connects and provides interactive services among the requestors and providers.

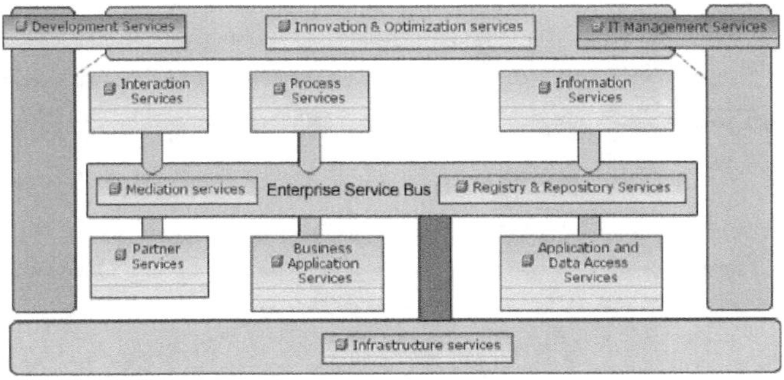

Fig. 1. Logical SOA reference architecture

The SOA pattern consists of an ESB infrastructure, with the service interaction points (SIPs), or end points. SIPs are as follows;

(1) **Interaction Services :** capabilities and functions to deliver content and data using a portal, or other related Web technologies, to consumers or users
(2) Process Services : Control capabilities to manage the message flow and interactions across multiple services according to business processes and flows.
(3) Information Services: Capabilities to federate, replicate, and transform disparate data sources
(4) **Business Application Services :** Capabilities for service consumers to be called by the business application services
(5) **Application and Data Access Services :** Capabilities to integrate core applications with external data repositories and packaged applications

The ESB serves as the connectivity entry point of the SOA model and provides the following services:

- Request and response services
- Transformations
- Content-based routing
- Customized logging
- Optimization
- Monitoring

ESB also provides the common connectivity and virtualization of services. To address the latest business application demand, the ESB leverages the Service Component Architecture (SCA) programming model.

In Figure 2 you can see an ESB supporting the latest SCA programming model, with a default messaging engine built on Java™ Message Service (JMS) specifications. The ESB uses a mediation component (module) that is based on SCA modules to mediate messages between service requestors and service providers. The mediation services in the ESB can thus be tailored to form complex mediation patterns that implement virtualization in the form of location and identity transparency.

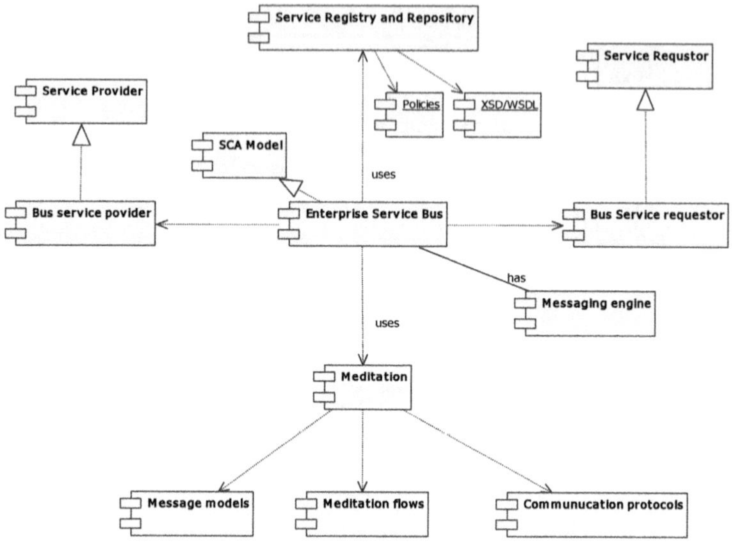

Fig. 2. Enterprise Service Bus

The mediation component is comprised of three components:

Message models
Based on the meta-model of the message under consideration (The ESB should be capable of supporting different types of message models flowing between the service provider and service requestor, thus creating a message-model-agnostic exchange.)

Mediation flows
Contain interfaces to invoke the mediation flows to perform mediation between service requestor and service provider, and to provide references to external services (The mediation flows support several mediation patterns: monitor, modifier, validator, cache, router, discovery clone, and so on.)

Communication protocols
Provide support for different communication protocols, such as MQ, Java Message Service (JMS), HTTP, and Remote Method Invocation (RMI), to connect the service providers with the service consumers (The communication protocols support several interactions patterns, such as request/response, publish/subscribe, and synchronous/asynchronous.)

The ESB uses the service registry and repository component as a dynamic look-up mechanism to provide information about service endpoints. The registry and repository service thus enables optimized access to service metadata and management of service interactions and policies. It also supports the integration and federation of other standard registries and repositories. In its most elemental state, it is composed of service metadata artifacts documents, such as XML Schema Definition Language (XSD) or Web Services Description Language (WSDL) files. These service metadata files are stored and managed by the service repository.

(1)Interaction services

The interaction services that have service integration points with the ESB are shown in Figure 3. The interaction services node serves as the SOA entry point for users. The interaction services provide the presentation layer for SOA that abstracts the interfaces and aggregates the information sources between the end user and the SOA applications.

Interaction services are cataloged into three main services:

User interface services
: Composed of a portal application that uses dashboards for decision making, as well as visibility into operations

User interaction services
: Composed of visualization, collaboration, composite applications, alerts and forms

Deployment services
: Comprised of mobile, browser, and rich clients

Interaction services use the support template components to easily create composite applications. The composite applications: -Provide the basis for outsourced or in-house service applications - Support rich clients and mobile end-user clients - Provide highly customized and dynamic data, which gives real-time visibility that link results to the underlying business process metrics - Serve as a dashboard, providing users with a real-time view of Key Performance Indicators (KPIs) on the project.

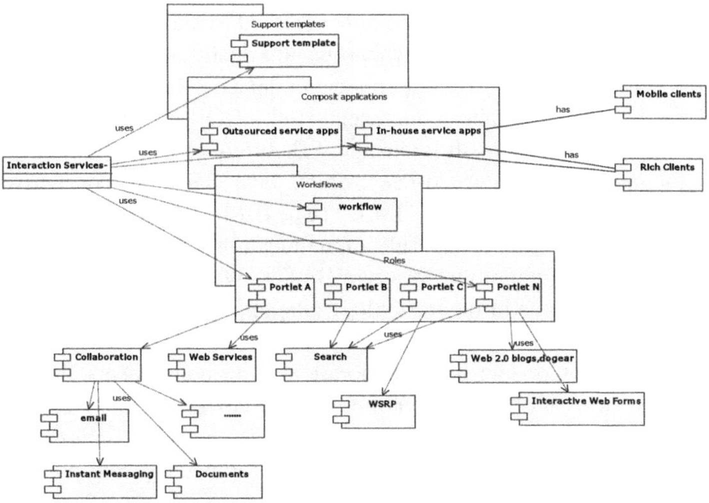

Fig. 3. Interaction services

Each of the composite applications may contain prebuilt portlets that have a specific function and an associated workflow. Interaction services could also have built-in filtering capabilities, browser-based configuration wizards, interactive Web forms, search, Web 2.0 technologies, and collaboration. For example, the collaboration service component is a completely integrated, portal-based collaborative environment that includes e-mail, calendaring and scheduling, instant messaging, Web conferencing, and document and Web content management.

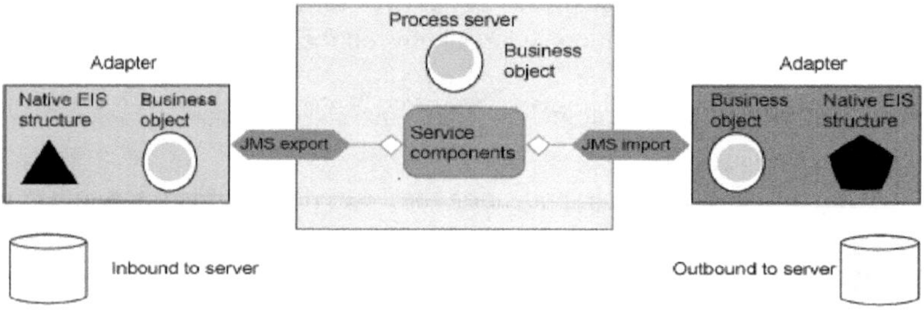

Fig. 4. Business integration adapter services

The center of Figure 4 shows the process server with a business integration application. The business integration application is made available for invocation to other services, outside of the SCA module, through a JMS export. The business integration application is able to invoke other services outside of the SCA module through the use of a JMS import. The adapters communicate with the back-end systems using the application-specific data structure or business object and are configured using the connector configuration file. When a business object is passed inbound to the process server through the export, it is converted to a format understood by the process server by a data binding that is part of the export. When a business object is passed outbound to the adapter, it is converted to a format understood by the adapter by a data binding that is part of the import. This data synchronization pattern can also incorporate mapping of the business object from an application-specific format to a generic format. Some of the technology adapter components are: ACORD XML, Microsoft® COM, CORBA, e-mail, EJB, Microsoft Exchange, FIX Protocol, IBM iSeries®, WebSphere Business Integration iSoft Peer-to-Peer Agent, Java Database Connectivity (JDBC) (SQL and stored procedure access), JMS, JText, IBM Lotus® Domino®, Society for Worldwide Interbank Financial Telecommunication (SWIFT), WebSphere MQ, WebSphere Business Integration Message Broker, WebSphere MQ Workflow, Web services, and XML. Some of the technology adapters can use data handlers, including data handlers for EDI, SOAP, XML, and various text formats. The business integration collaboration component has collaborations with components such as customer relationship management (CRM), Health Insurance Portability and Accountability Act (HIPAA), health care, order management, procurement, telecommunication, life insurance, and so on. Business integration collaboration is done with prebuilt templates that streamline and synchronize information and data related to the respective components. For example, collaborations for HIPAA transactions enable compliance with required specifications and standards, and ensure that all transactions and interactions interconnect across multiple applications and across enterprise boundaries. The broker plug-in component provides the necessary classes required for creating a user plug-in node. The micro broker plug-in component provides the necessary access-related information, such as broker name, queue name, data source, and so on.

(2) Business application services

Business application services constitute the reuse entry point for SOA. Business applications are loosely coupled to bring business value to the enterprise by using Web services. Web services reduce the cost of building expensive business applications and enable the deployment of new business models in the enterprise structure. Figure 5 shows the business application services that use the business process and policy management component to provide business security services to the business applications of the enterprise.

The business process and policy management component uses the following security components to fulfill its security obligations to the business applications.

Security governance framework

Addresses the need for effective governance structure and decision-making authority within an enterprise (This framework is used to establish the chain of command, responsibilities, and authority to ensure that enterprise business applications are controlled effectively from a security perspective.)

Trust management

Establishes trust between any two enterprises or organizations coming together to conduct secure business transactions (Trust is established with the two entities agreeing to abide by a set of relationship and liability management rules to conduct business.)

Trust is also established from a technology perspective using cryptographic methods, including encryption keys, private or public keys, digital signatures, or protocols.

Identity and access management

Provides the necessary ID management and access privileges across enterprises. This component uses the following additional components to fulfill its services:

- Approval component, to get the necessary management approval for modifications or updates to identity or information access
- User self-care component, to enable end users to carry out certain security administrative tasks without administrative supervision, such as periodically changing a password
- Delegation component, to provide the ability to delegate the IT security management functions to another individual
- Revalidation component, to provide access to systems that need to be approved at regular intervals

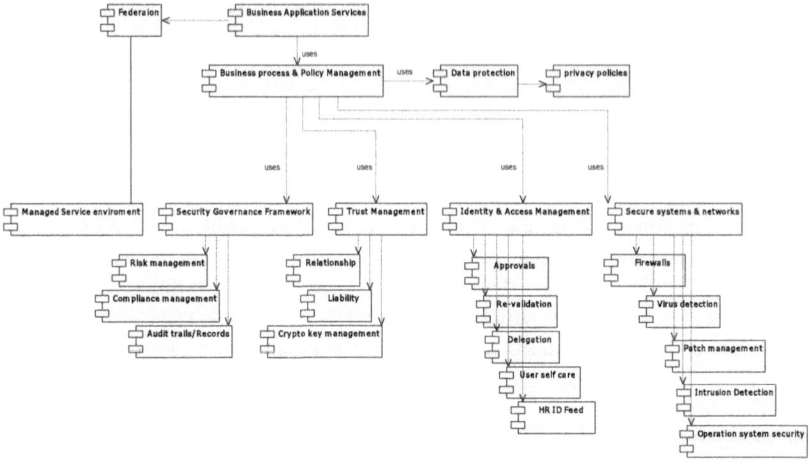

Fig. 5. Business application services

Secure systems and network

Provides security services such as firewalls, intrusion detection systems, virus detection, patch management, and operating and network security (The Business application services component uses a federated component to manage many different service environments of the enterprise.)

Data protection

Responsible for the security of the business information content during its transportation or at its destination (The data protection component establishes trust by managing privacy policies, obtaining detailed reports on sensitive information, publishing policies for review by users, and capturing and enforcing user preferences.)

Risk management

Determines the level of risk associated within the enterprise IT system and the need to take effective action to assess its impact on overall security operations based on a cost benefit analysis and its impact on the system.

Compliance management

Ensures compliance with external federal or state regulations and internal compliance with IT organization business security policies.

Audit trails and records

Reconciles and assesses how the different IT security policies introduced in the IT system are practically applied in day-to-day operations to ensure compliance that is set against internal and external policies. (This helps management and technical teams take quick corrective actions in case of policy divergence.)

4 Conclusion

Architects and stakeholders often find it challenging to articulate the SOA architecture pattern and to determine which entry point to choose. As a result, they may want to select several SOA entry points that can address the most pressing and challenging issues that face the enterprise. In this paper, we discuss the creation of such a model and its relevance for technical design of mobile software applications. The paper also reports from an empirical study where a methodology that combines both of these approaches was introduced and employed for modeling of the domain-dependent aspects that were relevant for the design of a mobile software component. The resulting models of domain-dependent aspects are presented, and the experiences from the modeling process are discussed. It strongly focus on the lightweight mobile service oriented common framework architectures for business applications running on mobile devices. It is concluded that a dual perspective based on both of the conventional approaches is relevant for capturing the aspects that are necessary for creating the domain-dependent models that are integrated in a mobile software system.

Acknowledgement. This work was supported by the Korea National Research Foundation (NRF) granted funded by the Korea Government (Scientist of Regional University No. 2011-0013259)

References

1. Lyytinen, K., Yoo, Y.: Research Commentary: The Next Wave of Nomadic Computing. Information Systems Research 13(4), 377–388 (2002)
2. Dey, A.K., Abowd, G.D.: Towards a Better Understanding of Context and Context-Awareness. Georgia Institute of Technology (1999)
3. Clemmensen, T., Nørbjerg, J.: Separation in theory, coordination in practice - teaching HCI and SE. Software Process: Improvement and Practice 8(2), 99–110 (2003)
4. Nielsen, P.A.: Reflections on development methods for information systems: a set of distinctions between methods. Office, Technology and People 5(2), 81–104 (1989)
5. Avison, D., Fitzgerald, G.: Information Systems Development: Methodologies, Techniques and Tools, 3rd edn. McGraw-Hill, London (2002)
6. DeMarco, T.: Structured Analysis and System Specification. Yourdon Inc. & Prentice-Hall, Englewood Cliffs (1979)
7. Yourdon, E.: Managing the System Life Cycle. Yourdon Inc., New York (1982)
8. Yourdon, E.: Modern Structured Analysis. Prentice-Hall, New York (1989)
9. Dahl, O.-J., Myhrhaug, B., Nygaard, K.: SIMULA 67 Common Base Language. Publikasjon nr. S-22. Norsk Regnesentral, Oslo (1971)
10. Jacobson, I., Booch, G., Rumbaugh, J.: The Unified Software Development Process. Addison-Wesley, Reading (1999)
11. Object Management Group: Unified Modeling Language Specification. Framingham, Massachusetts (1998)
12. Rumbaugh, J., Blaha, M., Premerlani, W., Eddy, S., Lorensen, W.: Object-Oriented Modelling and Design. Prentice-Hall, Englewood Cliffs (1991)

Double Layered Genetic Algorithm for Document Clustering

Lim Cheon Choi, Jung Song Lee, and Soon Cheol Park

Division of Electronics and Information Engineering,
Jeonbuk National University, Jeonju, Jeonbuk, Republic of Korea
{cis1124,ei200411147,scpark}@jbnu.ac.kr

Abstract. Genetic algorithm for document clustering(GC) shows good performance. However the genetic algorithm has problem of performance degradation by premature convergence phenomenon(PCP). In this paper, we propose double layered genetic algorithm for document clustering(DLGC) to solve this problem. The clustering algorithms including DLGC are tested and compared on Reuter-21578 data collection. The results show that our DLGC has the best performance among traditional clustering algorithms(K-means, Group Average Clustering) and GC in various experiments.

Keywords: Document Clustering, Genetic Algorithm, Premature Convergence Phenomenon.

1 Introduction

The document clustering is to group the documents which are similar in a set of documents without prior information[1,2,3]. Document clustering is used to analysis and conjugate large amount of information.

In recent years, Artificial intelligence algorithms are widely used to implement better performing Document clustering[4,5,6]. Genetic algorithm, one of the efficient artificial intelligence algorithms, is an optimal search algorithm which based on theory of evolution and survival of fittest[7,8]. Document clustering with genetic algorithm is implemented by substituting appropriate component required for document clustering in to the genetic algorithm[5,6].

Genetic algorithm has problem called premature convergence phenomenon (PCP) that is to converge a local optimal solution[9]. This problem is one of the biggest causes that lowered performance of genetic algorithm[10]. Genetic algorithm for document clustering has same problem.

In this paper, we proposed and applied double layer genetic algorithm for document clustering to solve underperformance caused by PCP .

This paper is organized as follows. The next section describes the genetic algorithm for document clustering. Section 3, Presents the principle of prosed algorithm. Section 4, explains experiment setting, evaluation approached, result, and analysis. Section 5 concludes and discusses future work.

T.-h. Kim et al. (Eds.): ASEA/DRBC/EL 2011, CCIS 257, pp. 212–218, 2011.

2 Genetic Algorithm for Document Clustering

Genetic Algorithm(GA) is based on the principles of the natural selection and the survival of the fittest[7]. Basic components of GA are gene, chromosome, individual and fitness function[8]. We need to define the individual structure and the gene operations for genetic algorithm applied to document clustering. Genetic algorithm for document clustering called GC(Genetic Clustering) in this paper.

2.1 Individual Structure

GC defined the individual structure using the information of cluster number that document belongs to[12]. Fig. 1 shows that the individual structure of GC

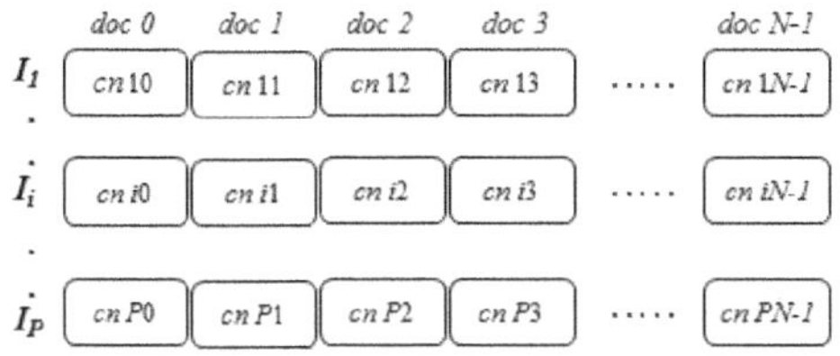

Fig. 1. The individual structure of Genetic Clustering

As shown the Fig. 1, GA has *P* individuals. Individual *I* has *N* genes. Index of gene means a document number and value of gene means a cluster number that document belongs to.

2.2 Genetic Operations

Genetic operations consist of selection, crossover, mutation, population initialization, and fitness function. Fig. 2 shows the progress of GC.

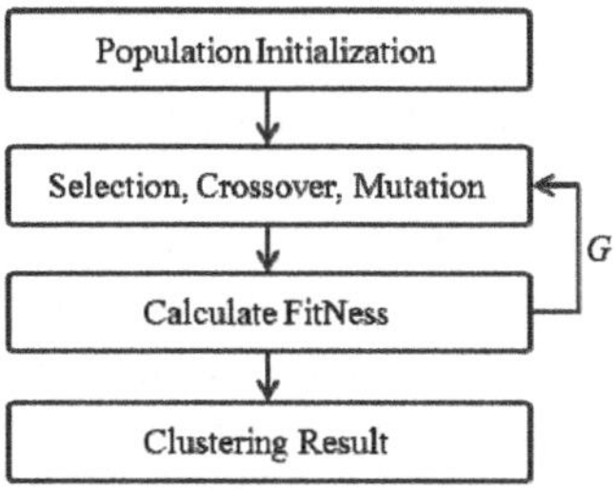

Fig. 2. The progress of Genetic Clustering

As shown the Fig. 2, until clustering result is generated GC performs *G* generation of genetic (Selection, crossover, Mutation) operation and calculation Fitness.

Selection, Crossover, Mutation. The roulette wheel selection, 0.5 threshold of uniform crossover algorithm and 0.015 threshold of typical variation mutation are adopted in GC[6,11].

Fitness Function. The fitness Function of GC is the *AveSim*. The *AveSim* use the average similarity of all documents in each cluster. Equation (1) shows that the formula of the *AveSim*[11,12].

$$AveSim = \frac{1}{K}\sum_{i=0}^{K} CluSim_i$$
$$where, CluSim_i = \sum_{j=0}^{NC_i \;\; 1} \sum_{k=j+1}^{NC_i} CosSim(d_{ij}, d_{jk}) \tag{1}$$

K means a number of cluster, NC_i means a number of documents in ith cluster, d_{ij} means jth document in ith cluster, *CosSim* means a cosine similarity function for similarity function[11].

In this paper the value of *AveSim* is called as Fitness.

3 Double Layered Genetic Algorithm for Document Clustering

In genetic algorithm, event which initially generated individual with value closest to the local optimal solution gets selected as product for the algorithm is called premature convergence phenomenon(PCP)[9].

The PCP is one of the main causes of underperformance in GA, and it is determined early stage of algorithm process[10]. PCP which happens during genetic algorithm in Document clustering has one more property and that is result of the PCP partially contains right information.

The two characteristics of the PCP in the document clustering are summarized as follows.

1. The PCP is decided in the early process of algorithm.
2. The result of PCP has right information partially.

With these two characteristics, we get the idea that retrieval of partially meaningful data from short-generation of GC is possible. We use this fact to apply genetic algorithm with double-layer which is more resistant against premature convergence than the conventional genetic algorithm, on the document clustering(DLGC). The following figure is a graphical representation of the structure of DLGC.

As shown in Fig. 3. DLGC is a two layer structure. Layer 1 which is M numbers of GC performing for generation $G1$. Layer 2 which obtain clustering result through genetic operation of generation $G2$.

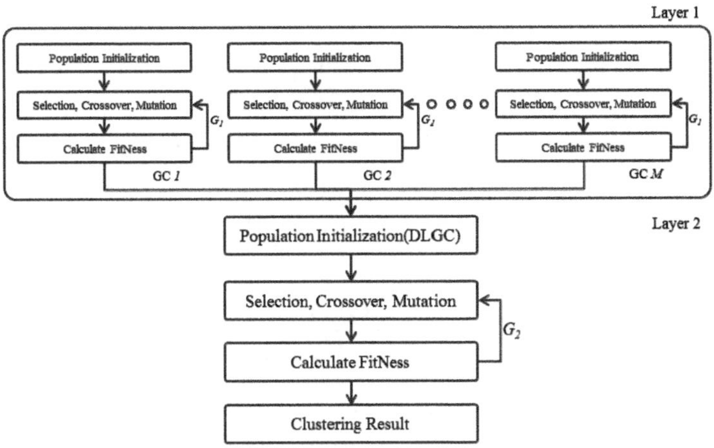

Fig. 3. The individual structure of Genetic Clustering

Genetic algorithm's execution time is determined by the number of individual and the number of generations[6]. DLGC uses same number of individual as GC so execution time of GC and DLGC are proportional to the number of generations. As Fig. 3 has shown, number of generations on DLGC can be expressed as $M*G1 + G2$. By assigning small number on $G1$, we made number of generations in DLGC and GC almost same and thus making them having almost same execution time.

Document clustering with PCP returns partial right information during layer 1 and with M number of execution we get diverse information.

4 Experiment and Result

This paper propose double layered genetic algorithm for document clustering. For estimating its performance, the Reuter-21578 text collection set is used. Two Topic-Sets are experimented and four subjects were allocated to each Topic-Set. Each subject has 50 doc1uments, so that a Topic-Set has 200 documents. Table 1. shows the subjects of Topic-Sets.

Table 1. Subjects of Topic-Sets

	Subjects
Topic-Set1	coffee, acq, trde, interest
Topic-Set2	earn, grain, crude, ship

Documents in Topic-Set are represented by VSM. The term weight as follow Equation 2[2,3].

$$w_{ij} = tf_{ij} \times \log \frac{N}{df_j} \tag{2}$$

w_{ij} means jth term frequency in ith document, tf_{ij} means a document frequency of j th term, N means number of documents in Topic-Set.

To evaluate the clustering performances, F-measure defined as in Equation 3 (Croft 2009) is used[2,3].

$$F \quad measure = \frac{2 \times precision \times recall}{precision + recall} \tag{3}$$

To evaluate performance of algorithms proposed in this paper, we measured Fitness and F-measure according to the GC and DLGC's generation number in each topic set. In GC, number of generation was set to 10,000. In DLGC, for layer 1, number of GC (M) is set to 2,3,5 and G1 was set to 300. For layer 2 G2 was set to 9000. As result, corresponding to M start point for DLGC is set to 600, 900, 1500 and end point is set to 9600, 9900, 10500.

Next Figures are shown the Fitness and the F-measure of GC and DLGC over the number of generation in Topic-Sets.

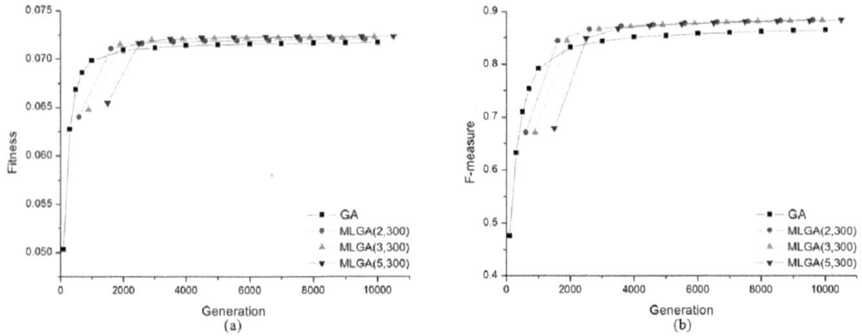

Fig. 4. (a) Fitness of GC and DLGC, (b) F-measure of GC and DLGC over the number of generation in Topic-Set1

As Fig. 4 shown, DLGC has 0.003~0.005 higher Fitness and 2~4% higher F-measure than GC in same generation. And DLGC converged to almost same Fitness and F-measure, regardless of M.

As Fig. 5 shown, DLGC has 0.003~0.005 higher Fitness and 4~7% higher F-measure than GC in same generation. And DLGC converged to the different Fitness and F-measure, according to the M.

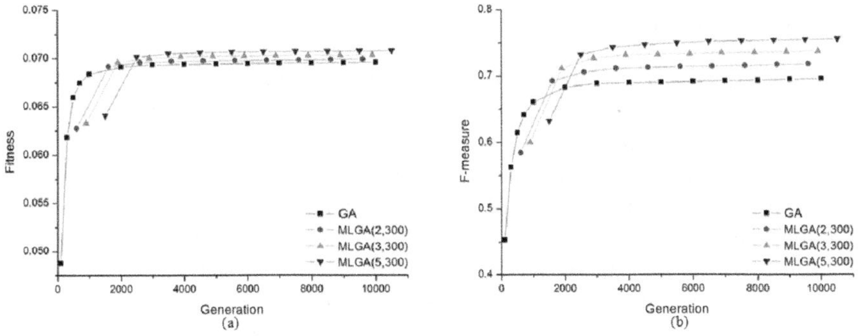

Fig. 5. (a) Fitness of GC and DLGC, (b) F-measure of GC and DLGC over the number of generation in Topic-Set2

The performance difference in GC and DLGC was small in the Topic-Set1 but in the Topic-Set2 differences was much bigger. This was caused because each data set has different local optimal solution that converges to. Data set with high degree of PCP, DLGC showed much better result than GC.

To objectively analyses algorithm proposed in this paper, we evaluated it with conventional clustering algorithms. The following table shows performance for each algorithm[3,13,14].

Table 2. Performances of Clustering Algorithms in all Topic-Sets

Cluster Algorithm	*Topic-Set1*		*Topic-Set2*	
	Precision	*Recall*	*Precision*	*Recall*
K-means	62.62	62.14	59.93	59.25
Group Average	56.38	55.25	72.38	73.21
Original GA	86.83	86.42	69.38	68.84
DLGA (2, 300)	87.49	86.66	71.57	72.03
DLGA (3, 300)	88.80	87.86	73.53	73.73
DLGA (5, 300)	88.79	87.85	75.38	75.74

As Table 2 shown, DLGA has 10~20% better performance than traditional clustering algorithms(K-means, Group Average Clustering) in all Topic-Sets. Also DLGA has 3 ~ 7% better performance than GA in all Topic-Sets.

5 Conclusion

In this paper, we propose the double layered genetic algorithm (DLGA) for document clustering. DLGC was implemented by using two characteristics of PCP which we get when genetic algorithm is applied on document clustering. Through various experiments performed in this paper, we have confirmed that DLGC is stronger against premature convergence phenomenon compared to the conventional GC. In addition, the document clustering using genetic algorithms performs better than the traditional clustering algorithms (K-means, Group Average). However, genetic algorithms still has its weakness as it is slower compare to the older algorithms. We will research more about characteristics of Document clustering using genetic algorithms to overcome this problem.

Acknowledgments. This research was supported by Basic Science Research Program through the National Research Foundation of Korea(NRF) funded by the Ministry of Education, Science and Technology(No. 2011-0004389) And Brain Korea 21 Project

References

1. Foster, I., Kesselman, C.: Modern information retrieval. Addison-Wesley (1999)
2. Manning, C.D., Raghavan, P., Schütze, H.: Introduction to Information Retrieval. Cambridge University Press (2008)
3. Croft, W.B., Metzler, D., Strohman, T.: Search Engines Information Retrieval in Practice. Addison Wesley (2009)
4. Maulik, U., Bandyopadhyay, S.: Genetic Algorithm-based Clustering Technique. Pattern Recognition 33(9), 1455–1465 (2000)
5. Bandyopadhyay, S., Mauilk, U.: Nonparametric genetic clustering: Comparison of validity indices. IEEE Trans. System Man Cybern.-Part C Applications and Reviews 31, 120–125 (2001)
6. Song, W., Park, S.C.: Genetic Algorithm-Based Text Clustering Technique. In: Jiao, L., Wang, L., Gao, X.-b., Liu, J., Wu, F. (eds.) ICNC 2006, Part I. LNCS, vol. 4221, pp. 779–782. Springer, Heidelberg (2006)
7. Goldberg, D.E.: The Grid: Genetic Algorithms in Search, Optimization and Machine Learning. Addison Wesley (1989)
8. David, L.D.: Handbook of Genetic Algorithms. Van Nostrand Reinhold (1991)
9. Andre, J., Siarry, P., Dognon, T.: An improvement of the standard genetic algorithm fighting premature convergence in continuous optimization. Advances in Engineering Software 32(1), 49–60 (2001)
10. Yao, X., Liu, Y., Lin, G.: Evolutionary programming made faster. Presented at IEEE Trans. Evolutionary Computation, 82–102 (1999)
11. Davies, D.L., Bouldin, D.W.: A cluster separation measure. IEEE Trans. Pattern Anal.l Intell. 1, 224–227 (1979)
12. Song, W., Park, S.C.: Genetic algorithm for text clustering based on latent semantic indexing. Presented at Computers & Mathematics with Applications, 1901–1907 (2009)
13. Selim, S.Z., Ismail, M.A.: K-Means-Type Algorithms: A Generalized Convergence Theorem and Characterization of Local Optimality. IEEE Trans. Pattern Anal. Mach. Intell., 81–87 (1984)
14. Zhao, Y., Karypis, G., Fayyad, U.M.: Hierarchical Clustering Algorithms for Document Datasets. Data Min. Knowl. Discov. 10(2), 141–167 (2006)

Multi-Objective Genetic Algorithms, NSGA-II and SPEA2, for Document Clustering

Jung Song Lee, Lim Cheon Choi, and Soon Cheol Park

Division of Electronics and Information Engineering,
Jeonbuk National University, Jeonju, Jeonbuk, Republic of Korea
{ei200411147,cis1124,scpark}@jbnu.ac.kr

Abstract. This paper proposes the multi-objective genetic algorithm (MOGA) for document clustering. The studied, hierarchical agglomerative algorithms, *k*-means algorithm and general genetic algorithm (GA) are more progressing in document clustering. However, in hierarchical agglomerative algorithms, efficiency is a problem ($O(n^2\log n)$), *k*-means algorithm depends on too much the initial centroids, and general GA can converge to the local optimal value when defining an objective function which is not suitable. In this paper, two of MOGA's algorithms, NSGA-II and SPEA2 are applied to document clustering in order to complete these disadvantages. We compare to NSGA-II, SPEA2 and the existing clustering algorithms (*k*-means, general GA). Our experimental results show the average values of NSGA-II and SPEA2 are about 28% higher the clustering performance than the *k*-means algorithm and about 17% higher the clustering performance than the general GA.

Keywords: Document Clustering, Genetic Algorithm, Multi-Objective Genetic Algorithm, NSGA-II, SPEA2.

1 Introduction

Clustering is an unsupervised technique to group the meaningful data from a large amount of data [1]. Document clustering, which is one part of a clustering is important in the information retrieval field [2]. Generally document clustering algorithms are hierarchical agglomerative algorithms, *k*-means algorithm and genetic algorithm (GA).

Hierarchical agglomerative algorithms differ in how they compute cluster similarity, i.e., Single-link, Average-link, and etc. Efficiency is a problem with all these algorithms. Because the complexity of these algorithms is $O(n^2\log n)$, where n is the number of documents [3].

k-means algorithm, one of the most widely used, is a family of partitional clustering algorithms. This algorithm is easy to implement and its complexity is linear in n, where n is the number of documents. However, it has a problem in which its performance much depends on the initial centroids [3].

T.-h. Kim et al. (Eds.): ASEA/DRBC/EL 2011, CCIS 257, pp. 219–227, 2011.

GA is randomized search and optimization techniques guided by the principles of evolution and natural genetics [4]. GA provide near optimal solutions for objective function in complex, large and multimodal landscapes [5]. Document clustering using general GA uses the cluster validity index as the objective function. It is thought as the optimization problem in which value of cluster validity index becomes the maximum or minimum. The performance of document clustering using general GA is better than other clustering algorithms [6]. However, it has the following problems: First, it can converge to the local optimal value when defining an objective function which is not suitable [7]. Second, the clustering result is optimal in one cluster validity index but it can't be optimal in the other cluster validity indices [8]. Third, the computational complexity is increased if the chromosome is encoded by centroid vector.

To solve these problems, we applied the multi-objective optimization problem (MOP) for document clustering. And to solve MOP for document clustering, we used multi-objective genetic algorithm (MOGA).

This paper is organized as follows. The next section describes about MOGA which is document clustering proposed in this paper. Section 3 explains experimental results of document clustering algorithms (*k*-means, general GA, NSGA-II, SPEA2). Section 4 concludes and discusses future work.

2 MOGA for Document Clustering

MOP is to find the solution by optimizing several objective functions. Generally it is almost impossible to simultaneously optimize all objective functions [9]. Various algorithms had been being suggested in order to solve MOP. However, there are certain limitations when tackling MOP. In order to solve these problems, GA was paid attention. GA can make various solutions which are close to the Pareto optimal solution set in a single run of the algorithm [10].

2.1 Overview of Document Clustering Using MOGA

MOGA for document clustering proposed in this paper is constructed of two steps as shown in Fig. 1. First, the document vector is constructed. Second, document is clustered by using MOGA.

In step for constructing the document vector, the feature of each document is extracted. Afterward, by using this, the document vector is constructed. In document clustering using MOGA, documents are clustered by using the evolution operator and objective function, gene structure which is suitable to document clustering.

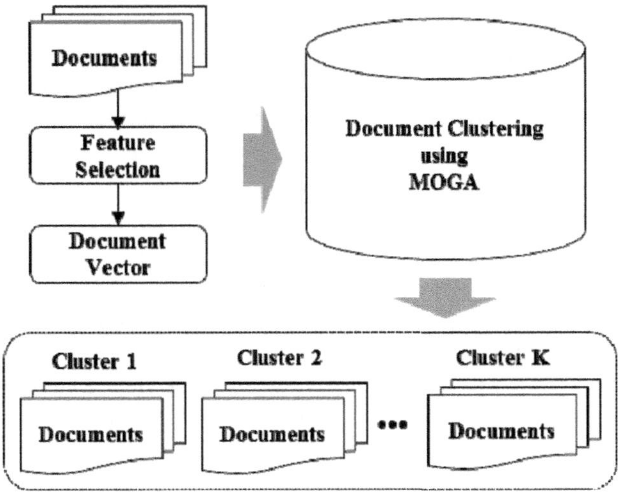

Fig. 1. Overview of document clustering using MOGA

Document vector. Document vector that represents character of document is formed by the weights of the terms indexed in a document. The nth the document vector whose size is 1 by t given by

$$d_n = \langle W_{n,1} \quad W_{n,2} \quad \cdots \quad W_{n,t} \rangle \tag{1}$$

where, t is the number of the total indexed terms in the corpus and W is the term weight. We extract the indexed terms by using stop word and Poter's stemming [11], and calculate the term weight by using Okapi rule [12].

Term weight. In our preprocessing algorithm, we adopt Okapi rule for term weight calculation. Okapi rule is defined as

$$W_{ij} = \frac{tf_{ij}}{tf_{ij} + 0.5 + 1.5 \times \frac{dl}{avgdl}} \times idf_j \tag{2}$$

where, idf_j=log(N/n), N is the total number of documents in the data sets, and n is the number of documents in which the ith term comprised. tf_{ij} is the term frequency of ith indexing term in document j. dl is the length of the document and $avgdl$ is average length of documents.

2.2 MOP for Document Clustering Using GA

In document clustering, general GA having a single objective function was thought as the problem of optimizing a single clustering validity index [6]. Occasionally, the optimal cluster solution which we get from general GA optimizes the cluster validity index of objective function, but it is unable to optimize the different cluster validity indices [8]. That is, all other cluster validity indices are unable to be optimized. Therefore, in this paper, document clustering was thought as MOP optimizing two cluster validity indices through this trade off relation. And, to solve MOP we use GA approach (MOGA).

Optimization for document clustering is defined as

$$\underset{C_i \in P}{\arg\max} \left(F_{CH}(C_i) \wedge F_{DB}(C_i)\right) \tag{3}$$

where, CH and DB are represented as CH index [13] and DB index [14] for the objective functions. P is the population and $P=\{C_1, C_2, \dots, C_i, \dots, C_n\}$. C_i is a chromosome and $C_i=\{CN_1, CN_2, \dots, CN_j, \dots, CN_m\}$. CN_j is the cluster number assigned to a document and $1 \le CN_j \le K$. n is the number of chromosome in a population, m is the number of documents and K is the number of cluster.

2.3 Chromosome Encoding and Evolution Operators

The chromosome has the size of m and was encoded by the integer of 1~K. Each gene represents a document. And the value of a gene represents a cluster number. That is, document clustering using MOGA finds the optimal cluster group of each document. Each chromosome which represents document cluster is computed by two objective functions (CH, DB index). And, we used to multi-point crossover and uniform mutation in the evolution operators [4].

2.4 Objective Functions

When the CH index [13] is the maximum value by using inter-group variance and between-group variance, clustering result is good cluster. The CH index given by

$$CH = \frac{B/(n \quad k)}{W/(k \quad 1)} \tag{4}$$

where, B stands for Between Group Sum of Squares and W stands for Within Group Sum of Squares. n is the number of documents, k is the number of clusters.

The DB index [14] is based on similarity measure of clusters (R_{ij}) whose bases are the dispersion measure of a cluster (s_i, s_j) and the cluster dissimilarity measure (d_{ij}). In similarity, maximum value is considered as the good cluster when the cluster is evaluating with the cosine similarity. The DB index given by

$$DB = \frac{1}{n_c} \sum_{i=1}^{n_c} R_i \,. \tag{5}$$

Subsequently, R_i is

$$R_i = \max(R_{ij}), i \text{ and } j = 1 \cdots n_c \,. \tag{6}$$

R_{ij} defined as

$$R_{ij} = \frac{s_i + s_j}{d_{ij}} \tag{7}$$

where, n_c is number of clusters. s_i and s_j are the average similarities of documents in cluster centroids, i and j respectively. d_{ij} is the dissimilarity between the cluster centroids, i and j.

2.5 Document Clustering Using NSGA-II and SPEA2

In this paper, NSGA-II [15] and SPEA2 [16] is used for document clustering among the MOGAs. The main criticisms of NSGA have been as follows: First, High computational complexity. Second, Lack of elitism. Third, Need for specifying the sharing parameter. For this, NSGA-II with Fast Non-Dominated Sort and Crowding Distance Assignment operation was proposed.

Under elite preserve strategy, SPEA stores the Pareto optimal solution set separately. However, the diversity cannot be maintained due to the fitness assignment problem. For this, SPEA2 with the new fitness assignment and archive truncation method was proposed.

Pseudo code of document clustering using NSGA-II and SPEA2 are as shown Fig. 2 and Fig. 3.

```
procedure : Document Clustering using Multi - Objective Genetic Algorithms (NSGA - II)
begin
  t ← 0
  CN ← RANDOM (K)  // k is the number of cluster
  C ← {CN_1, CN_2, ···, CN_j}  // j is the number of documents
  initialize population P(t)  // P(t) ← {C_1, C_2, ···, C_i}
  while(not termination condition) do
    P'(t) ← compute ovjective functions P(t) // ovjective functions are the CH index and DB index
    F'(t) ← fast nondominated sort P'(t)
    A'(t) ← fitness assignment F'(t)
    offspring Q(t) ← evolution operate A'(t)
    R(t) ← P(t)+Q(t)
    R'(t) ← fast nondominated sort R(t)
    P(t+1) ← fitness assignment R'(t)
    t ← t+1
  end
end
```

Fig. 2. Pseudo code of document clustering using NSGA-II

```
procedure : Document Clustering using Multi-Objective Genetic Algorithms (SPEA2)
begin
  t ← 0
  CN ← RANDOM(K)  // k is the number of cluster
  C ← {CN_1, CN_2, ..., CN_j}  // j is the number of documents
  initialize population P(t)  // P(t) ← {C_1, C_2, ..., C_i}
  while (not termination condition) do
    P'(t) ← compute ovjective functions P(t) // ovjective functions are the CH index and DB index
    achiveset update E(t)
    F'(t) ← fitness assignment P'(t)
    mating pool M(t) ← tournament select F'(t) ∪ E(t)
    P(t+1) ← evolution operate M(t)
    t ← t+1
  end
end
```

Fig. 3. Pseudo code of document clustering using SPEA2

3 Experimental Results

In this section, we will discuss the performance of document clustering using MOGA proposed in this paper. MOGA performance was compared with k-means, general GA in document clustering. And we use the F-measure [17] to evaluate the performance of these clustering algorithms.

To evaluate performance of clustering algorithm, we adopted Reuters-21578 data sets. In the current test data set 1 containing 200 documents from four topics (earn 50, gnp 50, cocoa 50, gas 50), data set 2 containing 200 documents form four topics (coffee 50, trade 50, crude 50, sugar 50), and data set 3 containing 300 documents from six topics (coffee 50, trade 50, crude 50, sugar 50, grain 50, ship 50) are selected. After being processed by word extraction, stop word removal, and Poter's stemming, there are respectively 2654, 3436 and 4210 index terms. And the term weight of the index terms which is extracted by using the Okapi rule was calculated.

The number of population in our general GA and MOGA is 300. These algorithms are terminated when the number of generations reaches to 1000 or when the iterations without improvement reach consecutive 20.

Fig. 4, Fig. 5, and Fig. 6 show the performances of clustering algorithms with the different data set. General GA is general genetic algorithm with a single objective function. NSGA-II and SPEA2 are MOGA with two objective functions. DB and CH are objective function applied in the clustering algorithm. DB is stands for DB index with cosine similarity and CH is stands for CH index.

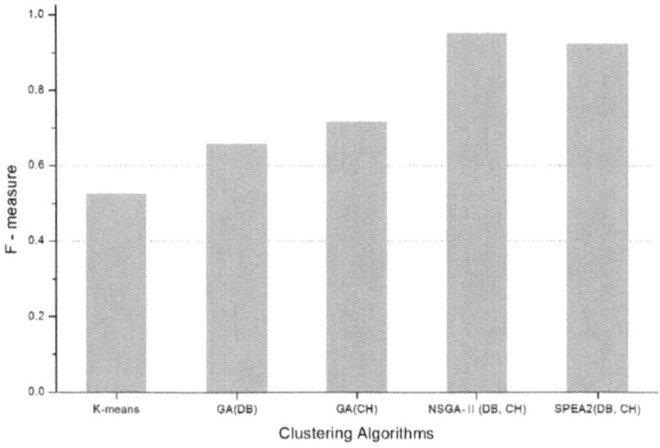

Fig. 4. The clustering performance for data set 1 (earn 50, gnp 50, cocoa 50, gas 50)

In Fig. 4, the F-measures of clustering algorithms (*k*-means, GA(DB), GA(CH), NSGA-II(DB,CH), SPEA2(DB,CH)) with data set 1 are 0.53, 0.66, 0.72, 0.95 and 0.92 respectively. The average of F-measure of document clustering using GA is 0.69 and using MOGA is 0.94. Especially, the F-measure of MOGA using NSGA-II with data set 1 is 0.95 which is much better than another clustering algorithm.

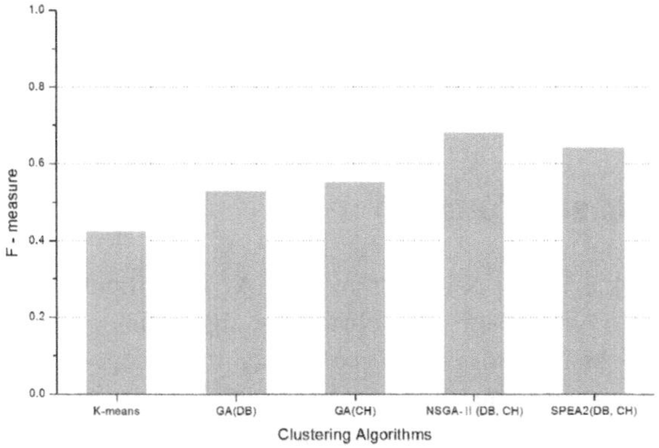

Fig. 5. The clustering performance for data set 2 (coffee 50, trade 50, crude 50, sugar 50)

From, Fig. 5 we can see that the respective F-measure of clustering algorithms, with data set 2, are 0.42, 0.53, 0.55, 0.68 and 0.64. The average of F-measure of document clustering using GA is 0.54 and using MOGA is 0.66. Especially, the F-measure of MOGA using NSGA-II with data set 2 is 0.68 which is much better than another clustering algorithm.

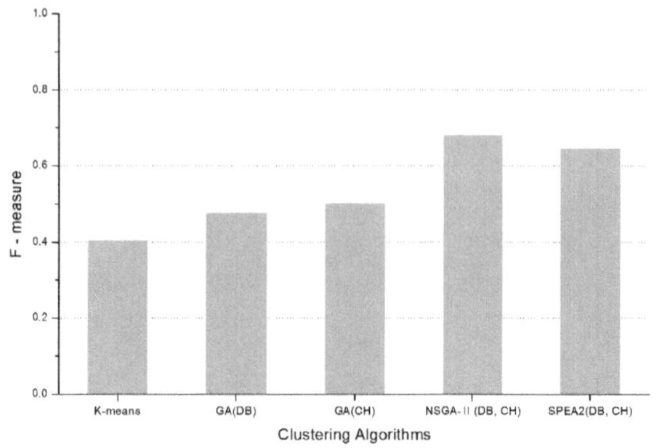

Fig. 6. The clustering performance for data set 3 (coffee 50, trade 50, crude 50, sugar 50, grain 50, ship 50)

From, Fig. 6 we can see that the respective F-measure of clustering algorithms, with data set 3, are 0.40, 0.47, 0.50, 0.68 and 0.64. The average of F-measure of document clustering using GA is 0.49 and using MOGA is 0.66. Especially, the F-measure of MOGA using NSGA-II with data set 3 is 0.68 which is much better than another clustering algorithm.

The clustering performances in all data sets shows highest F-measure when NSGA-II was used and next, SPEA2. For each data set, the average F-measure value of MOGA using NSGA-II and SPEA2 is 0.94, 0.66 and 0.66. Consequently, document clustering applying MOGA shows the performance about 28% better than the *k*-means, about 19% than GA(DB), and about 16% than the GA(CH).

4 Conclusion and Future Work

Two of MOGA's algorithms, NSGA-II and SPEA2 are proposed for document clustering and compare with the other clustering algorithms. NSGA-II and SPEA2 showed about 28% higher clustering performance than the k-means and about 17% higher the clustering performance than the general GA.

In the document clustering, the processing times of MOGA are little bit longer than the exiting other algorithms. So, we will apply the matrix factorization technique or parallel processing to the algorithms in near future. In addition, various cluster indices will be tried as objective functions to improve the performance of the algorithms.

Acknowledgments. This research was supported by Basic Science Research Program through the National Research Foundation of Korea(NRF) funded by the Ministry of Education, Science and Technology(No. 2011-0004389) And Brain Korea 21 Project.

References

1. Croft, W.B., Metzler, D., Strohman, T.: Search Engines Information Retrieval in Practice. Addison Wesley (2009)
2. Frigui, H., Krishnapuram, R.: A Robust Competitive Clustering Algorithm with Applications in Computer Vision. Pattern Analysis and Machine Intelligence 21(4), 450–465 (1999)
3. Pantel, P., Lin, D.: Document Clustering with Committees. In: 25th Annual International ACM SIGIR Conference on Research and Development in Information Retrieval, Finland (2002)
4. Maulik, U., Bandyopadhyay, S.: Genetic Algorithm-based Clustering Technique. Pattern Recognition 33(9), 1455–1465 (2000)
5. Srinivas, M., Patnaik, L.M.: Adaptive Probabilities of Crossover and Nutation in Genetic Algorithms. IEEE Trans. Syst. Man Cybern. 24(4), 656–667 (1994)
6. Song, W., Park, S.C.: Genetic Algorithm for Text Clustering based on Latent Semantic Indexing. Computers and Mathematics with Applications 57, 1901–1907 (2009)
7. Cha, S.M., Kwon, K.H.: A new Migration Method of the Multipopulation Genetic Algorithms. The Korea Institute of Information Scientists and Engineers (2001)
8. Halkidi, M., Batistakis, Y., Vazirgiannis, M.: On Clustering Validation Techniques. Intelligent Information Systems (2001)
9. Osyczka, A.: Multicriteria Optimization for Engineering Design. Design Optimization, 193–227 (1985)
10. Coello Coello, C.A.: Evolutionary multi-objective optimization: a historical view of the field. IEEE Computational Intelligence Magazine, 28–36 (2006)
11. Choi, L.C., Choi, K.U., Park, S.C.: An Automatic Semantic Term-Network Construction System. In: International Symposium on Computer Science and its Applications (2008)
12. Salton, G., Buckley, C.: Term-Weighting Approaches in Automatic Text Retrieval. Information Processing & Management (1988)
13. Calinski, T., Harabasz, J.: A Dendrite Method for Cluster Analysis. Communications in Statistics (1974)
14. Davies, D.L., Bouldin, D.W.: A Cluster Separation Measure. IEEE transactions on Pattern analysis and Machine Intelligence (1979)
15. Deb, K., Pratap, A., Agarwal, S., Meyarivan, T.: A Fast Elitist Multiobjective Genetic Algorithm: NSGA- II. IEEE Transaction on Evolutionary Computation 6(2), 182–197 (2002)
16. Zitzer, E., Laumanns, M., Thiele, L.: SPEA2: Improving the Strength Pareto Evolutionary Algorithm for Multiobjective Optimization. In: Proceedings of the EROGEN Conference, pp. 182–197 (2001)
17. Fragoudis, D., Meretakis, D., Likothanassis, S.: Best Terms: an Efficient Feature-Selection Algorithm for Text Categorization. Knowl. Inform. Syst. (2005)

Implementing a Coordination Algorithm for Parallelism on Heterogeneous Computers

Hao Wu[1] and Chia-Chu Chiang[2]

[1] Microsoft Corporation, 16011 Northeast 36th Way,
Redmond, Washington 98052, USA
[2] Department of Computer Science, University of Arkansas at Little Rock,
Little Rock, Arkansas 72204, USA
cxchiang@ualr.edu

Abstract. Writing parallel programs is not a simple task. Especially, writing parallel programs for a heterogeneous computing environment is even more difficult. In this paper, a coordination algorithm is implemented to support programmers to write implicitly parallel programs in a heterogeneous computing environment. The programs can be written in a sequential programming language that the programmers are familiar with and feel comfortable to write. In addition, the implicit parallelism allows programmers not to worry about how the tasks are to be performed in parallel. The programmers only focus on what the tasks are supposed to do.

Keywords: programming model, coordination, middleware, and parallelism.

1 Introduction

One obstacle to heterogeneous distributed programming for parallelism is that programmers are overwhelmed to consider the low-level details of programming including communication, synchronization, and data marshalling and un-marshalling. In addition, programmers are compelled to program at a low level with specific target platforms or are faced with unfamiliar programming models.

In this paper, we are implementing a coordination algorithm to support implicit parallel programming. The code implemented from the coordination algorithm will help synchronize the participating processes to accomplish parallel tasks. Therefore, the programmers are only required to implement what the tasks are supposed to do. The processes exchange messages through a communication infrastructure in CORBA. The details of communication issues handled in the CORBA environment reduce the burden of programmers. In addition, parallel programs can be written in a sequential programming language.

2 Related Work

The paper written by Joung and Smolka [8] introduces a taxonomy of languages for multiparty interaction that covers the complexity of the coordination implementation

T.-h. Kim et al. (Eds.): ASEA/DRBC/EL 2011, CCIS 257, pp. 228–236, 2011.

problem. Some languages and implementations for multiparty interactions can be found in the early articles [6-7]. However, they are closely related to the underlying computer and network architecture and they cannot be easily adapted to other architectures and networks. CAL [6-7] is one of the specification languages for multiparty interaction. It supports the proxy generation from the specification language. Java is used to implement the computations of interacting functions in participating objects. A tool called weaver combines both sources into a piece of code that can be compiled, linked, and executed on the top of a CORBA which contains a multiparty CORBA service (MPCS) to support coordination. Currently, the CAL approach only supports the mapping to Java.

IP (Interacting Processes) was proposed and developed by Francez and I. R. Forman [5]. They present IP as the basis of programming languages for multiparty interaction. IP provides language constructs for multiparty interactions, teams and superimpositions. A team consists of a set of participating processes. Superimposition facilitates separation of concerns by allowing for a stepwise refinement with correctness preserving transformations. The feasibility of implementing multiparty interactions in IP is also addressed by the authors.

Linda was developed by Nicholas Carriero and David Gelernter [1]. It is a coordination language that extends different programming languages such as C, FORTRAN, and Modula 2 for parallel programming with a shared data space. The shared data space is called tuple space and six basic operations for accessing the tuple space. The tuple space is shared by all processes. However, the operations for accessing the tuple space are low-level operations. Low-level language operations are considered harmful for distributed parallel programming [4].

Radestock and Eisenbach [9] present a coordination model based on intercepting messages. The model has been successfully integrated to a CORBA system. The two authors proposed a list of good properties to support coordination systems. The model of coordination presented in their paper enables the coordination of components in open adaptive systems, independently from the underlying distributed system platforms. However, the model suffers from performance problems due to infinite messages that may be stored in the message space.

The MANIFOLD [2] is a control-oriented coordination language. The language is based on the IWIM model (Idealized Worker Idealized Manager), which is a generic, abstract communication model that separates computation from communication and cooperation modules. But it directed to aspects such as processing or the flow of control, rather than large-scale data handling.

3 Coordination Algorithm

In this section, we present a coordination algorithm for the multiparty interaction expressed in IP, given by Chiang and Tang [3]. Since the processes participating interactions are not known until the run time, the coordination has to be centered on interactions. In our algorithm, a process is denoted as P and each multiparty interaction is denoted I. When a process is ready to participate in multiparty interactions, it starts a separate thread for each interaction in which it is prepared to participate. Let there be k interactions in which process P_j is ready to participate and let those interactions be $I_1, I_2, \ldots, I_k$. Also let the proxy thread created by P_j for I_r (1 <= r <= k) is denoted $T_{j,r}$ where the first subscript of T, j, is the index of the participating process and the second subscript of T, r, is the index of the interaction to communicate with. In addition, process P_j starts a thread manager denoted M_j to manage all the communications and coordinate proxy threads $T_{j,1}$, $T_{j,2}$, …, and $T_{j,k}$. Hence, there are three kinds of communicating processes and threads in the algorithm: proxy thread $T_{j,r}$, interaction process I_r and proxy thread manager M_j corresponding to the process P_j. Proxy thread $T_{j,r}$ communicates with process I_r and the proxy thread manager M_j. Proxy threads $T_{j,r}$ (r = 1…k) also communicate with each other. The underlying communication system is implemented as follows: 1) Communications are asynchronous and carried out through middleware CORBA, and 2) Each thread or process maintains a queue for the incoming messages. Figure 1 shows the relationships among two processes, two thread managers, five proxy threads, and three interactions.

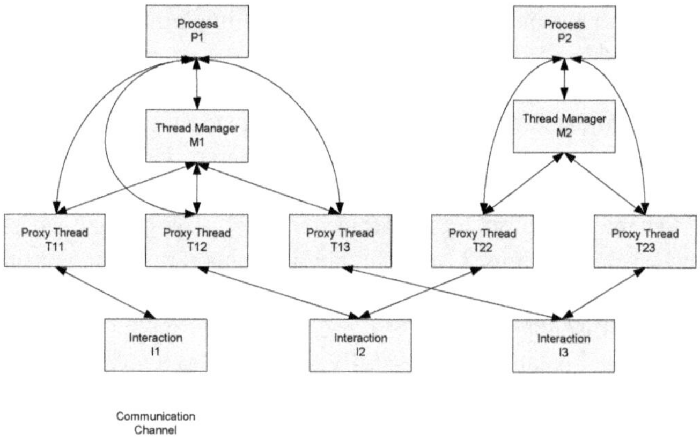

Fig. 1. Coordination relationships

The basic idea behind the algorithm is as following. The proxy thread $T_{j,r}$ first sends a request with its identity to I_r and then waits for a message called 'All-Met' back from it. I_r saves the request from $T_{j,r}$ and will not send 'All-Met' back until all the participating processes are committed to participating in the interaction. Upon receiving the commitment from all the participating processes, the $T_{j,r}$ proxy thread enters into the second phase. Depending on the states of other proxy threads of P_j, $T_{j,r}$ can either send a 'commitment' or 'withdrawal' to I_r. Since only one proxy thread of P_j is allowed to participate in one interaction at a time, thus the other proxy threads of P_j must withdraw. I_r sends a 'fail' message to a proxy thread if it has ever received a 'withdrawal' from its participating processes or another peer interaction has been selected for execution. Upon receiving the 'success' message, $T_{j,r}$ signals M_j to kill all other proxy threads of P_j. If $T_{j,r}$ receives the fail message, it continues to the next round of coordination.

According to the algorithm described above, the pseudo code of Interaction, I, Process, P, and Proxy Thread, T, can be found in [10]. Classes 'Interaction' and 'T' should be executed as threads that need to be synchronized during the runtime. Basically, both of them maintain a message queue for incoming messages. If the message queue is empty, the thread will block itself, and whoever sending a message to the thread will wake up the thread if necessary. The queue ensures the messages will be handled in the first-in and first-out (FIFO) order. And also note there are critical variables and critical functions in the code that can only be exclusively accessed by one thread at a time.

4 Implementation of the Coordination Algorithm

4.1 The IDL

An IDL file shown in Figure 2 is written to implement the coordination algorithm.

```
module CoordinationAlgorithm
{
interface T
{
void request_interaction();
void setTState(in long sta);
void addTMessage(in long mes);
};
                    interface Interaction
{
void addProcess(in T ot, in long state);
void set_Interaction_State(in T ot, in long state);
};
};
```

Fig. 2. Coordination algorithm in IDL

A CORBA module is a namespace that acts as a container for related interfaces and declarations. It corresponds closely to a Java package. So the IDL compiler will generate 'CoordinationAlgorithm' package for Java code. The 'interface' in the CORBA IDL will map to a Java interface statement. So after compiling the CORBA IDL, we will get two Java interfaces: 'T' and 'Interaction'. Each operation statement in the IDL generates a corresponding method statement in the generated Java interface. Those are methods will be invoked by a process. The 'T' IDL interface contains three operations: 'request_interaction()', 'setTState()', and 'addTMessage()'. A thread 'T' represents a process to show the interests in some interactions with other processes and selects an enabling interaction for the process to participate in. The 'request_interaction()' operation is called by a process when the process is interested in participating some interactions by having its proxy instances to request interactions respectively. The 'setTState()' operation is called by either the 'Process' or the 'Interaction' process to update the states of 'T'. The 'addTMessage()' operation is called by an 'Interaction' process to inform 'T' regarding the interaction state of coordination. The 'Interaction' interface contains two operations: 'set_Interaction_State()' and 'addProcess()'. The 'set_Interaction_State()' operation is called by the 'T' class to inform the 'Interaction' process about T's current state. The 'addProcess()' operation is invoked by the 'T' to register itself to the corresponding 'Interaction' processes of interest. The 'T' and 'Interaction' interface in IDL provides operations for the management of the interactions via coordination among the participating processes.

4.2 Mapping IDL to Java

J2SE v.1.5 provides a tool, idlj to compile the OMG IDL file. The tool idlj produces the stub and skeleton code that implements location transparency, along with the infrastructure code for connecting to the ORB. Use the -fall option when running the idlj compiler to get both the server and client side Java code. Some generated files are for both server and client use.

For the 'Interaction' interface, the following Java files are generated by the IDL compiler.

- InteractionPOA.java
  This is an abstract class which our server class should extend from. It is the stream-based server skeleton, including basic CORBA functionality such as '_invoke()' for marshalling /unmarshalling data. To implement the coordination algorithm, the server class, 'InteractionImpl' will extend 'InteractionPOA'.
- _InteractionStub.java
  This class is the client stub, providing CORBA functionality such as 'readObject()' and 'writeObject()' for marshalling/unmarshalling data. The two methods 'addProcess' and 'set_Interaction_State' are contained in this class.
- Interaction.Java
  This interface is to be used in both server and client code. This Java interface contains the empty methods defined in the IDL interface. The actual implementation of the methods is defined in 'InteractionOperations.java'.
- InteractionOperations.java
  This interface is to be used both server and client side. All of the operations defined in the 'Interaction' interface are included in this file. We are required to implement the 'addProcess' and 'set_Interaction_State' methods in this class.
- InteractionHelper.java
  This class provides auxiliary functionality, including the narrow() method required to cast CORBA object references to their proper types. The 'Helper' class is responsible for reading and writing the data type to CORBA streams.
- InteractionHolder.java
  This class holds a public instance member of the 'Interaction' class. The class delegates to the '_read' and '_write' methods in the 'Helper' class for reading and writing.

The 'T' interface also generates functions including TPOA.java, _TStub.java, T.java, TOperations.java, THelper.java, and THolder.java.

4.3 Add Implementation of the Coordination to the Code

The code of 'InteractionImpl', 'TImpl', and 'Process' needs to be implemented for completion. The logics of 'InteractionImpl', 'TImpl' and 'Process' are described in Section 3. Their implementations can be found in [10].

5 The Dining Philosophers Problem

In the dining philosopher problem, there are n philosophers and n forks. Each philosopher has to pick up both forks beside him/her in order to eat. We use the IP language to describe the problem.

```
1  DINING_PHILOSOPHERS :: [Philosopher_0 || Philosopher_1 ||…|| Philosopher_{n-1}
2     || Fork_0 || Fork_1 ||…|| Fork_{n-1}]
3     Philosopher_i :: i=0,n-1
4     *[S_i ='thinking' → S_i :='hungry'
5     □
6     S_i= 'hungry' & get_fork_i [] → S_i :='eating'
7     □
8     S_i :='eating' →  S_i := release_fork_i[] & 'thinking'
9     ]
10    Fork_i :: i=0,n-1
11    *[get_fork_i [] → release_fork_i []
12    □
13    get_fork_(i+1) mod n [] → release_fork_(i+1) mod n []
14    ]
```

In the program, lines 1 and 2 give the program name: DINING_PHILOSOPHERS, and define the processes of Philosophers and Forks. The statements from lines 3 to 9 define the process Philosopher_i. Philosopher is in one of the three states: 'thinking', 'hungry', and 'eating'. The Philosopher_i can move to 'hungry' from 'thinking' (line 4). The Philosopher_i can be in the 'hungry' state and try to get the forks by participating the 'get_fork_i' interaction. After the 'get_fork_i' interaction is executed, the state will change to 'eating' (line 6). After leaving the 'eating' state, the process executes the 'release_fork_i' and the state moves to 'thinking' (line 8). The statements from lines 10 to 14 define the process 'Fork_i'. 'Fork_i' is ready to attend two interactions, 'get_fork_i' and '$\text{get\_fork}_{(i+1) \bmod n}$', but the coordination protocol makes sure that it can only participate in one of them at a time. Therefore, the forks can only be picked up by one philosopher at a time.

5.1 A Solution to the Problem

With the auxiliary code generated from the coordination algorithm, the following code is the code required to be developed by the programmers for the solution of the problem.

5.1.1 Development of the 'RunInteraction' Class

Programmers develop the 'RunInteraction' class to initiate the interaction for coordination. The program performs the following steps,

a. Create and initialize an ORB instance,
b. Get a reference to the root POA and activate the POAManager,
c. Create an Interaction servant instance (the implementation of one CORBA Interaction object, that's 'InteractionImpl' object) and tell the ORB about it,
d. Get a CORBA object reference from the servant,
e. Get the root naming context,
f. Bind the new object in the naming context under a name, here we can use 'Interaction' followed by the interaction index,
g. Start the Interaction servant, and
h. Start ORB and wait for the invocations.

5.1.2 Development of the 'ForkProcess' Class

The 'ForkProcess' class extends from 'Process' class, and overrides the request_interaction () method to simulate the Forks behavior. Whenever fork is available, it will request an interaction.

5.1.3 Development of the 'PhilosopherProcess' Class

The 'PhilosopherProcess' class extends from 'Process' class, and overrides the request_interaction () method to simulate the Philosophers behavior. When a philosopher is started, he/she will think for a period of random time and then request an interaction.

5.1.4 Development of the 'RunForks' Class

Programmers develop the 'RunForks' class to register the forks to the interactions. The program performs the following steps,

a. Create and initialize the ORB,
b. Obtain the root Naming Context,
c. Find the Interaction servant by the name,
d. Narrow the object reference,
e. Register Forks to Interactions, and
f. Invoke the request_interaction() operation.

5.1.5 Development of the 'RunPhilosophers' Class

The 'RunPhilosophers' class register the philosophers to the interactions. The program performs the following steps,

a. Create and initialize the ORB,
b. Obtain the root Naming Context,
c. Find the Interaction servant by the name,
d. Narrow the object reference,
e. Register Philosophers to Interactions, and

f. Invoke the request_interaction() operation.

5.1.6 Compilation and Execution of the Programs

Use the NetBean IDE to compile all the generated files (InteractionPOA.java, _InteractionStub.java, Interaction.java, InteractionOperations.java, InteractionHelper.java, InteractionHolder.java, TPOA.java, _TStub.java, T.java, TOperations.java, THelper.java, and THolder.java), the coordination layer implementation files (InteractionImpl.java, Process.java, and TImpl.java) and the application layer implementation files (Services.java, ForkProcess.java, PhilosopherProcess.java, RunForks.java, and RunPhilosophers.java). The compiler will generate the byte code in class files. To execute the class files,

a. Start orbd (Object Request Broker Daemon)
   The orbd tool with Java SDK is used to enable clients to transparently locate and invoke persistent objects on servers in the CORBA environment.
   To start orbd from an MS-DOS system prompt (Windows), enter:
   orbd -ORBInitialPort 1050 -ORBInitialHost localhost
   where - ORBInitialHost is a required command-line argument. We can replace this with the name of the host, or the localhost if both client and server run on the same machine.
   - ORBInitialPort is also a required command-line argument. It is recommend to use a port number greater than 1024.
b. Start the Interaction services.
   To start the Interaction services from an MS-DOS system prompt (Windows), enter: java ApplicationLayer.Services
c. Start the Forks processes
   To start the Forks processes from an MS-DOS system prompt (Windows), enter:
   Java ApplicationLayer.RunForks
d. Start the Philosophers processes

To start the Philosophers processes from an MS-DOS system prompt (Windows), enter: Java ApplicationLayer.RunPhilosophers

6 Summary

We implemented a coordination algorithm to support the development of implicitly parallel programs in a heterogeneous computing environment. CORBAL IDL is used to implement the coordination algorithm as well as the underlying communication infrastructure. Thus, all the processes are communicating to each other through this communication infrastructure in a heterogeneous computing environment. The code implemented from the coordination algorithm will manage the synchronization of parallel processes.

To develop parallel programs, programmers create the template programs by extending the classes implemented from the coordination algorithm. The programmers complete the templates by implementing the tasks that are required to be done by coordination. Thus, our work of implicit parallel programming allows programmers to focus on the implementations of the tasks, not the details of parallelism. However, experiments have shown that programmers might have difficulty in expressing tasks to be synchronized. Currently, this work supports the IDL to Java mapping. Future work may include the IDL mapping to C and C++.

Acknowledgments. We would like to thank Dr. Peiyi Tang and Dr. Sean Geoghegan for their valuable comments.

References

1. Ahuja, S., Carriero, N., Gelernter, D.: Linda and Friends. Computer 19(8), 26–34 (1986)
2. Arbab, F.: The Coordination Language Manifold (March 18, 2011), retrieved from `http://www.ercim.org/publication/Ercim_News/enw35/arbab.html`
3. Chiang, C.-C., Tang, P.: Middleware Support for Coordination in Distributed Applications. In: Proceedings of the Fifth IEEE International Symposium on Multimedia Software Engineering (MSE 2003), pp. 148–155 (December 2003)
4. Chiang, C.-C.: Low-level language constructs considered harmful for distributed parallel programming. In: Proceedings of the 42nd Annual ACM Southeast Conference (ACM ACMSE 2004), April 2-3, pp. 279–284. Huntsville, Alabama (2004)
5. Francez, N., Forman, I.R.: Interacting Processes. Addison-Wesley (1996)
6. Garg, V., Ajmani, S.: An Efficient Algorithm for Multiprocess Shared Events. In: Proceedings of the 2nd Symposium on Parallel and Distributed Computing (1990)
7. Joung, Y.-J., Smolka, S.: A Completely Distributed and Message-Efficient Implementation of Synchronous Multiprocess Communication. In: Yew, P.-C. (ed.) Proceedings of the 19th International Conference on Parallel Processing, vol. 3, pp. 311–318 (August 1990)
8. Joung, Y.-J., Smolka, S.: A Comprehensive Study of the Complexity of Multiparty Interaction. Journal of the ACM 43(1), 75–115 (1996)
9. Radestock, M., Eisenbach, S.: Component Coordination in Middleware System. In: Proceedings of the 2nd International Conference of Coordination Languages and Models (September 1997)
10. Wu, H.: A Java Prototype Implementation of Coordination for Heterogeneous, Distributed, and Parallel Programming, M.S. Thesis, Department of Computer Science, University of Arkansas at Little Rock (May 2010)

Efficient Loop-Extended Model Checking of Data Structure Methods*

Qiuping Yi[1], Jian Liu[1], and Wuwei Shen[2]

[1] Institute of Software Chinese Academy of Sciences, Beijing, 100190, China
[2] Department of Computer Science Western Michigan Univarsity, Kalamazoo, 49009, MI
qiuping@nfs.iscas.ac.cn, liujian@iscas.ac.cn,
wuwei.shen@wmich.edu

Abstract. Many methods in data structures contain a loop structure on a collection type. These loops result in a large number of test cases and are one of the main obstacles to systematically test these methods. To deal with the loops in methods, in this paper, we propose a novel loop-extended model checking approach, abbreviated as LEMC, to efficiently test whether methods satisfy their own invariant. Our main idea is to combine dynamic symbolic execution with static analysis techniques. Specifically, a concrete execution of the method under test is initially done to collect dynamic execution information, which is used to statically identify the loop-extended similar paths of the concrete execution path. LEMC statically checks and prunes all the states which follow these loop-extended similar paths. The experiments on several case studies show that LEMC can dramatically reduce as many as 90% of the search space and achieve much better performance, compared with the existing approaches such as the Glass Box model checker and Korat.

Keywords: Model Checking, Loop-Extended, Symbolic Execution.

1 Introduction

While various software model checking approaches [5, 11, 8, 27, 16] have been proposed to test whether a program behaves properly on its all possible inputs within some given bounds, few approaches can handle the data-oriented program containing loop structures. They are one of the main obstacles to systematically test, and we think a technique for efficiently handling loop structures is desperately needed.

Many methods and techniques have been proposed to deal with state explosion in model checking, such as partial order reduction [12], and tools based on predicate abstraction [14] such as SLAM [2] or MAGIC [5]. However, none of them is effective in reducing the search space of data-oriented programs. Only a few existing approaches are based on data-oriented programs, such as Korat [4], which generates all valid states within some given bounds and then checks whether the method under

* This research was supported in part by the Key Project of Chinese Academy of Sciences (No.KGCX2-YW-125) and the National Science and Technology Major Project.

T.-h. Kim et al. (Eds.): ASEA/DRBC/EL 2011, CCIS 257, pp. 237–249, 2011.

```
class Node {
    int key;
    Node next;
}

Class SortedList {
    Node header;
    void insert(int data) {
    Node node = new Node();
    node.key = data;
    node.next = null;
    Node previous = null;
    if (header== null) {
          header = node;return ;
    }
    Node current = header;
    while (current!=null) {
          if (current.key< data) {
               previous = current;
               current = current.next;
          } else
               break;
          }
          if (previous == null)
               header = node;
          else
               previous.next = node;

          node.next = current;
    }
    @Declarative
    boolean repOK( ) {
          if (!isOrdered(header)) return false;
          return true;
    }
    @Declarative
    static boolean isOrdered(Node node) {
          if (node == null) return true;
          if (node.next != null && node.key>node.next.key)
               return false;
          if (!isOrdered(node.next)) return false;
          return true;
    }
}
```

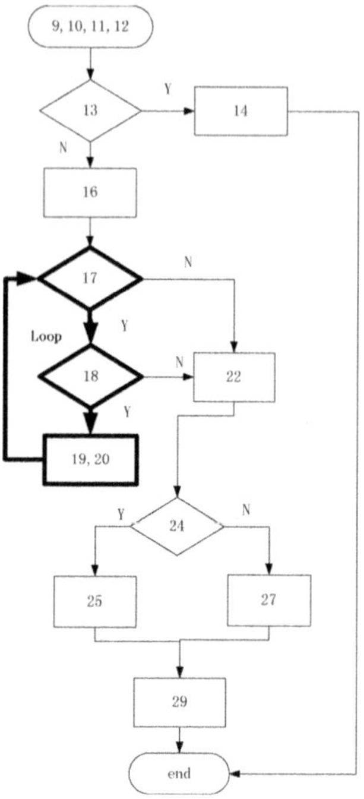

Fig. 1. The left graph is an implementation of the method *insert* of *SortedList*. The right graph is the control flow graph of the method *insert*.

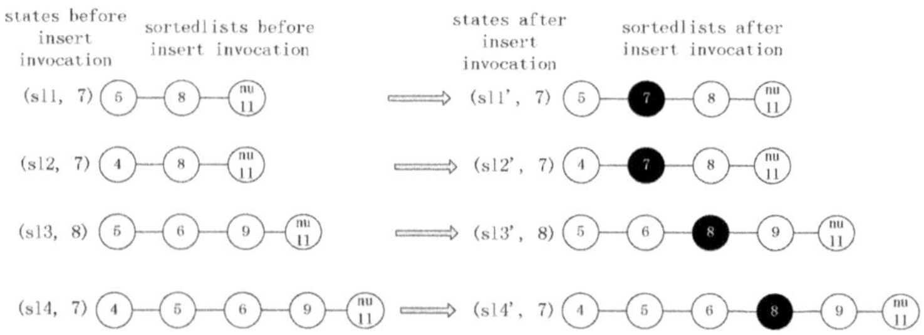

Fig. 2. Four states and their corresponding post states. Every state is constituted of a sorted list and a number to be inserted into the list. The new added nodes are highlighted.

test behaves properly on these states. However, data-oriented programs always have numerous valid states even when a small number of values for each variable are considered. The Glass Box model checker [25], PIPAL, identifies a set of similar states in the search space and checks these states at the same time.

Consider checking whether the method *insert* in *BinarySearchTree* class satisfies a post-condition. Existing model checking approaches, such as CMC [22], systematically generate all binary search trees within a given tree height *n*, and check every *insert* invocation on every tree. Since the number of trees with maximal height *n* is exponential in *n*, it is infeasible to separately check all the trees. The Glass Box model checkers [9, 25] find a set of similar binary search trees on which the *insert* invocations can be checked at the same time. But they don't exploit the loop information in the method under test. This paper presents a novel loop-extended model checking approach to dynamically find loop structures and quickly check and reduce the search space of programs containing loop structures on collection types.

The rest of this paper is organized as follows. Section 2 illustrates the idea of LEMC via a simple example. Section 3 describes our loop-extended model checking approach in detail. Some experimental results are shown in Section 4. Section 5 discusses some related work and we draw a conclusion in Section 6.

2 Example

In this section, we illustrate our approach via a simple example. Consider the implementation of *SortedList* in Fig. 1. A state *(sl, d)* represents a sorted list *sl* with parameter data *d*. Every invocation on *insert* is regarded as a transition from a pre-state *(sl, d)* to a post-state *(sl', d')*. As described in Section 1, the checkers, using black box technique, systematically generate all sorted lists within given bounds and check every *insert* invocation on them. Unfortunately, the search space is still huge even it is limited. For example, when sorted lists have at most ten nodes and each key value has ten different values at maximum, there are still (2^10)×(10^11) states.

Next, we show how LEMC efficiently and exhaustively tests *insert*. Considering *insert* is invoked on state *(sl1, 7)* in Fig. 2, state *(sl1', 7)* depicts the post-state after the invocation. Using line numbers to represent program statements, LEMC detects that the execution goes through path *p1*, {9, 10, 11, 12, 13, 16, 17, 18, 19, 20, 17, 18, 22, 24, 27, 29}, when the method *insert* is invoked on *(sl1, 7)*. It also discovers many other states, such as state *(sl2, 7)*, also go through *p1*. All the states which go through *p1* behave similarly, so LEMC checks and safely prune them at the same time.

Path *p3* {9, 10, 11, 12, 13, 16, 17, 18, 19, 20, 17, 18, 19, 20, 17, 18, 22, 24, 27, 29}, produced by the invocation on state *(sl3, 8)*, goes through the loop in bold twice, but covers the same program locations as *p1*. We call *p1* and *p3* are loop-extended similar paths. LEMC statically constructs *p3* with the information of *p1*, and statically checks and prunes the states, such as *(sl3, 8)*, which go through *p3*. Similarly, LEMC constructs another loop-extended similar paths *p4*, {9, 10, 11, 12, 13, 16, 17, 18, 19, 20, 17, 18, 19, 20, 17, 18, 19, 20, 17, 18, 22, 24, 27, 29}, which state *(sl4, 7)* goes through. Consequently, LEMC statically checks and prunes all the states which go through path *p1*, *p3*, *p4* after the invocation on state *(sl1, 7)*. LEMC repeats the above process until all the states in the bounded search space have been explored.

The method *repOK* in Fig. 1 implements the validity checking of a sorted list. LEMC only considers the valid states on which the method *repOK* returns true. A correct *insert* implementation guarantees that the sorted list after the *insert* invocation is also a valid sorted list. Therefore, after every invocation on state *s*, LEMC checks whether the post-state *s'* is a valid state. If *s'* is an invalid state, LEMC finds an error in *insert*, because the method *insert* translates a valid sorted list to an invalid one.

```
1 void check(Bounds b) {    // b bounds the search space
2     S = {s ∈ b|s.repOK() == True}// init the search space
3     while (S != ∅) {
4         s = selectFrom( S)   // select a state randomly
5         p = run(s)           // run a concrete execution
6         lbs = getPatterns(p);
7         sums = summaries(lbs);   // summarize loop bodies
8         n = sizeOf(lbs);

          // statical analysis
          // ti is the iteration of lbs[i] in p'
9         while (hasNextValuation(t1~tlb_n ))
             // set t1~tlb_n satisfying the given constraints
10           b = setUnderConstrs(t1~tlb_n)
11           if (!b)    break; // no valid valuations
12           p'= LESPOf()      // compute the LESP of  p
13           if (!isValid(p')) continue; // whether p' is a valid path
14           S' = similarStates (p')
15           if (some s' in S' fails check) { // check S'
16                print ("error" and a counterexample)
17           }
18           S = S - S'        // prune the search space
19        }
20    }
21 }
```

Fig. 3. Pseudo-code of the search algorithm in LEMC

3 Approach

3.1 Search Algorithm

Fig. 3 presents the search algorithm of LEMC. Based on some given bounds *b*, it first initializes the search space to all the valid states on which the method *repOK* returns true at line 2. Between line 3 and line 19, LEMC repeats the checking and pruning process until the search space is exhausted. In each iteration, LEMC randomly chooses an unchecked state *s* in search space *S* at line 4 and gets a concrete execution path *p* by invoking the method under check on *s* at line 5. They repeatedly compute the loop-extended similar path *p'* of *p* at line 12, and all the states *S'* that follow *p'* at line 14. LEMC checks whether the method under test works properly on states in *S'* during line 15 to line 17, and reports an error via a counterexample at line 16 when any state *s'* fails the check. Otherwise, LEMC safely prunes *S'* from *S* at line 18. The other unmentioned lines in the algorithm will be explained in the following sections.

3.2 Representation of the Search Space

LEMC represents the search space *S* as a formula and uses a SMT-based solver to find states in *S*. Every field in the bounded search space is represented as a solver variable with a constraint which specifies its domain. Consider the implementation of

Field	Domain	Field	Domain
header	{null, n0}	insert.data	{1,2,…,10}
ni.next(0<=i<=9)	{null, n1}	ni.key(0<=i<=9)	{1,2,…,10}

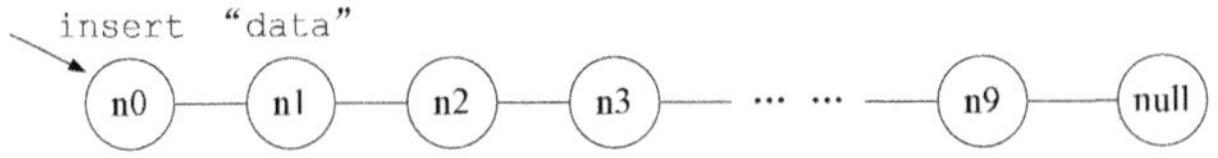

Fig. 4. The search space of the *insert* method of *SortedList*, which has ten nodes at most, and the key of every node and parameter *data* are between 1 and 10

the method *insert* in Fig. 1. When every list has at most ten nodes and each key value has ten different values from 1 to 10, the bounded search space is shown in Fig. 4. To test the method exhaustively, LEMC checks every state in the search space. Note that every node may be *null*, so the search space could include many invalid states, which are not taken into account by the algorithm in Fig. 3.

Every formula over the solver variables represents a set of states in the search space. For example, the valid states of the method *insert* of Fig. 1, which contain one node and the key of the node and parameter *data* are both limited to between 1 to 2, can be represented by the formula $header \neq null \wedge n0.next = null \wedge n0.key \geq 1 \wedge n0.key \leq 2 \wedge data \geq 1 \wedge data \leq 2$. A SMT-based solver can provide a satisfying assignment to the variables in the formula, and then the assignment is decoded into a concrete state in the search space. Generally, a formula, representing a subspace satisfying property p in the search space S, can be represented as $S \wedge p$.

3.3 Initialization of Search Space

LEMC only considers the valid states as input of the method under test. So LEMC finds a formula to describe all the valid states, and uses it to initialize the search space. To accomplish this goal, LEMC analyzes the method *repOK* and the methods invoked transitively by *repOK* to produce a formula representing all the valid states in the bounded search space. For example, all the valid lists which have two nodes at most, can be represented as the formula $header = null \vee (n0.next = null \vee (n0.key \leq n1.key \wedge n1.next = null))$. To efficiently translate the method *repOK* to a formula, we constraint the method *repOK* and the methods it transitively invokes to declarative methods [25]. A declarative method may not contain object creations, assignments, loops, exception handlers or other statements which have side effects.

3.4 Loop Body and Loop Pattern

A program path is a sequence of program locations, represented using line numbers, encountered along a particular execution. We use $b, \ldots, l_i, \ldots, l_j, \ldots, e$ to represent a complete path, where b and e are representing the beginning and ending of the path respectively. l_i and l_j represent the same program location if $l_i = l_j$. Any sub-sequence $l_i, \ldots, l_j$ of a path is a *loop body* if and only if $l_i = l_{j+1} \wedge l_k \neq l_i \ (i < k \leq j)$. LEMC relates every loop body with a unique tag. A *loop body* can iterate different times in different program path. We regard a complete path as a special loop body, the *top* loop body, which iterates one and only once. A loop body is *nested* when it contains other loop body(ies). LEMC records the line numbers that a concrete execution goes through and dynamically discovers loop bodies. Whenever a loop body is found, LEMC replaces it with its unique tag to discover a nested loop body.

The *loop pattern* of a loop body is a sequence of line numbers, which describe the loop structure the loop body go through. So the loop bodies which go through the same loop structure but different time share the same loop pattern. Consider path *p3* {9, 10, 11, 12, 13, 16, 17, 18, 19, 20, 17, 18, 19, 20, 17, 18, 22, 24, 27, 29}, getting from the invocation of the method *insert* in Fig. 1 on state *(sl3, 8)* in Fig. 2. LEMC discovers loop body {17, 18, 19, 20, 17, 18, 19, 20} with loop pattern {17, 18, 19, 20}. At ending, LEMC finds the *top* loop body {9, 10, 11, 12, 13, 16, *tag*, 17, 18, 22, 24, 27, 29}, whose loop pattern is also {9, 10, 11, 12, 13, 16, *tag*, 17, 18, 22, 24, 27, 29}, where tag represents the unique tag of the founded loop body.

We give the following definitions based on the description above.

- **LESP:** Path *p'* is a loop-extended similar path (LESP) of path *p* if and only if path *p'* and *p* have the same number of loop bodies, and for every loop body lb of *p*, *p'* has a loop body *lb'* which shares the same *loop pattern* with *lb*.
- **Similar states and LESSs:** Similar states are the states which go through the same path of a program, and loop-extended similar states (LESSs) are the states which go through one LESP sharing the same loop pattern.

3.5 Dynamic Analysis

To construct LESPs of a path statically, LEMC symbolically executes [20] the method under consideration along with its concrete execution to collect dynamic information, which will be used by the following static analysis. Specifically, when getting a concrete execution path *p* LEMC firstly computes its loop bodies and their *loop patterns* at line 6 of the algorithm as described before. Furthermore, LEMC summarizes the founded loop bodies at line 7 of the algorithm. A *summary* of loop body *lb* is constituted of its preconditions and post effects. Preconditions are the path conditions generated in the loop body, and post effects are the effects on the fields in the search space and the local variables of the program under test.

LESP uses two assistant structures. One is *Heap* which records the symbolic values of every field in the search space, and the other is *Stack* recording the symbolic values of the local variables in the program under test. Like [25], a concrete value is *null*, *true*, *false*, or any allocated object. Symbolic value *sv* is a set of guarded value such as$\alpha \rightarrow v$, where α is a formula, and *v* is a concrete value. Every guarded value $\alpha \rightarrow v$ represents the concrete value of *sv* is *v* when formula α is true, and true → v can be abbreviated as *v*. If a program statement changes the variables in *Heap* or *Stack*, the statement generates a post *effect*, which is a three-tuple *(ln, oldValue, newValue)* representing the symbolic value of *oldValue* (a variable in *Heap* or *Stack*) is changed to that of *newValue* at line *ln* when *oldValue* is not empty, and when *oldValue* is empty it represents a new concrete value *newValue* is generated at line *ln*. Fig. 5 shows the summaries of the path when invoking *inset* on *(sl1, 7)* of Fig. 2.

Loop Body	Summary	
	Preconditions	Post Effects
17, 18, 19, 20	17: current != null 18: current.key < data	(19, previous, current) (20, current, current.next)
9, 10, 11, 12, 13, 16, *tag*, 17, 18, 22, 24, 27, 29	13: header != null 17: current != null 18: current.key >= data 24: previous != null	(9, , node) (10, node.key, data) (11, node.next, null) (12, previous, null) (16, current, header) (27, previous.next, node) (29, node.next, current)

Fig. 5. The summaries of the loop bodies of the path getting from invoking the method *inset* of Fig. 1 on *(sl1, 7)* of Fig. 2. *tag* represent a tag of the first loop body.

Change on Heap	Symbolic Branch Conditions
node.key -> data	13: header != null
node.next -> null	17^1: header != null
n1.next -> node	18^1: n0.key < data
node.next -> n2	17^2: n0.next != null
	18^2: n1.key < data
	17^3: n1.next != null
	18^3: n2.key >= data
	24: n0.next != null

Fig. 6. The changes on *Heap* and collected symbolic branch conditions along constructing *p3*. The *i* in n^i represents the *i*-th occurrence of line number *n*.

3.6 Static Analysis

In static analysis, LEMC firstly constructs the LESPs of path *p* discovered by concrete execution, and then statically checks and prunes the LESSs of the LESPs from the search space. Assume *p* contains *n* loop bodies *lb1*, …, *lbi*, …, *lbn* besides the top loop body. LEMC limits the number of iterations of all the loop structures to [1, *t*], then *p* has t^n candidates of LESPs. Using t_i to represent the iterations of lb_i, every assignment to $(t_1, \ldots, t_i, \ldots, t_n)$ corresponds to a LESP candidate of *p*. To prevent generating vast invalid LESPs, LEMC puts some simple constraints on $t_1 \sim t_n$ based on the structure of the program under test when setting $t_1 \sim t_n$. Besides, LEMC checks the validity of the generated LESP before checking the states following it.

After setting a valuation, LEMC uses the loop patterns and the summaries of the founded loop bodies to construct the symbolic branch conditions representing a LESP *p'* of path *p* and its corresponding post-state. Consider path *p1*, whose summaries are shown in Fig. 5. Fig. 6 shows the changes on *Heap* and collected symbolic branch conditions along one of *p1*'s LESP, *p3*, which goes through the first loop body twice.

LEMC checks the correctness for all the similar states that go through the LESP at line 15 ~ 17 in Fig. 3 before pruning them, because a method works correctly on one state cannot assure it works correctly on all the similar states. Considering the following simple *class example,* when invoking method *test* on *x* = *2*, we get a path whose path constraint is *x* >= *0*. Although the execution works correctly on *x* = *2*, we cannot prune all the similar states following the path. Because when invoking *test* on

```
class example {
private int x, a;
public Boolean repOk() {
  if (x>0&&a!=10)    reurn false;
    if (x<=0&&a==10) return false;
    return true;
  }
  public void test(){if (x>=0) a = 10; }
}
```

x = *0*, we get a post-state on which the method *repOK()* returns false. In other words, we find an error in method *test* which can be triggered by setting *x* to 0.

Specifically, for every LESP *p'*, LEMC checks whether all similar states go through *p'* are error-free at line 15 of Fig. 3. LEMC constructs a formula $S' \rightarrow R$, where *S'* is the path constraint of *p'*, and *R* is a formula asserting that every state in *S'* is translated into a state satisfying the method *repOK()*. LEMC uses a SMT solver to find a solution of formula $\sim (S' \rightarrow R)$. If such a solution exists, we find a counterexample exposing an error, else no error is found (and then LEMC safely prunes *S'* from the search space). LEMC constructs the formula representing the method based on the symbolic values of all the fields described by *Heap*. In the *SortedList* example, after invoking the method *insert* on *(sl1, 7)* of Fig. 2, formula *R* will claim *n0.key* < *data* && *n1.key* >= *data*.

4 Experiments

We used ASM framework [18], an efficient toolkit for Java Bytecode Manipulation, to instrument the target program to perform the dynamic analysis, and used an incremental SMT solver, YICES[6], to manage the search space efficiently. Now LEMC only checked Java code. All the experiments were performed on a Linux Ubuntu 9.4 machine with dual core Pentium 2.2.GHz processor and 2 GB memory. We considered a test case time out if the test case either ran out of memory or produced no result within one hour.

To evaluate LEMC, we conducted two experiments. The first was used to check the efficiency of LEMC. We have conducted the following benchmarks: (a) checking the methods *insert, get, and remove* of *SortedList* partially presented in Fig. 1; (b) checking the methods *insert, find, and delete* of *BinarySearchTree* [25]. *SortedList* is structurally identical to single linked lists from the Java Collections Framework, but has sorted elements. Methods *insert*, *get* and *remove* inserts, finds, and removes an element from sorted lists respectively. *BinarySearchTree* is a binary search tree implementation including methods *insert*, *find*, and *delete*, which respectively inserts, finds, and deletes an element from a binary search trees.

All the methods were checked on the states within the bounded search space. In this experiment, the sorted lists (binary search trees) are bounded by *maximum number* (*height*) Both *key* value of nodes and *Int* parameters (such as parameter *data* in the

	Method	Maximum number	Number of states LEMC	Number of states PIPAL	Number of states Korat	Time(s) LEMC	Time(s) PIPAL	Time(s) Korat
Sorted List	insert	1	3	3	200	0.405	0.375	8.265
		2	4	5	3550	0.534	0.537	142.650
		4	4	9		0.741	0.945	time out
		8	4	17		1.146	1.685	time out
		16	4	32		1.971	3.202	time out
		32	4	65		4.043	7.216	time out
		64	4	129		9.668	19.893	time out
		128	4	257		18.712	71.602	time out
	get	1	4	4	200	0.370	0.338	0.679
		2	6	7	3550	0.458	0.508	5.865
		4	6	13		0.556	0.814	time out
		8	6	25		0.593	1.500	time out
		16	6	49		0.887	3.125	time out
		32	6	97		1.878	5.931	time out
		64	6	193		6.249	17.256	time out
		128	6	385		23.810	101.74	time out
	remove	1	4	4	200	0.374	0.346	1.017
		2	6	7	3550	0.497	0.522	13.110
		4	6	13		0.647	0.936	time out
		8	6	25		0.981	1.686	time out
		16	6	49		1.488	3.295	time out
		32	6	97		3.171	7.239	time out
		64	6	193		9.391	19.788	time out
		128	6	385		29.915	108.639	time out

	Method	Max height	Number of states LEMC	Number of states PIPAL	Number of states Korat	Time(s) LEMC	Time(s) PIPAL	Time(s) Korat
Binary Search Tree	insert	1	4	4	200	0.409	0.387	7.951
		2	10	10	60200	0.934	0.874	2331.321
		3	16	22		1.723	1.807	time out
		4	22	46		3.080	3.870	time out
		5	28	94		6.305	10.202	time out
		6	34	190		12.942	61.685	time out
		7	40	382		62.321	228.522	time out
	find	1	4	4	200	0.353	0.346	0.736
		2	8	10	60200	0.643	0.684	154.790
		3	12	22		0.847	1.262	time out
		4	16	46		1.488	2.894	time out
		5	20	94		3.240	7.919	time out
		6	24	190		7.297	56.280	time out
		7	28	382		51.107	216.582	time out
	delete	1	4	4	200	0.536	0.354	1.041
		2	11	13	60200	0.935	0.972	271.931
		3	22	32		2.108	2.348	time out
		4	34	71		3.914	5.497	time out
		5	46	150		8.362	15.595	time out
		6	58	309		31.365	184.558	time out
		7	70	628		177.008	747.476	time out

Fig. 7. The experimental results for the first experiment

method *insert*) were limited to have ten different integer values. When constructing LESPs, we limited the number of iterations to *maximum number* (*height*) for *SortedList* (*BinaySearchTree*). For comparison, we simulated the algorithm used by

	Method	Maximum number	Key scope	Number of mutants	Number of equivalent mutants	Number of killed mutants	Mutant score (%)
Sorted List	insert	1	[1,1]	23	1	12	52
		1	[1,2]			19	82
		2	[1,2]			20	86
		2	[1,3]			21	91
		3	[1,3]			22	95
	get	1	[1,1]	20	0	16	80
		1	[1,2]			18	90
		2	[1,2]			20	100
	remove	1	[1,1]	24	0	16	66
		1	[1,2]			22	91
		2	[1,2]			22	100
Binary Search Tree	Method	Maximum height	Key scope	Number of mutants	Number of equivalent mutants	Number of killed mutants	Mutant score (%)
	insert	1	[1,1]	41	1	27	65
		1	[1,2]			38	92
		2	[1,1]			27	65
		2	[1,2]			40	97
	find	1	[1,1]	34	1	14	41
		1	[1,2]			20	58
		2	[1,1]			14	41
		2	[1,2]			31	91
		2	[1,3]			33	97
	delete	1	[1,1]	57	0	18	31
		1	[1,2]			20	35
		2	[1,1]			39	68
		2	[1,2]			55	96
		3	[1,3]			57	100

Fig. 8. The result of mutation test on the methods tested in the first group of experiments

Korat [4] which separately checked every valid state and PIPAL [25], which separately checked every path in the method under test.

Fig. 7 presents the comparison result of the first experiment. The number of states explicitly checked by LEMC was affected by the loop structure(s) of the method under test. Noting that, for the methods of *SortedList*, LEMC checked only *O(1)* states regardless of the size of the search space. For the methods of *BinarySearchTree*, the number of states explicitly checked appeared to be roughly *O(n)* where *n* is maximum number of the nodes. Obviously, the larger the search space is, the more states can be implicitly checked by LEMC. Different from PIPAL, LEMC checked most states implicitly. Furthermore, it is extremely obvious that LEMC is more scalable than Korat.

To illustrate the soundness of the small scope hypothesis LEMC bases on, we conducted the second experiment, *mutation tests*. We used a java mutant test tool, *mujava* [21, 24], to generate and kill the mutants. Finally, *mujava* presented the mutant score, the ratio of the number of the killed mutants to the number of the total mutants. Known from Fig. 8, almost all the mutants except several equivalent mutants were killed by the test cases within a small scope. So LEMC can find almost all the errors in a method within a given bounds based on small scope hypothesis.

5 Related Work

In this section, we compare LEMC with some extremely related existing approaches. Only a few existing work are concentrated on data-oriented programs, such as Alloy [19], Korat [4] and Glass Box model checking [9, 25], etc. Alloy and Korat generate all valid inputs within some give bounds, and test every valid state with the given bounds explicitly. As shown in Section 2, valid states in a small bounded scope are also very enormous, so it's inefficient to check every valid state separately. The Glass Box model checker [9] uses similarity to efficiently reduce the search space. Different from the Glass Box technique in [9], Modular Glass Box model technique [25] uses path information to find similarity in the search space, and checks all the states that follow the same path at the same time. Different from the existing work, LEMC dynamically discovers its loop information, statically constructs LESPs for p, and checks and prunes all the LESSs that follow these LESPs statically. Our experiments show LEMC can explicitly check remarkable smaller states than PIPAL, and is significantly more scalable than Korat.

For the relevant work for handling loops, the approach in [26] relates every loop with a trip count, which is a symbolic variable representing the times executed by a loop, and then uses a static analysis to determine linear relations between program variables and trip counts. Through trip counts it discovers the indirect relation between inputs and program variables. The approach in [13] dynamically infers the linear relations among induction variables during a dynamic symbolic execution, and infers loop counts based on pattern matching. Unlike the two approaches before, our Loop-extended approach mainly handles the loops in data-oriented programs and these loops always have relations with the search space of the programs under check.

6 Conclusion

In this paper, a new loop-extended model checking method, LEMC, is proposed. LEMC can efficiently deal with the programs with complex data structures, especially with a loop structure which always has relation with its search space. Instead of checking every state in the search space separately as traditional techniques, LEMC statically checks the states which go through the same path in the method under test at the same time. Furthermore, LEMC collects dynamic information during a concrete execution path, and then uses the collected dynamic information to construct all the loop-extended similar paths of the path. Then LEMC statically checks and prunes all the states which follow these loop-extended similar paths. Our experiments show that LEMC, our loop-extended model checker, uses extremely fewer test cases and less time than the other techniques and approaches based on data-oriented programs. Moreover, based on the small scope hypothesis and our mutation test, LEMC increases the confidence of the correctness of the method under test.

References

1. Alur, R., Henzinger, T.A. (eds.): CAV 1996. LNCS, vol. 1102. Springer, Heidelberg (1996)
2. Ball, T., Majumdar, R., Millstein, T.D., Rajamani, S.K.: Automatic predicate abstraction of c programs. In: PLDI, pp. 203–213 (2001)
3. Bongartz, I., Conn, A.R., Gould, N.I.M., Toint, P.L.: Cute: Constrained and unconstrained testing environment. ACM Trans. Math. Softw. 21(1), 123–160 (1995)
4. Boyapati, C., Khurshid, S., Marinov, D.: Korat: automated testing based on java predicates. In: ISSTA, pp. 123–133 (2002)
5. Chaki, S., Clarke, E.M., Groce, A., Jha, S., Veith, H.: Modular verification of software components in c. In: ICSE, pp. 385–395 (2003)
6. Dutertre, B., Moura, L.D.: The YICES SMT Solver (2006), `http://citeseerx.ist.psu.edu/viewdoc/summary?`, do:=10.1.1.85.7567
7. Clarke, E.M., McMillan, K.L., Campos, S.V.A., Hartonas-Garmhausen, V.: Symbolic Model Checking. In: Alur, R., Henzinger, T.A. (eds.) CAV 1996. LNCS, vol. 1102, pp. 419–427. Springer, Heidelberg (1996)
8. Corbett, J.C., Dwyer, M.B., Hatcliff, J., Robby: Bandera: a source-level interface for model checking java programs. In: ICSE, pp. 762–765 (2000)
9. Darga, P.T., Boyapati, C.: Efficient software model checking of data structure properties. In: OOPSLA, pp. 363–382 (2006)
10. Dwyer, M.B., Hatcliff, J., Hoosier, M., Robby: Building Your Own Software Model Checker using the Bogor Extensible Model Checking Framework. In: Etessami, K., Rajamani, S.K. (eds.) CAV 2005. LNCS, vol. 3576, pp. 148–152. Springer, Heidelberg (2005)
11. Godefroid, P.: Partial-Order Methods for the Verification of Concurrent Systems. LNCS, vol. 1032. Springer, Heidelberg (1996)
12. Godefroid, P.: Model checking for programming languages using verisoft. In: POPL, pp. 174–186 (1997)
13. Godefroid, P., Luchaup, D.: Automatic Partial Loop Summarization in Dynamic Test Generation (2011), `http://research.microsoft.com/apps/pubs/?id=144788`
14. Graf, S., Saidi, H.: Construction of Abstract State Graphs with PVS. In: Grumberg, O. (ed.) CAV 1997. LNCS, vol. 1254, pp. 72–83. Springer, Heidelberg (1997)
15. Henzinger, T.A., Jhala, R., Majumdar, R., Sutre, G.: Lazy abstraction. In: POPL, pp. 58–70 (2002)
16. Holzmann, G.J.: The model checker spin. IEEE Trans. Software Eng. 23(5), 279–295 (1997)
17. Jackson, D., Damon, C.: Elements of style: Analyzing a software design feature with a counterexample detector. In: ISSTA, pp. 239–249 (1996)
18. Kuleshov, E.: Using the ASM Toolkit for Bytecode Manipulation (2004), `http://asm.ow2.org/doc/tutorial.html`
19. Khurshid, S., Marinov, D.: Testera: Specification-based testing of java programs using sat. Autom. Softw. Eng. 11(4), 403–434 (2004)
20. King, J.C.: Symbolic execution and program testing. Commun. ACM 19(7), 385–394 (1976)
21. Ma, Y.-S., Offutt, J., Kwon, Y.R.: Mujava: an automated class mutation system. Softw. Test., Verif. Reliab. 15(2), 97–133 (2005)
22. Musuvathi, M., Park, D.Y.W., Chou, A., Engler, D.R., Dill, D.L.: Cmc: A pragmatic approach to model checking real code. In OSDI (2002)

23. Musuvathi, M., Qadeer, S., Ball, T., Basler, G., Nainar, P.A., Neamtiu, I.: Finding and reproducing heisenbugs in concurrent programs. In: OSDI, pp. 267–280 (2008)
24. Offutt, A.J., Untch, R.H.: Mutation 2000: uniting the orthogonal. In: Wong, W.E. (ed.), pp. 34–44. Kluwer Academic Publishers (2001)
25. Roberson, M., Boyapati, C.: Efficient modular glass box software model checking. In: OOPSLA, pp. 4–21 (2010)
26. Saxena, P., Poosankam, P., McCamant, S., Song, D.: Loop-extended symbolic execution on binary programs. In: ISSTA, pp. 225–236 (2009)
27. Visser, W., Havelund, K., Brat, G.P., Park, S.: Model checking programs. In: ASE, pp. 3–12 (2000)

The Systematic Practice of Test Design Automation

Oksoon Jeong

LG Electronics, 221 Yangjae-dong, Seocho-gu, Seoul, Korea
oksoon.jeong@lge.com

Abstract. This paper proposes more practical guidelines for test case generation extending pairwise techniques including boundary value analysis and equivalence partitioning as a generic analysis technique of factors' values which can affect target features. That is, as a factor's values are also classified and any combination technique of them can be selectively applied, it is possible to create robust test cases which can detect interactive defects among factors. On top of that, single fault based test design can be applied to comprise test cases including invalid values of factors. Also, as defining test oracle and details of each factor's value at test design phase, enormous test efforts which should be always considered to create test oracles or to understand automated test data by testers when testing software can remarkably be removed.

Keywords: Pairwise testing, Test case generation, Practical test design, Systematic testing.

1 Introduction

Test design is categorized into black-box and white-box test design. The black-box test design is conducted based on requirements specification[1]. Therefore, the evaluation metric of the test design can be considered as requirements specification coverage. That is, if the implementation of a software product reflects well-defined requirements, the high code coverage can be expected to be achieved by executing test cases generated based on the requirements. On top of that, high defect detection rate can be acquired as skilled test engineers complement abnormal test cases not specified in the requirements specification.

Test design deals with analyzing factors which can affect any feature we want to validate and extracting various values of them, which are conducted investigating how to acquire high code coverage and defect detection rate. As the generic test design techniques, equivalence partitioning and boundary value analysis methods can analyze mutually exclusive and collectively exhaustive test data. Also, there have been some defects specially found by an interaction of two more than factors not by single factor. To detect these kinds of defects, Pairwise[2] and Orthogonal array techniques[3][4] are representative, which not only can combine values of factors of any feature but can generate not duplicated and minimum test cases.

In general, automated tools of black-box test case generation should provide not only how to analyze factors and their values of each feature, but also how to combine the values to generate robust and minimum test data.

T.-h. Kim et al. (Eds.): ASEA/DRBC/EL 2011, CCIS 257, pp. 250–255, 2011.

There are many test design tools using these kinds of test design techniques which are generic and intuitive. However, in practice, most practitioners have felt some kinds of difficulties when trying to apply them because these tools tend to focus on creating robust test data rather than considering how to practically apply them.

The main obstacles mentioned at test design automation are following.

- Many tools using Pairwise technique combine factors' values with the same level regardless any attribute of each value, which results in infeasible and tremendous test cases. As a result, needless review and execution of them could be required. With this point in view, some of these tools recommend to combine only valid values using Pairwise method and to separately comprise abnormal test cases with invalid values in order to generate feasible test cases as possible. But, even these test cases generated with only valid values are too enormous to execute in practice. It is also impossible to test selectively considering priorities of test cases due to limited test resources.
- After automatically generating test cases, manually defining test oracle defined as expected results every test cases, which features through executing the test cases bring out, should be required.
- In general, at automation tools such as Pairwise tools, expression forms of factors and their values are suggested as an item format, which makes combining them more convenient to generate test cases.

Consequently, it is likely to be hard for testers or a third party to understand and to execute these test cases because it is hard for someone who does not define them to understand these implied data.

This paper proposes resolutions to get over these limitations, goes further, and suggests a systematic and practical test design automatic environment which can adequately be applied by practitioners.

2 An Interaction Testing Technique

Defects have various types, one type among which is likely to be injected by developers' mistakes. In general, frequent mistakes of developers often happen when handling of boundary values of data domains of input factors.

As another defect type, a function sometimes has a different result from an expected result due to an interaction among values of factors. For an example, given a kind of Operating System and Printer model type as input factors for testing a printer application, supposing Windows 2000, Windows XP, and Windows 2003 Server as Operating System's values, and Model A and Model B as Printer model's values, test cases which can validate at least once all kinds of values of Operating System and Printer model can be assumed as follows: (Windows 2000, Model A), (Windows XP, Model B), (Windows 2003, Model A)

However, assuming there is an interaction on between Windows 2003 Server and Printer Model B for a feature of the printer application and the result of the combination is different from that of Windows XP and Printer model B, these three test cases are hard to detect the different results corresponding to the factors' interaction.

Therefore, in order to detect defects due to any interaction between factors, test cases should be generated by combining factors' values. The representative combination techniques are Pairwise and Othorgonal array. But, these kinds of combination techniques are usually suitable for only valid values without considering invalid values. In order to comprise abnormal test cases, not only valid values but also invalid values of factors should be analyzed. But, as these techniques combine the values regardless their attributes, test cases combined more than two factors which have an invalid value can be generated. In practice, most of which these cases are infeasible. Also, combining not only valid but also invalid values as the targets of combination results in tremendous test cases many of which are duplicated.

In general, in order to design test cases including any invalid value, as combining one invalid value of each factor and each valid value of the others, the test cases can verify test results according to an invalid value. As a commercial test design tool, AETG[5] includes features of this kind of test case design concept.

3 Single Fault Based Test Case Generation

In practice, considerable test efforts should also be required to execute test cases which deal with only valid values by Pairwise technique. Valid values of factors can be more categorized. That is, a nominal value and boundary values are analyzed according to boundary value analysis in each equivalence class which is classified by equivalence partitioning. Boundary values also consist of valid and invalid values. As valid values on boundary as well as a nominal value are considered as valid values and all of them are combined without distinction, many of these test cases are also infeasible and redundant. The test cases consisting of more than two valid values on boundary could not be infeasible, because they are valid but rare or special value.

Therefore, the valid values on boundary should also be handled like an invalid value when creating test cases. In otherwise, test cases can be comprised as combining one valid value on boundary of each factor and valid and nominal values of the others. The test result according to each valid value on boundary can be verified.

Consequently, the attributes of factors' values can be categorized into general, special and error class. That is, the nominal values are classified as general class, valid values on boundary as special class, and invalid values as error class. Therefore, the way to comprise values of factors can be differently applied based on each attribute. Test cases can be generated by Pairwise combination for the values in general class and by combining each special value or each error value and general values of others for special or error class. For decades, this approach has been studied to test specific hardware components such as combinatorial circuits[6]. At electronic circuits, various operators can be largely classified as AND and OR operator as the most fundamental operators. In hardware, only two things can go wrong with the logic of a circuit. One is that the circuit can be stuck at one and the other at zero. To detect a wrong signal of a circuit as an input, validating all the combination of all signals of input circuits as test data can check whether any fault happens, which tells that the number of test data is 2^n, given the number of the circuit as n. But, only the minimum set of test data can find out the same faults not considering all combinations. Given the AND gate with 2 input, A, B and 1 output C circuits, suppose to validate the result signal of C circuit after entering 0 or 1 signal to A and B circuits.

To find out the output signal of C circuit whether A or B circuit has stuck at fault, 0 or 1, the number of test data would be considered as 4, as 2^2. Let's examine the following case comparing C as an output to the expected result given a fault of A or B stuck at 0 or 1 as an input.

Table 1. The combination of A and B

A	B	C	C (if only A stuck at fault)	C (if only B stuck at fault)
0	0	0	0	0
1	0	0	0	1
0	1	0	1	0
1	1	1	0	0

4 Practical Test Design

Generally, test case design automation considers the efficiency of test case generation, but lacks considerations to acquire the readability or test oracles of test cases generated for testers' or 3rd party's executing. In practice, these lacks result in enormous efforts not only to review each test case and create each test oracle but also to let testers or third party be able to understand.

Therefore, to achieve more practical efficiency of test effort, comprising test oracles and description of factors' value in advance at the time of test design could be suggested.

At this kind of test design concept, test design can be defined as analyzing factors and their values for a certain function and classifying as general, special, and error type.

- First, at test design phase, the description for each general, special, and error value of any factor can be defined. This description can be expanded to comprise each test case with the detailed description according to combining factors' values.
- Second, according to each value's type, a test oracle can be supposed. That is, for special or error values, when comprising one special or error value and general values, it can be expected the result depends on the special or error value. When comprising only all general values, the result can be expected to be normal. Therefore, test oracles can be identified according to each factor's value at test design phase.

The practical template which can guide this kind of this test design is as follows. It has the Microsoft's Excel format which can provide flexibilities for practitioners.

1. List up target functions horizontally and write down the expected result just below each function when normally operating
2. Analyze and define factors and their values vertically.
3. Classify into general, special, or error type for each factor's value.
4. Define the value's description in details.
5. Define the expected result for each error value.
6. For features defined at the Feature area, mark as "x" at the cross cell of factors' values corresponding to each function.
7. At the Filter area, constraints and seeds can be defined with the prefix, [constraints] or [seeds].

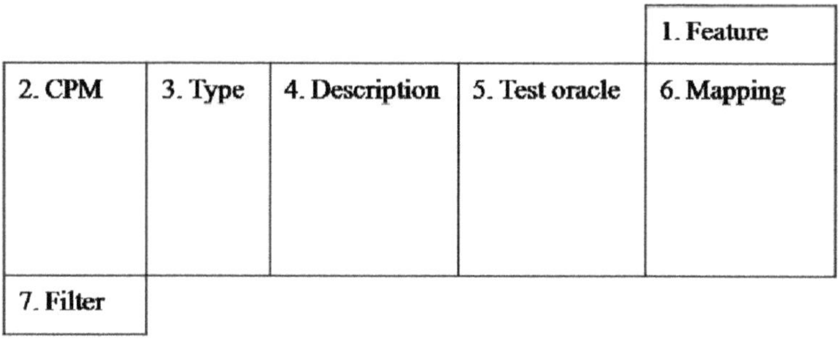

Fig. 1. The excel template for practical test design

5 Practical and Systematic Test Automation Process

Although many methods of test design automation are introduced, practitioners would feel difficulties to practice them if there are no practical guidelines.

In general, the software testing consists of various activities such as test planning, requirements analysis, test design, and test execution. But, in practice, a test engineer's role is assigned to overall test activities according of a unit of a software product rather than each test activity. That is, the methods to do these activities cannot be viewed and tend to depend on a test engineer's skills or experiences.

Therefore, a new test engineer who tests a same product would repeat the same trial and error because it is hard to share the know-how.

This paper also proposes not only a theoretical method for test design but also web-based system for overall activities of software testing using the method. To provide convenience of practical application of test design techniques, the following system can be proposed.

- At requirements analysis phase, the user interface menu can be provided to register target features to validate.
- At test design phase, the features to analyze and define factors, choices, constraints, and seeds are provided.
- At test case generation phase, when combining factors' choices, the amount of test cases can be controlled according to test resources. This can be possible through

Pairwise & Single fault combination(strong) and Pairwise & Single-fault combination(weak). That is, for the strong test case generation, general and special values are combined for Pairwise combination and error values for Single-fault combination. For the weak test case generation, only general values are combined for Pairwise combination and special and error values for Single-fault combination.

6 Conclusion

This paper proposed the resolutions of various limitations always mentioned at test case design automation such as the selective method of test case generation, early consideration of test oracle and high readability of test cases and web-based system for automated and practical testing using test design techniques. This approach helps test engineers to remove useless and enormous test efforts for testing, which leads them to focus on more efficient and effective test design. As a test activity among test activities which test engineers should concentrate on is identified, at test execution phase when manual test efforts should be consumed, outsourcing resources can be applied after test design and test case generation by test engineers.

7 Related Works

As a generic method of test case generation, analyzing factors and their values is based on black-box test design technique. Although considering the best combination method through analyzing interactions among factors, there must be redundancy test cases through combinations of unnecessary interactions or to detect defects injected by 2 more than interactions among factors would be missed.

That is, the most efficient test design can be achieved through combination of factors' values according to analyzing source code structures and identifying the correct interactions among factors.

References

[1] Richardson, D.J., Owen O'Malley, T.: Cindy Tittle: Approach to Specification-Based Testing. In: ACM SIGSOFT 1989, TAV3, pp. 86–96 (1989)

[2] Tai, K.C., Lei, Y.: A Test Generation Strategy for Pairwise Testing. IEEE Transactions on Software Engineering 28(1) (2002)

[3] Mandl, R.: Orthogonal Latin Squares: An Application of Experimental Design to Compiler Testing. Comm. ACM 28(10), 1054–1058 (1985)

[4] Lazic, L., Mastorakis, N.: Orthogonal Array application for optimal combination of software defect detection techniques choice. WEAS Trans. Computers 7(8) (August 2008)

[5] Cohen, D.M., Dalal, S.R., Fredman, M.L., Patton, G.C.: The AETG System: An Approach to Testing. IEEE Tran. Software Eng. 23(7) (July 1997)

[6] Armstrong, D.B.: On Finding a Nearly Minimal Set of Fault Detection Tests for Combinational Logic Nets. IEEE Tran. Electronic Computer EC-15(1) (February 1966)

Application Runtime Framework for Model-Driven Development

Nacha Chondamrongkul[1] and Rattikorn Hewett[2]

[1] School of Information Technology, Mah Fah Luang University, Chiang Rai, Thailand
[2] Department of Computer Science, Texas Tech University, Lubbock, Texas, USA
nacha.cho@mfu.ac.th, rattikorn.hewett@ttu.edu

Abstract. Model-driven development aims to overcome the complexity of software construction by allowing developers to work at the high-level models of software systems instead of low-level codes. Most studies have focused on model abstraction, deployment of modeling languages, and automated supports for transforming the models to implemented codes. However, current model-driven engineering (MDE) has little or no support for system evolution (e.g., platform, meta-model). This paper takes the vision of MDE to further transform models to running systems. We present a framework for developing an MDE runtime environment that supports the model-driven development of enterprise applications to automatically deploy the models and produce the running applications. Furthermore, the framework supports platform evolution by providing an infrastructure that is robust to changing requirements from new target platforms. The framework architecture, its underlying infrastructure and mechanisms are described and illustrated on a running enterprise application system for semi-automated price quotation approval service.

Keywords: model-driven engineering, enterprise applications, run-time environments.

1 Introduction

Technologies in network, communication and Internet have enabled highly sophisticated software that results in demanding requirements (e.g., operating in distributed, embedded computing environments with diverse devices and platforms). Software development becomes increasingly complex. *Model-driven engineering* (MDE) aims to shield software developers from the complexity of software construction by allowing software to be developed and maintained at the high-level models of software systems instead of low-level codes [4]. Most existing work has focused on deployment and integration of model artifacts (e.g., XML-based configuration files) [6] and producing implemented codes from detailed design models (e.g., WebML [3], AndroMDA [2]). However, current MDE tends to lock-in on the abstractions and technologies employed initially. This makes it hard for the systems developed by model-driven approaches to adapt to changes (e.g., platforms, meta-models) when the systems evolve through life cycles. Traditional software evolution typically assumes a

T.-h. Kim et al. (Eds.): ASEA/DRBC/EL 2011, CCIS 257, pp. 256–264, 2011.

fixed development platform but this is not always the case in MDE environments. To support platform evolution, the underlying MDE infrastructure (e.g., the application framework and code generator) needs to adapt to the changing requirements of new target platforms with minimum effects to the software models. Current MDE has little or no support for platform evolution [4].

Our research takes the vision of MDE software development to further transform models to running systems instead of codes [6]. To realize this vision, it is desirable to develop MDE environments where models are primary means for developers and systems to interact, configure and modify executing software systems in a controlled manner. Such environments should also provide mechanisms for runtime environment management and for adapting and evolving the systems produced. This raises two important questions: "*how can models be cost-effectively used to manage executing software?*" and "*how can models be used to effect changes to running systems in a controlled manner*?" [6]. Our work aims to study these issues.

This paper presents a framework for developing MDE runtime environments that support the development of enterprise applications from models by automatically generating codes and executing the codes to produce the results of the running applications. The framework provides an underlying infrastructure, interfaces and mechanisms to support 1) the deployment of light-weight models of integrated data, business logic, and organization, 2) semi-automated model transformations to interactive running enterprise applications, and 3) application robustness to evolving target platforms. Furthermore, unlike most model-driven enterprise application frameworks [7], [5], [13] our framework provides a combination of all three important capabilities of enterprise application development, namely integration of structured and unstructured data, incorporation of business process models, and supports for platform evolution.

The rest of the paper is organized as follows. Section 2 discusses our motivating scenario and its corresponding models. Section 3 describes the proposed application runtime framework including its architecture, components and mechanisms. Section 4 illustrates the proposed approach on an enterprise application for automated price quotation approval service as described in our scenario. Section 5 discusses related work. The paper concludes in Section 6.

2 Motivating Real-World Application

2.1 A Scenario

Consider a motivating scenario of a simple semi-automated enterprise application to support a request for quotation approval that we will use in this paper. Customers send price quotes of a product to a supplier company where a *sales representative* selects or proposes a quote and sends it for approval. A *sales manager* reviews the quote, cost/profit analysis and the quotation letter, makes a decision whether to reject or approve it, and sends an e-mail notification to the sales representative. Some quote may require a second approval (e.g., when the quote deviates from a listed price) and so a *sales director* examines a customer profile and repeats the approval process. A rejected quote is sent back to the sales representative for re-work. After the price quotation is approved, a detailed document of the quotation and a letter can be created and sent to the customer by a *business administrator*. Manual quotation approval is a time-consuming process that can cause a delay in product delivery. Model-driven development of such enterprise application system would be useful because different companies may have different product details while sharing the same business logic in the quotation approval process.

2.2 Application Blueprint

Based on the scenario describing what the enterprise application does and how it is to be used, we create an *application blueprint*, a set of models of important aspects of the enterprise application system to be developed in the MDE environment. The blueprint models are associated with a running application design represented by a graphical model or a workflow diagram. The application blueprint consists of three main models:

- *Data Model* representing data entities, each of which contains data fields with corresponding data types (e.g., integer, string), or values, which can be unstructured data (e.g., formatted file and image). Data model also represents relationships among data entities.
- *Process Model* representing business logic of the enterprise application process in terms of a workflow diagram, where each box represents an activity of the process and the logic follows sequences of activities from top to the bottom of the model. Each activity may be performed by a user of a certain role, or software components.
- *Organizational Model* representing a hierarchical structure of user roles within the organization that the application is to be deployed. This gives the scope of functionality they can perform.

Each model in the blueprint is transformed to an XML-based Intermediate Execution Language (IEL) by applying a set of syntactical mapping rules. The results serve as inputs for our proposed framework.

As an example, data entities and their relationships in the data model of the quotation approval scenario are shown in Figure 1 a). Each quote from a customer may have one or more quote entries for each product. The model omits details of data fields. For example, the customer entity may contain two data fields: first name and last name of type string, and a data field image whose value is an unstructured data file of the customer photo. Figure 1 b) shows a quotation approval process of the described scenario. Here a sales representative creates or retrieves a price quote, which is sent to a sales manager to review and decide if the quote is approved or rejected and so on. As shown in Figure 1 c), the enterprise application to be built involves three user roles, namely, sales representative, sales manager and sales director. Also, each sales manager can have one or more sales representatives.

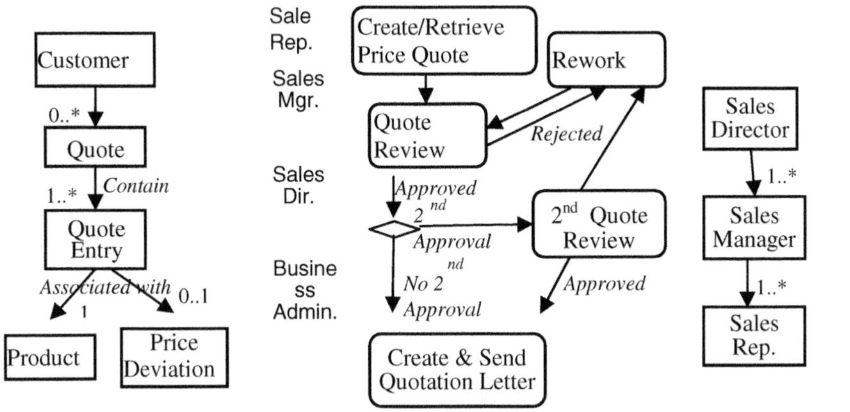

a) Data Model b) Process Model c) Organizational Model

Fig. 1. Quotation approval application blueprint

3 The Proposed Application Runtime Framework

3.1 The Architecture and Components

The proposed MDE runtime framework architecture contains multiple layers, namely *client, presentation, application* and *foundation services* as shown in Figure 2. The client layer includes devices and hardware that users use to access to and interact with the framework during the application development.

The presentation layer contains the *application presentation engine* (APE) that includes a pre-built user interface customized to presentation configurations defined by the application blueprint models. Theses configurations are loaded in the initialization and ready to be used by APE. The pre-built user interface has button controls for a variety of actions and function calls including authentication, create, update, delete data entity, and list tasks in user inbox.

The next layer is the application layer, which has three core components: *Data Runtime Engine* (DRE), *Process Runtime Engine* (PRE), and *Organization Runtime Engine* (ORE). These components facilitate a runtime environment that is customized to the application design as specified in the application blueprint. DRE manages the data and operations (e.g., create, store, view, delete) required by the running application, whereas PRE controls execution flows of the application based on the process model described in the blueprint. Finally, ORE controls access of users and subsystems based on their roles, authorities and usage of the running application.

Each core component is built on one or more native components to perform a certain function. For example, as shown on the right of Figure 2, the DRE core component contains two native components: Hibernate [10] and Alfrsco CMS [14] for handling data persistence. On the other hand, the PRE core component contains the jBPM [15] native component to route the workflow execution, while the ORE core

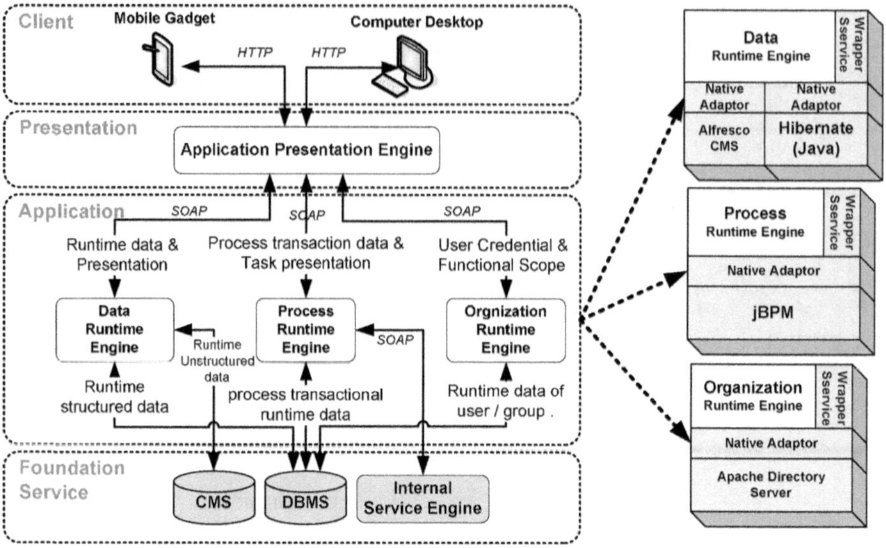

Fig. 2. Overview of the proposed application runtime architecture

component uses the Apache Directory Server [1] native component to verify user credentials and organizational structures. Each native component typically runs on a certain application server platform. By exploiting an appropriate adapter for each plug-in of the native component, the proposed architecture can be adapted to any platform. The adapter takes the blueprint models (specified by IEL or any modeling language) to generate appropriate configurations and codes required by its corresponding native component. Thus, our architecture supports platform evolution.

As shown on the right of Figure 2, each core component relies on its *wrapper service* to provide core functions to be used by its native components. Examples of these functions include creating, updating, and deleting a data entity and searching by a data field by the DRE wrapper service, or executing an activity and listing received activities in a user inbox by the PRE wrapper service, or authentication and authorization by the ORE wrapper service.

Finally, the foundation service layer provides basic supports for the application layer containing *Database management system* (DBMS), *Content Management System* (CMS) and *Internal Service Engine* (ISE). DBMS provides data to appropriate components in the application layer (e.g, structured and unstructured data for DRE, transactional data for workflow execution in PRE, and data for verifying user credentials and roles in ORE). CMS manages runtime unstructured data (e.g., document and images) to be cooperated with necessary structured data for the running application. ISE executes in-house developed functions (e.g., create formatted document, and export data) that are deployed as web services. This provides ease of integration with other external web services, which ISE may exploit. Thus, our architecture is flexible. The services interact by using a commonly used SOAP protocol [11] and are triggered by user actions during the application runtime, or PRE calls during the workflow execution.

3.2 Mechanisms for the Runtime Environment

We now describe mechanisms offered by the proposed application runtime framework for: 1) *generation of presentation configurations*, 2) *data entity integration*, and 3) *native code transformation*, respectively. First, when a user accesses a running application, the application engine retrieves relevant application runtime data and automatically renders a user interface according to the presentation configuration produced based on the blueprint models retrieved during system initialization. The data retrieval is performed over SOAP with wrapper services in the application core components. The framework can support multiple running applications by centralized runtime data storage that allows data sharing across multiple running applications.

Second, because the framework supports multiple running applications, it is possible that these applications may use the same data entities or user roles. The framework provides mechanisms to first check if there is any identical data entity or a user role. If so, it recursively merges them by adding uncommon attributes from each data entity to the merged data entity. Such a merge helps support data consistency in the application runtime framework.

Finally, during initialization, after the core component retrieves relevant models from the most updated application blueprint expressed in IEL, it transforms IEL into a desired native code. For example, the Hibernate native component deploys the two native codes: Hibernate mapping file and POJO Java class, while the jBPM native component deploys the BPMN XML native code. Similarly, the Apache Directory Server native component deploys the LDIF code. For each native component, the code is automatically transformed by using a corresponding native adapter's XSLT (Extensible Style-sheet Language Transformations) [16] style sheet and a built-in XSLT processor. The resulting native codes are compiled and deployed. Consequently, data entities and schemas are created on the DBMS (by Hibernate), process definition according to the workflow process model is deployed (by jBPM), and the role organization structure is defined. The framework is now ready for the application execution to produce the application outputs.

4 Illustration

In the scenario of the quotation approval application, if the framework handles multiple blueprints, it has to first perform data integration as described. Then the core components transform the application blueprint (as described in Section 3.2) into the native codes required by the corresponding target native components.

```
<hibernate-mapping package="nc">
 <class name="Customer"
     table="CUSTOMER">
  <id name="id" column="CUSTOMER_ID">
  <generator class="native" />
  </id>
  <property name="name" column="NAME"
      not-null="true" />
  <property name="address"
            column="ADDRESS" />
  <property name="registerDate"
      column="REGISTERDATE" />
  <property name="contactPerson"
      column="CONTACTPERSON" />
  <bag name="quotations"
       inverse="true"
       cascade="all">
   <key column="QUOTATIONID" />
   <one-to-many class="Quotation" />
  </bag>
 </class>
</hibernate-mapping>
```

a) Partial Hibernate mapping

```
<process id="quotationapproval"
         name="Quotation Approval">
    <startEvent id="start"/>
    <sequenceFlow id="flow1"
      name="fromStartToReview"
      sourceRef="start"
      targetRef="review"/>
    <userTask id="review"
       name="Review"
       groupId="salesmanager"/>
    <sequenceFlow id="flow2"
         sourceRef="review"
         targetRef="approve"/>
    ...
    <endEvent id="end" name="End"/>
</process>
```

b) Partial BPMN 2.0 XML

```
dn: ou=salesrep,o=abc
objectclass: organizationalUnit
objectclass: top
description: entries for salesrep
ou: groups
dn: ou=salesmanager,ou=salesrep,o=abc
objectclass: organizationalUnit
objectclass: top
description: entries for sales manager
ou: salesmanager
```

c) Partial LDIF

Fig. 3. Transformation from blueprint models to native codes.

For example, Figure 3 a) shows partial Hibernate mapping file native code where a customer entity is defined with its properties (e.g., *name*, *address*), which can be mapped into an actual database schema and relationships to other entities (e.g., *quotations*). The Java class is also generated but is not shown here. Similarly, the process model of the application blueprint is transformed into the BPMN XML file native code as partially shown in Figure 3 b). The file describes a sequence of activities in the XML elements, where `<userTask>` and `<serviceTask>` respectively represents an activity performed by a human and a web service (not shown in this scenario). Finally, the organizational model is transformed into the LDIF [8] file native code as partially shown in Figure 3 part c). An organization unit (ou) hierarchically defines roles of sales representative and sales manager.

When a sales representative signs on the quotation approval application and successfully passes credential checking, he can create a price quote and a price deviation, fill values in data fields rendering on the screen by APE. The quotation approval process instance is initiated; appropriate data (e.g., quotation letter) are attached and sent for review by PRE. The review activity arrives at the sales manager's inbox. The sales manager logs on, checks the incoming activity and reviews the attached quotation letter rendering on the screen by APE. The sales manager executes the activity by selecting either approved or rejected. The PRE continues on to the next activity and so on.

5 Related Work

Studies in MDE can be classified into two broad categories: *MDE code generator* ([2], [3], [9], [12], [17]) and *MDE runtime environment* ([5], [7], [13]). The former has focused on automating transformation from software design models to codes. While these approaches are useful, they tend to lack supports for round trip engineering, where changes at the code level must be propagated back to make relevant changes at the model level [4]. The lack of such support makes updating models error-prone and MDE code generator approaches difficult to deploy. The problem has motivated the idea of an MDE runtime environment that aims to systematically apply MDE approaches further to a software deployment level, instead of a code level, so that code modification can be avoided. Our framework fits in this category. Recent work in [7] is similar to ours in that it employs workflow models to represent business logic for developing enterprise application systems. However, unlike ours, most frameworks ([5], [7], [13]) use interlocked components for specific target platforms without a concrete way to adapt to other target platforms. Furthermore, they often support only data persistent or workflow alone. These features that are likely to be inadequate for vast enterprise applications have been eliminated in our proposed framework.

6 Conclusions

We present the application runtime framework that supports MDE enterprise application development to ease the typical requirements of a sophisticated infrastructure. Driven by the software design models, our framework includes a generic architecture and mechanisms for automating the development from code generation to software system deployment. The framework provides a robust and cost effective way to enterprise application development. It offers mechanisms that provide flexibility to adopt any platform of choice, giving support to platform evolution. The framework is partially implemented and is part of our ongoing research.

References

1. Apache Software Foundation: Apache DS User's Guide. Apache Software (2009)
2. AndroMDA. AndroMDA, `http://www.andromda.org`
3. Ceri, S., Fraternali, P., Bongio, A.: Web Modeling Language (WebML): A Modeling Language for Designing Web Sites. Computer Networks (2000)
4. Deursen, A.V., Visser, E., Warmer, J.: Model-Driven Software Evolution: A Research Agenda. In: International Workshop on Model-Driven Software Evolution (2007)
5. De Sousa Saraiva, J., da Silva, A.R.: CMS-Based Web-Application Development Using Model-Driven Languages. In: Software Engineering Advances 's 2009 (ICSEA). IEEE (2009)
6. France, R., Rumpe, B.: Model-driven Development of Complex Software: A Research Roadmap. In: Future of Software Engineering's 2007 (FOSE) (2007)

7. Freudenstein, P., Buck, J., Nussbaumer, M., Gaedke, M.: Model-driven Construction of Workflow-based Web Application with DSL. In: Model-Driven Web Engineering 2007 (MDWE) (2007)
8. Good, G.: RFC 2849 The LDAP Data Interchange Format (LDIF) - Technical Specification. iPlanet e-commerce Solutions (2000)
9. Heckel, R., Lohmann, M.: Model-Based Development of Web Applications Using Graphical Reaction Rules. In: Pezzé, M. (ed.) FASE 2003. LNCS, vol. 2621, pp. 170–183. Springer, Heidelberg (2003)
10. King, G., Bauer, C., Andersen, M.R., Bernard, E., Ebersole, S., Ferentschik, H.: Hibernate Reference Documentation 3.6.3 Final. JBoss Community (2011)
11. Li, Y., Xiong, Q.: Enterprise Application Rebuilding Framework Based on Semantic SOA and Workflow. In: Distributed Computing and Applications to Business Engineering and Science (DCABES) (2010)
12. Mattsson, A., Lundell, B., Lings, B., Fitzgerald, B.: Linking Model-Driven Development and Software Architecture: A Case Study. IEEE Transactions on Software Engineering 35 (2009)
13. Pleumann, J., Haustein, S.: A Model-Driven Runtime Environment for Web Applications. In: Stevens, P., Whittle, J., Booch, G. (eds.) UML 2003. LNCS, vol. 2863, pp. 190–204. Springer, Heidelberg (2003)
14. Potts, J.: Alfresco Developer Guide. Packt Publishing (2008)
15. Salatino, M.: jBPM Developers Guide. Packt Publishing (2010)
16. Tidwell, D.: Mastering XML Transformations XSLT, pp. 21–40. O'Reilly (2001)
17. Urban, P.: Getting started with IBM Rational Rhapsody. IBM Corporation (2009)

The Fractal Prediction Model of Software Reliability Based on Wavelet

Yong Cao, Youjie Zhao, and Huan Wang

School of Computer and Information Science, Southwest Forestry University, Kunming 650224, Yunnan, China
cn_caoyong@126.com

Abstract. Software failure time series analysis is an important part of the research of software reliability. Wavelet methods have been frequently used for time series analysis with high speed and accuracy. In this paper we apply the fractal model based on wavelet techniques to estimate software reliability. Analyzing the empirical failure data and comparison with the classical models validate the validity of the model. A new idea for the research of the software failure mechanism is provided.

Keywords: fractal, wavlet denoising, software reliability model, nolinear.

1 Introduction

Software reliability, namely the capability that a given component or system within a specified environment will operate correctly for a specified period of time, has been one of the most important qualities [1, 2, 3]. In general, the probability of correct operation is inversely related to the length of time specified; the longer a system operates, the greater the chance of failure. The software reliability model is used not only to estimate reliability, but also to measure and control the software test. The important problem of the software reliability model is to calculate and predict the next failure time in advance [2].

The term fractal, which means broken or irregular fragments are mathematical or natural objects that are made of parts similar to the whole in certain ways. It belongs to geometrical category. If time series also follow the laws of fractal geometry we can use fractal to analyze time series. According to [5] self-similarity exists in software failure time series Cao and Zhu have applied fractal to foresting software failures and provided software prediction model based on fractals. Please see [5] for a detailed exposition.

The wavelet transform tries to simultaneously capture the features of all window widths of the windowed Fourier transform. In order to construct a wavelet we should first construct the scaling function $\phi(t)$ from which an expression is derived for $\varphi(t) = \phi(2t) - \phi(t)$. A wavelet $\varphi(t)$ based on the scaling function $\phi(t)$ gives rise to decomposition (in the space of square integrable real valued functions) of the time series.

T.-h. Kim et al. (Eds.): ASEA/DRBC/EL 2011, CCIS 257, pp. 265–271, 2011.

$$f(t) = \phi_0 + \sum_{j=0}^{\infty} \varphi_j \tag{1}$$

where

$$\phi_0 = \sum_{k=-\infty}^{\infty} a_k \phi(t-k), \varphi_j = \sum_{k=-\infty}^{\infty} 2^{j/2} c_{j,k} \varphi(2^j - k) \tag{2}$$

and

$$c_{j,k} = \int_{-\infty}^{\infty} f(t)\varphi(2^j - k)dt \tag{3}$$

A simple calculus exercise shows that if $\varphi(t)$ vanishes outside of $[-N, N]$, then $c_{j,k}$ is completely determined by $f(t)$ during the time interval $(k - N)/2^j < t < (k + N)/2^j$. Thus, if $f(t) = 0$ for $(k - N) / 2^j < t < (k + N) / 2^j$, then $c_{j,k} = 0$. This is how wavelets provide time localization of phenomena. Basically, the window is compressed or expanded in time by factors of 2^j to provide varying degrees of localization.

In recent years there has been a considerable development in the use of wavelet-based statistical methods. To represent an arbitrary function, the series expansion in terms of orthogonal basis functions is familiar. On the other hand the wavelet bases used in wavelet expansion are applicable to a wide class of function spaces and are well known to be useful by virtue of their special structure. The wavelet-shrinkage techniques have emerged recently as powerful methods for the non-parametric estimation of objectives which may be characterized, mainly, as spatially variables. The observed noisy signal $X(t)$ is given by:

$$X(t) = S(t) + N(t) \tag{4}$$

contains the true signal $S(t)$ with additive noise $N(t)$ as functions in time t to be sampled. Let $w(\bullet)$ and $w^{-1}(\ )$ denote the forward and inverse wavelet transform operators. Let $D(\bullet, \lambda)$ denote the denoising operator with soft threshold λ. We intend to wavelet shrinkage denoise $X(t)$ in order to recover $\hat{S}(t)$ as an estimate of $S(t)$. Then the three steps

$$Y = w(X) \tag{5}$$

$$Z = D(Y, \lambda) \tag{6}$$

$$\hat{S} = w^{-1}(Z) \tag{7}$$

summarize the procedure. Of course, this summary of principles does not reveal the details involving implementation of the operators w or D, or selection of the threshold λ. Please see [6] for a detailed exposition.

Generally, software reliability is predicated by software reliability models. Many software reliability models based on wavelet denoising techniques have been proposed in the literature to estimate the relationship between software reliability and time and other factors.

Jin, Zhang and Ye etc [7] propose a novel approach based on wavelet transform and neural network (NN). Using this approach, the time series of software faults can be decomposed into four components information, and then predict them by NN respectively. The experience results show that the performance of novel software reliability prediction approach is satisfactory.

Using the wavelet basis in Recurrent Dynamic Neural Network (RDNN) can improve the failure event estimation of software defect. Smiarowski, Sherif and Hoda etc [8] have applied a wavelet based RDDN to provide intrinsic parameters to the model used for the defect discovery in a telecommunications network.

Xiao and Tadashi [9] apply the wavelet-based techniques to estimate software intensity functions in non-homogeneous Poisson process based software reliability models. They show that their wavelet-based estimation method can provide higher goodness-of-fit performances than the conventional maximum likelihood estimation and the least squares estimation in some cases.

The outline of this paper is the following: Section 2 presents the fractal software reliability model based on wavelet; Section 3 validates the model through analyzing the empirical failure data; Section 4 concludes this paper and describes the future research.

2 Fractal Software Reliability Model Based on Wavelet

Because software reliability prediction has only one dependent variable and no explanatory variable in strict sense and we have a time series, we followed the general time series predicting model in this paper, while is represented in the following form:

$$t = \{t_1, t2, \ \ldots , t_N\},$$

Where, failure time, of *i*th times, of software systems is t_i, and $t_0=0$. So, failure space time is $T_i=t_i-t_{i-1}$, $i \leq N$, and, N is maximum observation time domain. Thus, t and T are random sequence.

We focus on value of random sequence t, since it reflects evolving regularity of failure time of software systems. When a software system is tested, it is modified immediately whenever an error is found in software. Because software is changing irregularly, the sequence t is a non-stationary and nonlinear random sequence.

Recently, many linear and nonlinear techniques have been applied to the time series analysis. These techniques can be applied to the original time series, or in other words, to the signal in time domain and they can also be applied to the signal in frequency domain. In this paper, we applied fractal model based on wavelet to software failure time series. Suppose we model time series with E_t, and it can be represented as follow:

$$\ln(E_t) = \ln(\hat{F}_t) + \varepsilon_t \tag{8}$$

where $\hat{F}_t$ is the forecasting value and estimate it through fractal. ε_t is residual and it contains noise. Therefore, we can use wavelet to shrink noise and reconstruct signal to make our prediction more accurate . Therefore, the combined forecast is

$$\hat{E}_t = (\hat{F}_t)\exp(\hat{\varepsilon}_t) \tag{9}$$

where $\hat{\varepsilon}_t$ is the forecasting value of ε_t and $\hat{E}_t$ is the forecasting value of E_t.

Algorithm 1

```
Begin
  Initialization: suppose the size of slide window m, k=1
and A is a array of the number of failure corresponding
failure time;
  Repeat for i=k to m+k-1 {
        B(i)=log(A(i));/*the logarithm of practical failure time in the slide
window.*/
        C(i)=log(i);/*the logarithm of failure number in the slide window.*/
  }
        (1)         According to eq.(5) of literature [5]
                    and method of linear regression,
                    compute the slope of linear regression
                    in the slide window b=d=1/fractal dimension
                    and constant a=log(s)=-dlog(C);
        (2)         Using the above a and b and equation
                    c=b*ln(C(i))+a compute c of each point
                    in sliding window.
        (3)         Compute difference of c and actual
                    failure time of each point to produce a
                    difference series in sliding window.
        (4)         According to wavelet denosing method to
                    shrink the noise of the difference
                    series.
        (5)         According to eq.(8), eq.(9) and linear
                    regression method predict next failure
                    time.
        (6)         Add the practical failure time of the
                    next point to A;
   k++; /*the slide window move backwards.*/
   Until test over
End
```

3 Experiment

The forecasting algorithm and one-step-ahead forecasting policy are applied in Musa's data set 1 [6] (Table 1). The performance of the proposed model is compared

Table 1. The Musa's data set 1 of failure time series, and from left to right the time in each cell denotes the cumulate time of the ith software failure, i=1, 2, ……. Unit: second

3	33	146	227	342	351	353	444
556	571	709	759	836	860	968	1056
1726	1846	1872	1986	2311	2366	2608	2676
3098	3278	3288	4434	5034	5049	5085	5089
5089	5097	5324	5389	5565	5623	6080	6380
6477	6740	7192	7447	7644	7837	7843	7922
8738	10089	10237	10258	10491	10625	10982	11175
11411	11442	11811	12559	12559	12791	13121	13486
14708	15251	15261	15277	15806	16185	16229	16358
17168	17458	17758	18287	18568	18728	19556	20567
21012	21308	23063	24127	25910	26770	27753	28460
28493	29361	30085	32408	35338	36799	37642	37654
37915	39715	40580	42015	42045	42188	42296	42296
45406	46653	47596	48296	49171	49416	50145	52042
52489	52875	53321	53443	54433	55381	56463	56485
56560	57042	62551	62651	62661	63732	64103	64893
71043	74364	75409	76057	81542	82702	84566	88682

Table 2. Prediction results of different models of Musa's data set 1. Ak stands for adaptive Kalman filter, FW stands for fractal model based on wavelet.

	Error	FW	Fractal	ARIMA	AK
Musa 1	MAE	0.0244	0.0271	0.0432	0.0425
	NRMSE	0.0215	0.0312	0.0493	0.0481

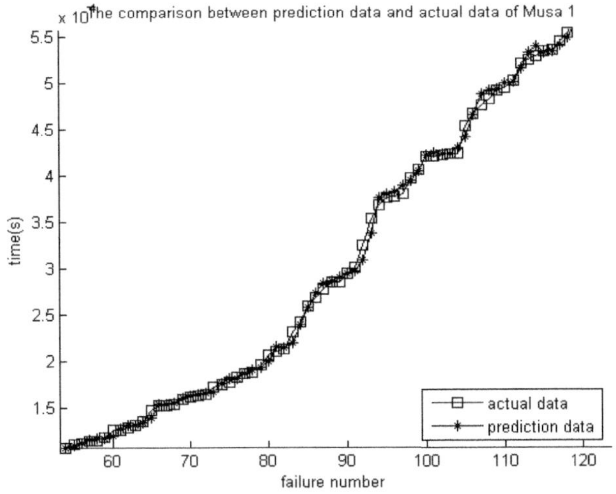

Fig. 1. The comparison between prediction data and actual data of Musa's data set 1 (sliding window size m=16)

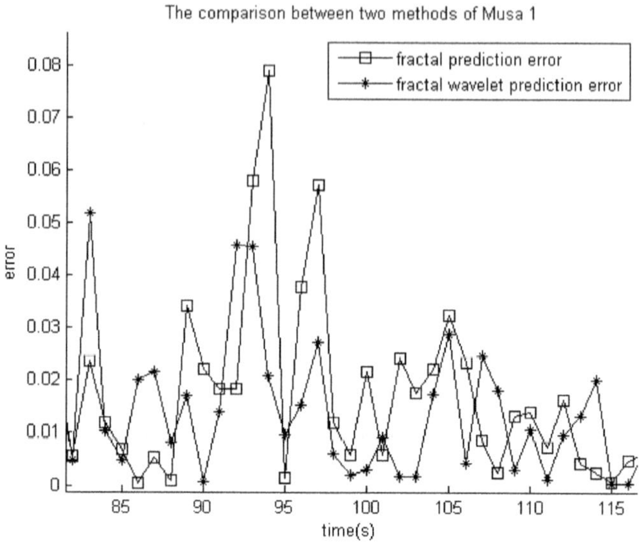

Fig. 2. The comparison of error between fractal prediction and fractal prediction based on wavelet of Musa's data set 1 (sliding window size m=16)

with fractal model [5], adaptive Kalman filter [5], and ARIMA [5] forecasting methods. The experimental results are shown in Fig.1, Fig.2 and Table.2. In Fig.2 70% of the forecasting errors using the fractal prediction model based on wavelet are less than 2%. Obviously our method is effective. In the investigation, the values of Mean Absolute Error MAE = $\frac{1}{n}\sum_{i=1}^{n} abs\frac{T_i - \overline{T}_i}{T_i}$ and Normal Root Mean Square Error NRMSE = $\sqrt{\frac{\sum_{i=1}^{n}(T_i - \overline{T}_i)^2}{\sum_{i=1}^{n} T_i^2}}$, where T_i is the ith actual failure time and $\overline{T}_i$ is prediction time (Table 2).

4 Conclusion

Reliability is one of the most important qualities of software, and failure analysis is an important part of the research of software reliability. The important problem of the software reliability model is to calculate and predict the next failure time in advance. This paper analyzes the empirical failure data, proposes the fractal software reliability model based on wavelet to predict the next software failure time which almost fit the practical failure time. Studying the empirical data (Musa's failure data set 1) and comparison with the classical models validate the proposed model. A new idea for the research of the software failure mechanism is provided. In the future, some other factors which affect the software reliability can be considered in the model to predict software reliability to improve forecasting accuracy. We will also research the mechanism behind fractals further and draw a clear conclusion.

References

1. Chen, H., Wang, J., Dong, W.: High Confidence Software Engineering Technologies. J. Acta Electronica Sinica 12 (2003)
2. Dick, S., Bethel, C.L., Kandel, A.: Software-Reliability Modeling: The Case for Deterministic Behavior. IEEE Transactions on Systems, Man, and Cybernetics—Part A: Systems and Humans 37(1) (January 2007)
3. Lewis, E.E.: Introduction to Reliability Engineering, 2nd edn. Wiley, New York (1996)
4. Zhan, K., Xiong, Q.: Software Defect Fractal Growing and Mechanism Analysis. J. Wu. Uni. Tech 1 (2004)
5. Cao, Y., Zhu, Q.: The software reliability model based on fractals. IEICE Trans. Inf. & Syst. E93-D(2), 376–379 (2010)
6. Musa, J.D.: Software Reliability Data, technical report available from Data Analysis Center for Software. Rome Air Development Center, New York (1979)
7. Jin, C., Jin, S.-W., Ye, J.-M., Zhang, Q.-G.: Software Reliability Prediction Based on Discrete Wavelet Transform and Neural Network. In: International Conference on Computational Intelligence and Software Engineering (CISE 2009) (December 2009)
8. Smiarowski Jr., A., Abdel-Aty-Zohdy, H.S., Sherif, M.H., Shah, H.: Wavelet Based RDNN for Software Reliability Estimation. In: Proceedings of the 11th IEEE Symposium on Computers and Communications, ISCC 2006 (2006)
9. Xiao, X., Dohi, T.: Wavelet-based Approach for Estimating Software Reliability. In: 20th International Symposium on Software Reliability Engineering (2009)

Source Code Metrics and Maintainability: A Case Study

Péter Hegedűs[1], Tibor Bakota[1], László Illés[1], Gergely Ladányi[2], Rudolf Ferenc[1], and Tibor Gyimóthy[1]

[1] University of Szeged, Department of Software Engineering
Árpád tér 2. H-6720 Szeged, Hungary
{hpeter,bakotat,Illes.Laszlo.2,ferenc,gyimothy}@inf.u-szeged.hu
[2] DEAK Cooperation Research Private Unlimited Company
Dugonics tér 13. H-6720 Szeged, Hungary
Ladanyi.Gergely@stud.u-szeged.hu

Abstract. Measuring high level quality attributes of operation-critical IT systems is essential for keeping the maintainability costs under control. International standards and recommendations, like ISO/IEC 9126, give some guidelines regarding the different quality characteristics to be assessed, however, they do not define unambiguously their relationship to the low level quality attributes. The vast majority of existing quality models use source code metrics for measuring low level quality attributes. Although, a lot of researches analyze the relation of source code metrics to other objective measures, only a few studies deal with their expressiveness of subjective feelings of IT professionals. Our research involved 35 IT professionals and manual evaluation results of 570 class methods of an industrial and an open source Java system. Several statistical models have been built to evaluate the relation of low level source code metrics and high level subjective opinions of IT experts. A decision tree based classifier achieved a precision of over 76% during the estimation of the *Changeability* ISO/IEC 9126 attribute.

Keywords: Metrics evaluation, Empirical quality model, ISO/IEC 9126, Software maintainability.

1 Introduction

Many important areas of our lives are supported and controlled by software systems. We rely on them, moreover, we entrust our lives to them in some cases (e.g. flight control systems or nuclear facilities). This fact has made the fields of software quality and reliability substantial and unavoidable research areas.

The internal quality of many industrial systems has deteriorated owing to long evolution phases of 10-20 years. Continuous quality monitoring in case of these systems is unavoidable for keeping the maintainability costs under control. Measuring different high level quality aspects allows the developers and managers to take the right decisions, to back up intuition, to estimate future costs and to assess risks. The international standards and recommendations like ISO/IEC

T.-h. Kim et al. (Eds.): ASEA/DRBC/EL 2011, CCIS 257, pp. 272–284, 2011.

9126 [16], ISO/IEC 25000/SQuaRE [17], ISO/IEC 15504/SPICE [15], Automotive SPICE (`http://www.automotivespice.com`) and CMMI [6] give guidelines regarding the different quality characteristics to be assessed.

In this paper our focus is on the ISO/IEC 9126 standard, which defines six high level product quality characteristics which are widely accepted both by industrial experts and academic researchers. These characteristics are: *Functionality, Reliability, Usability, Efficiency, Maintainability* and *Portability*. The characteristics are affected by low level quality properties, that can be *internal* (measured by looking inside the product, e.g. by analyzing the source code) or *external* (measured by executing the product, e.g. by performing testing). For the lowest level quality attributes, we used metrics, which quantify different attributes of the source code (e.g. size, complexity, coupling, coding rule violations, rate of code clones, etc.). Our research focuses on the relationship between the low level source code metrics and the high level quality characteristics defined by the standard.

Most of the related researches tackle the correlation of source code metrics with objective measures like failure rates during operation or bug numbers reported in an issue tracking system. Provided that it does not require a considerable manual work to be done, the reliability of the results highly depends on the reliability of the data collected during the operation or recorded in the issue tracking system.

In this research, contrary to the above mentioned approaches, we invested a large amount of manual work in order to gather reliable information regarding high level quality attributes of the systems' source code. The research involved 35 IT professionals and manual evaluation results of 570 class methods of an industrial and an open source Java system. Our aim was to find correlations between low level objective measures of source code elements (i.e. source code metrics) and high level subjective opinions of IT professionals. Beside drawing conclusions from the collected data, several machine learning models had been trained for estimating the high level quality characteristics. In the case of *Changeability*, a decision tree based classifier achieved a precision of over 76% during estimation, using the 10 fold cross-validation method. The paper focuses on the following two research questions:

RQ1: *How do the well-known source code metrics correlate individually with the subjective opinions of IT experts, regarding* Maintainability*?*

RQ2: *How do the well-known source code metrics perform together as predictors when using machine learning algorithms for assessing the subjective opinions of IT experts regarding* Maintainability*?*

The rest of the paper is structured as follows. In Section 2 we overview the related work. Then, in Section 3 we introduce the approach and technical details about the performed case study and the employed analysis methods. Section 4 presents the results of the case study. Afterwards, Section 5 discusses the known threats to the validity of our work. Finally, we conclude the paper and present future work in Section 6.

2 Related Work

The ISO/IEC 9126 standard is currently one of the most accepted standards for measuring software quality. Numerous adaptations and customizations have been developed for evaluating quality characteristics defined by the standard. Most of the researches utilize source code metrics as low level quality attributes and apply sophisticated methods for aggregating the values to higher levels. Alas, only a few papers tackle the connection between the metrics and the subjective feelings of IT professionals about the higher level characteristics.

Jung and Kim [19] examined the validity of the structure of the ISO/IEC 9126 standard based on a survey. They focused on the connection of characteristics and subcharacteristics by grouping the latter ones based on the answers of the evaluators. The authors found that most of the resulting groups corresponded to a characteristic defined by the standard. Here, we did not examine the connection between the subcharacteristics and characteristics but the code metrics and subcharacteristics.

Many researches use source code metrics for estimating software quality in terms of fault-proneness. For example, Olague et al. [20] studied the ability to predict fault-proneness by using the CK [5], QMOOD [3] and MOOD [13] metric suites. Basili et al. [4] and Gyimóthy et al. [11] calculated code metrics and used regression and machine learning techniques to predict fault-proneness. We used metrics and applied machine learning techniques to predict *maintainability* instead of fault-proneness.

Many researches propose maintainability models based on source code metrics. Bakota et al. [2] suggest a probabilistic approach for computing *maintainability* for a system. They use benchmark databases to ensure objectiveness, and apply probabilistic aggregation to capture the subjectiveness of high level characteristics. Heitlager et al. [14] also introduce a maintainability model. They transform metric value averages to the [-2,2] discrete scale and perform an aggregation to get a measure for *maintainability*. Bansiya and Davis [3] developed a hierarchical model (QMOOD) for assessment of high level design quality attributes and validated it on two large commercial framework systems. Our aim was not to aggregate metrics to high level attributes, but to reveal the connection between the low level metrics and high level characteristics given by IT experts. We built models for estimating high level attributes by applying a top-down approach. In our case, machine learning algorithms were trained with source code metrics as predictors and the results of manual assessment as the classes to be learned.

Many approaches try to quantify subcharacteristics by using surveys, before the aggregation to higher levels. Chua and Dyson [7] estimated the quality of an e-learning system merely based on end users' opinion. They demonstrated the validity of their model with a case study and showed how it could be used to detect design flaws. Others used both subjective opinions and metrics calculated from the code for estimating high level properties. Similarly, we also used expert opinions and code metrics, but we used the latter ones to learn the former ones by using machine learning techniques. We use the resulting models to predict *maintainability* based on source code metrics.

Bagheri and Gasevic [1] assessed the *maintainability* of software product line feature models based on structural metrics. They evaluated manually the high level maintainability attributes of different feature models. The authors studied the correlation between the low level structural metrics and the high level maintainability attributes. They also applied machine learning algorithms to predict the subjective opinions of these high level attributes using the structural metrics as predictors. Although their work is similar to ours, there are a number of differences. First of all, their focus is on the *maintainability* of product line feature models, while we studied the software product quality. It follows that the metrics suite we study is different. Our survey involved 35 IT experts who have more than 2 years programming experience on average, while they asked graduate students to answer their questions. They studied the *Analyzability*, *Changeability*, and *Understandability* attributes, while we investigated *Stability* and *Testability* as well.

3 Approach

In order to analyze the relationship between the source code metrics and the high level maintainability attributes, we performed a time-consuming manual evaluation task. IT experts evaluated 570 class methods of two Java systems from five different aspects of quality. The purpose of the evaluation was to collect subjective ranks for different quality attributes for a large number of methods.To ease the evaluation process, we developed a web-based framework to collect, store, and organize the evaluation results. In this section we give a brief overview of the evaluated systems, the evaluation process, and the developed framework itself.

3.1 Evaluated Systems

One of the evaluated systems was JEdit (`http://www.jedit.org`), a well-known text editor designed for programmers. It is a powerful tool written in Java to ease writing source code in several languages. It includes syntax highlight, built-in macros, plug-in support, etc. The system contains more than 700 methods (over 20,000 lines of code), from which we selected 320 to evaluate. The main aspect of the selection was the length of methods, e.g. we skipped the getter/setter methods and the generated ones.

The other evaluated system was an industrial software product, which contained more than 20,000 methods and over 200,000 lines of code. From this abundance of methods, we selected 250 to evaluate. The evaluation was performed by 35 experts, who varied in age and programming experience.

3.2 The Evaluation Framework

The developed *Metric Evaluation Framework* is a complex system, capable of analyzing Java source code, storing and visualizing artifacts, and guiding the user through the evaluation process. The system consists of four modules:

- *AnalyzeManager* - the module controls the Columbus analyzer tools [10,8,9] for computing low level source code metrics and other analysis results.
- *Uploader* - the module uploads the source code artifacts into a database.
- *AdminPages* - web interface to manage and control the analysis process.
- *EvalPages* - web interface providing necessary metrical information and allowing the users to evaluate the methods.

The Columbus analyzer tools produce metric information based on the source code and its structure. The results of this process are then handled by the *Uploader* component, which processes and uploads the information into a database. The *AnalyzeManager* and *Uploader* modules are hidden from the users (experts involved in the evaluation task). From the users' point of view, the other two modules are more important. The *AdminPages* module is a web interface where the users and the projects can be managed. The analysis of Java sources can also be initialized from this interface. The most important module is the *EvalPages*, where the user can evaluate the source code of the projects. First, the user has to select a method and an aspect from which the evaluation is performed. This can be done using the item (method) selector screen (see Figure 1(a)). The questions are organized into the following five categories:

- *Analyzability* - how easy it is to diagnose the system for deficiencies or to identify where to make a change
- *Changeability* - how easy it is to make a change in the system (includes designing, coding and documenting changes)
- *Stability* - how well does the system avoid unexpected effects after a change
- *Testability* - how easy it is to validate the software after a change
- *Comprehension* - how easy it is to comprehend the source code of a method (understanding its algorithm)

The first four aspects are defined by the ISO/IEC 9126 standard as subcharacteristics of the *Maintainability* characteristic. The standard defines a fifth subcharacteristic, which is the *Compliance*, but it has no practical meaning to a

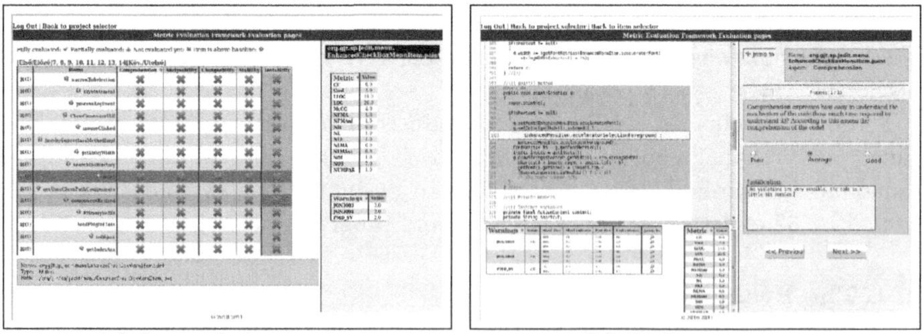

(a) Item selector screen (b) Evaluator screen

Fig. 1. Metric Evaluation Framework screens

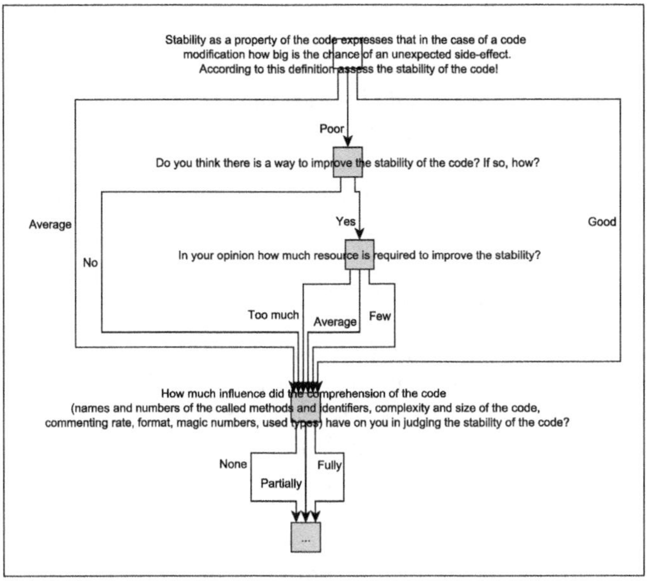

Fig. 2. Sample questions (Stability)

programmer so we left it out. Furthermore, *Comprehension* is not part of the standard but the experts agreed that it should be included.

After selecting an item and an aspect, the evaluator panel appears (see Figure 1(b)), where the evaluation can be performed. On the left-hand side of the screen, the item's source code can be seen. On the bottom left, there are two tables with the metric values and rule violations (if present) for the current item. On the right-hand side, the questions and text boxes for textual answers take place. With the help of these questions the user can form his own opinion regarding the item. It is important to note that every aspect has its own questions. Furthermore, the questions asked depend on the users' earlier answers. An example can be seen on Figure 2. Each node of the graph represents a question (starting from the white colored node) that is asked from the evaluators. The edges of the graph show the next question asked, based on the evaluator's answer (the possible answers are the labels of the edges). After the user finishes the evaluation, the given answers and rates will be stored in the project's database. The collected information is then used to build models that are able to predict high level quality characteristics based on metrical values.

4 Experimental Results

This section presents the results of our case study. During the evaluation process all of the previously mentioned 570 methods were evaluated one by one using the Metric Evaluation Framework and the results were stored in a database. Beside the code metric values we stored the high level attribute values (poor, average, good) assessed by one of the 35 IT experts involved in the evaluation process. We imported these data into the Weka Experimenter [12] to build models using different machine learning algorithms.

First, we assess the source code metrics that are calculated and used as predictors for the machine learning algorithms, and present the correlation of the metric values calculated for our test projects. Second, we examine the connection between the code metrics, then we try to answer our research questions through the experimental results.

4.1 The Applied Source Code Metrics

The method-level source code metrics that we examined and used as predictors for the machine learning algorithms in our case study are the following: Number of Outgoing Invocations (*NOI*); Lines Of Code (*LOC*); Logical Lines Of Code (*LLOC*); Number Of Statements (*NOS*); Number of Local Methods Accessed (*NLMA*); Nesting Level (*NL*); Number of Foreign Methods Accessed (*NFMA*); Number of Incoming Invocations (*NII*); Number of Parameters (*NPAR*); McCabe Cyclomatic Complexity (*McCC*); Clone Coverage (*CC*); Number of PMD warnings (`http://pmd.sourceforge.net`) in a method (*PMD*).

Table 1. Pearson Correlation between the code metrics

	NOI	LOC	LLOC	NOS	NLMA	NL	NFMA	NII	NPAR	McCC	CC	PMD
NOI	1.00	0.17	0.12	0.10	0.38	0.01	0.80	0.00	0.01	0.03	0.00	0.01
LOC		1.00	0.97	0.89	0.09	0.21	0.12	0.00	0.01	0.73	0.00	0.54
LLOC			1.00	0.95	0.08	0.20	0.07	0.00	0.01	0.82	0.00	0.64
NOS				1.00	0.08	0.19	0.05	0.00	0.00	0.86	0.00	0.72
NLMA					1.00	0.00	0.04	0.00	0.01	0.05	0.00	0.03
NL						1.00	0.00	0.00	0.00	0.17	0.03	0.03
NFMA							1.00	0.01	0.00	0.01	0.00	0.00
NII								1.00	0.01	0.00	0.00	0.00
NUMPAR									1.00	0.00	0.00	0.00
McCC										1.00	0.00	0.79
CC											1.00	0.00
PMD												1.00

Table 1 shows the Pearson correlation (R^2: coefficient of determination) between the metrical values measured for the methods of the Java projects (see Section 3.1). We found very high correlation between the following metrics: LOC, LLOC, NOS, McCC and PMD. The correlation between the LOC, LLOC and NOS metrics is not surprising, since they are similar size measures. The high correlation between the method size measures, McCC and PMD warnings is more interesting. It means that for our test projects the larger and more complex the code of a method was the more coding rule violations it contained and vice versa.

The NOI metric correlates well with NFMA. This is again not so surprising since NOI is a generalization of NFMA.

4.2 Relationship of Individual Metrics and High Level Attributes

To answer our first research question we examined the correlation matrix between the code metrics and the high level maintainability attributes.

Table 2. Pearson correlation between the code metrics and maintainability attributes

	NOI	LOC	LLOC	NOS	NLMA	NL	NFMA	NII	NPAR	McCC	CC	PMD
Analyzab.	-0.38	-0.41	-0.38	-0.34	-0.23	-0.16	-0.35	-0.03	-0.05	-0.27	0.12	-0.22
Changeab.	-0.35	-0.41	-0.38	-0.35	-0.20	-0.17	-0.33	-0.02	-0.10	-0.29	0.09	-0.21
Stability	-0.28	-0.35	-0.34	-0.31	-0.19	-0.13	-0.24	0.00	-0.06	-0.26	0.07	-0.22
Testab.	-0.25	-0.38	-0.37	-0.34	-0.16	-0.34	-0.22	0.01	-0.07	-0.29	-0.02	-0.24
Comprehen.	-0.34	-0.38	-0.36	-0.33	-0.22	-0.15	-0.30	0.02	-0.10	-0.26	0.09	-0.21

Table 2 shows that the assessed source code metrics have no statistically significant correlation with any of the maintainability properties. We note however, that almost all of the Pearson correlation (R) values are negative. This means that the smaller metric values indicate better subjective opinion about the maintainability properties. This is in accordance with our intuitive expectations.

4.3 Relationship of Metric-Based Models and High Level Attributes

To answer our second research question we have built several models using different machine learning algorithms and evaluated their prediction strength.

To perform the machine learning algorithms on the collected data we used the well-known data mining software package called *Weka*. It is a collection of machine learning algorithms for data mining tasks. It contains tools for data pre-processing, classification, regression, clustering, association rules, and visualization.

The main aim of this paper was to examine the connection between the code metrics and high level maintainability properties of methods. We showed in Section 4.2 that we haven't found any well-known source code metric that would be able to predict the subjective opinions of the IT experts by itself. In this section we are going to investigate how the basic multivariate machine learning algorithms perform in predicting these values. Before every classification process we executed a Principal Component Analysis (PCA) [18] which reduced the dimension of the problem. We used the Weka's PCA attribute selector function

Table 3. Rate of the correctly classified instances

	ZeroR	J48 Decision Tree	Log. Regression	Neural Network
Analyzability	67.93%	73.68%	70.97%	70.25%
Changeability	66.79%	76.65%	73.00%	74.26%
Stability	70.20%	73.12%	70.55%	70.92%
Testability	66.55%	64.72%	69.45%	70.54%
Comprehension	70.92%	76.68%	70.93%	73.99%

with the following parameters: *variance = 0.97*, *centerData = TRUE*. The latter parameter means that Weka subtracts the column's mean from each column, so each variable has zero mean. To get the proper number of dimensions we set the variance parameter to 0.97.

After applying PCA, we tested the well-known basic classifiers: logistic regression, J48 decision tree and neural network. We used the ZeroR algorithm as a baseline of the effectiveness in our experiment. This is the most simple classifier that chooses the class which has the most elements in the training data set. Table 3 shows the rate of correctly classified instances for each maintainability property. In our experiments, we used 10-fold cross-validation.

We found that the best classifier is the J48 (Weka implementation of C4.5) decision tree algorithm in four out of five cases. It performed very poorly in the classification of *Testability*, which was attributed to the fuzziness of the subcharacteristic's definition. The IT experts involved in the survey varied in testing skills, therefore it is possible that they interpreted the concept differently.

In the case of *Changeability* the precision of the J48 classifier was by 10% better than ZeroR. In this case the Logistic Regression and the Neural Network algorithms also performed well. Precision is a good way to measure the efficiency, but if we examine the precision and recall values separately for classes it appoints that the J48 algorithm is much more useful than ZeroR.

Table 4. Statistics by classes in the case of Changeability

	J48 decision tree				ZeroR			
Class	TP Rate	FP Rate	Precision	Recall	TP Rate	FP Rate	Precision	Recall
Bad	0.238	0.011	0.455	0.238	0	0	0	0
Average	0.640	0.160	0.624	0.640	0	0	0	0
Good	0.852	0.330	0.839	0.852	1	1	0.668	1

Table 4 shows detailed statistics about the precision and recall values of the ZeroR and J48 algorithms in the case of *Changeability*. The precision of the J48 algorithm is by 17 % higher for the *Good* class than ZeroR's. Moreover, it found 64% of the *Average* and 23.8 % of the *Poor* instances while ZeroR missed them completely.

During the evaluation, experts were asked to explain their opinion about the different maintainability properties in a textual format also. Based on their comments we created some new simple predictors (that were not covered by any of our metrics):

- *Indenting* - number of lines divided by the sum of the tabulate characters.
- *Logging* - *true* if there are "log", "logger", "Log" or "Logger" strings in the source code, *false* otherwise.
- *Comments* - sum of the lines starting with "/*" or "//".
- *Naming* - number of elements of the set of PMD naming related rule violations.

After adding these predictors to the learning process the results became slightly better, for example the precision of *Comprehension* rose up to 77.04%. This shows that there is a potential to extract more sophisticated predictors from the textual answers to increase the precision of the estimation.

5 Threats to Validity

The paper presents a case study involving 35 IT professionals and a manual evaluation of 570 methods of industrial and open source Java systems. The purpose of the case study is to reveal the relationship between the well-known source code metrics of methods and the high level *Maintainability* subcharacteristics defined by the ISO/IEC 9126 standard. We also built models with the help of machine learning algorithms for estimating the subjective opinions of the evaluators using source code metrics as low level predictors. Both the evaluation process and the data analysis approach bear some properties which may affect the validity of the results and the usability of the approach.

First of all, the 570 evaluated methods are not enough for drawing any general conclusions about the relationship between the source code metrics and the subjective evaluations of maintainability properties. But this number of evaluated methods is good enough for showing that there is a potential in our approach and it is worth putting more effort in further research.

The evaluators were asked to qualify methods on a scale of *Poor, Average, Good*. The three categories might seem scant but based on our experiences there would be no practical benefit from using a finer scale.

Another threat to the validity of the built prediction models is that the data used for training is very unbalanced. This is because most of the methods fell into the *Good* category in many aspects according to the evaluators.

It is also a threat to the validity that every method is evaluated by only one IT professional. Even in such way the evaluation required a lot of manual work. It is sure that more evaluations would increase the validity of our work, but we did not want to put more effort in it before it becomes clear that our approach is applicable and is worth investigating further.

Another problem is that the high level quality attributes defined by either the ISO/IEC 9126 standard or us are ambiguous, and different evaluators may interpret them differently. To minimize the risks of misunderstanding the concepts we held a briefing to the evaluators about the ISO/IEC 9126 standard. Moreover, the definitions of the basic concepts were available through the web framework used for the evaluation process.

Finally, the experience level and theoretical background of the evaluators were varying. But they were selected from IT professionals having knowledge about source code metrics and software quality.

6 Conclusions and Future Work

The current work tries to reveal the relationship between the well-known source code metrics and the subjective opinions of IT experts about different high level maintainability properties of the source code. There is a lot of work in the literature dealing with quality models. Most of them adapt the ISO/IEC 9126 standard and build hierarchical models in a bottom-up fashion using source code metrics at the lowest level and defining different aggregation operations to calculate higher level attributes.

We chose a top-down approach for adapting the standard meaning that we tried to develop models using machine learning algorithms and the subjective evaluations of many experts. To achieve our goal we performed a case study involving 35 IT experts and a manual evaluation of 570 methods of an industrial and an open source Java system. To help the process we have also developed a web-based application for collecting, storing, and organizing the evaluations.

We can conclude, that the results of the case study presented in the paper are very promising. It is clear, however, that the metrics we used for building our models are not enough by themselves. They simply do not bear enough information to describe the complex terms like *Comprehension* that a sophisticated human mind can understand. Some aspects can be predicted better by metrics, e.g. *Changeability*, while others cannot, e.g. *Testability.* We answered the following two research questions in the following way:

RQ1: *How do the well-known source code metrics correlate individually with the subjective opinions of IT experts, regarding* Maintainability*?*

We found no statistically significant correlation, however, almost every value was negative. It corresponds with our intuitive assumption that higher metrical values indicate lower maintainability feelings of experts.

RQ2: *How do the well-known source code metrics perform together as predictors when using machine learning algorithms for assessing the subjective opinions of IT experts regarding* Maintainability*?*

We applied three well-known machine learning techniques (decision tree, logistic regression, and neural network) to build prediction models using metrical values for predicting the human opinion. We found that metrics have the potential to predict high level quality indicators. In the case of the *Changeability* property the models performed with more than 76% precision (more than 10% better than the ZeroR algorithm). Although the results are promising, future research is needed to extract other factors that humans consider but the current metrics cannot measure. It can be done by analyzing the textual remarks of the evaluators and implementing appropriate predictors based on them.

Of course, the number of evaluated methods is too small for drawing any general conclusions. A larger number of data could help getting over this problem. Therefore, in the future we plan to extend the manual evaluation to much more methods of different systems.

It seems reasonable to group the evaluators by age, programming experience or other aspects, and examine the results for every group consecutively. After collecting more data we will also examine the distribution of the evaluations for different groups of IT experts.

During the evaluation lots of textual opinions have been collected also. Processing the answers is in progress currently. We hope that from the experts' remarks we can reveal some new properties that influence the subjective quality feeling of humans but are not measured by any of the investigated metrics yet. Based on these results and the opinions of the experts, we plan to define and implement new predictor metrics, which may increase the accuracy of the classification.

In this work, we used several well-known learning algorithms, but this does not mean that they are the only nor the best. On the contrary, a more complex algorithm may produce better results. Therefore, we plan to study much more machine learning algorithms and techniques to find the one that is the most suitable for the defined task.

Acknowledgements. This research was supported by the Hungarian national grants GOP-1.1.2-07/1-2008-0007, OTKA K-73688, TECH 08-A2/2-2008-0089, and by the János Bolyai Research Scholarship of the Hungarian Academy of Sciences.

References

1. Bagheri, E., Gasevic, D.: Assessing the maintainability of software product line feature models using structural metrics. Software Quality Journal 19(3), 579–612 (2011)
2. Bakota, T., Hegedűs, P., Körtvélyesi, P., Rudolf, F., Gyimóthy, T.: A Probabilistic Software Quality Model. In: Proceedings of the 27th IEEE International Conference on Software Maintenance, ICSM 2011, pp. 368–377. IEEE Computer Society, Williamsburg (2011)
3. Bansiya, J., Davis, C.: A Hierarchical Model for Object-Oriented Design Quality Assessment. IEEE Transactions on Software Engineering 28, 4–17 (2002)
4. Basili, V.R., Briand, L.C., Melo, W.L.: A Validation of Object-Oriented Design Metrics as Quality Indicators. IEEE Transactions on Software Engineering 22, 751–761 (1996)
5. Chidamber, S.R., Kemerer, C.F.: A Metrics Suite for Object Oriented Design. IEEE Trans. Softw. Eng., 476–493 (June 1994)
6. Chrissis, M.B., Konrad, M., Shrum, S.: CMMI Guidlines for Process Integration and Product Improvement. Addison-Wesley Longman Publishing Co., Inc., Boston (2003)
7. Chua, B., Dyson, L.: Applying the ISO9126 model to the evaluation of an e-learning system. In: Beyond the comfort zone: Proceedings of the 21st ASCILITE Conference, pp. 184–190. Citeseer, Perth (2004)
8. Ferenc, R., Beszédes, Á., Gyimóthy, T.: Extracting Facts with Columbus from C++ Code. In: Tools for Software Maintenance and Reengineering, Franco Angeli Milano, pp. 16–31 (2004)
9. Ferenc, R., Beszédes, Á., Tarkiainen, M., Gyimóthy, T.: Columbus – Reverse Engineering Tool and Schema for C++. In: Proceedings of the 18th International Conference on Software Maintenance (ICSM 2002), pp. 172–181. IEEE Computer Society (October 2002)

10. Ferenc, R., Siket, I., Gyimóthy, T.: Extracting Facts from Open Source Software. In: Proceedings of the 20th International Conference on Software Maintenance (ICSM 2004), pp. 60–69. IEEE Computer Society (September 2004)
11. Gyimóthy, T., Ferenc, R., Siket, I.: Empirical Validation of Object-Oriented Metrics on Open Source Software for Fault Prediction. IEEE Transactions on Software Engineering, 897–910 (2005)
12. Hall, M., Frank, E., Holmes, G., Pfahringer, B., Reutemann, P., Witten, I.H.: The WEKA Data Mining Software: An Update. SIGKDD Explorations (2009)
13. Harrison, R., Counsell, S., Nithi, R.: An evaluation of the mood set of object-oriented software metrics. IEEE Transactions on Software Engineering 24, 491–496 (1998)
14. Heitlager, I., Kuipers, T., Visser, J.: A Practical Model for Measuring Maintainability. In: Proceedings of the 6th International Conference on Quality of Information and Communications Technology, pp. 30–39 (2007)
15. International Organization for Standardization: ISO/IEC 15504:2004 Information technology – Process assessment – Part 3: Guidance on performing an assessment. Tech. rep., International Organization for Standardization (2004)
16. ISO/IEC: ISO/IEC 9126. Software Engineering – Product quality. ISO/IEC (2001)
17. ISO/IEC: ISO/IEC 25000:2005. Software Engineering – Software product Quality Requirements and Evaluation (SQuaRE) – Guide to SQuaRE. ISO/IEC (2005)
18. Jolliffe, I.: Principal Component Analysis. Springer, Heidelberg (1986)
19. Jung, H.W., Kim, S.G., Chung, C.S.: Measuring Software Product Quality: A Survey of ISO/IEC 9126. IEEE Software, 88–92 (2004)
20. Olague, H.M., Etzkorn, L.H., Gholston, S., Quattlebaum, S.: Empirical Validation of Three Software Metrics Suites to Predict Fault-Proneness of Object-Oriented Classes Developed Using Highly Iterative or Agile Software Development Processes. IEEE Transactions on Software Engineering, 402–419 (2007)

Systematic Verification of Operational Flight Program through Reverse Engineering

Dong-Ah Lee, Jong-Hoon Lee, Junbeom Yoo, and Doo-Hyun Kim

College of Information and Communication, KONKUK UNIVERSITY
New Millennium Hall, 1 Hwayang-dong, Gwangjin-gu, Seoul, 143-701, Korea
{ldalove,kirdess,jbyoo,doohyun}@konkuk.ac.kr

Abstract. Software reverse engineering is an engineering process analyzing a system for specific purposes such as identifying interrelationship between system components or reorganizing the system structure. The HELISCOPE project aims to develop an unmanned helicopter and its on-flight embedded computing system for navigation and real-time transmission of motion video using wireless communication schemes. The OFP (Operational Flight Program) in HELISCOPE project keeps only informal and non-standardized documents and has made us difficult to analyze and test it thoroughly. This paper introduces a verification plan through reverse engineering to get over the difficulties, and we share an experimentation about a small portion of the plan to the HELISCOPE OFP.

Keywords: Operational Flight Program, Verification, Reverse Engineering, Testing.

1 Introduction

HELISCOPE [1] project aims to develop on-flight computing system, embedded S/W, and related services for unmanned helicopter that shall be used for disaster response or recovery using real-time transmission of the motion video through wireless communication scheme. OFP (Operational Flight Program) of the HELISCOPE project [2] is a control program which provides real-time controls with various sensors and actuators equipped in the helicopter.

The OFP as a safety-critical and mission-critical system should be sufficiently verified through application of various validation and verification techniques. For instance, formal verification technique [3] plays an important role in demonstrating safety and correctness of the system. Our previous work we used two formal verification techniques to verify process communications and timing constraints of the OFP [4][5]. Testing is also one of widely used technique to verify structure or functionality of software. For applying testing techniques to a target system, well-formed specifications such as SRS (Software Requirement Specification) or SDD (Software Design Description) are mandatory. The OFP, however, didn't have sufficient specifications or documentations to apply test techniques. It had only a few documents such as informal specifications and non-standardized documents.

T.-h. Kim et al. (Eds.): ASEA/DRBC/EL 2011, CCIS 257, pp. 285–291, 2011.

We decided to do software reverse engineering against the OFP in order to develop formal specification and structure information, which are the prerequisite for software testing. Reverse engineering is a process of analyzing a target system for a specific subject to identify the system components and their interrelationships, and create representations of the system in another form or at a higher level of abstraction [6]. There are two subareas that are widely referred to: redocumentation, and design recovery. The redocumentation is the creation or revision of a semantically equivalent representation within in the same relative abstraction level. On the other hand, the design recovery adds domain knowledge, external information and deduction or fuzzy reasoning to the observations of the subject system.

Results of redocumentation, represented by data flows, data structures, or control flows, make us possible to understand a whole structure and flow of a target system. The information will be useful to perform structural testing [7]. For example, understanding data structures and flows helps us rise test case adequacy like coverage. We, therefore, decided to use structural testing technique against the OFP with the results of redocumentation.

This paper introduces our plan to verify the OFP through reverse engineering systematically, and we share an experimentation about a small portion of the plan. The remainder of the paper is organized as follows: Section 2 introduces background information on the target system, OFP in HELISCOPE project, and reverse engineering briefly. Section 3 shows the plan from the reverse engineering to the test of the OFP and Section 4 covers the experimentation. Finally we conclude the paper and sum up some unsolved problems in Section 5.

2 Background

2.1 Operational Flight Program

OFP is developed as a subpart of the HELISCOPE project and it is based on the well-known TMO scheme [8]. The OFP support the unmanned helicopter navigation that is done by commands on flight mode from GCS (Ground Control System). It operates servo motors using collected data from various sensors such as GPS (Global Positioning System), navigation, CGS, and SWM (Helicopter Servo Actuator Switching Module).

There are six threads, four readers, one controller, and one monitor, and they run simultaneously. Fig. 1 shows an overview of the OFP working with servo motor and sensors. The monitor thread catches a data packet from sensors and operates one of reader threads which is supposed to collect the data. If the monitor thread operates one of reader threads, then the reader thread reads the data and saves the data in ODS (Object Data Storage). The controller thread, otherwise, computes collected data to control the servo motors. The reader threads and controller thread share ODS (Object Data Store) to forward data collected from sensors. To avoid simultaneous use of the OSD by them, mutual exclusion algorithm is used.

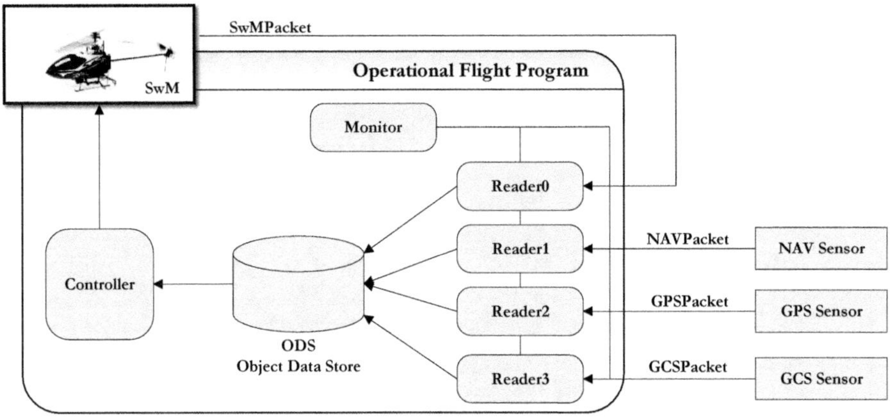

Fig. 1. An overview of Operational Flight Program with servo motor and sensors

2.2 Reverse Engineering

Origin of reverse engineering is in the analysis of hardware — where the practice of deciphering designs from finished products is commonplace. Reverse engineering of software is also the practice of analyzing a software system, either in whole or in part, to extract design and implementation information [9]. It can be performed any level of abstraction or at any stage of the life cycle. There are no changes or modifications about target system during performing reverse engineering. This performance only crates documents or abstract information about the target system.

3 A Testing Plan for the HELISCOPE OFP

The testing plan for the HELISCOPE OFP consists of two parts: *reverse engineering* and *testing*. Fig 2. describes the overall plan. Analysis on the source codes and informal/unstructured documents is the first step of our reverse engineering. It will progressively produce 4 different documents: data descriptions, structure charts [10][11], data flow diagrams, and control flow diagrams. Data descriptions are derived from definitions and uses of variables. The structure charts are also derived from the data descriptions and functions defining the relationship of data. The data flow and control flow diagrams are finally recovered from the structure charts. The more we perform the redocumentation, the more extractive the source code and informal documents become. All documents derived in this part become a source of activities in the testing part.

There are two activities in verification part. Test cases generation generates new test cases, while referring related documents produced from the reverse engineering (redocumentation) process. The other one is test execution with test cases including new test cases generated in test cases generation activity. We estimate that test case coverage (e.g. such as statement, branch, or MC/DC

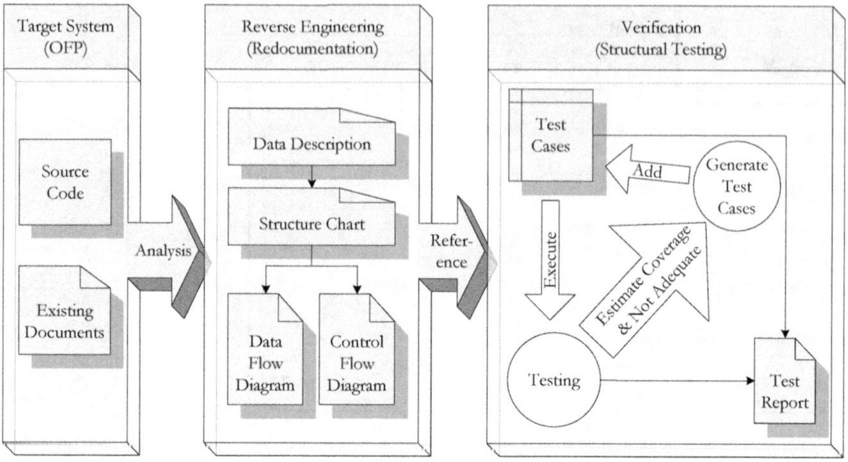

Fig. 2. The OFP verification plan through reverse engineering

(Modified Condition & Decision Condition) coverages) [12] is adequate. It means lack of test cases to cover the whole system that one of coverage which we decided to set a test criterion is not adequate sufficiently. We, thus, should generate new test cases until the coverage is adequate. Analysis of DFD or CFD makes flows the system, so we can discover uncovered area to generate new test cases. Test report include the results of the two activities.

4 Experimentation

In this section, we share our experiment with respect to the verification described in Section 3. We performed reverse engineering with source code and documents of OFP, and executed structural testing to its source code. To recover data description, first of all, we analyzed functions and its relationship using Doxygen [14] which is a documentation system. Next, we manually drew an outline of the structure chart, referring the generated relationship of function calls and the control flows and data flows are added on the structure chart. Fig. 3[1] shows the result of recovering structure chart used notations defined by Yourdon [13].

DFD (Data Flow Diagram) supports that we generate test cases, so we recovered DFD referring to the structure chart. Outlines of the DFD are derived from the structure chart, and detail data flows are referred from actual source code. We should derive the DFD starts from higher level which is level 0 expressing a outline of data flow roughly, because we only could refer the recovered structure of the target system. The deeper level of DFD is the more detailed analysis is progressed. Fig. 4[2] shows the DFD from level 0 to level 2. The whole of the

[1] Assumed names of all modules are substituted for original ones in source code for security reasons.

[2] Assumed names of all processes and flow labels under level 1 are substituted for original ones of source code for security reasons.

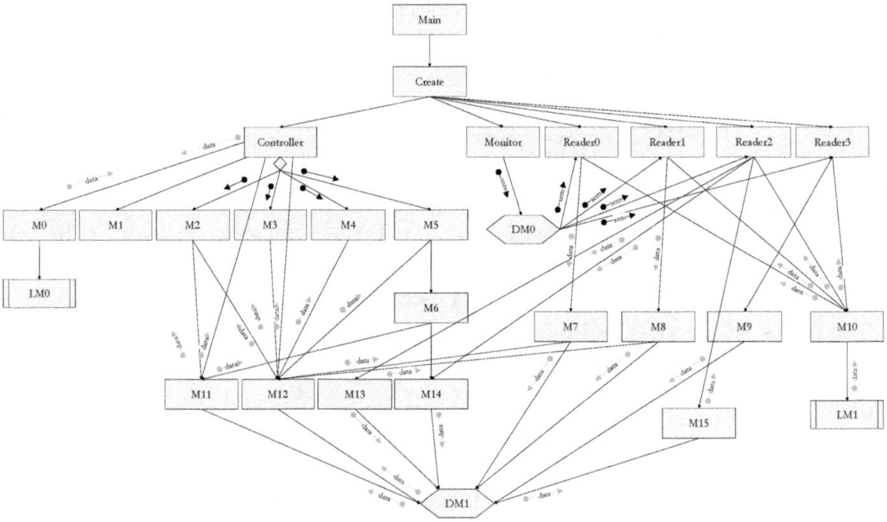

Fig. 3. Recovered structure chart of the Operational Flight Program

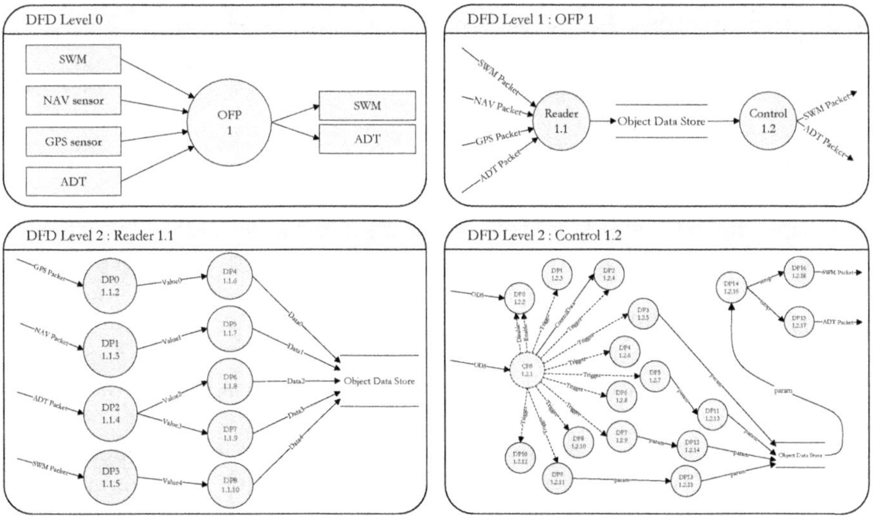

Fig. 4. Recovered data flow diagram of the Operational Flight Program

DFD consists of 5 levels and the last level, level 4, is made up of state transition diagram.

We focused on modules which affect control of unmanned helicopter without communicating sensors through serial ports. Testing environment within a PC, therefore, is sufficient without a embedded system environment in use. We set QNX Software Development Platform 6.5.0[15] as an operating system in virtual environment. The QNX is one of RTOS (Real-Time Operating System) which the OFP use. To check statement coverage, we used a test coverage program named gcov [16].

We, first of all, selected data referring related documents which are data descriptions and DFD. Next we generated initial test cases about the data and executed the test. Estimation of statement coverage was not adequate at first. We, therefore, executed test case generation and testing activities over 10 times, and could get adequate test cases coverage. Table 1 shows the result of the testing. Unfortunately, some of target modules don't have 100 % statement coverage, because they include a few unused codes or codes to access serial ports. Those statements, however, is not our consideration which we set before start the test, so we could make decision that the test cases are adequate.

Table 1. Result of structural testing

Module Name	Number of Test Cases	Statement Coverage
Module 0	11	99.47 %
Module 1	1	100.00 %
Module 2	17	100.00 %
Module 3	4	100.00 %
Module 4	3	93.33 %
Module 5	4	86.26 %

5 Conclusion

This paper introduced a systematic verification plan and parts of practical use of OFP in HELISCOPE project through reverse engineering. We identified that results of performing reverse engineering, derived from source code and informal documents, are useful information to analyze structure and execute structural testing about the target system. Our experimentation did not cover widely used coverages such as branch or MC/DC, so we plan to perform testing with different coverage criterias.

Functional testing is good to verify functionality, and it is available through design recovery technique mentioned above. The technique, however, needs very close collaboration with developers of the target system, because the design includes additional domain knowledge, external information, etc. We also plan the collaboration with the developer of the OFP, and expect that those additional verification techniques make the OFP more reliable.

Acknowledgments. This research was supported by the MKE(The Ministry of Knowledge Economy), Korea, under the ITRC(Information Technology Research Center) support program supervised by the NIPA(National IT Industry Promotion Agency) (NIPA-2011-C1090-1131-0003)

References

1. Kim, D.H., Nodir, K., Chang, C.H., Kim, J.G.: HELISCOPE Project: Research Goal and Survey on Related Technologies. In: The Proceeding of 12th IEEE International Symposium on Object /Component / Service-Oriented Real-Time Distributed Computing (ISORC), Tokyo, pp. 112–118 (2009)
2. Kim, S.-G., et al.: Design and Implementation of an Operational Flight Program for an Unmanned Helicopter FCC Based on the TMO Scheme. In: Lee, S., Narasimhan, P. (eds.) SEUS 2009. LNCS, vol. 5860, pp. 1–11. Springer, Heidelberg (2009)
3. Berard, B., Bidoit, M., Finkel, A., Laroussinie, F., Petit, A., Petrucci, L., Schnoebelen, P.: Systems and Software Verification: Model-Checking Techniques and Tools. Springer, Heidelberg (2001)
4. Lee, D.-A., Yoo, J., Kim, D.: Formal Verification of Process Communications in Operational Flight Program for a Small-Scale Unmanned Helicopter. In: The 6th International Conference on Intelligent Unmanned Systems (ICIUS 2010), Bali, Indonesia, pp. 91–96 (2010)
5. Lee, D.-A., Sung, S., Yoo, J., Kim, D.-H.: Formal Modeling and Verification of Operational Flight Program in a Small-Scale Unmanned Helicopter. Journal of Aerospace Engineering (accepted, 2011)
6. Chikofsky, E.J., Cross, J.H.: II: Reverse engineering and design recovery: a taxonomy. IEEE Software 7(1), 13–17 (1990)
7. Pezze, M., Young, M.: Software testing and analysis: process, principles, and techniques. Wiley (2008)
8. Kim, K.H., Kopetz, H.: A Real-Time Object Model RTO.k and an Experimental Investigation of Its Potentials. In: 18th IEEE Computer Software & Applications Conference, Los Alamitos, pp. 392–402 (1994)
9. Stavroulakis, P., Stamp, M.: Handbook of Information and Communication Security. Springer, Heidelberg (2010)
10. Martin, J., McClure, C.: Diagramming Techniques for Analysts and Programmers. Prentice-Hall, Englewood Cliffs (1985)
11. Yourdon, E.: Constantine, Structured Design. Prentice-Hall, Englewood (1979)
12. Zhu, H., Hall, P., May, J.: Software Unit Test Coverage and Adequacy. ACM Computing Surveys 29, 366–427 (1997)
13. Yourdon, E.: Modern structured analysis. Yourdon Press (1989)
14. Doxygen, `http://www.stack.nl/~dimitri/doxygen/index.html`
15. QNX Software Systems, `http://www.qnx.com`
16. gcov—a Test Coverage Program, `http://gcc.gnu.org/onlinedocs/gcc/Gcov.html`

A Study on UML Model Convergence Using Model Transformation Technique for Heterogeneous Smartphone Application

Woo Yeol Kim, Hyun Seung Son, and Robert Young Chul Kim

Dept. of CIC(Computer and Information Communication), Hongik University, Jochiwon, 339-701, Korea
{john,son,bob}@selab.hongik.ac.kr

Abstract. Smart phones have various types of platform such as Android, Cocoa touch, and Windows Phone. As software is developed in one specific platform, it is impossible to use this software on different platforms. To solve this problem, this paper suggests UML model convergence with model conversion method to develop heterogeneous software per each platform. The suggested method consists of two stages: one TIM(target independent model) stage to abstract a model independent on the particular platform and other TSM(target dependent model) stage to convert the independent model into several target models based on the Model-to-Model transformation method. As a case study, a calculator model on Android oriented Platform is converted into another model on Windows oriented Platform.

Keywords: Model Transformation, Model Convergence, UML, Heterogeneous Smartphone Application, Cross Platform.

1 Introduction

Many different development platforms included in smart phones, such as Symbian, OpenC, iPhone, Android, Windows Phone, and Palm operating systems contains various technologies such as widget, Web runtimes, Python, Lazarus, Brew, Java Mobile Edition (ME), .NET Compact Framework (CF), and Flash Lite [1]. These provide strong mobile contents such as audio, video, multimedia messaging, and Flash. For this reason, most software developers prefer the particular platform-based development. However, as software is developed based on a specific platform, it is impossible to reuse the software into other platforms.

In this paper, we adapt MDD (Model-Driven Development) approach [2] to develop heterogeneous software. The original MDD needs to make automation of the process from design model to code generation [3]. In this method, it is possible to convert one upper model to different lower models based on a basic top-down mechanism. With a platform independent model (upper model), it may generate several platform dependent models. Then model convergence through free movement with common elements between and among heterogeneous models might be difficult. In the previous studies [4,5,6,7,8], smart platform development was conducted with

T.-h. Kim et al. (Eds.): ASEA/DRBC/EL 2011, CCIS 257, pp. 292–297, 2011.

applied MDD mechanism, but it was not for model convergence. This paper suggests a way for model convergence for improving such results

The suggested method consists of two stages: one TIM(target independent model) stage to abstract a model independent on the particular platform and other TSM(target dependent model) stage to convert the independent model into several target models based on the Model-to-Model transformation method. This paper is organized as follows. Chapter 2 describes Model Transformation with related studies. Chapter 3 mentions model convergence for heterogeneous platforms. Chapter 4 presents a case study. Finally, Chapter 5 makes a conclusion.

2 Related Studies

The existing methods to convert models can be largely classified with Direct-Manipulation, Relational, Graph-Transformation, Structure-Driven, and Hybrid approaches [9]. The Direct-Manipulation approach provides internal model conversion and control API. This approach is also good in that there is no constraint on conversion. But its weakness is in that all parts must be materialized for conversion. The relational approach defines a constraint on the relationship between elements of the source model and the target model. Also while there are various connection methods on mapping rules, it is difficult to prepare for a conversion language. The Graph-Transformation approach uses graphs for easily understanding it. However, most conversions are complex, which is a weak point of these approaches. The Structure-Driven method is to provide meta-model definitions of each source and target model with model element structures. This weak point applies to the same model conversion. The Hybrid approach is a combination with two or more these approaches based on different strengths and weaknesses. The Hybrid approach enables various types of conversion, which may make the conversion process complex.

3 Model Conversion Methods for Heterogeneous Platforms

The basic model conversion for heterogeneous platforms is as shown in Figure 1. A model converted is selected in the model on an 'A' platform while the Model-to-Model transformation is applied to convert it into a 'B' Platform model.

The important technology for model convergence is the model-to-model conversion. The description for this is displayed in Figure 2. First, the model to be converted is selected. The selected model includes a library subject to the platform. What is important at this point is the process to separate a model dependent on the platform from that independent of the platform. The method to separate for design is described in detail with four example questions. In this paper, the process to convert this platform-dependent model into a platform-independent model will be called abstractization. This is applied because the conversion into platform-independent

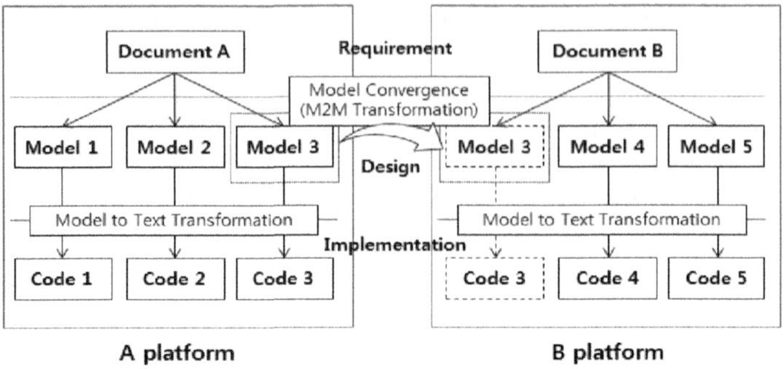

Fig. 1. Schematic diagram for model convergence

models is easier that that into the existing platform-dependent models. Also the abstracted model is converted into a platform subject to conversion. The conversion rule is prepared based on transformation language. The model generated finally through the conversion process is inserted into the model subject to convergence.

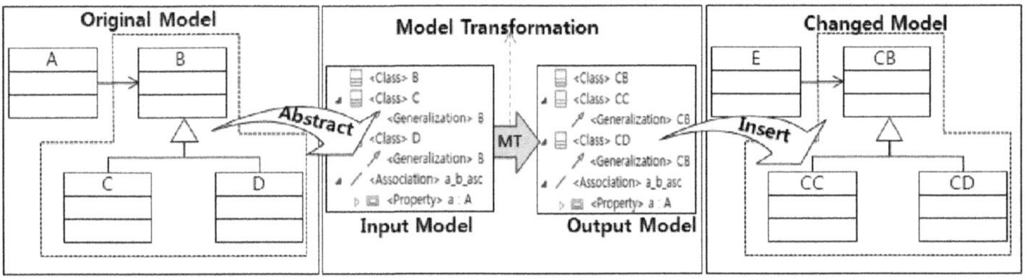

Fig. 2. Model-to-Model Transformation for Model Convergence

4 Case Study

The application model for Android platform, just like Figure 3, is prepared as a class diagram. The calculator class is the main class to play a role of calculators. The event processing in Android platform applies *Listener*. *ButtonListener* class was used to process many buttons at one time. *ResultViewer* class is a class to show the calculated result. The behavior processing when the calculator button is pressed is *ButtonAction* class. As for *ButtonAction* class, the roles were divided into *Backspace*, *Clear*, *ClearEach*, *Dot*, *Number*, and *Operation* classes. *Backspace* is a class to delete one letter when the "BS" button is pressed. *Clear* is a class to delete all data when the "C" button is pressed. *ClearEach* is a class to delete a formula when the "CE" is pressed. *Dot* is a class to feed decimal points when the "." button is pressed. *Number* is a class carrying out processing when number keys are pressed and *Operation* is a class applied when " + ", " - ", " * ", " / " keys are pressed.

Figure 4 is a diagram displaying the results from model conversion. Based on the model conversion process, the result shows that most of the independent model

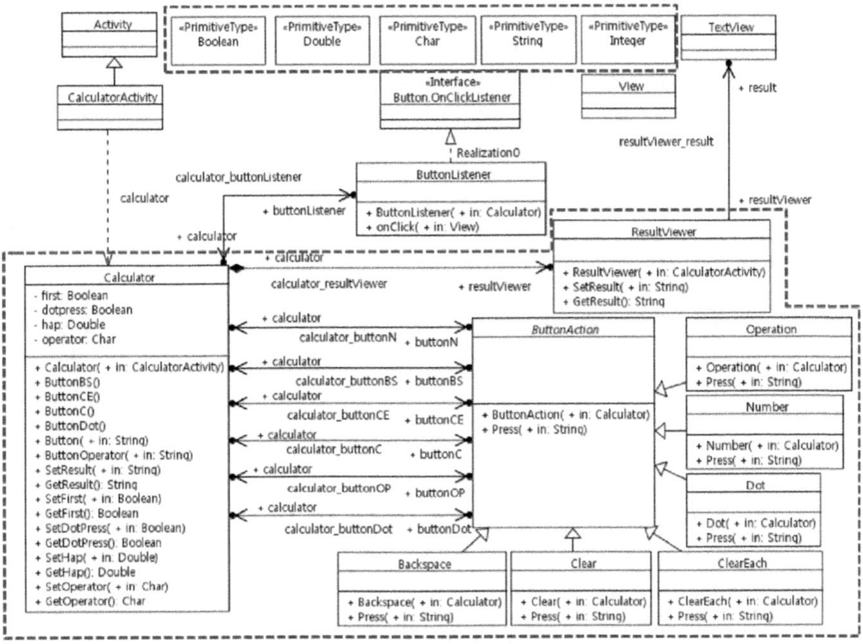

Fig. 3. Class Diagram of Android Platform

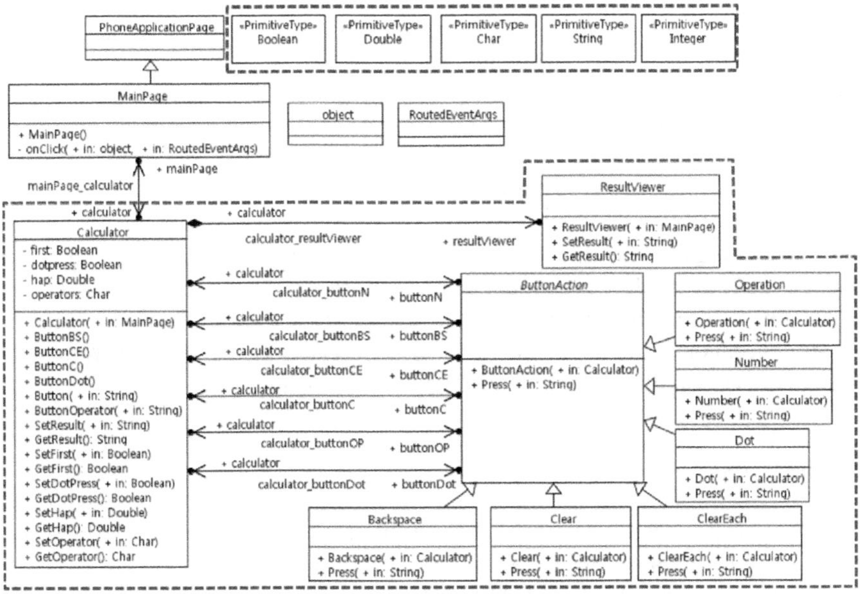

Fig. 4. Class Diagram of Windows Phone Platform

structures can be reused. Also the generation of *MainPage* and *PhoneApplicationPage* classes that are dependent on Windows Phone based on model conversion can be confirmed in the figure. As for Windows Phone, *MainPage* directly receives Event through Method and there is no *ButtonListener* class. In order to increase the reuse of models upon convergence, we can tell that based on the case study, it is important to separate platform-independent areas from platform-dependent ones upon designing model.

5 Conclusion

In the smart phone environment, the model convergence for heterogeneous platforms is more necessary than that for homogeneous ones. In this paper, for the model convergence in heterogeneous platform environment, the original MDD (Model-Driven Development) was adopted into smart phone area. The MDD is a method that automates the process from a software design model to software materialization, and enables the conversion of one upper model into lower models of different types. MDD is a very appropriate way for model conversion, but is not capable of horizontal movement between heterogeneous models. Thus, it is not advantageous in terms of model convergence. Therefore, this paper has suggested a method for model convergence that applies the Model Transformation.

The suggested method uses the Model Transformation as a major technology of MDD and conducts convergence of the existing model with the target model. The first stage is abstractization, separating the platform-dependent models from those platform-independent ones. The second stage is Model-to-Model Transformation, which converts the model from the abstracted model based on the correlation generation rules and class-generating templates into a subject model. The model generated based on abstractization is platform-independent while the dependent attribute of the subject model to be converted can be generated without revising the existing model. As such generation is repeated, we can create class-generating templates and correlation generation methods.

Acknowledgments. This research was supported by Basic Science Research Program through the National Research Foundation of Korea(NRF) funded by the Ministry of Education, Science and Technology(2011-0004203) and the Ministry of Education, Science Technology (MEST) and National Research Foundation of Korea(NRF) through the Human Resource Training Project for Regional Innovation.

References

1. Gavalas, D., Economou, D.: Development Platforms for Mobile Applications: Status and Trends. IEEE Software 28(1), 77–86 (2011)
2. Selic, B.: The pragmatics of model-driven development. IEEE Software 20(5), 19–25 (2003)

3. Czarnecki, K., Helsen, S.: Feature-based survey of model transformation approaches. IBM Systems Journal 45(3), 621–645 (2006)
4. Kim, W.Y., Son, H.S., Kim, J.S., Kim, R.Y.C.: Development of Windows Mobile Applications using Model Transformation techniques. Journal of KIISE: Computing Practices and Letters 16(11), 1091–1095 (2010)
5. Kim, W.Y., Son, H.S., Kim, R.Y.C.: Design of Code Template for Automatic Code Generation of Heterogeneous Smartphone Application. In: Kim, T.-h., Adeli, H., Robles, R.J., Balitanas, M. (eds.) ACN 2011. CCIS, vol. 199, pp. 292–297. Springer, Heidelberg (2011)
6. Kim, W.Y., Son, H.S., Kim, J.S., Kim, R.Y.C.: Adapting Model Transformation Approach for Android Smartphone Application. In: Kim, T.-h., Adeli, H., Robles, R.J., Balitanas, M. (eds.) ACN 2011. CCIS, vol. 199, pp. 421–429. Springer, Heidelberg (2011)
7. Kim, W.Y., Son, H.S., Yoo, J., Park, Y., Kim, R.Y.C.: A Study on Target Model Generation for Smartphone Applications using Model Transformation Technique. In: International Conference on Internet (ICONI) 2010, vol. 2, pp. 557–558 (2010)
8. Son, H.S., Kim, W.Y., Woo Sung J., Kim, R.Y.C.: Development Android Application using Model Transformation. In: Joint Workshop on Software Engineering Technology 2010, vol. 8(1), pp. 64–67 (2010)
9. Czarnecki, K., Helsen, S.: Classification of model transformation approaches. In: OOPSLA 2003 Workshop on Generative Techniques in the Context of Model-Driven Architecture (2003)

A Validation Process for Real Time Transactions

Kyu Won Kim[1], Woo Yeol Kim[2], Hyun Seung Son[2], and Robert Young Chul Kim[2]

[1] Deptatment of Information System, KOVEN Co.,Ltd,
Seoul, 135-270, Korea
kkw1206@kovan.com
[2] Dept. of CIC(Computer and Information Communication), Hongik University,
Jochiwon, 339-701, Korea
{john,son,bob}@selab.hongik.ac.kr

Abstract. Real financial transactions take place on a consecutive real-time serialization. They are carried out as dynamic transaction chains along with various related systems rather than with just one system. This paper suggests a process that generates a test case for the verification of such consecutive real-time transaction system. The suggested process generates a test case through mechanism applied with UML and ECA (Event/Condition/Action) rules. Through analyzing transactions, we generate UML modeling, then maps UML with ECA rules, which creates an ECA-decision table. A test scenario is generated with this table. That is, the test scenario is modeled from an ECA diagram based on the consecutive transaction chains, which generate a test case.

Keywords: transaction, modeling, ECA, test case.

1 Introduction

VAN companies are intermediates that connect affiliates using settlement systems with card companies as well as other various financial institutions. As for credit card settlement systems, credit card terminals, VAN (Value Added Network) companies, and card companies are interconnected [1,2]. Credit card settlement systems were followed by various settlement models such as transaction approvals via telephone wires and terminals, POS systems, and HOST servers [3,4,5].

Based on various settlement models, VAN companies' systems have become more complex. Also, the structure requires the acceptance of all requests from affiliates and financial institutions, resulting in frequent maintenance and repairs of the system [6]. As the number of system change increases, there are more tests on such systems. As for the testing by VAN companies, developers used to play a role of such testers. While a test case shall be provided in consideration of the relations between new requirements and the existing system, there is no systemic way for the preparation of test cases. Reliability of testing depends on the different maturity level with developer's capacity and experiences. Therefore, such a test case depends a lot on the tester's capacity.

This paper suggests a test case generation model to verify real-time transactions that occur in the VAN (Value Added Network) environment. The suggested process

T.-h. Kim et al. (Eds.): ASEA/DRBC/EL 2011, CCIS 257, pp. 298–304, 2011.

generates a test case by applying UML modeling and ECA (Event, Condition Action) rules. In order to generate a test case, real time transactions are analyzed and modeled UML and ECA diagrams, then generated test scenarios. With the test scenarios, we can generate test cases.

This paper consists of the following. Chapter 2 explains a related study. Chapter 3 explains about real-time transactions and suggests a method to generate a test case. Chapter 4 provides conclusions and tasks to be studied in the future.

2 Related Work

The Cause-Effect Graphing technique provides systemic methods to develop a statement prepared in a natural language into a decision table [7]. In the cause-effect graphing technique, it is selected a set of test cases in consideration of causes that have logical relations with effects for a test. This test can take place in the following order.

1. Every requirement is identified.
2. The requirements are analyzed for the identification of every cause and effect to assign a unique number to each cause-effect set.
3. Based on the analysis of requirements, a graph connected causes with effects is provided.
4. The graph is converted into a decision table.
5. Each row in the decision table is selected as a test case for testing.

Decision Table Testing is to describe all movements related to decisions, conditions, and processes required in the process and to prepare for a decision table that displays a movement occurring based on the combination of each decision and condition, which is an effective technique to find errors embedded in the materialization or statement[8]. Each row of the table consisting of combinations between the remaining decisions and actions are selected as a test case.

Finite-State Testing is to test the models of finite states, that is, behaviors of a system [9]. Input and output of every state are identified. The state table includes input combinations of all states and checks whether it can be reached or not before testing. In the finite-state testing stage, a state graph is prepared and converted a state table. Only those that can reach the state based on one specific state are selected like test scenarios (or paths) for testing.

3 Validation Process for Real-Time Transactions

Figure 1 is a process to generate a test case for real-time transaction chains. A use case is modeled based on the path, action and conditions for transactions acquired from analysis. The use case scenario based on the use case modeling is modeled through a sequence diagram. This diagram generates a table that decides ECA (Event, Condition, Action) and an ECA diagram.

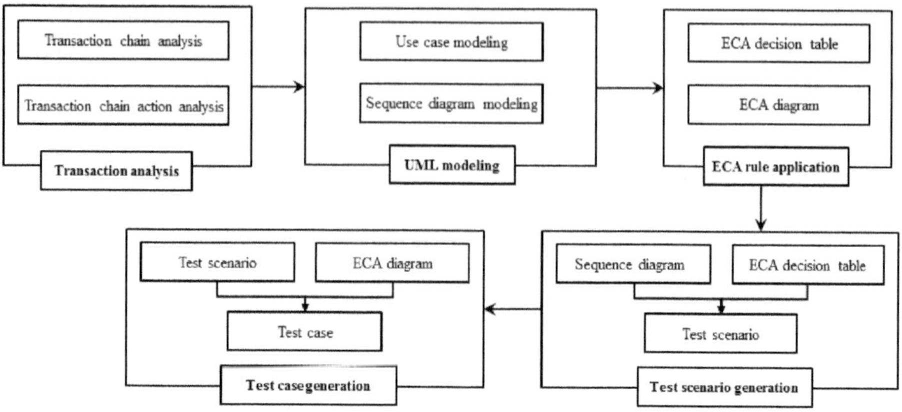

Fig. 1. Process to generate test cases for real-time transactions

Figure 2 is a process to analyze a simple transaction. Unit transactions, T1 (ACTOR), T2 (A), and T3 (B) are defined while unit transaction chain is organized. The transaction is analyzed based on dynamic diagram modeling of transaction chains. In order for T1 to be committed, T2 transaction is committed. In order for T2 transaction to be committed, T3 transaction shall be committed.

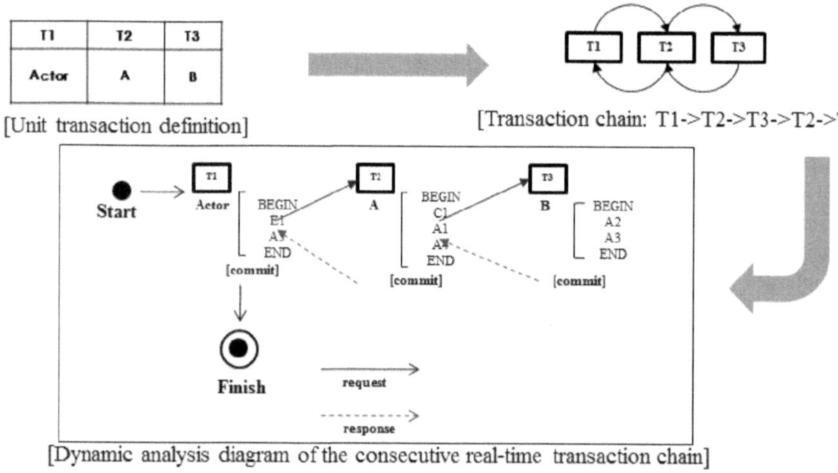

Fig. 2. Analysis of consecutive real-time transactions

Figure 3 shows the UML modeling of a transaction in Figure 2. A sequence diagram generated in the UML modeling can be expressed with an ECA rules. The objects that are organized in a sequence diagram are mapped to the unit transaction with an ECA rules in the ECA decision table. Through mapping Event/Condition/Action on messages between objects, and also assigning the number on them, this information is applied in the ECA decision table, respectively.

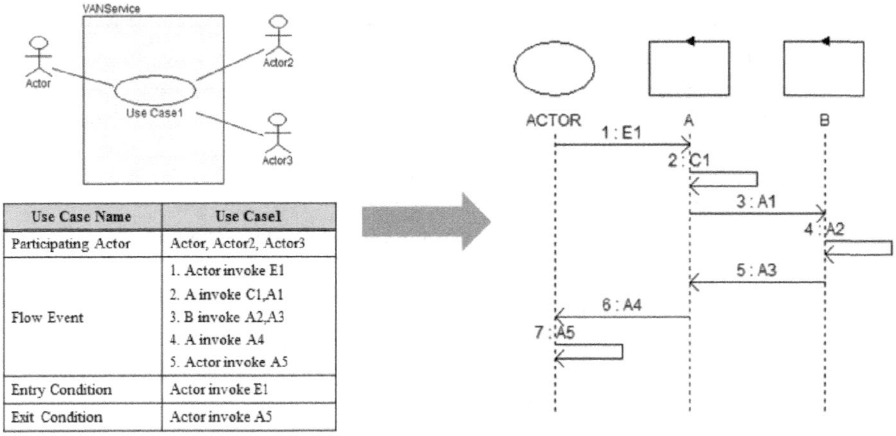

Use Case Name	Use Case1
Participating Actor	Actor, Actor2, Actor3
Flow Event	1. Actor invoke E1 2. A invoke C1,A1 3. B invoke A2,A3 4. A invoke A4 5. Actor invoke A5
Entry Condition	Actor invoke E1
Exit Condition	Actor invoke A5

Fig. 3. UML modeling

Table 1 is an ECA table with an expression of the sequence diagram. Actor's message numbers, 1(E1) and 7(A5) are applied to Event and Action of the unit transaction Actor. A's message numbers, 2(C1), 3(A1), and 6(A4) are applied to Condition and Action of unit transaction A. B's message numbers, 4(A2) and 5(A3) are applied to Action of unit transaction B. Figure 4 is an ECA transaction diagram. Table 1 represents based on the modeling of Figure 4.

Table 1. ECA Decision Table of consecutive real-time transactions

Transaction	EVENT	Condition	Action
Actor	1	-	7
A	-	2	3,6
B	-	-	4,5

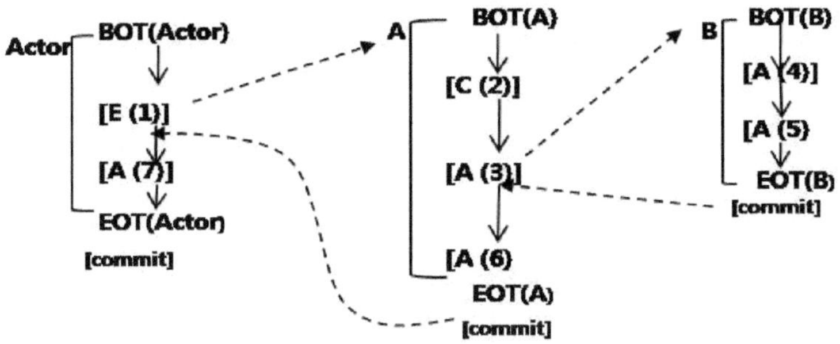

Fig. 4. ECA Diagram

Table 2. Test scenario of consecutive real-time transactions

Transaction	Test scenario
Actor	1- E1 is committed. A commits A4. 7- A5 committed (Actor commit)
A	Actor commits E1 (condition for starting) 2-C1 committed. 3-A1 committed. B commits A3. 6-A4is committed (A commit)
B	A commits A1(condition for starting) 4-A2 committed. 5-A3 committed (B commit)

Table 2 is a test scenario organized based on the combination with the sequence diagram in Figure 3 and the decision table in Table 2. Unit transactions of the decision table are applied to the transactions in Table 2 while Event, Condition, and Action of each unit transaction are applied to the test scenario. Messages pertaining to Event, Condition, and Action in the ECA decision table are represented from the sequence diagram for a test scenario. Figure 5 is a test case generated based on the combination with the ECA transaction diagram and the test scenario in Table 2. The ECA based Test Cases consist of the subject transaction, test case ID, conditions for starting, Action, and expected results.

Subject transaction	Test case	Conditions for starting	Action	Expected result
Actor	TC1	-	E1	A begin
Actor	TC2	-	A5	Actor commit
A	TC3	E1	C1	A1
A	TC4	C1	A1	A2
A	TC5	B commit	A4 execution	A Commit
B	TC6	A1	A2	A3
B	TC7	A2	A3	B commit

Fig. 5. ECA-based Test Case

Transactions of the test scenarios are applied to the subject transactions while the actions prior to those to be conducted are applied as for conditions to start. The actions following those to be conducted are applied for the expected results.

4 Examples of Application

As a case study, the application is for point card transactions that occur in the VAN environment. There are four transactions such as point view, point collection, point use, and point cancellation. As for the application to "point card" transactions, the information on test cards and test affiliates is necessary. For this, hypothetical test card numbers and affiliate numbers are to be set up. A real test case is generated based on this.

5 Conclusion

A functional test in real time transaction chains take place based on the statements of requirements. A test case is mainly based on functional requirement. As most companies in real time transaction environments do not have any methods to generate test cases, they prepare with this testing based on their accumulated experiences. In this paper, we suggest validation process to test consecutive real-time transactions from transaction analysis. The suggested process generates UML modeling and ECA (Event, Condition Action) rules, and makes ECA decision table. With sequence diagram and ECA decision table, we can generate test scenarios, and then extracts test cases through dynamic transaction analysis. We still research on test cases about parallel transactions.

Acknowledgments. This research was supported by the MKE(The Ministry of Knowledge Economy), Korea, under the ITRC(Information Technology Research Center) support program supervised by the NIPA(National IT Industry Promotion Agency)(NIPA-2011-(C1090-1131-0008)) and the Ministry of Education, Science Technology (MEST) and National Research Foundation of Korea(NRF) through the Human Resource Training Project for Regional Innovation.

References

1. Sam-saeng, H., Jae-young, Y., Hee-cheol, M.: A study on electronic transactions via VAN-based computers and networks. In: The Korean Academy of International Business Management, Symposium Proceeding 2001, pp. 159–185 (2001)
2. Seong-geun, K., Jae-beom, L., Joo-heon, L., Gwang-ho, C.: A study on inter-industry information network for the facilitation of VAN industrialization. The Korean Academic Society of Business Administration 2, 24 (1990)
3. Gi-hyeon, L., Hong-hoi, G.: The present and future of Korea's financial VAN. Communications of the Korea Information Science Society 6(5), 15–22 (1988)
4. Gi-yong, K.: The future prospect for VAN. Communications of the Korea Information Science Society 6(5), 5–10 (1988)
5. Geon-joong, K.: VAN and its use. Telcom 6(2), 71–79 (1990)

6. Kyu-Won, K., Bo-Kyung, P., Woo-Sung, J., So-Young, M., Kim, R.Y.C.: A Study on System Implementation through modeling the Financial VAN(Vale Added Network) Connected Service Based on Reverse engineering. In: Korea Computer Congress 2010, Jeju, Korea, vol. 37(1)(B), pp. 92–96 (2010)
7. Nursimulu, K., Probert, R.L.: Cause-Effect Graphing Analysis and Validation of Requirements. In: Proceeding of the 1995 Conference of the Centre for Advanced Studies on Collaborative Research, pp. 46–61 (1995)
8. Beizer, B.: Software Testing Techniques. Van Nostrand Reinhold Inc., New York (1990)
9. Ji-Hyun, L., Hye-Min, N., Cheol-Jung, Y., Ok-Bae, C., Jun-Wook, L.: Test Case Generation Technique for Interoperability Testing. Journal of KIISE: Software and Applications 33(1), 44–58 (2006)

A Test Management System for Operational Validation

Myoung Wan Kim[1], Woo Yeol Kim[2],
Hyun Seung Son[2], and Robert Young Chul Kim[2]

[1] Institute of Technology, Infnis, Inc.,
Seoul, 135-080, Korea
kimmw@infnis.com

[2] Dept. of CIC(Computer and Information Communication), Hongik University,
Jochiwon, 339-701, Korea
{john,son,bob}@selab.hongik.ac.kr

Abstract. NMS (Network Management System) is a central monitoring system that can manage equipment on network environments. This should be used for efficient and centralized management of network equipment. On NMS, it enables the real-time transmission and monitoring of the data on states, problems, composition, and statistics of equipment that make a network. But we need to verify whether it works on operations or functions of NMS operations or not. To do this, this paper suggests a test management system for the efficient verification of NMS environments. In order to develop a test management system, requirements from each NMS shall be extracted, and designed and materialized based on them. The suggested system enables efficient test management, result analysis, and comparative verification of test versions.

Keywords: NMS, test, test management system, verification.

1 Introduction

NMS (Network Management System) is a central monitoring system that can manage equipment on a network. This is used for efficient and centralized management of network equipment [1,2]. NMS enables to the real-time transmission and monitoring of the data on states, problems, composition, and statistics of equipment that make a network. When problems with the equipment are occurred, an alarm signal can be transmitted to a manager for a speedy measurement. Statistics and states of networks can also be analyzed based on the collected information [3].

Figure 1 shows the network of NSM. Each company manages its own network, which should make NMS system test system requirements, functions, and operations.

In order to verify NSM of various environments, the existing test has been conducted manually via a checklist with the managed results based on documentation [4,5,6]. There are the problems with manual operation of the test results in that it is difficult to integrate test results as various testers conduct testing simultaneously because the analysis and management of the test results does not appropriately executed. The version management of test cases is also not sufficient and the reuse of test cases is difficult.

T.-h. Kim et al. (Eds.): ASEA/DRBC/EL 2011, CCIS 257, pp. 305–313, 2011.

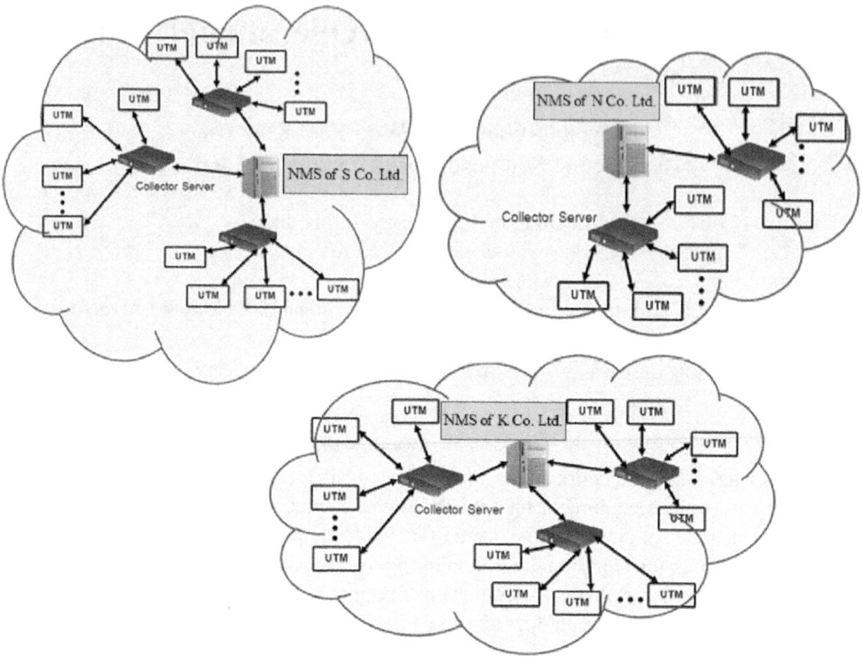

Fig. 1. Composition of NSM

This paper suggests test management system to solve such problems. In order to develop a test management system, each NMS environment is analyzed, which helps to extract requirements. Based on the extracted requirements, a test management system is designed and managed. The suggested system enables efficient test management, result analysis, and comparative verification of test versions. The currently used NMS tests were conducted as a case study and the results were applied to the suggested test management system.

This paper consists of the following. Chapter 2 explains about NMS as related studies. Chapter 3 describes the suggested test management system. Chapter 4 shows the application system of this suggested test management system as an applied case study. Finally, Chapter 5 provides conclusions and describes the future studies.

2 Network Management System

NMS centrally monitors communication networks on the network [7]. NMS consists of NMS servers providing main functions, which collect receiving data from equipment, sending them to NMS Server, and saving data to DB server. NMS is organized as Figure 2. Each UTM equipment on the network transmits system monitoring data, alarm data related to problems, log data, and equipment registration data to NMS system via collector server while NMS Server provides central management of the related network.

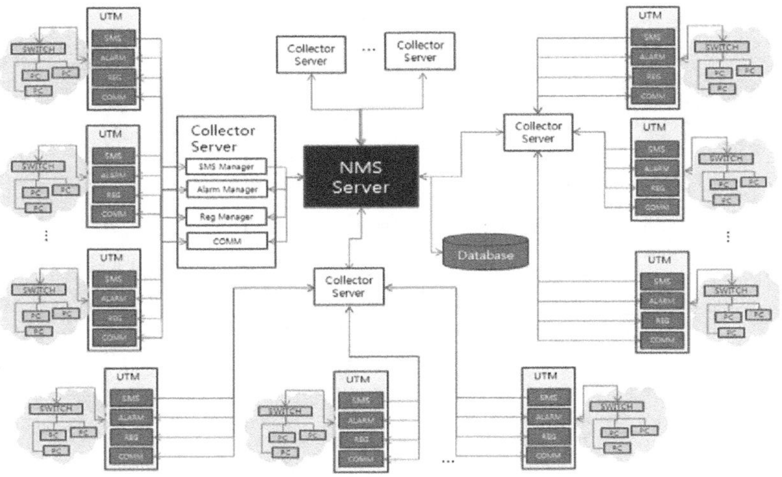

Fig. 2. NMS organization

NMS Server can centrally manage network equipment based on the information on UTM equipment states, problems, and log received from Collector Server. It provides with user management UI for managing Collector Server and UTM equipment. It analyzes the data received from UTM equipment and provides statistical information. Based on the collected and analyzed data, it organizes the status of interface links of UTM equipment and IPSEC tunnel links as well as the monitoring screen, generating a report.

Individual connecttion to each UTM equipment can bring the information of setup of interface, routing, NAT, firewall, IPS, web filter, and content filter and the setup change is available. Multiple UTM equipments can be grouped to order firewall rules, group IPS rules, group web filter rules, and content filter rules simultaneously.

3 Proposed Test Management System

3.1 The Test Management System Architecture

Figure 3 is architecture of the suggested test management system. The values to be fed firstly in the test management system include that the version information, types of test manuals, and test cases are extracted through analysis. The user authorization is implemented via the account management module. After authorization, the information is managed in the TESTID management mode.

After the test cases are extracted through analyses, the relevant test cases are tested while the results are managed through the test manual management module. The test manual management module can manage preconditions, testing steps, and actual results. Finally, the testing for test results is managed in the test result management module, which provides the functions such as the result document printing and preview.

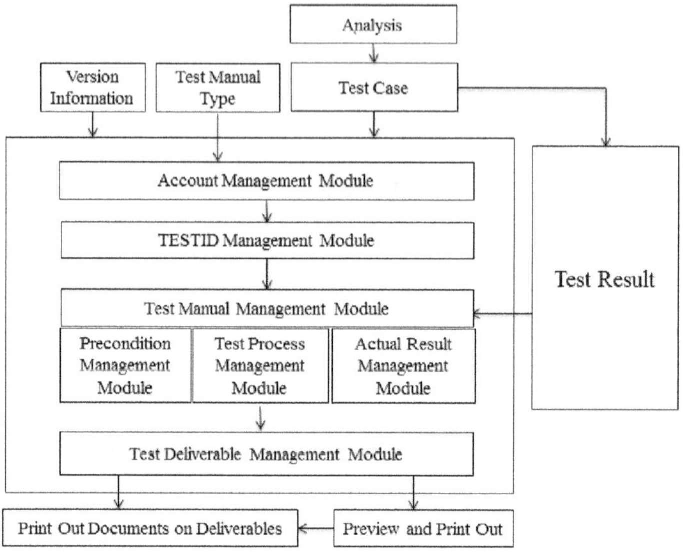

Fig. 3. Test Management System Architecture

3.2 Integrated data model

The integrated data model is to manage the data generated in the test management system. Figure 4 is an expression of this integrated data model in the E-R diagram.

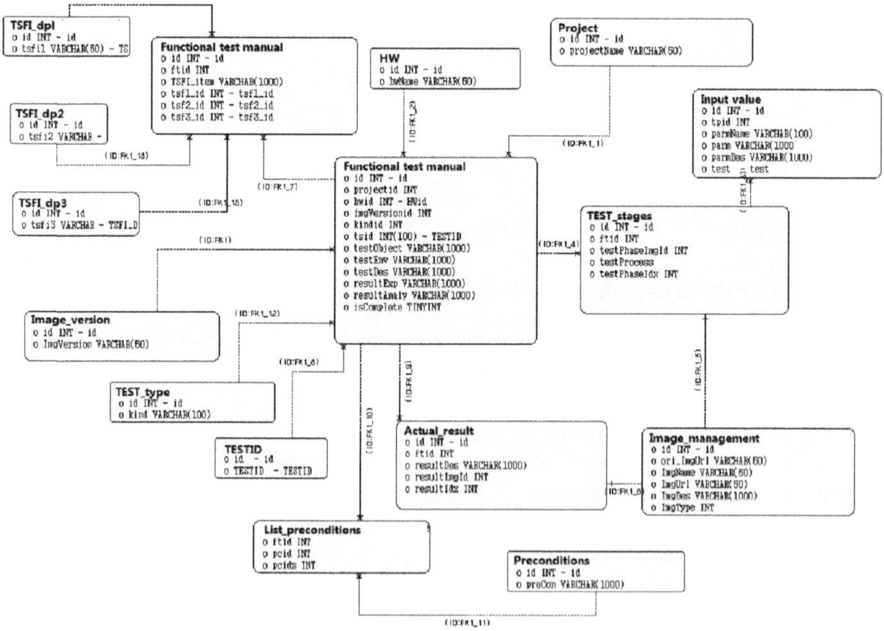

Fig. 4. Integrated data model for a test management system

The integrated data model integrates the basic TESTID information, list of preconditions, list of testing stages, and list of actual results, enabling the printing of test result forms through the test manual management module and the test deliverables management module in Figure 5.

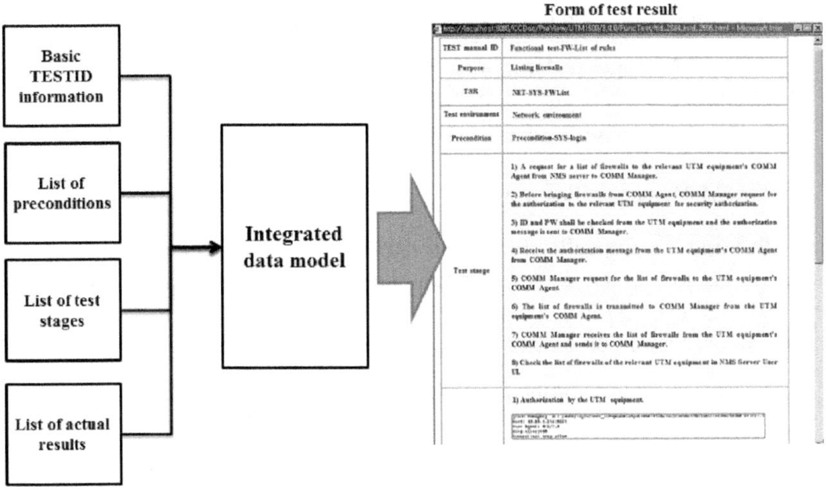

Fig. 5. Generation of the test results

The specifications on the basic TESTID information, list of preconditions, list of testing stages, and list of actual results were defined while the Pseudo Code of data-integrating algorithm in Figure 6 was prepared based on the defined classification codes. The data-integrating algorithm can lead to the extraction of test results.

```
String report = A1 + A2 + A5 + A3 + A4      }- Basic TESTID information
If( B1.length > 0 ){
        for( B1.length ){
report += B1                                 }- Information on preconditions
        }
}

If( C1.length > 0 ){
        for( C1.length ){
                report += C2 + C1
                If( D1.length > 0 ){
                for( D1.length ){
                 report += D3 + D2 + D1      }- Test stage and input values
                }
            }
        }
}

report += A7        }- Expected results

If( E1.length > 0 ){
        for( E1.length ){
              report += E2 + E1 + E3         }- Actual results
        }
}

Report += A8        }- Analysis of test information
```

Fig. 6. Data-integrating algorithm

4 NMS Verification Using the Test Management System

This chapter explores the functions of the developed test management system and verifies by it by using the test management system and carrying out NSM tests based on the actual test cases.

The followings take place to verify the test management system.

1) COMM Manager testing
2) Feeding the test results in the test management system
3) Confirming the printing of test results in the test management system

4.1 COMM Manager Testing

In order to bring the firewall rule setup list from NMS Server, the firewall rule list is transmitted based on the communication between COMM Manager in Collector Server and COMM Agent in UTM equipments. Afterwards, the test confirmation in NMS Server user's UI will be carried out.

1) Testing a request for the list of firewall rules to COMM Agent of the relevant UTM equipment from NMS Server to COMM Manager

```
[COMM Manager]  FilterCmd called!!!
[COMM Manager]  new create FWPolicyInfo called!!!
```

2) Before importing the firewall rules from COMM Agent, testing an authorization request from COMM Manager to the relevant UTM equipment for security authorization

```
[COMM Manager]  GET /auth/login?user_id=[redacted]&pwd=[redacted] HTTP/1.1
Host: 10.80.1.216:9221
User-Agent: WEB/2.0
Keep-Alive:300
Connection: keep-alive
```

3) ID and PW to be checked in the UTM equipment and testing the transmission of authorization messages to COMM Manager

```
13:40:37.595659 IP 10.80.1.61.2637 > 10.80.1.216.ipcg: S 601707624:601707624(0) win 65535 <ms
s 1460,nop,nop,sackOK>
13:40:37.595760 IP 10.80.1.216.ipcg > 10.80.1.61.2637: S 1256001678:1256001678(0) ack 6017076
25 win 5840 <mss 1460,nop,nop,sackOK>
13:40:37.596758 IP 10.80.1.61.2637 > 10.80.1.216.ipcg: . ack 1 win 65535
13:40:37.596807 IP 10.80.1.61.2637 > 10.80.1.216.ipcg: P 1:101(100) ack 1 win 65535
13:40:37.596834 IP 10.80.1.216.ipcg > 10.80.1.61.2637: . ack 101 win 5840
13:40:37.607723 IP 10.80.1.216.ipcg > 10.80.1.61.2637: P 1:855(854) ack 101 win 5840
13:40:37.610974 IP 10.80.1.61.2637 > 10.80.1.216.ipcg: P 101:240(139) ack 855 win 64681
13:40:37.654447 IP 10.80.1.216.ipcg > 10.80.1.61.2637: . ack 240 win 6432
13:40:37.655428 IP 10.80.1.61.2637 > 10.80.1.216.ipcg: P 240:283(43) ack 855 win 64681
13:40:37.655581 IP 10.80.1.216.ipcg > 10.80.1.61.2637: . ack 283 win 6432
13:40:37.655970 IP 10.80.1.216.ipcg > 10.80.1.61.2637: P 855:898(43) ack 283 win 6432
13:40:37.657562 IP 10.80.1.61.2637 > 10.80.1.216.ipcg: P 283:479(196) ack 898 win 64638
13:40:37.671175 IP 10.80.1.216.ipcg > 10.80.1.61.2637: P 898:1121(223) ack 479 win 7504
13:40:37.671446 IP 10.80.1.216.ipcg > 10.80.1.61.2637: FP 1121:1144(23) ack 479 win 7504
13:40:37.673730 IP 10.80.1.61.2637 > 10.80.1.216.ipcg: . ack 1145 win 64392
13:40:37.685085 IP 10.80.1.61.2637 > 10.80.1.216.ipcg: P 479:502(23) ack 1145 win 64392
13:40:37.685105 IP 10.80.1.61.2637 > 10.80.1.216.ipcg: F 502:502(0) ack 1145 win 64392
13:40:37.685265 IP 10.80.1.216.ipcg > 10.80.1.61.2637: . ack 503 win 7504
13:40:37.686212 IP 10.80.1.61.2637 > 10.80.1.216.ipcg: R 601708127:601708127(0) win 0
13:40:37.688717 IP 10.80.1.61.2639 > 10.80.1.216.ipcg: S 2759155723:2759155723(0) win 65535 <
mss 1460,nop,nop,sackOK>
13:40:37.688776 IP 10.80.1.216.ipcg > 10.80.1.61.2639: S 1250485726:1250485726(0) ack 2759155
724 win 5840 <mss 1460,nop,nop,sackOK>
```

4) Testing an authorization message receipt from COMM Agent of the UTM equipment in COMM Manager

```
[COMM Manager] Connect to Server : 10.80.1.216  Port: 9221
[COMM Manager] Client IP : 10.80.1.61
 Response    : <utm_rule><ret><val>0</val><msg>HTTP/1.1 [redacted]
Connection: close
Date: Sun Oct 24 13:36:13 2010
WWW-Authenticate: Digest realm="[redacted]", nonce="44fb0dc891d1f67b01e931d181f784ba1e1287894973", algorithm=[redacted],
qop="auth"</msg></ret></utm_rule>
[COMM Manager] GET /auth/login?user_id=[redacted]&pud=[redacted] HTTP/1.1
Host: 10.80.1.216:9221
User-Agent: WEB/2.0
Accept: */*
Connection: Keep-Alive
Authorization: Digest username="[redacted]", realm="[redacted]", nonce="44fb0dc891d1f67b01e931d181f784ba1e1287894973",
algorithm=RIPEMD160, qop="auth"</msg></ret></utm_rule>, nc=00000001, address="10.80.1.61", uri="/auth/login?
user_id=[redacted]&pud=[redacted]", cnonce="cnon",
response="5c9dca910ccaf7e0549185c733cda67390e8936b"
```

5) Testing a request for firewall rules from COMM Manager to the UTM equipment's COMM Agent

```
[COMM Manager] Connect to Server : 10.80.1.216  Port: 9221
[COMM Manager] Client IP : 10.80.1.61
[COMM Manager] session id=4a6bb6844551f4334118bf00f310f90641287895237
[COMM Manager] GET /fw/list_filter HTTP/1.1
Authorization: Digest utm_nonce="4a6bb6844551f4334118bf00f310f90641287895237", username="[redacted]", address="10.80.1.61"
Host: 10.80.1.216
User-Agent: WEB/2.0
Connection: close
```

6) Testing the transmission of the firewall list from the UTM equipment's COMM Agent to COMM Manager

```
13:40:37.816266 IP 10.80.1.61.2640 > 10.80.1.216.ipcg: S 2577325587:2577325587(0) win 65535 <
mss 1460,nop,nop,sackOK>
13:40:37.816330 IP 10.80.1.216.ipcg > 10.80.1.61.2640: S 1253272785:1253272785(0) ack 2577325
588 win 5840 <mss 1460,nop,nop,sackOK>
13:40:37.817324 IP 10.80.1.61.2640 > 10.80.1.216.ipcg: . ack 1 win 65535
13:40:37.817383 IP 10.80.1.61.2640 > 10.80.1.216.ipcg: P 1:101(100) ack 1 win 65535
13:40:37.817407 IP 10.80.1.216.ipcg > 10.80.1.61.2640: . ack 101 win 5840
13:40:37.828266 IP 10.80.1.216.ipcg > 10.80.1.61.2640: P 1:855(854) ack 101 win 5840
13:40:37.833120 IP 10.80.1.61.2640 > 10.80.1.216.ipcg: P 101:240(139) ack 855 win 64681
13:40:37.874433 IP 10.80.1.216.ipcg > 10.80.1.61.2640: . ack 240 win 6432
13:40:37.875410 IP 10.80.1.61.2640 > 10.80.1.216.ipcg: P 240:283(43) ack 855 win 64681
13:40:37.875480 IP 10.80.1.216.ipcg > 10.80.1.61.2640: . ack 283 win 6432
13:40:37.875764 IP 10.80.1.216.ipcg > 10.80.1.61.2640: P 855:898(43) ack 283 win 6432
13:40:37.877937 IP 10.80.1.61.2640 > 10.80.1.216.ipcg: P 283:517(234) ack 898 win 64638
13:40:37.918455 IP 10.80.1.216.ipcg > 10.80.1.61.2640: . ack 517 win 7504
13:40:37.982523 IP 10.80.1.216.ipcg > 10.80.1.61.2640: P 898:1786(888) ack 517 win 7504
13:40:37.983152 IP 10.80.1.216.ipcg > 10.80.1.61.2640: FP 1786:1809(23) ack 517 win 7504
13:40:37.983559 IP 10.80.1.61.2640 > 10.80.1.216.ipcg: . ack 1810 win 65535
13:40:37.984567 IP 10.80.1.61.2640 > 10.80.1.216.ipcg: P 517:540(23) ack 1810 win 65535
13:40:37.984586 IP 10.80.1.61.2640 > 10.80.1.216.ipcg: F 540:540(0) ack 1810 win 65535
```

7) After receiving the firewall rules from COMM Manager to the UTM equipment COMM Agent, testing the transmission to NMS Server

```
[COMM Manager] Connect to Server : 10.80.1.216  Port: 9221
[COMM Manager] Client IP : 10.80.1.61
-----------------------------------------------------------
Test Module name = UnDefined-Debug-Module
Contents **********************
RecvMsg =
<utm_rule>
<idxlist>
<idxnum>2</idxnum>
<idxnum>3</idxnum>
</idxlist>
<filter>
<id>1</id>
<name>a1111111111l</name>
<idxnum>2</idxnum>
<indev>any</indev>
```

8) Testing the confirmation of the relevant UTM equipment's firewall rule list in NMS Server user's UI

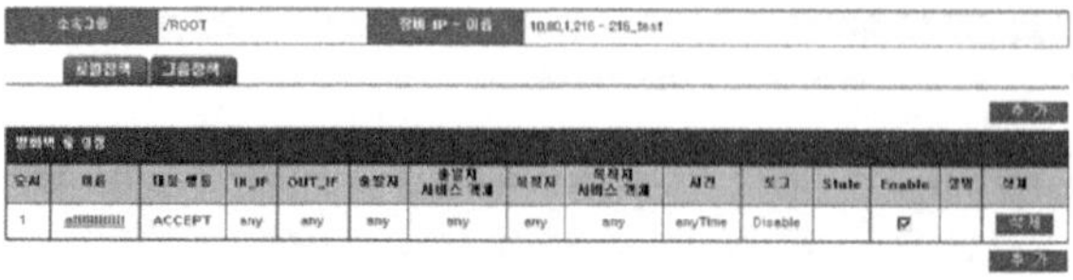

4.2 Confirmation of the Printing of Test Results

The results of tests of each stage are fed into the test management system. Pressing Preview or Print ensures printing based on the following form in Figure 7 through the test result management module.

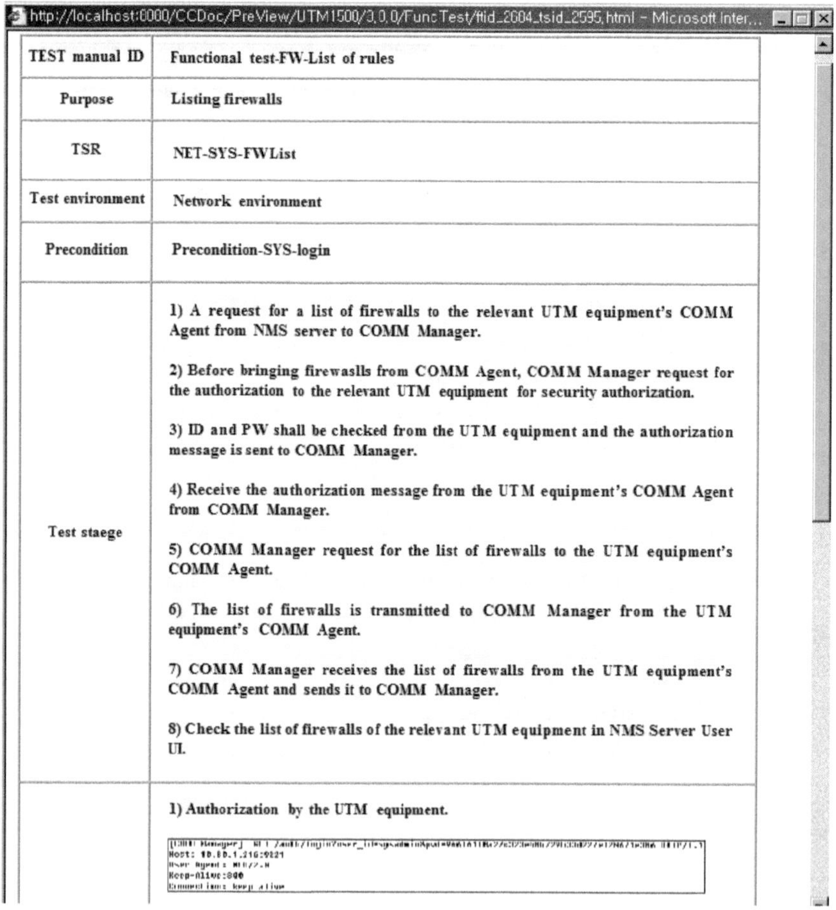

TEST manual ID	Functional test-FW-List of rules
Purpose	Listing firewalls
TSR	NET-SYS-FWList
Test environment	Network environment
Precondition	Precondition-SYS-login
Test staege	1) A request for a list of firewalls to the relevant UTM equipment's COMM Agent from NMS server to COMM Manager. 2) Before bringing firewaslls from COMM Agent, COMM Manager request for the authorization to the relevant UTM equipment for security authorization. 3) ID and PW shall be checked from the UTM equipment and the authorization message is sent to COMM Manager. 4) Receive the authorization message from the UTM equipment's COMM Agent from COMM Manager. 5) COMM Manager request for the list of firewalls to the UTM equipment's COMM Agent. 6) The list of firewalls is transmitted to COMM Manager from the UTM equipment's COMM Agent. 7) COMM Manager receives the list of firewalls from the UTM equipment's COMM Agent and sends it to COMM Manager. 8) Check the list of firewalls of the relevant UTM equipment in NMS Server User UI.
	1) Authorization by the UTM equipment.

Fig. 7. Test result form

5 Conclusion

The test to verify the efficient operation of NMS was manually conducted based on a documented checklist. The test results were managed in Excel or Word, requiring the analysis or management of test results. Many testers tested each assigned part and collected all the results, resulting in problems with integrated management. This produced requirements for the test caser version management and reuse.

This paper designed and materialized the test management system to overcome such problems with NMS. The integration became more convenient as many testers' test results were centrally managed via the test management system. As the test results were documented and kept after computation, the safe storage was ensured. The test management system enabled separate saving of test results by version while the test case reuse are helped with efficient testing. Also, the interrelatedness of test cases was found while the automated report printing for test results became possible.

While there is a system that manages erroneous operation (bugs, errors, or faults) by using a tool like Bugzilla in the existing open sources and Bugzilla tool can be conveniently used as a means for communication between developers and testers, the suggested test management system not only provides overall test management of the system but also organically derives the result documents according to circumstances.

The test management tool and the test automation tool can be integrated to derive a way to support more efficient testing as a future study.

Acknowledgments. This research was supported by 2010 Hongik University Research Fund and National Research Foundation of Korea(NRF) through the Human Resource Training Project for Regional Innovation.

References

1. Nam Su, K., Hye Kyoung, R., Jai Ho, C., Gi Moo, C.: NMS Trends and The Case of Application of NMS for Effective Network Management. In: KICS 2003, pp. 11–34 (2003)
2. YoungJin, P., YoungMin, K., JaeWon, P., ChiYoung, L., NamYong, L.: A Conceptual Quality Evaluation Model of NMS Software Systems. In: Proceedings of The 32th KIISE Fall Conference, vol. 32(2), pp. 391–393 (2005)
3. Seong-ho, K.: Design and Implementation of NMS Platform using Multithread. KNOM Reveiw 4(1), 39–47 (2001)
4. Seokhwan, J., Jeongdong, K., Doo-Kwon, B.: A Flexible Unit Testing Tool for Test Driven Development. Journal of KIISE: Computing Practices and Letters 15(2), 140–144 (2009)
5. Joong Hee, M., Seong Hee, J., Sung Hoon, K., Yong Rae, K.: The Experimental Comparison of Fault Detection Efficiency of Black Box Testing Methods. In: Korea Computer Congress 2007, vol. 34(1)(B), pp. 41–46 (2007)
6. Eunjung, C., Byoungju, C.: Test Process Execution Tool: Test PET. Journal of KIISE: Computing Practices and Letters 10(2), 125–133 (2004)
7. Myoung-Wan K., Kim, R.Y.C.: A Study on Modeling NMS for the Effective Management among the Security VPNs. In: The IWIT 2009 Fall Green IT Conference, vol. 7(2), pp. 196–200 (2009)

Mobile Application Compatibility Test System Design for Android Fragmentation

Hyung Kil Ham and Young Bom Park

Information Architecture Labority, Department of Computer Science and Engineering, Dankook University, Cheonan, Korea
fhipuer@naver.com, ybpark@dankook.ac.kr

Abstract. Android is an open operating system developed by the Open Handset Alliance (OHA) that Google-led. However, due to the nature of an open operating system, Android has the fragmentation problem which is mobile application behavior varies by device. And due to this problem, a developer has been consuming a lot of time and money to develop mobile app test. In this paper, we have designed mobile application compatibility test system for android fragmentation. This system is designed to compare code analysis result and API pre-testing to detect android fragmentation. By comparing the fragmentation in the code level and the API level, the time and cost of mobile application test can be reduced.

Keywords: Android Fragmentation Problem, Android Compatibility, Compatibility Test System.

1 Introduction

Since Android is an open operating system developed by the Open Handset Alliance (OHA) that is Google-led, it is different from existing mobile operating system. It is an open platform; source code is publicly available so that anyone can create software and can make embedded devices for Android [1]. For this reason, many manufacturers have been involved in the development of Android devices.

But recently, due to various devices which is developed in various manufacturers, Android has the fragmentation problem which is mobile application behavior varies by device [2]. As a developer, ensuring compatibility between Android devices is an important issue. But practically, full compatibility between devices from different manufactures and even from the same manufactures does not ensured [3]. According to the survey results of Baird Research, 86% of developers think that the Android fragmentation is a serious problem, and particularly, 24% of developers think that Android fragmentation is very serious problem. [4]

To deal with Android fragmentation problem, Google have been proposed the Android Compatibility Program [5] to maintain compatibility between Android devices. But fragmentation problem is still not resolved. Due to this problem, a developer is porting each mobile apps for each device and has been consuming a lot of time and money to develop mobile app test.

T.-h. Kim et al. (Eds.): ASEA/DRBC/EL 2011, CCIS 257, pp. 314–320, 2011.

In this paper, we have designed mobile application compatibility test system for android fragmentation. This system is designed to compare code analysis result and API pre-testing to detect android fragmentation. By comparing the fragmentation in the code level and the API level, fragmentation problems are detected without directly porting to the device. And the time and cost of mobile application test can be effectively reduced..

2 Related Work

2.1 Android Fragmentation

Android fragmentation has been recognized as a very important problem in among developers and has been mentioned a lot. However, it did not clearly define. Google's Open Source & Compatibility Program Manager Dan Morril said that many peoples have each different definition for android fragmentation. [2] For example, he said that too many mobile operating systems, others to refer to optional APIs causing inconsistent platform implementations, "locked down" device, existence of multiple versions of the software at the same time, and existence of different UI skins. In this paper, definition of android fragmentation is shown in figure 1.

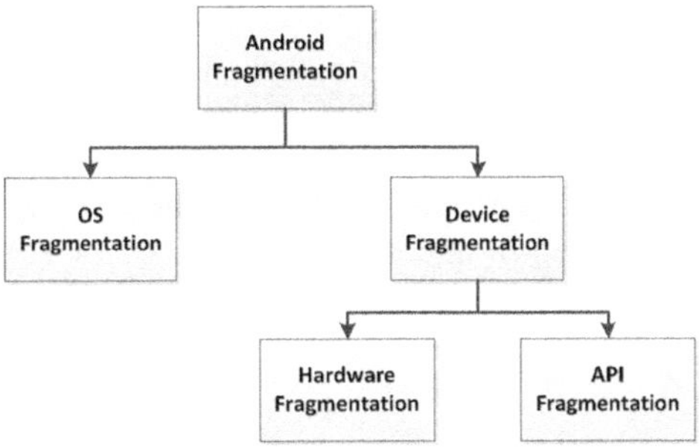

Fig. 1. Android Fragmentation Problem Category

Android fragmentation means that Apps behavior that is different on each android device. Android fragmentation is divided into the OS fragmentation and the device fragmentation. And device fragmentation is divided into the hardware fragmentation and the API fragmentation.

OS fragmentation means fragmentation due to different versions. This means version compatibility problem due to Android's frequent upgrade. However, OS Fragmentation problem has been resolved that reduced the proportion of older version device and updated android adjustment and ensured google's update. [6]

The major problem is device fragmentation. Hardware fragmentation means between devices are different hardware specifications. Typically, resolution is problematic. [7] API fragmentation is a problem to modifying the base Android API for the differentiation strategy of each manufacturer and service provider. [2]

Due to this problem, The Developers have conducted the test that each device is directly ported. And they were trying to solve the fragmentation problem.

However, this method is very time consuming to test. And this method had caused a lot of money from the process of collecting device, the process of building test workers. In addition, due to problems of time and money, the developer has a specific device supports. Or if you are switching to other mobile operating systems were also raised.

2.2 Google's Android Compatibility Program

Google also felt seriousness on the android fragmentation. As a solution, Android compatibility program was offered. Android compatibility program is program to support develop compatibility with the device in areas of a variety including software and hardware from mobile device manufacturers.

The following is composed of three elements:

- Android Source Code
- Compatibility Definition Document(**CDD**)
- Compatibility Test Suite(CTS)

Of these the CDD [8] is a document that describes the policy of the android compatibility, and CTS [9] is a set of test case to test compatibility for Android API. When manufacturer create the device without having to pass the CTS, they can deliver products to the market. But they cannot be mounted "Google Search", "Google Maps", "Google Market," and such Google Mobile services (GMS).

The major problem, android compatibility program properly does not resolved fragmentation problem. Precisely the criteria for passing the CTS has not been revealed, if tests are performed from commercial devices, most are not 100%. Above all, CTS is a program that checks for compatibility to android device. When developing the app, the current structure cannot be used.

3 Test Method Suggestion

In this paper, for fragmentation problem from a developer perspective, first study proposed two methods to replace test method which directly ported apps under development.

3.1 Code Level Test Method Suggestion

The first proposed Code Level Check Method is a method for the detection of fragmentation problem on the code level. The fragmentation problem to detect does not dependent on device, and appears in common. Often this appears when using the development method that does not recognize fragmentation problem.

Accordingly, source code analyses, and the source code that caused the fragmentation detect. This is idea of this method.

Example of the android layout source code

```
 <LinearLayout
xmlns:android="http://schemas.android.com/apk/res/android
"
      android:orientation="vertical"
      android:padding="10px"
      android:layout_width="fill_parent"
      android:layout_height="wrap_content">

      <TextView
          android:layout_width="fill_parent"
          android:layout_height="wrap_content"
          android:layout_marginBottom="10px"
```

As above, layout code using xml example. See section marked in bold. If used a pixel of fixed (px), does not display properly on the device to support the various resolutions. Thus, it should be replaced by the Density-Independent Pixel (dip).

3.2 Device API Level Test Method Suggestion

The second proposed Device API Level Check Method is a method for the detection of fragmentation problem on the API level. The fragmentation problem to detect is that Android API operates differently in the device. Primarily when it does not maintain compatibility between devices, it appears. Idea of this method is shown in figure 2.

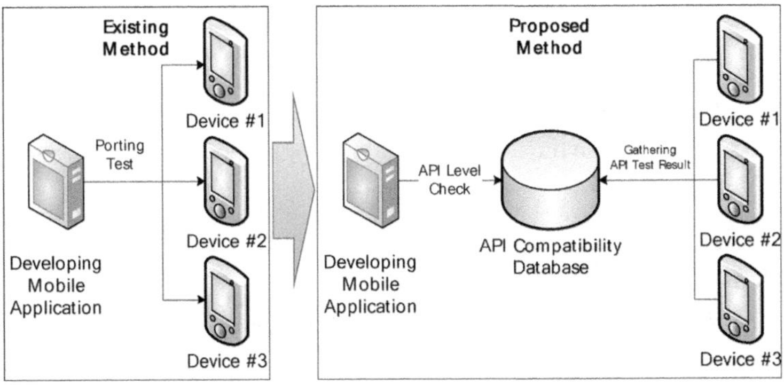

Fig. 2. Existing Method and Proposed Method

Existing method is directly ported apps under development. The test results of Android API of each device are pre-stored in the database. Since then, used Android API extracts apps analyzed. And API information compared with information stored in databases to detect the fragmentation problem.

Example of the android source code used Android API.

```
Switch (media)
{
      case LOCAL_AUDIO:
         mMediaPlayer = new MediaPlayer();
         mMediaPlayer.setDataSource(path);
         mMediaPlayer.prepare();
         mMediaPlayer.start();
      break;

      case RESOURCES_AUDIO:
         mMediaPlayer      =      MediaPlayer.create(this,
       R.raw.cbr);
         mMediaPlayer.start();
}
tx.setText("Playing audio...");
```

As above, the source code example. API of Device in order to compare, in the source code to be included in the Android API is composed of a list. Columns of list are class, method, argument and result. This is shown in table 2.

Table 1. Android API extract list

Class	Method	Argument	Result
Media Player	setDataSource	this	pass
	prepare	N/A	pass
	start	N/A	pass
	create	this,R.raw.cbr	MediaPlayer

After you configure a list, the information extracted API are compared with the test results of Android API of each device stored in a database. If you are not the same, as shown in table 2, which on the device does not work properly can be detected.

Table 2. Android API compatibility test

Test Method Information :

Class	Method	Argument	Result
MediaPlayer	setDataSoruce	this	pass

Device Test :

Device	Result	Check
Device #1	pass	not problem
Device #2	pass	not problem
Device #3	pass	not problem
Device #4	exception error	has problem

4 Mobile Application Compatibility Test System Design

Using the proposed two kinds of test methods, the proposed mobile application compatibility test system designed shown in figure 3.

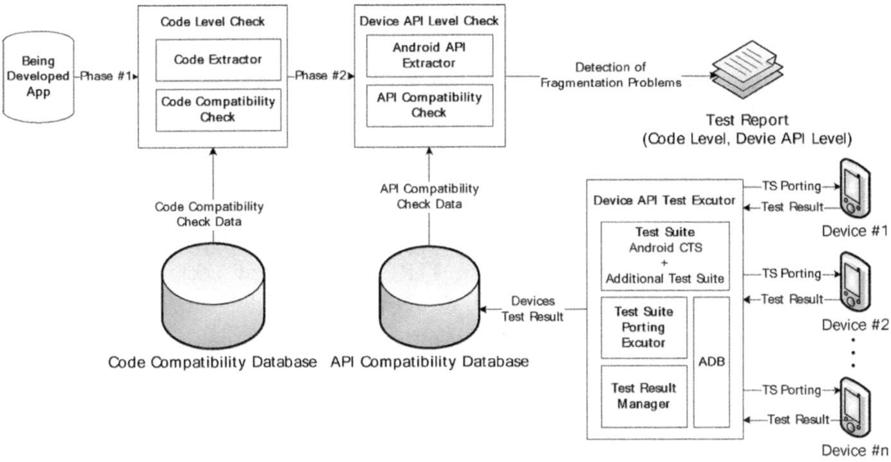

Fig. 3. Mobile Application Compatibility Test System Architecture.

The overall structure of the mobile application compatibility test system is as follows:

- Part of testing course for Apps under development
  - ✓ Code Level Check
  - ✓ Device API Level Check
  - ✓ Test Report Submit
- Device API Test Extractor
- Code Compatibility Database
- API Compatibility Database

At the part to precede test of app, it is detected android fragmentation through the following process. First step, source code analyses, and the source code that caused the fragmentation detect. Second step, after you configure a list, the information extracted API are compared with the test results of Android API of each device stored in a database. Finally, test results are recorded in the Test Report. Developers using test report is checked fragmentation problem and can fix this.

Through a system designed, developers do not need to directly ported apps on the device, does not work on the device is easy to find. It also is easy to see occurred problem in some code. Through which the time and cost of fragmentation problem detection can be effectively reduced.

5 Conclusion

Until now, the two methods were presented to solve the existing problem in mobile apps test techniques. And mobile application compatibility test system was designed using these techniques. In this way, Fragmentation problem could be solved by comparing the fragmentation in the code level and the API level. And using designed system, the time and cost of mobile application test could be effectively reduced.

As a future work, we do expect that designed system can be developed in plug-in form of Eclipse. This plug-in can be used in practical Android application development process. In future, proposed method can be used to solve similar fragmentation problem on other open-platform.

Acknowledgments. This research was supported by the MKE(The Ministry of Knowledge Economy), Korea, under the ITRC (Information Technology Research Center) support program supervised by the NIPA.(National IT Industry Promotion Agency(NIPA-2011-(C1090-1131-0008))).

References

1. Google Android, http://www.android.com/ (acceesed on September 14, 2011)
2. On Android Compatiblity, http://android-developers.blogspot.com/2010/05/on-android-compatibility.html (acceesed on September 14, 2011)
3. Hwang, B.S.: 2015 Future Scenario of Android, KT EBRI, June 27 (2011)
4. Powers, W.: Q1'11 - Do you view Android Fragmentation as a Problem? Baird Research (2011)
5. Android Compatibility Program, http://source.android.com/compatibility/index.html (acceesed on September 14, 2011)
6. Google Developer Conference 2011, http://www.google.com/events/io/2011/index-live.html (acceesed on September 19, 2011)
7. Screen Sizes and Densities, http://developer.android.com/resources/dashboard/screens.html (acceesed on September 19, 2011)
8. Compatibility Definition Document, http://static.googleusercontent.com/external_content/untrusted_dlcp/source.android.com/ko//compatibility/2.3/android-2.3.3-cdd.pdf (acceesed on September 19, 2011)
9. Compatibility Test Suite, http://source.android.com/compatibility/cts-intro.html (acceesed on September 19, 2011)

Efficient Image Identifier Composition for Image Database

Je-Ho Park and Young Bom Park

Department of Computer Science and Engineering, Dankook University, Cheonan, Republic of Korea
{dk_jhpark,ybpark}@dankook.ac.kr

Abstract. As devices with image acquisition functionality have became affordable, the amount of images produced in diverse applications is enormous. Hence, binding an image with a distinctive value for the purpose identification needs to be efficient in the perspective of cost and effective regarding the goal as well. In this paper, we present a novel approach to image identifier generation. The proposed identifier generation method is motivated by pursuing a simple but effective and efficient approach. Taking fundamental image feature extraction methods into account, we make use of distribution of line segment so as to compose identifiers that basically satisfy one-to-one relationship between an image and a corresponding identifier. The generated identifiers can be used for name composition mechanism in a storage system or indexing in a massive image database. Our experimental results on generation of constituent index values have shown favorable results.

Keywords: Database, Identifier, Image, Indexing.

1 Introduction

Technology in the field of image acquisition has been quietly enhanced regarding performance and applicability so as to provide a wide spectrum of selection that can satisfy various user's requirement. According to this, small personal devices with high-performance image functionality are widely being used among common people as well as a large number of applications utilizing image related technologies in diverse industrial fields. In storage level, the particular names are assigned to images in order to distinguish the identity of the images. Moreover, the names are also used as an intermediary between storage level and an image database in order to maintain relationships between the physical image file and the information. In the database, information for images might include various intrinsic features which are created for the goal of image search and retrieval.

The image names used in the storage level are generally composed by a user randomly or by a simple sequence-based methods that are implemented by device manufacturer or system provider. Such image names are clearly independent from images' physical property so that when the names are lost or modified, it is barely able to recover the original names. Different images, moreover, can share the same name or the duplicated images with the same name can be found in different storage area.

T.-h. Kim et al. (Eds.): ASEA/DRBC/EL 2011, CCIS 257, pp. 321–329, 2011.

Independently from identifying images by the image filenames, various image feature extraction methods that generate descriptions for images being based upon different perspectives were studied [1]. Through the last decade, comprehensive research for Content-based image retrieval (CBIR) [2] as well as indexing techniques [3] has been done utilizing various features obtained from visual content. A huge number of CBIR techniques concentrate on indexing and retrieval of image for queries composing clusters but on constructing one-to-one relationship between images and representing values. Unlike utilizing contents in images, color distribution histograms are also compressed and utilized in indexing [4]. The color histogram compression based feature and technique might need much processing time and might be not appropriate for composing a literal based filenames or indexing.

In the following sections, we will discuss how to compose identifiers using distribution of line segments. We also demonstrate the experimental evaluation that our approach is feasible in creating identifiers efficiently and effectively.

2 Image Identifier Generation

Image identifiers need to satisfy the following characteristic requirements:

- Uniqueness: an image identifier provides a unique description in the form of a set of values such that one-to-one correspondence relationship exists between the set of images and the corresponding identifiers.
- Efficient Representation: the constituent components of an image identifier need to be simple in terms of form of representation such that the resulting identifier can be manipulated and stored without complex process.
- Cost Effectiveness: the composition of an identifier needs to be completed within acceptable processing time.

The image identifier that we are proposing in this paper utilizes multiple values from a single context. In order to formalize our description of image identifier, we compose an image identifier based on the following form:

$$ID = (i_{0,}i_1, \ldots, i_k) \quad (1)$$

In the above processing model, the componential value ij can be an extracted value from an image or a predetermined value such as image size as well. Fig. 1 describes the overall process to generate an image identifier.

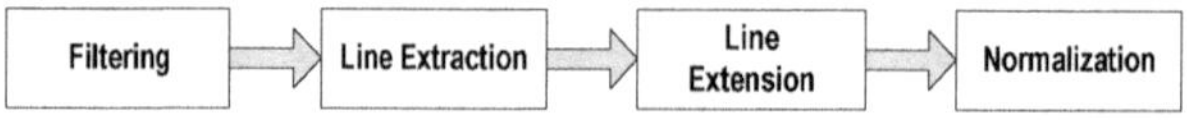

Fig. 1. Image Identifier Generation Process

The first step in the generation of an identifier is to preprocess an image before extraction of line segments after transforming the image into the grey scale image if necessary. In this step, we apply sharpening filter in order to increase the sharpness of lines that are contained in the image [5]. For the edge detection, we utilize Canny algorithm after sensitivity tests using multiple algorithms.

In the second step of the process, after the preparing the image for better identification of potential line segments, statistical hough transform [6] is applied to the image to extract the line segments that are used as the base for the longer line composition.

Fig. 2 illustrates the effect of hough transform. As seen in the result, the pixels in the line segments that are determined by hough transform are shown as white line segments. The extracted line segments are however rather short resulting in discontinuity of lines due to the existence of noisy elements.

Fig. 2. Effect of Hough Transform
(Left: Source image, Right: After applying Hough transform)

In the third step of the workflow, extension of extracted line segments to longer lines by linking short line segments is being performed preparing the determination of constituent elements for configuring an identifier. Fig. 3 shows an image with longer lines by linking short elementary line segments that are extracted by probabilistic hough transform.

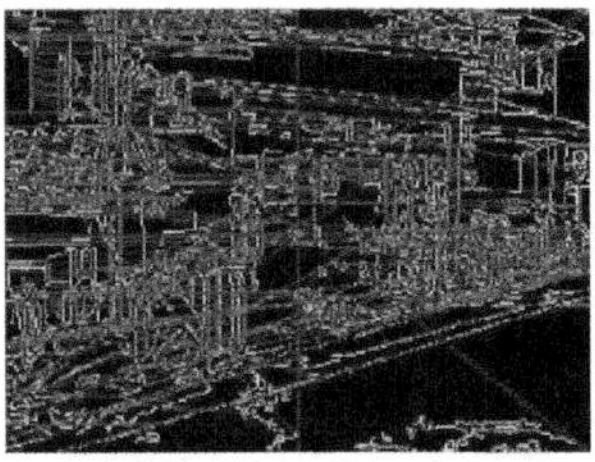

Fig. 3. Effect of Line Extension using Linking

For the normalization process, we utilize virtual lines over the preprocessed image in such a way that if a virtual line intersects a line segment in an image, we collect the location of intersecting point for the final composition of an identifier.

In the final step of an image identifier generation, the collected points of intersections between virtual lines and lines in an image are represented as a counting value. The counting value can be used as it is or can be transformed into a ratio to a predetermined value.

The virtual lines for our identifier generation start from the center of an image and extended to different directions. The four virtual lines from the center of an image to the four corners are considered as fundamental while the additional lines are generalized on demand. In the drawing process of additional virtual lines, the middle points of two adjacent end points on the boundary of an image that are determined in the previous step are regarded as the end points of new lines. Following the procedure, for kth step, the number of virtual lines can be obtained by following

$$\text{Number}_k = 4 + \sum_{i=1}^{k} 4^i \tag{2}$$

Fig. 4 illustrates the virtual lines for step 1 which contains eight lines. In the following, we demonstrate our experiments.

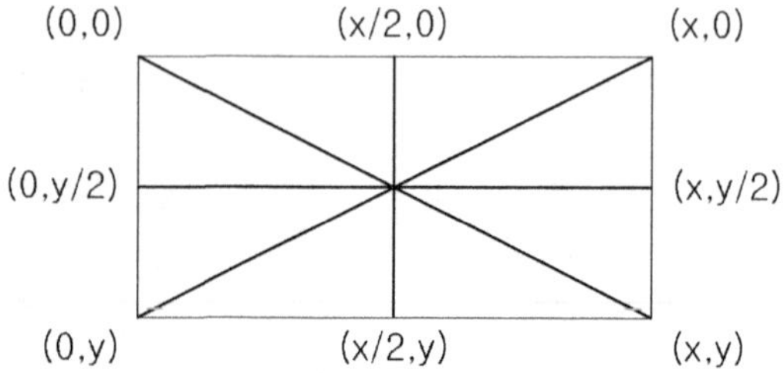

Fig. 4. Virtual lines for the First Step

3 Experiments

For the experimental evaluation of our proposed method, we developed a system that generates image identifiers using OpenCV [7]. The images used for the experiments are stored in the format of JPEG. For the clear and more reliable analysis, we composed by using only the extracted values from an image for the composition of image identifier, not using the predetermined image feature such as size. The drawing of virtual lines is implemented using Best-Fit DDA algorithm [Ref: D. Salomon, *Computer Graphics and Geometric Modeling*, New York: Springer-Verlag, 1999.]. Experiments were processed for the first step in terms of drawing virtual lines so that intersections with eight virtual lines were collected for the composition of image identifier.

3.1 Optimization of Hough Transform Processing

For the proper application of hough transform, we select 5 parameters in the implementation of probabilistic hough transform in order to evaluate the optimal setting for the process regarding hough space [8]:

- Rho: this value represents the distance between the line and the origin in the image plane.
- Theta: this value is the angle of the vector from the origin to the closest point.
- Line Threshold: this value is used for the determination of lines relating accumulator implementation.
- Minimum Line Length: this value is the minimum line length for the probabilistic hough transform.
- Maximum Gap: this value is finally the maximum gap between the line segments.

Before the experiments for sensitivity of image identifier generation, we performed a series of evaluation tests in order to analyze the effect of hough transform using different parameter values. For the evaluation, we applied statistical hough transform to 1600 random JPEG images. Fig.'s 5-8 demonstrate analyses of the effect of Rho, Theta, Line Threshold and Minimum Line Length values respectively by calculating the percentage value of the duplicated identifiers including NULL identifiers. Since determination of optimal values for multiple parameters is not our major focus, the analyses were performed in such a way that we figure out the value range which results in acceptable performance in the context of identifier composition. The experiments were performed by varying a specified parameter value while fixing the remaining parameters as best cases.

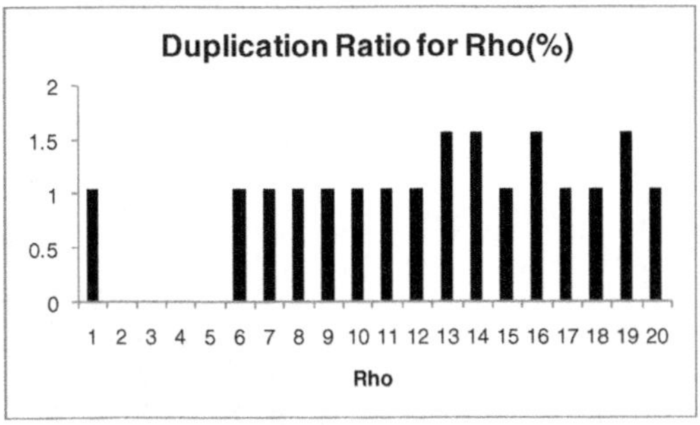

Fig. 5. Rho Value Optimality Analysis

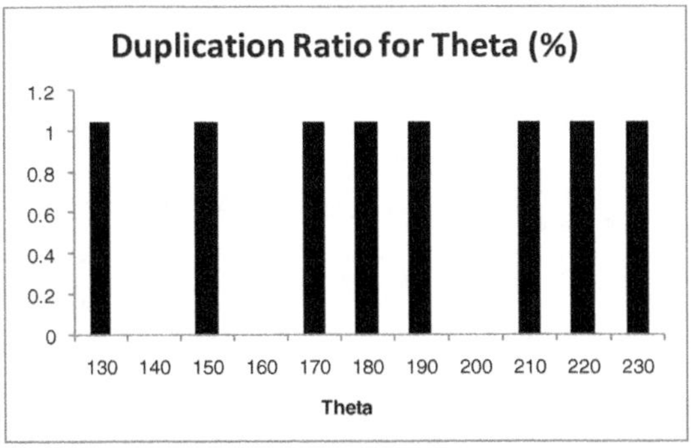

Fig. 6. Theta Value Optimality Analysis

Table 1 shows the parameter settings for hough transform in the cases of best and worst results regarding identifier generation. Even with the extensive experiments, the determination of the optimal parameter setting might not be achieved due to the hardness of the multi-dimensional space of the domain space. However, we conclude that in some range of parameter value, the evaluation shows acceptable performance.

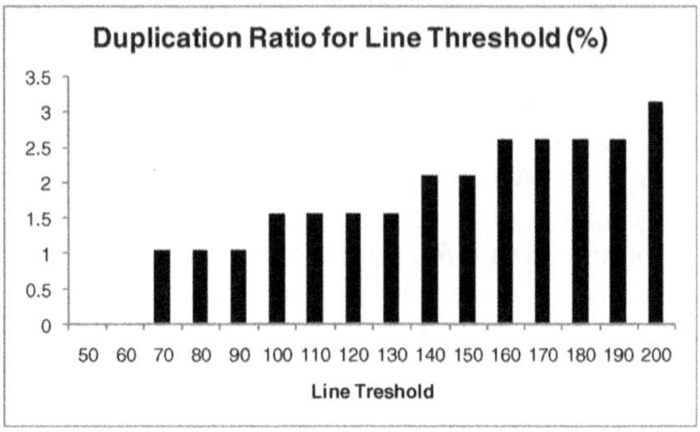

Fig. 7. Line Threshold Value Optimality Analysis

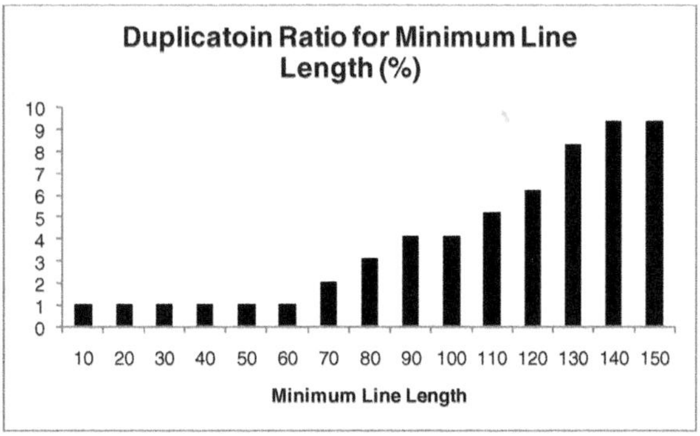

Fig. 8. Minimum Line Length Optimality Analysis

Table 1. Hought Transform Parameter Analysis

Parameter Category	Parameter Setting Results	
	Best	*Worst*
Rho	17	2
Theta	130	190
Line Threshold	170	50
Minimum Line Length	130	30
Maximum Gap	140	10

3.2 Analsys of Image Identifier Generation

The number of counting values derived from the identifier generation process affects the performance of identifier generation in terms of the effectiveness of the image identifier. When the number of componential elements is relatively large, the index size will increase in terms of storage and index processing time. On the contrary, when the information that is carried by the extracted values is small, the demanding property of uniqueness might be adversely affected.

To analyze the effect of the number of being used componential values, we applied the abovementioned process to 11,381 images extracting 8 values for each image. For the application of hough transform, we assigned used parameter values that shows the best performance. For the experiments, we generated identifiers considering all the combination of counting values varying cardinality from 2 to 8. For each combination, we built an index and used for the analysis of effectiveness. For example, for the cardinality 2, there exist ${}_2C_8$ resulting indexes.

For each index, we evaluated how many distinct index entries are found. For the same cardinality, we collect the average of unique identification ratio values comparing to the number of the sample images and standard deviation values. In the case that singular value is used, the ratio of distinct index entries to the number of overall images was as 12.57%.

Fig. 9 shows the resulting average unique identification ratio from the cardinality 2 to 8. Fig. 10 shows the corresponding standard deviation. Fig. 11 demonstrates the ratio of indexes that consist of invalid (NULL) componential values. Table 2 summarizes the experimental results that are shown in Fig. 9 and 10 in order to analyze the results in detail.

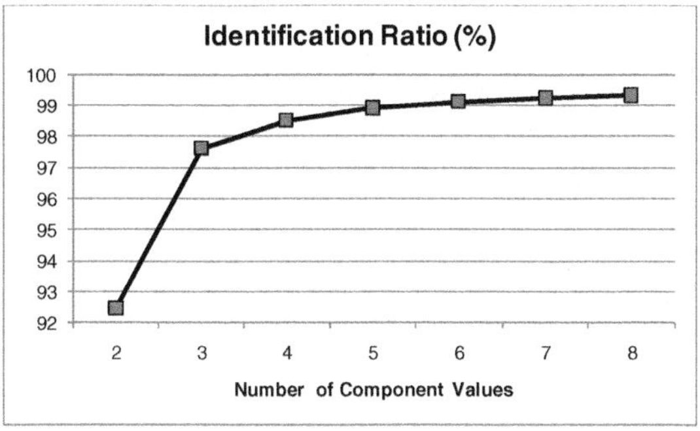

Fig. 9. Identification Ratio for Varying Cardinalities

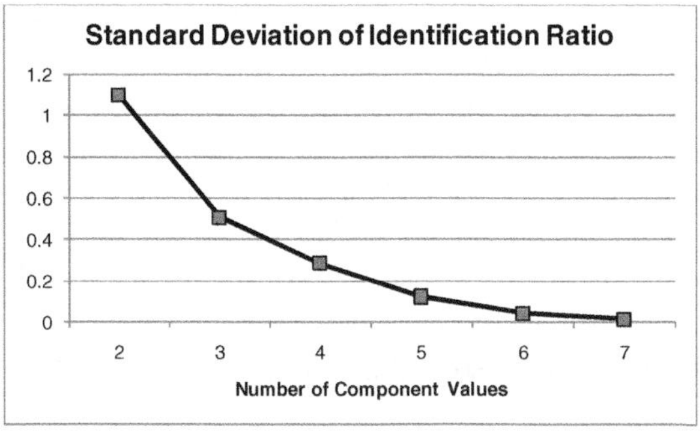

Fig. 10. Standard Deviation for Varying Cardinalities

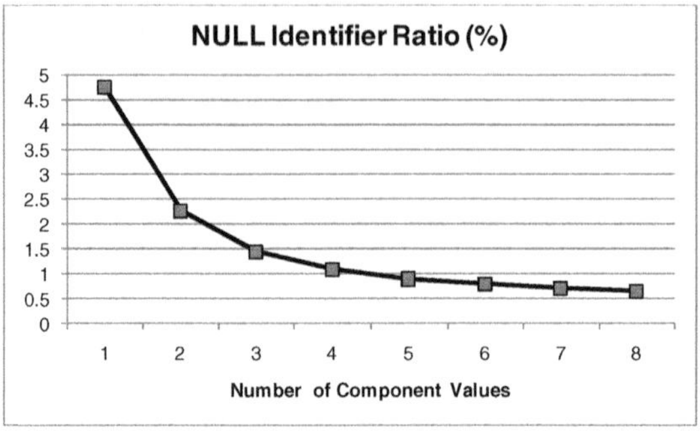

Fig. 11. NULL Identifier Ratio

From the experiments, it is clear that the successful identification ratio and the decreased NULL indexing ratio can be obtained when more componential values are being contained in the composition of identifiers. When an identifier consists of 6 componential values, the identification ratio is greater than 99%. For the case of that all the componential values are utilized, the identification ratio is 99.32%. Considering this result, we can conjecture that the practically effective composition of an image identifier does not need to include all the componential values.

From the result, we found that the identifier with NULL values is due to that little of linear components are extracted within an image. As seen in TABLE 2, the summation of NULL indexing ratio and identification ratio is 99.04% for three componential values, 99.93% for seven values and 99.96% for eight values. Hence if the NULL indexing problem can be resolved, the performance of the proposed identifier generation method will be enhanced significantly. The processing time for identifier generation is 207.15 milliseconds per Mbytes when 2.93GHz CPU is used in the experiments.

Table 2. Summary of Analysis

# of Componential Index	*Identification Ratio (IR)*	*NULL Identifier Ratio (NIR)*	*Sum of IR and NIR*
1	12.57 %	4.72 %	17.29 %
2	92.43 %	2.24 %	94.67 %
3	97.61 %	1.43 %	99.04 %
4	98.50 %	1.07 %	99.57 %
5	98.89 %	0.90 %	99.79 %
6	99.09 %	0.78 %	99.87 %
7	99.22 %	0.71 %	99.93 %
8	99.31 %	0.65 %	99.96 %

3.3 Line Segment vs. Short Edge Based Identifier Generation

The main focus of the final phase of identification composition is to examine the distribution of intersections between the virtual lines and the extracted line segments within an image. Acknowledging that the intersections occur within small areas, the whole part of line segment might be excessive in terms of minimal requirements of processing. In order to analyze this, we generated identifiers by using Canny, Sobel and Prewitt edge detection algorithms and measured identification ratio and processing time per Mbytes. TABLE 3 summarizes the result of the analysis among a number of experiments.

Table 3. Analysis with Edge Detection Algorithms

Methods	*Identification Ratio*	*Processing Time*
Hough transform	99.31 %	207 msec
Canny	51.66 %	64 msec
Sobel	0.2 %	52 msec
Prewitt	86.7 %	45 msec

4 Conclusions

Our approach was motivated for study of cost effective and efficient methods for image identification that can be utilized in storage system and in indexing very large database. The suggested approach utilizes the distribution of line segments within images and the counting of intersecting points with a number of virtual lines aiming simplification of quantization of discovered distribution pattern. As seen in the experimental results, the extracted line segments by applying probabilistic hough transform support successfully the generation of image identifiers satisfying the identifier's requirements. The disadvantage of application of hough transform to the identifier generation processing might be the processing time regarding the simpler edge detection algorithms even with superior performance. In addition, there are cases that extraction of line segments is barely achieved due to the nature of the given images.

References

1. Nixon, M.P., Aguado, A., Nixon, M., Aguado, A.S.: Feature Extraction & Image Processing for Computer Vision, 2nd edn. Academic Press (2008)
2. Bantum, M.G.: US Patent 5,887,081 (1999)
3. Pabboju, S., Reddy, A.V.G.: A novel approach for content-based image indexing and retrieval system using global and region features. IJCSNS 9(2), 119–130 (2009)
4. Berens, J., Finlayson, G.D., Qiu, G.: Image indexing using compressed color histograms. IEE Proc. of Vision, Image and Signal Processing 147(4), 349–355 (2000)
5. Gonzalez, R.C.: Digital Image Processing, 3rd edn. Prentice Hall (2007)
6. Kiryati, N., Eldar, Y., Bruckstein, A.M.: A probabilistic hough transform. Pattern Recognition 24(4), 303–316 (1991)
7. Bradski, G., Kaehler, A.: Learning OpenCV. O'Reily Media (2008)
8. Salomon, D.: Computer Graphics and Geometric Modeling. Springer, New York (1999)

A Note on Two-Stage Software Testing by Two Teams

Mitsuhiro Kimura[1,*] and Takaji Fujiwara[2]

[1] Department of Industrial & Systems Engineering,
Faculty of Science & Engineering, Hosei University
3-7-2, Kajino-cho, Koganei-shi, Tokyo 184-8584, Japan
kim@hosei.ac.jp

[2] SRATECH Laboratory Inc.
1949-24, Yamakuni, Katoh-shi, Hyogo 673-1421, Japan
fujiwara.takaji@nifty.com

Abstract. This paper reports our experience of software reliability evaluation in the actual software development which employs somewhat uncommon testing procedure. The procedure can be called as a two-stage testing by two teams. First we discuss the problems underlying the software testing. We explain the concept of the procedure of the two-stage testing by two teams, and then, a stochastic model which traces the procedure is derived. The model analyzes a data set which were obtained from the real testing activity. By using the result of data analysis, we show some numerical illustrations for the software reliability assessment and the evaluation of the skill level of the test teams.

Keywords: Software reliability, Software test, Two-stage testing, Binomial distribution model.

1 Introduction

Recall news reports on various electrical/electronic industrial products have been often made in the recent mass media. Almost all of the recall news reports alert severe problems which may affect our social life, if these problems could be actualized. For example, such problems have actually occurred in some braking equipment or the steering control system in automobiles, and in the other cases, somebody has experienced the problem in which he/she could not dial the emergency call of three figures in the mobile phone. One of the most conceivable causes is the lack of reliability in the program code included in these software systems and products.

In such a situation, in the testing activities in the software development process or the simulated operational testing, software developers verify the software which is to be implemented in terms of the conformity with the customer's requirements, by executing huge amount and various test cases in order to check whether the software behaves and performs without any problem.

* This work was partially supported by KAKENHI, the Grant-in-Aid of Scientific Research (C)(23510189).

T.-h. Kim et al. (Eds.): ASEA/DRBC/EL 2011, CCIS 257, pp. 330–337, 2011.

Today, the software developers test the software so as to find all of the malfunctions which may occur in the operational environment, by using the traceability matrix [1] made of the information on which test cases are tested and how those verify the customer's requirements.

Even though we release such precisely-tested software systems, we have often experienced the following phenomena:

- Some faults are still detected in the customer's acceptance testing.
- Some claims of the product are sent from the customers after purchasing in a mass market.

Although the software developers apply the traceability matrix to the software not to overlook the customer's requirements and sufficiently test it, why do the above-mentioned problems occur?

In order to solve these difficult problems, various testing methods have been studied and proposed by many researchers, real developers, and practitioners so far. These are for instance, capture-recapture method [2,3], two-stage editing method [4], and so on [1,5]. Also in recent years, Akiyama et al. have proposed the test case design method which is applied the Latin square approach (see e.g. [6]).

Recently we have obtained a development opportunity of a certain application software which runs on both of Windows7 OS of 32 bit and 64 bit versions. On the development, first of all we have carried out all tests on the 32 bit OS. After that, we have tested it again on the 64 bit OS, as a regression test. In these testing, we used the same test cases to this identical software program (i.e., object code). We first expected that any fault would not be detected in the regression testing, however, in fact, several faults have been detected.

Therefore we have investigated the causes of these faults detection in the regression testing. We thought such causes would surely lead to the software failure occurrence in the acceptance testing by the customer and in the users environment after the release. As the result, we have been able to divide the causes into two groups as follows:

- Lack of the testers' understanding of the contents of the assigned test cases.
- Lack of confirmation to the each result of the test by the testers.

About the first cause pointed above, the overlooking probability of a fault can be reduced by reflecting in the review check lists to the design specifications and the testing specifications. On the other hand, for the second point above, it becomes avoidable by introducing the automatic testing or applying the testing tool.

Hence in this research, we propose the reliability prediction method for assessing the testing activities based on the data which were collected in such testing environment. Especially, we show the prediction of the number of remaining faults and the evaluation of the testing skill, in order to clarify the appropriate testing activities which should be performed and estimate the number of faults which should be detected in the acceptance test phase.

2 Two-Stage Software Testing by Two Teams

As described in Section 1, we have obtained the opportunity of the application software development corresponding to both of Windows7 OS of the 32 bit and 64 bit versions lately. In this project, we have determined the outline of the development activities as follows (see Fig. 1):

1) Divide project members into two teams (i.e., Team A and B).
2) Divide customer's requirements into two functional groups (we call them Functions A and B) according to the activity 1).
3) From the requirement analysis to detailed design phase, both teams together carry out the analysis and design.
4) From the coding to software testing phase, Team A takes charge of Functions A, and Team B takes charge of Functions B.
5) Exchange the functional group of each team in charge, and carry out testing by using the same test cases again.

We call this testing procedure the *two-stage testing by two teams*.
Furthermore, the details of the testing activities after finishing the coding are shown as follows:

1) Compile the program on the 32 bit OS so that the application can be run on both OS of the 32 bit and 64 bit versions.
2) Design test cases in order to confirm that the software is implemented in accordance with the customer's requirements.
3) Confirm that the application is tested fully, the detected all faults were corrected, and the problems have been solved on the 32 bit version OS.
4) Run the application software on the 64 bit version OS, and test it again as the regression test by using the same test cases used in the 32 bit test, and confirm that no fault is detected.

We can regard this testing-procedure 4) as the acceptance test by the customer after the delivery of the software system. Accordingly, we construct a stochastic model in the following sections based on the data obtained by this testing procedure.

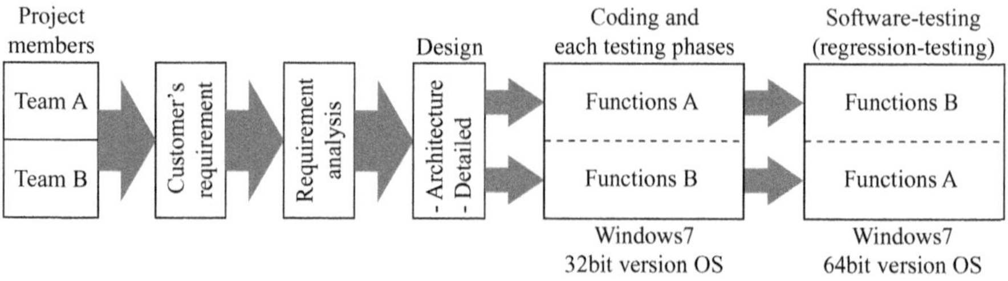

Fig. 1. Outline of software development activities

3 Model Description

First we show the following notation for our modeling.

N_{A}: Number of initial fault content in the program for Functions A.
N_{B}: Number of initial fault content in the program for Functions B.
$m_{1\mathrm{A}}$: Fault detection ratio at Stage 1 of Team A.
$m_{1\mathrm{B}}$: Fault detection ratio at Stage 1 of Team B.
$m_{2\mathrm{A}}$: Fault detection ratio at Stage 2 of Team A.
$m_{2\mathrm{B}}$: Fault detection ratio at Stage 2 of Team B.
$X_{1\mathrm{A}}$: Number of remaining faults after Stage 1 by Team A (r.v.[1]).
$X_{1\mathrm{B}}$: Number of remaining faults after Stage 1 by Team B (r.v).
$X_{2\mathrm{A}}$: Number of remaining faults after Stage 2 by Team A (r.v.).
$X_{2\mathrm{B}}$: Number of remaining faults after Stage 2 by Team B (r.v.).

Figure 2 illustrates the testing procedure discussed in this study.

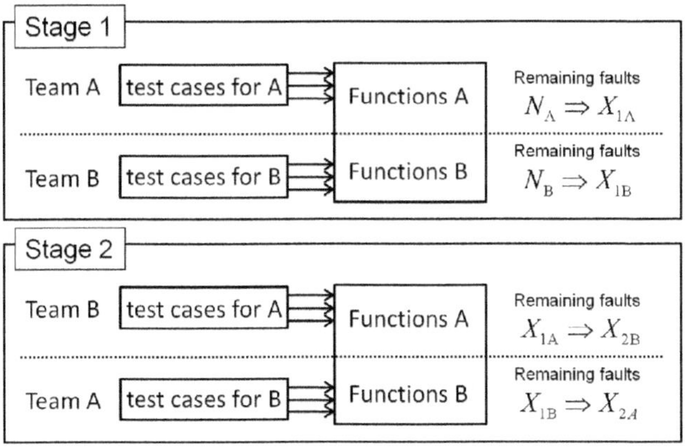

Fig. 2. Procedure of two-stage testing by two teams

Since we assume that the testing activity naturally obeys a binomial distribution, we have the following quantities for Stage 1, respectively.

$$\Pr[X_{1\mathrm{A}} = x_{1\mathrm{A}}] = \binom{N_{\mathrm{A}}}{x_{1\mathrm{A}}} (1 - m_{1\mathrm{A}})^{x_{1\mathrm{A}}} {m_{1\mathrm{A}}}^{N_{\mathrm{A}} - x_{1\mathrm{A}}}, \tag{1}$$

$$\Pr[X_{1\mathrm{B}} = x_{1\mathrm{B}}] = \binom{N_{\mathrm{B}}}{x_{1\mathrm{B}}} (1 - m_{1\mathrm{B}})^{x_{1\mathrm{B}}} {m_{1\mathrm{B}}}^{N_{\mathrm{B}} - x_{1\mathrm{B}}}, \tag{2}$$

where $x_{1\mathrm{A}}$ and $x_{1\mathrm{B}}$ are the realizations of $X_{1\mathrm{A}}$ and $X_{1\mathrm{B}}$, respectively.

[1] random variable

Therefore for Stage 2, we also have the following probability functions for the number of remaining faults X_{2A} and X_{2B}, respectively.

$$\begin{aligned}
\Pr[X_{2A} = x_{2A}] &= \sum_{k=x_{2A}}^{N_B} \binom{X_{1B}}{x_{2A}} (1-m_{2A})^{x_{2A}} {m_{2A}}^{X_{1B}-x_{2A}} \cdot \Pr[X_{1B} = k] \\
&= \sum_{k=x_{2A}}^{N_B} \left[\binom{k}{x_{2A}} (1-m_{2A})^{x_{2A}} {m_{2A}}^{k-x_{2A}} \right. \\
&\quad \left. \times \binom{N_B}{k} (1-m_{1B})^{k} {m_{1B}}^{N_B-k} \right] \\
&= \binom{N_B}{x_{2A}} \{(1-m_{2A})(1-m_{1B})\}^{x_{2A}} \\
&\quad \times \{1-(1-m_{2A})(1-m_{1B})\}^{N_B-x_{2A}}, \qquad (3)
\end{aligned}$$

$$\begin{aligned}
\Pr[X_{2B} = x_{2B}] &= \sum_{k=x_{2B}}^{N_A} \binom{X_{1A}}{x_{2B}} (1-m_{2B})^{x_{2B}} {m_{2B}}^{X_{1A}-x_{2B}} \cdot \Pr[X_{1A} = k] \\
&= \sum_{k=x_{2B}}^{N_A} \left[\binom{k}{x_{2B}} (1-m_{2B})^{x_{2B}} {m_{2B}}^{k-x_{2B}} \right. \\
&\quad \left. \times \binom{N_A}{k} (1-m_{1A})^{k} {m_{1A}}^{N_A-k} \right] \\
&= \binom{N_A}{x_{2B}} \{(1-m_{2B})(1-m_{1A})\}^{x_{2B}} \\
&\quad \times \{1-(1-m_{2B})(1-m_{1A})\}^{N_A-x_{2B}}. \qquad (4)
\end{aligned}$$

Appendix illustrates the derivation of Eq. (4) for instance. Thus we respectively obtain the expectations and variances of X_{2A} and X_{2B} as:

$$\mathrm{E}[X_{2A}] = N_B\{(1-m_{2A})(1-m_{1B})\}, \qquad (5)$$

$$\mathrm{E}[X_{2B}] = N_A\{(1-m_{2B})(1-m_{1A})\}, \qquad (6)$$

$$\mathrm{Var}[X_{2A}] = N_B\{(1-m_{2A})(1-m_{1B})\}\{1-(1-m_{2A})(1-m_{1B})\}, \qquad (7)$$

$$\mathrm{Var}[X_{2B}] = N_A\{(1-m_{2B})(1-m_{1A})\}\{1-(1-m_{2B})(1-m_{1A})\}. \qquad (8)$$

Hence we can evaluate the probability distribution of the number of remaining faults after Stage 2. These quantities can be used as software reliability evaluation. Also the testing skill level of each Team is presented by m_{1A}, m_{1B}, m_{2A}, and m_{2B}.

3.1 Parameter Estimation

We can easily obtain the maximum likelihood estimators for N_A, N_B, m_{1A}, m_{1B}, m_{2A}, and m_{2B}.

Let $d_{1\mathrm{A}}$ be the number of actually detected/corrected software faults during Stage 1 by Team A, and $d_{1\mathrm{B}}$ by Team B, respectively. Then,

$$N_{\mathrm{A}} m_{1\mathrm{A}} = d_{1\mathrm{A}}(> 0), \tag{9}$$

$$N_{\mathrm{B}} m_{1\mathrm{B}} = d_{1\mathrm{B}}(> 0). \tag{10}$$

For Stage 2, denoting that $d_{2\mathrm{A}}$ and $d_{2\mathrm{B}}$ respectively represent the number of actually detected/corrected software faults by Team A and B, we have

$$N_{\mathrm{B}}(1 - m_{1\mathrm{B}}) m_{2\mathrm{A}} = d_{2\mathrm{A}}, \tag{11}$$

$$N_{\mathrm{A}}(1 - m_{1\mathrm{A}}) m_{2\mathrm{B}} = d_{2\mathrm{B}}. \tag{12}$$

In addition, we assume that $m_{1\mathrm{A}} = m_{2\mathrm{A}}$ and $m_{1\mathrm{B}} = m_{2\mathrm{B}}$, i.e., the abilities in terms of software fault detection of each team are the same throughout Stage 1 and Stage 2. Therefore by solving Eqs. (9), (10), (11), and (12), we obtain the following estimators.

$$\widehat{N_{\mathrm{A}}} = \frac{(d_{1\mathrm{A}} + d_{2\mathrm{B}}) d_{1\mathrm{A}} d_{1\mathrm{B}}}{d_{1\mathrm{A}} d_{1\mathrm{B}} - d_{2\mathrm{A}} d_{2\mathrm{B}}}, \tag{13}$$

$$\widehat{N_{\mathrm{B}}} = \frac{(d_{1\mathrm{B}} + d_{2\mathrm{A}}) d_{1\mathrm{A}} d_{1\mathrm{B}}}{d_{1\mathrm{A}} d_{1\mathrm{B}} - d_{2\mathrm{A}} d_{2\mathrm{B}}}, \tag{14}$$

$$\widehat{m_{1\mathrm{A}}} = \widehat{m_{2\mathrm{A}}} = \frac{d_{1\mathrm{A}} d_{1\mathrm{B}} - d_{2\mathrm{A}} d_{2\mathrm{B}}}{(d_{1\mathrm{A}} + d_{2\mathrm{B}}) d_{1\mathrm{B}}}, \tag{15}$$

$$\widehat{m_{1\mathrm{B}}} = \widehat{m_{2\mathrm{B}}} = \frac{d_{1\mathrm{A}} d_{1\mathrm{B}} - d_{2\mathrm{A}} d_{2\mathrm{B}}}{(d_{1\mathrm{B}} + d_{2\mathrm{A}}) d_{1\mathrm{A}}}. \tag{16}$$

4 Numerical Examples

This section illustrates numerical examples. We actually performed a two-stage software testing by two teams which is mentioned in Sections 1 and 2. Table 1 shows the obtained data. From the results of the previous section, we have estimated the number of initial fault content of the software by

$$\widehat{N_{\mathrm{A}}} = 20.4, \tag{17}$$

$$\widehat{N_{\mathrm{B}}} = 20.4. \tag{18}$$

On the other hand, the testing skill of each team is calculated as

$$\widehat{m_{1\mathrm{A}}} = \widehat{m_{2\mathrm{A}}} = 0.688, \tag{19}$$

$$\widehat{m_{1\mathrm{B}}} = \widehat{m_{2\mathrm{B}}} = 0.786. \tag{20}$$

Table 1. Data set

Stage and Team	1-A	1-B	2-A	2-B
# of detected faults	$d_{1\mathrm{A}} = 14$	$d_{1\mathrm{B}} = 16$	$d_{2\mathrm{A}} = 3$	$d_{2\mathrm{B}} = 5$

From Eqs. (3) and (4), also we respectively obtain the mean number of remaining faults in the whole software system and its standard deviation by

$$\widehat{\mathrm{E}}[X_{2\mathrm{A}} + X_{2\mathrm{B}}] \simeq 2.8, \tag{21}$$

$$\sqrt{\widehat{\mathrm{Var}}}[X_{2\mathrm{A}} + X_{2\mathrm{B}}] \simeq 1.6. \tag{22}$$

N.B. that the above equations are true since we assume $m_{1\mathrm{A}} = m_{2\mathrm{A}}$ and $m_{1\mathrm{B}} = m_{2\mathrm{B}}$, i.e., the reproductive property of binomial distribution works.

Actually, after this testing procedure, we performed the acceptance test for this software. As a result, we received a report where 1 fault was newly detected. After its debugging, we have released the software. Up to the present, we have not received any information on the malfunctions of this software (over two months). This fact tells us that this reliability estimation works well at this time.

On the testing skill level of each team, we found the Team B is better than Team A from the results of Eqs. (19) and (20). If no faults are detected in the second stage of Team A, the testing skill of Team B becomes 1, and conversely, if no faults are detected in the second stage of Team B, the testing skill of Team A becomes 1. These mean that one test team of Stage 1 can detect all the inherent faults, the other team cannot detect any fault in Stage 2.

5 Concluding Remarks

This study has reported our experience of software testing, which employs two test teams and its procedure consists of two stages. This method purposes to squeeze out the remaining software faults at the final chance of software development. The model is simple but the estimation results in terms of the number of remaining software faults are acceptable in our case.

In the future, we plan to combine this method and the traditional time-series analysis approach for dynamic software reliability evaluation.

Appendix: Two-Stage Coin Tossing

In order to express how Eq. (4) can be derived, we depict Fig. 3. This shows a two-stage coin tossing experiment.

From the figure, it is apparent that $X_{2\mathrm{B}}$ described by

$$\begin{aligned}
\Pr[X_{2\mathrm{B}} = x_{2\mathrm{B}}] &= \sum_{k=x_{2\mathrm{B}}}^{N_\mathrm{A}} \binom{X_{1\mathrm{A}}}{x_{2\mathrm{B}}} (1 - m_{2\mathrm{B}})^{x_{2\mathrm{B}}} {m_{2\mathrm{B}}}^{X_{1\mathrm{A}} - x_{2\mathrm{B}}} \cdot \Pr[X_{1\mathrm{A}} = k] \\
&= \sum_{k=x_{2\mathrm{B}}}^{N_\mathrm{A}} \Bigg[\binom{k}{x_{2\mathrm{B}}} (1 - m_{2\mathrm{B}})^{x_{2\mathrm{B}}} {m_{2\mathrm{B}}}^{k - x_{2\mathrm{B}}} \\
&\quad \times \binom{N_\mathrm{A}}{k} (1 - m_{1\mathrm{A}})^{k} {m_{1\mathrm{A}}}^{N_\mathrm{A} - k} \Bigg],
\end{aligned}$$

originally comes from N_{A} by a binomial distribution with

$$\begin{cases} \Pr[\text{T at Stage 2}] = (1 - m_{1\mathrm{A}})(1 - m_{2\mathrm{B}}) \\ \Pr[\text{others}] \qquad\quad = 1 - (1 - m_{1\mathrm{A}})(1 - m_{2\mathrm{B}}) \end{cases}.$$

Therefore we have the following result.

$$\Pr[X_{2\mathrm{B}} = x_{2\mathrm{B}}] = \binom{N_{\mathrm{A}}}{x_{2\mathrm{B}}} \{(1 - m_{2\mathrm{B}})(1 - m_{1\mathrm{A}})\}^{x_{2\mathrm{B}}} \times \{1 - (1 - m_{2\mathrm{B}})(1 - m_{1\mathrm{A}})\}^{N_{\mathrm{A}} - x_{2\mathrm{B}}}.$$

Nothing to say, Eq. (3) can be obtained in the same manner.

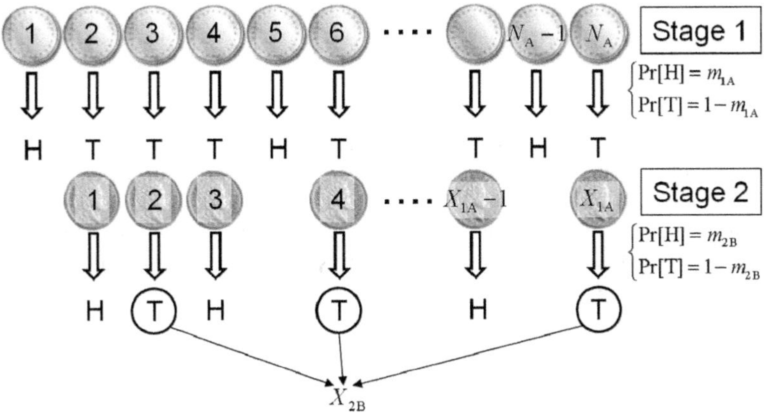

Fig. 3. Illustration of two-stage coin tossing based on Eq. (4)

References

1. Kimura, M., Fujiwara, T.: Software Reliability. JUSE Press, Tokyo (2011) (in Japanese)
2. Mills, H.D.: On the statistical validation of computer programs. Technical Report FSC-72-6015, IBM Federal Systems Division (1972)
3. Duran, J.W., Wiorkowski, J.J.: Capture-recapture sampling for estimating software error content. IEEE Transactions on Software Engineering SE-7(1), 147–148 (1981)
4. Basin, S.L.: Estimation of software error rates via capture-recapture sampling, Technical Report, Science Applications Inc. (1973)
5. Pham, H.: Software reliability. Springer, Heidelberg (1999)
6. Yoshizawa, M., Akiyama, K., Sengoku, T.: Introduction to Software Test by HAYST Method. JUSE Press, Tokyo (2007) (in Japanese)

Cumulative Damage Models with Replacement Last

Xufeng Zhao[1], Keiko Nakayama[2], and Syouji Nakamura[3]

[1] Department of Business Administration, Aichi Institute of Technology, 1247 Yachigusa, Yakusa-cho, Toyota 470-0392, Japan
g09184gg@aitech.ac.jp

[2] Faculty of Economics, Chukyo University, 101-2 Yagoto-Honmachi, Showa-ku, Nagoya, 466-8666, Japan
nakayama@mecl.chukyo-u.ac.jp

[3] Department of Human Life and Information, Kinjo Gakuin University, 1723 Omori 2-chome, Moriyama-ku, Nagoya 463-8521, Japan
snakam@kinjo-u.ac.jp

Abstract. This paper proposes a damage model with replacement last. First, the preventive replacement policies with a damage process is given: the unit is replaced at a damage level Z or a planned time T, whichever occurs last. Second, optimal Z for a given T is derived, and compare such an optimal policy with those of replacement first and standard replacement. It shows that the ratio of replacement costs plays an important role in determining which policy is better. Third, a numerical example is given in an exponential case.

Keywords: Replacement last, Replacement first, Damage model, Maintenance policy, Failure.

1 Introduction

The recent published books [1-4] collected many maintenance models and their optimal policies. Especially, Nakagawa [3] summarized sufficiently maintenance policies and their optimization problems for various shock and damage models which are called cumulative damage models. Such models have been applied successfully to backup policies and garbage collections in computer science [5, 6]. However, it has been assumed in all policies that the unit is replaced before failure at a planned time or when some amount of quantities exceed a threshold level, whichever occurs first. These policies are reasonable in practical fields if the replacement cost after failure might be much high. However, if such a cost would be estimated to be not so high, then the unit should be working as long as possible before failures. From such a viewpoint, the replacement policies, where the unit is replaced at a planned time or a working time, whichever occurs last, were proposed, and the expected cost rates were obtained [7, 8], optimization problems of such models, i.e., replacement last, and some extended models, were discussed in detail [9].

T.-h. Kim et al. (Eds.): ASEA/DRBC/EL 2011, CCIS 257, pp. 338–345, 2011.

In this paper, we apply a replacement last technique to cumulative damage models: First, the unit is replaced at a damage level Z or a planned time T, whichever occurs last. Second, because policy T is always considered in the maintenance strategy, we derive optimal Z for a given T, and compare the optimal policy with those of replacement first and standard replacement. We find theoretically how to determine which policy is better than the other according to the ratio of replacement costs. Third, such comparisons are shown by a numerical example.

2 Modeling and Optimization

It is assumed that X_j $(j = 1, 2, \cdots)$ are shock time intervals of the unit which are independent and have an identical distribution $F(t)$ with a finite mean $1/\lambda$, and each shock causes a random amount of damage Y_j $(j = 1, 2, \cdots)$ to the unit according to an identical distribution $G(x)$ with a finite mean $1/\mu$. These damages are additive, and the unit fails when the total damage exceeds a failure level K $(0 < K < \infty)$, its failure is immediately detected, and it is replaced with a new one. Then, the probability that shocks occur j times in $(0, t]$ is, from [3, p.17],

$$\Pr\{N(t) = j\} = F^{(j)}(t) - F^{(j+1)}(t) \qquad (j = 0, 1, 2, \cdots),$$

and the distribution of the total damage $Z(t)$ at time t is

$$\Pr\{Z(t) \leq x\} = \sum_{j=0}^{\infty} G^{(j)}(x)[F^{(j)}(t) - F^{(j+1)}(t)],$$

where $\Phi^{(j)}(t)$ denotes the j-fold Stieltjes convolution of any function $\Phi(t)$ with itself and $\Phi^{(0)}(t) \equiv 1$ for $t > 0$.

As the preventive replacement policies, the unit is replaced at a damage level Z $(0 < Z \leq K)$ or a planned time T $(0 < T < \infty)$, whichever occurs last, which is called *replacement last*. Then, the probability that the unit is replaced at level Z is

$$\sum_{j=0}^{\infty} \overline{F}^{(j+1)}(T) \int_0^Z [G(K-x) - G(Z-x)]\mathrm{d}G^{(j)}(x), \tag{1}$$

the probability that the unit is replaced at time T is

$$\sum_{j=0}^{\infty} [F^{(j)}(T) - F^{(j+1)}(T)][G^{(j)}(K) - G^{(j)}(Z)], \tag{2}$$

and the probability that the unit is replaced at failure is divided into three cases: The age of the unit reaches T when the damage level is less than Z and it is not replaced, however, the total damage exceeds K at the following some shock,

$$P_1 = \sum_{j=0}^{\infty} \overline{F}^{(j+1)}(T) \int_0^Z \overline{G}(K-x)\mathrm{d}G^{(j)}(x),$$

the damage level reaches Z at some shock and it is not replaced, however, the total damage exceeds K at the next shock when its age is less than T,

$$P_2 = \sum_{j=0}^{\infty} F^{(j+1)}(T) \int_Z^K \overline{G}(K-x) \mathrm{d}G^{(j)}(x),$$

the damage level is less than Z at some shock, however, the total damage exceeds K at the next shock when its age is also less than T,

$$P_3 = \sum_{j=0}^{\infty} F^{(j+1)}(T) \int_0^Z \overline{G}(K-x) \mathrm{d}G^{(j)}(x).$$

By summing up P_1, P_2 and P_3, we derive

$$\sum_{j=0}^{\infty} \overline{F}^{(j+1)}(T) \int_0^Z \overline{G}(K-x) \mathrm{d}G^{(j)}(x) + \sum_{j=0}^{\infty} F^{(j+1)}(T)[G^{(j)}(K) - G^{(j+1)}(K)], \quad (3)$$

where note that (1) + (2) + (3) $\equiv 1$. Then the mean time to replacement is

$$\frac{1}{\lambda}\left[\sum_{j=0}^{\infty} \overline{F}^{(j+1)}(T) G^{(j)}(Z) + \sum_{j=0}^{\infty} F^{(j+1)}(T) G^{(j)}(K)\right]. \quad (4)$$

Therefore, the expected cost rate is

$$\frac{C_1(Z)}{\lambda} = \frac{c_P + (c_F - c_P)\{\sum_{j=0}^{\infty} \overline{F}^{(j+1)}(T) \int_0^Z \overline{G}(K-x)\mathrm{d}G^{(j)}(x) + \sum_{j=0}^{\infty} F^{(j+1)}(T)[G^{(j)}(K) - G^{(j+1)}(K)]\}}{\sum_{j=0}^{\infty} \overline{F}^{(j+1)}(T) G^{(j)}(Z) + \sum_{j=0}^{\infty} F^{(j+1)}(T) G^{(j)}(K)}, \quad (5)$$

where c_P is the replacement cost at damage level Z or at time T which is done as a preventive policy, c_F is the replacement cost at failure which is done as a corrective policy, and $c_F > c_P$.

We find an optimal Z_1^* which minimizes $C_1(Z)$ for a given T. Differentiating $C_1(Z)/\lambda$ with respect to Z and setting it equal to zero,

$$-G(K-Z)\left[\sum_{j=0}^{\infty} \overline{F}^{(j+1)}(T) G^{(j)}(Z) + \sum_{j=0}^{\infty} F^{(j+1)}(T) G^{(j)}(K)\right] + \sum_{j=0}^{\infty} \overline{F}^{(j+1)}(T) \int_0^Z G(K-x)\mathrm{d}G^{(j)}(x) + \sum_{j=1}^{\infty} F^{(j)}(T) G^{(j)}(K) = \frac{c_P}{c_F - c_P}. \quad (6)$$

Denoting the left-hand side of (6) by $L_1(Z)$,

$$-\frac{\mathrm{d}G(K-Z)}{\mathrm{d}Z}\left[\sum_{j=0}^{\infty} \overline{F}^{(j+1)}(T) G^{(j)}(Z) + \sum_{j=0}^{\infty} F^{(j+1)}(T) G^{(j)}(K)\right], \quad (7)$$

which is greater than 0. Thus, $L_1(Z)$ increases from

$$\sum_{j=0}^{\infty} F^{(j+1)}(T) \int_0^K [\overline{G}(K) - \overline{G}(K-x)]\mathrm{d}G^{(j)}(x) < 0$$

to $M(K) \equiv \sum_{j=1}^{\infty} G^{(j)}(K)$, which means the expected number of shocks before the total damage exceeds K. Therefore, if $M(K) > c_P/(c_F - c_P)$, there exists a finite and unique Z_1^* $(0 < Z_1^* < K)$ that satisfies (6), and the resulting cost rate is

$$\frac{C_1(Z_1^*)}{\lambda} = (c_F - c_P)\overline{G}(K - Z_1^*). \tag{8}$$

If $M(K) \leq c_P/(c_F - c_P)$, $Z_1^* = K$, and the resulting cost rate is

$$\frac{C_1(K)}{\lambda} = \frac{c_F}{1 + M(K)}. \tag{9}$$

Further, let $L_1(Z) = \widetilde{L}_1(Z) + \sum_{j=1}^{\infty} F^{(j)}(T)G^{(j)}(K)$ and $\widetilde{Z}_1$ be a solution of

$$\widetilde{L}_1(Z) = \frac{c_P}{c_F - c_P}, \tag{10}$$

and let $L_1(Z) = \widehat{L}_1(Z) - \sum_{j=0}^{\infty} F^{(j+1)}(T)[G^{(j)}(K) - G^{(j+1)}(K)]$ and $\widehat{Z}_1$ be a solution of

$$\widehat{L}_1(Z) = \frac{c_P}{c_F - c_P}, \tag{11}$$

then $\widehat{Z}_1 < Z_1^* < \widetilde{Z}_1$, so that $\widetilde{Z}_1$ and $\widehat{Z}_1$ would be useful for computing an optimal Z_1^* as its upper and lower limits.

2.1 Comparison with Replacement First

Suppose that the unit is replaced at a damage level Z $(0 < Z \leq K)$, a planned time T $(0 < T < \infty)$, whichever occurs first, which is called *replacement first.* The expected cost rate is, from [3, p.53],

$$\frac{C_2(Z)}{\lambda} = \frac{c_P + (c_F - c_P)\sum_{j=0}^{\infty} F^{(j+1)}(T) \int_0^Z \overline{G}(K - x)\mathrm{d}G^{(j)}(x)}{\sum_{j=0}^{\infty} F^{(j+1)}(T)G^{(j)}(Z)}. \tag{12}$$

By similar method above, we discuss the optimal policy as follows: If there exists an optimal Z_2^* to minimize $C_2(Z)$, it should be satisfied

$$-G(K - Z)\sum_{j=0}^{\infty} F^{(j+1)}(T)G^{(j)}(Z) + \sum_{j=0}^{\infty} F^{(j+1)}(T) \int_0^Z G(K - x)\mathrm{d}G^{(j)}(x) = \frac{c_P}{c_F - c_P}. \tag{13}$$

Denoting the left-hand side of (13) by $L_2(Z)$,

$$-\frac{\mathrm{d}G(K - Z)}{\mathrm{d}Z}\sum_{j=0}^{\infty} F^{(j+1)}(T)G^{(j)}(Z), \tag{14}$$

which is greater than 0. Then, $L_2(Z)$ increases from 0 to

$$N(K) \equiv \sum_{j=1}^{\infty} F^{(j)}(T)G^{(j)}(K).$$

Therefore, if $N(K) > c_P/(c_F - c_P)$, there exists a finite and unique Z_2^* $(0 < Z_2^* < K)$ that satisfies (13), and the resulting cost rate is

$$\frac{C_2(Z_2^*)}{\lambda} = (c_F - c_P)\overline{G}(K - Z_2^*). \tag{15}$$

If $N(K) \leq c_P/(c_F - c_P)$, $Z_2^* = K$, and the resulting cost rate is

$$\frac{C_2(K)}{\lambda} = \frac{c_P - (c_F - c_P)N(K)}{\sum_{j=0}^{\infty} F^{(j+1)}(T)G^{(j)}(K)} + (c_F - c_P). \tag{16}$$

Suppose that there exist both finite and unique Z_1^* $(0 < Z_1^* < K)$ and Z_2^* $(0 < Z_2^* < K)$ which satisfy (6) and (13), respectively. Compare the left-hand side of (6) and (13) by denoting

$$A(Z) \equiv L_1(Z) - L_2(Z). \tag{17}$$

Then,

$$A(0) = \lim_{Z \to 0} A(Z) = \sum_{j=0}^{\infty} F^{(j+1)}(T) \int_0^K [\overline{G}(K) - \overline{G}(K - x)] \mathrm{d}G^{(j)}(x) < 0,$$

$$A(K) = \lim_{Z \to K} A(Z) = M(K) - N(K) = \sum_{j=1}^{\infty} \overline{F}^{(j)}(T)G^{(j)}(K) > 0.$$

From the above discussions and equations (7) and (14), differentiate $A(Z)$ with Z,

$$-\frac{\mathrm{d}G(K - Z)}{\mathrm{d}Z}\left[\sum_{j=0}^{\infty} \overline{F}^{(j+1)}(T)G^{(j)}(Z) + \sum_{j=0}^{\infty} F^{(j+1)}(T)[G^{(j)}(K) - G^{(j)}(Z)]\right],$$

which is greater than 0. Thus, there exists a finite and unique Z_A^* $(0 < Z_A^* < K)$ which satisfies $A(Z) = 0$.

From (13), denote that

$$L(Z_A^*) \equiv -G(K - Z_A^*) \sum_{j=0}^{\infty} F^{(j+1)}(T)G^{(j)}(Z_A^*) + \sum_{j=0}^{\infty} F^{(j+1)}(T) \int_0^{Z_A^*} G(K - x) \mathrm{d}G^{(j)}(x). \tag{18}$$

Then, it is easily shown that if $L(Z_A^*) < c_P/(c_F - c_P)$, then $Z_1^* < Z_2^*$, and hence, from (8) and (15), $C_1(Z_1^*) < C_2(Z_2^*)$, i.e., the replacement last is better than

Table 1. Optimal Z_1^*, Z_2^*, Z_3^*, and Z_A^* and $L(Z_A^*)$ when $K = 5.0$ and $\lambda T = 0.5$

$\frac{c_P}{c_F - c_P}$	$1/\mu = 1.0$			$1/\mu = 3.0$			$1/\mu = 5.0$		
	Z_1^*	Z_2^*	Z_3^*	Z_1^*	Z_2^*	Z_3^*	Z_1^*	Z_2^*	Z_3^*
0.1	0.07	0.13	0.01	0.21	0.43	0.04	0.35	0.81	0.08
0.2	0.09	0.28	0.02	0.26	0.93	0.08	0.44	1.73	0.17
0.3	0.10	0.44	0.03	0.30	1.49	0.12	0.54	2.77	0.25
0.4	0.11	0.64	0.04	0.35	2.12	0.16	0.63	3.89	0.34
0.5	0.13	0.87	0.06	0.39	2.83	0.20	0.73	5.00	0.42
0.6	0.13	1.16	0.07	0.43	3.58	0.24	0.82	5.00	0.51
0.7	0.15	1.53	0.08	0.48	4.31	0.28	0.92	5.00	0.59
0.8	0.16	2.05	0.09	0.52	4.99	0.32	1.01	5.00	0.68
0.9	0.17	2.79	0.10	0.57	5.00	0.36	1.11	5.00	0.77
1.0	0.18	3.57	0.11	0.61	5.00	0.41	1.21	5.00	0.86
2.0	0.30	5.00	0.22	1.07	5.00	0.82	2.27	5.00	1.80
Z_A^*		0.07			0.19			0.30	
$L(Z_A^*)$		0.05			0.05			0.04	

that of replacement first. Conversely, if $L(Z_A^*) \geq c_P/(c_F - c_P)$, then $Z_2^* < Z_1^*$, i.e., the replacement first is better than that of replacement last.

2.2 Comparison with Standard Replacement

Suppose that the unit is replaced at a damage level Z $(0 < Z \leq K)$, or at failure when the total damage exceeds level K $(0 < K < \infty)$, whichever occurs first. This is called *standard replacement*. The expected cost rate is, from [3, p.45],

$$\frac{C_3(Z)}{\lambda} = \frac{c_P + (c_F - c_P)[\int_0^Z \overline{G}(K-x)\mathrm{d}M(x) + \overline{G}(K)]}{M(Z)+1}. \tag{19}$$

It is easily shown that $C_3(Z) = \lim_{Z\to 0} C_1(Z) = \lim_{Z\to\infty} C_2(Z)$.

A finite and unique Z_3^* $(0 < Z_3^* < K)$ to minimize $C_3(Z)$ satisfies, from [3, p.45],

$$-G(K-Z)[M(Z)+1] + \int_0^Z G(K-x)\mathrm{d}M(x) + G(K) = \frac{c_P}{c_F - c_P}, \tag{20}$$

and the resulting cost rate is

$$\frac{C_3(Z_3^*)}{\lambda} = (c_F - c_P)\overline{G}(K - Z_3^*). \tag{21}$$

Denote the left-hand side of (20) by $L_3(Z)$ and $B_1(Z) \equiv L_3(Z) - L_1(Z)$. Then, $B_1(0) > 0$, $B_1(K) = 0$, and

$$\frac{\mathrm{d}B_1(Z)}{\mathrm{d}Z} = \frac{\mathrm{d}G(K-Z)}{\mathrm{d}Z}\sum_{j=0}^{\infty} F^{(j+1)}(T)[G^{(j)}(K) - G^{(j)}(Z)] < 0, \tag{22}$$

which follows that $Z_3^* < Z_1^*$. From (8) and (21), $C_3(Z_3^*) < C_1(Z_1^*)$, i.e., the standard replacement is better than that of replacement last.

Table 2. Optimal Z_1^*, Z_2^*, Z_3^*, and Z_A^* and $L(Z_A^*)$ when $K = 5.0$ and $\lambda T = 1.0$

$\frac{c_P}{c_F - c_P}$	$1/\mu = 1.0$ Z_1^*	Z_2^*	Z_3^*	$1/\mu = 3.0$ Z_1^*	Z_2^*	Z_3^*	$1/\mu = 5.0$ Z_1^*	Z_2^*	Z_3^*
0.1	0.16	0.04	0.01	0.44	0.15	0.04	0.68	0.30	0.08
0.2	0.18	0.09	0.02	0.49	0.30	0.08	0.79	0.61	0.17
0.3	0.19	0.13	0.03	0.54	0.47	0.12	0.90	0.94	0.25
0.4	0.21	0.18	0.04	0.60	0.64	0.16	1.01	1.29	0.34
0.5	0.22	0.23	0.06	0.65	0.81	0.20	1.13	1.67	0.42
0.6	0.23	0.28	0.07	0.70	1.00	0.24	1.24	2.08	0.51
0.7	0.25	0.33	0.08	0.76	1.20	0.28	1.36	2.51	0.59
0.8	0.26	0.39	0.09	0.81	1.41	0.32	1.47	2.98	0.68
0.9	0.28	0.44	0.10	0.86	1.62	0.36	1.59	3.48	0.77
1.0	0.29	0.50	0.11	0.92	1.85	0.41	1.71	4.03	0.86
2.0	0.43	1.29	0.22	1.45	4.90	0.82	2.99	5.00	1.80
Z_A^*		0.22			0.58			0.88	
$L(Z_A^*)$		0.48			0.37			0.28	

Further, denote $B_2(Z) \equiv L_3(Z) - L_2(Z)$. Then, $B_1(0) = 0$, $B_1(K) > 0$, and

$$\frac{\mathrm{d}B_2(Z)}{\mathrm{d}Z} = -\frac{\mathrm{d}G(K-Z)}{\mathrm{d}Z}\sum_{j=0}^{\infty}\overline{F}^{(j+1)}(T)G^{(j)}(Z) > 0, \tag{23}$$

which follows that $Z_3^* < Z_2^*$. From (15) and (21), $C_3(Z_3^*) < C_2(Z_2^*)$, i.e., the standard replacement is better than that of replacement first.

3 Numerical Example

Suppose that $F(t) = 1 - \mathrm{e}^{-\lambda t}$ and $G(x) = 1 - \mathrm{e}^{-\mu x}$. Tables 1-3 present optimal replacement damage level Z_1^*, Z_2^*, Z_3^*, and Z_A^* and $L(Z_A^*)$ when $K = 5.0$ for

Table 3. Optimal Z_1^*, Z_2^*, Z_3^*, and Z_A^* and $L(Z_A^*)$ when $K = 5.0$ and $\lambda T = 1.5$

$\frac{c_P}{c_F - c_P}$	$1/\mu = 1.0$ Z_1^*	Z_2^*	Z_3^*	$1/\mu = 3.0$ Z_1^*	Z_2^*	Z_3^*	$1/\mu = 5.0$ Z_1^*	Z_2^*	Z_3^*
0.1	0.29	0.03	0.01	0.74	0.09	0.04	1.09	0.18	0.08
0.2	0.31	0.05	0.02	0.81	0.18	0.08	1.23	0.37	0.17
0.3	0.33	0.08	0.03	0.87	0.28	0.12	1.37	0.56	0.25
0.4	0.35	0.10	0.04	0.94	0.37	0.16	1.51	0.76	0.34
0.5	0.37	0.13	0.06	1.00	0.47	0.20	1.65	0.97	0.42
0.6	0.38	0.16	0.07	1.07	0.57	0.24	1.79	1.19	0.51
0.7	0.40	0.19	0.08	1.13	0.67	0.28	1.93	1.41	0.59
0.8	0.42	0.21	0.09	1.20	0.78	0.32	2.07	1.65	0.68
0.9	0.43	0.24	0.10	1.26	0.89	0.36	2.22	1.90	0.77
1.0	0.45	0.27	0.11	1.32	1.00	0.41	3.36	2.16	0.86
2.0	0.62	0.60	0.22	1.96	2.32	0.82	3.98	5.00	1.80
Z_A^*		0.63			1.68			2.60	
$L(Z_A^*)$		2.01			1.56			1.16	

$\lambda T = 0.5, 1.0, 1.5$, $1/\mu = 1.0, 3.0, 5.0$ and $c_P/(c_F - c_P) = 0.1, 0.2, 0.3, 0.4, 0.5, 0.6, 0.7, 0.8, 0.9, 1.0, 2.0$.

4 Conclusions

We have proposed the cumulative damage models where the unit is replaced before failure at a damage level Z or a planned time T, whichever occurs last. Modeling and optimizations have been discussed analytically and numerically. Comparisons of replacement last with replacement first and standard replacement have been made, it has shown that we can determine which policy is better using the ratio of replacement costs. That is, if the replacement cost after failure would be lower, replacement last may be much better than replacement first, however, standard replacement is better than either replacement last or replacement first.

Acknowledgement. This work is partially supported by the Grant-in-Aid for Scientific Research (C) of Japan Society for the Promotion of Science under Grant No. 22500897 and 21530318.

References

1. Osaki, S.: Stochastic Models in Reliability and Maintenance. Springer, Berlin (2002)
2. Nakagwa, T.: Maintenance Theory of Reliability. Springer, London (2005)
3. Nakagwa, T.: Shock and Damage Models in Reliability Theory. Springer, London (2007)
4. Wang, H., Pham, H.: Reliability and Optimal Miantenance. Springer, London (2007)
5. Chen, M., Mizutani, S., Nakagawa, T.: Random and age replacement policies. International Journal of Reliability, Quality and Safety Engineering 17, 27–39 (2010)
6. Chen, M., Nakamura, S., Nakagawa, T.: Replacement and preventive maintenace models with random working times. IEICE Trans. Fundamentals E93-A, 500–507 (2010)
7. Zhao, X.F., Nakagawa, T.: Optimization problems of replacement first or last in reliability theory. Submitted to European Journal of Operational Research (2011)
8. Qian, C.H., Nakamura, S., Nakagawa, T.: Cumulative damage model with two kinds of shocks and its application to the backup policy. Journal of the Operations Research Society of Japan 42, 501–511 (1999)
9. Zhao, X.F., Nakamura, S., Nakagawa, T.: Two generational garbage collection models with major collection time. IEICE Transactions on Fundamentals of Electronics Communications and Computer Sciences E94-A, 1558–1566 (2011)

Periodic and Random Inspection Policies for Computer Systems

Mingchih Chen[1], Cunhua Qian[2], and Toshio Nakagawa[3]

[1] Graduate Institute of Business Administration, Fu Jen Catholic University, 510 Jhongjheng Rd., Sinjhuang City, Taipei County, 24205, Taiwan
081438@mail.fju.edu.tw

[2] School of Economics and Management, Nanjing University of Technology, 30 Puzhu Road, Nanjing 211816, China
qch64317@njut.edu.cn

[3] Department of Business Administration, Aichi Institute of Technology, 1247 Yachigusa, Yakusa-cho, Toyota 470-0392, Japan
toshi-nakagawa@aitech.ac.jp

Abstract. Faults in computer systems sometimes occur intermittently. This paper applies a standard inspection policy with imperfect inspection to a computer system: The system is checked at periodic times and its failure is detected at the next checking time with a certain probability. The expected cost until failure detection is obtained, and when the failure time is exponential, an optimal inspection time to minimize it is derived. Next, when the system executes computer processes, it is checked at random processing times and its failure is detected at the next checking time with a certain probability. The expected cost until failure detection is obtained, and when random processing times are exponential, an optimal inspection time to minimize it is derived. Finally, this paper compares optimal times for two inspection policies and shows that if the random inspection cost is the half of the periodic one, then two expected costs are almost the same.

Keywords: Periodic inspection, Random inspection, Imperfect, Checking time, Expected cost.

1 Introduction

It has been well-known that faults in computer systems sometimes occur intermittently [1, 2, 3, p.220]: Faults are hidden and become permanent failure when the duration of hidden faults exceeds a threshold level [4, 5, p.110]. To prevent such faults, some inspection policies for computer systems were considered [1, 6, 7] and summarized [3, p.220], and data transmission strategies for communication systems were considered [8].

We apply a standard inspection policy with imperfect inspection to a computer system: The system has to be operated for an infinite time span and fails. To detect the failure, the system is checked at periodic times. System failure is detected at the next checking time with a certain probability, and undetected

T.-h. Kim et al. (Eds.): ASEA/DRBC/EL 2011, CCIS 257, pp. 346–353, 2011.

failure is detected at the next checking time with the same probability. Such procedures are continued until the failure is detected. The expected cost until failure detection is obtained, and when the failure time is exponential, an optimal inspection time which minimizes it is derived.

Most systems in offices and industries successively execute computer processes. For such systems, it would be impossible to maintain them in a strictly periodic fashion. We consider the system which executes a job with random processing times and apply the inspection policy with imperfect inspection to the system [1, p.253]. Optimal periodic and random inspection policies were summarized in [9]. It is assumed that the system is checked at random processing times. System failure is detected at the next checking time with a certain probability. By the methods similar to the periodic inspection policy, the expected cost until failure detection is obtained, and when each processing time is exponential, an optimal random time which minimizes it is derived.

Finally, we compare optimal times for periodic and random inspection policies when both failure and processing times are exponential. It is shown that the periodic inspection is better than the random one, however, if the random inspection cost is the half of the periodic one, then two expected costs are almost the same.

2 Periodic Inspection

Consider a standard inspection policy [3, p.202] with imperfect inspection: A system should operate for an infinite time span and is checked at periodic times kT $(k = 1, 2, \cdots)$. System failure is detected at the next checking time with probability q $(0 < q \leq 1)$ and is replaced immediately, and is not done with probability $p \equiv 1-q$. The undetected failure is detected at the next checking time with the same probability q. Such procedures are continued until the failure is detected. It is assumed that the system has a failure distribution $F(t)$ with finite mean $1/\lambda$, irrespective of any inspection. All times for checks and replacement are negligible. Let c_T be the cost of one check and c_D be the loss cost per unit of time for the time elapsed between a failure and its detection at some checking time. Then, the probability that the system fails between the jth and $(j+1)$th $(j = 0, 1, 2, \cdots)$ checking times, and its failure is detected after the $(k+1)$th $(k = 0, 1, 2, \cdots)$ check, *i.e.*, at the $(j + k + 1)$th checking time, is

$$[F((j+1)T) - F(jT)]p^k q.$$

Clearly,

$$\sum_{j=0}^{\infty}[F((j+1)T) - F(jT)]\sum_{k=0}^{\infty}p^k q = 1.$$

Then, the expected number of checks until replacement is

$$\sum_{j=0}^{\infty} j[F((j+1)T) - F(jT)] + \sum_{k=0}^{\infty}(k+1)p^k q = \sum_{j=1}^{\infty}\overline{F}(jT) + \frac{1}{q}, \tag{1}$$

and the mean time from failure to its detection is

$$\sum_{j=0}^{\infty}\sum_{k=0}^{\infty}p^k q\int_{jT}^{(j+1)T}[(j+k+1)T-t]\mathrm{d}F(t)=T\left[\sum_{j=1}^{\infty}\overline{F}(jT)+\frac{1}{q}\right]-\frac{1}{\lambda}. \quad (2)$$

Therefore, the total expected cost until replacement is, from (1) and (2),

$$C_P(T)=(c_T+c_D T)\left[\sum_{j=1}^{\infty}\overline{F}(jT)+\frac{1}{q}\right]-\frac{c_D}{\lambda}. \quad (3)$$

In particular, when $F(t)=1-\mathrm{e}^{-\lambda t}$,

$$C_P(T)=(c_T+c_D T)\left(\frac{1}{1-\mathrm{e}^{-\lambda T}}+\frac{p}{q}\right)-\frac{c_D}{\lambda}. \quad (4)$$

Differentiating $C_P(T)$ with respect to T and setting it equal to zero,

$$\frac{p}{q}(1-\mathrm{e}^{-\lambda T})^2\mathrm{e}^{\lambda T}+\mathrm{e}^{\lambda T}-1-\lambda T=\frac{\lambda c_T}{c_D}, \quad (5)$$

whose left-hand side increases from 0 to ∞. Thus, there exists an optimal T^* ($0 < T^* < \infty$) which satisfies (5).

3 Random Inspection

Consider a random inspection policy [3, p.253] with imperfect inspection: Suppose that the system is checked at successive times S_j ($j=1,2,\cdots$), where $S_0 \equiv 0$ and $Y_j \equiv S_j - S_{j-1}$ ($j=1,2,\cdots$) are independently and identically distributed random variables, and also, independent of its failure time. It is assumed that each Y_j has an identical distribution $G(t)$ with finite mean $1/\mu$. The system is checked at successive times S_j and its cost for one check is c_R. The other assumptions are the same as those in Section 2.

The probability that the system fails between the jth and $(j+1)$th ($j=0,1,2,\cdots$) checking times and its failure is detected after the $(k+1)$th check is

$$\int_0^{\infty}\mathrm{d}G^{(j)}(t_1)\int_{t_1}^{\infty}[F(t_2)-F(t_1)]\mathrm{d}G(t_2-t_1)p^k q.$$

Clearly,

$$\begin{aligned}&\sum_{j=0}^{\infty}\int_0^{\infty}\mathrm{d}G^{(j)}(t_1)\int_{t_1}^{\infty}[F(t_2)-F(t_1)]\mathrm{d}G(t_2-t_1)\sum_{k=0}^{\infty}p^k q\\&=\sum_{j=0}^{\infty}\int_0^{\infty}\mathrm{d}G^{(j)}(t_1)\int_0^{\infty}[\overline{F}(t_1)-\overline{F}(t_1+t_2)]\mathrm{d}G(t_2)\\&=\sum_{j=0}^{\infty}\int_0^{\infty}\overline{F}(t)\mathrm{d}G^{(j)}(t)-\sum_{j=1}^{\infty}\int_0^{\infty}\overline{F}(t)\mathrm{d}G(t)=1.\end{aligned}$$

Then, the expected number of checks until replacement is

$$\sum_{j=0}^{\infty} j \int_0^{\infty} \mathrm{d}G^{(j)}(t_1) \int_{t_1}^{\infty} [F(t_2) - F(t_1)]\mathrm{d}G(t_2 - t_1) + \sum_{k=0}^{\infty} (k+1)p^k q$$
$$= \sum_{j=1}^{\infty} \int_0^{\infty} \overline{F}(t)\mathrm{d}G^{(j)}(t) + \frac{1}{q} = \int_0^{\infty} M(t)\mathrm{d}F(t) + \frac{1}{q}, \tag{6}$$

where $M(t) \equiv \sum_{j=1}^{\infty} G^{(j)}(t)$ which is the expected number of checks in $[0, t]$ and is called a renewal function in stochastic processes [10]. The mean time from failure to its detection is

$$\sum_{j=0}^{\infty} \int_0^{\infty} \mathrm{d}G^{(j)}(t_1) \int_{t_1}^{\infty} \mathrm{d}G(t_2 - t_1) \int_{t_1}^{t_2} \mathrm{d}F(t) \sum_{k=0}^{\infty} p^k q \int_{t_2}^{\infty} (t_3 - t)\mathrm{d}G^{(k)}(t_3 - t_2)$$
$$= \sum_{j=0}^{\infty} \int_0^{\infty} \mathrm{d}G^{(j)}(t_1) \int_{t_1}^{\infty} \mathrm{d}G(t_2 - t_1) \int_{t_1}^{t_2} \left(\frac{p}{q\mu} + t_2 - t\right) \mathrm{d}F(t)$$
$$= \frac{p}{q\mu} + \sum_{j=0}^{\infty} \int_0^{\infty} \mathrm{d}G^{(j)}(t_1) \int_0^{\infty} \mathrm{d}G(t_2) \int_{t_1}^{t_1+t_2} [\overline{F}(t_1) - \overline{F}(t)]\mathrm{d}t$$
$$= \frac{p}{q\mu} + \sum_{j=0}^{\infty} \int_0^{\infty} \mathrm{d}G^{(j)}(t_1) \int_0^{\infty} \overline{G}(t)[\overline{F}(t_1) - \overline{F}(t + t_1)]\mathrm{d}t$$
$$= \frac{1}{q\mu} + \frac{1}{\mu} \int_0^{\infty} M(t)\mathrm{d}F(t) - \frac{1}{\lambda}. \tag{7}$$

Therefore, the total expected cost until replacement is, from (6) and (7),

$$C_R(G) = \left(c_R + \frac{c_D}{\mu}\right) \left[\int_0^{\infty} M(t)\mathrm{d}F(t) + \frac{1}{q}\right] - \frac{c_D}{\lambda}. \tag{8}$$

In particular, when $G(t) = 1 - \mathrm{e}^{-\mu t}$, *i.e.*, $M(t) = \mu t$, the expected cost is a function of μ which is given by

$$C_R(\mu) = \left(c_R + \frac{c_D}{\mu}\right) \left(\frac{\mu}{\lambda} + \frac{1}{q}\right) - \frac{c_D}{\lambda}. \tag{9}$$

Differentiating $C_R(\mu)$ with respect to μ and setting it equal to zero,

$$\left(\frac{\lambda}{\mu}\right)^2 = \frac{q\lambda c_R}{c_D}. \tag{10}$$

Suppose that $F(t) = 1 - \mathrm{e}^{-\lambda t}$, $G(t) = 1 - \mathrm{e}^{-\mu t}$, $c_T = c_R$, and $q = 0.9$. Then, Table 1 presents optimal λT^*, λ/μ^* and their resulting costs for $\lambda c_T/c_D$. This indicates as estimated previously that $T^* > 1/\mu^*$ and $C_P(T^*) < C_R(\mu^*)$, *i.e.*, the periodic inspection time is larger than the random one, and hence, when $c_T = c_R$, the periodic policy is better than the random one.

Table 1. Optimal λT^*, λ/μ^*, and $\lambda C_P(T^*)/c_D$, $\lambda C_R(\mu^*)/c_D$ when $q = 0.9$

$\lambda c_T/c_D$	λT^*	$\lambda C_P(T^*)/c_D$	λ/μ^*	$\lambda C_R(\mu^*)/c_D$
0.001	0.0403	0.0502	0.0300	0.0678
0.002	0.0566	0.0714	0.0424	0.0965
0.005	0.0893	0.1143	0.0671	0.1546
0.010	0.1256	0.1639	0.0949	0.2219
0.020	0.1764	0.2363	0.1342	0.3204
0.050	0.2746	0.3879	0.2121	0.5270
0.100	0.3824	0.5716	0.3000	0.7778
0.200	0.5282	0.8556	0.4243	1.1650
0.500	0.7994	1.5052	0.6708	2.0463
1.000	1.0757	2.3807	0.9487	3.2193

4 Comparison of Periodic and Random Inspection Policies

We compare the periodic and random inspection policies theoretically and numerically when $F(t) = 1 - \mathrm{e}^{-\lambda t}$ and $G(t) = 1 - \mathrm{e}^{-\mu t}$. For the simplicity of notations, it is assumed that $q = 1$, $\lambda = 1$, $c_T = c_R$, and $c \equiv \lambda c_T/c_D \leq 1$ because the expected loss cost for the mean failure time $1/\lambda$ would be much higher than the cost c_T of one check for most inspection models.

Under the above assumptions, the total expected cost for the periodic inspection is, from (4),

$$\frac{C_P(T)}{c_D} = \frac{c + T}{1 - \mathrm{e}^{-T}} - 1. \tag{11}$$

An optimal T^* which minimizes $C_P(T)$ is given by a solution of the equation

$$\mathrm{e}^T - 1 - T = c, \tag{12}$$

and the resulting cost is

$$\frac{C_P(T^*)}{c_D} = c + T^* = \mathrm{e}^{T^*} - 1. \tag{13}$$

The total expected cost for the random inspection is, from (9),

$$\frac{C_R(\mu)}{c_D} = c(1 + \mu) + \frac{1}{\mu}. \tag{14}$$

An optimal μ^* which minimizes $C_R(\mu)$ is given by

$$\frac{1}{\mu^*} = \sqrt{c}, \tag{15}$$

and the resulting cost is

$$\frac{C_R(\mu^*)}{c_D} = c(1 + \mu^*) + \frac{1}{\mu^*} = \left(\frac{1}{\mu^*}\right)^2 + \frac{2}{\mu^*}. \tag{16}$$

When $c = 1$, $T^* = 1.1462$ from (12), and $1/\mu^* = 1$ from (15). Thus, it is easily proved that $0 < T^* < 1.1462$ and $0 < 1/\mu^* \leq 1$.

From (12) and (15), compute a solution of the equation

$$Q(T) \equiv \mathrm{e}^T - (1 + T + T^2) = 0. \tag{17}$$

Clearly, a solution of (17) is about 1.79. Thus, $Q(T) < 0$ for $0 < T < 1.79$, and hence,

$$0 < \frac{1}{\mu^*} < T^* \leq 1.1462.$$

Next, prove that $2/\mu^* > T^*$. From (12),

$$c = \mathrm{e}^T - (1 + T) > \frac{T^2}{2},$$

which follows that $T^* < \sqrt{2c}$. In addition, from (15),

$$\frac{2}{\mu^*} = 2\sqrt{c} > \sqrt{2c} > T^*.$$

Thus,

$$\frac{1}{\mu^*} < T^* < \frac{2}{\mu^*}.$$

Furthermore, from (13) and (16),

$$\begin{aligned}\frac{C_R(\mu^*) - C_T(T^*)}{c_D} &= c(1 + \mu^*) + \frac{1}{\mu^*} - c - T^* \\ &= c\mu^* + \frac{1}{\mu^*} - T^* > c\mu^* - \frac{1}{\mu^*} = 0.\end{aligned}$$

From the above results, $T^* > 1/\mu^*$ and $C_P(T^*) < C_R(\mu^*)$ when $c_T = c_R$, *i.e.*, the periodic inspection is better than the random one and the optimal interval T^* is greater than $1/\mu^*$.

It has been assumed until now that costs c_T and c_R for two inspection policies are the same. In general, cost c_R would be lower than c_T because the system is checked at random. We compute c_R when the expected costs of two inspection policies are the same. From (13) and (16), we compute $1/\widetilde{\mu}$ for $c = c_T/c_D$ which satisfies

$$\frac{C_R(T^*)}{c_D} = \mathrm{e}^{T^*} - 1 = \left(\frac{1}{\widetilde{\mu}}\right)^2 + \frac{2}{\widetilde{\mu}},$$

and compute

$$\frac{c_R}{c_D} = \left(\frac{1}{\widetilde{\mu}}\right)^2.$$

Table 2 presents $1/\widetilde{\mu}$, c_R/c_D and c_R/c_T, and indicates that c_R is a little more than the half of c_T. In other words, when $c_R \approx c_T/2$, two expected costs are almost the same.

It is noted from (12) and (15) that $T^* \to 0$ and $1/\mu^* \to 0$ as $c \to 0$. Thus, from (13) and (16),

$$\lim_{T\to 0} \frac{e^T - 1}{T^2 + 2T} = \frac{1}{2}.$$

This shows that if $c \to 0$, then $C_T(T^*) \to C_R(\mu^*)/2$. So that, it would be estimated that if $c \to 0$ and $c_R/c_T = 0.5$, then two expected costs of the periodic and random policies would be the same as shown in Table 2.

Table 2. Values of $1/\widetilde{\mu}$, c_R/c_D and c_R/c_T

c_T/c_D	$1/\widetilde{\mu}$	c_R/c_D	c_R/c_T
0.001	0.0224	0.0005	0.5039
0.002	0.0318	0.0010	0.5054
0.005	0.0504	0.0025	0.5086
0.010	0.0715	0.0051	0.5118
0.020	0.1016	0.0103	0.5160
0.050	0.1621	0.0263	0.5253
0.100	0.2313	0.0535	0.5352
0.200	0.3312	0.1097	0.5485
0.500	0.5355	0.2868	0.5735
1.000	0.7738	0.5987	0.5987

5 Conclusions

We have applied a standard inspection policy with imperfect inspection to a computer system. The expected costs of the periodic and random inspection policies are obtained and the optimal inspection times which minimize them are derived analytically, when the failure and random times are exponential. It is shown numerically that when the costs for periodic and random inspection are the same, the periodic policy is better than the random one. However, it is of interest that if the cost for random inspection is the half of the periodic one, two expected costs are almost the same.

Acknowledgement. This work is partially supported by National Natural Science Foundation of China (70471017, 70801036); Humanities and Social Science Research Foundation of China (05JA630027); Grant-in-Aid for Scientific Research (C) of Japan Society for the Promotion of Science under Grant No. 22500897.

References

1. Malaiya, Y.K., Su, S.Y.H.: Reliability Measure of Hardware Redundancy Fault-Tolerant Digital Systems with Intermittent Faults. IEEE Transactions on Computers C-30, 600–604 (1981)

2. Castillo, X., McConner, S.R., Siewiorek, D.P.: Derivation and Calibration of a Transient Error Reliability Model. IEEE Transactions on Computers C-31, 658–671 (1982)
3. Nakagawa, T.: Maintenance Theory of Reliability. Springer, London (2005)
4. Nakagawa, T., Yasui, K., Sandoh, H.: An Optimal Policy for a Data Transmission System with Intermittent Faults. IEICE Transactions on Fundamentals of Electronics, Communications and Computer Sciences J76-A, 1201–1206 (1993)
5. Nakagawa, T.: Adcanced Reliability Models and Maintennace Polices. Springer, London (2008)
6. Su, S.Y.H., Koren, T., Malaiya, Y.K.: A Continuous-paremeter Markov Model and Detection Procedures for Intermittent Faults. IEEE Transactions on Computers C-27, 567–570 (1978)
7. Malaiya, Y.K.: Linearly Corrected Intermittent Failures. IEEE Transactions on Reliability R-31, 211–215 (1982)
8. Yasui, K., Nakagawa, T., Sandoh, H.: Reliability Models in Reliability and Maintenance. In: Osaki, S. (ed.) Stochastic Models in Reliability and Maintenance, pp. 281–301. Springer, Berlin (2002)
9. Nakagawa, T., Mizutani, S., Chen, M.: A Summary of Periodic and Random Inspection Policies. Reliability Engineering & System Safety 95, 906–911 (2010)
10. Nakagawa, T.: Stochastic Processes with Applications to Reliability Theory. Springer, London (2011)

Software Reliability Growth Modeling with Change-Point and Its Goodness-of-Fit Comparisons

Shinji Inoue and Shigeru Yamada

Department of Social Management Engineering,
Graduate School of Engineering,
Tottori University,
4-101, Koyama-Minami, Tottori 680-8552, Japan
{ino,yamada}@sse.tottori-u.ac.jp

Abstract. In an actual testing-phase, software testing manager usually observes a change of the software failure-occurrence phenomenon due to some factors being related to the software reliability growth process. Testing-time when behavior of the software failure-occurrence time interval notably changes is called change-point. Such change influences accuracy of software reliability assessment based on a software reliability growth model. This paper discusses software reliability growth modeling with the influence of the change-point by using the environmental function. Then, we check goodness-of-fit of our change-point models to actual data by comparing with the existing non-change-point models.

1 Introduction

Quantitative assessment of software reliability is one of the important activities for ensure software reliability. As one of the quantitative assessment method for software reliability, software reliability growth models (abbreviated as SRGMs) [1, 2, 3] are known as mathematical models for quantitative software reliability assessment. Ordinarily, SRGMs are developed by treating the software failure-occurrence time or the fault-detection time intervals as random variables. And, it is assumed that the stochastic characteristics for these quantities are same throughout the testing phase in the usual software reliability growth modeling. However, such assumptions do not enable us to reflect an actual software failure-occurrence phenomenon to software reliability growth modeling because we often observe a change of the stochastic behavior for the software failure-occurrence time interval due to changing some factors being related to the software failure-occurrence phenomenon, e.g., changing of fault target, changing of testing-effort expenditure, and so forth. Testing-time when such phenomenon is observed is called change-point [4]. It is known that occurrence of the change-point influences accuracy of SRGM-based software reliability assessment. Under the background, software reliability growth modeling with the influence of the change-point has been discussed so far [4, 5, 6, 7].

T.-h. Kim et al. (Eds.): ASEA/DRBC/EL 2011, CCIS 257, pp. 354–361, 2011.

However, it is very difficult to find research results, which discuss software reliability growth modeling with a relationship between the software failure-occurrence time intervals before the change-point and those after the change-point. In an actual testing phase, it might be natural to consider that there exists the relationship between the time-intervals before change-point and those after change-point because a same software product is tested even if the change-point is occurred during the testing-phase for the software product. And it is very important to know how the stochastic characteristic of the software failure-occurrence time-interval changes at the change-point from the point of view of software development management. This paper discusses a framework for software reliability growth modeling with the effect of change-point. Concretely speaking, we incorporate the relationship between the software failure-occurrence time intervals before change-point and those after change-point into the usual modeling framework by using the testing-environmental function. Further, we check goodness-of-fit of our change-point models, which is developed by using our change-point modeling framework, for actual data by comparing with the existing non change-point models.

2 Software Reliability Modeling

2.1 Basic Modeling Framework

We discuss the nonhomogeneous Poisson process (NHPP)-based software reliability growth modeling approach, in which the total number of detectable faults is assumed to be finite [8, 9, 10, 11]. The modeling assumptions are

(A1) Whenever a software failure is observed, the fault which caused it will be detected immediately and no new faults are introduced in the fault-removing activities.
(A2) Each software failure occurs at independently and identically distributed random times with the probability distribution, $F(t) \equiv \Pr\{T \leq t\} = \int_0^t f(x)dx$, where $\Pr\{A\}$ represents the probability of event A and $f(t)$ the probability density function.
(A3) The initial number of faults in the software, $N_0(> 0)$, is finite, and is treated as a random variable.

Now, let $\{N(t),\, t \geq 0\}$ denote a counting process representing the total number of faults detected up to testing-time t. From the basic assumptions above, the probability that m faults are detected up to testing-time t is derived as

$$\begin{aligned}\Pr\{N(t) = m\} &= \sum_n \binom{n}{m} \{F(t)\}^m \{1 - F(t)\}^{n-m} \frac{\omega^n}{n!} \exp[-\omega] \\ &= \frac{\{\omega F(t)\}^m}{m!} \exp[-\omega F(t)] \qquad (m = 0, 1, 2, \cdots), \qquad (1)\end{aligned}$$

in which it is assumed that the initial fault content, N_0, follows a Poisson distribution with mean ω, Eq. (1) is equivalent to an NHPP with mean value function

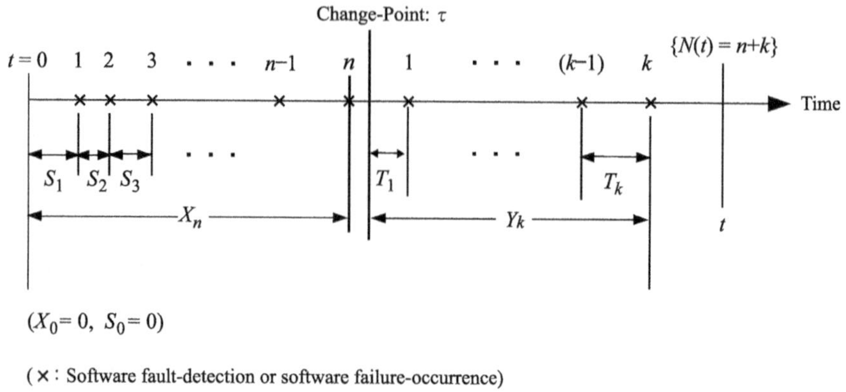

Fig. 1. Stochastic quantities for software failure-occurrence and fault-detection phenomena

$\mathrm{E}[N(t)] \equiv \Lambda(t) = \omega F(t)$. An NHPP model for software reliability assessment can be developed by assuming a suitable software failure-occurrence time distribution.

2.2 Modeling with Change-Point

In an actual testing phase, it might be natural to consider that there exists a relationship of the software failure-occurrence time-interval before and after change-point since we test an identical software product even if change-point occurs. And it is very important to get to know the quantitative aspect of the effect of the change being related to the software failure-occurrence phenomenon. In this paper, we develop software reliability growth modeling framework with the effect of the change-point for overcoming the problems mentioned above.

Now we define the following stochastic quantities being related to our modeling approach in this paper: X_i: the i-th software failure-occurrence time before change-point ($X_0 = 0, \quad i = 0, 1, 2, \cdots$), S_i: the i-th software failure-occurrence time-interval before change-point ($S_i = X_i - X_{i-1}, \quad S_0 = 0, \quad i = 1, 2, \cdots$), Y_i: the i-th software failure-occurrence time after change-point ($Y_0 = 0, \quad i = 0, 1, 2, \cdots$), T_i: the i-th software failure-occurrence time-interval after change-point ($T_i = Y_i - Y_{i-1}, \quad T_0 = 0, \quad i = 1, 2, \cdots$). Figure 1 shows the stochastic quantities for the software failure-occurrence or fault-detection phenomena with change-point.

We assume that the stochastic quantities before and those after the change-point have the following relationships:

$$\begin{cases} Y_i = \alpha(X_i), \\ T_i = \alpha(S_i), \\ K_i(t) = J_i(\alpha^{-1}(t)), \end{cases} \tag{2}$$

respectively, where $\alpha(t)$ is a test-environmental function representing the relationship between the stochastic quantities of the software failure-occurrence times or time-intervals before change-point and those after change-point, $J_i(t)$ and $K_i(t)$ the probability distribution functions with respect to the random variables S_i and T_i, respectively. In this paper, we assume that the test-environmental function is given as [12]

$$\alpha(t) = \alpha t \qquad (\alpha > 0), \tag{3}$$

where α is the proportional constant representing the relative magnitude of the effect of the change for the software reliability growth process. Eq. (3) is one of the examples for the testing-environmental function. However, we can get to know the effect of the change for the software reliability growth process simply by assuming Eq. (3) as the testing-environmental function.

Suppose that n faults have been detected up to the change-point and their fault-detection times from the test-beginning ($t = 0$) have been observed as $0 < x_1 < x_2 < \cdots < x_n \le \tau$. Then, the probability distribution function of T_1, a random variable representing the time-interval from change point to the 1-st software failure-occurrence after change-point, can be derived as

$$\begin{aligned} \bar{K}_1(t) \equiv \Pr\{T_1 > t\} &= \frac{\Pr\{S_{n+1} > \tau - x_n + t/\alpha\}}{\Pr\{S_{n+1} > \tau - x_n\}} \\ &= \frac{\exp[-\{M_B(\tau + t/\alpha) - M_B(x_n)\}]}{\exp[-M_B(\tau) - M_B(x_n)]}, \end{aligned} \tag{4}$$

where $\bar{K}_1(t)$ indicates the cofunction of the probability distribution function $K_1(t) \equiv \Pr\{T_1 \le t\}$, i.e., $\bar{K}_1(t) \equiv 1 - K_1(t)$, and $M_B(t)(\equiv \omega J_1(t))$ represents the expected number of faults detected up to change-point, i.e., a mean value function for the NHPP before the change-point. From Eq. (4), the expected number of faults detected up to $t \in (\tau, \infty]$ after change-point, $M_A(t)$, can be formulated as

$$\begin{aligned} M_A(t) &= -\log \Pr\{T_1 > t - \tau\} \\ &= -\log \bar{K}_1(t - \tau) \\ &= M_B\left(\tau + \frac{t - \tau}{\alpha}\right) - M_B(\tau) \end{aligned} \tag{5}$$

Then, the expected number of faults detected up to testing-time t ($t \in (0, \infty], 0 < \tau < t$) can be derived as

$$\Lambda(t) = \begin{cases} \Lambda_1(t) = M_B(t) & (0 \le t \le \tau) \\ \Lambda_2(t) = M_B(\tau) + M_A(t) & \\ \qquad\;\; = M_B\left(\tau + \frac{t-\tau}{\alpha}\right) & (\tau < t). \end{cases} \tag{6}$$

From Eq. (6), we can see that an NHPP-based SRGM with change-point can be developed by assuming a suitable probability distribution function for the software failure-occurrence time before the change-point.

Table 1. Results of goodness-of-fit comparisons of Model 1 and 2 based on MSE

	Exponential	Model 1	Delayed S-shaped	Model 1
DS1 (S-shpaed)	16.0848	21.6153	7.21958	**6.12918**
DS2 (S-shaped)	32.0834	58.3482	**19.3189**	22.1304
DS3 (Exponential)	2.40089	**2.19263**	6.87789	6.05874
DS4 (S-shaped)	0.348901	**0.331126**	1.70385	1.60806
DS5 (Exponential)	2.47239	**2.2943**	7.63319	7.49945

Table 2. Results of goodness-of-fit comparisons of Model B based on the predicted relative errors for DS2 and DS4

DS2				
TPR(%)	Exponential	Model 1	Delayed S-shaped	Model 1
85	1.279E-01	5.431E-02	6.845E-02	**4.826E-02**
90	8.158E-02	2.047E-02	4.352E-02	**1.951E-02**
95	2.048E-02	3.422E-03	1.083E-02	**3.380E-03**
100	-1.947E-16	-7.787E-16	1.947E-16	-3.893E-16

DS4				
TPR(%)	Exponential	Model 1	Delayed S-shaped	Model 1
85	**1.988E-02**	3.492E-02	-2.939E-02	-3.666E-02
90	2.542E-02	3.643E-02	-8.470E03	**-1.388E-02**
95	**-6.345E-03**	-7.578E-03	-1.864E-02	-2.099E-02
100	-2.757E-05	-4.263E-16	2.842E-16	O

(TPR: Testing progress ratio, E: Exponential in decimal)

3 Goodness-of-Fit Comparisons

We compare performance for software reliability assessment of our SRGMs with non change-point SRGMs in terms of a mean square error (abbreviated as MSE) [3] and predicted relative errors [2] by using the following actual data:

DS1 : $(t_i, y_i)(i = 1, 2, \cdots, 26\,;\ t_{26} = 26, y_{26} = 40\,;\ \tau = 18)$ where t_i is measured on the basis of weeks,

DS2 : $(t_i, y_i)(i = 1, 2, \cdots, 29\,;\ t_{29} = 29, y_{26} = 73\,;\ \tau = 24)$ where t_i is measured on the basis of weeks,

DS3 : $(t_i, y_i)(i = 1, 2, \cdots, 26\,;\ t_{26} = 26, y_{26} = 34\,;\ \tau = 17)$ where t_i is measured on the basis of weeks,

DS4 : $(t_i, y_i)(i = 1, 2, \cdots, 29\,;\ t_{29} = 29, y_{26} = 25\,;\ \tau = 18)$ where t_i is measured on the basis of weeks,

DS5 : $(t_i, y_i)(i = 1, 2, \cdots, 28\,;\ t_{28} = 29, y_{28} = 43\,;\ \tau = 18)$ where t_i is measured on the basis of weeks,

where DS3 and DS5 show exponential software reliability growth curves and the remainder (DS1, DS2, DS4) show S-shaped software reliability growth curves, respectively. And these actual data are fault count data collected from an actual testing phase for the Windows version software. Regarding the model comparison criteria, the MSE is calculated by dividing the sum of squared vertical distance between the observed and estimated cumulative numbers of faults, y_i and $\widehat{y}(t_i)$, detected during the time-interval $(0, t_i]$, respectively, by the number of observed data pairs. That is, supposing that N data pairs (t_i, y_i) $(i = 1, 2, \cdots, N\,;\, 0 < t_1 < t_2 < \cdots < t_N)$ are observed, we can formulate the MSE as

$$\mathrm{MSE} = \frac{1}{N}\sum_{i=1}^{N}\left[y_i - \widehat{y}(t_i)\right]^2. \tag{7}$$

The model having the smallest MSE fits best to the observed data set. The predicted relative error, $PRE[t_e]$, is calculated as

$$PRE[t_e] = \frac{\widehat{y}(t_e; t_q) - n_q}{n_q}, \tag{8}$$

where $\widehat{y}(t_e; t_q)$ is the estimated value of the number of detected faults at the testing-termination time, t_q, by using the observed data collected up to the arbitrary testing-time, t_e $(0 < t_e \leq t_q)$, and n_q the observed number of faults detected up to the termination time of the testing. Then, we can say that the SRGM whose value of the predicted relative errors at each testing-period or testing-time is closed to zero has better performance on the predictive accuracy.

We develop two-types of our change-point model, Model 1 and Model 2, by using our change-point modeling framework. Model 1 and Model 2 are developed as

$$\Lambda_1(t) = \begin{cases} \Lambda_B(t) = \omega\left\{1 - \exp\left[-bt\right]\right\} & (0 < t \leq \tau), \\ \Lambda_A(t) = \omega\left\{1 - \exp\left[-b\left(\tau + \frac{t-\tau}{\alpha}\right)\right]\right\} & (\tau < t), \end{cases} \tag{9}$$

and

$$\Lambda_2(t) = \begin{cases} \Lambda_B(t) = \omega\left\{1 - (1 + bt)\exp[-bt]\right\} & (0 < t \leq \tau), \\ \Lambda_A(t) = \omega\left[1 - \left\{1 + b\left(\tau + \frac{t-\tau}{\alpha}\right)\exp\left[-b\left(\tau + \frac{t-\tau}{\alpha}\right)\right]\right\}\right], & \\ & (\tau < t), \end{cases} \tag{10}$$

by assuming that the software failure-occurrence time distributions before change-point follow an exponential distribution with parameter b and a gamma distribution with parameter $(2, b)$, respectively.

Table 1 shows the results of model comparisons of our change-point models with existing SRGMs (an exponential and a delayed S-shaped SRGMs [1, 13]) based on the MSE. The parameter estimations are obtained by the method of maximum likelihood. From Table 1, we can say that Model 1 has the best fitting performance among other SRGMs for the actual data showing exponential software reliability growth curves, which are DS3 and DS5. Model 2 does not have the best performance for the data showing S-shaped software reliability growth curves. However, we can say that Model 2 has better fitting performance for DS1 and DS4 compared with the corresponding existing non change-point model, i.e., the delayed S-shaped SRGM. For DS4, Model 1 fits well to the actual data regardless of the shape of the software reliability growth curve because DS4 is not saturated with respect to the expected initial fault content and might be collected the middle of the software reliability growth process.

Further, we conduct calculating the predicted relative errors of these SRGMs for DS2 and DS4 for checking the predictive performance of Model 2. Table 2 shows the results of goodness-of-fit comparisons based on the predicted relative errors. In Table 2, we started calculating the predicted relative errors from 85% of the testing progress ratio because software reliability assessment is ordinarily conducted after 60 − 80% of the testing progress ratio. From Table 2, we can say that Model 2 has good predictive performance for DS2 and DS4 against to the results of model comparisons based on MSE in Table 1. From these results of model comparisons, we can say that our modeling approach contributes to improve accuracy of the software reliability assessment based on existing SRGMs.

4 Conclusion

This paper discusses software reliability growth modeling framework with change of the software failure-occurrence phenomenon in a testing-phase. Such change ordinarily observed in a testing-phase in an actual testing-phase of a software development process. Especially in this paper, we consider the relationship of the software failure-occurrence phenomenon before and after the change-point by using a testing-environmental function. By our modeling approach, we can get to know the quantitative aspect of the change for the software failure-occurrence phenomenon at the change-point. Further, this paper conducted goodness-of-fit comparisons of our models with existing SRGMs in terms of the MSE and the predicted relative errors by using actual data. From the goodness-of-fit comparisons, we checked that our modeling approach contributes to improve software reliability assessment accuracy based on existing non change-point SRGMs, such as an exponential and a delayed S-shaped SRGMs. In further studies, we need to check software reliability assessment performance of our models with existing change-point models by using actual data for checking usefulness of our change-point modeling approach.

Acknowledgement. This work was supported in part by the Grant-in-Aid for Scientific Research (C), Grant No. 22510150, from the Ministry of Education, Sports, Science, and Technology of Japan.

References

1. Yamada, S., Osaki, S.: Software reliability growth modeling: Models and applications. IEEE Trans. Soft. Eng. SE-11(12), 1431–1437 (1985)
2. Musa, J.D., Iannio, D., Okumoto, K.: Software Reliability: Measurement, Prediction, Application. McGraw-Hill, New York (1987)

3. Pham, H.: Software Reliability. Springer, Singapore (2000)
4. Zhao, M.: Change-point problems in software and hardware reliability. Commun. Statist. — Theory Meth. 22(3), 757–768 (1993)
5. Huang, C.Y.: Performance analysis of software reliability growth models with testing-effort and change-point. J. Sys. Soft. 76(2), 181–194 (2005)
6. Zou, F.Z.: A change-point perspective on the software failure process. Softw. Test., Verif. Reliab. 13(2), 85–93 (2003)
7. Zhao, J., Liu, H.W., Cui, G., Yang, X.Z.: Software reliability growth model with change-point and environmental function. J. Sys. Soft. 79(11), 1578–1587 (2006)
8. Langberg, N., Singpurwalla, N.D.: A unification of some software reliability models. SIAM J. Scien. Comput. 6(3), 781–790 (1985)
9. Miller, D.S.: Exponential order statistic models of software reliability growth. IEEE Trans. Soft. Eng. SE-12(1), 12–24 (1986)
10. Raftery, A.E.: Inference and prediction for a general order statistic model with unknown population size. J. ASA 82(400), 1163–1168 (1987)
11. Joe, H.: Statistical inference for general-order-statistics and nonhomogeneous-Poisson-process software reliability models. IEEE Trans. Soft. Eng. 15(11), 1485–1490 (1989)
12. Okamura, H., Dohi, T., Osaki, S.: A reliability assessment method for software products in operational phase? Proposal of an accelerated life testing model. Trans. IEICE J83-A(3), 294–301 (2000) (in Japanese)
13. Goel, A.L., Okumoto, K.: Time-dependent error-detection rate model for software reliability and other performance measures. IEEE Trans. Reliab. R-28(3), 206–211 (1979)

Replacement Policies with Interval of Dual System for System Transition

Satoshi Mizutani[1] and Toshio Nakagawa[2]

[1] Department of Media Informatics, Aichi University of Technology, 50-2 Manori, Nishihasama-cho, Gamagori, Aichi 443-0047, Japan
mizutani@aut.ac.jp

[2] Department of Business Administration, Aichi Institute of Technology, 1247 Yachigusa, Yakusa-cho, Toyota City, Aichi, 470-0392 Japan
toshi-nakagawa@aitech.ac.jp

Abstract. This study considers optimal replacement policies in which the system operates as a dual system from the beginning of new unit to the stopping of old unit. Especially, when a new unit begins to operate, it is in initial failure period. Then, the old unit is in random failure period or wearout failure period. When the system fails, minimal repair is done. Introducing the loss cost for a minimal repair and maintenance, we obtain the expected cost for a interval that the new unit is in initial failure period, and derive analytically optimal times of stopping of old unit. Numerical examples are given when the failure distribution of new unit is Weibull distribution and ones of old unit are exponential and Weibull distributions.

Keywords: Replacement, Maintenance Policy, Dual System, Minimal Repair, Initial Failure.

1 Introduction

In recent years, information systems with database and network have been greatly developed and become widely used. Especially, we consider the system is a enterprise system with database and network included web system. Some failures of such a system might incur great losses, and sometimes, might cause a social confusion. specially, such failures or accidents tend to occur when the system transition. Replacing from old unit o new unit, the new unit might be in initial failure period and lead to some failures. Further, the replacement cost of the system would be usually very expensive. Thus, planning system transition policy is very important and necessary from the viewpoint of reliability and economics.

We consider a system with minimal repair. The system has been operated for a long time and is in random failure period or wearout failure period. Then, we should replace the old unit with a new unit. However, the new unit might be in initial failure period. Therefore, it would be better to operate the system as a dual system for a while in order to decrease the cost of failures and ensure the reliability.

T.-h. Kim et al. (Eds.): ASEA/DRBC/EL 2011, CCIS 257, pp. 362–369, 2011.

There have been many studies of maintenance and replacement policies using reliability theory [1,2,3]. Periodic replacement with minimal repair was considered in [1]. The policy regarding the version that a unit is replaced at the Nth failure and $(N-1)$th previous failures are corrected with minimal repair [4]. The stochastic models to describe the failure pattern of repairable units subject to minimal maintenance are dealt with [5]. Periodic replacement with minimal repair is summarized in [6]. The periodic replacement model with two unit is consider in [7]. In the model, when unit 1 fails, it undergoes minimal repair, and when unit 2 fails, the system is replaced without repairing unit 2. Minimal repair when the failure occur at a non-homogeneous Poisson process are described in [8]. There have been also many studies of maintenance policies for multi-unit systems. Nakagawa considered optimal number of units was derived analytically [11]. Yasui and Nakagawa summarized optimum policies for a parallel system [15]. In the models, the number of units is given, and discussed the number of failed units to replace the system. Murthy and Nguyen proposed the model that the units fail with interaction [12,13]. Mizutani, Koike and Nakagawa considered the replacement policy that the system operate as a dual system from the beginning of new unit to the stopping of old unit. In the model, the old unit is in wearout failure period [18]. In this paper, we change the model to the old unit has a exponential failure distribution, because the time of replacement is decide by some reasons and the unit would be in random failure period. Further, we assume that, when the system operate as a dual system, failure cost of old unit and one of new unit is different.

In this study, we consider optimal replacement policies that the system operates as a dual system from the beginning of new unit to the stopping of old unit. When the old unit is in random or wearout failure period, the new system, which is in initial failure period, is introduced. Then, the system operates as a dual system to ensure the reliability for a while. In this case, we must decide the stopping operation of old unit. When the system fails, minimal repair is done. Introducing the loss cost for a minimal repair and replacement, we obtain the total expected cost for a interval that the new unit is in initial failure period. Further, we derive analytically optimal times of the stopping of old unit, which minimize the expected cost. Numerical examples are given when the failure distributions of the old unit is an exponential distribution and the new unit is a Weibull distribution.

2 Modeling

In this paper, we treat two models: (1) Old unit is in random failure period (Fig. 1), and (2) old unit is in wearout failure period (Fig. 2).

2.1 Old Unit in Random Failure Period

We make following assumptions:

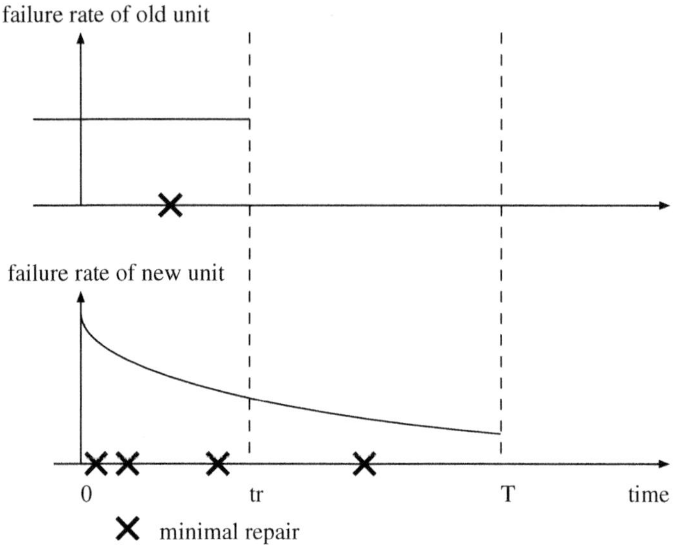

Fig. 1. Old unit in random failure period

(1) The new unit is introduced at time 0 and is in initial failure period from time 0 to T ($T > 0$). The operation of the old unit is stopped at time t_r ($0 \leq t_r \leq T$). After that, the system operates as a single unit (Fig. 1).
(2) The old unit is in random failure period at time t ($t > 0$) and has an exponential distribution $F_o(t) = 1 - e^{-\lambda t}$ with finite mean $1/\lambda$. Note that we assume the old unit has operated for a long time by time 0. From the memory less property of exponential distribution, we can decide the time 0 without considering the total operating time of the old unit.
(3) The new unit is introduced at time 0, that is, time t is a lapse time from the beginning of the new unit. Then the unit is in initial failure period at time t. The new unit has a failure distribution $F_n(t) = 1 - e^{-H(t)}$. Further, we assume that the failure rate $h(t)$ ($H(t) = \int_0^t h(x)dx$) is a monotonic decreasing function, i.e., $h'(t) < 0$ ($t > 0$).
(4) When the system fails, a minimal repair is done. That is, the failure rate remains undisturbed after the repair, i.e., the system after the repair has the same failure rate as before the failure.
(5) Cost c_1 (> 0) is the minimal repair cost when the system operates as a single system. Cost c_{21} is the minimal repair cost for the old unit when the system operates as a dual system. Cost c_{22} ($c_1 > c_{22} \geq c_{21} > 0$) is the minimal repair cost for the new unit when the system operates as a dual system. Further, cost c_3 (> 0) is a total replacement cost from old unit to new unit.

From above assumptions, the failure distribution $F(t)$ of a dual system at time t ($0 \leq t \leq t_r$) is given as

$$F(t) = 1 - [1 - F_o(t)][1 - F_n(t)] \\ = 1 - e^{-\lambda t - H(t)}. \tag{1}$$

The density function $f(t)$ of the failure distribution $F(t)$ is

$$f(t) = [\lambda + h(t)]e^{-\lambda t - H(t)}. \tag{2}$$

Therefore, we have the failure rate $r(t)$ as follows.

$$r(t) = \frac{f(t)}{1 - F(t)} = \lambda + h(t). \tag{3}$$

Next, we derive the expected cost for a interval that the new unit is in initial failure period. That is, as the new system is in initial failure period until T, we derive the expected cost $C(t_r)$ from time 0 to time T. The expected number of failures from 0 to t_r for the old unit is λt_r.

The expected number of failures from 0 to t_r for the new unit is $H(t_r)$. The expected number of failures from t_r to T is $H(T)-H(t_r)$. Therefore, the expected cost $C_1(t_r)$ from time 0 to time T is given by

$$C_1(t_r) = c_1[H(T)-H(t_r)] + c_{21}\lambda t_r + c_{22}H(t_r) + c_3 \qquad (0 \le t_r \le T). \tag{4}$$

Clearly,

$$C_1(0) = c_1[H(T) - H(0)] + c_{22}H(0) + c_3, \tag{5}$$

$$C_1(T) = c_{21}\lambda T + c_{22}H(T) + c_3. \tag{6}$$

2.2 Old Unit in Wearout Failure Period

We make following assumptions:

(1) The new unit is introduced at time t_n, and is in initial failure period from t_n to t_n+T. The operation of the old unit is stopped at time t_r ($t_n \le t_r \le T+t_n$) (Fig. 2).
(2) The old unit is in wearout failure period at time 0 and has a failure distribution $F_o(t) = 1 - e^{-H_o(t)}$. Further, we assume that the failure rate $h_o(t)$ ($H_o(t) = \int_0^t h_o(x)dx$) is a monotonic increasing function, i.e., $h_o'(t) > 0$ ($t > 0$).
(3) The new unit is introduced at time t_n (> 0), and is in initial failure period and has a failure distribution $F_n(t) = 1 - e^{-H_n(t-t_n)}$ at time t ($t_n \le t \le t_n + T$)Further, we assume that the failure rate $h_n(t)$ ($H_n(t) = \int_0^t h_n(x)dx$) is a monotonic decreasing function.
(4) When the system fails, a minimal repair is done. That is, the failure rate remains undisturbed after the minimal repair.
(5) Cost c_1 is the minimal repair cost when the system operates as a single system. Cost c_{21} is the minimal repair cost for the old unit when the system operates as a dual system. Cost c_{22} ($c_1 > c_{22} \ge c_{21}$) is the minimal repair cost for the new unit when the system operates as a dual system. Further, cost c_3 is a total replacement cost from old unit to new unit.

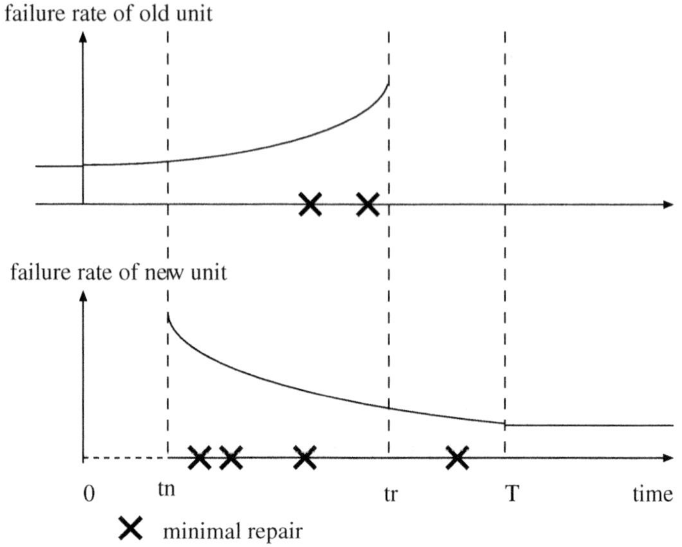

Fig. 2. Old unit in wearout failure period

Therefore, the expected cost $C_2(t_r)$ from time 0 to time $t_n + T$ is given by

$$C_2(t_r) = \frac{\begin{array}{c} c_1[H_o(t_n) + H_n(T) - H_n(t_r - t_n)] \\ + c_{21}[H_o(t_r) - H_o(t_n)] + c_{22}H_n(t_r - t_n) + c_3 \end{array}}{t_n + T} \quad (t_n \le t_r \le t_n + T). \tag{7}$$

Clearly,

$$C_2(t_n) = \frac{c_1[H_o(t_n) + H_n(T)] + c_3}{t_n + T}, \tag{8}$$

$$C_2(t_n + T) = \frac{c_1 H_o(t_n) + c_{21}[H_o(t_n + T) - H_o(t_n)] + c_{22}H_n(T) + c_3}{t_n + T}. \tag{9}$$

3 Optimal Policies

3.1 Old Unit in Random Failure Period

We find an optimal t_r^* $(0 \le t_r^* \le T)$ which minimizes the expected cost rate $C_1(t_r^*)$ in (4).

Differentiating $C_1(t_r)$ with respect to t_r and setting it equal to 0,

$$h(t_r^*) = \frac{\lambda c_{21}}{c_1 - c_{22}}. \tag{10}$$

Because $h(t_r^*)$ is a monotonic decreasing function , we have following optimal policy:

(i) If $\lambda c_{21}/(c_1 - c_{22}) \geq h(0)$ then $t_r^* = 0$, and the expected cost rate is given in (5). That is, we should immediately replace the old unit with the new unit without any interval for which the system operates as a dual system.
(ii) If $h(0) > \lambda c_{21}/(c_1 - c_{22}) > h(T)$ then there exists a finite and unique t_r^* $(0 < t_r^* < T)$ which satisfies (10).
(iii) If $h(T) \geq \lambda c_{21}/(c_1 - c_{22})$ then $t_r^* = T$, and the expected cost rate is given in (6).

3.2 Old Unit in Wearout Failure Period

Differentiating $C_2(t_r)$ in (7) with respect to t_r and setting it equal to 0,

$$\frac{h_n(t_r - t_n)}{h_o(t_r)} = \frac{c_{21}}{c_1 - c_{22}}. \tag{11}$$

Because the left hand side of above equation is a monotonic decreasing function, we have following optimal policy,

(i) If $h_n(0)/h_o(t_n) \leq c_{21}/(c_1 - c_{22})$ then $t_r^* = t_n$, and the expected cost rate is given in (8).
(ii) If $h_n(0)/h_o(t_n) > c_{21}/(c_1 - c_{22}) > h_n(T)/h_o(T + t_n)$ then there exists a finite and unique t_r^* $(t_n < t_r^* < T + t_n)$.
(iii) If $c_{21}/(c_1 - c_{22}) \leq h_n(T)/h_o(T + t_n)$ then $t_r^* = T + t_n$, and the expected cost rate is given (9).

4 Numerical Examples

We compute numerically optimal t_r^* when $F_n(t) = 1 - e^{-[\mu(t+\gamma_n)]^{\alpha_n}}$ $(\alpha_n < 1)$.

4.1 Old Unit in Random Failure Period

We suppose $F_o(t) = 1 - e^{-\lambda t}$. Table 1 gives optimal t_r^* which satisfy (10) for $c_1/c_{21} = 6, 7, 8, 9, 10$, $\alpha_n = 0.6, 0.7$, $c_{22}/c_{21} = 2, 3, 4, 5$ when $\gamma_n = 1$, $T = 100$, $\lambda = 0.01$, $\mu = 0.01$. In the table, †show the value is computed from optimal policy (i), and ‡show the value is computed from optimal policy (iii). We can see that if c_1/c_{21} is small and c_{22}/c_{21} is large, we should not have a interval as a dual system. Conversely, if c_1/c_{21} is large and c_{22}/c_{21} is small, we should select the optimal policy (iii) to have a interval as a dual system as long as possible.

4.2 Old Unit in Wearout Failure Period

We suppose $F_o(t) = 1 - e^{-[\lambda(t+\gamma_o)]^{\alpha_o}}$ $(\alpha_o > 1)$. Table 2 gives optimal t_r^* which satisfies (11) for $c_1/c_{21} = 6, 7, 8, 9, 10$, $\alpha_n = 0.6, 0.7$, $c_{22}/c_{21} = 2, 3, 4, 5$ when $\gamma_n = 1$, $T = 100$, $\lambda = 0.01$, $\mu = 0.01$, $\alpha_o = 1.2$. This indicates that optimal t_r* increase when c_1/c_{21} and α_n increase and c_{22}/c_{21} decrease. These tendencies are the same with Table 1.

Table 1. Optimal t_r^* when $\gamma_n = 1$, $T = 100$, $\lambda = 0.01$, $\mu = 0.01$ for old unit in random failure period

c_1/c_{21}	$\alpha_n = 0.6$				$\alpha_n = 0.7$			
	c_{22}/c_{21}							
	2	3	4	5	2	3	4	5
6	7.92	3.35	0.58	†0.00	29.94	10.86	2.07	†0.00
7	14.59	7.92	3.35	0.58	64.10	29.94	10.86	2.07
8	23.59	14.59	7.92	3.35	‡100.00	64.10	29.94	10.86
9	35.15	23.59	14.59	7.92	‡100.00	‡100.00	64.10	29.94
10	49.48	35.15	23.59	14.59	‡100.00	‡100.00	‡100.00	64.10

† : Optimal Policy (i), ‡ : Optimal Policy (ii)

Table 2. Optimal t_r^* when $\gamma_n = 1$, $T = 100$, $\lambda = 0.01$, $\mu = 0.01$, $\alpha_o = 1.2$ for old unit in wearout failure period

c_1/c_{21}	$\alpha_n = 0.6$				$\alpha_n = 0.7$			
	c_{22}/c_{21}							
	2	3	4	5	2	3	4	5
6	10.66	†10.00	†10.00	†10.00	12.04	10.28	†10.00	†10.00
7	11.77	10.66	†10.00	†10.00	14.66	12.04	10.28	†10.00
8	13.14	11.77	10.66	†10.00	18.11	14.66	12.04	10.28
9	14.77	13.14	11.77	10.66	22.33	18.11	14.66	12.04
10	16.62	14.77	13.14	11.77	27.29	22.33	18.11	14.66

† : Optimal Policy (i)

5 Conclusion

We have considered optimal replacement policies with a interval of dual system for two models: (1) old unit is in random failure period, and (2) old unit is in wearout failure period. We have obtained the expected cost for a interval that the new unit is in initial failure period. Further, we have derived analytically optimal policies of stopping old unit which minimizes the expected cost. Numerical examples have been given when the times to failure of old unit are exponential or Weibull distributions. These formulations and results would be applied to other real systems such as digital circuits or server system by suitable modifications.

Acknowledgments. This work was supported in part by the grand-in-aid for Scientific Research (C) of Japan Society for the Promotion of Science under Grand No. 22500897.

References

1. Barlow, R.E., Proschan, F.: Mathematical Theory of Reliability. John Wiley & Sons, New York (1965)
2. Osaki, S.: Applied Stochastic System Modeling. Springer, Berlin (1992)

3. Nakagawa, T.: Maintenance Theory of Reliability. Springer, London (2005)
4. Morimura, H.: On some preventive maintenance policies for IFR. Journal Operations Research Society Japan 12, 94–124 (1970)
5. Pulcicni, G.: Mechanical reliability and maintenance models. In: Pham, H. (ed.) Handbook of Reliability Engineering, pp. 317–348. Springer, London (2003)
6. Nakagawa, T.: A Summary of periodic replacement with minimal repair at failure. Journal Operations Research Society Japan 24, 213–227 (1981)
7. Nakagawa, T.: Optimum replacement policies for systems with two types of units. In: Osaki, S., Cao, J.H. (eds.) Reliability Theory and Applications Proceedings of the China-Japan Reliability Symposium, Shanghai, China (1987)
8. Murthy, D.N.P.: A note on minimal repair. IEEE Transactions Reliability 40, 245–246 (1991)
9. Nakagawa, T.: Replacement problem of a parallel system in random environment. Journal Applied Probability 16, 203–205 (1979)
10. Nakagawa, T.: Further results of replacement problem of a parallel system in random environment. Journal Applied Probability 16, 923–926 (1979)
11. Nakagawa, T.: Optimal number of units for a parallel system. Journal Applied Probability 21, 431–436 (1984)
12. Murthy, D.N.P., Nguyen, D.G.: Study of two-component system with failure interaction. Naval Research Logistics 32, 239–248 (1985)
13. Murthy, D.N.P., Nguyen, D.G.: Study of a multi-component system with failure interaction. European Journal of Operations Research 21, 330–338 (1985)
14. Pham, H., Suprasad, A., Misra, B.: Reliability and MTTF prediction of k-out-of-n complex systems with components subjected to multiple stages of degradation. International Journal System Science 27, 995–1000 (1996)
15. Yasui, K., Nakagawa, T., Osaki, S.: A summary of optimum replacement policies for a parallel redundant system. Microelectron Reliability 28, 635–641 (1988)
16. Nakagawa, T., Mizutani, S.: A summary of maintenance policies for a finite interval. Reliability Engineering & System Safety 94, 89–96 (2009)
17. Nakagawa, T., Mizutani, S., Chen, M.: A summary of random inspection policies. Reliability Engineering & System Safety 95, 906–911 (2010)
18. Mizutani, S., Nakagawa, T.: Optimal Maintenance Policy with an Interval of Duplex System. In: Chukova, S., Haywood, J., Dohi, T. (eds.) Advanced Reliability Modeling IV, pp. 496–503. McGraw-Hill, Taiwan (2010)

Probabilistic Analysis of a System with Illegal Access

Mitsuhiro Imaizumi[1] and Mitsutaka Kimura[2]

[1] College of Contemporary Management, Aichi Gakusen University, 1 Shiotori Ohike-Cho, Toyota 471-8532, Japan
imaizumi@gakusen.ac.jp

[2] Department of International Culture Studies, Gifu City Women's College, 7-1 Hitoichiba Kita-matchi, Gifu 501-0192, Japan
kimura@gifu-cwc.ac.jp

Abstract. As the Internet has been greatly developed, the demand for improvement of the reliability of the Internet has increased. Recently, there exists a problem in the illegal access which attacks a server intentionally. This paper considers two inspection policies. In Model 1, we assume that illegal access is checked at both random and periodic time. In Model 2, we assume that illegal access is checked by two types of random check. Optimal policies which minimize the expected cost are discussed. Finally, numerical examples are given.

Keywords: Random inspection, Illegal access, Security, Optimal policy.

1 Introduction

As computer systems have been widely used, the Internet has been greatly developed and rapidly spread on all over the world. Recently, the Internet plays an important role as the infrastructure in the information society, and the demands for improvement of the reliability and security of the Internet have increased.

Although various services are performed on the Internet, illegal access on the Internet has become a problem in recent years. Illegal access which attacks a server intentionally causes computers to malfunction. In order to cope with this problem, several schemes has been considered. As one of schemes to detect the illegal access, IDS (Intrusion Detection System) has been widely used. IDS can detect illegal access by monitoring packets which flow on the network. IDS judges an abnormal condition by comparing packets which flow on the network to the pattern of illegal access registered in advanced [1,2,3]. Generally, illegal access is performed so that it circumvents server monitoring. Therefore, if illegal access is checked irregularly, its detection probability is high compared to the case that it is checked regularly. The simulation about the policy for the monitoring and detection of illegal access has already introduced by [4,5,6], however, there are few formalized stochastic models.

This paper considers two inspection policies. In Model 1, we assume that illegal access is checked at both random and periodic time. In Model 2, we assume that

T.-h. Kim et al. (Eds.): ASEA/DRBC/EL 2011, CCIS 257, pp. 370–376, 2011.

illegal access is checked by two types of random check. The expected cost until the detection of illegal access is derived. Further, optimal policies which minimize the expected cost are discussed. Finally, numerical examples are given.

2 Model 1

We pay attention only to a server which is connected with the Internet. A server has the function of IDS.

(1) Illegal access repeats occurrence and disappearance at random. After a server begins to operate, illegal access occurs according to a general distribution $F(t)$ with finite mean $1/\lambda$.
(2) Illegal access is checked at successive times $Y_j (j = 1, 2, \cdots)$ (random check), where $Y_0 \equiv 0$, and at periodic times $kT (k = 1, 2, \cdots)$ (periodic check).
(3) The distribution of $Y_j - Y_{j-1} (j = 1, 2, \cdots)$ has an exponential distribution $G(t) = 1 - e^{-\mu t}$ with finite mean $1/\mu$. The distribution of Y_j is represented by the j-th fold convolution $G^{(j)}(t)$ of $G(t)$ with itself, i.e., $G^{(j)}(t) \equiv G^{(j-1)}(t) * G(t), G(t) * G(t) \equiv \int_0^t G(t-u)dG(u), G(t)^{(0)}(t) \equiv 1$, where the asterisk mark denotes the Stieltjes convolution.
(4) After illegal access occurs, it is detected by random check with probability 1, and it is detected by i-th periodic check with probability $p_i (0 < p_i \leq 1)(i = 1, 2, \cdots)$.

When $p_1 = p$ and $p_2 = 1$, the probability P_p that illegal access is detected by periodic check is

$$
\begin{aligned}
P_p = {} & p \sum_{k=0}^{\infty} \int_{kT}^{(k+1)T} \left\{ \sum_{j=0}^{\infty} \int_0^t \overline{G}[(k+1)T - x] dG^{(j)}(x) \right\} dF(t) \\
& + (1-p) \sum_{k=0}^{\infty} \int_{kT}^{(k+1)T} \left\{ \sum_{j=0}^{\infty} \int_0^t \overline{G}[(k+1)T - x] dG^{(j)}(x) \right\} dF(t) \\
& - (1-p) \\
& \times \sum_{k=0}^{\infty} \int_{(k+1)T}^{(k+2)T} \left(\int_{kT}^{(k+1)T} \left\{ \sum_{j=0}^{\infty} \int_0^t \overline{G}[(k+1)T - x] dG^{(j)}(x) \right\} dF(t) \right) dG(y).
\end{aligned}
\tag{1}
$$

Moreover, the probability P_r that illegal access is detected by random check is

$$
\begin{aligned}
P_r = {} & \sum_{k=0}^{\infty} \int_{kT}^{(k+1)T} \left(\sum_{j=0}^{\infty} \int_0^t \{G[(k+1)T - x] - G(t-x)\} dG^{(j)}(x) \right) dF(t) \\
& + (1-p) \\
& \times \sum_{k=0}^{\infty} \int_{(k+1)T}^{(k+2)T} \left(\int_{kT}^{(k+1)T} \left\{ \sum_{j=0}^{\infty} \int_0^t \overline{G}[(k+1)T - x] dG^{(j)}(x) \right\} dF(t) \right) dG(y).
\end{aligned}
\tag{2}
$$

3 Optimal Policy

We obtain the expected cost and discuss the optimal policy which minimizes it. Let c_p be the cost for periodic check, c_r be the cost for random check and c_1 is the cost per unit of time for the time elapsed between occurrence of illegal access and its detection. Then, the expected cost $C_1(T,\mu)$ [7,8,9] is

$$
\begin{aligned}
C_1(T,\mu) \equiv & \sum_{k=0}^{\infty}\int_{kT}^{(k+1)T}\Bigg(\sum_{j=0}^{\infty}\{(k+1)c_p + jc_r + c_1[(k+1)T-t]\} \\
& \times \int_0^t \overline{G}[(k+1)T-x]dG^{(j)}(x)\Bigg)dF(t) \\
& + \sum_{k=0}^{\infty}\int_{kT}^{(k+1)T}\Bigg(\sum_{j=0}^{\infty}\int_0^t\Bigg\{\int_{t-x}^{(k+1)T-x}[kc_p + (j+1)c_r \\
& + c_1(x+y-t)]dG(y)\Bigg\}dG^{(j)}(x)\Bigg)dF(t) \\
& + (1-p)\sum_{k=0}^{\infty}\int_{kT}^{(k+1)T}\Bigg\{\sum_{j=0}^{\infty}(c_p + c_1T) \\
& \times \int_0^t \overline{G}[(k+1)T-x]dG^{(j)}(x)\Bigg\}dF(t) \\
& - (1-p)\sum_{k=0}^{\infty}\int_{(k+1)T}^{(k+2)T}\Bigg(\int_{kT}^{(k+1)T}\Bigg\{\sum_{j=0}^{\infty}(c_p + c_1T) \\
& \times \int_0^t \overline{G}[(k+1)T-x]dG^{(j)}(x)\Bigg\}dF(t)\Bigg)dG(y) \\
& + (1-p)\sum_{k=0}^{\infty}\int_{(k+1)T}^{(k+2)T}\Bigg((c_r + c_1y) \\
& \times \int_{kT}^{(k+1)T}\Bigg\{\sum_{j=0}^{\infty}\int_0^t \overline{G}[(k+1)T-x]dG^{(j)}(x)\Bigg\}dF(t)\Bigg)dG(y). \quad (3)
\end{aligned}
$$

In particular, when $F(t) = 1 - e^{-\lambda t}$ for $\mu > \lambda$, the expected cost in (3) becomes

$$
\begin{aligned}
C_1(T,\mu) = & \frac{c_p}{1-e^{-\lambda T}} + c_r\frac{\mu}{\lambda} \\
& + \left(c_r - c_p + \frac{c_1}{\mu}\right)\left[1 - \frac{\lambda}{\mu-\lambda}\frac{e^{-\lambda T} - e^{-\mu T}}{1-e^{-\lambda T}}\right] \\
& + (1-p)(c_p + c_1T)\frac{\lambda}{\mu-\lambda}\frac{e^{-\lambda T} - e^{-\mu T}}{1-e^{-\lambda T}} \\
& + (1-p)(c_r - c_p - c_1T)\frac{\lambda}{\mu-\lambda}\frac{(e^{-\lambda T} - e^{-\mu T})(1-e^{-\mu T})e^{-\mu T}}{1-e^{-(\lambda+\mu)T}} \\
& + (1-p)c_1\frac{\lambda}{\mu-\lambda}(e^{-\lambda T} - e^{-\mu T})e^{-\mu T}
\end{aligned}
$$

$$\times \left\{ \frac{T(1-e^{-\mu T})e^{-(\lambda+\mu)T}}{[1-e^{-(\lambda+\mu)T}]^2} + \frac{T(1-2e^{-\mu T}) + \frac{1}{\mu}\left(1-e^{-\mu T}\right)}{1-e^{-(\lambda+\mu)T}} \right\}. \quad (4)$$

We seek an optimal T^* and μ^* which minimize $C_1(T,\mu)$ when $p=1$.

Differentiating (4) with respect to T and setting it equal to zero,

$$\frac{\mu}{\mu-\lambda}[1-e^{-(\mu-\lambda)T}] - (1-e^{-\mu T}) = \frac{c_p}{c_r - c_p + \dfrac{c_1}{\mu}}. \quad (5)$$

Denoting the left-hand side of (5) by $L_1(T)$,

$$L_1(0) = 0, \quad (6)$$

$$L_1(\infty) = \frac{\lambda}{\mu-\lambda}, \quad (7)$$

$$L_1'(T) = \mu e^{-\mu T}(e^{\lambda T}-1) \geq 0. \quad (8)$$

Hence, $L_1(T)$ is strictly increasing in T from 0 to $\lambda/(\mu-\lambda)$. Thus, we can characterize the optimal policy:

(1) If $\lambda/(\mu-\lambda) > c_p/(c_r - c_p + (c_1/\mu))$, i.e., $c_r + c_1/\mu > (\mu/\lambda)c_p$, then there exists a finite and unique optimal $T^*(0 < T^* < \infty)$ which satisfies (5).
(2) If $c_r + c_1/\mu \leq (\mu/\lambda)c_p$, then $T^* = \infty$.

4 Model 2

We modify Model 1.

(1) Illegal access repeats occurrence and disappearance at random. After a server begins to operate, illegal access occurs according to a general distribution $F(t)$ with finite mean $1/\lambda$.
(2) Illegal access is checked at successive times $Y_j(j=1,2,\cdots)$ (random check 1), where $Y_0 \equiv 0$, and at successive times $T_k(k=1,2,\cdots)$ (random check 2), where $T_0 \equiv 0$. We assume that there is a difference between random check 1 and random check 2.
(3) The distribution of $Y_j - Y_{j-1}(j=1,2,\cdots)$ has an exponential distribution $G(t) = 1-e^{-\mu t}$ with finite mean $1/\mu$.
(4) After illegal access occurs, it is detected by random check 1 with probability 1, and it is detected by i-th random check 2 with probability $p_i(0 < p_i \leq 1)(i=1,2,\cdots)$.

Let c_{r1} be the cost for random check 1, c_{r2} be the cost for random check 2 and c_1 is the cost per unit of time for the time elapsed between occurrence of illegal access and its detection. When $p_1 = p$ and $p_2 = 1$, the expected cost $C_2(T,\mu)$ is

$$C_2(T,\mu) \equiv \sum_{k=0}^{\infty} \int_{T_k}^{T_{k+1}} \left\{ \sum_{j=0}^{\infty} [(k+1)c_{r2} + jc_{r1} + c_1(T_{k+1}-t)] \right.$$

$$\times \int_0^t \overline{G}(T_{k+1}-x)dG^{(j)}(x)\Big\}dF(t)$$

$$+\sum_{k=0}^{\infty}\int_{T_k}^{T_{k+1}}\Big(\sum_{j=0}^{\infty}\int_0^t\Big\{\int_{t-x}^{T_{k+1}-x}[kc_{r2}+(j+1)c_{r1}$$

$$+c_1(x+y-t)]dG(y)\Big\}dG^{(j)}(x)\Big)dF(t)$$

$$+(1-p)\sum_{k=0}^{\infty}\int_{T_k}^{T_{k+1}}\Big\{\sum_{j=0}^{\infty}[c_{r2}+c_1(T_{k+2}-T_{k+1})]$$

$$\times \int_0^t \overline{G}(T_{k+1}-x)dG^{(j)}(x)\Big\}dF(t)$$

$$-(1-p)\sum_{k=0}^{\infty}\int_{T_{k+1}}^{T_{k+2}}\Big(\int_{T_k}^{T_{k+1}}\Big\{\sum_{j=0}^{\infty}[c_{r2}+c_1(T_{k+2}-T_{k+1})]$$

$$\times \int_0^t \overline{G}[T_{k+1}-x]dG^{(j)}(x)\Big\}dF(t)\Big)dG(y)$$

$$+(1-p)\sum_{k=0}^{\infty}\int_{(k+1)T}^{(k+2)T}\Big\{(c_{r1}+c_1y)$$

$$\times \int_{T_k}^{T_{k+1}}\Big[\sum_{j=0}^{\infty}\int_0^t \overline{G}(T_{k+1}-x)\Big]dG^{(j)}(x)\Big\}dF(t)dG(y). \quad (9)$$

In particular, when $p=1$, the expected cost in (9) becomes

$$C_2(T,\mu)=c_{r2}\sum_{k=0}^{\infty}\overline{F}(T_k)+c_{r1}\frac{\mu}{\lambda}+\left(c_{r1}-c_{r2}+\frac{c_1}{\mu}\right)$$

$$\times\sum_{k=0}^{\infty}\int_{T_k}^{T_{k+1}}[1-e^{-\mu(T_{k+1}-t)}]dF(t). \quad (10)$$

Differentiating (10) with respect to T_k and setting it equal to zero,

$$1-e^{-\mu(T_{k+1}-T_k)}-\frac{\int_{T_{k-1}}^{T_k}\mu e^{-\mu(T_k-t)}dF(t)}{f(T_k)}=-\frac{c_{r2}}{c_{r1}-c_{r2}+\frac{c_1}{\mu}}. \quad (11)$$

When $\mu\to 0$, (10) becomes

$$T_{k+1}-T_k-\frac{F(T_k)-F(T_{k-1})}{f(T_k)}=-\frac{c_{r2}}{c_1}. \quad (12)$$

The optimal inspection time T_k^* is derived by using Algorithm 1 [7, p. 203].

5 Numerical Examples

We compute numerically T^* and $1/\mu^*$ which minimize the expected cost $C_1(T,\mu)$. It is assumed that the mean time to illegal access occurrence is $1/\lambda=100$, the

Table 1. Optimal checking time T^* to minimize $C_1(T, \mu)$

$1/\mu$	$p = 1$			$p = 0.9$			$p = 0.8$		
	c_p								
	2	3	4	2	3	4	2	3	4
10	∞	∞	∞	∞	∞	∞	∞	∞	∞
40	23.62	30.63	37.38	22.18	28.95	35.48	20.89	27.42	33.73
60	21.93	27.68	32.87	20.47	26.08	31.17	19.15	24.61	29.59
80	21.20	26.47	31.11	19.61	24.77	29.36	18.20	23.22	27.72

Table 2. Optimal checking time $1/\mu^*$ to minimize $C_1(T, \mu)$

T	$p = 1$			$p = 0.9$			$p = 0.8$		
	c_p								
	2	3	4	2	3	4	2	3	4
40	15.95	15.27	14.68	13.74	13.26	12.85	12.27	11.93	11.61
60	12.24	12.06	11.89	11.29	11.14	11.00	10.56	10.44	10.32
80	11.24	11.15	11.06	10.60	10.54	10.46	10.09	10.03	9.96
100	10.80	10.74	10.70	10.32	10.27	10.22	9.91	9.86	9.82

mean time to random check is $1/\mu = 10 \sim 80$, the time to periodic check is $T = 40 \sim 80$, the probability that illegal access is detected by periodic check is $p = 0.8 \sim 1$, the cost for random check is $c_r = 1$, the cost per unit of time for the time elapsed between occurrence of illegal access and its detection is $c_1 = 1$, the cost for periodic check is $c_p = 2 \sim 4$.

Table 1. gives the optimal checking time T^* which minimizes the expected cost $C_1(T, \mu)$. This indicate that T^* decreases with $1/\mu$, however, increases with c_p and p. Table 1 presents that when $1/\mu$ is small, $T^* = \infty$. In this case, we should not perform the periodic check.

Table 2. gives the optimal checking time $1/\mu^*$ which minimizes the expected cost $C_1(T, \mu)$. This indicates that $1/\mu^*$ decreases with T and c_p, however, increases with p. For example, when $T = 60$, $c_p = 3$ and $p = 0.9$, the optimal checking time $1/\mu^* = 11.14$.

6 Conclusion

We have investigated two random inspection policies and have discussed optimal policies which minimize the expected cost until the detection of illegal access.

From the numerical example, we have shown the optimal periodic checking time decreases with the mean time to random check, however, increases with the cost for periodic check.

It would be very important to evaluate and improve the reliability of a server system with illegal access. The results derived in this paper would be applied in practical fields by making some suitable modification and extensions. Further studies for such subject would be expected.

References

1. Miyake, Y.: Attack Detection and Analysis on Internet. The Journal of Institute of Electronics, Information and Communication Engineers 89(4), 313–317 (2006)
2. Ohta, K., Mansfield, G.: Illegal Access Detection on the Internet -Present status and future directions. Transactions of Institute of Electronics, Information and Communication Engineers J83-B(9), 1209–1216 (2000)
3. Takei, Y., Ohta, K., Kato, N., Nemoto, Y.: Detecting and Tracing Illegal Access by using Traffic Pattern Matching Technique. Transactions of Institute of Electronics, Information and Communication Engineers J84-B(8), 1464–1473 (2001)
4. Sawada, A., Takakura, H., Okabe, Y.: A Support System for Monitoring Log Information of IDS Applied to Large Scaled Open Networks. Transactions of Information Processing Society of Japan 44(8), 1861–1871 (2003)
5. Kanaoka, A., Okamoto, E.: The Problems and Countermeasures of Intrusion Detection Exchange Format in IETF. Transactions of Information Processing Society of Japan 44(8), 1830–1837 (2003)
6. Ohya, H., Miyaji, R., Kawaguchi, N., Shigeno, H., Okada, K.: A Technique to Reduce False Positives of Network IDS with Machine Learning. Transactions of Information Processing Society of Japan 45(8), 2105–2112 (2004)
7. Nakagawa, T.: Maintenance Theory of Reliability. Springer, Heidelberg (2005)
8. Sugiura, T., Miszutani, S., Nakagawa, T.: Optimal random and periodic inspection policies. In: Ninth ISSAT International Conference on Reliability and Quality in Design, pp. 42–45 (2003)
9. Nakagawa, T., Mizutani, S., Chen, M.: A summary of periodic and random inspection policies. RESS 95, 906–911 (2010)

Bayesian Inference for Credible Intervals of Optimal Software Release Time

Hiroyuki Okamura[1], Tadashi Dohi[1], and Shunji Osaki[2,⋆]

[1] Department of Information Engineering, Graduate School of Engineering, Hiroshima University, 1–4–1 Kagamiyama, Higashi-Hiroshima 739-8527, Japan
http://www.rel.hiroshima-u.ac.jp/

[2] Faculty of Information Sciences and Engineering, Nanzan University, Seto 489–0863, Japan

Abstract. This paper deals with the estimation of a credible interval of the optimal software release time in the context of Bayesian inference. In the past literature, the optimal software release time was often discussed under the situation where model parameters are exactly known. However, in practice, we should evaluate effects of the optimal software release time on uncertainty of the model parameters. In this paper, we apply Bayesian inference to evaluating the uncertainty of the optimal software release time. More specifically, a Markov chain Monte Carlo (MCMC) method is proposed to compute a credible interval of the optimal software release time.

1 Introduction

Software release is one of the most important issues to manage software development projects. The software release time (SRT) is determined according to cost/load estimation incurred in software projects. Project managers make a schedule for the software development in order to meet the committed SRT at the planning phase. The optimal software release problem is helpful for the managers to make a decision of the software release from the economic point of view.

In general, the formulation of the optimal software release problem is based on software reliability growth models (SRGMs). The SRGM can estimate the quantitative software reliability from failure or fault detection data in testing phase. More precisely, SRGMs represent counting processes regarding the number of failures in testing and operational phase.

The non-homogeneous Poisson process (NHPP) based SRGM is one of the most popular classes of SRGMs due to its mathematical tractability. In fact, several of NHPP-based SRGMs are applied to the optimal software release problem. Okumoto and Goel [14] formulated the problem to find the optimal SRT in terms

⋆ This research was supported by the Ministry of Education, Science, Sports and Culture, Grant-in-Aid for Scientific Research (C), Grant No. 21510167 (2009-2011), Grant No. 23500047 (2011–2013) and Grant No. 23510171 (2011–2013).

T.-h. Kim et al. (Eds.): ASEA/DRBC/EL 2011, CCIS 257, pp. 377–384, 2011.

of cost criterion using the exponential-type NHPP-based SRGM. Yamada and Osaki [17] also considered a problem of determining the optimal SRT under both the expected cost and reliability criteria. Also, Dohi et al. [2] proposed the neural network model to determine the SRT based on the cost-based SRM. In the past literature, the authors mainly discussed how to determine the optimal SRT in which model parameters are given as point estimates. However, in practice, estimates of model parameters have uncertainty. It is very risky to make a decision under only the point value of optimal SRT, since the optimal SRT is sensitive to the uncertainty of model parameters. Thus we should evaluate dependency of the optimal SRT on the uncertainty of estimated model parameters. Xie and Hong [15] studied the sensitivity of estimated model parameters on the optimal SRT. They used the first two moments of estimated model parameters and illustrated their effects on the optimal SRT. However, such analytical approach is often infeasible if the model and problem formulation becomes complex.

This paper discusses how to evaluate uncertainty of the optimal SRT in the context of Bayesian inference. Bayesian estimation enables us to evaluate the uncertainty by means of posterior distributions. The interval estimation using posterior distributions is called *credible interval.* In particular, we propose a Markov chain Monte Carlo (MCMC) approach to compute a credible interval of the optimal SRT, and our proposed method does not require any of specific analytical techniques.

2 NHPP-Based Software Reliability Models

2.1 Model Description

The number of faults in the software at the beginning of testing, N, follows a Poisson distribution with mean value ω;

$$P(N = n) = \frac{\omega^n}{n!} \exp(-\omega) \qquad \text{for } n = 0, 1, ... \tag{1}$$

Moreover, it is assumed that failure times (fault detection times) $T_1, T_2, ..., T_N$ are independent and identically distributed (i.i.d.) random variables having a general distribution with a parameter vector $\boldsymbol{\theta}$, $F(t; \boldsymbol{\theta})$. These assumptions imply that the number of failures experienced in the time interval $(0, t]$, $M(t)$, has a Poisson probability mass function, i.e.,

$$P(M(t) = m) = \frac{\Lambda(t)^m}{m!} \exp(-\Lambda(t)), \tag{2}$$

with mean value

$$\Lambda(t) = \omega F(t; \boldsymbol{\theta}). \tag{3}$$

Hence, the mean value function of the NHPP-based SRGM can be completely characterized by only the failure time distribution $F(t; \boldsymbol{\theta})$. In particular, when the failure time distribution is given by an exponential distribution with mean $1/\beta$

$$G(t; \beta) = 1 - e^{-\beta t}, \tag{4}$$

Table 1. Relationship between existing NHPP-based SRGMs and failure time distributions

Distribution	References
Exponential	[4]
Gamma	[16][18]
Pareto	[7]
Normal	[1][13]
Logistic	[8][5]
Extreme-Value	[3][10]
Hyperexponential	[9]
Hyper-Erlang	[12]
Phase-Type	[11]

the corresponding NHPP-based SRGM is the exponential-type NHPP-based SRGM which is the first NHPP-based SRGM proposed by Goel and Okumoto [4]. Table 1 presents the relationship between existing NHPP-based SRGMs and fault-detection time distributions.

2.2 Optimal Software Release Problem

According to the formulation of NHPP-based SRGMs, we consider how to determine the optimal SRT. In the past literature, several kinds of problems have been formulated under respective criteria. In this paper, we focus on the cost-based SRT problem discussed by Okumoto and Goel [14].

Suppose that the software has a life cycle T_{LC}. The life cycle can be regarded as a warranty period of software. The life cycle T_{LC} is assumed to be a sufficiently large value. Then we denote the following cost parameters:

c_1 (> 0): the cost incurred by a debugging in testing phase,
c_2 ($> c_1$): the cost incurred by a debugging in operational phase,
c_3 (> 0): the testing cost per unit time incurred in testing phase.

When the software is released at time T, the expected total cost until T_{LC} is given by

$$V(T) = (c_1 - c_2)\Lambda(T) + c_2\Lambda(T_{LC}) + c_3 T. \tag{5}$$

Then the cost-based problem is to find the optimal SRT minimizing the total cost $V(T)$. Applying the exponential-type NHPP-based SRGM, i.e., $\Lambda(t) = \omega(1-e^{-\beta t})$, we obtain the optimal SRT analytically

$$T^* = \frac{1}{\beta}\log\left(\frac{\omega\beta(c_2 - c_1)}{c_3}\right). \tag{6}$$

3 Statistical Inference

3.1 Point Estimation

In order to evaluate the optimal SRT, we should know the values of NHPP-based SRGM parameters. The commonly used parameter estimation method for NHPP-based SRGMs is the maximum likelihood (ML) estimation. In the context of ML estimation, ML estimates (MLEs) are defined as maxima of the log-likelihood function of failure data.

Let $\mathcal{D} = \{X_1, \ldots, X_n\}$ denote grouped failure data on a time sequence $s_0 = 0 < s_1 < \cdots < s_n$, i.e., X_i represents the number of failures experienced during the time interval $(s_{i-1}, s_i]$. For such grouped failure data $\mathcal{D}$, the log-likelihood function (LLF) is written in the form:

$$\mathcal{L}(\omega, \boldsymbol{\theta}) = \log p(\mathcal{D}|\omega, \boldsymbol{\theta}) = \sum_{i=1}^{n} X_i \log \left(F(s_i; \boldsymbol{\theta}) - F(s_{i-1}; \boldsymbol{\theta}) \right) + \sum_{i=1}^{n} X_i \log \omega - \sum_{i=1}^{k} \log X_i! - \omega F(s_k; \boldsymbol{\theta}). \quad (7)$$

In Eq. (7), $p(A)$ denotes a probability density or mass function of the event A. MLEs can be obtained as the parameters maximizing the above LLF.

In the context of ML estimation, a point estimate of the optimal SRT is computed by substituting MLEs into Eq. (6). However, it should be noted that MLEs involve the statistical variation, i.e., uncertainty of model parameters. Thus we evaluate the effects of the uncertainty of estimated parameters on the optimal SRT.

3.2 Bayesian Estimation

Bayesian estimation is one of the most appropriate methods to estimate uncertainty of model parameters. The key idea behind Bayesian inference is to regard model parameters as random variables and to compute posterior distributions of parameters under the given prior information on the parameters. Let us consider ω and $\boldsymbol{\theta}$ as random variables. When the failure data $\mathcal{D}$ is given, Bayes theorem gives the following formula:

$$p(\omega, \boldsymbol{\theta}|\mathcal{D}) \propto p(\mathcal{D}|\omega, \boldsymbol{\theta}) p(\omega, \boldsymbol{\theta}), \quad (8)$$

where $p(\omega, \boldsymbol{\theta})$ and $p(\omega, \boldsymbol{\theta}|\mathcal{D})$ are called prior and posterior distributions, respectively. Equation (8) implies that the prior knowledge $p(\omega, \boldsymbol{\theta})$ is updated by using the observed information, namely, the likelihood function of observed data $p(\mathcal{D}|\omega, \boldsymbol{\theta})$.

If the posterior distribution is given, the interval estimates, say *credible intervals*, are derived by the quantile of posterior distribution. For instance, $100\alpha\%$ credible intervals of parameters are given by

$$\int_0^\infty \int_{\omega_L}^{\omega_U} p(\omega, \boldsymbol{\theta}|\mathcal{D}) d\omega d\boldsymbol{\theta} = \alpha, \quad (9)$$

$$\int_{\boldsymbol{\theta}_L}^{\boldsymbol{\theta}_U} \int_0^\infty p(\omega, \boldsymbol{\theta}|\mathcal{D}) d\omega d\boldsymbol{\theta} = \alpha. \quad (10)$$

4 Credible Interval of Optimal SRT

Markov chain Monte Carlo (MCMC) is a versatile method to evaluate posterior distributions in the Bayesian context. Generally speaking, the MCMC algorithm is a method to obtain samples drawn from the stationary distribution of a Markov chain. In the Bayesian estimation, the Markov chain is designed so that its stationary distribution equals a target posterior distribution. The typical MCMC algorithm is the Metropolis-Hastings (MH) algorithm. Moreover, as a special case of MH algorithm, the MCMC with Gibbs sampler is also one of the most famous MCMC algorithms.

This paper utilizes the MH method incorporating Gibbs sampling proposed by [6]. Without loss of any generality, we assume that the model parameter vector $\boldsymbol{\theta}$ consists of m parameters, and each of them is defined on the interval $[L_i, U_i]$ for $i = 1, \ldots m$. In particular, L_i and U_i are allowed to be $-\infty$ and ∞, respectively. Moreover, the prior distribution is supposed to be decomposed into factors with one parameter, i.e., $p(\omega, \boldsymbol{\theta}) = p(\omega) \prod_{i=1}^{m} p(\theta_i)$. The prior distribution of ω is given by a gamma distribution with parameter vector (m_ω, ϕ_ω):

$$p(\omega) = \frac{\phi_\omega^{m_\omega} \omega^{m_\omega - 1} e^{-\phi_\omega \omega}}{\Gamma(m_\omega)}. \tag{11}$$

According to Gibbs sampling and MH method, Hirata et al. [6] provided the following sampling scheme as an MCMC algorithm for NHPP-based SRGMs:

- S-1: Generate a new sample of ω drawn from the conditional posterior:

$$\omega \sim \text{Gamma}\left(m_\omega + \sum_{i=1}^{n} (u_i + z_i), \phi_\omega + F(t_n; \boldsymbol{\theta}) \right), \tag{12}$$

  where Gamma(m, ϕ) means the gamma distribution with parameter vector (m, ϕ).
- S-2: For $l = 1, \ldots, m$, execute S-2-1 through S-2-3.
- S-2-1: Generate a candidate $\tilde{\theta}_l$ using the following proposal distribution:

$$\tilde{\theta}_l = \theta_l + z_l, \tag{13}$$

  where z_l is a random variable having a normal distribution truncated at both boundaries L_l and U_l. Concretely, $\tilde{\theta}_l$ is generated from the following truncated normal density defined on $[L_l, U_l]$:

$$f_{\text{trunc}}(\tilde{\theta}_l; L_l, U_l, \theta_l, \sigma_l) = \frac{1}{\sqrt{2\pi}\sigma_l} e^{-\frac{(\tilde{\theta}_l - \theta_l)^2}{2\sigma_l^2}} / \Psi(L_l, U_l, \theta_l, \sigma_l), \tag{14}$$

$$\Psi(L_l, U_l, \theta_l, \sigma_l) = \int_{L_l}^{U_l} \frac{1}{\sqrt{2\pi}\sigma_l} e^{-\frac{(s - \theta_l)^2}{2\sigma_l^2}} ds. \tag{15}$$

– S-2-2: Compute the following acceptance probability $\alpha(\tilde{\theta}_l, \theta_l)$:

$$\alpha(\tilde{\theta}_l, \theta_l) = \min\left(1, \frac{\mathcal{L}(\omega, \theta_1, \ldots, \tilde{\theta}_l, \ldots, \theta_m)p(\tilde{\theta}_l)\Psi(L_l, U_l, \tilde{\theta}_l, \sigma_l)}{\mathcal{L}(\omega, \theta_1, \ldots, \theta_l, \ldots, \theta_m)p(\theta_l)\Psi(L_l, U_l, \theta_l, \sigma_l)}\right), \quad (16)$$

  where $p(\theta_l)$ is the decomposed prior density of θ_l.
– S-2-3: Choose a new sample of θ_l as $\tilde{\theta}_l$ with probability $\alpha(\tilde{\theta}_l, \theta_l)$. Otherwise, do not update the parameter θ_l.

By applying the above steps, we get a new sample vector, and can execute the above step with the new sample vector repeatedly. The set of parameter vectors drawn from the posterior distribution can be selected from long series of outcomes of the steps.

Based on the above MCMC sampling, we can evaluate the optimal SRTs by taking account of their uncertainty. The point estimation of optimal SRT is based on the expected value of Eq. (6). Let $\{(\hat{\omega}_1, \hat{\beta}_1), \ldots, (\hat{\omega}_m, \hat{\beta}_m)\}$ be parameter samples from the MCMC sampling. Then the point estimates are given by

$$\hat{T}^* = \frac{1}{m}\sum_{i=1}^{m}\frac{1}{\hat{\beta}_i}\log\left(\frac{\hat{\omega}_i\hat{\beta}_i(c_2 - c_1)}{c_3}\right), \quad (17)$$

On the other hand, the credible interval of the optimal SRT is defined as the quantile of posterior distribution of Eq. (6). The quantile can be estimated by order statistics of the samples. Therefore, let $\hat{T}^{[1]}, \ldots, \hat{T}^{[m]}$ be the order statistics of T^* corresponding to parameter samples $\{(\hat{\omega}_1, \hat{\beta}_1), \ldots, (\hat{\omega}_m, \hat{\beta}_m)\}$. The $100\alpha\%$ credible interval is given by $(\hat{T}^{[i_L]}, \hat{T}^{[i_U]})$, where i_L and i_U are indexes corresponding to $100\alpha\%$-quantiles;

$$i_L = m * (1 - \alpha)/2 \qquad \text{and} \qquad i_U = m * 1 - (1 - \alpha)/2. \quad (18)$$

5 A Numerical Example

We examine the statistical inference of SRTs. Here we use the System 17 data collected during the system test phase of a military application[1]. The exponential-type NHPP-based SRGM is applied to the above data set. Moreover, we assume the following scenario about prior information:

The prior information consists of good guesses of parameters. The mean and standard deviation of the prior distributions are (50, 15.8) for ω and (1.0e-5, 3.2e-6) for β.

Table 2 presents the point estimates and the 95% credible interval of T^*. Here we calculate the optimal SRTs for all 20000 parameter samples and derive the point estimate and the interval estimate as the sample mean and the respective

1 DACS: Data & Analysis Center for Software `http://www.dacs.dtic.mil/databases/sled/~swrel.shtml`

Table 2. Credible intervals of T^*

c_1	c_2	c_3	T^* (× 1000 seconds) point estimate (mean)	lower bound	upper bound
1	10	0.0004	213.7	166.7	280.7
1	2	0.0001	137.6	108.2	175.2
1	20	0.0001	413.9	305.6	576.2
1	5	0.01	71.5	42.9	96.7

order statistics of all values computed. Under the MCMC method, we generate samples of the posterior distribution from one long-range MCMC series. In order to prevent dependence on the starting values of the parameters, the first 10000 samples (so-called "burn-in samples") are discarded. Moreover, at only every 10th MCMC iteration a sample is collected to avoid auto-correlation between the samples taken. The quantiles of the posterior distribution are estimated by the corresponding order statistics.

From this table, we find that the optimal SRTs indicate wide intervals in the statistical sense. That is, when the software is released at the point estimate of the optimal SRT, we actually have the large risk in cost criterion. In this example, the System 17 has already tested for 282.6 (× 1000) seconds. Therefore the achievement of software test is enough, except for the case where $c_1 = 1$, $c_2 = 20$ and $c_3 = 0.001$, in terms of cost criterion. On the other hand, if the debugging cost in operation is $c_2 = 20$, we need at least 23.0 (= 305.6 – 282.6) ×1000 seconds for software testing.

6 Conclusions

This paper has investigated the interval estimation of the optimal SRT. In particular, we focus on the application of Bayesian estimation to the optimal SRT problem. In the numerical example, we have presented the simple estimates of the optimal SRT based on the real software system. The resulting intervals of SRTs are not so small, and therefore we have to take account of the risk to decide the timing of software release in practical situation.

In future, we will examine the interval estimation of the optimal SRT under different NHPP-based SRGMs and software release criteria. In addition, we will develop a statistical testing to decide the software release.

References

1. Achcar, J.A., Dey, D.K., Niverthi, M.: A Bayesian approach using nonhomogeneous Poisson processes for software reliability models. In: Basu, A.P., Basu, K.S., Mukhopadhyay, S. (eds.) Frontiers in Reliability, pp. 1–18. World Scientific, Singapore (1998)
2. Dohi, T., Nishio, Y., Osaki, S.: Optimal software release scheduling based on artifical neural networks. Annals of Software Engineering 8, 167–185 (1999)
3. Goel, A.L.: Software reliability models: Assumptions, limitations and applicability. IEEE Transactions on Software Engineering SE-11, 1411–1423 (1985)

4. Goel, A.L., Okumoto, K.: Time-dependent error-detection rate model for software reliability and other performance measures. IEEE Transactions on Reliability R-28, 206–211 (1979)
5. Gokhale, S.S., Trivedi, K.S.: Log-logistic software reliability growth model. In: Proc. 3rd IEEE Int'l. High-Assurance Systems Eng. Symp. (HASE 1998), pp. 34–41 (1998)
6. Hirata, T., Okamura, H., Dohi, T.: A Bayesian Inference Tool for NHPP-Based Software Reliability Assessment. In: Lee, Y.-h., Kim, T.-h., Fang, W.-c., Ślęzak, D. (eds.) FGIT 2009. LNCS, vol. 5899, pp. 225–236. Springer, Heidelberg (2009)
7. Littlewood, B.: Rationale for a modified duane model. IEEE Transactions on Reliability R-33(2), 157–159 (1984)
8. Ohba, M.: Inflection S-shaped software reliability growth model. In: Osaki, S., Hatoyama, Y. (eds.) Stochastic Models in Reliability Theory, pp. 144–165. Springer, Berlin (1984)
9. Ohba, M.: Software reliability analysis. IBM J. Research & Development 28, 428–443 (1984)
10. Ohishi, K., Okamura, H., Dohi, T.: Gompertz software reliability model: estimation algorithm and empirical validation. Journal of Systems and Software 82(3), 535–543 (2009)
11. Okamura, H., Dohi, T.: Building phase-type software reliability model. In: Proc. of the 17th Int'l Symp. on Software Reliab. Eng. (ISSRE 2006), pp. 289–298 (2006)
12. Okamura, H., Dohi, T.: Hyper-Erlang software reliability model. In: Proceedings of 14th Pacific Rim International Symposium on Dependable Computing (PRDC 2008), pp. 232–239. IEEE Computer Society Press, Los Alamitos (2008)
13. Okamura, H., Dohi, T., Osaki, S.: Software reliability growth model with normal distribution and its parameter estimation. In: Proceedings of the International Conference on Quality, Reliability, Maintenance and Safety Engieering (ICQR2MSE), pp. 424–429 (2011)
14. Okumoto, K., Goel, L.: Optimum release time for software systems based on reliability and cost criteria. Journal of Systems and Software 1, 315–318 (1980)
15. Xie, M., Hong, G.Y.: A study of the sensitivity of software release time. The Journal of Systems and Software 44, 163–168 (1998)
16. Yamada, S., Ohba, M., Osaki, S.: S-shaped reliability growth modeling for software error detection. IEEE Transactions on Reliability R-32, 475–478 (1983)
17. Yamada, S., Osaki, S.: Cost-reliability optimal release policies for software systems. IEEE Transactions on Reliability R-34, 422–424 (1985)
18. Zhao, M., Xie, M.: On maximum likelihood estimation for a general non-homogeneous Poisson process. Scand. J. Statist. 23, 597–607 (1996)

A Note on Replacement Policies in a Cumulative Damage Model

Won Young Yun

Department of Industrial Engineering
Pusan National University, Busan, 609-735, Korea
wonyun@pusan.ac.kr

Abstract. In this note, we consider a single unit system that should operate over an infinite time span. It is assumed that shocks occur in random times and each shock causes a random amount of to a unit. These damages are additive, and a unit fails when the total damage has exceeded a failure level *K*. We consider preventive maintenance to recover the cumulative damage before system failure. We assume that the shock process is independent of system maintenance and system replacement can not affect the shock process. We compare four typical policies for preventive maintenance (PM) by numerical examples: Time-based PM, number-based PM, damage-based PM, and modified time-based PM.

Keywords: Cumulative damage model, replacement policies, expected cost rate.

1 Introduction

In this paper, we consider a standard cumulative damage model [1] for an operating single unit system. An item is operated under shocks and suffers some damage from shocks. Suppose that a unit begins to operate at time 0 and its damage level is 0. Let $X_i (i = 1,2,...)$ be the inter-arrival time between ($i-1$) th and i th shock. They are independent and have an identical distribution $F(t)$ with finite mean $1/\lambda$ and $S_j = \sum_{i=1}^{j} X_i, F(0) = 0$.

Let $N(t)$ be the number of shocks in time t and $N(t)$ follows a renewal process. Let $F^{(i)}(t)$ be the j-fold convolution of distribution $F(t)$.

The probability that j shocks occur exactly in [0, t] is

$$\Pr\{N(t) = j\} = \Pr\{S_j \le t, S_{j+1} > t\} = F^{(j)}(t) - F^{(j+1)}(t), \quad j = 0,1,2.....$$

An amount W_j of damage due to the jth shock has an identical distribution $G(x) = P(W \le x)$ with finite mean $1/\mu$ and $\overline{G}(x) = 1 - G(x)$. Furthermore, the total damage is additive, and its level is investigated and is known only at shock times. The unit fails when the total damage has exceeded a failure level K at some shock, its failure is immediately detected, and it is replaced with a new one. The replacement cost at the failure is c_k. Fig. 1 shows a sample path of shock and damage to a failure.

T.-h. Kim et al. (Eds.): ASEA/DRBC/EL 2011, CCIS 257, pp. 385–391, 2011.

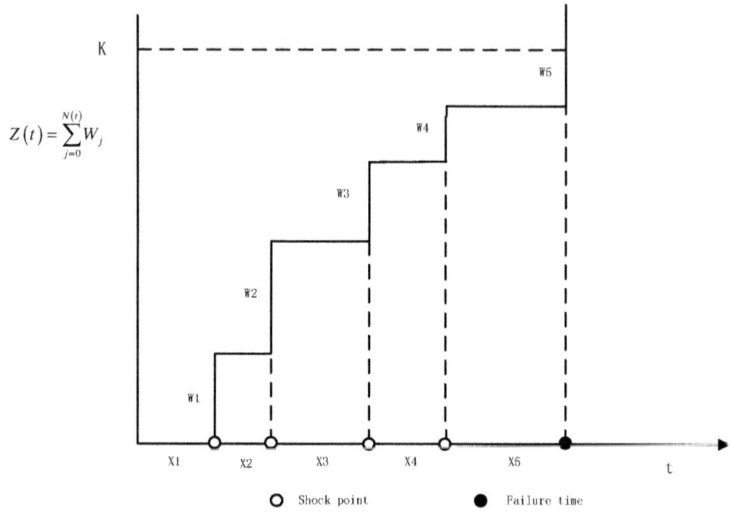

Fig. 1. Shock and damage model

We can replace the unit preventively before a failure and reduce the total cost to operate the unit for infinite horizon. In the next section, we consider several preventive replacement models.

2 Preventive Replacement Models

In this section, we consider four preventive replacement policies in Nakagawa [1] and compare the optimal policies to minimize the expected cost rate by numerical examples.

2.1 Replacement Model at Time *T*

In this model, the unit is replaced at time *T* or at failure, whichever occurs first. If the system is failed before *T*, the shock process is renewed. But in preventive maintenance case, the shock process is not renewed because we assume that the shock process is independent of the preventive maintenance. We consider failure times (corrective replacement points) as renewal points. First, the probability that the system does not fail before *T* is

$$P_T = \sum_{j=0}^{\infty}\left[F^{(j)}(T) - F^{(j+1)}(T)\right]G^{(j+1)}(K)$$

where $G^{(i)}(x)$ be the j-fold convolution of distribution $G(x)$. Let c_T be the preventive replacement cost at the time *T*. The expected cost of a renewal cycle is given approximately

$$EC(T) = (1-P_T)c_K + P_T(1-P_T)(c_K + c_T) + P_T^{\,2}(1-P_T)(c_K + 2c_T) + \cdots$$
$$= \sum_{i=0}^{\infty} P_T^{\,i}(1-P_T)(c_K + ic_T) = \frac{c_K - (c_K - c_T)P_T}{1-P_T}$$

Next, we consider the expected time to the first failure under preventive replacement based on T. The mean time to the first failure before T is

$$T_K = \sum_{j=0}^{\infty} \int_0^T t dF^{(j+1)}(t) \int_0^K \overline{G}(k-x) dG^{(j)}(x)$$

If a shock occurs at time 0, the mean time to the first failure before T is

$$DT_K = \sum_{j=0}^{\infty} \int_0^T t dF^{(j+1)}(t) \int_0^K \overline{G}(k-x) dG^{(j+1)}(x)$$

and $T_K = \dfrac{1}{\lambda} + DT_K$

The expected time to the first failure time is given

$$ET(K,T) = T_K + P_T[T + EY(T) + DT_K + P_T[T + EY(T) + DT_K + P_T[\cdots$$
$$= T_K + P_T[T + EY(T) + DT_K] + P_T^{\,2}[T + EY(T) + DT_K] + P_T^{\,3}[\cdots$$
$$= \frac{T_K + P_T(T + EY(T) + DT_K - T_K)}{1-P_T} = \frac{T_K + P_T(T + EY(T) - 1/\lambda)}{1-P_T}$$

where $Y(T)$ is the excess life of the renewal process of shocks at time T. Therefore, the expected cost rate is

$$C_1(T) = \frac{c_K + P_T(c_T - c_K)}{T_K + P_T(T + EY(T) - 1/\lambda)} \qquad (1)$$

2.2 Replacement Models at Number *N*, Damage *Z* and the First Shock after Time *T*

In this subsection, we consider three additional replacement models. First, the unit is replaced at shock N or at failure, whichever occurs first. Secondly, the unit is replaced at damage Z or at failure, whichever occurs first. Finally, the unit is replaced at the next shock after time T or at failure. In three replacement models, the system is replaced preventively at renewal points of the shock process. Thus, all preventive and corrective replacement points are renewal points and the expected cost rate are same as ones in Nakagawa [1] (refer to Nakagawa [1] for detail derivation). The expected cost rate of number based PM is

$$C_2(N) = \frac{c_K - (c_K - c_N) G^{(N)}(K)}{(1/\lambda) \sum_{j=0}^{N-1} G^{(j)}(K)} \tag{2}$$

where c_N is the preventive replacement cost at the number N.

The expected cost rate of damage based PM is

$$C_3(Z) = \frac{c_K - (c_K - c_Z)\left[G(K) - \int_0^Z \overline{G}(K-x)\, dM_G(x)\right]}{\left[1 + M_G(Z)\right]/\lambda} \tag{3}$$

where $M_G(x) = \sum_{j=1}^{\infty} G(x)$ and c_Z is the preventive replacement cost at the damage.

The expected cost rate of the modified time based PM in which the system is replaced preventively at the first shock after T is

$$C_4(T) = \frac{c_K - (c_K - c_T) \sum_{j=0}^{\infty} \left[F^{(j)}(T) - F^{(j+1)}(T)\right] G^{(j+1)}(K)}{(1/\lambda) \sum_{j=0}^{\infty} G^{(j)}(K) F^{(j)}(T)} \tag{4}$$

3 Numerical Examples

In this section, we compare the expected cost rates of four PM models by numerical examples. We assume that shock arrival follows a renewal process and the inter-arrival times follow an Erlang distribution. The density and distribution functions are given

$$f(t) = te^{-t}, F(t) = 1 - e^{-t} - te^{-t}$$

Then the renewal function is given

$$m(t) = \left(-\frac{1}{4}\right) + \frac{t}{2} + \frac{1}{4} e^{-2t}$$

The distribution function of jth shock is given

$$F^{(j)}(x) = \int_0^x \frac{t^{2j-1} e^{-t}}{(2j-1)!} dt$$

The expected excess life is given (Refer to Ross [2])

$$EY(t) = E[X - t \mid X > t]\overline{F}(t) + \int_0^t E[X - (x-y) \mid X > x-y]dm(y)$$
$$= \frac{2+t}{1+t}[e^{-t} + te^{-t}] + \int_0^t \frac{2+(t-y)}{1+(t-y)}\frac{1}{2}(1-e^{-2y})dy$$

It is also assumed that damage amount from each shock follows an Exponential distribution ($\mu = 1$). Thus,

$$G^{(j)}(x) = \int_0^x \frac{t^{j-1}}{(j-1)!}e^{-t}dt$$

We consider a simple case with $c_T = c_N = c_Z = 1, c_K = 4$.

For given values of model parameters, we obtain the expected cost rates and optimal solutions numerically. Fig. 2-4 show the expected cost rates for four models under different failure levels K. Let T_1^*, N^*, Z^*, T_4^* be the optimal solutions of four policies and then

$$\text{For } K = 2,\ C_1(T_1^*) \approx C_4(T_4^*) \approx C_2(N^*) > C_3(Z^*)$$
$$\text{For } K = 12,\ C_1(T_1^*) \approx C_4(T_4^*) \approx C_2(N^*) > C_3(Z^*)$$
$$\text{For } K = 20,\ C_1(T_1^*) \approx C_4(T_4^*) \approx C_2(N^*) > C_3(Z^*)$$

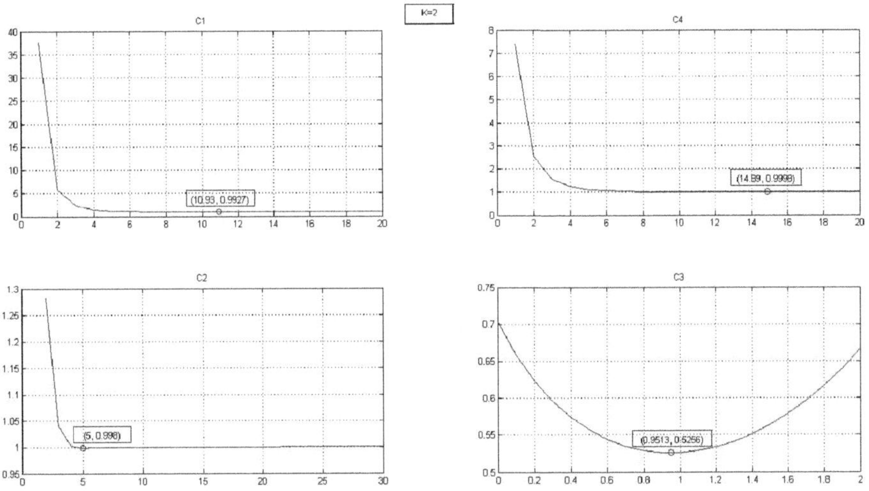

Fig. 2. Optimal solutions of four models (K=2)

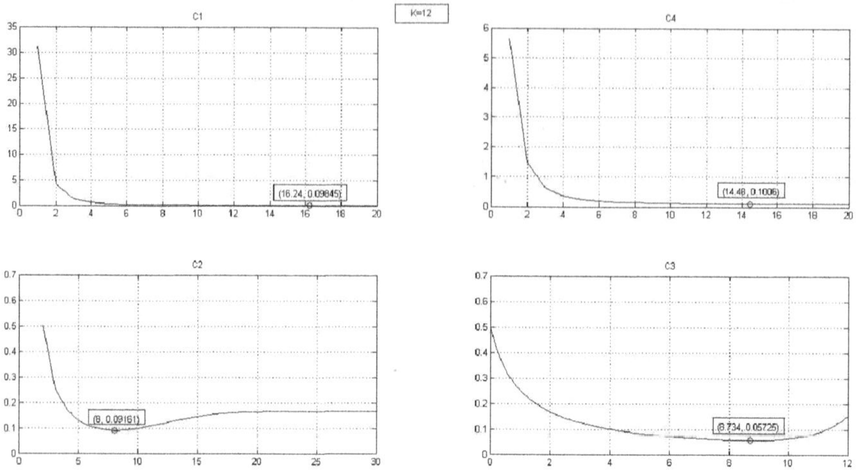

Fig. 3. Optimal solutions of four models (K=12)

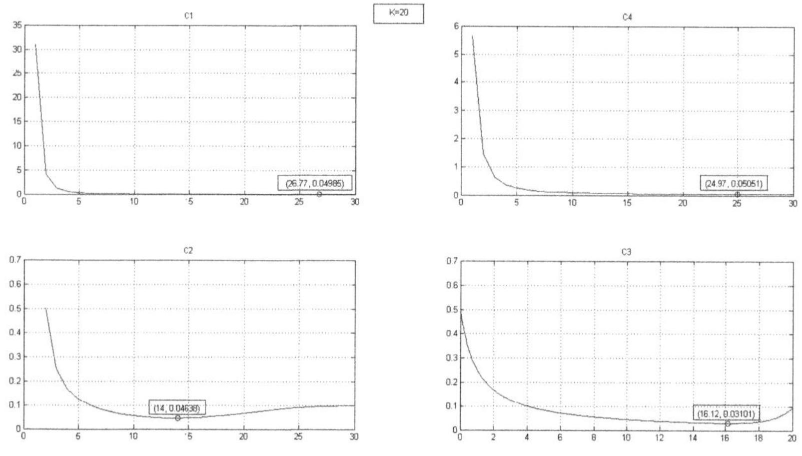

Fig. 4. Optimal solutions of four models (K=20)

4 Conclusions

In this note, we considered preventive maintenance models in which shocks occur in random times and each shock causes a random amount to a system. These damages are additive, and a system fails when the total damage exceeds a failure level K. Four basic preventive replacement policies based on age, shock numbers and damage amounts are studied. We assume that the shock process is independent of system maintenance and system replacement can not affect the shock process. Under this independence assumption, we cannot use the existing cost models in some cases (time based PM) but it depends on model assumptions. For example, if we assume Poisson processes as shock occurrence, all preventive and corrective replacement points are renewal points and cost models of four policies are same as existing ones in Nakagawa [1]. As an application area of this shock model, some interesting optimization models of garbage collection policies were studied in Satow et al. [3]. Non-homogeneous Poisson processes are assumed for shock arrivals and several replacement policies are applied. If the independence assumption is made in Non-homogeneous Poisson processes, it is difficult to derive the expected cost rates of four PM models because it is difficult to define renewal points and cycles.

Acknowledgments. This research was supported by Basic Science Research Program through the National Research Foundation of Korea(NRF) funded by the Ministry of Education, Science and Technology(No.2010-0025084).

References

1. Nakagawa, T.: Shock and Damage Models in Reliability Theory. Springer, Heidelberg (2007)
2. Ross, S.M.: Stochastic Processes, 2nd edn. Wiley, New York (1996)
3. Satow, T., Yasui, K., Nakagawa, T.: Optimal garbage collection policies for a database in a computer system. RAIRO Oper. Res. 30, 359–372 (1996)

Reliability Consideration of a Server System with Replication Buffering Relay Method for Disaster Recovery

Mitsutaka Kimura[1], Mitsuhiro Imaizumi[2], and Toshio Nakagawa[3]

[1] Department of International Culture Studies, Gifu City Women's College, 7-1 Hitoichiba Kita-matchi Gifu City, 501-0192 Japan
kimura@gifu-cwc.ac.jp

[2] College of Contemporary Management, Aichi Gakusen University, 1 Shiotori,Oike-Cho Toyota City, Aichi, 471-8532 Japan
imaizumi@gakusen.ac.jp

[3] Department of Business Administration, Aichi Institute of Technology, 1247 Yachigusa, Yakusa-cho, Toyota City, Aichi, 470-0392 Japan
toshi-nakagawa@aitech.ac.jp

Abstract. Recently, replication buffering relay method has been used in order to guarantee consistency of database content and reduce cost of replication. We consider the problem of reliability in server system using the replication buffering relay method. The server in a main site updates the storage database when a client requests the data update, and transfers the data and the address of the location updated data to a buffering relay unit. The server transmits all of the data in the buffering relay unit to a backup site after a constant number of data update. We derive the expected number of the replication and of updated data in buffering relay unit. Further, we calculate the expected cost and discuss optimal replication interval to minimize it. Finally, numerical examples are given.

Keywords: Server system, Disaster recovery, Replication Buffering Relay Method, Reliability.

1 Introduction

Recently, the server system with main and backup sites has been widely used in order to protect enterprise database and avoid out of service state. That is, the backup site stands by the alert when a main site has broken down due to electricity failure, hurricanes, earthquakes, and so on. The server in the main site transmits the database content to the backup site using a network link. This is called replication [1][2].

In order to guarantee consistency of database content and reduce cost of replication, some replication schemes have been proposed[1]∼[5]. For example, in the replication scheme using journaling file, the server takes checkpoint for all database transactions in the main site and transmits the database content from

T.-h. Kim et al. (Eds.): ASEA/DRBC/EL 2011, CCIS 257, pp. 392–398, 2011.

the main site to the backup site at any time. Further, the server in the main site transmits journaling files to the backup site as soon as the server updates the storage database when a client requests the data update[3]∼[5]. But, if the server in the backup site has received many journaling files, the replication scheme needs some time until the system resumes services in the backup site. To solve this problem, replication buffering relay method has been proposed [6][7].

In replication buffering relay method, the server system consists of a buffering relay unit as well as both main and backup sites in order to speed up the response time and smooth communication load [7]. The server in a main site updates the storage database when a client requests the data update, and transfers the data and the address of the physical location updated data on the storage to a buffering relay unit. The server transmits all of the data in the buffering relay unit to a backup site at any time (replication) [6][7]. When a disaster has occurred in the main site, the routine work is migrated from the main site to the backup site and is executed immediately. When a client requests the data update or the data read, the server confirm the address held in the buffering relay unit. If the address of the requested data corresponds with the address, it is transmitted from the buffering relay unit to the backup site instantly. In this paper, an optimal policy is proposed to reduce waste of costs for replication and transmitting the updated data in buffering relay unit. We formulate a stochastic model of a server system with the replication buffering relay method and derive the expected number of the replication and of updated data in buffering relay unit. Further, we calculate the expected cost and discuss optimal replication interval to minimize it. Finally, numerical examples are given.

2 Model and Analysis

A server system consists of a monitor, a buffering relay unit, a main site and a backup site as shown in Figure 1:

Both main and backup sites consist of identical server and storage. Both backup site and buffering relay unit stand by the alert when a disaster has occurred. The server in the main site performs the routine work and updates the storage database when a client requests the data update. Then, the monitor transmits the updated data and the address of the physical location updated

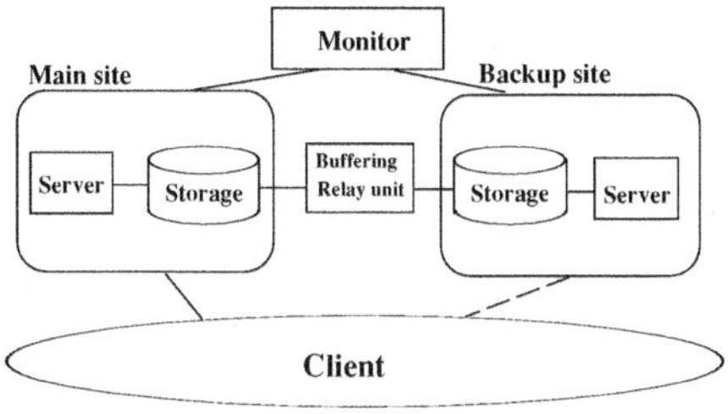

Fig. 1. Outline of a server system

data on the storage to the buffering relay unit immediately. Furthermore, the monitor orders the buffering relay unit to transmit all of the data to the backup site after a constant number of transmitting data update. Then, we formulate the stochastic model as follows:

(1) A client requests the data update to the storage. The request requires the time according to an exponential distribution $(1 - e^{-\alpha t})$. The server in the main site updates the storage database and transmits the updated data and the address of the physical location updated data on the storage. The data update and the transmission of the data and the address of the location updated data require the time according to an exponential distribution $(1 - e^{-\beta t})$.

(2) The monitor orders the buffering relay unit to transmit all of the data to the backup site, after the server in the main site updates the data by requesting from client and transmits the data at $n(n = 0, 1, 2, \cdots)$ times (replication).
   (a) The replication requires the time according to an exponential distribution $(1 - e^{-wt})$.
   (b) If a disaster occurs in the main site while the buffering relay unit transmits all of the data from the buffering relay unit to the backup site, the monitor immediately orders to migrate the routine work from the main site to the backup site and the system migration is executed.

(3) When a disaster has occurred in the main site, the routine work is migrated from the main site to the backup site, and the server performs the routine work in the backup site (system migration).
   (a) A disaster occurs according to an exponential distribution $(1 - e^{-\lambda t})$. A disaster does not occur in the monitor, the buffering relay unit and the backup site.
   (b) When the routine work is migrated from the main site to the backup site, the monitor orders the buffering relay unit to transfer the address of updated data held in it to the backup site.
   (c) When a client requests the data update or the data read, the server confirm the address held in the buffering relay unit. If the address of the requested data corresponds with the address, it is transmitted from the buffering relay unit to the backup site instantly.

Under the above assumptions, we define the following states of the network server system:

State 0: System begins to operate or restart.
State a_i $(i = 1, 2, \cdots, n)$:When a client requests the data update to the storage, the data update begins.
State b_i $(i = 1, 2, \cdots, n-1)$:Data update and the transmission of the data and the address of the location updated data is completed.
State b_n: When the server in the main site has transmitted the data and the address of the location updated data at $n(n = 0, 1, 2, \cdots)$ times, replication begins.
State F_i $(i = 0, 1, \cdots, n)$: Disaster occurs in the main site.

The system states defined above form a Markov renewal process [8][9], where $F_i(i = 0, 1, \cdots, n)$ is an absorbing state. A transition diagram between system states is shown in Figure 2.

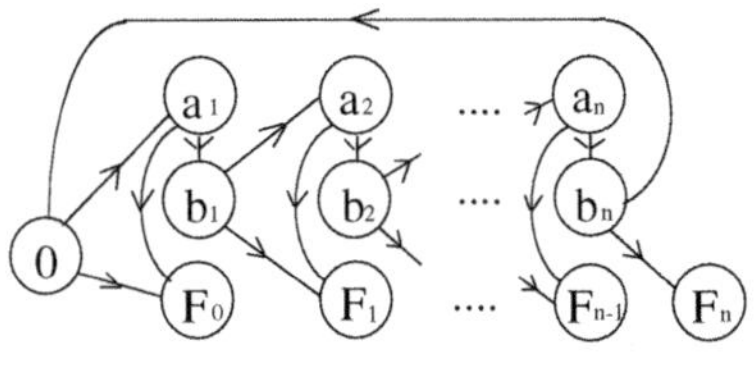

Fig. 2. Transition diagram between a server system states

Let $\phi(s)$ be the Laplace-Stieltjes (LS) transform of any function $\Phi(t)$, i.e., $\phi(s) \equiv \int_0^{\infty} e^{-st} d\Phi(t)$ for $Re(s) > 0$. The LS Transforms of transition probabilities $Q_{j,k}(t)(j = 0, a_i, b_i, b_n; k = 0, a_1, a_{i+1}, b_i, F_0, F_{i-1}, F_i, F_n)$ are given by the following equations :

$$q_{0,a_1}(s) = q_{b_i,a_{i+1}}(s) = \frac{\alpha}{s+\alpha+\lambda} \qquad (i = 1, 2, \cdots, n-1),$$

$$q_{0,F_0}(s) = q_{b_i,F_i}(s) = \frac{\lambda}{s+\alpha+\lambda} \qquad (i = 1, 2, \cdots, n-1),$$

$$q_{a_i,b_i}(s) = \frac{\beta}{s+\beta+\lambda} \qquad (i = 1, 2, \cdots, n),$$

$$q_{a_i,F_{i-1}}(s) = \frac{\lambda}{s+\beta+\lambda} \qquad (i = 1, 2, \cdots, n),$$

$$q_{b_n,0}(s) = \frac{w}{s+w+\lambda}, \qquad q_{b_n,F_n}(s) = \frac{\lambda}{s+w+\lambda}.$$

We derive the expected number M_R of replication. The LS transform $m_R(s)$ of the expected number distribution $M_R(t)$ in $[0, t]$ are

$$m_R(s) = \frac{\left(\frac{w}{s+w+\lambda}\right)\left[\frac{\alpha\beta}{(s+\alpha+\lambda)(s+\beta+\lambda)}\right]^n}{1 - \left(\frac{w}{s+w+\lambda}\right)\left[\frac{\alpha\beta}{(s+\alpha+\lambda)(s+\beta+\lambda)}\right]^n}.$$

Hence, the expected number M_R is

$$M_R \equiv \lim_{s \to 0}[m_R(s)] = \frac{\frac{w}{w+\lambda}X^n}{1 - \frac{w}{w+\lambda}X^n}, \qquad (1)$$

where $X \equiv \alpha\beta/[(\alpha+\lambda)(\beta+\lambda)]$.

We derive the expected number M_B of the updated data in buffering relay unit. The LS transform $p_{0,F_i}(s)(i = 1, 2, \cdots, n)$ of the probability distributions $P_{0,F_i}(t)(i = 1, 2, \cdots, n)$ from state 0 to state $F_i(i = 1, 2, \cdots, n)$ until time t are

$$p_{0,F_1}(s) = \frac{\frac{\lambda(s+\alpha+\beta+\lambda)}{(s+\alpha+\lambda)(s+\beta+\lambda)}\left[\frac{\alpha\beta}{(s+\alpha+\lambda)(s+\beta+\lambda)}\right]}{1-\frac{w}{w+\lambda}\left[\frac{\alpha\beta}{(s+\alpha+\lambda)(s+\beta+\lambda)}\right]^n},$$

$$p_{0,F_2}(s) = \frac{\frac{\lambda(s+\alpha+\beta+\lambda)}{(s+\alpha+\lambda)(s+\beta+\lambda)}\left[\frac{\alpha\beta}{(s+\alpha+\lambda)(s+\beta+\lambda)}\right]^2}{1-\frac{w}{w+\lambda}\left[\frac{\alpha\beta}{(s+\alpha+\lambda)(s+\beta+\lambda)}\right]^n},$$

$$\vdots$$

$$p_{0,F_{n-1}}(s) = \frac{\frac{\lambda(s+\alpha+\beta+\lambda)}{(s+\alpha+\lambda)(s+\beta+\lambda)}\left[\frac{\alpha\beta}{(s+\alpha+\lambda)(s+\beta+\lambda)}\right]^{n-1}}{1-\frac{w}{w+\lambda}\left[\frac{\alpha\beta}{(s+\alpha+\lambda)(s+\beta+\lambda)}\right]^n},$$

$$p_{0,F_n}(s) = \frac{\frac{\lambda}{s+w+\lambda}\left[\frac{\alpha\beta}{(s+\alpha+\lambda)(s+\beta+\lambda)}\right]^n}{1-\frac{w}{w+\lambda}\left[\frac{\alpha\beta}{(s+\alpha+\lambda)(s+\beta+\lambda)}\right]^n}.$$

Hence, the probability $P_{0,F_i}(i=1,2,\cdots,n)$ from state 0 to state $F_i(i=1,2,\cdots,n)$ is derived by $P_{0,F_i} \equiv \lim_{s\to 0}[p_{0,F_i}(s)](i=1,2,\cdots,n)$. Thereafter, the expected number M_B is

$$\begin{aligned} M_B &\equiv P_{0,F_1} + 2P_{0,F_2} + \cdots + (n-1)P_{0,F_{n-1}} + nP_{0,F_n} \\ &= \frac{\frac{X(1-X^{n-1})}{1-X} + X^n\left[1-n\left(\frac{w}{w+\lambda}\right)\right]}{1-\frac{w}{w+\lambda}X^n}. \end{aligned} \tag{2}$$

3 Optimal Policy

We propose an optimal policy to reduce waste of costs for replication and transmitting the updated data in buffering relay unit. That is, we calculate the cost and derive an optimal replication interval n^* to minimize it. Let c_B be the cost for transmitting the updated data in buffering relay unit and c_R the cost for replication. Further, let $M_R(n), M_B(n)$ denote M_R, M_B respectively because they are function of n. Then, we define the cost $C(n)$ as follows:

$$C(n) \equiv c_R M_R(n) + c_B M_B(n) \qquad (n=0,1,2,\cdots). \tag{3}$$

Clearly,

$$C(0) = \frac{c_R w}{\lambda}, \qquad C(\infty) \equiv \lim_{n\to\infty} C(n) = \frac{c_B X}{1-X}.$$

We seek an optimal replication interval $n^*(0 \le n^* \le \infty)$ which minimizes $C(n)$ in (3). From $C(n+1) - C(n) \ge 0$,

$$\left(\frac{\lambda - w}{w}\right)\left(\frac{X}{1-X}\right) + n + \left(\frac{w}{\lambda+w}\right)\left(\frac{X^{n+1}}{1-X}\right) \ge \frac{c_R}{c_B} \qquad (n=0,1,2,\cdots). \tag{4}$$

Denoting the left-hand side of (4) by $L(n)$,

$$L(n) - L(n-1) = 1 - \left(\frac{w}{\lambda + w}\right) X^n > 0.$$

Thus, $L(n)$ is strictly increasing in n from $L(0) = \lambda\alpha\beta/[w(\lambda + w)(\lambda + \alpha + \beta)]$ to ∞. Therefore, we have the following optimal policy:

(i) If $L(0) \geq c_R/c_B$, $n^* = 0$. That is, we should apply synchronous replication between main and backup sites.
(ii) If $c_R/c_B > L(0)$, there exists a finite and unique $n^* (1 \leq n^* < \infty)$ which satisfies (4).

Note that n^* increases with c_R/c_B and X, i.e., increases with α and β, and decreases with λ.

4 Numerical Example

We compute numerically an optimal replication interval n^* which minimizes $C(n)$ in (3). Suppose that the mean time $1/\beta$ required for the data update is a unit time. It is assumed that the mean generation interval of request the data update is $(1/\alpha)/(1/\beta) = 2 \sim 10$, the mean generation interval of a disaster is $(1/\lambda)/(1/\beta) = 1000, 5000$, the mean time required for the replication is $(1/w)/(1/\beta) = 10 \sim 40$, Further, we introduce the following costs : The cost for transmitting the data and the address of the location updated data is $c_B = 1$, the cost for replication is $c_R/c_B = 5, 10$.

Table 1 gives the optimal replication interval n^* which minimizes the cost $C(n)$. For example, when $c_B = 1, c_R = 5$ and $1/\beta = 1, 1/\alpha = 10, 1/w = 20, 1/\lambda = 1000$, the optimal replication interval is $n^* = 30$. This indicates that n^* increase with $1/\lambda$. Further, n^* increase with c_R/c_B. Thus, we should hold more amount of updated data in the buffering relay unit than execute replication. Moreover, n^* decrease with $1/\alpha$ and $1/w$. In this case, we should execute replication rather than hold large amounts of updated data in it.

Table 1. Optimal replication interval n^* to minimize $C(n)$

c_R/c_B	β/w	β/λ = 1000, β/α = 2	5	10	β/λ = 5000, β/α = 2	5	10
5	10	56	40	31	127	91	68
	20	52	39	30	123	89	67
	40	44	35	28	116	86	65
10	10	81	59	45	182	130	97
	20	78	57	44	179	129	97
	40	71	54	42	172	125	95

5 Conclusions

We have considered the problem of reliability in server system using the replication buffering relay method. We have formulated a stochastic model of the server system with replications using buffering relay unit, and derive the expected number of the replication and of the updated data in buffering relay unit. Further, we calculate the expected cost and discuss optimal replication interval to minimize it.

From numerical examples, we have shown that the optimal replication interval increases with the cost for replication and decrease with the interval of request for the data update and the time required the replication. That is, we have shown that the more the cost for replication, we should hold more amount of updated data in the buffering relay unit rather than execute replication and conversely the more interval of request for the data update and time required the replication, we should execute replication rather than hold large amounts of updated data in it.

Further, it would be important to evaluate and improve the reliability of a server system with replication schemes. Such study would be expected to apply to actual fields.

References

1. Yamato, J., Kan, M., Kikuchi, Y.: Storage based data protection for disaster recovery. The Journal of Institute of Electronics, Information and Communication Engineers 89(9), 801–805 (2006)
2. VERITAS Software corporation. VERITAS volume replication for UNIX datasheet, http://eval.veritas.com/mktginfo/products/Datasheets/High_Availability/vvr_datasheet_unix.pdf
3. Fujita, T., Yata, K.: Asynchronous remote mirroring with journaling file systems. Transactions of Information Processing Society of Japan 46 (SIG 16), 56–68 (2005)
4. Watabe, S., Suzuki, Y., Mizuno, K., Fujiwara, S.: Evaluation of speed-up methods of database redo processing for log-based disaster recovery systems. The Database Society of Japan Letters 6(1), 133–136 (2007)
5. Goda, K., Kitsuregawa, M.: A study on power reduction method of disk storage for log forwarding based disaster recovery systems. The Database Society of Japan Letters 6(1), 69–72 (2007)
6. Yamato, J., Kaneko, Y., Kan, M., Kikuchi, Y.: A Replication buffering relay method for disaster recovery. Technical Report of The Institute of Electronics, Information, and Communication Engineers, DC2004-20: 43–48 (2004)
7. Kan, M., Yamato, J., Kaneko, Y., Kikuchi, Y.: An approach of shortening the recovery time in the replication buffering relay method for disaster recovery. Technical Report of The Institute of Electronics, Information, and Communication Engineers, CPSY200519: 25–30 (2005)
8. Osaki, S.: Applied stochastic system modeling. Springer, Berlin (1992)
9. Yasui, K., Nakagawa, T., Sandoh, H.: Reliability models in data communication systems. In: Osaki, S. (ed.) Stochastic Models in Reliability and Maintenance, pp. 281–301. Springer, Berlin (2002)

Estimating Software Reliability Using Extreme Value Distribution

Xiao Xiao and Tadashi Dohi

Department of Information Engineering, Graduate School of Engineering,
Hiroshima University, 1–4–1 Kagamiyama, Higashi-Hiroshima, 739–8527, Japan
{xiaoxiao,dohi}@rel.hiroshima-u.ac.jp

Abstract. In this paper, we propose a novel modeling approach for the non-homogeneous Poisson process (NHPP) based software reliability models (SRMs) to describe the stochastic behavior of software fault-detection processes. Specifically, we apply the extreme value distribution to the software fault-detection time distribution. We study the effectiveness of extreme value distribution in software reliability modeling and compare the resulting NHPP-based SRMs with the existing ones.

Keywords: software reliability, NHPP, extreme value distribution, real data analysis, prediction analysis.

1 Introduction

Software reliability, which is the probability that the software system does not fail during a specified time period, is one of the most significant attributes of software quality. Up to now, a huge number of software reliability models (SRMs) ([7], [8], [9], [12]) have been proposed from various points of view to assess the software reliability. Among them, the SRMs based on non-homogeneous Poisson processes (NHPPs) have played a central role in describing stochastic behavior of the number of faults experienced over time. Goel and Okumoto [4], Yamada, Ohba and Osaki [13] and Goel [5] proposed representative SRMs based on the NHPP. More specifically, NHPP-based SRMs can be classified by their detection time distributions of software faults, and then the mean value functions (and their variances) are proportional to the fault-detection time distributions. That is, if the fault-detection time distribution is an exponential distribution, then the mean trend of fault-detection process increases like an exponential function and converges to a saturation level which can be regarded as the number of initial software fault contents. If the fault-detection time distribution is given by the Rayleigh distribution [5] and two-stage Erlang distribution [13], then the mean trends of the fault-detection processes exhibit S-shaped curves. Xiao and Dohi [11] proposed a generalized NHPP-based SRM by applying the so-called equilibrium distribution. Their models always provide the most representative pattern, an exponential curve, of software fault-detection process, and are proved much more attractive than the usual ones in the perspective of goodness-of-fit

T.-h. Kim et al. (Eds.): ASEA/DRBC/EL 2011, CCIS 257, pp. 399–406, 2011.

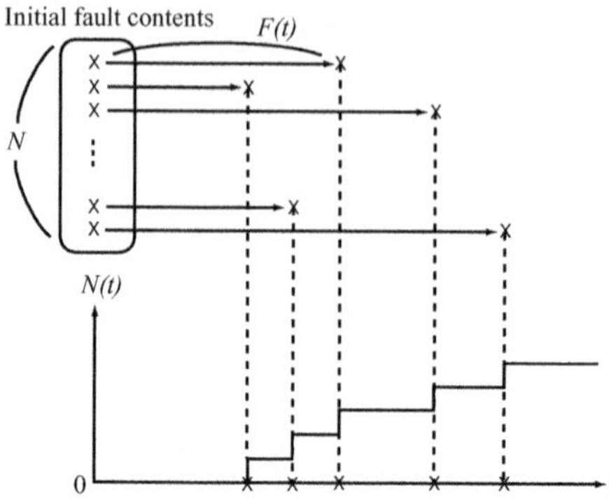

Fig. 1. Configuration of software debugging theory

and prediction performances. This work motivates us to study other distribution properties in the modeling of software fault-detection process.

In this paper, we propose a novel modeling approach for the NHPP-based SRMs to assess the software reliability. The fundamental idea is to apply the extreme value (EV) distribution to a fault-detection time distribution. EV distributions are known as the limiting distributions for the maximum or the minimum of a large collection of independent and identically distributed random variables from the same arbitrary distribution. In engineering field such as the study of floods [3] and equity risk [2], the EV distributions have been widely used. We study the effectiveness of EV distribution in software reliability modeling and compare the resulting NHPP-based SRMs with the existing ones.

The remainder of this paper is organized as follows. In Section 2, we introduce a basic modeling framework of NHPP-based SRMs. In Section 3, we describe the EV distribution and propose a new modeling approach based on the EV distribution. Section 4 is devoted to the real project data analysis, where we use 4 real project data [7] and investigate the goodness-of-fit performance of our new NHPP-based SRMs, where the maximum likelihood (ML) method is applied for estimating model parameters, and the Akaike information criterion (AIC) [1] and the Bayesian information criterion (BIC) [10] as well as the mean squares error (MSE) are used for model selection. We conduct the prediction analysis to investigate the prediction ability of the resulting NHPP-based SRMs with EV distributions and estimate the software reliability by both models. The paper is concluded in Section 5 with some remarks.

2 NHPP-Based Software Reliability Modeling

Let $N(t)$ denote the number of software faults detected by testing time t, and be a stochastic point process in continuous time. Suppose that software failures caused by software faults occur at independent and identically distributed (i.i.d.) random times having a cumulative distribution function (c.d.f.) $F(t)$ with a probability density function (p.d.f.) $f(t) = dF(t)/dt$. Figure 1 illustrates the

Table 1. Typical NHPP-based SRMs

Model	$\Lambda_1(t)$	$\Lambda_2(t)$	$\Lambda_3(t)$
EXP	$\omega(1-e^{-\beta t})$	$\omega[(1-e^{-\beta t})^n]$	$\omega(1-e^{-n\beta t})$
RAY	$\omega(1-e^{-\beta t^2})$	$\omega[(1-e^{-\beta t^2})^n]$	$\omega(1-e^{-n\beta t^2})$
WEB	$\omega(1-e^{-\beta t^\alpha})$	$\omega[(1-e^{-\beta t^\alpha})^n]$	$\omega(1-e^{-n\beta t^\alpha})$
TSE	$\omega(1-(1+\beta t)e^{-\beta t})$	$\omega[(1-(1+\beta t)e^{-\beta t})^n]$	$\omega[1-((1+\beta t)e^{-\beta t})^n]$

configuration of software debugging theory. The unknown initial number of software faults, N, is then appropriately assumed as a discrete (integer-valued) random variable. Langberg and Singpurwalla [6] proved that when the initial number of software faults N was a Poisson random variable with mean ω (> 0) , the number of software faults detected before time t is given by the following NHPP:

$$\Pr\{N(t)=n\} = \frac{\{\omega F(t)\}^n}{n!}e^{-\omega F(t)}. \tag{1}$$

Equation (1) is equivalent to the probability mass function of the NHPP having a mean value function $\mathrm{E}[N(t)] = \Lambda_1(t) = \omega F(t)$. From this modeling framework, almost all NHPP-based SRMs can be derived by choosing the software fault-detection time distribution $F(t)$. If $F(t) = 1 - e^{-\beta t}$, then we can derive the Goel and Okumoto SRM [4] with mean value function $\Lambda_1(t) = \omega(1 - e^{-\beta t})$. If the software fault-detection time distribution is given by the two-stage Erlang distribution or the Weibull distribution, then the resulting NHPP-based SRM becomes the delayed S-shaped SRM [13] or Goel SRM [5].

3 New Modeling Approach

Here we present a new NHPP-based SRM belonging to the general modeling framework described in Section 2. In the context of reliability modeling, extreme value distributions (EVDs) for the maximum and the minimum are frequently encountered in series and parallel systems. For example, if a system consists of n identical components in parallel, and the system fails when all the components fail, then system failure time is the maximum of n random component failure times. Similarly, if a system consists of n identical components in series, then the system failure time is the minimum of n random component failure times.

By applying the above two EVDs, maximum-extreme value distribution and minimum-extreme value distribution, we define the EVD-NHPP models as follows. Let T_i $(i = 1,\ 2, \ldots,\ n)$ be i.i.d. random variables with distribution function $F(t)$, which discribes the detection time of each software fault. Letting $Y_n = \max(T_1,\ T_2, \ldots, T_n)$ and $Z_n = \min(T_1,\ T_2, \ldots, T_n)$, the distribution of Y_n is $F_{\max}(t) = \Pr\{Y_n \le y\} = \Pr(T_1 \le y) \times \Pr(T_2 \le y) \times \cdots \times \Pr(T_n \le y) = \{F(t)\}^n$, and the distribution of Z_n is $F_{\min}(t) = \Pr\{Z_n \le z\} = 1 - \Pr(T_1 > z) = 1 - \Pr(T_1 \le z) \times \Pr(T_2 \le z) \times \cdots \times \Pr(T_n \le z) = 1 - \{1 - F(t)\}^n$. Suppose

Table 2. Goodness-of-fit test

DS1		AIC	BIC	MSE
EXP	MVF	288.142	292.396	0.666
	MAX	289.999	296.381	0.679
RAY	MVF	326.450	330.704	1.159
	MAX	289.312	295.693	0.681
WEB	MVF	290.028	296.409	0.679
	MAX	290.290	298.798	0.699
TSE	MVF	312.193	316.447	0.917
	MAX	289.996	296.378	0.679
	MIN	290.284	296.665	9.629

DS2		AIC	BIC	MSE
EXP	MVF	325.498	328.925	3.452
	MAX	292.207	297.348	2.439
RAY	MVF	314.617	318.045	2.768
	MAX	278.082	283.222	1.941
WEB	MVF	283.774	288.914	2.141
	MAX	276.949	283.803	1.828
TSE	MVF	291.441	294.868	2.384
	MAX	290.146	295.287	2.387
	MIN	292.632	297.773	2.440

DS3		AIC	BIC	MSE
EXP	MVF	491.258	494.915	1.962
	MAX	488.770	494.256	2.064
RAY	MVF	564.395	568.052	3.670
	MAX	488.548	494.034	2.008
WEB	MVF	489.153	494.639	2.047
	MAX	483.633	490.947	2.138
TSE	MVF	512.326	515.983	2.812
	MAX	488.652	494.138	2.062
	MIN	484.915	490.401	6.374

DS4		AIC	BIC	MSE
EXP	MVF	345.204	349.785	0.813
	MAX	338.564	345.435	0.997
RAY	MVF	396.936	401.516	2.930
	MAX	342.254	349.125	1.036
WEB	MVF	339.840	346.711	0.972
	MAX	335.942	345.104	0.872
TSE	MVF	353.591	358.172	1.874
	MAX	338.733	345.605	0.996
	MIN	335.362	342.233	0.908

that the software fault-detection time obeys $F_{\max}(t)$ or $F_{\min}(t)$, from the similar discussion to Section 2. Then, we have

$$\Pr\{N(t) = x\} = \frac{\{\omega F_{\max}(t)\}^x}{x!} e^{-\omega F_{\max}(t)}, \tag{2}$$

and

$$\Pr\{N(t) = x\} = \frac{\{\omega F_{\min}(t)\}^x}{x!} e^{-\omega F_{\min}(t)}. \tag{3}$$

In this paper we call the above models the EVDmax-NHPP and EVDmin-NHPP models with the mean value function $\Lambda_2(t) = \omega F_{\max}(t)$ and $\Lambda_3(t) = \omega F_{\min}(t)$, respectively. Table 1 summarizes the NHPP-based SRMs with different software fault-detection time distributions.

4 Numerical Study

4.1 Goodness-of-fit Test

In the numerical examples, we use 4 real project data sets [7] and compare the EVD-NHPP models with their associated existing NHPPs to 4 underlying distributions (EXP, RAY, WEB, TSE). The data used here are DS1 through DS4, and consist of 133, 351, 266 and 367 fault count data, which are all the group data (the number of software faults detected per each testing date). We estimate model parameters by means of the ML estimation, and calculate the information

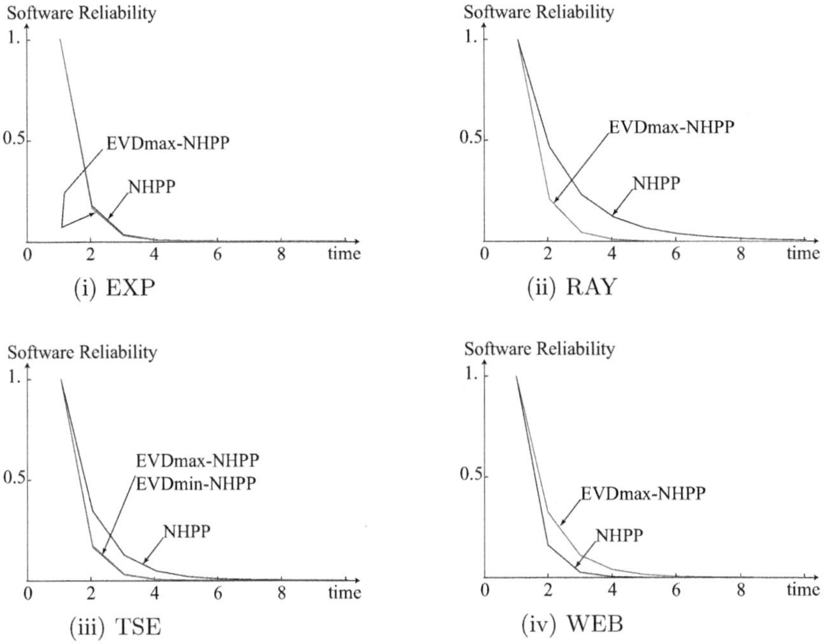

Fig. 2. Plotting software reliability function.

criteria; AIC and BIC as well as MSE. In addition to the model selection based on the information criteria, we take place the Kolmogorov-Smirnov (K-S) test with two significance levels (5% and 1%). If the K-S test was accepted, it means that the SRM assumed fits to the underlying data. Hence, for the accepted data sets through the K-S test, we compare AIC, BIC and MSE, and select the best SRM based on them.

Table 2 presents the goodness-of-fit results for all the data sets. Let MVF, MAX and MIN denote the SRM with mean value function $\omega F(t)$, $\omega F_{\max}(t)$ and $\omega F_{\min}(t)$, respectively. Note that in EXP, RAY and WEB, MIN essentially shows the same value with that of MVF. This is due to the fact that the model parameter n of MIN is absorbed by multipling it to the model parameter β. Therefore we omit the results of MIN when underlying distributions are assumed as EXP, RAY and WEB in the following tables. First, we compare MVF and MAX with EXP, RAY and WEB. Since MVF is completely involved in MIN, it is obvious that the EVD-NHPP model is much more appropriate than the usual one. Moreover, MAX could still fit to the software fault data better than MVF in DS2, DS3 and DS4. Next, when TSE is assumed, the EVD-NHPP model could minimize AICs/BICs as well as MSE in almost all cases except DS2. On K-S test, all EVD-NHPP models could be accept with significant level 5% and 1%. However, when the usual NHPP models are assumed, the K-S test could not accept MVF with EXP in DS3. Throughout the comparative study performed here, it can be concluded that the EVD-NHPP models can provide the satisfactory goodness-of-fit performance to the real software fault data.

We evaluate the quantitative software reliability, which is the probability that the software system does not fail during a specified time interval after release. Let t_n be the nth testing day. Suppose that the software test terminates at time t_n and the product is released at the same time to the user or market. Then, the software reliability for the operational period $[t_n, t_n + x)$ is defined by

$$R(x \mid t_n) = \exp\{-[\Lambda_1(t_n + x) - \Lambda_1(t_n)]\}, \tag{4}$$

where the reliability for EVD-NHPP models is derived by replacing $\Lambda_1(\cdot)$ with $\Lambda_2(\cdot)$ or $\Lambda_3(\cdot)$. Figure 2 shows the behavior of software reliability function with DS1. The EVD-NHPP models tend to under-estimate the usual NHPP-based SRMs except in the case where WEB is assumed. In other words, our NHPP-based SRMs provide pessimistic prediction in assessing the software reliability. Actually this property would be acceptable for practitioners, because the software reliability should be estimated smaller from the safety point of view in practice. As an empirical result throughout the numerical illustrations, we can conclude that our new SRMs based on the extreme value distributions outperform the existing NHPP-based SRMs in many data sets in terms of goodness-of-fit tests.

4.2 Prediction Analysis

Finally, we examine the prediction performance of the EVD-NHPP-based SRMs, where two prediction measures are used: predictive log likelihood (PLL) and predictive least square error (PLS). The PLL is defined as the logarithm of likelihood function with future data at an observation point, and the PLS is the residual sum of errors between the mean value function and the future data from an observation point.

Table 3 presents the prediction result at each observation point, 50%, 75% and 90% of a whole data and calculate the PLL and PLS for both NHPP-based SRMs with the same underlying fault-detection time distribution. In the 50% observation, it is checked that the EVD-NHPPs provide the larger PLL and the smaller PLS than the usual NHPPs in all data sets. Similar to this case, in 75% (90%) points, the EVD-NHPPs with TSE tend to outperform the usual NHPPs in most cases. Especially, our new model with the extreme distributions provides the best prediction performance in DS4 in spite of their observation points. Another advantage of the EVD-NHPP-based SRMs over the usual ones is that they provide considerably better prediction performance in the 50% observation point. This implies that our models are much helpful in the ealier period of the testing phase. In the long history of software reliability engineering it has been known that there was no uniquely best SRM which could be fitted to all the software failure data. In other words, the software reliability research suggested that the SRM used for analysis strongly depends on the kind of software fault data. In that sense, we can recommend that the EVD-NHPP based SRMs with the representative fault-detection time distributions should be applied at the same time when the usual NHPP-based SRMs are tried.

Table 3. Prediction performance

DS1		50%		75%		90%	
		PLL	PLSE	PLL	PLSE	PLL	PLSE
EXP	MVF	-138.071	1.050	-136.067	2.492	-139.528	2.550
	MAX	-137.095	0.762	-136.319	2.342	-139.050	2.366
RAY	MVF	-191.241	4.721	-151.081	5.090	-135.585	0.630
	MAX	-137.079	0.761	-136.312	2.350	-138.978	2.338
WEB	MVF	-137.095	0.762	-136.319	2.342	-139.050	2.366
	MAX	-137.095	0.762	-136.319	2.342	-139.050	2.366
TSE	MVF	-154.378	3.807	-141.994	4.330	-136.143	1.053
	MAX	-137.195	0.780	-136.312	2.336	-139.003	2.348
	MIN	-137.572	0.913	-136.222	2.099	-139.285	2.459
DS2		50%		75%		90%	
		PLL	PLSE	PLL	PLSE	PLL	PLSE
EXP	MVF	-419.714	20.393	-391.755	11.054	-367.970	6.206
	MAX	-421.675	21.476	-371.647	6.253	-360.826	3.806
RAY	MVF	-319.908	5.919	-358.796	1.193	-353.871	0.715
	MAX	-451.154	25.671	-359.925	2.709	-355.979	1.945
WEB	MVF	-428.378	22.471	-365.780	4.661	-357.948	2.755
	MAX	-418.744	20.725	-357.636	1.442	-354.980	1.465
TSE	MVF	-891.195	84.668	-361.419	3.116	-357.690	2.654
	MAX	-418.157	20.967	-370.325	5.914	-360.148	3.566
	MIN	-786.771	72.280	-375.783	7.301	-361.415	4.011
DS3		50%		75%		90%	
		PLL	PLSE	PLL	PLSE	PLL	PLSE
EXP	MVF	-265.067	1.988	-296.335	8.224	-267.243	1.333
	MAX	-262.252	3.872	-296.018	8.152	-266.331	0.914
RAY	MVF	-382.043	11.352	-273.005	0.841	-268.347	2.733
	MAX	-278.604	4.870	-303.902	9.916	-265.536	1.013
WEB	MVF	-262.041	2.745	-296.747	8.316	-266.264	0.898
	MAX	-266.216	5.055	-292.191	7.172	-267.180	1.256
TSE	MVF	-549.440	46.197	-274.752	2.081	-265.849	1.698
	MAX	-261.851	3.584	-296.274	8.213	-266.255	0.895
	MIN	-295.056	9.421	-333.843	16.389	-291.416	11.420
DS4		50%		75%		90%	
		PLL	PLSE	PLL	PLSE	PLL	PLSE
EXP	MVF	-272.217	1.598	-322.470	1.331	-346.961	0.370
	MAX	-400.406	12.185	-323.487	2.399	-347.297	1.491
RAY	MVF	-799.785	15.810	-363.309	7.432	-356.112	4.489
	MAX	-618.482	14.622	-323.655	2.315	-347.414	1.613
WEB	MVF	-516.521	13.837	-323.093	2.154	-347.244	1.427
	MAX	-375.329	11.530	-321.947	1.358	-346.963	0.943
TSE	MVF	-403.711	12.169	-334.324	5.081	-350.246	3.162
	MAX	-416.498	12.505	-323.463	2.377	-347.297	1.490
	MIN	-409.493	12.313	-322.243	1.635	-347.042	1.122

5 Conclusion

In this paper we have proposed a novel modeling framework for the NHPP-based SRMs by using the extreme value distribution of fault-detection time. In the numerical examples with 4 real software fault data we have compared our new NHPP-based SRMs with the existing ones. The numerical results have shown that the goodness-of-fit and prediction performance for the new SRMs were rather stable and could sometimes outperform the existing SRMs.

In the past literature, considerable attentions have been paid to select the fault-detection time distribution in the mean value function. Although we have just treated 4 types of EVD-NHPP models in this paper, of course, the other types of distribution can be applied to build the EVD-NHPP models. In future, we will study the other types of EVD-NHPP model with more flexible distributions such as Hyper-Erlang distribution, and investigate their applicability to the actual software reliability evaluation.

References

1. Akaike, H.: A new look at the statistical model identification. IEEE Trans. Autom. Contr. AC-19, 716–723 (1974)
2. Assaf, A.: Extreme observations and risk assessment in the equity markets of MENA region: Tail measures and Value-at-Risk. International Review of Financial Analysis 18, 109–116 (2009)
3. Escalante-Sandoval, C.: Application of Bivariate Extreme Value Distribution to Flood Frequency Analysis: A Case Study of Northwestern Mexico. Natural Hazards 42(1), 37–46 (2007)
4. Goel, A.L., Okumoto, K.: Time-dependent error-detection rate model for software reliability and other performance measures. IEEE Trans. on Reliab. R-28, 206–211 (1979)
5. Goel, A.L.: Software reliability models: assumptions, limitations and applicability. IEEE Trans. on Software Eng. SE-11, 1411–1423 (1985)
6. Langberg, N., Singpurwalla, N.D.: Unification of some software reliability models. SIAM J. Sci. Comput. 6, 781–790 (1985)
7. Lyu, M.R.: Handbook of Software Reliability Engineering. McGraw-Hill, New York (1996)
8. Musa, J.D., Iannino, A., Okumoto, K.: Software Reliability, Measurement, Prediction, Application. McGraw-Hill, New York (1987)
9. Pham, H.: Software Reliability. Springer, Singapore (2000)
10. Schwarz, G.: Estimating the dimension of a model. Ann. Statist. 6, 461–464 (1978)
11. Xiao, X., Dohi, T.: On equilibrium distribution properties in software reliability modeling. In: Proceedings of 4th International Conference on Availability, Reliability and Security (ARES 2009), pp. 158–165. IEEE CSP (2009)
12. Xie, M.: Software Reliability Modelling. World Scientific, Singapore (1999)
13. Yamada, S., Ohba, M., Osaki, S.: S-shaped reliability growth modeling for software error detection. IEEE Trans. on Reliab. R-32, 475–478 (1983)

Program Conversion for Detecting Data Races in Concurrent Interrupt Handlers*

Byoung-Kwi Lee[1], Mun-Hye Kang[1], Kyoung Choon Park[2], Jin Seob Yi[3], Sang Woo Yang[3], and Yong-Kee Jun[1,**]

[1] Department of Informatics, Gyeongsang National University, Jinju 660-701, The Republic of Korea
{lbk1116,kmh,jun}@gnu.ac.kr

[2] Aero Master Corporation, 668-1 Bangji-ri, Sanam-myeon, Sacheon-si, Gyeongsangnam-do, Korea
gilsion@amc21.co.kr

[3] Korea Aerospace Industriers, LTD., 802 Yucheon-ri, Sanam-myeon, Sacheon-si, Gyeongsangnam-do, Korea
{avionics,sangyang}@koreaaero.com

Abstract. Data races are one of the most notorious concurrency bugs in explicitly shared-memory programs including concurrent interrupt handlers, because these bugs are hard to reproduce and lead to unintended nondeterministic executions of the program. The previous tool for detecting races in concurrent interrupt handlers converts each original handler into a corresponding thread to use existing techniques that detect races in multi-threaded programs. Unfortunately, this tool reports too many false positives, because it uses a static technique for detecting races. This paper presents a program conversion tool that translates the program to be debugged into a semantically equivalent multi-threaded program considering real-time scheduling policies and interrupt priorities of processor. And then, we detect races in the converted programs using a dynamic tool which detects races in multi-threaded programs. To evaluate this tool, we used two flight control programs for unmanned aerial vehicle. The previous approach reported two and three false positives in these programs, respectively, while our approach did not report any false positive.

Keywords: Races, Concurrent Interrupt Handler, Threads, Embedded Software, Dynamic Analysis.

* This research was performed as a part of R&D program Air-BEST (Airborne Embedded System and Technology) funded by MKE (Ministry of Knowledge and Economy). This research was financially supported by the Ministry of Education, Science Technology (MEST) and National Research Foundation of Korea (NRF) through the Human Resource Training Project for Regional Innovation.

** Corresponding author: In Gyeongsang National University, he is also involved in the Research Institute of Computer and Information Communication (RICIC) and GNU Engineering Research Institute (ERI).

T.-h. Kim et al. (Eds.): ASEA/DRBC/EL 2011, CCIS 257, pp. 407–415, 2011.

1 Introduction

Data races [10] are one of the most notorious concurrency bugs in explicitly shared-memory concurrent programs, because these bugs are hard to reproduce and lead to unintended non-deterministic executions of the program. A data race is a pair of concurrent accesses to a shared variable which include at least one write access without appropriate synchronization. Since these races lead to unintended non-deterministic executions of the program, it is important to detect the races for effective debugging. These races may also occur in embedded software which often includes concurrent interrupt handlers. A previous program conversion tool [14] for detecting data races in concurrent interrupt handlers converts the program into a semantically equivalent multi-threaded program so that an existing thread verification tool can be used to find the races in the original program using static race detection. Unfortunately, this technique reports too many false positives without any false negative, because it uses a static technique.

This paper presents a novel conversion tool that converts an original program with concurrent interrupt handlers into a semantically equivalent POSIX threads [3] considering real-time scheduling policies and interrupt priorities of processor. And then, we detect races in the converted programs using a dynamic detection tool [1,6], called Helgrind+, developed for multi-threaded programs. Helgrind+ is an extension of the Helgrind tool which is a Valgrind tool [17] to detect synchronization errors in C, C++, and Fortran programs that use the POSIX threads. We empirically compared our approach with the previous one using two flight control programs of unmanned aerial vehicle (UAV). The previous approach reports two and three false positives in each program, respectively, while our approach does not report any false positive with still more false negatives than the previous static approach.

Section 2 introduces concurrent interrupt handlers and explains previous techniques for detecting races in multi-threaded programs. Section 3 presents our conversion tool that converts each concurrent interrupt handler into a semantically equivalent POSIX thread. Section 4 empirically shows our approach is practical with two flight control programs of UAV. The final section concludes our argument.

2 Background

An interrupt [14] is a hardware mechanism used to inform the CPU that an asynchronous event has occurred. When an interrupt is recognized, the CPU saves part or all of its context and jumps to a special subroutine called an *interrupt handler*. Microprocessors allow interrupts to be ignored or recognized through the use of two special machine instructions: *disable interrupt, or enable interrupt*, respectively. In a real-time environment, every period of interrupt disabling should be as shortly as possible. Interrupt disabling may affect interrupt processing to be delayed or ignored, and then cause such interrupts to be missed. Most processors allow interrupts to be nested.

The structure of common embedded software has two major components as shown in Figure 1: concurrent interrupt handlers called *foreground routines* [7], and the main routine, called the background routine, which is one infinite loop. These concurrent interrupt handlers may also involve data races. Data races [10] occur when two parallel threads access a shared memory location without proper inter-thread coordination, and at least one of these accesses is a write. Since these races lead to unintended non-deterministic executions of the program, it is important to detect the races for effective debugging.

The previous tool [14] for detecting races in concurrent interrupt handlers converts each handler into a corresponding thread to use existing techniques that detect races in multi-threaded program. Such the techniques can be classified into static and dynamic techniques. Static analysis [9,12,13] consider the entire program and warn about potential races in all possible execution orders. However, these techniques tend to make conservative assumptions that lead to a large number of false positives. Therefore, the previous approach reports too many false positives without any false negative, because it uses a static technique for detecting races. On the other hand, dynamic techniques [1,6,16] report still less false positives than static techniques, but their coverage is limited to the paths and thread interleaving explored at runtime. In practice, the coverage of dynamic techniques can be increased by running more tests. In addition, dynamic data races detectors are severely limited by their runtime overhead.

There are two different methods for dynamic race detection in multi-threaded programs: post-mortem and on-the-fly methods. A post-mortem technique records events that occur during a program execution, and then analyzes or

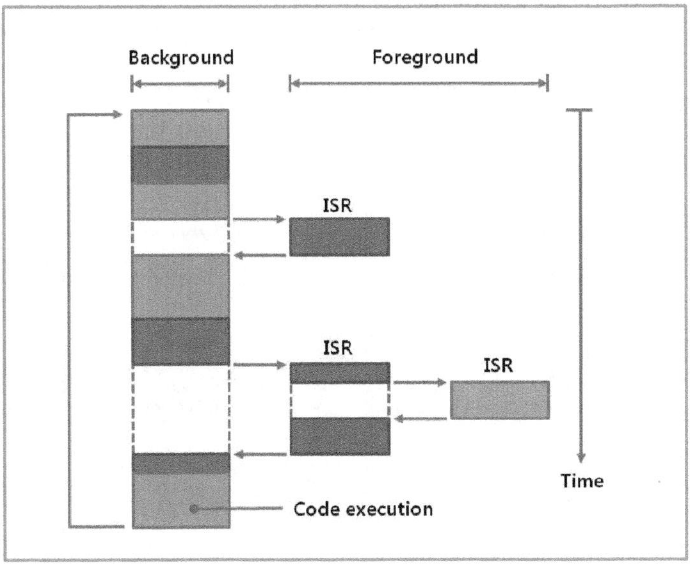

Fig. 1. A Dynamic Structure of Embedded Software

replays them after the program execution. An on-the-fly technique records and analyzes information during a program execution. This technique is based on *lockset* [4,6,15] or *happens-before algorithm* [2,4,11]. A lockset algorithm checks if two threads accessing a shared memory location hold a common lock. This algorithm is practically efficient, while it reports many false positives. A happens-before algorithm is based on Lamport's happens-before relation [8]. This algorithm may report still fewer false positives, while it incurs huge overhead in performance. Therefore, recent race detectors tend to combine happens-before techniques with lockset based ones to obtain the advantages of both algorithms.

3 A Program Conversion Tool

This paper presents a novel tool that converts an original program with concurrent interrupt handlers into the corresponding set of semantically equivalent POSIX thread [3] considering real-time scheduling policies and interrupt priorities of processor. Therefore, we detect the races in the converted programs using a dynamic detection tool for multi-treaded programs to reduce false positives. The dynamic tool is Helgrind+ that is an extension of Helgrind which combines the happens-before algorithm and the Lockset algorithm. Helgrind is a Valgrind tool [17] for detecting races in C, C++ and Fortran programs that use the POSIX threads. It uses an Eraser algorithm [15] which is improved based on the happens-before algorithm of VisualThreads [5] in order to reduce false positives.

Figure 2 shows the design of our tool which consists of three steps: a source scanner, a foreground conversion, and a background conversion. The original source code is scanned by source scanner module. The foreground one converts every interrupt handler into a POSIX thread using two modules: an interrupt handler exploration, and function pointer conversion. The interrupt handler exploration module explores the interrupt handlers using the *interrupt vector table*

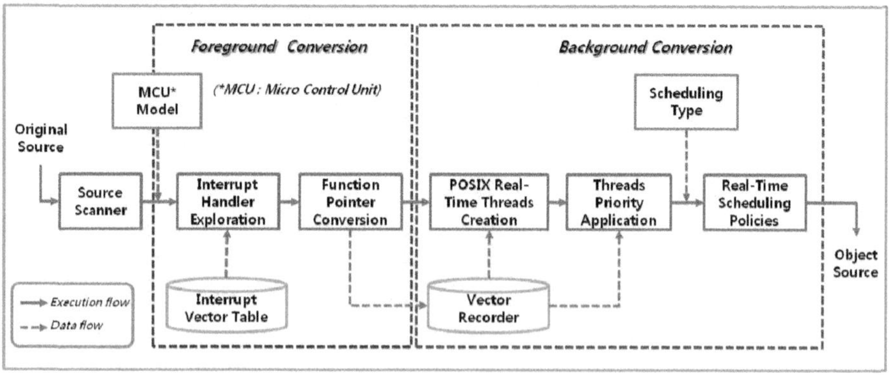

Fig. 2. Design of Program Conversion Tool

that defines interrupt priorities of processor and function names used at conversion time. The function pointer conversion converts the explored interrupt handlers into the corresponding function pointers, and records the results into the interrupt handler table. These results are used as the parameters to call `pthread_create()` which creates POSIX threads for concurrent interrupt handlers. To handle interrupts that occur asynchronously, the each handler function is converted to be included into an infinite loop.

The background conversion consists of three modules to apply priorities and real-time scheduling: POSIX thread creation, thread priority application, and real-time scheduling policies. Interrupts are activated and deactivated using `sei()` and `cil()` functions, respectively, in the processor developed by ATmel which provides the WinAVR compiler. Therefore, the POSIX thread creation module converts every code which calls `sei()` function into one `pthread_create()` calling. We use only two of four parameters needed in the function: the thread identifier and the function that will automatically run at the end of the thread creation process using the information stored in the interrupt handler table. Also, the module deletes or annotates every code that calls the `cil()` function, because the function is of no use in POSIX threads. To execute the converted program under the same condition with that of the original source code, we apply the thread priorities and real-time scheduling in the last two steps of conversion. The thread priority application module changes attributes of threads using the *interrupt handler table*. The real-time scheduling module sets its policies. We use the PHREAD_EXPLICIT_SCHED option provided in POSIX real-time threads to change the policy. A list of optional policies is as follows.

(1) The `SCHED_FIFO` option allows a thread to run until another thread becomes ready with a higher priority, or until it blocks voluntarily. When a thread with this option becomes ready, it begins executing immediately unless a thread with equal or higher priority is already executing.
(2) The `SCHED_RR` option is much the same as SCHED_FIFO policy except that the running thread will be preempted so that the ready thread can be executed, if a thread is ready with SCHED_RR policy executes for more than a fixed period of the time slice interval without blocking, and another

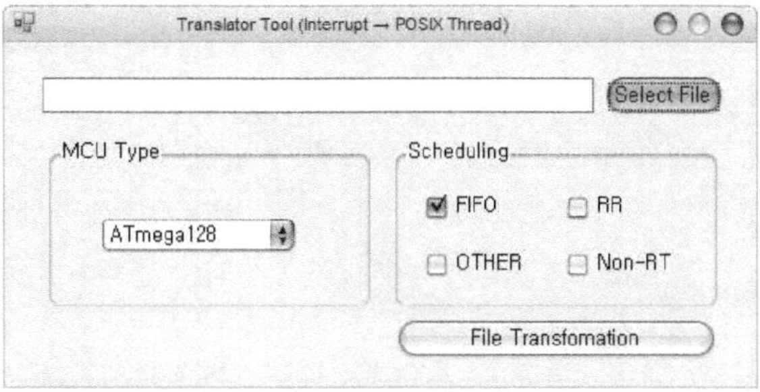

Fig. 3. User Interface of Program Conversion Tool

thread with SCHED_RR or SCHED_FIFO policy and the same priority. When threads with SCHED_FIFO or SCHED_RR policy wait on a condition variable or wait to lock a mutex, they will be awakened in priority order.

(3) The `SCHED_OTHER` option may be an alias for SCHED_FIFO, or it may be SCHED_RR, or it may be something entirely different. The real problem with this ambiguity is not that we do not know what SCHED_OTHER does, but that we have no way of knowing what scheduling parameters it might require.

4 Experimentation

Figure 3 shows the user interface of our tool that has been implemented in the C# language under the Windows operating system. Using the interface, the user selects the program to be debugged, the processor type, and the real-time scheduling policy to convert the program into a POSIX thread-based program.

To evaluate the accuracy of our tool, we use two programs with concurrent interrupt handlers for UAV flight control. These programs are parts of a UAV ground control station. The first program is the Knob Assembly Control (KAC) that is a firmware embedded into the micro controller unit of Knob assembly to execute autopilot commands by communicating with a real-time computer of the ground control station. KAC controls the altitude, the speed, the roll/heading and the azimuth angles of an aircraft. The part shown in dotted line in Figure 4 shows a Knob assembly. If the KAC gets commands to control aircraft by real-time computer, it outputs those values have been input by user using the Knob dials to the dot matrixes and the real-time computer. A micro controller unit communicates with a dot matrix using the Inter Integrated Circuit (I^2C) or the Two-wire Serial Interface (TWI), and communicates with the real-time computer using RS-232C. Commands or some feedback on the commands are transmitted

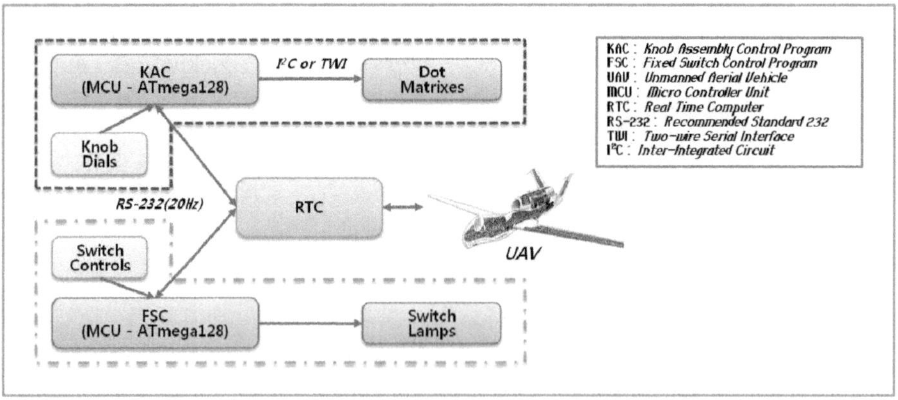

Fig. 4. Structure of KAC/FSC Program

on a cycle, 20Hz, by a timer interrupt and a serial communication interrupt. The second program is the Fixed Switch Control (FSC) that is also a firmware embedded in the micro controller unit of the Fixed Switch to control a parafoil or an engine for collecting an aircraft without runaway by communicating with the real-time computer. The part shown in dashed or dotted-line in Figure 4 represents the Fixed Switch. This program passes commands to the real-time computer and receives feedback from the real-time computer on a cycle. We assume that these programs are executed according to the scenarios denoted in Figure 5.

We translated these programs into thread-based programs using our tool implemented in C# language. We detect races in those programs using Helgrind+. We have performed experiments on Intel Pentium 4 with 2GB of RAM under Fedora 12 operating system. To empirically compare the accuracy, we installed Helgrind+ for dynamic race detection and Locksmith [13,14] for static race detection. We used the MSM-short (Memory State Machine for short-running application) option [1] provided in Helgrind+. This option is suitable for unit testing of program development or debugging of program with short execution time. We experimented for the race detection five times with each scheduling policy, because the result of race detection with Helgrind+ is affected by the real-time scheduling policy.

Figure 6 shows the result of race detection with Helgrind+ and Locksmith. The third and the fourth columns of Figure 6 show the number of races detected by Locksmith and Helgrind+, respectively. The fourth column is divided into four subcolumns according to the real-time scheduling policies: FIFO, RR, OTHER, and non-real time. In the KAC program, Locksmith detected one race toward each of ten shared variables. By source code analysis, we found that

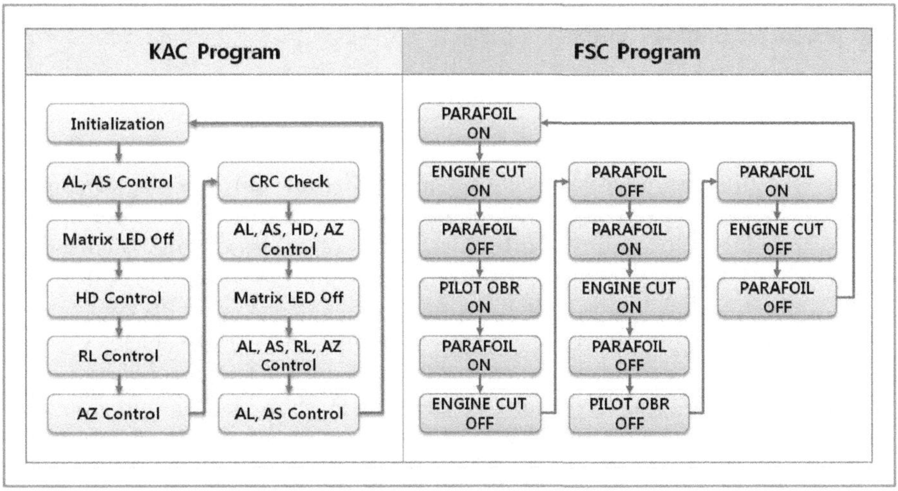

Fig. 5. Execution Scenario for Experimentation

Program	Result of Detection	Static Tool (Locksmith)	Dynamic Tool (Helgrind+)			
			FIFO	RR	OTHER	Non-RealTime
KAC	True Positives	8	3	1	3	6
	false positives	2	0	0	0	0
	false negatives	0	5	7	5	2
FSC	True Positives	5	2	2	3	3
	false positives	3	0	0	0	0
	false negatives	0	3	3	2	2

Fig. 6. Result of Data Race Detection

races detected toward two shared variables of them are false positives, because the source code involved in the races are executed once in a program execution to allocate memory before activating interrupt handlers. On the other hand, Helgrind+ detects one race toward each one of three, one, and three shared variables with FIFO, RR and OTHER, real-time scheduling, respectively. Also, the tool detects one race toward each one of six shared variables without any scheduling policy. Helgrind+ does not report a false positive. Thus, the results are different according to scheduling policies. The reason is that partial order executions of program depend on scheduling policies. In the FSC program, the two tools have also produced similar results.

5 Conclusion

This paper presents a program conversion tool that converts the concurrent interrupt handlers into semantically equivalent POSIX threads considering real-time scheduling policies and interrupt priorities of processor, and then detects the races in the converted programs using a dynamic detection tool, called Helgrind+, developed for multi-threaded programs.

By using two flight control programs of unmanned aerial vehicle, we were able to identify the existence of races in the embedded software with concurrent interrupt handlers. And the results of experiment show that the previous tool reports two and three false positives without any false negative in each software, while our tool does not report any false positive. However, our tool reports still more false negatives than the previous tool. There still remains more work which include additional effort to effectively improve the portability without among various hardware.

References

1. Jannesari, A., Bao, K., Pankratius, V., Tichy, W.F.: Helgrind+: An efficient dynamic race detector. In: Proceedings of the 2009 IEEE International Symposium on Parallel Distributed Processing, pp. 1–13. IEEE Computer Society Press, Washington, DC, USA (2009)
2. Banerjee, U., Bliss, B., Ma, Z., Petersen, P.: A theory of data race detection. In: Proceedings of the 2006 Workshop on Parallel and Distributed Systems: Testing and Debugging, PADTAD 2006, pp. 69–78. ACM, New York (2006)
3. Butenhof, D.R.: Programming with posix threads. Addison-Wesley Professional (1997)
4. Dinning, A., Schonberg, E.: Detecting access anomalies in programs with critical sections. In: Proceedings of the 1991 ACM/ONR Workshop on Parallel and Distributed Debugging, PADD 1991, pp. 85–96. ACM, New York (1991)
5. Edelstein, O., Farchi, E., Nir, Y., Ratsaby, G., Ur, S.: Multithreaded java program test generation. In: Proceedings of the 2001 Joint ACM-ISCOPE Conference on Java Grande, JGI 2001. ACM, New York (2001)
6. Jannesari, A., Tichy, W.F.: On-the-fly race detection in multi-threaded programs. In: Proceedings of the 6th Workshop on Parallel and Distributed Systems: Testing, Analysis, and Debugging, PADTAD, pp. 6:1–6:10. ACM, New York (2008)
7. Labrosse, J.J.: Microc/os-ii the real-time kernel, 2nd edn., pp. 32–66. CMP Books (2002)
8. Lamport, L.: Time, clocks, and the ordering of events in a distributed system. Communications of ACM, 558–565 (1978)
9. Le, W., Yang, J., Soffa, M.L., Whitehouse, K.: Lazy preemption to enable path-based analysis of interrupt-driven code. In: Proceeding of the 2nd Workshop on Software Engineering for Sensor Network Applications, SESENA 2011, pp. 43–48. ACM, New York (2011)
10. Netzer, R.H.B., Miller, B.P.: What are race conditions?: Some issues and formalizations. ACM Lett. Program. Lang. Syst. 1, 74–88 (1992)
11. Park, S.H., Park, M.Y., Jun, Y.K.: A Comparison of Scalable Labeling Schemes for Detecting Races in OpenMP Programs. In: Eigenmann, R., Voss, M.J. (eds.) WOMPAT 2001. LNCS, vol. 2104, pp. 68–80. Springer, Heidelberg (2001)
12. Pessanha, V., Dias, R.J., Lourenço, J.A.M., Farchi, E., Sousa, D.: Practical verification of high-level dataraces in transactional memory programs. In: Proceedings of the Workshop on Parallel and Distributed Systems: Testing, Analysis, and Debugging, PADTAD 2011, pp. 26–34. ACM, New York (2011)
13. Pratikakis, P., Foster, J.S., Hicks, M.: Locksmith: context-sensitive correlation analysis for race detection. SIGPLAN Not. 41, 320–331 (2006)
14. Regehr, J., Cooprider, N.: Interrupt verification via thread verification. Electron. Notes Theor. Comput. Sci. 174, 139–150 (2007)
15. Savage, S., Burrows, M., Nelson, G., Sobalvarro, P., Anderson, T.: Eraser: a dynamic data race detector for multithreaded programs. ACM Trans. Comput. Syst. 15, 391–411 (1997)
16. Tahara, T., Gondow, K., Ohsuga, S.: Dracula: Detector of data races in signals handlers. In: Asia-Pacific Software Engineering Conference, pp. 17–24 (2008)
17. Valgrind-project: Helgrind: a data-race detector (2007)

Implementation of an Integrated Test Bed for Avionics System Development

Hyeon-Gab Shin[1], Myeong-Chul Park[2], Jung-Soo Jun[1], Yong-Ho Moon[1], and Seok-Wun Ha[1,*]

[1] ERI, Dept. of Informatics, Gyeongsang National University, 900 GajwaDong, Jinju 660-701, Republic of Korea
hkshin2@gmail.com, {jjs,moon5,swha}@gnu.ac.kr
[2] Dept. Of Biomedical Electronics, Songho College, NamsanRi, HyeongseongEup, HoengseongGun 225-704, Republic of Korea
africa@songho.ac.kr

Abstract. An integrated test environment is required to test functions for development of avionics systems. In this paper we introduce an integrated test bed system which utilizes variety functions of the commercial flight simulator X-Plane and the model-based programming language LabView. The test system generates the flight data from X-Plane which linked a running gear and input the data to a display function as 3D map using Google Earth. Our proposed system could drive the flight operation in real time using generated flight data. We could trace the flying route of the simulated data based on the visualized results.

Keywords: Flight simulator, integrated test bed, manipulation system, data link, X-Plane, LabView.

1 Introduction

In recent the avionics system that is mounted on a variety of aircrafts including UAV have been developed in an integrated form for advancing their mission operation.[1-3] Avionics system is composed of hardware and software parts for aircraft operation and control software of LRUs(Line replaceable Unit), MC(Mission Computer), and FC(Flight Control Computer) can be developed as a unit system, In development of these unit systems, in order to verify communication, data flow, function operation and abnormal inspection and etc. the simulation flight data and the avionics communication interfaces should be ready for system linkage on the ground station.[1] In current UAV development the commercial flight simulator X-Plane is applied as a usage of flight data acquisition and processing for flight control test of the system's software functions.[2-3] And There are some cases that used as a test system of hardware in the loop for software test, a software-based cockpit visualization and a flight path information feeder.[4] The proposed integrated test bed system can earn a user-desired simulation flight data through specific functions of the commercial flight

* Corresponding author.

T.-h. Kim et al. (Eds.): ASEA/DRBC/EL 2011, CCIS 257, pp. 416–423, 2011.

simulator and an external manipulation system and verify the flight operation based on the generated manipulation data on the 3D map.

2 Related Concepts

2.1 Flight Simulator – X-Plane

X-Plane, a tool to acquire the simulation flight data on the test bed system, is a commercial flight simulator earned the FAA authentication and is easy to acquire a similar data with the real flight operation data. This simulator has various kinds of characteristics as follows:[5-6]

- Various types of flight model
- Function extension through plug-in
- FTD(Flight Training Device Level 2) authentication by FAA
- Providing of a variety forms of flight data

In this paper we utilize the above features of X-Plane for flight data acquisition from various aircraft models. Among each unit system there exist a packet middleware (PM) for processing flight data from X-Plane. The packet middleware eliminates head part of the input packet data and discriminates data index and eight values from the read data. Table 1 shows the packet format and a UDP packet is composed header data of 5 bytes and data segment of 36 bytes.

Table 1. Structure of X-Plane UDP packet

"data"	'0' or '1'	index	v0	v1	v2	v3	v4	v5	v6	v7
4	1	4	4	4	4	4	4	4	4	4
Header (5 bytes)		Data Segment (36 bytes)								

2.2 Model Programming - LabView

LabView is a type of graphical programming language and a tool which can develop a system by doing a design based on data processing flow. This tool provides virtual instruments for implementation of various functions such as signal condition processing to be necessary for data acquisition, A/D conversion, timing operation, storage and communication processing for data analysis, data visualization, and reporting [7].

Figure 1 shows a sample of data processing procedure using virtual instruments provided by LabView. In this paper we compose to enable the flight manipulation system to control a joystick input driver and implement the user interface for data acquisition and visualization using LabView.

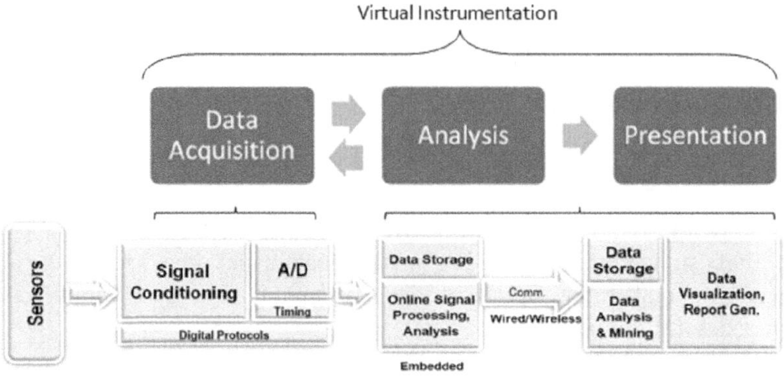

Fig. 1. Data processing procedure using virtual instruments provided by LabView

3 Integrated Test Bed System

3.1 System Structure

In this paper the proposed integrated test bed system is largely composed of flight simulation system (FSS), data link and distribution system (DLDS), flight manipulation system (FMS) and 3D map display system (3DMDS). Figure 2 shows the structure of the proposed integrated test bed system.

In figure 2, FSS generates and outputs the flight data and updates and visualizes the input flight data generated from user manipulation through FMS. DLDS receives the output data from FSS and distributes by UDP protocol. FMS processes the joystick input data and shows the output data from FSS. 3DMDS visualizes the current flight position information on 3D map-Google Earth.

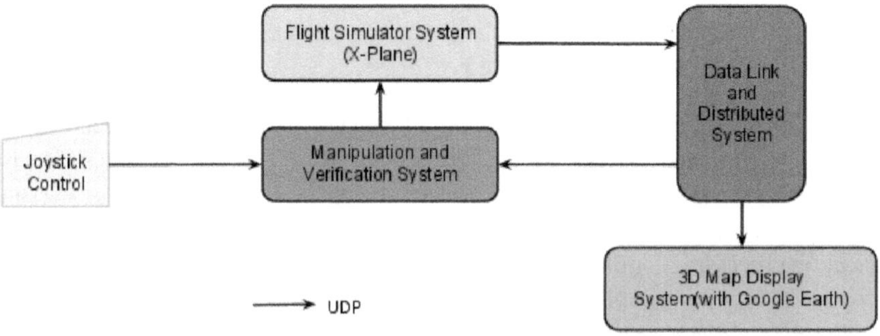

Fig. 2. Block diagram of the proposed integrated test bed system

3.2 Flight Simulation System

FSS is linked with FMS and DLDS as shown in figure 3, and the user data transferred from FMS is updated in a plug-in program and the output data of FSS outputs to DLDS through in/out set-up.

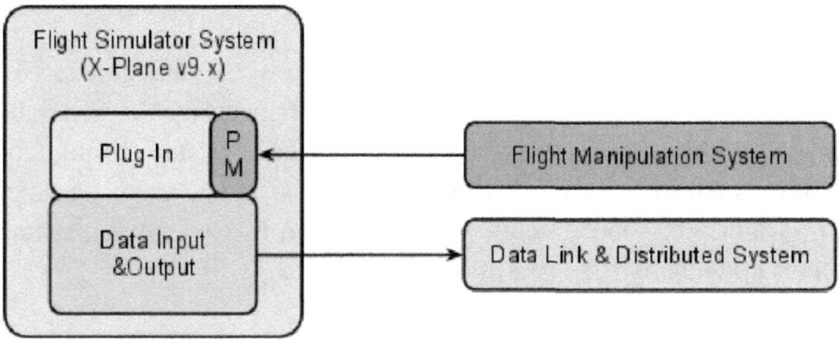

Fig. 3. Input/Output flow diagram of Flight Simulation System

Input data to FSS is processed by plug-in program. FSS has a package middleware (PM) for plug-in with FMS and it discriminates a UDP packet data stored in the UDP buffer to a flight parameter data referencing the packet format, and then it verifies the updating parameter in FSS and updates the corresponding value. And output data from FSS is selected by user-desired from the "Data Input/Output Setting" menu.

In X-Plane flight simulator the input data is processed to a suitable form to the aircraft information and the flight conditions and visualized, and then it is returned to UDP for the selected output data items.

3.3 Data Link and Distribution System

DLDS is linked with FSS, FMS, and 3DMDS, FSS by UDP as figure 4 and it distributes the UDP data to each system.

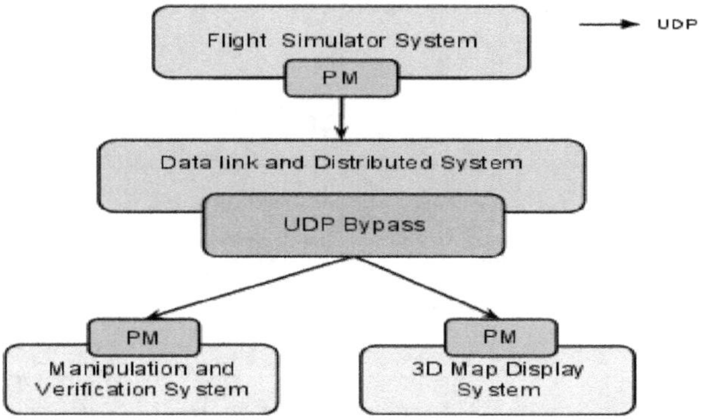

Fig. 4. Data flow diagram between DLDS and the other Systems

In figure 4, DLDS receives the UDP packet transmitted from FSS and then it transfers the received UDP packet to FMS and 3DMDS through UDP bypass task. And the transferred data to FMS and 3DMDS is converted to the parameter discriminated data through PM and used in their internal system.

3.4 Flight Manipulation System

FMS processes the view of data from FSS, the view of data generated by joystick control, and the re-transmission to FSS using multi-tasking. As the data processing diagram of FMS in figure 5, first, through the task for the simulated flight data processing the transferred data from DLDS is classified to each parameter, and the corresponding data is loaded to each parameter, and the avionics instruments are selected and then updates by the current updated values.

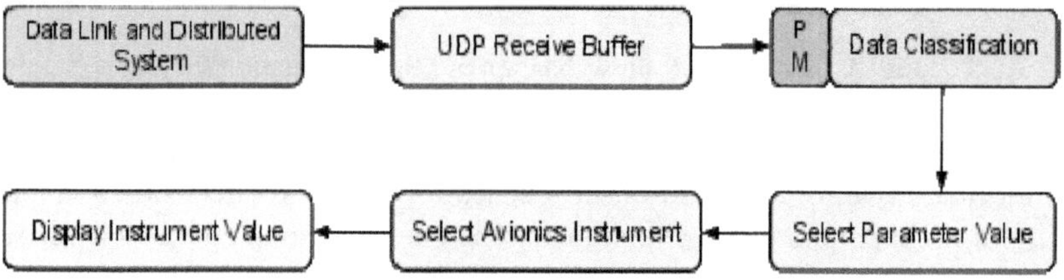

Fig. 5. Data processing diagram of Flight Manipulation System.

Next, in the task for input data processing from joystick device, when the input data from joystick device exists the corresponding data is stored in a buffer, and the data conversion for the display view and transmission to FSS are operated by using current joystick's position information and the button values, and then the converted data is viewed through the joystick indicator in the view screen and transmitted to FSS after a packet generation by UDP packet builder. Above two tasks for FMS operation are composed by multi-tasking environment provided LabView and they are implemented with the user interface. Figure 6 shows block diagram for joystick device input data processing.

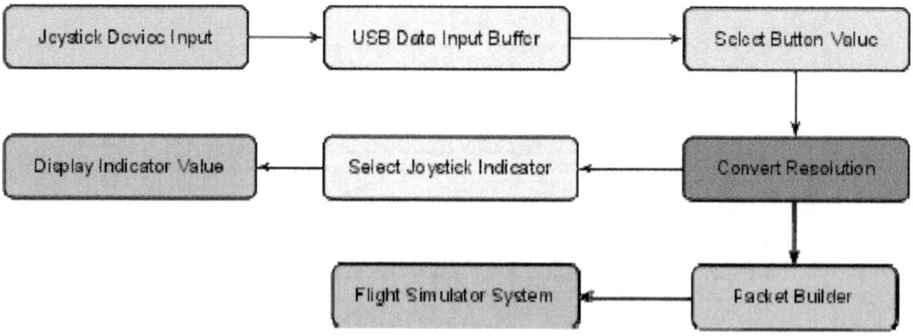

Fig. 6. Block diagram for joystick device input data processing

3.5 3D Map Display System

3DMDS matches the position and path information received from FSS to the corresponding position and path of Google Earth data system, and then displays the linked data by 3D on Google Earth. As figure 7, first for flight data processing 3DMDS receives the UDP packet from DLDS and classifies the flight data parameter through PM. And then for the path planning visualization it makes a KML file as a Google additional function using the path planning data received from FMS and visualizes the data on 3D Google Earth.

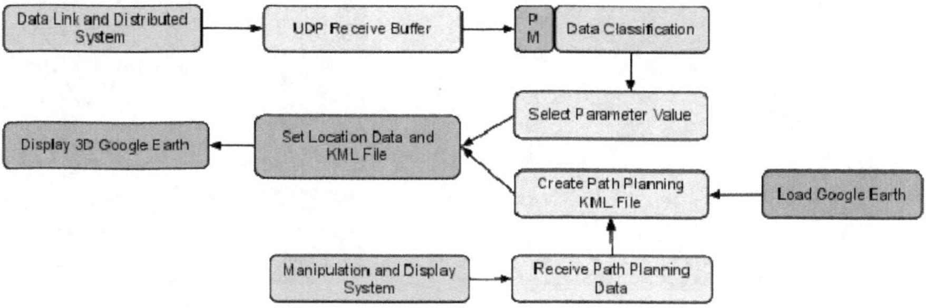

Fig. 7. Data processing diagram of 3D Map Display System

4 Results

The proposed integrated test bed system for avionics system development is composed as figure 8. Using the integrated test bad system implemented on the bases of X-Plane and LabView we tested the operation of the proposed system in real time. On the implemented user interface when the interfaced joystick device is operated the simulated flight data could be generated and utilized to the flight visualization.

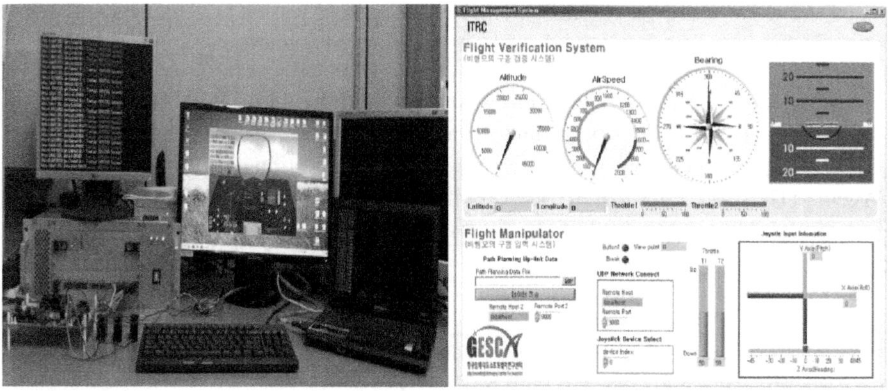

Fig. 8. Overall view of the proposed system and the result view of the implemented user interface

Figure 8 shows the overall view of the proposed integrated test bed for avionics system implementation and the result view of the implemented user interface linked with joystick device. And figure 9 represents the aircraft flight on Google Earth map and the manipulated flight data view.

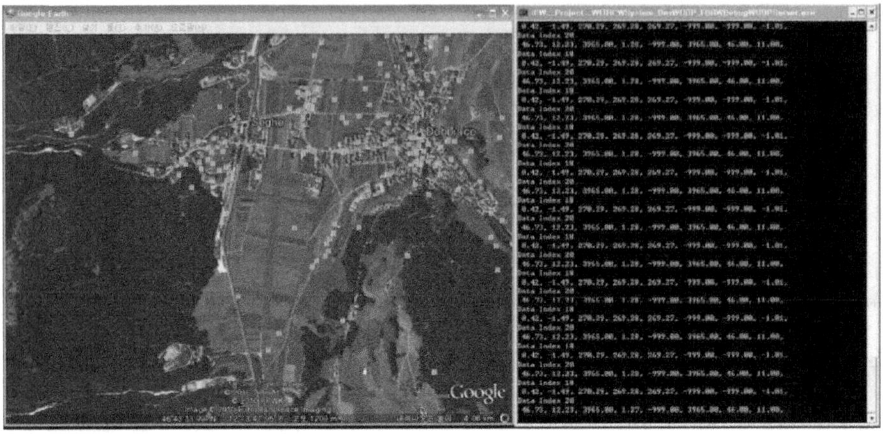

Fig. 9. The aircraft flight on Google Earth and the manipulated flight data view

5 Conclusion

The proposed integrated test bed system for avionics system development is composed as figure 8. Using the integrated test bad system implemented on the bases of X-Plane and LabView we tested the operation of the proposed integrated system in real time. By the manipulation system the selected aircraft was manipulated and controlled about necessary functions by plug-in module. We made certain that the generated simulation flight data could be well operated through 3D map and the manipulated view. In future we would extend this integrated test bed system by add several specific functions for LRU manipulation and external actuations.

Acknowledgement. This research was supported by the MKE (The Ministry of Knowledge Economy), Korea, under the ITRC (Information Technology Research Center) support program supervised by the NIPA (National IT Industry Promotion Agency) (NIPA-2011-C1090-1031-0007)

References

1. Pontzer, A.E., Lower, M.D., Miller, J.R.: Unique aspects of flight testing unmanned aircraft systems. Flight Test Technique Series, vol. 27, pp. 1–78 (2010)
2. Garcia, R., Barnes, L.: Multi-uav simulator utilizing x-plane. J. Intell. Robotics Syst. 57, 393–406 (2010)

3. Ribeiro, L., Oliveira, N.: Uav autopilot controllers test platform using matlab/simulink and x-plane. In: Frontiers in Education Conference (FIE), pp. S2H-1–S2H-6. IEEE (October 2010)
4. Park, M.-C., Ha, S.-W.: The Visualization Tool of the Open-Source Based for Flight Waypoint Tracking. In: Kim, T.-h., Adeli, H., Robles, R.J., Balitanas, M. (eds.) UCMA 2011, Part II. CCIS, vol. 151, pp. 153–161. Springer, Heidelberg (2011)
5. X-Plane Desktop Manual, `http://wiki.x-plane.com/Category:X-Plane_Desktop_Manual`
6. X-Plane SDK, `http://www.xsquawkbox.net/xpsdk/mediawiki/Main_Page`
7. Academic Research Using NI LabVIEW, `http://zone.ni.com/devzone/cda/tut/p/id/7429`

Efficient Thread Labeling for On-the-fly Race Detection of Programs with Nested Parallelism*

Ok-Kyoon Ha and Yong-Kee Jun**

Department of Informatics, Gyeongsang National University,
Jinju 660-701, The Republic of Korea
{jassmin,jun}@gnu.ac.kr

Abstract. It is quite difficult to detect data races in parallel programs, because they may lead to unintended nondeterministic executions of the program. To detect data races during an execution of program that may have nested parallelism, it is important to maintain thread information called label which is used to determine the logical concurrency between threads. Unfortunately, the previous schemes of thread labeling introduce a serious amount of overhead that includes serializing bottleneck to access centralized data structure or depends on the maximum parallelism or the depth of nested parallelism. This paper presents an efficient thread labeling, called *eNR Labeling*, which does not use any centralized data structure and creates thread labels on every thread operation in a constant amount of time and space even in its worst case. Furthermore, this technique allows to determine the logical concurrency between threads in a small amount of time that is proportional only to the depth of nested parallelism. Compared with three state-of-the-arts labeling schemes, our empirical results using OpenMP benchmarks show that eNR labeling reduces both time overhead by 10% and space overhead by more than 90% for on-the-fly race detection.

Keywords: Fork-join programs, nested parallelism, data races, on-the-fly detection, thread labeling, efficiency.

1 Introduction

Data races [4,9,17] in parallel programs is the most notorious class of concurrency bugs that may occur when two parallel threads access a shared memory location without proper inter-thread coordination, and at least one of the accesses is a write. The parallel program may not show the same execution instances with the same input, because execution order of threads is timing-dependent. It is still difficult for programmer to figure out when the program runs into data

* "This research was supported by Basic Science Research Program through the National Research Foundation of Korea(NRF) funded by the Ministry of Education, Science and Technology(2011-0026340)".

** Corresponding author: In Gyeongsang National University, he is also involved in the Research Institute of Computer and Information Communication (RICIC).

T.-h. Kim et al. (Eds.): ASEA/DRBC/EL 2011, CCIS 257, pp. 424–436, 2011.

races, because they may lead to unintended nondeterministic executions of the program.

On-the-fly race detection [7,11,16,19,20,21] dynamically detects data races with still less overhead in storage space than other dynamic techniques, because it removes unnecessary information for race detection during the execution of parallel program. To detect data races during an execution of program that may have nested parallelism, the Lamport's happens-before relation [15] is applied for maintaining thread labels to precisely determine if any pair of parallel accesses is logically concurrent with each other. Previous work [16,20], however, is not efficient in thread labeling, because its overhead includes serializing bottleneck to access centralized data structure or depends on the maximum parallelism or the depth of nested parallelism.

This paper presents an efficient thread labeling, called *eNR Labeling*, which does not use any centralized data structure. On every thread operation, this technique creates thread labels in a constant amount of time and space even in its worst case by inheriting a pointer to their shared component from the parent thread. Furthermore, the technique allows to determine the logical concurrency between threads in a small amount of time that is proportional only to the depth of nested parallelism just by traversing the linked list back through the inherited pointers. Compared with three state-of-the-arts labeling schemes, our empirical results using OpenMP benchmarks show that eNR labeling reduces both time overhead by 10% and space overhead by more than 90% for on-the-fly race detection.

The remainder of this paper is organized as follows. Section 2 explains important concepts and problems on the efficiency of on-the-fly thread labeling. We present our eNR Labeling in section 3 as a solution for the problems and evaluates it empirically in section 4 by comparing existing techniques of labeling with each other. We introduce the related work of thread labeling in section 5 and conclude our argument in the last section.

2 Background

This section introduces the importance of on-the-fly race detection for nested parallelism and defines the efficiency problems of previous thread labeling schemes developed to work in nested parallelism. This problem creates serious overhead in happens-before analysis for on-the-fly race detection.

2.1 On-the-fly Race Detection for Nested Parallelism

Parallel programs often employ a structured fork-join model of threads which can be implemented with loop-level parallelism. Nested parallelism [6,13] is a nestable fork-join model of parallel execution in which a parallel thread can generate a team of parallel threads. The main benefit of nested parallelism is the speedup of program execution which can be derived from Amdal's law:

$$Speedup(\alpha, p_1, H) = \frac{1}{(1-\alpha)/H + \alpha/(p_1 \times H)}$$

where α is the fraction of parallelized regions in the program code, p_i is the number of threads for the level i loop, and H is the maximum size of one thread team for a nested loop. This equation shows that the speedup is increased if H is larger than one [6]. For example, consider a parallel program in which α is 0.8 and the maximum parallelism T $(= \prod_{i=1}^{N} p_i)$ is four, where N is the depth of nested parallelism. In case of a non-nested parallelism where p_1 is four and H is one, the speedup is 2.5 according to the above equation. On the other hand, in case of a nested parallelism where p_1 is two and H is two, the speedup is about 3.3. Note that this law uses H even in the case that the nesting depth is greater than two.

On-the-fly race detection dynamically detects data races with still less overhead in storage space than other dynamic techniques, because it removes unnecessary information for race detection during the execution of parallel program. This technique uses one of the following methods: happens-before analysis, lock-set analysis, and hybrid analysis. The happens-before analysis [7,16,20] on-the-fly reports data races involving the current access and previous accesses maintained in a special kind of data structures. To determine the logical concurrency between two accesses, this technique generates thread labels which represent Lamport's happens-before relation [15]. Lock-set analysis [21] detects data races in the monitored program by checking violations of locking discipline. Compared with the happens-before analysis, this technique reports still more false positives, although it is simple and can be implemented with still less overhead. The hybrid analysis [11,19] tries to combine both two techniques to obtain both accuracy and performance.

2.2 On-the-fly Thread Labeling

Thread labeling for nested parallelism often reduce storage space of creating and maintaining thread information for logical concurrency. Generally, vector clocks [3,7,10] require $O(T)$ size of space for creating and maintaining a thread information, but the size of thread labels designed for nested parallelism is $O(N)$ [7,16,12,2] or $O(\sum_{i=1}^{N} p_i)$ [1]. Any technique to create thread labels for the happens-before analysis can be regarded as one of the following two cases: the *generalized* labelings [1,7] which extend vector clocks for nested parallelism, and the *specialized* labelings [2,12,16,18] which are customized for nested parallelism. The generalized labeling includes Task Recycling (TR) [7] and Clock Trees (CT) [1], and their overhead includes serializing bottleneck to access centralized data structure or depends on the maximum parallelism. The specialized labeling includes English Hebrew (EH) [18], Offset Span (OS) [16], Breadth Depth (BD) [2], and Nest Region (NR) [12]. Their overheads depend on the nesting depth N of fork-join constructs, not on the degree of parallelism because they use only local information of a thread.

Table 1 shows the efficiencies of each thread labeling which supports fork-join programs with nested parallelism. In the table, the most efficient technique for comparing logical concurrency among parallel threads is TR, a generalized technique, but it is most expensive to create and maintain thread labels whose sizes

Table 1. The efficiencies of thread labeling schemes

Techniques		Label Space	Labeling Time Fork/Join	Comparison
Generalized	TR	$O(T)$	$O(T)$	$O(1)$
	CT	$O(P)$	$O(P)$	$O(N)$
Specialized	EH	$O(N)$	$O(N)$	$O(N)$
	OS	$O(N)$	$O(N)$	$O(N)$
	BD	$O(N)$	$O(N)$	$O(N)$
	NR	$O(N)$	$O(N)$	$O(\log_2 N)$
	eNR	$O(1)$	$O(1)$	$O(N)$

depend on T, the maximum parallelism of program executions. Although CT requires a similar amount of comparison overhead to the specialized techniques, it requires a larger overhead for each thread operation depending on P, the sum of all p_i $(= \sum_{i=1}^{N} p_i)$. P is larger than the nesting depth N and less than or equal to T, if every p_i is larger than one. Among the specialized techniques, NR labeling requires the smallest overhead $O(\log_2 N)$ in time to determine the logical concurrency between a pair of two threads. For thread operations, all of the specialized techniques require smaller overheads than those of generalized techniques, which depends on the nesting depth N. NR labeling is applied to the Space-efficient NR (SNR) labeing [14] which creates labels for monitoring parallel programs sequentially using the original structure of NR labels. Since SNR also maintains the information of parent threads, the efficiency of SNR is as much as the original NR labeling.

For one special kind of multithreaded programs, EH labeling is applied to the SP-hybrid algorithm [5] whose bound is a constant for the size of each thread label. However, SP-hybrid is designed to run only with a Cilk-like work-stealing scheduler of threads, requiring a special input, called SP parse tree, used for order-maintenance and shared by all thread operations. We do not compare this SP-hybrid algorithm with our work in this paper, because this algorithm has not been applied to any general kind of parallel programs.

3 The Efficient Labeling

This section presents an efficient thread labeling, called eNR labeling, which improves the NR labeling [12] without using any centralized data structure. This technique generates thread labels on every thread operation in a constant amount of time and space even in its worst case, as shown in Table 1. Furthermore, eNR labeling allows comparing thread labels to determine the logical concurrency between two threads in a small amount of time that is proportional only to the depth of nested parallelism.

3.1 Generating Thread Labels

An eNR label of a thread T_i has two components: its thread identifier, called *one-way region* $OR(T_i) = OR_i$, and a structure of pointers to its ancestor threads,

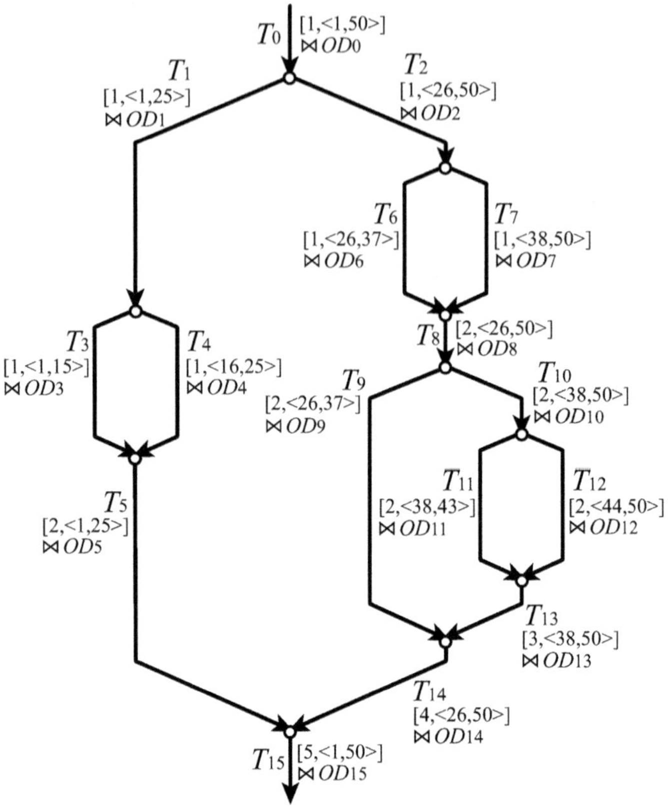

Fig. 1. An example of eNR labeling

called *one-way descriptor* $OD(T_i) = OD_i$. We use $OR_i \bowtie OD_i$ to denote these components of eNR label altogether.

A one-way region OR_i identifies a thread T_i with a pair of components: an integer, called the *join counter* λ_i of T_i, and a pair of integers, called the *nest region* $NR(T_i) = NR_i$ of T_i. We use $[\lambda_i, NR_i]$ to denote the components of OR_i altogether. We say a *joined* thread for a logical thread which is newly created by a join operation. A join counter of T_i means the number of the joined ancestor threads of T_i in the critical path from the initial thread to T_i. A nest region of T_i means an integer space which is divided by every fork operation and concatenated by every join operation. We use two integers $\langle \alpha_i, \beta_i \rangle$ to denote a nest region NR_i of T_i with its boundaries.

Figure 1 shows an example of the eNR labels generated during an execution of a program with nested parallelism using a directed acyclic graph called POEG (Partial Order Execution Graph) [7]. This graph effectively captures the logical concurrency of threads, because a vertex means a fork or join operation for a set of parallel threads, and an arc started from a vertex represents a logical thread started from a thread operation. The graph shows every eNR label of thread T_i as $[\lambda_i, \langle \alpha_i, \beta_i \rangle] \bowtie OD_i$.

T_i	m_i	L_i	T_i	m_i	L_i
T_0	$loc(OR_0)$	$null$	T_8	$loc(OR_8)$	$loc(OD_0)$
T_1	$loc(OR_0)$	$null$	T_9	$loc(OR_8)$	$loc(OD_0)$
T_2	$loc(OR_0)$	$null$	T_{10}	$loc(OR_8)$	$loc(OD_0)$
T_3	$loc(OR_0)$	$null$	T_{11}	$loc(OR_8)$	$loc(OD_0)$
T_4	$loc(OR_0)$	$null$	T_{12}	$loc(OR_8)$	$loc(OD_0)$
T_5	$loc(OR_5)$	$loc(OD_0)$	T_{13}	$loc(OR_{13})$	$loc(OD_8)$
T_6	$loc(OR_0)$	$null$	T_{14}	$loc(OR_{14})$	$loc(OD_0)$
T_7	$loc(OR_0)$	$null$	T_{15}	$loc(OR_{15})$	$null$

Fig. 2. One-way descriptors for Figure 1

Because the initial thread T_0 is assumed as a joined thread, its join counter λ_0 is illustrated as one just for readability. This initial join counter is initialized to *minint* in principle, where *minint* is the minimum integer that can be represented in a machine. The forked thread T_1 or T_2 just copies λ_0 to the value of its join counter. Whenever a join operation occurs, the join counter of the newly created thread is set to an integer which is one more than the largest join counter of its ancestor threads. For example, λ_{13} is three because the largest join counter of its ancestor threads is two. This means that there are three joined threads $\{T_0, T_8, T_{13}\}$ in its critical path from the initial thread T_0 to the current thread T_{13}.

The nest region of T_0 in the figure is illustrated as $\langle 1, 50\rangle$ just for readability. In principle, we initialized it to $\langle minint, maxint\rangle$, where *maxint* is the maximum integer that can be represented in a machine. The initial nest region is divided into two regions in the two child threads: $\langle 1, 25\rangle$ and $\langle 26, 50\rangle$. The nest region of the joined thread T_{13} is $\langle 38, 50\rangle$, since the two nest regions of its ancestors, T_{11} and T_{12}, are concatenated. This nest region of T_{13} can be regarded as being inherited from the latest ancestor thread T_{10} at the same nesting level.

A one-way descriptor allows the current thread to keep track of a special set of threads, called *one-way roots* of the thread. A one-way root of a thread T_i is defined as follows: T_i itself if T_i is a joined thread, or the latest joined ancestor T_x of T_i, or the latest joined ancestor of T_i at a nesting level which is higher than the nesting level of the joined ancestor T_x. A one-way descriptor OD_i is defined as a pair of pointers, denoted by (m_i, L_i), where m_i is a pointer to the latest one-way root T_x of T_i, and L_i is a pointer to the one-way descriptor of thread T_{x-1} which is the latest one-way root of T_i but T_x.

Figure 2 shows one-way descriptors of eNR labeled threads shown in Figure 1. The one-way descriptor OD_0 of the initial thread T_0 is initialized to (the location of OR_0, *null*), because T_0 is assumed to be a joined thread. A forked thread T_f inherits its one-way descriptor OD_f from its parent thread to refer to the one-way descriptor of the latest joined ancestor of T_f. For the one-way descriptor OD_j of a joined thread T_j, m_j of the current thread is updated to a pointer to its own OR_j, and L_j is updated as a pointer to the one-way descriptor of its parent thread. The overhead of eNR labeling for each thread operation is a constant in both space and time, because the size and the frequency of instructions for eNR labeling is constant as well.

3.2 Comparing Thread Labels

We can analyze the happens-before relation [15] between a pair of parallel threads by comparing their eNR labels with each other. By the relation, if a thread T_i must happen at an earlier time than a thread T_j, T_i *happens before* T_j, denoted by $T_i \rightarrow T_j$. If $T_i \rightarrow T_j$ or $T_j \rightarrow T_i$ is not satisfied, we say that T_i is *concurrent with* T_j, denoted by $T_i \parallel T_j$.

Given three eNR labeled threads T_i, T_j, and T_c, if T_c is the one-way root of T_j in the highest nesting level such that $\lambda_i < \lambda_c$, $T_i \rightarrow T_j$ is equivalent to

$$\begin{cases} (OR_i \supseteq OR_j) \quad or \\ \{(OR_i \not\supseteq OR_j) \ \wedge \ (OR_i \supseteq OR_c)\}, \end{cases}$$

where $OR_i \supseteq OR_j$ denotes that NR_i overlaps with NR_j or NR_j overlaps with NR_i, and $\lambda_i \leq \lambda_j$; and $OR_i \not\supseteq OR_j$ denotes that NR_i does not overlap with NR_j or NR_j does not overlap with NR_i, and $\lambda_i \leq \lambda_j$. For example, $T_8 \rightarrow T_{13}$ is satisfied in Figure 1, because $OR_8 \supseteq OR_{13}$ such that $NR_8 = \langle 26, 50 \rangle$ overlaps with $NR_{13} = \langle 38, 50 \rangle$, and the $\lambda_8 = 2$ is less than $\lambda_{13} = 3$.

To pinpoint T_c which is the one-way root of T_j in the highest nesting level such that $\lambda_i < \lambda_c$, we can traverse back through the linked list of one-way roots of T_j starting from the one-way descriptor of T_j, OD_j. Since a one-way descriptor $OD_j = (m_j, L_j)$ and L_j is a pointer to another one-way descriptor, the linked list pointed by OD_j can be represented with a linear list in string $(m_j, (m_x, (m_{x-1}, \cdots, (m_1, null)))$, and then the nest region OR_c of T_c can be found by traversing back through the list. By this linear search employed in finding a nest region of one-way root to be compared, eNR labeling allows to determine the logical concurrency between two threads in this amount of time that is proportional only to the depth N of nested parallelism.

We can conclude that two threads satisfy $T_i \parallel T_j$, if T_i and T_j do not satisfy $T_i \rightarrow T_j$ or $T_j \rightarrow T_i$. For example, if a join counter λ_i of thread T_i is larger than the λ_j of thread T_j, it does not satisfy $T_i \rightarrow T_j$. In case that T_j is the current thread in execution, two threads are concurrent with each other, because we do not have to consider if $T_j \rightarrow T_i$ is satisfied. For example, consider two thread T_5 and T_7 in Figure 1. If T_7 is the current thread, we can simply conclude $T_5 \parallel T_7$ because $\lambda_5 = 2$ is larger than $\lambda_7 = 1$.

4 Evaluation

This section empirically evaluates the efficiency of eNR labeling to compare it with those of other specialized labeling schemes: OS, BD, and NR labeling. The efficiencies are focused on the overhead in time and space for on-the-fly race detection.

4.1 Experimentation

To evaluate the efficiency of eNR labeling, we measured the execution time and the space consumed by execution instances of some instrumented benchmarks which support nested parallelism.

Table 2. The feature of three kernel applications

	Mandelbrot	FFT6	Jacobi
m-way degree	1	7	2
Nesting depth	2	3	2
Maximum Iteration	100K	10K	1000K

We implemented all labeling schemes as run-time libraries and compiled and executed the instrumented programs for on-the-fly race detection. For race detection methods that utilize the labeling schemes, we employed both Mellor-Crummey's method [16] for happens-before analysis and Jannesari and Tichy's method [11] for hybrid analysis. The Mellor-Crummey's method exploits a simple technique to compare any two threads, called left-of relation, and requires a small amount of overhead for race detection. The Jannesari and Tichy's method provides a lower rate of false positives and smaller performance overhead by consulting the happens-before relation whenever the lock-set algorithm indicates a possible race. These methods were also implemented as dynamic libraries for compilers.

For our benchmarks, we used OmpSCR (the OpenMP Source Code Repository) [8] which consists of kernel applications and complete applications with simple code under five thousands lines. We chose three kernel applications from the OmpSCR applications by considering nested parallelism. Their features are specified in Table 2, where *m-way degree* means the maximum number of loops in a nesting level of parallel loop. For example, `FFT6` has the nesting depth of three and a series of seven nested loops at a nesting level. The details of the applications are as follows:

- `Mandelbrot` computes an estimation to the Mandelbrot set area using Monte Carlo sampling. A Mandelbrot set is a fractal that is defined as the set of points in the complex plane. The input parameter for this program is the number of points in the complex plane to be explored. This application includes a one-way nested parallel loop with the nesting depth of two. In our experiments, we used a constant 100,000 to explore the points for the application.
- `FFT6` is a kind of the Fast Fourier Transform (FFT) algorithms, which uses the Bailey's 6-step. FFTs are used to solve the problems in digital signal processing, partial differential equations, quick multiplication of large integers, and so on. The 6-step FFT includes seven-way nested parallel loops with the nesting depth of three. We used 2^7 as the size of the input signal to store vectors and a complex array as the first parameter of the application.
- `Jacobi` solves a finite difference discretization of Helmholtz equation using the well known Jacobi iterative method. The program is implemented using two parallel loops inside one parallel region.

Each application has the maximum number of iterations for a parallel loop, which ranges from 10 to 1,000 thousands.

Table 3. The time and space overheads with FFT6

Labeling Schemes		Threads					
		2	4	8	16	32	64
eNR	Time(Sec)	33	47	43	37	36	37
	Space(MB)	420	419	416	413	406	388
NR	Time(Sec)	36	55	54	54	62	63
	Space(MB)	5.6K	5.6K	5.6K	5.5K	5.5K	5.5K
BD	Time(Sec)	35	60	61	61	69	68
	Space(MB)	5.7K	5.7K	5.6K	5.6K	5.6K	5.6K
OS	Time(Sec)	36	60	61	59	69	67
	Space(MB)	5.0K	5.0K	5.0K	4.9K	4.9K	4.9K

All applications were compiled with gcc 4.4.4 for OpenMP 3.0 which supports nested parallelism, and run on a system with Intel Quad-core 2 Xeon CPUs and 8GB RAM under the Kernel 2.6 of Linux operating system. The overhead of each instrumented application was measured for five executions in average, with the number of available parallel threads increasing from two to sixty-four.

4.2 Results and Analysis

We acquired three kinds of measured results: the overheads for `FFT6`, `Mandelbrot`, and `Jacobi`. Table 3 shows the results from the monitored executions of `FFT6`, which does not include the time and space of the original execution of `FFT6` without any instrumentation. In the results, eNR labeling slows down the executions of `FFT6` 6.8 times and requires about 410MB more storage space for on-the-fly race detection in the average case. The slowdown of eNR labeling is 1.5 times smaller than the previous three labeling schemes: the slowdown of NR labeling is 9.5 times, and those of BD labeling and OS labeling resulted in about 10 times. The space overhead of eNR labeling is moderated enough for large parallel applications, while the space overhead of others increases with a factor of 92% relatively to the eNR labeling's space overhead.

Figure 3 shows the results of run-time overhead to monitor parallel executions of two applications, `Mandelbrot` and `Jacobi`, for on-the-fly race detection. The Mellor-Crummey's method was used to detect races in `Mandelbrot`, and the Jannesari and Tichy's method was used for `Jacobi` which includes lock primitives. Race detection with eNR labeling shows a run-time overhead that were increased 2.2 times more than the original executions of `Mandelbrot`. On the other hand, the overhead of NR labeling was 3.2 times, and those of BD labeling and OS labeling were 4 times in average. The slowdown of eNR labeling is 14.8% to monitor thread accesses and races with `Jacobi` in the average case. The slowdown of NR labeling is 20%, BD labeling is 18.3%, and OS labeling is 18% in the average case. The results of `Jacobi` show that the run-time overhead of eNR labeling is reduced less than the results of `Mandelbrot`, because Jannesari and Tichy's method leads to lower overhead than Mellor-Crummey's method.

These empirical results from Table 3 and Figure 3 show that eNR labeling is more efficient than other specialized labeling schemes reducing both time

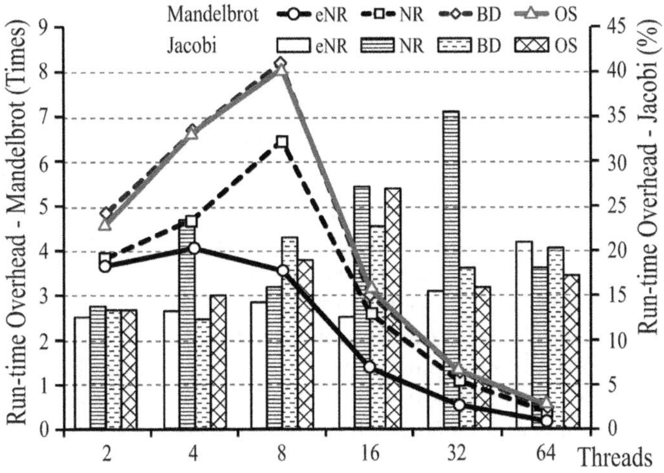

Fig. 3. Runtime overheads for benchmarks

overhead by 10% and space overhead by more than 90% for on-the-fly race detection.

5 Related Work

For on-the-fly race detection, Task Recycling (TR) [7] is the first vector clock that was extended for nested parallelism. A label generated by TR is a pair of thread identifier and its version number. The label is maintained using a parent vector associated with each executing thread and a centralized data structure to manage information about free thread identifiers. Since the size of a parent vector is proportional to the number of simultaneously active threads, TR introduces overhead depending on the maximum parallelism of the program in the worst case. Clock Tree (CT) [1] extends the vector clock for nested parallelism without centralized data structures using a tree of vector clocks. The tree maintains the version numbers which are associated with the current thread or its ancestor teams of threads. Thus, the size of clock tree is usually larger than the nesting depth of the program and less than or equal to the maximum parallelism of the program.

A thread label generated by the EH labeling [18] is a pair of the English (E) and the Hebrew (H) label: the label E produced by performing a left-to-right preorder numbering, and the label H created symmetrically from right-to-left preorder numbering. A thread label generated by the OS labeling [16] is a non-null sequence of ordered pairs each of which consists of two integers, offset (O) and span (S). The offset distinguishes among relatives descended from the same parent, and the span indicates the number of threads spawned by a fork operation. The size of a label by both labeling schemes increases along with the nesting level of fork-join constructs, thus their efficiencies depend on the nesting depth of the program. The difference between them is that the size of the EH label generated on a join operation is not decreased.

A BD label [2] is a pair of breadth (B) and depth (D) values, which is maintained using a list structure. The value B indicates the position of the current thread considering its sibling threads, and the value D counts the number of threads that happened before the current thread in the critical path from the initial thread. An NR label [12] is a pair of one join counter and the nest region of the current thread, which is also maintained using a list structure. A nest region is a range of number space created by thread operations. The join counter counts the number of joined threads in the critical path from the initial thread. The list structure of BD label or NR label maintains the required information of parent threads in the critical path. The size of the list in the BD labeling or the NR labeling depends on the nesting depth, thus the efficiencies of both labeling schemes depend on the nesting depth of the program.

6 Conclusion

This paper presented an efficient thread labeling, called eNR Labeling, which does not use any centralized data structure and creates thread labels on every thread operation in a constant amount of time and space even in its worst case. On every thread operation, this technique creates thread labels by inheriting a pointer to their shared one-way descriptor from the parent thread. Furthermore, this technique allows to determine the logical concurrency between threads in a small amount of time that is proportional only to the depth of nested parallelism just by traversing a linear linked list back through the inherited pointers from the current one-way descriptor. Compared with three state-of-the-arts labeling schemes, our empirical results using OpenMP benchmarks show that eNR labeling reduces both time overhead by 10% and space overhead by more than 90% for on-the-fly race detection.

This low-overhead of eNR labeling is significant, because a thread labeling scheme for nested parallelism can be used for on-the-fly detection based not only on the happens-before relation but also on a hybrid relation that combines the happens-before with the lockset , as this paper presents for empirical comparison of efficiencies. Future work includes additional improvement of the eNR labeling to make it possible to compare logical concurrency of parallel threads also in a constant amount of time, and additional enhancement of the labeling to extend its application to more general types of thread synchronizations including barriers, signal-waits, and others.

References

1. Audenaert, K.: Clock trees: logical clocks for programs with nested parallelism. IEEE Transactions on Software Engineering 23(10), 646–658 (1997)
2. Audenaert, K., D'Hollander, E., Joubert, F., Trottenberg, F.: Maintaining Concurrency Information for On-the-fly Data Race Detection. Advances in Parallel Computing, 319–326 (1998)

3. Baldoni, R., Klusch, M.: Fundamentals of distributed computing: A practical tour of vector clock systems. IEEE Distributed Systems Online 3 (February 2002)
4. Banerjee, U., Bliss, B., Ma, Z., Petersen, P.: A theory of data race detection. In: Proceedings of the 2006 Workshop on Parallel and Distributed Systems: Testing and Debugging, PADTAD 2006, pp. 69–78. ACM, New York (2006)
5. Bender, M.A., Fineman, J.T., Gilbert, S., Leiserson, C.E.: On-the-fly maintenance of series-parallel relationships in fork-join multithreaded programs. In: Proceedings of the 16th Annual ACM Symposium on Parallelism in Algorithms and Architectures, SPAA 2004, pp. 133–144. ACM, New York (2004)
6. Bücker, H.M., Rasch, A., Wolf, A.: A class of openmp applications involving nested parallelism. In: Proc. of the 2004 ACM Symp. on Applied Comput., SAC 2004, pp. 220–224. ACM, New York (2004)
7. Dinning, A., Schonberg, E.: An empirical comparison of monitoring algorithms for access anomaly detection. In: Proceedings of the 2nd ACM SIGPLAN Symposium on Principles & Practice of Parallel Prog., PPOPP 1990, pp. 1–10. ACM, New York (1990)
8. Dorta, A.J., Rodriguez, C., Sande, F.D., Gonzalez-Escribano, A.: The openmp source code repository. In: Proceedings of the 13th Euromicro Conference on Parallel, Distributed and Network-Based Processing, pp. 244–250. IEEE Computer Society, Washington, DC, USA (2005)
9. Farchi, E., Nir, Y., Ur, S.: Concurrent bug patterns and how to test them. In: Proceedings of the 17th International Symposium on Parallel and Distributed Processing, IPDPS 2003, p. 286. IEEE Computer Society, Washington, DC, USA (2003)
10. Flanagan, C., Freund, S.N.: Fasttrack: efficient and precise dynamic race detection. In: Proceedings of the 2009 ACM SIGPLAN Conference on Programming Language Design and Implementation, PLDI 2009, pp. 121–133. ACM, New York (2009)
11. Jannesari, A., Tichy, W.F.: On-the-fly race detection in multi-threaded programs. In: Proceedings of the 6th Workshop on Parallel and Distributed Systems: Testing, Analysis, and Debugging, PADTAD 2008, pp. 6:1–6:10. ACM, New York (2008)
12. Jun, Y.K., Koh, K.: On-the-fly detection of access anomalies in nested parallel loops. In: Proceedings of the 1993 ACM/ONR Workshop on Parallel and Distributed Debugging, PADD 1993, pp. 107–117. ACM, New York (1993)
13. Kejariwal, A., Nicolau, A., Veidenbaum, A.V., Banerjee, U., Polychronopoulos, C.D.: Efficient scheduling of nested parallel loops on multi-core systems. In: Proceedings of the 2009 International Conference on Parallel Processing, ICPP 2009, pp. 74–83. IEEE Computer Society, Washington, DC, USA (2009)
14. Kim, D.G., Jun, Y.K.: Space-efficient on-the-fly race detection for programs with nested parallelism. In: Parallel and Distributed Systems, pp. 245–250 (1997)
15. Lamport, L.: Time, clocks, and the ordering of events in a distributed system. Commun. ACM 21, 558–565 (1978)
16. Mellor-Crummey, J.: On-the-fly detection of data races for programs with nested fork-join parallelism. In: Proceedings of the 1991 ACM/IEEE Conference on Supercomputing, Supercomputing 1991, pp. 24–33. ACM, New York (1991)
17. Netzer, R.H.B., Miller, B.P.: What are race conditions?: Some issues and formalizations. ACM Lett. Program. Lang. Syst. 1, 74–88 (1992)

18. Nudler, I., Rudolph, L.: Tools for the efficient development of efficient parallel programs. In: Proceedings of 1st Israeli Conference on Computer System Engineering. IEEE (1988)
19. O'Callahan, R., Choi, J.D.: Hybrid dynamic data race detection. In: Proceedings of the Ninth ACM SIGPLAN Symposium on Principles and Practice of Parallel Programming, PPoPP 2003, pp. 167–178. ACM, New York (2003)
20. Ronsse, M., De Bosschere, K.: Recplay: a fully integrated practical record/replay system. ACM Trans. Comput. Syst. 17, 133–152 (1999)
21. Savage, S., Burrows, M., Nelson, G., Sobalvarro, P., Anderson, T.: Eraser: a dynamic data race detector for multithreaded programs. ACM Trans. Comput. Syst. 15, 391–411 (1997)

A Taxonomy of Concurrency Bugs in Event-Driven Programs*

Guy Martin Tchamgoue, Ok-Kyoon Ha,
Kyong-Hoon Kim, and Yong-Kee Jun**

Department of Informatics, Gyeongsang National University,
Jinju 660-701, South Korea
guymt@ymail.com, {jassmin,khkim,jun}@gnu.ac.kr

Abstract. Concurrency bugs are a well-documented topic in shared-memory programs including event-driven programs which handle asynchronous events. Asynchronous events introduce fine-grained concurrency into event-driven programs making them hard to be thoroughly tested and debugged. Unfortunately, previous taxonomies on concurrency bugs are not applicable to the debugging of event-driven programs or do not provide enough knowledge on event-driven concurrency bugs. This paper classifies the event-driven program models into low and high level based on event types and carefully examines and categorizes concurrency bug patterns in such programs. Additionally, we survey existing techniques to detect concurrency bugs in event-driven programs. To the best of our knowledge, this study provides the first detailed taxonomy on concurrency bugs in event-driven programs.

Keywords: Events, event handlers, signal, interrupt, event-driven programs, concurrency bugs, taxonomy, detection techniques.

1 Introduction

Caused by non-deterministic interleaving between shared memory accesses [28], concurrency bugs are a well-documented topic in shared-memory programs including event-driven programs which handle asynchronous events. Asynchronous events introduce fine-grained concurrency into these programs making them hard to be thoroughly tested and debugged. However, concurrency bugs such as unintended race conditions, atomicity and order violations and deadlocks are not only common, but also notoriously hard to uncover. Despite the numberless tools and techniques devised to detect concurrency bugs, they often remain undetectable

* This research was supported by the MKE (The Ministry of Knowledge Economy), Korea, under the ITRC (Information Technology Research Center) support program supervised by the NIPA (National IT Industry Promotion Agency), NIPA-2011-C1090-1131-0007.

** Corresponding Author: In Gyeongsang National University, he is also involved in the Research Institute of Computer and Information Communication (RICIC).

T.-h. Kim et al. (Eds.): ASEA/DRBC/EL 2011, CCIS 257, pp. 437–450, 2011.

until the exploitation phase leading the application into unpredictable executions sometimes with severe consequences. A typical example is the well-known accident of the Therac-25 [15] where, as the result of a race condition caused by the keyboard event handler, many people received fatal radiation doses.

Event-driven programs are becoming pervasive with applications ranging from web servers to operating system kernels and safety-critical embedded software. Understanding the causes and characteristics of concurrency bugs may ease the debugging process and can help creating new heuristics for some debugging tools as shown in [7] for shared-memory parallel programs. Unfortunately, previous taxonomies or studies are not applicable to the debugging of event-driven programs or do not provide enough knowledge on event-driven concurrency bugs. A taxonomy of concurrency bugs in shared-memory parallel programs is presented in [7] and used to create new heuristics for an existing detection tool. However, this taxonomy cannot only fit for event-driven software due to the differences in the concurrency models. A short taxonomy of bugs in device drivers is given in [23]. Although the classification is not centered on concurrency bugs, this work showed however that concurrency bugs accounts for 19% of the total number of bugs in device drivers. Many other existing works [16,17,24] focus on understanding the characteristics of concurrency bugs in real world programs and their impact on new testing and debugging tools. However, all these studies focus only on shared-memory parallel programs giving few or less attention to event-driven concurrency bugs.

This paper classifies the event-driven program models into low and high level based on event types and carefully examines and categorizes concurrency bug patterns in such programs. As software bugs represent the major cause for system failures, it is therefore important to deeply understand the causes and characteristics of bugs in order to effectively design tools and support for detecting and recovering from software failures [17]. Detecting concurrency bugs in event-driven programs is particularly difficult since they usually contain a very large number of executable paths [19] due to asynchronous events. Nevertheless, many tools and techniques [1,6,9,10,11,19,27] have been proposed for uncovering such bugs for various application domains. These detection techniques can be roughly classified into three major groups: testing methods, static analysis and dynamic analysis. Additionally to the taxonomy, this work also surveys the existing tools for detecting concurrency bugs in event-driven programs.

In the remainder of this paper, Section 2 describes the event-driven programs and gives our motivation. Section 3 provides details on the proposed taxonomy. Section 4 presents a survey of existing detection techniques and gives useful recommendations to avoid concurrency bugs in event-driven programs. Finally, our conclusion comes in Section 5.

2 Background

In order to understand the causes and to categorize the concurrency bugs in event-driven programs, it is crucial to have a look on their inner characteristics. Thus, this section describes the event-driven programs, presents the general properties of events and gives the motivation that sustains this work.

2.1 Events and Programs

Globally, events can be classified into two categories: the *low-level* events or interrupts and the *high level* events or signals (UNIX-like signals). Thus, in this paper, when not specifically mentioned, the term event refers to both interrupts and signals and not to the actions that generate them. A signal is a message sent by the kernel or another process (using the `kill` system call) to a process. Often referred to as *software interrupts*, signals are used as basic inter-process communication mechanisms. In the other hand, interrupts are defined as *hardware signals* as they are generated by the hardware in response to an external operation or environment change. These two classes of events share almost the same properties.

Event Handling: To service each event, an asynchronous callback subroutine called *event handler* is required. In the case of interrupts, the interrupt handler generally reside in the operating system kernel. However, for some embedded systems with a thin kernel layer like TinyOS [12], applications have to provide and manage their own interrupt handlers. Before its invocation, any signal handler must be carefully registered with the kernel using the `signal()` or `sigaction()` system calls. Each signal has a default handler or action and depending on the signal, the default action may be to terminate the receiving process, to suspend the process, or just to ignore the signal. When an event is received, it remains pending until it is delivered or handled.

Blocking, Preemption, Nesting, and Reentrancy: Contrarily to threads, event handlers cannot block: they run to completion except when preempted by another event handler [9,19]. Events have an asymmetric preemption relation with the non-event code: event handlers can preempt non-event code but not the contrary. Events are nested when they preempt each other. Nesting events are used to allow time-sensitive events to be handled with low latency [19]. An event is said to be reentrant when it directly or indirectly preempts itself.

Split-Phase Operations: In order to minimize the impact of event handlers on non-event code, all long-latency operations must run in split-phase. With this mechanism, event handlers immediately return after servicing critical operations and post heavy computations for later execution as a new task or process. This technique is known under different names according to the environment: deferred procedure call in Windows [3], bottom-half in Linux [4] or split-phase in TinyOS [9].

Synchronous or Asynchronous: As described in [19], asynchronous interrupts are signaled by external devices such as network interfaces and can fire at any time that the corresponding device is enabled. Synchronous interrupts, on the other hand, are those that arrive in response to a specific action taken by the processor, such as setting a timer. Similarly, signals may also be generated synchronously or asynchronously. A synchronous signal pertains to a specific action in the program and is generally generated by some errors in the program like the division by zero. Asynchronous signals are generated by actions outside the control of the process (e.g. resizing an application's window) that receives them and may arrive at unpredictable times during execution.

Disabling/Enabling: Event-driven programs present a very simple concurrency model which however allows high and complex concurrency at runtime with an exponentially increasing number of execution paths. Since the only way to share data between a program and its event handlers is through global variables, concurrency bugs like race conditions may show up. To protect sensitive parts of the program, events must be disabled before and enabled only after critical sections. However, it is not recommended to call non-reentrant functions or system calls within event handlers. In the case of signals, system calls like `getuid()` or `rmdir()` recommended to be invoked in signal handlers are referred to as *async-signal-safe*. Other system calls like `printf()` are classified non async-signal-safe.

Event-Driven Programs: A program is event-driven when a considerable amount of its computation is initiated and influenced by external events like interrupts and/or signals. As described above, depending on the environment, a program can be interrupt-driven or signal-based. For programs that implement only high level events, the operating system is responsible to handle the low-level event and to generate a corresponding high level event for them. In accordance with the type of events they handle, Fig.1 shows a classification of event-driven programs and their interaction with the operating system kernel.

2.2 Motivation

Event-driven programs are becoming pervasive with the vulgarization of embedded systems. For applications like those in embedded sensor networks which need to interact with the external world, events provide means to fastly respond to changes from the outside environment. Since parallel programs are difficult to implement and to debug, events have been viewed by many researchers as alternative to threads [2,14,18]. As event-driven software become more and more complex, there is a real need for more effective and robust tools for testing and debugging in order to reduce the number of bugs that escape in production runs [17]. Event-driven programs present a complex concurrency structure with an exponentially increasing number of execution paths at runtime. Since the only way to share data between an event handler and the non-event code is

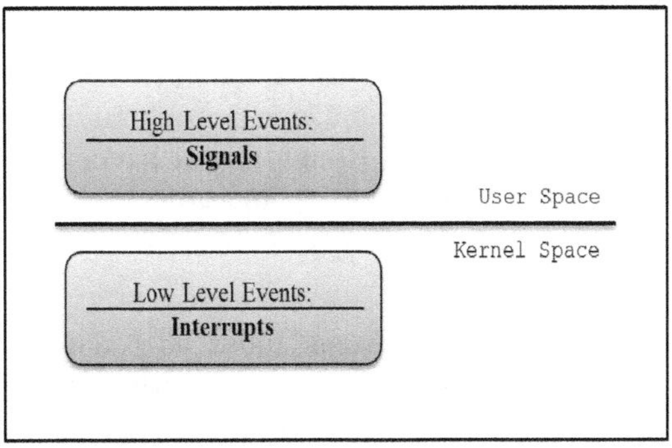

Fig. 1. Event-Driven Programs

through global variables, event-driven programs are also prone to concurrency bugs. Designing effective tools for improving the quality of software requires a good understanding of software bug characteristics [17]. However, understanding bug characteristics alone is not enough for designing effective tools for testing and debugging concurrency bugs. Additionally to bug characteristics, a deep understanding of the concurrency model and the bug root causes is also required. Having such knowledge on concurrency bugs certainly helps developers to avoid introducing them.

A taxonomy of concurrency bugs in shared-memory parallel programs is presented in [7] and used to create new heuristics for a concurrency bug detection tool. Unfortunately, this taxonomy cannot only fit for event-driven software due to the differences in the concurrency models. For example, the concurrency bugs due to the activation of dangerous event handlers when executing sensitive operations (cf. section 3.1) or to the use of unsafe functions in event handlers (cf. section 3.2) cannot be captured by the taxonomy in [7]. These bugs are directly related to the concurrency model of event-driven programs. A short taxonomy of bugs in device drivers is given in [23]. Although the classification is not centered on concurrency bugs, this work showed that concurrency bugs accounts for 19% of the total number of bugs in device drivers. Many other existing works [16,17,24] focused on understanding the characteristics of concurrency bugs in real world programs and their impact on new testing and debugging tools. However, all these taxonomies or studies cannot directly be applicable to event-driven programs or do not provide enough knowledge on event-driven concurrency bugs or other event-related bugs. This paper carefully examines and categorizes concurrency bug patterns and surveys existing tools for detecting them in event-driven programs. Since software bugs may have similar patterns, a taxonomy of concurrency bugs can also be useful to identify and reveal hidden bugs. Also, studies to understand the characteristics of software bugs provide useful insights and guidelines for software engineering tool designers and reliable system builders [17].

3 Concurrency Bug Classification

In this section, we present our taxonomy of concurrency bugs in event-driven programs. This classification tries as much as possible to highlight the potential causes and risks for each class of bugs. Roughly, concurrency can be classified into three main categories: data races, atomicity and order violations, and deadlocks.

3.1 Data Races

As with shared-memory parallel programs, unintended data races represent one of the most notorious concurrency bugs in event-driven programs. Data races happen when a shared memory is uncoordinately accessed with at least one write by both an event handler and a non-event code or by multiple event handlers. Event handlers introduce logical concurrency into event-driven programs and exponentially increase their execution paths at runtime. In [23], it is shown that concurrency bugs in device drivers are mostly introduced in situations where a sporadic event, such as a hot-unplug notification or a configuration request, occurs while the driver is handling a stream of data requests. Data races can lead to different other concurrency bugs, resulting on unpredictable output, loss or inconsistency of data, data corruption or even on a crash of a program. Following are some examples of bugs belonging to this category:

Double Free: It is common in event-driven to share data through global variables. This situation can sometimes lead to pointers or shared memory areas been freed by both the event handler and the non-event code, resulting to the well-known double free bug[1]. This bug can happen because the programmer is confused over which part of the program is responsible for freeing the memory area. Worst, this can also happen if the developer misunderstands the event handling mechanism or has wrong assumptions about the behavior of events. A typical example of such bug is shown in Fig.2 where the shared variable *ptr* can be subject to a double free. If the program receives a signal right before the instruction in line 17 is executed, *ptr* will be doubly freed.

As we can see with the program of Fig.2, this bug may remain hidden as the probability to reproduce it is very low. Therefore, once it shows up at runtime, there are possibilities for the program to crash or to face data corruption. The double free in this example is a consequence of a race condition between the event handler and the non-event code over the variable *ptr*.

Use After Free: This bug pattern is somehow similar to the double free bug. Only, in this case, we face a situation where a previously deallocated memory location is referenced for computations. However, this bug will not be caused only by the fact that the programmer is confused over which part of the program is responsible for freeing the memory area, but also because of his misunderstanding of the event handling mechanisms. The use after free bug[2] can have number

[1] http://cwe.mitre.org/data/definitions/415.html
[2] http://cwe.mitre.org/data/definitions/416.html

```
1:  #include <signal.h>
2:  #include <stdio.h>
3:  #include <stdlib.h>
4:
5:  void *ptr;
6:
7:  void sh(int sig){
8:      if(ptr!=NULL) free(ptr);
9:  }
10:
11: void main(int argc, char* argv[])
12: {
13:     ptr=strdup(argv[2]);
14:     signal(SIGTERM,sh);
15:
16:     if(ptr!=NULL)
17:         free(ptr); //ptr=strdup(argv[0]);
18: }
```

Fig. 2. An Example Program with a Double Free

of consequences ranging from data corruption to the execution of arbitrary code and the crash of the program.

An example of this bug can be observed in Fig.2 where the instruction in line 17 is replaced by the one in the comment (i.e. `ptr=strdup(argv[0])`).

Dangerous Event Handlers Enabled During Sensitive Operations: Asynchronous events can fire at any time preempting non-event code or other event handlers. A global variable shared by the program and its event handlers can be exposed to concurrency bugs. Thus, it is recommended to disable dangerous events before sensitive operations like accessing shared states and to enable them only after. Forgetting to do so might lead the program to unintended data races or other concurrency bugs like atomicity or order violations with severe consequences.

As an example, we can consider again the program in Fig.2 which exposes a double free bug. However, this bug happens because the signal handler is still enabled when the variable *ptr* is accessed in lines 16 and 17. For more precaution, the signal handler must be disabled in line 15 and enabled again only in line 18.

3.2 Atomicity and Order Violations

In this section, we consider concurrency bugs related to *atomicity violations* or to *order violations*. A method or a sequence of instructions is atomic if its execution is not affected by and does not interfere with concurrently executing threads [8]. In the other hand, the order violation bugs occur when a program fails to enforce the programmer's execution order intention [16]. Generally, developers tend to make wrong assumptions about the behavior of event handlers. These wrong assumptions come in different flavors and result in different concurrency bug patterns. The following bugs belong to this class of concurrency bugs:

Use of Unsafe Functions: Due to the fact that global variables are exposed to concurrency bugs, non-reentrant functions or system calls are not recommended in event handlers. A function is said reentrant if multiple instances of the same function can run in the same address space concurrently without creating the potential for inconsistent states [5]. For signals, only a reduced set of reentrant system calls referred to as *async-signal-safe* are recommended to be invoked within signal handlers.

An unsafe function in an event handler cannot guarantee the consistency of data structures when preempted. This may lead to data corruption, loss or inconsistency of data or to unpredictable program output. An example of such vulnerability in signal handler that would have been exploited to perform remote authentication on a server was reported and fixed in OpenSSH [5, Chapter 13]. Another example is the bug detected in Bash 3.0 [26] where the global variable `errno` is overwritten by the non async-signal-safe `ioctl()` called in a signal handler.

Non-Returning Event Handlers: In this scenario, a process is preempted by an event handler, but the execution control never returns back to the interrupted function. There are two ways this can happen [5]: the event handler can either explicitly terminate the process by calling `exit()`, or return to another part of the application in the specific case of signal handler using `longjmp()`. Jumping back to another part of a program might be risky and unsafe if the reachable code is not async-signal-safe. Examples of data races due to non-returning signal handlers were reported in the well-known Sendmail SMTP and WU-FTPD [5].

Non Atomic Instructions Assumed to be Atomic: This bug pattern is usually related to some non-atomic operations or instructions in high level programming languages like C/C++ that are viewed as atomic by developers. A classical example is the well-known increment operator ++ that is often considered atomic as it seems to consist of a single machine operation. However, during compilation, an $x{+}{+}$ operation corresponds to three machine instructions: (1) load the current value of x into memory, (2) increment the memory copy of x, and (3) store the memory value of x. An event can then preempt the execution of this operation after each of these machine instructions resulting to unpredictable results. An example of such bug was detected and reported in Bash 3.0 [26].

Interleaving Assumed Never to Occur: For some reasons, the programmer assumes that a certain program interleaving never occurs. This assumption might be, for example, the relative execution length of a given part of the program, considerations about the underlying hardware, the reentrancy or the repeatability of an event handler, or simply the arrival time of an event. This bug might also happen because a segment of code is wrongly assumed to always run before or after an event handler. In any case, this bug might result in severe data corruption.

An example of such was found in a TinyOS application an described in [19]. The reported bug effectively involved the analog-to-digital converter interrupt handler which was written under the assumption that every posted task runs before the interrupt handler next fires.

3.3 Deadlocks

In section, we classify all kind of concurrency bugs that manifest themselves as a hang of the system. This commonly happens when an instruction or interleaving contains a blocking operation that blocks indefinitely the execution of a program. In this category, we can enumerate the following bug patterns:

Blocking Synchronizations: In a multithreaded environment, it is recommended to protect accesses to shared variables using synchronization primitives like locks. However, misusing the locking mechanism can lead a program to deadlock. An event handler is supposed to run as fast as possible and returns the control to the main program. Accessing a lock in an event handler might not only block, but cause a deadlock that will surely hand the entire system since the handler might never return. As explained in [5] for example, the use of a mutex data type in a signal handler can cause a PThreads program to deadlock.

Blocking Operations: Event handlers always have higher priority than the non-event code with which they have an asymmetric preemption relation. Event handlers must therefore be written efficiently not to monopolize the processor and run as fast as possible since they can also preempt each other. Thus, in the context of event handlers, is not allowed to perform any potentially blocking operations [23].

Directly executing blocking operations like some system calls (e.g. `sleep()`) or other file system blocking operations (e.g. manipulating bulk data from an external storage) within an event handler can penalize and even paralyze the entire program execution. An important number of such bugs due to calls to blocking functions in an atomic context were reported in several commonly used Linux device drivers [23].

3.4 Stack Overflow

The stack overflow is an important issue in event-driven programs especially in embedded software. As the microcontrollers used for embedded systems generally have reduced memory, programmers should seriously consider the stack overflow problem. Stack safety, a guarantee that the call stack does not overflow, is considered to be an important correctness criterion for embedded software [21].

A stack overflow occurs when a program attempts to use more memory space than is available on the stack. The stack overflow can have many causes like a poor memory management policy, an infinite recursion or an excessive reentrant or nested events. This problem can happen also when a developer lacks information about the underlying hardware and the operating system. Stack overflows cause loss of data and memory corruption that can easily crash a system or otherwise lead to incorrect operations. However, there are tools [21] that analytically determine the worst-case stack depth of event-driven programs to guarantee that they will not execute out of the stack memory at runtime.

4 Debugging Event-Driven Programs

Detecting concurrency bugs is particularly difficult and generally requires sophisticated techniques and tools. In this section, we present a survey of existing techniques and tools to detect and avoid concurrency bugs in event-driven programs.

4.1 Detection Techniques

Concurrency bugs are an important issue in event-driven programs which are getting pervasive with the popularization of embedded systems like networked embedded systems. Ever since, there is an urgent need to explore more effective software testing and debugging tools and software engineering methods to minimize the number of bugs that escape into production runs [17]. This section provides a survey of tools and techniques devised for this purpose. Note that these techniques can also be classified into low level tools [1,6,9,10,11,13,19,20,25] and high level tools [22,26,27] according to the type of events they target.

Testing Methods: These methods mostly focus on generating test cases that can efficiently reveal general and concurrency bugs. Regehr [19] proposed a method to random test event-driven applications by randomly fire interrupts at random time intervals. The main challenge in this work is to obtain adequate interrupt schedules by solving the tradeoff between generating a dense or a sparse interrupt schedule. With a dense interrupt schedule, there are always many pending interrupts, making the processor busy in interrupt mode and starving non interrupt code. On the other hand, a sparse schedule provokes less preemption among interrupts, then no or only few bugs might be detected.

To be able to test for all race conditions in a program, Higashi et al. [11] propose to generate one interrupt after every instruction that accesses a shared variable and to substitute a corrupted memory with a value provided by the developer. The work in [13] models how operations on different contexts in an event-driven application may interleave as inter-context flow graphs. Two test adequacy criteria, one on inter-context data-flows and another on inter-context control-flows, are proposed for failures detection in TinyOS applications.

Static Analysis: Static analysis techniques must deal with exponential number of states during the analysis process. They are then less scalable and may produce both false positives and false negatives. Some programming languages for event-driven systems like nesC [9] contain a native concurrency bugs detection tool. Thus, every nesC program has to enforce a race-free invariant stating that any update to a shared variable must occur either in a synchronous code reachable only from tasks, or within an atomic section.

Regehr and Cooprider [20] propose to transform an interrupt handler code into a corresponding multithreaded code and to use existing static race checker to detect data races in the newly generated program. Contrarily to other tools that detect typical concurrency bugs like data races or atomicity violations, the work in [21] focuses only on statically determine the worst-case stack depth of event-driven programs in order to prevent stack overflows at runtime.

Dynamic Analysis: Dynamic analysis techniques focus only on the specific execution path followed at runtime given an input. These techniques statically or dynamically instrument a program to collect runtime data needed for detection. False negatives are inherent to dynamic analysis techniques since bugs in unexecuted paths cannot be detected. Dynamic analysis techniques are classified into two main methods.

***Post-Mortem Methods*:** These techniques instrument the program to record runtime information and data for a post-execution analysis. The runtime overhead may be small, but the size of the log file can be very huge. The main challenge of these techniques is to reduce the size of the log and to accurately record asynchronous events at runtime.

Audenaert and Levrouw [1] proposed a method based on software instruction counter to record and replay multithreaded programs in the presence of interrupts. In [10] two functions are devised to reduce the size of the log file in an event-driven program: the selector function to select parts of the code to be logged and the hashing function to normalize the size of collected data in the log file. A lightweight control flow tracing and encoding scheme to generate a highly compressed log file is presented for networked embedded software debugging in [25].

***On-the-fly Methods*:** These techniques will instrument a program for runtime detection. On-the-fly approaches can further be categorized into several methods.

- **Summary Methods:** report concurrency bugs with incomplete information about the references that caused them. Ronsse et al. [22] adapted an existing on-the-fly race detector for multithreaded programs to handle data races in sequential programs with concurrent signal handlers. This tool employs a two-phase technique for race detection. During the first pass, memory accesses are collected, concurrent threads detected and primary information about data races found, stored in a log file. The second phase is therefore necessary to refine the information collected during the first execution.

- **Access History Methods:** maintain an access history to precisely determine each of a pair of concurrent accesses to every shared variable. Tchamgoue et al. [27] proposed a labeling scheme for race detection in sequential programs that use concurrent signals. This scheme generates concurrency information, called label, with constant size for the sequential program or every instance of the concurrent signal handlers.
- **Watchpoint Methods:** use the watchpoint facilities to simplify the detection process. Tahara et al. [26] presented an approach for race detection in sequential programs that use signals. The technique is based on the */proc* system file (for Solaris 10) or the debug registers (for IA32 Linux) and uses watchpoints to monitor accesses to shared variables.
- **Sampling/Breakpoint Methods:** use the breakpoint facilities to simplify the detection process. Erickson et al. [6] presented a technique that aims to detect data races in low-level operating system kernel code. Their technique randomly samples parts of the program to be used as candidate for the race detection and uses data and code breakpoints to detect conflicting threads.

4.2 Correction Techniques

In general, there are simple basic rules to meet in order to avoid concurrency bugs in event-driven programs. In the case of signals, the developer has to enforce the following:

- Disable signals before accessing shared data and enable them after;
- Make sure to use only async-signal-safe or reentrant functions in signal handlers or within user-defined functions called from signal handlers;
- Avoid blocking operations or functions in signal handlers;
- Define an atomic data type *volatile sig_atomic_t* for shared variables accessed from signal handlers.

These basic rules for signal programming also hold in case of interrupt-driven programs although their concurrency model may differ from one platform to another. At least, it is usually suggested to disable interrupts before accessing shared variables and to enable them only after. In nesC applications [9] for example, any update to a shared variable must occur either in synchronous code reachable only from tasks, or within an atomic section.

In the special case of stack overflow, the developer must control every manipulated data to make sure that their sizes fit the allocated memory space. In addition, tools like the one proposed in [21] must be used to determine the worst-case stack depth of the application before the deployment process and to guarantee that the program will not execute out of stack memory at runtime.

5 Conclusion

Asynchronous event handling introduces fine-grained concurrency into event-driven programs and consequently concurrency bugs. Concurrency bugs are difficult to reproduce making event-driven programs hard to be thoroughly tested and debugged. Concurrency bugs are not only the consequence of a complex concurrency model due to event handlers, but are also due to programmers' mistakes. A programmer may, for example, misuse existing facilities like disabling/enabling events or make incorrect assumptions during programming; exposing the program to concurrency bugs.

In this paper, we classified the event-driven program models into low and high level based on event types and carefully examined and categorized concurrency bug patterns in such programs. We believe that such taxonomy can help the developer to understand the causes of concurrency bugs and to avoid introducing them. It can also ease the debugging process, and help developing heuristics for more precise detection tools. Parallelly, we surveyed and classified existing detection techniques for concurrency bugs in event-driven programs.

In the future, it might be interesting to investigate and provide useful statistics on bug characteristics including security issues in event-driven programs by conducting an empirical study on real world event-driven software.

References

1. Audenaert, K.M.R., Levrouw, L.J.: Interrupt Replay: A Debugging Method for Parallel Programs with Interrupts. Microprocessors and Microsystems 18(10), 601–612 (1994)
2. Adya, A., Howell, J., Theimer, M., Bolosky, W.J., Douceur, J.R.: Cooperative Task Management without Manual Stack Management. In: Proceedings of the 2002 Usenix Annual Technical Conference, pages 14, USENIX (2002)
3. Baker, A., Lozano, J.: The Windows 2000 Device Driver Book: A Guide for Programmers, 2nd edn., pages 480. Prentice Hall (2009)
4. Corbet, J., Rubini, A., Kroah-Hartman, G.: Linux Device Drivers, 3rd edn., pages 640. O'Reilly Media (2009)
5. Dowd, M., McDonald, J., Schuh, J.: The Art of Software Security Assessment: Identifying and Preventing Software Vulnerabilities, 1st edn. Addison-Wesley Professional, Massachusetts (2006)
6. Erickson, J., Musuvathi, M., Burckhardt, S., Olynyk, K.: Effective Data-Race Detection for the Kernel. In: The 9th USENIX Conference on Operating Systems Design and Implementation (OSDI 2010). USENIX (2010)
7. Farchi, E., Nir, Y., Ur, S.: Concurrent Bug Patterns and How to Test Them. In: Parallel and Distributed Processing Symposium (IPDPS 2003), pp. 22–26. IEEE (2003)
8. Flanagan, C., Freund, S.N.: Atomizer: A Dynamic Atomicity Checker for Multithreaded Programs. ACM SIGPLAN Notices 39(1), 256–267 (2004)
9. Gay, D., Levis, P., Behren, R.V., Welsh, M., Brewer, E., Culler, D.: The nesC Language: A holistic Approach to Networked Embedded Systems. In: Programming Language Design and Implementation (PLDI 2003), pp. 1–11. ACM (2003)
10. Gracioli, G., Fischmeister, S.: Tracing Interrupts in Embedded Software. In: International Conference on Languages, Compilers, and Tools for Embedded Systems (LCTES 2009), pp. 137–146. ACM (2009)
11. Higashi, M., Yamamoto, T., Hayase, Y., Ishio, T., Inoue, K.: An Effective Method to Control Interrupt Handler for Data Race Detection. In: 5th International Workshop on Automation of Software Test (AST 2010), pp. 79–86. ACM (2010)

12. Hill, J., Szewczyk, R., Woo, A., Hollar, S., Culler, D.E., Pister, K.S.J.: System Architecture Directions for Networked Sensors. In: Architectural Support for Programming Languages and Operating Systems, pp. 93–104. ACM (2000)
13. Lai, Z., Cheung, S.C., Chan, W.K.: Inter-Context Control-Flow and Data-Flow Test Adequacy Criteria for nesC Applications. In: The 16th International Symposium on Foundations of Software Engineering (SIGSOFT 2008/FSE-16), pp. 94–104. ACM (2008)
14. Lee, E.A.: The Problem with Threads. IEEE Computer 36(5), 33–42 (2006)
15. Leveson, N.G., Turner, C.S.: An Investigation of the Therac-25 Accidents. IEEE Computer 26(7), 18–41 (1993)
16. Lu, S., Park, S., Seo, E., Zhou, Y.: Learning from Mistakes? A Comprehensive Study on Real World Concurrency Bug Characteristics. In: International Conference on Architectural Support for Programming Languages and Operating Systems (ASPLOS 2008), pp. 329–339. ACM (2008)
17. Li, Z., Lin, T., Wang, X., Lu, S., Zhou, Y., Zhai, C.: Have Things Changed Now? - An Empirical Study of Bug Characteristics in Modern Open Source Software. In: The 9th Asian Symposium on Information Display (ASID 2006), pp. 25–33. ACM (2006)
18. Ousterhout, J.K.: Why Threads are a Bad Idea (for most purposes). In: Invited talk at the 1996 USENIX Technical Conference. USENIX (1996)
19. Regehr, J.: Random Testing of Interrupt-Driven Software. In: International Conference on Embedded Software (EMSOFT 2005), pp.290–298. ACM (2005)
20. Regehr, J., Cooprider, N.: Interrupt Verification via Thread Verification. Electronic Notes in Theoretical Computer Science 174, 139–150 (2007)
21. Regehr, J., Reid, A., Webb, K.: Eliminating Stack Overflow by Abstract Interpretation. ACM Transactions on Embedded Computing Systems 4(4), 751–778 (2005)
22. Ronsse, M., Maebe, J., De Bosschere, K.: Detecting Data Races in Sequential Programs with DIOTA. In: Danelutto, M., Vanneschi, M., Laforenza, D. (eds.) Euro-Par 2004. LNCS, vol. 3149, pp. 82–89. Springer, Heidelberg (2004)
23. Ryzhyk, L., Chubb, P., Kuz, I., Heiser, G.: Dingo: Taming Device Drivers. In: The 4th ACM European Conference on Computer Systems (EuroSys 2009), pp. 275–288. ACM (2009)
24. Sahoo, S.K., Criswell, J., Adve, V.: An Empirical Study of Reported Bugs in Server Software with Implications for Automated Bug Diagnosis. In: The International Conference on Software Engineering (ICSE 2010), pp. 485–494. ACM (2010)
25. Sundaram, V., Eugster, P., Zhang, X.: Lightweight Tracing for Wireless Sensor Networks Debugging. In: The Workshop on Middleware Tools, Services and Run-Time Support for Sensor Networks (MidSens 2009), pp. 13–18. ACM (2009)
26. Tahara, T., Gondow, K., Ohsuga, S.: Dracula: Detector of Data Races in Signals Handlers. In: The 15th IEEE Asia-Pacific Software Engineering Conference (APSEC 2008), pp. 17–24. IEEE (2008)
27. Tchamgoue, G.M., Ha, O.-K., Kim, K.-H., Jun, Y.-K.: Lightweight Labeling Scheme for On-the-fly Race Detection of Signal Handlers. In: Kim, T.-h., Adeli, H., Robles, R.J., Balitanas, M. (eds.) UCMA 2011, Part II. CCIS, vol. 151, pp. 201–208. Springer, Heidelberg (2011)
28. Zhang, W., Lim, J., Olichandran, R., Scherpelz, J., Jin, G.: ConSeq: Detecting Concurrency Bugs through Sequential Errors. ACM SIGPLAN Notices 46(3), 251–264 (2011)

Efficient Verification of First Tangled Races to Occur in Programs with Nested Parallelism*

Mun-Hye Kang and Young-Kee Jun**

Department of Informatics, Gyeongsang National University,
Jinju 660-701, The Republic of Korea
{kmh,jun}@gnu.ac.kr

Abstract. Since data races result in unintended nondeterministic executions of the programs, detecting the races is important for debugging shared memory programs with nested parallelism. Particularly, the first races to occur in an execution of a program must be detected, because they can potentially affect other races that occur later. Previous on-the-fly techniques are inefficient or can not guarantee to verify the existence of the first tangle of data races to occur. This paper presents an efficient two-pass on-the-fly technique in such a kind of programs. This technique is still efficient with regard to the execution time and memory space by keeping a constant number of accesses involved in the first races for each shared variable during the execution. We empirically compare our technique with previous techniques using a set of synthetic programs with OpenMP directives.

Keywords: shared memory programs, nested parallelism, data races, first races to occur, first tangle verification, on-the-fly race detection, efficiency.

1 Introduction

The data race [5,11] or simply a race is an access error which can arise in an execution of explicitly shared-memory program [2,12,1] in which the parallel threads use shared variables and include at least one write access without appropriate synchronization. Since such the races result in unintended non-deterministic executions of programs, it is important to efficiently detect the races, especially *the first races to occur* [4,8,13], for the effective debugging of such programs. Such the first races are unaffected by other races and may lead other races to appear or to be hidden.

There are only two previous on-the-fly techniques [4,13] to detect the first races to occur in programs with nested parallelism. A two-pass on-the-fly technique

* This research was supported by Basic Science Research Program through the National Research Foundation of Korea (NRF) funded by the Ministry of Education, Science and Technology (2011-0026340).

** Corresponding author: In Gyeongsang National University, he is also involved in the Research Institute of Computer and Information Communication (RICIC).

T.-h. Kim et al. (Eds.): ASEA/DRBC/EL 2011, CCIS 257, pp. 451–460, 2011.

[13] verifies the existence of the first races to occur including the first tangle. But, this technique keeps the history of the accesses for each shared variable, and checks the logical concurrency relation of each current access and the previous accesses stored in the access history whose size is as many as the maximum parallelism of the program in the worst case. The other technique [4] can not guarantee to verify the existence of the first tangle, because the technique detects only one race in the first tangle in the worst case. Therefore, this technique requests unpredictable the number of executions to determine a race-free portion of program which has tangles of races.

This paper presents an efficient two-pass on-the-fly technique for verifying the first tangle to occur in such a kind of programs. The first pass collects at most four accesses involved in the first races for a shared variable by examining the *happens-before relation* and the *left-of relation* between every two accesses to the shared variable. And the second pass detects all first races to occur including the tangled races using those accesses collected in the first pass. This technique is still efficient with regard to the execution time and memory space by keeping a constant number of accesses involved in the first races for each shared variable during an execution.

The rest of the paper is organized as follows. Section 2 introduces first races to occur in shared memory programs with nested parallelism and discusses the problems of previous techniques to detect such races. Section 3 presents an efficient technique that verifies the existence of the first races to occur including the tangle races. Section 4 analyzes the efficiency of the technique in terms of its time and space complexities and compares it with the previous techniques. The final section concludes the paper.

2 Background

We consider a shared memory program [2,12,1] such as an OpenMP Program with nested parallelism. To help user's understanding, the concurrency relation among threads in an execution of the shared-memory program can be represented by a directed acyclic graph called *Partial Order Execution Graph* (POEG) [3] as shown in Figure 1. In a POEG, a vertex indicates a fork or join operation, and an arc between vertices represents a forked or joined thread. The accesses named r and w drawn in the figure as small dots on the arcs represent a read and a write access that access the same shared variable, respectively. The numbers in the access names indicate the order in which those accesses are observed.

Concurrency determination is not dependent on the number or relative speeds of processors executing the program. Because the graph captures the *happens-before relation* [9], it represents a partial order over the set of events executed by the program and may be denoted as *Ordered*(e_i, e_j). An event e_i happened before another event e_j if there exists a path from e_i to e_j in the POEG and e_i is concurrent with e_j if neither one happened before the other. For example, consider the accesses in Figure 1, where $r0$ happened before $w6$ because there exists a path from $r0$ to $w6$, and $r0$ is concurrent with $w10$, because there is no

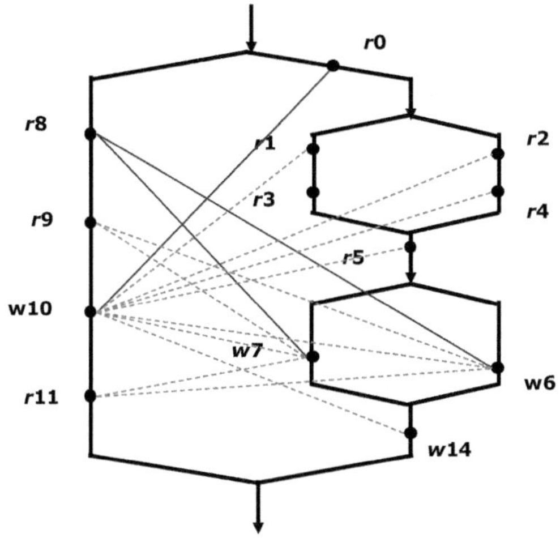

Fig. 1. The First Races to Occur in Shared-memory Programs: dotted lines represent races occurred in the programs, and solid lines represent the first races to occur in the programs

path between them. If two accesses e_i, e_j are conflicting and concurrent with each other then the two accesses are involved in a *race* denoted e_i-e_j.

An access e_j is affected by another access e_i, if e_i happened before e_j and e_i is involved in a race. A race e_i-e_j is unaffected, if neither e_i nor e_j are affected by any other accesses. A race is partially affected, if only one of e_i and e_j is affected by another access. A tangle is a set of partially affected races such that if e_i-e_j is a race in the tangle then exactly one of them is affected by e_k such that e_k is also involved in a race of the same tangle. A tangled race is a partially affected race that is involved in a tangle. A *first race to occur* [4,8,13] or simply *first race* is either an unaffected race or a tangled race. Fig 1 shows a POEG which includes seventeen races represented dotted lines and solid lines, but only three $\{r0\text{-}w10, r8\text{-}w6, r8\text{-}w7\}$ of the seventeen races indicated solid lines can be the first races which are tangled races. Eliminating the first race is very important for effective debugging, because it may make the other affected races disappear or appear.

There are only two previous on-the-fly techniques [4,13] to detect the first races to occur in programs with nested parallelism. The first technique [13] is a two-pass monitoring algorithm. The first pass collects a subset of first races by maintaining in a shared data structure called *access history* for the shared variable in order to collect a subset of *candidate access* [7,8,13] for being involved in a first race. And then the second pass reports all first races including the first tangle using the candidate subset already collected in the second pass. In Figure 1, the technique detects all first races $\{r0\text{-}w10, r8\text{-}w6, r8\text{-}w7\}$. Therefore, this technique can guarantee to verify the existence of the first race including the first tangle. However, this technique is inefficient with regard to the execution time and memory space that keeps the history of the accesses for each shared variable and checks the logical concurrency relation of an current access and the previous accesses stored in the access history, as many as the maximum parallelism of the program in the worst case.

The most efficient on-the-fly technique [4] is also a two-pass monitoring algorithm. In the first pass, the number of accesses stored is kept constant based on examining the *happens-before relation* [9] and the *left-of relation* [10] between every two accesses to the shared variable in order to collect a constant number of candidate accesses for being involved in first races. In the second pass, the candidates collected in the first pass are examined also based on the happens-before relation and the left-of relation with each current conflicting access in order to complete the set of candidate accesses. In Figure 1, the technique detects only one race $\{r0\text{-}w10\}$ included the tangle. Therefore, this technique can not guarantee to verify the existence of the first tangle, because the technique detects only one race in the first tangle in the worst case by reporting limited the number of first races.

3 Efficient Verification of First Tangle

This paper presents an efficient two-pass on-the-fly technique for verifying the first tangle in shared-memory programs with nested parallelism. The first pass collects at most four accesses involved in the first race into an *access history* and *first-race access history* for a shared variable by examining the *happened-before relation* and the *left-of relation* between every two accesses to the shared variable. And the second pass detects all first races to occur including the tangle race using those accesses in the first-race access history collected in the first pass.

3.1 First-Race Access

On-the-fly detection technique detects races at runtime by maintaining shared data structures to monitor every access to each shared variable in an execution instance. In other words, whenever an access accesses a shared variable, a runtime monitoring technique checks to determine whether there is a race between the current access and previous accesses by examining the *happened-before relation* [9] and the *left-of relation* between every two accesses to the shared variable. This technique uses the left-of relation of Mellor-crummey [10] redefined in the previous paper [4]. If an access e_i is left side of e_j, we denote the relation as $Leftof(e_i, e_j)$. To make check efficient by collecting at most four accesses, we need to define the notion of an *outer access* that is executed more outside than other accesses. Also, we need to define the notion of a *last outer access* in order not to miss any race involved a tangle.

Definition 3.1. *An access event e_i is left side of another event e_j, if they satisfy the boolean relation, $Leftof(e_i, e_j)$. An access event e_i is an* outer access, *if there does not exist any other access in the left or right side of e_i.*

Definition 3.2. *An access event e_i is a* last access, *if there does not exist any other access that happened after e_i. An access event e_i is a* last-outer access, *if e_i is an* outer access *and a* last access.

Definition 3.3. *A* first-race access *is one of two accesses involved in a first race to occur: a read (write) first-race access or a read-write first-race access.*

Definition 3.4. *A read or write access e_i involved in a race is a* first-race access, *if there does not exist any other access that is involved in a race and happened before e_i.*

Definition 3.5. *A write access event e_i is a* read-write first-race access, *if the following are satisfied: 1) there does not exist a write access that happened before e_i; 2) there exist a read access that happened before e_i and involved in a race; and 3) there does not exist another* write first-race access *that has concurrent relationship with e_i.*

For example, an access $r0$ is a read first-race access, because the access is involved in a race with $w10$ and there does not exist any other access that is involved in a race and happened before $r0$ in the Figure 1. An access $w6$ is a read-write first-race access, because there does not exist a write access that happened before the access, and there exist a read access $r0$ that happened before $w6$ and involved in a race. Also, there does not exist another write first-race access that has concurrent relationship with $w6$. Two accesses $w7$ and $w10$ that has concurrent relationship with $w6$ are read-write first-race access, too.

To verify the first races to occur including the first tangle, this technique maintains second shared data structures. The first shared data structure is an *access history* (*AH*) which stores at most three accesses involved in the first race for a shared variable, and the second shared data structure is an *first-race access history* (*FH*) which stores at most four accesses involved in the first race and executed as outer accesses at that time for a shared variable. The accesses are called the *first-race accesses.* An access history (AH_X) for a shared variable X is composed of two subsets of most recent accesses: $AH_X[R]$ and $AH_X[W]$. $AH_X[R]$ stores two read accesses (called *last outer accesses*) which were executed as outer accesses: $AH_X[R_L]$ and $AH_X[R_R]$. $AH_X[W]$ stores only one write access. FA consists of two subsets of unaffected access by any access for a shared variable X: $FA_X[R]$ and $FA_X[W]$. FA_X stores two accesses in each subset which were executed as outer accesses at that time and involved in a race with an access included in AH: $FA_X[R_L]$, $FA_X[R_R]$, $FA_X[W_L]$ and $FA_X[W_R]$.

3.2 The Efficient Verification Algorithm

The Fig 2 shows two procedures for the two types of accesses in the first monitoring pass: checkread_1st() and checkwrite_1st(). A *current* represents the current access to a shared variable X. In checkread_1st(), line 1-2 determines if the *current* is involved in a race by checking the happened-before relation with one write access stored previously in $AH_X[W]$. Line 3-6 checks the left-of relation between the *current* and every read stored in $AH_X[R]$ in order to maintain $AH_X[R]$ to store the only outside accesses. If the *current* was not involved in a race by line1, this procedure returns to exit in line 7-8. In line 9-14, it checks the left-of relations between the *current* and the previous first-race accesses stored

```
0 Checkread_1st(X, current)
1 if ¬ Ordered(AH_X[W], current) then
2     racing_current := true;
3 if ¬ Leftof(AH_X[R_L], current) then
4     AH_X[R_L] := current;
5 if ¬ Leftof(current, AH_X[R_R]) then
6     AH_X[R_R] := current;
7 if ¬ racing_current then
8     return;
9 if FH_X[R_L] = ∅ or
10    Leftof(current, FH_X[R_L]) then
11        FH_X[R_L]) := current;
12 if FH_X[R_R] = ∅ or
13    Leftof(FH_X[R_R], current) then
14        FH_X[R_R]) := current;
15 end Checkread_1st
```

```
0 Checkwrite_1st(X, current)
1 for all c in AH_X do
2     if ¬ Ordered(c, current) then
3         racing_current := true;
4 AH_X[W] := current;
5 if ¬ racing_current then
6     return;
7 if FH_X[W_L] = ∅ or
8     Leftof(current, FH_X[W_L]) then
9         FH_X[W_L]) := current;
10 if FH_X[W_R] = ∅ or
11    Leftof(FH_X[W_R], current) then
12        FH_X[W_R]) := current;
13 halt;
14 end Checkwrite_1st
```

Fig. 2. The First-Pass Algorithm

in $FH_X[R]$ to determine whether the current access is a new first-race access to replace the previous access there.

In checkwrite_1st(), line 1-3 determines if the *current* is involved in a race by checking the happened-before relations with tree previous accesses stored in AH_X. In line 4, the *current* is stored into $AH_X[W]$ unconditionally, because a future access that is involved in a race with the access stored previously in $AH_X[W]$. It the *current* is not involved in a race by line1-3, this procedure returns to exit in line 5-6. Because the access that not involved in a race is also not involved in a first-race. In line 7-12, it checks the left-of relations between the *current* and the previous first-race accesses stored in $FH_X[W]$ to determine if it becomes a new first-race access to replace the previous access there. In the last line, this current thread is halted to eliminate unnecessary monitoring time.

If these two procedures of the first pass monitoring algorithm are applied to an example shown in the Figure 1, it is stored $\{r9, r5, w10\}$ in AH_X and $\{r8, w10\}$ in FH_X.

The Figure 3 shows two procedures for the two types of accesses in the second monitoring pass: checkread_2nd() and checkwrite_2nd(). In line 1-2 of checkread_2nd(), this procedure returns to exit, if there exists a first-race access in a current thread. The reason is that already detected a first-race access in this current thread. Line 3-4 determines if the *current* is involved in a race by checking the happened-before relation with the all first-race accesses of $FH_X[W]$ collected in the first pass. If the *current* was not involved in a race by being checked in line 3-4, this procedure returns to exit in line 6-7 because the *current* is not a first-race access. Also, it checks in line 8-13 the left-of relations between the *current* and the previous first-race accesses stored in $FH_X[R]$ to determine if it becomes a new first-race access to replace the previous there. And, the racing *current* is added into $FS_X[R]$ to be reported, because the access is involved in a first race. In checkwrite_2nd(), line 1-3 determines if the *current* is involved in a race by checking the happened-before relations with all of the four first-race

```
0 Checkread_2nd(X, current)
1 if read_first_candidate then
2     return;
3 for all c in FH_X[W] do
4     if ¬ Ordered(c, current) then
5         racing_current := true;
6     if ¬ racing_current then
7         return;
8 if FH_X[R_L] = ∅ or
9     Leftof(current, FH_X[R_L]) then
10        FH_X[R_L]) := current;
11 if FH_X[R_R] = ∅ or
12    Leftof(FH_X[R_R], current) then
13        FH_X[R_R]) := current;
14 add current to FS_X[R];
15 read_first_candidate := true;
16 end Checkread_2nd
```

```
0 Checkwrite_2nd(X, current)
1 for all c in FH_X do
2     if ¬ Ordered(c, current) then
3         racing_current := true;
4 if ¬ racing_current then
5     return;
6 if FH_X[W_L] = ∅ or
7     Leftof(current, FH_X[W_L]) then
8         FH_X[W_L]) := current;
9 if FH_X[W_R] = ∅ or
10    Leftof(FH_X[W_R], current) then
11        FH_X[W_R]) := current;
12 add current to FS_X[W];
13 halt;
14 end Checkwrite_2nd
```

Fig. 3. The Second-Pass Algorithm

access stored in FH_X. And line 6-12 is similar to that in checkread_2nd(). Finally, this current thread is halted to eliminate unnecessary monitoring time. As a result, accesses $\{r8,\ r0,\ w10\}$ are stored in FH_X and accesses $\{r0,\ w10\}$ are stored in FS_X.

4 Efficiency Evaluation

In this section, we analyze complexities of our algorithm and empirically compare our technique with the previous techniques using a set of synthetic programs with OpenMP directives.

4.1 Analysis

This two-pass on-the-fly technique stores at most seven access information for each shared variable into the two kinds of collecting histories: three accesses for access history and four accesses for first race access history. The efficiency of our technique depends on the worst case complexities of two factors: (1) the memory space is required for each entry of the histories, and (2) the time is required for comparing an access with another accesses to determine the happened-before relation and the left-of relation. Since these two factors are dependent on the labeling schemes which generate a constant size of access information, the complexities of this technique are constant for both the space required for each monitoring history and the number of comparisons for each access to a shared variable.

Let V be the number of shared variables, N be the nesting depth, and T be the maximum parallelism of the parallel program. The worst case complexities of the technique include therefore $O(V)$ space for seven constant sized entries

	Synthetic	detected races: [13]	detected races: Our Technique
1	r1 r2 r3 w4	r1-w4	r1-w4
2	r1 r2 r3 r4 w5	r1-w5, r1-w4	r1-w5, r1-w4
3	r1 w2 r3 r4 w5	r1-w2	r1-w2
4	w1 r2 r3 r4 w5	w1-r2	w1-r2
5	r1 r2 r3 r4 r7 w5 r6	r1-w5, w5-r6	r1-w5, w5-r6
6	r1 r2 r3 w4 r7 w5 r6	r1-w4	r1-w4
7	r1 r2 r3 w4 r5 r6	w4-r2, w4-r3	w4-r2, w4-r3
8	r1 r2 r3 w4 r5 r6	r1-w6, r2-w4, r2-w6, r3-w4	r1-w6, r2-w4, r2-w6, r3-w4
9	r1 r2 r3 w4 w5	r1-w4, r1-w5, w4-w5	r1-w4, r1-w5, w4-w5
10	r1 r2 w3 w4 w5	r1-w4, r1w5, r2-w3	r1-w4, r1w5, r2-w3
11	r1 r2 r3 r4 w5 r6 r7	r1-w5, r4-w5	r1-w5, r4-w5
12	r1 r2 r3 r4 r5 r6 w7	r1-w7	r1-w7

Fig. 4. The Results for Accuracy

of collecting histories except the space to generate access information which is $O(NT)$ by NR-Labeling for all of the simultaneously active threads each of which has $O(N)$; and $O(log_2 N)$ time by NR-Labeling on every access for comparing with at most seven previous accesses in monitoring histories except the time to generate access information which is $O(N)$ by NR-Labeling at every fork or join operation.

4.2 Experimentation

We empirically compare our technique with the previous techniques using a set of synthetic programs with OpenMP directives [2,12,1]. We use NR-labeling [6] to check the logical concurrency relation of an current access and the previous accesses stored in an access history. The NR-labeling, our technique, and the previous techniques are implemented as run-time libraries written in C language. Synthetic programs were developed by varying the thread number, the nesting depth, and the location or number of write access events. And these programs were compiled with gcc 4.4.4 for OpenMP 3.0 which supports nested parallelism, and run on a system with Intel Quad-core 2Xeon CPUs and 8GB RAM under the Kernel 2.6 of Linux operating system.

To check the accuracy of our technique, we compared our technique with the previous technique [13] that verifies the existence of the first races to occur including the first tangle. Figure 4 shows the test results for accuracy using twelve types of synthetic programs. The first program shows two parallel threads using two columns and the next third program includes a nested thread in a second thread. The 7-8th programs execute three parallel threads. In the result, our technique and previous technique detected the number of first races in experimentation with simple programs. To check the verification ability, we compared our technique with the previous efficient technique [4]. Figure 5 shows the test

Type	Synthetic Program	The number of tangled race	The number of detected tangled race					
			Previous Technique			Our Technique		
			Maximum	Minimum	Average	Maximum	Minimum	Average
1		6	6	6	6	6	6	6
	r r r	12	9	12	11.1	12	12	12
		20	20	20	20	20	20	20
		30	25	30	28	30	30	30
		42	36	42	41.4	42	42	42
	w w w	56	56	56	56	56	56	56
		72	40	40	40	72	72	72
		90	36	45	44.1	90	90	90
2		3	3	3	3	3	3	3
	r r	10	6	10	9.6	12	12	12
		21	20	21	20.4	21	21	21
		36	28	36	32.8	36	36	36
		55	46	55	54.1	42	42	42
	w w w	78	78	78	78	78	78	78
		105	105	105	105	105	105	105
		136	30	76	66.7	136	136	136

Fig. 5. The Results for Tangle Verification

results with more complex programs including many tangles. We executed each program ten times and took the max, the min and the average of the total number of detected races. The third column of Figure 5 shows the total number of tangle race involved in each program. The first type of program, call a non-nested program, concurrently executes three threads and a write access after a read access in each thread to produce tangled races. And, to increase the number of tangle race, we increase the number of the last thread. Our technique detected all tangled races in the programs. On the other hand, the previous efficient technique detected only 36 races of 90 races in last row of the first program type. We can expect the number of races missed by the previous technique tzxo increase with the number of tangles. The second type of program, call a nested program, concurrently executes two threads. The second thread has two child threads. Like the first type, these threads execute a write access after a read access. The forth column of Figure 5 shows the number of tangled race that are actually detected by previous technique and our technique.

5 Conclusion

Previous on-the-fly techniques are inefficient or can not guarantee to verify the existence of the first tangle of data races to occur. This paper presents an efficient two-pass on-the-fly technique for verifying the first tangle to occur in shared memory programs with nested parallelism. The first pass collects at most three accesses involved in the first race into an access history and first-race access history for a shared variable by examining the happened-before relation and the left-of relation between every two accesses to the shared variable. And the second pass detects all first races to occur including the tangle race using those accesses in the first-race access history collected in the first pass. This technique guarantees to verify the existence of the first tangle and is still more efficient with regard to the execution time and memory space.

References

1. Chandra, R., Menon, R., Dagum, L., Kohr, D., Maydan, D., McDonald, D.: Parallel programming in openmp
2. Dagum, L., Menon, R.: Openmp: An industry-standard api for shared-memory programming. In: IEEE Computational Science, pp. 46–55. IEEE (January/March 1998)
3. Dinning, A., Schonberg, E.: An empirical comparison of monitoring algorithms for access anomaly detection. SIGPLAN Not. 25, 1–10 (1990)
4. Ha, K., Jun, Y.J., Yoo, K.: Efficient on-the-fly detection of first races in nested parallel programs. In: Proc. of Workshop on State-of-the-Art in Scientific Computing, PARA 2004. LNCS, pp. 75–84 (2004)
5. Helmbold, D.P., McDowell, C.E.: A taxonomy of race conditions. J. Parallel Distrib. Comput. 33, 159–164 (1996)
6. Jun, Y.K., Koh, K.: On-the-fly detection of access anomalies in nested parallel loops. SIGPLAN Not. 28, 107–117 (1993)
7. Jun, Y.K., McDowell, C.E.: On-the-fly detection of the first races in programs with nested parallelism. In: 2nd Conf. on Parallel and Distributed Processing Technique and Application, CSREA, pp. 1549–1560 (1996)
8. Kim, J.S., Jun, Y.K.: Scalable on-the-fly detection of the first races in parallel programs. In: Proceedings of the 12th International Conference on Supercomputing, ICS 1998, pp. 345–352. ACM, New York (1998)
9. Lamport, L.: Ti clocks, and the ordering of events in a distributed system. Commun. ACM 21, 558–565 (1978)
10. Mellor-Crummey, J.: On-the-fly detection of data races for programs with nested fork-join parallelism. In: Proceedings of the 1991 ACM/IEEE Conference on Supercomputing, Supercomputing 1991, pp. 24–33. ACM, New York (1991)
11. Netzer, R.H.B., Miller, B.P.: What are race conditions?: Some issues and formalizations. ACM Lett. Program. Lang. Syst. 1, 74–88 (1992)
12. Netzer, R.H.B., Miller, B.P.: Openmp architecture review board (2008)
13. Park, H.D., Jun, Y.K.: Two-pass on-the-fly detection of the first races in shared-memory parallel. In: Proceedings of the SIGMETRICS Symposium on Parallel and Distributed Tools, SPDT 1998, p. 158. ACM, New York (1998)

Implementation of Display Based on Pilot Preference

Chung-Jae Lee[1], Jin Seob Yi[2], and Ki-Il Kim[3,*]

[1] Department of Aerospace Enginerring, Gyeongsang National University, Jinju, Korea
[2] Korea Aerospace Industries, Ltd., Sacheon, Korea
[3] Department of Informatics, Engineering Research Institute, Gyeongsang National University, Jinju, Korea
kikim@gnu.ac.kr

Abstract. As the many functions on the aircraft are implemented through software, they provide the pilots with more flexible and extensible controls. Among them, display is one of the important instruments in that information on the aircraft is recognized through it. While previous display was static with fixed layout, a new display is dynamic by employing floating layout on the screen through the help of software. In this paper, we propose a new display method, which automatically returns to the layout of instruments on the aircraft according to the pilot preference. To achieve this, the software records current layout and suggests the best matching layout to the pilot whenever the same event occurs. We explain the design and implementation issues to add this function into the current system.

Keywords: Display, Pilot preference.

1 Introduction

Aeronautical instruments provide the pilots information about working status, warning for malfunctions, position and navigating path toward the destination. In general, aeronautical instrument is largely divided into following three categories, flight instruments, navigation instruments, and engine instruments. The requirement of them includes accuracy, light weight, small size and durability. In addition, there is regulation to place them on the aircraft such as FAR Part 23 Subpart F[1].

In the point of instrument placement, the noticeable current trend for them is known as glass cockpit[2-3] that features electronic instrument displays, typically large LCD screens, as opposed to the traditional style of analog dials and gauges[4]. This means that previous analog and stand-alone instruments are replaced by digital and integrated one. For example, navigation system through the GPS system is introduced in glass cockpit nowadays. This trend is led by software that is regarded to play a great role in aircraft system. In addition, by the help of software, many research works such as Enhanced Vision System, Synthetic Vision System, Combined Vision System, and Automatic Dependent Surveillance-Broadcast are going on. More

* Corresponding author.

T.-h. Kim et al. (Eds.): ASEA/DRBC/EL 2011, CCIS 257, pp. 461–466, 2011.

detailed for glass cockpit, more convenient and flexible functions are introduced in new aircraft system. One of them is flexible layout system. While previous display has the fixed layout system so the replacement of each instrument on the cockpit is not allowed. On the contrary, current glass cockpit supports movement of instruments according to the pilot's will. This system is known to be implemented in F-35made by Lockheed Martin. In this paper, we propose how to extend and add functions into this system. Even though current glass cockpit system supports dynamic layout and touch based interface on the display, there function is limited to follow the pilot's order. In addition to this function, our system is extended to suggest the most familiar layout according to pilot's preference. This function is achieved by recording current system status whenever interesting events happen.

The rest of this paper is organized as follows. In section 2, we briefly describe the touch based display system in F-35. And then, the proposed scheme and its prototype are explained in next section. Finally, we provide the conclusion and further works.

2 Touch Based Display

An 8"x20" Multi-Function Display System (MFDS) is the panoramic projection display for the F-35[5]. MFDS employs leading edge technology in projection engine architecture, video, compression, illumination module controls and processing memory – all of which will make the MFDS the most advanced tactical display. One-gigabyte-per-second data interfaces will enable the MFDS to display six full motion images simultaneously. The adaptable layout will be easily reconfigurable for different missions or mission segments. Projection display technology will provide a high-luminance, high-contrast, and high-resolution picture with no viewing angle effect. The display is changed by pressing a finger on different parts of the screen of the multi-function display, or MFD, to reconfigure or prioritize information or activate systems. The forest of toggle switches in previous fighter cockpits has been wiped clean from the F-35's interior landscape, with most of their functions moved to the touch screen. A few switches still sprout here and there, but the overall cockpit ambience is one of simplicity and calm. The Fig. 1 shows the example of display on F-35.

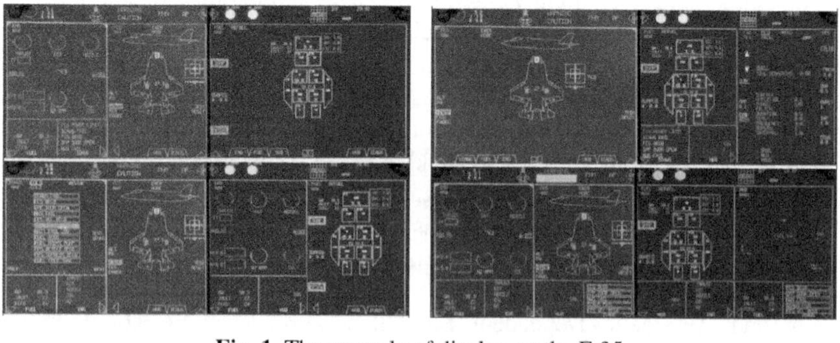

Fig. 1. The example of display on the F-35

As you can see in Fig. 1, different layout is easily reconfigurable for different missions and events through pilot touch interface. Multifunction display, created by combining two eight- by ten-inch displays, can be customized and divided into many different-sized screens through pilot-vehicle interface design. By touching the screen, the pilot can select a pair of eight- by ten-inch window displays, or four five- by eight-inch windows, or any combination of window sizes to project information based on its importance at any given moment. This ability to control formats eases the interpretation of complex data. However, the flexibility in display size and the diversity of data are not available in any other fighter aircraft.

This implies that pilot can make priority to situational awareness and to ensuring the information - not just raw data - the pilot receives is the most pertinent for any given moment instead of presenting the pilot with acres of gauges representing all systems and situations all the time.

3 Display Based on Pilot Preference

In this section, we explain how to extend current MFDS by proposing preferred display automatically according to events. The proposed scheme records the current layout and seeks the most preferred layout whenever the events happen. To achieve this, a new system employs database system and uses it to suggest the most preferred layout.

3.1 Software Architecture

The proposed scheme has the following software architecture. For generating events, we use Microsoft Flight Simulator[6] that is software providing an artificial re-creation of aircraft flight and various aspects of the flight environment. When a corresponding event occurs, event is notified to our display software. And then, Event ID and current layout is inserted into database as well as query with Event ID is delivered to system. Database system returns the result for query with recommended layout according to the mode. When a pilot selects it, the current display is replaced by suggested one. The SimConnect SDK is used to write add-on components for communicating Flight Simulator and display software.

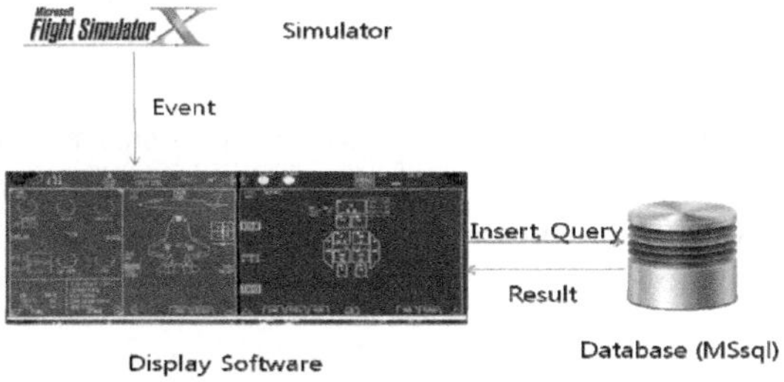

Fig. 2. The example of display on the F-35

3.2 Preferred Display

When an event happens, the predetermined Event ID is generated. With this ID, we search the database to check which layout is the most preferred. For the suggestion, three different policies are concerned.

Window Based. In this method, the entries with same Event ID are first extracted from the database. And then, the total number for each layout is counted. After this, we count Instrument ID appeared in each window. Upon completing this job, a system shows the candidate for layout at corresponding event.

Layout Based. Unlike the window based that is dependent on respective window in layout, this scheme records the layout as string, for example, "13452876" is for the first layout from up to down, left to right placement. After corresponding layer is selected, the counting is conducted with the string. And then, the layout with the largest number of recording is recommended to the pilot.

In addition to above two methods searching the most preferred display, we can add useful functions to proposed scheme. First, we can make use of time information to suggest the layout in a principle of time locality. According to configuration, a recent layout during defined duration will be concerned for selection. This is very useful when each pilot tends to move his preference. Also, we can modify the current system to suggest the pilot for each layout. That is, the most one preferred display for each layout is searched at window based or layout based.

3.3 Implementation

We implement display software by C#. In the design, we define four possible layouts in Fig. 3 and three events (take-off, landing, and encountering the enemy). We run many difference scenarios to collect the several cases. Fig. 4 shows the case when our fighter aircraft encounters the enemy. There are two different preferred displays according to mode, windows based or layout based. On the contrary, for the landing, two different modes suggest the same layout for the event. Fig. 5 illustrates the case for landing.

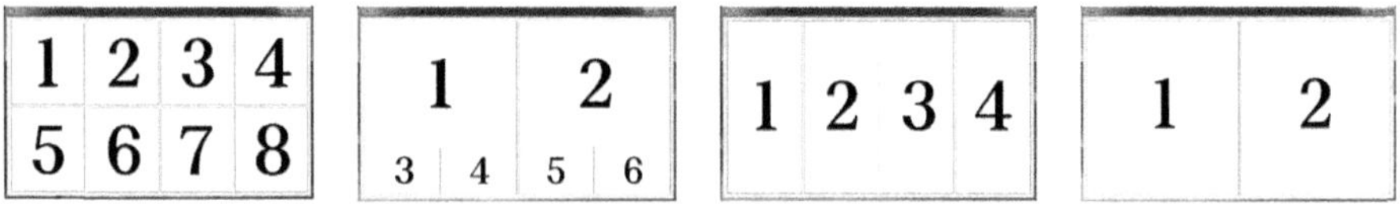

Fig. 3. Four layouts for display (Each windows are numbered)

Usually, even though pilot preference can vary for each event, there are some commons for large windows.

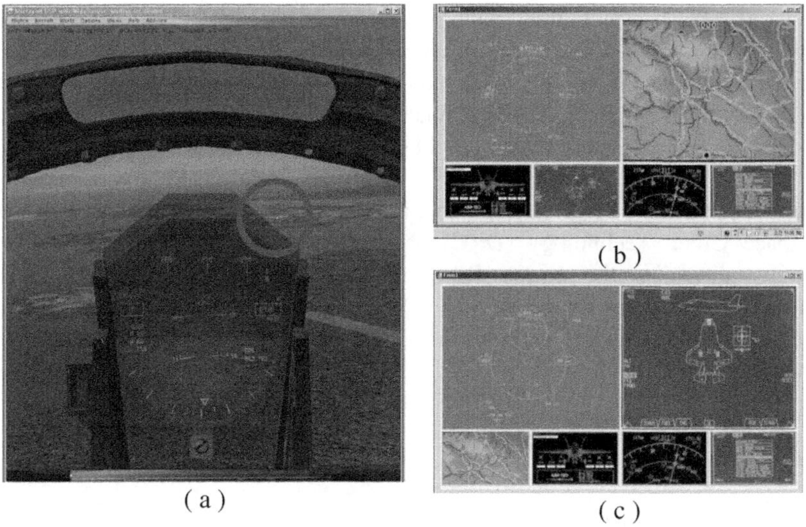

Fig. 4. (a) Event at encountering the enemy in Flight Simulator (b) windows based display (c) layout based display

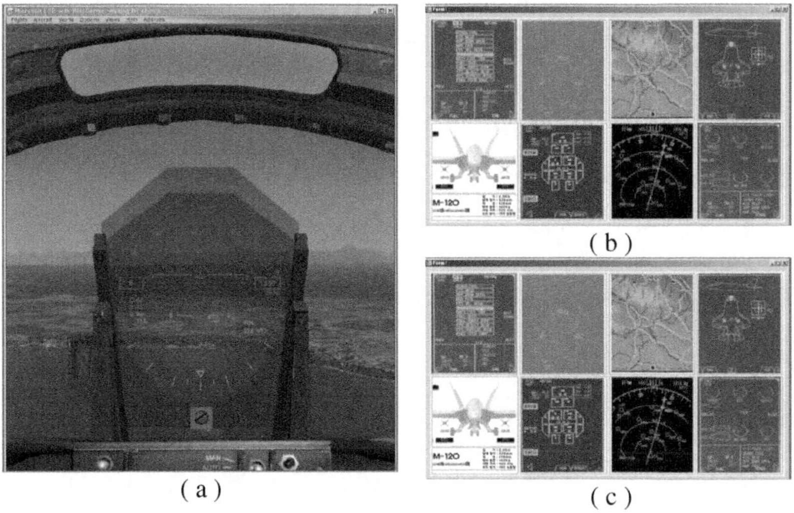

Fig. 5. (a) Landing in Flight Simulator (b) windows based display (c) layout based display

4 Conclusion and Further Works

Even though current glass cockpit system has evolved significantly from the previous one by the help of software on the integrated system, there are still some issues mentioned yet. For the rapid response, in this paper, we propose how to extend current MFDS by including pattern matching algorithm. Instead of manual configuration for the display, the proposed scheme automatically searches for the most preferred display for the happened event. Also, implementation through C# reveals that it can be good additional functionality for the pilot. Related to this work, improved display for each instrument will going on as further work.

Acknowledgments. This work was supported by the Degree and Research Center for Aerospace Green Technology (DRC) of the Korea Aerospace Research Institute (KARI) funded by the Korea Research Council of Fundamental Science & Technology (KRCF) and performed as a part of R&D program Air-BEST (Airborne Embedded System and Technology) funded by MKE (Ministry of Knowledge and Economy).

References

1. FAA FAR Part 23 (Subpart F)- Equipment, `http://www.astech-engineering.com/systems/avionics/aircraft/faapart23f.html`
2. Knight, J.: The Glass Cockpit. IEEE Comp., 92–95 (2007)
3. Inside The Glass Cockpit: IEEE Spectrum, `http://www.spectrum.ieee.org/publicaccess/0995ckpt.html`
4. Read, B.C.: Developing the Next Generation Cockpit Display System. IEEE AES Sys. Mag., 25–28 (1996)
5. F-35 Cockpit, `http://www.darkgovernment.com/news/f-35-cockpit/`
6. Microsoft Flight Simulator, `http://www.microsoft.com/games/fsinsider/`

A Study on WSN System Integration for Real-Time Global Monitoring

Young-Joo Kim[1], Sungmin Hong[1], Jong-uk Lee[2], Sejun Song[1], and Daeyoung Kim[3]

[1] Texas A&M University, Colleage Station, USA
{akates, ghitsh, song}@tamu.edu
[2] ETRI, Daejeon, South Korea
scinfuture@etri.re.kr
[3] KAIST,Daejeon, South Korea
kimd@kaist.ac.kr

Abstract. Since Wireless Sensor Networks (WSNs) have a lot of potential capability to provide diverse services to human by monitoring things scattered in real world, they are envisioned one of the core enabling technologies for ubiquitous computing. However, existing sensor network systems are designed for observing special zones or regional things by using small-scale, low power, and short range technologies. The seamless system integration in global scale is still in its infancy stage due to the lack of the fundamental integration technologies. In this paper, we present an effective integration avenue of real-time global monitoring system. The proposed technology includes design, integration, and operational strategies of IP-WSN based territorial monitoring system to ensure compatibility and interoperability. We especially offer the standardizations of sensing data formats and their database interfaces, which enable a spontaneous and systematic integration among the legacy WSN systems. The proposed technology would be a fundamental element for the practically deployable global territorial monitoring systems.

1 Introduction

The idea of ubiquitous computing has been envisioned to organize and mediate both physical and social interactions anytime and anywhere. The recent rapid evolution toward ubiquitous computing environment has been accelerated by enhanced sensors, advancement of cost effective wireless and mobile network technologies, improved computing powers, prolonged battery life, and open software architectures. One of the most important and essential technical building blocks of ubiquitous computing is WSNs (Wireless Sensor Networks) [1, 2, 3], which consist of self-powered, low-cost, and tiny processing nodes and can be deployed close to *things* [4, 5] of interest to create a cooperative and self-organizing wireless ad hoc network. Various public sectors (national, regional or local/municipal) have already deployed WSNs for the applications including structural health (bridge, building, dam, etc) monitoring, home safety and intrusion detection, industrial distribution management, and critical resource and environment (fire, flooding, earthquake, etc) surveillance. Recently, to

T.-h. Kim et al. (Eds.): ASEA/DRBC/EL 2011, CCIS 257, pp. 467–478, 2011.

deliver social security, organize national defense, ensure public safety, and rapidly respond natural disaster, the public sectors further focus on globally integrated monitoring systems and convergence technologies. However, existing WSN based monitoring systems are originally designed for observing special zones or regional things by using small-scale, low power, and short range stationary sensor nodes with proprietary or ZigBee [6, 7, 8, 9] communication technologies. Although many research efforts have been made to standardize the global network communication technologies such as IP-WSN (IP-based Wireless Sensor Network) [10, 11], the realization of seamless system integration in global scale is still in its infancy stage due to the lack of the fundamental integration technologies to handle heterogeneous and complicate WSN monitoring systems.

In this paper, we present an effective integration avenue of real-time global monitoring based on WSNs. The proposed technology includes design, integration, and operational strategies of IP-WSN based territorial monitoring system to ensure compatibility and interoperability. The system is designed to monitor ground, environment, and video (image) information of territory. In support of real-time monitoring capability, various wireless communication methods including CDMA, HSDPA, Wibro, and TRS are selectively used according to their availability on each geographical region. Our particular contribution is the standardizations of sensing data formats and their database interfaces, which enable a spontaneous and systematic integration among the legacy WSN systems to construct efficient and effective territorial monitoring systems. We envision that the proposed technology would be an essential element for the practically deployable global territorial monitoring systems.

The paper is organized as follows. Section 2 reviews existing technologies of legacy sensor network systems and their problems and investigates WSN communication protocols which can be used for the real-time territorial monitoring. Section 3 presents the hardware and software system designs of the proposed IP-WSN based real-time territorial monitoring integration system. In section 4, we propose the integration approaches among sensor network systems. Section 5 illustrates practical deployment scenarios of the proposed system. Finally, we offer conclusion and future work.

2 Background

In this section, we investigate existing technologies of legacy sensor network systems and their problems and study WSN communication protocols which can be used for the real-time territorial monitoring. We also point out the rational for the standardization of existing monitoring systems.

2.1 WSN Communication Technology for Real-time Monitoring

Most of legacy sensor networks have been using proprietary communication protocols, which intrinsically have several issues including expensive design cost, prolonged development time, high maintenance cost due to complicate operation and management, and limited scalability. Recent wireless communication technologies such as ZigBee and IP-WSN can be used to grapple with the legacy sensor network issues. ZigBee is a low-cost and low-power wireless mesh network standard which has been built upon the PHY and MAC layers defined in IEEE 802.15.4 [7]. It can construct a WSN system using low-power sensor nodes with the communication frequency of 800MHz ~ 2.4GHz and data rate of 20Kbps ~ 250Kbps. ZigBee, however, does not directly support IP connectivity. Their sensor nodes may equip various types of PHY/MAC including IEEE 802.15.4 PHY/MAC as an underlying layer beneath the adaptation layer and a lightweight TCP/IP layer since the adaptation layer specified in RFC 4944 [12] is not strongly dependent on the IEEE 802.15.4 standard unlike the ZigBee, which is tightly coupled with the current standard. Accordingly, a particular frequency band as well as 2.4 GHz can be chosen for various types of dedicated applications with IP-WSNs easier than with ZigBee. They can be easily interoperated with BcN (Broadband convergence Network) [13] since they run over a TCP/IP protocol. The IETF 6LoWPAN working group has been in progress of standardization for IP-WSNs since 2005.

2.2 Existing Monitor Systems

Sensor network monitoring applications include structural health (bridge, building, dam, etc) monitoring, home safety and intrusion detection, industrial distribution management, and critical resource and environment (fire, flooding, earthquake, etc) surveillance. Most of monitoring systems install stationary sensor nodes in small-scale points of interest and then collect necessary data to transmit it to the central computers for an information processing. For example, Figure 1 represents a legacy sensor network application (a reservoir remote monitoring system). A remote monitoring system for reservoir management [14] collects information related to a sluice gate, water quantity, and BOD (biochemical oxygen demand) from sensors installed in monitoring area around the sluice gate and then transmits collected information to the central monitoring computer. The computer saves and analyzes the information sent from plenty of places and then displays analyzed information as a GUI form. Communication between control devices such as sensor nodes and the monitoring system uses SMS (Short Message Service) through a cellphone. A building monitoring system [15] observes environmental information of temperature, humanity, CO_2, and crack information of buildings in real-time and stores their information into databases. This system can analyze variance in sensing values and environmental information of the special zone so that it can estimate energy consumption of buildings. Analyzed information or estimated information is displayed on PDA or WEB via the Internet. WSN applications related to ground environmental monitoring are a landslide prior warning system and real-time precise monitoring system for geological structures including fault plane around of primary national facilities. For example, Figure 2 illustrates a WSN based real-time landslide monitoring system [16]. A structural health monitoring system of Golden Gate Bridge in San Francisco is also designed and developed by UC Berkeley [17].

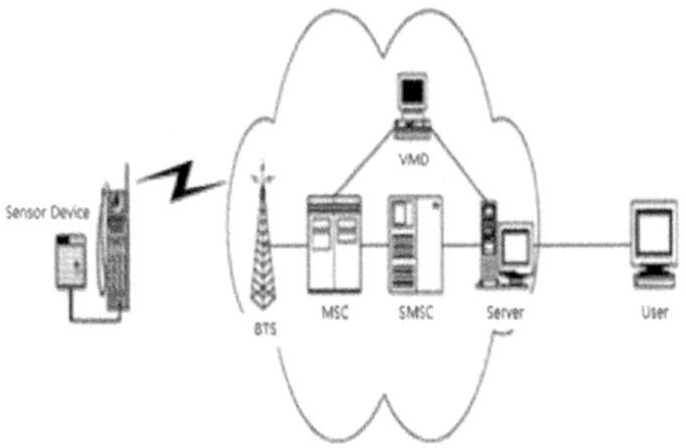

Fig. 1. Legacy Sensor Network Application

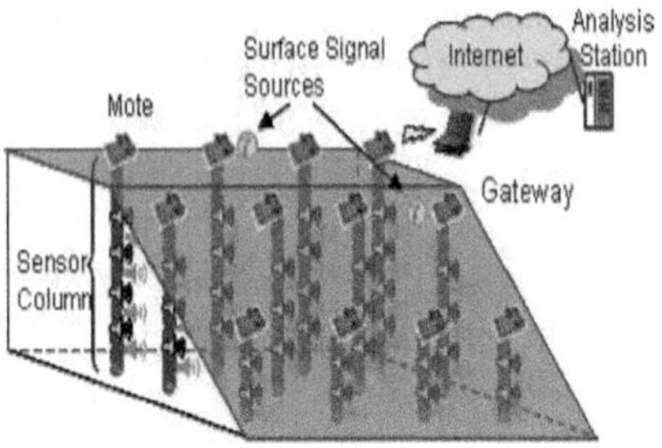

Fig. 2. WSN Application

2.3 Issues on WSN Based Monitor System Integration

Various public sectors (national, regional or local/municipal) focus on to construct globally integrated monitoring systems and to develop convergence technologies in order to deliver social security, organize national defense, ensure public safety, and rapidly respond natural disaster. However, existing sensor network approaches operate normally as a proxy to deliver sensing data to the central monitoring system and use local or proprietary protocols tailored to specific applications. If we directly integrate the systems with different proprietary protocols, as described in Figure 3, the integrated monitoring system may demand a complexity of interior structure in order to cope with several different network protocols, sensing formats, query commands, etc. The integration system structure shall be keep updated upon adding yet another proprietary sensor network. Although many research efforts have been made to standardize the global network communication protocols over the Internet such as IP-WSN, the realization of seamless system integration cannot be achieved alone due to the lack of the fundamental standards in such aspects of sensing data format and database interfaces. We envisioned to design a simplified integration approaches as presented in Figure 4. It can be achieved when standardized protocols are used on each WSN regardless of sensor network application.

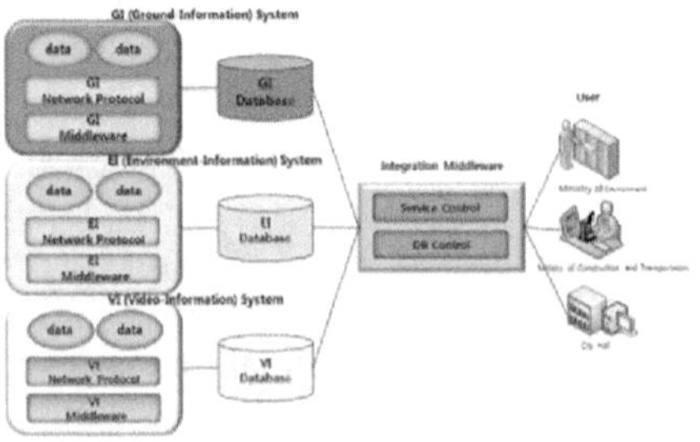

Fig. 3. Integration of Traditional Sensor Networks

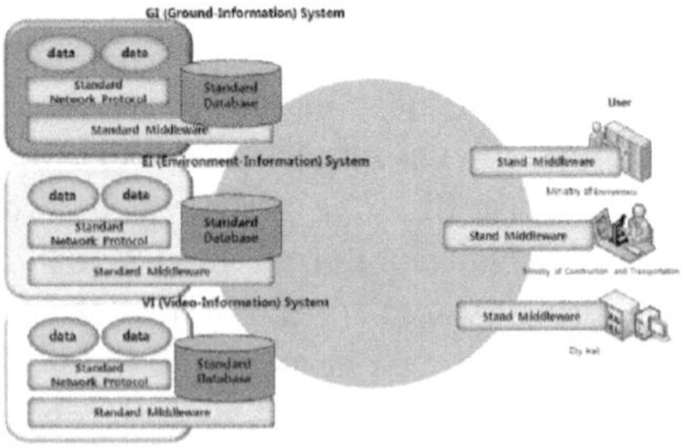

Fig. 4. Integration of Standardized Sensor Networks

3 Real-Time Global Monitoring Integration System

This section describes an overall system design for the real-time global monito ring and required components categorized by hardware and software.

3.1 IP-WSN Based Integration System

Figure 5 shows the real-time global monitoring integration system. The system consists of the ground/environment monitoring system, video collection system, and environmental monitoring system using ground mobility vehicles. The ground and environment monitoring system measures information on microseism, minute displacement, strain ratio, temperature, water level, water quality, exhaust/atmospheric gas, soil, etc. for chief national facilities. A star topology may be used for a flatland including a few types of farm fields and a multi-hop mesh topology is for trees, forests, hills, slanting surfaces, and winding areas. The 400 MHz band may be a better choice because of diffraction. The video collection system provides video information required for the global monitoring system in liaison with closed-circuit television (CCTV) systems built in a variety of public/private institutions. A star topology and peer-to-peer topology may be used for network cameras for the system. Also, it supports streaming services for real-time transport of video data and transformation services for streaming the types of existing CCTV videos. The environmental monitoring system using ground mobility vehicles monitors a wide scope of areas at runtime by compensating the limit

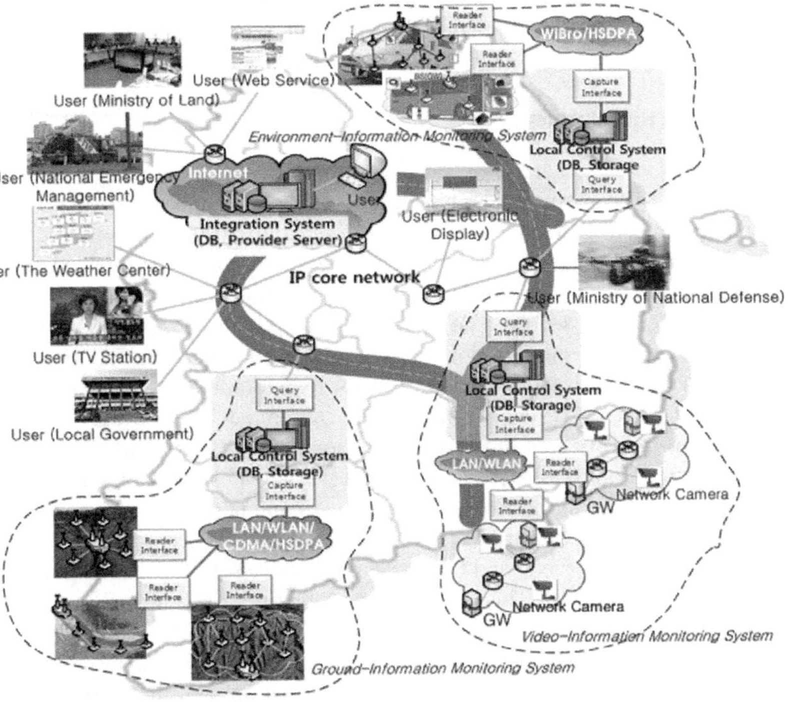

Fig. 5. Real-time Global Monitoring System

of fixed monitoring systems using special purpose vehicles or public transportations equipped with mobile IP-WSN gateways and sensors. Its targets to monitor include road conditions, road materials, road information, facilities near roads, information on the yellow dust, etc. A star topology may be mainly used in/on a vehicle, but a tree topology may be more useful due to the limit of communication coverage caused by the deployment of sensor nodes inside/outside the vehicle. The 2.4 GHz band may be a good choice for this system.

The real-time global monitoring integration system works as follows: In the video collection system, network cameras communicate each other via TCP/IP and a base station is connected to the Internet through LAN/WLAN. Whereas, other systems that deploy IP-WSNs and IP-WSN gateways may be connected to the Internet via a wireless communication medium (Wibro, HSDPA, CDMA, etc.) considering regional characteristics of their deployment. Information gathered from each system is managed by the local control system and it is stored in distributed databases in request to a query. The integrated control center manages those databases. The distributed databases can secure scalability, efficiency, and reliability since they logically integrate the databases which are distributed in multiple systems physically. In order for efficient management of system integration and national-scale network infrastructure, the network protocols may be standardized with IP-WSN for sensor networks and standardized Reader/Capture/Query interfaces may be applied for interoperation and integration of distributed databases and systems. In addition, standardized sensing data formats may be beneficial to unify existing territorial monitoring systems that have been operating separately. The system provides services facilitating integrated territorial information to government-related organizations, local governments, individuals, etc. in close liaison with systems distributed in the country.

3.2 Systems Requirement

Figure 6 and 7 describe hardware and software architecture for sensor networks and video networks. The hardware architecture consists of database servers that collect and store sensing and video data by regional groups, backup database servers, control servers, GIS servers, and web servers. The integrated control system comprises the integrated database server to consolidate local databases, the integrated GIS server, and the integrated web server. The local control system also interoperates with the databases that belong to other regions. In Figure 6, sensor networks adopt an IP-WSN to fulfill a global WSN and techniques easily to interoperate with existing CCTVs may be standardized for better support of integrated monitoring. The software architecture shows softwares required for sensor networks and camera networks and for the integrated control system and local servers. Gateways and sensor nodes are needed to build the sensor networks, and gateways and network cameras are required to form camera networks. Moreover, the integrated control server, streaming servers, web servers, database servers, and GIS servers are necessary for the integrated control system and local servers. This software architecture of figure 7 includes basic components about integrated control server and sensor network/network camera. According to need, additional softwares may be demanded because a variety of applications utilizing sensing data and video information form network cameras may appear in the future. Note that this paper proposes a guideline.

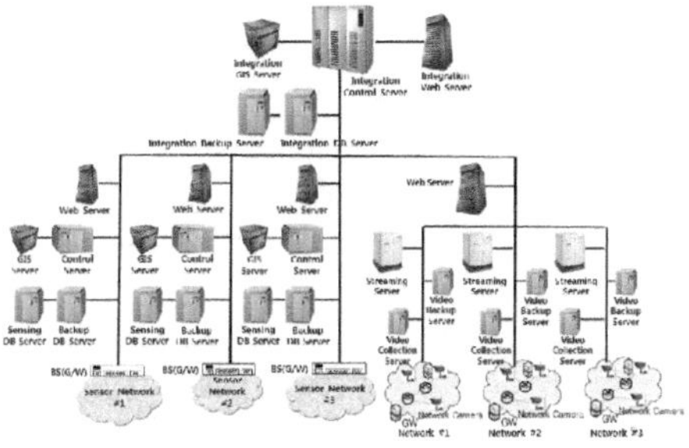

Fig. 6. Hardware Architecture for Sensor Networks and Video Networks

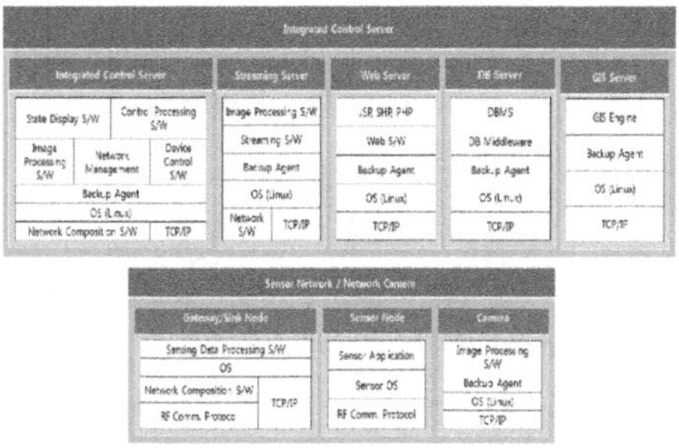

Fig. 7. Software Architecture for Sensor Networks and Video Networks

4 Integration Approaches of Existing WSNs

In order to operate the real-time territorial monitoring system based on a variety of sensors and provide the standardized interface, we propose a WSN integration approach which includes sensing data formats and databases to be used in various WSNs in common and to provide the interconnection among networks. This section presents sensing data format and databases for standardization.

4.1 Sensing Data Format

We provide sensing data formats for integration or linkage among various WSNs. These formats are able to help to integrate and manage a real-time territorial monitoring system for global monitoring. As shown in Figure 8, we suggest it to communication using UDP based on IEEE 802.15.4 data frame format. The available size including Network Header and Data Payload is 81 bytes and it is possible to compress network header by RFC 4944. When sensor nodes communicate each other within one PAN (Personal Area Network), Version, Priority, Flow Level, Payload Length, Next Header, Source Address, and Destination Address can be compressed in network header shown in Figure 9 and the total size of them is 2 bytes. The size of Source Port, Destination Port, and Length in UDP header can be minimized to 4 bytes and data of which the maximum size is 70 bytes can transmit. Meanwhile, if a sensor node communicates with other networks outside the PAN, Source Address and Destination Address must specify the 128-bit IPv6 address. Thus, the header compression is possible as the previous case excepting Source address and Destination Address and the data of which size is 54 bytes communication is available.

The sensing data message header and message payload format within the network header are presented in Figure 10. For the control of a flexible message size and data representation, it forms by separating two parts, and at most 4 sensing data of one packet can be transmitted for communicator with outside networks and at most 6 sensing data can be transmitted for communicator with the inside the network. Let's look at figure 11. Message Header is composed of Network ID (NWK ID), Node ID,

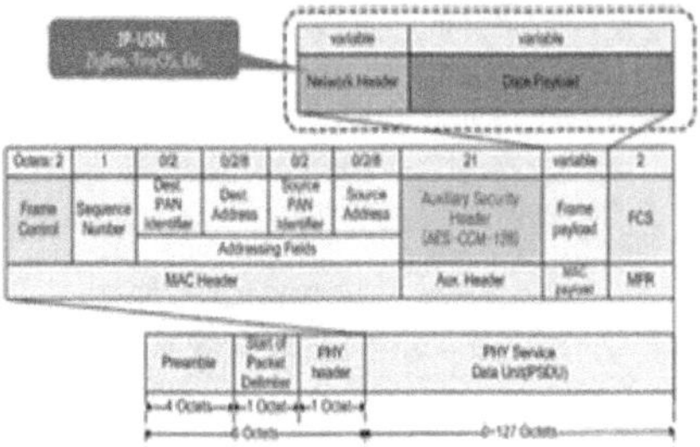

Fig. 8. UDP based on IEEE 802.15.4 Data frame Format

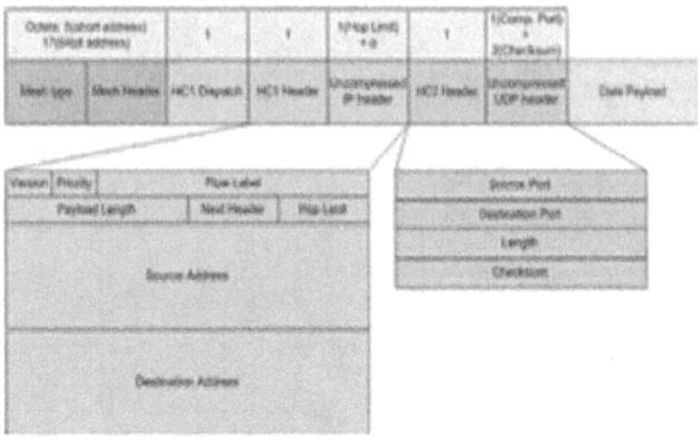

Fig. 9. Network Head of UDP

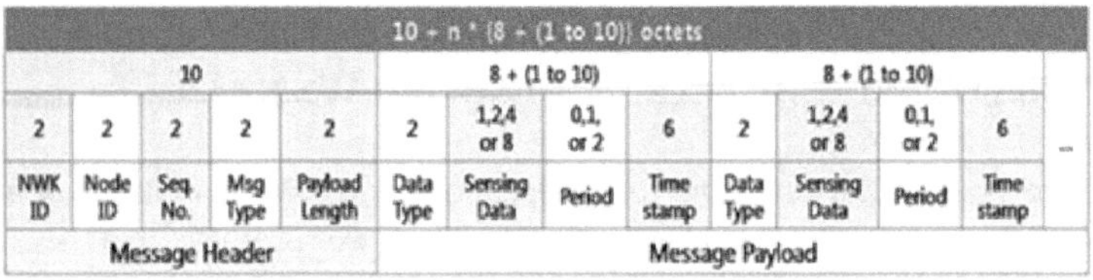

Fig. 10. Message Header and Payload Format

Sequence Number (Seq. No.), Message Type (Msg. Type), and Payload Length for representing attributes of the real message, and Message Payload has Data Type, Sensing Data, Period, and Timestamp for representing real sensing data. Message Header has Sequence Number to verify the arrival of a message using ID and UDP that distinguish networks and nodes. Moreover, several messages exchanged in sensor networks exist. For example, time synchronization request/response messages, alive request/response messages to monitor sensor nodes, sensing data messages to transmit sensing data, and so on. Message Header has also Message Type to distinguish them and Payload Length of Message Payload. Message Payload in which the real sensing data is included is composed of Data Type to distinguish the type of sensors per one sensing data, Sensing Data to present real sensing values, sensing period of the current sensing node (Period), and measured time (Timestamp). The first byte of Data

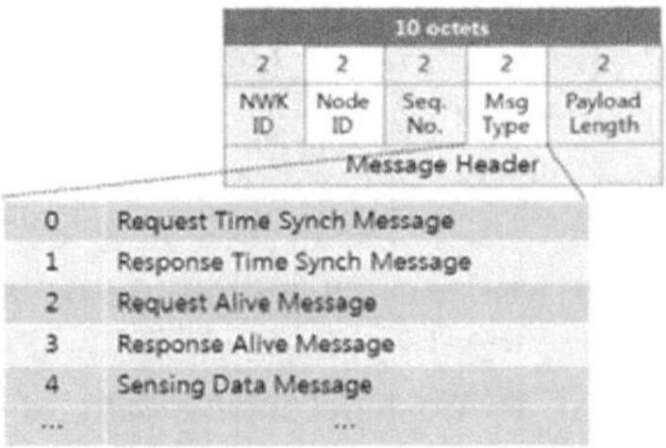

Fig. 11. Example of Message Header/Types

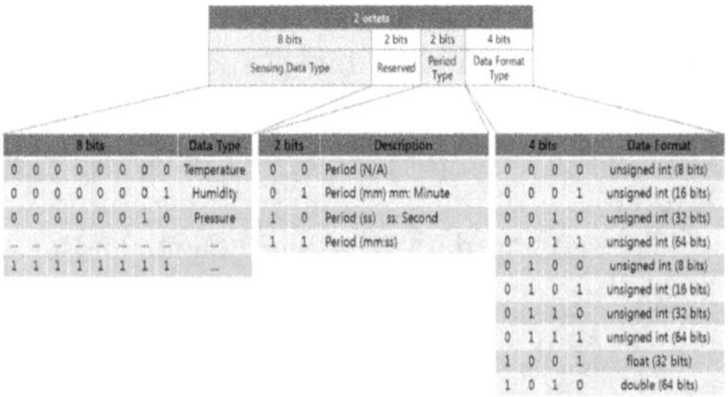

Fig. 12. Data Type in Message Payloal

2 octets															
1 octet								1 octet							
X	40	20	10	8	4	2	1	X	40	20	10	8	4	2	1
mm								ss							
Period															

6 octets											
1 octet		1 octet		1 octet		1 octet		1 octet		1 octet	
4 bits	4 bits	4 bits	4 bits	4 bits	4 bits	4 bits	4 bits	4 bits	4 bits	4 bits	4 bits
Y	Y	M	M	D	D	h	h	m	m	s	s
Timestamp											

Fig. 13. Period and Timestamp

Type means 256 sensing type, next two bits are reserved, next two bits determine the representation of sensing period (Period). This period type has four cases (the period is omitted by the sensor type, the period in minutes or seconds is used, or the period in minutes and seconds is used) and the period is transferred according to a setting of period type. The last 4 bits determine representation of sensing data and it supports 10 different representations for providing several sensing data representation depending on the scope and use.

The size of Sensing Data field in Figure 12 is 1, 2, 4, or 8 bytes by Data Format Type defined previously. The size of Period field in Figure 10 is also 0, 1, 2, bytes by Period Type and it stores the time by BCD code. Timestamp field in Figure 13 is similar, too. The size is 6 bytes and it is represented by BCD code from YY:MM:DD:hh:mm:ss (Year:Month:Day:Hour:Minute:Second). It is possible to use by characteristics of sensing data, provides the correctness of several integer and real number representations, and has an advantage that the conversion of existing variable representations into a specific defined representation is not necessary. It varies by the type of sensors, but the representation of most sensor information is applicable by the proposed sensing data representation. Also, it is based on SI units and modified by the domestic circumstance, and flexible sensing data format can be applied to sensor networks and the integrated monitoring system. Therefore, it is useful to exchange and store sensing information and it can be utilized systematically.

4.2 Sensing Database

For the management of standardized sensing data effectively, we propose database composition and sharing model with the standardized interface. The overall structure is that an independent database is constructed by each monitoring system and integrated servers and backup servers are also constructed to manage them. Then, all monitoring information becomes accessible. Also, heterogeneous sensor networks can be integrated, the multiple users are supported to share the database, and effective sharing of sensing data is achievable through the share by units of sensing data and distributed database.

Moreover, the database and interfaces should be provided to access database and store information, and thus the standardization of each interface would be required. First, Reader interface is the standardized interface to transmit data from a base station in sensor networks database and it is required to define sensing data formats for numerous types of sensors. Capture interface which enables to access the database is required to perform registration/process and subscription/publication of a variety of events including the database access interface. With these interfaces, we can integrate

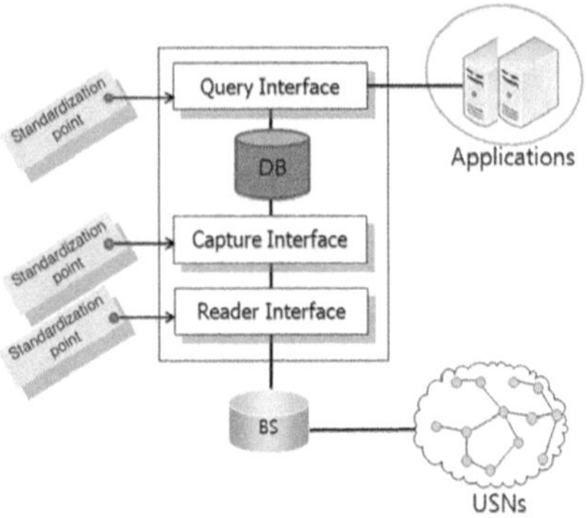

Fig. 14. Standard Interface for Sensing Database

several heterogeneous sensor networks and implement them using XML and Web-based. Finally, there is the Query interface is for the message interface between standardized databases and applications and integrated query technology may be required to support various kind of databases and queries. Figure 14 shows the standardized database interface.

5 System Deployment Scenarios

Figure 15 shows a snapshot of the scenario for the territorial monitoring system designed for applicable regions. The scenario depicts the integrated control center, IP-WSN based monitoring systems, and a network camera system. The information of target point of interest is monitored by sub-systems and collected to the control center, thereby providing various services at real-time such as web services, SMS, etc. Also, it enables service users to cope immediately with emergency situations. The environmental monitoring system using ground mobility vehicles (Figure 15-①,②) such as special purpose vehicles or public transportations sends information on the real-time volume of traffic, weather, exhaust gas, ozone, road conditions, etc. over a drive. The location of the ground mobility vehicles is used to monitor the status of a specific region and deliver useful information to residents in vicinity of the area at run-time. The information is exchanged with the integrated control center via the mobile IP-WSN gateway installed inside the vehicles. The network camera system (Figure 15-④) constantly monitors conditions of the volume of traffic, a parking lot, the status of environment, and so forth. For instance, cameras installed on a bridge observe the traffic on the bridge and water levels of a river at run-time in order to provide against emergencies. Furthermore, cameras in a parking lot check if there are empty spaces and notify drivers for ease of parking via the system. In addition, the system monitors (Figure 15-③) tunnels and the ground at risk so that it can prevent disasters at early stage. The system should be time synchronized for real-time communication and measured sensing data should be delivered in standardized formats to servers in order to make use of interoperability. Moreover, each system takes a command from administrators to manage the update of sensing intervals, check the status of sensor nodes, change network protocols, and so on, thereby enabling organizational configuration and management. From this approach, we can build the real-time monitoring system that can manage the whole country through interoperation with major cities and regions as well as limited areas. Figure 15-⑥ indicates that central control center of integrated IP-WSN and video monitoring systems.

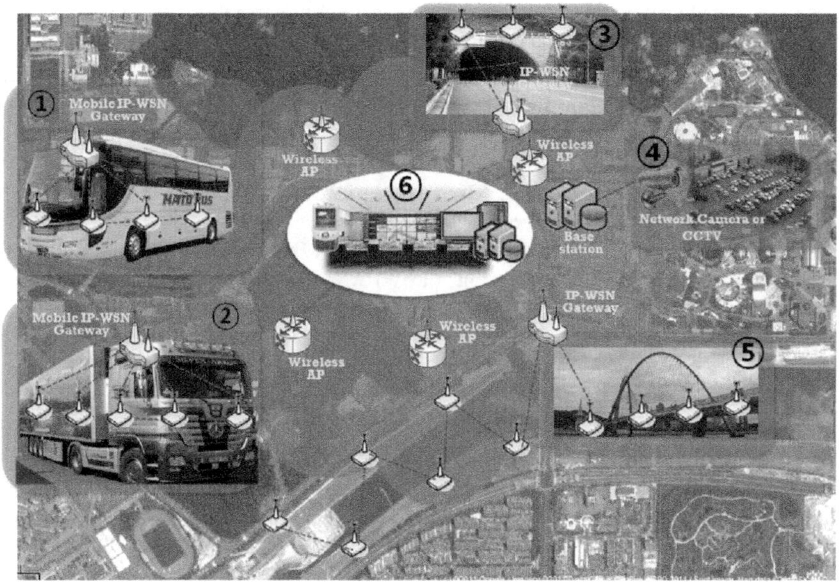

Fig. 15. Territorial Monitoring System Scenarios

6 Conclusion

We design IP-WSN based real-time global monitoring system to ensure compatibility and interoperability among various WSN systems. This system focuses on territorial monitoring: territorial ground/environment, and inner cities including downtown areas. For unstrained integration, sensing data formats and their database interfaces are suggested. Therefore, this enables a spontaneous and systematic integration among the legacy WSN systems to construct efficient and effective territorial monitoring systems. We envision that the proposed technology would be an essential element for the practically deployable global territorial monitoring systems. In the future, we plan to construct an IP-WSN based testbed system using an integration avenue of WSN systems for real-time global monitoring.

References

1. Garcia, C., Ibarguengoytia-Gonzalez, P., Garcia-Hernandez, J., Perez-Diaz, J.: Wireless Sensor Networks and Applications: a Survey. IJCSNS Intl. Journal of Computer Science and Network Security 7(3), 264–273 (2007)

2. Yick, J., Mukherjee, B., Ghosal, D.: Wireless sensor network survey. Computer Networks: Intl. Journal of Computer and Telecommunications Networking (ACM) 52(12), 2292–2330 (2008)
3. Kuorilehto, M., Hannikainen, M., Hamalainen, T.: A Survey of Application Distribution in Wireless Sensor Networks. EURASIP Journal on Wireless Communications and Networking (ACM) 5(5), 774–788 (2005)
4. Bae, S., Kim, D., Ha, M., Kim, S.: Browsing Architecture with Presentation metadata for the Internet of Things. In: IEEE International Conference on Parallel and Distributed Systems (ICPADS 2011), Tainan, Taiwan, December 7-9 (2011)
5. The Internet of Things, This ITU Internet Report (2005)
6. Wheeler, A.: Commercial Applications of Wireless Sensor Networks Using Zigbee. IEEE Communications Magazine 45(4), 70–77 (2007)
7. Ergen, S.: ZigBee/IEEE 802.15.4 Summary, 1-35, UC Berkeley (September 2004)
8. Texas Instruments, Inc., 2.4 GHz IEEE 802.15.4 / ZigBee-ready RF Transceiver (2007), `http://focus.ti.com/lit/ds/symlink/cc2420.pdf`
9. ZigBee Alliance, `http://www.zigbee.org/`
10. Ha, M., Kim, D., Kim, S., Hong, S.: Inter-MARIO: A Fast and Seamless Mobility Protocol to support Inter-PAN Handover in 6LoWPAN. In: IEEE Global Communications Conference (GLOBECOM 2010), Miami, USA (December 2010)
11. Hong, S., Kim, D., Ha, M., Bae, S., Park, S., Jung, W., Kim, J.: SNAIL: An IP-based Wireless Sensor Network Approach Toward the Internet of Things. IEEE Wireless Communications 17(6), 34–42 (2010)
12. Montenegro, G., Kushalnagar, N., et al.: Transmission of IPv6 Packets over IEEE 802.15.4 Networks, RFC 4944, IETF Network Working Group (2007)
13. Lee, K., Kim, S., Chung, T., Kim, Y.: Reference model of broadband convergence network in Korea. In: Proc. of Asia-Pacific Conference, pp. 219–222. IEEE (January 2008)
14. Cha, K.: Wireless Remote Monitoring System for Reservoir Management. In: Proc. of Industry-University Collaboration, vol. 4, pp. 99–106 (2001)
15. Dong, Q., Yu, L., Lu, H., Hong, Z., Chen, Y.: Design of Building Monitoring Systems Based on Wireless Sensor Networks. Wireless Sensor Network 2(9), 703–709 (2010)
16. Chen, Z., Zhang, J., Li, Z., Wu, F., Ho, K.: The technical concept within the Integrative Landslide Early Warning System. In: Proc. of Int'l. Symposium on Landslides and Engineered Slopes, pp. 1083–1088 (June 2008)
17. Melo, M., Taveras, J.: Structural Health Monitoring of the Golden Gate Bridge using Wireless Sensor Networks, Progress report, October 1-7 (2008)

The Modeling Approaches of Distributed Computing Systems

Susmit Bagchi

Department of Informatics, College of Natural Sciences
Gyeongsang National University, Jinju, South Korea
susmitbagchi@yahoo.co.uk

Abstract. The distributed computing systems have grown to a large scale having different applications such as, grid computing and cloud computing systems. It is important to model the architectures of large scale distributed computing systems in order to ensure stable dynamics of the computing systems as well as the reliability and performance. In general, the discrete event dynamical systems formalism is employed to construct the models of different dynamical systems. This paper proposes the constructions of models of distributed computing systems employing two different formalisms such as, discrete event dynamical systems and discrete dynamical systems. A comparative analysis illustrates that the discrete dynamical systems based model of distributed computing systems can be very effective to design and analyze the distributed computing architectures.

Keywords: distributed computing, discrete event dynamical systems, discrete dynamical systems, grid computing, cloud computing.

1 Introduction

Recently, the distributed computing systems have regained research attention due to the realizations of grid computing and cloud computing systems. The distributed computing architectures of grid and cloud computing systems are complex and difficult to implement as well as maintain. The large scale distributed computing systems employ complex communication protocols and synchronization of operations for maintaining data consistency. In general, the distributed computing systems are dynamic in nature, where the distributed processes may not have a complete as well as correct global knowledge about the entire system or processes [1]. The distributed processes communicate and coordinate among themselves through asynchronous messages to maintain consistency, which can be modeled as a partial order of the events generated by the distributed processes [5]. In general, the architectures of the large scale distributed computing systems are designed with the notion of local-knowledge, global-knowledge and communication direction in the network of distributed processes forming a directed graph [9, 10]. The controllability, stability and reliability of the distributed system architectures are important aspects of distributed computing systems design. The formal methods are the techniques to

T.-h. Kim et al. (Eds.): ASEA/DRBC/EL 2011, CCIS 257, pp. 479–488, 2011.

analyze the specifications, development and verification of design architectures of the distributed computing systems [2]. The discrete event dynamical systems (DEDS) and the discrete dynamical systems (DDS) are the mathematical formalisms, which can be effectively used in modeling and analyzing the distributed computing systems.

This paper describes the models of distributed computing systems based on the DEDS and DDS formalisms. The stability of distributed computing systems is analyzed using DDS model. A comparative analysis between DEDS and DDS models of distributed computing systems illustrates that, DDS model can be more effectively employed to model and analyze the distributed computing systems architecture, system stability and fault-tolerance. The rest of the paper is organized as follows. Section 2 explains the construction of DEDS model of a distributed computing system. The construction of DDS model of distributed computing systems is illustrated in section 3. The comparative analysis of DEDS model and DDS model of distributed computing systems is described in section 4. Section 5 describes related work. Section 6 concludes the paper.

2 DEDS Model of Distributed Computing Systems

The dynamic systems are generally modeled using finite state automata having partially observable events coupled with state transitions [4, 15]. The stability and error-recovery mechanisms can be modeled using DEDS by infinitely visiting the event-set (E) as well as by choosing a closed-loop system [4]. In general, a distributed computing system can be viewed as a dynamic system comprised of a set of distributed nodes (processes). The dynamic systems evolve in time, which is again true in case of distributed computing systems [1, 2]. In an evolvable dynamic system, such as a large scale distributed computing system, it is often required to predict and analyze the future trajectories of the system in order to ensure deterministic behaviour of the entire system. The DEDS is a mathematical formalism to construct the model of a dynamical system under control and to analyze the characteristics of the corresponding dynamical system. The DEDS model is often hybridized with Petri Nets (PN) to form DEDS-PN model of the dynamical systems in order to implement detailed analysis of the dynamics of the systems under deterministic control. Generally, the DEDS model can be constructed by using state-transition graph.

Let, a distributed computing system D is given by, $D = \{P_a : a = 1, 2, \ldots N\}$. The transition graph of process $P_a \in D$ is a four-tuple deterministic automation given by, $P_a = \langle S_a, E_a, T_a, s_{a0} \rangle$ where, S_a is the set of valid internal-states of process P_a, E_a is the set of events generated by P_a and, s_{a0} is initial state of process P_a. The state transition function T_a is given by, T_a: $S_a \times E_a \rightarrow S_a$ where, T_a is a partial transition function. Hence, the global set of valid events can be given as, $S_D = \cup_{a = 1,2,..N} S_a$. In DEDS model, P_a evolves either in isolation or in combination with the other processes. The isolated evolution and combinational evolution are illustrated in Fig. 1 and Fig. 2, respectively.

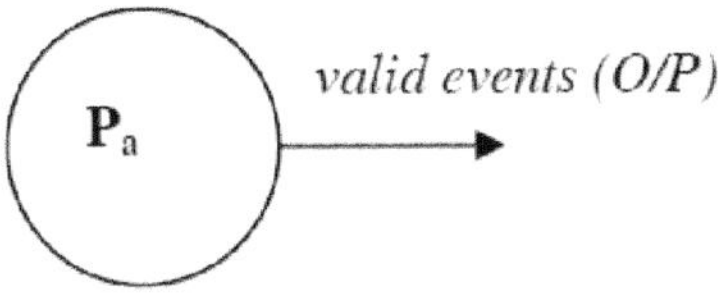

Fig. 1. Isolated Event-Process Model

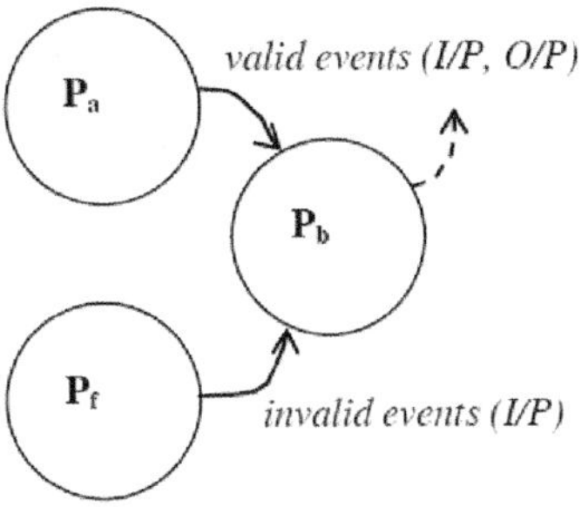

Fig. 2. General Event-Process Model

It is evident from Fig. 1 and Fig. 2 that, any valid process in DEDS model generates a set of valid events. However, the failed process (P_f in Fig. 2) may generate invalid events, which are filtered by other valid processes as illustrated in Fig. 2. Hence, $\forall P_a$, $P_x \in D$, the following implication holds in combinational evolution model of DEDS, $(e_i \in E_a : i \geq 1) \rightarrow (T_x(e_i, s_x) \neq s_\phi)$ where, $s_x \in S_x$, $s_\phi \notin S_D$ and, $P_a \neq P_f$. This mechanism ensures the failure-absorption and fault-tolerant behaviour of the distributed computing systems modeled as DEDS. However, the self-detection and filtering of invalid global events by the valid processes is having high computational complexities towards implementations. In addition, the complete and consistent global snapshots of D may not be available at P_a all the time.

2.1 Distributed Computing Systems as DEDS-PN

The PN is often incorporated into DEDS model for the purpose of analysis of whole system [13]. The DEDS-PN model can be constructed to extend the DEDS model of distributed computing systems further. The overall architecture of a distributed computing system can be represented as a directed bipartite graph given by, $A_D = \langle \vartheta, \Pi, F, G \rangle$, where ϑ is a finite set of computational states of entire distributed computing system D, Π is a finite set of state-transitions in D, $F \subseteq (\vartheta \times \Pi)$ and $G \subseteq (\Pi \times \vartheta)$. Hence, F and G represent the oriented edges entering and leaving to/from the transitions, respectively. If the computational states of entire system D is a set of ordered series of local-states of individual nodes then, $\vartheta \subset (S_D)^{|D|}$. Again, the F and G can be represented as the respective incident matrices, I_F and I_G respectively, such that,

$$\left.\begin{aligned} I_F &= \{f_{m,n} : 1 \leq m \leq |\vartheta|, 1 \leq n \leq |\Pi|\} \\ \text{and,} \quad & \\ I_G &= \{g_{m,n} : 1 \leq n \leq |\vartheta|, 1 \leq m \leq |\Pi|\} \end{aligned}\right\} \quad (1)$$

Thus, the structure of the entire distributed computing system A_D can be modified by following the definition of D and by using DEDS-PN model. The modified entire architecture of a distributed computing system can be represented as, $D_A = \langle X, U, \delta, x_0 \rangle$, $X \cap U = \phi$ where, X is a finite set of state-vectors, U is a finite set of elementary control-vectors and, δ is defined as, $\delta : X \times U \rightarrow X$ signifying the transition function of the model dynamics and, x_0 is the initial state-vector of the distributed computing system under consideration. Hence, the dynamics of the distributed computing systems following DEDS-PN model can be given by,

$$\left.\begin{aligned} & x_{k+1} = x_k + B.u_k, \ \ k = 0, 1, \ldots |D| \\ \text{and,} \quad & \\ & B = G^{\Pi} - I_F \end{aligned}\right\} \quad (2)$$

In Eq. 2, $F.u_k \leq x_k$ and $x_k \in X$ as well as $u_k \in U$.

The following set of properties can be derived from the DEDS-PN model of distributed computing systems,

- DEDS-PN model emulates the dynamic asynchronous distributed systems.
- The state-transitions in DEDS-PN model of distributed computing systems are initiated by events only.
- In DEDS-PN model of distributed computing systems, the events are discrete and occur in discrete time.
- The intervals of occurrences of events are not evenly distributed.

3 DDS Model of Distributed Computing Systems

The dynamics of any distributed computing systems closely follow the characteristics of DDS. The DDS model is a formal mechanism to capture, observe and control the behaviour of the evolvable dynamic systems [16]. In theory it is possible that, a distributed computing system may have infinitely many processes but each of the state transitions can only be finitely many [1]. In addition, a distributed system is synchronized through a monotonically increasing logical clock defined as a set of positive integers. This indicates that, there exists no bound on the number of processes for all valid state transitions. According to finite arrival model, a communication protocol cannot be designed using a defined upper bound on the number of processes in a distributed computing system [6, 14]. The DDS model allows the divergence of trajectory from any stable point to a boundary value and contracts the unstable system to a deterministic stable state through discrete transitions in time. Hence, the DDS model of distributed computing system should be constructed in a way such that, the end-point state transitions due to events (in a series) should be converging to the globally observable stable-states of the distributed processes. However, the intermediate local state-transitions at the distributed processes should be allowed due to divergent characteristics of any large scale distributed computing systems.

3.1 Constructing DDS Model of Distributed Systems

Let, a distributed computing system D contains m number of nodes (processes) denoted by a node-set $N = \{n_a : a = 1, 2, 3, \ldots .m\}$. Let, $\mathcal{E}$ is a set of events in D such that, $\mathcal{E} = (\cup_{a = 1,2,..m} E_a) \cup \{e_\phi\}$, where E_a is a series of events generated by node $n_a \in N$ and, $\{e_\phi\}$ is faulty event generated by any node in N during computation in D. Let, C $\in I^+$ is a set of globally consistent monotonically increasing positive integer logical clock values in D synchronizing the ongoing distributed computation. Let us consider that, s_ϕ is a unique terminal or halting point for all nodes in N of a D. Now, $\forall n_a \in N$, $S_a = \{s_a[x] : x \in C\} \cup \{s_\phi\}$ denotes the finite set of internal-states generated by a node n_a during the computation at different times inclusive of terminal point or halting point (s_ϕ). Hence, the set of internal-states of all the nodes of distributed computing system D is given by, $S_D = \cup_{a = 1,2,..m} S_a$. On the other hand, the globally observable states in a distributed computing system D can be given as, $S_\omega = \cap_{a = 1,2,..m} S_a$, where $S_\omega \neq \phi$ and, $|S_\omega| \geq 1$. The concept of distributed computing system D is illustrated in Fig. 3, where n_f is a halting node in D.

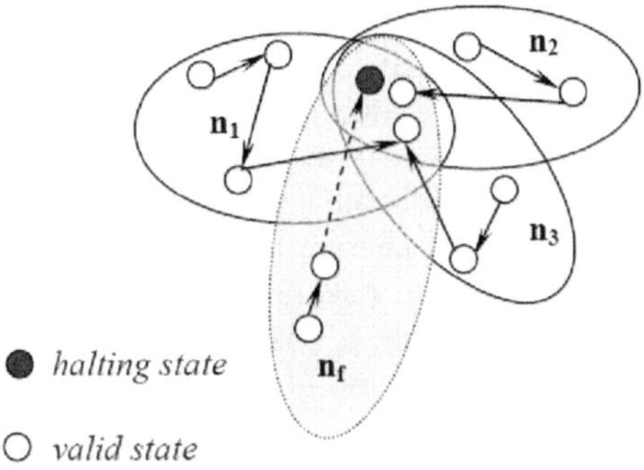

Fig. 3. A distributed computing system as DDS model

Let, R_a be a set of reactions at a node $n_a \in N$ in the distributed system D. The elements in R_a represent different outputs (reactions) of a node n_a through the distributed computation, where the outputs of a node is produced due to internal computation as well as due to inter-node message communications synchronized by the logical clock C. Hence, R_a can be represented as the relation, $R_a \subset (\mathcal{E} \text{ x } C)$ such that, $\exists e_i \in \mathcal{E}$, $R_a(e_i, x) \neq \phi$, $x \in C$. Now, $\forall n_a \in N$, a transition function τ_a can be defined as, $\tau_a : (S_D \text{ x } R_a) \rightarrow S_D$. Let, a global transition T is defined at every node in N as a relation on S_D given by, $T : S_D \rightarrow S_D$ in the distributed system D such that, T will constrain as well as control the overall state-transitions of all the nodes in N. Hence, a distributed system can be formally represented as four-tuple, $D = \langle N, S_D, \mathcal{E}, T \rangle$. Let, $\exists s_a[x], s_a[x+1] \in S_D$ for a node $n_a \in N$ in D such that, $s_a[x] \in \tau_a$ and $s_a[x+1] = T(s_a[x])$. Initially, at $x = 0$, $s_a[x] = s_a[0]$ be the initial stable internal-state of a node $n_a \in N$. So, $s_a[x]$ is a reactive intermediate internal-state of n_a, which makes transition to final state $s_a[x+1]$ in the next time instant in the logical clock time-series in D. This indicates that, $\forall n_a \in N$, $s_a[1] = T(s_a[0])$ and $s_a[x] = T^x(s_a[0])$. Hence, the valid execution trajectory of a node n_a in D at logical clock x is represented as, $\wp_a[x] = \langle s_a[k] : k = 0, 1, 2, \ldots x; s_a[k] \in S_\omega - \{s_\phi\} \rangle$. It is important to note that, T may contain globally non-conformal transitions in D executed by the nodes through the elements of S_D. In order to make convergence to the globally observable states, the $T^x(s_a[0])$ can be defined as,

$$\forall\, n_a \in N,\ T^x(s_a[0]) = \begin{cases} s_a[x] & \text{if } s_a[x] \in S_\omega \\ s_a[x\text{-}1] & \text{if } s_a[x] \notin S_\omega \\ s_\phi & \text{if } T^{x\text{-}1}(s_a[0]) = s_\phi \end{cases} \tag{3}$$

It is evident from the definition of $T^x(s_a[0])$ that, it will restrict the final transition states of the nodes in globally observable domain in the system D irrespective of any intermediate transitions executed by individual nodes in the system D due to internal (local) computations. The two properties of DDS model of distributed computing systems can be derived such as, (1) the space of system observation is limited to S_ω, which is global and, (2) the distributed computing system will terminate in S_ω even if the initial conditions are different at different nodes (i.e. DDS model of distributed computing systems has convergence to global states).

Interestingly, the DDS model of distributed computing systems allows divergence in trajectories of the nodes due to internal local-computations. However, the DDS model implements the deterministic convergence of the distributed computation at global stable points. The local halting points of the nodes are globally observable, which facilitates the distributed diagnosis of failures by the nodes.

3.2 Analyzing System Stability

A distributed system is stable if there exists a global converging state or a set of global states in the system under consideration. A monotonic divergence of all the nodes of a distributed computing system from the stable state(s) may lead to unreliability and instability of the system. Let, a globally observable equilibrium of a distributed computing system is $s_a[\beta] \in S_\omega$ for the node $n_a \in N$ of D, $\beta \in C$. The Taylor expansion of $T(s_a[x])$ considering first-order derivative at $s_a[\beta]$ is given by,

$$T(s_a[x]) = T(s_a[\beta]) + (s_a[x] - s_a[\beta]).\Delta_x T(s_a[\beta]) \tag{4}$$

Where, $\Delta_x T(s_a[\beta])$ is the discrete derivative of T in discrete time domain of logical clock at β and $(s_a[x] - s_a[\beta])$ represents shortest linear distance between the two states in $\wp_a[x]$ of the node n_a. It is clear that, $T(s_a[x])$ represents a discrete dynamical system in simple form. However, due to the stable equilibrium of D at logical clock β, the drift around β should be converging i.e., $\Delta_x T(s_a[\beta]) < 1$. Thus, around stability point the predicate $\boldsymbol{P}$ will hold true in D, where $\boldsymbol{P}$ is represented as, $\boldsymbol{P} \rightarrow ((s_a[x+1] = s_a[\beta]) \wedge (T(s_a[\beta]) = s_a[\beta]))$. As, $T(s_a[x]) = s_a[x+1]$ hence, at $s_a[\beta]$, $\Delta_x T(s_a[\beta]) = 0$ for the distributed computing system D. This indicates that Taylor expansion (Eq. 4) can be reduced to, $T(s_a[x]) = T(s_a[\beta])$. Deriving further following Eq. 3 and $\boldsymbol{P}$, it can be said that, $T^x(s_a[0]) = s_a[\beta]$, $x \in C$.

As $s_a[\beta] \in S_\omega$ thus, $s_a[\beta]$ is locally observable by all nodes in D. On the other hand, $\exists n_b \in N$ such that, stability point $s_b[\beta] \in S_\omega$, $s_b[\beta] \neq s_a[\beta]$ then, nodes n_a and n_b will be stable in D following Eq. 3 and Eq. 4, respectively. Hence, the distributed computing system D will be highly stable at $s_a[\beta]$, $\forall n_a \in N$, which is a globally observable stability in D. This indicates, the discrete dynamical behaviour of a distributed computing system would eventually lead to a globally observable and stable consistent state irrespective of any local intermediate state-transitions at the nodes. The convergence property of a discrete dynamical system makes a distributed computing system model globally stable.

4 Comparative Analysis

The DEDS model of distributed computing systems realizes the dynamic asynchronous characteristics of the large scale distributed systems. According to the DEDS model, the events at distributed processes enforce state transitions of nodes deterministically, where the delay of arrival time between any two events can have two classes namely, periodic and stochastic. Hence, a controlled DDS model of distributed computing systems can be viewed as a finite state machine (FSM) having deterministic state-transitions. The Petri Nets (PN) based DEDS model is widely used following the FSM model, where concepts of PN are incorporated within DEDS formalism [18].

However, the process model based dynamic systems are characterized by a succession of unstable states followed by stable states [1]. In the DDS model of the distributed computing systems, the toggling between divergence (instability) and convergence (stability) of computational states of the distributed processes are incorporated. The instantaneous divergence of the internal state transitions of the distributed processes is required in order to implement real-life execution environments of the distributed computing systems. However, the convergent transformation maps of the states of the distributed processes ensure that such instantaneous divergences are bounded within globally observable functional domains. It is interesting to note that the globally observable stable points within the functional maps have no internal partitions according to the local state-transitions of distributed processes during divergences. This enables the DDS model to encompass the possibilities of random state transitions across the domains of the distributed processes, which is a broad generalization of a distributed computing system without assuming any specifically rigid conditions.

Unlike the DDS model of distributed computing, the DEDS-PN hybrid model fails to provide any complete analytical solutions to distributed computing architectures [19]. The DEDS-PN model is too complex to realize [19]. Often, the computational or algorithmic complexities of DEDS model are very high. For example, the best polynomial time algorithms become slow under DEDS-PN model [19]. Lastly, unlike the DDS model, the DEDS model of distributed computing systems does not consider any provision of synchronizing logical clock [20]. However, the standard design architectures of distributed computing systems and distributed algorithms require a monotonically increasing logical clock in order to implement global snapshots and synchronization throughout the computation. Hence, DDS model performs better than DEDS and DEDS-PN models to construct and analyze the distributed computing systems architectures.

5 Related Work

The mathematical formalisms for constructing the dynamic systems can be employed to the distributed computing systems, because the characteristics of distributed computing systems resemble the dynamic systems. The dynamic model of an asynchronous message-oriented distributed computing system is proposed in [1]. In general, the process model having finite arrival rate is employed to design a distributed computing architecture [6, 14]. In the process model of distributed systems, the processes communicate using persistent and reliable broadcast semantics [8]. However, it is often not desired to design a distributed computing architecture based on such ideal or near to ideal operational environments in practice. For example, the network partitioning (permanent or transient) in a distributed system may lead to the failures. The distributed consensus mechanisms based upon the failure-detectors are explained in [11]. In static systems, the weak failure-detectors can be successfully employed [11]. However, the weak failure-detector model may not stabilize a dynamic system. In static systems, the leader election in a distributed system model assumes synchrony between process speed and message communication delays [7]. Hence, such synchronous model would fail in a dynamic asynchronous distributed computing environment.

In another direction, the concurrent computing systems are modeled based on the DDS formalism [2]. However, the DDS modeling of a large scale distributed computing system is not considered in the construction of the concurrent systems. Researchers have proposed to design load balancing mechanisms in distributed systems considering the dynamical discrete-time domain in the presence of time delays [3]. Apart from dynamic load-balancing in discrete-time, the mechanism does not model the overall characteristics of a distributed system as a single entity.

The applications of DEDS as a tool for modeling and controlling a distributed system are well researched [13, 15]. For example, the analysis of stability of any DEDS is explained in [4]. The DEDS model is applied to implement distributed diagnosis in a distributed computing system [12]. The DEDS model is often used in association with timed Petri Nets [18]. A detailed survey of supervised control of DEDS is described in [20]. However, one of the main difficulties of DEDS model with timed Petri Nets is the indeterminism of stability of the systems [17, 19]. In addition to the existing models, the DDS formalism [16] can be very effective and reliable mechanism to design and analyze the characteristics as well as execution trajectories of any distributed computing system. The DDS model successfully captures the uncertainties of large scale distributed computing systems and can serve as a concrete model to design fault-tolerant distributed systems architectures.

6 Conclusion

The design architectures of distributed computing systems are modeled employing various mathematical formalisms in order to verify and validate system stability and reliability. In general, DEDS and DEDS-PN models are used to analyze the large scale distributed computing systems. However, DDS formalism can be very effective to model and analyze the complex distributed computing systems architectures. The DDS model of distributed computing architectures offers more accurate analytical model of a dynamic distributed computing system as compared to the DEDS model. In addition, the computational complexity of DDS model is less than the DEDS-PN model.

References

1. Mostefaoui, A., Raynal, M., Travers, C., Patterson, S., Agrawal, D., Abbadi, E.A.: From Static Distributed Systems to Dynamic Systems. In: Proceedings of the 24th IEEE Symposium on Reliable Distributed Systems (SRDS). IEEE CS Press (2005)
2. Pelayo, L.F., Valverde, C.J., Pelayo, L.M., Cuartero, F.: Discrete Dynamical Systems for Encoding Concurrent Computing Systems. In: Proceedings of the 9th IEEE International Conference on Cognitive Informatics (ICCI). IEEE CS Press (2010)
3. Dhakal, S., Paskaleva, B.S., Hayat, M.M., Schamiloglu, E., Abdallah, C.T.: Dynamical Discrete-Time Load Balancing in Distributed Systems in the Presence of Time Delays. In: Proceedings of the 42nd IEEE International Conference on Decision and Control, Maui, Hawaii, USA (2003)
4. Ozveren, M.C., Willsky, A.S., Antsaklis, P.J.: Stability and Stabilizability of Discrete Event Dynamic Systems. Journal of the Association of Computing Machinery (ACM) 38(3) (1991)
5. Lamport, L.: Time, Clocks and the Ordering of Events in a Distributed System. Comm. of the ACM 21(7) (1978)
6. Aguilera, M.K.: A Pleasant Stroll through the Land of Infinitely Many Creatures. ACM SIGACT News, Distributed Computing Column 35(2) (2004)
7. Aguilera, M.K., Delporte-Gallet, C., Fauconnier, H., Toueg, S.: Communication-efficient Leader Election and Consensus with Limited Link Synchrony. In: Proceedings of the 23rd ACM Symposium on Principles of Distributed Computing (PODC). ACM Press (2004)
8. Friedman, R., Raynal, M., Travers, C.: Two Abstractions for Implementing Atomic Objects in Dynamic Systems. In: Proceedings of the 24th ACM Symposium on Principles of Distributed Computing (PODC). ACM Press (2005)
9. Chandy, K.M., Misra, J.: How Processes Learn. Distributed Computing 1(1) (1986)
10. Flocchini, P., Mans, B., Santoro, N.: Sense of Direction in Distributed Computing. In: Kutten, S. (ed.) DISC 1998. LNCS, vol. 1499, pp. 1–15. Springer, Heidelberg (1998)
11. Raynal, M.: A Short Introduction to Failure Detectors for Asynchronous Distributed Systems. ACM SIGACT News, Distributed Computing Column 36(1) (2005)
12. Fabre, E., Benveniste, A., Jard, C.: Distributed Diagnosis for Large Discrete Event Dynamic Systems. In: Proceedings of the IFAC World Congress (July 2002)
13. Capkovic, F.: Modelling and Control of Discrete Event Dynamic Systems, BRICS Technical Report, RS-00-26 (2000) ISSN: 0909-0878

14. Merritt, M., Taubenfeld, G.: Computing with Infinitely Many Processes. In: Herlihy, M.P. (ed.) DISC 2000. LNCS, vol. 1914, pp. 164–178. Springer, Heidelberg (2000)
15. Sobh, M.T.: Discrete Event Dynamic Systems: An Overview, Technical Report (CIS), MS-CIS-MS-CIS-91-39, University of Pennsylvania (1991)
16. Galor, O.: Discrete Dynamical Systems, JEL Classification numbers: C62, O40. Brown University (2005)
17. Konigsberg, R.Z.: The Stability Problem for Discrete Event Dynamical Systems Modeled with timed Petri Nets Using a Lyapunov-Max-Plus Algebra Approach. International Mathematical Forum 6(11) (2011)
18. Van Der Aalst, W.M.P., Colom, J.M., Kordon, F., Kotsis, G., Moldt, D.: Petri Net Approaches for Modelling and Validation. LINCOM Studies in Computer Science 1(1) (2003)
19. Ben-Naoum, L., Boel, R., Bongaerts, L., De Schutter, B., Peng, Y., Valckenaers, P., Vandewalle, J., Wertz, V.: Methodologies for Discrete Events Dynamic Systems: A Survey. Journal A 36(4) (1995) ISSN: 0771-1107
20. Charbonnier, F., Alla, H., David, R.: The Supervised Control of Discrete-Event Dynamic Systems. IEEE Transactions on Control Systems Technology 7(2) (1999)

Event-Centric Test Case Scripting Method for SOA Execution Environment

Youngkon Lee

e-Business Department, Korea Polytechnic University,
2121 Jeongwangdong, Siheung city, Korea
yklee777@kpu.ac.kr

Abstract. Electronic collaboration over the Internet between business partners appear to be converging toward well-established types of message exchange patterns that involve both user-defined standards and infrastructure standards. At the same time, the notion of event is increasingly promoted for asynchronous communication and coordination in SOA systems. In collaboration between partners or between components is achieved by the means of choreographed exchanges of discrete units of data - messages or events - over an Internet-based protocol. This paper presents an event-centric test case scripting method and execution model for such systems.

Keywords: SOA, event-driven, process invocation.

1 Introduction

While current Web Service technologies show much progress, current services are mainly limited to atomic services. Thus, they are not adequate to handle the autonomous and complex services in realistic settings. In dealing with this problem, some research works have developed languages to compose the individual Web Services into transactions or workflows. Web Services Flow Language (WSFL) [1] was designed for service compositions in the form of a workflow, and XLANG [2] for the behavior of a single Web Service. However, these works are not sufficient for providing the adaptive web Services generated from a particular context.

Electronic collaborations over the Internet between business partners (e-Business / e-Government) appear to be converging toward well-established types of message exchange patterns that involve both user-defined standards and infrastructure standards. At the same time, the notion of event is increasingly promoted for asynchronous communication and coordination in Event-Driven Architectures (EDA) that are considered as either complementary to or part of SOA systems. In both cases collaboration between partners or between components is achieved by the means of choreographed exchanges of discrete units of data - messages or events - over an Internet-based protocol. Such systems require an event-centric test case scripting markup and execution model.

T.-h. Kim et al. (Eds.): ASEA/DRBC/EL 2011, CCIS 257, pp. 489–496, 2011.

In e-Business transactions as in EDAs, partners or components must agree on the use of a combination of standards in order to interoperate with each other. Typically, these standards can be classified into three layers:

- Messaging infrastructure standards, ranging from transport level to higher-level messaging protocols and quality of service (QoS) including reliability and security, such as those defined as SOAP extensions, or REST (Representational State Transfer).
- Multi-message exchange standards as manifested in business processes and choreographies.
- Business document standards may be business content structure and semantics, taxonomies in use, code lists, semantic rules, or the XML schema modeling style. They are industry-specific (e.g. RosettaNet PIP schemas, AIAG Inventory Visibility and Interoperability schemas), horizontal document standards, or regional guidelines.

There have been conformance and interoperability test suites and testing tools for above layer individually. But the testing of integrations of standards has been ad-hoc, or limited mostly to standards in the messaging infrastructure.

Although the need for testing some form of integration of standards has been well recognized for infrastructure standards, there has been little support for testing integrations that extend to the use of standards specific to a business - e.g. for documents or choreographies. Such integrations can be construed as user-defined profiles. For example, the level of QoS required for a business transaction may depend on the nature of business data being exchanged, or on some property defined by the related business process.

Testing and monitoring these infrastructure layers and their integration also requires that test cases access a combination of contracts - agreements, policies or business transaction patterns - represented by meta-level documents.

This compliance objective goes beyond quality assurance for the messaging function: it requires the monitoring of live transactions in production environments, as well as verifying conformance of business endpoints in operation conditions. This calls for a flexible test execution model that can accommodate performance constraints as well as different timeliness constraints - e.g. where tests are either deferred over log data, or executed on live exchanges in a monitoring mode.

Consequently, the execution model of such test cases or monitoring cases, must accommodate dynamic conditions requiring real-time or near real-time error detection or measurement, allowing to correct and report on business exchanges as they proceed.

The output of a monitoring script also must provide more information than a report of the type pass / fail. Different ways of "passing" or "failing" must be reported on, as well as identifying the types of business transactions. The output must be easy to format and feed to another decision engine, such as a rule engine that will process this input in real-time. For example, a rule may decide to generate an alert if a business transaction lasts too long, depending on the nature of the transaction and on the SLA associated to these business partners.

This paper defines a testing and monitoring model, as well as a test script markup, so that test cases or monitoring cases can be fully automated, and portable across test environments. In section 2, we summarize the related works regarding the web service flow language for testing. Section 3 presents the concept of Event-Centric Test Case Script (EVEC), section 4 describes the implementation of EVEC, and we conclude in section 5.

2 Related Works

In fact, the automatic or semi-automatic management of service flows over the Web has not been achieved yet. In the Web Services model that is quite different from traditional one, there are a large number of similar or equivalent services which user can freely select and use for their application. Since the service is developed and deployed by the third party, the quality of service is not guaranteed. The services may not be adequate as per service requestor's requirements and kept evolving, without notification to service requestors, according to the provider's requirements and computing environment.

Thus, it is important to provide adaptability to evolving services as well as diverse context of services. Kammer et al. [3] suggested workflow to be dynamic, which allows changes with minimal impact to the ongoing execution of underlying workflow, as well as be reflexive, which provides knowledge about a workflow's applicability to the context and the effectiveness of its deployment evaluated over time. Understanding constraints and context associated with services may affect the quality of service. From this perspective, optimization may occur through the evaluation and refinement of a previous service flow.

Automatic composition of services is challenging, because it is difficult to capture semantics and context of services and measure the quality of services. One exemplary effort that aims for this function is DAML-based Web Service Ontology (DAML-S) [4], which describes the properties and capabilities of Web services.

Workflow technology has been around since a decade ago and has been successful in automating many complex business processes. A significant amount of work has been done in this field, which deals with different aspects of workflow technology process modeling, dynamic workflows, and distributed workflows. Process modeling languages such as IDEF, PIF, PSL or CIMOSA [5] and frame based models of services were used to design process typing, resource dependencies, ports, task decomposition and exception.

Current research on web services paves way for web service based workflows, which has obvious advantages pertaining to scalability, heterogeneity, reuse and maintenance of services. Major issues in such inter-organizational service based workflows are service discovery, service contracts and service composition. Web Services Flow Language (WSFL) was proposed to describe compositions of services in the form of a workflow, which describes the order of service invocation. Service composition aids such as BizTalk [6] were proposed to overcome the limitations of traditional workflow tools which manually specify the composition of programs to perform some tasks. Other industrial initiatives such as BPEL4WS [7], and XLANG concentrates on service representation issues to tackle the problems of service contracts, compositions and agreements. Current efforts are to automate the complete process of service discovery, composition and binding, using the machine understandable languages. Some other recent advances are WS-Transaction and WS-Coordination which define protocols for executing Transactions among web services. There is a research for modeling QoS of workflows [8], and defining a QoS based middleware for services associated with the underlying workflow [9], but it doesn't take into account QoS factors related to Internet based services. Some researchers describe QoS issues related to web services from the provider's perspective [10]. We believe that the current research has not delved into QoS issues related to Web Service based workflows, and many critical issues related to the availability, reliability, performance and security of Web Services need to be handled. Our approach tactfully utilizes and monitors these QoS parameters to provide a consistent service interface to other applications in the workflow through adaptive QoS based selection, binding and execution of Web Services.

3 Event-Centric Test Case Script

Event-centric test case script (EVEC) is designed so that the same scripts can be used either in live monitoring mode, or in analysis of past events from a log (referred to as deferred mode in this paper called hereafter the "deferred mode") or yet in mixed situation. Testing and Monitoring of Business Processes as well as more generally of systems the behaviour of which can be traced by events, fall in the following three categories:

- Compliance with specifications. Such specifications may be of a business transaction, business process definition, documents exchanged, or of infrastructure behaviour (e.g. messaging protocol). Enabling the automatic generation of EVEC scripts from such specifications when these specifications are formal – e.g. process definition, choreographies, document schema or rules – is part of the requirements although the methodology to achieve this is out of scope of this document. Some test assertion design and best practices, such as those in Test Assertions Guidelines [11] may be used for deriving scripts from such representations even when automatic generation is not possible.
- Compliance with agreements. Such agreements may be business agreements such as SLAs, or regulatory compliance rules. They may also be infrastructure configuration agreements (e.g. ebXML CPA, WS-Policy). This category of application includes SLA monitoring, business metrics and aspects of business activity monitoring (BAM) that are closest to operations, e.g. for regulatory compliance.
- Business Operation intelligence. Such monitoring is not directly related to compliance, but primarily intended for generating reports and various analytics of business activities. This includes analyzing the logs of processes and business transactions for reports and BI. This category of application includes BAM (business activity monitoring). In its dynamic aspect, this monitoring is addresses the

need for visibility in business processes and service-oriented systems, which include problem detection/anticipation, diagnostics and alarm generation. Each one of the above categories may be considered both in a real-time context (e.g. generation of alarms and notifications during operation) and a deferred, off-line analysis context (periodic generation of reports or metrics with no direct, automatic feedback loop to operations). In both cases, the same input – in form of events – is assumed.

From the viewpoint of script execution semantics, "live" and "deferred" are not distinguished: the same script is executable on input that is either live or logged. To ensure flexibility for handling various monitoring contexts and situations, mixing of both execution modes must be supported:

- A script may start executing "deferred mode" with its events already partially logged, and then catch-up with the on-going logging of events and continue "live".
- Conversely, a script may start live, and if its execution engine is interrupted for some reason, may resume its analysis of events that have already been logged while the test engine was stopped, in deferred mode. Then it may catch-up with events and eventually go live again. When events are consumed in a publish-subscribe mode, a simple queuing mechanism is sufficient to provide the above flexibility. However, EVEC must be able to correlate with past events.

4 Implementation of EVEC

The EVEC script language is designed for testing and monitoring processes or business transactions of various kinds, and more particularly for analyzing and validating event patterns that are generated by these processes. To this extent, EVEC may be described as an event-processing language. The content and structure of these events may be quite diverse, but a common XML wrapper is assumed. The top-level constructs are the script package and the scriplet:

- The script package, or "script": This is the main unit of execution. The script package contains an "execution context" (<execution-context> element) that defines various global constructs and bindings, e.g. for declaring event boards. The script package also contains one or more "scriplets". The execution context in a script package defines which scriplet to start execution with - or main scriplet. In case other scriplets are defined, the main scriplet is expected to invoke these directly or indirectly.
- The scriplet: A scriplet defines a flow (or thread) of execution for a sequence of atomic operations. Scriplets can execute either concurrently or not (see detailed meaning in the next section), and can be started in a blocking or non-blocking way.

EVEC is designed so that it leverages existing XML script languages for special features such as logical conditions and event selection. The default language for all logical expressions over XML content is XPath, along with its existing function libraries (e.g. advanced set of functions for time and duration management).

The concept of concurrency in EVEC is entirely dependent on the notion of "virtual present time" (VPtime). When a scriplet starts to execute, it is assigned a VP-time which will condition its event consumption and timestamp its event production. The default VP-time assignments are:

- The first scriplet of a script package is assigned the initial VP-time of this script, the default of which is in turn the actual present time (AP-time).
- The VP-time of a scriplet S2 started by a scriplet S1, is the value of VP-time in S1 when [start S2] is executed. These default values can be overriden by the <start> operation, which allows to set the VP-time of the started scriplet (see the start/@vptset attribute in section 4). Inside a scriplet, the VP-time may be progressed by two operations:
- <wait> : will add some predefined duration to the VP-time, or wait until some date, or yet until some other scriplets complete.
- <catch> : when waiting - virtually or really - for some event to occur, will advance the VP-time to the occurring date of events being caught.

Event catching in a scriplet is only considering (by default) events occurring at or after the current VP-time. Besides <wait> and <catch>, the execution duration of other EVEC operations is considered as negligible, as far as the VP-time is concerned: in other words, these operations do not affect the VP-time. The VP-time window of a scriplet execution is defined as the [starting VP-time, ending VP-time] time interval of the execution. Intuitively, concurrent execution is achieved when the VP-time windows of two scriplets overlap. Concurrency is entirely determined by the start VP-time assigned to these scriplets. When a scriplet S1 starts a scriplet S2, it can do so either in a blocking or non-blocking way:

- Blocking invocation: intuitively, the invoking scriplet (S1) will wait until the invoked scriplet (S2) terminates. The next statement in the invoking scriplet S1 (after <start>), will execute at a VP-time that is same as the VP-time set at the end of the invoked scriplet (S2). In other words, the VPtimes of S1 and S2 are "synchronized" after S2 completes (see start/@vptsync="true" in Section 4). More generally, to accommodate the case where a starting time is set at a date/time anterior to the invoking time (@vptset="a past date/time"), the VP-time of the next statement in S1 is either the last VP-time value of S2 or the last VP-time value in S1 (just before invoking S2), whichever occurs the latest.
- Non-blocking invocation: intuitively, the invoked scriplet (S2) will not cause the invoking scriplet (S1) to wait. In other words, the VP-times of S1 and S2 are not "synchronized" after S2 completes. (see start/@vptsync="false" in Section 4). The next statement in the invoking scriplet S1 will execute at a VP-time that is same as the VP-time value just before executing the <start> statement, this regardless of the value of start/@vptset. Non-blocking invocations should not be seen as only useful for actual concurrent (or multi-threaded) processing. In many cases, it makes scripting easier and more intuitive, even when execution is entirely deferred on past (logged) events that could otherwise be processed serially in a single-threaded way. Various cases of blocking and non-blocking invocations are illustrated below. The following figure illustrates both modes of scriplet invocations, and how the VP-time is affected – or not - in the invoking scriplet.

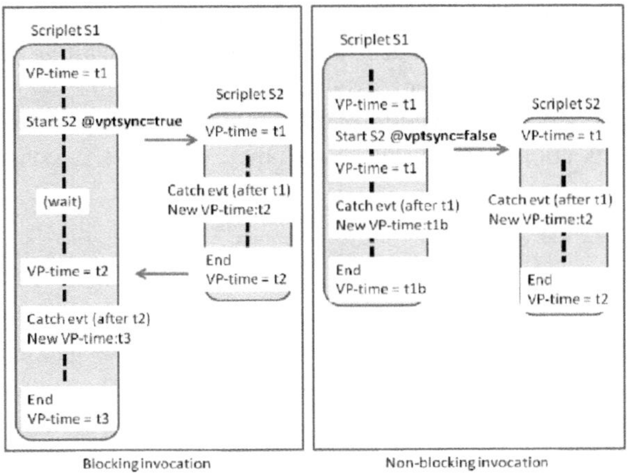

Fig. 1. Blocking and non-blocking modes of scriplet invocation

When a scriplet S1 does a blocking invocation of a scriplet S2, the VP-time of the invoked scriplet S2 is initiated at the current VP-time of the invoking scriplet S1 (unless a different VPtime value is given using start/@vptset as illustrated in the next figures). The scriplet S1 is then "blocked" until the VP-time at the end of S2 is known and assigned as current VP-time in S1.

In the non-blocking invocation (see Fig. 1.), S1 will ignore the ending time of S2. A single-threaded execution may still execute S2 first before executing the next statement in S1. The execution semantics would still allow "concurrent" catching (in terms of virtual present) of same events by S1 and S2, as both will select events starting from VP-time t1. In the above figure, S1 is catching an event at time t1b while S2 is catching an event at time t2. Depending on their respective selection expressions, these catches could capture either the same or different event, causing the new VPtime in S1 (t1b) to be either prior or after the new VP-time in S2 (t2).

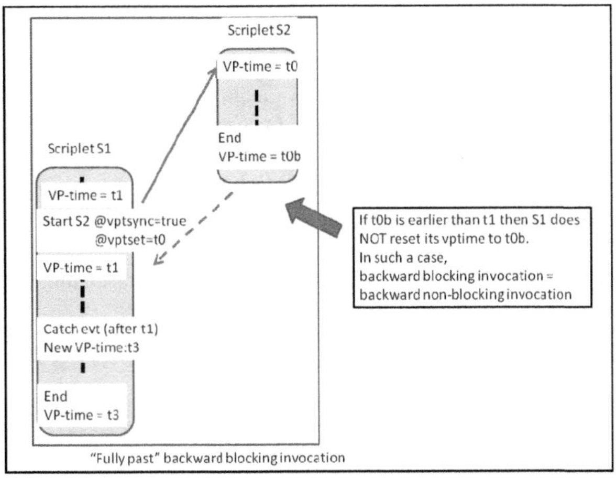

Fig. 2. Fully past backward blocking invocation

In a single-threaded execution of the non-blocking case that started "live" (VP-time = present time), S2 could be executed first live, then the remaining part of S1 can be executed "deferred" on the log of events, starting from time t1 now in the past. Clearly, more fine-grain serialization of S1 and S2 executions would be required if these two scriplets communicate with each other, e.g. if S1 is consuming an event posted by S2 or vice-versa.

5 Conclusion

In this paper, we present an event-centric test case scripting method and execution model, EVEC, for such systems. EVEC enables testing and monitoring of applications and business processes, the behavior of which can be traced and monitored via events. The notion of event in EVEC is broad, thus, it could cover all of the type of SOA business processes. Further study is required to define and classify the detailed test case metadata or artifacts that would complement EVEC in test environments.

References

1. Leymann, F.: Web services flow language, TR WSFL 1.0, IBM Software Group (May 2001)
2. Thatte, S.: XLANG Web Services for Business Process Design (2001), `http://www.gotdotnet.com/team/xmlwsspecs/xlang-c/default.htm`
3. Kammer, P., Bolcer, G.A., Taylor, R.N., Bergman, M.: Techniques for Supporting Dynamic and Adaptive Workflow. Journal of Computer Supported Cooperative Work (CSCW) 9, 269–292
4. DAML-S Specifications, `http://www.daml.org/services/`
5. Kosanke, K.: CIMOSA - Open System Architecture for CIM; ESPRIT Consortium AMICE. Springer, Heidelberg (1993)
6. Biztalk, `http://www.microsoft.com/biztalk/`
7. Business Process Execution Language for Web Services, Version 1.0 (July 2002), `http://www-106.ibm.com/developerworks/webservices/library/ws-bpel/`
8. Cardoso, J., Sheth, A., Miller, J.: Workflow Quality Of Service (2002)
9. Sheth, A., Cardoso, J., Miller, J., Koch, K.: QoS for Service-oriented Middleware. In: Web Services and Grid Computing. In: Proceedings of the Conference on Systemics, Cybernetics and Informatics, Orlando, FL (July 2002)
10. Mani, A., Nagarajan, A.: Understanding quality of service for Web services, `http://herzberg.ca.sandia.gov/jess/`
11. OASIS Test Assertions Guidelines (TAG) TC, Test Assertions Guidelines, `http://www.oasis-open.org/committees/tag/`

bQoS(business QoS) Parameters for SOA Quality Rating

Youngkon Lee

e-Business Department, Korea Polytechnic University,
2121 Jeongwangdong, Siheung city, Korea
yklee777@kpu.ac.kr

Abstract. With Web services starting to be deployed within organizations and being offered as paid services across organizational boundaries, quality of service (QoS) has become one of the key issues to be addressed by providers and clients. While methods to describe and advertise QoS properties have been developed, the main outstanding issue remains how to implement a service that lives up to promised QoS properties. This paper provides the service level agreement (SLA) parameters for QoS management applied to Web services and raises a set of research issues that originate in the virtualization aspect of services and are specific to QoS management in a services environment – beyond what is addressed so far by work in the areas of distributed systems and performance management.

Keywords: SOA, business context, SLA parameter.

1 Introduction

Whether offered within an organization or as a part of a paid service across organizational boundaries, quality-of-service (QoS) aspects of services are important in a service -oriented computing environment. Dealing with QoS is a sign of a technology going beyond its stage of initial experimentation to a production deployment and many recent activities related to QoS of Web services indicate that this is becoming an increasingly relevant topic.

Efforts in the past years mainly focused on describing, advertising and signing up to Web and Grid services at defined QoS levels. This includes HP's Web Services Management Framework (WSMF) [1], IBM's Web Service Level Agreement (WSLA) language [2][3], the Web Services Offer Language (WSOL) [4] as well as approaches based on WS-Policy [5]. These efforts enable us to describe quality metrics of services, such as response time, and the associated service level objectives flexibly and in a way that is meaningful for the business needs of a service client.

However, one of the challenging issues is to associate or derive a system configuration that delivers the QoS of a described Web service using the above mentioned approaches. In many cases, this is non-trivial. Sometimes we can rely on experience with tested, dedicated system configurations to decide, for example, the size of a cluster for a particular workload guaranteeing a particular response time for a given percentile of requests. In addition, managing a service at different QoS levels on the same infrastructure is not easy.

T.-h. Kim et al. (Eds.): ASEA/DRBC/EL 2011, CCIS 257, pp. 497–504, 2011.

While managing QoS in distributed systems is not a novel problem, a number of additional issues arise in the context of a service-oriented computing environment. Those issues arise from the specific properties of Web services. For example, cross-organizational Web services may be accessed through the public Internet and client side QoS metrics have to include network properties in addition to properties of the service-implementing application itself. In addition, composite and recursively aggregated services – and the ability to aggregate is seen as a key benefit of Web services – gain new QoS properties that are not always easily derived from their parts.

The objective of paper is to analyze the main QoS factors of Service-oriented Architecture (SOA) in a business context and to provide the service level agreement (SLA) parameters that affect critically the business performance.

According to OASIS Reference Model for Service Oriented Architecture [SOA-RM] [6], the Service Oriented Architecture (SOA) is a paradigm for organizing and utilizing distributed capabilities that may be under control of different ownership domains. The service within SOA is a mechanism to enable access to one or more capabilities, where the access is provided using a prescribed interface and is exercised consistent with constraints and policies as specified by the service description. This specification further defines the business service level agreement (bSLA) between the service requester and the service provider for the service which is defined in SOA-RM, within the end-to-end resource planning (EERP) technology [7]. The applications of EERP are any kind of business services, and they are not limited to Web Services only. This applies the well-known technique for service discovery and optimization in a novel way to improve business results. It models the business process and the range of potential services, and then guides the selection and deployment of services based on the end-to-end business value. Modeling the business service-level agreements to manage and evaluate services and establishing agreements about the business service is essential to long-term value chain improvement. The bSLA is different from the SLA in the software/IT world. The bSLA is the contact between the service requester and the service provider, and the SLA is the contract between the service provider and the network/system provider. The SLA is network/system oriented agreement that deals with network performance and system availability. The bSLA is a business oriented agreement that deals with price, time to deliver, and the quality/rating of the service.

In section 2, we summarize the related works about web service selection based on the QoS metrics. Section 3 presents the service process model which enables service performance optimization in the business respect and section 4 details the bSLA model including parties, parameters and obligations, and we conclude in section 5.

2 Related Works

The first step to manage Web service's quality is to define it. While this is important for Web services as well as in traditional distributed systems, explicit definition is particularly important in an environment transcending organizational boundaries. Quality is expressed referring to observable parameters relating to a non-functional property, for example, the response time of a request. A level of quality is agreed upon as a constraint over those parameters, potentially dependent on a precondition. Hence, the party offering a Web service, in agreement with its customers and users, will define the QoS parameters and the particular instances of the service to which these parameters relate. In the case of a Web service, a parameter such as response time can relate to an individual invocation of an operation or a class of operations, all having the same (individual) quality properties of having an aggregate property, e.g., the average response time of this class of operations or another stochastic metric.

A further step in managing Web services QoS is the definition of the semantics of the QoS parameters. A Web service and its subscribers and users must understand what it is meant. It is important what is measured where. For performance-oriented metrics this can be at different points, as Fig. 1 illustrates.

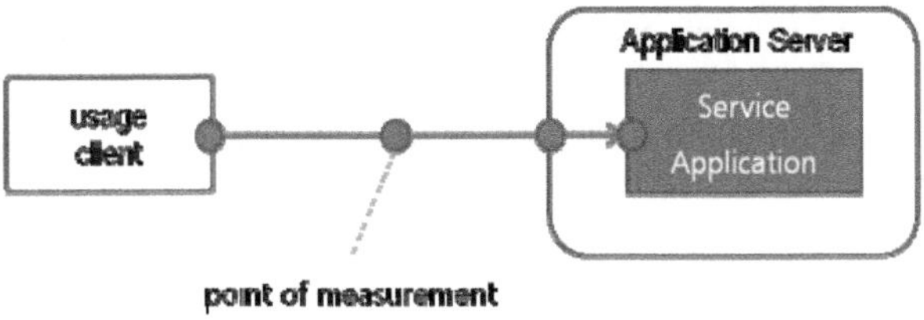

Fig. 1. Points of measurements defining semantics of metrics

The definition of QoS parameters corresponds to the establishment of ontology between a service provider and its clients. Ontology can be established in two approaches. (1) It can be a definition of terms and, potentially, or the semantics of the relationships between them, as facilitated by DAML and OIL [8]. This approach results in a fixed set of well understood terms – in our case the QoS parameters. (2) Another approach uses constructive ontology. Based on a set of well-know defined terms (as in 1) and a set of well-know composition operators, new terms' (QoS) parameters can be defined by composing new parameters out of existing ones using the operators.

Having established common understanding of quality of service parameters and the associated guarantees given by the provider, it also has to be established to which relationships between a client and a server a QoS guarantee applies. A service may provide the same quality to all requesting clients, to each client individually or to a defined set of clients that a provider organization and an organization requiring a QoS level for multiple clients agree upon in a contract, which is also called an SLA.

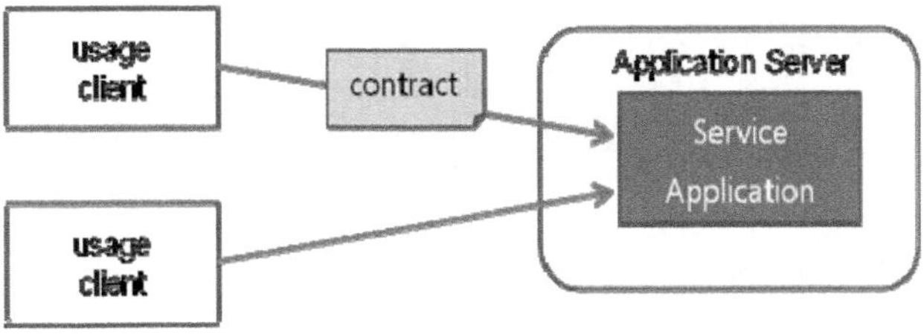

Fig. 2. Contracts defining the scope of quality guarantees

Clients will refer to the contract when requesting the service according to a particular quality level. The different scoping approaches of QoS guarantees require different means of establishing a particular quality level for a client: If a QoS level is associated with a service, a client searches for a suitable service in a directory, e.g., UDDI and retrieves its quality definition, e.g., stated as a WS-Policy expression. In the case of an individual client or a contract, a negotiation mechanism, which can be very simple, must be provided. Once the contract is established, the provider organization must provision a service-implementing system such that it behaves as it has been agreed upon. This involves deriving the amount of resources needed and the runtime management of resources.

However, this is not simple. While we have developed – improvable – approaches to the issues raised above, the issue of provisioning and runtime managing a Web service-implementing system is not equally well understood yet. In the next section, we discuss what distributed systems and performance management approaches can provide.

A number of performance management technologies, such as workload managers and network dispatchers, have been developed to control response times of individual systems and clusters and various availability management approaches. However, it is not straight-forward to configure, for example, workload managers to satisfy response time goals for a set of different scopes of quality – for Web services as well as for any distributed system. In this section, we outline some typical approaches of how today's QoS parameters are managed in distributed systems.

3 Service Process Model

This section describes the service process model conceptually. Fig. 3 shows the conceptual model, and of messages flows with brief descriptions. We also include timeline and sequence diagrams Fig. 4 to show how an implementation would use service messages and build a continuous business process improvement loop. In Figure 3, the business quality of Service is abbreviated as bQoS, business rating is abbreviated as Rating, and business service level agreement is abbreviated as bSLA.

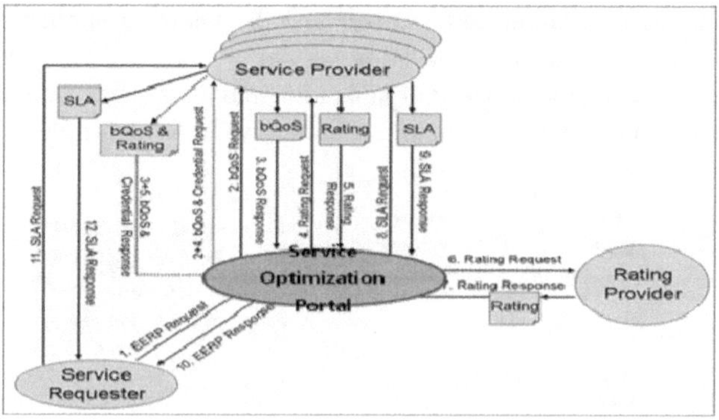

Fig. 3. Service Process Model

The service requester is the client system who tries to find an optimal solution provided by service optimization portal (SOP). Service providers provide business services. Each service provider may offer the same service but with different bQoS and Ratings. Services may be running on different platforms with different implementations, but they all support message exchanges of bQoS, Rating, and BSLA information in the XML formats.

The SOP accepts the request from the Service requester, performs bQoS and rating queries, calculates optimal solution(s), and then returns the result to the service requester. The Rating Provider is a party unaffiliated with either the requester or the target of the rating request, such as a third party rating organization, given a reference to a particular business service and provider, issues either a number or a classification description.

There can be another way to implement the service optimization without the SOP. For example, there can be a case for some services providers and service consumers using SOA Registry-Repository to find each other, to exchange business quality of services information among them, and to begin negotiations for establishing Service Level Agreements (SLAs). The results of messages 2 through 9 in Figure 4 are used to calculate the optimal deployment for a given set of services requests. A list of alternatives might be returned in message 10. Each step in the process would have a service provider determined for each service and for each alternative. Messages 11 and 12 are exchanged between the service requester and the selected service providers to define the BSLA.

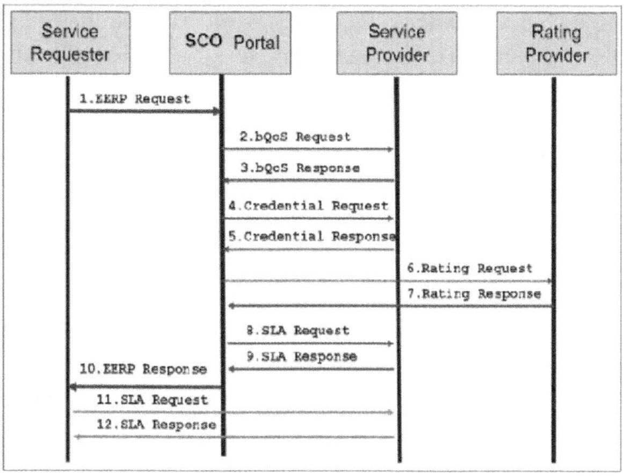

Fig. 4. Service message sequence without optional messages

4 bSLA Model

The bSLA model is for representing SLA parameters in the respect of business value. The BSLA is the root element for EERP- Business Service-level agreement (bSLA). The bSLA is a formal contract between a service provider and a client guaranteeing quantifiable business quality of service (bQoS) at defined levels. It can have one or more of the following elements:

```
<sla:BSLA   xmlns:sla="..."   xmlns:bqos="..."   ...>
  <sla:SLAParties   ...>sla:SLAPartiesTypeType</sla:SLAParties>
  <sla:SLAParameters   ...>sla:SLAParametersType</sla:SLAParameters>
  <sla:SLAObligations   ...>sla:SLAObligationsType</sla:SLAObligations>   ?
  <sla:SLATerms   ...>sla:SLATermsType</sla:SLATerms>   ?
</sla:BSLA>
```

Fig. 5. XML schema for bSLA

The following describes the attributes and elements listed in the schema outlined above:

- /sla:BSLA is a root element of Business Service-level agreement (bSLA) for EERP.
- SLAParties is a required element in bSLA that defines parties invoked in this bSLA for the service. SLAParties element has both the service provider and services requester elements.
- /sla:BSLA/sla:SLAParties/@{any} is an extensibility mechanism to allow additional attributes, based on schemas, to be added to the SLAParties element in the future. Unrecognized attributes may cause a fault or be silently ignored.
- /sla:BSLA/sla:SLAParameters is defined monitoring of bQoS metrics, including service profile uri, operations and other optional elements. It is a required element that uses sla:SLAParametersType.
- /sla:BSLA/sla:SLAParameters/@{any} is an extensibility mechanism to allow additional attributes, based on schemas, to be added to the SLAParameters element in the future.
- /sla:BSLA/sla:SLAObligations is agreed bSLA obligations aspect of the service, including obligations, action guarantees. It is a optional element that uses sla:SLAObligationsType.
- /sla:BSLA/sla:SLAObligations/@{any} is an extensibility mechanism to allow additional attributes, based on schemas, to be added to the SLA Obligations element in the future.
- /sla:BSLA/sla:SLATerms is agreed bSLA terms aspect of the service, including bSLA term elements.
- /sla:BSLA/sla:SLATerms/@{any} is an extensibility mechanism to allow additional attributes, based on schemas, to be added to the SLATerms element in the future.
- /sla:BSLA/@{any} is an extensibility mechanism to allow additional attributes, based on schemas, to be added to the root BSLA element in the future.
- /sla:BSLA/sla:BSLAExtension is an optional element that keeps different (extensible) elements to be specified in the future.
- /sla:BSLA/sla:BSLAExtension/{any} is an extensibility mechanism to allow different (extensible) elements to be specified in the future.

The SLAParties describes the list of parties invoked in the bSLA for the service. There should be one SLAParties element present in the bSLA of service. The following describes the attributes and elements listed in the schema outlined above:

- /sla:SLAParties, bSLA Parties aspect of the service, is for parties invoked in the bSLA for the service, including both service provider and service requester elements.
- /sla:SLAParties/sla:ServiceProvider represents the provider for parties. It is a required element for bSLA Parties.
- /sla:SLAParties/sla:ServiceProvider/sla:ServiceUri is a required element for Service Provider.
- /sla:SLAParties/sla:ServiceProvider/sla:ServiceProviderName is the name of the service provider. It is also a required element for Service Provider.
- /sla:SLAParties/sla:ServiceProvider/sla:ServiceProviderName/@languageID is an optional attribute in the ServiceProviderName element, using xsd:language type.

```
<sla:SLAParties   xmlns:sla="..."   ...>
<sla:ServiceProvider   ...>sla:ServiceProviderType
<sla:ServiceUri   ...>sla:SlaUriType</sla:ServiceUri>
<sla:ServiceProviderName
languageID="...">sla:ServiceProviderNameType</sla:ServiceProviderName>
</sla:ServiceProvider>
<sla:ServiceRequester   ...   >sla:ServiceRequesterType
<sla:ServiceRequesterUri   ...   >sla:SlaUriType</sla:ServiceRequesterUri>
<sla:ServiceRequesterName
languageID="...">sla:ServiceRequesterNameType</sla:ServiceRequesterName>
</sla:ServiceRequester>
...
</sla:SLAParties>
```

Fig. 6. XML schema for bSLA parties

- /sla:SLAParties/sla:ServiceProvider/@{any} is an extensibility mechanism to allow additional attributes, based on schemas, to be added to ServiceProvider element in the future. /sla:SLAParties/sla:ServiceRequester represents requester for the service, including requester's name and the URI that represents the requester. It is a required element for bSLA Parties.
- /sla:SLAParties/sla:ServiceRequester/sla:ServiceRequesterUri represents the requester's identifier in URI format for the service requester. It is a required element for Service Requester.
- /sla:SLAParties/sla:ServiceRequester/sla:ServiceRequesterName is requester's name for the service requester. It is a required element for Service Requester.
- /sla:SLAParties/sla:ServiceRequester/sla:ServiceRequesterName/@languageID is an optional attribute in the ServiceRequesterName element.
- /sla:SLAParties/sla:ServiceRequester/@{any} is an extensibility mechanism to allow additional attributes, based on schemas, to be added to the serviceRequester element in the future.
- /sla:SLAParties/{any} is an extensibility mechanism to allow different (extensible) elements to be specified in the future.

5 Conclusion

In this paper, we proposed a new concept of bSLA, whose items are proper to evaluate SOA service performance in the respect of service business benefit. The bSLA includes the service actor information, bSLA parties and the quality information, bSLA parameters, and bSLA obligations of the service parties. We also devised a service optimization portal which provides the best service composition by evaluating the value of bQoS of each service chain. Further study is required to define and classify the quality factor group for business case by case.

References

1. Catania, N., Kumar, P., Murray, B., Pourhedari, H., Vambenepe, W., Wurster, K.: Web Services Management Framework, Version 2.0, Hewlett-Packard (July 16, 2003), http://devresource.hp.com/drc/specifications/wsmf/WSMF-WSM.jsp
2. Ludwig, H., Keller, A., Dan, A., King, R., Franck, R.: A service level agreement language for dynamic electronic services. Electronic Commerce Research 3, 43–59 (2003)
3. Ludwig, H., Keller, A., Dan, A., King, R., Franck, R.: Web Service Level Agreement (WSLA) Language Specification, Version 1.0, IBM Corporation (January 28, 2003), http://www.research.ibm.com/wsla/WSLASpecV1-20030128.pdf
4. Tosic, V., Pagurek, B., Patel, K.: WSOL – A Language for the Formal Specification of Classes of Service for Web Services. In: Proc. of ICWS 2003 (The 2003 International Conference on Web Services), Las Vegas, USA, June 23-26, pp. 375–381. CSREA Press (2003)
5. Box, D., Curbera, F., Hondo, M., Kale, C., Langworthy, D., Nadalin, A., Nagaratnam, N., Nottingham, M., von Riegen, C., Shewchuk, J.: Web Services Policy Framework (WSPolicy) (May 28, 2003), http://www.ibm.com/developer-works/library/ws-policy
6. Mackenzie, C.M., et al.: Reference Model for Service Oriented Architecture 1.0. OASIS Committee draft (August 2006)
7. Cox, W., et al.: SOA-EERP Business Quality of Service Version. OASIS Committee draft (November 2010)
8. Connolly, D., van Harmelen, F., Horrocks, I., McGuinness, D.L., Patel-Schneider, P.F., Stein, L.A.: DAML+OIL (March 2001); Reference Description, W3C (December 18, 2001), http://www.w3.org/TR/daml+oil-reference

Business-Centric Test Assertion Model for SOA

Youngkon Lee

e-Business Department, Korea Polytechnic University,
2121 Jeongwangdong, Siheung city, Korea
yklee777@kpu.ac.kr

Abstract. This paper presents a design method for business-centric SOA test framework. The reference architecture of SOA system is usually layered: business process layer, service layer, and computing resource layer. In the architecture, there are so many subsystems affecting the system's performance, which relates with each other. As a result, in respect of overall performance, it is meaningless to measure each subsystem's performance separately. In SOA system, the performance of the business process layer with which users keep in contact usually depends on the summation of the performance of the other lower layers. Therefore, for testing SOA system, test cases describing business process activities should be prepared. We devised a business-centric SOA test assertion model which enables to semi-automatic transform test assertions into test cases by the concept of prescription level and normalized prerequisite definition. The model also minimizes the semantic distortion in the transformation process.

Keywords: SOA, business process, test assertions, test cases.

1 Introduction

Service Oriented Architecture (SOA) is generally defined as a business-centric IT architectural approach that supports integrating businesses as linked, repeatable business tasks, or services. SOA enables to solve integration complexity problem and facilitates broad-scale interoperability and unlimited collaboration across the enterprise. It also provides flexibility and agility to address changing business requirements in lower cost and lesser time to market via reuse.

SOA has a lot of promises of interoperability, however, at the cost of: lack of enterprise scale QoS, complex standards which are still forming, lack of tools and framework to support standards, and perform penalty. Recently, as SOA has been widely adopted in business system framework, performance issues in SOA are raised continuously from users and developers.

SOA system is generally composed of various subsystems, each of which relates intimately with others. Therefore, if performances are issued, it is very difficult to find out the reason clearly. For example, if a business process in SOA system has longer response time than before, there could be various reasons: cache overflow in a business processor, wrapping overhead in service interface, or exceptions in computing resources, etc. One thing clear is that the performance of business process layer

T.-h. Kim et al. (Eds.): ASEA/DRBC/EL 2011, CCIS 257, pp. 505–513, 2011.

depends on the lower layer and measuring the performance of business layer includes indirectly measuring the performance of all the lower layers. But, most of the test frameworks developed focus on measuring SOA messaging performance, as we present in chapter 2. They almost adopt batch-style testing where all the test cases are executed in a sequence.

OMG recommended a standard SOA reference model, MDA (Model Driven Architecture) [1]. It is widely adopted in real world because it is normative and enables SOA system to be implemented in a business-centric approach. In the MDA, a business process is designed firstly in a way for satisfying business requirements and later services are bounded to the activities in the business process. Business processes are described in a standardized language (e.g. WSBPEL) and they are executed generally on a business process management (BPM) system.

For testing SOA systems implemented according to the MDA reference model in business-centric way, test harness should have business process simulation functionality so that it can behave as BPM and test overall performance at the same time. This means that the test harness can execute business process, perform tests, and gather metric values. The performance of the business process layer with which users keep in contact usually depends on the summation of the performance of the other lower layers. Therefore, for testing SOA system, test cases describing business process activities should be prepared.

In SOA system, test assertions may help develop tighter test cases which could be used as an input for SOA test harness. Any ambiguities, contradictions and statements which require excessive resources for testing can be noted as they become apparent during test assertion creation. Test assertions should be reviewed and approved to improve both the quality and time-to-deployment of the test cases. Therefore, best results are achieved when assertions are developed in parallel with the test cases.

Test assertions provide a starting point for writing conformance test cases or interoperability test cases. They simplify the distribution of the test development effort between different organizations while maintaining consistent test quality. Test assertions improve confidence in the resulting test and provide a basis for coverage analysis.

In section 2, we present some related works. Section 3 provides the concept of test assertion. In section 4, we describe a test assertion model. Section 5 presents cases of the test assertion and section 6 shows complex predicates of test assertions. Conclusions are presented in the last section.

2 Related Works

This section presents some test frameworks and script languages developed or proposed for SOA system.

Web Services Quality Management System

This system has been developed by NIA in order to measure Web services' quality on the criteria of WSQM (Web Services Quality Model) quality factors [2]:

interoperability, security, manageability, performance, business processing capability, and business process quality. This system contributes to consolidate the quality factors of SOA. However, it requires expanding its architecture to apply SOA, system, because it targets only to Web services system.

ebXML Test Framework

This framework has been implemented by NIST and KorBIT for testing ebXML system according to OASIS IIC Specification [3]. It could test packaging, security, reliability, and transport protocol of ebXML messaging system implemented by ebMS specification [4]. The main purpose of this framework is to test conformance and interoperability of ebXML messaging system, and it is not proper for testing service oriented systems. Besides, it cannot test ad hoc status resulting from various events, because it is not event-driven but batch-style test framework.

JXUnit and JXU

JXUnit [5] and JXU [6] is a general scripting system (XML based) for defining test suites and test cases aimed at general e-business application testing. Test steps are written as Java classes. There is neither built-in support for business process test nor support for the event-driven features. However, as a general test scripting platform that relies on a common programming language, this system could be used as an implementation platform for general e-business tests.

ATML (Automatic Test Mark-up Language)

In its requirements, ATML provides XML Schemata and support information that allows the exchange of diagnostic information between conforming software components applications [7]. The overall goal is to support loosely coupled open architectures that permit the use of advanced diagnostic reasoning and analytical applications. The objective of ATML is focusing on the representation and transfer of test artifacts: diagnostics, test configuration, test description, instruments, etc.

Test Choreography Languages

These are standards for specifying the orchestration of business processes and/or transactional collaborations between partners. Although a markup like XPDL [8] is very complete from a process definition and control viewpoint, it is lacking the event-centric design and event correlation / querying capability required by testing and monitoring exchanges. Also, a design choice has been here to use a very restricted set of control primitives, easy to implement and validate, sufficient for test cases of modest size. Other languages or mark-ups define somehow choreographies of messages and their properties: ebBP, WS-BPEL, WS-Choreography[9]. The general focus of these dialects is either the operational aspect of driving business process or business transactions, and/or the contractual aspect, but not monitoring and validation. Although they may express detailed conformance requirements, they fall short of covering the various aspects of an exhaustive conformance check, e.g. the generation of intentional errors or simulation of uncommon behaviors. In addition, the focus of these languages is mainly on one layer of the choreography – they for instance, ignore lower-level message exchanges entailed by quality of service concerns such as reliability, or binding patterns with the transport layer.

3 Concept of Test Assertion

A test assertion is a testable or measurable expression for evaluating the adherence of an implementation (or part of it) to a normative statement in a specification.

A set of test assertions may be associated with a conformance clause in order to define more precisely what conformance entails. Test assertions lie between the specification and any suite of tests to be conducted to determine conformance (See Fig. 1). Such a test suite is typically comprised of a set of test cases. These test cases may be derived from test assertions which address the normative statements of the specification.

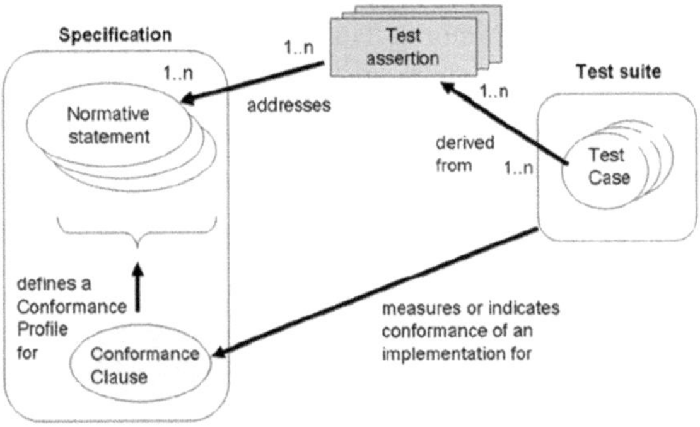

Fig. 1. Role of Test Assertion

Judging whether the test assertion is testable may require some knowledge about testing capabilities and resource constraints. Sometimes there is little knowledge of what actual testing conditions will be. In such cases the prime objective of writing test assertions is to provide a better understanding of what is expected from implementations, in order to fulfill the requirements. In other cases, the test assertions are designed to reflect a more precise knowledge of testing conditions. Such test assertions can more easily be used as a blueprint for test suites.

4 Test Assertion Model

This section aims to cover the simpler aspects of test assertions. Some more complex aspects are covered later in this section. Fig. 2 below shows the anatomy of a typical test assertion, and how its parts relate to the specification being addressed, as well as to the implementations under test. Some optional parts are not shown in the figure.

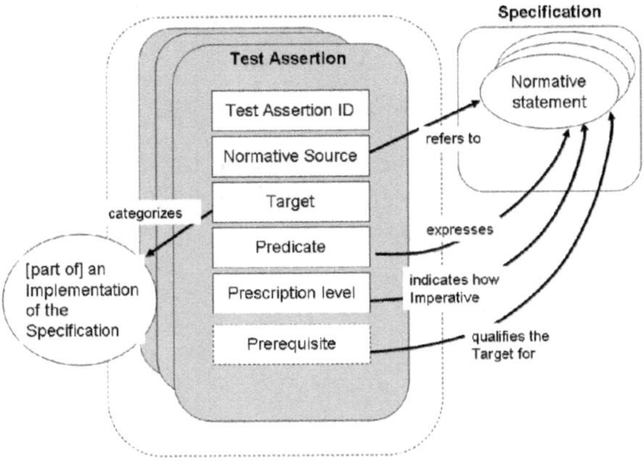

Fig. 2. General Anatomy of a Test Assertion

Some of the elements which comprise a test assertion are considered core while others are optional. A test assertion includes, implicitly or explicitly:

Identifier

A unique identifier of the test assertion facilitates tools development and the mapping of assertions to specification statements. It is recommended that the identifier be made universally unique.

Normative Sources

These refer to the precise specification requirements or normative statements that the test assertion addresses.

Target

The target categorizes an implementation or a part of an implementation of the referred specification, which is the main object of the test assertion and of its Normative Sources.

Predicate

A predicate asserts, in the form of an expression, the feature (a behavior or a property) described in the specification statement(s) referred by the Normative Sources. If the predicate is an expression which evaluates to "true" over the test assertion target, this means that the target exhibits this feature. "False" means the target does not exhibit this feature.

In addition, a test assertion may optionally include following components.

Description

This is an informal definition of the role of the test assertion with some optional details on some of its parts. This description must not alter the general meaning of the test assertion and its parts. This description may be used to annotate the test assertion with any information useful to its understanding. It does not need to be an exhaustive description of the test assertion.

Prescription Level

This is a keyword that indicates how imperative it is that the Normative Statement referred to in the Normative Source, be met. See possible keyword values in the Glossary.

Prerequisite

A test assertion Prerequisite is a logical expression (similar to a Predicate) which further qualifies the Target for undergoing the core test (expressed by the Predicate) that addresses the Normative Statement. It may include references to the outcome of other test assertions. If the Prerequisite evaluates to "false" then the Target instance is not qualified for evaluation by the Predicate.

Tags

Test assertions may be assigned 'tags' or 'keywords', which may in turn be given values. These tags provide you with an opportunity to categorize the test assertions. They enable you to group the test assertions; based on the type of test they assume or based on their target properties.

Variables

Test assertions may also include variables for convenience in storing values for reuse and shared use, as well as for parameterization.

As a test assertion has parts that can be evaluated over a Target instance (i.e. the Prerequisite and the Predicate), the following semantics apply to a test assertion:

- "Target not qualified": if the Prerequisite (if any) evaluates to "false" over a Target instance.
- "Normative statement fulfilled [by the Target]": if the Prerequisite (if any) evaluates to "true" over a Target instance, and the Predicate evaluates to "true".
- "Normative statement not fulfilled [by the Target]": if the Prerequisite (if any) evaluates to "true" over a Target instance, and the Predicate evaluates to "false".

5 Case Study of Test Assertion

Consider the following statement in the widget specification:

[requirement 101] "A widget of medium size MUST use exactly one AA battery encased in a battery holder."

There are actually two requirements here that can be tested separately:

(requirement 101, part 1) A medium-size widget MUST use exactly one AA battery.

(requirement 101, part 2) A medium-size widget MUST have a battery holder encasing the battery.

Because of this it is possible to write two test assertions:

- **TA id**: widget-TA101-1a
  Normative Source: specification requirement 101, part 1 Target: medium-size widget
  Predicate: [the widget] uses exactly one AA battery. Prescription Level: mandatory

and

- **TA id**: widget-TA101-1b
  Normative Source: specification requirement 101, part 2 Target: medium-size widget
  Predicate: [the widget] has a battery holder encasing the battery. Prescription Level: mandatory

The granularity of a test assertion is a matter of judgment. A single test assertion instead of two can be written here, with the predicate: "[the widget] uses exactly one AA battery AND has a battery holder, encasing the battery".

This choice may later have an impact on the outcome of a test suite written to verify the conformance of widgets. With a single test assertion, a test case derived from this test assertion will not be expected to distinguish between the two failure cases. Using two test assertions - one for each sub-requirement - will ensure that a test suite can assess and report independently about the fulfillment of each sub-requirement. Other considerations such as the different nature of tests implied or the reuse of a test assertion in different conformance profiles [VAR], may also lead to the adoption of "fine-grained" instead of "coarse-grained" test assertions. Usage considerations will dictate the best choice.

6 Complex Predicates

Recall the previous example of [requirement 101]. The target can be defined as "a medium-size widget" or as just "a widget". The latter is a natural decision if the specification requirement uses the wording: "[requirement 101] If a widget is medium size, then it MUST use exactly one AA battery and be encased in a battery holder." For the simplicity of this example, if the two test assertion predicates for widget-TA101-1a and widget-TA101-1b are combined into one example, one possible outcome is:

TA id: widget-TA101-2a

Normative Source: requirement 101 Target: widget

Predicate: if [the widget] is medium-size, then [the widget] uses exactly one AA battery AND the battery is encased in a battery holder.

Prescription Level: mandatory

The target category is broad, but the predicate part is really of interest only for a subset of this category (the medium-size widgets). Usage considerations should again drive the decision here: a test suite that is designed to verify all widgets, and does not assume a prior categorization of these into small / medium / large sizes, would be improved with test assertions that only use "widget" as the target, such as widget-TA101-2a.

A test assertion predicate may, then, be a Boolean expression - a composition of atomic predicates using logical operators AND, OR, NOT. A test assertion predicate may also be of the kind: "if (condition) then (expression)".

The predicate is worded in an abstract way, still close to the wording of the specification. No indication of what kind of test procedure will be used, such as how to determine the number and type of batteries, is given. Detailed criteria for the condition evaluation, such as what kind of battery holder is acceptable, are also not provided. These details are normally left to the test cases that can be derived from the test assertions. These test cases will determine the precise criteria for conforming to the specification. However, if a precise criterion for interpreting the battery holder requirement is provided in an external specification, either referred to directly by the widget specification or by a related conformance clause, then a test assertion must use this criterion in its predicate. Such a test assertion must then refer not only to the specification requirement in its reference property, but also to the external specification or to the conformance clause that refers to this specification.

Another case where a predicate is more complex is when its conditional expression involves more than one part of an implementation (or implementations). In some cases it is clear which one of these objects must be considered the target, while others are just accessory objects. Consider the following predicate: "the [widget price tag] matches the price assigned to the widget in its [catalog entry]", where price tags and catalog entries are both items that must follow the store policy (in effect the specification). In this case it may be reasonably assumed that the "catalog" content is authoritative over the price tag. The price tag can then be considered as the test target, while the accessory object may be identified by a variable which is then used in the predicate.

7 Conclusion

We presented a SOA test assertion model, which facilitates to make test cases in normalized form. In the model, we devised the concept of prescription level and normalized prerequisite for preparing test cases. By the concepts, test assertion can be transformed into test cases without semantic distortion. The model minimizes the human intervention in preparing test cases by automating some processes for translating test assertions into test cases. We showed two cases of complex predicates. Further studies are required to develop a test framework to check out automatically that test cases are conformed to test assertions.

References

1. Miller, J., Mukerji, J.: MDA Guide Version 1.0.1., OMG (June 2003), `http://www.omg.org/docs/omg/03-06-01.pdf`
2. Lee, Y., et al.: Web Services Quality Model 1.1. OASIS WSQM TC (October 2008)
3. Durand, J., et al.: ebXML Test Framework v1.0. OASIS IIC TC (October 2004)
4. Wenzel, P., et al.: ebXML Messaging Services 3.0. OASIS ebMS TC (July 2007)
5. Java XML Unit (JXUnit), `http://jxunit.sourceforge.net`
6. JUnit, Java for Unit Test, `http://junit.sourceforge.net`
7. ATML, Standard for Automatic Test Markup Language (ATML) for Exchanging Automatic Test Equipment and Test Information via XML. IEEE (December 2006)
8. XPDL: XML Process Definition Language) (Workflow Management Coalition) Document Number WFMC-TC-1025: Version 1.14 (October 3, 2005)
9. OASIS, Business Process Specification Schema 1.0.1, May 2001 and ebBP, v2.0.4 (October 2006)

Application of Systemability to Software Reliability Evaluation

Koichi Tokuno and Shigeru Yamada

Department of Social Management Engineering,
Graduate School of Engineering, Tottori University
4-101, Koyama, Tottori-shi, 680-8552 Japan
{toku,yamada}@sse.tottori-u.ac.jp

Abstract. This paper applies the concept of systemability, which is defined as the reliability characteristic subject to the uncertainty of the field operational environment, to the operational software reliability evaluation. We take the position that the software reliability characteristic in the testing phase is originally different from that in the user operation. First we introduce the environmental factor to consistently bridge the gap between the software failure-occurrence characteristics during the testing and the operation phases. Then we consider the randomness of the environmental factor, i.e., the environmental factor is treated as a random-distributed variable. We use the hazard rate-based model focusing on the software failure-occurrence time to describe the software reliability growth phenomena in the testing and the operation phases. We derive several operational software reliability assessment measures. Finally, we show several numerical illustrations to investigate the impacts of the consideration of systemability on the field software reliability evaluation.

Keywords: systemability, environmental factor, randomness of operational environment, hazard rate-based model, software reliability growth.

1 Introduction

It has been often reported that the software reliability characteristics emerging in the field operation after release are quite different from the original predictions in the testing phase of the software development process, which are conducted with the software reliability models (SRMs). One of the main causes of this prediction gap is thought to be the underlying assumption for constructing SRMs that the software failure-occurrence phenomenon in the testing phase is similar to that in the user operation phase. Therefore, there exist some negative opinions about the above assumption, and several studies on field-oriented software reliability assessment have been conducted. Okamura et al. [1], Morita et al. [2], and Tokuno and Yamada [3] have discussed the operation-oriented software reliability assessment models by introducing the concept of the accelerated life testing (ALT) model [4] which is often applied to the reliability assessment for hardware products. They have characterized the difference between the testing

T.-h. Kim et al. (Eds.): ASEA/DRBC/EL 2011, CCIS 257, pp. 514–521, 2011.

and the field-operation environments by assuming that the software failure time intervals between in the testing and the operation phases bear a proportional relation from the viewpoint that the severities of both usage conditions are different generally. They have called the proportional constant the environmental factor.

However, the practical and reasonable estimation of the environmental factor remains the outstanding problem in even Refs. [1,2]. Originally it is impossible to apply the usual procedure for estimating the environmental factor since the software failures data in the operation phase observed from the software system in question are never obtained in advance. Accordingly, in the present circumstance, we have to decide the value of the environmental factor empirically and subjectively based on the similar software systems developed before. On the other hand, Pham [5] has presented the new mathematical reliability function, called **systemability**. The systemability function is defined as the probability that the system will perform its intended functions for a specified mission time subject to the uncertainty of the operating environment. Ref. [5] assumes that the hazard rate function in the field operation is proportional to one in the controlled in-house testing phase, and then considers the variation of the field environment by regarding the environmental factor as a random variable. As to the case of the software system, the operating environment in the testing phase is well-controlled one with less variation compared with the field operation environment. In other words, the field operation environment includes the more uncertain factors than the testing environment in terms of the pattern of the execution load, the compatibility between the software system and the hardware platform, the operational profile, and so on [6]. It is almost impossible to prepare the test cases assuming all possible external disturbances. Therefore, the consideration of the randomness of the environmental factor can not only describe the actual operating environment more faithfully, but also reflect the subjective value of the environmental factor to the field operational software reliability evaluation with a certain level of rationality.

In this paper, we expand the meaning of systemability from the definition of Ref. [5] into the system reliability characteristic considering the uncertainty and the variability of the field operating environment. Then we apply the idea of systemability to operational software reliability measurement. We use the hazard rate-based model to describe the software reliability growth phenomena in the testing and the operation phases as the based model. We derive several operation-oriented software reliability assessment measures with systemability and show several numerical examples of the measures.

2 Hazard Rate-Based Model

Let X_k ($k = 1,\ 2,\ \ldots;\ X_0 \equiv 0$) be the random variable representing the time interval between the $(k-1)$-st and the k-th software failure-occurrences. Then the hazard rate of X_k is defined as

$$z_k(t) \equiv \frac{f_k(t)}{1 - F_k(t)}, \tag{1}$$

Table 1. Representative hazard rate-based models $z_k(t) \equiv \lambda_k t^{m-1}$

type	name	λ_k
exponential	Jelinski-Moranda[7]	$\phi(N-k+1) \quad (N>0, \phi>0)$
($m = 1$)	Moranda[8]	$Dc^{k-1} \quad (D>0, 0<c<1)$
	Xie[9]	$\phi(N-k+1)^{\alpha} \quad (N>0, \phi>0, \alpha>1)$
Weibull ($m = 2$)	Schick-Wolverton[10]	$\phi(N-k+1) \quad (N>0, \phi>0)$
Weibull ($m > 0$)	Wagoner[11]	$\phi(N-k+1) \quad (N>0, \phi>0)$

where $F_k(t) \equiv \Pr\{X_k \leq t\}$ and $f_k(t) \equiv \mathrm{d}F_k(t)/\mathrm{d}t$ are the cumulative distribution and the probability density functions of X_k, respectively. $z_k(t)\Delta t$ gives the conditional probability that the k-th software failure occurs in the small time-interval $(t,\ t+\Delta t]$ on the conditions that the k-th software failure has not occurred in the time-interval $(0,\ t]$ and that the $(k-1)$-st software failure occurred at time point $t = 0$. The hazard rate-based models in the software reliability model have been constructed by characterizing the hazard rate defined in Eq. (1). The unified description of the existing hazard rate-based models can be given by

$$z_k(t) \equiv \lambda_k t^{m-1} \quad (t \geq 0;\ k = 1,\ 2,\ \ldots;\ m > 0;\ \lambda_k > 0), \tag{2}$$

where λ_k is a non-increasing function of k, and the cases of $m = 1$ and $m \neq 1$ represent the exponential- and the Weibull-type hazard rate models, respectively. Table 1 summarizes the representative hazard rate-based models.

We obtain several software reliability assessment measures based on Eq. (2). The reliability function of X_k is given by

$$R_k(t) \equiv \Pr\{X_k > t\} = \exp\left[-\int_0^t z_k(s)\mathrm{d}s\right] = \exp\left[-\frac{\lambda_k}{m}t^m\right]. \tag{3}$$

Eq. (3) is called the software reliability which is defined as the probability that the k-th software failure does not occur in the time-interval $(0,\ t]$ after the $(k-1)$-st software failure-occurrence. Furthermore, the expectation of X_k is given by

$$\mathrm{E}[X_k] \equiv \int_0^\infty R_k(t)\mathrm{d}t = \left(\frac{m}{\lambda_k}\right)^{1/m} \Gamma\left(1+\frac{1}{m}\right), \tag{4}$$

where $\Gamma(y)$ is a gamma function defined as

$$\Gamma(y) \equiv \int_0^\infty x^{y-1}e^{-x}\mathrm{d}x \quad (y > 0). \tag{5}$$

Eq. (4) is called the mean time between software failures (MTBSF).

3 Introduction of Environmental Factor

In Sect. 2, we have treated the time domain regardless of whether the testing or the user operation phases. Hereafter, we discriminate the time domains between the testing and the operation phases. Let the superscript ^{O} and no superscript refer to the operation phase and the testing phase, respectively. For example, X_k^O and X_k denote the random variables representing the time intervals between the $(k-1)$-st and the k-th software failure-occurrences in the operation phase and the testing phase, respectively. Then we assume the following relationship between $z_k^O(t)$ and $z_k(t)$:

$$z_k^O(t) = \alpha \cdot z_k(t) \quad (\alpha > 0), \tag{6}$$

where α is called the environmental factor. From the viewpoint of the software reliability assessment, $0 < \alpha < 1$ ($\alpha > 1$) means that the testing phase is severer (milder) in the usage condition than the operation phase, and $\alpha = 1$ means that the testing environment is equivalent to the operational one.

From Eq. (6), the software reliability function and the MTBSF in the operation phase where the environmental factor is treated as a constant, are given by

$$R_k^O(t|\alpha) = \exp\left[-\int_0^t z_k^O(s)\mathrm{d}s\right] = \exp\left[-\frac{\alpha\lambda_k}{m}t^m\right], \tag{7}$$

$$\mathrm{E}[X_k^O|\alpha] = \int_0^\infty R_k^O(t|\alpha)\mathrm{d}t = \left(\frac{m}{\alpha\lambda_k}\right)^{1/m} \Gamma\left(1+\frac{1}{m}\right), \tag{8}$$

respectively.

4 Consideration of Systemability

In general, the actual operating environment in the field is quite different from the controlled testing environment, and it is natural to consider that the external factors affecting software reliability characteristics fluctuate. Therefore, it is not appropriate that the environmental factor, α, introduced to bridge the gap between the software failure characteristics in the testing and the operation phases, is constant. Hereafter, we treat α as a random variable, i.e., we introduce the concept of systemability into the model discussed in Sect. 3. In this paper, we consider the following two cases [12]: the first is the model whose α follows the gamma distribution (G-model) and the second is the beta distribution (B-model).

4.1 G-Model

The G-model is assumed that the environmental factor α follows the gamma distribution whose density function is denoted as

$$f_\alpha(x) \equiv f_\alpha^G(x) = \frac{\theta^\eta \cdot x^{\eta-1} \cdot e^{-\theta x}}{\Gamma(\eta)} \quad (x \geq 0;\ \theta > 0,\ \eta \geq 1), \tag{9}$$

where θ and η are called the scale and the shape parameters, respectively. The G-model can be used to evaluate and predict the software reliability characteristic in the operation phase where the usage condition is severer than ($\alpha > 1$), equivalent to ($\alpha = 1$), or milder than ($0 < \alpha < 1$) the testing environment. Then the mean and the variance of α are given by

$$\mathrm{E}[\alpha] = \frac{\eta}{\theta}, \quad \mathrm{Var}[\alpha] = \frac{\eta}{\theta^2}, \tag{10}$$

respectively.

Then the posterior reliability function of X_k^O based on the G-model is given by

$$\begin{aligned} R_k^{OG}(t) &= \int_0^\infty R_k^O(t|x) f_\alpha^G(x) \mathrm{d}x \\ &= \frac{1}{([\lambda_k/(m\theta)] \cdot t^m + 1)^\eta}. \end{aligned} \tag{11}$$

In particular, X_k^O follows the Pareto distribution when $m = 1$. Furthermore, the posterior MTBSF is given by

$$\begin{aligned} \mathrm{E}^G\left[X_k^O\right] &= \int_0^\infty R_k^{OG}(t) \mathrm{d}t \\ &= \frac{B\left(\frac{1}{m}, \eta - \frac{1}{m}\right)}{(\lambda_k/\theta)^{1/m} \cdot m^{1-1/m}}, \end{aligned} \tag{12}$$

where $B(y_1, y_2)$ is the beta function defined as

$$B(y_1, y_2) \equiv \int_0^1 x^{y_1 - 1}(1-x)^{y_2 - 1} \mathrm{d}x = \frac{\Gamma(y_1)\Gamma(y_2)}{\Gamma(y_1 + y_2)} \quad (y_1 > 0,\ y_2 > 0), \tag{13}$$

and it is noted that $\mathrm{E}^G\left[X_k^O\right]$ exists only when $\eta m > 1$.

4.2 B-Model

The B-model is assumed that the environmental factor follows the beta distribution whose density function is denoted as

$$\begin{aligned} f_\alpha(x) \equiv f_\alpha^B(x) &= \frac{1}{B(\beta_1, \beta_2)} x^{\beta_1 - 1}(1-x)^{\beta_2 - 1} \\ &(0 < x < 1;\ \beta_1 > 0,\ \beta_2 > 0), \end{aligned} \tag{14}$$

where β_1 and β_2 are the shape parameters. A beta-distributed random variable ranges between 0 and 1. Therefore, the B-model is appropriate to describe the operational software reliability characteristic only where the usage condition is estimated to be milder than the testing environment. Then the mean and the variance of α are given by

$$\mathrm{E}[\alpha] = \frac{\beta_1}{\beta_1 + \beta_2}, \quad \mathrm{Var}[\alpha] = \frac{\beta_1 \beta_2}{(\beta_1 + \beta_2)^2(\beta_1 + \beta_2 + 1)}, \tag{15}$$

respectively.

Then the posterior reliability function of X_k^O based on the B-model is given by

$$\begin{aligned} R_k^{OB}(t) &= \int_0^1 R_k^O(t|x) f_\alpha^B(x)\mathrm{d}x \\ &= \exp\left[-\frac{\lambda_k}{m}t^m\right] \cdot \mathrm{M}\left(\beta_2, \beta_1+\beta_2; \frac{\lambda_k}{m}t^m\right), \end{aligned} \tag{16}$$

where

$$\mathrm{M}(c_1, c_2; z) \equiv \sum_{l=0}^{\infty} \frac{(c_1)_l}{(c_2)_l l!} z^l \quad \Big((c_1)_l \equiv \Gamma(c_1+l)/\Gamma(c_1)\Big), \tag{17}$$

is the Kummer function which is a kind of confluent hypergeometric functions [13]. Furthermore, the posterior MTBSF is given by

$$\begin{aligned} \mathrm{E}^B\left[X_k^O\right] &= \int_0^\infty R_k^{OB}(t)\mathrm{d}t \\ &= \left(\frac{m}{\lambda_k}\right)^{1/m} \Gamma\left(1+\frac{1}{m}\right) \cdot \frac{B\left(\beta_1 - \frac{1}{m}, \beta_2\right)}{B(\beta_1, \beta_2)}, \end{aligned} \tag{18}$$

where $\mathrm{E}^B\left[X_k^O\right]$ exists only when $\beta_1 m > 1$.

5 Numerical Examples

We present several numerical examples on the operational software reliability analysis based on the above measures. We use the data set consisting of 31 software failure-occurrence times, cited by Goel and Okumoto [14]; the first 26 (referred to as DATA-I) were observed in the production (checkout) phase (referred to as PHASE-I) and the next 5 (referred to as DATA-II) were observed in the testing phase (referred to as PHASE-II). Here we regard DATA-I as the data set in the testing phase and DATA-II as in the user operation phase since DATA-I and DATA-II show different trends obviously although DATA-II is not the data set observed in the actual operation phase. We apply the model of Moranda [8] to the hazard rate $z_k(t)$ in the numerical examples, i.e., $\lambda_k \equiv Dc^{k-1}$ and $m \equiv 1$, and use the following maximum likelihood estimates based on DATA-I as the values of D and c:

$$\widehat{D} = 0.202, \ \widehat{c} = 0.955.$$

Furthermore, applying DATA-II retrospectively and based on Eq. (7), we can estimate the value of α when regarded as a constant as $\widehat{\alpha} = 0.312$. We assume that $\widehat{\alpha} = 0.312$ is known as the prior information on the environmental factor in the numerical examples below.

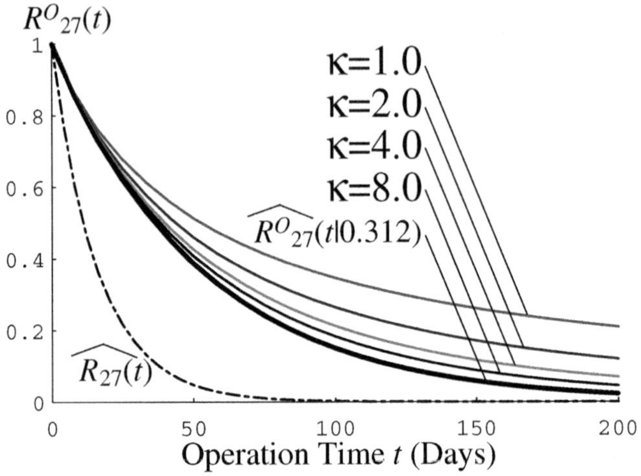

Fig. 1. Dependence of $\theta = \kappa\theta_0$ and $\eta = \kappa\eta_0$ on $R_{27}^{OG}(t)$, given $\eta/\theta = 0.312$ ($\theta_0 = 3.21$, $\eta_0 = 1.0$)

Figure 1 shows the dependence of the value of κ on the posterior reliability function for the first software failure-occurrence time-interval in PHASE-II, X_{27}^{O}, $R_{27}^{OG}(t)$ in the G-model in Eq. (11), along with $\widehat{R_{27}^{O}}(t|\widehat{\alpha})$ in Eq. (7) and $\widehat{R_{27}}(t)$ in Eq. (3), where we set $\theta = \kappa\theta_0$ and $\eta = \kappa\eta_0$, and then $\mathrm{E}[\alpha] = \eta/\theta = \widehat{\alpha}$ in any value of κ. On the other hand, the coefficient of variation (cv) of α is given by $\mathrm{cv}^G[\alpha] \equiv \sqrt{\mathrm{Var}[\alpha]}/\mathrm{E}[\alpha] = 1/\sqrt{\kappa}$ from Eq. (10). The larger value of κ means that the degree of conviction in terms of information on the environmental factor is higher. Figure 1 tells us that the higher degree of conviction of prior information on the environmental factor brings in more accurate reliability prediction in the operation phase, and that the lower degree of conviction gives more optimistic evaluation. We confirm that the B-model also displays the similar tendency to the G-model.

6 Concluding Remarks

In this paper, defining the concept of systemability as the system reliability characteristic considering the uncertainty and the variability of the field environment, we have constructed the operation-oriented SRM with systemability. We have introduced the environmental factor representing the conversion ratio of the hazard rate between the testing and the user operation phases, and then considered the randomness of the environmental factor. Using the hazard rate-based model, we have derived a couple of operational software reliability assessment measures.

Acknowledgments. This work was supported in part by Grant-in-Aid for Scientific Research (C) of Japan Society for the Promotion of Science under Grant Nos. 23510170 and 22510150.

References

1. Okamura, H., Dohi, T., Osaki, S.: A Reliability Assessment Method for Software Products in Operational Phase — Proposal of an Accelerated Life Testing Model. Electronics and Communications in Japan (Part III: Fundamental Electronic Science) 84, 25–33 (2001)
2. Morita, H., Tokuno, K., Yamada, S.: Markovian Operational Software Reliability Measurement Based on Accelerated Life Testing Model. In: 11th ISSAT Int. Conf. Reliability and Quality in Design, pp. 204–208 (2005)
3. Tokuno, K., Yamada, S.: User-Oriented and -Perceived Software Availability Measurement and Assessment with Environmental Factors. J. Opr. Res. Society of Japan 50, 444–462 (2007)
4. Elsayed, E.A.: Reliability Engineering. Addison Wesley Longman, Massachusetts (1996)
5. Pham, H.: A New Generalized Systemability Model. Int. J. Performability Eng. 1, 145–155 (2005)
6. Lyu, M.R. (ed.): Handbook of Software Reliability Engineering. IEEE CS Press, McGraw-Hill, Los Alamitos, California (1996)
7. Jelinski, Z., Moranda, P.B.: Software Reliability Research. In: Freiberger, W. (ed.) Statistical Computer Performance Evaluation, pp. 465–484. Academic Press, New York (1972)
8. Moranda, P.B.: Event-Altered Rate Models for General Reliability Analysis. IEEE Trans. Reliability R-28, 376–381 (1979)
9. Xie, M.: Software Reliability Models — Past, Present and Future. In: Limnios, N., Nikulin, M. (eds.) Recent Advances in Reliability Theory: Methodology, Practice, and Inference, pp. 325–340. Birkhäuser, Boston (2000)
10. Schick, G.J., Wolverton, R.W.: An Analysis of Competing Software Reliability Models. IEEE Trans. Software Engineering SE-4, 104–120 (1978)
11. Wagoner, W.L.: The Final Report on a Software Reliability Measurement Study. Aerospace Corporation, Report TOR-0074(4112)-1 (1973)
12. Teng, X., Pham, H.: A New Methodology for Predicting Software Reliability in the Random Field Environments. IEEE Trans. Reliability 55, 458–468 (2006)
13. Oldham, K.B., Myland, J.C., Spanier, J.: An Atlas of Functions: with Equator, the Atlas Function Calculator, 2nd edn. Springer, New York (2008)
14. Goel, A.L., Okumoto, K.: Time-Dependent Error-Detection Rate Model for Software Reliability and Other Performance Measures. IEEE Trans. Reliability R-28, 206–211 (1979)

'Surge Capacity Evaluation of an Emergency Department in Case of Mass Casualty'

Young Hoon Lee, Heeyeon Seo, Farrukh Rasheed, Kyung Sup Kim, Seung Ho Kim, and Incheol Park

Department of Information and Industrial Engineering,
Yonsei University, 134 - Shinchon Dong, Seodaemoon - Gu, Seoul, South Korea
youngh@yonsei.ac.kr, s893456@nate.com,
farrukhaccount@gmail.com, kyungkim@yonsei.ac.kr

Abstract. Health care has experienced many silos efforts to address mitigation and preparedness for large scale emergencies or disasters that can bring catastrophic consequences. All professionals and experts in this area have each developed relatively independent efforts to enhance emergency response of a health care facility in case of some disaster, but the need of the time is to integrate all these crucially important initiatives. A comprehensive surge management plan that provides coherent strategic guidance and tactical directions should be developed and implemented on priority in each health care installation on facility level followed by its integration with state surge management plan for optimum use or high utilization of space, resources and services. This research uses the concept of daily surge status and capacity of a health care facility, its relationship and the need of its effective integration with state level surge management plan which is a relatively new area to be considered. The simulation modeling and analysis technique is used for the modeling of an emergency department of a health care facility under consideration and after having an insight of the prevailing situation, few crowding indices were developed while considering resource capacities for the purpose of using them appropriately to reflect facility's daily surge status when required. The crowding indices as developed will highlight health care facility AS-IS situation after a specific time interval as defined by the management and will actuate relevant surge control measures in the light of developed surge management plan to effectively and efficiently cater for the surge and for restoration of normal facility working and operation.

1 Introduction

Disaster is an event or a situation, natural or manmade, responsible for occurrences of human death, suffering, and change in the community environment or social system that overwhelms a community health care system's ability to respond with its limited number of available resources. In medical terms, these types of disasters are named as health care surge defined as 'a sizeable increase in demand for resources compared with a baseline demand' or more comprehensively defined as 'an excess in demand over capacity in hospitals, long-term care facilities, community care clinics, public

T.-h. Kim et al. (Eds.): ASEA/DRBC/EL 2011, CCIS 257, pp. 522–531, 2011.

health departments, other primary and secondary care providers, resources and/or emergency medical services'. Components defining surge include influx of patients measured in terms of arrival rate or volume, specific type of surge event, the scale to which it cause damage, total surge duration and finally, requirement of resource demand consumption or degradation. Surge capacity is the maximum potential ability of any health care facility in delivery of required resources for recovery either through augmentation of existing resources or modification of resource management and allocation. Capacity of surge is measured in terms of four most influential factors such as system integrity, size and the quality of space i.e. acute care or critical care beds, number and the skill level of staff i.e. licensed healthcare professionals and support staff, and volume and the quality of medical related supplies i.e. pharmaceuticals, portable and fixed decontamination systems, isolation beds, personal protective equipment, ventilators, masks etc [1].

The development of a good surge plan takes into account the importance of separating elements of a group into subgroups that are mutually exclusive, unambiguous, and taken together, include all possibilities such as a good surge plan must be in its taxonomy simple, easy to remember, easy to use or implementable. The severity of surge may be different under different situations as experienced. In some cases, surge level of patients presented to the emergency department may result in significant stress to hospital limited resources but does not require waivers for normal patient care services. However, in some cases, surge in patients may affect all medical service providers such as they are required to co-ordinate, collaborate, strategize and communicate among all community health services, emergency medical system agencies, public health care services, fire departments, and office of emergency services (OES) representatives etc to come actively onboard. This surge level result in a lack of capacity to provide impacted service or services and as a consequence, state of emergency is being sought in order to meet the medical and health needs of the victims usually using pre-approved and well defined alternate care protocols.

In a nut shell, term such as surge response capability is generally used in practice to define or evaluate the ability of a health care facility referred to as its surge capacity in terms of the resources that can be made available during or after disaster to accommodate the surge or demand for resources. The ability of health care facility to respond to surge based situation is also referred to as its preparedness and as a matter of fact, preparedness can only be achieved through adequate and appropriate planning based on emphasizing solely on the desired context and functioning of the target facility and its specific environment by identifying gaps and priority areas for bringing improvements and successful integration of the individual facility with the 'State Surge Management Plan' if exists. The intended target is to enhance the ability of the health care system to expand beyond normal operations to meet a sudden increased demand such as in a result of above mentioned reasons like large scale public health emergency due to natural or man-made disaster etc. The system must be capable, flexible and well versed to respond to immediate short term surge and sustain response for extended period of times hence meeting the public health and medical needs during and following disasters.

2 Literature Review

A lot of valuable research is going on in the field of disaster medicine and emergency response preparedness. F. M. Burjle et. al. [2] addresses a population approach to SEIRV-based triage in which decision making falls under a two-phase system with specific measures of effectiveness to increase likelihood of medical success, epidemic control, and conservation of scarce resources in case of some bio-based disaster. Brent R. Aspin et. al. [3] comprehensively describes the overlap between the research agendas on daily surge capacity and patient flow. Next, they propose two models that have potential applications for surge capacity and hospital wide patient-flow research. Finally, they identify potential research questions that are based on applications of the proposed research models. M. Traub et. al. [4] demonstrates that physical assets in Australasian public hospitals do not meet US hospital preparedness benchmarks for mass casualty incidents. They recommend national agreement on disaster preparedness benchmarks and periodic publication of hospital performance indicators to enhance disaster preparedness and suggest the same for other stakeholders.

J. L. Hick et. al. [5] highlights the existence of few surplus resources in a country's existing health care system to accommodate surge casualties and the importance of plans for surge capacity to accommodate a large number of patients. They emphasized that surge planning should allow activation of multiple levels of capacity from the health care facility level to the federal level and the need for the plans to be scalable and flexible to cope with the many types and varied timelines of disasters. Y. Raiter et. al. [6] draws some lessons from a disaster concerning the management of the event, primary triage, evacuation priorities and the rate and characteristics of casualty arrival at the nearby hospitals. A. G. Macintyre et. al. [7] presents the concept that a broader conceptual foundation, health care emergency management, encompasses and interrelates all of the critical initiatives regarding surge management. Based upon long-standing emergency management principles and practices, health care emergency management can provide standardized, widely accepted management principles, application concepts, and terminology that effectively bridge the many current initiatives. This approach can also promote health care integration into the larger community emergency response system through the use of long-established concepts that have been validated through experience in these sectors.

3 Simulation Modeling and Validation

S Hospital' is a Korean urban 700 bed tertiary care teaching hospital located in Seoul. Its ED deals 66,000 patients on an annual basis – approx. 5,500 patients per month. An eventual observational study in an emergency department for a period of one and a half month (for a period starting from March 15, 2010 to April 30, 2010) was conducted and the data was gathered during different hours of the day and days of the week for the whole study period using on-site sampling technique and through patient information system. The data was analyzed using statistical software and simulation model input parameters were generated as in Table-1.

Table 1. Details of Service Times, Resources and Patient Classifications

Process	Distribution	Process	Distribution
Triage	Expo (10)	1st Treatment	TRIA (5,7,10)
Triage (Pediatric)	TRIA (5,8,10)	X-Ray	NORM (5,10)
Registration	TRIA (3,5,7)	CT	LOGN (25,10)
Detoxication	TRIA (5,8,10)	Consultation	NORM (84,25)
2nd Treatment	TRIA (5,8,10)	Resource (Nurse)	6 No.
Patient Arrival (Ambu)	25 %	Pediatric Patients	30 %
Patient Arrival (Walk)	75 %	Not Registered	20 %
Adult Patients	70 %	Admissions	36 %
Lab Tests	95 %	X-Ray	99 %
Consultation	60 %	Resource (Specialist)	13 No.
Adult Treatment Bays	39 No.	Pediatric Treatment Bays	14 No.
X-Ray Equipment	01 No.	CT Scanner	01 No.

Arrival mode of patients is either by ambulance or in a walk-in manner accounting for 25% and 75% of total arrivals respectively. The ambulance arrivals are led straight to the resuscitation station being critical while walk-in arrivals are received by the triage station where triage nurse assigns acuity to arriving patients based on severity of the illness, such as life threatening injuries/illness and vital signs. Acuity level is assigned as per universally accepted emergency severity index in a range of 1 to 5 (where ESI score of 1 means highly acuity patients and ESI score of 5 means lowest acuity patients). After triage, adult patients are routed to adult examination room whereas pediatric patients are routed to pediatric registration desk where non-medical staff is appointed. Patients routed straight to resuscitation room also join these patients at their respective registration desks after receiving preliminary acute care.

After registration and examination, few patients are found stable and are discharged to home or to hospital and remaining patients are routed to the treatment station. Adult patients are further divided into two categories at the treatment station such as acute and semi-acute patients. During treatment, 95% patients are required to have lab test and 99% patients are required to undergo X-Ray. After X-Ray, 60% of the patients are further required to undergo co-treatment in which medical specialists are invited as per the nature of the case complexity. Remaining 40% patients are routed straight to the diagnostic station where they are joined by co-treatment patients after getting expert opinion. Patients will be discharged to leave the hospital if treatment is completed. Patients admitted to the hospital usually need to wait until a bed is available on the appropriate hospital unit. The flow chart of the whole process is shown in Figure 1.

Before proceeding with further analysis, it was required to validate and verify the developed simulation model to make sure that it is an accurate representation of the real system or not? The simulation model was validated with respect to various parameters such as LOS of patients and several other parameters as in Table-2 along with

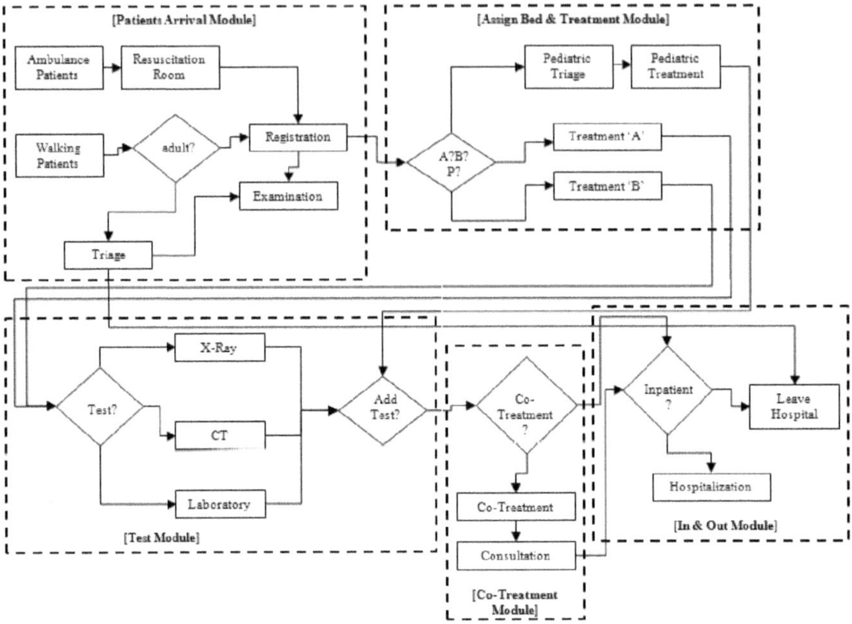

Fig. 1. ED Process Flow

validation trend as shown graphically in Figure-2. Real system stats were calculated using statistical software by analyzing the data set and the same parameters as estimated by the simulation model were also generated. Statistics of Table-2 shows that the system is working as intended.

Verification of the model is required to ensure that it behaves as intended and can perform without errors. Sensitivity analysis is performed to analyze the change in the input, which causes the output value to change accordingly. We alter the number of entities decreasing in one and increasing in another such as on the basis of the average arrival rate, amounts equal to half and double of this rate were considered for the

Table 2. Model Validation Stats

Item #	Real System Stats Avg. (Std. Dev.)	Simulation Output Stats Avg. (Std. Dev.)
Registration LOS[1]	19.76 min (53.85)	25.03 min (31.20)
Assign bed & Treat LOS	11.70 min (44.11)	41.71 min (35.89)
Test LOS	83.43 min (118.77)	81.41 min (101.94)
Consultation LOS	75.29 min (188.60)	77.79 min (73.50)
In-Out LOS	527.64 min (577.16)	656.85 min (119.26)
Total LOS	368.81 min (346.97)	360.83 min (310.28)

[1] LOS stands for 'Length of Stay'.

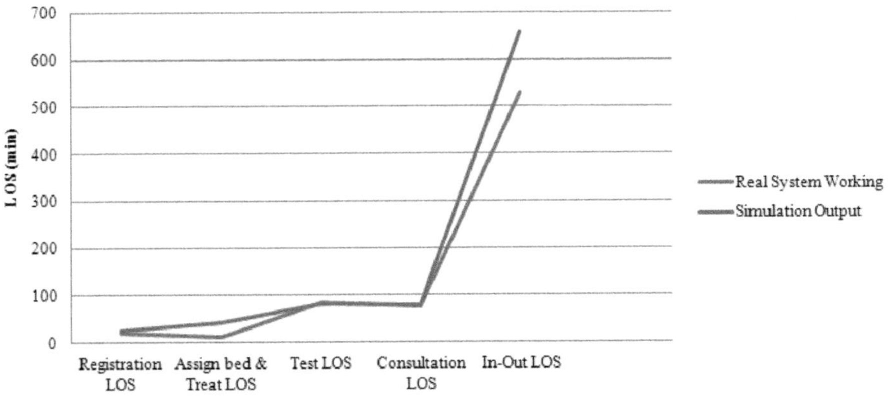

Fig. 2. Simulation Model - Validation Trend

decrease and increase in the number of patients entering the system. Afterwards, results were compared with the real system and it was found that by decreasing the arrival rate to half, all parameters such as LOS, WIP and throughput are decreased and vice versa thus verifying the simulation model.

After model verification and validation, the crowding indices were incorporated in the model by making modifications accordingly for the purpose of predicting surge status and crowdedness levels during different hours of the day and days of the week as per facility's surge management plan. Detail of the crowding indices and the surge status predictors based on these crowding indices is as under:

3.1 Surge Index for Resource Type (Bed):

$$SI^B{}_t = P_{t-1} + I_t * r_{area} / B$$

Where;

$SI^B{}_t$ = Bed Surge Index at time 't'
P_t = The number of bed occupancy patients at time 't'
I_t = The number of patients hospitalized at time 't'
r_{area} = The transition rate by area
B = Total Number of Treatment Bays

3.2 Surge Index for Resource Type (Specialist):

$$SI^S{}_t = \alpha_{t-1} + I_t * r_{area} / D_t * F$$

Where,

$$\alpha_{t-1} = \max [I_{t-1} + \alpha_{t-2} - D_{t-1} * F, 0]$$

And;

SI^S_t = Specialist Surge Index at time 't'
α_t = The number of patients did not receiving treatment at time 't'
I_t = The number of patients hospitalized at time 't'
r_{area} = The transition rate by area
D_t = The number of specialist at time 't'
F = The number of patients' doctors can handle per hour

3.3 Surge Index for Resource Type (Facility):

$$SI^F_t = \alpha_{t-1} + I_t * r_{test} / C_m$$

Where,

$$\alpha_{t-1} = \max [I_{t-1} + \alpha_{t-2} - C_m, 0]$$

And;

SI^F_t = Facility Surge Index at time 't'
α_t = The number of patients did not receive test service at time 't'
I_t = The number of patients hospitalized at time 't'
r_{test} = The transition rate by test
C_m = The number of patients facility 'm' can handle per hour

3.4 Surge Status Predictor

$$SIP_{t+\Delta t} = SI_t * \alpha_1 + [\Sigma^{t+\Delta t}_{t+1} I_t * \alpha_2 / \text{capacity}]$$

Thus;

$$SIP^B_t = [(P_{t-1} + I_t) * \alpha_1 / B] + [(I_{t+3} * \alpha_2) / B]$$
$$SIP^S_t = [(\alpha_{t-1} + I_t) * \beta_1 / (D_t * B)] + [(I_{t+3} * \beta_2) / B]$$
$$SIP^B_t = [(\alpha_{t-1} + I_t) * \gamma_1 / C_m] + [(I_{t+3} * \gamma_2) / B]$$

Where,

$SIP_{t+\Delta t}$ = Daily Surge Predictor after time interval Δt
SIP^B_t = Bed Surge Index to predict Surge Status
SIP^S_t = Specialist Surge Index to predict Surge Status
SIP^F_t = Facility Surge Index to predict Surge Status
α_1, α_2 = Constant Values
I_t = The number of patients hospitalized at time 't'
SI_t = Current Surge Index at time 't'
α, β, γ = Weight Values

4 Discussion and Surge Evaluation and Prediction Framework

Emergency department high patient surge or surge load is a situation in which the identified need for emergency services outstrips available resources in the emergency department. Many surge indices are used to predict emergency department surge status and patient surge load with an objective to take adequate relevant remedial actions. Results have demonstrated that these indices are an effective measure of surge status. The indices as suggested in this research calculate variables found to be statistically significant in emergency department surge situation and the values corresponds to a given level of operational capacity. Emergency department and hospital have limited number of beds, staff and related supplies as available for patient care. The corresponding operational capacity or surge situation and patient surge load will be interpreted as follows such as not busy, busy, extremely busy and collapse as in Figure-3.

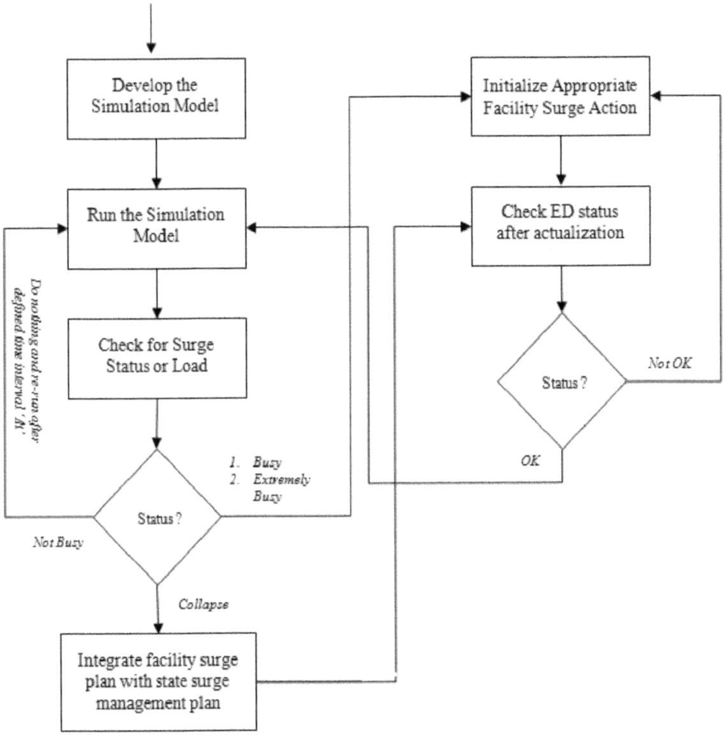

Fig. 3. Surge Evaluation and Management Framework

The surge evaluation and management plan or framework as suggested in this research represent a daily routine facility operational plan for 'S Hospital Emergency Department' and also serves as an integral part of the overall emergency disaster management plan named here as 'State Surge Management Plan'. The objective of the developed surge plan is to measure surge load in the emergency department as per suggested surge indices in terms of three inherent system characteristics measured in terms of bed capacity, staff capacity and facility capacity. The state of system during different hours of the day and days of the week measured in terms of relevant surge indices represents surge status or surge load on the system in terms of these three performance measures and automatically initiate appropriate network response ensuring rapid and appropriate counter measures or remedial action and their implementation as per 'Facility Surge Management Plan'. The aim to develop surge indices as in this paper is to design a system that can be updated, improved, and refined to maximize the delivery of patient care through all levels of patient surge by identifying additional resources required to control the disaster situation and bringing system to normal working mode on priority.

As per the procedure and framework adapted in this research as in Figure-3, the planner evaluates emergency department surge situation after defined time interval (say after every 2 or 3 hours) and the relevant surge status predictors are calculated. If the surge load or status as measured in terms of surge indices will rise above certain defined threshold (certain threshold level will be defined for all three surge categories as mentioned above), the emergency department use the emergency preparation system to alert the appropriate and pre-designated personnel. The level of actions to be undertaken by all concerned personnel depends on the level of surge as identified in the system. A preparation chart is established for this purpose and includes those components of hospital administration, nursing, medical staff, and auxiliary services that require alert notifications as per the level of surge identified and this strategy will also serve as an integral part of the overall emergency disaster management plan or 'State Surge Management Plan'. Moreover, approval for proceeding with the mandated response will be inherently given by the pre-defined nature of the system. The system automatically responds with the appropriate interventions to cope up with the disaster situation.

5 Conclusion – Surge Effective Spectrum

The actual effective spectrum of surge or health care system surge capacity is very wide. It must be addressed on state or country level. That is why; we have clearly identified and highlighted the difference between 'Individual Facility Surge Management Plan' and 'State Surge Management Plan' and the importance of link between the two. The surge indices as observed in emergency departments are used as a means to represent the surge load as faced by the facility and they trigger corresponding remedial actions accordingly as mentioned earlier such as on the basis of surge indices values or the surge load levels as identified defines that either the situation is under control of facility surge management or it demands additional support or help by exploring the link with state's surge management resources. Moreover, the surge indices as suggested in this research work have enhanced scope such as they are not representing just an individual health care facility situation and related remedial actions; they are also connecting or serving as a link to seek help from state's surge management plan and associated resources if required.

Moreover, a lot of dependent factors are required to be considered to manage against disasters or surges and this fact necessitates the consideration of these factors on both individual and aggregate basis. At first place, all health care facilities should identify those activities which can lessen the severity and impact of a potential surge emergency. It includes capacity building and the identification of resources, both internal and external, that may be needed if an emergency incident occurs. Some policies, procedures and protocols are required to be developed mutually to respond effectively to some disastrous situations. The ultimate objective must be to bring hospital operations to a stable and reliable level of performance during and after an emergency surge has occurred. Like all planning processes, disaster and emergency preparedness planning demands an on-going effort to measure performance and implement improvements as may be necessary to meet established performance objectives. The former text highlights the fact that surge management needs to collaborate and plan with a variety of community, civic, governmental and private organizations. The management should be familiar with the 'States Surge Management Plan' and critical aspect is to develop relationships to facilitate collaboration, coordination, strong communication and mutual interaction. It is a fact that each hospital will have its own unique issues and circumstances, but there are a number of common characteristics and considerations that should be addressed in preparation of a hospital's surge demand plans.

References

1. Hick, J.L., Barbera, J.A., Kelen, G.D.: Refining Surge Capacity: Conventional, Contigency and Crisis Capacity. Disaster Medicine and Public Health Preparedness 3(suppl. 1) (2009)
2. Burjle, F.M.: Population based Triage Management in Response to Surge Capacity Requirements during Large Scale Bioevent Disaster. Society for Academic Emergency Medicine 12(11) (2006)
3. Aspin, B.R., Flottemesch, T.J., Gordon, B.D.: Developing Models for Patient Flow and Daily Surge Capacity Research. Society for Academic Emergency Medicine 13, 1109–1113 (2006)
4. Traub, M., Bradt, D.A., Joseph, A.P.: The Surge Capacity for People in Emergencies (SCOPE) study in Australian Hospitals. MJA 186, 394–398 (2007)
5. Hick, J.L., Hanfling, D., et al.: Health Care Facility and Community Strategies for Patient Care Surge Capacity. Annals of Emergency Medicine 44, 253–261 (2004)
6. Raiter, Y., Farfel, A., Lehavi, O., et al.: Mass Casualty Incident Management, Triage, Injury distribu-tion of Casualities and rate of arrival of casualities at the hospital. Emergency Medicine Journal 25, 225–229 (2008)
7. Macintyre, A.G., Barbera, J.A., Brewster, P.: Health Care Emergency Management: Establishing the Science of Managing Mass Casuality and Mass Effect Incident. Disaster Medicine and Public Health Preparedness 3(suppl. 1) (2009)

Business Continuity after the 2003 Bam Earthquake in Iran

Alireza Fallahi and Solmaz Arzhangi

Shahid Beheshty University, Tehran, Iran
alifallahi30@gmail.com,
arzhangi.so@gmail.com

Abstract. In disaster prone countries, such as Iran, business continuity are one of the most important challenges in relation to disaster recovery operations. Iranian experiences indicate that following natural disasters, small business recovery has been faced with a number of problems. It seems that in the light of the lack of business continuity planning, disruption of small business operations may cause the affected community with a number of difficulties.

The 2003 Bam Earthquake resulted in huge physical destruction and significant impacts on small businesses. Following the disruption of economic activities, decision makers considered many issues in small-business recovery. However in the process of post-earthquake business continuity recovery, problems were arisen not only for shopkeepers but citizens. For instance, In the case of Bam, lack of specific organization and having a ready plan for pre-plan on business continuity management and also inefficient cooperation between the stockholders and the planners caused the problems of small business district reconstruction program reach a peak. So reconstruction planners endeavored to decrease the negative effects of shopping arcades reconstruction on the local community. In addition, the allocation of low interest loans to small business recovery resulted in some satisfaction among the stockholders. However in some aspects implemented plans were not able to facilitate the economic recovery completely. The present paper examines the reconstruction process of small businesses after Bam earthquake and discusses the main aspects of Business Continuity Planning. It concludes that an integration of Business Continuity Planning and reconstruction master plan may pave the way of better disaster recovery planning in Iran.

Keywords: earthquake, small business continuity planning, reconstruction, Bam.

1 Introduction

Disaster, such as an earthquake, is a one of the most significant events that can disrupt business process activities. On the other hand, small business provides marketplace, occupation and services to citizenry. So earthquake impression survey on business continuity and set pre-plan to support it both during and after an earthquake are considerable.

In this regard, the small business resilience is an important requirement after most catastrophes especially on local scale. It seems that in order to stay in the market in

T.-h. Kim et al. (Eds.): ASEA/DRBC/EL 2011, CCIS 257, pp. 532–540, 2011.

crisis situation, small businesses need to be able to quickly respond to changing situations such as after an earthquake. The Business Continuity Management (BCM) is required to make small-business resilience and keep businesses active in crisis conditions. Furthermore, it seems that affected urban community will be vulnerable when BCM has not been set down.

In the light of business importance and historical bazaar as a heritage in the city of Bam, the primary objective of rehabilitation after the 2003 destructive earthquake was small business recovery and shops structure reconstruction. But the lack of pre-business continuity plan in applied approach to small business recovery, stockholders, shopkeepers and heirs have been challenged.

This paper analyzes Bam small business recovery compares it with business continuity plan principles. The present is folded in three sections. The first part reviews the literature and relevant issues that could be used in the case of Bam. The second part provides information about Bam small business recovery. The last section is a comparison analysis with a number of comments in order to optimize business recovery process in future Iranian earthquakes.

2 Study Context

Investigation into literatures on business continuity after natural disasters show that small business recovery is crucial for livelihood rehabilitation. So from the small business continuity point of view, the economic, social and physical aspects are worth to be considered. On the other words, a comprehensive master plan is required to plan and implement an effective plan.

Past experience indicate that BCM complemented with risk management is an accepted approach that has been established to coordinate key aspects of business recovery in response to crisis (figure 1).

Source: (modified from Business Continuity Management, Commonwealth of Australia, 2000).

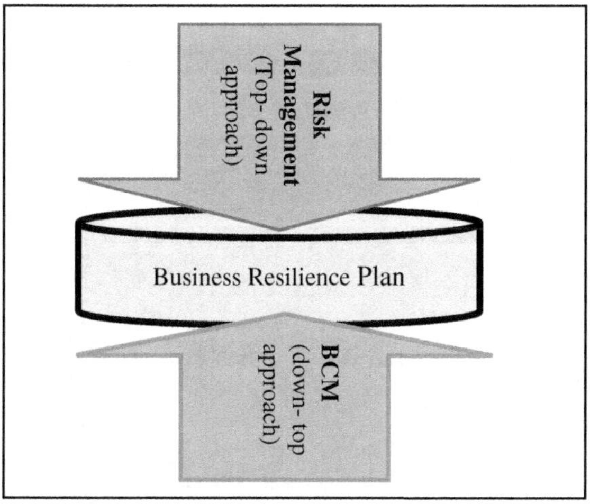

Fig. 1. BCM and Risk Management Approach in Business Recovery

2.1 Business Continuity Management (BCM)

Experience indicates that management commitment to business continuity provides a holistic system to business recovery after natural disasters. The first step toward the following management is BCM organization establishment [2].In this regard, the challenging question is how small businesses can be resilient with BCM. To achieve this purpose, after business impact analysis and risk livelihood mitigation, the response strategies are to be adjusted and the business continuity plan (BCP), set down, based on all analytic processes and strategies. Finally, BCP may be examined and it`s culture should be spread around the community. It is notable that disaster awareness, education and training are expletive components of the BCM process (figure 2).

In addition, BCM emphasizes on technology, people and all useful resources, therefore applies to most of potential to business recovery. In general, the holistic view of BCM provides a basis for planning to continue small businesses trading running following destroying earthquakes.

Source: (modified from Ken Doughty, CISA, CBCP)

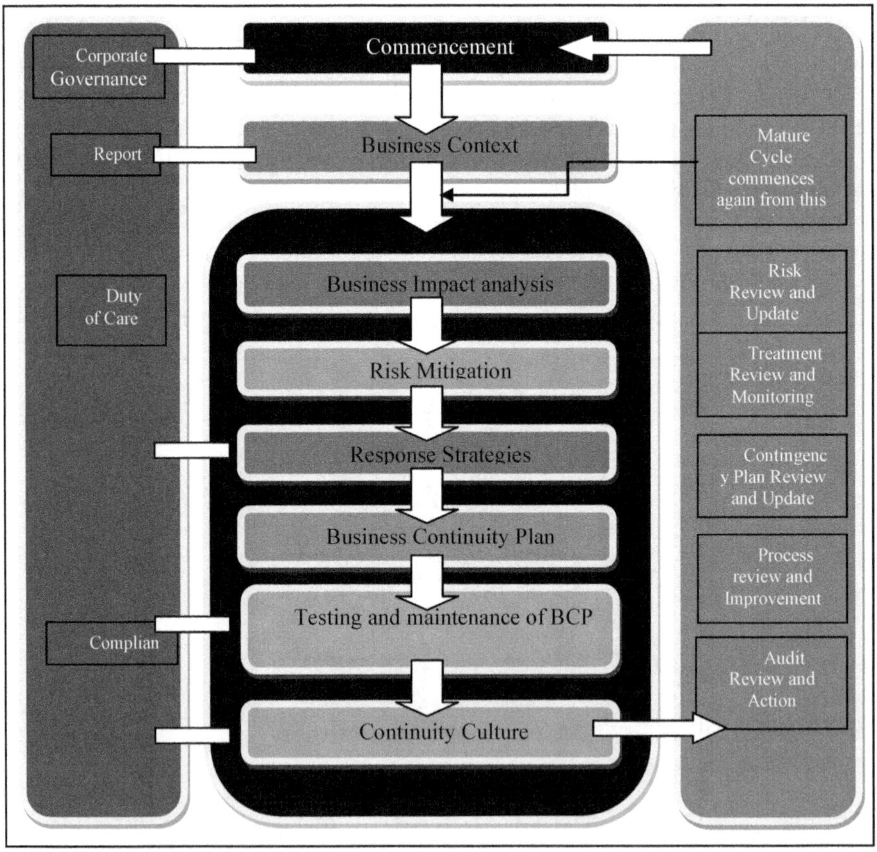

Fig. 2. Overview of Business Continuity Management

2.2 Business Continuity Planning (BCP)

The most significant output of the BCM process is a Business Continuity Planning (BCP). A BCP process consists of risk assessment, contingency planning and the actual disaster recovery. "In fact, a business continuity plan addresses actions to be taken before, during, and after a disaster "[11]. Planning includes several phases that lead to identify based measures (figure 3). It appears that testing and maintenance of plans should be implemented in order to gain more confidence in the crisis situation. In this regard, awareness and training of community and small business help plan set and enhance maintenance and test business continuity planning [6][3].

In the case of small business recovery, in post earthquake reconstruction, BCP determines small business reconstruction priorities. In order to achieve that, plan execution requires finance to be spent, which one of the most important aspects in business continuity plan is Support process [4]. Therefore, financial resource management should be done and the disruptions of this activity become investigated. In this manner, barriers such as inadequate executive protection and lack of fund allocation should be taken into consideration

Source: http://360ap.com/wp-content/uploads/2009/07/bcplifecycle_000.jpg

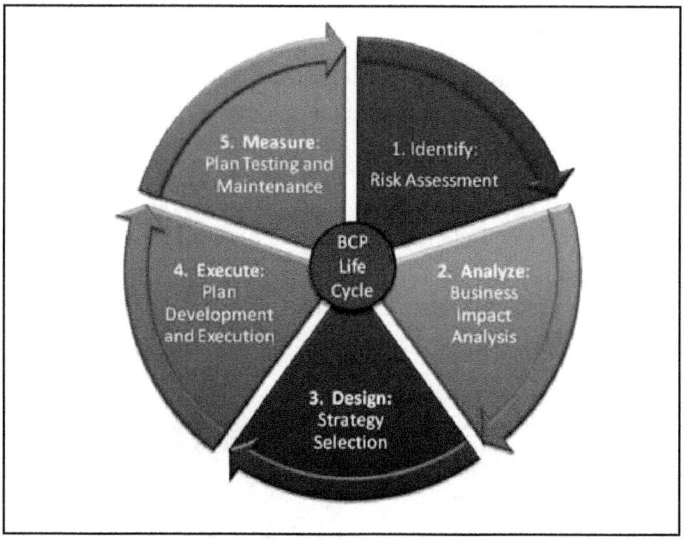

Fig. 3. Business Continuity Planning

2.3 Insurance and legal Issues

"Earthquake is one of the Top Ten Causes of Business interruptions disruptions "[10]. Following earthquake, in most cases, interrupted activities need to return to the normal situation. As a consequence, sufficient funding and supporting organizations are essential. In this respect, insurance coverage and insuring small businesses is a key factor in recovery activity. Furthermore, from the risk management viewpoint, establishing insurance organizations is fundamental for the recovery process. However, BCP is a down-top approach in planning and people should accept small business insurance culture. On the other hand, after an unexpected disaster, there is a value classification of small businesses property. In this regard, reconstruction master plan takes account business insurance and allocated fund such as low-interest and long-term loans are made available to small business reconstruction [7].

In terms of legal issues and Based on global research, it seems that addressing land issues and disaster response laws, rules and principles after natural disaster are inevitable. Also small business property is one of the most important raised issues in the post disaster reconstruction plan. Experiences show that in developing and under-developed countries, disaster legal Services are in a challenge. The problems were made worse by legal uncertainty after disaster and community relationship influenced by adjudication of land rights. In this sense the available literature shows that to decrease contradictions, pre-plan, data gathering, security of land tenure and flexible planning are appropriate solution. Also in relation to land security legitimacy and rights to land should be come from one source. Therefore, legal legitimacy and social legitimacy should be approach in one direction [1].

3 Bam Earthquake

Bam was situated on the earthquake-prone ground. Since the city of Bam was located on Trade route, local business was thriving and Bam old bazaar shoed business boom until 2003 earthquake in Iran. The devastating earthquake of 26 December 2003 caused widespread damage and 90 percent of shopping centers structure collapsed. Furthermore, the cultural heritage, Bam bazaar, was absolutely demolishes. This is why, local business interruption affected Bam livelihood during and after the disaster.

Post Source: endisaster reconstruction documt, Shahid Beheshti

Picture 2. Temporary shop

Source: http://www.mehrnews.com

Picture 2. Temporary shop

Execution activities to small business recovery after Bam earthquake begun with fencing and allocating prefabricated units and containers as temporary accommodations. In this regard, governor, municipality and the reconstruction headquarters were engaged in small business reconstruction. Government allocated low-interest and limited loans for store reconstruction per square meter [6].

Source: http://inlinethumb02.webshots.com

Picture 3. Reconstructed shopping center

4 Research Methodology

It was learned from literature review that BCM principles could be used in all business planning. A data analysis was based on descriptive analyses so a qualitative approach was selected to this comparative study. Data gathering in this project was based on personal observation and communications with local and also conducted a survey and interviews with the relevant stakeholders, authorities and shopkeepers in the city of Bam.

5 Finding Result

This article has investigated small businesses reconstruction process in the city of Bam after a major earthquake and has also focused on the Business Continuity Planning principles that could be applied in Bam. Several results emerge from the analysis evidence as below (table 1):

The followings emerged from personal communications with local business people:

- Shopkeeper Desire to take more from reconstruction funding.
- Bazaar has not been completed until now.
- People decided to complete reconstruction themselves.

Table 1. Findings

Addressed approach	All challenges	
✓ Business Continuity Management (BCM)	According to the surveys, there is no BCM in Iran. So in the light of loss of business continuity plan, Bam business recovery measures confronted with issues as a blow:	
	Bam issues	
	• lack of data	• Because of inadequate data, Properties limitation was unknown. So shopping center reconstruction has faced challenges and shops areas are not be accurate. • Heirs' problems were appeared in the light of insufficient data in relation to shops area and their heirs after earthquake and loss shopkeeper. • Since there were not sufficient losses data, Shop owners desired to take more. • As there are not suitable data in relation to shopkeepers dept and demand, debts have been remained and have not collected. In some cases the people of Bam pay their depts. themselves.
	• facilities allocation	• Inconsistent the bank facility during reconstruction led to tensions. • Equal facilities allocation without considering shops areas and their properties. • Facility Raised by increase Shopkeepers demand to take more.
✓ Business Continuity Management (BCM)	• role of organization in reconstruction	• During reconstruction, contractors have been changing by organization. So there was no stable plan. • There was any business organization and lack of BCP after 2003 bam earthquake.

Table 1. (*Continued*)

✓ Business Continuity Management (BCM)		
	• legal issue	• Bam small businesses reconstruction faced to inheritance problems. Therefore, the crucial question was which heir should be addressed in small businesses reconstruction. • The impact of restoration theory on property and land tenure is an important issue. In this regard, because of the role of collapse buildings at community memory, several shops at bazaar did not reconstruct. Hence shop owner have been facing to challenges. • Architectural design without considering land tenure and shop owners properties. Hence several shops relocated and became smaller after reconstruction.
	• insurance	• There were not any supporter systems as insurance in Bam business recovery.
	• upper management	• Bazaar was a heritage. So applied approach to bazaar reconstruction was top-down. As a consequence shop owner did not found themselves at the flexible plan.
	• people participation	• Migrant labor and non indigenous experts in reconstruction process led to unfamiliar implementation in the city of Bam for local community. • Shop owner participation was limited and their orders have participated in reconstruction.

According to a number of small businesses, BCM is very important in the context of Iran. It adjusts shopping center reconstruction after an earthquake and helps the businesses original states to be restored and the tension caused by the earthquake lessened. In this regard, specific organizations should be established and small business insurance system in disaster-prone cities should be enforced. Also insurance system provides an appropriate context for data gathering before disaster and sufficient funding would have been allocated in business recovery.

Furthermore, it was observed that local service providers such as experts, local governor and internal resources have not been applied in business recovery implementations in the city of Bam. Therefore BCP should takes account local supporters and sets awareness, education and training system at public culture. Also to achieve resilient businesses, there are some obstacles such as legal issues and lack of during disaster laws. It seems that flexible inherent law and land tenure system that cover all feasible conditions is a best solution.

As a consequence, business continuity plan must to be integrated with reconstruction master plan and all businesses recovery decisions would have been referred to above integration.

References

1. David, M.: With the supervision of Adriana Herrera Garibay: Assessing and Responding to Land Tenure Issues in Disaster Risk Management. In: FAO 2011 (2011)
2. Schumacher, H.J.: Disaster Recovery Planning: Insuring Business Continuity, Imperial Consulting, Inc., Strategic Research Institute 12/95; published in EERI Newsletter 8/96-&. Planning 'public seminars and 'customized learning solutions' including
3. Australian National Audit Office. Business Continuity Management, Guide to Effective Control (2000)
4. Williamson, J.: Business Continuity Planning (2002)
5. Federal Financial Institutions Examination Council; Business Continuity planning. FFIEC (2003)
6. `http://inlinethumb02.webshots.com`
7. Iran Reconstruction Head quarter's documents
8. Herrera Garibay, A., de Wit, P., Eleazar, L., Jordan Bucheli, F., Norfolk, S., Sanchez Mena, R., Shafi, S.A.: Land tenure and natural disasters. In: FAO 2010 (2010)
9. `http://www.mehrnews.com`
10. Source: Strategic Research Institute 12/95; published in EERI Newsletter 8/96
11. Texas Department of Information Resources Rev., Austin, Texas (December 2004)
12. `http://360ap.com/wp-content/uploads/2009/07/bcplifecycle_000.jpg`

Emergency-Affected Population Identification and Notification by Using Online Social Networks

Huong Pho, Soyeon Caren Han, and Byeong Ho Kang

School of Computing and Information System,
Tasmania 7005, Australia
{hhpho,soyeonh,Byeong.Kang}@utas.edu.au

Abstract. Natural disasters have been a major cause of huge losses for both people's life and property. There is no doubt that the importance of Emergency Warning System (EWS) has been considered more seriously than ever. Unfortunately, most EWSs do not provide acceptable service to identify people who might be affected by a certain disasters. In this project, we propose an approach to identify possibly affected users of a target disaster by using online social networks. The proposed method consists of three phases. First of all, we collect location information from social network websites, such as Twitter. Then, we propose a social network analysis algorithm to identify potential victims and communities. Finally, we conduct an experiment to test the accuracy and efficiency of the approach. Based on the result, we claim that the approach can facilitate identifying potential victims effectively based on data from social networking systems.

Keywords: Emergency Warning System, Online Social Network, User Extraction.

1 Introduction

Online Social Network (OSN) is currently providing people with virtual communities where can communicate with each other and share their interest [10]. With the rise of online social networking, many researchers have been worked on the use of OSNs for broadcasting emergency warnings [14]. However, many fields are facing the difficulty of discovering the potential victim groups accurately by using OSNs.

In this paper, the proposed approach enables to collect related information from OSNs, and detect possibly affected individual users. After that, the system of this approach analyzes and visualizes the correlation between social relationships and users' location in different virtual communities. The followings outline how the approach identifies the impact of the disaster by using OSNs. Firstly, when disaster occurred, the system collects the possibly affected user on Twitter. After that, the system searches groups that is related to collected users. At the end of this research, several experiments have also been conducted. The result of those experiments represents which elements can maximize and increase the accuracty of the algorithm and system. In this research, we assume that affected people may share similar

T.-h. Kim et al. (Eds.): ASEA/DRBC/EL 2011, CCIS 257, pp. 541–550, 2011.

attributes such as location, hobby and religion. These common attributes can help us to find the indirect-relationships between events and groups of individuals. As a result, we can calculate virtual relationship's metrics and identify the affected population based on the relationship's metrics.

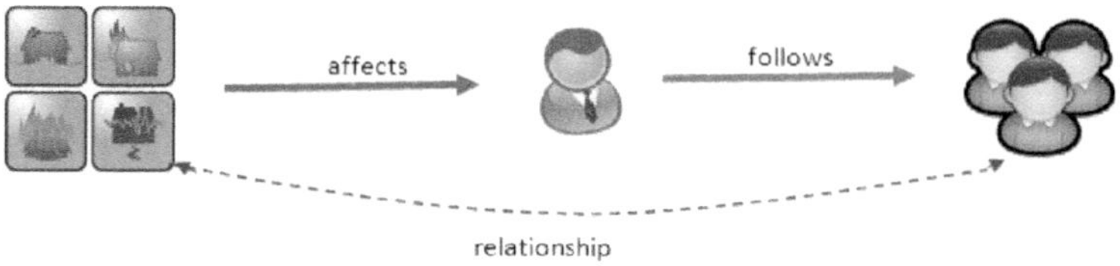

Fig. 1. The virtual relationship between the event and this group of individual

In this thesis, there are two major contributions. First of all, an investigation of relationships between status on OSNs and groups of users has been conducted. The accuracy of the introduced relationship metric equation has been evaluated in the investigation. Secondly, a group affection estimation equation has been developed to prove the accuracy of introduced metric and figure out the elements affect the metric's accuracy through several experiments.

The rest of the paper is arranged as follows. In related work, we review some related literatures in the field of OSNs, Social Network Analysis and Emergency Warning System. In addition, we point out some limitations of current Emergency Warning System. To overcome limitations found, we propose a basic concept and framework of affected people identification system in Chapter 3. The framework that is major components of system is described in detail. We scope this project as designing a framework to identify possibly affected people of a natural disaster by analyzing information from OSNs. In the experiment part, we indicate some results of conducted experiments. These experiments represent several elements that enable to increase and maximize the accuracy of result in the system. This paper is concluded in Chapter 5 that is summarized the contribution and limitations of the proposed system and the future studies.

2 Related Work

There are several kinds of Emergency Warning Systems including: the Standard Emergency Warning Signal (SEWS) and Australian Emergency Alert System. The SEWS was firstly used in Australia in 1985 by Emergency Management Australia as the result of needs for national emergency warning signal. The SWE is defined as "a distinctive audio signal that has been adopted to alert the community to the broadcast of an urgent safety message relating to a major emergency. It is meant to attract listeners' attention to the fact that they should take notice of the emergency message." [12]. Australian Emergency Alert System is a telephone warning system that originally Emergency Broadcast System (EBS) was used in from 1963 to 1997. After that, new Emergency Alert System replaced EBS since 1 Dec 2009. The new system sends a voice message on landline and a text message on mobile service. The landline service is based on the billing address and the mobile service is based on the location of hand set.

The alert is only issued by authorities such as fire, emergency service, and police. It supplies official and authorized information and action. Moreover, it provides further information after SEWS [2]. A modern notification system is a combination of software and hardware. It provides a message delivery to a set of recipients. Notification systems are used in many industries for security purposes, such as emergency service, financial institution, information technology, government, education, sport, and healthcare [7]. It is required to keep attempting to contact by various methods until being done. There are several kinds of contacting method, such as telephone, email, instant messaging, pagers, SMS and Fax. To communicate effectively, it is required the accurate and direct connection. It requires not only traditional and generic messages but also the tailor specific message to specific groups or individuals.

A social network is defined as a social structure made by individuals and organization called 'nodes'. The connection among several nodes is linked by one or more specific types of interdependency, such as friendship, common interest, and relationships of beliefs [1]. From 2000s, online social network has become more popular and played a vital role in modern societies. OSNs have brought the users' real life into virtual communities in online. For example, Facebook is the one of the best social network site developed by Mark Zuckerberg of Harvard University in 2004. By using this website, people can easily connect with their friends and maintain a friendship, even long-lost friends. People can share their personal interest with their friends and communicate with each other. Twitter can be another example of website that offers a social networking and micro-blogging service. User can send and read messages called tweets in this website. It enables people to search the information of keywords. Tweets are text-based posts that allows up to 140 characters on the user's profile page. Twitter has more than 200 million users on June 2011and it is generating 190 million tweets per day [6].

Social network analysis is defined as the measuring and mapping the relationships between people, organizations, groups, or other knowledge/information processing entities. Along with changing in organization, the continuous formations of blogs, online communities, and social networking site contribute to emergence of Social Networking Analysis from the academic closet [13]. Social network analysis is the study of social relationship or mathematical method among a set of actors: individual actors (nodes) in the network and relationship between actors (ties). In the network, the nodes are the people and groups and the links/ties show relationships or flows between the nodes. There are several metrics that is measured in social network analysis including: Betweenness centrality, Degree centrality, Closeness centrality, Eigenvector centrality. Social network analysis is the way that number of nodes can communicate to each other affect some important features of that small social network of its group. In parallel, it provides both a visual and a mathematical analysis of complex human systems. Social network analysis can help master when, why, and how they best function.

3 An Online Social Networks Based Approach for Identifying Emergency-Effected Population

As mentioned before, it is an important issue to identify proper people who may be affected by a natural disaster. OSNs, especially Twitter, are suitable to identify affected people. Surprisingly, the number of user in Twitter is over 200 million on June 2011 [3]. Moreover, the survey from the Nielsen Company proves that people are spending more and more time in using OSNs [8]. Twitter supplies various application programming interfaces (API) to do this project. In addition, Twitter opens their data to the public. This idea gave us a great amount of advantages on studying the relationship between users as well. In twitter, there is special relationship that is called 'follower'. Followers are the people who have agreed to receive and subscribe your status in the real time.

In this section, we introduce the concept idea of the methodology. Firstly, when disaster occurred, the system discovers the possibly affected user on Twitter by comparing user's status with three criterias including: 1) keyword that is related to a disaster 2) the location of the posed status 3) the time that the status posted. After that, the system searches groups that are followed by collected users. Finally, three Social Network Analysis (SNA) metrics are applied to the result.

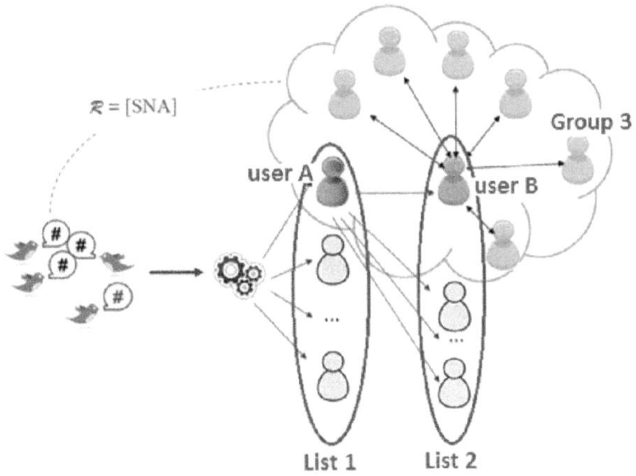

Fig. 2. System concept description

The detail of the above figure will be described as follows. From figure 2, the system collects a list of possibly affected users (List 1) by using users' statuses. After that, it also collects other users (List 2) who are followed by the list of possible affected users (List 1). Group 3 is the group of users who is following or followed by the collected users in List 2.

The undertaken approach has three main components including: Database server, HTTP server, and web interface. Database server communicates with HTTP server to save the retrieved information to MySQL database. HTTP server interacts with Twitter, MySQL database server, and five web-interfaces. The third component is web interface. There are five web pages in web interface as follows. (1) The system collected the list of affected users. It identifies impacted users by comparing their status with keywords, location and time. (2) It discovers a list of groups who are followed by already collected users. (3) The HTTP server uncovers the other users by using the discovered groups. (4) The collected groups will be analyzed the social network metrics: Degree centrality, Betweenness centrality and Closeness centrality. To analyze and visualize the social network, the system uses following two SNA tools: Text2Pajek and SocNetV. Text2Pagjek is for converting the raw text to Pajek format. It can be used as input for SocNetV. SocNetV is for analyzing and computing the SNA metrics. (5) The system retrieves location of all members in discovered groups. Each of the three interactions described below is pictured as system architecture in figure 3.

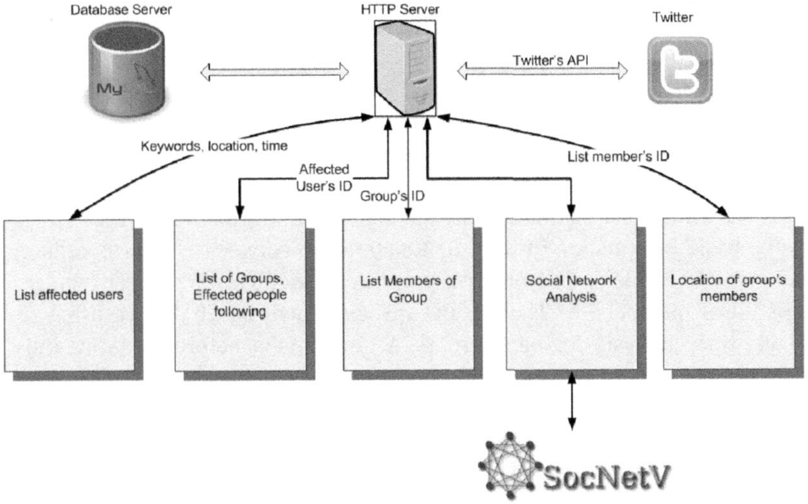

Fig. 3. System architecture

We introduce the detailed description of this framework for identifying emergency-affected population based on OSNs. Moreover, it will be applied not only the data collection but also data analysis. First of all, the system interacts with Twitter API to create searching interface that enables to find the status related to the entered keywords, geospatial information, and timeline. If certain user's status contains all three components (keywords, location, and time) that are related to disaster, the system assumes that the user is possibly affected by the disaster. The next step for this system is to find relationships of affected users. It is performed with the support of Twitter API that enables to build social graph by extracting the friend-list based on user id. Each followers of an affected user can also be considered as a seed user to build a small social network. In order to discover other members following this group, the system again uses considered user's identification to find other members' identification and stored to database as information of group users. The collected data is converted to Pajek format by Text2Pajek tool [9]. Pajek format is a popular format that mainly used for analyzing and visualizing social graph [5]. The structure of Pajek format represents all nodes and present relationship between nodes and the weight of relation. After that, the generated Pajek file imports to SocNetV that is a flexible tool for SNA and Social Relationship Visualization (SRV). SocNetV can handle Pajek file and analyze social networks in the file. It also measures three SNA metrics: centrality degree, centrality closeness, and centrality betweenness in this project. This tool enables user to interact with social network analysis through Graphic User Interface (GUI). The result of analysis stores to database. The final step of the framework is to demonstrate the correlation between social measure metrics and the group of possibly affected people. The group of affected people is defined as users in group have registered their location that is around the path of disaster. It is required to check all users' location in group in order to get value more accurately. Therefore, we developed an application interface to retrieve a list of user locations and time zone by interacting with Twitter API. The interface enables users to import a list of identification so that the retrieved result will be extracted by the list of users' geospatial information. With the collected list, the accuracy of result is calculated by counting the number of people in the way of disaster over that of list members. The system can evaluate the correlations between SNA metrics and the accuracy of result. In this project, the database has five main tables. 1) Status of User (tb_status): it contains basic information about searched status. 2) Information of User (tb_user): it stores the basic information of user. 3) Relationship between Users (tb_relationship): it records the relationship of stored user. 4) Information Group of Users (tb_group): it keep list id of members. 5) The Result of Social Analysis (tb_SNA): it has result of social network analysis for each group. As mentioned before, we uses only three metrics for SNA: centrality degree, closeness degree and betweenness degree.

The system is implemented in three steps: collecting data, analyzing data and evaluating the result. We collected the record of two recent disasters happened in Australia and New Zealand: 1) Christchurch earthquake in New Zealand on 22 February 2011. 2) Cyclone Yasi in Australia on February 2 and February 3 2011. After gathering information of two events, we randomly selected 10 affected individuals for each event. Each individual is randomly selected if he/she follows more than 7 groups. To ensure the diversity, it is applied in various social structure types and group sizes. After collecting data, we analyzed collected data by using three SNA metrics including: degree centrality, betweenness centrality and closeness centrality. The detailed description will be indicated in figure 4.

v^* : the node has highest degree centrality in graph G
n : number of vertices
σ_{st} : a number of shortest paths going between s and t
$\sigma_{st}(v)$ number of shortest paths going between s and t in through vertex v.
dG(v,t) : the geodesic distance from vertex v to vertex t

Degree centrality $$C_D(G) = \frac{\sum_{i=1}^{|V|} [C_D(v*) - C_D(v_i)]}{(n-1)(n-2)}$$

Betweeness centrality $$C_B(v) = \sum_{s \neq v \neq t \in V} \frac{\sigma_{st}(v)}{\sigma_{st}}$$

Closeness centrality $$C_C(v) = \sum_{t \in V \backslash v} 2^{-d_G(v,t)}.$$

Fig. 4. Three SNA metrics of centrality

Degree centrality is a simple metric that is defined as the number of links to a node incidentally. Degree centrality of social network contains two measurements: in-degree and out-degree. In-degree is the number of ties that direct-connected to the node and out-degree is the number of the ties that the node linked directly to others [4]. Betweenness centrality represents the ratio of the number of shortest paths going through the node to the total number of shortest paths existing in network. Closeness is used as a centrality measurement of a vertex inside a graph which reflects the access ability to information through the network members' grapevine [11].

The next step is to extract the group from database and presented in raw file. The raw file format need to use the following format: <identification of user A> [space] <identification of user B >.In this format, user A is a Twitter user and user B is a follower of user A. The raw file is converted to the Pajek format by the Text2Pajek tool which allows convert from raw text file descripted the user relationship to Pajek format. After analyzing, the result from SocNetV will be copied and stored back into database. The group information after used as input for SocNetV tool, it will be reuse to evaluate the accuracy by using developed application interface to calculate the accuracy value for each group. The evaluation of the system will be detailed below.

We assume that a user might be affected by a disaster if he/she is directly in the path of an event. In this way, we states that the accuracy of approach metric will be based on how many users in affected location at the time disaster happen. The number of user in the path of disaster (n) divided by the total member in group (N) gives the accuracy value. The figure 5 indicates the correlation between value of R and approach's accuracy. The R that is considered as all three measure metrics of social network analysis: Degree centrality, Betweenness centrality and Closeness centrality. Figure 5 shows that the accuracy values of Degree centrality and Closeness centrality are stably increasing, unlike that of Betweenness centrality.

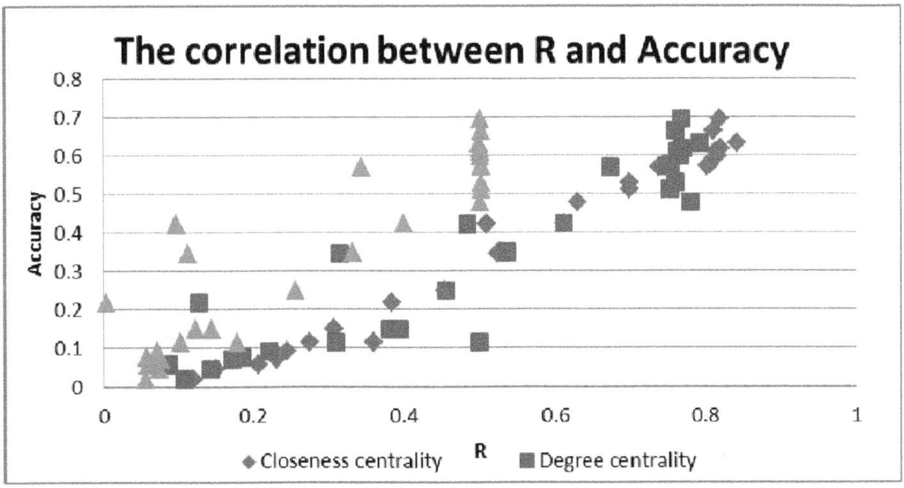

Fig. 5. Accuracy of R calculated on degree, betweenness, and closeness centrality

In the next section, we will introduce some experiments that conducted to indicate that some elements enable to increase and maximize the accuracy value.

4 Experiment and Discussion

In this project, some experiments have been conducted. The aim of those experiments is to estimate the accuracy of the system approach. Moreover, we intend to discover the way to maximize the accuracy of user's location identification. As mentioned before, the system finds the possibly affected user by comparing their status with three different elements: keywords, time of posting status, and location of posting his/her status. After collecting a list of affected users, we interact with Twitter API to retrieve the groups by using each affected users' Identification (user ID). All members in discovered groups go through the same procedure as well. Thirdly, the correlation between accuracy of groups' location identification and the SNA metrics will be generated in last step.

In this section, the accuracy of this methodology can be evaluated by two following experiment topic: 1) the size of affected user group 2) two elements (time and location) to find the accurate affected users. Firstly, as a list of possibly affected users is collected, each user in a list is considered as a seed user to discover the groups that he/she is following. The main goal of the experiment on discovered group is to investigate which size of group has the highest accuracy. Each group is classified in to four categories: 1) has 0 to 200 members 2) 200 to 400 3) 400 to 600 4) over 600 members. The correlation between categories and accuracy is resented in Figure 6.

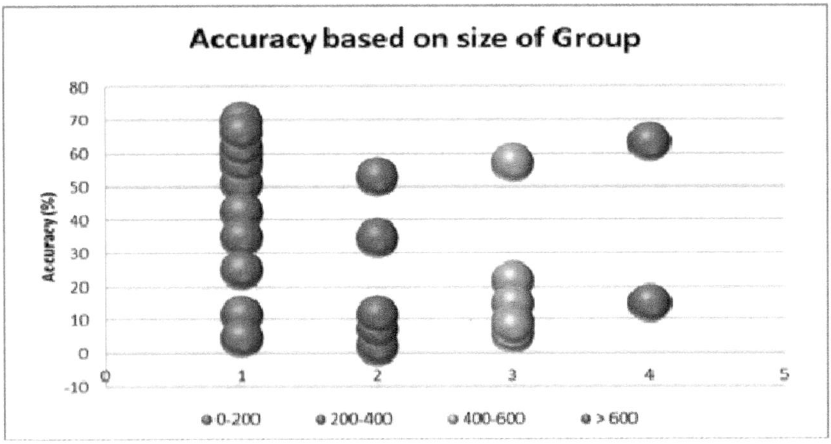

Fig. 6. The accuracy of four categories

The category 0 – 200 gets the highest density of group's size. Moreover, there is a very important issue that the highest accuracy value of group arrangement is located in the category 0 – 200. It implies that we need to pay more attention to the groups that have members between 0 and 200. However, as mentioned earlier, category 0 - 200 has the higher density so that it does not enough to form a definite conclusion. Therefore, we decided to divide the category 0-200 into four different sub-categories. These sub-categories are represented in the Figure 7. According to the figure 7, it indicates that the highest accuracy is located in the group who has members between 50 and 100. Conclusively, the total member in group is one of element affect the preciseness of identifying group's location method.

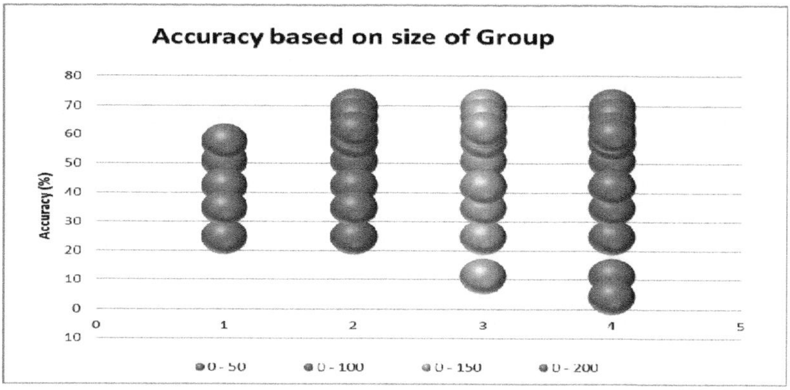

Fig. 7. The accuracy of four sub-categories

Secondly, the system collects a list of possibly affected users by using three elements which are keywords, time and location of posted status. If the system extracts irrelevant people who do not have any relation to disaster, the warning information will be considered as a spam message. In this section, we discuss whether time scale and location will maximize the accuracy of identifying users. The time period plays a huge role to filter and retrieve Twitter statuses. For this experiment, we applied the system to Christchurch earthquake in New Zealand that is happened in 22 February 2011 12:51 NZDT. After applied this data, the system indicated that there is the highest accuracy of user in three days before disaster. Another query element used in the system is the location of the posted status. As the system interacts with Twitter API, it is easy to customize the area by searching. Therefore, relevant Twitter status can be extracted by using the path of disaster.

5 Conclusion

The major objective of this project is to identify possibly affected people by using OSN. Moreover, it can be used to support the current Emergency Warning System. We indicate that there are three contributions in this research. Firstly, OSNs can be used in Emergency Warning Systems to extract the possibly affected people. This has been discovered in the Literature Review. Secondly, we introduce to the concept idea of the methodology and framework for Emergency Warning based on OSNs. Finally, more detailed information of design and experiment has also been provided in this research. The outcomes can also be referred for future development. We also evaluated several factors that enable to increase the efficiency and accuracy of the system. There are several directions for this research in the future. Due to time limitation, only two disasters had been applied to this system. Therefore, more events should be implemented to experiment and evaluate the convergence of this system. The future study should be focused on how to deliver Emergency Warning information to physical impacted user within the required time as well.

References

1. Te Ara - the Encyclopedia of New Zealand: Natural Hazards and Disasters (2011)
2. Australian Emergency Alert 2011, Emergency Alert. Be Warned. Be Informed: Frequently Asked Question (FAQs) (2011), http://www.emergencyalert.gov.au/frequently-asked-questions.html
3. Carlson, N.: Facebook Has More Than 600 Million Users, Goldman Tells Clients, Business Insider (2011)
4. Diestel, R.: Graph Theory, 3rd edn. Springer, Berlin (2005) ISBN 978-3-540-26183-4
5. Jünger, M., Mutzel, P.: Graph Drawing Software, pp. 77–103. Springer, Berlin (2003)
6. Maggie, S.: Twitter co-founder Jack Dorsey Rejoins Company. BBC News (2011)
7. New South Wales Government 2011, New South Wales Government - Online Notification System: ONS Frequently Asked Questions (2011), https://notifications.workcover.nsw.gov.au/FAQ.aspx
8. Nielsen: Nine Million Australians Use Social Networks, Wentworth Avenue Sydney, NSW (2010)
9. Pfeffer, J.: Networks / Pajek Package for Large Network Analysis (2004)
10. Sean, D.Y., Rice, E.: Online social networking Tips on using online social networks for development. Participatory Learning and Action 59(1), 112–114 (2009)
11. Stephenson, K.A., Zelen, M.: Rethinking centrality: Methods and examples. Social Networks 11, 1–37 (1989)
12. The Standard Emergency Warning Signal 2011, Standard Emergency Warning Signal (SEWS) (2011), http://www.ema.gov.au/www/emaweb/rwpattach.nsf/VAP%28FC77CAE5F7A38CF2EBC5832A6FD3AC0C%29~SEWS_DL+Brochure_HR.PDF/$file/SEWS_DL+Brochure_HR.PDF
13. Thompson, K.: Ken Thompson the Bumble Bee - Social Network Analysis: an introduction (2011)
14. White, C., Plotnick, C., Kushma, J., Hiltz, R., Turoff, M.: An Online Social Network for Emergency Management (2009)

Development and Application of an m-Learning System That Supports Efficient Management of 'Creative Activities' and Group Learning

Myung-suk Lee[1] and Yoo-ek Son[2]

[1] College of Liberal Education, Keimyung University
mslee@kmu.ac.kr
[2] Dept. Of Computer Engineering, Keimyung University
yeson@kmu.ac.kr

Abstract. In this paper, we developed an App of SNS-based mobile learning system where students can interact anytime and anywhere and the teacher can five a real-time feedback. By activating the developed App at Smartphones, users can store a variety of data at a web server without accessing to the website. In addition, if the teacher and students are at a different place, problems can be solved real-time via the SNS of the system, with feedback from the teacher. Therefore, when used for other activities like 'creative activity' classes and group lessons, the developed App can be used for self-directed learning and as a medium of real-time communication to raise the performance and interest of students. Also, the teacher can have an in-depth understanding of the level of each student from accumulated data, and students can develop various portfolios.

Keywords: Creative Activities, Data Accumulation, self-directed Learning, m-Learning, Social Network Service.

1 Introduction

Social changes amid the development of information and communication technology have brought about many changes to the education environment. To focus on diverse experience-centered education, 'the 2009 Revised Curriculum' has introduced 'creative activity' for the first time. The revised curriculum, therefore, seeks national unity and the polymorphism of regions, schools and individuals and increase the autonomy and creativity of students [1-2]. The curriculum also helps students find what is the focus of a given question by themselves, make a decision by means of doing research on related fields, and sharpen their problem-solving skills and judgement [3]. In particular, the 'creative activity' is designed for schools to develop well organized activities so that students can perform tasks of 'creative activity' in a self-directed manner [4-5].

With the help of the development of information communication technology, Apps(applications) are available, which allows for collaborative learning online without constraints of time and space outside the classroom. Although we attempted to use

T.-h. Kim et al. (Eds.): ASEA/DRBC/EL 2011, CCIS 257, pp. 551–558, 2011.

various features of web like board and blog for education [6-7], the participation of students remained sluggish over time and there was no big influence on academic performance of students, as they were used in a one-way communication means to check teaching materials and submit assignments [8]. Afterwards, a variety of ways have been attempted to use Smartphones for education, but problems remain in terms of data building and interactivity due to the separate operation of Apps from web[9-10].

Therefore, this study aims to develop an m-learning (mobile learning) system which enables real-time collaborative learning and building-up of diverse data to raise the interest and performance of students. The system has the following advantages for learning;

First, since the system is SNS-based(Social Network Service-based), students can exchange their opinions real-time, interact with the teacher more easily, and solve problems through immediate feedback and interaction, which results in improved problem-solving skills and advantages for group learning.

Second, SNS as one of the most popular services is widely used today. Accordingly, students can more easily adapt themselves to the system, which leads to enhanced interest in learning and academic performance.

Third, in an SNS-based system, all students become students and teachers at the same time, which helps reduce a sense of inferiority among students and ensures a higher level of academic performance.

Fourth, SNS system helps students re-study by developing a DB of the group's problem-solving process and materials of every activity including 'creative activity'. In this system, the teacher can teach students by carefully examining students' learning process, and from the data students can automatically make a portfolio which they need.

2 Related Studies

SNS has played a role in forming the concept of community in a virtual space beyond constraints of time and space as the Internet began to affect interactions of people in the concept of community, not individuals. People interact with others via email, real-time chats, board, online games and thereby build diverse human networks. As real communities such as local communities, workplace, family, friends, and clubs and virtual communities like Minihompy, clubs, blog, and cafe exist together, real communities began to be formed in a virtual space to communicate without constraints of time and space [11-12].

In web 2.0 services, the key word is 'share' with a focus on showing data, and SNS is designed to focus easier and more convenient sharing of data through relationships among people, and data is a media for communications among people[13]. Accordingly, if used for education, SNS is expected to create a collaborative environment that helps students relate themselves to others more intimately, exchange ideas, and give feedback, and thereby strengthen their knowledge base and interact with each other more actively by means of data sharing.

In addition, 'creative activity' can be used variously. As an extracurricular activity, 'creative activity' complements subjects and is designed to help students become a future-oriented creative and decent talent who puts into practice what they have learned, share things with and be kind to others. 'Creative activity' is in nature the autonomous group activity and reflects educational efforts to enhance individuality and creativity of group members. The 'creative activity' curriculum consists of four areas; voluntary activities, club activities, volunteer works, and career development activities as in <Table 1> [1].

Table 1. Overview of 'Creative Activities'

Category	Characteristics	Activity
Voluntary Activities	The school promotes student-centered voluntary activities, and students actively participate in various educational activities.	- Adaptation activity - Autonomous activity - Events - Creative special activity
Club Activities	Students participate in group activities voluntarily to sharpen a cooperative mindset and develop their hobby and specialty.	- Academic activity - Culture and art activity - Sports activity - Practice and elaboration activity - Youth club activity etc.
Volunteer Works	Students do sharing and kindness activities for neighbors and the community and preserve natural environment.	- On-campus volunteer work - Community volunteer work - Nature preservation work - Campaign work, etc.
Career Development Activities	Students find and design their career path via self-development activities fit to their interest, specialty, and aptitude.	- Self-understanding activity - Career Info search activity - Career planning activity, etc - Career experience activity etc.

Activities by category may vary depending on characteristics of individual students, classes, grades, schools, and communities. Activity categories and specific activities presented above are for recommendation purposes only, and schools may choose more creative intensive curriculum than this. Therefore, schools are allowed to develop well-organized activities so as to help students do each 'creative activity' in a self-directed manner. The developed SNS system aims to help this activity become student-oriented.

3 Analysis of Students and Design of the System

3.1 Analysis of Students

Prior to the design of the study, we carried out a questionnaire survey of 77 first-grade students of two classes of a high school located in Daegu, who learned the Information/Computer subject with the following results. In this study, we used a questionnaire consisting of questions to understand the present situations of the participants of a liberal arts high school who learned Information/Computer subject as shown in <Table 2>.

Table 2. Question for the analysis of students

Category	Question	Question No	Number of Questions
Use of Computer	•Do have a computer and use the Internet at home? •Do you have a computer-related license?	1~2	2
Use of Homepage	•Do you utilize your class homepage? •Do you use a personal blog and cafe (board)?	3~4	2
Use of Smart phones	•Do you have a Smartphone? • (If you have a Smartphone,) do you use an SNS?	5~6	2
Need for Studies	•How do you exchange and receive opinions in case of collaborative learning tasks? • (If you have a Smartphone,) do you want to use an SNS which can be used for a collaborative learning task, if any? • (If you have a Smartphone,) if you want to use an SNS for a collaborative learning task as above	7~9	3

We found that every participant had a computer, which indicates that the participants had good access to web in general. 30% of them were found to have a computer-related license, which shows that there is a wide gap in background knowledge on and use of computer of students.

Regarding the use of class homepage, it was found that few students used the class homepage, although there was one. Personal blog and cafe (board) was found to be used by around 95% of them, indicating that they thought of making friends at a personal blog and cafe more important than at the school homepage.

Smartphones were found to be owned by 62% or so, and more than 80% of them responded that they use SNS, which means that they frequently used Smartphones. When it comes to exchanging and receiving opinions about collaborative learning tasks, 59% of the participants were found to exchange and receives opinions on campus, 0% of them was found to use the class homepage for this purpose, 33% to use messengers, 0% to use blog, and 8% to use SNS network services, which indicates that most of them exchanged and received opinions on campus or used messengers after school.

When asked whether to use an SNS for collaborative learning, if any, more than 65% of the participants who had a Smartphone gave a positive answer. They added that currently available SNS has them talk about news and hobbies shared by many users, distracting them from learning. Some of the participants said, 'SNS saves them time and money,' while others responded, 'SNS seems like fun.' These results support the need of this study.

3.2 Flowchart of System Data

Overall, the system consists of Web-server and App Client. Main of the server is composed of User Management and Group Management, and data flows in the entire system as depicted in Fig. 1.

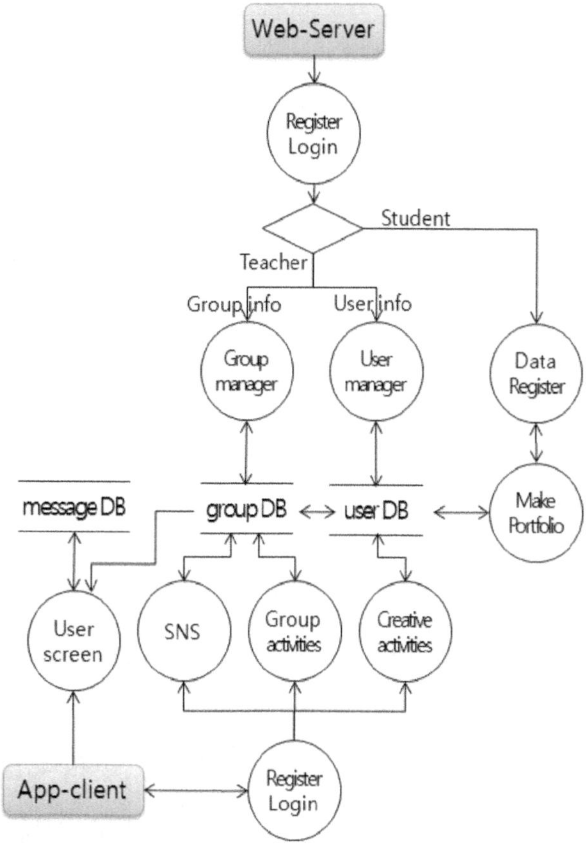

Fig. 1. Flowchart of system data

App Client is an android-based app which is activated at a Smartphone and allows for real-time interactions through web communication. For group learning, SNS allows for real-time problem solving in a group only, and for 'creative activity,' students can save their activity outcome, photos, and videos in a DB. Here, without a web login, users can add data to the DB with a click. Those students who do no have a Smartphone also can save data in the web, and all the students can create a portfolio in the web.

3.3 User Management Mode

User Management Mode of the serve is as shown in Fig. 2. In this mode, the teacher can give an approval of membership requests, add, modify, and delete members.

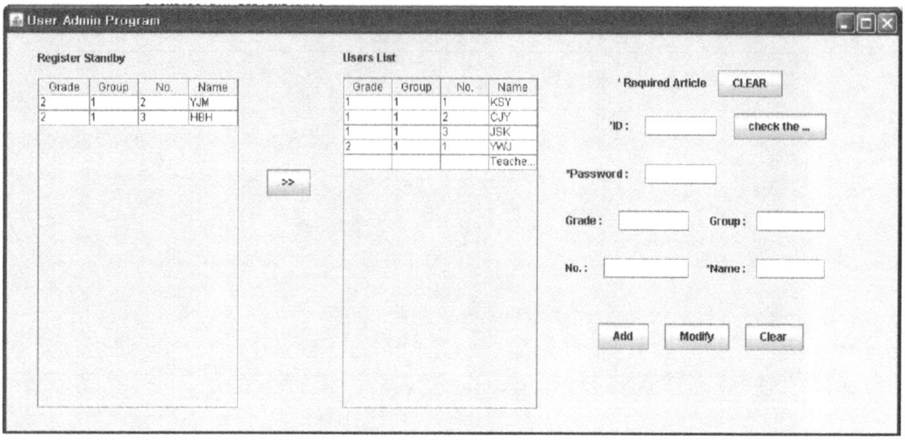

Fig. 2. User Management Mode

3.4 App Client

App-Client program is SNS_Client, which is activated only when the SNS_Client.apk file is installed on the Smartphone first. To install the apk file, file management application for android called Astro is needed, and App-Client program is activated as in Fig. 3.

Fig. 3. Install the program and opinions exchanged and feedback

Exchange Opinions and Feedback menu displays opinions exchanged among students and feedback from the teacher. With a Smartphones, users can check messages anytime and anywhere using SNS_Client to interact for problem solving.

The teacher can check messages from students anytime and anywhere using a Smartphone and give feedback to those students who are having trouble solving problems depending on what kinds of problems they are struggling with. In short, the teacher can check how much students understand what they learn without constraints of time and space via SNS. Fig. 4 shows the window of the app for 'creative activity.'

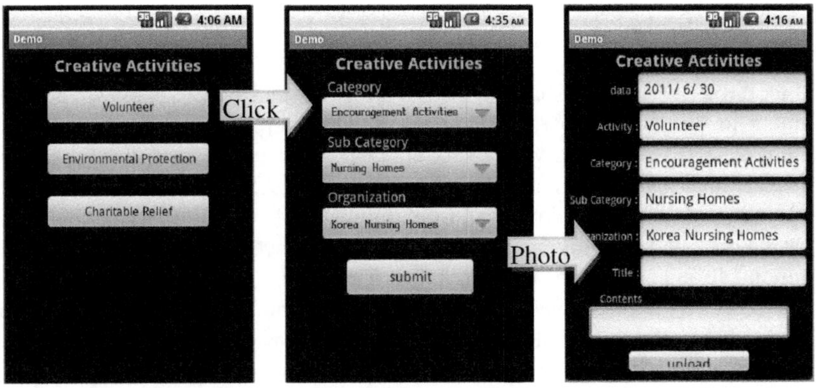

Fig. 4. 'Creative activity' App screen

3.5 Web Server

This system was able to register the data on the App as well as web server. Therefore, Lerner's did not own a Smarphone or easy to use web server can easily do all the works using a web server. The activity registration screen of the web server is as shown in Fig. 5.

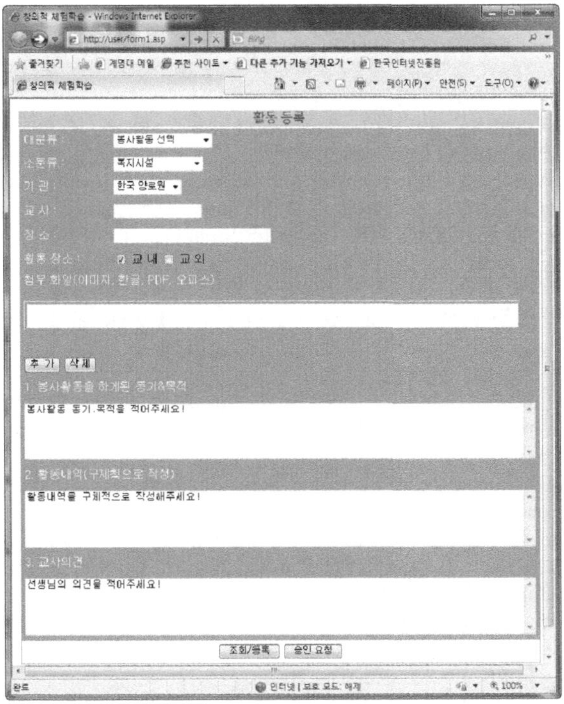

Fig. 5. Activity registration screen in the web server

4 Conclusion

Collaborative learning to sharpen socializing skills and boost seamless interaction is common in web-based board or blog today. This web-based environment requires a computer, and if accessing via a Smartphone, users need to visit the website and log in to see information and up and download data. Although web-based blogs and boards are widely used to download teaching materials or submit assignments, limited environment and inconvenience of accessing the website discourages active communication between the teacher and students.

Therefore, an application installed in a Smartphone that helps interaction anytime and anywhere allows for interaction between users via SNS and real-time feedback from the teacher. So, problem-solving via real-time access was found to help increase the interest in learning and academic performance. Moreover, diverse data of 'creative activity' can be saved anytime and anywhere using Smartphones to send photos, videos, and other data real-time to the web-server, leading to easier building-up of data and thereby ensuring self-directed learning.

There is a need of a study on how to analyze problems with the system and develop better self-directed teaching and learning methods by using apps for classes in link to the school homepage.

References

1. Ministry of Education, Science and Technology. Notice No. 2009-41 (2009)
2. edupot (2011), `http://www.edupot.go.kr/eduInfoMain.do`
3. Korea-Creative Problem Solving Center (2011), `http://www.k-cps.co.kr/edu/edu2.php`
4. Kim, D.: Comparison of Academic Achievement between Individual and Cooperative Learning in Web-Based Environment according to each level. Education Technology Major Graduate School of Education Andong National University (2004)
5. Kim, H., Lim, B.: Contents Development Strategies for Field Trips with Creative Activities using Smart Devices. Korea Association of Information Education (Winter 2011)
6. Choi, E.: The effect of cooperative learning and Individual Learning on Academic Achievement in Web-based Instruction. The Graduate School of Education Yonsei University 49, 121–133 (2001)
7. Yun, K.: The Study on the Improvement of Self-directed Learning Competency using Blog Systems in Elementary School. The Graduate School of Gyeongin National University of Education (2008)
8. Jang, J.: A Self-Directed Learning Model Using Social Networks. The Graduate School of Education Hannam University (2011)
9. Lee, G., Lee, J.: Comparison Study of Web Application Development Environments in Smartphone. The Journal of the Korea Contents Association 10(12), 155–163 (2010)
10. Lee, S.: Developer of Smartphone Application Program for Field Experience Activity Support System. The Graduate School of Ewha Womans University (2011)
11. Paek, I.: A Study on video contents usage for social network based on metadata. The Graduate School of Hongik University (2007)
12. Lee, M., Son, Y.: A Study on a SNS_based Learning Support System for Efficient Peer Tutoring. Korea Information Processing Sociaty 35 (Spring 2011)
13. Jung, Y.: Web Planning. Hanbit Media, Seoul (2004)

The Good and the Bad: The Effects of Excellence in the Internet and Mobile Phone Usage

Hyung Chul Kim[1], Chan Jung Park[1,*], Young Min Ko[1], Jung Suk Hyun[2], and Cheol Min Kim[1]

[1] Dept. of Computer Education, Jeju National University, Ara-dong 1, Jeju-si, Jeju-do, 690-756, South Korea
{callan,cjpark,libra109,cmkim}@jejunu.ac.kr
[2] Dept. of Management Information Systems, Jeju National University, Ara-dong 1, Jeju-si, Jeju-do, 690-756, South Korea
jshyun@jejunu.ac.kr

Abstract. Advanced InformationTechnology brings not only good effects but also bad effects to people's lives. In this paper, we analyze the relationship between Korean Information Culture Index (KICI) and the Internet and mobile phone addiction for Korean adolescent. KICI represents a quantitative value that measures people's information literacy levels. Thus, KICI measures how well people use the Internet, whereas the Internet and mobile phone addiction levels represent how badly people use them. In order to achieve our research goal, we firstly diagnose KICI and the Internet and mobile phone addiction level of Korean adolescent by using our questionnaire. Next, we analyze the relationships between KICI and the two addiction levels with regression analysis to see how KICI affects the two addictions. We also find out which questions are more influential to Korean adolescent in KICI measurement. Finally, we propose a better educational way to improve KICI level and to decrease the two addiction levels for Korean adolescent.

Keywords: Technology addiction, Korean information culture index, Information etiquette, Data mining application, Cyber ethics education.

1 Introduction

Recently, people cannot live without various kinds of technologies, especially the Internet or hand-held digital devices, in their daily lives. However, technology has both sides. In many schools and institutes, teachers or instructors have been using and teaching newer technology at the same time. On the other hand, parents have been worried about their children's technology addiction. Thus, for many years, there have been two types of research works about how to use technology. One is about making new measurements that can measure how well people, especially students, use the technology [1][2]. The other is about developing new ways to measure how serious people are addicted to technology [3][4].

* Corresponding author.

T.-h. Kim et al. (Eds.): ASEA/DRBC/EL 2011, CCIS 257, pp. 559–568, 2011.

The Internet is a good example to discuss as one of the most frequently used technologies by people. In Korea, an Index, namely *Korean Information Culture Index (KICI)*, is used to measure people's synthetic information literacy in terms of knowledge, ethics, emotion, and practice [5]. According to two reports in 2009 and 2010 [5][6], 99.1% of the Internet users can retrieve information from the Internet, 72.7% can operate blogs, 82.5% can purchase items on the Internet, and 72.8% can configure the Internet security set-ups on their computers. By contrast, the activities such as sharing good contents with other people, participating in valuable on-line activities, and contributing to on-line society were not performed well in Korea. The previous studies have showed the dark side or the bright side of the Internet separately. Despite the fact that there are growing needs of understanding the good and the bad of the Internet, the previous research has rarely considered both sides of the Internet technology together. In addition, the research about mobile phone addiction has started recently. Even though mobile phone addiction becomes much more serious than the Internet addiction, the research that deals with two addictions at the same time rarely exists.

In this paper, we deal with the both sides of the Internet and mobile phone at the same time. In order to achieve the purpose of this paper, we figure out the correlations between KICI and the Internet and mobile phone addiction levels for Korean adolescent. We firstly prepare questions for measuring KICI, the Internet addiction level, and mobile phone addiction level respectively. The questions, which were basically brought from the previous research works, are modified so that they are suitable for Korean adolescent. Next, we survey 783 primary, middle, and high school students. And then, we describe how KICI is related to the Internet addiction and mobile phone addiction by performing factor analysis and regression analysis. In addition, in order to find out which questions are more important to classify these two addiction levels, we perform tree-based and rule-based classification analyses with a data mining tool, called *Weka* [7], which is a collection of machine learning algorithms for data mining tasks. Finally, based on our analysis, we propose a better way to increase KICI and decrease the two addiction levels for Korean adolescent.

The rest of our paper is organized as follows. In Section 2, we introduce the questions for measuring KICI and the Internet and mobile phone addictions. In Section 3, we first perform factor analysis and regression analysis to test which factors of KICI affect the two addiction levels. In Section 4, we perform two classification analyses with *J48* and *JRIP* algorithms. Finally, we conclude our paper in Section 5.

2 Backgrounds

In this Section, we describe the questions for measuring KICI and the Internet and mobile phone addictions. Table 1 contains the questions for KICI, which originally came from [5]. Table 2 describes the questions for the Internet addiction, which originally came from Young's measurement [8][9].

Table 1. Questions for KICI

List of questions	
k1.	I can distinguish file types and run programs.
k2.	I can upload files and articles on the Internet.
k3.	I can operate blogs and cafés on the Internet.
k4.	I can do on-line shopping for books.
k5.	I can set up or change security settings and install programs for security.
k6.	I frequently post my opinion on boards.
k7.	I post my opinion to help other people understand well.
k8.	I read the opposite opinion about my ideas carefully and then persuade other people to understand.
k9.	I believe that the use of curse and slang on the Internet is bad.
k10.	I read the regulations about the usage of the Internet carefully.
k11.	I try to practice good manners towards other Internet users.
k12.	I have to keep the Internet related rules and regulations.
k13.	I have some experiences in using other people's personal information or posting it on the Internet inaccurately.
k14.	I have some experiences in using slang or in cursing other people.
k15.	I have some experiences in downloading videos for free.
k16.	I have some experiences in using document on the Internet without indicating the source of the document.
k17.	I trust companies in cyber space.
k18.	I trust content, people, and unions on the Internet.
k19.	It is important for me to read or write articles in the Internet.
k20.	I sometimes want to upload pictures and videos to share with other people.
k21.	I frequently get academic material on the Internet.
k22.	I usually collect the information about my club activities on the Internet.
k23.	I frequently watch videos on the Internet.
k24.	I frequently get the information about on-line games on the Internet.
k25.	I frequently make reservations for restaurants or theaters via the Internet.
k26.	I frequently purchase home appliances on the Internet.
k27.	I frequently participate in on-line surveys.
k28.	I frequently participate in signature campaigns for useful social purposes.
k29.	I frequently report illegal activities on the Internet.
k30.	I have experience on providing useful information on the Internet.

The questions for measuring mobile phone addiction came from [10]. They are similar to the questions for the Internet addiction test since they are based on Young's measurement. In summary, the questions are about self-control, emotion-control about anxiety, depression, and obsession, and obstacles in daily life.

To calculate KICI and the Internet and mobile phone addiction levels, we assign the *Likert* scale from 1 point (rarely) to 5 point (always) to each question. Next, we get 4 scores from KICI components with their weighting factors [5]. The 4 components are information knowledge (weighting factor: .3), information ethics (weighting factor: .3), information emotion (weighting factor: .2), and information practice (weighting factor: .2). And then, we can get the total by adding up the 4 scores.

For the Internet and mobile phone addiction levels, we add all the scores of 20 questions to find out the total. The maximum value of the total is 100, i.e., 5(always) $\times$ 20 = 100. If the total score lies between 20-49 points, then the person is a *normal* user. If the total score lies in 50-79, the person is experiencing occasional problems on the Internet, namely a *potential* user. If the total score is higher than 80, the person is a *highly addicted* user to the Internet.

Table 2. Questions for the Internet measurement [9]

List of questions	
c1.	How often do you find that you stay on-line longer than you intended?
c2.	How often do you neglect household chores to spend more time on-line?
c3.	How often do you prefer the excitement of the Internet to intimacy with your partner?
c4.	How often do you form new relationships with fellow on-line users?
c5.	How often do other people in your real life complain to you about the amount of time you spend on-line?
c6.	How often do you suffer from your grades or school work because of the amount of time you spend on-line?
c7.	How often do you check your e-mail before something else that you need to do?
c8.	How often does your job performance or productivity suffer because of the Internet?
c9.	How often do you become defensive or secretive when anyone asks you what you do during your Internet surfing?
c10.	How often do you block out disturbing thoughts about your life with soothing thoughts of the Internet?
c11.	How often do you find yourself anticipating when you will go on-line again?
c12.	How often do you fear that life without the Internet would be boring, empty, and joyless?
c13.	How often do you snap, yell, or act annoyed if someone bothers you while you are on-line?
c14.	How often do you lose sleep due to late-night log-ins?
c15.	How often do you feel preoccupied with the Internet when off-line, or fantasize about being on-line?
c16.	How often do you find yourself saying "just a few more minutes" when on-line?
c17.	How often do you fail to cut down the amount of time you spend on-line and fail?
c18.	How often do you try to hide how long you've been on-line?
c19.	How often do you choose to spend more time on-line instead of going out with others?
c20.	How often do you feel depressed or nervous when you are off-line, which goes away once you are back on-line?

3 Statistical Approach for Examining the Relationship between KICI and Two Addictions

In this section, we firstly performed a factor analysis to cluster the 30 questions of KICI and to reduce the number of questions to the small number of major factors. And then, we performed a regression test to identify which factors influence the Internet and mobile phone addition level. In this paper, SPSS 12.0 was used for our analyses. The demographic data of our respondents is shown in Table 3. We performed two cross tabulation analyses on KICI level, the Internet addiction level, and mobile phone addiction level over gender and academic year.

Table 3. Demographic data about the respondents

	Male	**Female**	**Total**
Primary school students	107	99	**206**
Middle school students	108	124	**232**
High school students	195	150	**345**
Total	**450**	**373**	**783**

KICI consists of 5 levels; level 1 is the lowest (poor) and level 5 is the highest (excellent). In our experiment, there was no student at level 1. The female students mainly belonged to level 3 (level 2 (.8%) < level 3 (66.2%) < level 4 (31.9%) < level 5(1.1%)) and the male students had a higher average level than female students (level 2 (4.4%) < level 3 (62.0%) < level 4 (32.4%) < level 5 (1.2%)). For the Internet addiction, the male students were more addicted than the female students (male: normal (30.5%) < potential (59.3%) < highly addicted (10.2%), female: normal (42.1%) < potential (40.1%) < highly addicted (7.8%)). However, for mobile phone addiction, the female students were more addicted than the male students (male: normal (36.6%) < potential (45.9%) < highly addicted (17.6%), female: normal (17.4%) < potential (52.8%) < highly addicted (29.8%)).

Next, we describe the differences among academic years. For KICI, most students belonged to level 3 or level 4. However, the primary school students had the highest percentage at level 4 (primary: level 2 (3.9%) < level 3 (51.9%) < level 4 (42.7%) < level 5 (1.5%), middle: level 2 (3.4%) < level 3 (67.7%) < level 4 (27.2%) < level 5 (1.7%), high: level 2 (1.4%) < level 3 (68.7%) < level 4 (29.3%) < level 5 (.6%)). For the Internet addiction, as the academic year went up, the percentage of potentially addicted group increased rapidly (primary: normal (52.9%) < potential (39.3%) < highly addicted (7.8%), middle: normal (35.8%) < potential (53.4%) < highly addicted (10.8%), high: normal (26.1%) < potential (65.2%) < highly addicted (8.1%)). For mobile phone addiction, the result was similar to the result of the Internet addiction (primary: normal (45.1%) < potential (34.5%) < highly addicted (20.4%), middle: normal (25.4%) < potential (51.3%) < highly addicted (23.3%), high: normal (18.3%) < potential (56.2%) < highly addicted (25.2%)).

In summary, for KICI, the male students had a little bit higher level than the female students. In case of the academic year, the distributions were similar, but the number of primary school students who belonged to good KICI level (level 4) was much more than that of middle school students. For the Internet addiction, the male students had a higher level than the female students. However, in case of mobile phone addiction, the female students had a much higher level than the male students. In case of the academic year, the distributions for the Internet and mobile phone were similar, but as their academic year increased, mobile phone addiction was severer than the Internet addiction.

Next, according to our factor analysis, the 30(k1 ~ k30) questions were clustered as 8 factors: ability for Information usage(k1 ~ k5), on-line society participation (k26 ~ k29), information exchange(k6 ~ k8), information gathering and sharing(k19 ~ k23), information etiquette(k9 ~ k12), information regulation(k15, k16), reliability about cyberspace(k17, k18), and illegal use of information or entertaining(k13, k14, k24). The cronbach, α, which represents a coefficient of reliability is .78. With the 8 factors, we performed a regression analysis. Table 4 (a) shows that among the 8 factors of KICI, on-line society participation (+), information etiquette and regulation (-), and the illegal use of information or entertaining factors (+) influenced the Internet addiction score positively or negatively. In particular, the lower the degrees of information etiquette and regulation were, the higher the Internet addiction score was. However, the higher the degrees of on-line society participation and illegal use of information were, the higher the Internet addiction score was. On the other hand, Table 4 (b) shows the relationship between the 8 KICI factors and mobile phone addiction. All factors except information usage ability and information exchange degree affected the mobile phone addiction scores.

One important thing is the relationship between on-line society participation and two addictions. Basically, national organizations give a higher point to the students who participate in on-line votes, surveys, or signature campaign. However, the students' addiction scores are higher than the scores of the other students who rarely participate in on-line votes, surveys, or campaign. It is a conflict between KICI and the levels of the two addictions.

We can solve the above conflict by education. In fact, due to emphasis on the importance of cyber ethics education, the students who have a higher level of the Internet etiquette have the higher KICI. Therefore, we knew that the cyber etiquette education for the students could partly solve the conflict between KICI and the two addictions. We also knew that the education which gives our students the right direction how to participate in on-line society participation should be performed in schools and institutes.

Table 4. Regression analysis for KICI and the two addictions

	Non-standardized coefficient		Standardized coefficient	t	Statistical significance
	B	Standard error	Beta		at p = .05
(constant)	55.13	.53		103.63	.00
Ability for Information Usage	.89	.53	.05	1.68	.09
On-line Society Participation	2.83	.53	.16	5.32	.00
Information Exchange	.22	.53	.01	.42	.68
Information Gathering and Sharing	-.18	.53	-.01	-.34	.73
Information Etiquette	-1.91	.53	-.11	-3.58	.00
Information Regulation	-5.50	.53	-.31	-10.32	.00
Reliability about Cyberspace	.24	.53	.01	.44	.66
Illegal Use or Entertaining	7.30	.53	.41	13.71	.00

(a) Dependant variable: the Internet addiction score

	Non-standardized coefficient		Standardized coefficient	t	Statistical significance
	B	Standard error	Beta		at p = .05
(constant)	49.22	.58		85.28	.00
Ability for Information Usage	.26	.58	.01	.44	.66
On-line Society Participation	4.08	.58	.22	7.07	.00
Information Exchange	.95	.58	.05	1.64	.10
Information Gathering and Sharing	2.37	.58	.13	4.10	.00
Information Etiquette	-3.26	.58	-.18	-5.64	.00
Information Regulation	-6.40	.58	-.34	-11.09	.00
Reliability about Cyberspace	1.31	.58	.07	2.26	.02
Illegal Use or Entertaining	3.37	.58	.18	5.83	.00

(b) Dependant variable: mobile phone addiction score

4 Data Mining Approach for Examining the Relationship between KICI and Two Addictions

In this section, we performed two types of classification analyses by using J48 and JRIP algorithms to figure out which questions of KICI measurement are more important to classify the two addiction levels. J48 [11] is a tree-based classification algorithm and JRIP [12] is a rule-based classification algorithm. Both algorithms are implemented on Weka. Both results from J48 and JRIP analyses for the Internet addiction are described in Figure 1 (a) and (b).

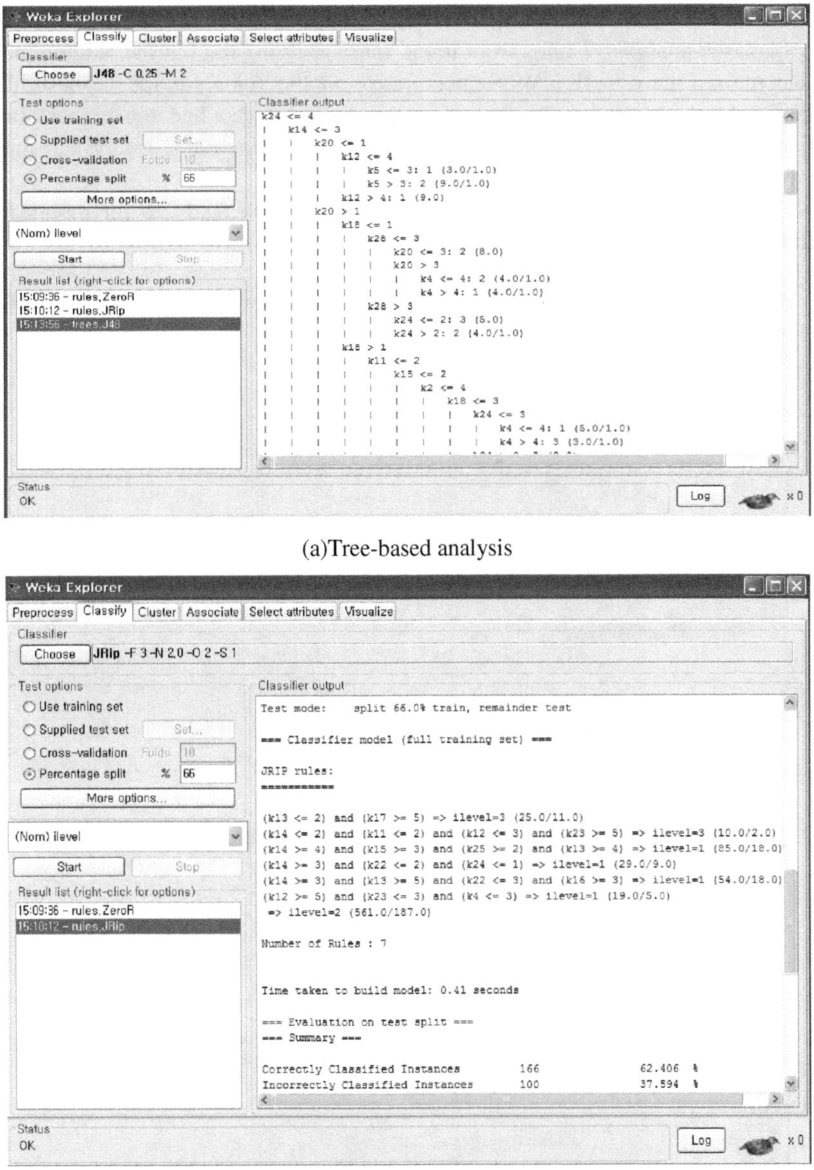

(a)Tree-based analysis

(b)Rule-based analysis

Fig. 1. The Internet addiction

As shown in Figure 1 (a), the questions, k23, k7, and k3, were more important when we classified the Internet addiction levels. The root question of the decision tree was k23, which is related to games. In other words, the students who collect information about games on the Internet can be classified as the group having the highest Internet addiction level. Thus, in order to measure KICI more accurate, students' attitude towards games should be considered more in the future. In case of the rule-based analysis, 7 rules were found for classifying the Internet addiction levels as shown in Figure 1 (b). We concentrated on the rules for the highest Internet addiction level. According to the rules, the students who had the highest Internet addiction level hardly followed the regulations of on-line sites, rarely had manners and etiquettes, and frequently watched on-line videos.

Next, Figure 2 shows the results of two classification analyses for mobile phone addiction.

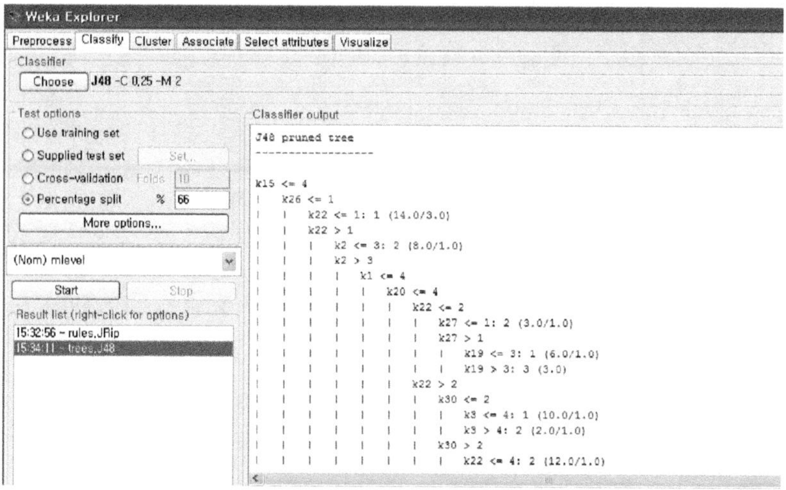

(a)Tree-based analysis

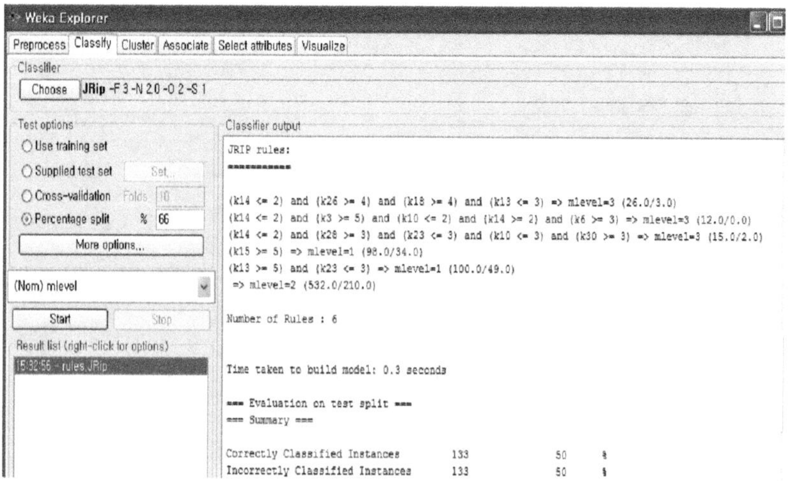

(b)Rule-based analysis

Fig. 2. Mobile phone addiction

Figure 2 (a) shows the decision tree for mobile phone addiction. In order to classify three mobile phone addiction levels, the questions, *k15, k4*, and *k10*, were more important. The root question of the decision tree was *k15*. It means that the students who had much more experience (degree 4 or more) on downloading free videos and a little experience (degree 2 or more) on on-line shopping had the highest mobile phone addiction level. Also, the students who did not read the regulations about the usage on a specific website had the highest mobile phone addiction level.

In Figure 2 (b), we found 6 rules for classifying mobile phone addiction levels. We focused on the highest mobile phone addiction level. Among questions, the students who had a lot of experience on purchasing something on the Internet and on running blogs or café had the highest mobile phone addiction level. Compared with the Internet addiction, mobile phone addicted students wanted to communicate more with other students. In fact, the current KICI focuses only on the Internet so far. Thus, KICI should be enhanced to cover more various kinds of digital devices as a better accurate measurement.

According to these results, we found out that KICI had statistically meaningful influence on the Internet and mobile phone addiction. However, even though KICI included the questions about on-line society participation, our schools did not educate how our students can participate in on-line activities in a desirable way. Currently, our education focuses only on the manners and etiquettes for browsing and getting information. Thus, we can increase the KICI level of Korean adolescent if schools and institutes teach students about how to participate and contribute to our society on the Internet more actively and practically. Also, their two addiction levels can be reduced as well.

5 Conclusion

In this paper, we compared KICI with the Internet or mobile phone addiction test measurements to identify if there is any conflict between two measures. KICI is used to measure the positive side of the Internet, whereas the Internet and mobile phone addiction level measurement items represent the negative side of the digital device. By doing this research, we figured out that there were positive or negative relationships between KICI and the two addictions and there was one important conflict among them. Also, we found out that among the questions of KICI, the Internet addiction could be highly influenced by gaming and on-line video factors and bad etiquette and the ignorance of regulations on the Internet. However, for mobile phone addiction, the experiences on purchasing something on the Internet and on running blogs or café were more important.

In summary, schools and institutes have been emphasizing the education only for getting information from the Internet in a right way. However, there has rarely been performing the education for putting information on the Internet and participating in on-line society on the Internet in a right way. Thus, future education should also focus on how to participate in our on-line society more actively and correctly. In addition, education for Korean adolescent should be also focused on how to contribute properly as well as how to keep the rules firmly on the Internet.

References

1. Huffaker, D. The Educated Blogger: Using Weblogs to Promote Literacy in the Classroom. AACE Journal, vol. 13, no. 2, pp. 91—98. (2005)
2. Elisheva, F. G., J. Juvonen, and S. L. Gable: Internet Use and Well-Being in Adolescence. Journal of Social Issues, vol. 58, no. 1. pp. 75—90. (2002)
3. Christakis, D. A. and Moreno, M. A.: Trapped in the Net: Will Internet Addiction Become a 21st-Century Epidemic? Arch Pediatr Adolesc Med. vol. 163, no. 10. pp. 959 – 960 (2009)
4. Jenaro, C., Flores, N., Gomez-vela, M., Gonzalez-Gil, F. and Caballo, C.: Problematic Internet and Cell-Phone Use: Psychological, Behavioral, and Health Correlates. Addiction Research and Theory, vol. 15, no. 3. pp. 309—320. (2007)
5. Information Culture Department: Report on Korean Information Culture Index 2009. Korean Ministry of Public Administration and Security. (2010) (Korean)
6. Digital Times: Information Culture Index 66, http://www.dt.co.kr/ contents.html?article_no= 2010100102010460634004. (2010) (Korean)
7. Witten, I. and E. Frank: Data Mining : Practical Machine Learning Tools and Techniques. Elsevier. (2005)
8. Young, Kimberly S.: Internet Addiction: The Emergence of a New Clinical Disorder. Cyber Psychology & Behavior, vol. 1, no. 3. pp. 237—244 (1998)
9. http://www.netaddiction.com/index.php?option=com_bfquiz&view=onepage&catid=46&itemid=106
10. Yang, S.: Research on Cell Phone Addiction for High School Adolescent. Korean Youth Policy Institute. (2002) (Korean)
11. I. H. Witten and E. Frank: Data Mining: Practical Machine Learning Tools and Techniques with Java Implementations. Morgan Kaufmann. (1999)
12. Stewart Yang, Jianping Song, Rajamani, H., Taewon Cho, Yin Zhang and Mooney, R.: Fast and Effective Worm Fingerprinting via Machine Learning. Proceedings of the 2006 IEEE International Conference on Autonomic Computing, pp. 311—313 (2006)

Trends in Social Media Application: The Potential of Google+ for Education Shown in the Example of a Bachelor's Degree Course on Marketing

Alptekin Erkollar[1] and Birgit Oberer[2]

[1] Halic University, Istanbul, Turkey
erkollar@etcop.com
[2] Kadir Has University, Cibali, Istanbul, Turkey
birgit.oberer@khas.edu.tr

Abstract. Google Plus has the potential to improve students' collaboration through circles, conduct research for projects with sparks, improve the student-instructor relationship by using this kind of social media to get in touch with each other, and support blended learning with the hang out functionality. The course concept, which is shown as an example, offers a concrete approach for integrating Google Plus functionalities in education. The results of the forthcoming analysis of the concept in use will show advantages and potential for improvement, both of the system and the use of it in education.

Keywords: social media, Google Plus, education, course content, marketing.

1 Introduction

Almost any web service can be adapted for educational use. Although some instructors do use social media, such as Facebook or Twitter, for their courses, they are not ideal for university settings. Privacy concerns always throttle the 'need' of instructors for social media. Too many public elements show too much private information about instructors to all their friends or followers, without any possibility to filter or group them and decide who is allowed to see which message. Some kind of privilege classes would be great, such as distinguishing between limited access, full access, and access on demand for individual friends or followers. Google Plus seems to offer the possibility to overcome this privacy issue, in using a methodology to group one's contacts. Other features available should attract people using this social network for communicating and sharing information. The main features of Google Plus are introduced below, followed by a first analysis of how to use these features in education and designing a concrete course framework, in turn integrating Google Plus functionalities. The results of the forthcoming analysis of this concept in use will be communicated after the concept that is introduced in this article has been in use for at least two courses.

2 Social Media

Social media focus on social interaction and use accessible and scalable communication techniques. Social media has begun influencing businesses and

T.-h. Kim et al. (Eds.): ASEA/DRBC/EL 2011, CCIS 257, pp. 569–578, 2011.

knowledge sharing processes in many organizations [10]. Implementing social media in education is an innovative process at many levels of universities. ELearning developers and course instructors have to be aware of changing user preferences, technological issues, and the new tools available in order to be able to determine how to benefit from them [10]. Social network sites are 'web-based services that allow individuals to (1) construct a public or semi-public profile within a bounded system, (2) articulate a list of other users with whom they share a connection, and (3) view and traverse their list of connections and those made by others within the system' [13]. Social media are popular for education, not least because young adults, who attend courses at university, are familiar with these systems and mostly use it frequently. Social media have been integrated into the daily practices of many users, supported by different websites, tools, and networks [11]. Everyone can add or edit information on social media, supported by digital tools enabling you to create, change, and publish dynamic content [12,14,15].

3 GOOGLE Plus and Education

Google Plus is a social media tool that was released in July 2011. The features offered by this tool should attract people sharing their thoughts, ideas, and information on the Web. The main features of Google Plus, which could be of interest for education, are its circles, hangouts, sparks, and huddle. Circles are contacts that you can group, using different criteria for grouping, such as interests, types of contact (business, family, friends, former colleagues, interest related contacts). Circles follow a relationship-based approach. Contacts can be added to the circle by drag and drop. The benefit is that you can manage your appearance on the Web, enabling you to not show all the content to all followers but rather to a selected circle. As an instructor, you can use Google Plus to add a circle for a course that you give and add your students to that circle. What you do not want to do is to share your private posts with your students. Therefore, you can select which user group can access which post by sorting them into circles, which provides support for direct communication to personalized groups [1, 2, 3,4,5].

Hangouts can be generated and used as an instant videoconferencing tool with circles, or selected contacts in circles. Hangouts offer video conferencing with multiple users; small groups can interact on video. This feature could be used in education for the online office hours of instructors, explaining assignments, talking about projects, group work or communicating with students completing a project in a company for one semester, facing problems, or needing some kind of support [1,2,4,5,9].

Sparks is a customized way of searching and sharing and follows an interest-based approach. Sparks offers the possibility to enter keywords and shows a list of results matching these keywords, showing beside the title of the article or contribution a short excerpt from the content as well, making it easier for users to select contributions that are relevant for their search. Sparks can be stored and the user can get updates on the stored keyword, in case new contributions are available. An important feature is that the results of such sparks can also be shared with circles or selected people. This feature could be used in class for searching and sharing course relevant content [4,5,6].

Huddle offers group chat possibilities. It is 'a group messaging experience that lets everyone inside the circle know what's going on, right this second'. For education, integrating this feature could offer benefits for both students and instructors. Huddle is part of the 'mobile' feature, offering services using a mobile phone, including other services as well, such as instant upload (for pictures and videos from a mobile phone to a private folder in Google Plus) and location (a service to add one's current location to every post) [6,7].

Google Plus could offer 'possibilities for students to share links and build a classroom community. Teachers could post homework information, project links, and hold class discussions, all while keeping the circle strictly education related' [1]. Social feeds can be tailored to different types of contacts (grouped in circles). Whenever something is posted, you can choose who gets to read it [3]. By using Google Plus, instructors can open their social networks to their students: they have to create a circle, add their students, and share school-related information.
The flexibility that Google Plus offers is that one can decide to follow someone who has the possibility to limit the updates to specific circles.

Google Plus could become a 'one stop tool for personal and professional social networking needs' [3].

4 Development of a Marketing Course Integrating Google Plus

4.1 Course Environment

The potential of Google Plus for education should be examined on its use for an interdisciplinary marketing course at the bachelor's degree level. The audience for the marketing course is students from different university departments, such as business administration, information technology, industrial engineering, tourism management, new media, or graphic design. This interdisciplinary approach makes it necessary to offer participating students information and communication structures sufficient to co-operate on course related topics and receive information that is needed to fulfill the requirements of the course. Currently, Blackboard is used to provide information to students, place announcements, and hand in homework. Information exchange using email is only allowed in case students have limited access to the Blackboard system or face other technical or organizational restrictions. In the past, students learned to use this system because it was mandatory for the course. Nevertheless, infrequent access to the system was recognized and although necessary information was available online and (partly) email announcements were sent, students were not informed about issues, homework, course requirements in general, or exam related questions. The reason for this lack of knowledge could be that students did not want to access an additional system frequently and in case email announcements were used, a weak management of students' email addresses (mainly because students did not update the changing of email addresses in the system) caused information packages to not be received. As an instructor, new ways to close this gap should be found. One way could be using a system that students are used to working with in order to communicate. In the past, the social network Facebook was an option to support, at least partly, an instructor in communicating with students. Generally, at some universities or schools, adding students as a friend on social networks is not allowed or undesired. That is mainly because there is a mixture between the private sphere and the school's sphere, such as you cannot separate between friends being your students, your family added as friends, or members of a research community, added as friends. All of them see everything you post, in case you have not defined restrictions that should be able to see the posts. It is important to mention that you can distinguish between 'friends', 'friends of your friends', and 'all'. You cannot define further categories for your friends, dividing them according to your relationship, interests, demographic data, or other attributes. For the marketing course in the past the instructor accepted 'be a friend enquiries' of students and added them to their friends list.

The privacy issue was not a problem for instructors because they use their Facebook account not for posting private topics, comments, pictures, or statements, but mainly for following friends. Nevertheless, using a social network like Facebook leads to the need for the controlled use of the instructor's account, always keeping in mind that students are following and will keep the statement you posted in mind when they meet for the next class.

On the whole, whenever the instructor was online and students asked questions regarding the course, these were answered. In case they were of relevance for not only the individual student but for more or all of them, the questions were answered as well using the Blackboard to ensure that all the students receive an answer to that question. Therefore, the instructor had to overcome communication restrictions, knowing that there is still at least one media break and increased effort still facing the limitations mentioned before.

The basic functions of Google Plus could support instructors in keeping students updated or getting in touch with them. Assuming that, in the nearer future, after being available, Google Plus will be used by an increasing community and become a common tool, such as other social networks (Facebook or Twitter), this system could support instructors, and some tasks that are currently fulfilled by other systems, such as course contents systems or social networks, could be shifted to Google Plus.

4.2 Course Content

The main focus of the course (Marketing M1, 14 weeks) is to give an introduction to the basic concepts of marketing and to provide an understanding for the marketing process as part of strategic planning. Marketing strategies like market segmentation, product strategies, pricing, or competition approaches are explained. The elements of the marketing mix will be examined in developing marketing strategies. Table 1 shows the planned content for the course and table 2 the drafted syllabus.

Generally, there course is designed in three main streams. The first one is the traditional lecture along with class work. The instructor and students meet in class and work on selected topics. The second stream focuses on a project undertaken by students. They are working in groups of 3-5 (depending on the class size) and start their projects (an example is given in table 3), which has to be finalized and the

Table 1. Course content and teaching methods

week	Topics	Teaching method
1	Introduction	lecture
2	marketing environment	lecture
3	Strategic planning, marketing process	Lecture, group work
4-5	Consumer markets, consumer buying behavior, decision making	Lecture, group work, field analysis, role play
6	Market segmentation, marketing strategies	Lecture, student project (week 6-14)
7-8	Products, product development	Lecture
9	Product lifecycle management	lecture
10	Services, branding	Lecture, field analysis on branding, social media activities (blogs, social networks)
11-12	Marketing research, pricing	Lecture, group work
13	Pricing, competition	lecture
14	Special issues	Student presentations

Table 2. Drafted syllabus

Syllabus: Marketing M1	
Course objective	The main focus of this course is to give an introduction to the basic concepts of marketing and to provide an understanding for the marketing process as part of strategic planning. Marketing strategies, such as market segmentation, product strategies, pricing, or competition approaches are explained. The elements of the marketing mix will be examined.
Content / week	1 introduction to marketing 2 marketing environment 3 strategic planning and marketing process 4-5 consumer markets, consumer buyer behavior, decision making 6 market segmentation and marketing strategies 7-8 products 9 product development, product life cycle 10 Services, branding 11-12 marketing research, pricing 13 pricing, competition 14 special issues
Reading resources	Kotler P, Armstrong G (2010). Principles of Marketing, Prentice Hall International Handouts, case studies, project resources
Tools, systems	Blackboard, Google Plus, Internet
Student evaluation criteria	Midterm exam 20% Projects 50% Final exam 20% Assignments 10%
Class attendance mandatory (physical, virtual)	

results presented in week 14, in week 6, after an instructor's introduction in market segmentation and marketing strategies. The project contains the development of a marketing strategy for a concrete product and the testing of this strategy among some friendly customers (in the school environment, other groups of students are 'friendly customers' for each other group and evaluate the group's outcome). For this project, students have to collaborate in a structured way and keep the instructor updated. Because of the interdisciplinary character of the course time constrains caused by different timetables of students often harm the outcome of such projects. To overcome these difficulties it is planned to use Google Plus for structured work on projects (student-student, group-instructor, instructor-groups).

Table 3. Sample of a student driven project

Marketing M1: Student project (sample)	
Project environment	
Your position	You are marketing managers at a national telecommunications company selling cell phones and offering phone, TV, and Internet services.
Your team	Each of you is an experienced marketing manager, responsible for different products to be offered to (different) target customers
The product	Cell phone, branded by the company XX
What should be sold?	Your company wants to offer the cell phone AND your phone services. Product bundles have already been developed by the product managers responsible for this new launched phone.
Your task	Your new task is to develop a strategy for attracting especially young adults (teenagers between 13 and 21) to buy a special cell phone, which was recently launched on the market. This product is branded by an international company.
Required steps	
Form your team	All of you are team members, define one team leader
Team meetings	Organize team meetings to agree on a strategy as to how to market your product (bundle). Consider how to use the brand of the cell phone for your marketing strategy
Prepare a strategy	Show the information on marketing strategies and customer behavior that you obtained during class (a documentation is available on the Blackboard). Prepare a draft of the strategy, after having received an OK from your team leader (use Google+), hand in documentation of the strategy (use Blackboard) and wait for your sponsor's feedback (Google+)
Go live for pre-testing	In case the sponsor agreed with the strategy, plan the go live.

Table 3. (*Continued*)

Contact 'friendly customer' for a field analysis	Your classmates are your friendly customers, contact them (use Google+) and arrange some kind of field test (you have to find out whether your strategy works or not). Use the information you obtained about field tests during class (a summary is available on the Blackboard).
Summarize customer feedback	Hand in a feedback report for sponsors (Blackboard)
Go live	Plan the final go live of the strategy and define the needed distribution channels (guidelines are available on the Blackboard)
Communication rules	
Before you start the project	Communicate the team leader's name to the company's management [your instructor]. Use Google+
Team meetings	Daily (online), use Google+
Sponsor meeting	Once a week (team + management), use Google +
In case there are urgent questions to be answered, contact your sponsor (the management), use Google+.	

Basically, the features offered by Google Plus could be integrated in this course. In a first steps, the instructor has to define a circle for this course on Google Plus, the 'Marketing M1 circle 2012'. Then, all the students have to be added to this circle. One requirement is that all the students have a Google Plus account and can be added. Open questions from the instructor (OQI): OQI 1: 'Can students without an active Google Plus account be added, such as sending an invitation message to the students email addresses, registered in the students database?'. OQI 2: 'Can a student be added to several circles, such as a student attending more than one course in one semester?' OQ3: 'After the end of the course, circles can be deleted. Can they be stored in an archive as well?' OQ4: 'How can the instructor use the course related content, generated using Google Plus store for upcoming courses?' OQ5: 'Can a content generated in one circle (course) be shifted or copied to another course?'. For the online office hours, the Google Plus functionality 'hangouts' can be used. In case students have questions regarding the course or their projects they can contact their instructor whenever available, independently from office hours during the day, using this real-time video functionality.

These hangouts can be used for group meetings as well. Up to ten people can join the real time video communication and get in touch with each other. This could be helpful for students, such as starting a successful project management for their semester projects, to discuss open issues, discuss critical paths, or prepare group presentations. The same functionality, hangouts, can be used for group meetings with the instructor, or for meetings of the instructor and selected students, like the designated project managers for the term projects. The integration with Gmail can prohibit students from missing course related information. In case the new announcements are placed on Blackboard, there are two options that an instructor can choose: to add the announcement and as an additional service, send a message to all students registered for the course. The second option seems to be appropriate, because without entering Blackboard students receive at least a header message stating that there is a new announcement available, to be considered. This requires that the students email addresses are up to date and maintained in the students' management system (mostly by students themselves). Using Gmail Google Plus messages are shown on the Gmail main page.For the practical part of the course, some 'offline' assignments are planned: students receive an assignment, work on parts of this assignment in groups, have to put together their results, and give a presentation on the whole assignment. Therefore, one assignment is spited; students are grouped and have to work on parts of the assignment. When finished, they have to prepare a complete view of the assignment, all the parts have to fit each other, and one presentation is given. To support this offline work conducted by the students, they can use Google Plus huddle to keep in touch with each other and groups could coordinate their results, although they are not working together directly. With Google Plus huddle all groups (such as one student per group) can use this group chat to communicate, such as decide on the main topic for the presentation, all the groups that have to give, based on the findings all groups had in their separate meetings on their topics. Table 4 gives an example for the use of Google Plus huddle.

Table 4. Use of Google Plus huddle for a sample students' project

Marketing M1: group project	
Topic	Marketing process
Assignment	Work out the main steps of a marketing process. What are the requirements, resources required, departments involved, company related restrictions? As a marketing manager, what are your duties? With whom do you have to co-operate within the company? What are frameworks that you can use?
Assignm. type:	Group work
Groups/topic	
Student 1-5	Situation analysis
Student 6-10	Marketing strategy
Student 11-15	Marketing mix decisions
Student 16-20	Implementation & control
outcome	One presentation: 'the marketing process'
What to do?	Work in groups on your topic, use Google Plus functionalities to communicate Prepare one (1) presentation 1. Step: you have 1 hour to make a draft of your presentation. Each group works on the assigned sub topic. Use Google Plus huddle to communicate with the other groups. Note: there should not be repetitions in the draft. Communicate with the other groups to avoid that.
Reading resources	Kotler P, Armstrong G (2010). Principles of Marketing, Prentice Hall International Sandhusen, R.L. (2008). Marketing. Barron's Business Review, 4th edition, Barron's Educational Series Handouts, case studies, project resources
Important dates	See handout

By using the Sparks functionality provided by Google Plus, the instructor has the possibility to add the main topics of the course to his or her sparks, getting the latest updates on these topics and being able to share them with the course circle. OQ5: 'Can sparks be shared with multiple circles?'. The benefit that sparks offers is that one part of every entry is shown and the instructor can easily scroll down a list of articles that could be of benefit when used in class, without the need to read all of them before selecting them for sharing. After sparks have been screened, the relevant ones can be selected, read, and shared as well. At the end of the course, related sparks can be removed easily.

For students, discussions, exam studying, and book reading could occur in a circle, where all the students of one course are grouped in.

5 Conclusions

Almost any web service can be adapted for educational use. Google Plus promises more structured control over sharing, with circles as one dominant feature. As this hype grows, increasingly more people will receive invitations to that social network and a discussion started on how to use Google Plus for education. Instructors could teach new material, review information from class, share it, or answer questions all in a virtual class meeting. Google Plus could offer an opportunity for distance learning or at least adding facets to the traditional in-class-studying by using course content systems for more or less offline learning. It needs some play from educators and research to find out ways to use Google Plus to improve education and to become aware of some kind of restrictions or limitations.

References

1. Venosdale, K.: Google Plus: What does it mean for education, Missouri State TeachersAssociation (2011), http://mostateteachers.typepad.com/missouri_state_teachers_a/2011/07/googleplus-what-does-it-mean-for-education.html
2. Smith, P.: Google+: First Thoughts and Potential Use in Education, edSocial Media (2011), http://www.edsocialmedia.com/2011/07/google-first-thoughts-and-potential-use-in-education/
3. Lewis, S.: Google Plus and Education (2011), http://anseo.net, http://www.anseo.net/2011/07/google-plus-and-education/
4. Spencer, J.T.: What Google Plus Could Teach Us About Education Reform, Teach Paperless (2011), http://teachpaperless.blogspot.com/2011/07/what-google-plus-could-teach-us-about.html
5. Google: The Google+ Project (2011), http://www.google.com/intl/en/+/learnmore/

6. Watters, H.: Google Plus and the Future of Sharing Educational Resources (2011), http://www.hackeducation.com/2011/07/15/google-plus-and-the-future-of-sharing-educational-resources/
7. Google: Google Blog. Introducing the Google + project: Real-life sharing, rethought the web (2011), http://googleblog.blogspot.com/2011/06/introducing-google-project-real-life.html
8. Watters, H.: Will Google+ Replace Twitter or Facebook for Teachers? Mind Shift (2011), http://mindshift.kqed.org/2011/07/will-google-replace-twitter-or-facebook-for-teachers/
9. Moran, M.: Google Plus and Education, Teaching, Learning and Technology (2011), http://learningedtech.wordpress.com/2011/07/01/google-plus-and-education/
10. Kurkela, L.J.: Systemic Approach to Learning Paradigms and the Use of Social Media in Higher Education. iJET 6, 14–20 (2011)
11. Shafique, F., Anwar, M., Bushra, M.: Exploitation of social media among university students: a case study. Webology 7(2), article 79 (2010), http://www.webology.org/2010/v7n2/a79.html
12. Aharony, N.: Web 2.0 in U.S. LIS schools: are they missing a boat? Ariadne 54 (2008), http://www.ariadne.ac.uk/issue54/aharony/#28
13. Boyd, D.M., Ellison, N.B.: Social network sites: Defintition, history and scholarship. J. of Comp.-Med. Comm. 13, article 11 (2007), http://jcmc.indiana.edu/vol13/issue1/boyd.ellison.html
14. Silius, K., Miilumäki, T., Huhtamäki, J., Meriläinen, J., Pohjolainen, S.: Students' Motivations for Social Media Enhanced Studying and Learning. Knowl. Man & eLearn. 2, 51–67 (2010)
15. Knoke, D., Yang, S.: Social Network Analysis, 2nd edn. Sage Publications, Los Angeles (2008)

Learning Preferences and Self-Regulation – Design of a Learner-Directed E-Learning Model

Stella Lee[1], Trevor Barker[2], and Vive Kumar[3]

[1] Computer Science Department, University of Hertfordshire, Hatfield, UK;
Golder Associates Inc., Calgary, Canada
[2] Computer Science Department, University of Hertfordshire, Hatfield, UK
[3]School of Computing & Information Systems, Athabasca University, Edmonton, Canada
stellal@athabascau.ca/stella_lee@golder.com
t.l.barker@herts.ac.uk
vive@athabascau.ca

Abstract. In e-learning, questions concerned how one can create course material that motivate and support students in guiding their own learning have attracted an increasing number of research interests ranging from adaptive learning systems design to personal learning environments and learning styles/preferences theories. The main challenge of learning online remains how learners can accurately direct and regulate their own learning without the presence of tutors to provide instant feedback. Furthermore, learning a complex topic structured in various media and modes of delivery require learners to make certain instructional decisions concerning what to learn and how to go about their learning. In other words, learning requires learners to self-regulate their own learning[1]. Very often, learners have difficulty self-directing when topics are complex and unfamiliar. It is not always clear to the learners if their instructional decisions are optimal.[2] Research into adaptive e-learning systems has attempted to facilitate this process by providing recommendations, classifying learners into different preferred learning styles, or highlighting suggested learning paths[3]. However, system-initiated learning aid is just one way of supporting learners; a more holistic approach, we would argue, is to provide a simple, all-in-one interface that has a mix of delivery modes and self-regulation learning activities embedded in order to help individuals learn how to improve their learning process. The aim of this research is to explore how learners can self-direct and self-regulate their online learning both in terms of domain knowledge and meta knowledge in the subject of computer science. Two educational theories: experiential learning theory (ELT) and self-regulated learning (SRL) theory are used as the underpinning instructional design principle. To assess the usefulness of this approach, we plan to measure: changes in domain-knowledge; changes in meta-knowledge; learner satisfaction; perceived controllability; and system usability. In sum, this paper describes the research work being done on the initial development of the e-learning model, instructional design framework, research design as well as issues relating to the implementation of such approach.

Keywords: learning theory, learning preferences, self-regulated learning, E-Learning, instructional design, learning design.

T.-h. Kim et al. (Eds.): ASEA/DRBC/EL 2011, CCIS 257, pp. 579–589, 2011.

1 Introduction

In e-learning, questions concerned how one can create online material that support and motivate students in guiding their own learning and make meaningful instructional decisions have attracted an increasing number of research interests ranging from areas in adaptive learning systems design to personal learning environments and learning styles/preferences theories. The main challenge of learning online remains how learners can self-regulate their own learning without the presence of tutors to provide instant feedback. It is especially difficult when topics are complex and unfamiliar and it is not always clear to the learners if their learning decisions are optimal[2]. Research into adaptive e-learning systems has attempted to facilitate the learning process by providing recommendations with respect to classifying learners into preferred learning styles and by associating recommended learning paths with these learning styles[3]. Indeed, research has shown the importance of adapting online course material to support learners with different background knowledge and skills[3, 4]. Another work has described a user modeling approach that is beneficial to learners who are interacting with complex learning applications in an online environment[5]. However, system-initiated learning aid is just one way of supporting learners; a more holistic approach, we would argue, is to provide a simple, all-in-one interface that has a mix of delivery modes and self-regulation learning activities embedded in order to help individuals learn how to improve their learning process.

Broadly speaking, user modeling is a technique employed to provide users with options with respect to performing tasks and interacting with systems differentially. The common variables to model include the user's personalities, abilities, prior knowledge, preferences, performances and intentions[6]. User modeling can also be defined as a model of users residing inside a system or computational environment[7]. However, many of these models attempt to "match" students with a certain learning styles or learner characteristics that it falls short on placing the initiative on the learners themselves and encourage them to take control of their learning. In fact, there has been no evidence in matching teaching to learning styles as the best way to improve learning. Instead, there is an optimal way to teach chunk of content to all students[8]. In this study, our design approach is centered on the constructive cognitive model - a model that helps students to self-direct their own learning, makes learning constructive while providing adaptive feedback. A simple, all-in-one interface for e-learning has been designed that has a mix of delivery modes and self-regulated learning activities embedded in order to help individuals learn how to improve their learning process. Self-regulated learning activities are provided contextually in the form of key study skills. Information and tools relating to these study skills are provided alongside the course material. Adaptive feedback is provided at the end in the form of a self-quiz to evaluate whether the learners have progress through their learning with adequate domain and meta learning knowledge. The domain we have chosen for this study is in computer programming. Specifically, we are conducting our study within an online introductory Java programming course (COMP 268) in a Western Canadian university. Two relevant educational theories:

experiential learning theory (ELT) and self-regulated learning (SRL) have been selected as the underlining instructional design principles for this approach.

This paper aims to describe the design and development of such a learner-directed model in an e-learning environment, with the focus on how the two educational theories are being applied, the overall research design and data collection plan as well as discussions on issues and challenges. To assess the usefulness of this approach, we plan to measure: changes in domain-knowledge; changes in meta-knowledge; learner satisfaction; perceived controllability; and system usability.

2 Literature Review

2.1 Experiential Learning Theory (ELT)

Experiential Learning Theory (ELT) emphasizes experience as the central focus in learning [9]. Learning-styles theories[10] raised questions about what learning strategies we operate with and how we use learning strategies to enhance student learning. By studying these theories, one would also attempt to gain insights into what motivates learners and how to help them to understand more about their own strengths and weaknesses as learners. Kolb's model of learning styles could be represented as "flexible stable learning preferences" [10] as ELT is not about fixed learner traits, but rather a "differential preference for learning, which changes slightly from situation to situation" [10]. For instance, a student working in a group setting during a field trip for geo-caching might prefer to take a turn at hands-on interaction with the device even though he would normally prefer reading textual instruction at home alone. In his research, Kolb observed that some students have a definite preference for certain learning activities [9]. For example, one student might prefer reading lecture notes whilst another student might prefer working on an interactive simulation. "From this emerged the idea of an inventory that would identify these preferences by capturing individual learning differences." [11]

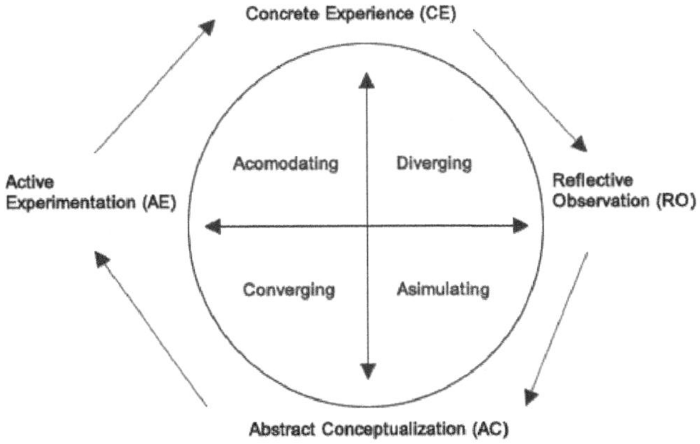

Fig. 1. Kolb's Experiential Learning Cycle

ELT sees learning as "the process whereby knowledge is created through the transformation of experience. Knowledge results from the combination of grasping and transforming experience" [11]. Figure 1 shows how a learner can progress through the experiential learning cycle: experience is translated through reflection into concepts, which are in turn used as guides for active experimentation and the choice of new experience. Kolb (1984) stated that a learner could begin the learning cycle at any one of the four modes, but that learning should be carried on as a continuous spiral. As a result, knowledge is constructed through the creative tension among the four modes and learners will be exposed to all aspects of learning: experiencing, reflecting, thinking and acting.

Furthermore, there are four dominant learning styles that are associated with these modes [9]

The four learning styles are:

- Converging (AC and AE focus) - interested in practical applications of concepts and theories. A learner who has this preference is good at problem solving, decision making and practical application of ideas.
- Diverging (CE and RO focus) - interested in observation and collection of a wide range of information. A learner who is strong in this preference is imaginative and aware of meanings and values. They are interested in people and are socially inclined.
- Assimilating (AC and RO focus) - interested in presentation and creation of theoretical models. A learner leaning toward this preference is more concerned with ideas and abstract concepts than with people.
- Accommodating (CE and AE focus) - interested in hands-on experiences. A learner with this preference likes doing things; carry out plans and trial-and-error method.

Two practical suggestions came out of ELT. First, teachers and learners should "explicitly share their respective theories of learning, a process which would help personalization and adaptation of learning" [10].The second suggestion is that "there is a need to individualize instruction and Kolb believes that information technology will provide the breakthrough" in this area [10].

Our research is grounded in individualized instruction. To further Kolb's take on distinctive learning preferences and to be able to provide options on learning activities accordingly, the four modes in the learning cycle has been used to design task-level content in the Java programming course in our research design. However, it is important to note that it is not our intention to prescribe and match a learner with a particular learning preference, as every learner uses a mix of learning styles, and not just one.

2.2 Self-Regulated Learning (SRL) Theory

Self-Regulated Learning (SRL) fits in well with our learner-initiated e-learning approach because in an individualized learning environment, learners are often left to their own devices, and a flexible e-learning system can help make them aware of their own thinking, monitoring, planning and evaluating personal progress against a standard, and motivation to learn[12-16]. When learners adapt their approaches to learning, learning is said to be self-regulated[17]. Self-regulated learning (SRL) states that learners not only need to regulate their performance, but also how they learn. Literature shows that self-regulation can positively affect learners' achievement[18]. Self-regulated learning (SRL) is "an active, constructive process whereby learners set goals for their learning and then attempt to monitor, regulate, and control their cognition, motivation, and behavior" [19]. Furthermore, [20] revealed that 'ordinary' collaboration (as found in traditional online forums and chats) is insufficient to transform learners' everyday "reflection" into productive "regulation".

What sets self-regulated learners apart is their awareness of when they know a skill or fact and when they do not, at a meta knowledge level - i.e. they plan, set goals, organize, self-monitor, and self-evaluate thorough out their studies[16]. In addition, self-regulation works best when learners are provided with continual feedback concerning the effectiveness of their learning approach. This is something that an adaptive system can provide as it can support and reinforce self-monitoring techniques as well as self-regulated learning strategies. We mainly focus on this aspect of self-regulation in relation to the design of an e-learning system wherein students can receive feedback if they choose to do so.

Our model's SRL interface includes components that allow students to self-reflect along with components that engage them in self-regulation. On one hand of the spectrum, self-reflection could be as simple as a thinking process made self aware, the intangible 'ah ha' moment of a conceptual breakthrough; on the other hand, self-regulation could be more tangible as a system or a tutor can observe what students do after they self-reflect. For example, in debugging, a student can self-reflect on errors identified by the compiler at the end of each compile of the program being developed. The system can track/record the number of errors and warnings faced by the student at the end of each compile. The system can also classify the types of errors encountered by a single student over multiple sessions of program development. Looking at this list of errors is an act of self-reflection. However, self-regulation takes it one step further. The student may try to identify most common errors and warnings he/she faced, take notes on how he/she resolved these common errors and warnings, and refer to these notes when he/she encounters these common errors and warnings when writing another program. This "proactive self-reflection" is what we identified as self-regulation even thought at this stage, we are not planning on tracking the end results of using the study skill tools, it is the provision of these "how to" study skill guides and tools embedded as options for students to assist them in becoming better self-regulated, self-reflected learners that we are interested in.

3 Methodology

3.1 E-Learning Model Design Approach

The e-learning model we created is a learner-directed model. This is a model that places full learning control in the hands of the learner. The model does not automatically adapt or assign any differentiated content to the learner[21]. Simply put, the model provides multiple options to the learner where he/she can make instructional decisions based on these options. Learners can pick and choose their learning activities and paths. This approach enables personal autonomy, active involvement and engagement with the content and serves as a motivational factor for online learning. For learning styles, learners will self-select from the multiple learning content representations, so there is no need for an automated system intervention. For prior knowledge and skills, the comparisons of the pre-test and post-test results will help inform the instructor as to what to recommend and adapt in class, online or both. The post-quiz we provided for the experimental unit also provide adaptive feedback. However, the feedbacks are not prescribed, it is served more as a guide than a mandate.

3.2 Participants

Estimated 60-80 voluntary participants are currently undergoing the research study. We recruited from students who enroll in COMP 268 - Introduction to Java Programming course started July 1, 2011. The participants are adult learners in various age groups with various programming skills. This is a *100 level* (all introductory computer science courses start with the number "2" at this institution) course and there is no prerequisite. Their age will be roughly ranging from 21 - 50. The majority of the students enrolled in this course in the past are computer science majors or minors, so we would expect that they would at least have some background and basic knowledge of computer science and technical ability to comprehend the content as well as navigating the course. Students who volunteer to be participants have received a complete debriefing at the beginning of the experiment and ethics approval has been sought prior to the start of the experiment.

3.3 Research Design

The e-learning model has been developed in Moodle (an open source Learning Management System currently in use at the authors' home institution) providing alternative content for Unit 3 of the course for the experiment.

After the redesigned of the unit, unit 3 composes of five learning concepts and each concept starts with the same home page interface that present the four modes of learning. The five learning concepts are: *If-Else Statement; Loops; Break, Continue, and Return; Switch, Try-Catch-Finally, and Labels*; and *Recursion*. Figure 2 below illustrates the Unit 3 layout design for the course while Figure 3 shows the home page of each learning concepts.

Once a student access the learning concept home page, a circular wheel interface with four quadrants will be presented to them. Each quadrant is linked to a different but comparable learning activity based on Kolb's experiential learning cycle learning modes: *experiencing, reflecting, thinking* and *acting*. We have translated the modes into the following four activities: Watching (videos), Discussing (forums), Conceptualizing (visual diagrams), and Trying Out (coding). For instance, the experiencing, the learning activity is presented as a series of tutorial videos on YouTube on how to program If-Statements (see figure 4).

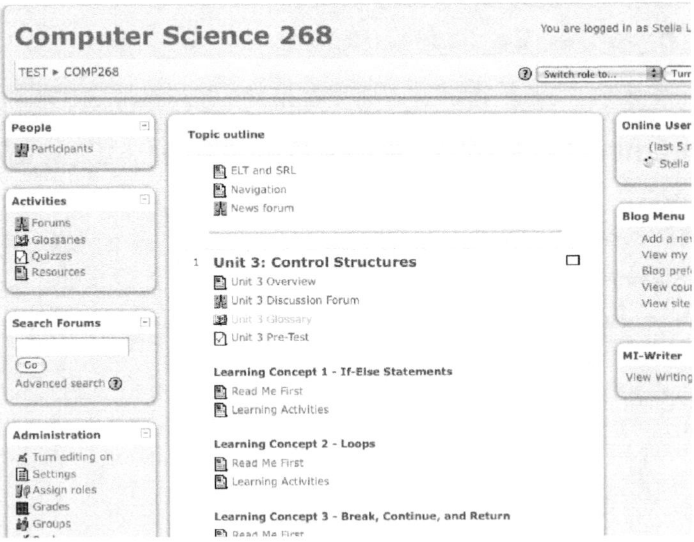

Fig. 2. Unit 3 home page as viewed by students entering into the experiment

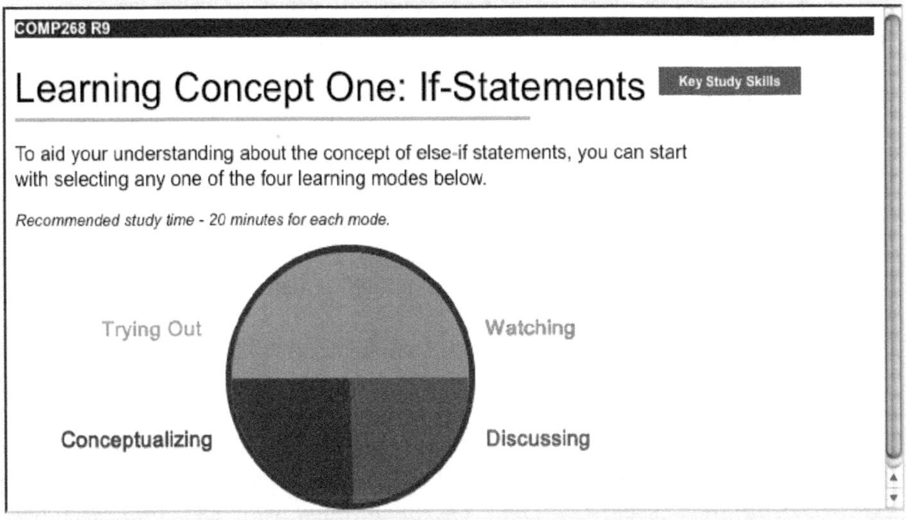

Fig. 3. Home page for learning concept 1 - If-Else Statement

A learner is free to choose any of the learning activities to begin his/her study. The system doesn't initiate or suggest any particular learning paths. According to ELT [9], a learner can begin at any stage of the learning cycle, but it is most beneficial for acquiring new knowledge if he/she would go through them all eventually to fully understand and apply this new knowledge. He/she might or might not choose to go through them all; the decision is his/her to make. If at the end of any chosen learning

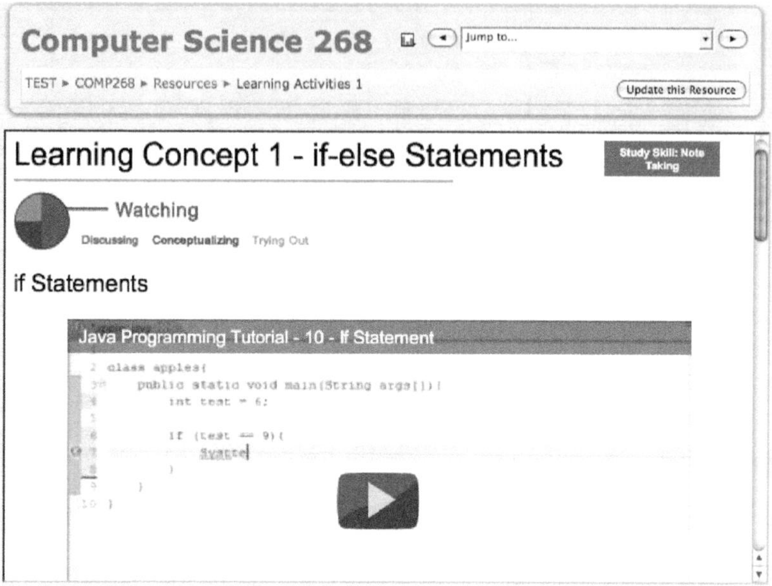

Fig. 4. YouTube tutorial videos on how to program If-Statements under the "Watching" quadrant learning activity

activity, the learner feels that he/she has a good grasp of the material, he/she can opt to skip the rest of the cycle and go to the next topic. A post-test is available at the end of the unit for learner to self-assess his/her knowledge both at the domain and meta level. In another word, learners can test how well they have learn a certain programming concepts in Java as well as whether the associated key study skills are helpful to them in regulating their own learning and deploying them as learning strategies. The post-test is a formative test and it will not affect the participants' grade in their overall course performance.

To help with self-regulation at a meta learning level based on the SRL theory, twenty study skills – five successive skills for each of the four learning modes -have been developed. These "Key Study Skills" is available on the upper right-hand corner of the webpage to assist with learning about meta knowledge. Meta knowledge in terms of key study skills for studying programming has been selected as: *note taking skill, reflection and discussion skill, conceptualization skill*, and *problem solving skill.* For example, within the "Watching" activity, the key study skill we emphases is "note taking". Learners can choose to access this supplementary material at any given time during his/her study. The design consideration is that the key study skills appear as an unobtrusive interface that sits on the upper-right-hand-corner of the main content. Learners can choose to engage and learn how the "note taking" skill helps with the "watching" activity (i.e. how to take better notes while watching a tutorial video online and what are the appropriate tool to use for note taking), or he/she can just ignore it and carry on with watching the YouTube tutorial video on its own. Figure 5 shows that the Note Taking skill is being presented with Evernote, a note-taking software. The rest of the study skills are paired with the following: Communications – Moodle discussion forum; Conceptualizing – FreeMap (mind mapping tool); and Problem Solving – BlueJ (an integrated development environment tool).

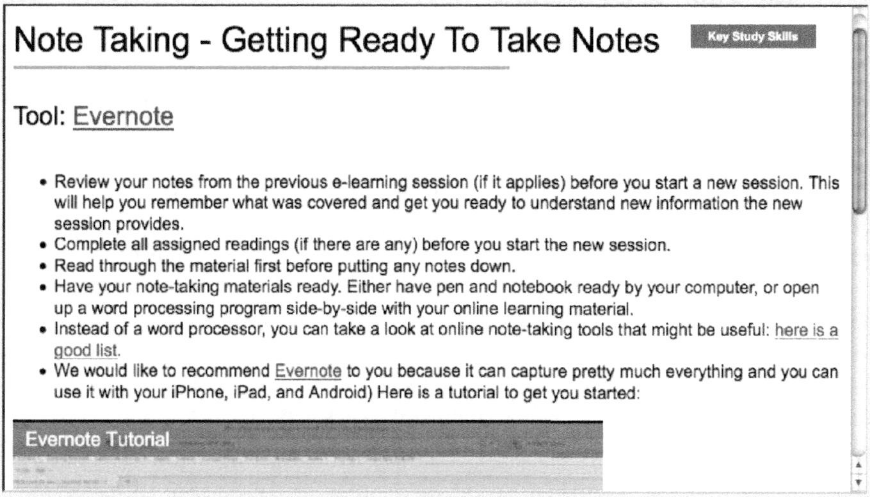

Fig. 5. One of the key study skills – Note taking skill

3.4 Measurement

One pre-test has been developed with 25 questions for domain-knowledge and 20 questions for meta-knowledge (study skills). Similar to the pre-test, one post test is available with 25 questions for domain knowledge and 20 questions for meta-knowledge (study skills). It is designed to measure the efficacy of each learning mode. Questions are generated based on the content from select mode of each learning concept. For each answer, the system will then give feedback and suggestions according to the test results, and direct the student to focus more in the learning mode in which the student is weak. The aim is to help learners to become more efficient and aware in self-monitoring their learning.

In addition, there is an end-of-unit survey and follow-up structured interviews with 6-10 participants two weeks upon the completion of the study. The survey aims to measure learner experience, usability, user satisfaction and perceived controllability of the e-learning model. At the end of the survey, we invite participants to take part in a 40-min structured interview using Adobe Connect. Participation in the interview is entirely voluntary and has no effect on their grades. The purpose of the interview is to discover more details about the learners' attitudes and impression about the experiment, and give learners a chance to elaborate on the survey results. Questions will also be geared towards whether they find the system and the options provided helpful, in both the domain specific content as well as the meta-cognitive activities, i.e., study skills. It is anticipated that the experiment will conclude by the end of this calendar year (December 2011) and will begin the data analysis phase of this research.

4 Issues and Conclusion

This paper has summarized the initial framework of the design of a self-directed e-learning model. Two learning theories - self-regulated learning theory (SRL) and experiential learning theory (ELT) serve as the instructional design structure. The next step in this research will be the continuous monitoring of the actual experiment, collecting and analyzing data. This experiment has been running since July 1, 2011 and will continue to run for six months. Undergraduate students in computer science are participating in the experiment in which we aim to examine the effect on how an adaptive system can affect learners' skills at both a domain-knowledge and metacognitive levels. Data concerning learning competency, user satisfaction, system usability, learners' experience, and perceived controllability will be collected and analyzed. As a result of this study, we hope to gain an understanding of how this learning approach and model may be of benefit to learners.

Some of the challenges and issues concerning this research project are listed as follow:

- The target course, COMP 268 - Introduction to Java Programming, is geared towards individualized, self-paced study. There are marginal collaborative activities using discussion forums but the course does not lend itself to explore task-specific collaborative activities. Hence, Co-Regulated Learning (CRL) cannot be investigated as part of this experiment and it is out of scope of this research.
- Only one unit (Unit 3) has been offered with multiple content types and students are invited to choose between the regular unit that is mostly text-based and the experimental unit that has multiple types of contents, including text-based content, for the same set of topics. Some participants may choose the experimental unit out of curiosity rather than for its projected values. The experimental unit also contains study activities outside the scope of what students normally do as part of the regular unit. Thus, participants are expected to spend a significant amount of time in the experimental unit as opposed to the regular unit, which will have a significant impact on the outcomes of the experiment.
- Different participants may have different learning styles such as kinesthetic, visual, and audio, among others. This study does not attempt to correlate learning styles with content types, even though learning style is a major variable in the selection of content types. This offers an opportunity to expand the scope of this research.
- While correlational results are targeted, if the experiment is run for longer periods of time, say 12 month to 2 years, the number of data points can be used to derive causal conclusions. Such a longitudinal experimental design offers another dimension of scope for this research.

References

1. Hadwin, F.H., Winne, P.H.: CoNoteS2: A Software Tool for Promoting Self-Regulation. Educational Research and Evaluation 7, 313–334 (2001)
2. Azevedo, R., Cromley, J.G., Seibert, D., Tron, M.: The role of co-regulated learning during students' understanding of complex systems with hypermedia. In: Annual Meeting of the American Educational Research Association, Chicago, IL (2003)
3. Brusilovsky, P.: Adaptive educational systems on the World-Wide-Web. In: Ayala, G. (ed.) Proc. of Workshop Current Trends and Applications of Artificial Intelligence in Education at 4th World Congress on Expert Systems, Mexico City, Mexico. ITESM, pp. 9–16 (1998)
4. Weber, G.: Adaptive learning systems in the World Wide Web. In: Kay, J. (ed.) 7th International Conference on User Modeling, UM 1999, Banff, Canada (1999)
5. Adisen, A., Barker, T.: Supporting the diversity of the E-learning 2.0 learners: The development of a psychological student model. In: E-Learn 2007 Conference, Quebec City, Canada (2007)
6. Barker, T., Adisen, A.: Experiments on visual and verbal skills: The development and testing of a skills profile. In: Proceedings of the European Learning Styles Information Network Conference, Univerity of Surrey, Surrey, England (2005)
7. Fischer, G.: User modeling in human-computer interaction. User Modeling and User Adapted Interaction 11, 65–86 (2001)
8. Pashler, H., McDaniel, M., Rohrer, D., Bjork, R.: Learning Styles: Concepts and Evidence. Psychological Science in the Public Interest 9, 105–119 (2008)
9. Kolb, D.: Experiential learning: Experience as the source of learning and development. Prentice-Hall, Englewood Cliffs (1984)
10. Coffield, F., Moseley, D., Hall, E., Ecclestone, K.: Learning styles and pedagogy in post-16 learning: A systematic and critical review. Learning and Skills Research Centre, London (2004)
11. Kolb, A., Kolb, D.: Learning styles and learning spaces: Enhancing experiential learning in higher education. Academy of Management Learning & Education 4 (2005)
12. Boekaerts, M., Corno, L.: Self-regulation in the classroom: A perspective on assessment and intervention. Applied Psychology: An International Review 54, 199–231 (2005)
13. Perry, N.E., Phillips, L., Hutchinson, L.R.: Preparing student teachers to support for self-regulated learning. Elementary School Journal 106, 237–254 (2006)
14. Winne, P.H., Perry, N.E.: Measuring self-regulated learning. In: Pintrich, P., Boekaerts, M., Seidner, M. (eds.) Handbook of Self-Regulation, pp. 531–566. Academic Press, Orlando (2000)
15. Butler, D.L., Winne, P.H.: Feedback and self-regulated learning: A theoretical synthesis. Review of Educational Research 65, 245–281 (1995)
16. Zimmerman, B.J.: Self-regulated learning and academic achievement: An overview. Educational Psychologist 25, 3–17 (1990)
17. Winne, P.H.: Experimenting to bootstrap self-regulated learning. Journal of Educational Psychology 89, 397–410 (1997)
18. Azevedo, R.: Using Hypermedia as a Metacognitive Tool for Enhancing Student Learning? The Role of Self-Regulated Learning. Educational Psychologist 40, 199–209 (2005)
19. Pintrich, P.R.: The role of goal orientation in self-regulated learning. In: Boekaerts, M., Pintrich, P.R., Ziedner, M. (eds.) Handbook of Self-Regulation, pp. 451–502. Academic Press, San Diego (2000)
20. Hadwin, A.F., Wozney, L., Pontin, O.: Scaffolding the appropriation of self-regulatory activity: A socio-cultural analysis of changes in teacher-student discourse about a graduate research portfolio. Instructional Science 33, 413–450 (2005)
21. Marzano, R.J.: A different kind of classroom: Teaching with dimensions of learning. Association for Supervision and Curriculum Development, Alexandria (1992)

Project Based Learning in Higher Education with ICT: Designing and Tutoring Digital Design Course at M S R I T, Bangalore

Satyadhyan Chickerur* and M. Aswatha Kumar

Department of Information Science and Engineering,
M S Ramaiah Institute of Technology, Bengaluru, India
{chickerursr,maswatha}@gmail.com

Abstract. This paper presents an approach to develop digital design curricula using modified Bloom's Taxonomy for making it more appealing to the students. The proposed approach uses the *Project Based Learning* strategy for increasing the attractiveness of the course. The case study also explores the use of ICT for effective teaching and learning. The developed curriculum has been evaluated successfully for the last three academic years. The students have shown increased interest in the digital design course, have acquired new skills and obtained good academic results. An important observation during the conduction of the course was that all the students have developed innovative digital systems, exhibited team work and have made a poster presentation during their second year of engineering undergraduate course.

Keywords: Project Based Learning, Modified Bloom's Taxonomy, Outcome Based Education, ICT4education, Information and Communication Technology.

1 Introduction

In the present day digital age, where every sphere of life is getting dominated by digital gadgets and digital systems, the digital design curricula in engineering education must focus not only on theoretical basis and lab experiments. The focus rather should be more on how this theoretical aspects and experiments can aid students to have a firm grounding for developing whole systems, involving multidisciplinary knowledge, for solving real life problems[1]; thus giving students a holistic approach of digital design course in real sense can be termed as outcome based education. This practical skill of solving real life problem is what many industries and companies look for in their new recruits during the recruitment process. In this context,project based learning PBL[2] appears as one of the most interesting instructional strategies. PBL encourages the students to become autonomous learners, to appreciate others point of view and become critical thinkers, develop team working skills, thus ensuring enhanced

* Corresponding author.

T.-h. Kim et al. (Eds.): ASEA/DRBC/EL 2011, CCIS 257, pp. 590–597, 2011.

learning and engaging students to solve real world tasks. PBL is student centric where students are organized in groups and instructors are facilitators ensuring that the course objectives are met. This approach not only helps develop the technical and intellectual capabilities of the students but also practical skills as follows:

a) *Library research for gathering information:* The students need to gather information for generating the requirements specification and need to design projects from incomplete or imprecise information available with each of the group students. The students as a collective group need to come with the design of the project which technically would be able to solve the real life problem the group is addressing.
b) *Data analysis and representation:*The students during the course of the project need to analyze the data and get to know the methods and means to represent the problem and solution in a correct manner.
c) *Written and oral communication skills:* The students during the duration of the projects will learn the way the project life cycle evolves. They learn the skills of preparing various reports and presentations from their peers during presentation and brain storming.
d) *Team work skills:* Team work plays a very important role in deciding the final output submission by the group. The students will learn to work in team, delegation of the work and coordination among themselves.
e) *Ethics:* Academic honesty and ethics involving referencing the work of others and abstaining from plagiarism will inculcate professional ethics in the students.
f) *Entrepreneurship:* Since the projects will generally involve survey for deciding the real life projects, which will include cost budget analysis, market survey, feasibility study etc, students will learn initial skills needed for exploring the domain of entrepreneurship.
g) *Reinforcing concepts by application:*The implementation of the project will reinforce the concepts studied during the duration of the course.
h) *Cross-cultural understanding:* Generally the students group will have members from varied background and countries cross cultural understanding gets developed which will increase the global outlook of the students.

Modified Bloom's taxonomy has proved to be successful in designing outcome based education and has been successful in assisting educational practices and teaching learning process. Assessment of learning outcomes for digital design course can be improved through proper application of the taxonomy. The modified Bloom's taxonomy for engineering courses is as shown in Fig.1. From the figure it is evident that the course design should start from a phase which revolves around remembering and ends up at a stage where students should be able to create a solution for a problem, using all the knowledge and information gathered during attending the course.

In the proposed approach, modified Blooms taxonomy [3][4] along with PBL has been used to guide the development of the digital design curricula. An complete view of the Digital Design Curriculum is presented with evaluation over

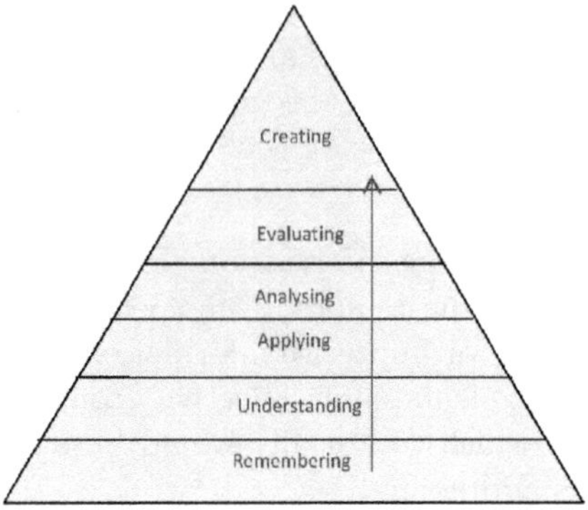

Fig. 1. Modified Bloom's Taxonomy for Engineering Education

three consecutive academic years.The paper is organized as follows: Section 2 details the method used and the design of curriculum structure. Section 3 discusses the evaluation results, and finally Section 4 summarizes the conclusions.

2 Applying Modified Bloom's Taxonomy for Digital Design Curricula

The course delivery was spread over a 14 week period and consisted of four hours per week contact time with the instructor and at least two hours per week independent work. The learning environment during the course delivery was such that the students could feel free to ask questions and consult instructor on any issue. This was made more informal by the way of using forums and discussion board using the ICT based Modular Object Oriented Developmental Learning Environment(*Moodle*). The initial session with the students centered around explaining the teaching philosophy of the course, the course objectives, concept of project based learning and motivational aspects of team working and learning. The curricula designed was delivered after the following steps were completed.

2.1 Grouping the Students as Teams

All the students were given a psychometric questionnaire designed using Myers-Briggs Type Indicator (*MBTI*) assessment to measure psychological preferences of their approach to making decisions. The results of this test [5] categorized each student into one of the 16 types. The students are grouped into groups of three or maximum four. Each group was allocated a faculty mentor who acted as a facilitator during the entire course of the project.

2.2 Weekly Status Reports and Presentation

All the groups where supposed to submit a weekly status report endorsed by the faculty coordinator, for the duration of the course. The format of the weekly status report to be submitted by the groups is as shown in Fig.2.

Format of the weekly status report

Project Status Report for Week Ending:

Project Name:

Faculty Incharge: **Team Members:**

Weekly Project Summary:

Enter a very brief summary of the project status, noting any key issues for the week. Comment on major deliverables completed, milestones reached and percent complete. Is project on time?

Example: Team started producing detailed design documents. Resources from the XYZ team will be available to match.

Key Milestones: *Should refer to major deliverables from WBS and Milestone Chart.*

ID	Title [Description]	Original planned completion date (this date should not change) [dd-mmm-yy]	Current forecast completion date [dd-mmm-yy]	Actual completion date [dd-mmm-yy]
1				
2				

Key Accomplishments:

Provide a brief list of key accomplishments for the past week. This could be in the form of a bulleted list.

Top Priorities for the coming week (2-6 items):

Priority #	Description	Individual responsible

Top 5 Risks for this Period

List the current high-risk issues, and identify them as type. Quality, Schedule, or Cost.

Risk ID	Risk Type	Description	Probability (L/M/H)	Impact (L/M/H)

M.S.Ramaiah Institute of Technology, Bangalore - 560054

Fig. 2. Weekly Status Report Format

The whole course was designed using the modified Bloom's taxonomy. We now look at each level of taxonomy and demonstrate suitable examples.

2.3 Remembering Level

At this level the students ability to recall concepts that they have learnt in the class and previous courses is evaluated. Below are some sample questions that fall under this level:

- List the household items which run with AC signals and digital signals.
- Name as many different types of equipment which run on AC and DC.
- Write down all the familiar digital waveforms.

2.4 Understanding Level

At this level the students ability to understand and restate or describe a concept in his own words is tested using various questions. Samples under this level are:

- Exemplify how memory elements are used to store digital information on hard disk drives.
- Explain the methods used to simplify Boolean expressions.
- Explain the difference between the sequential circuits and combinational circuits.

2.5 Applying Level

At this level the students skills in using the theories learnt to solve new problems is judged. Samples under this level are:

- Carry out experiments that demonstrate relationship between a Boolean function and implementing a counter using flip-flops.
- Implement combinational logic circuits using NAND gates, XOR gates.
- Implement Code converters using universal gates.

2.6 Analysing Level

At this level the students ability to separate a whole into various component parts is judged. Samples under this level are:

- Compare the present day scenario with the scenario a decade back; and attribute reasons how digital design has changed it.
- Integrate the various logic components to build a digital Voltmeter.
- Structure the design flow that the designer experiences when designing, implementing, and testing a digital circuit.

2.7 Evaluating Level

At this level the students ability to judge, critic and decide on value of ideas and materials is checked. Some sample questions under this level are:

- What criteria would you set up to evaluate the logic families?
- How would you use these criteria to select the components for designing a traffic light simulation?
- Test the design of the system by arriving at the design using various design methods ;(for ex use basic Boolean laws, POS, SOP, Tabular method).

2.8 Creating Level

At this level the students ability to create some solution to a real life problem is judged. Some sample questions under this level are:

- Construct an electronic game of handball using shift registers and other components.
- Use IC timer units to produce clock pulses at a given frequency.
- Devise a digital logic based solution for a real life problem which you encounter.

3 Evaluation

Every month the students were given opportunity to present their work in front of the instructors and peers. This was also some kind of brain storming where students discussed about the pros and cons of their approaches and methodology. The evaluation was carried out using various approaches described below.

3.1 Continuous Evaluation model

The course was designed keeping in mind the traditional model of evaluation and a mix of project based learning so that the students felt it easy to adapt. The course had a semester end exams where they were evaluated for 50 marks.The other 50 marks were given to students based on tests(25 marks) and projects(25 marks).

3.2 Final Demonstration and Poster Presentation

One of the components where students were evaluated was in the front of other faculty and students during the Final demonstration and poster presentation. Some snapshots of the students presenting their work is shown in Fig.3 and Fig.4

Fig. 3. Students presenting during their Final Demonstration

3.3 Feedback:

The students were free to give feedbacks to the instructors thorough various communications channels. One of the important medium was the use of forums and discussion board on Moodle. The other was Email exchanges between instructor and students. Apart from this the oral discussion with the peers and instructor was also useful. Analysis of various feedback questions and some sample results are shown in Fig 5.

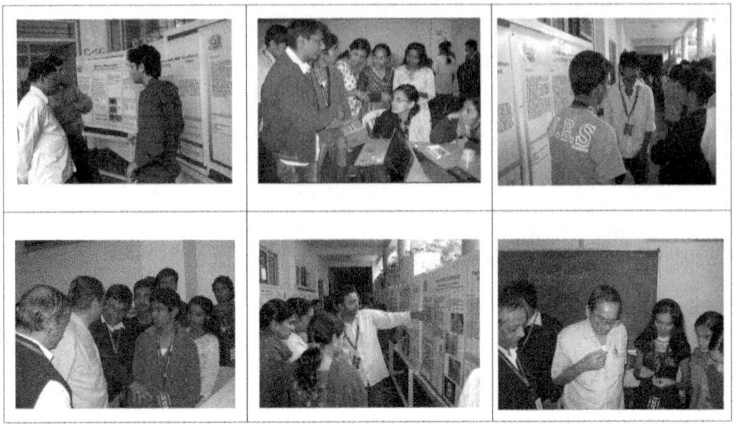

Fig. 4. Students presenting their Poster

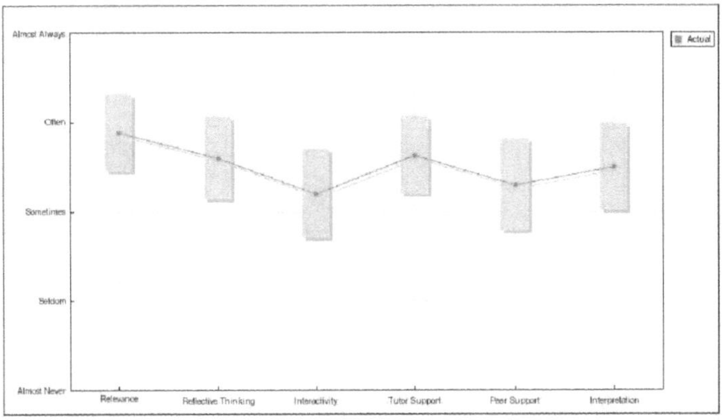

Fig. 5. Analysis of the feedback for various questions

4 Conclusions

During the of delivery of this course since last three years, it was felt and observed that the students have appreciated this attempt and model of teaching and learning. Lot of feedbacks have been received from the instructor which point to the advantages of the proposed approach. Some drawback's when multiple instructors are handling the course have been observed. This analysis is under process and a modified approach is under preparation.

Acknowledgments. The authors would like to acknowledge the support from the workshop of Professor Alice M. Agogino on Project Based learning at IUCEE 2008. The authors would also like to thank the Instructors at Faculty of Department of Information Science and Engineering,i.e N Ramesh, George Philip C,

Mohana Kumar S and Sandeep B L for taking part in this effort. The authors appreciate the advice and encouragement given by Dr K Rajanikanth, Advisor(Academic and Research), MSRIT during implementation of this approach.

References

1. Eide, A.R., Johnson, R.D., Mashaw, L.H., Northup, L.L.: Engineering Fundamentals and Problem Solving, 4th edn. McGraw-Hill (2002)
2. Solomon, G.: Project-Based learning: A Primer. Technol. Learn. 23(6), 20–30 (2003)
3. Anderson, L., Krathwohl, D.: A Taxonomy for Learning, Teaching, and Assessing: A Revision of Bloom's Taxonomy of Educational Objectives. Addison Wesley (2002)
4. Yadin, A.: Implementation of Bloom's Taxonomy on Systems Analysis Workshops. In: Proceedings of the AIS SIG-ED IAIM 2007 Conference (2007)
5. Jung Typology Test, http://www.humanmetrics.com/cgi-win/JTypes2.asp

A Case Study on Improvement of Student Evaluation of University Teaching

Sung-Hyun Cha[1] and Kum-Tack Seo[2]

[1] Korean Educational Development Institute, Baumoe 1Rd 35, Seocho-gu, Seoul 137-791 Korea
[2] WooSuk University, 443 Samnye-ro, Samnye-eup, Wnaju-Gun, Jeollabuk-do 565-701 Korea

Abstract. The study is to bring up the current issues on student evaluation of university teaching and to find a way to improve the evaluation. For this, the survey was conducted with a sample of 1,690 students and 24 professors were interviewed from W university. The results are as follows. Most of students and instructors agreed to the necessity of the course evaluation and revelation of the evaluation results. However, the evaluation method and the use of the evaluation results are recognized as problematic. Findings suggest that development of valid evaluation instruments, provision of full information related to course evaluation and the active use of evaluation results by establishing a supporting and management system.

Keywords: university teaching evaluation, course satisfaction.

1 Introduction

The paradigm of higher education reform has changed recently and quickly from teacher-centered to student-centered, weighting on teaching competency that are inseparable from research. Many universities in Korea have designed and implemented a variety of student course evaluation policy for improvement of quality of teaching despite the following concerns.

First of all, students are not mature enough to evaluate their instructors ' lectures. Second, instructors are unlikely to admit the fact that they are judged even from immature students under the Confucian tradition. Third, both students and instructors should be fully informed of the purpose and methods of evaluation, share with them, and further students need to be trained to be elaborated evaluators [1]. Indeed, Mckeachie(1997) suggested a solid qualitative study revealing how the students felt when they evaluate their instructors and classes, which would be of use to the development of teaching evaluation tools [2].

A current method based on students' rating on the courses they take is subject to be problematic. The first step to improve the current course evaluation is to examine how key participants, i.e., students and instructors perceive this evaluation policy and what they recognize to be problematic in the process of evaluation. To delve into such

T.-h. Kim et al. (Eds.): ASEA/DRBC/EL 2011, CCIS 257, pp. 598–603, 2011.

things, this study carried out a survey targeting students and instructors in W university in Korea.

2 Research Method

2.1 Sample

A sample of the study is a total of 1,690 students from 54 departments in W university in J province. In May 2011, three thousands of survey questionnaires were distributed to the departments, collected for one month, and finally 1,690 completed survey questionnaires returned. A total of 24 instructors were selected randomly from 6 colleges for face-to face interviews and interviews lasted for about 2 months.

Table 1. Characteristics of a Sampled Students and Instructors

Classification			Frequency (%)	Total (%)
Student	Gender	Male	837(49.5)	1,690(100)
		Female	853(50.5)	
	College	College of science and technology	246(14.6)	1,690(100)
		College of food science	76(4.5)	
		College of physical education science	85(5.0)	
		College of education	87(5.1)	
		College of pharmacy	80(4.7)	
		College of oriental medicine	109(6.4)	
		College of health and welfare	613(36.3)	
		College of culture and society	394(23.3)	
	Grade (prior Semester)	Above 95	121(7.2)	1,690(100)
		90~94	388(23.0)	
		85~89	438(25.9)	
		80~84	204(12.1)	
		75~79	88(5.2)	
		70~74	51(3.0)	
		65~69	30(1.8)	
		Below 65	41(2.4)	
		Freshmen	329(19.5)	
Instructor	College	College of science and technology	4(16.5)	24(100)
		College of culture and society	5(21.0)	
		College of health and welfare	4(16.5)	
		College of education	5(21.0)	
		College of oriental medicine	3(12.5)	
		College of liberal arts	3(12.5)	
	Position	Full-time instructor	3(12.5)	24(100)
		Assistant professor	4(16.5)	
		Associate professor	4(16.5)	
		Professor	13(54.5)	

As illustrated in Table 1, Among the 1,690 students, half of the students are female (50.5%) and the majority of students (68.2%) obtained more than 80 points out of a possible 100 points in their grades prior semester. About 60% students are from College of health and welfare and College of culture and society. Among the 24 instructors, 13 (or about 55%) are professors.

2.2 Survey Instrument

The survey questionnaires consist of 9 domains with 15 questions, excluding items asking respondents' background (See Table 2). Reliability (Cronbach α) of the Likert scale items is .633.

Table 2. A Summary of Survey Items

Domain	Items	Scale
Necessity	• Do you think the course evaluation is necessary?	Yes-No
Objectivity	• Do you think the university is operating the course evaluation properly? • Did you evaluate the lecture sincerely based on objective facts?	Yes-No 5 Likert
Lecture Improvement	• How much do you think the contents and teaching skills of the evaluated class have improved after the course evaluation?	5 Likert
Factors affecting evaluation	• Lecture style • Experiments or practices • Size of lecture • Required or elective course • Course for major	5 Likert
Release scores	• Do you think the course evaluation score should be open? • How much do you think the course evaluation score should be revealed?	Yes-No Multiple
Participating reasons	• What makes you participate in the course evaluation?	Multiple
	• What do you think is the biggest problem in the current course evaluation?	Multiple
Demand	• Choose one that is the most urgent thing to improve the course evaluation	Multiple
Utility	• Which do you think is the most appropriate use of the evaluation outcome?	Multiple

2.3 Data analysis

A descriptive statistical analysis with the survey data of students was performed to see how students perceive each question in general. The data from the interview with instructors was transcribed and categorized by the key words, considering the domain of the survey questionnaires.

3 Result

3.1 Survey Result of Student Perception of the Course Evaluation

Regarding necessity and proper operation of the course evaluation, about 83% of the students answered "yes", but 54% of the students answered "no" as showed in Table 3. When asked if the students evaluate the course in an objective way, about 83% answered positively, however about 36% responded negatively about the degree of improvement of the class through the course evaluation. Although there is a little difference, the students are affected by the instructional materials, type of main instruction (i.e., experiments or practices), and class size.

In the meanwhile, about 63% of the students responded positively when asked whether the result of course evaluation is open. In addition, half of the students participated in the evaluation because they expect the improvement of the class by providing useful information of the lecture. With regard to the biggest problem that the students recognized, about 30% of the students pointed that "the indifference of students" and about 22% did "unrevealed course evaluation result", which is the most responses.

Table 3. Result of Student Perception by Items

Questions		Frequency (%)	Total (%)
Do you think the course evaluation is necessary?	Yes	1,410(83.4)	1,690 (100)
	No	280(16.6)	
Do you think the university is operating the evaluation properly?	Yes	769(45.5)	1,690 (100)
	No	921(54.5)	
Did you evaluate the lecture sincerely based on objective facts?	Not very much	101(6.0)	1,690 (100)
	Not much	185(10.9)	
	Somewhat	574(34.0)	
	A little	338(20.0)	
	Very much	492(29.1)	
How much do you think the contents and teaching skills of the evaluated class have improved after the course evaluation?	Not very much	271(16.0)	1,690 (100)
	Not much	345(20.4)	
	Somewhat	825(48.8)	
	A little	182(10.8)	
	Very much	67(4.0)	
How much do you think your evaluation is affected by teaching materials (ppt, hand-outs)?	Not very much	108(6.4)	1,690 (100)
	Not much	175(10.4)	
	Somewhat	653(38.6)	
	A little	546(32.3)	
	Very much	208(12.3)	
How much do you think your evaluation is affected by ways of the delivery (experiments or practices)?	Not very much	92(5.4)	1,690 (100)
	Not much	203(12.0)	
	Somewhat	738(43.7)	
	A little	475(28.1)	
	Very much	182(10.8)	
How much do you think your evaluation is affected by the class size?	Not very much	119(7.1)	1,690 (100)
	Not much	234(13.8)	
	Somewhat	780(46.2)	
	A little	392(23.2)	
	Very much	165(9.8)	
How much do you think your evaluation is affected by whether the course is required or elective?	Not very much	115(6.8)	1,690 (100)
	Not much	202(12.0)	
	Somewhat	764(45.2)	
	A little	445(26.3)	
	Very much	164(9.7)	
How much do you think your evaluation is affected by whether the course is liberal arts or for major?	Not very much	121(7.2)	1,690 (100)
	Not much	185(10.9)	
	Somewhat	708(41.9)	
	A little	464(27.5)	
	Very much	212(12.5)	
Do you think the course evaluation score should be revealed?	Yes	1078(63.8)	1,690 (100)
	No	612(36.2)	
How much do you think the course evaluation score of instructors is revealed?	Every single subjects	611(56.7)	1,078 (100)
	Top 10%	184(17.0)	
	Bottom 10%	57(5.3)	
	Top 10% and bottom 10%	226(21.0)	
What makes you participate in the course evaluation?	For improvement of instruction	846(50.1)	1,690 (100)
	To give my opinions to instructors	844(49.9)	
What do you think is the biggest problem in the current course evaluation?	unrevealed course evaluation score	377(22.3)	1,690 (100)
	Invalid survey questions	282(16.7)	
	Indifference of students	506(29.9)	
	Indifference of professors	245(14.5)	
	Lack of administrative support	280(16.6)	
Choose one that is the most urgent thing to improve the course evaluation	Reveal evaluation score	419(24.8)	1,690 (100)
	Improve evaluation survey questions	298(17.6)	
	Obligatory reflect opinions on the evaluation	570(33.7)	
	Promote the course evaluation	229(13.6)	
	Extend incentive to the excellent instructors	174(10.3)	
Which do you think is the most appropriate use of the course evaluation outcome?	Open the evaluation score of the instructor's subject	527(31.2)	1,690 (100)
	Open the average score of the GPA of the subject	381(22.5)	
	Consider the result of evaluation in the process of instructors' performance evaluation	477(28.2)	
	Make instructors below average evaluation scores take some courses related teaching methods	305(18.0)	

When asked what the most urgent things to be done for the improvement of the course evaluation, about 34% of the student responded that their opinions on should be reflected on the next course evaluation and about 25% said that the result of the evaluation should be revealed. Additionally, for the uses of the course evaluation outcome, the largest number of the students said that the course evaluation result needs to be open to the students so that they would be advised in choosing better classes (31%) and followed by reflection of the course evaluation result on the instructors' performance evaluation (28%).

The open-ended question of reasons why the course evaluation is not properly running, overall students pointed out "inadequate system of the course evaluation operation" as a main reason and further students pointed out that the evaluation system needs to include "easy access of the evaluation result", "assurance of confidential evaluation," and "active promotion of the course evaluation policy" for the more participation.

3.2 Interview Result of Instructor Perception of Course Evaluation

Similar to the students' response above, overall instructors answered the course evaluation results including specific class scores should be revealed for the course improvement. However, they responded negatively that the resulted would be used as a stick (e.g., cutting wages), not a carrot for the betterment of the course, saying concerns on revelation of the evaluation results;

> If the evaluation results are revealed by individual instructors, the lectures will go in a way to get popularity from students. Instructors are more likely to avoid difficult parts of the subjects or even passing it to part-time lecturers who are not obliged to be evaluated. In addition, instructors are less likely to do collaborative teaching due to the revelation of the results (Interview with a full-time instructor).

The large number of instructors also pointed out the limited evaluation instrument that mainly depends on the student survey as one of the biggest problem of the current evaluation. Particularly, instructors mentioned the following things

- A small number of open-end questions that will provide more useful information for the improvement of the course
- Survey items that mainly consist of questions asking the present, not future (e.g., long-term effect of student's future)
- Invalid survey items that does not consider characteristics of particular subjects or courses; for example, the adequacy of the load of homework

In addition, instructors suggest the following for the better course evaluation policy and the resulting improvement of the course. First, the course evaluation needs to be performed at not only individual instructor level but also at the program-, department-, and college-level. Second, the full information of the course evaluation should be provided with individual instructors, including content, procedure, and the specific result. Third, a support and management system for the course evaluation should be established within the university, handling planning, operating, supporting, promoting, reporting.

4 Conclusion

Considering not much literature on the course evaluation in Korea, the study investigated how students and instructors perceive the course evaluation at W university, employing survey and interview methods. Overall, the research results show that most of the students and instructors all agreed with the necessity of the course evaluation and the revelation of the evaluation result. At the same time, however, they pointed out that the evaluation method and the use of the evaluation result; especially, the survey instrument of the course evaluation is invalid and the evaluation result that are not much used for the improvement of the university teaching. In addition, the study found that students' evaluation is affected by instructional materials, class style, and size of class. For more effective course evaluation, we suggest that development of valid evaluation instruments, active promotion of the course evaluation policy, and more use of evaluation results through a supporting and management are necessary. Future studies need to investigate more and deeper various factors affecting students' course evaluation.

References

1. Moon, K.B.: Problems and improvements of course evaluations -in view of mathematics education-. Korea Society of Mathematical Education Proceedings 45, 59–71 (2010)
2. McKeachie, W.J.: Student ratings: The validity of use. American Psychologist 52(11), 1218–1225 (1997)

An Inquiry into the Learning Principles Based on the Objectives of Self-directed Learning

Gi-Wang Shin

Korean Educational Development Institute (KEDI)
The Korean Federation of Teachers Association Building,
142 Woomyeon-dong, Seocho-gu, Seoul, Korea
gwshin@kedi.re.kr

Abstract. Self-directed learning has been utilized as a method used to increase class participation rates of students in education plans and has been advocated as a target of school education in order to cultivate the 'self-directed student'. It is not apparent whether it is the advancement of self-directed learning competency that is the objective, or whether it is merely to be utilized as a method to help accomplish certain study objectives. self-directed learning requires differentiating between self-directed learning that seeks to better understand the characteristics and principles of a course of education and self-directed learning that aims to elevate self-directed learning competency depending on the objectives being pursued. These two forms of objectives in self-directed learning are executed using different learning systems and methods. In order to execute both self-directed learning and to evaluate self-directed learning competency in schools, a close investigation needs to begin into whether these two different objectives are able to co-exist with one another or not.

Keywords: Self-directed learning, Self-directedness, Autonomy.

1 Introduction

Self-directed learning first entered public discourse in the realm of adult education beginning in the late 1960's and has now expanded to cover even children's education. It has been utilized as a method used to increase class participation rates of students in education plans and has been advocated as a target of school education in order to cultivate the 'self-directed student'. Within Korean 2011 high-school entrance examination 'Self-directed learning competency' was emphasized as an important provision of evaluation. In international foreign language high schools as well as other special and autonomous private schools, there has been an attempt to evaluate self-directed learning competency as evidenced through the self-directed learning form that includes English competency records and attendance records in the first stage while the second stage reviews the self-directed learning plan of a student, volunteer activities, and reading as presented in grade books and study plans (Park. H.J., 2001).

What is missing in this current trend of thought is that advancing self-directed learning stems from its unclear objectives. It is not apparent whether it is the

T.-h. Kim et al. (Eds.): ASEA/DRBC/EL 2011, CCIS 257, pp. 604–612, 2011.

advancement of self-directed learning competency that is the objective, or whether it is merely to be utilized as a method to help accomplish certain study objectives. Before any evaluation of self-directed learning can be undertaken, it is imperative to first clarify the objective it is pursuing. Candy (1991) stated that self-directed learning is at once both an objective of study and a course of study. This would literally imply that any learning undertaken by an individual would fall under this vague notion of self directed study. Ultimately, any unfounded method could then be perpetrated under the guise of 'self-directed learning'.

Researchers have been debating and interpreting 'self-directed learning' by utilizing various disparate meanings that have arisen due to the conceptual discrepancy regarding the term itself. self-directed learning can be seen as an organizational method, as characteristic of particular learners, as an individual quality, and as a strategy for increasing the learner's self-directed competency among other notions that all fall into the conceptual framework of this single term.

Only when the objective of self-directed learning is clarified will it become apparent how to evaluate self-directed learning competency: whether it is something that can be enhanced through education or whether it is utilized as a special method of instruction for those with self-directed learning competency is what needs to be clarified.

From here, through investigation into the objective of self-directed learning and related study principles, this report endeavors to elucidate what practical designs and strategies regarding self-directed learning may serve to best contribute towards materializing the objective of self-directed learning.

2 The Relationship between Self-direction and Learning Objectives

Self-directed learning 's point of view in respect to the learners is not as a passive participant in the learning activities but rather as an independent participant within learning activity The point of divergence concerning a learner's autonomy and self-directedness stems from the postulate regarding both human and ego concepts rooted in humanistic psychology[1].

The debate regarding human autonomy for the most part has been one of philosophical and political definition. Such definitions regarding the existence of human autonomy presuppose freedom from internal and external restrictions and emerge through the consistent individual values and beliefs in one's life. However, as the individual is but a part of the overarching social community and thus being subjected to the rule of language, standards, and normative behavior, it becomes nearly impossible to maintain one's individual autonomy completely. Moreover as autonomy differs regarding the interaction between individual and situational variables, any actualization into one current conceptual stream is unable to occur making any judgments of individual autonomy impossible as well(Candy, 1991).

The autonomy that arises from self-directed learning can be seen in the same vein as the self-directedness that arises from learning. As opposed to universal human

---

[1] In humanistic theory man is acknowledged as a trustworthy subject. This refers to the fact that man is good, autonomous, and possesses the unlimited latent potential for growing and desiring realization of the ego. (Hiemstra & Brockett, 1991).

autonomy, the autonomy arising out of self-directed learning denotes autonomous study that is performed in learning activities by active learners and is apparent while one is participating in active study. The autonomy arising from self-directed learning is treated as being conceptually analogous with self-directedness; however, from the perspective of a learning strategy, autonomy is merely one part of self-directedness. Self-directedness denotes the Learner Control of organizational study, ability governing learning objectives and necessary resources, as well as the autonomy of learning (Candy, 1991).

Self-directedness affects the subject and learning objectives matched to each learner. Learning objectives seek to discover what should be studied at the beginning course of learning. self-directed learning can only commence once all necessary components required to aid study and proper learning objectives are established. The establishment of learning objectives may be divided into two study objectives: one is to accomplish the objectives of subjects and projects provided in a systematic and organized school learning environment and the other is to elevate self-directed learning competency that may be useful in an unstructured and systematically unregulated education environment. These two forms of self-directed learning objectives share a deep relationship with the concept of a learner's self-directedness.

In an organized and systematically controlled school education, specific activity objectives are determined and proposed under concrete education objectives. Subjects of study in systemized and organized school education consist of material deemed necessary by providers and learning objectives need to maintain a thorough understanding of the characteristics inherent in the various subjects. The objective of learning in systematically controlled schools is generally defined as study designed to increase the results of learning. Some examples are knowledge accumulation, memorization, other types of mastering activities, abstraction of definitions, and interpretations for realistic understanding.

It follows that according to the education objectives demanded on top of education objectives, the self-directedness of learners in their attendant study will also differ based on one's current level of study as well as the given learning objectives coupled together with its own individual meaning. Self-directedness results in autonomous selection regarding the methods of study and self-directed learning competency in the individual is something that is possessed from the beginning of one's current starting point of study. The self-directedness of the learner constitutes one object of consideration in the course of teaching and is one of the specific characteristics demanded by the learner in the various stages that study progresses upon. As opposed to something that can be intentionally developed through study, self-directedness should be regarded as something that accumulates secondarily within a course of study.

On the other hand, those subjects of learning in unstructured and systematically unregulated education are more individually based and the learners themselves decide upon learning objectives. This type of study falls into a category denoting private and individual study which does not require supervision or approval from others. The subject of study is contained within one's own study aims and will appear as the natural result of pursuing more knowledge or different interests. Therefore, at the initial outset of study, a learning objective or learning objectives may be unclear; however, through the gradual elaboration of itself or through a reformulation of the learning objectives, it should become more readily apparent (Spear, 1988). A learner's self-directedness is one characteristic of an individual learner; however, it is not something that is fixed, but rather developed during a course of study in addition to being an objective in an overall course of education. Study denotes a process in which a learner sees experiences and accepts the world, and is also something that should give rise to qualitative change. The results of study are not found solely in knowledge accumulation but in discovering real meaning; not in how much one studies, but what one has studied and the meaning of that study.

3 Learning Principles Based on Self-directed Learning Objectives

Self-directed learning can be carried out based on two different points of view. First, focusing on self-directedness that can be discovered amongst adult characteristics, there is the perspective that what self-directedness is can be clarified and elevated. The second perspective searches for methods of study that are learner led as a means to overcome learning methods centered upon teachers in an organized and systematized education system.

These two perspectives of self-directed learning present two forms of self-directed learning: one is to aim to better understand principles and characteristics in a course of education, while the other is to aim to elevate self-directed learning competency itself.

From here, a closer look will be given to the divisions inherent within the two different forms of self-directed learning objectives: class of knowledge, focal point of study, special characteristics of learners, and teacher strategy.

3.1 Scope of Knowledge

Hitherto positivist perspectives have dominated knowledge. Knowledge is something to be ascertained through observation and experimentation and meant to be independent, objective and stockpiled as positively verified facts. Conversely, from the life-long education perspective, any form of experience is regarded as knowledge. The perception of knowledge from a life-long education perspective is like a constructivist view of knowledge that organizes thought and meaning on the basis of experience

In self-directed learning, the class of knowledge is applied differently according to what the objectives are. self-directed learning whose aim is to better understand the special characteristics and principles of a course of study falls into the rational and objective class of knowledge. On the other hand, the class of knowledge in self-directed learning whose objective is to elevate the learner's self-directed learning competency employs a relatively broader definition which not only includes organized knowledge, designed and planned knowledge, but also humanist beliefs, value systems and attitudes as well.

3.2 The Focal Point of Learning

The learning in the self-directed learning is a relatively broad conception of learning that moves beyond simply knowing more and refers to knowledge, abilities, emotions, attitudes, motivation, social behaviors, and even character changes. The concept of learning contains both knowledge accumulation and behavioral changes, but depending on which part is emphasized the focal point of learning changes.

In self-directed learning that maintains an objective to better understand the special characteristics and principles of a course of study, emphasis is usually then placed on planned and structured processes that serve to develop knowledge and skills. The focal point of self-directed learning is provided by specifying methods that lead to students' voluntary study behavior in order to achieve the learning objectives presented by a clear structure. self-directed learning is carried out based on an organic reciprocal interaction between self-fulfillment and self-accomplishments on the basis of self-perception and self-monitoring (Zimmerman, 2000). From here, the meaning of self-directed learning presents the problem regarding what method educators use to provide learners with knowledge as well as the fact that self-study itself does not rely on any material from a curriculum to educate or help the student learn. On the basis of constructivist learning theory, it materializes methods for student's participation in spontaneous study activity and emphasizes student's autonomy.

self-directed learning that maintains an objective to elevate self-directed learning competency places more emphasis on internal change in learners. This process depends on a learner's internal motivation and aims to bring about internal change as well. This is founded upon changing learning that emphasizes a learner's internal meaning and change and also lays emphasis upon a learner's self-directedness. Learning is not formed by the isolated connections that form one's life or by social or cultural currents. On the contrary, learning is handled within the current of a student's life. Learning in a situation lacking planned or structured processes is possible where self-directed learning competency or a learner's internal conscious change is emphasized.

3.3 Special Characteristics of Learners

According to self-directed learning theory, it is emphasized that from even the most dependent juveniles and young children all the way to the other side of the spectrum with the most independent and autonomous adults all possess self-directedness. While adults characteristically are seen as exhibiting self-directedness and children's ego conceptions are viewed as being dependent, the current trend is that of viewing self-directedness not as something that distinguishes adults from children, but rather as an essential universal human characteristic.

Guglielmino (1977) listed 8 elements he observed in individuals possessing skills or attitudes related with self-directed learning [2]. Oddi (1985) attempted to examine continuing and ongoing individual characteristics during a course of study by means of various study methods over the course of his life. However, while it was significant that the research identified characteristics of self-directed learners since it indicated the ideal appearance that self-directed learning needs to aim for, there was

---

[2] Eight elements of self-directed learning: 1) Self concept as an effective learner 2) Openness to learning opportunities 3) Initiative and independence in learning 4) Acceptance of responsibility for one's own learning 5) Love of learning 6) Creativity 7) Ability to use basic skills and problem-solving skills 8) Positive orientation to the future (Guglielmino, 1977).

no indication regarding any characteristics of learners that could be useful in establishing strategies for self-directed learning. Identifying the special characteristics of learners is useful because it seeks to thoroughly understand by what processes learners study in order to better establish strategies that are appropriate for learners. Research regarding the influence of an individual's personality on one's study is being conducted on a wide scale currently within the HRD sector[3]. Special characteristics of learners in self-directed learning which aims to better understand the characteristics and principles of a course of study are regarded as fixed characteristics of learners in the state of study that must be considered. Moreover, the interests or characteristics of learners may be excluded during the establishment of study targets. Conversely, characteristics of learners in self-directed learning that aims to elevate one's self-directed learning competency are regarded not as fixed, but rather as changing and that through self-directed learning need to be developed further. self-directed learning will emerge differently based on the different situations it is conducted in and self-directedness is not an inflexible state, but rather an on-going process of development making it difficult to regulate in any clearly defined manner.

3.4 Study Activities

self-directed learning is formed based on the primary elements of the learner. For example, one's individual characteristics, process of recognition, and study pattern among other examples. (Bae, 2008). self-directed learning is a series of unfolding activities that seek to impart learning that employs continuing inspection and reflection regarding all study activities as well as learning that seeks to find meaning and self-evaluation regarding the results of study. (Bae, 2008) A few specific strategies aimed at promoting self-directed learning activities that have been presented include, but are not limited to, opening oneself up to others, learning contracts designed to heighten responsibility in learners regarding the study process, self-evaluation of one's learning situation or behavior, and lastly forming study groups in order to improve co-operation and mutually beneficial relationships in and amongst constituents.

Study activities within self-directed learning that aims to better understand the characteristics and principles regarding a course of study center upon special teaching skills and methods proposed in order to aid learners in more effectively acquiring material that needs to be accomplished. Study accomplished in school is determined unilaterally according to patterns or principles of education plans regarding projects or material that learners must study. Even in states that don't impart any interest or effect on an entire study plan, the study activities of others are still able to be embarked upon. (Bae, 2008) Educators that seek to harmonize organized study subjects, learners' motivations, and an interest in learning are all helpful in evaluating, executing and planning the study of a learner.

Evaluation in self-directed learning that aims to better understand characteristics and principles of a course of study are conducted in order to verify whether the system and logic presented in the objectives and material of a class is understood or

---

[3] Honey & Numford (1992) separated learners into 4 types. Activists types enjoy participation and experiencing. Reflector types prefer data collection and systematic thinking. Theorists like analysis and thinking founded on theoretical facts. Pragmatists like carrying out ideas. (Honey & Numford, 1992).

not. Schools conduct evaluations in accordance with scholastic achievement; however, evaluation results can become elements hindering the progress of self-directed learning.

Self-directed learning that aims to elevate the competency of self-directed learning proposes self-directed learning activities from a humanistic perspective. Educators provide less structured subjects, as co-participants provide strength and inspiration, and also take on the role of facilitator in the study of students they are advising. This is not a process of study aimed at acquiring structured knowledge, but rather aims to bring about qualitative and internal change through a learner's participation and self-reflection. Change in a learner's way of seeing and attitude towards one's own world as well as new experiences regarding one's beliefs and values, all serve to elevate one's problem solving ability, responsibility towards learning, and active self-conception.

Study results are measurements in the degree of increase in one's self-directed learning competency[4]. That being said, these quantified results are an extremely individual phenomena in regards to self-directedness and it is hard to agree that they are generalized results that provide uniform rules. Table 1 compares self-directed learning that aims to better understand the characteristics and principles of a course of study alongside self-directed learning that aims to elevate the competency of self-directed learning that have been discussed thus far.

Table 1. Self-directed learning objectives and study principles

	Objectives of self-directed learning	
	'Understanding characteristics and principles of a course of study'	'Elevating self-directed learning competency'
Application	Structured and systematically regulated education	Un-structured study
Scope of Knowledge	Rational, objective and structured knowledge	Contains human beliefs, value systems and attitudes
Focal Point of Study	Materialization of student's voluntary study activity participation methods	Internal conscious change of learners
Individual Characteristic	Characteristics to consider regarding learners present stage of study	Characteristic of developing future of learner through self-directed learning
Learning Activity	Special teaching skills and methods for learners effective obtainment of necessary material	Learning course for internal and qualitative change in learner
Learning Results	Understand system and logic of objectives and materials presented in class	Elevate self-directed learning competency

[4] Two tools related with the quantitative measurement of self-directed learning are the OCLI(Oddi Continuing Learning Inventory) and SDLRS (Self-Directed Learning Readiness Scale). The OCLI is Likert's 24 part evaluation and is used in evaluating self-directedness and measuring individual self-directedness. The SDLRS handles a broader range including work satisfaction, job, ego concept and life satisfaction. (Marriam, 2007).

As we have seen up until this point self-directed learning that aims to better understand the characteristics and principles of a course of study and self-directed learning that aims to elevate the self-directed learning competency apply their principles of learning differently. In order to apply self-directed learning in schools or other similarly structured education systems there necessitates an approach to the essential problems as opposed to fundamental change of the school system being attendant.

4 Conclusion

self-directed learning requires differentiating between self-directed learning that seeks to better understand the characteristics and principles of a course of education and self-directed learning that aims to elevate self-directed learning competency depending on the objectives being pursued. These two forms of objectives in self-directed learning are executed using different learning systems and methods.

Self-directed learning that aims to better understand the characteristics and principles in a course of education is not determined by rigid methods or measures stemming from the strengthening or understanding of self-directedness, but is rather executed by measures that aim to acquire structured and systematized knowledge. On the other hand, self-directed learning that aims to elevate self-directed learning competency pursues internal change in individual's beliefs, value systems, and attitudes. This process contains the objective to strengthen and understand an individual's self-directedness.

Presently in Korea there are diverse attempts to cultivate more creative and self-directed learners as opposed to simple knowledge acquisition in schools. Moreover, the OECD has requested efforts towards developing juvenile and teenage self-directed learning competency as well as qualitative strengthening of educators in order to accomplish the former objective alongside a reforming of learning methods and teachers within schools.

This is then not simply using self-directed learning as a special learning method to be executed amongst learners possessing self-directed learning competency, but rather is something that is found upon the awareness that it is a learning ability that needs to be cultivated through education beginning from juvenile ages. Self-directed learning competency contains all of the elements that 21st century education needs to aim for including openness, curiosity, forward thinking, independence, responsibility, creativity, and problem solving ability in addition to being a concept that remains broad and not entirely clear. What is more is that self-directed learning within the context of a school system or school education can be utilized as a target in order to execute effective and efficient courses of education directly dictated by national governments.

In order to apply self-directed learning competency in schools or standard education systems there necessitates an approach to the essential problems as opposed to fundamental change of the school system being attendant. To be able to both execute self-directed learning as well as evaluate self-directed learning competency in schools, a close investigation needs to begin into whether these two different objectives are able to co-exist with one another or not.

References

1. Bae, Y.J.: A Study of Developing and Implementing Self-directed Learning Model for Schooling. The Journal of Curriculum Studies 26(3), 97–119 (2008)
2. Brockett, R.G., Hiemstra, R.: Self-direction in adult learning: Perspective on theory, research, and practice. Routledge, New York (1991)
3. Candy, P.C.: Self-direction for lifelong learning. Jossey-Bass, San Francisco (1991)
4. Gulielmino, L.M.: Development Self-directed learning readiness scale. Doctoral dissertation. Univ. of Georgia (1977)
5. Grow, G.: Teaching learners to be self-directed: A stage approach. Adult Education Quarterly 41(3), 125–149 (1991)
6. Marriam, S.B., Caffarella, R.S., Gaumgartner, L.M.: Learning in Adulthood, 3rd edn. Jossey-Bass, San Francisco (2007)
7. Mezirow, J., et al.: Fostering Critical Reflection in Adulthood: a Guide to Transformative and Emancipatory Learning. Jossey-Bass, San Francisco (1990)
8. Oddi, L.F.: Development and validation of an instrument to identify self-directed continuing learners. Adult Education Quarterly 36(2), 97–107 (1986)
9. OECD. Educational policy analysis 2001 Paris: OECD Center for Educational Research and Innovation (2001)
10. Park, H.J.: Policy Research of a Self-directed admissions system in School (2001)
11. Spear, G.E., Mocker, D.W.: The organizing circumstance: Environmental determinants in self-directed learning. Adult Education Quarterly 35(1), 1–10 (1984)
12. Zimmerman, B.J.: Attaining self-regulation: A social cognitive perspective. In: Handbook of Self-Regulation, pp. 13–19. Academic Press, CA (2000)

Bioethics Curriculum Development for Nursing Students in South Korea Based on Debate as a Teaching Strategy

Kwisoon Choe[1,*], Myeong-kuk Sung[2], and Sangyoon Park[3]

[1] Department of Nursing, Woosuk University, Samnye-eup, Wanju-gun, Jeollabuk-do, 565-701, Republic of Korea
choe1201@hanmail.net
[2] Center for Teaching and Learning, Chonbuk National university, Jeollabuk-do, Republic of Korea
[3] Department of psychology, Vassar College, New York

Abstract. Bioethics became a major field of discourse in medical education. This study aims to develop bioethics curriculum in nursing education for nursing students. The survey of nursing students and educators revealed that they think the bioethics curriculum should be a major requirement in the form of a two-credit, semester-long course open to all grades. The curriculum's learning contents consist of 8 categories and 29 subcategories. The curriculum utilizes both lecture and debate for effective education. Lecture is used mainly to teach contents of theoretical nature, and debate is used for other case-based contents. The finding of this study will provide a basis of bioethics education program for nursing students.

Keywords: Curriculum development, bioethics, nursing student.

1 Introduction

Rapid development in biology and medical technology in the past several decades brought up new ethical concerns that had not existed before, and this led to the birth of a new field called bioethics during the 1970s in the United States [1]. This relatively young field, which "examines the ethical issues at both the heart and the cutting edge of technology in health care and the life sciences," has rapidly grown since its birth, and became a major field of discourse in modern society [2]. In South Korea, the field received nationwide attention in 2006 through the controversy of Dr. Woo-Suk Hwang, who was once renowned for his cutting-edge research in stem cell technology but got disgraced for various ethical violations in the research process. The scandal alerted both the government and the public to the importance of bioethics, resulting in the establishment of many relevant policies and organizations such as Bioethics Policy Research Center [3].

Bioethics is significant for nurses as well as for researchers in life sciences because it provides nurses with broad ethical perspectives that help them take ethically desirable actions in patient care. A prior study indicates that enhancing ethical

* Corresponding author.

T.-h. Kim et al. (Eds.): ASEA/BRBC/EL 2011, CCIS 257, pp. 613–621, 2011.

knowledge and skills of nurses can increase their ability to deal with ethical issues and thus enable better performance in caring for patients [4]. One essential way to make nurses have sufficient knowledge of bioethics is teaching bioethics to students in nursing programs. For example, a healthcare ethics research center supports bioethics education for nursing students at Miami Dade College in Florida [5]; and ethicists with rich clinical experiences and degrees in philosophy teach bioethics to undergraduate nursing students at the University of Pennsylvania School of Nursing [6]. Also, bioethics education is a major part of the curriculum in most graduate level nursing programs in the United States [7].

In Korea, bioethics education for nursing students is relatively weak. It is mainly because ethics education for nursing students is focused on preparation for the national certification exam for RN [8] and these exams primarily test ethical principles and barely treat bioethical issues directly. But the knowledge of bioethics is significant for successful nursing practice as mentioned above, so it is necessary that nursing students in Korea receive adequate education of bioethics.

The present study addresses this issue and aims to develop a bioethics curriculum for nursing students in Korea. The development process focuses on: 1) selection and organization of learning contents; 2) selection of proper debate topics for the curriculum; and 3) development of effective and applicable class format. The developed curriculum is expected to provide a foundation for bioethics education in nursing and other medical professions.

2 Method

Hilda Taba's curriculum development model [9] served the framework for bioethics curriculum development. Taba's model was chosen because it presents simple steps to apply to practice and has a systematic organizing power. Details of the development process are as follows.

Stage 1: Diagnosis of learners' needs and expectations. Learners' needs and expectations were assessed through the survey of nursing students and educators in Korea. The survey examined various aspects of bioethics education including: the profile of current bioethics education (part of major or not, required or elective, number of credits, teaching strategies used, etc.); adequacy and helpfulness of current bioethics education; and directions for bioethics education in the future (part of major or not, required or elective, number of credits, teaching strategies, contents, etc.).

Stage 2: Formulation of learning objectives. Learning objectives of the curriculum were set based on literature review and advice from the experts.

Stages 3 & 4: Selection and organization of learning contents. Curriculum contents were selected from bioethics literature based on the established learning objectives. Advice was sought from experts on nursing ethics to remove topics with little relevance to the curriculum (e.g., environmental issues, protection of animals, etc.) and to prioritize the remained topics in order of relevance to nursing. Relevant topics were grouped together to form categories and subcategories and the categories were ordered in an educationally effective and helpful sequence.

Stages 5 & 6: Selection and organization of learning activities. Moon and Kim's debate-based class model [10] was used to develop the class format because it presents a systematic and effective method for value inquiry in scientific realms. The model suggests seven steps for value inquiry. First, students ask themselves the following three questions: 1) "What is the issue at hand?"; 2) "What are the perspectives on the issue?"; and 3) "What are the arguments of each perspective?". These questions help the students clarify and better understand value aspects of the given issue.

Next, students research and collect relevant information and data they can use to make alternative solutions to the issue. Third, students identify fundamental value(s) of each perspective on the issue. This helps them better understand the nature of value conflicts in the issue. Then students make and present alternative solutions to the issue based on the collected information and data (step 4). They should present each solution with its anticipated consequences, both positive and negative, and the anticipation must be based on various considerations—ethical, legal, political, social, economic, etc. Thus students come to produce concrete and realistic solutions. Next, students choose the best among these various solutions (step 5). Then they evaluate the chosen solution in various aspects (step 6). Both positive and negative aspects are considered of the solution and if the latter predominates without corresponding resolutions the next best solution replaces the initial choice. Finally, each student makes his/her own judgment on the issue and presents it in the form of writing (step 7).

For debate, the cross-examination debate style was adopted because a prior study suggests it is the most appropriate method for bioethics education [11]. And debate topics were selected by a case analysis of bioethical issues that are currently controversial in Korea.

Stage 7: Determination of what and how to evaluate. Various evaluation tools, such as the Ethical Reasoning Tool (ERT), were adopted for assessing the developed curriculum's effectiveness, which was defined as the extent of success in fulfilling the learning objectives.

3 Results

The survey of nursing students and educators revealed that they think the bioethics curriculum should be a major requirement in the form of a two-credit, semester-long course open to all grades.

3.1 Learning Contents

The curriculum's learning contents consist of 8 categories and 29 subcategories. These categories are presented in Table 1.

3.2 Class format

The curriculum utilizes both lecture and debate for effective education. Lecture is used mainly to teach contents of theoretical nature, and debate is used for other case-based contents. Debate topics are presented in Table 2.

Table 1. Learning contents of the bioethics curriculum for nursing students

Learning contents	
Categories	Subcategories
Ethical philosophies and theories	• Concepts of ethics and bioethics • Ethical theories and approaches
Religious and cultural perspectives on bioethics	• Bioethical perspectives of Buddhism, Taoism, Confucianism, Protestantism, Catholicism, and Jehovah's Witnesses • Feminism and bioethics
Ethical principles	• Principles of biomedical ethics • Information problems: Informed consent, truth telling, and confidentiality
Ethical concepts in nursing	• Ethical concepts for nursing practice: Advocacy, accountability, cooperation, and caring • Code of ethics for nurses • Critical thinking and ethical decision making
Beginning-of-life issues	• Western and Eastern perspectives on life • Artificial reproduction • Human cloning • Bioethics and the law • Fetus and newborn's rights to life • Early diagnosis of genetic anomalies • Abortion
End-of-life issues	• Definitions of death • Organ and tissue transplantation • Euthanasia • Hospice
Bioethical issues in nursing care	• Bioethical issues in Pediatrics • Bioethical issues in intensive care unit (ICU) • Bioethical issues in emergency room (ER) • Bioethical issues in hospice • Bioethical issues in psychiatric and mental health • Bioethical issues in community health • Bioethical issues in AIDS
Bioethical issues in research	• Research on human subjects • Biotechnology and bioethics

Table 3 presents the debate format for the curriculum. Based on the cross-examination debate style, it consists of three phases: 1) the constructive/cross-examination phase; 2) the rebuttal phase; and 3) the final speech phase. Between the two phases is given a preparation time of two minutes.

Table 2. Debate topics for the bioethics curriculum for nursing students

Categories	Topics for debate
Religious and cultural perspectives on bioethics	• Patient's refusal of treatments due to his/her religious belief should be accepted even if the patient will die without treatments.
Ethical principles	• Compulsory treatments are justifiable for patients with mental illness. • Significant other's request not to inform the truth to the patient should be accepted. • Prescribing placebos to relieve patients' symptoms is a justifiable act.
Beginning-of-life issues	• Surrogate parents should be legalized. • Human cloning should be legalized. • Screening test of fetus' gene is justifiable. • Abortion should be legalized.
End-of-life issues	• The use of executed prisoners' organs should be legalized. • Euthanasia (assisted suicide) has to be legalized.

3.3 Curriculum Evaluation

Three tools are used to evaluate the curriculum's effectiveness: 1) students' reports on debate topics; 2) debate evaluations from the audience; and 3) various educational evaluation scales such as the Ethical Reasoning Tool (ERT). The first two tools are implemented during the curriculum. First, each student is asked to write a brief report on the topic he/she will debate, considering and representing both affirmative and negative positions. Students submit their reports at least a week before they debate. During debates, students who are not debating write evaluations on peer debaters' performance and arguments.

The collected reports and evaluations are used to check and evaluate students' progress in learning and thus the curriculum's effectiveness eventually. Unlike these two tools, the third tool is implemented before and after the curriculum: students complete the scales before and after the curriculum, and the results are compared to assess the curriculum's contribution to students' improvement in desired aspects such as critical thinking skills and ethical reasoning abilities.

Table 3. Debate format for the bioethics curriculum for nursing students

Debate steps	Negative team				Affirmative team			
	1	2	3	4	1	2	3	4
1. First negative constructive (2 minutes)	●							
2. Second affirmative cross-examination (2 minutes)						●		
3. First affirmative constructive (2 minutes)					●			
4. Second negative cross-examination (2 minutes)		●						
5. Third negative constructive (2 minutes)			●					
6. Fourth affirmative cross-examination (2 minutes)								●
7. Third affirmative constructive (2 minutes)							●	
8. Fourth negative cross-examination (2 minutes)				●				
Preparation time (2 minutes)								
9. First negative rebuttal (2 minutes)	●							
10. First affirmative rebuttal (2 minutes)					●			
11. Second negative rebuttal (2 minutes)		●						
12. Second affirmative rebuttal (2 minutes)						●		
Preparation time (2 minutes)								
13. Third negative final speech (2 minutes)			●					
14. Third affirmative final speech (2 minutes)							●	

4 Discussions

Prior studies suggest that the developed curriculum will certainly improve nursing in Korea. First, bioethics education itself is reported to have a positive impact on nursing: nurses improved in ethical decision making abilities after participating in bioethics programs [12]; and students' ethical judgments were more rational if they took a bioethics class [13].

The developed curriculum has another merit in that it employs debate as its teaching strategy. In fact, various teaching strategies can be used for bioethics education, including lecture, problem-based learning, and simulation as well as debate. Lecture is advantageous in that it can deliver much information to many students in a relatively short time [14]. But it is quite disadvantageous when it comes to interaction with students. Problem-based learning is a relatively new teaching strategy and it was shown to be more effective than lecture, especially in situations with personnel and resource constraints [15]. Simulation is another new teaching strategy and it found its way to application in bioethics education in several cases. For example, simulation provided nursing students with opportunities to enhance their critical thinking skills [16] and ethical decision making abilities [17]. It is educationally effective because "simulators can provide safe, realistic learning environments for repeated practice, underpinned by feedback and objective metrics of performance" [18]. But high costs and much labor make it difficult to freely apply to actual practice in education.

Debate is a formal contest of argumentation between two teams or individuals. But more importantly, debate is an essential tool for developing and maintaining democracy and open societies. It is because "debate embodies the ideals of reasoned argument, tolerance for divergent points of view, and rigorous self-examination" [19].

The use of debate is a very helpful teaching and learning strategy for nursing students and nurses to comprehend the nature of ethical issues and apply the ethical knowledge to the practice [20]. Our initial survey on the need for bioethics education of this study supports that debate was the most efficient education strategy. Debates enhance critical thinking skills through studying issues and developing a stance that can be supported in scientific literature. Many students changed their views during the debates. Students evaluated the debates as a positive learning experience [20]. An ability of critical thinking in students who have participation experience in a debate tournament is higher than those without experience of debate [21].

5 Conclusions

The present study developed a debate-based bioethics curriculum for nursing students in Korea. For this is just the first step toward its direction, further research is much needed. Although Korean teachers of colleges and universities recognized the importance of debate-based education, the debate-based education was not widely implemented in Korea. Nevertheless, the education of ethics and bioethics in schools of nursing has to be implemented based on debate to improve nursing students' critical thinking and ethical reflective attitudes. This study will provide a basis of bioethics education program for nursing students.

Our study has some implications for nursing research and education. In nursing research, further research is needed to verify the effect of the debate-based education or web-based debate education of bioethics for nursing students. Also, essential content for ethical decision making in nursing practice need be identified, and the instrument to measure the essential content of ethical decision-making skills have to be developed. In nursing education, a systematic ethical debate training program for nursing faculties is needed to improve teacher's teaching skills to apply debate to education. The continuing education program of bioethics for nurses in hospital or community is also needed to be developed.

Acknowledgments. This research was supported by Basic Science Research Program through the National Research Foundation of Korea (NRF) funded by the Ministry of Education, Science and Technology (No. 2011-0005725).

References

1. Ravitsky, V., Fiester, A., Caplan, A.L.: The Penn center guide to bioethics. Springer Publishing Company, New York (2009)
2. Shannon, T.A., Kockler, N.J.: An introduction to bioethics, 4th edn. Paulist Press, New Jersey (2009)
3. Kim, J.: Bioethics policy research center' will be established. Kyunghyang Newspaper (May 7, 2005), http://news.khan.co.kr/kh_news/khan_art_view.html?artid=200505270820401&code=930401
4. Mckneally, M.F., Singer, P.A.: Teaching bioethics in medical students and postgraduate trainees in the clinical setting. In: Singer, P.A., Viens, A.M. (eds.) The Cambridge Textbook of Bioethics, pp. 329–335. Cambridge University Press, Cambridge (2008)
5. Petrozella, C.: Bioethics focus group survey results. The Florida Nurse 50(4), 30 (2002)
6. Perlman, D.: Experiential ethics education: one successful model of ethics education for undergraduate nursing students in the United States. Monash Bioethics Review 27(1-2), 9–32 (2008)
7. Pinch, W.J., Graves, J.K.: Using web-based discussion as a teaching strategy: bioethics as an exemplar. Journal of Advanced Nursing 32(3), 704–712 (2000)
8. Han, S.S., Kim, Y.S., Um, Y.R., Ahn, S.H.: The status of nursing ethics education in Korea 4-year-college of nursing. The Journal of Korean Academic Society of Nursing Education 5(2), 376–387 (1999)
9. Taba, H.: Curriculum development: theory and practice. Harcourt, Brace & World, New York (1962)
10. Moon, K., Kim, Y.: Development of web-based discussion model for value inquiry in biology education. The Korean Journal of Biological Education 33(3), 358–369 (2005)
11. Lee, K.: The CEDA academic debate for a bioethics class. Journal of Korean Ethics Education Research 19, 67–89 (2009)
12. Gerlach, C.J.: Relationships between moral reasoning and perception of moral behavior and participation in bioethics case study discussion by a select group of acute care staff registered nurses. Unpublished doctoral dissertation, Spalding University (1996)
13. Alves, F.D., Biogongiari, A., Mochizuki, S., Hossne, W.S., de Almeida, M.: Bioethical education in physical therapy undergraduate course. Fisioterapia e Pesquisa 15(2), 149–156 (2008)
14. Chiappetta, E.L., Koballa, T.R.: Science Instruction in the Middle and Secondary Schools: Developing Fundamental Knowledge and Skills, 7th edn. Merrill, Upper Saddle River (2009)
15. Lin, C., Lu, M., Chung, C., Yang, C.: A comparison of problem-based learning and conventional teaching in nursing ethics education. Nursing Ethics 17(3), 373–382 (2010)
16. Ravert, P.: Patient simulator sessions and critical thinking. Journal of Nursing Education 47(12), 557–562 (2008)

17. Gropelli, T.M.: Using active simulation to enhance learning of nursing ethics. The Journal of Continuing Education in Nursing 41(3), 104–105 (2010)
18. Kneebone, R.: Simulation in surgical training: educational issues and practical implications. Medical Education 37, 267–277 (2003)
19. IDEA: international debate education association (August 20, 2011), about debate: what is debate `http://www.idebate.org/debate/what.php`
20. Candela, L., Michael, S.R., Mitchell, S.: Ethical debates: enhancing critical thinking in nursing students. Nurse Educator 28(1), 37–39 (2003)
21. Colbert, K.R.: The effects of debate participation on argumentativeness and verbal aggression. Communication Education 42, 206–214 (1993)

A Case Study on SUID in Child-Care Facilities

Soon-Jeoung Moon, Chang-Suk Kang, Hyun-Hee Jung, Myoung-Hee Lee,
Sin-Won Lim, Sung-Hyun Cha, and Kum-Taek Seo

Abstract. This study investigates a healing process of parents who suddenly lose their child through observing their psychological changes reflected in parents behavioral characteristics based on recent SUID cases. The analysis method used in this study is performed based on the characteristics of a condolence process presented in a case in which a mother loses her child and overcomes her sadness of bereavement through creative painting. In the results of this study, three different periods are presented in the behavioral characteristics of the parent. First, the parent does not accept the death of their child after 1~2 months since their child was passed away and represents anger and violence. Second, although the parent shows certain rational behaviors after 3~4 months since their child was passed away, their emotion still represents unstable states. Third, after 4 months since their child was passed away the parent shows rational judgements and tries to set up new relationships and goals through some efforts to give meaning to the death of their child.

Keywords: SUID(Sudden Unexpected Infant Death) case, child-care facilities, healing process.

1 Introduction

Recently newspaper articles on some deaths estimated as SUID (SUID: Sudden Unexpected Infant Death) have been presented. Although there are some news about such deaths, it has been exposed to the media due to some accidents in child-care facilities in 2010 [1]. The death of a child in child-care facilities is usually estimated as SUID and the exact cause is concluded by the post-mortem examination. Based on the post-mortem, the cause of the death is cleared or determined as an unknown cause or SUID (Sudden Infant Death Syndrome). According to these results the child-care facility takes the criminal responsibility of the death. The criminal responsibility will be relieved if the misfeasance, i.e., SIDS or unknown SUID, of the child-care facility is not proved.

However, the case of SUID is not finished even though the criminal responsibility is relieved. The case will be finished as the civil compromise between the child-care facility and the parent is realized. However, it is difficult to draw an easy compromise between them. The reasons are the compromise is usually processed during the period of sadness and anger and some practical issues that a director of the facility may suffer from a personal insult during the compromise and prepares a settlement at a time. By investigating the behavioral characteristics of the parent who has the right about deciding on the key issue during the compromise, it is necessary to recommend a reasonable way for the compromise according to the healing process of the parent. As there are very few studies on such SUID cases in Korea, it is not possible to

T.-h. Kim et al. (Eds.): ASEA/DRBC/EL 2011, CCIS 257, pp. 622–626, 2011.

provides some helps for achieving the reasonable compromise between the parent and the director. Therefore it will remain lots of scratches for both sides.

Thus, in this study, a healing process of parents who suddenly lose their child through is investigated through observing their psychological changes reflected in parents behavioral characteristics based on some recent SUID cases.

2 Analysis Method

In the analysis method used in this study, the characteristics in a condolence process presented in a case in which a mother loses her child and overcomes her sadness of bereavement through creative painting [2].

Table 1. Characteristics and behaviors in a condolence process

Stage	Characteristics	Behaviors	Emotion
1	A painting in a stage that does not accept the situation	. A stage that represents intense emotion and anger and a release in initial shocks	Denying the reality
2	A painting in a stage that rushes emotions	. Unstableness and aggressiveness, anger at loss of a child	Rushing emotions
3	A painting in a stage that seeks, finds, and separates again	. Seeking a child through internal conversation and finds it . Presenting an intense complication with internal communication with a lost child . Accepting the present situation for setting up self and world relationships escape from the past	Controlling emotions
4	A painting in a stage that builds new self and world relationships	. Accepting the bereavement and the separation between the past and the present ego . Building a new relationship between the present ego and the world	Accepting the reality/Setting up new relationships (goals)

As shown in Table 1, the psychological characteristics of a mother who loses her child represent four different stages. The first stage shows denying the death of her child, the second stage represents her anger at the lose of her child as aggressiveness, the third stage shows an adjustment between the present denying and the reality, and the fourth stage accepts the reality and sets up new relationships and goals. Thus, in this study, some cases are analyzed according to these four stages.

3 Results

3.1 Results of the Analysis of the Day

The case presented in this study was the sudden death of an infant (18 month old, boy) at a child-care facility in K city, March 2011. The situation of the day was reconfigured according to the passage of time. Also, the situation after the infant death was described based on the details presented by the parent of the infant and relatives in an Internet cafe including the testimony of the director of the facility and surroundings. The analysis of this case was performed by different researchers using a cross tabulation analysis method.

Table 2. Situation of the day

Time	Description	Situation	Symptoms
Around 09:53 am	Attending the facility		. Taking medicine for snuffles
Around 10:03 am	. Laying the infant down to one side and watching	. The infant was laid at the side for about nine minutes.	
Around 10:05 am	. Taking off an overwear of the infant and cleaning face and hands	. The infant was moved to another side while he is crying.	
Around 10:10 am	. Moving the infant by his homeroom teacher to a blind spot of CCTV	. The infant left alone.	
Around 10:11 am	. The teacher stayed with the infant for 18 minutes.	. The infant was wrapped up in a blanket and laid at a blind side.	
Around 10:29 am	. The infant left alone.	. It is not clear whether the infant fall asleep.	
Around 10:30 am	. The teacher watches the condition of the infant at a distance.	. The infant left alone for about 17 minutes without considerations.	
Around 10:47 am	. A co-teacher finds the infant.	. The infant shows a difficulty in breathing but is still sensed.	. Dyspnoea
Around 11:00 am	. The infant was moved to a nearby hospital.	. Calling to the parent of the infant	. Applying a cardio-pulmonary resuscitation
Around 11:40 am	. The infant was moved to a University hospital.		. Death

As noted in Table 2, the infant visited a pediatry with his mother at the morning of the day, March 17, and took medicine. Then, the infant attended the child-care facility at 09:53 am. The infant played with some toys as usual but cried and fretted differed from the usual at around 10:00 am. Then, a teacher soothes the infant with some candies but it did not work. Then, the teacher laid the infant down at the floor.

Infants were cared by a homeroom teacher and co-teacher in a classroom. The infant was wrapped up in a blanket and slept at around 10:10 am. The co-teacher watched the infant with a nasty feeling and the infant showed a difficulty in breathing (around 10:50 am). The infant was immediately moved to a nearby S hospital (semi-general hospital) and treated by a cardio-pulmonary resuscitation. However, the infant showed no heartbeat and moved to the J University hospital. However, the infant has already passed away.

3.2 Results of the Analysis after the Death

As noted in Table 3, in this study, the condolence stage and state of emotion were investigated after the infant death based on the behavioral characteristics of the parent. As a result, the behavioral characteristic at the day was a stage that does not accept the death (Stage 1) and the state of emotion was denying the reality. After 1~2 weeks since the infant was passed away, it was determined as a stage that rushes emotions (Stage 2) and the state of emotion was rushing emotions. After 1~2 months since the infant was passed away, it was determined as a coupled stage of denying the reality (Stage 1) and rushing emotions (Stage 2) and the state of emotion represented two stages simultaneously. After 3~4 months since the infant was passed away, it was determined as a mix-up stage of rationality vs irrationality and can be considered as a period to make a rational behavior and to control emotions. After 4 months since the infant was passed away, the parent was attended to the meeting with a rational attitude and tried to effort for preventing the same accident. The state of emotion was accepting the reality and setting up new goals.

Table 3. Behaviors of the parent after the infant death and its stage

Period	Behavior and Characteristic	Stage	State of Emotion
The day	. Conversation for the recent specific reason "why the infant was died?" between the mother and the director of the facility	. Stage 1: Denying the reality	. Denying the reality
After 1~2 weeks	. The mother did violence to the director and teacher due to their attitudes. . Appeal to the public through Internet . Installing an incense altar in front of the facility	. Stage 2: Rushing emotions	. Rushing emotions
After 1~2 months	. Denying the final autopsy report . Inquiring a reinvestigation . Request for verifying the CCTV at the day . Putting in a claim for the death . One-man protest	. Stage 1: Denying the reality . Stage 2: Rusing emotions	. Denying the reality . Rushing emotions
After 3~4 months	. Inquiring a group meeting . Requiring an interview with the mayor, an improvement in the facility, and a preparation for preventing the same accident . Request for opening the CCTV at the day	. Mix-up of rationality vs irrationality . Stage 3: Seeking, finding, and separating again	. Controlling emotions
After 4 months	. Arguing parents opinions in a conference of the upbringing policy in K city . Bring about an agreement by the arbitration of the mayor's office and city association	. Stage 4: Setting up new self and world relationships	. Accepting the reality/Setting up new relationships (goals)

4 Conclusion

First, in the behavioral characteristics of the parent after the infant death, the parent denied the reality and showed anger and violence after 1~2 months since the infant was passed away. It is important to share the sadness and to soothe the emotion of the parent because the parent represents emotional attitudes in this period instead of showing rational behaviors. Thus, it is necessary to convey sincere condolences and install an incense altar at the facility for the healing of such emotions together with all members including the bereaved family.

Second, although the parent showed certain rational behaviors after 3~4 months since the infant was passed away, the state of emotion was still unstable. It was possible to find an attitude that the parent tries to give meaning to the death of their child. Thus, it is necessary to prepare a method that prevents such an accident and similar accidents in child-care facilities and describes it to the parent for giving meaning to the death even though it was very sad to the parent.

Third, after 4 months since the infant was passed away, it was a period that represents reasonable behaviors. The parent tried to find some meanings for the death of their child and was setting up new relationships and goals in this period. In this period, the parent considered the justice and value of the death based on rational behaviors. Therefore, it is necessary to help the parent in order to accept the reality and to contribute to the society.

References

1. Seo, K.T., Cha, S.H., Jung, H.H., Kim, M.H., Jung, G.H., Lim, S.W.: The study on BCP strategy for SIDS risk. Journal of Security Engineering 8(2), 299–308 (2011)
2. Henzler, C., Riedel, I.: Malen um zu überleben. Kreuz Verlag GmbH & Co. KG (2003)

Frames of Creativity-DESK Model; Its Application to 'Education 3.0'

Seon-ha Im

KoREC, Kongju National University, Team Researcher, 56 Kongjudaehakro, Kongjusi, Chungnamdo, Korea
imcreative@hanmail.net

Abstract. Recently, creativity education has been becoming the central trend of education in Korea. In this situation, we should critically review the understanding of and approach to existing creativity education and should suggest alternative ideas if any problem is found. This paper takes notice of the fact that the concept of creativity that has been dominantly accepted thus far does not reflect the cultural background of Korea. This research is proposing ideas of the understanding of and education on creativity based on agrarian culture which is the cultural base of the Eastern countries such as Korea, Japan, and China etc. In agrarian culture, the contents of education are accepted more importantly than the methods of education. As contents for creativity education, this researcher proposes 114 elements of creativity (DESK model of creativity) and discusses quite concrete methods to develop creativity education programs and teach creativity utilizing these elements with 'education 3.0' that is newly introduced approach to education.

Keywords: agrarian culture, creativity, model of the elements of creativity, DESK model, creativity education program, education 3.0.

1 Introduction

In the background of the rapid economic growth of Korea is education. This sentence which is beyond doubt at least in Korea is underlying the recent pan-national efforts for creativity education. The efforts indicate the intention of Korea that has succeeded in advancing into industrial society later than other countries to write another success story through education suitable to creative society. In the background of the idea is the 5.31 education reform plan announced in 1995. If the creativity education plan declared at that time is assumed to be a seed, the recent creativity·character education can be said to be flowers in full bloom. To enable these flowers to bear fruits, concrete guidelines and activity plans are being intensively researched and developed. The '2009 revised curriculum' to be applied to schools from 2011 embraces creativity·character education and integrated creativity and character. It does not set creativity and character as different educational objectives but sets creativity and character as an integrated educational objective termed creativity·character educational objective. The core objective of creativity·character education presented by the Korean Ministry of Education,

T.-h. Kim et al. (Eds.): ASEA/DRBC/EL 2011, CCIS 257, pp. 627–642, 2011.

Science and Technology(MEST) is 'creating new added values useful to society'. This is to go further from knowing knowledge to strengthen the function of much more 'advanced thinking'. To this end, the curriculum is also switching toward education to develop students' potential competences and reinforce key competences that are practically helpful to life. However, this policy measure cannot be immediately implemented in school education settings. Not only the entrance examination oriented education that has been solidified as practice but also lessons that are busy follow the progress are obstacles. The 2009 revised curriculum support unit schools to reduce the contents of course education and practice experience oriented education. In particular, the creative experiencing activities that have become mandatory in elementary/middle schools to be implemented for three hours a week and in high schools to be implemented for four hours a week are the core of creativity education. The creative experiencing activities are excluded from the subjects of time increases/decreases permitted in the 2009 revised curriculum and schools are obligated to enable practical experiencing activities.

What are the theory and philosophy underlying this creativity education that is being reinforced as such? To our sorry, the basic theories of the studies and practice of creativity conducted in Korea have been imported from foreign countries, mainly from the USA. Although it seems natural as the history of significant acceptance of creativity by the educational world began in the USA, since the frame of culture underlying the theory of creativity in the USA is fundamentally different from the frame of Korean culture, serious review and reflection are necessary before we accept the theories. This paper is intended to present the creativity conceptualized based on the characteristics of Korean traditional culture and its contents and introduce cases where creativity activity programs are developed and utilized based on the concept.

2 Culture Based Understanding of Creativity

One's thinking is quite dependent to the culture in which the person lives. Culture is a set of shared attitudes, values, goals, and practices that characterizes an institution, organization or group(wikipedia,2011). Therefore, it can be inferred that the understanding of creativity in one cultural area will be different from the understanding of creativity in another cultural area. If so, elucidating the origin of Korean culture will become a prerequisite of elucidating the concept of creativity in Korea. The reason why it is still not easy is that the origin of culture can be addressed from many directions. For instance, culture can be reviewed from the viewpoint of economy or from the viewpoint of art. This researcher will find the origin of Korean culture from settlement based agrarian culture. The culture in contrast to agrarian culture is set as nomadic culture.

Agrarian culture is formed over a long period of time by people who have settled in a region. Accordingly, the culture becomes to have a core. Centering the one core, the contents of the culture are organically structuralized over time. Therefore, the density of the culture becomes very high and since the density of the culture is high the quantity of the culture cannot but be small. Unlike agrarian culture, nomadic culture is formed while people move around wide spaces. Therefore, the culture becomes to have diverse cores and contents that are not related with each other exist superficially. Accordingly, the density of the culture becomes low and since the density of the culture is low, the quantity of the culture becomes large.

Table 1. Characteristics of agrarian culture and nomadic culture

Type of culture	Culture 1 - agrarian	Culture 2 - nomadic
Characteristic of the culture	Settlement	Movement
Determination of the culture	Time	Space
Core of the culture	Single core	Multi core
Formation of the culture	Structural(organic)	Superficial(no mutual relationship)
Density of the culture	High density	Low density
Quantity of the culture	Small quantity	Large quantity

*revised and expanded version of Im(1993)

Table 2. The characteristics of education in agrarian culture and those in nomadic culture

Type of culture	Culture 1 -agrarian	Culture 2 - nomadic
Contents and composition of education	Structuralization of small quantities	Listing of large quantities
Method to construct the contents	High degree of abstraction	Plain narration
Education channel	Teachers' teaching	Individuals' initiative
Educational method	Repeated recitation-grasping the essence of a matter	Free exploration - understanding
Educational objective	Mastery	Understanding

*revised and expanded version of Im(1993)

The different characteristics of agrarian culture and nomadic culture are connected to the different characteristics of education in the two cultures. In agrarian culture, since the quantity of the culture is small, the culture in the small quantity is organized as the contents of education using highly abstract methods. Since the contents of education are highly abstract, learners require teachers' teaching. Teachers have learners recite the abstract contents in order to grasp the physics. In this process, strict training and thorough imitation are essential. Through this process, the learners become to reach mastery. Mastery is an objective that is considered to be the utmost ideal in agrarian culture based education. Unlike agrarian culture, in nomadic culture, since the quantity of culture formed during movements is large, the culture cannot but be plainly organized as time series based contents. Since the components of the contents are plain, the contents can be studies under individual learners' initiatives. Learners become to understand the contents while freely exploring the subjects by themselves. The two types of education backed by two different culture move in quite different directions.

The differences between cultures in education can be applied as they are to situations where creativity is taught. Differences in creativity education between cultures are summarized as follows. In agrarian culture, in order to make learners have creativity, learners are made to go through thorough training or experience from the lowest level of certain areas. When a certain level has been reached as a result, the learners reach a free state. This free state is the very origin of creativity and the energy of creative thinking. As a result, the learners become to reach a state where they become to think creatively even when they don't make efforts to produce creative ideas(Torrance, 1979). Unlike agrarian culture, in nomadic culture, creativity is understood to be something that can produce as large as possible quantities of ideas even without any separate special training when one is stimulated to produce ideas after forming surrounding environments to enable the production of creative ideas. From these large quantities of ideas, good quality ideas, that is, original ideas are extracted. In other words, quantities determine quality(For instance, there is brain storming).

These processes are illustrated by figures as follows. The understanding and education of creativity in agrarian culture are achieved through the following courses.

Learners are made to go through thorough training or experience from the lowest level of certain areas(to master the contents) ⇨ Learners obtain freedom when they have reach a certain level ⇨ This freedom is the very origin of creativity ⇨ creative life and thinking

Example) apprenticeship training, Zen meditation

The understanding and education of creativity in nomadic culture are achieved through the following courses.

Satisfied with the formation of circumstances without any separate training(understanding of circumstances) ⇨ Produce large quantities of ideas ⇨ Extract good quality ideas[Quantities determine quality]

Example) brain storming

The different approaches to education and creativity that have been understood in contract based on culture clearly divide methods to educate on creativity. Agrarian culture based creativity education and nomadic culture based creativity education are greatly different in their bases.

3 Approach to the Contents of Creativity

Nomadic culture based creativity education utilizes the formation of atmospheres or methods to think creatively. They are approaches that have been dominant thus far. Then, how should agrarian culture based creativity education be implemented? If the above discussion is accepted, contents that are believed to constitute creativity should be taught instead of forming atmospheres for creative thinking or teaching creative thinking methods. However, such an approach has not been attempted. Im(1989,1993,1998) has been continuously making efforts to understand creativity centering on the contents that constitute it. His standpoint is that if the contents of creativity which is an abstract concept are extracted and the contents are structuralized and mastered, creative thinking will be automatically enabled. Unlike approaches that emphasize methods that have mainly come from the West which have been forming the main stream thus far, this standpoint places emphasis on securing the contents of creativity. Im(1989) defined the factors of creativity hierarchically as follows.

A. Domain

Creativity is divided into four domains(D,E,S,K).

- Disposition as an element of attitudes
- Individuals' experience as materials for thinking
- Skills that are techniques to think creatively
- Knowledge related to the subjects of thinking or knowledge related to creativity

B. Factor

There are 24 factors that constitute individual domains.

C. Element

There are a total of 114 concrete elements of individual factors.

These are domains, factors and elements that act in making people become creative which are relatively dividable. Using the first letters of these domains, the following formula can be established.

Im Seonha's creativity formula

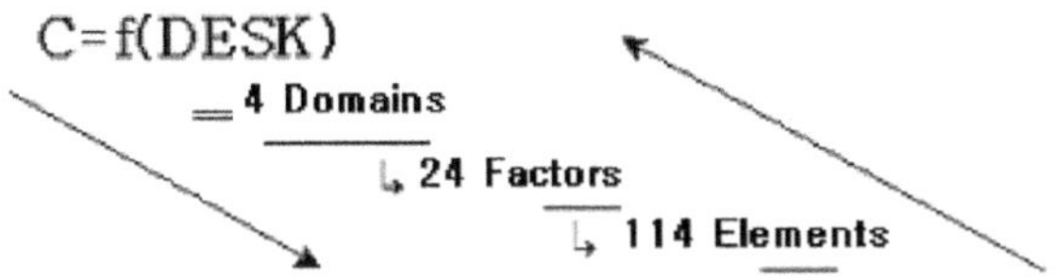

C=Creativity, D=Disposition, E=Experience, S=Skill, K=Knowledge

The Processes of converting experiences into creative ideas within the DESK model of creative thinking are as follows;

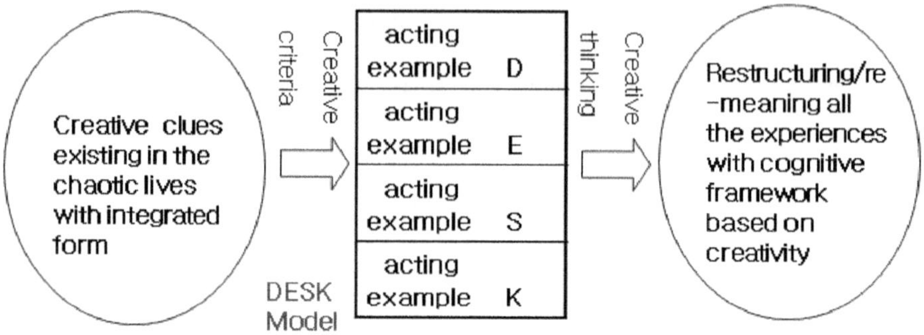

Fig. 1. Process of converting experiences into creative ideas

The factors and elements of the individual domains are reviewed as follows.

Domain D - creative thinking related disposition Humans' internal cognitive characteristics that are defining or attitudinal features required to individuals in processes for creative thinking functions to act for the ultimate achievement of humans. Feeling, attitude, character, temperament	
Factors(8)	**Elements(34)**
1.Curiosity	(1)Consciously raising questions such as 'Why is it so?' or "What is the matter?' about things or situations in surroundings. (2) Having curiosity about the hidden sides of things or phenomena too. (3)Enjoying 'new things'
2.The spirit of inquiry	(1)Searching for as much as possible information related with problems in problematic situations (2) Observing natural phenomena (3) Exploring the characteristics of objects (4) Observing the processes of changes in things
3. Confidence	(1) Accepting oneself as a positive and active being (2) Predicting self maturation (3) Having optimistic view of life

4.Spontaneity	(1) Accepting problems in surroundings as one's own problems (2) Doing disagreeable things first (3) Planning solutions and solving problems by oneself without external compensation such as compliments or prizes (4) Having active attitudes in life (5) Reconciling hobbies and interest with problematic situations (6) Setting the pursuit of newness as the goal of life (7) Having future oriented attitudes
5.Honesty	(1) Believing and expressing things known through the actions of one's five sensory organs as they are (2) Applying what has been felt through one's five sensory organs to certain situations for thinking (3) Accepting conclusions reached through one's thinking as they are (4) Checking the accuracy of one's own processes of cognition
6.Openness	(1) Accepting that this world will be changed into different states from its state of now (2) Bearing costs that may be incurred from accepting new ideas (3) Modestly accepting criticisms from others (4) Getting out of stereotypes or prejudice
7.Identity	(1) Continuously developing even ideas that have been negatively evaluated (2) Consciously suggesting ideas different from others' ideas in the process of producing ideas (3) Thinking beyond general common ideas in society in problematic situations (4)Getting out of the loneliness and fear of 'being left alone'
8.Concentricity	(1) Practicing impulse control (2) Treating things (phenomena) with concentration (3) Attempting to solve even difficult and boring problems or failing problems to the end with persistent passions (4) Continuously following up the results of problems even when the problems have been tentatively solved (5) Accepting given problems as being significant to oneself

Domain E – creative thinking related experience

Creative thinking related experiences include both positive experiences and negative experiences. Creative thinking begins from accepting those experiences as being significant and utilizing them. Ruminating on experiences, planning new experiences, analyzing the experiences

Factors(5)	Elements(18)
1.Reflecting on one's experiences	(1) Respecting one's past experiences (2) Reviving experiences in creative thinking (3) Giving creative meanings to one's past experiences (4) Abundantly experiencing creative thinking (5) Receiving positive feedback by oneself
2. Positioning oneself in the future to think	(1) Positioning oneself at a certain time point in future (2) Judging on one's current experiences at future time points
3. Searching for creative things in surroundings	(1) Experiencing in searching for creative persons (2) Experiencing in searching for creative artifacts (3) Searching for natural objects that make people have creative illusions
4.Stimulating one's creativity through others' behaviors	(1) Finding creative things from others' behaviors (2) Finding things that can be creatively improved from others' behaviors (3) Further developing others' creative behaviors observed by oneself (4) Comparing others' creative behaviors with my behaviors
5.Obtaining creative ideas from experiences with media	(1) Recording what are seen and heard (2) Criticising the contents of mass media (3) Participating firsthand in media (4) Creatively processing raw materials

Domain S – creative thinking skills The basic in the aspect of abilities that enables creative thinking is the very skills.	
Factors(7)	**Elements(47)**
1.Sensitivity	(1) Finding out problems even from phenomena that appear to be self-evident (2) Carefully grasping changes in surroundings (3) Finding out things that are not common from surroundings (4) Finding out things hidden in ambiguous situations (5) Trying to think familiar things as strange things (6) Trying to think strange things as familiar things(Thinking unfamiliar things as familiar things)

2.Inferring	(1) While seeing certain objects, recalling things of similar forms (2) When coming into contact with certain objects, recalling things with similar principles (3) When coming into contact with certain objects, recalling relative objects (4) When coming into contact with certain objects, recalling objects in the surroundings of relative objects (5) When seeing the entirety of certain objects, recalling their parts (6) When seeing parts of certain objects, recalling their appearances (7) When seeing certain objects, recalling their attributes (8) Finding out rules or principles in given situations (9) Giving consistency to things that exist separately (10) Inferring causes and results (11) Predicting
3.Fluency	(1) Freely recalling things related with certain objects (2) Intentionally changing viewpoints when thinking about objects (3) Associating as many things as possible from certain objects (language, figures) or phenomena (4) Presenting as many as solutions as possible in certain problematic situations
4. Flexibility	(1) Changing viewpoints for objects to grasp hidden aspects (2) While thinking about certain things, recalling other things together (3) Finding out relationships between things or phenomena that appear to be not related to combine time (4) Thinking about things or phenomena by their attribute (5) Symbolizing certain objects or phenomena to express them (6) Thinking in reverse order beginning from results (7) Switching ideas themselves to think (idea switching) (8) Expressing things in measures different from existing ones
5.Originality	(1) Thinking differently from others (2) Denying existing thinking or values of things before thinking (3) Applying existing thoughts to new situations to think
6.Elaboration	(1) Talking to oneself while doing something (2) Classifying and assembling things in surroundings (3) Concretizing rough ideas that rise unconsciously (4) Indicating the process of formation of thoughts or ideas in detail (5) Developing ideas considering their actual values

7.Imagination	(1) Recalling visual images with exaggerations (2) Recalling auditory images with exaggerations (3) Recalling past thoughts with exaggerations (4) Recalling stories in dreams as if they are real ones (5) Thinking things that exist now as if they do not exist (6) Thinking things that do not exist now as if they exist (7) Thinking things that exist now as if they have been reduced (8) Thinking things that exist now as if they are at other locations (9) Thinking certain objects after personifying them (10) Thinking at the outside of general processes of formation(generating)

Domain K – creative thinking related <u>knowledge</u> If one has professional knowledge of creativity, he/she will be able to creatively explain his/her thinking or others' thinking. It is important to know what creativity is and what meanings the activity, thinking creatively has.	
Factors(4)	**Elements(15)**
1. All theories about humans' cognition	(1) Understanding the history of studies of cognition (2) Understanding that studies of human cognition are being expanded (3) Knowing differences between computers' cognition and human cognition
2.Processes of thinking of those who think creatively	(1) Grasping the achievements left by those who think creatively (2) Understanding the characteristics of creative thinking (3) Getting out of interest in creative scientists as geniuses
3.Relationship between brain functions and thinking	(1) Knowing thinking related characteristics of the left/right brains (2) Knowing and utilizing the meaning of meta cognition (3) Knowing about the theory of multilateral intelligence theory (4) Knowing about the relationship between plays and thinking
4. Relationship between emotion and thinking	(1) Perceiving the state of one's own emotion (2) Adjusting and controlling one's own emotion (3) Efforts to develop potential abilities and utilizing described methods (4) Bringing in others' emotions (5) Forming social relationships with others

The domains, factors and elements as the content structures of creativity are arranged hierarchically based on the grade levels of learners.

Table of affiliation by the element of the contents of creativity(part/example)
(Disposition: skill)

Elements of thinking	Kindergarten (3:7)	Elementary school grades 1-2 (4:6)	Elementary school grades 3-4 (5:5)	Elementary school grades 5-6 (6:4)	Middle school (7:3)
A. creative thinking skill					
I. Sensitivity					
1. Finding out problems from self-evident phenomena	■5■	■5■	■5■	░	■
2. Gasping changes in surroundings	■5■	■5■	■5■	░	■
3. Thinking familiar things as strange things	■5■	■5■	■5■	■	■
4. Thinking strange things as familiar things	■5■	■5■	■5■	■ 5	■
II. Inferring					
1. Recalling similar forms	■				■
2. Recalling similar principles	■				■
III. Fluency					
1. Thinking from different viewpoints			■5■	■5■	■
2. Associating from objects	■5■	■10■	■5■	■5■	■10■
3. Presenting possible solutions			■5■	■5■	■
IV. Flexibility					
1. Changing viewpoints	■5■		■5■	■	■
2. Recalling different things				■ 10	■
3. Finding out relationships between phenomena			■5■	■	■
4. Extracting attributes to think			■5■	■5■	■
5. Switching ideas			■5■	■5■	■

4 Programs Approaching to the Contents of Creativity

A. Methods to Support Approaches to the Contents of Creativity

The most core principle among the principles of education in agrarian culture reviewed above is enabling learners to master the contents of education. To make learners master selected contents, it is better to fix the material that deals with the contents of creativity set as the goal of unit hour as one. Doing this will enable learners to grasp all the attributes of the material given in relation to the goal of learning.

When the relationship between goals and materials has been set up, now, mastery should be derived in the processes for learners to study. Creative ideas are the results of mental actions that occur when experiences and knowledge have been exhausted in order to fill the empty space. Therefore, teachers should induce experiences to be exhausted as soon as possible for more efficient and fast creativity education(Example; the use of paper cups). To explain this more easily, the structuralized system as follows is utilized.

Table 3. Relationship between goals and materials

Division		Goal	
		Fluid	Fixed
Material	Fixed	Goals are fluid, materials are fixed	Goals are fixed, materials are fixed
	Fluid	Goals are fluid, materials are fluid	Goals are fixed, materials are fluid

Number of reactions 30		Number of reactions 30
⇩		⇩
Continue the activity	Teachers are involved	Continue the activity
⇩		⇩
Number of reactions 10		Number of reactions 10
⇩		⇩
40 ideas	Teachers' judgment	40 experiences
⇩		⇩
Finish the creativity education		Continue the education(reconstruction of experiences)
		⇩
		Produce ideas
		⇩
		Finish the creativity education
Express 40 experiences	Result	Produce some ideas

Experience fixing creativity education	Idea oriented creativity education

Fig. 2. Differences between experience fixation and idea oriented education
[Problem] Tell new uses of paper cups freely.

B. Development of Programs to Approach the Contents of Creativity

Programs considering approaches to the contents of creativity were developed. Factors were set up as the goals of studies and then, materials suitable to the goals were selected(that is, by fixing the goals and materials) to develop study programs for around 120 minutes.

Table 4. List of the activity programs to approach the contents of creativity(part)

Factor	Title	Contents of activities	Time
Curiosity	An ascetic in a cave, Dudori	Recalling experiences in going underground roads, learners acquire the tendency to consciously raising a question, 'Why is that so?'. In the process of answering to this question, the learners become to obtain new knowledge and think.	120 minutes
Sensitivity	Green frogs and weather	Learners are enabled to grasp changes in surroundings sensitively through diverse problems related with many natural objects including green frogs.	120 minutes
Flexibility	Hands that have become foxes and feet that have become bears	Diverse solutions can be found in problem situations related with the body by changing fixed ways of thinking or viewpoints.	120 minutes
Spontaneity	Yellow mother, blue me	Through activities to think processes to actively respond to diverse situations occurring during camp activities, attitudes for spontaneous behaviors in real life can be brought up.	120 minutes
The spirit of inquiry	Good friends, trees	By inquiring about various phenomena and characteristics related with trees, as much as possible related information can be found.	120 minutes
Imagination	A travel of a white cloud	By having children who bring up imagination while seeing clouds that change from time to time face diverse cloud related situations, their imagination can be brought up to become rich.	120 minutes
Fluency	Fruit story	Diverse methods to use the tastes and appearances of fruits are examined and learners are encouraged to suggest as many ideas as possible about new approaches (for gift, new fruits)using fruits.	120 minutes
Elaboration	Stone family	Various thoughts that can be made with stones can be refined more concretely.	120 minutes

Table 4. (*Continued*)

Sensitivity	Lurulara, wearing dark glasses	Through activities such as observing colors in surroundings, saying feelings about colors and coloring in accordance with feelings, common things can be accepted specially and sensitively and expressed in peculiar methods.	120 minutes
Flexibility	Whether in the past or now	In diverse situations related with Korean traditional plays, learners can solve problems through various methods.	120 minutes
Flexibility	Transformation of paper	Fixed viewpoints can be changed by examining the diverse natures of paper and finding out many things that can be done with paper and things that can replace paper in order to find diverse methods to solve problems.	120 minutes
Confidence	The ants and grasshoppers	In various problematic situations that may occur when areas of interest are faced, learners can solve problems with confidence in themselves.	120 minutes
Honesty	Rain with feelings	In diverse situations related with rain, learners can believe the outcomes sensed by the five sensory organs as they are and apply them to certain situations to think about and accept the situations.	120 minutes
Curiosity	The moon, which moon is the moon?	Learners can observe changes in the moon to answer to various questions	120 minutes
Inferring	Finding fire	The discovery, storage and diverse methods to use fire can be inferred.	120 minutes
Imagination	A festival in a monkey village	Learners can freely exert their imagination for various problematic situations that do not actually exist to find interesting solutions.	120 minutes
Fluency	Green sea	Many ideas can be produced through diverse activities related with the sea.	120 minutes
Elaboration	Dudu's leaf pants and the superman's tight pants	Learners review the processes of development of clothes that were leaves or leather wrapping the body into the form of clothes and can expresses ideas to develop clothes suitable to various uses in details.	120 minutes

Table 4. (*Continued*)

Inferring	Kimchi is the best	Learners can bring up their inferring ability by doing activities to think about various kimchi related situations in connection with each other.	120 minutes
Originality	Diplomats of countries, foods	Using foods which are the summations of a country's weathers, geography and culture as materials, the originality to develop thoughts different from those of others can be brought up.	120 minutes

*Im(1998), creativity development program creativity school, Seoul: Hyundai Institute for Creativity Education

D. 'Education 3.0' as a Support System

The method of creativity education based on the education 3.0 paradigm can be an alternative solution for the problems raised from the present approach of making the student passive. Nearly all of the present education system was designed to teach something valuable, not creative. In this system the teacher who keeps the present value determines the newly forming value of students. This is the problem. Under the situation of education 3.0 paradigm all the students can be a master of their own learning for creativity.

Table 5. Education 3.0 paradigm

domain	1.0	2.0	3.0
Fundamental relationships	simple	Complex	Complex creative (teleological)
Conceptualization of order	Heterarchic	Heterarchic	Intentional, self-organizing
Relationships of parts	Mechanical	Holographic	Synergetic
Worldview	Deterministic	Indeterminate	Design
Causality	Linear	Mutual	Anticausal
Change process	Assembly	Morphogenic	Creative destruction
Reality	Objective	Perspectival	Contextual
Place	Local	Globalizing	Globalized

* John Moravec(2009)

5 Conclusion

What we need along with the global spreading of creativity education is the identification of its cultural basis in the theory of creativity and in education. Culture is a variable that determines the contents of education but it is also a variable that determines the effect of education in processes through which the contents are delivered. This is a basis of the argument of this writer that creativity education in Korea will be better if it is based on Korean culture. Through a study for a long time, this researcher draw an idea of 'approaches to the contents of creativity' based on agrarian culture. The creativity education based on approaches to the contents of creativity is an approach quite different from the methods to approach creativity that have been mainly conceptualized and developed mainly in the West. The approach to the contents of creativity is meaningful in that the current cultures are all based on settlement regardless of whether in the West or in the Orient. Now, this researcher is planning to broaden the width of approaches to the contents of creativity to find the possibility for it to be spread to the world in the era of 'education 3.0' paradigm.

References

Im, S.: Understanding and educating creativity based on the agrarian culture. A paper presented at the 2nd ISFIRE (KNU), Feburary 7-9 (2011)

Im, S.: Frames of creativity-DESK model. Hyundai Institute for Creativity Education, Seoul (2004)

Im, S.: Creativity Development Program, Creativity School. Hyundai Institute for Creativity Education, Seoul (1998)

Im, S.: Invitation to Creativity. Kyobobooks, Seoul (1993)

Im, S.: Creative thinking as a content of education, Education Development, 11-6. Korean Educational Development Institute, pp. 4–9 (December 1989)

Moravec, J.: Designing education 3.0 (2009), http://www.educationfutures.com/2009/04/19/designing-education-30/

Torrance, P.: The Search for Satori and Creativity. CEF, NY (1979)

Wikipedia (2011), http://www.wikipedia.org (searched on January 17, 2011)

Blended Nurture

Robert J. Wierzbicki

University of Applied Sciences Mittweida,
robert@wierzbicki.org

Abstract. There are numerous offerings on the media landscape which deal with the topic of upbringing, whereby the quality and usefulness of these media varies greatly. In particular the portrayal of educational concepts on television is questionable because here the line separating reality from fiction is blurred. This paper discusses the possibility of using a new, converged media format in the development of educationally oriented games and summarizes a number of parameters for the creation of interactive, virtual environments, which serve educational purposes. The concept of *Blended Nurture* will be introduced, which combines computer-delivered content with live interaction and arranges it in the new format.

Keywords: Blended Nurture, Nurture Games, pedagogics, upbringing, moral, ethics, good behavior, collective intelligence, neuroscience, converged media, GAMECAST.

1 Introduction

Young people today are growing up in a globalized world in which the weaker have barely a chance of surviving. Permanent stress and a fear of failure accompany our society every day. The focus when bringing up children is primarily on the achieving of an acceptable status in society and financial security for the future. Accompanying children as they develop their personality in a climate of moral and ethical values is something which is left to the schools. Parents are unable to cope with the active upbringing of their children. The efficient, educational dialogue often fails because of deficits in the psychological contact with the children. Parenting measures are often based on experiences of parenting methods from one's own childhood. However, these are no longer suitable in today's world and we talk about a conflict of generations.

2 Upbringing

2.1 Morals, Ethics and Good Behavior

In school, in the subjects ethics and religion, attempts are made to explain the concepts of morality and ethics and to introduce them into the context of pupils' lives. In doing so, also relevant, practical questions and their connection with ethics and

T.-h. Kim et al. (Eds.): ASEA/DRBC/EL 2011, CCIS 257, pp. 643–650, 2011.

morality are discussed. The aim – the discovery and realization of the proper values – is in most cases not achieved. More and more young people are fleeing into a world of virtual friendships and social networks, thereby detaching themselves from the real world. For the most part this is even accepted by the parents because that way they are left in peace – those who are sitting in front of the computer cannot cause any damage in the real world.

I am often annoyed by the behavior of young people who throw rubbish on the ground, or show no respect by taking the last seat on the bus instead of offering it to an old lady. They have failed to master the simplest rules of a good upbringing such as saying "please" and "thank you" and showing respect to others. What annoys me more, however, is the behavior of the parents, in particular that of some young mothers, who even encourage bad behavior by their children by not reacting to their bad behavior, or reacting with half-hearted judgment – after all the child should be allowed to do as it pleases. The modern-day passion for the child has quite serious consequences. The addictive drug love results in the child being brought up without any displacement, and only by emotions, something which is actually not possible. And that is why nobody wants to do it any more today [1].

Nowadays good behavior seems to be a scarce commodity. I often experience students who will say hello to me as long as they still need a grade, but as soon as they have passed the subject they don't know me anymore. Something isn't quite right with the way our children are being brought up. We blame the schools and the education system for this. The fact is that we don't make enough effort ourselves to instill and maintain the correct behavioral patterns within our own families and pass these on to the younger generation as something important. In any case everything is more complicated than it looks at first glance, since the value systems of different families are not the same and are dependent on their cultural backgrounds.

The poor behavior of young people is regularly addressed in the media. School pupils rebel against teachers and there has been an increase in violence among minors. The public are made aware time and again through the media of the powerlessness of the teachers due to the situation in school classes.

2.2 Collective-Intelligent Behavior?

Upbringing requires an active intervention in the process of children growing up. The creation of an atmosphere of mutual respect plays an important role in this, as it shapes the relationship of the individual with the outside world. It would be desirable that schools would cooperate more closely with families. In practice this doesn't seem to work, or at least not as well as it could. Institutions such as kindergartens and schools must therefore be entrusted with more responsibility for the upbringing of our children. It is not about completely new tasks for the schools but about restructuring and extending educational-didactic concepts and at the same time adapting and essentially reducing curricula which implement and dream of the myth of general knowledge. What we produce with the idea of a broad general knowledge is stress and demotivated pupils by overburdening them with learning resources.[2].

In the age of the internet it is necessary to employ new, up-to-date methods when it comes to education and didactics in order to achieve and sustainably establish certain learning effects. Traditional methods such as classroom discussions do not work because they aim to have an effect on a level which is not as accessible to the young people of today in the way it was to their parents. The new, purely virtual didactic methods on their own do not fulfill the purpose of effective teaching either, as they cannot be established cognitively or constructivistically. They replicate real situations but are unable to analyze the cognitive abilities of the learner and consider these in learning processes. Didactics and education also don't work in the context of virtual, social communities. The advocates of collective intelligence [3] assume the best talents of the individual develop to become an optimal achievement of the group, and assume optimistically that the collective intelligence resulting from the aggregation of the intelligence of several individuals will ensue by itself. In ethics we ask ourselves what is right and base our preferences and therefore also our behavior on objective moral standards [4]. Our conscience is seen as the ultimate appeal possibility for our decisions. Can social communities develop something like an objective conscience? The behavior of the individual can be adapted to the collective behavior, but who can ensure that this behavior corresponds to the orientation towards the objective value standards and that the correct normative decision basis can even develop in the group? Is the decision which enjoys the group's consensus automatically the best one? The desire for consensus can dominate the individual sense of reason and lead to irrational decisions (i.e. the desire for harmony in a decision-making group overrides a realistic appraisal of alternatives) [5].

3 Blended Nurture

3.1 Upbringing in the Context of Social-Cognitive Learning Theory

Bringing up a child, which can be understood as passing on norms and moral concepts, is a type of communication: The sender attempts to effect a change (of behavior) in the recipient. The majority (57%) of children and young people aged 6 to 13 regularly use computer games and games consoles; After the CD player, at 57% the games console is the second most frequently used piece of media equipment children get hold of [6]. Games have nowadays become a permanent part of the lives of digital natives and are therefore particularly suitable for conveying messages and examples of an educational nature which would otherwise possibly not reach their target audience on a purely traditional communication level.

The social-cognitive learning theory, also known as learning from observing, maintains that people, in particular children, learn effectively by observing behavior [7], [8], [9]. Actions that children observe through the media become an example to follow (every behavior witnessed can change a person's way of thinking (cognition)). In particular violence in the media is addressed in the context of the social-cognitive learning theory. Proponents of the theory believe that behavioral patterns come about as a result of the continuous consumption of media violence, which have long-term, largely negative consequences [10], [23]. It is known from behavioral research that 'learning by doing' is considerably more effective than the shaping of behavior purely by way of observation ('learning from observing'). This principle is also contained in Bandura's social-cognitive theory, which postulates that guided practice in a new behavior can lead to increased self-efficacy and to greater behavior change [11].

New neuroscientific findings demonstrate that people, in particular children, only learn those things effectively which are fun for them [12]. Emotional centers are thereby activated in the middle brain. This occurs through the release of so-called neuroplastic substances (dopamine, neuropeptides, encephalin). Neuroplasticity is the ability of synapses, nerve cells and entire cerebral areas to change both structurally and functionally depending on their use [13]. Dopamine is a neurotransmitter (a chemical in the brain) that either increases or reduces the activity of nerve cells. Dopamine formed in the brain is associated with pleasurable activity. It is released when people do naturally rewarding activities like having sex. Recent research suggests that dopamine is also released in reward-anticipation activities and when people are motivated to do something [13], [14], [15]. Merely thinking about something pleasurable can activate the reward centers in the brain and stimulate the production of dopamine. The result is an effective stabilization and facilitation of active neuronal nexuses and synaptic relays in the brain, which ensures a permanent, sustainable entrenchment of what has been experienced or learned.

3.2 Blended Nurture Arrangement

Experiences are neurobiologically entrenched in the brain. Emotions are an excellent prerequisite for the entrenchment of conscious behavioral patterns. In addition, they leave unconscious engrams in the memory, thereby influencing the conscious processing of stimuli [16].

Taking the comments in the previous chapter as a starting point, it is possible to establish some parameters for the conception and establishing of virtual education rooms. Players (children) should experience stories in a collective, virtual setting, which appeals to them both emotionally and in a multimodal way. Emotional storytelling is needed as the basic frame for this, which conveys realistic and profound experiences in an interactive context. Digital protagonists who can be controlled in the dramaturgic production of the game either by way of artificial intelligence or by real people (potentially real actors) would essentially be tasked with provoking specific conflict situations in the virtual room, thereby creating the basis for the acting out of dramaturgically appropriate plots. Essentially game environments set up in this way can be classified in the genre of serious, multiplayer games [17], [18], [19]. The conception of conflict situations and plot points must, however, be adapted to fulfill an educational purpose and therefore it is imperative that there is also cooperation with psychologists. At the same time it must be ensured that playing is linked to fun, as that way, as mentioned above, learning effects can be sustainably stored. The narration can essentially follow the usual rules of digital storytelling [20]. What is important is the implementation of psychological scenarios, the most important of which are summarized in the following table:

Challenge for the player	*Psychological scenario*
Observe events and plan one's own actions	*Players must be able to go through and carry out their actions in their minds.*
Make a decision in conflict situations	*Players must learn to appreciate the consequences of their actions and make decisions which have specific, but not always absolutely determinable and foreseeable consequences.*
Learn to deal with consequences	*The consequences of an action need not always prove to be absolutely and objectively right or wrong. The assessment as to whether something is right or wrong can be made dependent on the context (situation) and from the point of view.*
Learn to make moral judgments	*Decisions can have several outcomes and at the same time both positive and negative consequences.*
Put yourself in another person's position (change of the point of view)	*In a virtual setting it should be possible to take on the role of another person, experience the story from their point of view and to thereby learn how to qualify their own actions.*
Experience the strengths of communities	*Players must have trust in their own abilities, but also in friends. Some problems and conflict situations should only be able to be resolved with the help of others.*

Fig. 1. Scenarios and challenges for the player in "Nurture Games"

The morals that players develop in virtual educational scenarios and on which basis decisions are made, as well as consequences that result from these decisions, don't necessarily sustain objective ethical criteria. Children and young people cannot always distinguish between good and evil or between right and wrong. In the old fairytales we can find examples of clear situations, but life today is too complex for education to be based solely on fairytales with simple metaphors and abstract elements.

Contemporary educational methods require adaptations which, like modern "Blended Learning" consist of a number of components. They need to combine moderated face-to-face methods with modern computer-mediated activities. In the same way as blended learning we could talk about "Blended Nurture" or "Augmented Nurture" (Fig. 1).

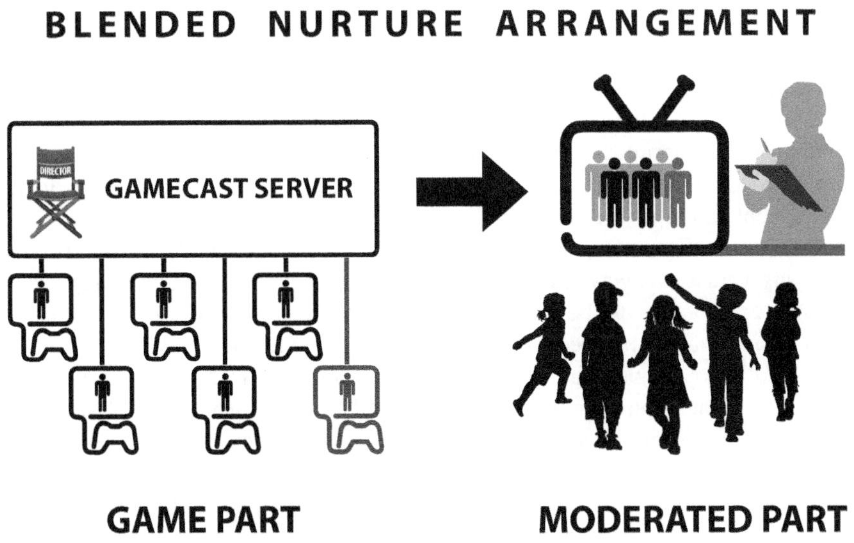

Fig. 2. "Blended Nurture" arrangement

A live phase moderated by a psychologist (coach) appears to be an essential component which supports the reflection on what has been experienced and decisions that were made, and helps with understanding difficult coherences. Players always consider and experience actions within an entirely individual context. The coach can, if necessary, qualify and correct their perception of game situations.

3.3 The Game System

In previous papers a promising, convergent system was introduced, which can, amongst other things, be used for pedagogical purposes: GAMECAST [21], [22]. With GAMECAST a range of stories can be told and sensitive scenarios can be acted out. Gamecast provides an opportunity, amongst other things, to record the players' actions (as log files) and subsequently convert them into a film (3D animation) and play them back (staging function in Gamecast). By switching from the actor's position to the observer's position the role behavior of individuals and groups can be called into question and the effects of their actions can be reflected emotionally. The strength of using such a system in the educational context is obvious. First, the system enables a variety of scenarios to be acted out like in a typical multiplayer game system, whereby relevant actions can be automatically combined in a film which serves as the basis for a concluding discussion with a deeper sociological, psycho-analytical and psychological background. Computer networks which consist of only a few game clients (<=7) are best suited as multiplayer game environments. The narrative construction of an interactive story can in this way be simplified and therefore also structured very efficiently.

4 Summary

In this paper the concept of "Blended Nurture" has been introduced, a concept which aims at changing social or personal behavior through participation in virtual reality based games ("Nurture Games") combined with a moderated live part. What distinguishes the approach from that of the other serious, multiplayer games is the use of an innovative, converged media system which is able to record actions in the game environment and reproduce them in the form of a film.

In "Nurture Games" a number of approaches are combined for the purpose of conveying values in a way which has educational value. The three most important are allowing experiences to be collected by an individual, being able to experience actions from another perspective and discussing the outcome of the game under the direction of a coach and together with the players from a psychological point of view. Playing the game on its own is not sufficient for behavioral patterns to be stored in the brain correctly. What is needed is an adaptation which contains both virtual and real components. A coach (psychologist) must ensure that experiences are correctly classified and that the correct behavioral patterns become fixed in the mind.

References

1. Thompson, C.: La violence de l'amour. Hachette Littératures, Paris (2006)
2. Städtler, T.: Die Bildungs-Hochstapler: Warum unsere Lehrpläne um 90% gekürzt werden müssen. Spektrum Akademischer Verlag (2010)
3. Kennedy, J., Eberhart, R.C., Shi, Y.: Swarm Intelligence. Morgan Kaufmann, Academic Press, San Francisco (2001)
4. von Kutschera, F.: Grundlagen der Ethik, 2nd edn. de Gruyter, Berlin (1999)
5. Janis, I.L.: Victims of Groupthink: A psychological study of foreign policy decisions and fiascoes. Houghton Mifflin, Boston (1972)
6. Behrens, P., Rathgeb, T.: KIM-Studie 2010, Kinder + Medien, Computer + Internet, Medienpädagogischer Forschungsverbund Südwest, Stuttgart (2010), http://www.mpfs.de/fileadmin/KIM-pdf10/KIM2010.pdf (October 6, 2011)
7. Miller, N.E., Dollard, J.: Social Learning and Imitation. Yale University Press, New Haven (1941)
8. Bandura, A.: Social Foundations of Thought and Action: A Social Cognitive Theory. Prentice-Hall, Englewood Cliffs (1986)
9. Bandura, A.: Social cognitive theory: An agentic perspective. Annual Review of Psychology 52, 1–26 (2001)
10. Kunczik, M., Zipfel, A.: Gewalt und Medien – Ein Studienhandbuch, 5 Auflage, UTB (2006)
11. Farquhar, J.W.: Health Interventions: Community-based. In: Smelser, N.J., Baltes, P.B. (eds.) International Encyclopedia of the Social and Behavioral Sciences, pp. 6576–6581. Elsevier Science, Oxford (2002)
12. 3sat, nano (October 6, 2011), http://www.3sat.de/page/?source=/nano/gesellschaft/152463/index.html
13. Doidge, N.: The Brain That Changes Itself: Stories of Personal Triumph from the Frontiers of Brain Science. Penguin Books, New York (2007)
14. Storch, M., Cantieni, B., Hüther, G., Tschacher, W.: Embodiment. Die Wechselwirkung von Körper und Psyche verstehen und nutzen, 2nd edn. Huber Verlag, Bern (2010)
15. Waelti, P., Dickinson, A., Schultz, W.: Dopamine Responses Comply with Basic Assumptions of Formal Learning Theory. Nature 412(6842), 43–48 (2001), http://www.nature.com/nature/journal/v412/n6842/full/412043a0.html (October 6, 2011)
16. Freud, S.: An Outline of Psychoanalysis (trans. Strachey J). Hogarth Press, London (1949)
17. Shaffer, D., Halverson, R., Squire, K., Gee, J.: Video Games and the Future of Learning. WCER Working Paper No. 2005-4, University of Wisconsin (2005), http://www.wcer.wisc.edu/publications/workingpapers/working_paper_no_2005_4.pdf (October 7, 2011)
18. Keitt, T.J.: It's Time to Take Games Seriously. Forrester Research, Cambridge (2008)
19. Ritterfeld, U., Cody, M.J., Vorderer, P. (eds.): Serious Games: Mechanisms and Effects. Routledge (2009)
20. Perry, D., DeMaria, R.: David Perry on Game Design: A Brainstorming ToolBox. Charles River Media (2009)

21. Blom, K., Beckhaus, S.: Emotional Storytelling. In: IEEE Virtual Reality 2005 Conference, Workshop Virtuality Structure, pp. 23–27. IEEE, Bonn (2005), http://imve.informatik.uni-hamburg.de/files/18-EmotionalStorytelling-VR2005-BlomBeckhaus.pdf (October 7, 2011)
22. Schmieder, T., Wierzbicki, R.J., Lugmayr, A.R.: GAMECAST®: A Cross-Media Game And Entertainment System. In: Lugmayr, A., et al. (eds.) TICSP Adjunct Proceedings of EuroITV 2008, Changing Television Environments, Salzburg, Austria, July 3-4, pp. 157–161 (2008)
23. Wierzbicki, R.J., Kermer, K., Röbisch, K, Schmieder, T., Straßburger, T.: Media Pedagogics in Converged Environments of the Future. In: Proc. iTV 2010, Tampere, Finland (2009)

University-Industry Ecosystem: Factors for Collaborative Environment

Muhammad Fiaz[1] and Baseerat Rizran[2]

[1] School of Management, Northwestern Polytechnical University, Xi'an, China
fiaz_42@yahoo.com
[2] Department of Management, Hazara University, Pakistan
baseeratrizwan@gmail.com

Abstract. This research contribution is an effort to figure out the root causes that leads to the integration and disintegration of Research & Development (R&D) collaborations between University and Industry. R&D has been in practice since many years in nearly all kinds of organizations from developed and developing nations. Educational institutions with strong and state –of-the-art research knowledge base have shown more intentions for R&D collaborations. Literature has presented many reasons for the execution of these joint ventures and elaborated the key issues to make them more profitable and feasible. University-Industry R&D collaboration has got an important research status and becoming an emerging field due to the global wave of commercialization, cooperation and mergers.

The purpose of this research is to find out those raison d'êtres that lead the firms to collaborate with other firms and academia. The authors suggest the road map that leads to strong, long lasting, productive, and effective collaboration ventures. This paper also marks the reasons which are the cause of cleavage in these collaborations of university-Industry endeavors. This earnest and conscientious activity has also highlighted the challenges for University-Industry (U-I) R&D Collaborations and devises a plan to overcome these mistrust paradigm of conflict.

Keywords: R&D, U-I Collaborations, Academia, Industry.

1 Introduction

Research & Development (R&D) is not a new concept and Collaboration in the R&D projects has also a long history. It has been in practice for many decades in developed nations. Now it is becoming an emerging field followed by the large national and international enterprises all over the world in both developed and developing countries. As the rapid growth of scientific knowledge imposes new challenges for companies that need to maintain their research and development capacity and keep track of current advances. R&D collaboration is widespread in developed countries like US, China and European countries. USA firms have been reported in literature to establish

T.-h. Kim et al. (Eds.): ASEA/DRBC/EL 2011, CCIS 257, pp. 651–661, 2011.

collaborations with universities from early 19s and contributing in the national economy and academic development on large scales. Correspondingly, in Europe, European Framework Programs (FPs) on Research and Technological Development (RTD) is an example of R&D Collaboration where the European Union has funded thousands of worldwide collaborative R&D projects.

The empirical research shows that how trends were changed from Industry-Industry collaboration to University-Industry collaboration. Since the 1980s, various countries have implemented policies to promote and sustain University-Industry partnerships. Currently, it is understood that the creation and application of new ideas and knowledge are the essential factors that stimulate the growth of an economy. Universities are the major sources of this new knowledge particularly in science and technology. Therefore, researchers have put great efforts to examine the nature and significance of university-industry relationships. There can be various reasons for this change: firms seek to get more R&D benefits but want to spend very less. Secondly, it is not possible to execute all the R&D activities by a single firm especially for SMEs. One more, in addition to former is that firms give more importance to innovation for creating and maintaining values. So, in-house R&D and R&D Collaboration have become increasingly important for firms to enhance their competitiveness. Trends were changed due to fast technological changes and global competition, which led the firms to start sharing R&D with other industries on national and international level. It was very difficult and expensive to manage all R&D by a single company due to limited resources specially allocated for Research & Development. It is also quite difficult to manage R&D related risks. Although, some multinational firms have their proper R&D cells, but still it is a challenge for large firms and SMEs. Globalization of R&D also has forced such big and multinational organizations to get benefits from collaborations. These changes resulted in a paradigm shift in R&D Collaboration to University-Industry R&D collaboration during last decades.

The purpose of this study is to depict the importance of R&D Collaboration, its positive and negative aspects, importance of University-Industry R&D Collaboration and the risks involved in R&D collaboration. Core theme is to find out crux which makes collaboration successful. On the basis of literature, author has also pointed out those clues that lead to collaboration failures.

2 Cognitive Contents for R&D Collaborations

R&D efforts of a firm play a significant role in improving its knowledge reserves, innovations and getting competitive advantages All these R&D efforts are not possible for a single company to carry out particularly when a firm is facing the shortage of resources for R&D. Trends for R&D alliances among business jargons have been increased due to commercialization, globalization and rapid growth of technology. Collaborations among partners are in practice with different names like, clustering, alliances, joint ventures and collaborations. Many organizations are found to increase their internal R&Ds, as well approaching external R&Ds. Nevertheless, gobs of barriers have been observed facing by SMEs and others as, manufacturing, chemical, medicine, pharmaceutical industry where R&D can play vital role. Collaborative relations are the direct and intentional involvement of two or more firms in crafting and developing a product, process or service [1]. Literature streams and numerous scholars have been widely investigated the significance of collaboration in the development of R&D activities. Nevertheless, a variety of reasons are found in literature for the obvious augmentation in innovations and technology coalition but basically firms that favour the collaborative associations for effectiveness and innovation, have insufficient essential resources (including knowledge) or yearn to lessen the risks related to the innovation (mainly the risk of technological spillovers) [2].

The formation of these arrangements and their strength depends on the core competencies of partners, knowledge intensity and R&D resources. Literature depicts that collaborations and alliances are affected also by knowledge spillover capacity and collaborative inclinations of partners. A broad range of causes affecting the alliances among the contributors have been discussed in the literature but the most imperative of them is the low budget specified for R&D and lack of knowledge. The period of time that is happening now, it is apparent that the introduction and implementation of novel knowledge are the key factors that compel the economic growth. For the reason, firms seek partners for carrying out R&D projects.

In the field of R&D collaborations, variety of work has been done and different researchers have pointed out diverse perspectives of it. [3] Presents the R&D collaboration as the Particular course of various modes of inter-firm collaboration, where firms share their R&D activities by staying sovereign economic agents and organizations. Innovation is also considered to be an affective motive for alliance establishment. Knowledge sharing and management is the main challenge faced by organizations these days. Technological complexities and race forced organizations to increase the articulated knowledge reserves. Scholars [4] also supported the arguments that growing range of collaborative measures and agreements among the innovating firms has been emerged since the 1980s. Fast and complex technologies and mutually making the dissemination of information easier are the causes for innovating firms to collaborate on R&D with other firms or R&D institutes. Other motives include cost sharing, uncertainties inherent in developing new technologies, and access to tacit knowledge [5].

In a concise manner, knowledge production, Knowledge sharing, reuse of this knowledge to achieve innovative goals and overcome technological complexities, competitive advantages, firms growth, R&D cost and resource sharing, reducing the uncertainties and risks in developing new technologies and so on are the major motives for organizations to collaborate with other firms or institutes.

3 U-I Collaboration Epitomes

Considering the objects of R&D collaborations, discussed in earlier section, organizations wants more benefits from R&D by spending less budgets. So trends were changes and a paradigm shift from Organization-Organization collaboration towards University-Industry R&D collaboration has been observed in the last few decades. U-I collaboration played an important role for innovation and researchers believed that lacking of academic research contribution have led many innovations unrealized or have followed much later [6], [7]. In the past 20 years, the collaboration between universities and the private sector has become too much trite and banal in the society [8] because the interaction between the creators and users of knowledge within a society is the major origin of ideas and technologies driving and facilitating the innovative process.

Industry-University collaboration is known as the vital form of learning association where university tendency is more towards knowledge contribution while companies are involved in dealing with the uncertainties of innovation and accessing exploration. It is universally acknowledged that universities are major sources of new knowledge, ideas and novelty, particularly in the field of sciences and technology [9]. Thus, researchers have put immense efforts to examine the nature and importance of the associations between universities and industry, building clear image of mechanism which may support this interaction; resulting in advancing knowledge transfer and acquisition.

Recently, the significance of R&D collaboration as a source to enhance the impact of R&D on economic growth by improving the R&D productivity and technological dissemination has focused by many researchers. Particularly, R&D relationship between the innovating firms and public R&D institutions i.e. universities are considered as a channel that supports knowledge sharing and R&D spillovers which leads towards the realization of it by associated innovating firms. In china, universities can own profit-making firms, while in the U.S., a university's direct ownership of a commercial firm would invalidate its tax-exempt status [10]. In china, state promotes the institutions for U-I research collaborations. Chinese government has consistently been in the favor of use-driven science policy requiring URIs to serve the national economy by solving practical problems for industry [11].

There are numerous factors that force firms to collaborate with others, specifically in knowledge-intensive industries that always seek those partners that have capacity to introduce new knowledge (spillovers). A series of empirical studies confirms that technological development, innovations and growth in private sector, novel theoretical insights, new techniques and skills that usually difficult for companies to find and access, can be made possible by the academic knowledge and contribution [12], [13].

While examining the importance of academic knowledge to the business growth, [14] heralded it a complex phenomenon. Nevertheless, it has also been noticed that areas with research-intensive universities have better opportunities to attract and support innovative firms than other areas.

4 Academe Enticement for U-I R&D Collaborations

Empirical studies portrays several reasons that support and promote U-I collaborations. Literature enlightens why the firms favor and seek the collaboration with academic institutions. Julio Alberto [15] demonstrates that industry supports the collaboration with university researchers because,

1) Universities Introduce novel solutions to problems
2) Academic Institutions are Valuable origin of knowledge spillovers about new technology and its executions

3) The academe possesses imperative competencies to fulfill the business needs of industry.

On the contrary, firms are primarily accessing universities in their craving for knowledge, novelty and proficiency. In fact, the kind of partnership and communications between industry and universities is majorly affected by the involvement and motivation by both actors [16]. Reasons for U to collaborate with industries are research funds and assistance. Researchers in U are required more financial supports for latest equipped labs, access external knowledge, and to establish consortiums for researchers to meet with the technological challenges. Therefore, the creation, exploitation and transfer of knowledge are contributing as emerging important factors in modern economies. Researchers as [17] also pronounces the collaborative incentives in a way that University-Industry research collaborations alleviate the researchers to get access to Industrial R&D facilities to improve their technical quotients along with other financial ads. These funds are always helpful for attaining new instrumentality and additional research personnel needs. Additionally, in order to increase the revenues from public and private sources universities are gradually getting more involved in research, exploration and other activities to chase the academic excellence and researchers [8]. The universities that share the royalties with researchers– inventors become successful in technology transfer and gain higher royalties as compare to those that do not share.[17].

According to Lee [17], the basic stimulant for industrial firms to collaborate is to approach the novelty in knowledge (76%) motivational for innovation (61%). Siegel [20] admitted that working in the collaboration with industrial scientists have made him better and effective researcher.

The intensity of funds generated and provided by private sources to universities is directly related to the extent and capacity of research endeavored at the universities [21]. Similarly, firms competing in international market are relatively more stimulated to collaborate with universities than firms facing only local market [22, 23].

Overall, increasing research funds, equipping research labs with latest technology, sharing practical expertise with practitioners, access of latest techniques to resolve a technological complex issues, finding jobs and internships for own university graduates and new business opportunities are major incentives that force academia to collaborate with industry.

5 Industry Enticement for R&D Collaborations

The importance of university–industry collaboration has greatly increased in the industrialized world since the late 1970s [24], [25]. Universities are equipped with latest knowledge reserves, researchers armed with latest researches and cheap research labor in the form of university graduates with their final thesis and projects based on latest technology. Empirical research depicts motives and causes for industry to collaborate with university. The main factor for this collaboration is to support an organization to become an effective and substantial innovator. Academia support can help the firms to achieve rapid innovative goals by facilitating technology transfer from academic institutes to the industry. As a result, it can boost up the firm's regional and national growth. In modern industrial economies, the basic reason of economic growth is the replacement of exploitation of natural resources and labor-intensive industries with the new knowledge [8]. Accordingly, universities contribute a key social and economic role [26]. In his research, Cohen [27] identifies that in order to meet the targets of improving excellence, prestige and reputation in introduction and dissemination of knowledge, the university is basically pushed by the need to seek funds for the purpose [28].

The streams of literature on university–industry collaborations are majorly supported by the range of empirical research, case studies, patent and bibliometric analyses. One part of the whole literature on the university–industry points out and supports the positive effect of scientific outcomes on the economic field. Scientific outcomes pursued to boost up the sales and higher research productivity and patenting process for companies [26]. The next string of literature analyzes the relative significance of PROs (Public Research Organizations) from the firms' perspective, as an external means of information both for novel ideas and innovation completion and application.

In 1990s, [6] anticipated in his study that without the contribution of academic research in last 15 years, 10% of innovations could not have been realized during 1975-1985 period or would have been pursued too late. A German study following Mansfield's approach argued that in the period of 1993–1996 40% of German companies introduced innovations that could not have been developed without the guideline of modern university research [7].

Literature exhibits that U-I collaboration is a form of bidirectional relationship where knowledge is transferred and exchanged from both partners. While managing these collaborations, there are so many problems encounters. The most important is trust among the partners. There is another main problem that industries need a quick response but research is continues process. On the other hand, universities are mostly impelled by the scientific research having academic culture that is facilitated with openness and relaxed working environment, whereas firms are shaped by comparatively inflexible, standardized processes and culture [29]. In spite of the literature support and evidences on a positive effect, various researchers emphasize that their knowledge on the interactions and relations between universities and industries is still inadequate, limited and vague.

6 U-I Collaboration Stimulating Dynamics

Followings are main features discussed in the literature by different authors that stimulate universities and industries to collaborate for smooth execution of joint R&D projects.

A. Innovation

Innovation is considered as the most important feature that pushes the organizations to establish cooperation. Organizations with innovative tendencies have to face the ever-growing technological challenges and complexities. These challenges can be met by proceeding in a certain circumstances for R&D activities. Innovation may be of different type depending upon the strategy used by the firm; [1]Product innovation, process innovation, innovation for the market and innovation for firm. Collaboration propensity for R&D projects is affected by the type of innovation. Innovation for the market and innovation for firm are alternatively distinguished forms of innovations [30].

B. Firm Size

Bidirectional argues have been observed in term of affect of firm size as a motivating factor for University-I R&D collaborations. Some author support that bigger the firm size, more will be collaboration among partners, on the other hand, some historical views are against as firm size has no affect for innovation and collaboration. In German, universities have been reported to prefer collaborations with big firms and universities. Reason is their better financing capacity and the scientific orientation of their research [7]. The frequency of innovation is directly proportionate to the firm size [22]. Nearly one fifth of firms employing more than 500 employees engaged in a collaboration agreement with a university or a college during the period of 1997–1999. Large firms are considered more reliable for R&D collaboration due to having core competencies for a specific product or service and allocation of large budgets under R&D budget heads. Supports for large firms have also been inclined by [30] that large firms are better able to carry R&D activities than smaller ones, since they benefit from economies of scale and scope. In Canada, large firms are also more inclined, compared to small firms, to get involved in partnerships with universities [22].

C. Openness of the firms

Collaborating firms mostly like to use the exiting knowledgebase for easiness and reusability of articulated R&D intellectual property. Proper agreements among partners and patenting techniques are useful tools for on organization to become open. Firms having more tendencies towards using exiting knowledge domains for innovation process have been observed to make more alliances. Knowledge spillover (incoming or outgoing) is also attractive for the other firms to participate in this collaborating structure. Research work of [32] and [33] believe that external knowledge flows have on decision to collaborate in R&D projects with the other firms. Contrastively, [34] has belief that the incoming spillovers reflect the importance of available public knowledge. There is a significant relation between incoming spillovers and the decision to collaborate in R&D. In addition, the higher the incoming spillovers are, the greater the scope for learning within R&D collaborations, and hence the greater is the marginal profit to be derived from collaboration [33].

D. Firm's R&D capacity

R&D Capacity is internal knowledge flows and R&D tendency of the firm to collaborate with the other firms. Empirical research analysis for choice of collaboration in

---

[1] Product innovation (related with goals and services), process innovation (Related with Technological innovations).

Belgian manufacturing firms suggests that R&D capacity affects the decision to collaborate with universities. R&D capacity of a firm can be assessed by scrutinizing the internal sources of knowledge owned by the firm. The Presence of sources by a firm in great quantity is the indication of great internal knowledge reserves that is good for R&D capacity development.

The other way to asses R&D capacity is firm's R&D intensity. R&D intensity is an indicator of the firm's absorptive capacity [35]. Empirical studies, have shown that firms' absorptive capacity depends on their own R&D intensity and the benefits from R&D collaboration depend on the absorptive capacity of the firm [33]. References as [36]and [37] also has illustrated a positive impact of R&D intensity of firms on R&D collaboration. Another line of empirical research has specifically taken into account the symbiotic relationship between R&D collaboration and in-house R&D activities. [38].

E. Innovation Barriers

A paradigm shift of R&D collaboration is to facilitate a firm to overcome the barriers or difficulties that arise due to technological complexities and innovative activities during execution of joint R&D projects. So, collaboration leads to reduce and overcome these barriers or difficulties. Different reasons for collaboration have been discussed but the ability to share cost and risks is important for the success of R&D collaboration [39]. Studies of [32] weighed three measures for innovation hampering faced by a firm and these potentially push the firm to collaborate: cost constraints, risk constraints, and organizational capability. Theter [2] presented the list of innovation process difficulties and use of collaboration to reduce these difficulties: stakeholders' response to innovation, organizational behavior and inadequacies, availability and cost of finance for innovation, difficulties with regulations or standards, and a lack of information on technologies major items for this list.

7 U-I Collaboration Disintigrating Factors

Many authors have highlighted the important factors and determinants that are necessary for U-I R&D collaboration. A few articles have discussed the reasons that leads towards U-I collaborations failures This section will discuss those stimulating situation that can lead to disintegration of U-I collaborations. If these challenges are kept in mind while making R&D Collaborations especially among partners like academia and industry, such alliances may be protected for long time and strategic benefits.

- *Lack of trust among the partners while applying mitigation and negotitiation skills*
- *Lower tendenciesof R&D activities*
- *Interfaring secrecy and privacyof the other partners*
- *Avoiding quality and other standardizations during collaboration*
- *Bypassing professional ethics and etiquettes*
- *Poor communication while develop project proposals for collaborating R&D projects.*

- *shortage of trainings for students with latest tools of technology and softwares used by the industryfor collaboration*
- *insufficient meetings among industry magnates and researchers at universities*
- *Sharing the modules of project rathar than complete project*
- *Defeciency in documentations for intellectual and technological copyrights*
- *Any knowledge piracy/frogry record in past*
- *Illegitimate Transfer of technology and knowledge reserves for competitive advantages*
- *Reducing the ratio between total employement and R&D emloyment*
- *Unpredictable results/outcomes weakens the realtion among partners*
- *Lack of core competencies*
- *Lack of oppenness of a firm or university*
- *Improper knowledge protecting techniques from any partner*
- *Obscured time lines and schedulesfor R&D projects being exicuted as U-Icollaboration*

8 Conclusion

This research article has highlighted the two important domains of University-Industry R&D collaborations. Firstly, it has marked out the factors that stimulate and steer the successful U-I collaboration. Secondly, the disintegrating factors are addressed that become the cause of collaboration termination without achieving the goals for alliances. This article also points out the attractors for both partners for successful collaborations. The academe tycoons are directed towards such alliances due to the raise in their academic research funds, practicalities for a core competencies and new business directions. In return, entrepreneurs' gain latest technology and knowledge access to overcome technological complexities and attaining innovative goals at lower R&D budgets. At the end, a road map for effective joint ventures is provided while highlighting the menaces for collaboration breakups.

Acknowledgment. The author is thankful to China Scholarship Council and NPU for research grants for this contribution

References

[1] Polenske, K.R.: Competition, collaboration and cooperation: an uneasy triangle in networks of firms and regions. Regional Studies 38, 1029–1104 (2004)
[2] Theter, B.S.: Who co-operates for innovation, and why. An empirical analysis. Res. Policy 31, 947–967 (2002)
[3] Hagedoorn, J.: Inter-firm R&D partnerships: an overview of major trends and patterns since 1960. Research Policy 31, 477–492 (2002)
[4] Baumol, W.J.: The Free-Market Innovation Machine. Princeton University Press, Princeton

[5] Hagedoorn, J.: Understanding the Rationale of Strategic Technology Partnering: Interorganizational Modes of Cooperation and Sectoral differences. Strategic Management Journal 14, 371–385 (1993)
[6] Mansfield, E.: Academic research and industrial innovation. Research Policy 26, 1–12 (1991)
[7] Beise, M., Stahl, H.: Public research and industrial innovation in Germany. Research Policy 28, 397–422 (1999)
[8] Hanel, P., St-Pierre, M.: Industry–University Collaboration by Canadian Manufacturing Firms. Journal of Technology Transfer 31, 485–499 (2006)
[9] Etzkowitz, H., Leydesdorff, L.: The dynamics of innovation: from national systems and.Mode 2.to a Triple Helix of university.industry.government relations. Research Policy 29(2), 109–123 (2000)
[10] Chen, K., Kenney, M.: Universities/research institutes and regional innovation systems: The case of Beijing and Shenzhen. World Dev. 35(6), 1056–1074 (2007)
[11] Li, J.: Global R&D Alliances in China: Collaborations With Universities and Research Institutes. IEEE Transactions on Engineering Management 57(1) (2010)
[12] Nelson, R.R.: Institutions Supporting Technical Advance in Industry. American Economic Review 762, 186–189 (1986)
[13] Zucker, L.G., Darby, M.R.: Socio-economic Impact of Nanoscale Science: Initial Results and NanoBank, NBER Working Papers 1118 (2005)
[14] Griliches, Z.: Productivity, R&D and the Data Constraint. American Economic Review 84, 1–23 (1994)
[15] Julio Alberto Pertuze Salas' Thesis; requirement for the degree of Master of Sciences in Technology and Policy at the Massachusetts Institute of Technology (June 2009)
[16] Poyago-Theotoky, J., Beath, J., Siegel, D.: Universities and Fundamental Research: Reflections on the Growth (2002)
[17] Breschi, S., Lissoni, F., Montobbio, F.: The scientific productivity of academic inventors: New evidence from Italian data. Economics of Innovation and New Technology 16(2), 101–118 (2007)
[18] Friedman, J., Silberman, J.: University Technology transfer: Do Incentives, Management, and Location Matter? The Journal of Technology Transfer 28, 17–30 (2003)
[19] Lee, J.-Y.: The Sustainability of University–Industry Research Collaboration: An Empirical Assessment. Journal of Technology Transfer 25(2), 111–133 (2000)
[20] Siegel, D.S., Waldman, D.A., Atwater, L.E., Link, A.N.: Commercial knowledge transfers from universities to firms: Improving the effectiveness of university–industry collaboration. Journal of High Technology Management Research 14(1), 111–133 (2003)
[21] Berman, E.M.: The Economic Impact of Industry-Funded University R&D. Research Policy 19, 349–355 (1990)
[22] Warda, J.: Perspectives on R&D Collaboration: A Survey of University and Industry Leaders. Conference Board of Canada, Ottawa (1995)
[23] Baldwin, J.R., Hanel, P.: Innovation and Knowledge Creation in an Open Economy. Cambridge University Press, Cambridge (2003)
[24] Cohen, W.M., Nelson, R.R., Walsh, J.P.: Links and impacts: The influence of public research on industrial R&D. Manage. Sci. 48, 1–23 (2002)
[25] Mowery, D., Rosenberg, N.: The U.S. national innovation system. In: Nelson, R.R. (ed.) National Innovation Systems: A Comparative Analysis, pp. 29–75. Oxford Univ. Press, New York (1993)
[26] Feller, I.: Universities as Engines of R&D-based Economic Growth: They Think They Can. Research Policy 19, 335–348 (1990)

[27] Cohen, W.M., Levinthal, D.A.: Innovation and Learning: Two Faces of R&D. The Economic Journal 99, 569–596 (1989)
[28] OCDE, Trends in University–Industry Research Partnerships. STI Review 23, 39–65 (1998)
[29] Schartinger, D., Schibany, A., Gassler, H.: Interactive relations between universities and firms: Empirical evidence for Austria. Journal of Technology Transfer 26, 255–268 (2001)
[30] Annique Un, C., et al.: Determinants of R&D collaboration of service firms. Serv. Bus. 3, 373–394 (2009)
[31] Cohen, W.M., Klepper, S.: Firm Size and the Nature of Innovation within Industries: The Case of Process and Product Data. The Review of Economics and Statistics 78(2), 232–243 (1996)
[32] Mansfield, E.: Academic research and industrial innovation: An update of empirical findings. Research Policy 26(7-8), 773–776 (1998)
[33] Belderbos, R., Carree, M., Diederen, B., Lokshin, B., Veugelers, R.: Heterogeneity in R&D cooperation strategies. Int. J. Ind. Organ. 22, 1237–1263 (2004)
[34] López, A.: Determinants of R&D cooperation: Evidence form Spanish manufacturing firms. Int. J. Ind. Organ. 26, 113–136 (2008)
[35] Cassiman, B., Veugelers, R.: R&D cooperation and spillovers: some empirical evidence from Belgium. Am. Econ. Rev. 92(4), 1169–1184 (2002)
[36] Cohen, W.M., Levinthal, D.A.: Absorptive capacity: a new perspective on learning and innovation. Adm. Sci. Q 35(1), 128–152 (1990)
[37] Fritsch, M., Lukas, R.: Who cooperates on R&D? Res. Policy 30, 297–312 (2001)
[38] Colombo, M.G., Gerrone, P.: Technological cooperative agreements and firm R&D intensity. A note on casuality relations. Res. Policy 25(6), 923–932 (1996)
[39] Becker, W., Dietz, J.: R&D cooperation and innovation activities of firms-evidence for the German manufacturing industry. Res. Policy 33, 209–223 (2004)
[40] Tyler, B.B., Steensma, K.H.: Evaluating technological collaborative opportunities: a cognitive modelling perspective. Strateg. Manag. J. 16, 43–70 (1995)

Role Playing for Scholarly Articles

Bee Bee Chua

University of Technology, Sydney, Australia
beebee.chua@uts.edu.au

Abstract. In attempting to read a scholarly article, learners (students) often struggle with problems of comprehension. It is likely that when a scholar writes a paper and discusses a new idea or a method within a particular discipline, they assume that readers have a scholarly background enabling them to understand the paper content in detail. Such an assumption is not justified, and there is evidence that students who are learning to carry out research for the first time find that understanding scholars' papers is not always an easy task. Deciding which RE (Requirement Elicitation) technique and tool to apply to issues can become complicated for educators constructing a learning approach which emphasises that group learners should read scholarly articles in a short time and be able to summarise the content from the article, while at the same time allowing learners to devise solutions that will, enhance their creativity and innovation, allowing them to explore how an idea in a paper could be integrated into an industry application. A case study in this paper introduces a university framework, which can be applied to aid students in their decision-making on selecting a presentation technique; that is, choosing role-playing as the appropriate technique for an effective learning outcome.

Keywords: Role Playing, Scholarly Articles, Requirement Elicitation techniques.

1 Introduction

A scholarly article is defined in many ways. A standard definition describes it as an original research or experimentation written by a researcher or an expert in the field who is often affiliated with a college or university [1]. California State University, Chico [2] conducted a research study to compare and contrast scholarly articles with other article types and established that the language used in scholarly articles is a technical terminology appropriate to the discipline. It is assumed that readers will have a similar scholarly background, but despite this assumption, there is unfortunately no evidence that the process of reading and understanding scholarly articles is easy.

Learners want the simplest possible solution in understanding scholars' papers to keep them at the cutting edge of a knowledge-based economy [3, 4]. This paper highlights a case study using role-playing as a collaborative technique for information gathering from a paper in terms of translating emerging concepts into practical knowledge with the aid of supports to understanding.

T.-h. Kim et al. (Eds.): ASEA/DRBC/EL 2011, CCIS 257, pp. 662–674, 2011.

The paper is structured as follows: the introduction provides an overview of definitions of scholarly articles and a discussion of the access of scholarly articles by readers. Section 2 is a brief outline of educators' feedback on scholarly articles and Section 3 is a discussion of scholarly papers and role playing. Section 4 discusses related works on learning techniques. Section 5 highlights a case study using the role play technique for implementation. Section 6 reports the case study findings and Section 7 discusses the analysis and evaluation of the results. Section 8 is the conclusion and proposal for future work.

2 Educators' Feedback on Scholarly Articles

As an educator, I have always wanted to gather a holistic view from other educators as to what they expect from learners after reading scholarly articles. I surveyed at least ten educators in a faculty of a large city university to understand what their aims were for learners who have to read scholarly papers. Every educator has different expectations and requirements; for example, some educators provide scholarly articles for learners to read, but their requirement is for learners to summarize the article in their own words. This means writing a short version of the research paper, from which the educator can assess the learner's writing and analytical skills. The process is similar to a 'requirements elicitation' technique, that is, requirement analysis.

One group of educators does not ask for a summary page but wants to know how the learners judge the scholarly articles, to test their evaluative skills. This process is similar to the requirement gathering technique called 'prototyping'. Two out of ten educators want learners to answer questions in response to scholarly articles. The aim is to test their critical analysis in problem solving; this process is similar to the interview technique. Four other educators want learners to discuss what the article is about, a process which is similar to the agile methodology of story-telling. One commonality of these approaches for scholarly papers is managing and eliciting requirements.

None of the educators' approaches has flaws, unfortunately, no educator claims that their technique is so useful that every student finds reading scholarly articles interesting. Similarly, there is no disagreement among educators on the need to investigate the development of a useful technique to help students understand scholarly articles effectively.

Interestingly, students know how to extract important data and facts from papers, but when asked to relate the theories that are discussed in a paper and put them into practice using a real world example, the process becomes quite difficult. Certain requirements elicitation techniques such as brainstorming, prototyping, interviews, agile methodology and role playing are used to clarify, elicit and confirm requirement needs with users [5,6,7,8,9,10,11] in a project environment. Some of these techniques are thought to be worth introducing into the academic environment to promote learning effects by encouraging learning between students via socialization and interaction. These techniques are useful for group discussion and for promoting a group synergy and subsequent effects on student learning.

According to Ambler [5], agile methodology highlights story telling from an unclear scenario. It is effective for eliciting users' or customers' requirements, and is useful for helping users to clarify their knowledge through an implicit method, by putting their ideas into a narrative to help the developer understand their requirements. Applying agile methodology in the context of scholarly articles helps the explicit understanding of a paper rather than the implicit gathering of knowledge from a case study. On the other hand, the use of role-playing promotes critical review by introducing active learning [12] and this technique obviously gives learners access to knowledge both explicitly and implicitly. There is very minimal literature which considers using role playing technique as a learning tool for understanding scholarly articles.

3 Scholarly Papers and Role Playing

Scholarly articles need to be succinct in order to sustain the reader's interest. Papers are usually circulated within academic institutions and are available to industry because they not only contribute to the body of knowledge, but also to the development of new products and services, new processes and new technology, all of which benefit organizations and society as a whole. They drive innovation and change. The three largest groups of people who frequently need to access, retrieve and read scholarly papers are educators, researchers, and students. They read scholarly papers to: 1) conduct new research, 2) collect information, 3) advance knowledge, and 4) collect ideas and translate them into projects. Developing scholarly articles, however, is compelling and challenging. Introducing them in the classroom may frequently be even more challenging, especially if they are to attract students' interest as a support for their learning [32,36].

The reasons are essentially two fold. Firstly, some articles are not easily read and understood due to the technical nature of the language used, and secondly, the students' lack of critical research skills disadvantages them in understanding the methodologies used in the development of the articles It is therefore recommended that an RE technique be applied in order to facilitate a good learning process to help students understand scholarly articles. Using role-playing, according to my evidence, can definitely improve this process. The technique has been widely discussed in literature for teaching social-technical subjects such as software engineering and project management [12,13,14,15,16,17]. Its emphasis is on dealing with human issues; for example, establishing communication, collaboration, motivation, work environment, team harmony, sense of purpose, engagement, training and education.

The technique is used in environments where software inspection is carried out, in the process of debating, and in the involvement of panel discussions that require role-playing [18,19,20]. McGuffee [19] used role playing to help students understand concepts of object oriented design. Integrating scholarly papers into any learning activity can facilitate the student learning process and can help to increase learners' interest and excitement [32] A number of traditional teaching and learning methods fail to demonstrate explicitly how to introduce research into practice-based learning. Many learning methods focus on theory-based and practical-based components, but very few have integrated research-based components into their learning processes. Few researchers could imagine how the mapping of scholarly papers enables learners to improve their learning performance and even to experience joy in reading them, particularly when achieved by means of role-playing.

4 Related Works on Learning Techniques

The term 'learning' is broad. Buchanan and Huczynski [21] define learning as 'the process of acquiring knowledge through experience which leads to a change in behaviour'. In other words, learning is not just the acquisition of knowledge, but its application by doing something different in the world.Case based learning is not a new concept in education. It is effective, but it can be challenging. These challenges have been discussed widely in research that focuses on achieving better learning experiences by recognizing the depth of the subject content while increasing the capacity of the learner to develop skills, including problem solving skills [22,23,24,25,26,27,28].

Case based learning can be conducted either by individuals or by groups. Traditionally, the method involves face-to-face teaching. Although some researchers claim that face-to-face teaching of case based reasoning is one of the most traditional and effective learning methods, it demonstrates a lack of learning innovation. Face-to-face teaching is usually conducted in a classroom environment where one or more learners absorb the concepts or theories directly from an educator. The learner can clarify immediate doubts directly with the educator. Such a method promotes a dual learning loop: questions from learners and feedback from educators. The drawback of this approach is that not all learners are able to accept and adapt to an educator's teaching techniques. In particular, the technique used in case based reasoning does not promote student learning through the sharing of ideas and knowledge among individuals in the class. Hence, some students find learning difficult, rather than enjoyable or fun. In the worst case, students can become bored with a single and lengthy case study, and instead of their learning horizons being widened, their thinking narrows to focus solely on the case.

A familiar scenario that has incorporated changes can drive us to learn something new, or adjust to a new way of operating, or to unlearn something. From an organizational learning point of view [28], learning is associated with two important concepts: the first is the power of knowledge acquisition, and the second is the power of knowledge sharing. Understanding scholarly articles provides readers with knowledge, and thus increases their ability to knowledge-share with others [29,30].

5 An Adapted Framework in Support of Choosing Presentation Techniques for Understanding Scholarly Articles

All universities have their own teaching philosophy, as does my university. A teaching framework constructed on THINK, CHANGE and DO (see Figure. 1) promotes a philosophical view in higher education to seek better teaching and learning [35]. My university enrolls approximately 60% students from international backgrounds and 40% local students. As result of the students' diverse educational backgrounds, educators seek ways to improve their teaching and learning techniques.

A subject that I coordinated recently advised my postgraduate students to use a university framework (Figure. 1) as a basis to help them decide on a presentation technique for providing learners with an understanding of scholarly articles and the use of a learning tool evaluated by Chua and Dyson [31] for group and class discussions. As the articles focus on organizational changes and change management, the understanding of each page in the paper discussion is important. Students took the subject coordinator's advice seriously. The ten groups adapted this framework to help them frame their thinking in selecting a presentation technique. Nine groups chose agile methods like story-telling to present their findings. One particular group interestingly chose role playing instead.

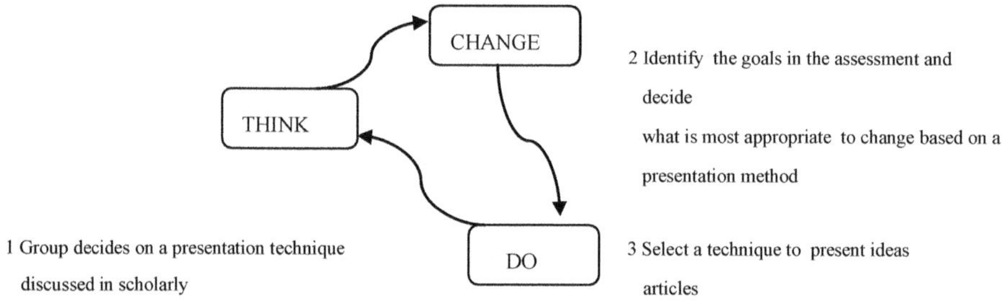

Fig. 1. Adopted UTS framework, THINK. CHANGE. DO

According to reviews of role playing [17,18,19,20], it promotes effective interpersonal relations and social transactions among participants. "In order for a simulation to occur the participants must accept the duties and responsibilities of their roles and functions, and do the best they can in the situation in which they find themselves" [17]. To fulfill their role responsibilities, students must relate to others in the simulation, utilizing effective social skills. The other aspect of role playing is that of allowing members to reflect what they have learned by reinforcing ideas to easily remember the concepts and ideas in papers. It achieves that in the memory of both participatory and non-participatory learners more quickly than using any RE methods

6 Findings

Nine groups chose common presentation techniques to discuss ideas addressed in a paper in class. Figure. 2 shows the subject coordinator's assessment criteria against which students will be tested. Of the three main assessment criteria, the component of research skill has the highest mark on innovation and invention.

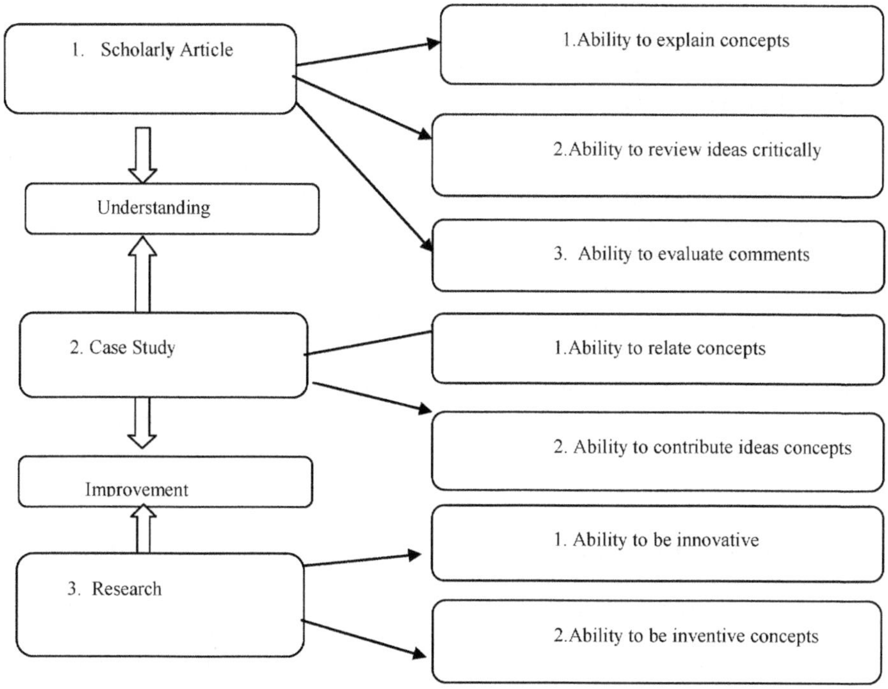

Fig. 2. Subject Assessment Criteria

It was assumed that students would review this criterion carefully and decide on a presentation technique.

This was not the primary concern for nine groups as they did not prioritize a good presentation as their first criterion to aim for; only the group using role playing did this (see Table 1).

Table 1. Groups Goal Prioritization

	Groups Criteria Prioritization								
Structure	1	2	3	4	5	6	7	8	9
Scholarly article	1	1	1	1	2	1	1	1	1
Case Study	2	3	2	2	3	3	2	2	2
Research	3	2	3	3	1	2	3	3	3

The role playing team (group 5) had six members. All are international students and from different cultural backgrounds. They were asked to read the scholarly paper 'Choosing strategies for change' [33], to understand the concept, put ideas into a case study and discuss an innovative and inventive approach. This paper is sixteen pages long and discusses methods for managing resistance. If six members read a scholarly article, it is unlikely that they will all achieve a consistent understanding and knowledge from the paper, especially given the cultural differences and language problems of this group. The group discussed and carefully reviewed the content of the paper and decided what they needed to present in class. They remembered being told by the subject coordinator that important points highlighted in a paper must relate to a practical case study.

They looked at the paper and selected two tables in the paper that discussed 1) methods for managing resistance (see Figure 3) and 2) methods for dealing with resistance to change (see Figure. 4). The group discussed among themselves the methods that are often used in organizations and decided that the way to present their ideas was by role playing. This corresponds with Skehan's finding [14] on using the role playing method: that it is a goal which needs to be worked towards, the activity is

Methods	How to use	When to Use	Advantages	Drawbacks
Education	Communicate with desire for changes and reasons for them	Employees lack information about the implications of the change	Once persuaded, people often help to implement the change	Time consuming if many people are involved
Participation	Involving potential resistors in designing and implementing change	Change initiators lack sufficient information to design the change	People feel more committed to making the change happen	Time consuming, and employees may design inappropriate change
Facilitation	Provide skilled training and emotional support	People are resistant because they can't make the adjustments needed	No other approach works as well with adjustment problems	Can be time consuming and expensive; can still fail
Negotiation	Offer incentives for making the change	People will lose out in the change and have considerable power to resist	A relatively easy way to defuse major resistance	Can be expensive and expose managers to the possibility of blackmail
Coercion	Threaten loss of jobs or promotion opportunities; fire those who can't or won't change	Speed is essential and change imitators possess considerable power	Works quickly and can overcome any kind of resistance	Can spark intense resentment toward change initiators

Fig. 3. Methods for managing resistance cited from [33]

outcome-evaluated and there is a real-world relationship. Activities in role playing do not focus on language, but on the goals and activities in particular.

The goal is to relate concepts of methods suitable for managing resistance and change in a medium sized IT organization. The scenario for the role play is as follows: A director is appointed, a manager, two help desk users, one consultant and one supplier. The player who acts as a director will need to review costing. The IT manager needs to find a method to educate staff in how to overcome change and manage resistance the two helpdesk users have and in addition to search for an appropriate solution. The consultant's task is to provide ideas about how to improve helpdesk work and the supplier's is to provide a solution to the organization.

Approach	Commonly used in these situations	Advantages	Drawbacks
Education + Communication	Where there is a lack of information or inaccurate information and analysis	Once persuaded, people will often help with implementation of the change	Can be very time consuming if many people are involved
Participation and Involvement	When the initiators do not have all the information they need to design the change, and where others have considerable power to resist	People who participate will be committed to implementing change and any relevant information they have will be integrated into the change plan	Can be very time consuming if participators design an inappropriate change
Facilitation + Support	When people are resisting because of adjustment problems	No other approach works as well with adjustment problems	Can be very time consuming, expensive, and can still fail
Manipulation + Cooperation	When other tactics will not work or are too expensive	Can be a relatively quick and inexpensive solution to resistance problems	Can lead to future problems if people feel manipulated
Explicit + Implicit Coercion	When speed is essential, and the change initiators posses considerable power	Is speedy and can overcome any kind of resistance	Can be risky if it leaves people mad at the initiators

Fig. 4. Methods for dealing with resistance to change cited from [33]

7 Results Analysis

An anonymous survey was distributed to all students to evaluate and comment on their responses to the role play technique. Nearly 90% students completed and returned the survey. Nine students did not complete it as they did not attend the class. The survey findings are shown in Table 2, Figure. 5 and Figure. 6.

Table 2. Survey Findings

Group Completed Survey Form									
Group	1	2	3	4	5	6	7	8	9
Mem	5	6	6	5	6	5	5	6	5
Number of survey returned	5	6	5	5	NA	4	5	4	3
Students in each group watching the role play presentation and rated their like and dislike as per below									
Like	5	5	5	5	NA	3	5	3	2
Dislike	0	1	0	0	NA	1	0	1	1

N.A. NOT REQUIRED

Figure 5 and 6 show a high percentage of student satisfaction and I consolidated some of their feedback, explaining what they like about role playing, is given below (actual quotes):

1. 'Role playing provides valuable information.'
2. 'A technique reinforcing paper materials being read.'
3. 'Scholarly paper is presented in a creative way.'
4. 'Role playing helps us remember the content of the paper and never to forget it specially because the article was one of the most useful and interesting in Change Management.'
5. 'Role playing is unique for team unity and collaboration. Paper summarization cannot be done by one person but as a group.'
6. 'Role playing is a good way of presenting ideas.'
7. 'It gives us an impressive view who responsible what in each role.'
8. 'It is an interesting process to develop and find out relevant issues on presentation.'

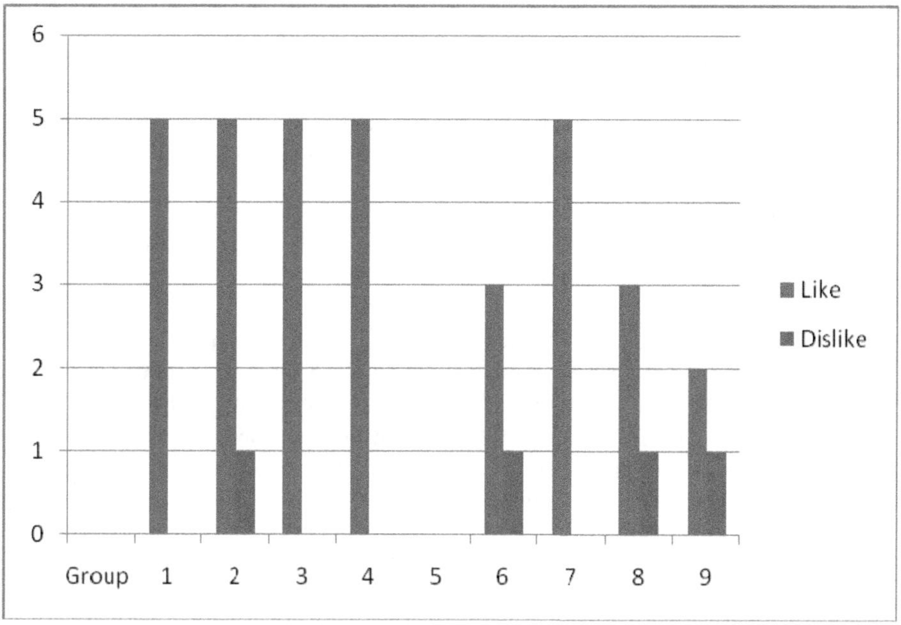

Fig. 5. Class response to role playing technique

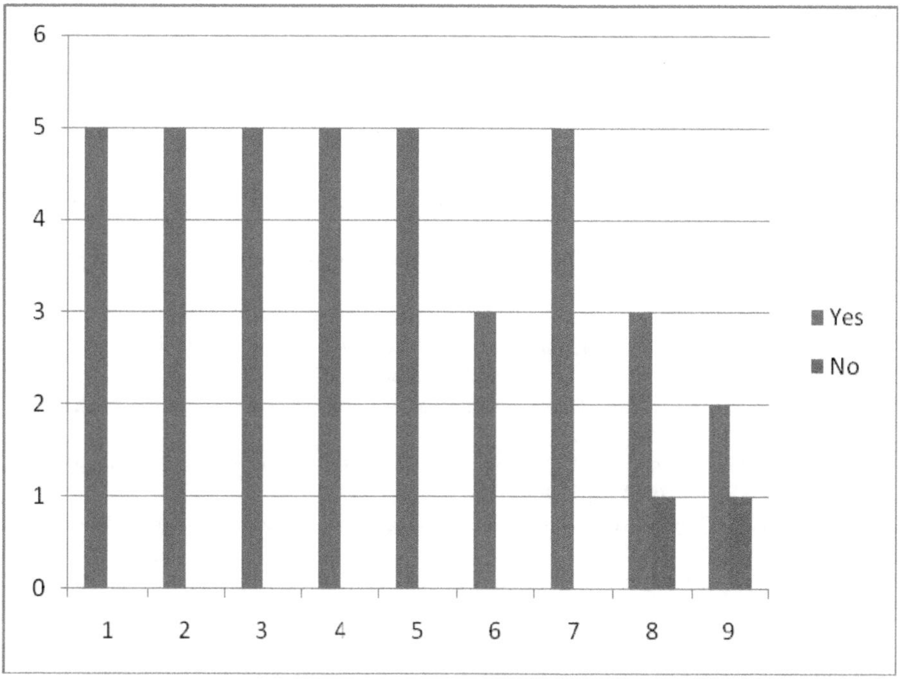

Fig. 6. Does role playing technique help students to understand scholarly articles?

Figure 6 shows a minority of students did not like the role playing techniques recommend for role playing improvements included the language problem. As the group members are non-English speaking, some students found understanding their presentation somewhat difficult. Kaplan [34] argues against role-plays that focus solely on prescriptive themes emphasizing specific fields of vocabulary, as they do not capture the spontaneous, real-life flow of conversation.

8 Conclusion and Future Works

The case study demonstrates that using the role-playing technique is effective for helping students to understand scholarly articles. The university framework that is based on allow students to stimulate their thinking in choosing an RE technique appropriately. Role- playing shows strong student engagement in deep learning, and establishes strong team collaboration in spite of the different cultural backgrounds from which the team members come. Nonetheless, role-playing needs strategic planning, and further evaluation is important. Although the group presented their scholarly article well, using role playing, a feedback mechanism is not evaluated. My next step is to evaluate role-playing effects from different groups which will be sufficient to determine whether it is appropriate to introduce it in big classes.

References

[1] Anonymous. What is a scholarly article or book? `http://instructional1.calstaela.edu/tclim/definition-boxes/scholarly_article.htm` (accessed on November 25, 2010)
[2] California State University, Chico Meriam Library `http://www.csuchico.edu/lins/handouts/scholarly.pdf` (accessed on November 25, 2010)
[3] Hussein, R., Goodman, J.: Leading with Knowledge: The Nature of Competition in the 21st Century. Sage, Thousand Oaks (1998)
[4] Sommerville, I.: Software Engineering. Addison Wesley, Wokingham (1983)
[5] Ambler, S.W.: Agile Modelling: Extreme Practices for eXtreme Programming and the Unified Process. John Wiley and Sons, New York (2002)
[6] Cockburn, A., Highsmith, J.: Agile software development: The people factor. IEEE Computer 34(11), 131–133 (2001)
[7] Kotonya, G., Sommerville, I.: Requirements Engineering Processes and Techniques. John Wiley and Sons, New York (1998)
[8] Kotonya, G., Sommerville, I.: Requirements engineering with viewpoints. Software Engineering 1(11), 5–18 (1996)
[9] Vonk, R.: Prototyping: The Effective Use of CASE Technology. Prentice Hall, New York (1990)
[10] Young, R.R.: Effective Requirements Practices. Addison-Wesley, Boston (2001)
[11] Tyson, R.H., LaFrance, J.: Integrating Role-Play into Software Engineering Courses. Journal of Computing Sciences in Colleges 22(2), 32–38 (2006)

[12] Berstein, L., Klappholz, D., Kelley, C.: Eliminating adversion to software process in computer science students and measuring the results. In: Proceedings of the 15th Conference on Software Engineering Education and Training (2002)

[13] Sullivan, S.A.: A software project management course role play team project approach emphasizing written and oral communication skills. In: Proceedings of the 24th SIGCSE Technical Symposium on Computer Science Education (1993)

[14] Skehan, P.: A Cognitive Approach To Language Learning. Oxford University Press, Oxford (1998)

[15] Henry, T.R., LaFrance, J.: Integrating role-play into software engineering courses. Journal of Computing Science in Colleges 22(2), 32–88 (2006)

[16] Ludi, S., Natarajan, S., Reichlmayr, T.: An introductory software engineering course that facilitates active learning. In: Proceedings of the 36th SIGCSE Technical Symposium on Computer Science Education, pp. 302–306 (2005)

[17] Jones, J.: Participatory teaching methods in computer science. In: Proceedings of the 18th SIGCSE Technical Symposium On Computer Science Education (1987)

[18] Andrianoff, S., Levine, D.: Role playing in an object-oriented world. In: Proceedings of the 33rd SIGCSE Technical Symposium on Computer Science Education (2002)

[19] McGuffee, J.: Drama in the computer science classroom. Journal of Computing Sciences in Colleges 19(4), 292–298 (2004)

[20] Kane, L.: Learners and active learning methodologies. International Journal of Lifelong Education 23(3), 275–286 (2004)

[21] Buchanan, D., Huczynski, A.: Organizational Behaviour. Prentice Hall, London (1995)

[22] Kheong, L.S.: Framework for structuring learning in problem-based learning, `http://pbl.tp.edu.sg/Understanding%20PBL/Articles/lyejayarartna.pdf` (accessed December 6, 2009)

[23] Clarke, S., Thomas, R., Adams, M.: Developing case studies to enhance student learning, `http://crpit.com/confpapers/CRPITV42Clarke.pdf` (accessed December 6, 2009)

[24] Aha, D.W.: Case-based learning algorithms. In: Proceedings of DARPA Workshop on Case-Based Reasoning, pp. 147–157. Morgan Kaufmann, San Mateo (1991)

[25] Cardie, C.: Using decision trees to improve case-based learning, fMJ:http://www.cs.cornell.edu/home/cardie/papers/ml-93.ps+8.+C.+Cardie,+1991.+%E2%80%9CUsing+Decision+Trees+to+Improve+Case-Based+Learning&cd=1&hl=en&ct=clnk&gl=sg (accessed December 6, 2009)

[26] Drummond, C.: Using a case base of surfaces to speed-up reinforcement learning. In: Proceedings of the 2nd International Conference on Case-Based Reasoning Research and Development, pp. 435–444. Springer, London (1997)

[27] Kolodner, J.L.: Case-Based Learning. Morgan-Kaufmann, San Mateo (1993)

[28] Drucker, P.F.: The coming of the new organization. Harvard Business Review on Knowledge Management, 1–19 (1998)

[29] Hussein, R., Goodman, J.: Leading with Knowledge: The Nature of Competition in the 21st Century. Sage, Thousand Oaks (1998)

[30] Davenport, T., Prusak, L.: Working Knowledge: How Organizations Manage What They Know. Harvard Business School Press, Boston (1998)

[31] Chua, B.B., Dyson, L.E.: Applying the ISO 9126 model to the evaluation of an e-learning System. In: Proceedings of the 21st ASCILITE Conference, pp. 184–190 (2004)

[32] Chua, B.B., Bernardo, D.V.: Introducing scholarly articles: A way for attaining educational sustainability. In: 2nd International IEEE Conference on Mobile, Hybrid, and On-Line Learning (2010)

[33] Kotter, J.P., Schlesinger, L.A.: Choosing strategies for change. Harvard Business Review, 1–13 (2008)

[34] Kaplan, M.A.: Learning to converse in a foreign language: the Reception Game. Simulation and Gaming, 149–163 (2008)

[35] University of Technology, Sydney, Think. Change. Do, `http://www.uts.edu.au/` (accessed November 26, 2010)

[36] Chua, B.B., Bernardo, D.V.: Integrating scholarly articles within e-learning courses: a framework. In: Proceedings of the 16th Annual SIGCSE Conference on Innovation and Technology in Computer Science Education, ITiCSE 2011, Darmstadt, Germany, June 27-29. ACM (2011)

Statistical Analysis and Prior Distributions of Significant Software Estimation Factors Based on ISBSG Release 10

Abou Bakar Nauman[1], Jahangir khan[1], Zubair A. Shaikh[2],
Abdul Wahid Shaikh[3], and Khisro khan[3]

[1] Department of computer science & Information Technology,
Sarhad university of science & Information Technology, peshawar 25000, pakistan
[2] Department of computer science,
FAST National university of computer & Emerging Sciences, karachi, pakistan
[3] Department of computer science,
Shah Abdul Latif university, Mirpur sukkar sindh, pakistan
{jahangir.csit,abubakar.csit}@suit.edu.pk,
zubair@nu.edu.pk, ashaikh@salu.edu.pk, khisrp2k5@hotmail.com

Abstract. Software estimation is an active research area with researchers working on areas like accuracy, new model development and statistical analysis. Estimates are probabilistic values and can be represented with a degree of uncertainty. Prior distributions are one of the way to represent the historical and organizational data which can be used by researchers to conduct further estimations. In this paper we introduce the software estimation landscape and prior distributions of significant factors, determined from ISBSG data set. These priors can be used for development of estimation models e.g. Bayesian networks. The paper make contributions in number of ways, it provides a brief overview of quality of data set. It also provides statistics of vital factors from dataset. This paper also provides prior distributions of productivity for Architecture e.g. Standalone, Client server and mixture of architectures.

Keywords: Software estimation, Statistical analysis, ISBSG data set, Prior distribution.

1 Introduction

Software estimation: Estimates are foundation of project management [1]. Two major estimates are conducted in the software engineering, size and effort. Size is the measure of functionalities of a software solution. Opposite to the physical volume like in physical commodity, in software engineering the size of software indicates the number of functionalities developed in a software project. As there are no tangible objects, the size estimation is itself a complex task. The effort estimates are mainly concerned with the amount of time required to develop software of a given size. Schedule and cost can be by-products of effort estimates. Effort estimation is also replaced by the term cost estimation due to the proportionality in effort and cost. Different factors, techniques and tools are used for both the size and effort estimates. Size estimates are

T.-h. Kim et al. (Eds.): ASEA/DRBC/EL 2011, CCIS 257, pp. 675–686, 2011.

used as an input for effort estimates. There are many factors which affect the accuracy and acceptability of the software engineering estimates. As the software engineering product, processes and project are not in physical form, they are always really hard to measure. The units, in which these estimates are presented, also become complex to understand e.g. function points or use-case point. Another factor is the amount of information available at the early stages of the project, lesser the amount of information lesser is the chances of accuracy of estimates. This phenomenon is represented as cone of uncertainty in literature. As the project goes further the uncertainty in estimates lessens. However it is required to be understood that the cone doesn't converges itself, it depends on the right application of management tools and techniques.

1.1 Estimates as Probability Statements

Software estimators acknowledge that software projects are full of uncertainty from all related external and internal factors [1,2]. This requires attaching the level of uncertainty with the estimates. Another method is to present Prediction Interval rather than a single value. Some estimation techniques e.g. SEER-M also represent the estimation in terms of probability distribution. Need of probability priors in this context is thus more important than having a single central tendency value. The traditional effort datasets e.g COCOMO are smaller in size and older in terms of time period. The inference techniques e.g. Bayesian Networks also require prior data distributions which can be used to inference and decision making. This research is thus significant in context with providing statistics based on ISBSG data set, as well as priors based on varying factors. In this paper we had made discussion on the factors in software estimation, dataset of ISBSG and availability of data in data set.

1.2 Estimation Factors

The software development is not a closed environment activity; it includes a lot of activities with their own factors affecting the whole software development project cost and schedule. The libraries are rich with the articles discussing the software development projects and factors involved in the estimation; however some of the representative articles are discussed here. There exist a large set of factors which affects the whole software development project; here we try to identify the most significant factors. The basic factors involved in the estimation process are Size, development productivity and environmental costs; however each factor is dependent on many other factors or sub factors.

There are more or less 100 factors which have been considered by researchers [4], however different researchers have focused on diverse set of factors, considering dissimilar viewpoints. Walston and Felix [5] used 36 factors in their research, the set of 36 factors consists of the areas of customer, experience, development environment, complexity , hardware and design techniques. In [4] 72 factors were considered, these 72 factors are categorizes in the methodology, complexity and experience. Some of the factors were later considered insignificant and a total of 21 factors were considered in the further research. In one of the significant research articles the author

[6] proposed a management model, which identified four subsystems in software development activity or organization. This model is not for estimation; however highlights the major factors in software development, the subsystems named as Human resource, software product, planning and control. These subsystems can be considered as the group of factors, as factors can be easily categorized by the each subsystem. The subsystems are shown to communicate with each other in the macro level, however existence and connectivity of 20 or more factors is also evident.

In another paper [7] the authors analyzed the data of software estimation and applied statistical techniques and methods to identify the most significant variables or factors in the software estimation. They started with a set of 20 factors and concluded with the identification of six most significant factors which are size, time, development platform, effort recording method, organization type and counting technique for function point. It is found by [8] that there are up-to 20 different factors which exist in different estimation models and most of them are commonly used in these models.

The discussion above concludes that there is no definite set of factors which are used for effort estimation in estimation models. The researchers have proposed the models based on the data sets available and the approach adopted for building the estimation models. However size is considered as most significant factor. There exist different sources of error in the estimation process which make the estimation results in accurate and the project manager has to deal with these sources [3]. It also depends who is performing the estimation process and what is his skill level in the area. The estimation techniques are not independent of the human interaction, these techniques involve human input in less or more amount [9-13]. Even in the mathematical models the human has to select values of different factors, which are mostly uncertain[9-13].

2 The ISBSG Data Set

The ISBSG group collects data of software projects and develops benchmarking standards, according to the available data (ISBSG 2007) [14]. The group has also developed some benchmark equations to represent the regress ional relationship among project factors. The group has also developed an estimation tool, namely "Estimate Checker", based on these regress ional equations. The group has launched the release 10 of Data CD, in year 2007, which provides a data set of more than 4000 software projects. The data is provided in Microsoft Excel sheet, which can be easily used.

The contribution of this research is

- a Quality matrix is constructed about the given data.
- b This document reviews the available data set, and explores the significance of provided factors.
- c Availability and scattered-ness of data is analyzed.
- d Prior distribution for different type of data is constructed.

2.1 Quality of Data

To establish the confidence level, the data has been tagged by quality indicators. The show credibility of data received from different project submitters, two factors, namely Data integration and Function Point quality are used. Four classes (A,B,C & D, where A is best in quality and D is lowest) are used to indicate the quality of data, as established by ISBSG team. Above 90% of the data has the rating B for data quality. The table below, provides the snapshot of the number of data items in each quality rating.

Table 1. Quality Values Frequency

Quality Parameters			**Function Point quality**		
Data Integration Quality		All	A	B	C
	A	847	631	160	4
	B	2964	1508	637	633
	C	154	75	26	34

The data set consists of 8 major factors, namely Data Quality, Size, Effort, Productivity, Schedule, Project Type, Architecture, Technology factors. Each of these factors has different attributes to describe the characteristics of each project. This data set has been used in number of researches including new model development, data analysis, review as well as accuracy gain [15-31]. Different projects has different level of response from the data providers, hence different degree of availability exists in different factors. Although some significant factors of the project management is available up to 95% of total population, however there are many factors which have below 50% response. The data is collection of response from project submitters, each record representing one project, in many cases data about all the fields was not provided, 50% availability means that from whole population 50% records had data, remaining 50% were left blank. The data provides more than 4000 projects data collected in last few years. The major factors are Sizing, effort, productivity, schedule, Software quality and project grouping factors. Project grouping factors are used to identify the type of project with respect to platform, architecture, user and development type. There also exist some factors which indicate the methodologies adopted to collect the data about major factors, or the metrics used. The availability of major factors like Size, Effort and productivity is more than 95%, however other factors have lesser data availability, which even comes down to 50%.

a) Size

The sizing factor has attributes of count approach, function points, adjusted functional point. Approximately 80% of the projects used IFPUG (International Function Point User Group) as count approach; however in cases where IFPUG is not used the value is converted in adjusted function points, to provide a single unit for size. Approximately 95% of the data for function point or adjusted function point is available in the data set. There also exist other variables which inform how the values of the function point are recorded; however a very low availability of data in these factors exists.

b) Effort

The next major factor is effort, it is described with three attributes, Normalized Work Effort Level1(NWE1) Normalised Work Effort(NWE) and Summary Work Effort(SWE). The NWE1 provides the hours consumed by Development team for full life cycle, where as the NWE provides the effort of whole project team. The Summary Work effort is more suitable as it provides a sum of all phased and un-phased work effort consumed in a project. The availability of these factors is more than 95%. In the data set, the effort is also provided with respect to different phases of project e.g. planning design, implementation; however this division is not provided for majority of projects.

Table 2. Parameters of Size factor

Factors	**Size**		
Attributes	**Description**	**Unit**	**Availability**
Count approach	Method of counting the size of software.	IFPUG/FiSMA	95%.
Functional size	The size of software according to count approach	Depends on counting approach	95%
Adjusted function point	The size in other than FP, is converted into Function point	Function point	95%
Value adjustment factor	A adjustment factor, provided by the project data submitter, to convert data into function point. The factor depends on technical and organizational factors	Default=1.0 Min: 0.65 Max : 1.30	In aprox 40% the value is not submitted, hence considered the default value i.e.1.0.
Other factors	Input count, output count, file count, Cosmic FFP factors, Size other than FSM, LOC.		

Table 3. Parameters of Effort factor

Factors	**Effort**		
Attributes	**Description**	**Unit/choice**	**Availability**
Normalized Work effort Level1	Full life cycle effort by development team	Hours	95%.
Normalized Work Effort	All teams effort for full life cycle	Hours	95%
Summary work effort	Total effort recorded	Hours	95%
Other factors	Recording method, Resource level, Maximum team size, Average team size (Most of the projects had team size 5-9i.e. 37%, where as 9.7% had team size 20+) Ratio to project effort to non project effort, Percentage of non collected work effort ,Effort (planning, design, implementation etc), un-phased effort		

c) Productivity

The factor of Productivity is provided with three variables, Normalized Level 1, normalized productivity and productivity pre 2002. The main formulae for calculating the productivity is Effort divided by size, i.e P = hours/fp, the same formulae is used for all the three types of productivity. Availability of this factor is also above 95%. An other significant factor is the schedule; it describes the time line of the project, e.g. project elapsed time in months, in active time, implementation dates. The elapsed time is most significant factor, and its availability is approximately 90%.

Table 4. Parameters of Productivity factor

Factors	**Productivity**		
Attributes	**Description**	**Unit/choice**	**Availability**
Normalized Level 1	Productivity rate calculated from normalized level 1 effort for the development team only	Effort/size Hours/FP	95 %
Normalized	Productivity rate calculated from normalized effort.	Effort/size Hours/FP	95%
Pre 2002	Before 2002, calculated productivity with different formulae.		95%

d) Grouping Attributes

There are some grouping factors which are used to indicate the type of project e.g. organization type, development type, application type. The data is also collected to determine the architecture of software e.g. client/server or stand alone. In most of the cases the data is available regarding this factor, and availability is upto 70%. The data set also provides information regarding grouping of projects according to platform and languages. The technical attributes, which are collected, provides information related to the development and implementation platform, data base, language, operation system.

Table 5. Factors of Grouping attributes

Factors	**Grouping Attributes**		
Project type	**Architecture**	**Schedule**	**Technical factors**
Development Type Organization type Business Area Type Package Customization	Client/Server Roles of server and client. Web development	Project elapsed time Implementation date Project activity scope	Platform Language type Programming language Hardware Operating system Database

3 Analysis of Data

Although some analysis of data had been conducted in above, however the major contribution of this paper is in terms of presenting the data in terms of prior distributions. For this research not all the factors are selected. We have used some significant factors as listed below. It is worth mentioning that the analysis is based on Adjusted Function Point instead of Unadjusted function point, which has already been used in some researches based on the same data set. The below scatter plot (fig. 1) shows the distribution of the data of three top factors i.e. Effort, size and Productivity. It can be seen that the data set contains many scattered (extreme) values. To deal with this issue the data set was reduced by shedding these extreme values.

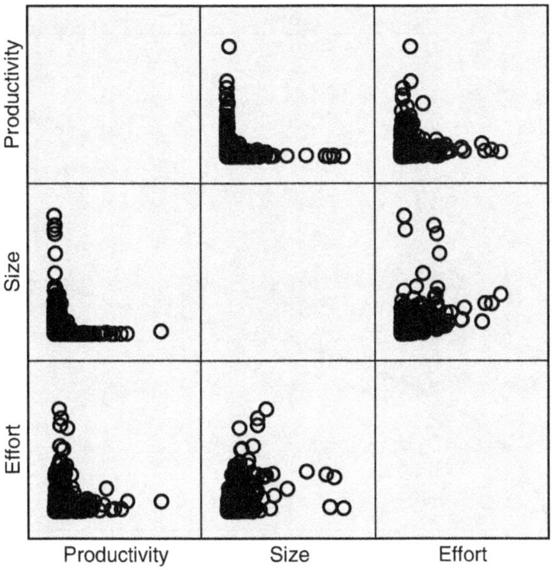

Fig. 1. Scatter Plot of significant factors ISBSG Release 10

After removing the extreme values the data set was reduced to 3529 records. The table below (table 6) provides a brief overview of Size, Effort and Productivity factors.

Table 6. Statistics of Factors

			Skew ness		Kurtosis	
Variable	Mean	Std. Dev	Statistic	Std Error	Statistic	Std Error
Effort	3623.38	5299.90	3.220	.041	12.848	.082
Productivity	13.24	13.53	2.458	.041	7.795	.082
Size	362.26	460.82	2.570	.041	7.390	.082

3.1 Prior Distributions

Prior distributions are helpful to apply probabilistic estimation techniques e.g Bayesian inference. Prior distributions provide efficient way to develop decision support systems to estimate a future value. Prior can be developed using different shapes or Probability Density Functions e.g. Beta, Gamma or Normal. To construct the priors we have used following procedure

a One way to estimate the prior distribution is to run Q-Q plot. We have executed the Q-Q plot using SPSS software.

b Normal distribution and Gamma distribution are presented based on Q-Q plot

c A triangular distribution is presented on the basis of expert opinion. We have termed it as triangular-A.

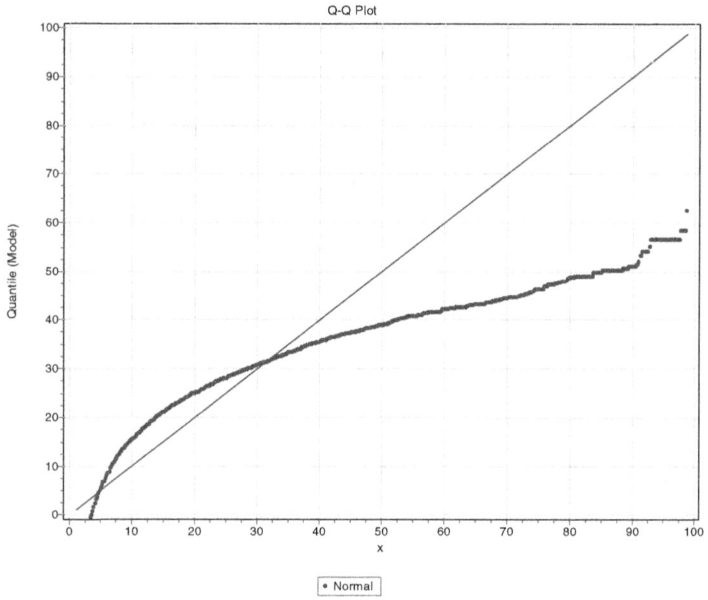

Fig. 2. Q-Q Plot for Normal PDF

Although the distributions are skewed and Gamma distributions are also suitable prior, however we also present Normal prior distributions, which are easier to understand. The Q-Q plot of productivity data for Normal distribution can be seen below. It can be observed that the actual values tend to distance after 30. This means the normal distribution is not much suitable prior for the said data.

It can be observed that Q-Q plot for Gamma distribution provides a better match between expected and actual values. Thus Gamma distribution is more suitable for the productivity value. It is interesting to note that when these distributions are plotted with histogram, The graphs seems to reflect opposite scenarios in the 0-10 section Fig X. Gamma shows that there would be tendency of lower productivity values e.g 0-1, which can be considered impossible in known software development processes. Meanwhile Normal PDF shows a "bell" shape curve which actually doesn't exist in data and cant be justified viewing the Q-Q plot. We thus propose a self created triangular distribution where m = 8, a = 2 and b = 40. This is a more realistic prior for productivity of software development projects. This prior is named as Triangular-A, where A shows first letter of authors name.

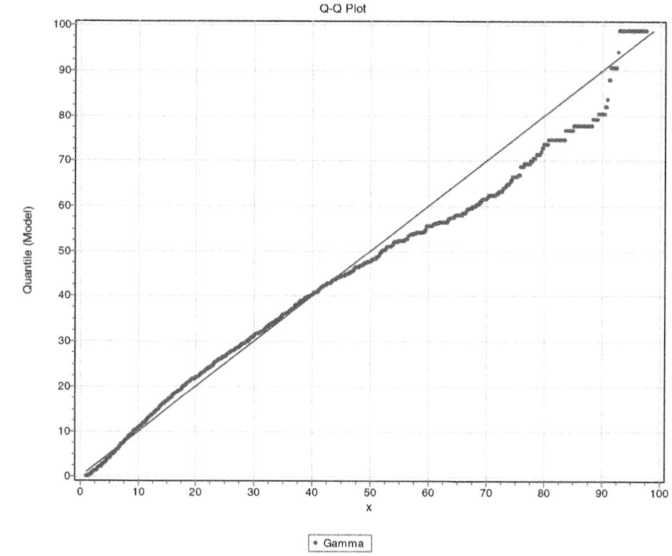

Fig. 3. Q-Q plot for Gamma PDF

Similarly we have estimated Normal, Gamma and Triangular-A priors for subsets of productivity values. These subsets are selected against the Architecture type.

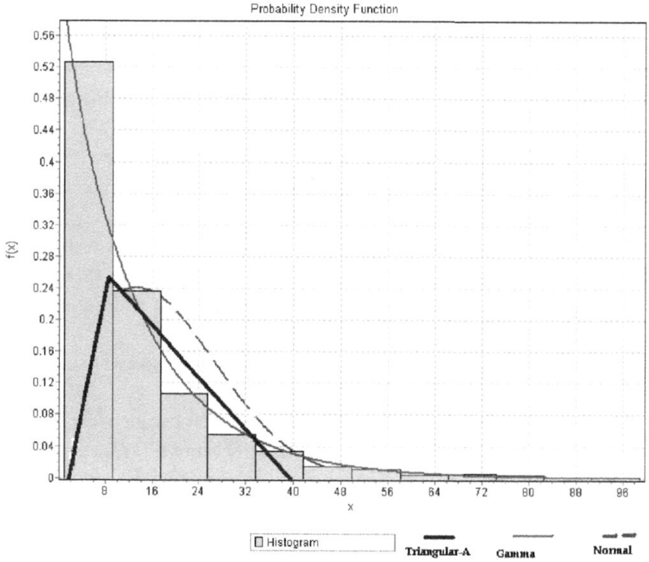

Fig. 4. Comparision of PDF priors

Fig. 5. Prior for Architecture types

Projects Architecture type	Normal		Gamma		Triangle-A Prior		
	Location	Scale	α	β	a	m	b
Stand Alone	13.0896	12.30688	0.957	13.01	-5	12.1	30
Client Server	12.6376	13.21344	0.921	12.75	-5	11.5	30
MIX	13.5090	12.87599	0.930	13.2	-5	12.5	30

4 Conclusion

This research provides a lot of information for the researchers to work in the area of software estimation using ISBSG release 10. This paper also provides theoretical review of software effort estimation factors and their status in ISBSG dataset. We also explain the issues in prior development for productivity factor and provide a method to estimate a realistic prior. The prior distributions provided in this research can be used to develop further estimation models. The data can be used to develop models using Bayesian Networks as well as developing fuzzy rules.

References

1. Bechtold, R.: Essentials of software project management. Management Concepts Inc. (1999)
2. Website COCOMO, `http://sunset.usc.edu/research/COCOMOII/cocomo_main.html` (accessed on February 18, 2009)
3. McConnell, S.: Software Estimation: Demystifying the Black Art. Microsoft Press (2006)
4. Bittner, K., Spence, I.: Managing Iterative Software Development Projects. Addison Wesley Professional (2006)
5. Jalote, P.: Software project management in practice. Addison Wesley (2002)
6. Galorath, D.D., Evans, M.W.: Software sizing, estimation, and risk management: when performance is measured performance improves. Aurbech Publications (2006)
7. Abrahmasson, P., Salo, O., Ronkainem, J., Warts, J.: Agile Software Development Methods, Review and Analysis. In: Espoo 2002, VTT publications 478 (2002)
8. Boehm, B., Abts, C., Chulani, S.: Software development cost estimation approaches—A survey. Annals of Software Engineering 10, 177–205 (2000)
9. Jorgensen, M.: A review of studies on expert estimation of software development effort. The Journal of Systems & Software (2002)
10. Jorgensen, M., Shepperd, M.: A Systematic Review of Software Development Cost Estimation Studies. IEEE Transactions on Software Engineering (2007)
11. Boehm, B., Abts, C., Chulani, S.: Software development cost estimation approaches—A survey. Annals of Software Engineering 10, 177–205 (2000)

12. Witting, G., Finnie, G.: Estimating software development effort with connectionist models. In: Proceedings of the Information and Software Technology Conference, pp. 469–476 (1997)
13. Benediktsson, O., Dalcher, D., Reed, K., Woodman, M.: COCOMO Based Effort Estimation for Iterative and Incremental Software Development. Software Quality Journal 11, 265–281 (2003)
14. ISBSG data release 10 (2007) http://www.isbsg.org (accessed on February 18, 2009)
15. Gencel, C., Buglione, L., Abran, A.: Improvement Opportunities and Suggestions for Benchmarking. In: Abran, A., Braungarten, R., Dumke, R.R., Cuadrado-Gallego, J.J., Brunekreef, J. (eds.) IWSM 2009. LNCS, vol. 5891, pp. 144–156. Springer, Heidelberg (2009)
16. Lokan, C., Mendes, E.: Using Chronological Splitting to Compare Cross- and Single-company Effort Models: Further Investigation. In: ACSC 2009, 32nd Australasian Computer Science Conference, Wellington, New Zealand (January 2009)
17. Lokan, C., Mendes, E.: Investigating the Use of Chronological Splitting to Compare Software Cross-company and Single-company Effort Predictions. In: EASE 2008, 12th International Conference on Evaluation and Assessment in Software Engineering, Bari, Italy (June 2008)
18. Mendes, E., Lokan, C.: Replicating Studies on Cross- vs. Single-company Effort Models using the ISBSG Database. Empirical Software Engineering 13(1), 3–37 (2008)
19. Buglione, L., Gencel, C.: Impact of Base Functional Component Types on Software Functional Size Based Effort Estimation. In: Jedlitschka, A., Salo, O. (eds.) PROFES 2008. LNCS, vol. 5089, pp. 75–89. Springer, Heidelberg (2008)
20. Buglione, L., Abran, A.: Performance calculation and estimation with QEST/LIME using ISBSG r10 data. In: Proceedings of the 5th Software Measurement European Forum (SMEF 2008), Milan, Italy, May 28-30, pp. 175–192 (2008) ISBN 9-788870-909999
21. Deng, K.: The value and validity of software effort estimation models built from a multiple organization data set, Masters thesis, University of Auckland (2008)
22. Abran, A., Ndiaye, I., Bourque, P.: Evaluation of a black-box estimation tool: a case study. Software Process Improvement and Practice 12, 199–218 (2007)
23. Cuadrado-Gallego, J.J., Sicilia, M.-A.: An Algorithm for the Generation of Segmented Parametric Software Estimation Models and its Empirical Evaluation. Computing and Informatics 26, 1–15 (2007)
24. Cheikhi, L., Abran, A., Buglione, L.: ISBSG Software Project Repository & ISO 9126: An Opportunity for Quality Benchmarking. European Journal for the Informatics Professional 7(1), 46–52 (2006)
25. Desharnais, J.-M., Abran, A., Cuadrado, J.: Convertibility of Function Points to COSMIC-FFP: Identification and Analysis of Functional Outliers (2006), http://www.cc.uah.es/cubit/CuBITIFPUG/MENSURA2006.pdf
26. Cuadrado-Gallego, J.J., Sicilia, M.-A., Garre, M., Rodrýguez, D.: An empirical study of process related attributes in segmented software cost estimation relationships. The Journal of Systems and Software 79, 353–361 (2006)
27. Mendes, E., Lokan, C., Harrison, R., Triggs, C.: A Replicated Comparison of Cross-company and Within-company Effort Estimation Models using the ISBSG Database
28. Garre, M., Cuadrado, J.J., Sicilia, M.A., Charro, M., Rodríguez, D.: Segmented Parametric Software Estimation Models: Using the EM Algorithm with the ISBSG 8 Database

29. Santillo, L., Lombardi, S., Natale, D.: Advances in Statistical Analysis from the ISBSG Benchmarking Database, GUFPI-ISMA SBC (Software Benchmarking Committee). In: SMEF 2005, Rome, Italy (March 2005)
30. Sensitivity of results to different data quality meta-data criteria in the sample selection of projects from the ISBSG dataset. In: Proceedings of the 6th International Conference on Predictive Models in Software Engineering, PROMISE 2010 (2010)
31. Lokan, C., Mendes, E.: Applying moving windows to software effort estimation. In: Proceedings of the 2009 3rd International Symposium on Empirical Software Engineering and Measurement, October 15-16, pp. 111–122 (2009)

Virtual FDR Based Frequency Monitoring System for Wide-Area Power Protection

Kwang-Ho Seok[1], Junho Ko[1], Chul-Won Park[2], and Yoon Sang Kim[1]

[1] Dept. of Computer Science and Engineering,
Korea University of Technology and Education, Cheonan, Korea
mono,lich126,yoonsang}@kut.ac.kr
[2] Dept. of Electrical Engineering, Gangneung-Wonju National University, Wonju, Korea
cwpark1@gwnu.ac.kr

Abstract. There have been recent research activities on GPS-based FNET to prevent wide-area blackouts by monitoring frequency deviation. This paper presented a virtual FDR based monitoring system for monitoring regional frequencies in power grid modeling as an advanced research project for implementing intelligent wide-area protective relaying of South Korea. The system was implemented by modeling an actual 345 kV transmission system using EMTP-RV and by measuring voltages and currents at 5 regions. The frequencies were estimated with a frequency estimation algorithm using gain compensation. The virtual FDR based monitoring system was implemented and simulated in various failure conditions.

Keywords: Frequency Monitoring, Wide-Area Protection, Virtual FDR.

1 Introduction

Recently, time synchronized frequency estimation methods for GPS-based FNET(Frequency Monitoring Network) and GPS(Global Positioning System)-based PMU(Phasor Measurement Unit) have been attracted. In the 1980s, researchers began studies on the FDR (frequency disturbance recorder), PSDM (power system disturbance monitor), and PMU (phasor measurement unit) based on GPS (global positioning system) to prevent wide-area blackout and to monitor, analyze, and control wide-area power grids [1-4]. In the U.S., the FNET (frequency monitoring network) has been constructed and is being operated by the Electric Power Research Institute, TVA (Tennessee Valley Authority), and the IT Research Center at Virginia Tech University [5-7]. FNET uses the FDR to measure power system frequencies in more than 40 regions across the U.S. in real time. The measurements are synchronized by GPS and transmitted over the Internet to the central server. FNET is inexpensive and simple to implement.

In Korea, K-WAMS (Korea-Wide Area Measurement System) has been developed by KERI (Korea Electrotechnology Research Institute), KEPCO KDN, and LS Industrial Systems. K-WAMS is currently in its trial operation. K-WAMS monitors and

T.-h. Kim et al. (Eds.): ASEA/DRBC/EL 2011, CCIS 257, pp. 687–694, 2011.

evaluates wide-area power grids using the synchro-phasor of the voltages and currents measured by the I-PIU (intelligent power system information unit). However, considering the convenience of collecting data from power grids, it is believed that FNET, which monitors frequencies and frequency deviations, can be applied for examining the dynamic characteristics of power grids during transient states and failures [8].

In this paper, a virtual FDR based monitoring system developed for monitoring regional frequencies in power grid modeling as an intelligent wide-area protective relaying in South Korea was introduced. The system was implemented by modeling an actual 345 kV transmission system using EMTP-RV and by measuring voltages and currents at 5 regions. The frequencies were estimated with a frequency estimation algorithm using gain compensation. Furthermore, the virtual FDR based monitoring system was implemented and simulated in various failure conditions.

2 Frequency Estimation Using Power Grid Modeling Data

In order to compile objective and reliable data, we used the EMTP-RV transient phenomenon analytical tool to model the 345 kV power grid in Korea. We studied and modeled the generators and controllers installed in Korea to analyze their frequency characteristics. The power grid was modeled based on the data from the PSS/E program using EMPT-RV with the 345 kV power grid as the target. The 345 kV model consists of 154 generators that generate 57,654.76 MVA of power. Fig. 1 displays the model of the 345 kV grid.

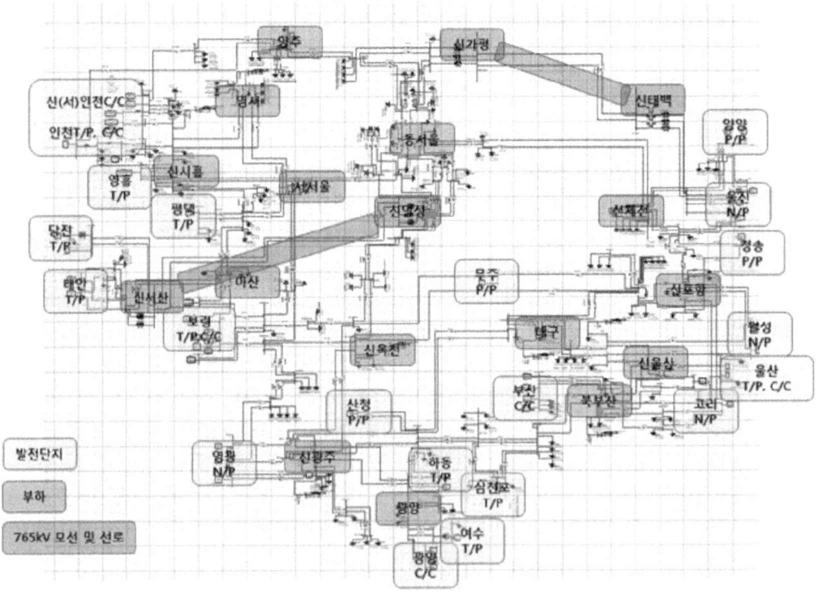

Fig. 1. 345kV Power grid model

In order to simulate various disturbances in the model depicted in Fig. 1 and measure the corresponding parameters of the power grid, we hypothesized that FDRs are installed in the 5 regions (Seoul, Daejeon, Gwangju, Daegu, and Busan) and collected all the data from each location. The selected regions are five major cities in Korea that require analysis of effects from various forms of disturbance.

Most conventional techniques for measuring frequency and estimating frequency deviation require digital filtering and preprocessing. In addition, a trade-off between accuracy and calculation speed must be considered for real-time implementation. A frequency estimation algorithm must be able to measure not only regular frequencies under a normal state, but also irregular frequencies under transient states such as failure and load variation. However, widely used frequency estimation techniques based on DFT filters are not capable of accurately measuring frequencies when they monotonically increase/decrease or transform into sinusoidal waves, creating estimation errors. In other words, frequency variation causes gain error, which undermines accuracy [10-14].

This paper used a frequency estimation algorithm[9] that incorporates gain compensation of real and imaginary filters during frequency variation to improve the accuracy and allow real-time implementation of conventional frequency estimation techniques based on DFT filters.

3 Implementation of Proposed Virtual FDR Based Frequency Monitoring System

3.1 Frequency Monitoring S/W

The implemented monitoring software uses frequency visualization technique to display frequencies in color codes and major parameters (voltage, current, and frequency) in graphs. We used voltage and current data measured at 5 regions (Seoul, Daejeon, Daegu, Gwangju, and Busan). Frequencies were calculated with the frequency estimation algorithm based on measured voltages.

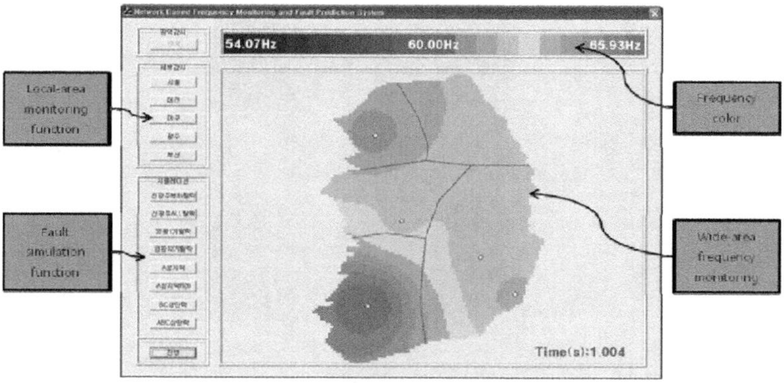

Fig. 2. A snapshot of wide-area monitoring

Fig. 3 is the client-side operation display, which provides the operator with data regarding wide-area power grids. The output of the algorithm for monitoring wide-area power grids is presented as a highly legible display. The monitoring software shows regional stability in color on a 2D map, enabling operators to monitor the overall status of the power grids and the process of a failure being propagated.

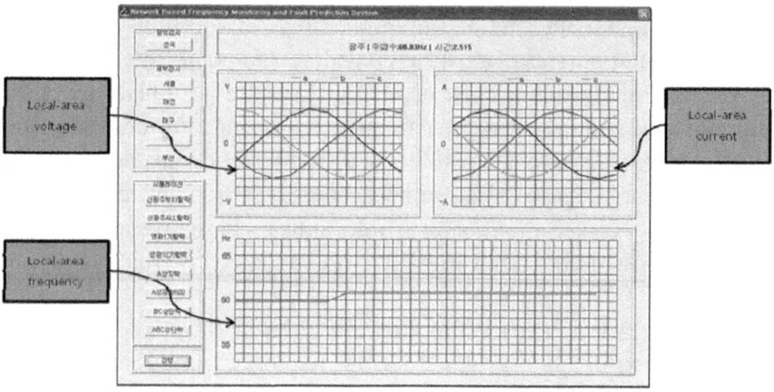

Fig. 3. A snapshot of local-area monitoring

Fig. 3 is the power grid data display of a local area. Voltages, currents, and frequencies are presented in graphics to allow the operator to examine their variations in local areas. In the present study, the fast frequency contour algorithm[20] was applied for frequency visualization. The fast frequency contour algorithm provides good visualization effects when there is limited a number of measurement devices. The fast frequency contour algorithm calculates the frequency by assigning weight factors based on the distance to the measurement device, as shown in Equation. Fig. 4 displays the visualization screen of the monitoring system implemented by applying the fast frequency contour algorithm.

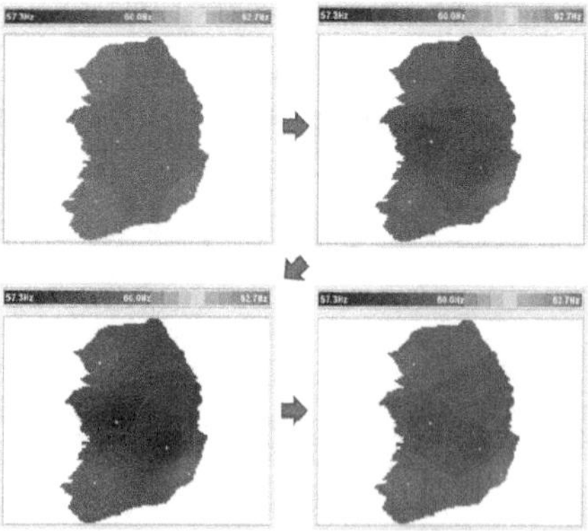

Fig. 4. Visualization of the implemented monitoring system

3.2 Frequency Monitoring Simulation Using Virtual FDR

For frequency monitoring simulation, real data from actual power grid is required. However, it is not easy to connect and obtain real-time power data. Thus in this section, a concept of "virtual FDR" is introduced, which is a sub-system of frequency monitoring network (FNET) for monitoring data. The virtual FDR has roles in measuring the gird frequency from data of modeled grid and sending them to a server.

Data acquired from the EMTP-RV is used into the virtual FDR. The virtual FDR has a MCU(micro controller unit) and GPS. The MCU of the virtual FDR has a role in monitoring and communicating with a server, and the GPS has a role in time synchronization. Fig. 5 shows the overall structure of FNET with multiple virtual FDRs, and Fig. 6 shows a snapshot of frequency monitoring simulation using a virtual FDR.

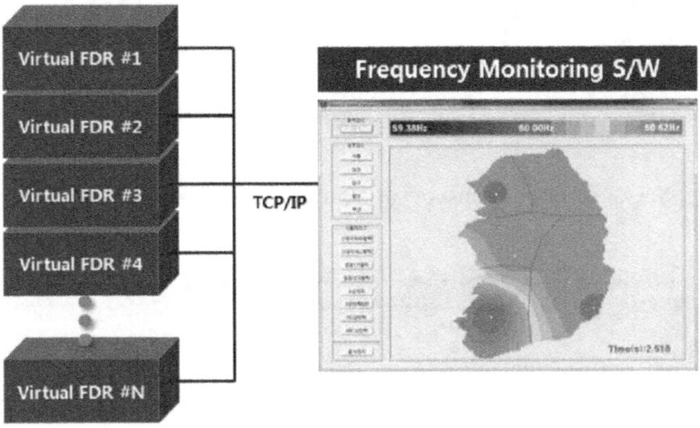

Fig. 5. FNET Structure

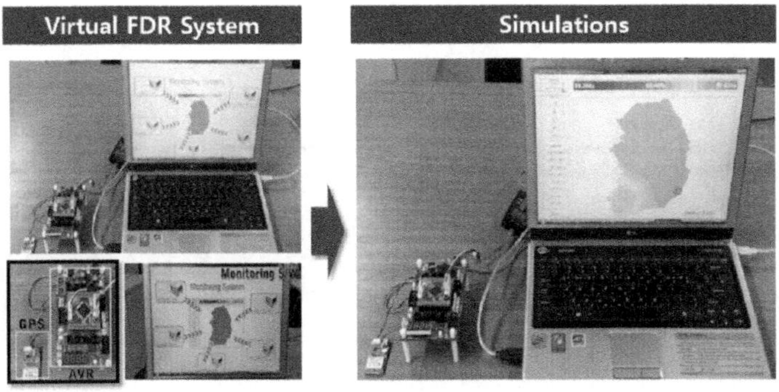

Fig. 6. Simulation using virtual FDR

Various fault conditions (including generator rejection, load rejection, single line-to-ground fault, double line-to-ground fault, triple line-to-ground fault) are studied for the simulation based on the proposed monitoring system with virtual FDR. The following figures show frequency propagations corresponding to the faults.

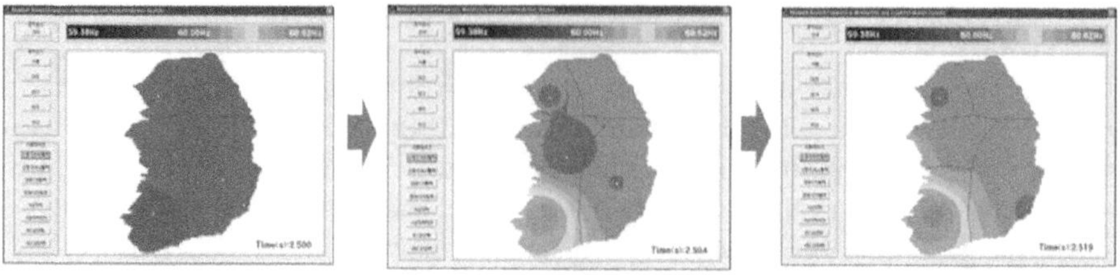

Fig. 7. Consecutive snapshots of generator rejection in Yeonggwang

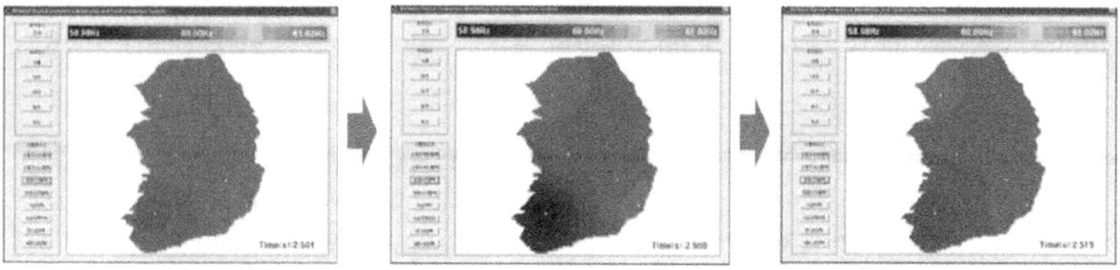

Fig. 8. Consecutive snapshots of 500mW load rejection in Shinkwangju

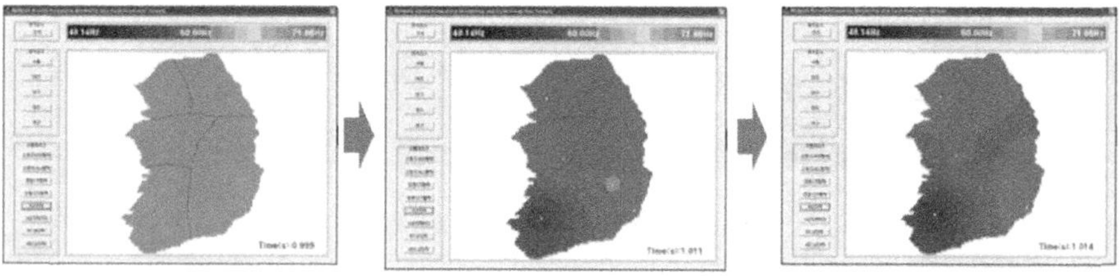

Fig. 9. Consecutive snapshots of single line-to-ground fault in Yeonggwang between Shingwangju

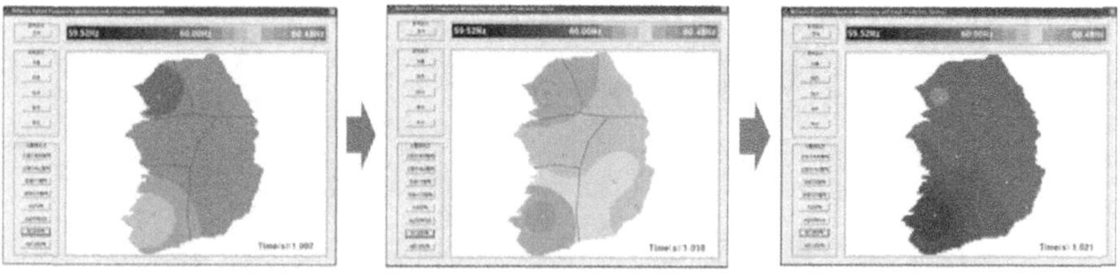

Fig. 10. Consecutive snapshots of double line-to-ground fault in Yeonggwang between Shingwangju

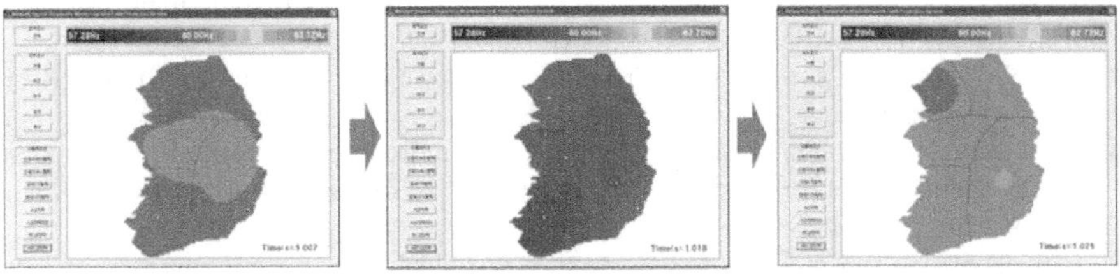

Fig. 11. Consecutive snapshots of triple line-to-ground fault in Yeonggwang between Shingwangju

4 Conclusions

A virtual FDR based monitoring system for monitoring regional frequencies in power grid modeling was introduced in this paper, which is developed as an advanced research project for implementing intelligent wide-area protective relaying of South Korea. The system was implemented by modeling an actual 345 kV transmission system using EMTP-RV and by measuring voltages and currents at 5 regions. The frequencies were estimated with a frequency estimation algorithm using gain compensation. The virtual FDR based monitoring system introduced in this paper was reviewed by the simulation processes considering various failure conditions. The objective of this paper was to develop a FNET sub-system for monitoring power grids by improving accuracy in frequency estimation and analyzing the properties of frequency variation. In addition, this paper is an outcome of next-generation technology research that incorporates information technology into the power domain. We were able to implement a prototype of the frequency monitoring system to assess feasibility of application in actual power grids, and also analyze system's functionality and further requirements.

Acknowledgments. This work has been supported by KESRI (2008T10010013 1), which is funded by MKE (Ministry of Knowledge Economy).

References

1. Martin, K.E., et al.: IEEE Standard For Synchrophasors for Power Systems. IEEE Transactions on Power Delivery 13(1), 73–77 (1998)
2. Phadke, A.G.: Synchronized Phasor Measurements, A Historical Overview. In: IEEE PES Summer Meeting, pp. 476–479 (2002)
3. Fan, D., Centeno, V., Zhang, H.: Aspects on Relative Phase Angle Measurement. In: IEEE PES, pp. 1–4 (2007)
4. Power System Relaying Committee of the IEEE PES. IEEE Standard for Synchrophasors for Power Systems, IEEE Std 1344-1995(R2001), pp. 1–36 (2006)
5. Qiu, B., Chen, L., Centeno, V.A., Dong, X., Liu, Y.: Internet Based Frequency Monitoring Network (FNET). In: IEEE Power Engineering Society Winter Meeting, vol. 3, pp. 1166–1171 (2001)

6. Zhong, Z., et al.: Power System Frequency Monitoring Network (FNET) Implementation. IEEE Transactions on Power Delivery 20(4), 1914–1921 (2005)
7. Liu, Y.: A US-wide power systems frequency monitoring network. In: IEEE Power Engineering Society General Meeting, pp. 18–22 (2006)
8. Kook, K.S., et al.: Global behaviour of power system frequency in Korean power system for the application of frequency monitoring network. IET Generation Transmission Distribution 2(5), 764–774 (2008)
9. Park, C.-W.: Advanced Frequency Estimation Technique using Gain Compensation. Journal of KIEE 59(2) (2010)
10. Sidhu, T.S., Sachdev, M.S.: An Iterative Technique for Fast and Accurate Measurement of Power System Frequency. IEEE Trans. on P.D. 13(1), 109–115 (1998)
11. Sidhu, T.S.: Accurate measurement of power system frequency using a digital signal processing technique. IEEE Trans. on I&M 48(1), 75–81 (1999)
12. Moore, P.J., Carranza, R.D., Johns, A.T.: A new numeric technique for high speed evaluaton of power system frequency. IEE Proc. -Gener. Transm. Distrib. 141(5), 529–536 (1994)
13. Moore, P.J., Allmeling, J.H., Johns, A.T.: Frequency Relaying Based on Instantaneous Frequency Measurement. IEEE Trans. on P.D. 11(4), 1737–1742 (1996)
14. Girgis, A.A., Peterson, W.L.: Adaptive Estimation of Power System Deviation and Its Rate of Change for Calculating Sudden Power System Overloads. IEEE Trans. on P.D. 5(2), 585–594 (1990)
15. Moore, P.J., Carranza, R.D., Johns, A.T.: Model System Tests on a New Numeric Method of Power System Frequency Measurement. IEEE Trans. on PD. 11(2), 696–701 (1996)
16. Park, J.-C., Kim, B.-J.: The Design of UFR with Fast Frequency Measurement Technique. Journal of KIEE 55(1), 1–5 (2006)
17. Nam, S.-R., Kang, S.-H., Park, J.-K.: An algorithm for Power Frequency Estimation Using the Difference between the Gains of Cosine and Sine Filters. Journal of KIEE 55(6), 249–254 (2006)
18. Zhang, G., Hirsch, P., Lee, S.: Wide Area Frequency Visualization using Smart Client Technology. In: IEEE PES (2007)

Engaging and Effective Asynchronous Online Discussion Forums

Jemal Abawajy[1] and Tai-hoon Kim[2]

[1] School of Information Technology,
Deakin University, Victoria, Australia
jemal@deakin.edu.au

[2] Department of Multimedia Engineering, Hannam University, Daejeon, Korea
taihoonn@empal.com

Abstract. Discussion is usually considered a powerful tool for the development of pedagogical skills such as critical thinking, collaboration and reflection. In the last few years, an online asynchronous discussion forum has become an integral part of teaching and learning in tertiary education. However, there are considerable challenges involved in designing discussion forum for learning and teaching arrangements that can support desired learning outcomes. The study analysed the factors that affect the level of the student participation in the online discussion forums with emphases on some of the critical issues that should be taken into account when designing online discussions forums that can support desired learning outcomes. We show that the course instructor roles and level of participations in the discussion forum particularly determines the overall level of discussion among the learning communities.

Keywords: Student learning support, online discussion environments, Online learning, Asynchronous discussion forums.

1 Introduction

A learning management system with asynchronous online discussion forums is becoming more and more pervasive in tertiary institutions. Asynchronous online discussion forum facilitates interaction beyond the constraints of time and physical classroom boundaries. It is capable of saving, arranging and presenting the discussion topics into various discussion threads, it is thus provides a key component of flexible learning. It provides a virtual space to the participants where they can ask questions regarding assessment tasks, lectures or concepts as well as discuss issues raised in class or the assigned readings. Students are able to access the online discussion forum from anywhere at any time and post messages that others can read and comment on at their convenience. As a result, asynchronous online discussion forums have increasingly become an integral part of university courses, online or otherwise, to teach and engage students.

A growing body of research indicates that asynchronous online discussion forums can enhance learning outcomes. A number of studies have shown a strong positive

T.-h. Kim et al. (Eds.): ASEA/DRBC/EL 2011, CCIS 257, pp. 695–705, 2011.

correlation between the levels of engagement in online discussion forums and final grade performance [5]. Picciano [32] who found that students perceived greater quality and quantity of learning as a result of participating in the discussions. Meyer [27] observed that students involved in a threaded, asynchronous online discussion tend to exhibit a higher level of thinking that may not be seen in the classroom, particularly when they contribute comments that are exploratory in nature.

The discussion forums offer a unique opportunity where some of the most important learning such as engagement in learning task, deeper levels of understanding, increased metacognition, increased motivation and divergent thinking can happen. The discussion forum affords students to exchange messages and network with people beyond those they would normally interact with. It promotes active thinking and interaction with others, allow more intimidated and shy students to participate [1, 12]. This would only happen if the students do take part in the discussion both as contributors and consumers to the topic at hand. Hrastinski [16] defines online learner participation as "a process of learning by taking part and maintaining relations with others. It is a complex process comprising doing, communicating, thinking, feeling and belonging, which occurs both online and offline." Therefore, it is important to find out the extent to which students participate in the discussion forum.

In this paper, we explore the purported value of the online discussion forum in light of research into factors that influence students' engagement in online discussions. This is important as research shows that online discussion forums may not be utilized to their full potential in enhancing the effectiveness and efficiency of teaching due to a lower than expected student participation rate ([14]. Current research suggests that there are a number of factors that affect the participation rate of learners in asynchronous discussion forums [3, 11]. Moreover, in order to design effective asynchronous online discussion forums, we need to know the components of successful asynchronous discussion forums. Also, understanding the nature and the determinants of effective learning, an asynchronous online discussion forum is critical because these discussions are the equivalent to the face-to-face discussions common in the traditional classroom [3]. Therefore, based on variables found in the literature that are relevant to understanding the participation patterns of students in online discussions forums, learner participation patterns were systematically analysed.

2 Components of Asynchronous Discussion Forums

Although research shows that asynchronous discussion forums can achieve high levels of learning in some subjects, the online discussion forum designers and mediators must be aware of the conditions for this to occur. The role and presence of the instructor and assessing participation have emerged in the literature as being particularly important for a successful asynchronous discussion forum. In this section, we focus on the following two research questions:

- How much the course instructor participation in the discussion forum determines the overall level of discussion among the learning communities?

- Does assessing the discussion encourage learners to engage in the learning activity?

Woods [39] stated that both quality and quantity of interaction with the instructor and peers are much more crucial to the student success.

2.1 The Instructor Role and Presence

Every educator is interested in establishing a successful asynchronous discussion forum for his/her course. Research shows that high and consistent interaction levels amongst the students as well as between the students and their lecturers as a positive variable in developing student skills and in ensuring that they master the course content [36]. Hew et al [13] identified not understanding the need for online discussion and not knowing what to contribute to be two main factors leading to poor participation in online discussions.

The instructors' role and presence are central to the effectiveness of online learning. Instructors take on a variety of roles as a component of good teaching practice to successfully promote online discussions. The role of instructors' support feedback in promoting and moderating discussion forum has also been identified as success factors [29]. The instructors should focus on how to get students to participate thoughtfully and frequently by guiding students, providing encouragement, motivation, and support to students. They also clarity expectations, respond promptly to student concerns and create a climate of open communication, offering summaries of the discussions and providing resources to support discussions and thus enhance participants' learning experience.

The extent in which the instructor's participate in discussion forums is a vital component of the online learning experience as students weigh the importance and relevance of the discussion form by the instructor's level of participation [24]. Generally, students feel they learned more from the class when they were satisfied with the perceived availability of their course instructor. Therefore, instructors must actively participate in the course to avoid the perception of being invisible or absent [4, 32]. The active involvement of instructors in the online discussion could promote increased student participation in the discussion. The presence of the lecturers in the discussion forum is commonly associated with high levels of learners' satisfaction [19].

Although instructor participation is vital in the overall success of student learning, care must be taken to ensure that the instructors are not overwhelmed with messages. For example, McLain [26] indicates that online students attempted to contact their instructors twenty-four hours per day, seven days per week, at least every fourteen hours. This also suggests that students find it important that teachers were involved in the interaction. Although this means that teacher presence has a central role in student responsiveness and engagement in discussion [19, 18], setting limits and being explicit with students as to the availability of the instructor right from the start is very important. For practical purposes, the instructors may act as facilitators of the discussion at the start of each main topic and kept to a minimum the instructor's interaction afterwards.

Although many research shows that instructor presence is paramount for high level engagement in online discussion forums, there are opposing views on the level of participation of the lecturer. Vonderwell et al.'s [37] study showed mixed findings on the participation of the instructors in the discussion forums. Zhu [40] indicates that the instructor's presence in the discussion forum may negatively affect student participation. Similarly, Gerbic [12] suggests that students take responsibility for the discussion with the absence of the instructor, "creating a democratic space." In contrast, Lim and Cheah [30] argue for more assertive roles of instructors for more effective online discussion, such as answering queries, providing feedback, keeping the discussion focused and posting conflicting views to elicit thinking or reflection. In contrast, Oren et al. [42] suggests that a decrease in teachers' involvement is an important factor in the development of social climate in virtual discussion groups. Social interaction developed more easily when students' discussion postings not moderated. Although a successful discussion forum contains a good portion of socialisation, unless the discussion forum is carefully moderated it is possible that a social strain could spin out of control detracting from the learning process.

The major issue for instructors is how to strike a balance between being overly active facilitator and completely absent. These studies simply assert that instructors should focus on encouraging student-to-student interaction and avoid dominating the content discussion. Therefore, the developers of the asynchronous online discussion forums should aim to make most students believe that their knowledge, understanding, and critical ability will be enhanced by getting involved in the discussion forum. Most of the time, the lecturers need to put their energy into drawing out the quiet students and encouraging more of the kind of participation they want to see in their students.

2.2 Overt Reward or Punishment System

Asynchronous online discussion forums enable collaboration and open discussion that can increase the flexibility of learning while motivating the learners. The discussion forums support student learning by enabling them to access the forum from anywhere at any time and post messages that others can read and comment on at their convenience. Postings messages to the forum will encourage learners to come up with new perspectives on the issue or topic under discussion independently. Comments on the posting of others are also important in terms of promoting critical thinking on the part of students and ensuring that they were able to appreciate and evaluate alternative perspectives. However, it is important that the instructors and moderators of the discussion forum ensure that the discussion forum is conducive to learning while supporting collaboration.

Assessing the discussion is widely acknowledged as influencing student participation rate and encouraging them to engage in the learning activity. Existing study suggests that grading contributions is one cause of increased engagement of the learners in the discussion forum. Gerbic [12] suggests that learners need to be motivated to participate in online discussions, with well-planned and structured learning and assessment activities. This is supported by Vonderwell, Liang and Alder-man [37], who suggest that the structure of a discussion influences student participation and subsequently how they value the assessment in the online learning environment. Macdonald [21] states that with online discussions it is possible to assess individual contributions. Therefore, participation level in asynchronous discussions forums can be used as metrics to evaluate the progress of interaction and collaboration in online courses [33]. Andressen [3] indicates that "many learners need an incentive to participate," suggesting that the degree of participation be included in the assessment. This is supported by Vonderwell, Liang and Alder-man [37] as well as Gerbic [12], who suggest that the structure of a discussion influences student participation and subsequently how they value the assessment in the online learning environment.

When assessing learner contributions to the discussion forum, many aspects of student learning need to be looked at. Currently, students are simply provided with instructions at the beginning of the course for how they would be graded on the discussion. Generally, students are asked to make a minimum number of original posts as well as commenting to a posting made by other students. Instructors need to be aware not only of the specifics, deadlines, and weighting of an asynchronous discussion question or topic, but whether or not that type of topic or question is appropriate in an asynchronous environment. Also, the instructor need to be aware of the fact that in some cases, such assessment can represent an onerous task both to the instructor and the learners particularly when class sizes are large and individual discussion contributions are numerous.

Deciding how to assess the quality of interactions is another important issue that the instructors need to address. There are several possible ways of determining the effectiveness of student participation in discussion forums. One way is by reading the students' posts and categorising them according to Bloom's taxonomy to determine the learning outcomes associated with the level of discourse. An alternative approach is to utilise the content analysis model proposed by Henri [41] in which transcripts of the discussions are analysed according to four educational dimensions - interactive, social, cognitive and meta-cognitive - as well as the frequency, structure and type of on-line participation.

Although many research shows that assessment of the discussion could act as a vehicle for increased participation, there are opposing research results on the level of influence. For example, Oliver [29] is critical about the usage of assessment as a means to increase students' participation. This is because students could simply play the "game of assessment", making postings that earned marks but rarely contributed otherwise. Moreover, students differ in their participation. Some students simply posted questions always most of which are directed to the lecturers whereas some others always gave feedbacks. Masters and Oberprieler [23] tried to promote student participation by asking questions that were important to students' course of study and structured in a way to encourage free and open debate and allowing unhindered debate. These strategies obtained large-scale and equitable participation across the student body despite the lack of immediate assessment incentives.

3 Factors Affecting Participation

Research shows that most students respond extremely positively to the use of discussion forums to aid learning and for assessment. Although the importance of participation in online discussion forums is extensive in the literature, in reality the participation rate is often mediocre at best. Many students tend to make inadequate contributions on the discussion forum and the online discussion forum designers and mediators must be aware of the factors for this to occur. Specifically, we must answer the question: "What are the major factors that could possible hinder the level of learners' engagement in asynchronous online discussions? "

Inadequate student contribution is defined as "students making few or no postings, or students exhibiting surface-level thinking or low-level knowledge construction in online discussions." [13] The factors that determine the level of learners' engagement in asynchronous online discussions are many and well researched in the literature. We reviewed numerous empirical studies in order to identify the major factors that influence student contribution on discussion forums. In this section, we will analyse some of the major variables that influence the degree of the learner contribution to the discussion.

3.1 Feedback or Response Delays

Feedback enables the students to understand their weakness and adjust their learning strategies accordingly. As feedback is essential to students' learning, students normally expect to receive timely, constructive and meaningful feedback on their coursework [33]. The lack of visual and auditory cues in an asynchronous online discussion forum makes feedback in online environments even more important than in traditional classrooms [20]. Higgins, Hartley, and Skelton [15] note that feedback that is meaningful, of high quality, and timely helps students become cognitively engaged in the content under study, as well as in the learning environment in which they are studying.

For some students, the delay in receiving feedback or responses to their messages is perceived to be a major problem and may lead to problems such as procrastination to participate [13]. The lack of both visual and auditory cues could also contribute to more unrestrained behaviour on the part of the participants. The use of constructive feedback that is prompt, consistent, and ongoing can act as a catalyst for increasing the quality of student discussion responses. However, this is practically impossible as it requires the instructress to be constantly available.

3.2 Gender Differences

Are there differences in online participation on the basis of gender? Although gender is considered to be the major influencing variable for participation patterns in terms of both quantity and quality [9], research results to date are not conclusive as to whether or not there are differences in online participation on the basis of gender. Wishart and Guy (2009) suggest that e-learning furnishes environment for equitable communication across genders. Some research results indicate that women are more active than their male counterparts in posting and reading messages online [33]. Others find no significant difference in number of postings or readings on the basis of gender [23, 29].

3.3 Information Overload

Generally, learners especially adults have several responsibilities, such as, jobs and families. Thus, one major concern that needs to be considered in the design of the discussion forum is information overload. For example, as the number of the produced postings with variable quality increase, it becomes difficult to keep up with the postings and become difficult to decide which postings are valuable and thus worth reading from others of modest (or no) importance, and which poster should be avoided. Thus, students must invest a significant amount of time and effort to access and read the messages. In other words, increased effectiveness comes at the price of an increased workload. Another serious problem is that high levels of participation without focus or coherence creates confusion and information overload for other learners.

It is important that the forum has a focus on learning and is interesting enough to attract learners into the discussion, but at the same time is not so demanding that learners are overwhelmed. In addition to making the interactions on the forum enriching and relevant, the course lecturer must also manage effectively the time that the learners spend interacting on the forum. Therefore, the instructor can provide time guidelines for each task to help students manage their time appropriately. The course instructor needs to manage the workload more effectively.

3.4 Cultural Differences

Culturally diverse class are increasingly becoming a norm. Overall, the asynchronous online discussion was perceived as a valuable learning strategy that resulted in increased confidence to interact in a collaborative online environment. Bassett [31] is contended that an asynchronous online discussion can facilitate an inclusive learning environment. Giannini-Gachago and Seleka [9] suggest that culture or membership of a specific group did not seem to influence participation patterns. According to Bassett [31], the online discussion increased ESL students' confidence; they felt less shy and had time to think about and outline their contributions, alleviating the fear of a poorly phrased answer [31]. More recently Coldwell, Craig and Goold (2006) have found that there is little cultural impact on online activities at the undergraduate level and yet Smith, Smith, Coldwell and Murphy (2005) found that the perceptions and level of engagement of Chinese heritage students was significantly different from local students in a wholly online unit.

Online learning is particularly challenging for international students and mature professionals returning to study. Previous studies found that, while many English as a second language (ESL) students lack confidence and are hesitant to participate in face-to-face discussions, these factors are alleviated in collaborative asynchronous online discussions [1, 12]. In contrast, Mazzolini & Maddison [24] found that the non-native English speakers posted and replied less often than did native English speakers and had a tendency to be pessimistic about how articulate they were in forums. Most of these students appear reluctant to participate in online activities due to the exposure of their written communication skills (or lack of) to the scrutiny of lecturers and peers [10].

In fact, some students seem to be intimidated in posting questions online if it is not anonymous. Note that student contributions to an online class discussion are not anonymous and therefore postings are clearly tied to a particular student. Recent anecdotal evidence suggests that, at the postgraduate level at least, international students do not engage in online activities to the same extent as local students, thus impacting negatively on their learning experience and learning outcomes.

4 Discussion and Conclusion

Asynchronous online discussion has increasingly become common means to facilitate discussion between instructors and students, as well as students and students beyond the boundaries of their physical classrooms. For asynchronous online discussion forums to be used well, the discussion forum designers and lecturers should be aware of some of the main factors that influence student participation. In this paper, we reviewed numerous empirical studies in order to identify the factors leading to few or no postings, or students exhibiting surface-level thinking or low-level knowledge construction in online discussions. Several studies examined factors that affect learner participation in online asynchronous discussion forums [6]. Past studies which investigated interaction in asynchronous online discussion found that limited student interaction is a persistent and wide-spread problem [14, 25]. Current research suggests that there are several key variables that are relevant to understanding the participation patterns of students in online discussions forums [3, 11]. Since there is no conclusive evidence as to the level of influences of these variables, further research on the impact of these variables on the asynchronous online discussion is needed.

The participation of the instructors in the discussion forum is the most widely discussed factor in successful asynchronous discussion forums. Although the instructors need to be "seen" in order to be perceived by their students as present in the course just as do face-to-face course instructors [4], depending on the number of the students and the quantity of the discussion messages, one can draw a conclusion that the lecturers should strike a balance between being overly active and completely absent. They should ask more questions than they give answers, and put the bulk of their energy into drawing out the quiet students and encouraging more of the kind of participation they want to see. Also, it is very important that the instructors set specific limits and be explicit with the students from the very beginning.

Although some of the researchers such as Andresen [3] and Gerbic [11] have examined some of the factors that influence learner participation in the discussion forums, the literature on this topic is largely inconclusive. We believe that exiting research findings are based on a single course and small-scale studies. Therefore, one area of further studies is examining more than one course participation to quantify the factors affecting participation. Also, the research discussed in the literature does not really indicate the type of asynchronous discussion forum the course was taught. An implication for instructors is to provide several types of asynchronous communication so that appropriate means are available for different learning activities. The combination of the different types of discussion forum supports several ways for learners and teachers to exchange information, collaborate on work, and get to know each other.

The relationship between participation and interaction and learning outcomes is a complex phenomenon and further research is needed to develop a greater understanding of the nature of the relationship. Another direction of future study is to provide unambiguous evidence that investment in the participation of the discussions forum will indeed 'pay-off' in terms of improved student performance in the subject. Exiting literatures generally give cursory attention to the link between the various components of the curriculum. For instance, although many exiting forums certainly integrated learning and assessment activities in achieving the learning outcomes [40], but further research is required to explore whether the linkage between the various learning and assessment components is fully realized. Research is also needed to develop a greater understanding of the nature of online collaboration especially in the pretense of cross-culture variables; in particular, the concept of inclusion and its relationship to collaboration. There is a need for investigating how the asynchronous online discussion forum is impacting the learning experience of cohorts that include more linguistically and culturally diverse student populations, particularly in the achievement of graduate attributes.

References

1. Al-Salman, S.M.: The role of the asynchronous discussion forum in online communication. Journal of Instruction Delivery Systems 23(2), 8–13 (2009)
2. Anderson, T.: Getting the Mix Right Again: An updated and theoretical rationale for interaction. The International Review of Research in Open and Distance Learning 4(2) (2003)
3. Andresen, M.A.: Asynchronous discussion forums: success factors, outcomes, assessments, and limitations. Educational Technology & Society 12(1), 249–257 (2009)
4. Jean Mandernach, B., Gonzales, R.M., Garrett, A.L.: An Examination of Online Instructor Presence via Threaded Discussion Participation. MERLOT Journal of Online Learning and Teaching 2(4) (2006)
5. Bliuc, A., Goodyear, P., Ellis, R.: Blended learning in higher education: How students perceive integration of face-to-face and online learning experiences in a foreign policy course. In: Research and Development in Higher Education: Reshaping Higher Education, Melbourne, July 6–9, vol. 33, pp. 73–81 (2010)
6. Cheung, W.S., Hew, K.F.: Examining facilitators' habits of mind and learners' participation. In: Hello! Where are you in the landscape of educational technology? Proceedings ascilite Melbourne (2008)
7. Coldwell, J., Craig, A., Goold, A.: Student perspectives of online learning. In: Proceedings of ALT-C 2006: the Next Generation, pp. 97–107. Association for Learning Technology, Oxford (2006)
8. Wishart, C., Guy, R.: Analyzing responses, moves, and roles in online discussions, interdisciplinary. Journal of e-Learning and learning Objects 5, 129–144 (2009)

9. Giannini-Gachago, D., Seleka, G.: Experiences with international online discussions: Participation patterns of Botswana and American students in an Adult Education and Development course at the University of Botswana. International Journal of Education and Development using Information and Communication Technology (IJEDICT) 1(2), 163–184 (2005)
10. De Fazio, G., Gilding, A., Zorzenon, G.: Student Learning Support in an Online Learning Environment. In: Proceedings of ASCILITE 2000, Harbour, December 9-14 (2000)
11. Gerbic, P.: Chinese learners and online discussions: New opportunities for multi-cultural classrooms. Research and Practice in Technology Enhanced Learning 1(3), 221–237 (2006)
12. Gerbic, P.: Getting the blend right in new learning environments: A complementary approach to online discussions. Education and Information Technologies 15, 125–137 (2010)
13. Hew, K.F., Cheung, W.S., Ng, C.S.L.: Student contribution in asynchronous online discussion: A review of the research and empirical exploration. Instructional Science 38, 571–606 (2010)
14. Hewitt, J.: Toward an understanding of how threads die in asynchronous computer conferences. The Journal of the Learning Sciences 14(4), 567–589 (2005)
15. Higgins, R., Hartley, P., Skelton, A.: The conscientious consumer: Reconsidering the role of assessment feedback in student learning. Studies in Higher Education 27(1), 53–64 (2002)
16. Hrastinski, S.: What is online learner participation? A literature review. Computers & Education 51(4), 1755–1765 (2008)
17. Im, Y., Lee, O.: Pedagogical Implications of Online Discussion for Preservice Teacher Training. Journal of Research of Technology in Education 36(2), 155–170 (2003)
18. Jahnke, J.: Student perceptions of the impact of online discussion forum participation on learning outcomes. Journal of Learning Design 3(2), 27–34 (2010)
19. Lowes, S., Lin, P., Wang, Y.: Studying the Effectiveness of the Discussion Forum in Online Professional Development Courses. Journal of Interactive Online Learning 6(3) (Winter 2007), http://www.ncolr.org/jiol
20. Lynch, M.M.: The Online Educator: A Guide to Creating the Virtual Classroom. Routledge Falmer, NewYork (2002)
21. Macdonald, J.: Blended learning and online tutoring: Planning learner support and activity design. Gower Publishing, Aldershot (2008)
22. Malikowski, S., Thompson, M., Theis, J.: External factors associated with adopting a CMS in resident college courses. The Internet and Higher Education, 163–174 (2006)
23. Masters, K., Oberprieler, G.: Encouraging equitable online participation through curriculum articulation. Computers and Education (42) (2004)
24. Mazzolini, M., Maddison, S.: Education without frontiers? International participation in an online astronomy program. In: Proceedings of the 21st ASCILITE Conference, Perth, December 5-8, pp. 606–615 (2004)
25. Wozniak, H., Silveira, S.: Online discussions: Promoting effective student to student interaction. In: Proceedings of the 21st ASCILITE Conference, Perth, December 5-8, pp. 956–960 (2004)
26. McLain, B.: Estimating faculty and student workload for interaction in online graduate music courses. Journal of Asynchronous Learning Networks 9(3) (2005)
27. Meyer, K.: Face-to-face versus threaded discussions: The role of time and higher-order thinking. Journal of Asynchronous Learning Networks 7(3), 55–65 (2003)
28. Meyer, K.: Does Feedback Influence Student Postings to Online Discussions? The Journal of Educators Online 4(1) (January 2007)

29. Oliver, M.: Asynchronous Discussion in Support of Medical Education. Journal of Asynchronous Learning Networks 7(1) (2003)
30. Lim, P., Cheah, P.T.: The role of the tutor in asynchronous discussion boards: A case study of a pre-service teacher course. Educational Media International 40(2), 33–47 (2003)
31. Bassett, P.: How do students view asynchronous online discussions as a learning Experience? Interdisciplinary Journal of E-Learning and Learning Objects (2011)
32. Picciano, A.G.: Beyond student perceptions: Issues of interaction, presence, and performance in an online course. Journal of Asynchronous Learning Networks 6(1), 2140 (2002)
33. Prinsen, F., Volman, M.L.L., Terwel, J.: The influence of learner characteristics on degree and type of participation in a CSCL environment. British Journal of Educational Technology 38(6), 1037–1055 (2007)
34. Schulte, A.: The development of an asynchronous computer-mediated course. College Teaching 52(1), 6–10 (2004)
35. Simonson, M., Smaldino, S., Albright, M., Zvacek, S.: Teaching and Learning at a Distance: Foundations of distance education, 4th edn. Prentice-Hall, Columbus (2009)
36. Vonderwell, S.: An examination of asynchronous communication experiences and perspectives of students in an online course: A case study. Internet and Higher Education 6, 77–90 (2003)
37. Vonderwell, S., Liang, X., Alderman, K.: Asynchronous discussions and as-sessment in online learning. Research on Technology in Education 39(3), 309–328 (2007)
38. Williams, M., Wache, D.: Just link and leave' a recipe for disaster for online discussions. In: Breaking the Boundaries: The International Experience in Open, Distance and Flexible Education, Adelaide, November 9-11 (2005)
39. Woods, R.H.J.: How much communication is enough in online courses? Exploring the relationship between frequency of instructor-initiated personal email and learners's perceptions of and participation in online learning. International Journal of Instructional Media 29(4), 377–394 (2002)
40. Zhu, E.: Interaction and cognitive engagement: An analysis of four asynchronous online discussions. Instructional Science 34, 451–480 (2006)
41. Henri, F.: Computer conferencing and content analysis. In: Kaye, A.R. (ed.) Collaborative Learning Through Computer Conferencing, pp. 117–136. Springer, Berlin (1992)
42. Oren, A., Mioduser, D., Nachmias, R.: The Development of Social Climate in Virtual Learning Discussion Groups. Review of Research in Open and Distance Learning 3(1) (2002)

Online Learning Environment: Taxonomy of Asynchronous Online Discussion Forums

Jemal Abawajy[1] and Tai-hoon Kim[2]

[1] School of Information Technology, Deakin University, Victoria, Australia
jemal@deakin.edu.au
[2] Department of Multimedia Engineering, Hannam University, Daejeon, Korea
taihoonn@empal.com

Abstract. Due to its perceived benefits, asynchronous discussion forums have become progressively popular in higher education. The ultimate goal of developing an asynchronous discussion forum is to create an online learning environment that will achieve high levels of learning. This paper reviews the exiting literature and develops taxonomy of the asynchronous discussion forums with the aims of increasing the understanding and awareness of various types of asynchronous discussion forums. The taxonomy will help increase the online course designers' ability to design more effective learning experiences for student success and satisfaction. It will also help researchers to understand the features of the various asynchronous discussion forums.

Keywords: Asynchronous discussion forums, Taxonomy, Online discussion environments, On-line learning.

1 Introduction

It is well known that discussion is a critical facet of the learning process. In the last few years, there has been a proliferation of asynchronous online discussion forums in tertiary education. Asynchronous online discussion forums have opened up the possibilities for learners to exchange ideas for the purpose of discussing a topic related to the objective of the course. In addition to allowing the learners to have learning experiences beyond the physical classroom settings, asynchronous online discussion forums provide the learners with a new perspective, giving them more time to think formulate response to the topics. Through collaboration and social negotiation in an asynchronous online environment, individuals are able to construct knowledge and relate what they learn to their prior knowledge [6].

Online learning is being used increasingly for both on-campus and distance education students. Asynchronous online discussion forums have changed the way students have traditionally engaged with course content, with teachers and other students. Students can participate in the asynchronous online discussion any time and from any place, giving them more time to think about the issues and/or problems before responding to them [8]. Moreover, they allow learners to express their thoughts and ideas

T.-h. Kim et al. (Eds.): ASEA/DRBC/EL 2011, CCIS 257, pp. 706–714, 2011.

with more freedom and ease as well as increasing their own reflection and interactions with others [8]. By collaboration and social negotiation in an asynchronous online forum, the learners will be able to create knowledge and connect what they learn to their prior knowledge [6].

There is a growing body of literature that discusses the effectiveness of online discussion forums. For example, Webb et al. [19] finds that as participation in the asynchronous discussion forums increases so do the measured grades for the learners. Although there are various types of asynchronous discussion forums, creating a successful asynchronous discussion is probably the most important aspect for an instructor to consider [1]. In order to create appropriate and relevant online discussion forums, the various types of asynchronous discussion forums must be specifically analysed with the aim to select the discussion forum that is effective and appropriate to the objectives of the course in question.

This paper reviews the exiting literature and develops taxonomy of the asynchronous discussion forums with the aims of increasing the understanding and awareness of various types of asynchronous discussion forums. Simply establishing an asynchronous discussion forum, providing the technology, and a question or topic of discussion is not enough to ensure success in an asynchronous discussion [7]. Although the lecturers and learners are increasingly comfortable with the use of information technology for communication, they are still grappling with strategies to ensure their effective use and achievement of quality learning outcomes. Without appropriate asynchronous discussion forums, only lower levels of cognitive engagement will occur and the learners may end up feel a sense of isolation. The core basis for this research study was that understanding the various classes of online discussion forums is a key to create an online learning environment that will achieve high levels of learning. The taxonomy will help increase the online course designers' ability to design more effective learning experiences for student success and satisfaction. It will also help researchers to understand the features of the various asynchronous discussion forums as well associated strengths and shortcomings.

2 Online Discussion Forum Classification

Discussion is usually considered a powerful tool for the development of pedagogical skills such as critical thinking, collaboration and reflection. As a result, online asynchronous discussion forums have become an integral part of teaching and learning in colleges and universities. The discussion forum can be used in a range of ways, from being primarily for optional student-to-student communication only, through to being a formally assessable element of the unit. One of the main advantages of asynchronous discussion forums is that there is a record of nearly everything that occurs in that environment. All materials, correspondence, and interactions can be electronically archived and accessible to students at anytime and from anywhere.

As shown in Table 1, the online discussion forums can be generally classified into three predominant models, namely auxiliary forum, hybrid forum and embedded forum. Asynchronous online discussions can be structured with defined topics and procedures or unstructured allowing students to make free expressions of issues and ideas. Table 1 also details the main features that distinguish these online discussion forums. The common characteristics of all discussion forums are that the participants post messages to a permanent location where they are preserved for others to read and comment at their convenience.

Table 1. Taxonomy of the asynchronous online discussion forums

Points	Auxiliary	Hybrid	Embedded
Participation	Optional	Mandatory	mandatory
Instructor		Visible	Visible
Major Interaction	learner-to-learner	learner-to-learner, learner-to-instructor	learner-to-learner, learner-to-instructor
Participation assessment	None	Explicit assessment	Explicit assessment
Lecturers engagement	Mostly optional	Essential	Required
Message quantity	Low	Medium	High
Topic Time-to-Live	None	Maybe	Maybe
Receiving feedback	None/slow	Slow	
Learning	Instructor-led learning	Blended learning	student-led learning
Activity	Open, self-directed and unstructured	Single topic decided by the lecturer and semi-structure	Single topic decided by the lecturer and highly structured

2.1 Auxiliary Discussion Forum

The simplest model is what we call auxiliary discussion forum in which asynchronous discussion forum is provided to the students as supplement to the traditional face-to-face delivery model. The model is based on recognition that knowledge is an individual construct that is developed through interaction with other group members. Self-directed and open discussions with peers about content facilitate not only knowledge construction but also awareness due to multiple perspectives. Thus, the model is mainly focused on the learner-to-learner interaction for the students to support one another.

Students will engage in the learning out of their own interest. The students have the freedom to choose to contribute to the online discussion and if they do, the students clarify their own understanding of key concepts, and further develop their communication skills by answering each other's questions. Rather than seeking to take on the role of a disseminator of knowledge, the instructors sparingly respond to the student queries so that they tend not to be scholastic, but supportive. Students can feed off each other's knowledge and limited social presence of the instructors. Research revealed certain limitations toward the content and behavior of students' discussion without teachers' guidance. The instructor needs to intervene only in order to keep the discussion on track and to motivate the discussion, guide, moderate, scaffold and support the learners as they transition from prior knowledge and understanding towards construction of new learning.

This type of asynchronous discussion forum is characterised by different levels of participation. The main issue with this type of the forum is that, without explicit requirements for participation, students may elect not to engage in the discussion for various reasons such as time management, passivity, interest, and disregard. Since participation is not compulsory, a small vocal group may naturally emerge as discussion leaders and consistently contribute. A second small group may be moderately active, while the remaining students will participate less frequently. One way to ameliorate this situation is for the instructors to encourage discussion by responding to posts in a timely manner to show that student comments are being read while at the same time making sure that the comments don't inhibit further student responses. In addition, unlike in face-to-face discussion where learners can have responses to their queries impromptu, the learners may have to wait for responses on some ideas that they wished to clarify urgently. The feedback or response may not come either. This may lead to the participant frustration and subsequently discourage participation.

2.2 Hybrid Discussion Forum

The hybrid discussion forum is the most widely used online discussion forum. For example, Bassett [12] explored postgraduate business students' perceptions of the value of hybrid asynchronous online discussion forum. Similarly, Naranjo et. al. [15] analysed the relationships between participation in an online discussion forum and the cognitive quality of the contributions made.

In the hybrid model, online discussion forum is considered as a major component of the face-to-face classroom learning. The discussion forum is designed to enhance the learning experience of students by providing an opportunity to work in groups to collaborate on assessable tasks such as term projects. Each group may have a student facilitator who would be in charge of leading the discussion. Empirical research indicates that the structure of groups has an impact on the quality of the online discussions in terms of the relative responsiveness of individuals. When discussion groups are relatively small (6-8 people), high-quality sharing are more common [2] whereas larger groups are likely to cause student frustration and a feeling of discussion 'overload' [11].

Lecturers act as facilitator and provide explicit assessment activities for student engagements. Discussion activity is often based on a single topic developed by the lecturer. Requirements for participation such as length or quantity of posts, expectations for content (e.g., relevance and quality), are also provided by the lecturers. Moreover, each topic will have a specific deadline and students must contribute before the deadline expires. In a sense, the learners will not necessarily engage in the discussion forum out of their own interest. The forum may generate large amounts of text which can make grading for participation extremely time consuming. Also, the quality and quantity of student discussion may vary widely. Moreover, when discussion topics were specific and related to a concept or idea within the course readings, the discussions were more successful in generating complex interaction between learners than those discussions that were begun with open-ended and broad questions [5]. In addition, class attendance may be affected as most of the course materials are provided online. Another concern is that some students may be less enthusiastic in mandatory participation, as they may find that the online engagement to an unnecessary burden given they attend lectures, have active discussions in class and can talk to the lecturer [2].

2.3 Embedded Discussion Forum

The embedded model is fast becoming the dominant online discussion forum. This is because, in the embedded model, the course is wholly online and learners rely solely on online communication methods to interact with their lecturers as well as the classmates. In 'wholly online' delivery mode, all teaching is occurred online and it requires students to be actively involved with and take more responsibility for their own learning. Also, all communication and interactions between instructors and students are integrated and delivered online. Many people have investigated the relationships between the online participation level and academic performance of students in course that was taught wholly online [4].

Collaborative learning is created through the discussion forum, where students engaged in open dialogue with the instructor and each other about the topical questions. Within the wholly-online course, the asynchronous discussion forum replaces the face-to-face interaction of the traditional classroom [1]. The loss of face-to-face contact renders the relationship between the instructor and the learner to be changed. Similarly, instructors needed to find new ways to express emotion, or passion for the subject matter, when communicating ideas to the learners. Picciano [21] found that students perceived greater quality and quantity of learning as a result of participating in the online discussions.

As in the hybrid model, the instructor posts threaded discussion topics and each topic will have a specific deadline and students must contribute before the deadline expires. The threaded discussions represent class participation, which usually is evaluated based upon the quality and quantity of each student's postings. The forum requires explicit and clear articulation of guidelines in order to promote participation and quality postings for online discussions. A wide range of weighting for participation is used in the literature. Usually, a ten percent was chosen for discussion participation. Gilbert and Dabbagh [6] developed a rubric that awarded a point value to excellent, good, average and poor postings. Chang [3] developed a five-point grading scale to examine the quality of online discussions. The evaluation form focused on four aspects: depth, appropriateness, correctness, completeness, and usefulness.

The instructors must be aware that the number of possible responses to a particular topic depends on the nature of the question and the number of the learners enrolled in the course. Thus, required regular discussions with a large class can result in long conversations, perhaps too long to maintain interest or focus. Also, usually, students have other commitments and may be very busy with other course modules. Thus, instructors must take into account the limited amount of time the learners have in using the asynchronous online discussion in order to minimize student discouragement from fully participating in the discussion. Similar to the hybrid model, student participation in the online discussion was made 'mandatory' in the sense that marks were assigned to participation.

Another possible problem is that students may feel like "everything has already been said" by the time it's their turn to post. This could possibly be handled by ensuring that when students enter the forum, they cannot see any other posts until they make a new post of their own. This way everyone is forced to post an original thought, even if it has already been generated in the discussion.

3 Discussion and Conclusions

In this paper, we discussed the opportunities, the constraints and the value of a asynchronous online discussion forums. We also developed taxonomy of the online discussion forums. The learning experience has been shown to be enhanced through the regular participation in discussions regardless of where (i.e., in a classroom or through online forums) these discussions take place. Specifically, the amounts of time students spend reading postings on the forum and engaged in virtual conversation with their classmates have positive influences on their achievement of course objectives [22]. However, compared to face-to-face discussion, the asynchronous discussion forum affords time to participate and contribute to a discussion. Moreover, a transcript of the discussion is archived and accessible at anytime and from anywhere. Regardless of how the discussion forum is used in a course, it is important that it be actively managed. This includes ensuring that initial information that explains the purpose of the forum is made available to the students. Also, the role of the instructors and the extent to which the instructors will be contributing to the discussion must be made available to the learners. All is said, it is important to ensure that the content of the discussion to be regularly monitored to ensure that it is not being inappropriately used by students.

Regardless of the type of the asynchronous discussion forum types, they all provide the participants an alternative way to interact with one another. Within the wholly-online course, the asynchronous discussion forum replaces the face-to-face interaction of the traditional classroom [1]. Both quality and quantity of interaction with the instructor and peers are much more crucial to the success of online courses and student satisfaction than to success and satisfaction in traditional courses (Woods, 2002) and successful students in the online course were generally active participants in discussion forum. The design of online discussion activities imposes great influence on the quality of online discussion, message quantity and others [17]. Equally important in the design of the asynchronous discussion forums is the role of the instructors.

Although countless course designers and educators recognise the value of online discussions, keeping the discussion threads lively and informative is a challenge.

In the embedded model, the quantity of the message can overwhelm the learners to navigate through [8]. Also, the use of 'threaded' discussions increases the amount of time students spend on course objectives and on reflection [14]. Proponents of threaded discussions view it as an integral part of the learning process, where students seek knowledge and express understanding. Consequently, they deem it essential to assess participation.

There is an ongoing debate about the value and utility of grading discussions to ensure and assess full participation in the online classroom. Palmer et. al. [16] recommend an approach that include both quantitative (i.e., number of postings, length of posting, number of messages read, etc.) and qualitative terms (i.e., does the posting exhibit cognitive/social/teaching presence?). Their implementation indicates that assessing online discussions positively impacted students' participation and final grades. Similarly, Levenburg and Major [22] suggest that assessing participation recognises students' workload and time commitment with respect to online discussions and encourages students to participate in required learning activities associated with the discussions. However, as noted in Houghton [23], some students' tend to "structure their learning activities to optimise their assessment performance. This means, some learners will not participate while others, once they had, may not follow up their arguments because they felt they had already posted enough to get their marks.

Although both the embedded and hybrid model are becoming pervasive, establishing effective opportunities for peer learning in online environments requires care in creating groups, structuring learning activities, and facilitating group interactions. The question initiating each of the online discussions influenced the level of the responses from students. Unless care is taken, the lecturer-led selection of the topic for discussion may restrict innovative discussion and fewer interactions of discussion behaviours may occur. One way to address this problem for the lecturers to drafted only the scope of topics for students' questions and allowed the students to raise questions and perform problem-solving discussions themselves [10]. Moreover, successful discussion topics must be related to the learning objectives with clarity in due dates, expectations, and the weighting of grades so that learning objectives may become learning outcomes [7, 13].

With proper design, the auxiliary discussion forum can furnish the learners with more conducive and productive way of learning. This is because student will engage in the learning out of their own interest without feeling threatened. Apart from cursory involvements of the lecturer, the learners have total freedom to discuss what they want. However, in general, learners may experience bottlenecks, such as insufficient information or inadequate deduction. When this occurs, lecturer participation will be needed. In fact, Swan and Shih [18] find that the perceived presence of an instructor is more important than the perceived presence of peers in student satisfaction. Therefore, unless proper balance is made, the instructor can decrease learner – learner interaction because the learners begin to rely on the instructor to answer questions [7].

References

1. Andresen, M.A.: Asynchronous discussion forums: success factors, outcomes, assessments, and limitations. Educational Technology & Society 12(1), 249–257 (2009)
2. Beckmann, E.A., Kilby, P.: On-line, Off-campus but in the Flow: Learning from Peers in Development Studies. Journal of Peer Learning 1(1), 61–69 (2008)
3. Chang, C.: A case study on the relationships between participation in online discussion and achievement of project work. Journal of Educational Multimedia and Hypermedia 17(4), 477–509 (2008)
4. Coldwell, J., Craig, A., Paterson, T., Mustard, J.: Online Students: Relationships between Participation, Demographics and Academic Performance. The Electronic Journal of e-Learning 6(1), 19–30 (2008)
5. Fung, Y.H.: Collaborative online learning: Interaction patterns and limiting factors. Open Learning 19(2), 136–149 (2004)
6. Gilbert, P.K., Dabbagh, N.: How to structure online discussions for meaningful discourse: A case study. British Journal of Educational Technology 36(1), 5–18 (2005)
7. Guldberg, K., Pilkington, R.M.: Tutor roles in facilitating reflection on practice through online discussion. Educational Technology & Society 10(1), 61–72 (2007)
8. Hew, K.F., Cheung, W.S.: An exploratory study on the use of asynchronous online discussion in hypermedia design. Journal of Instructional Science& Technology 6(1) (2003) (retrieved September 23, 2005)
9. Holley, D.: Which room is the virtual seminar in please? Education and Training 44(3), 112–121 (2002)
10. Hou, H.-T., Chang, K.-E., Sung, Y.-T.: Analysis of problem-solving-based online asynchronous discussion pattern. Educational Technology & Society 11(1), 17–28 (2008)
11. Kimball, L.: Managing distance learning: new challenges for faculty. In: Hazemi, R., Hailes, S., Wilbur, S. (eds.) The Digital University: Building a Learning Community, pp. 27–40. Springer, London (2001)
12. Bassett, P.: How Do Students View Asynchronous Online Discussions As A Learning Experience? Interdisciplinary Journal of E-Learning and Learning Objects 7 (2011)
13. Majeski, R., Stover, M.: Theoretically based pedagogical strategies leading to deep learning in asynchronous online gerontology courses. Educational Gerontology 33(3), 171–185 (2007)
14. Meyer, K.A.: Face-to-face versus threaded discussions: the role of time and higher-order thinking. Journal of Asynchronous Learning Networks 7(3), 55–65 (2003)
15. Naranjo, M., Onrubia, J., Teresa, M.: Participation and cognitive quality profiles in an online discussion forum. British Journal of Educational Technology (2011)
16. Palmer, S., Holt, D., Bray, S.: Does the discussion help? the impact of a formally assessed online discussion on final student results. British Journal of Educational Technology 39(5), 847–858 (2008)
17. Patricia, K.G., Dabbagh, N.: How to structure online discussions for meaningful discourse: a case study. British Journal of Educational Technology 36(1), 5–18 (2005)
18. Swan, K., Shih, L.F.: On the nature and development of social presence in online course discussions. Journal of Asynchronous Learning Networks 9(3), 115–136 (2005)
19. Webb, E., Jones, A., Barker, P., van Schaik, P.: Using e-learning dialogues in higher education. Innovations in Education and Teaching International 41(1), 93–103 (2004)

20. Wood, E.: A dilemma beyond discussion – increasing student interaction in external study modes. In: Bunker, A., Swan, G. (eds.) Focussing on the student, pp. 153–157. Edith Cowan University, Mount Lawley, Western Australia (2002)
21. Picciano, A.G.: Beyond student perceptions: Issues of interaction, presence, and performance in an online course. Journal of Asynchronous Learning Networks 6(1), 2140 (2002)
22. Levenburg, N., Major, H.: Motivating the online learner: The effect of frequency of online postings and time spent online on achievement of learning goals and objectives (2000)
23. Houghton, W. (2004). Constructive Alignment—why it is important to the learning process. Engineering Subject Centre Guide: Learning and Teaching Theory for Engineering Academics

Erratum: University-Industry Ecosystem: Factors for Collaborative Environment

Muhammad Fiaz[1] and Baseerat Rizran[2]

[1] School of Management, Northwestern Polytechnical University, Xi'an, China
fiaz_42@yahoo.com
[2] Department of Management, Hazara University, Pakistan
baseeratrizwan@gmail.com

T.-h. Kim et al. (Eds.): ASEA/DRBC/EL 2011, CCIS 257, pp. 651–661, 2011.

DOI 10.1007/978-3-642-27207-3_77

In the original version, the second name of the author is incorrect. Instead of "Baseerat Rizran" it should be read as "Baseerat Rizwan".

The original online version for this chapter can be found at
http://dx.doi.org/10.1007/978-3-642-27207-3_71

Author Index

GPSR Compliance

The European Union's (EU) General Product Safety Regulation (GPSR) is a set of rules that requires consumer products to be safe and our obligations to ensure this.

If you have any concerns about our products, you can contact us on ProductSafety@springernature.com

In case Publisher is established outside the EU, the EU authorized representative is:

Springer Nature Customer Service Center GmbH
Europaplatz 3
69115 Heidelberg, Germany

Batch number: 10844611

Printed by Printforce, the Netherlands